PENNSYLVANIA RULES OF COURT

VOLUME II – FEDERAL

2016
REVISED EDITION

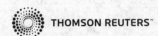
THOMSON REUTERS™

Mat #41778527

ISBN: 978–0–314–68182–9

PREFACE

Designed for use in the office or courtroom, this pamphlet contains Pennsylvania federal rules.

WHAT'S NEW

Pennsylvania Rules of Court, Volume II – Federal, 2016 Revised Edition, includes rules and associated material governing practice before the Pennsylvania federal courts. It is current with amendments received through June 1, 2016.

CONTACT US

For additional information or research assistance, call the reference attorneys at 1-800-REF-ATTY (1-800-733-2889). Contact our U.S. legal editorial department directly with your questions and suggestions by e-mail at editors.us-legal@tr.com.

Thank you for subscribing to this product. Should you have any questions regarding this product please contact Customer Service at 1-800-328-4880 or by fax at 1-800-340-9378. If you would like to inquire about related publications, or to place an order, please contact us at 1-888-728-7677 or at legalsolutions.thomsonreuters.com.

THE PUBLISHER

July 2016

TABLE OF CONTENTS

FEDERAL RULES OF CIVIL PROCEDURE

Including Amendments Effective December 1, 2016, Absent Contrary Congressional Action

---

TITLE I. SCOPE OF RULES; FORM OF ACTION

RULE 1. SCOPE AND PURPOSE

These rules govern the procedure in all civil actions and proceedings in the United States district courts, except as stated in Rule 81. They should be construed, administered, and employed by the court and the parties to secure the just, speedy, and inexpensive determination of every action and proceeding.

(Amended December 29, 1948, effective October 20, 1949; February 28, 1966, effective July 1, 1966; April 22, 1993, effective December 1, 1993; April 30, 2007, effective December 1, 2007; April 29, 2015, effective December 1, 2015.)

RULE 2. ONE FORM OF ACTION

There is one form of action—the civil action.

(Amended April 30, 2007, effective December 1, 2007.)

TITLE II. COMMENCING AN ACTION; SERVICE OF PROCESS, PLEADINGS, MOTIONS, AND ORDERS

RULE 3. COMMENCING AN ACTION

A civil action is commenced by filing a complaint with the court.

(Amended April 30, 2007, effective December 1, 2007.)

RULE 4. SUMMONS

(a) Contents; Amendments.

(1) *Contents.* A summons must:

(A) name the court and the parties;

(B) be directed to the defendant;

(C) state the name and address of the plaintiff's attorney or—if unrepresented—of the plaintiff;

(D) state the time within which the defendant must appear and defend;

(E) notify the defendant that a failure to appear and defend will result in a default judgment against the defendant for the relief demanded in the complaint;

(F) be signed by the clerk; and

(G) bear the court's seal.

(2) *Amendments.* The court may permit a summons to be amended.

(b) **Issuance.** On or after filing the complaint, the plaintiff may present a summons to the clerk for signature and seal. If the summons is properly completed, the clerk must sign, seal, and issue it to the plaintiff for service on the defendant. A summons—or a copy of a summons that is addressed to multiple defendants—must be issued for each defendant to be served.

(c) **Service.**

(1) *In General.* A summons must be served with a copy of the complaint. The plaintiff is responsible for having the summons and complaint served within the time allowed by Rule 4(m) and must furnish the necessary copies to the person who makes service.

(2) *By Whom.* Any person who is at least 18 years old and not a party may serve a summons and complaint.

(3) *By a Marshal or Someone Specially Appointed.* At the plaintiff's request, the court may order that service be made by a United States marshal or deputy marshal or by a person specially appointed by the court. The court must so order if the plaintiff is authorized to proceed in forma pauperis under 28 U.S.C. § 1915 or as a seaman under 28 U.S.C. § 1916.

(d) **Waiving Service.**

(1) *Requesting a Waiver.* An individual, corporation, or association that is subject to service under Rule 4(e), (f), or (h) has a duty to avoid unnecessary expenses of serving the summons. The plaintiff may notify such a defendant that an action has been commenced and request that the defendant waive service of a summons. The notice and request must:

(A) be in writing and be addressed:

  (i) to the individual defendant; or

  (ii) for a defendant subject to service under Rule 4(h), to an officer, a managing or general agent, or any other agent authorized by appointment or by law to receive service of process;

(B) name the court where the complaint was filed;

(C) be accompanied by a copy of the complaint, 2 copies of the waiver form appended to this Rule 4, and a prepaid means for returning the form;

(D) inform the defendant, using the form appended to this Rule 4, of the consequences of waiving and not waiving service;

(E) state the date when the request is sent;

(F) give the defendant a reasonable time of at least 30 days after the request was sent—or at least 60 days if sent to the defendant outside any judicial district of the United States—to return the waiver; and

(G) be sent by first-class mail or other reliable means.

(2) *Failure to Waive.* If a defendant located within the United States fails, without good cause, to sign and return a waiver requested by a plaintiff located within the United States, the court must impose on the defendant:

(A) the expenses later incurred in making service; and

(B) the reasonable expenses, including attorney's fees, of any motion required to collect those service expenses.

(3) *Time to Answer After a Waiver.* A defendant who, before being served with process, timely returns a waiver need not serve an answer to the complaint until 60 days after the request was sent—or until 90 days after it was sent to the defendant outside any judicial district of the United States.

(4) *Results of Filing a Waiver.* When the plaintiff files a waiver, proof of service is not required and these rules apply as if a summons and complaint had been served at the time of filing the waiver.

(5) *Jurisdiction and Venue Not Waived.* Waiving service of a summons does not waive any objection to personal jurisdiction or to venue.

(e) **Serving an Individual Within a Judicial District of the United States.** Unless federal law provides otherwise, an individual—other than a minor, an incompetent person, or a person whose waiver has been filed—may be served in a judicial district of the United States by:

(1) following state law for serving a summons in an action brought in courts of general jurisdiction in the state where the district court is located or where service is made; or

(2) doing any of the following:

(A) delivering a copy of the summons and of the complaint to the individual personally;

(B) leaving a copy of each at the individual's dwelling or usual place of abode with someone of suitable age and discretion who resides there; or

(C) delivering a copy of each to an agent authorized by appointment or by law to receive service of process.

(f) **Serving an Individual in a Foreign Country.** Unless federal law provides otherwise, an individual—other than a minor, an incompetent person, or a person whose waiver has been filed—may be served at a place not within any judicial district of the United States:

(1) by any internationally agreed means of service that is reasonably calculated to give notice, such as those authorized by the Hague Convention on the Service Abroad of Judicial and Extrajudicial Documents;

(2) if there is no internationally agreed means, or if an international agreement allows but does not specify other means, by a method that is reasonably calculated to give notice:

(A) as prescribed by the foreign country's law for service in that country in an action in its courts of general jurisdiction;

(B) as the foreign authority directs in response to a letter rogatory or letter of request; or

(C) unless prohibited by the foreign country's law, by:

(i) delivering a copy of the summons and of the complaint to the individual personally; or

(ii) using any form of mail that the clerk addresses and sends to the individual and that requires a signed receipt; or

(3) by other means not prohibited by international agreement, as the court orders.

(g) Serving a Minor or an Incompetent Person. A minor or an incompetent person in a judicial district of the United States must be served by following state law for serving a summons or like process on such a defendant in an action brought in the courts of general jurisdiction of the state where service is made. A minor or an incompetent person who is not within any judicial district of the United States must be served in the manner prescribed by Rule 4(f)(2)(A), (f)(2)(B), or (f)(3).

(h) Serving a Corporation, Partnership, or Association. Unless federal law provides otherwise or the defendant's waiver has been filed, a domestic or foreign corporation, or a partnership or other unincorporated association that is subject to suit under a common name, must be served:

(1) in a judicial district of the United States:

(A) in the manner prescribed by Rule 4(e)(1) for serving an individual; or

(B) by delivering a copy of the summons and of the complaint to an officer, a managing or general agent, or any other agent authorized by appointment or by law to receive service of process and—if the agent is one authorized by statute and the statute so requires—by also mailing a copy of each to the defendant; or

(2) at a place not within any judicial district of the United States, in any manner prescribed by Rule 4(f) for serving an individual, except personal delivery under (f)(2)(C)(i).

(i) Serving the United States and Its Agencies, Corporations, Officers, or Employees.

(1) *United States.* To serve the United States, a party must:

(A)(i) deliver a copy of the summons and of the complaint to the United States attorney for the district where the action is brought—or to an assistant United States attorney or clerical employee whom the United States attorney designates in a writing filed with the court clerk—or

(ii) send a copy of each by registered or certified mail to the civil-process clerk at the United States attorney's office;

(B) send a copy of each by registered or certified mail to the Attorney General of the United States at Washington, D.C.; and

(C) if the action challenges an order of a nonparty agency or officer of the United States, send a copy of each by registered or certified mail to the agency or officer.

(2) *Agency; Corporation; Officer or Employee Sued in an Official Capacity.* To serve a United States agency or corporation, or a United States officer or employee sued only in an official capacity, a party must serve the United States and also send a copy of the summons and of the complaint by registered or certified mail to the agency, corporation, officer, or employee.

(3) *Officer or Employee Sued Individually.* To serve a United States officer or employee sued in an individual capacity for an act or omission occurring in connection with duties performed on the United States' behalf (whether or not the officer or employee is also sued in an official capacity), a party must serve the United States and also serve the officer or employee under Rule 4(e), (f), or (g).

(4) *Extending Time.* The court must allow a party a reasonable time to cure its failure to:

(A) serve a person required to be served under Rule 4(i)(2), if the party has served either the United States attorney or the Attorney General of the United States; or

(B) serve the United States under Rule 4(i)(3), if the party has served the United States officer or employee.

(j) Serving a Foreign, State, or Local Government.

(1) *Foreign State.* A foreign state or its political subdivision, agency, or instrumentality must be served in accordance with 28 U.S.C. § 1608.

(2) *State or Local Government.* A state, a municipal corporation, or any other state-created governmental organization that is subject to suit must be served by:

   (A) delivering a copy of the summons and of the complaint to its chief executive officer; or

   (B) serving a copy of each in the manner prescribed by that state's law for serving a summons or like process on such a defendant.

(k) Territorial Limits of Effective Service.

(1) *In General.* Serving a summons or filing a waiver of service establishes personal jurisdiction over a defendant:

   (A) who is subject to the jurisdiction of a court of general jurisdiction in the state where the district court is located;

   (B) who is a party joined under Rule 14 or 19 and is served within a judicial district of the United States and not more than 100 miles from where the summons was issued; or

   (C) when authorized by a federal statute.

(2) *Federal Claim Outside State–Court Jurisdiction.* For a claim that arises under federal law, serving a summons or filing a waiver of service establishes personal jurisdiction over a defendant if:

   (A) the defendant is not subject to jurisdiction in any state's courts of general jurisdiction; and

   (B) exercising jurisdiction is consistent with the United States Constitution and laws.

(l) Proving Service.

(1) *Affidavit Required.* Unless service is waived, proof of service must be made to the court. Except for service by a United States marshal or deputy marshal, proof must be by the server's affidavit.

(2) *Service Outside the United States.* Service not within any judicial district of the United States must be proved as follows:

   (A) if made under Rule 4(f)(1), as provided in the applicable treaty or convention; or

   (B) if made under Rule 4(f)(2) or (f)(3), by a receipt signed by the addressee, or by other evidence satisfying the court that the summons and complaint were delivered to the addressee.

(3) *Validity of Service; Amending Proof.* Failure to prove service does not affect the validity of service. The court may permit proof of service to be amended.

[Text of subdivision (m) effective until December 1, 2016, absent contrary Congressional action.]

(m) Time Limit for Service. If a defendant is not served within 90 days after the complaint is filed, the court — on motion or on its own after notice to the plaintiff — must dismiss the action without prejudice against that defendant or order that service be made within a specified time. But if the plaintiff shows good cause for the failure, the court must extend the time for service for an appropriate period. This subdivision (m) does not apply to service in a foreign country under Rule 4(f) or 4(j)(1) or to service of a notice under Rule 71.1(d)(3)(A).

[Text of subdivision (m) effective December 1, 2016, absent contrary Congressional action.]

(m) Time Limit for Service. If a defendant is not served within 90 days after the complaint is filed, the court—on motion or on its own after notice to the plaintiff—must dismiss the action without prejudice against that defendant or order that service be made within a specified time. But if the plaintiff shows good cause for the failure, the court must extend the time for service for an appropriate period. This subdivision (m) does not apply to service in a foreign country under Rule 4(f), 4(h)(2), or 4(j)(1).

(n) Asserting Jurisdiction over Property or Assets.

(1) *Federal Law.* The court may assert jurisdiction over property if authorized by a federal statute. Notice to claimants of the property must be given as provided in the statute or by serving a summons under this rule.

(2) *State Law.* On a showing that personal jurisdiction over a defendant cannot be obtained in the district where the action is brought by reasonable efforts to serve a summons under this rule, the court may assert jurisdiction over the defendant's assets found in the district. Jurisdiction is acquired by seizing the assets under the circumstances and in the manner provided by state law in that district.

Rule 4   Notice of a Lawsuit and Request to Waive Service of Summons.

(Caption)

To (*name the defendant or — if the defendant is a corporation, partnership, or association — name an officer or agent authorized to receive service*):

Why are you getting this?

A lawsuit has been filed against you, or the entity you represent, in this court under the number shown above. A copy of the complaint is attached.

This is not a summons, or an official notice from the court. It is a request that, to avoid expenses, you waive formal service of a summons by signing and returning the enclosed waiver. To avoid these expenses, you must return the signed waiver within (*give at least 30 days or at least 60 days if the defendant is outside any judicial district of the United States*) from the date shown below, which is the date this notice was sent. Two copies of the waiver form are enclosed, along with a stamped, self-addressed envelope or other prepaid means for returning one copy. You may keep the other copy.

What happens next?

If you return the signed waiver, I will file it with the court. The action will then proceed as if you had been served on the date the waiver is filed, but no summons will be served on you and you will have 60 days from the date this notice is sent (see the date below) to answer the complaint (or 90 days if this notice is sent to you outside any judicial district of the United States).

If you do not return the signed waiver within the time indicated, I will arrange to have the summons and complaint served on you. And I will ask the court to require you, or the entity you represent, to pay the expenses of making service.

Please read the enclosed statement about the duty to avoid unnecessary expenses.

I certify that this request is being sent to you on the date below.

Date: _____

_____
(Signature of the attorney
or unrepresented party)

_____
(Printed name)

_____
(Address)

_____
(E–mail address)

_____
(Telephone number)

Rule 4   Waiver of the Service of Summons.

(Caption)

To (*name the plaintiff's attorney or the unrepresented plaintiff*):

I have received your request to waive service of a summons in this action along with a copy of the complaint, two copies of this waiver form, and a prepaid means of returning one signed copy of the form to you.

I, or the entity I represent, agree to save the expense of serving a summons and complaint in this case.

I understand that I, or the entity I represent, will keep all defenses or objections to the lawsuit, the court's jurisdiction, and the venue of the action, but that I waive any objections to the absence of a summons or of service.

I also understand that I, or the entity I represent, must file and serve an answer or a motion under Rule 12 within 60 days from _____, the date when this request was sent (or 90 days if it was sent outside the United States). If I fail to do so, a default judgment will be entered against me or the entity I represent.

Date: _____

_____
(Signature of the attorney
or unrepresented party)

_____
(Printed name)

_____
(Address)

_____
(E–mail address)

_____
(Telephone number)

(Attach the following)

Duty to Avoid Unnecessary Expenses of Serving a Summons

Rule 4 of the Federal Rules of Civil Procedure requires certain defendants to cooperate in saving unnecessary expenses of serving a summons and complaint. A defendant who is located in the United States and who fails to return a signed waiver of service requested by a plaintiff located in the United States will be required to pay the expenses of service, unless the defendant shows good cause for the failure.

"Good cause" does not include a belief that the lawsuit is groundless, or that it has been brought in an improper venue, or that the court has no jurisdiction over this matter or over the defendant or the defendant's property.

If the waiver is signed and returned, you can still make these and all other defenses and objections, but you cannot object to the absence of a summons or of service.

If you waive service, then you must, within the time specified on the waiver form, serve an answer or a motion under Rule 12 on the plaintiff and file a copy with the court. By signing and returning the waiver form, you are allowed more time to respond than if a summons had been served.

(Amended January 21, 1963, effective July 1, 1963; February 28, 1966, effective July 1, 1966; April 29, 1980, effective August 1, 1980; amended by Pub.L. 97-462, § 2, January 12, 1983, 96 Stat. 2527, effective 45 days after January 12, 1983; amended March 2, 1987, effective August 1, 1987; April 22, 1993, effective December 1, 1993; April 17, 2000, effective December 1, 2000; April 30, 2007, effective December 1, 2007; April 29, 2015, effective December 1, 2015; April 28, 2016, effective December 1, 2016, absent contrary Congressional action.)

RULE 4.1. SERVING OTHER PROCESS

(a) In General. Process—other than a summons under Rule 4 or a subpoena under Rule 45—must be served by a United States marshal or deputy marshal or by a person specially appointed for that purpose. It may be served anywhere within the territorial limits of the state where the district court is located and, if authorized by a federal statute, beyond those limits. Proof of service must be made under Rule 4(*l*).

(b) Enforcing Orders: Committing for Civil Contempt. An order committing a person for civil contempt of a decree or injunction issued to enforce federal law may be served and enforced in any district. Any other order in a civil-contempt proceeding may be served only in the state where the issuing court is located or elsewhere in the United States within 100 miles from where the order was issued.

(Adopted April 22, 1993, effective December 1, 1993; amended April 30, 2007, effective December 1, 2007.)

RULE 5. SERVING AND FILING PLEADINGS AND OTHER PAPERS

(a) Service: When Required.

(1) *In General.* Unless these rules provide otherwise, each of the following papers must be served on every party:

(A) an order stating that service is required;

(B) a pleading filed after the original complaint, unless the court orders otherwise under Rule 5(c) because there are numerous defendants;

(C) a discovery paper required to be served on a party, unless the court orders otherwise;

(D) a written motion, except one that may be heard ex parte; and

(E) a written notice, appearance, demand, or offer of judgment, or any similar paper.

(2) *If a Party Fails to Appear.* No service is required on a party who is in default for failing to appear. But a pleading that asserts a new claim for relief against such a party must be served on that party under Rule 4.

(3) *Seizing Property.* If an action is begun by seizing property and no person is or need be named as a defendant, any service required before the filing of an appearance, answer, or claim must be made on the person who had custody or possession of the property when it was seized.

(b) Service: How Made.

(1) *Serving an Attorney.* If a party is represented by an attorney, service under this rule must be made on the attorney unless the court orders service on the party.

(2) *Service in General.* A paper is served under this rule by:

(A) handing it to the person;

(B) leaving it:

(i) at the person's office with a clerk or other person in charge or, if no one is in charge, in a conspicuous place in the office; or

(ii) if the person has no office or the office is closed, at the person's dwelling or usual place of abode with someone of suitable age and discretion who resides there;

(C) mailing it to the person's last known address—in which event service is complete upon mailing;

(D) leaving it with the court clerk if the person has no known address;

(E) sending it by electronic means if the person consented in writing—in which event service is complete upon transmission, but is not effective if the serving party learns that it did not reach the person to be served; or

(F) delivering it by any other means that the person consented to in writing—in which event service is complete when the person making service delivers it to the agency designated to make delivery.

(3) *Using Court Facilities.* If a local rule so authorizes, a party may use the court's transmission facilities to make service under Rule 5(b)(2)(E).

(c) Serving Numerous Defendants.

(1) *In General.* If an action involves an unusually large number of defendants, the court may, on motion or on its own, order that:

(A) defendants' pleadings and replies to them need not be served on other defendants;

(B) any crossclaim, counterclaim, avoidance, or affirmative defense in those pleadings and replies to them will be treated as denied or avoided by all other parties; and

(C) filing any such pleading and serving it on the plaintiff constitutes notice of the pleading to all parties.

(2) *Notifying Parties.* A copy of every such order must be served on the parties as the court directs.

(d) Filing.

(1) *Required Filings; Certificate of Service.* Any paper after the complaint that is required to be served—together with a certificate of service—must be filed within a reasonable time after service. But disclosures under Rule 26(a)(1) or (2) and the following discovery requests and responses must not be filed until they are used in the proceeding or the court orders filing: depositions, interrogatories, requests for documents or tangible things or to permit entry onto land, and requests for admission.

(2) *How Filing Is Made—In General.* A paper is filed by delivering it:

(A) to the clerk; or

(B) to a judge who agrees to accept it for filing, and who must then note the filing date on the paper and promptly send it to the clerk.

(3) *Electronic Filing, Signing, or Verification.* A court may, by local rule, allow papers to be filed, signed, or verified by electronic means that are consistent with any technical standards established by the Judicial Conference of the United States. A local rule may require electronic filing only if reasonable exceptions are allowed. A paper filed electronically in compliance with a local rule is a written paper for purposes of these rules.

(4) *Acceptance by the Clerk.* The clerk must not refuse to file a paper solely because it is not in the form prescribed by these rules or by a local rule or practice.

(Amended January 21, 1963, effective July 1, 1963; March 30, 1970, effective July 1, 1970; April 29, 1980, effective August 1, 1980; March 2, 1987, effective August 1, 1987; April 30, 1991, effective December 1, 1991; April 22, 1993, effective December 1, 1993; April 23, 1996, effective December 1, 1996; April 17, 2000, effective December 1, 2000; April 23, 2001, effective December 1, 2001; April 12, 2006, effective December 1, 2006; April 30, 2007, effective December 1, 2007.)

RULE 5.1. CONSTITUTIONAL CHALLENGE TO A STATUTE—NOTICE, CERTIFICATION, AND INTERVENTION

(a) Notice by a Party. A party that files a pleading, written motion, or other paper drawing into question the constitutionality of a federal or state statute must promptly:

(1) file a notice of constitutional question stating the question and identifying the paper that raises it, if:

(A) a federal statute is questioned and the parties do not include the United States, one of its agencies, or one of its officers or employees in an official capacity; or

(B) a state statute is questioned and the parties do not include the state, one of its agencies, or one of its officers or employees in an official capacity; and

(2) serve the notice and paper on the Attorney General of the United States if a federal statute is questioned—or on the state attorney general if a state statute is questioned—either by certified or registered mail or by sending it to an electronic address designated by the attorney general for this purpose.

(b) Certification by the Court. The court must, under 28 U.S.C. § 2403, certify to the appropriate attorney general that a statute has been questioned.

(c) Intervention; Final Decision on the Merits. Unless the court sets a later time, the attorney general may intervene within 60 days after the notice is filed or after the court certifies the challenge, whichever is earlier. Before the time to intervene expires, the court may reject the constitutional challenge, but may not enter a final judgment holding the statute unconstitutional.

(d) No Forfeiture. A party's failure to file and serve the notice, or the court's failure to certify, does not forfeit a constitutional claim or defense that is otherwise timely asserted.

(Adopted April 12, 2006, effective December 1, 2006; amended April 30, 2007, effective December 1, 2007.)

RULE 5.2. PRIVACY PROTECTION FOR FILINGS MADE WITH THE COURT

(a) Redacted Filings. Unless the court orders otherwise, in an electronic or paper filing with the court that contains an individual's social-security number, taxpayer-identification number, or birth date, the name of an individual known to be a minor, or a financial-account number, a party or nonparty making the filing may include only:

(1) the last four digits of the social-security number and taxpayer-identification number;

(2) the year of the individual's birth;

(3) the minor's initials; and

(4) the last four digits of the financial-account number.

(b) Exemptions from the Redaction Requirement. The redaction requirement does not apply to the following:

(1) a financial-account number that identifies the property allegedly subject to forfeiture in a forfeiture proceeding;

(2) the record of an administrative or agency proceeding;

(3) the official record of a state-court proceeding;

(4) the record of a court or tribunal, if that record was not subject to the redaction requirement when originally filed;

(5) a filing covered by Rule 5.2(c) or (d); and

(6) a pro se filing in an action brought under 28 U.S.C. §§ 2241, 2254, or 2255.

(c) Limitations on Remote Access to Electronic Files; Social–Security Appeals and Immigration Cases. Unless the court orders otherwise, in an action for benefits under the Social Security Act, and in an action or proceeding relating to an order of removal, to relief from removal, or to immigration benefits or detention, access to an electronic file is authorized as follows:

(1) the parties and their attorneys may have remote electronic access to any part of the case file, including the administrative record;

(2) any other person may have electronic access to the full record at the courthouse, but may have remote electronic access only to:

    (A) the docket maintained by the court; and

    (B) an opinion, order, judgment, or other disposition of the court, but not any other part of the case file or the administrative record.

(d) Filings Made Under Seal. The court may order that a filing be made under seal without redaction. The court may later unseal the filing or order the person who made the filing to file a redacted version for the public record.

(e) Protective Orders. For good cause, the court may by order in a case:

(1) require redaction of additional information; or

(2) limit or prohibit a nonparty's remote electronic access to a document filed with the court.

(f) Option for Additional Unredacted Filing Under Seal. A person making a redacted filing may also file an unredacted copy under seal. The court must retain the unredacted copy as part of the record.

(g) Option for Filing a Reference List. A filing that contains redacted information may be filed together with a reference list that identifies each item of redacted information and specifies an appropriate identifier that uniquely corresponds to each item listed. The list must be filed under seal and may be amended as of right. Any reference in the case to a listed identifier will be construed to refer to the corresponding item of information.

(h) Waiver of Protection of Identifiers. A person waives the protection of Rule 5.2(a) as to the person's own information by filing it without redaction and not under seal.

(Adopted April 30, 2007, effective December 1, 2007.)

RULE 6. COMPUTING AND EXTENDING TIME; TIME FOR MOTION PAPERS

(a) Computing Time. The following rules apply in computing any time period specified in these rules, in any local rule or court order, or in any statute that does not specify a method of computing time.

(1) *Period Stated in Days or a Longer Unit.* When the period is stated in days or a longer unit of time:

    (A) exclude the day of the event that triggers the period;

    (B) count every day, including intermediate Saturdays, Sundays, and legal holidays; and

    (C) include the last day of the period, but if the last day is a Saturday, Sunday, or legal holiday, the period continues to run until the end of the next day that is not a Saturday, Sunday, or legal holiday.

(2) *Period Stated in Hours.* When the period is stated in hours:

    (A) begin counting immediately on the occurrence of the event that triggers the period;

    (B) count every hour, including hours during intermediate Saturdays, Sundays, and legal holidays; and

    (C) if the period would end on a Saturday, Sunday, or legal holiday, the period continues to run until the same time on the next day that is not a Saturday, Sunday, or legal holiday.

(3) *Inaccessibility of the Clerk's Office.* Unless the court orders otherwise, if the clerk's office is inaccessible:

    (A) on the last day for filing under Rule 6(a)(1), then the time for filing is extended to the first accessible day that is not a Saturday, Sunday, or legal holiday; or

    (B) during the last hour for filing under Rule 6(a)(2), then the time for filing is extended to the same time on the first accessible day that is not a Saturday, Sunday, or legal holiday.

(4) *"Last Day" Defined.* Unless a different time is set by a statute, local rule, or court order, the last day ends:

    (A) for electronic filing, at midnight in the court's time zone; and

    (B) for filing by other means, when the clerk's office is scheduled to close.

(5) *"Next Day" Defined.* The "next day" is determined by continuing to count forward when the period is measured after an event and backward when measured before an event.

(6) *"Legal Holiday" Defined.* "Legal holiday" means:

(A) the day set aside by statute for observing New Year's Day, Martin Luther King Jr.'s Birthday, Washington's Birthday, Memorial Day, Independence Day, Labor Day, Columbus Day, Veterans' Day, Thanksgiving Day, or Christmas Day;

(B) any day declared a holiday by the President or Congress; and

(C) for periods that are measured after an event, any other day declared a holiday by the state where the district court is located.

(b) Extending Time.

(1) *In General.* When an act may or must be done within a specified time, the court may, for good cause, extend the time:

(A) with or without motion or notice if the court acts, or if a request is made, before the original time or its extension expires; or

(B) on motion made after the time has expired if the party failed to act because of excusable neglect.

(2) *Exceptions.* A court must not extend the time to act under Rules 50(b) and (d), 52(b), 59(b), (d), and (e), and 60(b).

(c) Motions, Notices of Hearing, and Affidavits.

(1) *In General.* A written motion and notice of the hearing must be served at least 14 days before the time specified for the hearing, with the following exceptions:

(A) when the motion may be heard ex parte;

(B) when these rules set a different time; or

(C) when a court order—which a party may, for good cause, apply for ex parte—sets a different time.

(2) *Supporting Affidavit.* Any affidavit supporting a motion must be served with the motion. Except as Rule 59(c) provides otherwise, any opposing affidavit must be served at least 7 days before the hearing, unless the court permits service at another time.

[Text of subdivision (d) effective until December 1, 2016, absent contrary Congressional action.]

(d) Additional Time After Certain Kinds of Service. When a party may or must act within a specified time after service and service is made under Rule 5(b)(2)(C), (D), (E), or (F), 3 days are added after the period would otherwise expire under Rule 6(a).

[Text of subdivision (d) effective December 1, 2016, absent contrary Congressional action.]

(d) Additional Time After Certain Kinds of Service. When a party may or must act within a specified time after being served and service is made under Rule 5(b)(2)(C) (mail), (D) (leaving with the clerk), or (F) (other means consented to), 3 days are added after the period would otherwise expire under Rule 6(a).

(Amended December 27, 1946, effective March 19, 1948; January 21, 1963, effective July 1, 1963; February 28, 1966, effective July 1, 1966; December 4, 1967, effective July 1, 1968; March 1, 1971, effective July 1, 1971; April 28, 1983, effective August 1, 1983; April 29, 1985, effective August 1, 1985; March 2, 1987, effective August 1, 1987; April 29, 1999, effective December 1, 1999; April 23, 2001, effective December 1, 2001; April 25, 2005, effective December 1, 2005; April 30, 2007, effective December 1, 2007; March 26, 2009, effective December 1, 2009; April 28, 2016, effective December 1, 2016, absent contrary Congressional action.)

TITLE III. PLEADINGS AND MOTIONS

RULE 7. PLEADINGS ALLOWED; FORM OF MOTIONS AND OTHER PAPERS

(a) Pleadings. Only these pleadings are allowed:

(1) a complaint;

(2) an answer to a complaint;

(3) an answer to a counterclaim designated as a counterclaim;

(4) an answer to a crossclaim;

(5) a third-party complaint;

(6) an answer to a third-party complaint; and

(7) if the court orders one, a reply to an answer.

(b) Motions and Other Papers.

(1) *In General.* A request for a court order must be made by motion. The motion must:

(A) be in writing unless made during a hearing or trial;

(B) state with particularity the grounds for seeking the order; and

(C) state the relief sought.

(2) *Form.* The rules governing captions and other matters of form in pleadings apply to motions and other papers.

(Amended December 27, 1946, effective March 19, 1948; January 21, 1963, effective July 1, 1963; April 28, 1983, effective August 1, 1983; April 30, 2007, effective December 1, 2007.)

RULE 7.1. DISCLOSURE STATEMENT

(a) Who Must File; Contents. A nongovernmental corporate party must file two copies of a disclosure statement that:

(1) identifies any parent corporation and any publicly held corporation owning 10% or more of its stock; or

(2) states that there is no such corporation.

(b) Time to File; Supplemental Filing. A party must:

(1) file the disclosure statement with its first appearance, pleading, petition, motion, response, or other request addressed to the court; and

(2) promptly file a supplemental statement if any required information changes.

(Adopted April 29, 2002, effective December 1, 2002; April 30, 2007, effective December 1, 2007.)

RULE 8. GENERAL RULES OF PLEADING

(a) Claim for Relief. A pleading that states a claim for relief must contain:

(1) a short and plain statement of the grounds for the court's jurisdiction, unless the court already has jurisdiction and the claim needs no new jurisdictional support;

(2) a short and plain statement of the claim showing that the pleader is entitled to relief; and

(3) a demand for the relief sought, which may include relief in the alternative or different types of relief.

(b) Defenses; Admissions and Denials.

(1) *In General.* In responding to a pleading, a party must:

  (A) state in short and plain terms its defenses to each claim asserted against it; and

  (B) admit or deny the allegations asserted against it by an opposing party.

(2) *Denials—Responding to the Substance.* A denial must fairly respond to the substance of the allegation.

(3) *General and Specific Denials.* A party that intends in good faith to deny all the allegations of a pleading—including the jurisdictional grounds—may do so by a general denial. A party that does not intend to deny all the allegations must either specifically deny designated allegations or generally deny all except those specifically admitted.

(4) *Denying Part of an Allegation.* A party that intends in good faith to deny only part of an allegation must admit the part that is true and deny the rest.

(5) *Lacking Knowledge or Information.* A party that lacks knowledge or information sufficient to form a belief about the truth of an allegation must so state, and the statement has the effect of a denial.

(6) *Effect of Failing to Deny.* An allegation—other than one relating to the amount of damages—is admitted if a responsive pleading is required and the allegation is not denied. If a responsive pleading is not required, an allegation is considered denied or avoided.

(c) Affirmative Defenses.

(1) *In General.* In responding to a pleading, a party must affirmatively state any avoidance or affirmative defense, including:

- accord and satisfaction;
- arbitration and award;
- assumption of risk;
- contributory negligence;
- duress;
- estoppel;
- failure of consideration;
- fraud;
- illegality;
- injury by fellow servant;
- laches;
- license;
- payment;
- release;
- res judicata;
- statute of frauds;
- statute of limitations; and
- waiver.

(2) *Mistaken Designation.* If a party mistakenly designates a defense as a counterclaim, or a counterclaim as a defense, the court must, if justice requires, treat the pleading as though it were correctly designated, and may impose terms for doing so.

(d) Pleading to Be Concise and Direct; Alternative Statements; Inconsistency.

(1) *In General.* Each allegation must be simple, concise, and direct. No technical form is required.

(2) *Alternative Statements of a Claim or Defense.* A party may set out 2 or more statements of a claim or defense alternatively or hypothetically, either in a single count or defense or in separate ones. If a party makes alternative statements, the pleading is sufficient if any one of them is sufficient.

(3) *Inconsistent Claims or Defenses.* A party may state as many separate claims or defenses as it has, regardless of consistency.

(e) Construing Pleadings. Pleadings must be construed so as to do justice.

(Amended February 28, 1966, effective July 1, 1966; March 2, 1987, effective August 1, 1987; April 30, 2007, effective December 1, 2007; April 28, 2010, effective December 1, 2010.)

RULE 9.   PLEADING SPECIAL MATTERS

(a) Capacity or Authority to Sue; Legal Existence.

(1) *In General.* Except when required to show that the court has jurisdiction, a pleading need not allege:

(A) a party's capacity to sue or be sued;

(B) a party's authority to sue or be sued in a representative capacity; or

(C) the legal existence of an organized association of persons that is made a party.

(2) *Raising Those Issues.* To raise any of those issues, a party must do so by a specific denial, which must state any supporting facts that are peculiarly within the party's knowledge.

(b) Fraud or Mistake; Conditions of Mind. In alleging fraud or mistake, a party must state with particularity the circumstances constituting fraud or mistake. Malice, intent, knowledge, and other conditions of a person's mind may be alleged generally.

(c) Conditions Precedent. In pleading conditions precedent, it suffices to allege generally that all conditions precedent have occurred or been performed. But when denying that a condition precedent has occurred or been performed, a party must do so with particularity.

(d) Official Document or Act. In pleading an official document or official act, it suffices to allege that the document was legally issued or the act legally done.

(e) Judgment. In pleading a judgment or decision of a domestic or foreign court, a judicial or quasi-judicial tribunal, or a board or officer, it suffices to plead the judgment or decision without showing jurisdiction to render it.

(f) Time and Place. An allegation of time or place is material when testing the sufficiency of a pleading.

(g) Special Damages. If an item of special damage is claimed, it must be specifically stated.

(h) Admiralty or Maritime Claim.

(1) *How Designated.* If a claim for relief is within the admiralty or maritime jurisdiction and also within the court's subject-matter jurisdiction on some other ground, the pleading may designate the claim as an admiralty or maritime claim for purposes of Rules 14(c), 38(e), and 82 and the Supplemental Rules for Admiralty or Maritime Claims and Asset Forfeiture Actions. A claim cognizable only in the admiralty or maritime jurisdiction is an admiralty or maritime claim for those purposes, whether or not so designated.

(2) *Designation for Appeal.* A case that includes an admiralty or maritime claim within this subdivision (h) is an admiralty case within 28 U.S.C. § 1292(a)(3).

(Amended February 28, 1966, effective July 1, 1966; December 4, 1967, effective July 1, 1968; March 30, 1970, effective July 1, 1970; March 2, 1987, effective August 1, 1987; April 11, 1997, effective December 1, 1997; April 12, 2006, effective December 1, 2006; April 30, 2007, effective December 1, 2007.)

RULE 10.   FORM OF PLEADINGS

(a) Caption; Names of Parties. Every pleading must have a caption with the court's name, a title, a file number, and a Rule 7(a) designation. The title of the complaint must name all the parties; the title of other pleadings, after naming the first party on each side, may refer generally to other parties.

(b) Paragraphs; Separate Statements. A party must state its claims or defenses in numbered paragraphs, each limited as far as practicable to a single set of circumstances. A later pleading may refer by number to a paragraph in an earlier pleading. If doing so would promote clarity, each claim founded on a separate transaction or occurrence—and each defense other than a denial—must be stated in a separate count or defense.

(c) Adoption by Reference; Exhibits. A statement in a pleading may be adopted by reference elsewhere in the same pleading or in any other pleading or motion. A copy of a written instrument that is an exhibit to a pleading is a part of the pleading for all purposes.

(Amended April 30, 2007, effective December 1, 2007.)

RULE 11. SIGNING PLEADINGS, MOTIONS, AND OTHER PAPERS; REPRESENTATIONS TO THE COURT; SANCTIONS

(a) Signature. Every pleading, written motion, and other paper must be signed by at least one attorney of record in the attorney's name—or by a party personally if the party is unrepresented. The paper must state the signer's address, e-mail address, and telephone number. Unless a rule or statute specifically states otherwise, a pleading need not be verified or accompanied by an affidavit. The court must strike an unsigned paper unless the omission is promptly corrected after being called to the attorney's or party's attention.

(b) Representations to the Court. By presenting to the court a pleading, written motion, or other paper—whether by signing, filing, submitting, or later advocating it—an attorney or unrepresented party certifies that to the best of the person's knowledge, information, and belief, formed after an inquiry reasonable under the circumstances:

(1) it is not being presented for any improper purpose, such as to harass, cause unnecessary delay, or needlessly increase the cost of litigation;

(2) the claims, defenses, and other legal contentions are warranted by existing law or by a nonfrivolous argument for extending, modifying, or reversing existing law or for establishing new law;

(3) the factual contentions have evidentiary support or, if specifically so identified, will likely have evidentiary support after a reasonable opportunity for further investigation or discovery; and

(4) the denials of factual contentions are warranted on the evidence or, if specifically so identified, are reasonably based on belief or a lack of information.

(c) Sanctions.

(1) *In General.* If, after notice and a reasonable opportunity to respond, the court determines that Rule 11(b) has been violated, the court may impose an appropriate sanction on any attorney, law firm, or party that violated the rule or is responsible for the violation. Absent exceptional circumstances, a law firm must be held jointly responsible for a violation committed by its partner, associate, or employee.

(2) *Motion for Sanctions.* A motion for sanctions must be made separately from any other motion and must describe the specific conduct that allegedly violates Rule 11(b). The motion must be served under Rule 5, but it must not be filed or be presented to the court if the challenged paper, claim, defense, contention, or denial is withdrawn or appropriately corrected within 21 days after service or within another time the court sets. If warranted, the court may award to the prevailing party the reasonable expenses, including attorney's fees, incurred for the motion.

(3) *On the Court's Initiative.* On its own, the court may order an attorney, law firm, or party to show cause why conduct specifically described in the order has not violated Rule 11(b).

(4) *Nature of a Sanction.* A sanction imposed under this rule must be limited to what suffices to deter repetition of the conduct or comparable conduct by others similarly situated. The sanc-

tion may include nonmonetary directives; an order to pay a penalty into court; or, if imposed on motion and warranted for effective deterrence, an order directing payment to the movant of part or all of the reasonable attorney's fees and other expenses directly resulting from the violation.

(5) *Limitations on Monetary Sanctions.* The court must not impose a monetary sanction:

(A) against a represented party for violating Rule 11(b)(2); or

(B) on its own, unless it issued the show-cause order under Rule 11(c)(3) before voluntary dismissal or settlement of the claims made by or against the party that is, or whose attorneys are, to be sanctioned.

(6) *Requirements for an Order.* An order imposing a sanction must describe the sanctioned conduct and explain the basis for the sanction.

(d) Inapplicability to Discovery. This rule does not apply to disclosures and discovery requests, responses, objections, and motions under Rules 26 through 37.

(Amended April 28, 1983, effective August 1, 1983; March 2, 1987, effective August 1, 1987; April 22, 1993, effective December 1, 1993; April 30, 2007, effective December 1, 2007.)

RULE 12. DEFENSES AND OBJECTIONS: WHEN AND HOW PRESENTED; MOTION FOR JUDGMENT ON THE PLEADINGS; CONSOLIDATING MOTIONS; WAIVING DEFENSES; PRETRIAL HEARING

(a) Time to Serve a Responsive Pleading.

(1) *In General.* Unless another time is specified by this rule or a federal statute, the time for serving a responsive pleading is as follows:

(A) A defendant must serve an answer:

(i) within 21 days after being served with the summons and complaint; or

(ii) if it has timely waived service under Rule 4(d), within 60 days after the request for a waiver was sent, or within 90 days after it was sent to the defendant outside any judicial district of the United States.

(B) A party must serve an answer to a counterclaim or crossclaim within 21 days after being served with the pleading that states the counterclaim or crossclaim.

(C) A party must serve a reply to an answer within 21 days after being served with an order to reply, unless the order specifies a different time.

(2) *United States and Its Agencies, Officers, or Employees Sued in an Official Capacity.* The United States, a United States agency, or a United States officer or employee sued only in an official capacity must serve an answer to a complaint, counterclaim, or crossclaim within 60 days after service on the United States attorney.

(3) *United States Officers or Employees Sued in an Individual Capacity.* A United States officer or employee sued in an individual capacity for an act or omission occurring in connection with duties performed on the United States' behalf must serve an answer to a complaint, counterclaim, or crossclaim within 60 days after service on the officer or employee or service on the United States attorney, whichever is later.

(4) *Effect of a Motion.* Unless the court sets a different time, serving a motion under this rule alters these periods as follows:

(A) if the court denies the motion or postpones its disposition until trial, the responsive pleading must be served within 14 days after notice of the court's action; or

(B) if the court grants a motion for a more definite statement, the responsive pleading must be served within 14 days after the more definite statement is served.

(b) How to Present Defenses. Every defense to a claim for relief in any pleading must be asserted in the responsive pleading if one is required. But a party may assert the following defenses by motion:

(1) lack of subject-matter jurisdiction;

(2) lack of personal jurisdiction;

(3) improper venue;

(4) insufficient process;

(5) insufficient service of process;

(6) failure to state a claim upon which relief can be granted; and

(7) failure to join a party under Rule 19.

A motion asserting any of these defenses must be made before pleading if a responsive pleading is allowed. If a pleading sets out a claim for relief that does not require a responsive pleading, an opposing party may assert at trial any defense to that claim. No defense or objection is waived by joining it with one or more other defenses or objections in a responsive pleading or in a motion.

(c) Motion for Judgment on the Pleadings. After the pleadings are closed—but early enough not to delay trial—a party may move for judgment on the pleadings.

(d) Result of Presenting Matters Outside the Pleadings. If, on a motion under Rule 12(b)(6) or 12(c), matters outside the pleadings are presented to and not excluded by the court, the motion must be treated as one for summary judgment under Rule 56. All parties must be given a reasonable opportunity to present all the material that is pertinent to the motion.

(e) Motion for a More Definite Statement. A party may move for a more definite statement of a pleading to which a responsive pleading is allowed but which is so vague or ambiguous that the party cannot reasonably prepare a response. The motion must be made before filing a responsive pleading and must point out the defects complained of and the details desired. If the court orders a more definite statement and the order is not obeyed within 14 days after notice of the order or within the time the court sets, the court may strike the pleading or issue any other appropriate order.

(f) Motion to Strike. The court may strike from a pleading an insufficient defense or any redundant, immaterial, impertinent, or scandalous matter. The court may act:

(1) on its own; or

(2) on motion made by a party either before responding to the pleading or, if a response is not allowed, within 21 days after being served with the pleading.

(g) Joining Motions.

(1) *Right to Join.* A motion under this rule may be joined with any other motion allowed by this rule.

(2) *Limitation on Further Motions.* Except as provided in Rule 12(h)(2) or (3), a party that makes a motion under this rule must not make another motion under this rule raising a defense or objection that was available to the party but omitted from its earlier motion.

(h) Waiving and Preserving Certain Defenses.

(1) *When Some Are Waived.* A party waives any defense listed in Rule 12(b)(2)-(5) by:

(A) omitting it from a motion in the circumstances described in Rule 12(g)(2); or

(B) failing to either:

(i) make it by motion under this rule; or

(ii) include it in a responsive pleading or in an amendment allowed by Rule 15(a)(1) as a matter of course.

(2) *When to Raise Others.* Failure to state a claim upon which relief can be granted, to join a person required by Rule 19(b), or to state a legal defense to a claim may be raised:

(A) in any pleading allowed or ordered under Rule 7(a);

(B) by a motion under Rule 12(c); or

(C) at trial.

(3) *Lack of Subject–Matter Jurisdiction.* If the court determines at any time that it lacks subject-matter jurisdiction, the court must dismiss the action.

(i) Hearing Before Trial. If a party so moves, any defense listed in Rule 12(b)(1)-(7)—whether made in a pleading or by motion—and a motion under Rule 12(c) must be heard and decided before trial unless the court orders a deferral until trial.

(Amended December 27, 1946, effective March 19, 1948; January 21, 1963, effective July 1, 1963; February 28, 1966, effective July 1, 1966; March 2, 1987, effective August 1, 1987; April 22, 1993, effective December 1, 1993; April 17, 2000, effective December 1, 2000; April 30, 2007, effective December 1, 2007; March 26, 2009, effective December 1, 2009.)

RULE 13.   COUNTERCLAIM AND CROSSCLAIM

(a) Compulsory Counterclaim.

(1) *In General.* A pleading must state as a counterclaim any claim that—at the time of its service—the pleader has against an opposing party if the claim:

(A) arises out of the transaction or occurrence that is the subject matter of the opposing party's claim; and

(B) does not require adding another party over whom the court cannot acquire jurisdiction.

(2) *Exceptions.* The pleader need not state the claim if:

(A) when the action was commenced, the claim was the subject of another pending action; or

(B) the opposing party sued on its claim by attachment or other process that did not establish personal jurisdiction over the pleader on that claim, and the pleader does not assert any counterclaim under this rule.

(b) Permissive Counterclaim. A pleading may state as a counterclaim against an opposing party any claim that is not compulsory.

(c) Relief Sought in a Counterclaim. A counterclaim need not diminish or defeat the recovery sought by the opposing party. It may request relief that exceeds in amount or differs in kind from the relief sought by the opposing party.

(d) Counterclaim Against the United States. These rules do not expand the right to assert a counterclaim—or to claim a credit—against the United States or a United States officer or agency.

(e) Counterclaim Maturing or Acquired After Pleading. The court may permit a party to file a supplemental pleading asserting a counterclaim that matured or was acquired by the party after serving an earlier pleading.

(f) [Abrogated]

(g) Crossclaim Against a Coparty. A pleading may state as a crossclaim any claim by one party against a coparty if the claim arises out of the transaction or occurrence that is the subject matter of the original action or of a counterclaim, or if the claim relates to any property that is the subject matter of the original action. The crossclaim may include a claim that the coparty is or may be liable to the cross-claimant for all or part of a claim asserted in the action against the cross-claimant.

(h) Joining Additional Parties. Rules 19 and 20 govern the addition of a person as a party to a counterclaim or crossclaim.

(i) Separate Trials; Separate Judgments. If the court orders separate trials under Rule 42(b), it may enter judgment on a counterclaim or crossclaim under Rule 54(b) when it has jurisdiction to do so, even if the opposing party's claims have been dismissed or otherwise resolved.

(Amended December 27, 1946, effective March 19, 1948; January 21, 1963, effective July 1, 1963; February 28, 1966, effective July 1, 1966; March 2, 1987, effective August 1, 1987; April 30, 2007, effective December 1, 2007; March 26, 2009, effective December 1, 2009.)

RULE 14.   THIRD–PARTY PRACTICE

(a) When a Defending Party May Bring in a Third Party.

(1) *Timing of the Summons and Complaint.* A defending party may, as third-party plaintiff, serve a summons and complaint on a nonparty who is or may be liable to it for all or part of the claim against it. But the third-party plaintiff must, by motion, obtain the court's leave if it files the third-party complaint more than 14 days after serving its original answer.

(2) *Third–Party Defendant's Claims and Defenses.* The person served with the summons and third-party complaint—the "third-party defendant":

(A) must assert any defense against the third-party plaintiff's claim under Rule 12;

(B) must assert any counterclaim against the third-party plaintiff under Rule 13(a), and may assert any counterclaim against the third-party plaintiff under Rule 13(b) or any crossclaim against another third-party defendant under Rule 13(g);

(C) may assert against the plaintiff any defense that the third-party plaintiff has to the plaintiff's claim; and

(D) may also assert against the plaintiff any claim arising out of the transaction or occurrence that is the subject matter of the plaintiff's claim against the third-party plaintiff.

(3) **Plaintiff's Claims Against a Third–Party Defendant.** The plaintiff may assert against the third-party defendant any claim arising out of the transaction or occurrence that is the subject matter of the plaintiff's claim against the third-party plaintiff. The third-party defendant must then assert any defense under Rule 12 and any counterclaim under Rule 13(a), and may assert any counterclaim under Rule 13(b) or any cross-claim under Rule 13(g).

(4) **Motion to Strike, Sever, or Try Separately.** Any party may move to strike the third-party claim, to sever it, or to try it separately.

(5) **Third–Party Defendant's Claim Against a Nonparty.** A third-party defendant may proceed under this rule against a nonparty who is or may be liable to the third-party defendant for all or part of any claim against it.

(6) **Third–Party Complaint In Rem.** If it is within the admiralty or maritime jurisdiction, a third-party complaint may be in rem. In that event, a reference in this rule to the "summons" includes the warrant of arrest, and a reference to the defendant or third-party plaintiff includes, when appropriate, a person who asserts a right under Supplemental Rule C(6)(a)(i) in the property arrested.

(b) **When a Plaintiff May Bring in a Third Party.** When a claim is asserted against a plaintiff, the plaintiff may bring in a third party if this rule would allow a defendant to do so.

(c) **Admiralty or Maritime Claim.**

(1) **Scope of Impleader.** If a plaintiff asserts an admiralty or maritime claim under Rule 9(h), the defendant or a person who asserts a right under Supplemental Rule C(6)(a)(i) may, as a third-party plaintiff, bring in a third-party defendant who may be wholly or partly liable— either to the plaintiff or to the third-party plaintiff—for remedy over, contribution, or otherwise on account of the same transaction, occurrence, or series of transactions or occurrences.

(2) **Defending Against a Demand for Judgment for the Plaintiff.** The third-party plaintiff may demand judgment in the plaintiff's favor against the third-party defendant. In that event, the third-party defendant must defend under Rule 12 against the plaintiff's claim as well as the third-party plaintiff's claim; and the action pro-

ceeds as if the plaintiff had sued both the third-party defendant and the third-party plaintiff.

(Amended December 27, 1946, effective March 19, 1948; January 21, 1963, effective July 1, 1963; February 28, 1966, effective July 1, 1966; March 2, 1987, effective August 1, 1987; April 17, 2000, effective December 1, 2000; April 12, 2006, effective December 1, 2006; April 30, 2007, effective December 1, 2007; March 26, 2009, effective December 1, 2009.)

RULE 15. AMENDED AND SUPPLEMENTAL PLEADINGS

(a) **Amendments Before Trial.**

(1) **Amending as a Matter of Course.** A party may amend its pleading once as a matter of course within:

(A) 21 days after serving it, or

(B) if the pleading is one to which a responsive pleading is required, 21 days after service of a responsive pleading or 21 days after service of a motion under Rule 12(b), (e), or (f), whichever is earlier.

(2) **Other Amendments.** In all other cases, a party may amend its pleading only with the opposing party's written consent or the court's leave. The court should freely give leave when justice so requires.

(3) **Time to Respond.** Unless the court orders otherwise, any required response to an amended pleading must be made within the time remaining to respond to the original pleading or within 14 days after service of the amended pleading, whichever is later.

(b) **Amendments During and After Trial.**

(1) **Based on an Objection at Trial.** If, at trial, a party objects that evidence is not within the issues raised in the pleadings, the court may permit the pleadings to be amended. The court should freely permit an amendment when doing so will aid in presenting the merits and the objecting party fails to satisfy the court that the evidence would prejudice that party's action or defense on the merits. The court may grant a continuance to enable the objecting party to meet the evidence.

(2) **For Issues Tried by Consent.** When an issue not raised by the pleadings is tried by the parties' express or implied consent, it must be treated in all respects as if raised in the pleadings. A party may move—at any time, even after judgment—to amend the pleadings to conform them to the evidence and to raise an unpleaded issue. But failure to amend does not affect the result of the trial of that issue.

(c) Relation Back of Amendments.

 (1) *When an Amendment Relates Back.* An amendment to a pleading relates back to the date of the original pleading when:

  (A) the law that provides the applicable statute of limitations allows relation back;

  (B) the amendment asserts a claim or defense that arose out of the conduct, transaction, or occurrence set out—or attempted to be set out—in the original pleading; or

  (C) the amendment changes the party or the naming of the party against whom a claim is asserted, if Rule 15(c)(1)(B) is satisfied and if, within the period provided by Rule 4(m) for serving the summons and complaint, the party to be brought in by amendment:

   (i) received such notice of the action that it will not be prejudiced in defending on the merits; and

   (ii) knew or should have known that the action would have been brought against it, but for a mistake concerning the proper party's identity.

 (2) *Notice to the United States.* When the United States or a United States officer or agency is added as a defendant by amendment, the notice requirements of Rule 15(c)(1)(C)(i) and (ii) are satisfied if, during the stated period, process was delivered or mailed to the United States attorney or the United States attorney's designee, to the Attorney General of the United States, or to the officer or agency.

(d) Supplemental Pleadings. On motion and reasonable notice, the court may, on just terms, permit a party to serve a supplemental pleading setting out any transaction, occurrence, or event that happened after the date of the pleading to be supplemented. The court may permit supplementation even though the original pleading is defective in stating a claim or defense. The court may order that the opposing party plead to the supplemental pleading within a specified time.

(Amended January 21, 1963, effective July 1, 1963; February 28, 1966, effective July 1, 1966; March 2, 1987, effective August 1, 1987; April 30, 1991, effective December 1, 1991; amended by Pub.L. 102–198, § 11, December 9, 1991, 105 Stat. 1626; amended April 22, 1993, effective December 1, 1993; April 30, 2007, effective December 1, 2007; March 26, 2009, effective December 1, 2009.)

RULE 16. PRETRIAL CONFERENCES; SCHEDULING; MANAGEMENT

(a) Purposes of a Pretrial Conference. In any action, the court may order the attorneys and any unrepresented parties to appear for one or more pretrial conferences for such purposes as:

 (1) expediting disposition of the action;

 (2) establishing early and continuing control so that the case will not be protracted because of lack of management;

 (3) discouraging wasteful pretrial activities;

 (4) improving the quality of the trial through more thorough preparation; and

 (5) facilitating settlement.

(b) Scheduling.

 (1) *Scheduling Order.* Except in categories of actions exempted by local rule, the district judge—or a magistrate judge when authorized by local rule—must issue a scheduling order:

  (A) after receiving the parties' report under Rule 26(f); or

  (B) after consulting with the parties' attorneys and any unrepresented parties at a scheduling conference.

 (2) *Time to Issue.* The judge must issue the scheduling order as soon as practicable, but unless the judge finds good cause for delay, the judge must issue it within the earlier of 90 days after any defendant has been served with the complaint or 60 days after any defendant has appeared.

 (3) *Contents of the Order.*

  (A) *Required Contents.* The scheduling order must limit the time to join other parties, amend the pleadings, complete discovery, and file motions.

  (B) *Permitted Contents.* The scheduling order may:

   (i) modify the timing of disclosures under Rules 26(a) and 26(e)(1);

   (ii) modify the extent of discovery;

   (iii) provide for disclosure, discovery, or preservation of electronically stored information;

   (iv) include any agreements the parties reach for asserting claims of privilege or of protection as trial-preparation material after information is produced, including agreements reached under Federal Rule of Evidence 502;

   (v) direct that before moving for an order relating to discovery, the movant must request a conference with the court;

   (vi) set dates for pretrial conferences and for trial; and

   (vii) include other appropriate matters.

 (4) *Modifying a Schedule.* A schedule may be modified only for good cause and with the judge's consent.

1

(c) Attendance and Matters for Consideration at a Pretrial Conference.

  (1) *Attendance.* A represented party must authorize at least one of its attorneys to make stipulations and admissions about all matters that can reasonably be anticipated for discussion at a pretrial conference. If appropriate, the court may require that a party or its representative be present or reasonably available by other means to consider possible settlement.

  (2) *Matters for Consideration.* At any pretrial conference, the court may consider and take appropriate action on the following matters:

    (A) formulating and simplifying the issues, and eliminating frivolous claims or defenses;

    (B) amending the pleadings if necessary or desirable;

    (C) obtaining admissions and stipulations about facts and documents to avoid unnecessary proof, and ruling in advance on the admissibility of evidence;

    (D) avoiding unnecessary proof and cumulative evidence, and limiting the use of testimony under Federal Rule of Evidence 702;

    (E) determining the appropriateness and timing of summary adjudication under Rule 56;

    (F) controlling and scheduling discovery, including orders affecting disclosures and discovery under Rule 26 and Rules 29 through 37;

    (G) identifying witnesses and documents, scheduling the filing and exchange of any pretrial briefs, and setting dates for further conferences and for trial;

    (H) referring matters to a magistrate judge or a master;

    (I) settling the case and using special procedures to assist in resolving the dispute when authorized by statute or local rule;

    (J) determining the form and content of the pretrial order;

    (K) disposing of pending motions;

    (L) adopting special procedures for managing potentially difficult or protracted actions that may involve complex issues, multiple parties, difficult legal questions, or unusual proof problems;

    (M) ordering a separate trial under Rule 42(b) of a claim, counterclaim, crossclaim, third-party claim, or particular issue;

    (N) ordering the presentation of evidence early in the trial on a manageable issue that might, on the evidence, be the basis for a judgment as a matter of law under Rule 50(a) or a judgment on partial findings under Rule 52(c);

    (O) establishing a reasonable limit on the time allowed to present evidence; and

    (P) facilitating in other ways the just, speedy, and inexpensive disposition of the action.

(d) Pretrial Orders. After any conference under this rule, the court should issue an order reciting the action taken. This order controls the course of the action unless the court modifies it.

(e) Final Pretrial Conference and Orders. The court may hold a final pretrial conference to formulate a trial plan, including a plan to facilitate the admission of evidence. The conference must be held as close to the start of trial as is reasonable, and must be attended by at least one attorney who will conduct the trial for each party and by any unrepresented party. The court may modify the order issued after a final pretrial conference only to prevent manifest injustice.

(f) Sanctions.

  (1) *In General.* On motion or on its own, the court may issue any just orders, including those authorized by Rule 37(b)(2)(A)(ii)-(vii), if a party or its attorney:

    (A) fails to appear at a scheduling or other pretrial conference;

    (B) is substantially unprepared to participate—or does not participate in good faith—in the conference; or

    (C) fails to obey a scheduling or other pretrial order.

  (2) *Imposing Fees and Costs.* Instead of or in addition to any other sanction, the court must order the party, its attorney, or both to pay the reasonable expenses—including attorney's fees—incurred because of any noncompliance with this rule, unless the noncompliance was substantially justified or other circumstances make an award of expenses unjust.

(Amended April 28, 1983, effective August 1, 1983; March 2, 1987, effective August 1, 1987; April 22, 1993, effective December 1, 1993; April 12, 2006, effective December 1, 2006; April 30, 2007, effective December 1, 2007; April 29, 2015, effective December 1, 2015.)

TITLE IV.   PARTIES

RULE 17.   PLAINTIFF AND DEFENDANT; CAPACITY; PUBLIC OFFICERS

(a) Real Party in Interest.

(1) *Designation in General.* An action must be prosecuted in the name of the real party in interest. The following may sue in their own names without joining the person for whose benefit the action is brought:

   (A) an executor;

   (B) an administrator;

   (C) a guardian;

   (D) a bailee;

   (E) a trustee of an express trust;

   (F) a party with whom or in whose name a contract has been made for another's benefit; and

   (G) a party authorized by statute.

(2) *Action in the Name of the United States for Another's Use or Benefit.* When a federal statute so provides, an action for another's use or benefit must be brought in the name of the United States.

(3) *Joinder of the Real Party in Interest.* The court may not dismiss an action for failure to prosecute in the name of the real party in interest until, after an objection, a reasonable time has been allowed for the real party in interest to ratify, join, or be substituted into the action. After ratification, joinder, or substitution, the action proceeds as if it had been originally commenced by the real party in interest.

(b) Capacity to Sue or Be Sued. Capacity to sue or be sued is determined as follows:

(1) for an individual who is not acting in a representative capacity, by the law of the individual's domicile;

(2) for a corporation, by the law under which it was organized; and

(3) for all other parties, by the law of the state where the court is located, except that:

   (A) a partnership or other unincorporated association with no such capacity under that state's law may sue or be sued in its common name to enforce a substantive right existing under the United States Constitution or laws; and

   (B) 28 U.S.C. §§ 754 and 959(a) govern the capacity of a receiver appointed by a United States court to sue or be sued in a United States court.

(c) Minor or Incompetent Person.

(1) *With a Representative.* The following representatives may sue or defend on behalf of a minor or an incompetent person:

   (A) a general guardian;

   (B) a committee;

   (C) a conservator; or

   (D) a like fiduciary.

(2) *Without a Representative.* A minor or an incompetent person who does not have a duly appointed representative may sue by a next friend or by a guardian ad litem. The court must appoint a guardian ad litem—or issue another appropriate order—to protect a minor or incompetent person who is unrepresented in an action.

(d) Public Officer's Title and Name. A public officer who sues or is sued in an official capacity may be designated by official title rather than by name, but the court may order that the officer's name be added.

(Amended December 27, 1946, effective March 19, 1948; December 29, 1948, effective October 20, 1949; February 28, 1966, effective July 1, 1966; March 2, 1987, effective August 1, 1987; April 25, 1988, effective August 1, 1988; amended by Pub.L. 100–690, Title VII, § 7049, November 18, 1988, 102 Stat. 4401 (although amendment by Pub.L. 100–690 could not be executed due to prior amendment by Court order which made the same change effective August 1, 1988); April 30, 2007, effective December 1, 2007.)

RULE 18.   JOINDER OF CLAIMS

(a) In General. A party asserting a claim, counterclaim, crossclaim, or third-party claim may join, as independent or alternative claims, as many claims as it has against an opposing party.

(b) Joinder of Contingent Claims. A party may join two claims even though one of them is contingent on the disposition of the other; but the court may grant relief only in accordance with the parties' relative substantive rights. In particular, a plaintiff may state a claim for money and a claim to set aside a conveyance that is fraudulent as to that plaintiff, without first obtaining a judgment for the money.

(Amended February 28, 1966, effective July 1, 1966; March 2, 1987, effective August 1, 1987; April 30, 2007, effective December 1, 2007.)

RULE 19.   REQUIRED JOINDER OF PARTIES

(a) Persons Required to Be Joined if Feasible.

(1) *Required Party.* A person who is subject to service of process and whose joinder will not

deprive the court of subject-matter jurisdiction must be joined as a party if:

(A) in that person's absence, the court cannot accord complete relief among existing parties; or

(B) that person claims an interest relating to the subject of the action and is so situated that disposing of the action in the person's absence may:

(i) as a practical matter impair or impede the person's ability to protect the interest; or

(ii) leave an existing party subject to a substantial risk of incurring double, multiple, or otherwise inconsistent obligations because of the interest.

(2) *Joinder by Court Order.* If a person has not been joined as required, the court must order that the person be made a party. A person who refuses to join as a plaintiff may be made either a defendant or, in a proper case, an involuntary plaintiff.

(3) *Venue.* If a joined party objects to venue and the joinder would make venue improper, the court must dismiss that party.

(b) **When Joinder Is Not Feasible.** If a person who is required to be joined if feasible cannot be joined, the court must determine whether, in equity and good conscience, the action should proceed among the existing parties or should be dismissed. The factors for the court to consider include:

(1) the extent to which a judgment rendered in the person's absence might prejudice that person or the existing parties;

(2) the extent to which any prejudice could be lessened or avoided by:

(A) protective provisions in the judgment;

(B) shaping the relief; or

(C) other measures;

(3) whether a judgment rendered in the person's absence would be adequate; and

(4) whether the plaintiff would have an adequate remedy if the action were dismissed for nonjoinder.

(c) **Pleading the Reasons for Nonjoinder.** When asserting a claim for relief, a party must state:

(1) the name, if known, of any person who is required to be joined if feasible but is not joined; and

(2) the reasons for not joining that person.

(d) **Exception for Class Actions.** This rule is subject to Rule 23.

(Amended February 28, 1966, effective July 1, 1966; March 2, 1987, effective August 1, 1987; April 30, 2007, effective December 1, 2007.)

RULE 20. PERMISSIVE JOINDER OF PARTIES

(a) **Persons Who May Join or Be Joined.**

(1) *Plaintiffs.* Persons may join in one action as plaintiffs if:

(A) they assert any right to relief jointly, severally, or in the alternative with respect to or arising out of the same transaction, occurrence, or series of transactions or occurrences; and

(B) any question of law or fact common to all plaintiffs will arise in the action.

(2) *Defendants.* Persons—as well as a vessel, cargo, or other property subject to admiralty process in rem—may be joined in one action as defendants if:

(A) any right to relief is asserted against them jointly, severally, or in the alternative with respect to or arising out of the same transaction, occurrence, or series of transactions or occurrences; and

(B) any question of law or fact common to all defendants will arise in the action.

(3) *Extent of Relief.* Neither a plaintiff nor a defendant need be interested in obtaining or defending against all the relief demanded. The court may grant judgment to one or more plaintiffs according to their rights, and against one or more defendants according to their liabilities.

(b) **Protective Measures.** The court may issue orders—including an order for separate trials—to protect a party against embarrassment, delay, expense, or other prejudice that arises from including a person against whom the party asserts no claim and who asserts no claim against the party.

(Amended February 28, 1966, effective July 1, 1966; March 2, 1987, effective August 1, 1987; April 30, 2007, effective December 1, 2007.)

RULE 21. MISJOINDER AND NONJOINDER OF PARTIES

Misjoinder of parties is not a ground for dismissing an action. On motion or on its own, the court may at any time, on just terms, add or drop a party. The court may also sever any claim against a party.

(Amended April 30, 2007, effective December 1, 2007.)

RULE 22. INTERPLEADER

(a) **Grounds.**

(1) *By a Plaintiff.* Persons with claims that may expose a plaintiff to double or multiple liability

may be joined as defendants and required to interplead. Joinder for interpleader is proper even though:

(A) the claims of the several claimants, or the titles on which their claims depend, lack a common origin or are adverse and independent rather than identical; or

(B) the plaintiff denies liability in whole or in part to any or all of the claimants.

(2) *By a Defendant.* A defendant exposed to similar liability may seek interpleader through a crossclaim or counterclaim.

(b) **Relation to Other Rules and Statutes.** This rule supplements—and does not limit—the joinder of parties allowed by Rule 20. The remedy this rule provides is in addition to—and does not supersede or limit—the remedy provided by 28 U.S.C. §§ 1335, 1397, and 2361. An action under those statutes must be conducted under these rules.

(Amended December 29, 1948, effective October 20, 1949; March 2, 1987, effective August 1, 1987; April 30, 2007, effective December 1, 2007.)

RULE 23. CLASS ACTIONS

(a) **Prerequisites.** One or more members of a class may sue or be sued as representative parties on behalf of all members only if:

(1) the class is so numerous that joinder of all members is impracticable;

(2) there are questions of law or fact common to the class;

(3) the claims or defenses of the representative parties are typical of the claims or defenses of the class; and

(4) the representative parties will fairly and adequately protect the interests of the class.

(b) **Types of Class Actions.** A class action may be maintained if Rule 23(a) is satisfied and if:

(1) prosecuting separate actions by or against individual class members would create a risk of:

(A) inconsistent or varying adjudications with respect to individual class members that would establish incompatible standards of conduct for the party opposing the class; or

(B) adjudications with respect to individual class members that, as a practical matter, would be dispositive of the interests of the other members not parties to the individual adjudications or would substantially impair or impede their ability to protect their interests;

(2) the party opposing the class has acted or refused to act on grounds that apply generally to the class, so that final injunctive relief or corresponding declaratory relief is appropriate respecting the class as a whole; or

(3) the court finds that the questions of law or fact common to class members predominate over any questions affecting only individual members, and that a class action is superior to other available methods for fairly and efficiently adjudicating the controversy. The matters pertinent to these findings include:

(A) the class members' interests in individually controlling the prosecution or defense of separate actions;

(B) the extent and nature of any litigation concerning the controversy already begun by or against class members;

(C) the desirability or undesirability of concentrating the litigation of the claims in the particular forum; and

(D) the likely difficulties in managing a class action.

(c) **Certification Order; Notice to Class Members; Judgment; Issues Classes; Subclasses.**

(1) *Certification Order.*

(A) *Time to Issue.* At an early practicable time after a person sues or is sued as a class representative, the court must determine by order whether to certify the action as a class action.

(B) *Defining the Class; Appointing Class Counsel.* An order that certifies a class action must define the class and the class claims, issues, or defenses, and must appoint class counsel under Rule 23(g).

(C) *Altering or Amending the Order.* An order that grants or denies class certification may be altered or amended before final judgment.

(2) *Notice.*

(A) *For (b)(1) or (b)(2) Classes.* For any class certified under Rule 23(b)(1) or (b)(2), the court may direct appropriate notice to the class.

(B) *For (b)(3) Classes.* For any class certified under Rule 23(b)(3), the court must direct to class members the best notice that is practicable under the circumstances, including individual notice to all members who can be identified through reasonable effort. The notice must clearly and concisely state in plain, easily understood language:

(i) the nature of the action;

(ii) the definition of the class certified;

(iii) the class claims, issues, or defenses;

(iv) that a class member may enter an appearance through an attorney if the member so desires;

(v) that the court will exclude from the class any member who requests exclusion;

(vi) the time and manner for requesting exclusion; and

(vii) the binding effect of a class judgment on members under Rule 23(c)(3).

(3) *Judgment.* Whether or not favorable to the class, the judgment in a class action must:

  (A) for any class certified under Rule 23(b)(1) or (b)(2), include and describe those whom the court finds to be class members; and

  (B) for any class certified under Rule 23(b)(3), include and specify or describe those to whom the Rule 23(c)(2) notice was directed, who have not requested exclusion, and whom the court finds to be class members.

(4) *Particular Issues.* When appropriate, an action may be brought or maintained as a class action with respect to particular issues.

(5) *Subclasses.* When appropriate, a class may be divided into subclasses that are each treated as a class under this rule.

(d) Conducting the Action.

(1) *In General.* In conducting an action under this rule, the court may issue orders that:

  (A) determine the course of proceedings or prescribe measures to prevent undue repetition or complication in presenting evidence or argument;

  (B) require—to protect class members and fairly conduct the action—giving appropriate notice to some or all class members of:

    (i) any step in the action;

    (ii) the proposed extent of the judgment; or

    (iii) the members' opportunity to signify whether they consider the representation fair and adequate, to intervene and present claims or defenses, or to otherwise come into the action;

  (C) impose conditions on the representative parties or on intervenors;

  (D) require that the pleadings be amended to eliminate allegations about representation of absent persons and that the action proceed accordingly; or

  (E) deal with similar procedural matters.

(2) *Combining and Amending Orders.* An order under Rule 23(d)(1) may be altered or amended from time to time and may be combined with an order under Rule 16.

(e) Settlement, Voluntary Dismissal, or Compromise. The claims, issues, or defenses of a certified class may be settled, voluntarily dismissed, or compromised only with the court's approval. The following procedures apply to a proposed settlement, voluntary dismissal, or compromise:

(1) The court must direct notice in a reasonable manner to all class members who would be bound by the proposal.

(2) If the proposal would bind class members, the court may approve it only after a hearing and on finding that it is fair, reasonable, and adequate.

(3) The parties seeking approval must file a statement identifying any agreement made in connection with the proposal.

(4) If the class action was previously certified under Rule 23(b)(3), the court may refuse to approve a settlement unless it affords a new opportunity to request exclusion to individual class members who had an earlier opportunity to request exclusion but did not do so.

(5) Any class member may object to the proposal if it requires court approval under this subdivision (e); the objection may be withdrawn only with the court's approval.

(f) Appeals. A court of appeals may permit an appeal from an order granting or denying class-action certification under this rule if a petition for permission to appeal is filed with the circuit clerk within 14 days after the order is entered. An appeal does not stay proceedings in the district court unless the district judge or the court of appeals so orders.

(g) Class Counsel.

(1) *Appointing Class Counsel.* Unless a statute provides otherwise, a court that certifies a class must appoint class counsel. In appointing class counsel, the court:

  (A) must consider:

    (i) the work counsel has done in identifying or investigating potential claims in the action;

    (ii) counsel's experience in handling class actions, other complex litigation, and the types of claims asserted in the action;

    (iii) counsel's knowledge of the applicable law; and

    (iv) the resources that counsel will commit to representing the class;

  (B) may consider any other matter pertinent to counsel's ability to fairly and adequately represent the interests of the class;

  (C) may order potential class counsel to provide information on any subject pertinent to the appointment and to propose terms for attorney's fees and nontaxable costs;

(D) may include in the appointing order provisions about the award of attorney's fees or nontaxable costs under Rule 23(h); and

(E) may make further orders in connection with the appointment.

(2) *Standard for Appointing Class Counsel.* When one applicant seeks appointment as class counsel, the court may appoint that applicant only if the applicant is adequate under Rule 23(g)(1) and (4). If more than one adequate applicant seeks appointment, the court must appoint the applicant best able to represent the interests of the class.

(3) *Interim Counsel.* The court may designate interim counsel to act on behalf of a putative class before determining whether to certify the action as a class action.

(4) *Duty of Class Counsel.* Class counsel must fairly and adequately represent the interests of the class.

(h) Attorney's Fees and Nontaxable Costs. In a certified class action, the court may award reasonable attorney's fees and nontaxable costs that are authorized by law or by the parties' agreement. The following procedures apply:

(1) A claim for an award must be made by motion under Rule 54(d)(2), subject to the provisions of this subdivision (h), at a time the court sets. Notice of the motion must be served on all parties and, for motions by class counsel, directed to class members in a reasonable manner.

(2) A class member, or a party from whom payment is sought, may object to the motion.

(3) The court may hold a hearing and must find the facts and state its legal conclusions under Rule 52(a).

(4) The court may refer issues related to the amount of the award to a special master or a magistrate judge, as provided in Rule 54(d)(2)(D).

(Amended February 28, 1966, effective July 1, 1966; March 2, 1987, effective August 1, 1987; April 24, 1998, effective December 1, 1998; March 27, 2003, effective December 1, 2003; April 30, 2007, effective December 1, 2007; March 26, 2009, effective December 1, 2009.)

RULE 23.1. DERIVATIVE ACTIONS

(a) Prerequisites. This rule applies when one or more shareholders or members of a corporation or an unincorporated association bring a derivative action to enforce a right that the corporation or association may properly assert but has failed to enforce. The derivative action may not be maintained if it appears that the plaintiff does not fairly and adequately represent the interests of shareholders or members who are similarly situated in enforcing the right of the corporation or association.

(b) Pleading Requirements. The complaint must be verified and must:

(1) allege that the plaintiff was a shareholder or member at the time of the transaction complained of, or that the plaintiff's share or membership later devolved on it by operation of law;

(2) allege that the action is not a collusive one to confer jurisdiction that the court would otherwise lack; and

(3) state with particularity:

(A) any effort by the plaintiff to obtain the desired action from the directors or comparable authority and, if necessary, from the shareholders or members; and

(B) the reasons for not obtaining the action or not making the effort.

(c) Settlement, Dismissal, and Compromise. A derivative action may be settled, voluntarily dismissed, or compromised only with the court's approval. Notice of a proposed settlement, voluntary dismissal, or compromise must be given to shareholders or members in the manner that the court orders.

(Adopted February 28, 1966, effective July 1, 1966; amended March 2, 1987, effective August 1, 1987; April 30, 2007, effective December 1, 2007.)

RULE 23.2. ACTIONS RELATING TO UNINCORPORATED ASSOCIATIONS

This rule applies to an action brought by or against the members of an unincorporated association as a class by naming certain members as representative parties. The action may be maintained only if it appears that those parties will fairly and adequately protect the interests of the association and its members. In conducting the action, the court may issue any appropriate orders corresponding with those in Rule 23(d), and the procedure for settlement, voluntary dismissal, or compromise must correspond with the procedure in Rule 23(e).

(Adopted February 28, 1966, effective July 1, 1966; amended April 30, 2007, effective December 1, 2007.)

RULE 24. INTERVENTION

(a) Intervention of Right. On timely motion, the court must permit anyone to intervene who:

(1) is given an unconditional right to intervene by a federal statute; or

(2) claims an interest relating to the property or transaction that is the subject of the action, and is so situated that disposing of the action may as a practical matter impair or impede the movant's ability to protect its interest, unless existing parties adequately represent that interest.

(b) Permissive Intervention.

(1) *In General.* On timely motion, the court may permit anyone to intervene who:

(A) is given a conditional right to intervene by a federal statute; or

(B) has a claim or defense that shares with the main action a common question of law or fact.

(2) *By a Government Officer or Agency.* On timely motion, the court may permit a federal or state governmental officer or agency to intervene if a party's claim or defense is based on:

(A) a statute or executive order administered by the officer or agency; or

(B) any regulation, order, requirement, or agreement issued or made under the statute or executive order.

(3) *Delay or Prejudice.* In exercising its discretion, the court must consider whether the intervention will unduly delay or prejudice the adjudication of the original parties' rights.

(c) Notice and Pleading Required. A motion to intervene must be served on the parties as provided in Rule 5. The motion must state the grounds for intervention and be accompanied by a pleading that sets out the claim or defense for which intervention is sought.

(Amended December 27, 1946, effective March 19, 1948; December 29, 1948, effective October 20, 1949; January 21, 1963, effective July 1, 1963; February 28, 1966, effective July 1, 1966; March 2, 1987, effective August 1, 1987; April 30, 1991, effective December 1, 1991; April 12, 2006, effective December 1, 2006; April 30, 2007, effective December 1, 2007.)

RULE 25. SUBSTITUTION OF PARTIES

(a) Death.

(1) *Substitution if the Claim Is Not Extinguished.* If a party dies and the claim is not extinguished, the court may order substitution of the proper party. A motion for substitution may be made by any party or by the decedent's successor or representative. If the motion is not made within 90 days after service of a statement noting the death, the action by or against the decedent must be dismissed.

(2) *Continuation Among the Remaining Parties.* After a party's death, if the right sought to be enforced survives only to or against the remaining parties, the action does not abate, but proceeds in favor of or against the remaining parties. The death should be noted on the record.

(3) *Service.* A motion to substitute, together with a notice of hearing, must be served on the parties as provided in Rule 5 and on nonparties as provided in Rule 4. A statement noting death must be served in the same manner. Service may be made in any judicial district.

(b) Incompetency. If a party becomes incompetent, the court may, on motion, permit the action to be continued by or against the party's representative. The motion must be served as provided in Rule 25(a)(3).

(c) Transfer of Interest. If an interest is transferred, the action may be continued by or against the original party unless the court, on motion, orders the transferee to be substituted in the action or joined with the original party. The motion must be served as provided in Rule 25(a)(3).

(d) Public Officers; Death or Separation from Office. An action does not abate when a public officer who is a party in an official capacity dies, resigns, or otherwise ceases to hold office while the action is pending. The officer's successor is automatically substituted as a party. Later proceedings should be in the substituted party's name, but any misnomer not affecting the parties' substantial rights must be disregarded. The court may order substitution at any time, but the absence of such an order does not affect the substitution.

(Amended December 29, 1948, effective October 20, 1949; April 17, 1961, effective July 19, 1961; January 21, 1963, effective July 1, 1963; March 2, 1987, effective August 1, 1987; April 30, 2007, effective December 1, 2007.)

TITLE V. DISCLOSURES AND DISCOVERY

RULE 26. DUTY TO DISCLOSE; GENERAL PROVISIONS GOVERNING DISCOVERY

(a) Required Disclosures.

(1) *Initial Disclosure.*

(A) *In General.* Except as exempted by Rule 26(a)(1)(B) or as otherwise stipulated or ordered by the court, a party must, without awaiting a discovery request, provide to the other parties:

(i) the name and, if known, the address and telephone number of each individual likely to have discoverable information—along with the subjects of that information—that the disclosing party may use to support its claims or defenses, unless the use would be solely for impeachment;

(ii) a copy—or a description by category and location—of all documents, electronically stored information, and tangible things that the disclosing party has in its possession, custody, or control and may use to support its claims or defenses, unless the use would be solely for impeachment;

(iii) a computation of each category of damages claimed by the disclosing party—who must also make available for inspection and copying as under Rule 34 the documents or other evidentiary material, unless privileged or protected from disclosure, on which each computation is based, including materials bearing on the nature and extent of injuries suffered; and

(iv) for inspection and copying as under Rule 34, any insurance agreement under which an insurance business may be liable to satisfy all or part of a possible judgment in the action or to indemnify or reimburse for payments made to satisfy the judgment.

(B) *Proceedings Exempt from Initial Disclosure.* The following proceedings are exempt from initial disclosure:

(i) an action for review on an administrative record;

(ii) a forfeiture action in rem arising from a federal statute;

(iii) a petition for habeas corpus or any other proceeding to challenge a criminal conviction or sentence;

(iv) an action brought without an attorney by a person in the custody of the United States, a state, or a state subdivision;

(v) an action to enforce or quash an administrative summons or subpoena;

(vi) an action by the United States to recover benefit payments;

(vii) an action by the United States to collect on a student loan guaranteed by the United States;

(viii) a proceeding ancillary to a proceeding in another court; and

(ix) an action to enforce an arbitration award.

(C) *Time for Initial Disclosures—In General.* A party must make the initial disclosures at or within 14 days after the parties' Rule 26(f) conference unless a different time is set by stipulation or court order, or unless a party

objects during the conference that initial disclosures are not appropriate in this action and states the objection in the proposed discovery plan. In ruling on the objection, the court must determine what disclosures, if any, are to be made and must set the time for disclosure.

(D) *Time for Initial Disclosures—For Parties Served or Joined Later.* A party that is first served or otherwise joined after the Rule 26(f) conference must make the initial disclosures within 30 days after being served or joined, unless a different time is set by stipulation or court order.

(E) *Basis for Initial Disclosure; Unacceptable Excuses.* A party must make its initial disclosures based on the information then reasonably available to it. A party is not excused from making its disclosures because it has not fully investigated the case or because it challenges the sufficiency of another party's disclosures or because another party has not made its disclosures.

(2) *Disclosure of Expert Testimony.*

(A) *In General.* In addition to the disclosures required by Rule 26(a)(1), a party must disclose to the other parties the identity of any witness it may use at trial to present evidence under Federal Rule of Evidence 702, 703, or 705.

(B) *Witnesses Who Must Provide a Written Report.* Unless otherwise stipulated or ordered by the court, this disclosure must be accompanied by a written report—prepared and signed by the witness—if the witness is one retained or specially employed to provide expert testimony in the case or one whose duties as the party's employee regularly involve giving expert testimony. The report must contain:

(i) a complete statement of all opinions the witness will express and the basis and reasons for them;

(ii) the facts or data considered by the witness in forming them;

(iii) any exhibits that will be used to summarize or support them;

(iv) the witness's qualifications, including a list of all publications authored in the previous 10 years;

(v) a list of all other cases in which, during the previous 4 years, the witness testified as an expert at trial or by deposition; and

(vi) a statement of the compensation to be paid for the study and testimony in the case.

(C) *Witnesses Who Do Not Provide a Written Report.* Unless otherwise stipulated or ordered by the court, if the witness is not required to provide a written report, this disclosure must state:

  (i) the subject matter on which the witness is expected to present evidence under Federal Rule of Evidence 702, 703, or 705; and

  (ii) a summary of the facts and opinions to which the witness is expected to testify.

(D) *Time to Disclose Expert Testimony.* A party must make these disclosures at the times and in the sequence that the court orders. Absent a stipulation or a court order, the disclosures must be made:

  (i) at least 90 days before the date set for trial or for the case to be ready for trial; or

  (ii) if the evidence is intended solely to contradict or rebut evidence on the same subject matter identified by another party under Rule 26(a)(2)(B) or (C), within 30 days after the other party's disclosure.

(E) *Supplementing the Disclosure.* The parties must supplement these disclosures when required under Rule 26(e).

(3) *Pretrial Disclosures.*

(A) *In General.* In addition to the disclosures required by Rule 26(a)(1) and (2), a party must provide to the other parties and promptly file the following information about the evidence that it may present at trial other than solely for impeachment:

  (i) the name and, if not previously provided, the address and telephone number of each witness—separately identifying those the party expects to present and those it may call if the need arises;

  (ii) the designation of those witnesses whose testimony the party expects to present by deposition and, if not taken stenographically, a transcript of the pertinent parts of the deposition; and

  (iii) an identification of each document or other exhibit, including summaries of other evidence—separately identifying those items the party expects to offer and those it may offer if the need arises.

(B) *Time for Pretrial Disclosures; Objections.* Unless the court orders otherwise, these disclosures must be made at least 30 days before trial. Within 14 days after they are made, unless the court sets a different time, a party may serve and promptly file a list of the following objections: any objections to the use under Rule 32(a) of a deposition designated by another party under Rule 26(a)(3)(A)(ii); and any objection, together with the grounds for it, that may be made to the admissibility of materials identified under Rule 26(a)(3)(A)(iii). An objection not so made—except for one under Federal Rule of Evidence 402 or 403—is waived unless excused by the court for good cause.

(4) *Form of Disclosures.* Unless the court orders otherwise, all disclosures under Rule 26(a) must be in writing, signed, and served.

(b) Discovery Scope and Limits.

(1) *Scope in General.* Unless otherwise limited by court order, the scope of discovery is as follows: Parties may obtain discovery regarding any nonprivileged matter that is relevant to any party's claim or defense and proportional to the needs of the case, considering the importance of the issues at stake in the action, the amount in controversy, the parties' relative access to relevant information, the parties' resources, the importance of the discovery in resolving the issues, and whether the burden or expense of the proposed discovery outweighs its likely benefit. Information within this scope of discovery need not be admissible in evidence to be discoverable.

(2) *Limitations on Frequency and Extent.*

(A) *When Permitted.* By order, the court may alter the limits in these rules on the number of depositions and interrogatories or on the length of depositions under Rule 30. By order or local rule, the court may also limit the number of requests under Rule 36.

(B) *Specific Limitations on Electronically Stored Information.* A party need not provide discovery of electronically stored information from sources that the party identifies as not reasonably accessible because of undue burden or cost. On motion to compel discovery or for a protective order, the party from whom discovery is sought must show that the information is not reasonably accessible because of undue burden or cost. If that showing is made, the court may nonetheless order discovery from such sources if the requesting party shows good cause, considering the limitations of Rule 26(b)(2)(C). The court may specify conditions for the discovery.

(C) *When Required.* On motion or on its own, the court must limit the frequency or extent of discovery otherwise allowed by these rules or by local rule if it determines that:

  (i) the discovery sought is unreasonably cumulative or duplicative, or can be obtained from some other source that is more convenient, less burdensome, or less expensive;

(ii) the party seeking discovery has had ample opportunity to obtain the information by discovery in the action; or

(iii) the proposed discovery is outside the scope permitted by Rule 26(b)(1).

(3) *Trial Preparation: Materials.*

(A) *Documents and Tangible Things.* Ordinarily, a party may not discover documents and tangible things that are prepared in anticipation of litigation or for trial by or for another party or its representative (including the other party's attorney, consultant, surety, indemnitor, insurer, or agent). But, subject to Rule 26(b)(4), those materials may be discovered if:

(i) they are otherwise discoverable under Rule 26(b)(1); and

(ii) the party shows that it has substantial need for the materials to prepare its case and cannot, without undue hardship, obtain their substantial equivalent by other means.

(B) *Protection Against Disclosure.* If the court orders discovery of those materials, it must protect against disclosure of the mental impressions, conclusions, opinions, or legal theories of a party's attorney or other representative concerning the litigation.

(C) *Previous Statement.* Any party or other person may, on request and without the required showing, obtain the person's own previous statement about the action or its subject matter. If the request is refused, the person may move for a court order, and Rule 37(a)(5) applies to the award of expenses. A previous statement is either:

(i) a written statement that the person has signed or otherwise adopted or approved; or

(ii) a contemporaneous stenographic, mechanical, electrical, or other recording—or a transcription of it—that recites substantially verbatim the person's oral statement.

(4) *Trial Preparation: Experts.*

(A) *Deposition of an Expert Who May Testify.* A party may depose any person who has been identified as an expert whose opinions may be presented at trial. If Rule 26(a)(2)(B) requires a report from the expert, the deposition may be conducted only after the report is provided.

(B) *Trial–Preparation Protection for Draft Reports or Disclosures.* Rules 26(b)(3)(A) and (B) protect drafts of any report or disclosure

required under Rule 26(a)(2), regardless of the form in which the draft is recorded.

(C) *Trial–Preparation Protection for Communications Between a Party's Attorney and Expert Witnesses.* Rules 26(b)(3)(A) and (B) protect communications between the party's attorney and any witness required to provide a report under Rule 26(a)(2)(B), regardless of the form of the communications, except to the extent that the communications:

(i) relate to compensation for the expert's study or testimony;

(ii) identify facts or data that the party's attorney provided and that the expert considered in forming the opinions to be expressed; or

(iii) identify assumptions that the party's attorney provided and that the expert relied on in forming the opinions to be expressed.

(D) *Expert Employed Only for Trial Preparation.* Ordinarily, a party may not, by interrogatories or deposition, discover facts known or opinions held by an expert who has been retained or specially employed by another party in anticipation of litigation or to prepare for trial and who is not expected to be called as a witness at trial. But a party may do so only:

(i) as provided in Rule 35(b); or

(ii) on showing exceptional circumstances under which it is impracticable for the party to obtain facts or opinions on the same subject by other means.

(E) *Payment.* Unless manifest injustice would result, the court must require that the party seeking discovery:

(i) pay the expert a reasonable fee for time spent in responding to discovery under Rule 26(b)(4)(A) or (D); and

(ii) for discovery under (D), also pay the other party a fair portion of the fees and expenses it reasonably incurred in obtaining the expert's facts and opinions.

(5) *Claiming Privilege or Protecting Trial-Preparation Materials.*

(A) *Information Withheld.* When a party withholds information otherwise discoverable by claiming that the information is privileged or subject to protection as trial-preparation material, the party must:

(i) expressly make the claim; and

(ii) describe the nature of the documents, communications, or tangible things not produced or disclosed—and do so in a manner that, without revealing information itself privileged or protected, will enable other parties to assess the claim.

(B) *Information Produced.* If information produced in discovery is subject to a claim of privilege or of protection as trial-preparation material, the party making the claim may notify any party that received the information of the claim and the basis for it. After being notified, a party must promptly return, sequester, or destroy the specified information and any copies it has; must not use or disclose the information until the claim is resolved; must take reasonable steps to retrieve the information if the party disclosed it before being notified; and may promptly present the information to the court under seal for a determination of the claim. The producing party must preserve the information until the claim is resolved.

(c) Protective Orders.

(1) *In General.* A party or any person from whom discovery is sought may move for a protective order in the court where the action is pending — or as an alternative on matters relating to a deposition, in the court for the district where the deposition will be taken. The motion must include a certification that the movant has in good faith conferred or attempted to confer with other affected parties in an effort to resolve the dispute without court action. The court may, for good cause, issue an order to protect a party or person from annoyance, embarrassment, oppression, or undue burden or expense, including one or more of the following:

(A) forbidding the disclosure or discovery;

(B) specifying terms, including time and place or the allocation of expenses, for the disclosure or discovery;

(C) prescribing a discovery method other than the one selected by the party seeking discovery;

(D) forbidding inquiry into certain matters, or limiting the scope of disclosure or discovery to certain matters;

(E) designating the persons who may be present while the discovery is conducted;

(F) requiring that a deposition be sealed and opened only on court order;

(G) requiring that a trade secret or other confidential research, development, or commercial information not be revealed or be revealed only in a specified way; and

(H) requiring that the parties simultaneously file specified documents or information in sealed envelopes, to be opened as the court directs.

(2) *Ordering Discovery.* If a motion for a protective order is wholly or partly denied, the court may, on just terms, order that any party or person provide or permit discovery.

(3) *Awarding Expenses.* Rule 37(a)(5) applies to the award of expenses.

(d) Timing and Sequence of Discovery.

(1) *Timing.* A party may not seek discovery from any source before the parties have conferred as required by Rule 26(f), except in a proceeding exempted from initial disclosure under Rule 26(a)(1)(B), or when authorized by these rules, by stipulation, or by court order.

(2) *Early Rule 34 Requests.*

(A) **Time to Deliver.** More than 21 days after the summons and complaint are served on a party, a request under Rule 34 may be delivered:

(i) to that party by any other party, and

(ii) by that party to any plaintiff or to any other party that has been served.

(B) *When Considered Served.* The request is considered to have been served at the first Rule 26(f) conference.

(3) *Sequence.* Unless the parties stipulate or the court orders otherwise for the parties' and witnesses' convenience and in the interests of justice:

(A) methods of discovery may be used in any sequence; and

(B) discovery by one party does not require any other party to delay its discovery.

(e) Supplementing Disclosures and Responses.

(1) *In General.* A party who has made a disclosure under Rule 26(a)—or who has responded to an interrogatory, request for production, or request for admission—must supplement or correct its disclosure or response:

(A) in a timely manner if the party learns that in some material respect the disclosure or response is incomplete or incorrect, and if the additional or corrective information has not otherwise been made known to the other parties during the discovery process or in writing; or

(B) as ordered by the court.

(2) *Expert Witness.* For an expert whose report must be disclosed under Rule 26(a)(2)(B), the party's duty to supplement extends both to information included in the report and to information given during the expert's deposition.

Any additions or changes to this information must be disclosed by the time the party's pretrial disclosures under Rule 26(a)(3) are due.

(f) Conference of the Parties; Planning for Discovery.

(1) *Conference Timing.* Except in a proceeding exempted from initial disclosure under Rule 26(a)(1)(B) or when the court orders otherwise, the parties must confer as soon as practicable—and in any event at least 21 days before a scheduling conference is to be held or a scheduling order is due under Rule 16(b).

(2) *Conference Content; Parties' Responsibilities.* In conferring, the parties must consider the nature and basis of their claims and defenses and the possibilities for promptly settling or resolving the case; make or arrange for the disclosures required by Rule 26(a)(1); discuss any issues about preserving discoverable information; and develop a proposed discovery plan. The attorneys of record and all unrepresented parties that have appeared in the case are jointly responsible for arranging the conference, for attempting in good faith to agree on the proposed discovery plan, and for submitting to the court within 14 days after the conference a written report outlining the plan. The court may order the parties or attorneys to attend the conference in person.

(3) *Discovery Plan.* A discovery plan must state the parties' views and proposals on:

(A) what changes should be made in the timing, form, or requirement for disclosures under Rule 26(a), including a statement of when initial disclosures were made or will be made;

(B) the subjects on which discovery may be needed, when discovery should be completed, and whether discovery should be conducted in phases or be limited to or focused on particular issues;

(C) any issues about disclosure, discovery, or preservation of electronically stored information, including the form or forms in which it should be produced;

(D) any issues about claims of privilege or of protection as trial-preparation materials, including — if the parties agree on a procedure to assert these claims after production — whether to ask the court to include their agreement in an order under Federal Rule of Evidence 502;

(E) what changes should be made in the limitations on discovery imposed under these rules or by local rule, and what other limitations should be imposed; and

(F) any other orders that the court should issue under Rule 26(c) or under Rule 16(b) and (c).

(4) *Expedited Schedule.* If necessary to comply with its expedited schedule for Rule 16(b) conferences, a court may by local rule:

(A) require the parties' conference to occur less than 21 days before the scheduling conference is held or a scheduling order is due under Rule 16(b); and

(B) require the written report outlining the discovery plan to be filed less than 14 days after the parties' conference, or excuse the parties from submitting a written report and permit them to report orally on their discovery plan at the Rule 16(b) conference.

(g) Signing Disclosures and Discovery Requests, Responses, and Objections.

(1) *Signature Required; Effect of Signature.* Every disclosure under Rule 26(a)(1) or (a)(3) and every discovery request, response, or objection must be signed by at least one attorney of record in the attorney's own name—or by the party personally, if unrepresented—and must state the signer's address, e-mail address, and telephone number. By signing, an attorney or party certifies that to the best of the person's knowledge, information, and belief formed after a reasonable inquiry:

(A) with respect to a disclosure, it is complete and correct as of the time it is made; and

(B) with respect to a discovery request, response, or objection, it is:

(i) consistent with these rules and warranted by existing law or by a nonfrivolous argument for extending, modifying, or reversing existing law, or for establishing new law;

(ii) not interposed for any improper purpose, such as to harass, cause unnecessary delay, or needlessly increase the cost of litigation; and

(iii) neither unreasonable nor unduly burdensome or expensive, considering the needs of the case, prior discovery in the case, the amount in controversy, and the importance of the issues at stake in the action.

(2) *Failure to Sign.* Other parties have no duty to act on an unsigned disclosure, request, response, or objection until it is signed, and the court must strike it unless a signature is promptly supplied after the omission is called to the attorney's or party's attention.

(3) *Sanction for Improper Certification.* If a certification violates this rule without substantial justification, the court, on motion or on its own, must impose an appropriate sanction on the signer, the party on whose behalf the signer was acting, or both. The sanction may include an order to pay the reasonable expenses, including attorney's fees, caused by the violation.

(Amended December 27, 1946, effective March 19, 1948; January 21, 1963, effective July 1, 1963; February 28, 1966, effective July 1, 1966; March 30, 1970, effective July 1, 1970; April 29, 1980, effective August 1, 1980; April 28, 1983, effective August 1, 1983; March 2, 1987, effective August 1, 1987; April 22, 1993, effective December 1, 1993; April 17, 2000, effective December 1, 2000; April 12, 2006, effective December 1, 2006; April 30, 2007, effective December 1, 2007; April 28, 2010, effective December 1, 2010; April 29, 2015, effective December 1, 2015.)

RULE 27. DEPOSITIONS TO PERPETUATE TESTIMONY

(a) Before an Action Is Filed.

(1) *Petition.* A person who wants to perpetuate testimony about any matter cognizable in a United States court may file a verified petition in the district court for the district where any expected adverse party resides. The petition must ask for an order authorizing the petitioner to depose the named persons in order to perpetuate their testimony. The petition must be titled in the petitioner's name and must show:

(A) that the petitioner expects to be a party to an action cognizable in a United States court but cannot presently bring it or cause it to be brought;

(B) the subject matter of the expected action and the petitioner's interest;

(C) the facts that the petitioner wants to establish by the proposed testimony and the reasons to perpetuate it;

(D) the names or a description of the persons whom the petitioner expects to be adverse parties and their addresses, so far as known; and

(E) the name, address, and expected substance of the testimony of each deponent.

(2) *Notice and Service.* At least 21 days before the hearing date, the petitioner must serve each expected adverse party with a copy of the petition and a notice stating the time and place of the hearing. The notice may be served either inside or outside the district or state in the manner provided in Rule 4. If that service cannot be made with reasonable diligence on an expected adverse party, the court may order service by publication or otherwise. The court must appoint an attorney to represent persons not served in the manner provided in Rule 4 and to cross-examine the deponent if an unserved person is not otherwise represented. If any expected adverse party is a minor or is incompetent, Rule 17(c) applies.

(3) *Order and Examination.* If satisfied that perpetuating the testimony may prevent a failure or delay of justice, the court must issue an order that designates or describes the persons whose depositions may be taken, specifies the subject matter of the examinations, and states whether the depositions will be taken orally or by written interrogatories. The depositions may then be taken under these rules, and the court may issue orders like those authorized by Rules 34 and 35. A reference in these rules to the court where an action is pending means, for purposes of this rule, the court where the petition for the deposition was filed.

(4) *Using the Deposition.* A deposition to perpetuate testimony may be used under Rule 32(a) in any later-filed district-court action involving the same subject matter if the deposition either was taken under these rules or, although not so taken, would be admissible in evidence in the courts of the state where it was taken.

(b) Pending Appeal.

(1) *In General.* The court where a judgment has been rendered may, if an appeal has been taken or may still be taken, permit a party to depose witnesses to perpetuate their testimony for use in the event of further proceedings in that court.

(2) *Motion.* The party who wants to perpetuate testimony may move for leave to take the depositions, on the same notice and service as if the action were pending in the district court. The motion must show:

(A) the name, address, and expected substance of the testimony of each deponent; and

(B) the reasons for perpetuating the testimony.

(3) *Court Order.* If the court finds that perpetuating the testimony may prevent a failure or delay of justice, the court may permit the depositions to be taken and may issue orders like those authorized by Rules 34 and 35. The depositions may be taken and used as any other deposition taken in a pending district-court action.

(c) Perpetuation by an Action. This rule does not limit a court's power to entertain an action to perpetuate testimony.

(Amended December 27, 1946, effective March 19, 1948; December 29, 1948, effective October 20, 1949; March 1, 1971, effective July 1, 1971; March 2, 1987, effective August 1, 1987; April 25, 2005, effective December 1, 2005; April 30, 2007, effective December 1, 2007; March 26, 2009, effective December 1, 2009.)

RULE 28. PERSONS BEFORE WHOM DEPOSITIONS MAY BE TAKEN

(a) Within the United States.

(1) *In General.* Within the United States or a territory or insular possession subject to United States jurisdiction, a deposition must be taken before:

  (A) an officer authorized to administer oaths either by federal law or by the law in the place of examination; or

  (B) a person appointed by the court where the action is pending to administer oaths and take testimony.

(2) *Definition of "Officer".* The term "officer" in Rules 30, 31, and 32 includes a person appointed by the court under this rule or designated by the parties under Rule 29(a).

(b) In a Foreign Country.

(1) *In General.* A deposition may be taken in a foreign country:

  (A) under an applicable treaty or convention;

  (B) under a letter of request, whether or not captioned a "letter rogatory";

  (C) on notice, before a person authorized to administer oaths either by federal law or by the law in the place of examination; or

  (D) before a person commissioned by the court to administer any necessary oath and take testimony.

(2) *Issuing a Letter of Request or a Commission.* A letter of request, a commission, or both may be issued:

  (A) on appropriate terms after an application and notice of it; and

  (B) without a showing that taking the deposition in another manner is impracticable or inconvenient.

(3) *Form of a Request, Notice, or Commission.* When a letter of request or any other device is used according to a treaty or convention, it must be captioned in the form prescribed by that treaty or convention. A letter of request may be addressed "To the Appropriate Authority in [name of country]." A deposition notice or a commission must designate by name or descriptive title the person before whom the deposition is to be taken.

(4) *Letter of Request—Admitting Evidence.* Evidence obtained in response to a letter of request need not be excluded merely because it is not a verbatim transcript, because the testimony was not taken under oath, or because of any similar departure from the requirements for depositions taken within the United States.

(c) Disqualification. A deposition must not be taken before a person who is any party's relative, employee, or attorney; who is related to or employed by any party's attorney; or who is financially interested in the action.

(Amended December 27, 1946, effective March 19, 1948; January 21, 1963, effective July 1, 1963; April 29, 1980, effective August 1, 1980; March 2, 1987, effective August 1, 1987; April 22, 1993, effective December 1, 1993; April 30, 2007, effective December 1, 2007.)

RULE 29. STIPULATIONS ABOUT DISCOVERY PROCEDURE

Unless the court orders otherwise, the parties may stipulate that:

(a) a deposition may be taken before any person, at any time or place, on any notice, and in the manner specified—in which event it may be used in the same way as any other deposition; and

(b) other procedures governing or limiting discovery be modified—but a stipulation extending the time for any form of discovery must have court approval if it would interfere with the time set for completing discovery, for hearing a motion, or for trial.

(Amended March 30, 1970, effective July 1, 1970; April 22, 1993, effective December 1, 1993; April 30, 2007, effective December 1, 2007.)

RULE 30. DEPOSITIONS BY ORAL EXAMINATION

(a) When a Deposition May Be Taken.

(1) *Without Leave.* A party may, by oral questions, depose any person, including a party, without leave of court except as provided in Rule 30(a)(2). The deponent's attendance may be compelled by subpoena under Rule 45.

(2) *With Leave.* A party must obtain leave of court, and the court must grant leave to the extent consistent with Rule 26(b)(1) and (2):

  (A) if the parties have not stipulated to the deposition and:

    (i) the deposition would result in more than 10 depositions being taken under this rule or Rule 31 by the plaintiffs, or by the defendants, or by the third-party defendants;

    (ii) the deponent has already been deposed in the case; or

    (iii) the party seeks to take the deposition before the time specified in Rule 26(d), unless the party certifies in the notice, with supporting facts, that the deponent is expected to leave the United States and be unavailable for examination in this country after that time; or

  (B) if the deponent is confined in prison.

(b) Notice of the Deposition; Other Formal Requirements.

(1) *Notice in General.* A party who wants to depose a person by oral questions must give reasonable written notice to every other party. The notice must state the time and place of the deposition and, if known, the deponent's name and address. If the name is unknown, the notice must provide a general description sufficient to identify the person or the particular class or group to which the person belongs.

(2) *Producing Documents.* If a subpoena duces tecum is to be served on the deponent, the materials designated for production, as set out in the subpoena, must be listed in the notice or in an attachment. The notice to a party deponent may be accompanied by a request under Rule 34 to produce documents and tangible things at the deposition.

(3) *Method of Recording.*

(A) *Method Stated in the Notice.* The party who notices the deposition must state in the notice the method for recording the testimony. Unless the court orders otherwise, testimony may be recorded by audio, audiovisual, or stenographic means. The noticing party bears the recording costs. Any party may arrange to transcribe a deposition.

(B) *Additional Method.* With prior notice to the deponent and other parties, any party may designate another method for recording the testimony in addition to that specified in the original notice. That party bears the expense of the additional record or transcript unless the court orders otherwise.

(4) *By Remote Means.* The parties may stipulate—or the court may on motion order—that a deposition be taken by telephone or other remote means. For the purpose of this rule and Rules 28(a), 37(a)(2), and 37(b)(1), the deposition takes place where the deponent answers the questions.

(5) *Officer's Duties.*

(A) *Before the Deposition.* Unless the parties stipulate otherwise, a deposition must be conducted before an officer appointed or designated under Rule 28. The officer must begin the deposition with an on-the-record statement that includes:

(i) the officer's name and business address;

(ii) the date, time, and place of the deposition;

(iii) the deponent's name;

(iv) the officer's administration of the oath or affirmation to the deponent; and

(v) the identity of all persons present.

(B) *Conducting the Deposition; Avoiding Distortion.* If the deposition is recorded non-stenographically, the officer must repeat the items in Rule 30(b)(5)(A)(i)-(iii) at the beginning of each unit of the recording medium. The deponent's and attorneys' appearance or demeanor must not be distorted through recording techniques.

(C) *After the Deposition.* At the end of a deposition, the officer must state on the record that the deposition is complete and must set out any stipulations made by the attorneys about custody of the transcript or recording and of the exhibits, or about any other pertinent matters.

(6) *Notice or Subpoena Directed to an Organization.* In its notice or subpoena, a party may name as the deponent a public or private corporation, a partnership, an association, a governmental agency, or other entity and must describe with reasonable particularity the matters for examination. The named organization must then designate one or more officers, directors, or managing agents, or designate other persons who consent to testify on its behalf; and it may set out the matters on which each person designated will testify. A subpoena must advise a nonparty organization of its duty to make this designation. The persons designated must testify about information known or reasonably available to the organization. This paragraph (6) does not preclude a deposition by any other procedure allowed by these rules.

(c) Examination and Cross–Examination; Record of the Examination; Objections; Written Questions.

(1) *Examination and Cross–Examination.* The examination and cross-examination of a deponent proceed as they would at trial under the Federal Rules of Evidence, except Rules 103 and 615. After putting the deponent under oath or affirmation, the officer must record the testimony by the method designated under Rule 30(b)(3)(A). The testimony must be recorded by the officer personally or by a person acting in the presence and under the direction of the officer.

(2) *Objections.* An objection at the time of the examination—whether to evidence, to a party's conduct, to the officer's qualifications, to the manner of taking the deposition, or to any other aspect of the deposition—must be noted on the record, but the examination still proceeds; the testimony is taken subject to any objection. An objection must be stated concisely in a nonargumentative and nonsuggestive manner. A person may instruct a deponent not to answer only when necessary to preserve a privilege, to en-

force a limitation ordered by the court, or to present a motion under Rule 30(d)(3).

(3) ***Participating Through Written Questions.*** Instead of participating in the oral examination, a party may serve written questions in a sealed envelope on the party noticing the deposition, who must deliver them to the officer. The officer must ask the deponent those questions and record the answers verbatim.

(d) Duration; Sanction; Motion to Terminate or Limit.

(1) ***Duration.*** Unless otherwise stipulated or ordered by the court, a deposition is limited to one day of 7 hours. The court must allow additional time consistent with Rule 26(b)(1) and (2) if needed to fairly examine the deponent or if the deponent, another person, or any other circumstance impedes or delays the examination.

(2) ***Sanction.*** The court may impose an appropriate sanction—including the reasonable expenses and attorney's fees incurred by any party—on a person who impedes, delays, or frustrates the fair examination of the deponent.

(3) ***Motion to Terminate or Limit.***

(A) *Grounds.* At any time during a deposition, the deponent or a party may move to terminate or limit it on the ground that it is being conducted in bad faith or in a manner that unreasonably annoys, embarrasses, or oppresses the deponent or party. The motion may be filed in the court where the action is pending or the deposition is being taken. If the objecting deponent or party so demands, the deposition must be suspended for the time necessary to obtain an order.

(B) *Order.* The court may order that the deposition be terminated or may limit its scope and manner as provided in Rule 26(c). If terminated, the deposition may be resumed only by order of the court where the action is pending.

(C) *Award of Expenses.* Rule 37(a)(5) applies to the award of expenses.

(e) Review by the Witness; Changes.

(1) ***Review; Statement of Changes.*** On request by the deponent or a party before the deposition is completed, the deponent must be allowed 30 days after being notified by the officer that the transcript or recording is available in which:

(A) to review the transcript or recording; and

(B) if there are changes in form or substance, to sign a statement listing the changes and the reasons for making them.

(2) ***Changes Indicated in the Officer's Certificate.*** The officer must note in the certificate prescribed by Rule 30(f)(1) whether a review

was requested and, if so, must attach any changes the deponent makes during the 30–day period.

(f) Certification and Delivery; Exhibits; Copies of the Transcript or Recording; Filing.

(1) ***Certification and Delivery.*** The officer must certify in writing that the witness was duly sworn and that the deposition accurately records the witness's testimony. The certificate must accompany the record of the deposition. Unless the court orders otherwise, the officer must seal the deposition in an envelope or package bearing the title of the action and marked "Deposition of [witness's name]" and must promptly send it to the attorney who arranged for the transcript or recording. The attorney must store it under conditions that will protect it against loss, destruction, tampering, or deterioration.

(2) ***Documents and Tangible Things.***

(A) *Originals and Copies.* Documents and tangible things produced for inspection during a deposition must, on a party's request, be marked for identification and attached to the deposition. Any party may inspect and copy them. But if the person who produced them wants to keep the originals, the person may:

(i) offer copies to be marked, attached to the deposition, and then used as originals—after giving all parties a fair opportunity to verify the copies by comparing them with the originals; or

(ii) give all parties a fair opportunity to inspect and copy the originals after they are marked—in which event the originals may be used as if attached to the deposition.

(B) *Order Regarding the Originals.* Any party may move for an order that the originals be attached to the deposition pending final disposition of the case.

(3) ***Copies of the Transcript or Recording.*** Unless otherwise stipulated or ordered by the court, the officer must retain the stenographic notes of a deposition taken stenographically or a copy of the recording of a deposition taken by another method. When paid reasonable charges, the officer must furnish a copy of the transcript or recording to any party or the deponent.

(4) ***Notice of Filing.*** A party who files the deposition must promptly notify all other parties of the filing.

(g) Failure to Attend a Deposition or Serve a Subpoena; Expenses. A party who, expecting a deposition to be taken, attends in person or by an attorney may recover reasonable expenses for attending, including attorney's fees, if the noticing party failed to:

(1) attend and proceed with the deposition; or

(2) serve a subpoena on a nonparty deponent, who consequently did not attend.

(Amended January 21, 1963, effective July 1, 1963; March 30, 1970, effective July 1, 1970; March 1, 1971, effective July 1, 1971; November 20, 1972, effective July 1, 1975; April 29, 1980, effective August 1, 1980; March 2, 1987, effective August 1, 1987; April 22, 1993, effective December 1, 1993; April 17, 2000, effective December 1, 2000; April 30, 2007, effective December 1, 2007; April 29, 2015, effective December 1, 2015.)

RULE 31. DEPOSITIONS BY WRITTEN QUESTIONS

(a) When a Deposition May Be Taken.

(1) *Without Leave.* A party may, by written questions, depose any person, including a party, without leave of court except as provided in Rule 31(a)(2). The deponent's attendance may be compelled by subpoena under Rule 45.

(2) *With Leave.* A party must obtain leave of court, and the court must grant leave to the extent consistent with Rule 26(b)(1) and (2):

(A) if the parties have not stipulated to the deposition and:

(i) the deposition would result in more than 10 depositions being taken under this rule or Rule 30 by the plaintiffs, or by the defendants, or by the third-party defendants;

(ii) the deponent has already been deposed in the case; or

(iii) the party seeks to take a deposition before the time specified in Rule 26(d); or

(B) if the deponent is confined in prison.

(3) *Service; Required Notice.* A party who wants to depose a person by written questions must serve them on every other party, with a notice stating, if known, the deponent's name and address. If the name is unknown, the notice must provide a general description sufficient to identify the person or the particular class or group to which the person belongs. The notice must also state the name or descriptive title and the address of the officer before whom the deposition will be taken.

(4) *Questions Directed to an Organization.* A public or private corporation, a partnership, an association, or a governmental agency may be deposed by written questions in accordance with Rule 30(b)(6).

(5) *Questions from Other Parties.* Any questions to the deponent from other parties must be served on all parties as follows: cross-questions, within 14 days after being served with the notice and direct questions; redirect questions, within 7 days after being served with cross-questions; and recross-questions, within 7 days after being served with redirect questions. The court may, for good cause, extend or shorten these times.

(b) Delivery to the Officer; Officer's Duties. The party who noticed the deposition must deliver to the officer a copy of all the questions served and of the notice. The officer must promptly proceed in the manner provided in Rule 30(c), (e), and (f) to:

(1) take the deponent's testimony in response to the questions;

(2) prepare and certify the deposition; and

(3) send it to the party, attaching a copy of the questions and of the notice.

(c) Notice of Completion or Filing.

(1) *Completion.* The party who noticed the deposition must notify all other parties when it is completed.

(2) *Filing.* A party who files the deposition must promptly notify all other parties of the filing.

(Amended March 30, 1970, effective July 1, 1970; March 2, 1987, effective August 1, 1987; April 22, 1993, effective December 1, 1993; April 30, 2007, effective December 1, 2007; April 29, 2015, effective December 1, 2015.)

RULE 32. USING DEPOSITIONS IN COURT PROCEEDINGS

(a) Using Depositions.

(1) *In General.* At a hearing or trial, all or part of a deposition may be used against a party on these conditions:

(A) the party was present or represented at the taking of the deposition or had reasonable notice of it;

(B) it is used to the extent it would be admissible under the Federal Rules of Evidence if the deponent were present and testifying; and

(C) the use is allowed by Rule 32(a)(2) through (8).

(2) *Impeachment and Other Uses.* Any party may use a deposition to contradict or impeach the testimony given by the deponent as a witness, or for any other purpose allowed by the Federal Rules of Evidence.

(3) *Deposition of Party, Agent, or Designee.* An adverse party may use for any purpose the deposition of a party or anyone who, when deposed, was the party's officer, director, managing agent, or designee under Rule 30(b)(6) or 31(a)(4).

(4) *Unavailable Witness.* A party may use for any purpose the deposition of a witness, whether or not a party, if the court finds:

(A) that the witness is dead;

(B) that the witness is more than 100 miles from the place of hearing or trial or is outside the United States, unless it appears that the witness's absence was procured by the party offering the deposition;

(C) that the witness cannot attend or testify because of age, illness, infirmity, or imprisonment;

(D) that the party offering the deposition could not procure the witness's attendance by subpoena; or

(E) on motion and notice, that exceptional circumstances make it desirable—in the interest of justice and with due regard to the importance of live testimony in open court—to permit the deposition to be used.

(5) *Limitations on Use.*

(A) *Deposition Taken on Short Notice.* A deposition must not be used against a party who, having received less than 14 days' notice of the deposition, promptly moved for a protective order under Rule 26(c)(1)(B) requesting that it not be taken or be taken at a different time or place—and this motion was still pending when the deposition was taken.

(B) *Unavailable Deponent; Party Could Not Obtain an Attorney.* A deposition taken without leave of court under the unavailability provision of Rule 30(a)(2)(A)(iii) must not be used against a party who shows that, when served with the notice, it could not, despite diligent efforts, obtain an attorney to represent it at the deposition.

(6) *Using Part of a Deposition.* If a party offers in evidence only part of a deposition, an adverse party may require the offeror to introduce other parts that in fairness should be considered with the part introduced, and any party may itself introduce any other parts.

(7) *Substituting a Party.* Substituting a party under Rule 25 does not affect the right to use a deposition previously taken.

(8) *Deposition Taken in an Earlier Action.* A deposition lawfully taken and, if required, filed in any federal- or state-court action may be used in a later action involving the same subject matter between the same parties, or their representatives or successors in interest, to the same extent as if taken in the later action. A deposition previously taken may also be used as allowed by the Federal Rules of Evidence.

(b) **Objections to Admissibility.** Subject to Rules 28(b) and 32(d)(3), an objection may be made at a hearing or trial to the admission of any deposition testimony that would be inadmissible if the witness were present and testifying.

(c) **Form of Presentation.** Unless the court orders otherwise, a party must provide a transcript of any deposition testimony the party offers, but may provide the court with the testimony in nontranscript form as well. On any party's request, deposition testimony offered in a jury trial for any purpose other than impeachment must be presented in nontranscript form, if available, unless the court for good cause orders otherwise.

(d) **Waiver of Objections.**

(1) *To the Notice.* An objection to an error or irregularity in a deposition notice is waived unless promptly served in writing on the party giving the notice.

(2) *To the Officer's Qualification.* An objection based on disqualification of the officer before whom a deposition is to be taken is waived if not made:

(A) before the deposition begins; or

(B) promptly after the basis for disqualification becomes known or, with reasonable diligence, could have been known.

(3) *To the Taking of the Deposition.*

(A) *Objection to Competence, Relevance, or Materiality.* An objection to a deponent's competence—or to the competence, relevance, or materiality of testimony—is not waived by a failure to make the objection before or during the deposition, unless the ground for it might have been corrected at that time.

(B) *Objection to an Error or Irregularity.* An objection to an error or irregularity at an oral examination is waived if:

(i) it relates to the manner of taking the deposition, the form of a question or answer, the oath or affirmation, a party's conduct, or other matters that might have been corrected at that time; and

(ii) it is not timely made during the deposition.

(C) *Objection to a Written Question.* An objection to the form of a written question under Rule 31 is waived if not served in writing on the party submitting the question within the time for serving responsive questions or, if the question is a recross-question, within 7 days after being served with it.

(4) *To Completing and Returning the Deposition.* An objection to how the officer transcribed the testimony—or prepared, signed, certified, sealed, endorsed, sent, or otherwise dealt with the deposition—is waived unless a motion to suppress is made promptly after the error or irregularity becomes known or, with reasonable diligence, could have been known.

(Amended March 30, 1970, effective July 1, 1970; November 20, 1972, effective July 1, 1975; April 29, 1980, effective August 1, 1980; March 2, 1987, effective August 1, 1987; April 22, 1993, effective December 1, 1993; April 30, 2007, effective December 1, 2007; March 26, 2009, effective December 1, 2009.)

RULE 33.　INTERROGATORIES TO PARTIES

(a) In General.

(1) *Number.* Unless otherwise stipulated or ordered by the court, a party may serve on any other party no more than 25 written interrogatories, including all discrete subparts. Leave to serve additional interrogatories may be granted to the extent consistent with Rule 26(b)(1) and (2).

(2) *Scope.* An interrogatory may relate to any matter that may be inquired into under Rule 26(b). An interrogatory is not objectionable merely because it asks for an opinion or contention that relates to fact or the application of law to fact, but the court may order that the interrogatory need not be answered until designated discovery is complete, or until a pretrial conference or some other time.

(b) Answers and Objections.

(1) *Responding Party.* The interrogatories must be answered:

(A) by the party to whom they are directed; or

(B) if that party is a public or private corporation, a partnership, an association, or a governmental agency, by any officer or agent, who must furnish the information available to the party.

(2) *Time to Respond.* The responding party must serve its answers and any objections within 30 days after being served with the interrogatories. A shorter or longer time may be stipulated to under Rule 29 or be ordered by the court.

(3) *Answering Each Interrogatory.* Each interrogatory must, to the extent it is not objected to, be answered separately and fully in writing under oath.

(4) *Objections.* The grounds for objecting to an interrogatory must be stated with specificity. Any ground not stated in a timely objection is waived unless the court, for good cause, excuses the failure.

(5) *Signature.* The person who makes the answers must sign them, and the attorney who objects must sign any objections.

(c) Use. An answer to an interrogatory may be used to the extent allowed by the Federal Rules of Evidence.

(d) Option to Produce Business Records. If the answer to an interrogatory may be determined by examining, auditing, compiling, abstracting, or summarizing a party's business records (including electronically stored information), and if the burden of deriving or ascertaining the answer will be substantially the same for either party, the responding party may answer by:

(1) specifying the records that must be reviewed, in sufficient detail to enable the interrogating party to locate and identify them as readily as the responding party could; and

(2) giving the interrogating party a reasonable opportunity to examine and audit the records and to make copies, compilations, abstracts, or summaries.

(Amended December 27, 1946, effective March 19, 1948; March 30, 1970, effective July 1, 1970; April 29, 1980, effective August 1, 1980; April 22, 1993, effective December 1, 1993; April 12, 2006, effective December 1, 2006; April 30, 2007, effective December 1, 2007; April 29, 2015, effective December 1, 2015.)

RULE 34.　PRODUCING DOCUMENTS, ELECTRONICALLY STORED INFORMATION, AND TANGIBLE THINGS, OR ENTERING ONTO LAND, FOR INSPECTION AND OTHER PURPOSES

(a) In General. A party may serve on any other party a request within the scope of Rule 26(b):

(1) to produce and permit the requesting party or its representative to inspect, copy, test, or sample the following items in the responding party's possession, custody, or control:

(A) any designated documents or electronically stored information—including writings, drawings, graphs, charts, photographs, sound recordings, images, and other data or data compilations—stored in any medium from which information can be obtained either directly or, if necessary, after translation by the responding party into a reasonably usable form; or

(B) any designated tangible things; or

(2) to permit entry onto designated land or other property possessed or controlled by the responding party, so that the requesting party may inspect, measure, survey, photograph, test, or sample the property or any designated object or operation on it.

(b) Procedure.

(1) *Contents of the Request.* The request:

(A) must describe with reasonable particularity each item or category of items to be inspected;

(B) must specify a reasonable time, place, and manner for the inspection and for performing the related acts; and

(C) may specify the form or forms in which electronically stored information is to be produced.

(2) *Responses and Objections.*

  (A) *Time to Respond.* The party to whom the request is directed must respond in writing within 30 days after being served or — if the request was delivered under Rule 26(d)(2) — within 30 days after the parties' first Rule 26(f) conference. A shorter or longer time may be stipulated to under Rule 29 or be ordered by the court.

  (B) *Responding to Each Item.* For each item or category, the response must either state that inspection and related activities will be permitted as requested or state with specificity the grounds for objecting to the request, including the reasons. The responding party may state that it will produce copies of documents or of electronically stored information instead of permitting inspection. The production must then be completed no later than the time for inspection specified in the request or another reasonable time specified in the response.

  (C) *Objections.* An objection must state whether any responsive materials are being withheld on the basis of that objection. An objection to part of a request must specify the part and permit inspection of the rest.

  (D) *Responding to a Request for Production of Electronically Stored Information.* The response may state an objection to a requested form for producing electronically stored information. If the responding party objects to a requested form—or if no form was specified in the request—the party must state the form or forms it intends to use.

  (E) *Producing the Documents or Electronically Stored Information.* Unless otherwise stipulated or ordered by the court, these procedures apply to producing documents or electronically stored information:

    (i) A party must produce documents as they are kept in the usual course of business or must organize and label them to correspond to the categories in the request;

    (ii) If a request does not specify a form for producing electronically stored information, a party must produce it in a form or forms in which it is ordinarily maintained or in a reasonably usable form or forms; and

    (iii) A party need not produce the same electronically stored information in more than one form.

(c) **Nonparties.** As provided in Rule 45, a nonparty may be compelled to produce documents and tangible things or to permit an inspection.

(Amended December 27, 1946, effective March 19, 1948; March 30, 1970, effective July 1, 1970; April 29, 1980, effective August 1, 1980; March 2, 1987, effective August 1, 1987; April 30, 1991, effective December 1, 1991; April 22, 1993, effective December 1, 1993; April 12, 2006, effective December 1, 2006; April 30, 2007, effective December 1, 2007; April 29, 2015, effective December 1, 2015.)

RULE 35.   PHYSICAL AND MENTAL EXAMINATIONS

(a) **Order for an Examination.**

(1) *In General.* The court where the action is pending may order a party whose mental or physical condition—including blood group—is in controversy to submit to a physical or mental examination by a suitably licensed or certified examiner. The court has the same authority to order a party to produce for examination a person who is in its custody or under its legal control.

(2) *Motion and Notice; Contents of the Order.* The order:

  (A) may be made only on motion for good cause and on notice to all parties and the person to be examined; and

  (B) must specify the time, place, manner, conditions, and scope of the examination, as well as the person or persons who will perform it.

(b) **Examiner's Report.**

(1) *Request by the Party or Person Examined.* The party who moved for the examination must, on request, deliver to the requester a copy of the examiner's report, together with like reports of all earlier examinations of the same condition. The request may be made by the party against whom the examination order was issued or by the person examined.

(2) *Contents.* The examiner's report must be in writing and must set out in detail the examiner's findings, including diagnoses, conclusions, and the results of any tests.

(3) *Request by the Moving Party.* After delivering the reports, the party who moved for the examination may request—and is entitled to receive—from the party against whom the examination order was issued like reports of all earlier or later examinations of the same condition. But those reports need not be delivered by the party with custody or control of the person examined if the party shows that it could not obtain them.

(4) *Waiver of Privilege.* By requesting and obtaining the examiner's report, or by deposing the examiner, the party examined waives any privilege it may have—in that action or any other action involving the same controversy—concerning testimony about all examinations of the same condition.

(5) *Failure to Deliver a Report.* The court on motion may order—on just terms—that a party deliver the report of an examination. If the report is not provided, the court may exclude the examiner's testimony at trial.

(6) *Scope.* This subdivision (b) applies also to an examination made by the parties' agreement, unless the agreement states otherwise. This subdivision does not preclude obtaining an examiner's report or deposing an examiner under other rules.

(Amended March 30, 1970, effective July 1, 1970; March 2, 1987, effective August 1, 1987; amended by Pub.L. 100–690, Title VII, § 7047(b), November 18, 1988, 102 Stat. 4401; amended April 30, 1991, effective December 1, 1991; April 30, 2007, effective December 1, 2007.)

RULE 36.   REQUESTS FOR ADMISSION

(a) Scope and Procedure.

(1) *Scope.* A party may serve on any other party a written request to admit, for purposes of the pending action only, the truth of any matters within the scope of Rule 26(b)(1) relating to:

(A) facts, the application of law to fact, or opinions about either; and

(B) the genuineness of any described documents.

(2) *Form; Copy of a Document.* Each matter must be separately stated. A request to admit the genuineness of a document must be accompanied by a copy of the document unless it is, or has been, otherwise furnished or made available for inspection and copying.

(3) *Time to Respond; Effect of Not Responding.* A matter is admitted unless, within 30 days after being served, the party to whom the request is directed serves on the requesting party a written answer or objection addressed to the matter and signed by the party or its attorney. A shorter or longer time for responding may be stipulated to under Rule 29 or be ordered by the court.

(4) *Answer.* If a matter is not admitted, the answer must specifically deny it or state in detail why the answering party cannot truthfully admit or deny it. A denial must fairly respond to the substance of the matter; and when good faith

requires that a party qualify an answer or deny only a part of a matter, the answer must specify the part admitted and qualify or deny the rest. The answering party may assert lack of knowledge or information as a reason for failing to admit or deny only if the party states that it has made reasonable inquiry and that the information it knows or can readily obtain is insufficient to enable it to admit or deny.

(5) *Objections.* The grounds for objecting to a request must be stated. A party must not object solely on the ground that the request presents a genuine issue for trial.

(6) *Motion Regarding the Sufficiency of an Answer or Objection.* The requesting party may move to determine the sufficiency of an answer or objection. Unless the court finds an objection justified, it must order that an answer be served. On finding that an answer does not comply with this rule, the court may order either that the matter is admitted or that an amended answer be served. The court may defer its final decision until a pretrial conference or a specified time before trial. Rule 37(a)(5) applies to an award of expenses.

(b) Effect of an Admission; Withdrawing or Amending It. A matter admitted under this rule is conclusively established unless the court, on motion, permits the admission to be withdrawn or amended. Subject to Rule 16(e), the court may permit withdrawal or amendment if it would promote the presentation of the merits of the action and if the court is not persuaded that it would prejudice the requesting party in maintaining or defending the action on the merits. An admission under this rule is not an admission for any other purpose and cannot be used against the party in any other proceeding.

(Amended December 27, 1946, effective March 19, 1948; March 30, 1970, effective July 1, 1970; March 2, 1987, effective August 1, 1987; April 22, 1993, effective December 1, 1993; April 30, 2007, effective December 1, 2007.)

RULE 37.   FAILURE TO MAKE DISCLOSURES OR TO COOPERATE IN DISCOVERY; SANCTIONS

(a) Motion for an Order Compelling Disclosure or Discovery.

(1) *In General.* On notice to other parties and all affected persons, a party may move for an order compelling disclosure or discovery. The motion must include a certification that the movant has in good faith conferred or attempted to confer with the person or party failing to make disclosure or discovery in an effort to obtain it without court action.

(2) *Appropriate Court.* A motion for an order to a party must be made in the court where the action is pending. A motion for an order to a nonparty must be made in the court where the discovery is or will be taken.

(3) *Specific Motions.*

(A) *To Compel Disclosure.* If a party fails to make a disclosure required by Rule 26(a), any other party may move to compel disclosure and for appropriate sanctions.

(B) *To Compel a Discovery Response.* A party seeking discovery may move for an order compelling an answer, designation, production, or inspection. This motion may be made if:

(i) a deponent fails to answer a question asked under Rule 30 or 31;

(ii) a corporation or other entity fails to make a designation under Rule 30(b)(6) or 31(a)(4);

(iii) a party fails to answer an interrogatory submitted under Rule 33; or

(iv) a party fails to produce documents or fails to respond that inspection will be permitted — or fails to permit inspection — as requested under Rule 34.

(C) *Related to a Deposition.* When taking an oral deposition, the party asking a question may complete or adjourn the examination before moving for an order.

(4) *Evasive or Incomplete Disclosure, Answer, or Response.* For purposes of this subdivision (a), an evasive or incomplete disclosure, answer, or response must be treated as a failure to disclose, answer, or respond.

(5) *Payment of Expenses; Protective Orders.*

(A) *If the Motion Is Granted (or Disclosure or Discovery Is Provided After Filing).* If the motion is granted—or if the disclosure or requested discovery is provided after the motion was filed—the court must, after giving an opportunity to be heard, require the party or deponent whose conduct necessitated the motion, the party or attorney advising that conduct, or both to pay the movant's reasonable expenses incurred in making the motion, including attorney's fees. But the court must not order this payment if:

(i) the movant filed the motion before attempting in good faith to obtain the disclosure or discovery without court action;

(ii) the opposing party's nondisclosure, response, or objection was substantially justified; or

(iii) other circumstances make an award of expenses unjust.

(B) *If the Motion Is Denied.* If the motion is denied, the court may issue any protective order authorized under Rule 26(c) and must, after giving an opportunity to be heard, require the movant, the attorney filing the motion, or both to pay the party or deponent who opposed the motion its reasonable expenses incurred in opposing the motion, including attorney's fees. But the court must not order this payment if the motion was substantially justified or other circumstances make an award of expenses unjust.

(C) *If the Motion Is Granted in Part and Denied in Part.* If the motion is granted in part and denied in part, the court may issue any protective order authorized under Rule 26(c) and may, after giving an opportunity to be heard, apportion the reasonable expenses for the motion.

(b) Failure to Comply with a Court Order.

(1) *Sanctions Sought in the District Where the Deposition Is Taken.* If the court where the discovery is taken orders a deponent to be sworn or to answer a question and the deponent fails to obey, the failure may be treated as contempt of court. If a deposition-related motion is transferred to the court where the action is pending, and that court orders a deponent to be sworn or to answer a question and the deponent fails to obey, the failure may be treated as contempt of either the court where the discovery is taken or the court where the action is pending.

(2) *Sanctions Sought in the District Where the Action Is Pending.*

(A) *For Not Obeying a Discovery Order.* If a party or a party's officer, director, or managing agent—or a witness designated under Rule 30(b)(6) or 31(a)(4)—fails to obey an order to provide or permit discovery, including an order under Rule 26(f), 35, or 37(a), the court where the action is pending may issue further just orders. They may include the following:

(i) directing that the matters embraced in the order or other designated facts be taken as established for purposes of the action, as the prevailing party claims;

(ii) prohibiting the disobedient party from supporting or opposing designated claims or defenses, or from introducing designated matters in evidence;

(iii) striking pleadings in whole or in part;

    (iv) staying further proceedings until the order is obeyed;

    (v) dismissing the action or proceeding in whole or in part;

    (vi) rendering a default judgment against the disobedient party; or

    (vii) treating as contempt of court the failure to obey any order except an order to submit to a physical or mental examination.

  (B) *For Not Producing a Person for Examination.* If a party fails to comply with an order under Rule 35(a) requiring it to produce another person for examination, the court may issue any of the orders listed in Rule 37(b)(2)(A)(i)-(vi), unless the disobedient party shows that it cannot produce the other person.

  (C) *Payment of Expenses.* Instead of or in addition to the orders above, the court must order the disobedient party, the attorney advising that party, or both to pay the reasonable expenses, including attorney's fees, caused by the failure, unless the failure was substantially justified or other circumstances make an award of expenses unjust.

(c) Failure to Disclose, to Supplement an Earlier Response, or to Admit.

  (1) *Failure to Disclose or Supplement.* If a party fails to provide information or identify a witness as required by Rule 26(a) or (e), the party is not allowed to use that information or witness to supply evidence on a motion, at a hearing, or at a trial, unless the failure was substantially justified or is harmless. In addition to or instead of this sanction, the court, on motion and after giving an opportunity to be heard:

  (A) may order payment of the reasonable expenses, including attorney's fees, caused by the failure;

  (B) may inform the jury of the party's failure; and

  (C) may impose other appropriate sanctions, including any of the orders listed in Rule 37(b)(2)(A)(i)-(vi).

  (2) *Failure to Admit.* If a party fails to admit what is requested under Rule 36 and if the requesting party later proves a document to be genuine or the matter true, the requesting party may move that the party who failed to admit pay the reasonable expenses, including attorney's fees, incurred in making that proof. The court must so order unless:

  (A) the request was held objectionable under Rule 36(a);

  (B) the admission sought was of no substantial importance;

  (C) the party failing to admit had a reasonable ground to believe that it might prevail on the matter; or

  (D) there was other good reason for the failure to admit.

(d) Party's Failure to Attend Its Own Deposition, Serve Answers to Interrogatories, or Respond to a Request for Inspection.

  (1) *In General.*

  (A) *Motion; Grounds for Sanctions.* The court where the action is pending may, on motion, order sanctions if:

    (i) a party or a party's officer, director, or managing agent—or a person designated under Rule 30(b)(6) or 31(a)(4)—fails, after being served with proper notice, to appear for that person's deposition; or

    (ii) a party, after being properly served with interrogatories under Rule 33 or a request for inspection under Rule 34, fails to serve its answers, objections, or written response.

  (B) *Certification.* A motion for sanctions for failing to answer or respond must include a certification that the movant has in good faith conferred or attempted to confer with the party failing to act in an effort to obtain the answer or response without court action.

  (2) *Unacceptable Excuse for Failing to Act.* A failure described in Rule 37(d)(1)(A) is not excused on the ground that the discovery sought was objectionable, unless the party failing to act has a pending motion for a protective order under Rule 26(c).

  (3) *Types of Sanctions.* Sanctions may include any of the orders listed in Rule 37(b)(2)(A)(i)-(vi). Instead of or in addition to these sanctions, the court must require the party failing to act, the attorney advising that party, or both to pay the reasonable expenses, including attorney's fees, caused by the failure, unless the failure was substantially justified or other circumstances make an award of expenses unjust.

(e) Failure to Preserve Electronically Stored Information. If electronically stored information that should have been preserved in the anticipation or conduct of litigation is lost because a party failed to take reasonable steps to preserve it, and it cannot be restored or replaced through additional discovery, the court:

  (1) upon finding prejudice to another party from loss of the information, may order measures no greater than necessary to cure the prejudice; or

(2) only upon finding that the party acted with the intent to deprive another party of the information's use in the litigation may:

(A) presume that the lost information was unfavorable to the party;

(B) instruct the jury that it may or must presume the information was unfavorable to the party; or

(C) dismiss the action or enter a default judgment.

(f) **Failure to Participate in Framing a Discovery Plan.** If a party or its attorney fails to participate in good faith in developing and submitting a proposed discovery plan as required by Rule 26(f), the court may, after giving an opportunity to be heard, require that party or attorney to pay to any other party the reasonable expenses, including attorney's fees, caused by the failure.

(Amended December 29, 1948, effective October 20, 1949; March 30, 1970, effective July 1, 1970; April 29, 1980, effective August 1, 1980; amended by Pub.L. 96–481, Title II, § 205(a), October 21, 1980, 94 Stat. 2330, effective October 1, 1981; amended March 2, 1987, effective August 1, 1987; April 22, 1993, effective December 1, 1993; April 17, 2000, effective December 1, 2000; April 12, 2006, effective December 1, 2006; April 30, 2007, effective December 1, 2007; April 16, 2013, effective December 1, 2013; April 29, 2015, effective December 1, 2015.)

TITLE VI. TRIALS

RULE 38. RIGHT TO A JURY TRIAL; DEMAND

(a) **Right Preserved.** The right of trial by jury as declared by the Seventh Amendment to the Constitution—or as provided by a federal statute—is preserved to the parties inviolate.

(b) **Demand.** On any issue triable of right by a jury, a party may demand a jury trial by:

(1) serving the other parties with a written demand—which may be included in a pleading—no later than 14 days after the last pleading directed to the issue is served; and

(2) filing the demand in accordance with Rule 5(d).

(c) **Specifying Issues.** In its demand, a party may specify the issues that it wishes to have tried by a jury; otherwise, it is considered to have demanded a jury trial on all the issues so triable. If the party has demanded a jury trial on only some issues, any other party may—within 14 days after being served with the demand or within a shorter time ordered by the court—serve a demand for a jury trial on any other or all factual issues triable by jury.

(d) **Waiver; Withdrawal.** A party waives a jury trial unless its demand is properly served and filed. A proper demand may be withdrawn only if the parties consent.

(e) **Admiralty and Maritime Claims.** These rules do not create a right to a jury trial on issues in a claim that is an admiralty or maritime claim under Rule 9(h).

(Amended February 28, 1966, effective July 1, 1966; March 2, 1987, effective August 1, 1987; April 22, 1993, effective December 1, 1993; April 30, 2007, effective December 1, 2007; March 26, 2009, effective December 1, 2009.)

RULE 39. TRIAL BY JURY OR BY THE COURT

(a) **When a Demand Is Made.** When a jury trial has been demanded under Rule 38, the action must be designated on the docket as a jury action. The trial on all issues so demanded must be by jury unless:

(1) the parties or their attorneys file a stipulation to a nonjury trial or so stipulate on the record; or

(2) the court, on motion or on its own, finds that on some or all of those issues there is no federal right to a jury trial.

(b) **When No Demand Is Made.** Issues on which a jury trial is not properly demanded are to be tried by the court. But the court may, on motion, order a jury trial on any issue for which a jury might have been demanded.

(c) **Advisory Jury; Jury Trial by Consent.** In an action not triable of right by a jury, the court, on motion or on its own:

(1) may try any issue with an advisory jury; or

(2) may, with the parties' consent, try any issue by a jury whose verdict has the same effect as if a jury trial had been a matter of right, unless the action is against the United States and a federal statute provides for a nonjury trial.

(Amended April 30, 2007, effective December 1, 2007.)

RULE 40. SCHEDULING CASES FOR TRIAL

Each court must provide by rule for scheduling trials. The court must give priority to actions entitled to priority by a federal statute.

(Amended April 30, 2007, effective December 1, 2007.)

RULE 41. DISMISSAL OF ACTIONS

(a) Voluntary Dismissal.

(1) *By the Plaintiff.*

(A) *Without a Court Order.* Subject to Rules 23(e), 23.1(c), 23.2, and 66 and any applicable federal statute, the plaintiff may dismiss an action without a court order by filing:

(i) a notice of dismissal before the opposing party serves either an answer or a motion for summary judgment; or

(ii) a stipulation of dismissal signed by all parties who have appeared.

(B) *Effect.* Unless the notice or stipulation states otherwise, the dismissal is without prejudice. But if the plaintiff previously dismissed any federal- or state-court action based on or including the same claim, a notice of dismissal operates as an adjudication on the merits.

(2) *By Court Order; Effect.* Except as provided in Rule 41(a)(1), an action may be dismissed at the plaintiff's request only by court order, on terms that the court considers proper. If a defendant has pleaded a counterclaim before being served with the plaintiff's motion to dismiss, the action may be dismissed over the defendant's objection only if the counterclaim can remain pending for independent adjudication. Unless the order states otherwise, a dismissal under this paragraph (2) is without prejudice.

(b) Involuntary Dismissal; Effect. If the plaintiff fails to prosecute or to comply with these rules or a court order, a defendant may move to dismiss the action or any claim against it. Unless the dismissal order states otherwise, a dismissal under this subdivision (b) and any dismissal not under this rule—except one for lack of jurisdiction, improper venue, or failure to join a party under Rule 19—operates as an adjudication on the merits.

(c) Dismissing a Counterclaim, Crossclaim, or Third–Party Claim. This rule applies to a dismissal of any counterclaim, crossclaim, or third-party claim. A claimant's voluntary dismissal under Rule 41(a)(1)(A)(i) must be made:

(1) before a responsive pleading is served; or

(2) if there is no responsive pleading, before evidence is introduced at a hearing or trial.

(d) Costs of a Previously Dismissed Action. If a plaintiff who previously dismissed an action in any court files an action based on or including the same claim against the same defendant, the court:

(1) may order the plaintiff to pay all or part of the costs of that previous action; and

(2) may stay the proceedings until the plaintiff has complied.

(Amended December 27, 1946, effective March 19, 1948; January 21, 1963, effective July 1, 1963; February 28, 1966, effective July 1, 1966; December 4, 1967, effective July 1, 1968; March 2, 1987, effective August 1, 1987; April 30, 1991, effective December 1, 1991; April 30, 2007, effective December 1, 2007.)

RULE 42. CONSOLIDATION; SEPARATE TRIALS

(a) Consolidation. If actions before the court involve a common question of law or fact, the court may:

(1) join for hearing or trial any or all matters at issue in the actions;

(2) consolidate the actions; or

(3) issue any other orders to avoid unnecessary cost or delay.

(b) Separate Trials. For convenience, to avoid prejudice, or to expedite and economize, the court may order a separate trial of one or more separate issues, claims, crossclaims, counterclaims, or third-party claims. When ordering a separate trial, the court must preserve any federal right to a jury trial.

(Amended February 28, 1966, effective July 1, 1966; April 30, 2007, effective December 1, 2007.)

RULE 43. TAKING TESTIMONY

(a) In Open Court. At trial, the witnesses' testimony must be taken in open court unless a federal statute, the Federal Rules of Evidence, these rules, or other rules adopted by the Supreme Court provide otherwise. For good cause in compelling circumstances and with appropriate safeguards, the court may permit testimony in open court by contemporaneous transmission from a different location.

(b) Affirmation Instead of an Oath. When these rules require an oath, a solemn affirmation suffices.

(c) Evidence on a Motion. When a motion relies on facts outside the record, the court may hear the matter on affidavits or may hear it wholly or partly on oral testimony or on depositions.

(d) Interpreter. The court may appoint an interpreter of its choosing; fix reasonable compensation to be paid from funds provided by law or by one or more parties; and tax the compensation as costs.

(Amended February 28, 1966, effective July 1, 1966; November 20, 1972, and December 18, 1972, effective July 1, 1975; March 2, 1987, effective August 1, 1987; April 23, 1996, effective December 1, 1996; April 30, 2007, effective December 1, 2007.)

RULE 44. PROVING AN OFFICIAL RECORD

(a) Means of Proving.

(1) *Domestic Record.* Each of the following evidences an official record—or an entry in it—that is otherwise admissible and is kept within the United States, any state, district, or commonwealth, or any territory subject to the administrative or judicial jurisdiction of the United States:

(A) an official publication of the record; or

(B) a copy attested by the officer with legal custody of the record—or by the officer's deputy—and accompanied by a certificate that the officer has custody. The certificate must be made under seal:

(i) by a judge of a court of record in the district or political subdivision where the record is kept; or

(ii) by any public officer with a seal of office and with official duties in the district or political subdivision where the record is kept.

(2) *Foreign Record.*

(A) *In General.* Each of the following evidences a foreign official record—or an entry in it—that is otherwise admissible:

(i) an official publication of the record; or

(ii) the record—or a copy—that is attested by an authorized person and is accompanied either by a final certification of genuineness or by a certification under a treaty or convention to which the United States and the country where the record is located are parties.

(B) *Final Certification of Genuineness.* A final certification must certify the genuineness of the signature and official position of the attester or of any foreign official whose certificate of genuineness relates to the attestation or is in a chain of certificates of genuineness relating to the attestation. A final certification may be made by a secretary of a United States embassy or legation; by a consul general, vice consul, or consular agent of the United States; or by a diplomatic or consular official of the foreign country assigned or accredited to the United States.

(C) *Other Means of Proof.* If all parties have had a reasonable opportunity to investigate a foreign record's authenticity and accuracy, the court may, for good cause, either:

(i) admit an attested copy without final certification; or

(ii) permit the record to be evidenced by an attested summary with or without a final certification.

(b) Lack of a Record.
A written statement that a diligent search of designated records revealed no record or entry of a specified tenor is admissible as evidence that the records contain no such record or entry. For domestic records, the statement must be authenticated under Rule 44(a)(1). For foreign records, the statement must comply with (a)(2)(C)(ii).

(c) Other Proof.
A party may prove an official record—or an entry or lack of an entry in it—by any other method authorized by law.

(Amended February 28, 1966, effective July 1, 1966; March 2, 1987, effective August 1, 1987; April 30, 1991, effective December 1, 1991; April 30, 2007, effective December 1, 2007.)

RULE 44.1. DETERMINING FOREIGN LAW

A party who intends to raise an issue about a foreign country's law must give notice by a pleading or other writing. In determining foreign law, the court may consider any relevant material or source, including testimony, whether or not submitted by a party or admissible under the Federal Rules of Evidence. The court's determination must be treated as a ruling on a question of law.

(Adopted February 28, 1966, effective July 1, 1966; amended November 20, 1972, effective July 1, 1975; March 2, 1987, effective August 1, 1987; April 30, 2007, effective December 1, 2007.)

RULE 45. SUBPOENA

(a) In General.

(1) *Form and Contents.*

(A) *Requirements—In General.* Every subpoena must:

(i) state the court from which it issued;

(ii) state the title of the action and its civil-action number;

(iii) command each person to whom it is directed to do the following at a specified time and place: attend and testify; produce designated documents, electronically stored information, or tangible things in that person's possession, custody, or control; or permit the inspection of premises; and

(iv) set out the text of Rule 45(d) and (e).

(B) *Command to Attend a Deposition—Notice of the Recording Method.* A subpoena commanding attendance at a deposition must state the method for recording the testimony.

(C) *Combining or Separating a Command to Produce or to Permit Inspection; Specifying the Form for Electronically Stored Information.* A command to produce documents, electronically stored information, or tangible things or to permit the inspection of premises may be included in a subpoena commanding attendance at a deposition, hearing, or trial, or may be set out in a separate subpoena. A subpoena may specify the form or forms in which electronically stored information is to be produced.

(D) *Command to Produce; Included Obligations.* A command in a subpoena to produce documents, electronically stored information, or tangible things requires the responding person to permit inspection, copying, testing, or sampling of the materials.

(2) *Issuing Court.* A subpoena must issue from the court where the action is pending.

(3) *Issued by Whom.* The clerk must issue a subpoena, signed but otherwise in blank, to a party who requests it. That party must complete it before service. An attorney also may issue and sign a subpoena if the attorney is authorized to practice in the issuing court.

(4) *Notice to Other Parties Before Service.* If the subpoena commands the production of documents, electronically stored information, or tangible things or the inspection of premises before trial, then before it is served on the person to whom it is directed, a notice and a copy of the subpoena must be served on each party.

(b) **Service.**

(1) *By Whom and How; Tendering Fees.* Any person who is at least 18 years old and not a party may serve a subpoena. Serving a subpoena requires delivering a copy to the named person and, if the subpoena requires that person's attendance, tendering the fees for 1 day's attendance and the mileage allowed by law. Fees and mileage need not be tendered when the subpoena issues on behalf of the United States or any of its officers or agencies.

(2) *Service in the United States.* A subpoena may be served at any place within the United States.

(3) *Service in a Foreign Country.* 28 U.S.C. § 1783 governs issuing and serving a subpoena directed to a United States national or resident who is in a foreign country.

(4) *Proof of Service.* Proving service, when necessary, requires filing with the issuing court a statement showing the date and manner of service and the names of the persons served. The statement must be certified by the server.

(c) **Place of Compliance.**

(1) *For a Trial, Hearing, or Deposition.* A subpoena may command a person to attend a trial, hearing, or deposition only as follows:

(A) within 100 miles of where the person resides, is employed, or regularly transacts business in person; or

(B) within the state where the person resides, is employed, or regularly transacts business in person, if the person

(i) is a party or a party's officer; or

(ii) is commanded to attend a trial and would not incur substantial expense.

(2) *For Other Discovery.* A subpoena may command:

(A) production of documents, electronically stored information, or tangible things at a place within 100 miles of where the person resides, is employed, or regularly transacts business in person; and

(B) inspection of premises at the premises to be inspected.

(d) **Protecting a Person Subject to a Subpoena; Enforcement.**

(1) *Avoiding Undue Burden or Expense; Sanctions.* A party or attorney responsible for issuing and serving a subpoena must take reasonable steps to avoid imposing undue burden or expense on a person subject to the subpoena. The court for the district where compliance is required must enforce this duty and impose an appropriate sanction—which may include lost earnings and reasonable attorney's fees—on a party or attorney who fails to comply.

(2) *Command to Produce Materials or Permit Inspection.*

(A) *Appearance Not Required.* A person commanded to produce documents, electronically stored information, or tangible things, or to permit the inspection of premises, need not appear in person at the place of production or inspection unless also commanded to appear for a deposition, hearing, or trial.

(B) *Objections.* A person commanded to produce documents or tangible things or to permit inspection may serve on the party or attorney designated in the subpoena a written objection to inspecting, copying, testing, or sampling any or all of the materials or to inspecting the premises—or to producing electronically stored information in the form or forms requested. The objection must be served before the earlier of the time specified for compliance or 14 days after the subpoena is served. If an objection is made, the following rules apply:

(i) At any time, on notice to the commanded person, the serving party may move the court for the district where compliance is required for an order compelling production or inspection.

(ii) These acts may be required only as directed in the order, and the order must protect a person who is neither a party nor a party's officer from significant expense resulting from compliance.

(3) *Quashing or Modifying a Subpoena.*

(A) *When Required.* On timely motion, the court for the district where compliance is required must quash or modify a subpoena that:

(i) fails to allow a reasonable time to comply;

(ii) requires a person to comply beyond the geographical limits specified in Rule 45(c);

(iii) requires disclosure of privileged or other protected matter, if no exception or waiver applies; or

(iv) subjects a person to undue burden.

(B) *When Permitted.* To protect a person subject to or affected by a subpoena, the court for the district where compliance is required may, on motion, quash or modify the subpoena if it requires:

(i) disclosing a trade secret or other confidential research, development, or commercial information; or

(ii) disclosing an unretained expert's opinion or information that does not describe specific occurrences in dispute and results from the expert's study that was not requested by a party.

(C) *Specifying Conditions as an Alternative.* In the circumstances described in Rule 45(d)(3)(B), the court may, instead of quashing or modifying a subpoena, order appearance or production under specified conditions if the serving party:

(i) shows a substantial need for the testimony or material that cannot be otherwise met without undue hardship; and

(ii) ensures that the subpoenaed person will be reasonably compensated.

(e) Duties in Responding to a Subpoena.

(1) *Producing Documents or Electronically Stored Information.* These procedures apply to producing documents or electronically stored information:

(A) *Documents.* A person responding to a subpoena to produce documents must produce them as they are kept in the ordinary course of business or must organize and label them to correspond to the categories in the demand.

(B) *Form for Producing Electronically Stored Information Not Specified.* If a subpoena does not specify a form for producing electronically stored information, the person responding must produce it in a form or forms in which it is ordinarily maintained or in a reasonably usable form or forms.

(C) *Electronically Stored Information Produced in Only One Form.* The person responding need not produce the same electronically stored information in more than one form.

(D) *Inaccessible Electronically Stored Information.* The person responding need not provide discovery of electronically stored information from sources that the person identifies as not reasonably accessible because of undue burden or cost. On motion to compel discovery or for a protective order, the person responding must show that the information is not reasonably accessible because of undue burden or cost. If that showing is made, the court may nonetheless order discovery from such sources if the requesting party shows good cause, considering the limitations of Rule 26(b)(2)(C). The court may specify conditions for the discovery.

(2) *Claiming Privilege or Protection.*

(A) *Information Withheld.* A person withholding subpoenaed information under a claim that it is privileged or subject to protection as trial-preparation material must:

(i) expressly make the claim; and

(ii) describe the nature of the withheld documents, communications, or tangible things in a manner that, without revealing information itself privileged or protected, will enable the parties to assess the claim.

(B) *Information Produced.* If information produced in response to a subpoena is subject to a claim of privilege or of protection as trial-preparation material, the person making the claim may notify any party that received the information of the claim and the basis for it. After being notified, a party must promptly return, sequester, or destroy the specified information and any copies it has; must not use or disclose the information until the claim is resolved; must take reasonable steps to retrieve the information if the party disclosed it before being notified; and may promptly present the information under seal to the court for the district where compliance is required for a determination of the claim. The person who produced the information must preserve the information until the claim is resolved.

(f) Transferring a Subpoena–Related Motion. When the court where compliance is required did not issue the subpoena, it may transfer a motion under this rule to the issuing court if the person subject to the subpoena consents or if the court finds exceptional circumstances. Then, if the attorney for a person subject to a subpoena is authorized to practice in the court where the motion was made, the attorney may file papers and appear on the motion as an officer of the issuing court. To enforce its order, the issuing court may transfer the order to the court where the motion was made.

(g) Contempt. The court for the district where compliance is required—and also, after a motion is transferred, the issuing court—may hold in contempt a person who, having been served, fails without adequate excuse to obey the subpoena or an order related to it.

(Amended December 27, 1946, effective March 19, 1948; December 29, 1948, effective October 20, 1949; March 30, 1970, effective July 1, 1970; April 29, 1980, effective August 1, 1980; April 29, 1985, effective August 1, 1985; March 2, 1987, effective August 1, 1987; April 30, 1991, effective December 1, 1991; April 25, 2005, effective December 1, 2005; April 12, 2006, effective December 1, 2006; April 30, 2007, effective December 1, 2007; April 16, 2013, effective December 1, 2013.)

RULE 46. OBJECTING TO A RULING OR ORDER

A formal exception to a ruling or order is unnecessary. When the ruling or order is requested or made, a party need only state the action that it wants the court to take or objects to, along with the grounds for the request or objection. Failing to object does not prejudice a party who had no opportunity to do so when the ruling or order was made.

(Amended March 2, 1987, effective August 1, 1987; April 30, 2007, effective December 1, 2007.)

RULE 47. SELECTING JURORS

(a) Examining Jurors. The court may permit the parties or their attorneys to examine prospective jurors or may itself do so. If the court examines the jurors, it must permit the parties or their attorneys to make any further inquiry it considers proper, or must itself ask any of their additional questions it considers proper.

(b) Peremptory Challenges. The court must allow the number of peremptory challenges provided by 28 U.S.C. § 1870.

(c) Excusing a Juror. During trial or deliberation, the court may excuse a juror for good cause.

(Amended February 28, 1966, effective July 1, 1966; April 30, 1991, effective December 1, 1991; April 30, 2007, effective December 1, 2007.)

RULE 48. NUMBER OF JURORS; VERDICT; POLLING

(a) Number of Jurors. A jury must begin with at least 6 and no more than 12 members, and each juror must participate in the verdict unless excused under Rule 47(c).

(b) Verdict. Unless the parties stipulate otherwise, the verdict must be unanimous and must be returned by a jury of at least 6 members.

(c) Polling. After a verdict is returned but before the jury is discharged, the court must on a party's request, or may on its own, poll the jurors individually. If the poll reveals a lack of unanimity or lack of assent by the number of jurors that the parties stipulated to, the court may direct the jury to deliberate further or may order a new trial.

(Amended April 30, 1991, effective December 1, 1991; April 30, 2007, effective December 1, 2007; March 26, 2009, effective December 1, 2009.)

RULE 49. SPECIAL VERDICT; GENERAL VERDICT AND QUESTIONS

(a) Special Verdict.

   (1) *In General.* The court may require a jury to return only a special verdict in the form of a special written finding on each issue of fact. The court may do so by:

      (A) submitting written questions susceptible of a categorical or other brief answer;

      (B) submitting written forms of the special findings that might properly be made under the pleadings and evidence; or

      (C) using any other method that the court considers appropriate.

   (2) *Instructions.* The court must give the instructions and explanations necessary to enable the jury to make its findings on each submitted issue.

   (3) *Issues Not Submitted.* A party waives the right to a jury trial on any issue of fact raised by the pleadings or evidence but not submitted to the jury unless, before the jury retires, the party demands its submission to the jury. If the party does not demand submission, the court may make a finding on the issue. If the court makes

no finding, it is considered to have made a finding consistent with its judgment on the special verdict.

(b) General Verdict with Answers to Written Questions.

  (1) *In General.* The court may submit to the jury forms for a general verdict, together with written questions on one or more issues of fact that the jury must decide. The court must give the instructions and explanations necessary to enable the jury to render a general verdict and answer the questions in writing, and must direct the jury to do both.

  (2) *Verdict and Answers Consistent.* When the general verdict and the answers are consistent, the court must approve, for entry under Rule 58, an appropriate judgment on the verdict and answers.

  (3) *Answers Inconsistent with the Verdict.* When the answers are consistent with each other but one or more is inconsistent with the general verdict, the court may:

    (A) approve, for entry under Rule 58, an appropriate judgment according to the answers, notwithstanding the general verdict;

    (B) direct the jury to further consider its answers and verdict; or

    (C) order a new trial.

  (4) *Answers Inconsistent with Each Other and the Verdict.* When the answers are inconsistent with each other and one or more is also inconsistent with the general verdict, judgment must not be entered; instead, the court must direct the jury to further consider its answers and verdict, or must order a new trial.

(Amended January 21, 1963, effective July 1, 1963; March 2, 1987, effective August 1, 1987; April 30, 2007, effective December 1, 2007.)

RULE 50. JUDGMENT AS A MATTER OF LAW IN A JURY TRIAL; RELATED MOTION FOR A NEW TRIAL; CONDITIONAL RULING

(a) Judgment as a Matter of Law.

  (1) *In General.* If a party has been fully heard on an issue during a jury trial and the court finds that a reasonable jury would not have a legally sufficient evidentiary basis to find for the party on that issue, the court may:

    (A) resolve the issue against the party; and

    (B) grant a motion for judgment as a matter of law against the party on a claim or defense that, under the controlling law, can be maintained or defeated only with a favorable finding on that issue.

  (2) *Motion.* A motion for judgment as a matter of law may be made at any time before the case is submitted to the jury. The motion must specify the judgment sought and the law and facts that entitle the movant to the judgment.

(b) Renewing the Motion After Trial; Alternative Motion for a New Trial. If the court does not grant a motion for judgment as a matter of law made under Rule 50(a), the court is considered to have submitted the action to the jury subject to the court's later deciding the legal questions raised by the motion. No later than 28 days after the entry of judgment—or if the motion addresses a jury issue not decided by a verdict, no later than 28 days after the jury was discharged—the movant may file a renewed motion for judgment as a matter of law and may include an alternative or joint request for a new trial under Rule 59. In ruling on the renewed motion, the court may:

  (1) allow judgment on the verdict, if the jury returned a verdict;

  (2) order a new trial; or

  (3) direct the entry of judgment as a matter of law.

(c) Granting the Renewed Motion; Conditional Ruling on a Motion for a New Trial.

  (1) *In General.* If the court grants a renewed motion for judgment as a matter of law, it must also conditionally rule on any motion for a new trial by determining whether a new trial should be granted if the judgment is later vacated or reversed. The court must state the grounds for conditionally granting or denying the motion for a new trial.

  (2) *Effect of a Conditional Ruling.* Conditionally granting the motion for a new trial does not affect the judgment's finality; if the judgment is reversed, the new trial must proceed unless the appellate court orders otherwise. If the motion for a new trial is conditionally denied, the appellee may assert error in that denial; if the judgment is reversed, the case must proceed as the appellate court orders.

(d) Time for a Losing Party's New-Trial Motion. Any motion for a new trial under Rule 59 by a party against whom judgment as a matter of law is rendered must be filed no later than 28 days after the entry of the judgment.

(e) Denying the Motion for Judgment as a Matter of Law; Reversal on Appeal. If the court denies the motion for judgment as a matter of law, the prevailing party may, as appellee, assert grounds entitling it to a new trial should the appellate court conclude that the trial court erred in denying the motion. If the appellate court reverses the judgment, it may order a new trial, direct the trial court to determine whether a new trial should be granted, or direct the entry of judgment.

(Amended January 21, 1963, effective July 1, 1963; March 2, 1987, effective August 1, 1987; April 30, 1991, effective December 1, 1991; April 22, 1993, effective December 1, 1993; April 27, 1995, effective December 1, 1995; April 12, 2006, effective December 1, 2006; April 30, 2007, effective December 1, 2007; March 26, 2009, effective December 1, 2009.)

RULE 51. INSTRUCTIONS TO THE JURY; OBJECTIONS; PRESERVING A CLAIM OF ERROR

(a) Requests.

(1) *Before or at the Close of the Evidence.* At the close of the evidence or at any earlier reasonable time that the court orders, a party may file and furnish to every other party written requests for the jury instructions it wants the court to give.

(2) *After the Close of the Evidence.* After the close of the evidence, a party may:

(A) file requests for instructions on issues that could not reasonably have been anticipated by an earlier time that the court set for requests; and

(B) with the court's permission, file untimely requests for instructions on any issue.

(b) Instructions. The court:

(1) must inform the parties of its proposed instructions and proposed action on the requests before instructing the jury and before final jury arguments;

(2) must give the parties an opportunity to object on the record and out of the jury's hearing before the instructions and arguments are delivered; and

(3) may instruct the jury at any time before the jury is discharged.

(c) Objections.

(1) *How to Make.* A party who objects to an instruction or the failure to give an instruction must do so on the record, stating distinctly the matter objected to and the grounds for the objection.

(2) *When to Make.* An objection is timely if:

(A) a party objects at the opportunity provided under Rule 51(b)(2); or

(B) a party was not informed of an instruction or action on a request before that opportunity to object, and the party objects promptly after learning that the instruction or request will be, or has been, given or refused.

(d) Assigning Error; Plain Error.

(1) *Assigning Error.* A party may assign as error:

(A) an error in an instruction actually given, if that party properly objected; or

(B) a failure to give an instruction, if that party properly requested it and—unless the court rejected the request in a definitive ruling on the record—also properly objected.

(2) *Plain Error.* A court may consider a plain error in the instructions that has not been preserved as required by Rule 51(d)(1) if the error affects substantial rights.

(Amended March 2, 1987, effective August 1, 1987; March 27, 2003, effective December 1, 2003; April 30, 2007, effective December 1, 2007.)

RULE 52. FINDINGS AND CONCLUSIONS BY THE COURT; JUDGMENT ON PARTIAL FINDINGS

(a) Findings and Conclusions.

(1) *In General.* In an action tried on the facts without a jury or with an advisory jury, the court must find the facts specially and state its conclusions of law separately. The findings and conclusions may be stated on the record after the close of the evidence or may appear in an opinion or a memorandum of decision filed by the court. Judgment must be entered under Rule 58.

(2) *For an Interlocutory Injunction.* In granting or refusing an interlocutory injunction, the court must similarly state the findings and conclusions that support its action.

(3) *For a Motion.* The court is not required to state findings or conclusions when ruling on a motion under Rule 12 or 56 or, unless these rules provide otherwise, on any other motion.

(4) *Effect of a Master's Findings.* A master's findings, to the extent adopted by the court, must be considered the court's findings.

(5) *Questioning the Evidentiary Support.* A party may later question the sufficiency of the evidence supporting the findings, whether or not the party requested findings, objected to them, moved to amend them, or moved for partial findings.

(6) *Setting Aside the Findings.* Findings of fact, whether based on oral or other evidence, must not be set aside unless clearly erroneous, and the reviewing court must give due regard to the trial court's opportunity to judge the witnesses' credibility.

(b) Amended or Additional Findings. On a party's motion filed no later than 28 days after the entry of judgment, the court may amend its findings—or make additional findings—and may amend the judgment accordingly. The motion may accompany a motion for a new trial under Rule 59.

(c) Judgment on Partial Findings. If a party has been fully heard on an issue during a nonjury trial and the court finds against the party on that issue, the court may enter judgment against the party on a claim or defense that, under the controlling law, can be maintained or defeated only with a favorable finding on that issue. The court may, however, decline to render any judgment until the close of the evidence. A judgment on partial findings must be supported by findings of fact and conclusions of law as required by Rule 52(a).

(Amended December 27, 1946, effective March 19, 1948; January 21, 1963, effective July 1, 1963; April 28, 1983, effective August 1, 1983; April 29, 1985, effective August 1, 1985; April 30, 1991, effective December 1, 1991; April 22, 1993, effective December 1, 1993; April 27, 1995, effective December 1, 1995; April 30, 2007, effective December 1, 2007; March 26, 2009, effective December 1, 2009.)

RULE 53.   MASTERS

(a) Appointment.

(1) *Scope.* Unless a statute provides otherwise, a court may appoint a master only to:

(A) perform duties consented to by the parties;

(B) hold trial proceedings and make or recommend findings of fact on issues to be decided without a jury if appointment is warranted by:

(i) some exceptional condition; or

(ii) the need to perform an accounting or resolve a difficult computation of damages; or

(C) address pretrial and posttrial matters that cannot be effectively and timely addressed by an available district judge or magistrate judge of the district.

(2) *Disqualification.* A master must not have a relationship to the parties, attorneys, action, or court that would require disqualification of a judge under 28 U.S.C. § 455, unless the parties, with the court's approval, consent to the appointment after the master discloses any potential grounds for disqualification.

(3) *Possible Expense or Delay.* In appointing a master, the court must consider the fairness of imposing the likely expenses on the parties and must protect against unreasonable expense or delay.

(b) Order Appointing a Master.

(1) *Notice.* Before appointing a master, the court must give the parties notice and an opportunity to be heard. Any party may suggest candidates for appointment.

(2) *Contents.* The appointing order must direct the master to proceed with all reasonable diligence and must state:

(A) the master's duties, including any investigation or enforcement duties, and any limits on the master's authority under Rule 53(c);

(B) the circumstances, if any, in which the master may communicate ex parte with the court or a party;

(C) the nature of the materials to be preserved and filed as the record of the master's activities;

(D) the time limits, method of filing the record, other procedures, and standards for reviewing the master's orders, findings, and recommendations; and

(E) the basis, terms, and procedure for fixing the master's compensation under Rule 53(g).

(3) *Issuing.* The court may issue the order only after:

(A) the master files an affidavit disclosing whether there is any ground for disqualification under 28 U.S.C. § 455; and

(B) if a ground is disclosed, the parties, with the court's approval, waive the disqualification.

(4) *Amending.* The order may be amended at any time after notice to the parties and an opportunity to be heard.

(c) Master's Authority.

(1) *In General.* Unless the appointing order directs otherwise, a master may:

(A) regulate all proceedings;

(B) take all appropriate measures to perform the assigned duties fairly and efficiently; and

(C) if conducting an evidentiary hearing, exercise the appointing court's power to compel, take, and record evidence.

(2) *Sanctions.* The master may by order impose on a party any noncontempt sanction provided by Rule 37 or 45, and may recommend a contempt sanction against a party and sanctions against a nonparty.

(d) Master's Orders. A master who issues an order must file it and promptly serve a copy on each party. The clerk must enter the order on the docket.

(e) Master's Reports. A master must report to the court as required by the appointing order. The master must file the report and promptly serve a copy on each party, unless the court orders otherwise.

(f) Action on the Master's Order, Report, or Recommendations.

(1) *Opportunity for a Hearing; Action in General.* In acting on a master's order, report, or recommendations, the court must give the parties notice and an opportunity to be heard; may receive evidence; and may adopt or affirm, modify, wholly or partly reject or reverse, or resubmit to the master with instructions.

(2) *Time to Object or Move to Adopt or Modify.* A party may file objections to—or a motion to adopt or modify—the master's order, report, or recommendations no later than 21 days after a copy is served, unless the court sets a different time.

(3) *Reviewing Factual Findings.* The court must decide de novo all objections to findings of fact made or recommended by a master, unless the parties, with the court's approval, stipulate that:

  (A) the findings will be reviewed for clear error; or

  (B) the findings of a master appointed under Rule 53(a)(1)(A) or (C) will be final.

(4) *Reviewing Legal Conclusions.* The court must decide de novo all objections to conclusions of law made or recommended by a master.

(5) *Reviewing Procedural Matters.* Unless the appointing order establishes a different standard of review, the court may set aside a master's ruling on a procedural matter only for an abuse of discretion.

(g) **Compensation.**

(1) *Fixing Compensation.* Before or after judgment, the court must fix the master's compensation on the basis and terms stated in the appointing order, but the court may set a new basis and terms after giving notice and an opportunity to be heard.

(2) *Payment.* The compensation must be paid either:

  (A) by a party or parties; or

  (B) from a fund or subject matter of the action within the court's control.

(3) *Allocating Payment.* The court must allocate payment among the parties after considering the nature and amount of the controversy, the parties' means, and the extent to which any party is more responsible than other parties for the reference to a master. An interim allocation may be amended to reflect a decision on the merits.

(h) **Appointing a Magistrate Judge.** A magistrate judge is subject to this rule only when the order referring a matter to the magistrate judge states that the reference is made under this rule.

(Amended February 28, 1966, effective July 1, 1966; April 28, 1983, effective August 1, 1983; March 2, 1987, effective August 1, 1987; April 30, 1991, effective December 1, 1991; April 22, 1993, effective December 1, 1993; March 27, 2003, effective December 1, 2003; April 30, 2007, effective December 1, 2007; March 26, 2009, effective December 1, 2009.)

TITLE VII.   JUDGMENT

RULE 54.   JUDGMENT; COSTS

(a) **Definition; Form.** "Judgment" as used in these rules includes a decree and any order from which an appeal lies. A judgment should not include recitals of pleadings, a master's report, or a record of prior proceedings.

(b) **Judgment on Multiple Claims or Involving Multiple Parties.** When an action presents more than one claim for relief—whether as a claim, counterclaim, crossclaim, or third-party claim—or when multiple parties are involved, the court may direct entry of a final judgment as to one or more, but fewer than all, claims or parties only if the court expressly determines that there is no just reason for delay. Otherwise, any order or other decision, however designated, that adjudicates fewer than all the claims or the rights and liabilities of fewer than all the parties does not end the action as to any of the claims or parties and may be revised at any time before the entry of a judgment adjudicating all the claims and all the parties' rights and liabilities.

(c) **Demand for Judgment; Relief to Be Granted.** A default judgment must not differ in kind from, or exceed in amount, what is demanded in the pleadings. Every other final judgment should grant the relief to which each party is entitled, even if the party has not demanded that relief in its pleadings.

(d) **Costs; Attorney's Fees.**

(1) *Costs Other Than Attorney's Fees.* Unless a federal statute, these rules, or a court order provides otherwise, costs—other than attorney's fees—should be allowed to the prevailing party. But costs against the United States, its officers, and its agencies may be imposed only to the extent allowed by law. The clerk may tax costs on 14 days' notice. On motion served within the next 7 days, the court may review the clerk's action.

(2) *Attorney's Fees.*

  (A) *Claim to Be by Motion.* A claim for attorney's fees and related nontaxable expenses must be made by motion unless the substantive law requires those fees to be proved at trial as an element of damages.

(B) *Timing and Contents of the Motion.* Unless a statute or a court order provides otherwise, the motion must:

  (i) be filed no later than 14 days after the entry of judgment;

  (ii) specify the judgment and the statute, rule, or other grounds entitling the movant to the award;

  (iii) state the amount sought or provide a fair estimate of it; and

  (iv) disclose, if the court so orders, the terms of any agreement about fees for the services for which the claim is made.

(C) *Proceedings.* Subject to Rule 23(h), the court must, on a party's request, give an opportunity for adversary submissions on the motion in accordance with Rule 43(c) or 78. The court may decide issues of liability for fees before receiving submissions on the value of services. The court must find the facts and state its conclusions of law as provided in Rule 52(a).

(D) *Special Procedures by Local Rule; Reference to a Master or a Magistrate Judge.* By local rule, the court may establish special procedures to resolve fee-related issues without extensive evidentiary hearings. Also, the court may refer issues concerning the value of services to a special master under Rule 53 without regard to the limitations of Rule 53(a)(1), and may refer a motion for attorney's fees to a magistrate judge under Rule 72(b) as if it were a dispositive pretrial matter.

(E) *Exceptions.* Subparagraphs (A)-(D) do not apply to claims for fees and expenses as sanctions for violating these rules or as sanctions under 28 U.S.C. § 1927.

(Amended December 27, 1946, effective March 19, 1948; April 17, 1961, effective July 19, 1961; March 2, 1987, effective August 1, 1987; April 22, 1993, effective December 1, 1993; April 29, 2002, effective December 1, 2002; March 27, 2003, effective December 1, 2003; April 30, 2007, effective December 1, 2007; March 26, 2009, effective December 1, 2009.)

RULE 55. DEFAULT; DEFAULT JUDGMENT

(a) Entering a Default. When a party against whom a judgment for affirmative relief is sought has failed to plead or otherwise defend, and that failure is shown by affidavit or otherwise, the clerk must enter the party's default.

(b) Entering a Default Judgment.

(1) *By the Clerk.* If the plaintiff's claim is for a sum certain or a sum that can be made certain by computation, the clerk—on the plaintiff's request, with an affidavit showing the amount due—must enter judgment for that amount and costs against a defendant who has been defaulted for not appearing and who is neither a minor nor an incompetent person.

(2) *By the Court.* In all other cases, the party must apply to the court for a default judgment. A default judgment may be entered against a minor or incompetent person only if represented by a general guardian, conservator, or other like fiduciary who has appeared. If the party against whom a default judgment is sought has appeared personally or by a representative, that party or its representative must be served with written notice of the application at least 7 days before the hearing. The court may conduct hearings or make referrals—preserving any federal statutory right to a jury trial—when, to enter or effectuate judgment, it needs to:

  (A) conduct an accounting;

  (B) determine the amount of damages;

  (C) establish the truth of any allegation by evidence; or

  (D) investigate any other matter.

(c) Setting Aside a Default or a Default Judgment. The court may set aside an entry of default for good cause, and it may set aside a final default judgment under Rule 60(b).

(d) Judgment Against the United States. A default judgment may be entered against the United States, its officers, or its agencies only if the claimant establishes a claim or right to relief by evidence that satisfies the court.

(Amended March 2, 1987, effective August 1, 1987; April 30, 2007, effective December 1, 2007; March 26, 2009, effective December 1, 2009; April 29, 2015, effective December 1, 2015.)

RULE 56. SUMMARY JUDGMENT

(a) Motion for Summary Judgment or Partial Summary Judgment. A party may move for summary judgment, identifying each claim or defense—or the part of each claim or defense—on which summary judgment is sought. The court shall grant summary judgment if the movant shows that there is no genuine dispute as to any material fact and the movant is entitled to judgment as a matter of law. The court should state on the record the reasons for granting or denying the motion.

(b) Time to File a Motion. Unless a different time is set by local rule or the court orders otherwise, a party may file a motion for summary judgment at any time until 30 days after the close of all discovery.

(c) Procedures.

(1) *Supporting Factual Positions.* A party asserting that a fact cannot be or is genuinely disputed must support the assertion by:

(A) citing to particular parts of materials in the record, including depositions, documents, electronically stored information, affidavits or declarations, stipulations (including those made for purposes of the motion only), admissions, interrogatory answers, or other materials; or

(B) showing that the materials cited do not establish the absence or presence of a genuine dispute, or that an adverse party cannot produce admissible evidence to support the fact.

(2) *Objection That a Fact Is Not Supported by Admissible Evidence.* A party may object that the material cited to support or dispute a fact cannot be presented in a form that would be admissible in evidence.

(3) *Materials Not Cited.* The court need consider only the cited materials, but it may consider other materials in the record.

(4) *Affidavits or Declarations.* An affidavit or declaration used to support or oppose a motion must be made on personal knowledge, set out facts that would be admissible in evidence, and show that the affiant or declarant is competent to testify on the matters stated.

(d) When Facts Are Unavailable to the Nonmovant. If a nonmovant shows by affidavit or declaration that, for specified reasons, it cannot present facts essential to justify its opposition, the court may:

(1) defer considering the motion or deny it;

(2) allow time to obtain affidavits or declarations or to take discovery; or

(3) issue any other appropriate order.

(e) Failing to Properly Support or Address a Fact. If a party fails to properly support an assertion of fact or fails to properly address another party's assertion of fact as required by Rule 56(c), the court may:

(1) give an opportunity to properly support or address the fact;

(2) consider the fact undisputed for purposes of the motion;

(3) grant summary judgment if the motion and supporting materials—including the facts considered undisputed—show that the movant is entitled to it; or

(4) issue any other appropriate order.

(f) Judgment Independent of the Motion. After giving notice and a reasonable time to respond, the court may:

(1) grant summary judgment for a nonmovant;

(2) grant the motion on grounds not raised by a party; or

(3) consider summary judgment on its own after identifying for the parties material facts that may not be genuinely in dispute.

(g) Failing to Grant All the Requested Relief. If the court does not grant all the relief requested by the motion, it may enter an order stating any material fact—including an item of damages or other relief—that is not genuinely in dispute and treating the fact as established in the case.

(h) Affidavit or Declaration Submitted in Bad Faith. If satisfied that an affidavit or declaration under this rule is submitted in bad faith or solely for delay, the court—after notice and a reasonable time to respond—may order the submitting party to pay the other party the reasonable expenses, including attorney's fees, it incurred as a result. An offending party or attorney may also be held in contempt or subjected to other appropriate sanctions.

(Amended December 27, 1946, effective March 19, 1948; January 21, 1963, effective July 1, 1963; March 2, 1987, effective August 1, 1987; April 30, 2007, effective December 1, 2007; March 26, 2009, effective December 1, 2009; April 28, 2010, effective December 1, 2010.)

RULE 57. DECLARATORY JUDGMENT

These rules govern the procedure for obtaining a declaratory judgment under 28 U.S.C. § 2201. Rules 38 and 39 govern a demand for a jury trial. The existence of another adequate remedy does not preclude a declaratory judgment that is otherwise appropriate. The court may order a speedy hearing of a declaratory-judgment action.

(Amended December 29, 1948, effective October 20, 1949; April 30, 2007, effective December 1, 2007.)

RULE 58. ENTERING JUDGMENT

(a) Separate Document. Every judgment and amended judgment must be set out in a separate document, but a separate document is not required for an order disposing of a motion:

(1) for judgment under Rule 50(b);

(2) to amend or make additional findings under Rule 52(b);

(3) for attorney's fees under Rule 54;

(4) for a new trial, or to alter or amend the judgment, under Rule 59; or

(5) for relief under Rule 60.

(b) **Entering Judgment.**

(1) *Without the Court's Direction.* Subject to Rule 54(b) and unless the court orders otherwise, the clerk must, without awaiting the court's direction, promptly prepare, sign, and enter the judgment when:

(A) the jury returns a general verdict;

(B) the court awards only costs or a sum certain; or

(C) the court denies all relief.

(2) *Court's Approval Required.* Subject to Rule 54(b), the court must promptly approve the form of the judgment, which the clerk must promptly enter, when:

(A) the jury returns a special verdict or a general verdict with answers to written questions; or

(B) the court grants other relief not described in this subdivision (b).

(c) **Time of Entry.** For purposes of these rules, judgment is entered at the following times:

(1) if a separate document is not required, when the judgment is entered in the civil docket under Rule 79(a); or

(2) if a separate document is required, when the judgment is entered in the civil docket under Rule 79(a) and the earlier of these events occurs:

(A) it is set out in a separate document; or

(B) 150 days have run from the entry in the civil docket.

(d) **Request for Entry.** A party may request that judgment be set out in a separate document as required by Rule 58(a).

(e) **Cost or Fee Awards.** Ordinarily, the entry of judgment may not be delayed, nor the time for appeal extended, in order to tax costs or award fees. But if a timely motion for attorney's fees is made under Rule 54(d)(2), the court may act before a notice of appeal has been filed and become effective to order that the motion have the same effect under Federal Rule of Appellate Procedure 4(a)(4) as a timely motion under Rule 59.

(Amended December 27, 1946, effective March 19, 1948; January 21, 1963, effective July 1, 1963; April 22, 1993, effective December 1, 1993; April 29, 2002, effective December 1, 2002; April 30, 2007, effective December 1, 2007.)

RULE 59. NEW TRIAL; ALTERING OR AMENDING A JUDGMENT

(a) **In General.**

(1) *Grounds for New Trial.* The court may, on motion, grant a new trial on all or some of the issues—and to any party—as follows:

(A) after a jury trial, for any reason for which a new trial has heretofore been granted in an action at law in federal court; or

(B) after a nonjury trial, for any reason for which a rehearing has heretofore been granted in a suit in equity in federal court.

(2) *Further Action After a Nonjury Trial.* After a nonjury trial, the court may, on motion for a new trial, open the judgment if one has been entered, take additional testimony, amend findings of fact and conclusions of law or make new ones, and direct the entry of a new judgment.

(b) **Time to File a Motion for a New Trial.** A motion for a new trial must be filed no later than 28 days after the entry of judgment.

(c) **Time to Serve Affidavits.** When a motion for a new trial is based on affidavits, they must be filed with the motion. The opposing party has 14 days after being served to file opposing affidavits. The court may permit reply affidavits.

(d) **New Trial on the Court's Initiative or for Reasons Not in the Motion.** No later than 28 days after the entry of judgment, the court, on its own, may order a new trial for any reason that would justify granting one on a party's motion. After giving the parties notice and an opportunity to be heard, the court may grant a timely motion for a new trial for a reason not stated in the motion. In either event, the court must specify the reasons in its order.

(e) **Motion to Alter or Amend a Judgment.** A motion to alter or amend a judgment must be filed no later than 28 days after the entry of the judgment.

(Amended December 27, 1946, effective March 19, 1948; February 28, 1966, effective July 1, 1966; April 27, 1995, effective December 1, 1995; April 30, 2007, effective December 1, 2007; March 26, 2009, effective December 1, 2009.)

RULE 60. RELIEF FROM A JUDGMENT OR ORDER

(a) **Corrections Based on Clerical Mistakes; Oversights and Omissions.** The court may correct a clerical mistake or a mistake arising from oversight or omission whenever one is found in a judgment, order, or other part of the record. The court may do so on motion or on its own, with or without notice. But after an appeal has been docketed in the appellate court and while it is pending, such a mistake may be corrected only with the appellate court's leave.

(b) Grounds for Relief from a Final Judgment, Order, or Proceeding. On motion and just terms, the court may relieve a party or its legal representative from a final judgment, order, or proceeding for the following reasons:

(1) mistake, inadvertence, surprise, or excusable neglect;

(2) newly discovered evidence that, with reasonable diligence, could not have been discovered in time to move for a new trial under Rule 59(b);

(3) fraud (whether previously called intrinsic or extrinsic), misrepresentation, or misconduct by an opposing party;

(4) the judgment is void;

(5) the judgment has been satisfied, released or discharged; it is based on an earlier judgment that has been reversed or vacated; or applying it prospectively is no longer equitable; or

(6) any other reason that justifies relief.

(c) Timing and Effect of the Motion.

(1) *Timing.* A motion under Rule 60(b) must be made within a reasonable time—and for reasons (1), (2), and (3) no more than a year after the entry of the judgment or order or the date of the proceeding.

(2) *Effect on Finality.* The motion does not affect the judgment's finality or suspend its operation.

(d) Other Powers to Grant Relief. This rule does not limit a court's power to:

(1) entertain an independent action to relieve a party from a judgment, order, or proceeding;

(2) grant relief under 28 U.S.C. § 1655 to a defendant who was not personally notified of the action; or

(3) set aside a judgment for fraud on the court.

(e) Bills and Writs Abolished. The following are abolished: bills of review, bills in the nature of bills of review, and writs of coram nobis, coram vobis, and audita querela.

(Amended December 27, 1946, effective March 19, 1948; December 29, 1948, effective October 20, 1949; March 2, 1987, effective August 1, 1987; April 30, 2007, effective December 1, 2007.)

RULE 61. HARMLESS ERROR

Unless justice requires otherwise, no error in admitting or excluding evidence—or any other error by the court or a party—is ground for granting a new trial, for setting aside a verdict, or for vacating, modifying, or otherwise disturbing a judgment or order. At every stage of the proceeding, the court must disregard all errors and defects that do not affect any party's substantial rights.

(Amended April 30, 2007, effective December 1, 2007.)

RULE 62. STAY OF PROCEEDINGS TO ENFORCE A JUDGMENT

(a) Automatic Stay; Exceptions for Injunctions, Receiverships, and Patent Accountings. Except as stated in this rule, no execution may issue on a judgment, nor may proceedings be taken to enforce it, until 14 days have passed after its entry. But unless the court orders otherwise, the following are not stayed after being entered, even if an appeal is taken:

(1) an interlocutory or final judgment in an action for an injunction or a receivership; or

(2) a judgment or order that directs an accounting in an action for patent infringement.

(b) Stay Pending the Disposition of a Motion. On appropriate terms for the opposing party's security, the court may stay the execution of a judgment—or any proceedings to enforce it—pending disposition of any of the following motions:

(1) under Rule 50, for judgment as a matter of law;

(2) under Rule 52(b), to amend the findings or for additional findings;

(3) under Rule 59, for a new trial or to alter or amend a judgment; or

(4) under Rule 60, for relief from a judgment or order.

(c) Injunction Pending an Appeal. While an appeal is pending from an interlocutory order or final judgment that grants, dissolves, or denies an injunction, the court may suspend, modify, restore, or grant an injunction on terms for bond or other terms that secure the opposing party's rights. If the judgment appealed from is rendered by a statutory three-judge district court, the order must be made either:

(1) by that court sitting in open session; or

(2) by the assent of all its judges, as evidenced by their signatures.

(d) Stay with Bond on Appeal. If an appeal is taken, the appellant may obtain a stay by supersedeas bond, except in an action described in Rule 62(a)(1) or (2). The bond may be given upon or after filing the notice of appeal or after obtaining the order allowing the appeal. The stay takes effect when the court approves the bond.

(e) Stay Without Bond on an Appeal by the United States, Its Officers, or Its Agencies. The court must not require a bond, obligation, or other security from the appellant when granting a stay on an appeal by the United States, its officers, or its agencies or on an appeal directed by a department of the federal government.

(f) Stay in Favor of a Judgment Debtor Under State Law. If a judgment is a lien on the judgment debtor's property under the law of the state where the court is located, the judgment debtor is entitled to the same stay of execution the state court would give.

(g) Appellate Court's Power Not Limited. This rule does not limit the power of the appellate court or one of its judges or justices:

    (1) to stay proceedings—or suspend, modify, restore, or grant an injunction—while an appeal is pending; or

    (2) to issue an order to preserve the status quo or the effectiveness of the judgment to be entered.

(h) Stay with Multiple Claims or Parties. A court may stay the enforcement of a final judgment entered under Rule 54(b) until it enters a later judgment or judgments, and may prescribe terms necessary to secure the benefit of the stayed judgment for the party in whose favor it was entered.

(Amended December 27, 1946, effective March 19, 1948; December 29, 1948, effective October 20, 1949; April 17, 1961, effective July 19, 1961; March 2, 1987, effective August 1, 1987; April 30, 2007, effective December 1, 2007; March 26, 2009, effective December 1, 2009.)

RULE 62.1. INDICATIVE RULING ON A MOTION FOR RELIEF THAT IS BARRED BY A PENDING APPEAL

(a) Relief Pending Appeal. If a timely motion is made for relief that the court lacks authority to grant because of an appeal that has been docketed and is pending, the court may:

    (1) defer considering the motion;

    (2) deny the motion; or

    (3) state either that it would grant the motion if the court of appeals remands for that purpose or that the motion raises a substantial issue.

(b) Notice to the Court of Appeals. The movant must promptly notify the circuit clerk under Federal Rule of Appellate Procedure 12.1 if the district court states that it would grant the motion or that the motion raises a substantial issue.

(c) Remand. The district court may decide the motion if the court of appeals remands for that purpose.

(Added March 26, 2009, effective December 1, 2009.)

RULE 63. JUDGE'S INABILITY TO PROCEED

If a judge conducting a hearing or trial is unable to proceed, any other judge may proceed upon certifying familiarity with the record and determining that the case may be completed without prejudice to the parties. In a hearing or a nonjury trial, the successor judge must, at a party's request, recall any witness whose testimony is material and disputed and who is available to testify again without undue burden. The successor judge may also recall any other witness.

(Amended March 2, 1987, effective August 1, 1987; April 30, 1991, effective December 1, 1991; April 30, 2007, effective December 1, 2007.)

TITLE VIII. PROVISIONAL AND FINAL REMEDIES

RULE 64. SEIZING A PERSON OR PROPERTY

(a) Remedies Under State Law—In General. At the commencement of and throughout an action, every remedy is available that, under the law of the state where the court is located, provides for seizing a person or property to secure satisfaction of the potential judgment. But a federal statute governs to the extent it applies.

(b) Specific Kinds of Remedies. The remedies available under this rule include the following—however designated and regardless of whether state procedure requires an independent action:

    • arrest;

    • attachment;

    • garnishment;

    • replevin;

    • sequestration; and

    • other corresponding or equivalent remedies.

(Amended April 30, 2007, effective December 1, 2007.)

RULE 65. INJUNCTIONS AND RESTRAINING ORDERS

(a) Preliminary Injunction.

    (1) *Notice.* The court may issue a preliminary injunction only on notice to the adverse party.

    (2) *Consolidating the Hearing with the Trial on the Merits.* Before or after beginning the hearing on a motion for a preliminary injunction, the court may advance the trial on the merits and consolidate it with the hearing. Even when consolidation is not ordered, evidence that is received on the motion and that would be admissible at trial becomes part of the trial record and need not be repeated at trial. But the court must preserve any party's right to a jury trial.

(b) Temporary Restraining Order.

(1) *Issuing Without Notice.* The court may issue a temporary restraining order without written or oral notice to the adverse party or its attorney only if:

(A) specific facts in an affidavit or a verified complaint clearly show that immediate and irreparable injury, loss, or damage will result to the movant before the adverse party can be heard in opposition; and

(B) the movant's attorney certifies in writing any efforts made to give notice and the reasons why it should not be required.

(2) *Contents; Expiration.* Every temporary restraining order issued without notice must state the date and hour it was issued; describe the injury and state why it is irreparable; state why the order was issued without notice; and be promptly filed in the clerk's office and entered in the record. The order expires at the time after entry—not to exceed 14 days—that the court sets, unless before that time the court, for good cause, extends it for a like period or the adverse party consents to a longer extension. The reasons for an extension must be entered in the record.

(3) *Expediting the Preliminary–Injunction Hearing.* If the order is issued without notice, the motion for a preliminary injunction must be set for hearing at the earliest possible time, taking precedence over all other matters except hearings on older matters of the same character. At the hearing, the party who obtained the order must proceed with the motion; if the party does not, the court must dissolve the order.

(4) *Motion to Dissolve.* On 2 days' notice to the party who obtained the order without notice—or on shorter notice set by the court—the adverse party may appear and move to dissolve or modify the order. The court must then hear and decide the motion as promptly as justice requires.

(c) **Security.** The court may issue a preliminary injunction or a temporary restraining order only if the movant gives security in an amount that the court considers proper to pay the costs and damages sustained by any party found to have been wrongfully enjoined or restrained. The United States, its officers, and its agencies are not required to give security.

(d) **Contents and Scope of Every Injunction and Restraining Order.**

(1) *Contents.* Every order granting an injunction and every restraining order must:

(A) state the reasons why it issued;

(B) state its terms specifically; and

(C) describe in reasonable detail—and not by referring to the complaint or other document—the act or acts restrained or required.

(2) *Persons Bound.* The order binds only the following who receive actual notice of it by personal service or otherwise:

(A) the parties;

(B) the parties' officers, agents, servants, employees, and attorneys; and

(C) other persons who are in active concert or participation with anyone described in Rule 65(d)(2)(A) or (B).

(e) **Other Laws Not Modified.** These rules do not modify the following:

(1) any federal statute relating to temporary restraining orders or preliminary injunctions in actions affecting employer and employee;

(2) 28 U.S.C. § 2361, which relates to preliminary injunctions in actions of interpleader or in the nature of interpleader; or

(3) 28 U.S.C. § 2284, which relates to actions that must be heard and decided by a three-judge district court.

(f) **Copyright Impoundment.** This rule applies to copyright-impoundment proceedings.

(Amended December 27, 1946, effective March 19, 1948; December 29, 1948, effective October 20, 1949; February 28, 1966, effective July 1, 1966; March 2, 1987, effective August 1, 1987; April 23, 2001, effective December 1, 2001; April 30, 2007, effective December 1, 2007; March 26, 2009, effective December 1, 2009.)

RULE 65.1. PROCEEDINGS AGAINST A SURETY

Whenever these rules (including the Supplemental Rules for Admiralty or Maritime Claims and Asset Forfeiture Actions) require or allow a party to give security, and security is given through a bond or other undertaking with one or more sureties, each surety submits to the court's jurisdiction and irrevocably appoints the court clerk as its agent for receiving service of any papers that affect its liability on the bond or undertaking. The surety's liability may be enforced on motion without an independent action. The motion and any notice that the court orders may be served on the court clerk, who must promptly mail a copy of each to every surety whose address is known.

(Adopted February 28, 1966, effective July 1, 1966; amended March 2, 1987, effective August 1, 1987; April 12, 2006, effective December 1, 2006; April 30, 2007, effective December 1, 2007.)

RULE 66.   RECEIVERS

These rules govern an action in which the appointment of a receiver is sought or a receiver sues or is sued. But the practice in administering an estate by a receiver or a similar court-appointed officer must accord with the historical practice in federal courts or with a local rule. An action in which a receiver has been appointed may be dismissed only by court order.

(Amended December 27, 1946, effective March 19, 1948; December 29, 1948, effective October 20, 1949; April 30, 2007, effective December 1, 2007.)

RULE 67.   DEPOSIT INTO COURT

(a) **Depositing Property.** If any part of the relief sought is a money judgment or the disposition of a sum of money or some other deliverable thing, a party—on notice to every other party and by leave of court—may deposit with the court all or part of the money or thing, whether or not that party claims any of it. The depositing party must deliver to the clerk a copy of the order permitting deposit.

(b) **Investing and Withdrawing Funds.** Money paid into court under this rule must be deposited and withdrawn in accordance with 28 U.S.C. §§ 2041 and 2042 and any like statute. The money must be deposited in an interest-bearing account or invested in a court-approved, interest-bearing instrument.

(Amended December 29, 1948, effective October 20, 1949; April 28, 1983, effective August 1, 1983; April 30, 2007, effective December 1, 2007.)

RULE 68.   OFFER OF JUDGMENT

(a) **Making an Offer; Judgment on an Accepted Offer.**   At least 14 days before the date set for trial, a party defending against a claim may serve on an opposing party an offer to allow judgment on specified terms, with the costs then accrued. If, within 14 days after being served, the opposing party serves written notice accepting the offer, either party may then file the offer and notice of acceptance, plus proof of service.   The clerk must then enter judgment.

(b) **Unaccepted Offer.** An unaccepted offer is considered withdrawn, but it does not preclude a later offer. Evidence of an unaccepted offer is not admissible except in a proceeding to determine costs.

(c) **Offer After Liability is Determined.** When one party's liability to another has been determined but the extent of liability remains to be determined by further proceedings, the party held liable may make an offer of judgment. It must be served within a reasonable time—but at least 14 days—before the date set for a hearing to determine the extent of liability.

(d) **Paying Costs After an Unaccepted Offer.** If the judgment that the offeree finally obtains is not more favorable than the unaccepted offer, the offeree must pay the costs incurred after the offer was made.

(Amended December 27, 1946, effective March 19, 1948; February 28, 1966, effective July 1, 1966; March 2, 1987, effective August 1, 1987; April 30, 2007, effective December 1, 2007; March 26, 2009, effective December 1, 2009.)

RULE 69.   EXECUTION

(a) **In General.**

   (1) *Money Judgment; Applicable Procedure.* A money judgment is enforced by a writ of execution, unless the court directs otherwise. The procedure on execution—and in proceedings supplementary to and in aid of judgment or execution—must accord with the procedure of the state where the court is located, but a federal statute governs to the extent it applies.

   (2) *Obtaining Discovery.* In aid of the judgment or execution, the judgment creditor or a successor in interest whose interest appears of record may obtain discovery from any person—including the judgment debtor—as provided in these rules or by the procedure of the state where the court is located.

(b) **Against Certain Public Officers.** When a judgment has been entered against a revenue officer in the circumstances stated in 28 U.S.C. § 2006, or against an officer of Congress in the circumstances stated in 2 U.S.C. § 118, the judgment must be satisfied as those statutes provide.

(Amended December 29, 1948, effective October 20, 1949; March 30, 1970, effective July 1, 1970; March 2, 1987 effective August 1, 1987; April 30, 2007, effective December 1, 2007.)

RULE 70.   ENFORCING A JUDGMENT FOR A SPECIFIC ACT

(a) **Party's Failure to Act; Ordering Another to Act.** If a judgment requires a party to convey land, to deliver a deed or other document, or to perform any other specific act and the party fails to comply within the time specified, the court may order the act to be done—at the disobedient party's expense—by another person appointed by the court. When done, the act has the same effect as if done by the party.

(b) **Vesting Title.** If the real or personal property is within the district, the court—instead of ordering a conveyance—may enter a judgment divesting any party's title and vesting it in others. That judgment has the effect of a legally executed conveyance.

(c) Obtaining a Writ of Attachment or Sequestration. On application by a party entitled to performance of an act, the clerk must issue a writ of attachment or sequestration against the disobedient party's property to compel obedience.

(d) Obtaining a Writ of Execution or Assistance. On application by a party who obtains a judgment or order for possession, the clerk must issue a writ of execution or assistance.

(e) Holding in Contempt. The court may also hold the disobedient party in contempt.

(Amended April 30, 2007, effective December 1, 2007.)

RULE 71. ENFORCING RELIEF FOR OR AGAINST A NONPARTY

When an order grants relief for a nonparty or may be enforced against a nonparty, the procedure for enforcing the order is the same as for a party.

(Amended March 2, 1987, effective August 1, 1987; April 30, 2007, effective December 1, 2007.)

TITLE IX. SPECIAL PROCEEDINGS

RULE 71.1. CONDEMNING REAL OR PERSONAL PROPERTY

(a) Applicability of Other Rules. These rules govern proceedings to condemn real and personal property by eminent domain, except as this rule provides otherwise.

(b) Joinder of Properties. The plaintiff may join separate pieces of property in a single action, no matter whether they are owned by the same persons or sought for the same use.

(c) Complaint.

(1) *Caption.* The complaint must contain a caption as provided in Rule 10(a). The plaintiff must, however, name as defendants both the property—designated generally by kind, quantity, and location—and at least one owner of some part of or interest in the property.

(2) *Contents.* The complaint must contain a short and plain statement of the following:

(A) the authority for the taking;

(B) the uses for which the property is to be taken;

(C) a description sufficient to identify the property;

(D) the interests to be acquired; and

(E) for each piece of property, a designation of each defendant who has been joined as an owner or owner of an interest in it.

(3) *Parties.* When the action commences, the plaintiff need join as defendants only those persons who have or claim an interest in the property and whose names are then known. But before any hearing on compensation, the plaintiff must add as defendants all those persons who have or claim an interest and whose names have become known or can be found by a reasonably diligent search of the records, considering both the property's character and value and the interests to be acquired. All others may be made defendants under the designation "Unknown Owners."

(4) *Procedure.* Notice must be served on all defendants as provided in Rule 71.1(d), whether they were named as defendants when the action commenced or were added later. A defendant may answer as provided in Rule 71.1(e). The court, meanwhile, may order any distribution of a deposit that the facts warrant.

(5) *Filing; Additional Copies.* In addition to filing the complaint, the plaintiff must give the clerk at least one copy for the defendants' use and additional copies at the request of the clerk or a defendant.

(d) Process.

(1) *Delivering Notice to the Clerk.* On filing a complaint, the plaintiff must promptly deliver to the clerk joint or several notices directed to the named defendants. When adding defendants, the plaintiff must deliver to the clerk additional notices directed to the new defendants.

(2) *Contents of the Notice.*

(A) *Main Contents.* Each notice must name the court, the title of the action, and the defendant to whom it is directed. It must describe the property sufficiently to identify it, but need not describe any property other than that to be taken from the named defendant. The notice must also state:

(i) that the action is to condemn property;

(ii) the interest to be taken;

(iii) the authority for the taking;

(iv) the uses for which the property is to be taken;

(v) that the defendant may serve an answer on the plaintiff's attorney within 21 days after being served with the notice;

(vi) that the failure to so serve an answer constitutes consent to the taking and to the court's authority to proceed with the action and fix the compensation; and

(vii) that a defendant who does not serve an answer may file a notice of appearance.

(B) *Conclusion.* The notice must conclude with the name, telephone number, and e-mail address of the plaintiff's attorney and an address within the district in which the action is brought where the attorney may be served.

(3) *Serving the Notice.*

(A) *Personal Service.* When a defendant whose address is known resides within the United States or a territory subject to the administrative or judicial jurisdiction of the United States, personal service of the notice (without a copy of the complaint) must be made in accordance with Rule 4.

(B) *Service by Publication.*

(i) A defendant may be served by publication only when the plaintiff's attorney files a certificate stating that the attorney believes the defendant cannot be personally served, because after diligent inquiry within the state where the complaint is filed, the defendant's place of residence is still unknown or, if known, that it is beyond the territorial limits of personal service. Service is then made by publishing the notice—once a week for at least 3 successive weeks—in a newspaper published in the county where the property is located or, if there is no such newspaper, in a newspaper with general circulation where the property is located. Before the last publication, a copy of the notice must also be mailed to every defendant who cannot be personally served but whose place of residence is then known. Unknown owners may be served by publication in the same manner by a notice addressed to "Unknown Owners."

(ii) Service by publication is complete on the date of the last publication. The plaintiff's attorney must prove publication and mailing by a certificate, attach a printed copy of the published notice, and mark on the copy the newspaper's name and the dates of publication.

(4) *Effect of Delivery and Service.* Delivering the notice to the clerk and serving it have the same effect as serving a summons under Rule 4.

(5) *Amending the Notice; Proof of Service and Amending the Proof.* Rule 4(a)(2) governs amending the notice. Rule 4(*l*) governs proof of service and amending it.

(e) **Appearance or Answer.**

(1) *Notice of Appearance.* A defendant that has no objection or defense to the taking of its property may serve a notice of appearance designating the property in which it claims an interest. The defendant must then be given notice of all later proceedings affecting the defendant.

(2) *Answer.* A defendant that has an objection or defense to the taking must serve an answer within 21 days after being served with the notice. The answer must:

(A) identify the property in which the defendant claims an interest;

(B) state the nature and extent of the interest; and

(C) state all the defendant's objections and defenses to the taking.

(3) *Waiver of Other Objections and Defenses; Evidence on Compensation.* A defendant waives all objections and defenses not stated in its answer. No other pleading or motion asserting an additional objection or defense is allowed. But at the trial on compensation, a defendant—whether or not it has previously appeared or answered—may present evidence on the amount of compensation to be paid and may share in the award.

(f) **Amending Pleadings.** Without leave of court, the plaintiff may—as often as it wants—amend the complaint at any time before the trial on compensation. But no amendment may be made if it would result in a dismissal inconsistent with Rule 71.1(i)(1) or (2). The plaintiff need not serve a copy of an amendment, but must serve notice of the filing, as provided in Rule 5(b), on every affected party who has appeared and, as provided in Rule 71.1(d), on every affected party who has not appeared. In addition, the plaintiff must give the clerk at least one copy of each amendment for the defendants' use, and additional copies at the request of the clerk or a defendant. A defendant may appear or answer in the time and manner and with the same effect as provided in Rule 71.1(e).

(g) **Substituting Parties.** If a defendant dies, becomes incompetent, or transfers an interest after being joined, the court may, on motion and notice of hearing, order that the proper party be substituted. Service of the motion and notice on a nonparty must be made as provided in Rule 71.1(d)(3).

(h) **Trial of the Issues.**

(1) *Issues Other Than Compensation; Compensation.* In an action involving eminent domain under federal law, the court tries all issues, including compensation, except when compensation must be determined:

(A) by any tribunal specially constituted by a federal statute to determine compensation; or

(B) if there is no such tribunal, by a jury when a party demands one within the time to answer or within any additional time the court sets, unless the court appoints a commission.

(2) *Appointing a Commission; Commission's Powers and Report.*

(A) *Reasons for Appointing.* If a party has demanded a jury, the court may instead appoint a three-person commission to determine compensation because of the character, location, or quantity of the property to be condemned or for other just reasons.

(B) *Alternate Commissioners.* The court may appoint up to two additional persons to serve as alternate commissioners to hear the case and replace commissioners who, before a decision is filed, the court finds unable or disqualified to perform their duties. Once the commission renders its final decision, the court must discharge any alternate who has not replaced a commissioner.

(C) *Examining the Prospective Commissioners.* Before making its appointments, the court must advise the parties of the identity and qualifications of each prospective commissioner and alternate, and may permit the parties to examine them. The parties may not suggest appointees, but for good cause may object to a prospective commissioner or alternate.

(D) *Commission's Powers and Report.* A commission has the powers of a master under Rule 53(c). Its action and report are determined by a majority. Rule 53(d), (e), and (f) apply to its action and report.

(i) Dismissal of the Action or a Defendant.

(1) *Dismissing the Action.*

(A) *By the Plaintiff.* If no compensation hearing on a piece of property has begun, and if the plaintiff has not acquired title or a lesser interest or taken possession, the plaintiff may, without a court order, dismiss the action as to that property by filing a notice of dismissal briefly describing the property.

(B) *By Stipulation.* Before a judgment is entered vesting the plaintiff with title or a lesser interest in or possession of property, the plaintiff and affected defendants may, without a court order, dismiss the action in whole or in part by filing a stipulation of dismissal. And if the parties so stipulate, the court may vacate a judgment already entered.

(C) *By Court Order.* At any time before compensation has been determined and paid, the court may, after a motion and hearing, dismiss the action as to a piece of property. But if the plaintiff has already taken title, a lesser interest, or possession as to any part of it, the court must award compensation for the title, lesser interest, or possession taken.

(2) *Dismissing a Defendant.* The court may at any time dismiss a defendant who was unnecessarily or improperly joined.

(3) *Effect.* A dismissal is without prejudice unless otherwise stated in the notice, stipulation, or court order.

(j) Deposit and Its Distribution.

(1) *Deposit.* The plaintiff must deposit with the court any money required by law as a condition to the exercise of eminent domain and may make a deposit when allowed by statute.

(2) *Distribution; Adjusting Distribution.* After a deposit, the court and attorneys must expedite the proceedings so as to distribute the deposit and to determine and pay compensation. If the compensation finally awarded to a defendant exceeds the amount distributed to that defendant, the court must enter judgment against the plaintiff for the deficiency. If the compensation awarded to a defendant is less than the amount distributed to that defendant, the court must enter judgment against that defendant for the overpayment.

(k) Condemnation Under a State's Power of Eminent Domain. This rule governs an action involving eminent domain under state law. But if state law provides for trying an issue by jury—or for trying the issue of compensation by jury or commission or both—that law governs.

(l) Costs. Costs are not subject to Rule 54(d).

(Adopted April 30, 1951, effective August 1, 1951; amended January 21, 1963, effective July 1, 1963; April 29, 1985, effective August 1, 1985; March 2, 1987, effective August 1, 1987; April 25, 1988, effective August 1, 1988; amended by Pub.L. 100–690, Title VII, § 7050, November 18, 1988, 102 Stat. 4401 (although amendment by Pub.L. 100–690 could not be executed due to prior amendment by Court order which made the same change effective August 1, 1988); amended April 22, 1993, effective December 1, 1993; March 27, 2003, effective December 1, 2003; April 30, 2007, effective December 1, 2007; March 26, 2009, effective December 1, 2009.)

RULE 72. MAGISTRATE JUDGES: PRETRIAL ORDER

(a) Nondispositive Matters. When a pretrial matter not dispositive of a party's claim or defense is referred to a magistrate judge to hear and decide, the magistrate judge must promptly conduct the required proceedings and, when appropriate, issue a written order stating the decision. A party may serve and file objections to the order within 14 days after being served with a copy. A party may not assign as error a defect in the order not timely objected to. The district judge in the case must consider timely objections and modify or set aside any part of the order that is clearly erroneous or is contrary to law.

(b) Dispositive Motions and Prisoner Petitions.

(1) *Findings and Recommendations.* A magistrate judge must promptly conduct the required proceedings when assigned, without the parties' consent, to hear a pretrial matter dispositive of a claim or defense or a prisoner petition challenging the conditions of confinement. A record must be made of all evidentiary proceedings and may, at the magistrate judge's discretion, be made of any other proceedings. The magistrate judge must enter a recommended disposition, including, if appropriate, proposed findings of fact. The clerk must promptly mail a copy to each party.

(2) *Objections.* Within 14 days after being served with a copy of the recommended disposition, a party may serve and file specific written objections to the proposed findings and recommendations. A party may respond to another party's objections within 14 days after being served with a copy. Unless the district judge orders otherwise, the objecting party must promptly arrange for transcribing the record, or whatever portions of it the parties agree to or the magistrate judge considers sufficient.

(3) *Resolving Objections.* The district judge must determine de novo any part of the magistrate judge's disposition that has been properly objected to. The district judge may accept, reject, or modify the recommended disposition; receive further evidence; or return the matter to the magistrate judge with instructions.

(Former Rule 72 abrogated December 4, 1967, effective July 1, 1968; new Rule 72 adopted April 28, 1983, effective August 1, 1983; amended April 30, 1991, effective December 1, 1991; April 22, 1993, effective December 1, 1993; April 30, 2007, effective December 1, 2007; March 26, 2009, effective December 1, 2009.)

RULE 73. MAGISTRATE JUDGES: TRIAL BY CONSENT; APPEAL

(a) Trial by Consent. When authorized under 28 U.S.C. § 636(c), a magistrate judge may, if all parties consent, conduct a civil action or proceeding, including a jury or nonjury trial. A record must be made in accordance with 28 U.S.C. § 636(c)(5).

(b) Consent Procedure.

(1) *In General.* When a magistrate judge has been designated to conduct civil actions or proceedings, the clerk must give the parties written notice of their opportunity to consent under 28 U.S.C. § 636(c). To signify their consent, the parties must jointly or separately file a statement consenting to the referral. A district judge or magistrate judge may be informed of a party's response to the clerk's notice only if all parties have consented to the referral.

(2) *Reminding the Parties About Consenting.* A district judge, magistrate judge, or other court official may remind the parties of the magistrate judge's availability, but must also advise them that they are free to withhold consent without adverse substantive consequences.

(3) *Vacating a Referral.* On its own for good cause—or when a party shows extraordinary circumstances—the district judge may vacate a referral to a magistrate judge under this rule.

(c) Appealing a Judgment. In accordance with 28 U.S.C. § 636(c)(3), an appeal from a judgment entered at a magistrate judge's direction may be taken to the court of appeals as would any other appeal from a district-court judgment.

(Former Rule 73 abrogated December 4, 1967, effective July 1, 1968; new Rule 73 adopted April 28, 1983, effective August 1, 1983; amended March 2, 1987, effective August 1, 1987; April 22, 1993, effective December 1, 1993; April 11, 1997, effective December 1, 1997; April 30, 2007, effective December 1, 2007.)

RULE 74. METHOD OF APPEAL FROM MAGISTRATE JUDGE TO DISTRICT JUDGE UNDER TITLE 28, U.S.C. § 636(c)(4) AND RULE 73(d) [ABROGATED]

(Former Rule 74 abrogated December 4, 1967, effective July 1, 1968; new Rule 74 adopted April 28, 1983, effective August 1, 1983; amended April 22, 1993, effective December 1, 1993; abrogated April 11, 1997, effective December 1, 1997; April 30, 2007, effective December 1, 2007.)

RULE 75. PROCEEDINGS ON APPEAL FROM MAGISTRATE JUDGE TO DISTRICT JUDGE UNDER RULE 73(d) [ABROGATED]

(Former Rule 75 abrogated December 4, 1967, effective July 1, 1968; new Rule 75 adopted April 28, 1983, effective August 1, 1983; amended March 2, 1987, effective August 1, 1987; April 22, 1993, effective December 1, 1993; abrogated April 11, 1997, effective December 1, 1997; April 30, 2007, effective December 1, 2007.)

TITLE X. DISTRICT COURTS AND CLERKS: CONDUCTING BUSINESS; ISSUING ORDERS

RULE 77. CONDUCTING BUSINESS; CLERK'S AUTHORITY; NOTICE OF AN ORDER OR JUDGMENT

(a) When Court Is Open. Every district court is considered always open for filing any paper, issuing and returning process, making a motion, or entering an order.

(b) Place for Trial and Other Proceedings. Every trial on the merits must be conducted in open court and, so far as convenient, in a regular courtroom. Any other act or proceeding may be done or conducted by a judge in chambers, without the attendance of the clerk or other court official, and anywhere inside or outside the district. But no hearing—other than one ex parte—may be conducted outside the district unless all the affected parties consent.

(c) Clerk's Office Hours; Clerk's Orders.

    (1) *Hours.* The clerk's office—with a clerk or deputy on duty—must be open during business hours every day except Saturdays, Sundays, and legal holidays. But a court may, by local rule or order, require that the office be open for specified hours on Saturday or a particular legal holiday other than one listed in Rule 6(a)(6)(A).

    (2) *Orders.* Subject to the court's power to suspend, alter, or rescind the clerk's action for good cause, the clerk may:

        (A) issue process;

        (B) enter a default;

        (C) enter a default judgment under Rule 55(b)(1); and

        (D) act on any other matter that does not require the court's action.

(d) Serving Notice of an Order or Judgment.

    (1) *Service.* Immediately after entering an order or judgment, the clerk must serve notice of the entry, as provided in Rule 5(b), on each party who is not in default for failing to appear. The clerk must record the service on the docket. A party also may serve notice of the entry as provided in Rule 5(b).

    (2) *Time to Appeal Not Affected by Lack of Notice.* Lack of notice of the entry does not affect the time for appeal or relieve—or authorize the court to relieve—a party for failing to appeal within the time allowed, except as allowed by Federal Rule of Appellate Procedure (4)(a).

(Amended December 27, 1946, effective March 19, 1948; January 21, 1963, effective July 1, 1963; December 4, 1967, effective July 1, 1968; March 1, 1971, effective July 1, 1971; March 2, 1987, effective August 1, 1987; April 30, 1991, effective December 1, 1991; April 23, 2001, effective December 1, 2001; April 30, 2007, effective December 1, 2007; April 25, 2014, effective December 1, 2014.)

RULE 78. HEARING MOTIONS; SUBMISSION ON BRIEFS

(a) Providing a Regular Schedule for Oral Hearings. A court may establish regular times and places for oral hearings on motions.

(b) Providing for Submission on Briefs. By rule or order, the court may provide for submitting and determining motions on briefs, without oral hearings.

(Amended March 2, 1987, effective August 1, 1987; April 30, 2007, effective December 1, 2007.)

RULE 79. RECORDS KEPT BY THE CLERK

(a) Civil Docket.

    (1) *In General.* The clerk must keep a record known as the "civil docket" in the form and manner prescribed by the Director of the Administrative Office of the United States Courts with the approval of the Judicial Conference of the United States. The clerk must enter each civil action in the docket. Actions must be assigned consecutive file numbers, which must be noted in the docket where the first entry of the action is made.

    (2) *Items to be Entered.* The following items must be marked with the file number and entered chronologically in the docket:

        (A) papers filed with the clerk;

        (B) process issued, and proofs of service or other returns showing execution; and

        (C) appearances, orders, verdicts, and judgments.

    (3) *Contents of Entries; Jury Trial Demanded.* Each entry must briefly show the nature of the paper filed or writ issued, the substance of each proof of service or other return, and the substance and date of entry of each order and judgment. When a jury trial has been properly demanded or ordered, the clerk must enter the word "jury" in the docket.

(b) Civil Judgments and Orders. The clerk must keep a copy of every final judgment and appealable order; of every order affecting title to or a lien on real or personal property; and of any other order that the court directs to be kept. The clerk must keep these in the form and manner prescribed by the Director of the Administrative Office of the United States Courts with the approval of the Judicial Conference of the United States.

(c) Indexes; Calendars. Under the court's direction, the clerk must:

 (1) keep indexes of the docket and of the judgments and orders described in Rule 79(b); and

 (2) prepare calendars of all actions ready for trial, distinguishing jury trials from nonjury trials.

(d) Other Records. The clerk must keep any other records required by the Director of the Administrative Office of the United States Courts with the approval of the Judicial Conference of the United States.

(Amended December 27, 1946, effective March 19, 1948; December 29, 1948, effective October 20, 1949; January 21, 1963, effective July 1, 1963; April 30, 2007, effective December 1, 2007.)

RULE 80. STENOGRAPHIC TRANSCRIPT AS EVIDENCE

If stenographically reported testimony at a hearing or trial is admissible in evidence at a later trial, the testimony may be proved by a transcript certified by the person who reported it.

(Amended December 27, 1946, effective March 19, 1948; April 30, 2007, effective December 1, 2007.)

TITLE XI. GENERAL PROVISIONS

RULE 81. APPLICABILITY OF THE RULES IN GENERAL; REMOVED ACTIONS

(a) Applicability to Particular Proceedings.

 (1) *Prize Proceedings.* These rules do not apply to prize proceedings in admiralty governed by 10 U.S.C. §§ 7651–7681.

 (2) *Bankruptcy.* These rules apply to bankruptcy proceedings to the extent provided by the Federal Rules of Bankruptcy Procedure.

 (3) *Citizenship.* These rules apply to proceedings for admission to citizenship to the extent that the practice in those proceedings is not specified in federal statutes and has previously conformed to the practice in civil actions. The provisions of 8 U.S.C. § 1451 for service by publication and for answer apply in proceedings to cancel citizenship certificates.

 (4) *Special Writs.* These rules apply to proceedings for habeas corpus and for quo warranto to the extent that the practice in those proceedings:

  (A) is not specified in a federal statute, the Rules Governing Section 2254 Cases, or the Rules Governing Section 2255 Cases; and

  (B) has previously conformed to the practice in civil actions.

 (5) *Proceedings Involving a Subpoena.* These rules apply to proceedings to compel testimony or the production of documents through a subpoena issued by a United States officer or agency under a federal statute, except as otherwise provided by statute, by local rule, or by court order in the proceedings.

 (6) *Other Proceedings.* These rules, to the extent applicable, govern proceedings under the following laws, except as these laws provide other procedures:

  (A) 7 U.S.C. §§ 292, 499g(c), for reviewing an order of the Secretary of Agriculture;

  (B) 9 U.S.C., relating to arbitration;

  (C) 15 U.S.C. § 522, for reviewing an order of the Secretary of the Interior;

  (D) 15 U.S.C. § 715d(c), for reviewing an order denying a certificate of clearance;

  (E) 29 U.S.C. §§ 159, 160, for enforcing an order of the National Labor Relations Board;

  (F) 33 U.S.C. §§ 918, 921, for enforcing or reviewing a compensation order under the Longshore and Harbor Workers' Compensation Act; and

  (G) 45 U.S.C. § 159, for reviewing an arbitration award in a railway-labor dispute.

(b) Scire Facias and Mandamus. The writs of scire facias and mandamus are abolished. Relief previously available through them may be obtained by appropriate action or motion under these rules.

(c) Removed Actions.

 (1) *Applicability.* These rules apply to a civil action after it is removed from a state court.

 (2) *Further Pleading.* After removal, repleading is unnecessary unless the court orders it. A defendant who did not answer before removal must answer or present other defenses or objections under these rules within the longest of these periods:

(A) 21 days after receiving—through service or otherwise—a copy of the initial pleading stating the claim for relief;

(B) 21 days after being served with the summons for an initial pleading on file at the time of service; or

(C) 7 days after the notice of removal is filed.

(3) *Demand for a Jury Trial.*

(A) *As Affected by State Law.* A party who, before removal, expressly demanded a jury trial in accordance with state law need not renew the demand after removal. If the state law did not require an express demand for a jury trial, a party need not make one after removal unless the court orders the parties to do so within a specified time. The court must so order at a party's request and may so order on its own. A party who fails to make a demand when so ordered waives a jury trial.

(B) *Under Rule 38.* If all necessary pleadings have been served at the time of removal, a party entitled to a jury trial under Rule 38 must be given one if the party serves a demand within 14 days after:

(i) it files a notice of removal; or

(ii) it is served with a notice of removal filed by another party.

(d) Law Applicable.

(1) *"State Law" Defined.* When these rules refer to state law, the term "law" includes the state's statutes and the state's judicial decisions.

(2) *"State" Defined.* The term "state" includes, where appropriate, the District of Columbia and any United States commonwealth or territory.

(3) *"Federal Statute" Defined in the District of Columbia.* In the United States District Court for the District of Columbia, the term "federal statute" includes any Act of Congress that applies locally to the District.

(Amended December 28, 1939, effective April 3, 1941; December 27, 1946, effective March 19, 1948; December 29, 1948, effective October 20, 1949; April 30, 1951, effective August 1, 1951; January 21, 1963, effective July 1, 1963; February 28, 1966, effective July 1, 1966; December 4, 1967, effective July 1, 1968; March 1, 1971, effective July 1, 1971; March 2, 1987, effective August 1, 1987; April 23, 2001, effective December 1, 2001; April 29, 2002, effective December 1, 2002; April 30, 2007, effective December 1, 2007; March 26, 2009, effective December 1, 2009.)

RULE 82. JURISDICTION AND VENUE UNAFFECTED

[Text of Rule 82 effective until December 1, 2016, absent contrary Congressional action.]

These rules do not extend or limit the jurisdiction of the district courts or the venue of actions in those courts. An admiralty or maritime claim under Rule 9(h) is not a civil action for purposes of 28 U.S.C. §§ 1391–1392.

[Text of Rule 82 effective December 1, 2016, absent contrary Congressional action.]

These rules do not extend or limit the jurisdiction of the district courts or the venue of actions in those courts. An admiralty or maritime claim under Rule 9(h) is governed by 28 U.S.C. § 1390.

(Amended December 29, 1948, effective October 20, 1949; February 28, 1966, effective July 1, 1966; April 23, 2001, effective December 1, 2001; April 30, 2007, effective December 1, 2007; April 28, 2016, effective December 1, 2016, absent contrary Congressional action.)

RULE 83. RULES BY DISTRICT COURTS; JUDGE'S DIRECTIVES

(a) Local Rules.

(1) *In General.* After giving public notice and an opportunity for comment, a district court, acting by a majority of its district judges, may adopt and amend rules governing its practice. A local rule must be consistent with—but not duplicate—federal statutes and rules adopted under 28 U.S.C. §§ 2072 and 2075, and must conform to any uniform numbering system prescribed by the Judicial Conference of the United States. A local rule takes effect on the date specified by the district court and remains in effect unless amended by the court or abrogated by the judicial council of the circuit. Copies of rules and amendments must, on their adoption, be furnished to the judicial council and the Administrative Office of the United States Courts and be made available to the public.

(2) *Requirement of Form.* A local rule imposing a requirement of form must not be enforced in a way that causes a party to lose any right because of a nonwillful failure to comply.

(b) Procedure When There Is No Controlling Law. A judge may regulate practice in any manner consistent with federal law, rules adopted under 28 U.S.C. §§ 2072 and 2075, and the district's local rules. No sanction or other disadvantage may be imposed for noncompliance with any requirement not in federal law, federal rules, or the local rules unless the alleged violator has been furnished in the particular case with actual notice of the requirement.

(Amended April 29, 1985, effective August 1, 1985; April 27, 1995, effective December 1, 1995; April 30, 2007, effective December 1, 2007.)

RULE 84. FORMS [ABROGATED]

(Amended December 27, 1946, effective March 19, 1948; April 30, 2007, effective December 1, 2007; abrogated April 29, 2015, effective December 1, 2015.)

RULE 85. TITLE

These rules may be cited as the Federal Rules of Civil Procedure.

(Amended April 30, 2007, effective December 1, 2007.)

RULE 86. EFFECTIVE DATES

(a) In General. These rules and any amendments take effect at the time specified by the Supreme Court, subject to 28 U.S.C. § 2074. They govern:

(1) proceedings in an action commenced after their effective date; and

(2) proceedings after that date in an action then pending unless:

  (A) the Supreme Court specifies otherwise; or

  (B) the court determines that applying them in a particular action would be infeasible or work an injustice.

(b) December 1, 2007 Amendments. If any provision in Rules 1–5.1, 6–73, or 77–86 conflicts with another law, priority in time for the purpose of 28 U.S.C. § 2072(b) is not affected by the amendments taking effect on December 1, 2007.

(Amended December 27, 1946, effective March 19, 1948; December 29, 1948, effective October 20, 1949; April 17, 1961, effective July 19, 1961; January 21, 1963, and March 18, 1963, effective July 1, 1963; April 30, 2007, effective December 1, 2007.)

APPENDIX OF FORMS [Abrogated]

[Abrogated (Apr. 29, 2015, eff. Dec. 1, 2015).]

SUPPLEMENTAL RULES FOR ADMIRALTY OR MARITIME CLAIMS AND ASSET FORFEITURE ACTIONS

RULE A. SCOPE OF RULES

(1) These Supplemental Rules apply to:

(A) the procedure in admiralty and maritime claims within the meaning of Rule 9(h) with respect to the following remedies:

(i) maritime attachment and garnishment,

(ii) actions in rem,

(iii) possessory, petitory, and partition actions, and

(iv) actions for exoneration from or limitation of liability;

(B) forfeiture actions in rem arising from a federal statute; and

(C) the procedure in statutory condemnation proceedings analogous to maritime actions in rem, whether within the admiralty and maritime jurisdiction or not. Except as otherwise provided, references in these Supplemental Rules to actions in rem include such analogous statutory condemnation proceedings.

(2) The Federal Rules of Civil Procedure also apply to the foregoing proceedings except to the extent that they are inconsistent with these Supplemental Rules.

(Added Feb. 28, 1966, eff. July 1, 1966; amended Apr. 12, 2006, eff. Dec. 1, 2006.)

RULE B. IN PERSONAM ACTIONS: ATTACHMENT AND GARNISHMENT

(1) When Available; Complaint, Affidavit, Judicial Authorization, and Process. In an in personam action:

(a) If a defendant is not found within the district when a verified complaint praying for attachment and the affidavit required by Rule B(1)(b) are filed, a verified complaint may contain a prayer for process to attach the defendant's tangible or intangible personal property—up to the amount sued for—in the hands of garnishees named in the process.

(b) The plaintiff or the plaintiff's attorney must sign and file with the complaint an affidavit stating that, to the affiant's knowledge, or on information and belief, the defendant cannot be found within the district. The court must review the complaint and affidavit and, if the conditions of this Rule B appear to exist, enter an order so stating and authorizing process of attachment and garnishment. The clerk may issue supplemental process enforcing the court's order upon application without further court order.

(c) If the plaintiff or the plaintiff's attorney certifies that exigent circumstances make court review impracticable, the clerk must issue the summons and process of attachment and garnishment. The plaintiff has the burden in any post-attachment hearing under Rule E(4)(f) to show that exigent circumstances existed.

(d)(i) If the property is a vessel or tangible property on board a vessel, the summons, process, and any supplemental process must be delivered to the marshal for service.

(ii) If the property is other tangible or intangible property, the summons, process, and any supplemental process must be delivered to a person or organization authorized to serve it, who may be (A) a marshal; (B) someone under contract with the United States; (C) someone specially appointed by the court for that purpose; or, (D) in an action brought by the United States, any officer or employee of the United States.

(e) The plaintiff may invoke state-law remedies under Rule 64 for seizure of person or property for the purpose of securing satisfaction of the judgment.

(2) Notice to Defendant. No default judgment may be entered except upon proof—which may be by affidavit—that:

(a) the complaint, summons, and process of attachment or garnishment have been served on the defendant in a manner authorized by Rule 4;

(b) the plaintiff or the garnishee has mailed to the defendant the complaint, summons, and process of attachment or garnishment, using any form of mail requiring a return receipt; or

(c) the plaintiff or the garnishee has tried diligently to give notice of the action to the defendant but could not do so.

(3) Answer.

(a) By Garnishee. The garnishee shall serve an answer, together with answers to any interrogatories served with the complaint, within 21 days after service of process upon the garnishee. Interrogatories to the garnishee may be served with the complaint without leave of court. If the garnishee refuses or neglects to answer on oath as to the debts, credits, or effects of the defendant in the garnishee's hands, or any interrogatories concerning such debts, credits, and effects that may be propounded by the plaintiff, the court may award compulsory process against the garnishee. If the garnishee admits any debts, credits, or effects, they shall be held in the garnishee's hands or paid into the registry of the court, and shall be held in either case subject to the further order of the court.

(b) By Defendant. The defendant shall serve an answer within 30 days after process has been executed, whether by attachment of property or service on the garnishee.

(Added Feb. 28, 1966, eff. July 1, 1966; amended Apr. 29, 1985, eff. Aug. 1, 1985; Mar. 2, 1987, eff. Aug. 1, 1987; Apr. 17, 2000, eff. Dec. 1, 2000; Apr. 25, 2005, eff. Dec. 1, 2005; Mar. 26, 2009, eff. Dec. 1, 2009.)

RULE C. IN REM ACTIONS: SPECIAL PROVISIONS

(1) When Available. An action in rem may be brought:

(a) To enforce any maritime lien;

(b) Whenever a statute of the United States provides for a maritime action in rem or a proceeding analogous thereto.

Except as otherwise provided by law a party who may proceed in rem may also, or in the alternative, proceed in personam against any person who may be liable.

Statutory provisions exempting vessels or other property owned or possessed by or operated by or for the United States from arrest or seizure are not affected by this rule. When a statute so provides, an action against the United States or an instrumentality thereof may proceed on in rem principles.

(2) Complaint. In an action in rem the complaint must:

(a) be verified;

(b) describe with reasonable particularity the property that is the subject of the action; and

(c) state that the property is within the district or will be within the district while the action is pending.

(3) Judicial Authorization and Process.

(a) Arrest Warrant.

(i) The court must review the complaint and any supporting papers. If the conditions for an in rem action appear to exist, the court must issue an order directing the clerk to issue a warrant for the arrest of the vessel or other property that is the subject of the action.

(ii) If the plaintiff or the plaintiff's attorney certifies that exigent circumstances make court review impracticable, the clerk must promptly issue a summons and a warrant for the arrest of the vessel or other property that is the subject of the action. The plaintiff has the burden in any post-arrest hearing under Rule E(4)(f) to show that exigent circumstances existed.

(b) Service.

(i) If the property that is the subject of the action is a vessel or tangible property on board a vessel, the warrant and any supplemental process must be delivered to the marshal for service.

(ii) If the property that is the subject of the action is other property, tangible or intangible, the warrant and any supplemental process must be delivered to a person or organization authorized to enforce it, who may be: (A) a marshal; (B) someone under contract with the United States; (C) someone specially appointed by the court for that purpose; or, (D) in an action brought by the United States, any officer or employee of the United States.

(c) Deposit in Court. If the property that is the subject of the action consists in whole or in part of freight, the proceeds of property sold, or other intangible property, the clerk must issue—in addition to the warrant—a summons directing any person controlling the property to show cause why it should not be deposited in court to abide the judgment.

(d) Supplemental Process. The clerk may upon application issue supplemental process to enforce the court's order without further court order.

(4) Notice. No notice other than execution of process is required when the property that is the subject of the action has been released under Rule E(5). If the property is not released within 14 days after execution, the plaintiff must promptly—or within the time that the court allows—give public notice of the action and arrest in a newspaper designated by court order and having general circulation in the district, but publication may be terminated if the property is released before publication is completed. The notice must specify the time under Rule C(6) to file a statement of interest in or right against the seized property and to answer. This rule does not affect the notice requirements in an action to foreclose a preferred ship mortgage under 46 U.S.C. §§ 31301 et seq., as amended.

(5) Ancillary Process. In any action in rem in which process has been served as provided by this rule, if any part of the property that is the subject of the action has not been brought within the control of the court because it has been removed or sold, or because it is intangible property in the hands of a person who has not been served with process, the court may, on motion, order any person having possession or control of such property or its proceeds to show cause why it should not be delivered into the custody of the marshal or other person or organization having a warrant for the arrest of the property, or paid into court to abide the judgment; and, after hearing, the court may enter such judgment as law and justice may require.

(6) Responsive Pleading; Interrogatories.

(a) Statement of Interest; Answer. In an action in rem:

(i) a person who asserts a right of possession or any ownership interest in the property that is the subject of the action must file a verified statement of right or interest:

(A) within 14 days after the execution of process, or

(B) within the time that the court allows;

(ii) the statement of right or interest must describe the interest in the property that supports the person's demand for its restitution or right to defend the action;

(iii) an agent, bailee, or attorney must state the authority to file a statement of right or interest on behalf of another; and

(iv) a person who asserts a right of possession or any ownership interest must serve an answer within 21 days after filing the statement of interest or right.

(b) Interrogatories. Interrogatories may be served with the complaint in an in rem action without leave of court. Answers to the interrogatories must be served with the answer to the complaint.

(Added Feb. 28, 1966, eff. July 1, 1966; amended Apr. 29, 1985, eff. Aug. 1, 1985; Mar. 2, 1987, eff. Aug. 1, 1987; Apr. 30, 1991, eff. Dec. 1, 1991; Apr. 17, 2000, eff. Dec. 1, 2000; Apr. 29, 2002, eff. Dec. 1, 2002; Apr. 25, 2005, eff. Dec. 1, 2005; Apr. 12, 2006, eff. Dec. 1, 2006; Apr. 23, 2008, eff. Dec. 1, 2008; Mar. 26, 2009, eff. Dec. 1, 2009.)

RULE D. POSSESSORY, PETITORY, AND PARTITION ACTIONS

In all actions for possession, partition, and to try title maintainable according to the course of the admiralty practice with respect to a vessel, in all actions so maintainable with respect to the possession of cargo or other maritime property, and in all actions by one or more part owners against the others to obtain security for the return of the vessel from any voyage undertaken without their consent, or by one or more part owners against the others to obtain possession of the vessel for any voyage on giving security for its safe return, the process shall be by a warrant of arrest of the vessel, cargo, or other property, and by

notice in the manner provided by Rule B(2) to the adverse party or parties.

(Added Feb. 28, 1966, eff. July 1, 1966.)

RULE E. ACTIONS IN REM AND QUASI IN REM: GENERAL PROVISIONS

(1) Applicability. Except as otherwise provided, this rule applies to actions in personam with process of maritime attachment and garnishment, actions in rem, and petitory, possessory, and partition actions, supplementing Rules B, C, and D.

(2) Complaint; Security.

(a) Complaint. In actions to which this rule is applicable the complaint shall state the circumstances from which the claim arises with such particularity that the defendant or claimant will be able, without moving for a more definite statement, to commence an investigation of the facts and to frame a responsive pleading.

(b) Security for Costs. Subject to the provisions of Rule 54(d) and of relevant statutes, the court may, on the filing of the complaint or on the appearance of any defendant, claimant, or any other party, or at any later time, require the plaintiff, defendant, claimant, or other party to give security, or additional security, in such sum as the court shall direct to pay all costs and expenses that shall be awarded against the party by any interlocutory order or by the final judgment, or on appeal by any appellate court.

(3) Process.

(a) In admiralty and maritime proceedings process in rem or of maritime attachment and garnishment may be served only within the district.

(b) Issuance and Delivery. Issuance and delivery of process in rem, or of maritime attachment and garnishment, shall be held in abeyance if the plaintiff so requests.

(4) Execution of Process; Marshal's Return; Custody of Property; Procedures for Release.

(a) In General. Upon issuance and delivery of the process, or, in the case of summons with process of attachment and garnishment, when it appears that the defendant cannot be found within the district, the marshal or other person or organization having a warrant shall forthwith execute the process in accordance with this subdivision (4), making due and prompt return.

(b) Tangible Property. If tangible property is to be attached or arrested, the marshal or other person or organization having the warrant shall take it into the marshal's possession for safe custody. If the character or situation of the property is such that the taking of actual possession is impracticable, the marshal or other person executing the process shall affix a copy thereof to the property in a conspicuous place and leave a copy of the complaint and process with the person having possession or the person's agent. In furtherance of the marshal's custody of any vessel the marshal is authorized to make a written request to the collector of customs not to grant clearance to such vessel until notified by the marshal or deputy marshal or by the clerk that the vessel has been released in accordance with these rules.

(c) Intangible Property. If intangible property is to be attached or arrested the marshal or other person or organization having the warrant shall execute the process by leaving with the garnishee or other obligor a copy of the complaint and process requiring the garnishee or other obligor to answer as provided in Rules B(3)(a) and C(6); or the marshal may accept for payment into the registry of the court the amount owed to the extent of the amount claimed by the plaintiff with interest and costs, in which event the garnishee or other obligor shall not be required to answer unless alias process shall be served.

(d) Directions With Respect to Property in Custody. The marshal or other person or organization having the warrant may at any time apply to the court for directions with respect to property that has been attached or arrested, and shall give notice of such application to any or all of the parties as the court may direct.

(e) Expenses of Seizing and Keeping Property; Deposit. These rules do not alter the provisions of Title 28, U.S.C., § 1921, as amended, relative to the expenses of seizing and keeping property attached or arrested and to the requirement of deposits to cover such expenses.

(f) Procedure for Release From Arrest or Attachment. Whenever property is arrested or attached, any person claiming an interest in it shall be entitled to a prompt hearing at which the plaintiff shall be required to show why the arrest or attachment should not be vacated or other relief granted consistent with these rules. This subdivision shall have no application to suits for seamen's wages when process is issued upon a certification of sufficient cause filed pursuant to Title 46, U.S.C. §§ 603 and 604 or to actions by the United States for forfeitures for violation of any statute of the United States.

(5) Release of Property.

(a) Special Bond. Whenever process of maritime attachment and garnishment or process in rem is issued the execution of such process shall be stayed, or the property released, on the giving of security, to be approved by the court or clerk, or by stipulation of the parties, conditioned to answer the judgment of the court or of any appellate court.

The parties may stipulate the amount and nature of such security. In the event of the inability or refusal of the parties so to stipulate the court shall fix the principal sum of the bond or stipulation at an amount sufficient to cover the amount of the plaintiff's claim fairly stated with accrued interest and costs; but the principal sum shall in no event exceed (i) twice the amount of the plaintiff's claim or (ii) the value of the property on due appraisement, whichever is smaller. The bond or stipulation shall be conditioned for the payment of the principal sum and interest thereon at 6 per cent per annum.

(b) General Bond. The owner of any vessel may file a general bond or stipulation, with sufficient surety, to be approved by the court, conditioned to answer the judgment of such court in all or any actions that may be brought thereafter in such court in which the vessel is attached or arrested. Thereupon the execution of all such process against such vessel shall be stayed so long as the amount secured by such bond or stipulation is at least double the aggregate amount claimed by plaintiffs in all actions begun and pending in which such vessel has been attached or arrested. Judgments and remedies may be had on such bond or stipulation as if a special bond or stipulation had been filed in each of such actions. The district court may make necessary orders to carry this rule into effect, particularly as to the giving of proper notice of any action against or attachment of a vessel for which a general bond has been filed. Such bond or stipulation shall be indorsed by the clerk with a minute of the actions wherein process is so stayed. Further security may be required by the court at any time.

If a special bond or stipulation is given in a particular case, the liability on the general bond or stipulation shall cease as to that case.

(c) Release by Consent or Stipulation; Order of Court or Clerk; Costs. Any vessel, cargo, or other property in the custody of the marshal or other person or organization having the warrant may be released forthwith upon the marshal's acceptance and approval of a stipulation, bond, or other security, signed by the party on whose behalf the property is detained or the party's attorney and expressly authorizing such release, if all costs and charges of the court and its officers shall have first been paid. Otherwise no property in the custody of the marshal, other person or organization having the warrant, or other officer of the court shall be released without an order of the court; but such order may be entered as of course by the clerk, upon the giving of approved security as provided by law and these rules, or upon the dismissal or discontinuance of the action; but the marshal or other person or organization having the warrant shall not deliver any property so released until the costs and charges of the officers of the court shall first have been paid.

(d) Possessory, Petitory, and Partition Actions. The foregoing provisions of this subdivision (5) do not apply to petitory, possessory, and partition actions. In such cases the property arrested shall be released only by order of the court, on such terms and conditions and on the giving of such security as the court may require.

(6) Reduction or Impairment of Security. Whenever security is taken the court may, on motion and hearing, for good cause shown, reduce the amount of security given; and if the surety shall be or become insufficient, new or additional sureties may be required on motion and hearing.

(7) Security on Counterclaim.

(a) When a person who has given security for damages in the original action asserts a counterclaim that arises from the transaction or occurrence that is the subject of the original action, a plaintiff for whose benefit the security has been given must give security for damages demanded in the counterclaim unless the court for cause shown, directs otherwise. Proceedings on the original claim must be stayed until this security is given unless the court directs otherwise.

(b) The plaintiff is required to give security under Rule E(7)(a) when the United States or its corporate instrumentality counterclaims and would have been required to give security to respond in damages if a private party but is relieved by law from giving security.

(8) Restricted Appearance. An appearance to defend against an admiralty and maritime claim with respect to which there has issued process in rem, or process of attachment and garnishment, may be expressly restricted to the defense of such claim, and in that event is not an appearance for the purposes of any other claim with respect to which such process is not available or has not been served.

(9) Disposition of Property; Sales.

(a) Interlocutory Sales; Delivery.

(i) On application of a party, the marshal, or other person having custody of the property, the court may order all or part of the property sold—with the sales proceeds, or as much of them as will satisfy the judgment, paid into court to await further orders of the court—if:

(A) the attached or arrested property is perishable, or liable to deterioration, decay, or injury by being detained in custody pending the action;

(B) the expense of keeping the property is excessive or disproportionate; or

(C) there is an unreasonable delay in securing release of the property.

(ii) In the circumstances described in Rule E(9)(a)(i), the court, on motion by a defendant or a person filing a statement of interest or right under Rule C(6), may order that the property, rather than being sold, be delivered to the movant upon giving security under these rules.

(b) Sales; Proceeds. All sales of property shall be made by the marshal or a deputy marshal, or by other person or organization having the warrant, or by any other person assigned by the court where the marshal or other person or organization having the warrant is a party in interest; and the proceeds of sale shall be forthwith paid into the registry of the court to be disposed of according to law.

(10) Preservation of Property. When the owner or another person remains in possession of property attached or arrested under the provisions of Rule E(4)(b) that permit execution of process without taking actual possession, the court, on a party's motion or on its own, may enter any order necessary to preserve the property and to prevent its removal.

(Added Feb. 28, 1966, eff. July 1, 1966; amended Apr. 29, 1985, eff. Aug. 1, 1985; Mar. 2, 1987, eff. Aug. 1, 1987; Apr. 30, 1991, eff. Dec. 1, 1991; Apr. 17, 2000, eff. Dec. 1, 2000; Apr. 12, 2006, eff. Dec. 1, 2006.)

RULE F.   LIMITATION OF LIABILITY

(1) Time for Filing Complaint; Security. Not later than six months after receipt of a claim in writing, any vessel owner may file a complaint in the appropriate district court, as provided in subdivision (9) of this rule, for limitation of liability pursuant to statute. The owner (a) shall deposit with the court, for the benefit of claimants, a sum equal to the amount or value of the owner's interest in the vessel and pending freight, or approved security therefor, and in addition such sums, or approved security therefor, as the court may from time to time fix as necessary to carry out the provisions of the statutes as amended; or (b) at the owner's option shall transfer to a trustee to be appointed by the court, for the benefit of claimants, the owner's interest in the vessel and pending freight, together with such sums, or approved security therefor, as the court may from time to time fix as necessary to carry out the provisions of the statutes as amended. The plaintiff shall also give security for costs and, if the plaintiff elects to give security, for interest at the rate of 6 percent per annum from the date of the security.

(2) Complaint. The complaint shall set forth the facts on the basis of which the right to limit liability is asserted and all facts necessary to enable the court to determine the amount to which the owner's liability shall be limited. The complaint may demand exoneration from as well as limitation of liability. It shall state the voyage if any, on which the demands sought to be limited arose, with the date and place of its termination; the amount of all demands including all unsatisfied liens or claims of lien, in contract or in tort or otherwise, arising on that voyage, so far as known to the plaintiff, and what actions and proceedings, if any, are pending thereon; whether the vessel was damaged, lost, or abandoned, and, if so, when and where; the value of the vessel at the close of the voyage or, in case of wreck, the value of her wreckage, strippings, or proceeds, if any, and where and in whose possession they are; and the amount of any pending freight recovered or recoverable. If the plaintiff elects to transfer the plaintiff's interest in the vessel to a trustee, the complaint must further show any prior paramount liens thereon, and what voyages or trips, if any, she has made since the voyage or trip on which the claims sought to be limited arose, and any existing liens arising upon any such subsequent voyage or trip, with the amounts and causes thereof, and the names and addresses of the lienors, so far as known; and whether the vessel sustained any injury upon or by reason of such subsequent voyage or trip.

(3) **Claims Against Owner; Injunction.** Upon compliance by the owner with the requirements of subdivision (1) of this rule all claims and proceedings against the owner or the owner's property with respect to the matter in question shall cease. On application of the plaintiff the court shall enjoin the further prosecution of any action or proceeding against the plaintiff or the plaintiff's property with respect to any claim subject to limitation in the action.

(4) **Notice to Claimants.** Upon the owner's compliance with subdivision (1) of this rule the court shall issue a notice to all persons asserting claims with respect to which the complaint seeks limitation, admonishing them to file their respective claims with the clerk of the court and to serve on the attorneys for the plaintiff a copy thereof on or before a date to be named in the notice. The date so fixed shall not be less than 30 days after issuance of the notice. For cause shown, the court may enlarge the time within which claims may be filed. The notice shall be published in such newspaper or newspapers as the court may direct once a week for four successive weeks prior to the date fixed for the filing of claims. The plaintiff not later than the day of second publication shall also mail a copy of the notice to every person known to have made any claim against the vessel or the plaintiff arising out of the voyage or trip on which the claims sought to be limited arose. In cases involving death a copy of such notice shall be mailed to the decedent at the decedent's last known address, and also to any person who shall be known to have made any claim on account of such death.

(5) **Claims and Answer.** Claims shall be filed and served on or before the date specified in the notice provided for in subdivision (4) of this rule. Each claim shall specify the facts upon which the claimant relies in support of the claim, the items thereof, and the dates on which the same accrued. If a claimant desires to contest either the right to exoneration from or the right to limitation of liability the claimant shall file and serve an answer to the complaint unless the claim has included an answer.

(6) **Information to be Given Claimants.** Within 30 days after the date specified in the notice for filing claims, or within such time as the court thereafter may allow, the plaintiff shall mail to the attorney for each claimant (or if the claimant has no attorney to the claimant) a list setting forth (a) the name of each claimant, (b) the name and address of the claimant's attorney (if the claimant is known to have one), (c) the nature of the claim, i.e., whether property loss, property damage, death, personal injury etc., and (d) the amount thereof.

(7) **Insufficiency of Fund or Security.** Any claimant may by motion demand that the funds deposited in court or the security given by the plaintiff be increased on the ground that they are less than the value of the plaintiff's interest in the vessel and pending freight. Thereupon the court shall cause due appraisement to be made of the value of the plaintiff's interest in the vessel and pending freight; and if the court finds that the deposit or security is either insufficient or excessive it shall order its increase or reduction. In like manner any claimant may demand that the deposit or security be increased on the ground that it is insufficient to carry out the provisions of the statutes relating to claims in respect of loss of life or bodily injury; and, after notice and hearing, the court may similarly order that the deposit or security be increased or reduced.

(8) **Objections to Claims: Distribution of Fund.** Any interested party may question or controvert any claim without filing an objection thereto. Upon determination of liability the fund deposited or secured, or the proceeds of the vessel and pending freight, shall be divided pro rata, subject to all relevant provisions of law, among the several claimants in proportion to the amounts of their respective claims, duly proved, saving, however, to all parties any priority to which they may be legally entitled.

(9) **Venue; Transfer.** The complaint shall be filed in any district in which the vessel has been attached or arrested to answer for any claim with respect to which the plaintiff seeks to limit liability; or, if the vessel has not been attached or arrested, then in any district in which the owner has been sued with respect to any such claim. When the vessel has not been attached or arrested to answer the matters aforesaid, and suit has not been commenced against the owner, the proceedings may be had in the district in which the vessel may be, but if the vessel is not within any district and no suit has been commenced in any district, then the complaint may be filed in any district. For the convenience of parties and witnesses, in the

interest of justice, the court may transfer the action to any district; if venue is wrongly laid the court shall dismiss or, if it be in the interest of justice, transfer the action to any district in which it could have been brought. If the vessel shall have been sold, the proceeds shall represent the vessel for the purposes of these rules.

(Added Feb. 28, 1966, eff. July 1, 1966; amended Mar. 2, 1987, eff. Aug. 1, 1987.)

RULE G. FORFEITURE ACTIONS IN REM

(1) Scope. This rule governs a forfeiture action in rem arising from a federal statute. To the extent that this rule does not address an issue, Supplemental Rules C and E and the Federal Rules of Civil Procedure also apply.

(2) Complaint. The complaint must:

(a) be verified;

(b) state the grounds for subject-matter jurisdiction, in rem jurisdiction over the defendant property, and venue;

(c) describe the property with reasonable particularity;

(d) if the property is tangible, state its location when any seizure occurred and—if different—its location when the action is filed;

(e) identify the statute under which the forfeiture action is brought; and

(f) state sufficiently detailed facts to support a reasonable belief that the government will be able to meet its burden of proof at trial.

(3) Judicial Authorization and Process.

(a) **Real Property.** If the defendant is real property, the government must proceed under 18 U.S.C. § 985.

(b) **Other Property; Arrest Warrant.** If the defendant is not real property:

(i) the clerk must issue a warrant to arrest the property if it is in the government's possession, custody, or control;

(ii) the court—on finding probable cause—must issue a warrant to arrest the property if it is not in the government's possession, custody, or control and is not subject to a judicial restraining order; and

(iii) a warrant is not necessary if the property is subject to a judicial restraining order.

(c) **Execution of Process.**

(i) The warrant and any supplemental process must be delivered to a person or organization authorized to execute it, who may be: (A) a marshal or any other United States officer or employee; (B) someone under contract with the United States; or (C) someone specially appointed by the court for that purpose.

(ii) The authorized person or organization must execute the warrant and any supplemental process on property in the United States as soon as practicable unless:

(A) the property is in the government's possession, custody, or control; or

(B) the court orders a different time when the complaint is under seal, the action is stayed before the warrant and supplemental process are executed, or the court finds other good cause.

(iii) The warrant and any supplemental process may be executed within the district or, when authorized by statute, outside the district.

(iv) If executing a warrant on property outside the United States is required, the warrant may be transmitted to an appropriate authority for serving process where the property is located.

(4) Notice.

(a) **Notice by Publication.**

(i) **When Publication Is Required.** A judgment of forfeiture may be entered only if the government has published notice of the action within a reasonable time after filing the complaint or at a time the court orders. But notice need not be published if:

(A) the defendant property is worth less than $1,000 and direct notice is sent under Rule G(4)(b) to every person the government can reasonably identify as a potential claimant; or

(B) the court finds that the cost of publication exceeds the property's value and that other means of notice would satisfy due process.

(ii) **Content of the Notice.** Unless the court orders otherwise, the notice must:

(A) describe the property with reasonable particularity;

(B) state the times under Rule G(5) to file a claim and to answer; and

(C) name the government attorney to be served with the claim and answer.

(iii) **Frequency of Publication.** Published notice must appear:

(A) once a week for three consecutive weeks; or

(B) only once if, before the action was filed, notice of nonjudicial forfeiture of the same property was published on an official internet government forfeiture site for at least 30 consecutive days, or in a newspaper of general circulation for three consecutive weeks in a district where publication is authorized under Rule G(4)(a)(iv).

(iv) Means of Publication. The government should select from the following options a means of publication reasonably calculated to notify potential claimants of the action:

(A) if the property is in the United States, publication in a newspaper generally circulated in the district where the action is filed, where the property was seized, or where property that was not seized is located;

(B) if the property is outside the United States, publication in a newspaper generally circulated in a district where the action is filed, in a newspaper generally circulated in the country where the property is located, or in legal notices published and generally circulated in the country where the property is located; or

(C) instead of (A) or (B), posting a notice on an official internet government forfeiture site for at least 30 consecutive days.

(b) Notice to Known Potential Claimants.

(i) Direct Notice Required. The government must send notice of the action and a copy of the complaint to any person who reasonably appears to be a potential claimant on the facts known to the government before the end of the time for filing a claim under Rule G(5)(a)(ii)(B).

(ii) Content of the Notice. The notice must state:

(A) the date when the notice is sent;

(B) a deadline for filing a claim, at least 35 days after the notice is sent;

(C) that an answer or a motion under Rule 12 must be filed no later than 21 days after filing the claim; and

(D) the name of the government attorney to be served with the claim and answer.

(iii) Sending Notice.

(A) The notice must be sent by means reasonably calculated to reach the potential claimant.

(B) Notice may be sent to the potential claimant or to the attorney representing the potential claimant with respect to the seizure of the property or in a related investigation, administrative forfeiture proceeding, or criminal case.

(C) Notice sent to a potential claimant who is incarcerated must be sent to the place of incarceration.

(D) Notice to a person arrested in connection with an offense giving rise to the forfeiture who is not incarcerated when notice is sent may be sent to the address that person last gave to the agency that arrested or released the person.

(E) Notice to a person from whom the property was seized who is not incarcerated when notice is sent may be sent to the last address that person gave to the agency that seized the property.

(iv) When Notice Is Sent. Notice by the following means is sent on the date when it is placed in the mail, delivered to a commercial carrier, or sent by electronic mail.

(v) Actual Notice. A potential claimant who had actual notice of a forfeiture action may not oppose or seek relief from forfeiture because of the government's failure to send the required notice.

(5) Responsive Pleadings.

(a) Filing a Claim.

(i) A person who asserts an interest in the defendant property may contest the forfeiture by filing a claim in the court where the action is pending. The claim must:

(A) identify the specific property claimed;

(B) identify the claimant and state the claimant's interest in the property;

(C) be signed by the claimant under penalty of perjury; and

(D) be served on the government attorney designated under Rule G(4)(a)(ii)(C) or (b)(ii)(D).

(ii) Unless the court for good cause sets a different time, the claim must be filed:

(A) by the time stated in a direct notice sent under Rule G(4)(b);

(B) if notice was published but direct notice was not sent to the claimant or the claimant's attorney, no later than 30 days after final publication of newspaper notice or legal notice under Rule G(4)(a) or no later than 60 days after the first day of publication on an official internet government forfeiture site; or

(C) if notice was not published and direct notice was not sent to the claimant or the claimant's attorney:

(1) if the property was in the government's possession, custody, or control when the complaint was filed, no later than 60 days after the filing, not counting any time when the complaint was under seal or when the action was stayed before execution of a warrant issued under Rule G(3)(b); or

(2) if the property was not in the government's possession, custody, or control when the complaint was filed, no later than 60 days after the government complied with 18 U.S.C. § 985(c) as to real property, or 60 days after process was executed on the property under Rule G(3).

(iii) A claim filed by a person asserting an interest as a bailee must identify the bailor, and if filed on the bailor's behalf must state the authority to do so.

(b) Answer. A claimant must serve and file an answer to the complaint or a motion under Rule 12 within 21 days after filing the claim. A claimant waives an objection to in rem jurisdiction or to venue if the objection is not made by motion or stated in the answer.

(6) Special Interrogatories.

(a) Time and Scope. The government may serve special interrogatories limited to the claimant's identity and relationship to the defendant property without the court's leave at any time after the claim is filed and before discovery is closed. But if the claimant serves a motion to dismiss the action, the government must serve the interrogatories within 21 days after the motion is served.

(b) Answers or Objections. Answers or objections to these interrogatories must be served within 21 days after the interrogatories are served.

(c) Government's Response Deferred. The government need not respond to a claimant's motion to dismiss the action under Rule G(8)(b) until 21 days after the claimant has answered these interrogatories.

(7) Preserving, Preventing Criminal Use, and Disposing of Property; Sales.

(a) Preserving and Preventing Criminal Use of Property. When the government does not have actual possession of the defendant property the court, on motion or on its own, may enter any order necessary to preserve the property, to prevent its removal or encumbrance, or to prevent its use in a criminal offense.

(b) Interlocutory Sale or Delivery.

(i) Order to Sell. On motion by a party or a person having custody of the property, the court may order all or part of the property sold if:

(A) the property is perishable or at risk of deterioration, decay, or injury by being detained in custody pending the action;

(B) the expense of keeping the property is excessive or is disproportionate to its fair market value;

(C) the property is subject to a mortgage or to taxes on which the owner is in default; or

(D) the court finds other good cause.

(ii) Who Makes the Sale. A sale must be made by a United States agency that has authority to sell the property, by the agency's contractor, or by any person the court designates.

(iii) Sale Procedures. The sale is governed by 28 U.S.C. §§ 2001, 2002, and 2004, unless all parties, with the court's approval, agree to the sale, aspects of the sale, or different procedures.

(iv) Sale Proceeds. Sale proceeds are a substitute res subject to forfeiture in place of the property that was sold. The proceeds must be held in an interest-bearing account maintained by the United States pending the conclusion of the forfeiture action.

(v) Delivery on a Claimant's Motion. The court may order that the property be delivered to the claimant pending the conclusion of the action if the claimant shows circumstances that would permit sale under Rule G(7)(b)(i) and gives security under these rules.

(c) Disposing of Forfeited Property. Upon entry of a forfeiture judgment, the property or proceeds from selling the property must be disposed of as provided by law.

(8) Motions.

(a) Motion To Suppress Use of the Property as Evidence. If the defendant property was seized, a party with standing to contest the lawfulness of the seizure may move to suppress use of the property as evidence. Suppression does not affect forfeiture of the property based on independently derived evidence.

(b) Motion To Dismiss the Action.

(i) A claimant who establishes standing to contest forfeiture may move to dismiss the action under Rule 12(b).

(ii) In an action governed by 18 U.S.C. § 983(a)(3)(D) the complaint may not be dismissed on the ground that the government did not have adequate evidence at the time the complaint was filed to establish the forfeitability of the property. The sufficiency of the complaint is governed by Rule G(2).

(c) Motion To Strike a Claim or Answer.

(i) At any time before trial, the government may move to strike a claim or answer:

(A) for failing to comply with Rule G(5) or (6), or

(B) because the claimant lacks standing.

(ii) The motion:

(A) must be decided before any motion by the claimant to dismiss the action; and

(B) may be presented as a motion for judgment on the pleadings or as a motion to determine after a hearing or by summary judgment whether the claimant can carry the burden of establishing standing by a preponderance of the evidence.

(d) Petition To Release Property.

(i) If a United States agency or an agency's contractor holds property for judicial or nonjudicial forfeiture under a statute governed by 18 U.S.C. § 983(f), a person who has filed a claim to the property may petition for its release under § 983(f).

(ii) If a petition for release is filed before a judicial forfeiture action is filed against the property, the petition may be filed either in the district where the property was seized or in the district where a warrant to seize the property issued. If a judicial forfeiture action against the property is later filed in another district—or if the government shows that the action will be filed in another district—the petition may be transferred to that district under 28 U.S.C. § 1404.

(e) Excessive Fines. A claimant may seek to mitigate a forfeiture under the Excessive Fines Clause of the Eighth Amendment by motion for summary judgment or by motion made after entry of a forfeiture judgment if:

(i) the claimant has pleaded the defense under Rule 8; and

(ii) the parties have had the opportunity to conduct civil discovery on the defense.

(9) Trial. Trial is to the court unless any party demands trial by jury under Rule 38.

(Added Apr. 12, 2006, eff. Dec. 1, 2006; amended Mar. 26, 2009, eff. Dec. 1, 2009.)

INDEX TO
FEDERAL RULES OF CIVIL PROCEDURE

FEDERAL RULES OF EVIDENCE

Including Amendments Received Through May 1, 2016

ARTICLE I. GENERAL PROVISIONS

RULE 101. SCOPE; DEFINITIONS

(a) **Scope.** These rules apply to proceedings in United States courts. The specific courts and proceedings to which the rules apply, along with exceptions, are set out in Rule 1101.

(b) **Definitions.** In these rules:

(1) "civil case" means a civil action or proceeding;

(2) "criminal case" includes a criminal proceeding;

(3) "public office" includes a public agency;

(4) "record" includes a memorandum, report, or data compilation;

(5) a "rule prescribed by the Supreme Court" means a rule adopted by the Supreme Court under statutory authority; and

(6) a reference to any kind of written material or any other medium includes electronically stored information.

(Pub.L. 93–595, § 1, Jan. 2, 1975, 88 Stat. 1929; Mar. 2, 1987, eff. Oct. 1, 1987; Apr. 25, 1988, eff. Nov. 1, 1988; Apr. 22, 1993, eff. Dec. 1, 1993; Apr. 26, 2011, eff. Dec. 1, 2011.)

RULE 102. PURPOSE

These rules should be construed so as to administer every proceeding fairly, eliminate unjustifiable expense and delay, and promote the development of evidence law, to the end of ascertaining the truth and securing a just determination.

(Pub.L. 93–595, § 1, Jan. 2, 1975, 88 Stat.1929; Apr. 26, 2011, eff. Dec. 1, 2011.)

RULE 103. RULINGS ON EVIDENCE

(a) **Preserving a Claim of Error.** A party may claim error in a ruling to admit or exclude evidence only if the error affects a substantial right of the party and:

(1) if the ruling admits evidence, a party, on the record:

(A) timely objects or moves to strike; and

(B) states the specific ground, unless it was apparent from the context; or

(2) if the ruling excludes evidence, a party informs the court of its substance by an offer of proof, unless the substance was apparent from the context.

(b) **Not Needing to Renew an Objection or Offer of Proof.** Once the court rules definitively on the record—either before or at trial—a party need not renew an objection or offer of proof to preserve a claim of error for appeal.

(c) **Court's Statement About the Ruling; Directing an Offer of Proof.** The court may make any statement about the character or form of the evidence, the objection made, and the ruling. The court may direct that an offer of proof be made in question-and-answer form.

(d) **Preventing the Jury from Hearing Inadmissible Evidence.** To the extent practicable, the court must conduct a jury trial so that inadmissible evidence is not suggested to the jury by any means.

(e) **Taking Notice of Plain Error.** A court may take notice of a plain error affecting a substantial right, even if the claim of error was not properly preserved.

(Pub.L. 93–595, § 1, Jan. 2, 1975, 88 Stat. 1929; Apr. 17, 2000, eff. Dec. 1, 2000; Apr. 26, 2011, eff. Dec. 1, 2011.)

RULE 104. PRELIMINARY QUESTIONS

(a) **In General.** The court must decide any preliminary question about whether a witness is qualified, a privilege exists, or evidence is admissible. In so deciding, the court is not bound by evidence rules, except those on privilege.

(b) **Relevance That Depends on a Fact.** When the relevance of evidence depends on whether a fact exists, proof must be introduced sufficient to support a finding that the fact does exist. The court may admit the proposed evidence on the condition that the proof be introduced later.

(c) **Conducting a Hearing So That the Jury Cannot Hear It.** The court must conduct any hearing on a preliminary question so that the jury cannot hear it if:

(1) the hearing involves the admissibility of a confession;

(2) a defendant in a criminal case is a witness and so requests; or

(3) justice so requires.

(d) **Cross–Examining a Defendant in a Criminal Case.** By testifying on a preliminary question, a defendant in a criminal case does not become subject to cross-examination on other issues in the case.

(e) Evidence Relevant to Weight and Credibility. This rule does not limit a party's right to introduce before the jury evidence that is relevant to the weight or credibility of other evidence.

(Pub.L. 93–595, § 1, Jan. 2, 1975, 88 Stat.1930; Mar. 2, 1987, eff. Oct. 1, 1987; Apr. 26, 2011, eff. Dec. 1, 2011.)

RULE 105. LIMITING EVIDENCE THAT IS NOT ADMISSIBLE AGAINST OTHER PARTIES OR FOR OTHER PURPOSES

If the court admits evidence that is admissible against a party or for a purpose—but not against another party or for another purpose—the court, on timely request, must restrict the evidence to its proper scope and instruct the jury accordingly.

(Pub.L. 93–595, § 1, Jan. 2, 1975, 88 Stat. 1930; Apr. 26, 2011, eff. Dec. 1, 2011.)

RULE 106. REMAINDER OF OR RELATED WRITINGS OR RECORDED STATEMENTS

If a party introduces all or part of a writing or recorded statement, an adverse party may require the introduction, at that time, of any other part—or any other writing or recorded statement—that in fairness ought to be considered at the same time.

(Pub.L. 93–595, § 1, Jan. 2, 1975, 88 Stat. 1930; Mar. 2, 1987, eff. Oct. 1, 1987; Apr. 26, 2011, eff. Dec. 1, 2011.)

ARTICLE II. JUDICIAL NOTICE

RULE 201. JUDICIAL NOTICE OF ADJUDICATIVE FACTS

(a) Scope. This rule governs judicial notice of an adjudicative fact only, not a legislative fact.

(b) Kinds of Facts That May Be Judicially Noticed. The court may judicially notice a fact that is not subject to reasonable dispute because it:

   (1) is generally known within the trial court's territorial jurisdiction; or

   (2) can be accurately and readily determined from sources whose accuracy cannot reasonably be questioned.

(c) Taking Notice. The court:

   (1) may take judicial notice on its own; or

   (2) must take judicial notice if a party requests it and the court is supplied with the necessary information.

(d) Timing. The court may take judicial notice at any stage of the proceeding.

(e) Opportunity to Be Heard. On timely request, a party is entitled to be heard on the propriety of taking judicial notice and the nature of the fact to be noticed. If the court takes judicial notice before notifying a party, the party, on request, is still entitled to be heard.

(f) Instructing the Jury. In a civil case, the court must instruct the jury to accept the noticed fact as conclusive. In a criminal case, the court must instruct the jury that it may or may not accept the noticed fact as conclusive.

(Pub.L. 93–595, § 1, Jan. 2, 1975, 88 Stat. 1930; Apr. 26, 2011, eff. Dec. 1, 2011.)

ARTICLE III. PRESUMPTIONS IN CIVIL CASES

RULE 301. PRESUMPTIONS IN CIVIL CASES GENERALLY

In a civil case, unless a federal statute or these rules provide otherwise, the party against whom a presumption is directed has the burden of producing evidence to rebut the presumption. But this rule does not shift the burden of persuasion, which remains on the party who had it originally.

(Pub.L. 93–595, § 1, Jan. 2, 1975, 88 Stat. 1931; Apr. 26, 2011, eff. Dec. 1, 2011.)

RULE 302. APPLYING STATE LAW TO PRESUMPTIONS IN CIVIL CASES

In a civil case, state law governs the effect of a presumption regarding a claim or defense for which state law supplies the rule of decision.

(Pub.L. 93–595, § 1, Jan. 2, 1975, 88 Stat. 1931; Apr. 26, 2011, eff. Dec. 1, 2011.)

ARTICLE IV. RELEVANCE AND ITS LIMITS

RULE 401. TEST FOR RELEVANT EVIDENCE

Evidence is relevant if:

(a) it has any tendency to make a fact more or less probable than it would be without the evidence; and

(b) the fact is of consequence in determining the action.

(Pub.L. 93–595, § 1, Jan. 2, 1975, 88 Stat.1931; Apr. 26, 2011, eff. Dec. 1, 2011.)

RULE 402. GENERAL ADMISSIBILITY OF RELEVANT EVIDENCE

Relevant evidence is admissible unless any of the following provides otherwise:

- the United States Constitution;
- a federal statute;
- these rules; or
- other rules prescribed by the Supreme Court.

Irrelevant evidence is not admissible.

(Pub.L. 93–595, § 1, Jan. 2, 1975, 88 Stat. 1931; Apr. 26, 2011, eff. Dec. 1, 2011.)

RULE 403. EXCLUDING RELEVANT EVIDENCE FOR PREJUDICE, CONFUSION, WASTE OF TIME, OR OTHER REASONS

The court may exclude relevant evidence if its probative value is substantially outweighed by a danger of one or more of the following: unfair prejudice, confusing the issues, misleading the jury, undue delay, wasting time, or needlessly presenting cumulative evidence.

(Pub.L. 93–595, § 1, Jan. 2, 1975, 88 Stat. 1932; Apr. 26, 2011, eff. Dec. 1, 2011.)

RULE 404. CHARACTER EVIDENCE; CRIMES OR OTHER ACTS

(a) Character Evidence.

(1) Prohibited Uses. Evidence of a person's character or character trait is not admissible to prove that on a particular occasion the person acted in accordance with the character or trait.

(2) Exceptions for a Defendant or Victim in a Criminal Case. The following exceptions apply in a criminal case:

    (A) a defendant may offer evidence of the defendant's pertinent trait, and if the evidence is admitted, the prosecutor may offer evidence to rebut it;

    (B) subject to the limitations in Rule 412, a defendant may offer evidence of an alleged victim's pertinent trait, and if the evidence is admitted, the prosecutor may:

        (i) offer evidence to rebut it; and

        (ii) offer evidence of the defendant's same trait; and

    (C) in a homicide case, the prosecutor may offer evidence of the alleged victim's trait of peacefulness to rebut evidence that the victim was the first aggressor.

(3) Exceptions for a Witness. Evidence of a witness's character may be admitted under Rules 607, 608, and 609.

(b) Crimes, Wrongs, or Other Acts.

(1) Prohibited Uses. Evidence of a crime, wrong, or other act is not admissible to prove a person's character in order to show that on a particular occasion the person acted in accordance with the character.

(2) Permitted Uses; Notice in a Criminal Case. This evidence may be admissible for another purpose, such as proving motive, opportunity, intent, preparation, plan, knowledge, identity, absence of mistake, or lack of accident. On request by a defendant in a criminal case, the prosecutor must:

    (A) provide reasonable notice of the general nature of any such evidence that the prosecutor intends to offer at trial; and

    (B) do so before trial—or during trial if the court, for good cause, excuses lack of pretrial notice.

(Pub.L. 93–595, § 1, Jan. 2, 1975, 88 Stat.1932; Mar. 2, 1987, eff. Oct. 1, 1987; Apr. 30, 1991, eff. Dec. 1, 1991; Apr. 17, 2000, eff. Dec. 1, 2000; Apr. 12, 2006, eff. Dec. 1, 2006; Apr. 26, 2011, eff. Dec. 1, 2011.)

RULE 405. METHODS OF PROVING CHARACTER

(a) By Reputation or Opinion. When evidence of a person's character or character trait is admissible, it may be proved by testimony about the person's reputation or by testimony in the form of an opinion. On cross-examination of the character witness, the court may allow an inquiry into relevant specific instances of the person's conduct.

(b) By Specific Instances of Conduct. When a person's character or character trait is an essential element of a charge, claim, or defense, the character or trait may also be proved by relevant specific instances of the person's conduct.

(Pub.L. 93–595, § 1, Jan. 2, 1975, 88 Stat. 1932; Mar. 2, 1987, eff. Oct. 1, 1987; Apr. 26, 2011, eff. Dec. 1, 2011.)

RULE 406. HABIT; ROUTINE PRACTICE

Evidence of a person's habit or an organization's routine practice may be admitted to prove that on a particular occasion the person or organization acted in accordance with the habit or routine practice. The court may admit this evidence regardless of whether it is corroborated or whether there was an eyewitness.

(Pub.L. 93–595, § 1, Jan. 2, 1975, 88 Stat. 1932; Apr. 26, 2011, eff. Dec. 1, 2011.)

RULE 407. SUBSEQUENT REMEDIAL MEASURES

When measures are taken that would have made an earlier injury or harm less likely to occur, evidence of the subsequent measures is not admissible to prove:

- negligence;
- culpable conduct;
- a defect in a product or its design; or
- a need for a warning or instruction.

But the court may admit this evidence for another purpose, such as impeachment or—if disputed—proving ownership, control, or the feasibility of precautionary measures.

(Pub.L. 93–595, § 1, Jan. 2, 1975, 88 Stat. 1932; Apr. 11, 1997, eff. Dec. 1, 1997; Apr. 26, 2011, eff. Dec. 1, 2011.)

RULE 408. COMPROMISE OFFERS AND NEGOTIATIONS

(a) Prohibited Uses. Evidence of the following is not admissible—on behalf of any party—either to prove or disprove the validity or amount of a disputed claim or to impeach by a prior inconsistent statement or a contradiction:

(1) furnishing, promising, or offering—or accepting, promising to accept, or offering to accept—a valuable consideration in compromising or attempting to compromise the claim; and

(2) conduct or a statement made during compromise negotiations about the claim—except when offered in a criminal case and when the negotiations related to a claim by a public office in the exercise of its regulatory, investigative, or enforcement authority.

(b) Exceptions. The court may admit this evidence for another purpose, such as proving a witness's bias or prejudice, negating a contention of undue

delay, or proving an effort to obstruct a criminal investigation or prosecution.

(Pub.L. 93–595, § 1, Jan. 2, 1975, 88 Stat. 1933; Apr. 12, 2006, eff. Dec. 1, 2006; Apr. 26, 2011, eff. Dec. 1, 2011.)

RULE 409. OFFERS TO PAY MEDICAL AND SIMILAR EXPENSES

Evidence of furnishing, promising to pay, or offering to pay medical, hospital, or similar expenses resulting from an injury is not admissible to prove liability for the injury.

(Pub.L. 93–595, § 1, Jan. 2, 1975, 88 Stat.1933; Apr. 26, 2011, eff. Dec. 1, 2011.)

RULE 410. PLEAS, PLEA DISCUSSIONS, AND RELATED STATEMENTS

(a) Prohibited Uses. In a civil or criminal case, evidence of the following is not admissible against the defendant who made the plea or participated in the plea discussions:

(1) a guilty plea that was later withdrawn;

(2) a nolo contendere plea;

(3) a statement made during a proceeding on either of those pleas under Federal Rule of Criminal Procedure 11 or a comparable state procedure; or

(4) a statement made during plea discussions with an attorney for the prosecuting authority if the discussions did not result in a guilty plea or they resulted in a later-withdrawn guilty plea.

(b) Exceptions. The court may admit a statement described in Rule 410(a)(3) or (4):

(1) in any proceeding in which another statement made during the same plea or plea discussions has been introduced, if in fairness the statements ought to be considered together; or

(2) in a criminal proceeding for perjury or false statement, if the defendant made the statement under oath, on the record, and with counsel present.

(Pub.L. 93–595, § 1, Jan. 2, 1975, 88 Stat. 1933; Pub.L. 94–149, § 1(9), Dec. 12, 1975, 89 Stat. 805; Apr. 30, 1979, eff. Dec. 1, 1980; Apr. 26, 2011, eff. Dec. 1, 2011.)

RULE 411. LIABILITY INSURANCE

Evidence that a person was or was not insured against liability is not admissible to prove whether the person acted negligently or otherwise wrongfully. But the court may admit this evidence for another purpose, such as proving a witness's bias or prejudice or proving agency, ownership, or control.

(Pub.L. 93–595, § 1, Jan. 2, 1975, 88 Stat.1933; Mar. 2, 1987, eff. Oct. 1, 1987; Apr. 26, 2011, eff. Dec. 1, 2011.)

RULE 412. SEX–OFFENSE CASES: THE VICTIM'S SEXUAL BEHAVIOR OR PREDISPOSITION

(a) Prohibited Uses. The following evidence is not admissible in a civil or criminal proceeding involving alleged sexual misconduct:

(1) evidence offered to prove that a victim engaged in other sexual behavior; or

(2) evidence offered to prove a victim's sexual predisposition.

(b) Exceptions.

(1) Criminal Cases. The court may admit the following evidence in a criminal case:

(A) evidence of specific instances of a victim's sexual behavior, if offered to prove that someone other than the defendant was the source of semen, injury, or other physical evidence;

(B) evidence of specific instances of a victim's sexual behavior with respect to the person accused of the sexual misconduct, if offered by the defendant to prove consent or if offered by the prosecutor; and

(C) evidence whose exclusion would violate the defendant's constitutional rights.

(2) Civil Cases. In a civil case, the court may admit evidence offered to prove a victim's sexual behavior or sexual predisposition if its probative value substantially outweighs the danger of harm to any victim and of unfair prejudice to any party. The court may admit evidence of a victim's reputation only if the victim has placed it in controversy.

(c) Procedure to Determine Admissibility.

(1) Motion. If a party intends to offer evidence under Rule 412(b), the party must:

(A) file a motion that specifically describes the evidence and states the purpose for which it is to be offered;

(B) do so at least 14 days before trial unless the court, for good cause, sets a different time;

(C) serve the motion on all parties; and

(D) notify the victim or, when appropriate, the victim's guardian or representative.

(2) Hearing. Before admitting evidence under this rule, the court must conduct an in camera hearing and give the victim and parties a right to attend and be heard. Unless the court orders otherwise, the motion, related materials, and the record of the hearing must be and remain sealed.

(d) Definition of "Victim." In this rule, "victim" includes an alleged victim.

(Added Pub.L. 95–540, § 2(a), Oct. 28, 1978, 92 Stat. 2046; amended Pub.L. 100–690, Title VII, § 7046(a), Nov. 18, 1988, 102 Stat. 4400; Apr. 29, 1994, eff. Dec. 1, 1994; Pub.L. 103–322, Title IV, § 40141(b), Sept. 13, 1994, 108 Stat. 1919; Apr. 26, 2011, eff. Dec. 1, 2011.)

RULE 413. SIMILAR CRIMES IN SEXUAL–ASSAULT CASES

(a) Permitted Uses. In a criminal case in which a defendant is accused of a sexual assault, the court may admit evidence that the defendant committed any other sexual assault. The evidence may be considered on any matter to which it is relevant.

(b) Disclosure to the Defendant. If the prosecutor intends to offer this evidence, the prosecutor must disclose it to the defendant, including witnesses' statements or a summary of the expected testimony. The prosecutor must do so at least 15 days before trial or at a later time that the court allows for good cause.

(c) Effect on Other Rules. This rule does not limit the admission or consideration of evidence under any other rule.

(d) Definition of "Sexual Assault." In this rule and Rule 415, "sexual assault" means a crime under federal law or under state law (as "state" is defined in 18 U.S.C. § 513) involving:

(1) any conduct prohibited by 18 U.S.C. chapter 109A;

(2) contact, without consent, between any part of the defendant's body—or an object—and another person's genitals or anus;

(3) contact, without consent, between the defendant's genitals or anus and any part of another person's body;

(4) deriving sexual pleasure or gratification from inflicting death, bodily injury, or physical pain on another person; or

(5) an attempt or conspiracy to engage in conduct described in subparagraphs (1)–(4).

(Added Pub.L. 103–322, Title XXXII, § 320935(a), Sept. 13, 1994, 108 Stat. 2136; Apr. 26, 2011, eff. Dec. 1, 2011.)

RULE 414. SIMILAR CRIMES IN CHILD–MOLESTATION CASES

(a) Permitted Uses. In a criminal case in which a defendant is accused of child molestation, the court may admit evidence that the defendant committed any other child molestation. The evidence may be considered on any matter to which it is relevant.

(b) Disclosure to the Defendant. If the prosecutor intends to offer this evidence, the prosecutor must disclose it to the defendant, including witnesses' statements or a summary of the expected testimony. The prosecutor must do so at least 15 days before trial or at a later time that the court allows for good cause.

(c) Effect on Other Rules. This rule does not limit the admission or consideration of evidence under any other rule.

(d) Definition of "Child" and "Child Molestation." In this rule and Rule 415:

(1) "child" means a person below the age of 14; and

(2) "child molestation" means a crime under federal law or under state law (as "state" is defined in 18 U.S.C. § 513) involving:

(A) any conduct prohibited by 18 U.S.C. chapter 109A and committed with a child;

(B) any conduct prohibited by 18 U.S.C. chapter 110;

(C) contact between any part of the defendant's body—or an object—and a child's genitals or anus;

(D) contact between the defendant's genitals or anus and any part of a child's body;

(E) deriving sexual pleasure or gratification from inflicting death, bodily injury, or physical pain on a child; or

(F) an attempt or conspiracy to engage in conduct described in subparagraphs (A)–(E).

(Added Pub.L. 103–322, Title XXXII, § 320935(a), Sept. 13, 1994, 108 Stat. 2135; Apr. 26, 2011, eff. Dec. 1, 2011.)

RULE 415. SIMILAR ACTS IN CIVIL CASES INVOLVING SEXUAL ASSAULT OR CHILD MOLESTATION

(a) Permitted Uses. In a civil case involving a claim for relief based on a party's alleged sexual assault or child molestation, the court may admit evidence that the party committed any other sexual assault or child molestation. The evidence may be considered as provided in Rules 413 and 414.

(b) Disclosure to the Opponent. If a party intends to offer this evidence, the party must disclose it to the party against whom it will be offered, including witnesses' statements or a summary of the expected testimony. The party must do so at least 15 days before trial or at a later time that the court allows for good cause.

(c) Effect on Other Rules. This rule does not limit the admission or consideration of evidence under any other rule.

(Added Pub.L. 103–322, Title XXXII, § 320935(a), Sept. 13, 1994, 108 Stat. 2137; Apr. 26, 2011, eff. Dec. 1, 2011.)

ARTICLE V. PRIVILEGES

RULE 501. PRIVILEGE IN GENERAL

The common law—as interpreted by United States courts in the light of reason and experience—governs a claim of privilege unless any of the following provides otherwise:

- the United States Constitution;
- a federal statute; or
- rules prescribed by the Supreme Court.

But in a civil case, state law governs privilege regarding a claim or defense for which state law supplies the rule of decision.

(Pub.L. 93–595, § 1, Jan. 2, 1975, 88 Stat. 1933; Apr. 26, 2011, eff. Dec. 1, 2011.)

RULE 502. ATTORNEY–CLIENT PRIVILEGE AND WORK PRODUCT; LIMITATIONS ON WAIVER

The following provisions apply, in the circumstances set out, to disclosure of a communication or information covered by the attorney-client privilege or work-product protection.

(a) Disclosure Made in a Federal Proceeding or to a Federal Office or Agency; Scope of a Waiver. When the disclosure is made in a federal proceeding or to a federal office or agency and waives the attorney-client privilege or work-product protection, the waiver extends to an undisclosed communication or information in a federal or state proceeding only if:

(1) the waiver is intentional;

(2) the disclosed and undisclosed communications or information concern the same subject matter; and

(3) they ought in fairness to be considered together.

(b) Inadvertent Disclosure. When made in a federal proceeding or to a federal office or agency, the disclosure does not operate as a waiver in a federal or state proceeding if:

(1) the disclosure is inadvertent;

(2) the holder of the privilege or protection took reasonable steps to prevent disclosure; and

(3) the holder promptly took reasonable steps to rectify the error, including (if applicable) following Federal Rule of Civil Procedure 26(b)(5)(B).

(c) Disclosure Made in a State Proceeding. When the disclosure is made in a state proceeding and is not the subject of a state-court order concerning waiver, the disclosure does not operate as a waiver in a federal proceeding if the disclosure:

(1) would not be a waiver under this rule if it had been made in a federal proceeding; or

(2) is not a waiver under the law of the state where the disclosure occurred.

(d) Controlling Effect of a Court Order. A federal court may order that the privilege or protection is not waived by disclosure connected with the litigation pending before the court—in which event the disclosure is also not a waiver in any other federal or state proceeding.

(e) Controlling Effect of a Party Agreement. An agreement on the effect of disclosure in a federal proceeding is binding only on the parties to the agreement, unless it is incorporated into a court order.

(f) Controlling Effect of This Rule. Notwithstanding Rules 101 and 1101, this rule applies to state proceedings and to federal court-annexed and federal court-mandated arbitration proceedings, in the circumstances set out in the rule. And notwithstanding Rule 501, this rule applies even if state law provides the rule of decision.

(g) Definitions. In this rule:

(1) "attorney-client privilege" means the protection that applicable law provides for confidential attorney-client communications; and

(2) "work-product protection" means the protection that applicable law provides for tangible material (or its intangible equivalent) prepared in anticipation of litigation or for trial.

(Pub.L. 110–322, § 1(a), Sept. 19, 2008, 122 Stat. 3537; Apr. 26, 2011, eff. Dec. 1, 2011.)

ARTICLE VI. WITNESSES

RULE 601. COMPETENCY TO TESTIFY IN GENERAL

Every person is competent to be a witness unless these rules provide otherwise. But in a civil case, state law governs the witness's competency regarding a claim or defense for which state law supplies the rule of decision.

(Pub.L. 93–595, § 1, Jan. 2, 1975, 88 Stat.1934; Apr. 26, 2011, eff. Dec. 1, 2011.)

RULE 602. NEED FOR PERSONAL KNOWLEDGE

A witness may testify to a matter only if evidence is introduced sufficient to support a finding that the witness has personal knowledge of the matter. Evidence to prove personal knowledge may consist of the witness's own testimony. This rule does not apply to a witness's expert testimony under Rule 703.

(Pub.L. 93–595, § 1, Jan. 2, 1975, 88 Stat. 1934; Mar. 2, 1987, eff. Oct. 1, 1987; Apr. 25, 1988, eff. Nov. 1, 1988; Apr. 26, 2011, eff. Dec. 1, 2011.)

RULE 603. OATH OR AFFIRMATION TO TESTIFY TRUTHFULLY

Before testifying, a witness must give an oath or affirmation to testify truthfully. It must be in a form designed to impress that duty on the witness's conscience.

(Pub.L. 93–595, § 1, Jan. 2, 1975, 88 Stat. 1934; Mar. 2, 1987, eff. Oct. 1, 1987; Apr. 26, 2011, eff. Dec. 1, 2011.)

RULE 604. INTERPRETER

An interpreter must be qualified and must give an oath or affirmation to make a true translation.

(Pub.L. 93–595, § 1, Jan. 2, 1975, 88 Stat. 1934; Mar. 2, 1987, eff. Oct. 1, 1987; Apr. 26, 2011, eff. Dec. 1, 2011.)

RULE 605. JUDGE'S COMPETENCY AS A WITNESS

The presiding judge may not testify as a witness at the trial. A party need not object to preserve the issue.

(Pub.L. 93–595, § 1, Jan. 2, 1975, 88 Stat. 1934; Apr. 26, 2011, eff. Dec. 1, 2011.)

RULE 606. JUROR'S COMPETENCY AS A WITNESS

(a) At the Trial. A juror may not testify as a witness before the other jurors at the trial. If a juror is called to testify, the court must give a party an opportunity to object outside the jury's presence.

(b) During an Inquiry Into the Validity of a Verdict or Indictment.

(1) **Prohibited Testimony or Other Evidence.** During an inquiry into the validity of a verdict or indictment, a juror may not testify about any statement made or incident that occurred during the jury's deliberations; the effect of anything on that juror's or another juror's vote; or any juror's mental processes concerning the verdict or indictment. The court may not receive a juror's affidavit or evidence of a juror's statement on these matters.

(2) **Exceptions.** A juror may testify about whether:

(A) extraneous prejudicial information was improperly brought to the jury's attention;

(B) an outside influence was improperly brought to bear on any juror; or

(C) a mistake was made in entering the verdict on the verdict form.

(Pub.L. 93–595, § 1, Jan. 2, 1975, 88 Stat. 1934; Pub.L. 94–149, § 1(10), Dec. 12, 1975, 89 Stat. 805; Mar. 2, 1987, eff. Oct. 1, 1987; Apr. 12, 2006, eff. Dec. 1, 2006; Apr. 26, 2011, eff. Dec. 1, 2011.)

RULE 607. WHO MAY IMPEACH A WITNESS

Any party, including the party that called the witness, may attack the witness's credibility.

(Pub.L. 93–595, § 1, Jan. 2, 1975, 88 Stat.1934; Mar. 2, 1987, eff. Oct. 1, 1987; Apr. 26, 2011, eff. Dec. 1, 2011.)

RULE 608. A WITNESS'S CHARACTER FOR TRUTHFULNESS OR UNTRUTHFULNESS

(a) Reputation or Opinion Evidence. A witness's credibility may be attacked or supported by testimony about the witness's reputation for having a character for truthfulness or untruthfulness, or by testimony in the form of an opinion about that character. But evidence of truthful character is admissible only after the witness's character for truthfulness has been attacked.

(b) Specific Instances of Conduct. Except for a criminal conviction under Rule 609, extrinsic evidence is not admissible to prove specific instances of a witness's conduct in order to attack or support the witness's character for truthfulness. But the court may, on cross-examination, allow them to be inquired into if they are probative of the character for truthfulness or untruthfulness of:

(1) the witness; or

(2) another witness whose character the witness being cross-examined has testified about.

By testifying on another matter, a witness does not waive any privilege against self-incrimination for testimony that relates only to the witness's character for truthfulness.

(Pub.L. 93–595, § 1, Jan. 2, 1975, 88 Stat.1935; Mar. 2, 1987, eff. Oct. 1, 1987; Apr. 25, 1988, eff. Nov. 1, 1988; Mar. 27, 2003, eff. Dec. 1, 2003; Apr. 26, 2011, eff. Dec. 1, 2011.)

RULE 609. IMPEACHMENT BY EVIDENCE OF A CRIMINAL CONVICTION

(a) In General. The following rules apply to attacking a witness's character for truthfulness by evidence of a criminal conviction:

(1) for a crime that, in the convicting jurisdiction, was punishable by death or by imprisonment for more than one year, the evidence:

(A) must be admitted, subject to Rule 403, in a civil case or in a criminal case in which the witness is not a defendant; and

(B) must be admitted in a criminal case in which the witness is a defendant, if the probative value of the evidence outweighs its prejudicial effect to that defendant; and

(2) for any crime regardless of the punishment, the evidence must be admitted if the court can readily determine that establishing the elements of the crime required proving—or the witness's admitting—a dishonest act or false statement.

(b) Limit on Using the Evidence After 10 Years. This subdivision (b) applies if more than 10 years have passed since the witness's conviction or release from confinement for it, whichever is later. Evidence of the conviction is admissible only if:

(1) its probative value, supported by specific facts and circumstances, substantially outweighs its prejudicial effect; and

(2) the proponent gives an adverse party reasonable written notice of the intent to use it so that the party has a fair opportunity to contest its use.

(c) Effect of a Pardon, Annulment, or Certificate of Rehabilitation. Evidence of a conviction is not admissible if:

(1) the conviction has been the subject of a pardon, annulment, certificate of rehabilitation, or other equivalent procedure based on a finding that the person has been rehabilitated, and the person has not been convicted of a later crime punishable by death or by imprisonment for more than one year; or

(2) the conviction has been the subject of a pardon, annulment, or other equivalent procedure based on a finding of innocence.

(d) Juvenile Adjudications. Evidence of a juvenile adjudication is admissible under this rule only if:

(1) it is offered in a criminal case;

(2) the adjudication was of a witness other than the defendant;

(3) an adult's conviction for that offense would be admissible to attack the adult's credibility; and

(4) admitting the evidence is necessary to fairly determine guilt or innocence.

(e) Pendency of an Appeal. A conviction that satisfies this rule is admissible even if an appeal is pending. Evidence of the pendency is also admissible.

(Pub.L. 93–595, § 1, Jan. 2, 1975, 88 Stat.1935; Mar. 2, 1987, eff. Oct. 1, 1987; Jan. 26, 1990, eff. Dec. 1, 1990; Apr. 12, 2006, eff. Dec. 1, 2006; Apr. 26, 2011, eff. Dec. 1, 2011.)

RULE 610. RELIGIOUS BELIEFS OR OPINIONS

Evidence of a witness's religious beliefs or opinions is not admissible to attack or support the witness's credibility.

(Pub.L. 93–595, § 1, Jan. 2, 1975, 88 Stat.1936; Mar. 2, 1987, eff. Oct. 1, 1987; Apr. 26, 2011, eff. Dec. 1, 2011.)

RULE 611. MODE AND ORDER OF EXAMINING WITNESSES AND PRESENTING EVIDENCE

(a) Control by the Court; Purposes. The court should exercise reasonable control over the mode and order of examining witnesses and presenting evidence so as to:

(1) make those procedures effective for determining the truth;

(2) avoid wasting time; and

(3) protect witnesses from harassment or undue embarrassment.

(b) Scope of Cross–Examination. Cross-examination should not go beyond the subject matter of the direct examination and matters affecting the witness's credibility. The court may allow inquiry into additional matters as if on direct examination.

(c) Leading Questions. Leading questions should not be used on direct examination except as necessary to develop the witness's testimony. Ordinarily, the court should allow leading questions:

(1) on cross-examination; and

(2) when a party calls a hostile witness, an adverse party, or a witness identified with an adverse party.

(Pub.L. 93–595, § 1, Jan. 2, 1975, 88 Stat. 1936; Mar. 2, 1987, eff. Oct. 1, 1987; Apr. 26, 2011, eff. Dec. 1, 2011.)

RULE 612. WRITING USED TO REFRESH A WITNESS'S MEMORY

(a) Scope. This rule gives an adverse party certain options when a witness uses a writing to refresh memory:

(1) while testifying; or

(2) before testifying, if the court decides that justice requires the party to have those options.

(b) Adverse Party's Options; Deleting Unrelated Matter. Unless 18 U.S.C. § 3500 provides otherwise in a criminal case, an adverse party is entitled to have the writing produced at the hearing, to inspect it, to cross-examine the witness about it, and to introduce in evidence any portion that relates to the witness's testimony. If the producing party claims that the writing includes unrelated matter, the court must examine the writing in camera, delete any unrelated portion, and order that the rest be delivered to the adverse party. Any portion deleted over objection must be preserved for the record.

(c) Failure to Produce or Deliver the Writing. If a writing is not produced or is not delivered as ordered, the court may issue any appropriate order. But if the prosecution does not comply in a criminal case, the court must strike the witness's testimony or—if justice so requires—declare a mistrial.

(Pub.L. 93–595, § 1, Jan. 2, 1975, 88 Stat. 1936; Mar. 2, 1987, eff. Oct. 1, 1987; Apr. 26, 2011, eff. Dec. 1, 2011.)

RULE 613. WITNESS'S PRIOR STATEMENT

(a) Showing or Disclosing the Statement During Examination. When examining a witness about the witness's prior statement, a party need not show it or disclose its contents to the witness. But the party must, on request, show it or disclose its contents to an adverse party's attorney.

(b) Extrinsic Evidence of a Prior Inconsistent Statement. Extrinsic evidence of a witness's prior inconsistent statement is admissible only if the witness is given an opportunity to explain or deny the statement and an adverse party is given an opportunity to examine the witness about it, or if justice so requires. This subdivision (b) does not apply to an opposing party's statement under Rule 801(d)(2).

(Pub.L. 93–595, § 1, Jan. 2, 1975, 88 Stat.1936; Mar. 2, 1987, eff. Oct. 1, 1987; Apr. 25, 1988, eff. Nov. 1, 1988; Apr. 26, 2011, eff. Dec. 1, 2011.)

RULE 614. COURT'S CALLING OR EXAMINING A WITNESS

(a) Calling. The court may call a witness on its own or at a party's request. Each party is entitled to cross-examine the witness.

(b) Examining. The court may examine a witness regardless of who calls the witness.

(c) Objections. A party may object to the court's calling or examining a witness either at that time or at the next opportunity when the jury is not present.

(Pub.L. 93–595, § 1, Jan. 2, 1975, 88 Stat.1937; Apr. 26, 2011, eff. Dec. 1, 2011.)

RULE 615. EXCLUDING WITNESSES

At a party's request, the court must order witnesses excluded so that they cannot hear other witnesses' testimony. Or the court may do so on its own. But this rule does not authorize excluding:

(a) a party who is a natural person;

(b) an officer or employee of a party that is not a natural person, after being designated as the party's representative by its attorney;

(c) a person whose presence a party shows to be essential to presenting the party's claim or defense; or

(d) a person authorized by statute to be present.

(Pub.L. 93–595, § 1, Jan. 2, 1975, 88 Stat.1937; Mar. 2, 1987, eff. Oct. 1, 1987; Apr. 25, 1988, eff. Nov. 1, 1988; Pub.L. 100–690, Nov. 18, 1988, Title VII, § 7075(a), 102 Stat. 4405; Apr. 24, 1998, eff. Dec. 1, 1998; Apr. 26, 2011, eff. Dec. 1, 2011.)

ARTICLE VII. OPINIONS AND EXPERT TESTIMONY

RULE 701. OPINION TESTIMONY BY LAY WITNESSES

If a witness is not testifying as an expert, testimony in the form of an opinion is limited to one that is:

(a) rationally based on the witness's perception;

(b) helpful to clearly understanding the witness's testimony or to determining a fact in issue; and

(c) not based on scientific, technical, or other specialized knowledge within the scope of Rule 702.

(Pub.L. 93–595, § 1, Jan. 2, 1975, 88 Stat.1937; Mar. 2, 1987, eff. Oct. 1, 1987; Apr. 17, 2000, eff. Dec. 1, 2000; Apr. 26, 2011, eff. Dec. 1, 2011.)

RULE 702. TESTIMONY BY EXPERT WITNESSES

A witness who is qualified as an expert by knowledge, skill, experience, training, or education may testify in the form of an opinion or otherwise if:

(a) the expert's scientific, technical, or other specialized knowledge will help the trier of fact to understand the evidence or to determine a fact in issue;

(b) the testimony is based on sufficient facts or data;

(c) the testimony is the product of reliable principles and methods; and

(d) the expert has reliably applied the principles and methods to the facts of the case.

(Pub.L. 93–595, § 1, Jan. 2, 1975, 88 Stat. 1937; Apr. 17, 2000, eff. Dec. 1, 2000; Apr. 26, 2011, eff. Dec. 1, 2011.)

RULE 703. BASES OF AN EXPERT'S OPINION TESTIMONY

An expert may base an opinion on facts or data in the case that the expert has been made aware of or personally observed. If experts in the particular field would reasonably rely on those kinds of facts or data in forming an opinion on the subject, they need not be admissible for the opinion to be admitted. But if the facts or data would otherwise be inadmissible, the proponent of the opinion may disclose them to the jury only if their probative value in helping the jury evaluate the opinion substantially outweighs their prejudicial effect.

(Pub.L. 93–595, § 1, Jan. 2, 1975, 88 Stat.1937; Mar. 2, 1987, eff. Oct. 1, 1987; Apr. 17, 2000, eff. Dec. 1, 2000; Apr. 26, 2011, eff. Dec. 1, 2011.)

RULE 704. OPINION ON AN ULTIMATE ISSUE

(a) In General—Not Automatically Objectionable. An opinion is not objectionable just because it embraces an ultimate issue.

(b) Exception. In a criminal case, an expert witness must not state an opinion about whether the defendant did or did not have a mental state or condition that constitutes an element of the crime charged or of a defense. Those matters are for the trier of fact alone.

(Pub.L. 93–595, § 1, Jan. 2, 1975, 88 Stat. 1937; Pub.L. 98–473, Title IV, § 406, Oct. 12, 1984, 98 Stat. 2067; Apr. 26, 2011, eff. Dec. 1, 2011.)

RULE 705. DISCLOSING THE FACTS OR DATA UNDERLYING AN EXPERT'S OPINION

Unless the court orders otherwise, an expert may state an opinion—and give the reasons for it—without first testifying to the underlying facts or data. But the expert may be required to disclose those facts or data on cross-examination.

(Pub.L. 93–595, § 1, Jan. 2, 1975, 88 Stat. 1938; Mar. 2, 1987, eff. Oct. 1, 1987; Apr. 22, 1993, eff. Dec. 1, 1993; Apr. 26, 2011, eff. Dec. 1, 2011.)

RULE 706. COURT–APPOINTED EXPERT WITNESSES

(a) Appointment Process. On a party's motion or on its own, the court may order the parties to show cause why expert witnesses should not be appointed and may ask the parties to submit nominations. The court may appoint any expert that the parties agree on and any of its own choosing. But the court may only appoint someone who consents to act.

(b) Expert's Role. The court must inform the expert of the expert's duties. The court may do so in writing and have a copy filed with the clerk or may do so orally at a conference in which the parties have an opportunity to participate. The expert:

(1) must advise the parties of any findings the expert makes;

(2) may be deposed by any party;

(3) may be called to testify by the court or any party; and

(4) may be cross-examined by any party, including the party that called the expert.

(c) Compensation. The expert is entitled to a reasonable compensation, as set by the court. The compensation is payable as follows:

(1) in a criminal case or in a civil case involving just compensation under the Fifth Amendment, from any funds that are provided by law; and

(2) in any other civil case, by the parties in the proportion and at the time that the court directs— and the compensation is then charged like other costs.

(d) Disclosing the Appointment to the Jury. The court may authorize disclosure to the jury that the court appointed the expert.

(e) Parties' Choice of Their Own Experts. This rule does not limit a party in calling its own experts.

(Pub.L. 93–595, § 1, Jan. 2, 1975, 88 Stat.1938; Mar. 2, 1987, eff. Oct. 1, 1987; Apr. 26, 2011, eff. Dec. 1, 2011.)

ARTICLE VIII. HEARSAY

RULE 801. DEFINITIONS THAT APPLY TO THIS ARTICLE; EXCLUSIONS FROM HEARSAY

(a) Statement. "Statement" means a person's oral assertion, written assertion, or nonverbal conduct, if the person intended it as an assertion.

(b) Declarant. "Declarant" means the person who made the statement.

(c) Hearsay. "Hearsay" means a statement that:

(1) the declarant does not make while testifying at the current trial or hearing; and

(2) a party offers in evidence to prove the truth of the matter asserted in the statement.

(d) Statements That Are Not Hearsay. A statement that meets the following conditions is not hearsay:

(1) **A Declarant–Witness's Prior Statement.** The declarant testifies and is subject to cross-examination about a prior statement, and the statement:

(A) is inconsistent with the declarant's testimony and was given under penalty of perjury at a trial, hearing, or other proceeding or in a deposition;

(B) is consistent with the declarant's testimony and is offered:

(i) to rebut an express or implied charge that the declarant recently fabricated it or acted from a recent improper influence or motive in so testifying; or

(ii) to rehabilitate the declarant's credibility as a witness when attacked on another ground; or

(C) identifies a person as someone the declarant perceived earlier.

(2) **An Opposing Party's Statement.** The statement is offered against an opposing party and:

(A) was made by the party in an individual or representative capacity;

(B) is one the party manifested that it adopted or believed to be true;

(C) was made by a person whom the party authorized to make a statement on the subject;

(D) was made by the party's agent or employee on a matter within the scope of that relationship and while it existed; or

(E) was made by the party's coconspirator during and in furtherance of the conspiracy.

The statement must be considered but does not by itself establish the declarant's authority under (C); the existence or scope of the relationship under (D); or the existence of the conspiracy or participation in it under (E).

(Pub.L. 93–595, § 1, Jan. 2, 1975, 88 Stat.1938; Pub.L. 94–113, § 1, Oct. 16, 1975, 89 Stat. 576; Mar. 2, 1987, eff. Oct. 1, 1987; Apr. 11, 1997, eff. Dec. 1, 1997; Apr. 26, 2011, eff. Dec. 1, 2011; Apr. 25, 2014, eff. Dec. 1, 2014.)

RULE 802. THE RULE AGAINST HEARSAY

Hearsay is not admissible unless any of the following provides otherwise:

- a federal statute;
- these rules; or
- other rules prescribed by the Supreme Court.

(Pub.L. 93–595, § 1, Jan. 2, 1975, 88 Stat. 1939; Apr. 26, 2011, eff. Dec. 1, 2011.)

RULE 803. EXCEPTIONS TO THE RULE AGAINST HEARSAY—REGARDLESS OF WHETHER THE DECLARANT IS AVAILABLE AS A WITNESS

The following are not excluded by the rule against hearsay, regardless of whether the declarant is available as a witness:

(1) Present Sense Impression. A statement describing or explaining an event or condition, made while or immediately after the declarant perceived it.

(2) Excited Utterance. A statement relating to a startling event or condition, made while the declarant was under the stress of excitement that it caused.

(3) Then–Existing Mental, Emotional, or Physical Condition. A statement of the declarant's then-existing state of mind (such as motive, intent, or plan) or emotional, sensory, or physical condition (such as mental feeling, pain, or bodily health), but not including a statement of memory or belief to prove the fact remembered or believed unless it relates to the validity or terms of the declarant's will.

(4) Statement Made for Medical Diagnosis or Treatment. A statement that:

(A) is made for—and is reasonably pertinent to—medical diagnosis or treatment; and

(B) describes medical history; past or present symptoms or sensations; their inception; or their general cause.

(5) Recorded Recollection. A record that:

(A) is on a matter the witness once knew about but now cannot recall well enough to testify fully and accurately;

(B) was made or adopted by the witness when the matter was fresh in the witness's memory; and

(C) accurately reflects the witness's knowledge.

If admitted, the record may be read into evidence but may be received as an exhibit only if offered by an adverse party.

(6) Records of a Regularly Conducted Activity. A record of an act, event, condition, opinion, or diagnosis if:

(A) the record was made at or near the time by—or from information transmitted by—someone with knowledge;

(B) the record was kept in the course of a regularly conducted activity of a business, organization, occupation, or calling, whether or not for profit;

(C) making the record was a regular practice of that activity;

(D) all these conditions are shown by the testimony of the custodian or another qualified witness, or by a certification that complies with Rule 902(11) or (12) or with a statute permitting certification; and

(E) the opponent does not show that the source of information or the method or circumstances of preparation indicate a lack of trustworthiness.

(7) Absence of a Record of a Regularly Conducted Activity. Evidence that a matter is not included in a record described in paragraph (6) if:

(A) the evidence is admitted to prove that the matter did not occur or exist;

(B) a record was regularly kept for a matter of that kind; and

(C) the opponent does not show that the possible source of the information or other circumstances indicate a lack of trustworthiness.

(8) Public Records. A record or statement of a public office if:

(A) it sets out:

(i) the office's activities;

(ii) a matter observed while under a legal duty to report, but not including, in a criminal case, a matter observed by law-enforcement personnel; or

(iii) in a civil case or against the government in a criminal case, factual findings from a legally authorized investigation; and

(B) the opponent does not show that the source of information or other circumstances indicate a lack of trustworthiness.

(9) Public Records of Vital Statistics. A record of a birth, death, or marriage, if reported to a public office in accordance with a legal duty.

(10) Absence of a Public Record. Testimony—or a certification under Rule 902—that a diligent search failed to disclose a public record or statement if:

(A) the testimony or certification is admitted to prove that

(i) the record or statement does not exist; or

(ii) a matter did not occur or exist, if a public office regularly kept a record or statement for a matter of that kind; and

(B) in a criminal case, a prosecutor who intends to offer a certification provides written notice of that intent at least 14 days before trial, and the defendant does not object in writing within 7 days of receiving the notice—unless the court sets a different time for the notice or the objection.

(11) Records of Religious Organizations Concerning Personal or Family History. A statement of birth, legitimacy, ancestry, marriage, divorce, death, relationship by blood or marriage, or similar facts of personal or family history, contained in a regularly kept record of a religious organization.

(12) Certificates of Marriage, Baptism, and Similar Ceremonies. A statement of fact contained in a certificate:

    (A) made by a person who is authorized by a religious organization or by law to perform the act certified;

    (B) attesting that the person performed a marriage or similar ceremony or administered a sacrament; and

    (C) purporting to have been issued at the time of the act or within a reasonable time after it.

(13) Family Records. A statement of fact about personal or family history contained in a family record, such as a Bible, genealogy, chart, engraving on a ring, inscription on a portrait, or engraving on an urn or burial marker.

(14) Records of Documents That Affect an Interest in Property. The record of a document that purports to establish or affect an interest in property if:

    (A) the record is admitted to prove the content of the original recorded document, along with its signing and its delivery by each person who purports to have signed it;

    (B) the record is kept in a public office; and

    (C) a statute authorizes recording documents of that kind in that office.

(15) Statements in Documents That Affect an Interest in Property. A statement contained in a document that purports to establish or affect an interest in property if the matter stated was relevant to the document's purpose—unless later dealings with the property are inconsistent with the truth of the statement or the purport of the document.

(16) Statements in Ancient Documents. A statement in a document that is at least 20 years old and whose authenticity is established.

(17) Market Reports and Similar Commercial Publications. Market quotations, lists, directories, or other compilations that are generally relied on by the public or by persons in particular occupations.

(18) Statements in Learned Treatises, Periodicals, or Pamphlets. A statement contained in a treatise, periodical, or pamphlet if:

    (A) the statement is called to the attention of an expert witness on cross-examination or relied on by the expert on direct examination; and

    (B) the publication is established as a reliable authority by the expert's admission or testimony, by another expert's testimony, or by judicial notice.

If admitted, the statement may be read into evidence but not received as an exhibit.

(19) Reputation Concerning Personal or Family History. A reputation among a person's family by blood, adoption, or marriage—or among a person's associates or in the community—concerning the person's birth, adoption, legitimacy, ancestry, marriage, divorce, death, relationship by blood, adoption, or marriage, or similar facts of personal or family history.

(20) Reputation Concerning Boundaries or General History. A reputation in a community—arising before the controversy—concerning boundaries of land in the community or customs that affect the land, or concerning general historical events important to that community, state, or nation.

(21) Reputation Concerning Character. A reputation among a person's associates or in the community concerning the person's character.

(22) Judgment of a Previous Conviction. Evidence of a final judgment of conviction if:

    (A) the judgment was entered after a trial or guilty plea, but not a nolo contendere plea;

    (B) the conviction was for a crime punishable by death or by imprisonment for more than a year;

    (C) the evidence is admitted to prove any fact essential to the judgment; and

    (D) when offered by the prosecutor in a criminal case for a purpose other than impeachment, the judgment was against the defendant.

The pendency of an appeal may be shown but does not affect admissibility.

(23) Judgments Involving Personal, Family, or General History, or a Boundary. A judgment that is admitted to prove a matter of personal, family, or general history, or boundaries, if the matter:

    (A) was essential to the judgment; and

    (B) could be proved by evidence of reputation.

(24) [Other Exceptions.] [Transferred to Rule 807.]

(Pub.L. 93–595, § 1, Jan. 2, 1975, 88 Stat. 1939; Pub.L. 94–149, § 1(11), Dec. 12, 1975, 89 Stat. 805; Mar. 2, 1987, eff. Oct. 1, 1987; Apr. 11, 1997, eff. Dec. 1, 1997; Apr. 17, 2000, eff. Dec. 1, 2000; Apr. 26, 2011, eff. Dec. 1, 2011; Apr. 16, 2013, eff. Dec. 1, 2013; Apr. 25, 2014, eff. Dec. 1, 2014.)

RULE 804. EXCEPTIONS TO THE RULE AGAINST HEARSAY—WHEN THE DECLARANT IS UNAVAILABLE AS A WITNESS

(a) Criteria for Being Unavailable. A declarant is considered to be unavailable as a witness if the declarant:

(1) is exempted from testifying about the subject matter of the declarant's statement because the court rules that a privilege applies;

(2) refuses to testify about the subject matter despite a court order to do so;

(3) testifies to not remembering the subject matter;

(4) cannot be present or testify at the trial or hearing because of death or a then-existing infirmity, physical illness, or mental illness; or

(5) is absent from the trial or hearing and the statement's proponent has not been able, by process or other reasonable means, to procure:

(A) the declarant's attendance, in the case of a hearsay exception under Rule 804(b)(1) or (6); or

(B) the declarant's attendance or testimony, in the case of a hearsay exception under Rule 804(b)(2), (3), or (4).

But this subdivision (a) does not apply if the statement's proponent procured or wrongfully caused the declarant's unavailability as a witness in order to prevent the declarant from attending or testifying.

(b) The Exceptions. The following are not excluded by the rule against hearsay if the declarant is unavailable as a witness:

(1) Former Testimony. Testimony that:

(A) was given as a witness at a trial, hearing, or lawful deposition, whether given during the current proceeding or a different one; and

(B) is now offered against a party who had—or, in a civil case, whose predecessor in interest had—an opportunity and similar motive to develop it by direct, cross-, or redirect examination.

(2) Statement Under the Belief of Imminent Death. In a prosecution for homicide or in a civil case, a statement that the declarant, while believing the declarant's death to be imminent, made about its cause or circumstances.

(3) Statement Against Interest. A statement that:

(A) a reasonable person in the declarant's position would have made only if the person believed it to be true because, when made, it was so contrary to the declarant's proprietary or pecuniary interest or had so great a tendency to invalidate the declarant's claim against someone else or to expose the declarant to civil or criminal liability; and

(B) is supported by corroborating circumstances that clearly indicate its trustworthiness, if it is offered in a criminal case as one that tends to expose the declarant to criminal liability.

(4) Statement of Personal or Family History. A statement about:

(A) the declarant's own birth, adoption, legitimacy, ancestry, marriage, divorce, relationship by blood, adoption, or marriage, or similar facts of personal or family history, even though the declarant had no way of acquiring personal knowledge about that fact; or

(B) another person concerning any of these facts, as well as death, if the declarant was related to the person by blood, adoption, or marriage or was so intimately associated with the person's family that the declarant's information is likely to be accurate.

(5) [Other Exceptions.] [Transferred to Rule 807.]

(6) Statement Offered Against a Party That Wrongfully Caused the Declarant's Unavailability. A statement offered against a party that wrongfully caused—or acquiesced in wrongfully causing—the declarant's unavailability as a witness, and did so intending that result.

(Pub.L. 93–595, § 1, Jan. 2, 1975, 88 Stat. 1942; Pub.L. 94–149, § 1(12), (13), Dec. 12, 1975, 89 Stat. 806; Mar. 2, 1987, eff. Oct. 1, 1987; Pub.L. 100–690, Title VII, § 7075(b), Nov. 18, 1988, 102 Stat. 4405; Apr. 11, 1997, eff. Dec. 1, 1997; Apr. 28, 2010, eff. Dec. 1, 2010; Apr. 26, 2011, eff. Dec. 1, 2011.)

RULE 805. HEARSAY WITHIN HEARSAY

Hearsay within hearsay is not excluded by the rule against hearsay if each part of the combined statements conforms with an exception to the rule.

(Pub.L. 93–595, § 1, Jan. 2, 1975, 88 Stat. 1943; Apr. 26, 2011, eff. Dec. 1, 2011.)

RULE 806. ATTACKING AND SUPPORTING THE DECLARANT'S CREDIBILITY

When a hearsay statement—or a statement described in Rule 801(d)(2)(C), (D), or (E)—has been admitted in evidence, the declarant's credibility may be attacked, and then supported, by any evidence that would be admissible for those purposes if the declarant had testified as a witness. The court may admit evidence of the declarant's inconsistent statement or conduct, regardless of when it occurred or whether the declarant had an opportunity to explain or deny it. If the party against whom the statement was admitted calls the declarant as a witness, the party may examine the declarant on the statement as if on cross-examination.

(Pub.L. 93–595, § 1, Jan. 2, 1975, 88 Stat. 1943; Mar. 2, 1987, eff. Oct. 1, 1987; Apr. 11, 1997, eff. Dec. 1, 1997; Apr. 26, 2011, eff. Dec. 1, 2011.)

RULE 807. RESIDUAL EXCEPTION

(a) In General. Under the following circumstances, a hearsay statement is not excluded by the rule against hearsay even if the statement is not specifically covered by a hearsay exception in Rule 803 or 804:

    (1) the statement has equivalent circumstantial guarantees of trustworthiness;

    (2) it is offered as evidence of a material fact;

    (3) it is more probative on the point for which it is offered than any other evidence that the proponent can obtain through reasonable efforts; and

    (4) admitting it will best serve the purposes of these rules and the interests of justice.

(b) Notice. The statement is admissible only if, before the trial or hearing, the proponent gives an adverse party reasonable notice of the intent to offer the statement and its particulars, including the declarant's name and address, so that the party has a fair opportunity to meet it.

(Added Apr. 11, 1997, eff. Dec. 1, 1997; Apr. 26, 2011, eff. Dec. 1, 2011.)

ARTICLE IX. AUTHENTICATION AND IDENTIFICATION

RULE 901. AUTHENTICATING OR IDENTIFYING EVIDENCE

(a) In General. To satisfy the requirement of authenticating or identifying an item of evidence, the proponent must produce evidence sufficient to support a finding that the item is what the proponent claims it is.

(b) Examples. The following are examples only—not a complete list—of evidence that satisfies the requirement:

    (1) Testimony of a Witness with Knowledge. Testimony that an item is what it is claimed to be.

    (2) Nonexpert Opinion About Handwriting. A nonexpert's opinion that handwriting is genuine, based on a familiarity with it that was not acquired for the current litigation.

    (3) Comparison by an Expert Witness or the Trier of Fact. A comparison with an authenticated specimen by an expert witness or the trier of fact.

    (4) Distinctive Characteristics and the Like. The appearance, contents, substance, internal patterns, or other distinctive characteristics of the item, taken together with all the circumstances.

    (5) Opinion About a Voice. An opinion identifying a person's voice—whether heard firsthand or through mechanical or electronic transmission or recording—based on hearing the voice at any time under circumstances that connect it with the alleged speaker.

    (6) Evidence About a Telephone Conversation. For a telephone conversation, evidence that a call was made to the number assigned at the time to:

        (A) a particular person, if circumstances, including self-identification, show that the person answering was the one called; or

        (B) a particular business, if the call was made to a business and the call related to business reasonably transacted over the telephone.

    (7) Evidence About Public Records. Evidence that:

        (A) a document was recorded or filed in a public office as authorized by law; or

        (B) a purported public record or statement is from the office where items of this kind are kept.

    (8) Evidence About Ancient Documents or Data Compilations. For a document or data compilation, evidence that it:

        (A) is in a condition that creates no suspicion about its authenticity;

        (B) was in a place where, if authentic, it would likely be; and

        (C) is at least 20 years old when offered.

    (9) Evidence About a Process or System. Evidence describing a process or system and showing that it produces an accurate result.

(10) Methods Provided by a Statute or Rule. Any method of authentication or identification allowed by a federal statute or a rule prescribed by the Supreme Court.

(Pub.L. 93–595, § 1, Jan. 2, 1975, 88 Stat.1943; Apr. 26, 2011, eff. Dec. 1, 2011.)

RULE 902.   EVIDENCE THAT IS SELF–AUTHENTICATING

The following items of evidence are self-authenticating; they require no extrinsic evidence of authenticity in order to be admitted:

(1) Domestic Public Documents That Are Sealed and Signed. A document that bears:

(A) a seal purporting to be that of the United States; any state, district, commonwealth, territory, or insular possession of the United States; the former Panama Canal Zone; the Trust Territory of the Pacific Islands; a political subdivision of any of these entities; or a department, agency, or officer of any entity named above; and

(B) a signature purporting to be an execution or attestation.

(2) Domestic Public Documents That Are Not Sealed but Are Signed and Certified. A document that bears no seal if:

(A) it bears the signature of an officer or employee of an entity named in Rule 902(1)(A); and

(B) another public officer who has a seal and official duties within that same entity certifies under seal—or its equivalent—that the signer has the official capacity and that the signature is genuine.

(3) Foreign Public Documents. A document that purports to be signed or attested by a person who is authorized by a foreign country's law to do so. The document must be accompanied by a final certification that certifies the genuineness of the signature and official position of the signer or attester—or of any foreign official whose certificate of genuineness relates to the signature or attestation or is in a chain of certificates of genuineness relating to the signature or attestation. The certification may be made by a secretary of a United States embassy or legation; by a consul general, vice consul, or consular agent of the United States; or by a diplomatic or consular official of the foreign country assigned or accredited to the United States. If all parties have been given a reasonable opportunity to investigate the document's authenticity and accuracy, the court may, for good cause, either:

(A) order that it be treated as presumptively authentic without final certification; or

(B) allow it to be evidenced by an attested summary with or without final certification.

(4) Certified Copies of Public Records. A copy of an official record—or a copy of a document that was recorded or filed in a public office as authorized by law—if the copy is certified as correct by:

(A) the custodian or another person authorized to make the certification; or

(B) a certificate that complies with Rule 902(1), (2), or (3), a federal statute, or a rule prescribed by the Supreme Court.

(5) Official Publications. A book, pamphlet, or other publication purporting to be issued by a public authority.

(6) Newspapers and Periodicals. Printed material purporting to be a newspaper or periodical.

(7) Trade Inscriptions and the Like. An inscription, sign, tag, or label purporting to have been affixed in the course of business and indicating origin, ownership, or control.

(8) Acknowledged Documents. A document accompanied by a certificate of acknowledgment that is lawfully executed by a notary public or another officer who is authorized to take acknowledgments.

(9) Commercial Paper and Related Documents. Commercial paper, a signature on it, and related documents, to the extent allowed by general commercial law.

(10) Presumptions Under a Federal Statute. A signature, document, or anything else that a federal statute declares to be presumptively or prima facie genuine or authentic.

(11) Certified Domestic Records of a Regularly Conducted Activity. The original or a copy of a domestic record that meets the requirements of Rule 803(6)(A)–(C), as shown by a certification of the custodian or another qualified person that complies with a federal statute or a rule prescribed by the Supreme Court. Before the trial or hearing, the proponent must give an adverse party reasonable written notice of the intent to offer the record—and must make the record and certification available for inspection—so that the party has a fair opportunity to challenge them.

(12) Certified Foreign Records of a Regularly Conducted Activity. In a civil case, the original or a copy of a foreign record that meets the requirements of Rule 902(11), modified as follows: the certification, rather than complying with a federal statute or Supreme Court rule, must be signed in a manner that, if falsely made, would subject the maker to a criminal penalty in the country where the certification is signed. The proponent must also meet the notice requirements of Rule 902(11).

(Pub.L. 93–595, § 1, Jan. 2, 1975, 88 Stat. 1944; Mar. 2, 1987, eff. Oct. 1, 1987; Apr. 25, 1988, eff. Nov. 1, 1988; Apr. 17, 2000, eff. Dec. 1, 2000; Apr. 26, 2011, eff. Dec. 1, 2011.)

RULE 903. SUBSCRIBING WITNESS'S TESTIMONY

A subscribing witness's testimony is necessary to authenticate a writing only if required by the law of the jurisdiction that governs its validity.

(Pub.L. 93–595, § 1, Jan. 2, 1975, 88 Stat.1945; Apr. 26, 2011, eff. Dec. 1, 2011.)

ARTICLE X. CONTENTS OF WRITINGS, RECORDINGS, AND PHOTOGRAPHS

RULE 1001. DEFINITIONS THAT APPLY TO THIS ARTICLE

In this article:

(a) A "writing" consists of letters, words, numbers, or their equivalent set down in any form.

(b) A "recording" consists of letters, words, numbers, or their equivalent recorded in any manner.

(c) A "photograph" means a photographic image or its equivalent stored in any form.

(d) An "original" of a writing or recording means the writing or recording itself or any counterpart intended to have the same effect by the person who executed or issued it. For electronically stored information, "original" means any printout—or other output readable by sight—if it accurately reflects the information. An "original" of a photograph includes the negative or a print from it.

(e) A "duplicate" means a counterpart produced by a mechanical, photographic, chemical, electronic, or other equivalent process or technique that accurately reproduces the original.

(Pub.L. 93–595, § 1, Jan. 2, 1975, 88 Stat. 1945; Apr. 26, 2011, eff. Dec. 1, 2011.)

RULE 1002. REQUIREMENT OF THE ORIGINAL

An original writing, recording, or photograph is required in order to prove its content unless these rules or a federal statute provides otherwise.

(Pub.L. 93–595, § 1, Jan. 2, 1975, 88 Stat. 1946; Apr. 26, 2011, eff. Dec. 1, 2011.)

RULE 1003. ADMISSIBILITY OF DUPLICATES

A duplicate is admissible to the same extent as the original unless a genuine question is raised about the original's authenticity or the circumstances make it unfair to admit the duplicate.

(Pub.L. 93–595, § 1, Jan. 2, 1975, 88 Stat. 1946; Apr. 26, 2011, eff. Dec. 1, 2011.)

RULE 1004. ADMISSIBILITY OF OTHER EVIDENCE OF CONTENT

An original is not required and other evidence of the content of a writing, recording, or photograph is admissible if:

(a) all the originals are lost or destroyed, and not by the proponent acting in bad faith;

(b) an original cannot be obtained by any available judicial process;

(c) the party against whom the original would be offered had control of the original; was at that time put on notice, by pleadings or otherwise, that the original would be a subject of proof at the trial or hearing; and fails to produce it at the trial or hearing; or

(d) the writing, recording, or photograph is not closely related to a controlling issue.

(Pub.L. 93–595, § 1, Jan. 2, 1975, 88 Stat. 1946; Mar. 2, 1987, eff. Oct. 1, 1987; Apr. 26, 2011, eff. Dec. 1, 2011.)

RULE 1005. COPIES OF PUBLIC RECORDS TO PROVE CONTENT

The proponent may use a copy to prove the content of an official record—or of a document that was recorded or filed in a public office as authorized by law—if these conditions are met: the record or document is otherwise admissible; and the copy is certified as correct in accordance with Rule 902(4) or is testified to be correct by a witness who has compared it with the original. If no such copy can be obtained by reasonable diligence, then the proponent may use other evidence to prove the content.

(Pub.L. 93–595, § 1, Jan. 2, 1975, 88 Stat. 1946; Apr. 26, 2011, eff. Dec. 1, 2011.)

RULE 1006. SUMMARIES TO PROVE CONTENT

The proponent may use a summary, chart, or calculation to prove the content of voluminous writings, recordings, or photographs that cannot be conveniently examined in court. The proponent must make the originals or duplicates available for examination or copying, or both, by other parties at a reasonable time and place. And the court may order the proponent to produce them in court.

(Pub.L. 93–595, § 1, Jan. 2, 1975, 88 Stat. 1946; Apr. 26, 2011, eff. Dec. 1, 2011.)

RULE 1007. TESTIMONY OR STATEMENT OF A PARTY TO PROVE CONTENT

The proponent may prove the content of a writing, recording, or photograph by the testimony, deposition, or written statement of the party against whom the evidence is offered. The proponent need not account for the original.

(Pub.L. 93–595, § 1, Jan. 2, 1975, 88 Stat. 1947; Mar. 2, 1987, eff. Oct. 1, 1987; Apr. 26, 2011, eff. Dec. 1, 2011.)

RULE 1008. FUNCTIONS OF THE COURT AND JURY

Ordinarily, the court determines whether the proponent has fulfilled the factual conditions for admitting other evidence of the content of a writing, recording, or photograph under Rule 1004 or 1005. But in a jury trial, the jury determines—in accordance with Rule 104(b)—any issue about whether:

(a) an asserted writing, recording, or photograph ever existed;

(b) another one produced at the trial or hearing is the original; or

(c) other evidence of content accurately reflects the content.

(Pub.L. 93–595, § 1, Jan. 2, 1975, 88 Stat. 1947; Apr. 26, 2011, eff. Dec. 1, 2011.)

ARTICLE XI. MISCELLANEOUS RULES

RULE 1101. APPLICABILITY OF THE RULES

(a) To Courts and Judges. These rules apply to proceedings before:

- United States district courts;
- United States bankruptcy and magistrate judges;
- United States courts of appeals;
- the United States Court of Federal Claims; and
- the district courts of Guam, the Virgin Islands, and the Northern Mariana Islands.

(b) To Cases and Proceedings. These rules apply in:

- civil cases and proceedings, including bankruptcy, admiralty, and maritime cases;
- criminal cases and proceedings; and
- contempt proceedings, except those in which the court may act summarily.

(c) Rules on Privilege. The rules on privilege apply to all stages of a case or proceeding.

(d) Exceptions. These rules—except for those on privilege—do not apply to the following:

(1) the court's determination, under Rule 104(a), on a preliminary question of fact governing admissibility;

(2) grand-jury proceedings; and

(3) miscellaneous proceedings such as:

- extradition or rendition;
- issuing an arrest warrant, criminal summons, or search warrant;
- a preliminary examination in a criminal case;
- sentencing;
- granting or revoking probation or supervised release; and
- considering whether to release on bail or otherwise.

(e) Other Statutes and Rules. A federal statute or a rule prescribed by the Supreme Court may provide for admitting or excluding evidence independently from these rules.

(Pub.L. 93–595, § 1, Jan. 2, 1975, 88 Stat. 1947; Pub.L. 94–149, § 1(14), Dec. 12, 1975, 89 Stat. 806; Pub.L. 95–598, Title II, § 251, Nov. 6, 1978, 92 Stat. 2673; Pub.L. 97–164, Title I, § 142, Apr. 2, 1982, 96 Stat. 45; Mar. 2, 1987, eff. Oct. 1, 1987; Apr. 25, 1988, eff. Nov. 1, 1988; Pub.L. 100–690, Title VII, § 7075(c), Nov. 18, 1988, 102 Stat. 4405; Apr. 22, 1993, eff. Dec. 1, 1993; Apr. 26, 2011, eff. Dec. 1, 2011.)

RULE 1102. AMENDMENTS

These rules may be amended as provided in 28 U.S.C. § 2072.

(Pub.L. 93–595, § 1, Jan. 2, 1975, 88 Stat.1948; Apr. 30, 1991, eff. Dec. 1, 1991; Apr. 26, 2011, eff. Dec. 1, 2011.)

RULE 1103. TITLE

These rules may be cited as the Federal Rules of Evidence.

(Pub.L. 93–595, § 1, Jan. 2, 1975, 88 Stat.1948; Apr. 26, 2011, eff. Dec. 1, 2011.)

INDEX TO
FEDERAL RULES OF EVIDENCE

FEDERAL RULES OF APPELLATE PROCEDURE

Including Amendments Effective December 1, 2016, Absent Contrary Congressional Action

---

7. Declaration of Inmate Filing.

APPENDIX

TITLE I. APPLICABILITY OF RULES

RULE 1. SCOPE OF RULES; DEFINITION; TITLE

(a) Scope of Rules.

(1) These rules govern procedure in the United States courts of appeals.

(2) When these rules provide for filing a motion or other document in the district court, the procedure must comply with the practice of the district court.

(b) Definition.
In these rules, "state" includes the District of Columbia and any United States commonwealth or territory.

(c) Title.
These rules are to be known as the Federal Rules of Appellate Procedure.

(As amended Apr. 30, 1979, eff. Aug. 1, 1979; Apr. 25, 1989, eff. Dec. 1, 1989; Apr. 29, 1994, eff. Dec. 1, 1994; Apr. 24, 1998, eff. Dec. 1, 1998; Apr. 29, 2002, eff. Dec. 1, 2002; Apr. 28, 2010, eff. Dec. 1, 2010.)

RULE 2. SUSPENSION OF RULES

On its own or a party's motion, a court of appeals may—to expedite its decision or for other good cause—suspend any provision of these rules in a particular case and order proceedings as it directs, except as otherwise provided in Rule 26(b).

(As amended Apr. 24, 1998, eff. Dec. 1, 1998.)

TITLE II. APPEAL FROM A JUDGMENT OR ORDER OF A DISTRICT COURT

RULE 3. APPEAL AS OF RIGHT— HOW TAKEN

(a) Filing the Notice of Appeal.

(1) An appeal permitted by law as of right from a district court to a court of appeals may be taken only by filing a notice of appeal with the district clerk within the time allowed by Rule 4. At the time of filing, the appellant must furnish the clerk with enough copies of the notice to enable the clerk to comply with Rule 3(d).

(2) An appellant's failure to take any step other than the timely filing of a notice of appeal does not affect the validity of the appeal, but is ground only for the court of appeals to act as it considers appropriate, including dismissing the appeal.

(3) An appeal from a judgment by a magistrate judge in a civil case is taken in the same way as an appeal from any other district court judgment.

(4) An appeal by permission under 28 U.S.C. § 1292(b) or an appeal in a bankruptcy case may be taken only in the manner prescribed by Rules 5 and 6, respectively.

(b) Joint or Consolidated Appeals.

(1) When two or more parties are entitled to appeal from a district-court judgment or order, and their interests make joinder practicable, they may file a joint notice of appeal. They may then proceed on appeal as a single appellant.

(2) When the parties have filed separate timely notices of appeal, the appeals may be joined or consolidated by the court of appeals.

(c) Contents of the Notice of Appeal.

(1) The notice of appeal must:

(A) specify the party or parties taking the appeal by naming each one in the caption or body of the notice, but an attorney representing more than one party may describe those parties with such terms as "all plaintiffs," "the defendants," "the plaintiffs A, B, et al.," or "all defendants except X";

(B) designate the judgment, order, or part thereof being appealed; and

(C) name the court to which the appeal is taken.

(2) A pro se notice of appeal is considered filed on behalf of the signer and the signer's spouse and minor children (if they are parties), unless the notice clearly indicates otherwise.

(3) In a class action, whether or not the class has been certified, the notice of appeal is sufficient if it names one person qualified to bring the appeal as representative of the class.

(4) An appeal must not be dismissed for informality of form or title of the notice of appeal, or for failure to name a party whose intent to appeal is otherwise clear from the notice.

(5) Form 1 in the Appendix of Forms is a suggested form of a notice of appeal.

(d) Serving the Notice of Appeal.

(1) The district clerk must serve notice of the filing of a notice of appeal by mailing a copy to each party's counsel of record—excluding the appellant's—or, if a party is proceeding pro se, to the party's last known address. When a defendant in a criminal case appeals, the clerk must also serve a copy of the notice of appeal on the defendant, either by personal service or by mail addressed to the defendant. The clerk must promptly send a copy of the notice of appeal and of the docket entries—and any later docket entries—to the clerk of the court of appeals named in the notice. The district clerk must note, on each copy, the date when the notice of appeal was filed.

(2) If an inmate confined in an institution files a notice of appeal in the manner provided by Rule 4(c), the district clerk must also note the date when the clerk docketed the notice.

(3) The district clerk's failure to serve notice does not affect the validity of the appeal. The clerk must note on the docket the names of the parties to whom the clerk mails copies, with the date of mailing. Service is sufficient despite the death of a party or the party's counsel.

(e) Payment of Fees. Upon filing a notice of appeal, the appellant must pay the district clerk all required fees. The district clerk receives the appellate docket fee on behalf of the court of appeals.

(As amended Apr. 30, 1979, eff. Aug. 1, 1979; Mar. 10, 1986, eff. July 1, 1986; Apr. 25, 1989, eff. Dec. 1, 1989; Apr. 22, 1993, eff. Dec. 1, 1993; Apr. 29, 1994, eff. Dec. 1, 1994; Apr. 24, 1998, eff. Dec. 1, 1998.)

[RULE 3.1 APPEAL FROM A JUDGMENT OF A MAGISTRATE JUDGE IN A CIVIL CASE (ABROGATED APR. 24, 1998, EFF. DEC. 1, 1998)]

RULE 4. APPEAL AS OF RIGHT— WHEN TAKEN

[Text of subdivision (a) effective until December 1, 2016, absent contrary Congressional action.]

(a) Appeal in a Civil Case.

(1) Time for Filing a Notice of Appeal.

(A) In a civil case, except as provided in Rules 4(a)(1)(B), 4(a)(4), and 4(c), the notice of appeal required by Rule 3 must be filed with the district clerk within 30 days after entry of the judgment or order appealed from.

(B) The notice of appeal may be filed by any party within 60 days after entry of the judgment or order appealed from if one of the parties is:

(i) the United States;

(ii) a United States agency;

(iii) a United States officer or employee sued in an official capacity; or

(iv) a current or former United States officer or employee sued in an individual capacity for an act or omission occurring in connection with duties performed on the United States' behalf—including all instances in which the United States represents that person when the judgment or order is entered or files the appeal for that person.

(C) An appeal from an order granting or denying an application for a writ of error coram nobis is an appeal in a civil case for purposes of Rule 4(a).

(2) Filing Before Entry of Judgment. A notice of appeal filed after the court announces a decision or order—but before the entry of the judgment or order—is treated as filed on the date of and after the entry.

(3) Multiple Appeals. If one party timely files a notice of appeal, any other party may file a notice of appeal within 14 days after the date when the first notice was filed, or within the time otherwise prescribed by this Rule 4(a), whichever period ends later.

(4) Effect of a Motion on a Notice of Appeal.

(A) If a party timely files in the district court any of the following motions under the Federal Rules of Civil Procedure, the time to file an appeal runs for all parties from the entry of the order disposing of the last such remaining motion:

(i) for judgment under Rule 50(b);

(ii) to amend or make additional factual findings under Rule 52(b), whether or not granting the motion would alter the judgment;

(iii) for attorney's fees under Rule 54 if the district court extends the time to appeal under Rule 58;

(iv) to alter or amend the judgment under Rule 59;

(v) for a new trial under Rule 59; or

(vi) for relief under Rule 60 if the motion is filed no later than 28 days after the judgment is entered.

(B)(i) If a party files a notice of appeal after the court announces or enters a judgment—but before it disposes of any motion listed in Rule 4(a)(4)(A)—the notice becomes effective to appeal a judgment or order, in whole or in part, when the order disposing of the last such remaining motion is entered.

(ii) A party intending to challenge an order disposing of any motion listed in Rule 4(a)(4)(A), or a judgment's alteration or amendment upon such a motion, must file a notice of appeal, or an amended notice of appeal—in compliance with Rule 3(c)—within the time prescribed by this Rule measured from the entry of the order disposing of the last such remaining motion.

(iii) No additional fee is required to file an amended notice.

(5) Motion for Extension of Time.

(A) The district court may extend the time to file a notice of appeal if:

(i) a party so moves no later than 30 days after the time prescribed by this Rule 4(a) expires; and

(ii) regardless of whether its motion is filed before or during the 30 days after the time prescribed by this Rule 4(a) expires, that party shows excusable neglect or good cause.

(B) A motion filed before the expiration of the time prescribed in Rule 4(a)(1) or (3) may be ex parte unless the court requires otherwise. If the motion is filed after the expiration of the prescribed time, notice must be given to the other parties in accordance with local rules.

(C) No extension under this Rule 4(a)(5) may exceed 30 days after the prescribed time or 14 days after the date when the order granting the motion is entered, whichever is later.

(6) Reopening the Time to File an Appeal. The district court may reopen the time to file an appeal for a period of 14 days after the date when its order to reopen is entered, but only if all the following conditions are satisfied:

(A) the court finds that the moving party did not receive notice under Federal Rule of Civil Procedure 77(d) of the entry of the judgment or order sought to be appealed within 21 days after entry;

(B) the motion is filed within 180 days after the judgment or order is entered or within 14 days after the moving party receives notice under Federal Rule of Civil Procedure 77(d) of the entry, whichever is earlier; and

(C) the court finds that no party would be prejudiced.

(7) Entry Defined.

(A) A judgment or order is entered for purposes of this Rule 4(a):

(i) if Federal Rule of Civil Procedure 58(a) does not require a separate document, when the judgment or order is entered in the civil docket under Federal Rule of Civil Procedure 79(a); or

(ii) if Federal Rule of Civil Procedure 58(a) requires a separate document, when the judgment or order is entered in the civil docket under Federal Rule of Civil Procedure 79(a) and when the earlier of these events occurs:

● the judgment or order is set forth on a separate document, or

● 150 days have run from entry of the judgment or order in the civil docket under Federal Rule of Civil Procedure 79(a).

(B) A failure to set forth a judgment or order on a separate document when required by Federal Rule of Civil Procedure 58(a) does not affect the validity of an appeal from that judgment or order.

[Text of subdivision (a) effective December 1, 2016, absent contrary Congressional action.]

(a) Appeal in a Civil Case.

(1) Time for Filing a Notice of Appeal.

(A) In a civil case, except as provided in Rules 4(a)(1)(B), 4(a)(4), and 4(c), the notice of appeal required by Rule 3 must be filed with the district clerk within 30 days after entry of the judgment or order appealed from.

(B) The notice of appeal may be filed by any party within 60 days after entry of the judgment or order appealed from if one of the parties is:

(i) the United States;

(ii) a United States agency;

(iii) a United States officer or employee sued in an official capacity; or

(iv) a current or former United States officer or employee sued in an individual capacity for an act or omission occurring in connection with duties performed on the United States' behalf—including all instances in which the United States represents that person when the judgment or order is entered or files the appeal for that person.

(C) An appeal from an order granting or denying an application for a writ of error coram nobis is an appeal in a civil case for purposes of Rule 4(a).

(2) Filing Before Entry of Judgment. A notice of appeal filed after the court announces a decision or order—but before the entry of the judgment or order—is treated as filed on the date of and after the entry.

(3) Multiple Appeals. If one party timely files a notice of appeal, any other party may file a notice of appeal within 14 days after the date when the first notice was filed, or within the time otherwise prescribed by this Rule 4(a), whichever period ends later.

(4) Effect of a Motion on a Notice of Appeal.

(A) If a party files in the district court any of the following motions under the Federal Rules of Civil Procedure—and does so within the time allowed by those rules—the time to file an appeal runs for all parties from the entry of the order disposing of the last such remaining motion:

(i) for judgment under Rule 50(b);

(ii) to amend or make additional factual findings under Rule 52(b), whether or not granting the motion would alter the judgment;

(iii) for attorney's fees under Rule 54 if the district court extends the time to appeal under Rule 58;

(iv) to alter or amend the judgment under Rule 59;

(v) for a new trial under Rule 59; or

(vi) for relief under Rule 60 if the motion is filed no later than 28 days after the judgment is entered.

(B)(i) If a party files a notice of appeal after the court announces or enters a judgment—but before it disposes of any motion listed in Rule 4(a)(4)(A)—the notice becomes effective to appeal a judgment or order, in whole or in part, when the order disposing of the last such remaining motion is entered.

(ii) A party intending to challenge an order disposing of any motion listed in Rule 4(a)(4)(A), or a judgment's alteration or amendment upon such a motion, must file a notice of appeal, or an amended notice of appeal—in compliance with Rule 3(c)—within the time prescribed by this Rule measured from the entry of the order disposing of the last such remaining motion.

(iii) No additional fee is required to file an amended notice.

(5) Motion for Extension of Time.

(A) The district court may extend the time to file a notice of appeal if:

(i) a party so moves no later than 30 days after the time prescribed by this Rule 4(a) expires; and

(ii) regardless of whether its motion is filed before or during the 30 days after the time prescribed by this Rule 4(a) expires, that party shows excusable neglect or good cause.

(B) A motion filed before the expiration of the time prescribed in Rule 4(a)(1) or (3) may be ex parte unless the court requires otherwise. If the motion is filed after the expiration of the prescribed time, notice must be given to the other parties in accordance with local rules.

(C) No extension under this Rule 4(a)(5) may exceed 30 days after the prescribed time or 14 days after the date when the order granting the motion is entered, whichever is later.

(6) Reopening the Time to File an Appeal. The district court may reopen the time to file an appeal for a period of 14 days after the date when its order to reopen is entered, but only if all the following conditions are satisfied:

(A) the court finds that the moving party did not receive notice under Federal Rule of Civil Procedure 77(d) of the entry of the judgment or order sought to be appealed within 21 days after entry;

(B) the motion is filed within 180 days after the judgment or order is entered or within 14 days after the moving party receives notice under Federal Rule of Civil Procedure 77(d) of the entry, whichever is earlier; and

(C) the court finds that no party would be prejudiced.

(7) Entry Defined.

(A) A judgment or order is entered for purposes of this Rule 4(a):

(i) if Federal Rule of Civil Procedure 58(a) does not require a separate document, when the judgment or order is entered in the civil docket under Federal Rule of Civil Procedure 79(a); or

(ii) if Federal Rule of Civil Procedure 58(a) requires a separate document, when the judgment or order is entered in the civil docket under Federal Rule of Civil Procedure 79(a) and when the earlier of these events occurs:

• the judgment or order is set forth on a separate document, or

• 150 days have run from entry of the judgment or order in the civil docket under Federal Rule of Civil Procedure 79(a).

(B) A failure to set forth a judgment or order on a separate document when required by Federal Rule of Civil Procedure 58(a) does not affect the validity of an appeal from that judgment or order.

(b) Appeal in a Criminal Case.

(1) Time for Filing a Notice of Appeal.

(A) In a criminal case, a defendant's notice of appeal must be filed in the district court within 14 days after the later of:

(i) the entry of either the judgment or the order being appealed; or

(ii) the filing of the government's notice of appeal.

(B) When the government is entitled to appeal, its notice of appeal must be filed in the district court within 30 days after the later of:

(i) the entry of the judgment or order being appealed; or

(ii) the filing of a notice of appeal by any defendant.

(2) Filing Before Entry of Judgment. A notice of appeal filed after the court announces a decision, sentence, or order—but before the entry of the judgment or order—is treated as filed on the date of and after the entry.

(3) Effect of a Motion on a Notice of Appeal.

(A) If a defendant timely makes any of the following motions under the Federal Rules of Criminal Procedure, the notice of appeal from a judgment of conviction must be filed within 14 days after the entry of the order disposing of the last such remaining motion, or within 14 days after the entry of the judgment of conviction, whichever period ends later. This provision applies to a timely motion:

(i) for judgment of acquittal under Rule 29;

(ii) for a new trial under Rule 33, but if based on newly discovered evidence, only if the motion is made no later than 14 days after the entry of the judgment; or

(iii) for arrest of judgment under Rule 34.

(B) A notice of appeal filed after the court announces a decision, sentence, or order—but before it disposes of any of the motions referred to in Rule 4(b)(3)(A)—becomes effective upon the later of the following:

(i) the entry of the order disposing of the last such remaining motion; or

(ii) the entry of the judgment of conviction.

(C) A valid notice of appeal is effective—without amendment—to appeal from an order disposing of any of the motions referred to in Rule 4(b)(3)(A).

(4) Motion for Extension of Time. Upon a finding of excusable neglect or good cause, the district court may—before or after the time has expired, with or without motion and notice—extend the time to file a notice of appeal for a period not to exceed 30 days from the expiration of the time otherwise prescribed by this Rule 4(b).

(5) Jurisdiction. The filing of a notice of appeal under this Rule 4(b) does not divest a district court of jurisdiction to correct a sentence under Federal Rule of Criminal Procedure 35(a), nor does the filing of a motion under 35(a) affect the validity of a notice of appeal filed before entry of the order disposing of the motion. The filing of a motion under Federal Rule of Criminal Procedure 35(a) does not suspend the time for filing a notice of appeal from a judgment of conviction.

(6) Entry Defined. A judgment or order is entered for purposes of this Rule 4(b) when it is entered on the criminal docket.

[Text of subdivision (c) effective until December 1, 2016, absent contrary Congressional action.]

(c) Appeal by an Inmate Confined in an Institution.

(1) If an inmate confined in an institution files a notice of appeal in either a civil or a criminal case, the notice is timely if it is deposited in the institution's internal mail system on or before the last day for filing. If an institution has a system designed for legal mail, the inmate must use that system to receive the benefit of this rule. Timely filing may be shown by a declaration in compliance with 28 U.S.C. § 1746 or by a notarized statement, either of which must set forth the date of deposit and state that first-class postage has been prepaid.

(2) If an inmate files the first notice of appeal in a civil case under this Rule 4(c), the 14–day period provided in Rule 4(a)(3) for another party to file a notice of appeal runs from the date when the district court dockets the first notice.

(3) When a defendant in a criminal case files a notice of appeal under this Rule 4(c), the 30–day period for the government to file its notice of appeal runs from the entry of the judgment or order appealed from or from the district court's docketing of the defendant's notice of appeal, whichever is later.

[Text of subdivision (c) effective December 1, 2016, absent contrary Congressional action.]

(c) Appeal by an Inmate Confined in an Institution.

(1) If an institution has a system designed for legal mail, an inmate confined there must use that system to receive the benefit of this Rule 4(c)(1). If an inmate files a notice of appeal in either a civil or a criminal case, the notice is timely if it is deposited in the institution's internal mail system on or before the last day for filing and:

(A) it is accompanied by:

(i) a declaration in compliance with 28 U.S.C. § 1746—or a notarized statement—setting out the date of deposit and stating that first-class postage is being prepaid; or

(ii) evidence (such as a postmark or date stamp) showing that the notice was so deposited and that postage was prepaid; or

(B) the court of appeals exercises its discretion to permit the later filing of a declaration or notarized statement that satisfies Rule 4(c)(1)(A)(i).

(2) If an inmate files the first notice of appeal in a civil case under this Rule 4(c), the 14–day period provided in Rule 4(a)(3) for another party to file a notice of appeal runs from the date when the district court dockets the first notice.

(3) When a defendant in a criminal case files a notice of appeal under this Rule 4(c), the 30–day period for the government to file its notice of appeal runs from the entry of the judgment or order appealed from or from the district court's docketing of the defendant's notice of appeal, whichever is later.

(d) Mistaken Filing in the Court of Appeals. If a notice of appeal in either a civil or a criminal case is mistakenly filed in the court of appeals, the clerk of that court must note on the notice the date when it was received and send it to the district clerk. The notice is then considered filed in the district court on the date so noted.

(As amended Apr. 30, 1979, eff. Aug. 1, 1979; Nov. 18, 1988, Pub.L. 100–690, Title VII, § 7111, 102 Stat. 4419; Apr. 30, 1991, eff. Dec. 1, 1991; Apr. 22, 1993, eff. Dec. 1, 1993; Apr. 27, 1995, eff. Dec. 1, 1995; Apr. 24, 1998, eff. Dec. 1, 1998; Apr. 29, 2002, eff. Dec. 1, 2002; Apr. 25, 2005, eff. Dec. 1, 2005; Mar. 26, 2009, eff. Dec. 1, 2009; Apr. 28, 2010, eff. Dec. 1, 2010; Apr. 26, 2011, eff. Dec. 1, 2011; Apr. 28, 2016, eff. Dec. 1, 2016, absent contrary Congressional action.)

RULE 5.   APPEAL BY PERMISSION

(a) Petition for Permission to Appeal.

(1) To request permission to appeal when an appeal is within the court of appeals' discretion, a party must file a petition for permission to appeal. The petition must be filed with the circuit clerk with proof of service on all other parties to the district-court action.

(2) The petition must be filed within the time specified by the statute or rule authorizing the appeal or, if no such time is specified, within the time provided by Rule 4(a) for filing a notice of appeal.

(3) If a party cannot petition for appeal unless the district court first enters an order granting permission to do so or stating that the necessary conditions are met, the district court may amend its order, either on its own or in response to a party's motion, to include the required permission or statement. In that event, the time to petition runs from entry of the amended order.

(b) Contents of the Petition; Answer or Cross–Petition; Oral Argument.

(1) The petition must include the following:

(A) the facts necessary to understand the question presented;

(B) the question itself;

(C) the relief sought;

(D) the reasons why the appeal should be allowed and is authorized by a statute or rule; and

(E) an attached copy of:

(i) the order, decree, or judgment complained of and any related opinion or memorandum, and

(ii) any order stating the district court's permission to appeal or finding that the necessary conditions are met.

(2) A party may file an answer in opposition or a cross-petition within 10 days after the petition is served.

(3) The petition and answer will be submitted without oral argument unless the court of appeals orders otherwise.

[Text of subdivision (c) effective until December 1, 2016, absent contrary Congressional action.]

(c) Form of Papers; Number of Copies. All papers must conform to Rule 32(c)(2). Except by the court's permission, a paper must not exceed 20 pages, exclusive of the disclosure statement, the proof of service, and the accompanying documents required by Rule 5(b)(1)(E). An original and 3 copies must be filed unless the court requires a different number by local rule or by order in a particular case.

[Text of subdivision (c) effective December 1, 2016, absent contrary Congressional action.]

(c) Form of Papers; Number of Copies; Length Limits. All papers must conform to Rule 32(c)(2). An original and 3 copies must be filed unless the court requires a different number by local rule or by order in a particular case. Except by the court's permission, and excluding the accompanying documents required by Rule 5(b)(1)(E):

(1) a paper produced using a computer must not exceed 5,200 words; and

(2) a handwritten or typewritten paper must not exceed 20 pages.

(d) Grant of Permission; Fees; Cost Bond; Filing the Record.

(1) Within 14 days after the entry of the order granting permission to appeal, the appellant must:

(A) pay the district clerk all required fees; and

(B) file a cost bond if required under Rule 7.

(2) A notice of appeal need not be filed. The date when the order granting permission to appeal is entered serves as the date of the notice of appeal for calculating time under these rules.

(3) The district clerk must notify the circuit clerk once the petitioner has paid the fees. Upon receiving this notice, the circuit clerk must enter the appeal on the docket. The record must be forwarded and filed in accordance with Rules 11 and 12(c).

(As amended Apr. 30, 1979, eff. Aug. 1, 1979; Apr. 29, 1994, eff. Dec. 1, 1994; Apr. 24, 1998, eff. Dec. 1, 1998; Apr. 29, 2002, eff. Dec. 1, 2002; Mar. 26, 2009, eff. Dec. 1, 2009; Apr. 28, 2016, eff. Dec. 1, 2016, absent contrary Congressional action.)

[RULE 5.1 APPEAL BY LEAVE UNDER 28 U.S.C. § 636(C)(5) (ABROGATED APR. 24, 1998, EFF. DEC. 1, 1998)]

RULE 6. APPEAL IN A BANKRUPTCY CASE

(a) Appeal From a Judgment, Order, or Decree of a District Court Exercising Original Jurisdiction in a Bankruptcy Case. An appeal to a court of appeals from a final judgment, order, or decree of a district court exercising jurisdiction under 28 U.S.C. § 1334 is taken as any other civil appeal under these rules.

(b) Appeal From a Judgment, Order, or Decree of a District Court or Bankruptcy Appellate Panel Exercising Appellate Jurisdiction in a Bankruptcy Case.

(1) Applicability of Other Rules. These rules apply to an appeal to a court of appeals under 28 U.S.C. § 158(d)(1) from a final judgment, order, or decree of a district court or bankruptcy appellate panel exercising appellate jurisdiction under 28 U.S.C. § 158(a) or (b), but with these qualifications:

(A) Rules 4(a)(4), 4(b), 9, 10, 11, 12(c), 13–20, 22–23, and 24(b) do not apply;

(B) the reference in Rule 3(c) to "Form 1 in the Appendix of Forms" must be read as a reference to Form 5;

(C) when the appeal is from a bankruptcy appellate panel, "district court," as used in any applicable rule, means "appellate panel"; and

(D) in Rule 12.1, "district court" includes a bankruptcy court or bankruptcy appellate panel.

(2) Additional Rules. In addition to the rules made applicable by Rule 6(b)(1), the following rules apply:

(A) Motion for Rehearing.

(i) If a timely motion for rehearing under Bankruptcy Rule 8022 is filed, the time to appeal for all parties runs from the entry of the order disposing of the motion. A notice of appeal filed after the district court or bankruptcy appellate panel announces or enters a judgment, order, or decree—but before disposition of the motion for rehearing—becomes effective when the order disposing of the motion for rehearing is entered.

(ii) If a party intends to challenge the order disposing of the motion—or the alteration or amendment of a judgment, order, or decree upon the motion—then the party, in compliance with Rules 3(c) and 6(b)(1)(B), must file a notice of appeal or amended notice of appeal. The notice or amended notice must be filed within the time prescribed by Rule 4—excluding Rules 4(a)(4) and 4(b)—measured from the entry of the order disposing of the motion.

(iii) No additional fee is required to file an amended notice.

(B) The Record on Appeal.

(i) Within 14 days after filing the notice of appeal, the appellant must file with the clerk possessing the record assembled in accordance with Bankruptcy Rule 8009—and serve on the appellee—a statement of the issues to be presented on appeal and a designation of the record to be certified and made available to the circuit clerk.

(ii) An appellee who believes that other parts of the record are necessary must, within 14 days after being served with the appellant's designation, file with the clerk and serve on the appellant a designation of additional parts to be included.

(iii) The record on appeal consists of:

- the redesignated record as provided above;
- the proceedings in the district court or bankruptcy appellate panel; and
- a certified copy of the docket entries prepared by the clerk under Rule 3(d).

(C) Making the Record Available.

(i) When the record is complete, the district clerk or bankruptcy-appellate-panel clerk must number the documents constituting the record and promptly make it available to the circuit clerk. If the clerk makes the record available in paper form, the clerk will not send documents of unusual bulk or weight, physical exhibits other than documents, or other parts of the record designated for omission by local rule of the court of appeals, unless directed to do so by a party or the circuit clerk. If unusually bulky or heavy exhibits are to be made available in paper form, a party must arrange with the clerks in advance for their transportation and receipt.

(ii) All parties must do whatever else is necessary to enable the clerk to assemble the record and make it available. When the record is made available in paper form, the court of appeals may provide by rule or order that a certified copy of the docket entries be made available in place of the redesignated record. But any party may request at any time during the pendency of the appeal that the redesignated record be made available.

(D) Filing the Record. When the district clerk or bankruptcy-appellate-panel clerk has made the record available, the circuit clerk must note that fact on the docket. The date noted on the docket serves as the filing date of the record. The circuit clerk must immediately notify all parties of the filing date.

(c) Direct Review by Permission Under 28 U.S.C. § 158(d)(2).

(1) Applicability of Other Rules. These rules apply to a direct appeal by permission under 28 U.S.C. § 158(d)(2), but with these qualifications:

(A) Rules 3–4, 5(a)(3), 6(a), 6(b), 8(a), 8(c), 9–12, 13–20, 22–23, and 24(b) do not apply;

(B) as used in any applicable rule, "district court" or "district clerk" includes—to the extent appropriate—a bankruptcy court or bankruptcy appellate panel or its clerk; and

(C) the reference to "Rules 11 and 12(c)" in Rule 5(d)(3) must be read as a reference to Rules 6(c)(2)(B) and (C).

(2) Additional Rules. In addition, the following rules apply:

(A) The Record on Appeal. Bankruptcy Rule 8009 governs the record on appeal.

(B) Making the Record Available. Bankruptcy Rule 8010 governs completing the record and making it available.

(C) Stays Pending Appeal. Bankruptcy Rule 8007 applies to stays pending appeal.

(D) Duties of the Circuit Clerk. When the bankruptcy clerk has made the record available, the circuit clerk must note that fact on the docket. The date noted on the docket serves as the filing date of the record. The circuit clerk must immediately notify all parties of the filing date.

(E) Filing a Representation Statement. Unless the court of appeals designates another time, within 14 days after entry of the order granting permission to appeal, the attorney who sought permission must file a statement with the circuit clerk naming the parties that the attorney represents on appeal.

(Added Apr. 25, 1989, eff. Dec. 1, 1989; amended Apr. 30, 1991, eff. Dec. 1, 1991; Apr. 22, 1993, eff. Dec. 1, 1993; Apr. 24, 1998, eff. Dec. 1, 1998; Mar. 26, 2009, eff. Dec. 1, 2009; Apr. 25, 2014, eff. Dec. 1, 2014.)

RULE 7. BOND FOR COSTS ON APPEAL IN A CIVIL CASE

In a civil case, the district court may require an appellant to file a bond or provide other security in any form and amount necessary to ensure payment of costs on appeal. Rule 8(b) applies to a surety on a bond given under this rule.

(As amended Apr. 30, 1979, eff. Aug. 1, 1979; Apr. 24, 1998, eff. Dec. 1, 1998.)

RULE 8. STAY OR INJUNCTION PENDING APPEAL

(a) Motion for Stay.

(1) Initial Motion in the District Court. A party must ordinarily move first in the district court for the following relief:

(A) a stay of the judgment or order of a district court pending appeal;

(B) approval of a supersedeas bond; or

(C) an order suspending, modifying, restoring, or granting an injunction while an appeal is pending.

(2) Motion in the Court of Appeals; Conditions on Relief. A motion for the relief mentioned in Rule 8(a)(1) may be made to the court of appeals or to one of its judges.

(A) The motion must:

(i) show that moving first in the district court would be impracticable; or

(ii) state that, a motion having been made, the district court denied the motion or failed to afford the relief requested and state any reasons given by the district court for its action.

(B) The motion must also include:

(i) the reasons for granting the relief requested and the facts relied on;

(ii) originals or copies of affidavits or other sworn statements supporting facts subject to dispute; and

(iii) relevant parts of the record.

(C) The moving party must give reasonable notice of the motion to all parties.

(D) A motion under this Rule 8(a)(2) must be filed with the circuit clerk and normally will be considered by a panel of the court. But in an exceptional case in which time requirements make that procedure impracticable, the motion may be made to and considered by a single judge.

(E) The court may condition relief on a party's filing a bond or other appropriate security in the district court.

(b) **Proceeding Against a Surety.** If a party gives security in the form of a bond or stipulation or other undertaking with one or more sureties, each surety submits to the jurisdiction of the district court and irrevocably appoints the district clerk as the surety's agent on whom any papers affecting the surety's liability on the bond or undertaking may be served. On motion, a surety's liability may be enforced in the district court without the necessity of an independent action. The motion and any notice that the district court prescribes may be served on the district clerk, who must promptly mail a copy to each surety whose address is known.

(c) **Stay in a Criminal Case.** Rule 38 of the Federal Rules of Criminal Procedure governs a stay in a criminal case.

(As amended Mar. 10, 1986, eff. July 1, 1986; Apr. 27, 1995, eff. Dec. 1, 1995; Apr. 24, 1998, eff. Dec. 1, 1998.)

RULE 9.   RELEASE IN A CRIMINAL CASE

(a) **Release Before Judgment of Conviction.**

(1) The district court must state in writing, or orally on the record, the reasons for an order regarding the release or detention of a defendant in a criminal case. A party appealing from the order must file with the court of appeals a copy of the district court's order and the court's statement of reasons as soon as practicable after filing the notice of appeal. An appellant who questions the factual basis for the district court's order must file a transcript of the release proceedings or an explanation of why a transcript was not obtained.

(2) After reasonable notice to the appellee, the court of appeals must promptly determine the appeal on the basis of the papers, affidavits, and parts of the record that the parties present or the court requires. Unless the court so orders, briefs need not be filed.

(3) The court of appeals or one of its judges may order the defendant's release pending the disposition of the appeal.

(b) **Release After Judgment of Conviction.** A party entitled to do so may obtain review of a district-court order regarding release after a judgment of conviction by filing a notice of appeal from that order in the district court, or by filing a motion in the court of appeals if the party has already filed a notice of appeal from the judgment of conviction. Both the order and the review are subject to Rule 9(a). The papers filed by the party seeking review must include a copy of the judgment of conviction.

(c) **Criteria for Release.** The court must make its decision regarding release in accordance with the applicable provisions of 18 U.S.C. §§ 3142, 3143, and 3145(c).

(As amended Apr. 24, 1972, eff. Oct. 1, 1972; Oct. 12, 1984, Pub.L. 98–473, Title II, § 210, 98 Stat. 1987; Apr. 29, 1994, eff. Dec. 1, 1994; Apr. 24, 1998, eff. Dec. 1, 1998.)

RULE 10.   THE RECORD ON APPEAL

(a) **Composition of the Record on Appeal.** The following items constitute the record on appeal:

(1) the original papers and exhibits filed in the district court;

(2) the transcript of proceedings, if any; and

(3) a certified copy of the docket entries prepared by the district clerk.

(b) **The Transcript of Proceedings.**

(1) **Appellant's Duty to Order.** Within 14 days after filing the notice of appeal or entry of an order disposing of the last timely remaining motion of a type specified in Rule 4(a)(4)(A), whichever is later, the appellant must do either of the following:

(A) order from the reporter a transcript of such parts of the proceedings not already on file as the appellant considers necessary, subject to a local rule of the court of appeals and with the following qualifications:

(i) the order must be in writing;

(ii) if the cost of the transcript is to be paid by the United States under the Criminal Justice Act, the order must so state; and

(iii) the appellant must, within the same period, file a copy of the order with the district clerk; or

(B) file a certificate stating that no transcript will be ordered.

(2) **Unsupported Finding or Conclusion.** If the appellant intends to urge on appeal that a finding or conclusion is unsupported by the evidence or is contrary to the evidence, the appellant must include in the record a transcript of all evidence relevant to that finding or conclusion.

(3) **Partial Transcript.** Unless the entire transcript is ordered:

(A) the appellant must—within the 14 days provided in Rule 10(b)(1)—file a statement of the issues that the appellant intends to present on the appeal and must serve on the appellee a copy of both the order or certificate and the statement;

(B) if the appellee considers it necessary to have a transcript of other parts of the proceedings, the appellee must, within 14 days after the service of the order or certificate and the statement of the issues, file and serve on the appellant a designation of additional parts to be ordered; and

(C) unless within 14 days after service of that designation the appellant has ordered all such parts, and has so notified the appellee, the appellee may within the following 14 days either order the parts or move in the district court for an order requiring the appellant to do so.

(4) Payment. At the time of ordering, a party must make satisfactory arrangements with the reporter for paying the cost of the transcript.

(c) Statement of the Evidence When the Proceedings Were Not Recorded or When a Transcript Is Unavailable. If the transcript of a hearing or trial is unavailable, the appellant may prepare a statement of the evidence or proceedings from the best available means, including the appellant's recollection. The statement must be served on the appellee, who may serve objections or proposed amendments within 14 days after being served. The statement and any objections or proposed amendments must then be submitted to the district court for settlement and approval. As settled and approved, the statement must be included by the district clerk in the record on appeal.

(d) Agreed Statement as the Record on Appeal. In place of the record on appeal as defined in Rule 10(a), the parties may prepare, sign, and submit to the district court a statement of the case showing how the issues presented by the appeal arose and were decided in the district court. The statement must set forth only those facts averred and proved or sought to be proved that are essential to the court's resolution of the issues. If the statement is truthful, it—together with any additions that the district court may consider necessary to a full presentation of the issues on appeal—must be approved by the district court and must then be certified to the court of appeals as the record on appeal. The district clerk must then send it to the circuit clerk within the time provided by Rule 11. A copy of the agreed statement may be filed in place of the appendix required by Rule 30.

(e) Correction or Modification of the Record.

(1) If any difference arises about whether the record truly discloses what occurred in the district court, the difference must be submitted to and settled by that court and the record conformed accordingly.

(2) If anything material to either party is omitted from or misstated in the record by error or accident, the omission or misstatement may be corrected and a supplemental record may be certified and forwarded:

(A) on stipulation of the parties;

(B) by the district court before or after the record has been forwarded; or

(C) by the court of appeals.

(3) All other questions as to the form and content of the record must be presented to the court of appeals.

(As amended Apr. 30, 1979, eff. Aug. 1, 1979; Mar. 10, 1986, eff. July 1, 1986; Apr. 30, 1991, eff. Dec. 1, 1991; Apr. 22, 1993, eff. Dec. 1, 1993; Apr. 27, 1995, eff. Dec. 1, 1995; Apr. 24, 1998, eff. Dec. 1, 1998; Mar. 26, 2009, eff. Dec. 1, 2009.)

RULE 11. FORWARDING THE RECORD

(a) Appellant's Duty. An appellant filing a notice of appeal must comply with Rule 10(b) and must do whatever else is necessary to enable the clerk to assemble and forward the record. If there are multiple appeals from a judgment or order, the clerk must forward a single record.

(b) Duties of Reporter and District Clerk.

(1) Reporter's Duty to Prepare and File a Transcript. The reporter must prepare and file a transcript as follows:

(A) Upon receiving an order for a transcript, the reporter must enter at the foot of the order the date of its receipt and the expected completion date and send a copy, so endorsed, to the circuit clerk.

(B) If the transcript cannot be completed within 30 days of the reporter's receipt of the order, the reporter may request the circuit clerk to grant additional time to complete it. The clerk must note on the docket the action taken and notify the parties.

(C) When a transcript is complete, the reporter must file it with the district clerk and notify the circuit clerk of the filing.

(D) If the reporter fails to file the transcript on time, the circuit clerk must notify the district judge and do whatever else the court of appeals directs.

(2) District Clerk's Duty to Forward. When the record is complete, the district clerk must number the documents constituting the record and send them promptly to the circuit clerk together with a list of the documents correspondingly numbered and reasonably identified. Unless directed to do so by a party or the circuit clerk, the district clerk will not send to the court of appeals documents of unusual bulk or weight, physical exhibits other than documents, or other parts of the record designated for omission by local rule of the court of appeals. If the exhibits are unusually bulky or heavy, a party must arrange with the clerks in advance for their transportation and receipt.

(c) Retaining the Record Temporarily in the District Court for Use in Preparing the Appeal. The parties may stipulate, or the district court on motion may order, that the district clerk retain the record temporarily for the parties to use in preparing the papers on appeal. In that event the district clerk must certify to the circuit clerk that the record on appeal is complete. Upon receipt of the appellee's brief, or earlier if the court orders or the parties agree, the appellant must request the district clerk to forward the record.

(d) [Abrogated.]

(e) Retaining the Record by Court Order.

(1) The court of appeals may, by order or local rule, provide that a certified copy of the docket entries be forwarded instead of the entire record. But a party may at any time during the appeal request that designated parts of the record be forwarded.

(2) The district court may order the record or some part of it retained if the court needs it while the appeal is pending, subject, however, to call by the court of appeals.

(3) If part or all of the record is ordered retained, the district clerk must send to the court of appeals a copy of the order and the docket entries together with the parts of the original record allowed by the district court and copies of any parts of the record designated by the parties.

(f) Retaining Parts of the Record in the District Court by Stipulation of the Parties. The parties may agree by written stipulation filed in the district court that designated parts of the record be retained in the district court subject to call by the court of appeals or request by a party. The parts of the record so designated remain a part of the record on appeal.

(g) Record for a Preliminary Motion in the Court of Appeals. If, before the record is forwarded, a party makes any of the following motions in the court of appeals:

- for dismissal;

- for release;

- for a stay pending appeal;

- for additional security on the bond on appeal or on a supersedeas bond; or

- for any other intermediate order—

the district clerk must send the court of appeals any parts of the record designated by any party.

(As amended Apr. 30, 1979, eff. Aug. 1, 1979; Mar. 10, 1986, eff. July 1, 1986; Apr. 24, 1998, eff. Dec. 1, 1998.)

RULE 12. DOCKETING THE APPEAL; FILING A REPRESENTATION STATEMENT; FILING THE RECORD

(a) Docketing the Appeal. Upon receiving the copy of the notice of appeal and the docket entries from the district clerk under Rule 3(d), the circuit clerk must docket the appeal under the title of the district-court action and must identify the appellant, adding the appellant's name if necessary.

(b) Filing a Representation Statement. Unless the court of appeals designates another time, the attorney who filed the notice of appeal must, within 14 days after filing the notice, file a statement with the circuit clerk naming the parties that the attorney represents on appeal.

(c) Filing the Record, Partial Record, or Certificate. Upon receiving the record, partial record, or district clerk's certificate as provided in Rule 11, the circuit clerk must file it and immediately notify all parties of the filing date.

(As amended Apr. 30, 1979, eff. Aug. 1, 1979; Mar. 10, 1986, eff. July 1, 1986; Apr. 22, 1993, eff. Dec. 1, 1993; Apr. 24, 1998, eff. Dec. 1, 1998; Mar. 26, 2009, eff. Dec. 1, 2009.)

RULE 12.1 REMAND AFTER AN INDICATIVE RULING BY THE DISTRICT COURT ON A MOTION FOR RELIEF THAT IS BARRED BY A PENDING APPEAL

(a) Notice to the Court of Appeals. If a timely motion is made in the district court for relief that it lacks authority to grant because of an appeal that has been docketed and is pending, the movant must promptly notify the circuit clerk if the district court states either that it would grant the motion or that the motion raises a substantial issue.

(b) Remand After an Indicative Ruling. If the district court states that it would grant the motion or that the motion raises a substantial issue, the court of appeals may remand for further proceedings but retains jurisdiction unless it expressly dismisses the appeal. If the court of appeals remands but retains jurisdiction, the parties must promptly notify the circuit clerk when the district court has decided the motion on remand.

(Added Mar. 26, 2009, eff. Dec. 1, 2009.)

TITLE III. APPEALS FROM THE UNITED STATES TAX COURT

RULE 13. APPEALS FROM THE TAX COURT

(a) Appeal as of Right.

(1) How Obtained; Time for Filing a Notice of Appeal.

(A) An appeal as of right from the United States Tax Court is commenced by filing a notice of appeal with the Tax Court clerk within 90 days after the entry of the Tax Court's decision. At the time of filing, the appellant must furnish the clerk with enough copies of the notice to enable the clerk to comply with Rule 3(d). If one party files a timely notice of appeal, any other party may file a notice of appeal within 120 days after the Tax Court's decision is entered.

(B) If, under Tax Court rules, a party makes a timely motion to vacate or revise the Tax Court's decision, the time to file a notice of appeal runs from the entry of the order disposing of the motion or from the entry of a new decision, whichever is later.

(2) Notice of Appeal; How Filed. The notice of appeal may be filed either at the Tax Court clerk's office in the District of Columbia or by mail addressed to the clerk. If sent by mail the notice is considered filed on the postmark date, subject to § 7502 of the Internal Revenue Code, as amended, and the applicable regulations.

(3) Contents of the Notice of Appeal; Service; Effect of Filing and Service. Rule 3 prescribes the contents of a notice of appeal, the manner of service, and the effect of its filing and service.

Form 2 in the Appendix of Forms is a suggested form of a notice of appeal.

(4) The Record on Appeal; Forwarding; Filing.

(A) Except as otherwise provided under Tax Court rules for the transcript of proceedings, the appeal is governed by the parts of Rules 10, 11, and 12 regarding the record on appeal from a district court, the time and manner of forwarding and filing, and the docketing in the court of appeals.

(B) If an appeal is taken to more than one court of appeals, the original record must be sent to the court named in the first notice of appeal filed. In an appeal to any other court of appeals, the appellant must apply to that other court to make provision for the record.

(b) Appeal by Permission. An appeal by permission is governed by Rule 5.

(As amended Apr. 30, 1979, eff. Aug. 1, 1979; Apr. 29, 1994, eff. Dec. 1, 1994; Apr. 24, 1998, eff. Dec. 1, 1998; Apr. 16, 2013, eff. Dec. 1, 2013.)

RULE 14. APPLICABILITY OF OTHER RULES TO APPEALS FROM THE TAX COURT

All provisions of these rules, except Rules 4, 6–9, 15–20, and 22–23, apply to appeals from the Tax Court. References in any applicable rule (other than Rule 24(a)) to the district court and district clerk are to be read as referring to the Tax Court and its clerk.

(As amended Apr. 24, 1998, eff. Dec. 1, 1998; Apr. 16, 2013, eff. Dec. 1, 2013.)

TITLE IV. REVIEW OR ENFORCEMENT OF AN ORDER OF AN ADMINISTRATIVE AGENCY, BOARD, COMMISSION, OR OFFICER

RULE 15. REVIEW OR ENFORCEMENT OF AN AGENCY ORDER—HOW OBTAINED; INTERVENTION

(a) Petition for Review; Joint Petition.

(1) Review of an agency order is commenced by filing, within the time prescribed by law, a petition for review with the clerk of a court of appeals authorized to review the agency order. If their interests make joinder practicable, two or more persons may join in a petition to the same court to review the same order.

(2) The petition must:

(A) name each party seeking review either in the caption or the body of the petition—using such terms as "et al.," "petitioners," or "respondents" does not effectively name the parties;

(B) name the agency as a respondent (even though not named in the petition, the United States is a respondent if required by statute); and

(C) specify the order or part thereof to be reviewed.

(3) Form 3 in the Appendix of Forms is a suggested form of a petition for review.

(4) In this rule "agency" includes an agency, board, commission, or officer; "petition for review" includes a petition to enjoin, suspend, modify, or otherwise review, or a notice of appeal, whichever form is indicated by the applicable statute.

(b) Application or Cross–Application to Enforce an Order; Answer; Default.

(1) An application to enforce an agency order must be filed with the clerk of a court of appeals authorized to enforce the order. If a petition is filed to review an agency order that the court may enforce, a party opposing the petition may file a cross-application for enforcement.

(2) Within 21 days after the application for enforcement is filed, the respondent must serve on the applicant an answer to the application and file it with the clerk. If the respondent fails to answer in time, the court will enter judgment for the relief requested.

(3) The application must contain a concise statement of the proceedings in which the order was entered, the facts upon which venue is based, and the relief requested.

(c) Service of the Petition or Application. The circuit clerk must serve a copy of the petition for review, or an application or cross-application to enforce an agency order, on each respondent as prescribed by Rule 3(d), unless a different manner of service is prescribed by statute. At the time of filing, the petitioner must:

(1) serve, or have served, a copy on each party admitted to participate in the agency proceedings, except for the respondents;

(2) file with the clerk a list of those so served; and

(3) give the clerk enough copies of the petition or application to serve each respondent.

(d) Intervention. Unless a statute provides another method, a person who wants to intervene in a proceeding under this rule must file a motion for leave to intervene with the circuit clerk and serve a copy on all parties. The motion—or other notice of intervention authorized by statute—must be filed within 30 days after the petition for review is filed and must contain a concise statement of the interest of the moving party and the grounds for intervention.

(e) Payment of Fees. When filing any separate or joint petition for review in a court of appeals, the petitioner must pay the circuit clerk all required fees.

(As amended Apr. 22, 1993, eff. Dec. 1, 1993; Apr. 24, 1998, eff. Dec. 1, 1998; Mar. 26, 2009, eff. Dec. 1, 2009.)

RULE 15.1 BRIEFS AND ORAL ARGUMENT IN A NATIONAL LABOR RELATIONS BOARD PROCEEDING

In either an enforcement or a review proceeding, a party adverse to the National Labor Relations Board proceeds first on briefing and at oral argument, unless the court orders otherwise.

(Added Mar. 10, 1986, eff. July 1, 1986; amended Apr. 24, 1998, eff. Dec. 1, 1998.)

RULE 16. THE RECORD ON REVIEW OR ENFORCEMENT

(a) Composition of the Record. The record on review or enforcement of an agency order consists of:

(1) the order involved;

(2) any findings or report on which it is based; and

(3) the pleadings, evidence, and other parts of the proceedings before the agency.

(b) Omissions From or Misstatements in the Record. The parties may at any time, by stipulation, supply any omission from the record or correct a misstatement, or the court may so direct. If necessary, the court may direct that a supplemental record be prepared and filed.

(As amended Apr. 24, 1998, eff. Dec. 1, 1998.)

RULE 17. FILING THE RECORD

(a) Agency to File; Time for Filing; Notice of Filing. The agency must file the record with the circuit clerk within 40 days after being served with a petition for review, unless the statute authorizing review provides otherwise, or within 40 days after it files an application for enforcement unless the respondent fails to answer or the court orders otherwise. The court may shorten or extend the time to file the record. The clerk must notify all parties of the date when the record is filed.

(b) Filing—What Constitutes.

(1) The agency must file:

(A) the original or a certified copy of the entire record or parts designated by the parties; or

(B) a certified list adequately describing all documents, transcripts of testimony, exhibits, and other material constituting the record, or describing those parts designated by the parties.

(2) The parties may stipulate in writing that no record or certified list be filed. The date when the stipulation is filed with the circuit clerk is treated as the date when the record is filed.

(3) The agency must retain any portion of the record not filed with the clerk. All parts of the

record retained by the agency are a part of the record on review for all purposes and, if the court or a party so requests, must be sent to the court regardless of any prior stipulation.

(As amended Apr. 24, 1998, eff. Dec. 1, 1998.)

RULE 18. STAY PENDING REVIEW

(a) Motion for a Stay.

(1) Initial Motion Before the Agency. A petitioner must ordinarily move first before the agency for a stay pending review of its decision or order.

(2) Motion in the Court of Appeals. A motion for a stay may be made to the court of appeals or one of its judges.

(A) The motion must:

(i) show that moving first before the agency would be impracticable; or

(ii) state that, a motion having been made, the agency denied the motion or failed to afford the relief requested and state any reasons given by the agency for its action.

(B) The motion must also include:

(i) the reasons for granting the relief requested and the facts relied on;

(ii) originals or copies of affidavits or other sworn statements supporting facts subject to dispute; and

(iii) relevant parts of the record.

(C) The moving party must give reasonable notice of the motion to all parties.

(D) The motion must be filed with the circuit clerk and normally will be considered by a panel of the court. But in an exceptional case in which time requirements make that procedure impracticable, the motion may be made to and considered by a single judge.

(b) Bond. The court may condition relief on the filing of a bond or other appropriate security.

(As amended Apr. 24, 1998, eff. Dec. 1, 1998.)

RULE 19. SETTLEMENT OF A JUDGMENT ENFORCING AN AGENCY ORDER IN PART

When the court files an opinion directing entry of judgment enforcing the agency's order in part, the agency must within 14 days file with the clerk and serve on each other party a proposed judgment conforming to the opinion. A party who disagrees with the agency's proposed judgment must within 10 days file with the clerk and serve the agency with a proposed judgment that the party believes conforms to the opinion. The court will settle the judgment and direct entry without further hearing or argument.

(As amended Mar. 10, 1986, eff. July 1, 1986; Apr. 24, 1998, eff. Dec. 1, 1998; Mar. 26, 2009, eff. Dec. 1, 2009.)

RULE 20. APPLICABILITY OF RULES TO THE REVIEW OR ENFORCEMENT OF AN AGENCY ORDER

All provisions of these rules, except Rules 3–14 and 22–23, apply to the review or enforcement of an agency order. In these rules, "appellant" includes a petitioner or applicant, and "appellee" includes a respondent.

(As amended Apr. 24, 1998, eff. Dec. 1, 1998.)

TITLE V. EXTRAORDINARY WRITS

RULE 21. WRITS OF MANDAMUS AND PROHIBITION, AND OTHER EXTRAORDINARY WRITS

(a) Mandamus or Prohibition to a Court: Petition, Filing, Service, and Docketing.

(1) A party petitioning for a writ of mandamus or prohibition directed to a court must file a petition with the circuit clerk with proof of service on all parties to the proceeding in the trial court. The party must also provide a copy to the trial-court judge. All parties to the proceeding in the trial court other than the petitioner are respondents for all purposes.

(2)(A) The petition must be titled "In re [name of petitioner]."

(B) The petition must state:

(i) the relief sought;

(ii) the issues presented;

(iii) the facts necessary to understand the issue presented by the petition; and

(iv) the reasons why the writ should issue.

(C) The petition must include a copy of any order or opinion or parts of the record that may be essential to understand the matters set forth in the petition.

(3) Upon receiving the prescribed docket fee, the clerk must docket the petition and submit it to the court.

(b) Denial; Order Directing Answer; Briefs; Precedence.

(1) The court may deny the petition without an answer. Otherwise, it must order the respondent, if any, to answer within a fixed time.

(2) The clerk must serve the order to respond on all persons directed to respond.

(3) Two or more respondents may answer jointly.

(4) The court of appeals may invite or order the trial-court judge to address the petition or may invite an amicus curiae to do so. The trial-court judge may request permission to address the petition but may not do so unless invited or ordered to do so by the court of appeals.

(5) If briefing or oral argument is required, the clerk must advise the parties, and when appropriate, the trial-court judge or amicus curiae.

(6) The proceeding must be given preference over ordinary civil cases.

(7) The circuit clerk must send a copy of the final disposition to the trial-court judge.

(c) Other Extraordinary Writs. An application for an extraordinary writ other than one provided for in Rule 21(a) must be made by filing a petition with the circuit clerk with proof of service on the respondents. Proceedings on the application must conform, so far as is practicable, to the procedures prescribed in Rule 21(a) and (b).

[Text of subdivision (d) effective until December 1, 2016, absent contrary Congressional action.]

(d) Form of Papers; Number of Copies. All papers must conform to Rule 32(c)(2). Except by the court's permission, a paper must not exceed 30 pages, exclusive of the disclosure statement, the proof of service, and the accompanying documents required by Rule 21(a)(2)(C). An original and 3 copies must be filed unless the court requires the filing of a different number by local rule or by order in a particular case.

[Text of subdivision (d) effective December 1, 2016, absent contrary Congressional action.]

(d) Form of Papers; Number of Copies; Length Limits. All papers must conform to Rule 32(c)(2). An original and 3 copies must be filed unless the court requires the filing of a different number by local rule or by order in a particular case. Except by the court's permission, and excluding the accompanying documents required by Rule 21(a)(2)(C):

(1) a paper produced using a computer must not exceed 7,800 words; and

(2) a handwritten or typewritten paper must not exceed 30 pages.

(As amended Apr. 29, 1994, eff. Dec. 1, 1994; Apr. 23, 1996, eff. Dec. 1, 1996; Apr. 24, 1998, eff. Dec. 1, 1998; Apr. 29, 2002, eff. Dec. 1, 2002; Apr. 28, 2016, eff. Dec. 1, 2016, absent contrary Congressional action.)

TITLE VI. HABEAS CORPUS; PROCEEDINGS IN FORMA PAUPERIS

RULE 22. HABEAS CORPUS AND SECTION 2255 PROCEEDINGS

(a) Application for the Original Writ. An application for a writ of habeas corpus must be made to the appropriate district court. If made to a circuit judge, the application must be transferred to the appropriate district court. If a district court denies an application made or transferred to it, renewal of the application before a circuit judge is not permitted. The applicant may, under 28 U.S.C. § 2253, appeal to the court of appeals from the district court's order denying the application.

(b) Certificate of Appealability.

(1) In a habeas corpus proceeding in which the detention complained of arises from process issued by a state court, or in a 28 U.S.C. § 2255 proceeding, the applicant cannot take an appeal unless a circuit justice or a circuit or district judge issues a certificate of appealability under 28 U.S.C. § 2253(c). If an applicant files a notice of appeal, the district clerk must send to the court of appeals the certificate (if any) and the statement described in Rule 11(a) of the Rules Governing Proceedings

Under 28 U.S.C. § 2254 or § 2255 (if any), along with the notice of appeal and the file of the district-court proceedings. If the district judge has denied the certificate, the applicant may request a circuit judge to issue it.

(2) A request addressed to the court of appeals may be considered by a circuit judge or judges, as the court prescribes. If no express request for a certificate is filed, the notice of appeal constitutes a request addressed to the judges of the court of appeals.

(3) A certificate of appealability is not required when a state or its representative or the United States or its representative appeals.

(As amended Pub.L. 104–132, Title I, § 103, Apr. 24, 1996, 110 Stat. 1218; Apr. 24, 1998, eff. Dec. 1, 1998; Mar. 26, 2009, eff. Dec. 1, 2009.)

RULE 23. CUSTODY OR RELEASE OF A PRISONER IN A HABEAS CORPUS PROCEEDING

(a) Transfer of Custody Pending Review. Pending review of a decision in a habeas corpus proceeding commenced before a court, justice, or judge of the United States for the release of a prisoner, the person having custody of the prisoner must not transfer custody to another unless a transfer is directed in accordance with this rule. When, upon application, a custodian shows the need for a transfer, the court, justice, or judge rendering the decision under review may authorize the transfer and substitute the successor custodian as a party.

(b) Detention or Release Pending Review of Decision Not to Release. While a decision not to release a prisoner is under review, the court or judge rendering the decision, or the court of appeals, or the Supreme Court, or a judge or justice of either court, may order that the prisoner be:

(1) detained in the custody from which release is sought;

(2) detained in other appropriate custody; or

(3) released on personal recognizance, with or without surety.

(c) Release Pending Review of Decision Ordering Release. While a decision ordering the release of a prisoner is under review, the prisoner must—unless the court or judge rendering the decision, or the court of appeals, or the Supreme Court, or a judge or justice of either court orders otherwise—be released on personal recognizance, with or without surety.

(d) Modification of the Initial Order on Custody. An initial order governing the prisoner's custody or release, including any recognizance or surety, continues in effect pending review unless for special reasons shown to the court of appeals or the Supreme Court, or to a judge or justice of either court, the order is modified or an independent order regarding custody, release, or surety is issued.

(As amended Mar. 10, 1986, eff. July 1, 1986; Apr. 24, 1998, eff. Dec. 1, 1998.)

RULE 24.   PROCEEDING IN FORMA PAUPERIS

(a) Leave to Proceed In Forma Pauperis.

(1) Motion in the District Court. Except as stated in Rule 24(a)(3), a party to a district-court action who desires to appeal in forma pauperis must file a motion in the district court. The party must attach an affidavit that:

(A) shows in the detail prescribed by Form 4 of the Appendix of Forms the party's inability to pay or to give security for fees and costs;

(B) claims an entitlement to redress; and

(C) states the issues that the party intends to present on appeal.

(2) Action on the Motion. If the district court grants the motion, the party may proceed on appeal without prepaying or giving security for fees and costs, unless a statute provides otherwise. If the district court denies the motion, it must state its reasons in writing.

(3) Prior Approval. A party who was permitted to proceed in forma pauperis in the district-court action, or who was determined to be financially unable to obtain an adequate defense in a criminal case, may proceed on appeal in forma pauperis without further authorization, unless:

(A) the district court—before or after the notice of appeal is filed—certifies that the appeal is not taken in good faith or finds that the party is not otherwise entitled to proceed in forma pauperis and states in writing its reasons for the certification or finding; or

(B) a statute provides otherwise.

(4) Notice of District Court's Denial. The district clerk must immediately notify the parties and the court of appeals when the district court does any of the following:

(A) denies a motion to proceed on appeal in forma pauperis;

(B) certifies that the appeal is not taken in good faith; or

(C) finds that the party is not otherwise entitled to proceed in forma pauperis.

(5) Motion in the Court of Appeals. A party may file a motion to proceed on appeal in forma pauperis in the court of appeals within 30 days after service of the notice prescribed in Rule 24(a)(4). The motion must include a copy of the affidavit filed in the district court and the district court's statement of reasons for its action. If no affidavit was filed in the district court, the party must include the affidavit prescribed by Rule 24(a)(1).

(b) Leave to Proceed In Forma Pauperis on Appeal from the United States Tax Court or on Appeal or Review of an Administrative–Agency Proceeding. A party may file in the court of appeals a motion for leave to proceed on appeal in forma pauperis with an affidavit prescribed by Rule 24(a)(1):

(1) in an appeal from the United States Tax Court; and

(2) when an appeal or review of a proceeding before an administrative agency, board, commission, or officer proceeds directly in the court of appeals.

(c) Leave to Use Original Record. A party allowed to proceed on appeal in forma pauperis may request that the appeal be heard on the original record without reproducing any part.

(As amended Apr. 30, 1979, eff. Aug. 1, 1979; Mar. 10, 1986, eff. July 1, 1986; Apr. 24, 1998, eff. Dec. 1, 1998; Apr. 29, 2002, eff. Dec. 1, 2002; Apr. 16, 2013, eff. Dec. 1, 2013.)

TITLE VII. GENERAL PROVISIONS

RULE 25. FILING AND SERVICE

[Text of subdivision (a) effective until December 1, 2016, absent contrary Congressional action.]

(a) Filing.

(1) Filing with the Clerk. A paper required or permitted to be filed in a court of appeals must be filed with the clerk.

(2) Filing: Method and Timeliness.

(A) In general. Filing may be accomplished by mail addressed to the clerk, but filing is not timely unless the clerk receives the papers within the time fixed for filing.

(B) A brief or appendix. A brief or appendix is timely filed, however, if on or before the last day for filing, it is:

(i) mailed to the clerk by First–Class Mail, or other class of mail that is at least as expeditious, postage prepaid; or

(ii) dispatched to a third-party commercial carrier for delivery to the clerk within 3 days.

(C) Inmate filing. A paper filed by an inmate confined in an institution is timely if deposited in the institution's internal mailing system on or before the last day for filing. If an institution has a system designed for legal mail, the inmate must use that system to receive the benefit of this rule. Timely filing may be shown by a declaration in compliance with 28 U.S.C. § 1746 or by a notarized statement, either of which must set forth the date of deposit and state that first-class postage has been prepaid.

(D) Electronic filing. A court of appeals may by local rule permit or require papers to be filed, signed, or verified by electronic means that are consistent with technical standards, if any, that the Judicial Conference of the United States establishes. A local rule may require filing by electronic means only if reasonable exceptions are allowed. A paper filed by electronic means in compliance with a local rule constitutes a written paper for the purpose of applying these rules.

(3) Filing a Motion with a Judge. If a motion requests relief that may be granted by a single judge, the judge may permit the motion to be filed with the judge; the judge must note the filing date on the motion and give it to the clerk.

(4) Clerk's Refusal of Documents. The clerk must not refuse to accept for filing any paper presented for that purpose solely because it is not presented in proper form as required by these rules or by any local rule or practice.

(5) Privacy Protection. An appeal in a case whose privacy protection was governed by Federal Rule of Bankruptcy Procedure 9037, Federal Rule of Civil Procedure 5.2, or Federal Rule of Criminal Procedure 49.1 is governed by the same rule on appeal. In all other proceedings, privacy protection is governed by Federal Rule of Civil Procedure 5.2, except that Federal Rule of Criminal Procedure 49.1 governs when an extraordinary writ is sought in a criminal case.

[Text of subdivision (a) effective December 1, 2016, absent contrary Congressional action.]

(a) Filing.

(1) Filing with the Clerk. A paper required or permitted to be filed in a court of appeals must be filed with the clerk.

(2) Filing: Method and Timeliness.

(A) In general. Filing may be accomplished by mail addressed to the clerk, but filing is not timely unless the clerk receives the papers within the time fixed for filing.

(B) A brief or appendix. A brief or appendix is timely filed, however, if on or before the last day for filing, it is:

(i) mailed to the clerk by First–Class Mail, or other class of mail that is at least as expeditious, postage prepaid; or

(ii) dispatched to a third-party commercial carrier for delivery to the clerk within 3 days.

(C) Inmate Filing. If an institution has a system designed for legal mail, an inmate confined there must use that system to receive the benefit of this Rule 25(a)(2)(C). A paper filed by an inmate is timely if it is deposited in the institution's internal mail system on or before the last day for filing and:

(i) it is accompanied by:

● a declaration in compliance with 28 U.S.C. § 1746—or a notarized statement—setting out the date of deposit and stating that first-class postage is being prepaid; or

● evidence (such as a postmark or date stamp) showing that the paper was so deposited and that postage was prepaid; or

(ii) the court of appeals exercises its discretion to permit the later filing of a declaration or notarized statement that satisfies Rule 25(a)(2)(C)(i).

(D) Electronic filing. A court of appeals may by local rule permit or require papers to be filed, signed, or verified by electronic means that are consistent with technical standards, if any, that the Judicial Conference of the United States establishes. A local rule may require filing by electronic means only if reasonable exceptions are allowed. A paper filed by electronic means in compliance with a local rule constitutes a written paper for the purpose of applying these rules.

(3) Filing a Motion with a Judge. If a motion requests relief that may be granted by a single judge, the judge may permit the motion to be filed with the judge; the judge must note the filing date on the motion and give it to the clerk.

(4) Clerk's Refusal of Documents. The clerk must not refuse to accept for filing any paper presented for that purpose solely because it is not presented in proper form as required by these rules or by any local rule or practice.

(5) Privacy Protection. An appeal in a case whose privacy protection was governed by Federal Rule of Bankruptcy Procedure 9037, Federal Rule of Civil Procedure 5.2, or Federal Rule of Criminal Procedure 49.1 is governed by the same rule on appeal. In all other proceedings, privacy protection is governed by Federal Rule of Civil Procedure 5.2, except that Federal Rule of Criminal Procedure 49.1 governs when an extraordinary writ is sought in a criminal case.

(b) Service of All Papers Required. Unless a rule requires service by the clerk, a party must, at or before the time of filing a paper, serve a copy on the other parties to the appeal or review. Service on a party represented by counsel must be made on the party's counsel.

(c) Manner of Service.

(1) Service may be any of the following:

(A) personal, including delivery to a responsible person at the office of counsel;

(B) by mail;

(C) by third-party commercial carrier for delivery within 3 days; or

(D) by electronic means, if the party being served consents in writing.

(2) If authorized by local rule, a party may use the court's transmission equipment to make electronic service under Rule 25(c)(1)(D).

(3) When reasonable considering such factors as the immediacy of the relief sought, distance, and cost, service on a party must be by a manner at least as expeditious as the manner used to file the paper with the court.

(4) Service by mail or by commercial carrier is complete on mailing or delivery to the carrier. Service by electronic means is complete on transmission, unless the party making service is notified that the paper was not received by the party served.

(d) Proof of Service.

(1) A paper presented for filing must contain either of the following:

(A) an acknowledgment of service by the person served; or

(B) proof of service consisting of a statement by the person who made service certifying:

(i) the date and manner of service;

(ii) the names of the persons served; and

(iii) their mail or electronic addresses, facsimile numbers, or the addresses of the places of delivery, as appropriate for the manner of service.

(2) When a brief or appendix is filed by mailing or dispatch in accordance with Rule 25(a)(2)(B), the proof of service must also state the date and manner by which the document was mailed or dispatched to the clerk.

(3) Proof of service may appear on or be affixed to the papers filed.

(e) Number of Copies. When these rules require the filing or furnishing of a number of copies, a court may require a different number by local rule or by order in a particular case.

(As amended Mar. 10, 1986, eff. July 1, 1986; Apr. 30, 1991, eff. Dec. 1, 1991; Apr. 22, 1993, eff. Dec. 1, 1993; Apr. 29, 1994, eff. Dec. 1, 1994; Apr. 23, 1996, eff. Dec. 1, 1996; Apr. 24, 1998, eff. Dec. 1, 1998; Apr. 29, 2002, eff. Dec. 1, 2002; Apr. 12, 2006, eff. Dec. 1, 2006; Apr. 30, 2007, eff. Dec. 1, 2007; Mar. 26, 2009, eff. Dec. 1, 2009; Apr. 28, eff. Dec. 1, 2016, absent contrary Congressional action.)

RULE 26. COMPUTING AND EXTENDING TIME

[Text of subdivision (a) effective until December 1, 2016, absent contrary Congressional action.]

(a) Computing Time. The following rules apply in computing any time period specified in these rules, in any local rule or court order, or in any statute that does not specify a method of computing time.

(1) Period Stated in Days or a Longer Unit. When the period is stated in days or a longer unit of time:

(A) exclude the day of the event that triggers the period;

(B) count every day, including intermediate Saturdays, Sundays, and legal holidays; and

(C) include the last day of the period, but if the last day is a Saturday, Sunday, or legal holiday, the period continues to run until the end of the next day that is not a Saturday, Sunday, or legal holiday.

(2) Period Stated in Hours. When the period is stated in hours:

(A) begin counting immediately on the occurrence of the event that triggers the period;

(B) count every hour, including hours during intermediate Saturdays, Sundays, and legal holidays; and

(C) if the period would end on a Saturday, Sunday, or legal holiday, the period continues to run until the same time on the next day that is not a Saturday, Sunday, or legal holiday.

(3) Inaccessibility of the Clerk's Office. Unless the court orders otherwise, if the clerk's office is inaccessible:

(A) on the last day for filing under Rule 26(a)(1), then the time for filing is extended to the first accessible day that is not a Saturday, Sunday, or legal holiday; or

(B) during the last hour for filing under Rule 26(a)(2), then the time for filing is extended to the same time on the first accessible day that is not a Saturday, Sunday, or legal holiday.

(4) "Last Day" Defined. Unless a different time is set by a statute, local rule, or court order, the last day ends:

(A) for electronic filing in the district court, at midnight in the court's time zone;

(B) for electronic filing in the court of appeals, at midnight in the time zone of the circuit clerk's principal office;

(C) for filing under Rules 4(c)(1), 25(a)(2)(B), and 25(a)(2)(C)—and filing by mail under Rule 13(b)—at the latest time for the method chosen for delivery to the post office, third-party commercial carrier, or prison mailing system; and

(D) for filing by other means, when the clerk's office is scheduled to close.

(5) "Next Day" Defined. The "next day" is determined by continuing to count forward when the period is measured after an event and backward when measured before an event.

(6) "Legal Holiday" Defined. "Legal holiday" means:

(A) the day set aside by statute for observing New Year's Day, Martin Luther King Jr.'s Birthday, Washington's Birthday, Memorial Day, Independence Day, Labor Day, Columbus Day, Veterans' Day, Thanksgiving Day, or Christmas Day;

(B) any day declared a holiday by the President or Congress; and

(C) for periods that are measured after an event, any other day declared a holiday by the state where either of the following is located: the district court that rendered the challenged judgment or order, or the circuit clerk's principal office.

[Text of subdivision (a) effective December 1, 2016, absent contrary Congressional action.]

(a) Computing Time. The following rules apply in computing any time period specified in these rules, in any local rule or court order, or in any statute that does not specify a method of computing time.

(1) Period Stated in Days or a Longer Unit. When the period is stated in days or a longer unit of time:

(A) exclude the day of the event that triggers the period;

(B) count every day, including intermediate Saturdays, Sundays, and legal holidays; and

(C) include the last day of the period, but if the last day is a Saturday, Sunday, or legal holiday, the period continues to run until the end of the next day that is not a Saturday, Sunday, or legal holiday.

(2) Period Stated in Hours. When the period is stated in hours:

(A) begin counting immediately on the occurrence of the event that triggers the period;

(B) count every hour, including hours during intermediate Saturdays, Sundays, and legal holidays; and

(C) if the period would end on a Saturday, Sunday, or legal holiday, the period continues to run until the same time on the next day that is not a Saturday, Sunday, or legal holiday.

(3) Inaccessibility of the Clerk's Office. Unless the court orders otherwise, if the clerk's office is inaccessible:

(A) on the last day for filing under Rule 26(a)(1), then the time for filing is extended to the first accessible day that is not a Saturday, Sunday, or legal holiday; or

(B) during the last hour for filing under Rule 26(a)(2), then the time for filing is extended to the same time on the first accessible day that is not a Saturday, Sunday, or legal holiday.

(4) "Last Day" Defined. Unless a different time is set by a statute, local rule, or court order, the last day ends:

(A) for electronic filing in the district court, at midnight in the court's time zone;

(B) for electronic filing in the court of appeals, at midnight in the time zone of the circuit clerk's principal office;

(C) for filing under Rules 4(c)(1), 25(a)(2)(B), and 25(a)(2)(C)—and filing by mail under Rule 13(a)(2)—at the latest time for the method chosen for delivery to the post office, third-party commercial carrier, or prison mailing system; and

(D) for filing by other means, when the clerk's office is scheduled to close.

(5) "Next Day" Defined. The "next day" is determined by continuing to count forward when the period is measured after an event and backward when measured before an event.

(6) "Legal Holiday" Defined. "Legal holiday" means:

(A) the day set aside by statute for observing New Year's Day, Martin Luther King Jr.'s Birthday, Washington's Birthday, Memorial Day, Independence Day, Labor Day, Columbus Day, Veterans' Day, Thanksgiving Day, or Christmas Day;

(B) any day declared a holiday by the President or Congress; and

(C) for periods that are measured after an event, any other day declared a holiday by the state where either of the following is located: the district court that rendered the challenged judgment or order, or the circuit clerk's principal office.

(b) Extending Time. For good cause, the court may extend the time prescribed by these rules or by its order to perform any act, or may permit an act to be done after that time expires. But the court may not extend the time to file:

(1) a notice of appeal (except as authorized in Rule 4) or a petition for permission to appeal; or

(2) a notice of appeal from or a petition to enjoin, set aside, suspend, modify, enforce, or otherwise review an order of an administrative agency, board, commission, or officer of the United States, unless specifically authorized by law.

[Text of subdivision (c) effective until December 1, 2016, absent contrary Congressional action.]

(c) Additional Time after Service. When a party may or must act within a specified time after service, 3 days are added after the period would otherwise expire under Rule 26(a), unless the paper is delivered on the date of service stated in the proof of service. For purposes of this Rule 26(c), a paper that is served electronically is not treated as delivered on the date of service stated in the proof of service.

[Text of subdivision (c) effective December 1, 2016, absent contrary Congressional action.]

(c) Additional Time after Certain Kinds of Service. When a party may or must act within a specified time after being served, 3 days are added after the period would otherwise expire under Rule 26(a),

unless the paper is delivered on the date of service stated in the proof of service. For purposes of this Rule 26(c), a paper that is served electronically is treated as delivered on the date of service stated in the proof of service.

(As amended Mar. 1, 1971, eff. July 1, 1971; Mar. 10, 1986, eff. July 1, 1986; Apr. 25, 1989, eff. Dec. 1, 1989; Apr. 30, 1991, eff. Dec. 1, 1991; Apr. 23, 1996, eff. Dec. 1, 1996; Apr. 24, 1998, eff. Dec. 1, 1998; Apr. 29, 2002, eff. Dec. 1, 2002; Apr. 25, 2005, eff. Dec. 1, 2005; Mar. 26, 2009, eff. Dec. 1, 2009; Apr. 28, 2016, eff. Dec. 1, 2016, absent contrary Congressional action.)

RULE 26.1   CORPORATE DISCLOSURE STATEMENT

(a) Who Must File. Any nongovernmental corporate party to a proceeding in a court of appeals must file a statement that identifies any parent corporation and any publicly held corporation that owns 10% or more of its stock or states that there is no such corporation.

(b) Time for Filing; Supplemental Filing. A party must file the Rule 26.1(a) statement with the principal brief or upon filing a motion, response, petition, or answer in the court of appeals, whichever occurs first, unless a local rule requires earlier filing. Even if the statement has already been filed, the party's principal brief must include the statement before the table of contents. A party must supplement its statement whenever the information that must be disclosed under Rule 26.1(a) changes.

(c) Number of Copies. If the Rule 26.1(a) statement is filed before the principal brief, or if a supplemental statement is filed, the party must file an original and 3 copies unless the court requires a different number by local rule or by order in a particular case.

(Added Apr. 25, 1989, eff. Dec. 1, 1989; amended Apr. 30, 1991, eff. Dec. 1, 1991; Apr. 29, 1994, eff. Dec. 1, 1994; Apr. 24, 1998, eff. Dec. 1, 1998; Apr. 29, 2002, eff. Dec. 1, 2002.)

RULE 27.   MOTIONS

(a) In General.

(1) Application for Relief. An application for an order or other relief is made by motion unless these rules prescribe another form. A motion must be in writing unless the court permits otherwise.

(2) Contents of a Motion.

(A) Grounds and relief sought. A motion must state with particularity the grounds for the motion, the relief sought, and the legal argument necessary to support it.

(B) Accompanying documents.

(i) Any affidavit or other paper necessary to support a motion must be served and filed with the motion.

(ii) An affidavit must contain only factual information, not legal argument.

(iii) A motion seeking substantive relief must include a copy of the trial court's opinion or agency's decision as a separate exhibit.

(C) Documents barred or not required.

(i) A separate brief supporting or responding to a motion must not be filed.

(ii) A notice of motion is not required.

(iii) A proposed order is not required.

(3) Response.

(A) Time to file. Any party may file a response to a motion; Rule 27(a)(2) governs its contents. The response must be filed within 10 days after service of the motion unless the court shortens or extends the time. A motion authorized by Rules 8, 9, 18, or 41 may be granted before the 10–day period runs only if the court gives reasonable notice to the parties that it intends to act sooner.

(B) Request for affirmative relief. A response may include a motion for affirmative relief. The time to respond to the new motion, and to reply to that response, are governed by Rule 27(a)(3)(A) and (a)(4). The title of the response must alert the court to the request for relief.

(4) Reply to Response. Any reply to a response must be filed within 7 days after service of the response. A reply must not present matters that do not relate to the response.

(b) Disposition of a Motion for a Procedural Order. The court may act on a motion for a procedural order—including a motion under Rule 26(b)—at any time without awaiting a response, and may, by rule or by order in a particular case, authorize its clerk to act on specified types of procedural motions. A party adversely affected by the court's, or the clerk's, action may file a motion to reconsider, vacate, or modify that action. Timely opposition filed after the motion is granted in whole or in part does not constitute a request to reconsider, vacate, or modify the disposition; a motion requesting that relief must be filed.

(c) Power of a Single Judge to Entertain a Motion. A circuit judge may act alone on any motion, but may not dismiss or otherwise determine an appeal or other proceeding. A court of appeals may provide by rule or by order in a particular case that only the court may act on any motion or class of motions. The court may review the action of a single judge.

[Text of subdivision (d) effective until December 1, 2016, absent contrary Congressional action.]

(d) Form of Papers; Page Limits; and Number of Copies.

(1) Format.

(A) Reproduction. A motion, response, or reply may be reproduced by any process that yields a clear black image on light paper. The paper must be opaque and unglazed. Only one side of the paper may be used.

(B) Cover. A cover is not required, but there must be a caption that includes the case number, the name of the court, the title of the case, and a brief descriptive title indicating the purpose of the motion and identifying the party or parties for whom it is filed. If a cover is used, it must be white.

(C) Binding. The document must be bound in any manner that is secure, does not obscure the text, and permits the document to lie reasonably flat when open.

(D) Paper size, line spacing, and margins. The document must be on 8½ by 11 inch paper. The text must be double-spaced, but quotations more than two lines long may be indented and single-spaced. Headings and footnotes may be single-spaced. Margins must be at least one inch on all four sides. Page numbers may be placed in the margins, but no text may appear there.

(E) Typeface and type styles. The document must comply with the typeface requirements of Rule 32(a)(5) and the type-style requirements of Rule 32(a)(6).

(2) Page Limits. A motion or a response to a motion must not exceed 20 pages, exclusive of the corporate disclosure statement and accompanying documents authorized by Rule 27(a)(2)(B), unless the court permits or directs otherwise. A reply to a response must not exceed 10 pages.

(3) Number of Copies. An original and 3 copies must be filed unless the court requires a different number by local rule or by order in a particular case.

[Text of subdivision (d) effective December 1, 2016, absent contrary Congressional action.]

(d) Form of Papers; Length Limits; Number of Copies.

(1) Format.

(A) Reproduction. A motion, response, or reply may be reproduced by any process that yields a clear black image on light paper. The paper must be opaque and unglazed. Only one side of the paper may be used.

(B) Cover. A cover is not required, but there must be a caption that includes the case number, the name of the court, the title of the case, and a brief descriptive title indicating the purpose of the motion and identifying the party or parties for whom it is filed. If a cover is used, it must be white.

(C) Binding. The document must be bound in any manner that is secure, does not obscure the text, and permits the document to lie reasonably flat when open.

(D) Paper size, line spacing, and margins. The document must be on 8½ by 11 inch paper. The text must be double-spaced, but quotations more than two lines long may be indented and single-spaced. Headings and footnotes may be single-spaced. Margins must be at least one inch on all four sides. Page numbers may be placed in the margins, but no text may appear there.

(E) Typeface and type styles. The document must comply with the typeface requirements of Rule 32(a)(5) and the type-style requirements of Rule 32(a)(6).

(2) Length Limits. Except by the court's permission, and excluding the accompanying documents authorized by Rule 27(a)(2)(B):

(A) a motion or response to a motion produced using a computer must not exceed 5,200 words;

(B) a handwritten or typewritten motion or response to a motion must not exceed 20 pages;

(C) a reply produced using a computer must not exceed 2,600 words; and

(D) a handwritten or typewritten reply to a response must not exceed 10 pages.

(3) Number of Copies. An original and 3 copies must be filed unless the court requires a different number by local rule or by order in a particular case.

(e) Oral Argument. A motion will be decided without oral argument unless the court orders otherwise.

(As amended Apr. 30, 1979, eff. Aug. 1, 1979; Apr. 25, 1989, eff. Dec. 1, 1989; Apr. 29, 1994, eff. Dec. 1, 1994; Apr. 24, 1998, eff. Dec. 1, 1998; Apr. 29, 2002, eff. Dec. 1, 2002; Apr. 25, 2005, eff. Dec. 1, 2005; Mar. 26, 2009, eff. Dec. 1, 2009; Apr. 28, 2016, eff. Dec. 1, 2016, absent contrary Congressional action.)

RULE 28. BRIEFS

[Text of subdivision (a) effective until December 1, 2016, absent contrary Congressional action.]

(a) Appellant's Brief. The appellant's brief must contain, under appropriate headings and in the order indicated:

(1) a corporate disclosure statement if required by Rule 26.1;

(2) a table of contents, with page references;

(3) a table of authorities—cases (alphabetically arranged), statutes, and other authorities—with references to the pages of the brief where they are cited;

(4) a jurisdictional statement, including:

(A) the basis for the district court's or agency's subject-matter jurisdiction, with citations to applicable statutory provisions and stating relevant facts establishing jurisdiction;

(B) the basis for the court of appeals' jurisdiction, with citations to applicable statutory provisions and stating relevant facts establishing jurisdiction;

(C) the filing dates establishing the timeliness of the appeal or petition for review; and

(D) an assertion that the appeal is from a final order or judgment that disposes of all parties' claims, or information establishing the court of appeals' jurisdiction on some other basis;

(5) a statement of the issues presented for review;

(6) a concise statement of the case setting out the facts relevant to the issues submitted for review, describing the relevant procedural history, and identifying the rulings presented for review, with appropriate references to the record (see Rule 28(e));

(7) a summary of the argument, which must contain a succinct, clear, and accurate statement of the arguments made in the body of the brief, and which must not merely repeat the argument headings;

(8) the argument, which must contain:

(A) appellant's contentions and the reasons for them, with citations to the authorities and parts of the record on which the appellant relies; and

(B) for each issue, a concise statement of the applicable standard of review (which may appear in the discussion of the issue or under a separate heading placed before the discussion of the issues);

(9) a short conclusion stating the precise relief sought; and

(10) the certificate of compliance, if required by Rule 32(a)(7).

[Text of subdivision (a) effective December 1, 2016, absent contrary Congressional action.]

(a) Appellant's Brief. The appellant's brief must contain, under appropriate headings and in the order indicated:

(1) a corporate disclosure statement if required by Rule 26.1;

(2) a table of contents, with page references;

(3) a table of authorities—cases (alphabetically arranged), statutes, and other authorities—with references to the pages of the brief where they are cited;

(4) a jurisdictional statement, including:

　(A) the basis for the district court's or agency's subject-matter jurisdiction, with citations to applicable statutory provisions and stating relevant facts establishing jurisdiction;

　(B) the basis for the court of appeals' jurisdiction, with citations to applicable statutory provisions and stating relevant facts establishing jurisdiction;

　(C) the filing dates establishing the timeliness of the appeal or petition for review; and

　(D) an assertion that the appeal is from a final order or judgment that disposes of all parties' claims, or information establishing the court of appeals' jurisdiction on some other basis;

(5) a statement of the issues presented for review;

(6) a concise statement of the case setting out the facts relevant to the issues submitted for review, describing the relevant procedural history, and identifying the rulings presented for review, with appropriate references to the record (see Rule 28(e));

(7) a summary of the argument, which must contain a succinct, clear, and accurate statement of the arguments made in the body of the brief, and which must not merely repeat the argument headings;

(8) the argument, which must contain:

　(A) appellant's contentions and the reasons for them, with citations to the authorities and parts of the record on which the appellant relies; and

　(B) for each issue, a concise statement of the applicable standard of review (which may appear in the discussion of the issue or under a separate heading placed before the discussion of the issues);

(9) a short conclusion stating the precise relief sought; and

(10) the certificate of compliance, if required by Rule 32(g)(1).

(b) Appellee's Brief. The appellee's brief must conform to the requirements of Rule 28(a)(1)–(8) and (10), except that none of the following need appear unless the appellee is dissatisfied with the appellant's statement:

　(1) the jurisdictional statement;

(2) the statement of the issues;

(3) the statement of the case; and

(4) the statement of the standard of review.

(c) Reply Brief. The appellant may file a brief in reply to the appellee's brief. Unless the court permits, no further briefs may be filed. A reply brief must contain a table of contents, with page references, and a table of authorities—cases (alphabetically arranged), statutes, and other authorities—with references to the pages of the reply brief where they are cited.

(d) References to Parties. In briefs and at oral argument, counsel should minimize use of the terms "appellant" and "appellee." To make briefs clear, counsel should use the parties' actual names or the designations used in the lower court or agency proceeding, or such descriptive terms as "the employee," "the injured person," "the taxpayer," "the ship," "the stevedore."

(e) References to the Record. References to the parts of the record contained in the appendix filed with the appellant's brief must be to the pages of the appendix. If the appendix is prepared after the briefs are filed, a party referring to the record must follow one of the methods detailed in Rule 30(c). If the original record is used under Rule 30(f) and is not consecutively paginated, or if the brief refers to an unreproduced part of the record, any reference must be to the page of the original document. For example:

● Answer p. 7;

● Motion for Judgment p. 2;

● Transcript p. 231.

Only clear abbreviations may be used. A party referring to evidence whose admissibility is in controversy must cite the pages of the appendix or of the transcript at which the evidence was identified, offered, and received or rejected.

(f) Reproduction of Statutes, Rules, Regulations, etc. If the court's determination of the issues presented requires the study of statutes, rules, regulations, etc., the relevant parts must be set out in the brief or in an addendum at the end, or may be supplied to the court in pamphlet form.

(g) [Reserved]

(h) [Deleted]

(i) Briefs in a Case Involving Multiple Appellants or Appellees. In a case involving more than one appellant or appellee, including consolidated cases, any number of appellants or appellees may join in a brief, and any party may adopt by reference a part of another's brief. Parties may also join in reply briefs.

(j) Citation of Supplemental Authorities. If pertinent and significant authorities come to a party's attention after the party's brief has been filed—or after oral argument but before decision—a party may promptly advise the circuit clerk by letter, with a copy to all other parties, setting forth the citations. The letter must state the reasons for the supplemental citations, referring either to the page of the brief or to a point argued orally. The body of the letter must not exceed 350 words. Any response must be made promptly and must be similarly limited.

(As amended Apr. 30, 1979, eff. Aug. 1, 1979; Mar. 10, 1986, eff. July 1, 1986; Apr. 25, 1989, eff. Dec. 1, 1989; Apr. 30, 1991, eff. Dec. 1, 1991; Apr. 22, 1993, eff. Dec. 1, 1993; Apr. 29, 1994, eff. Dec. 1, 1994; Apr. 24, 1998, eff. Dec. 1, 1998; Apr. 29, 2002, eff. Dec. 1, 2002; Apr. 25, 2005, eff. Dec. 1, 2005; Apr. 16, 2013, eff. Dec. 1, 2013; Apr. 28, 2016, eff. Dec. 1, 2016, absent contrary Congressional action.)

RULE 28.1   CROSS–APPEALS

(a) Applicability. This rule applies to a case in which a cross-appeal is filed. Rules 28(a)-(c), 31(a)(1), 32(a)(2), and 32(a)(7)(A)-(B) do not apply to such a case, except as otherwise provided in this rule.

(b) Designation of Appellant. The party who files a notice of appeal first is the appellant for the purposes of this rule and Rules 30 and 34. If notices are filed on the same day, the plaintiff in the proceeding below is the appellant. These designations may be modified by the parties' agreement or by court order.

(c) Briefs. In a case involving a cross-appeal:

(1) Appellant's Principal Brief. The appellant must file a principal brief in the appeal. That brief must comply with Rule 28(a).

(2) Appellee's Principal and Response Brief. The appellee must file a principal brief in the cross-appeal and must, in the same brief, respond to the principal brief in the appeal. That appellee's brief must comply with Rule 28(a), except that the brief need not include a statement of the case unless the appellee is dissatisfied with the appellant's statement.

(3) Appellant's Response and Reply Brief. The appellant must file a brief that responds to the principal brief in the cross-appeal and may, in the same brief, reply to the response in the appeal. That brief must comply with Rule 28(a)(2)–(8) and (10), except that none of the following need appear unless the appellant is dissatisfied with the appellee's statement in the cross-appeal:

(A) the jurisdictional statement;

(B) the statement of the issues;

(C) the statement of the case; and

(D) the statement of the standard of review.

(4) Appellee's Reply Brief. The appellee may file a brief in reply to the response in the cross-appeal. That brief must comply with Rule 28(a)(2)–(3) and (10) and must be limited to the issues presented by the cross-appeal.

(5) No Further Briefs. Unless the court permits, no further briefs may be filed in a case involving a cross-appeal.

(d) Cover. Except for filings by unrepresented parties, the cover of the appellant's principal brief must be blue; the appellee's principal and response brief, red; the appellant's response and reply brief, yellow; the appellee's reply brief, gray; an intervenor's or amicus curiae's brief, green; and any supplemental brief, tan. The front cover of a brief must contain the information required by Rule 32(a)(2).

[Text of subdivision (e) effective until December 1, 2016, absent contrary Congressional action.]

(e) Length.

(1) Page Limitation. Unless it complies with Rule 28.1(e)(2) and (3), the appellant's principal brief must not exceed 30 pages; the appellee's principal and response brief, 35 pages; the appellant's response and reply brief, 30 pages; and the appellee's reply brief, 15 pages.

(2) Type-Volume Limitation.

(A) The appellant's principal brief or the appellant's response and reply brief is acceptable if:

(i) it contains no more than 14,000 words; or

(ii) it uses a monospaced face and contains no more than 1,300 lines of text.

(B) The appellee's principal and response brief is acceptable if:

(i) it contains no more than 16,500 words; or

(ii) it uses a monospaced face and contains no more than 1,500 lines of text.

(C) The appellee's reply brief is acceptable if it contains no more than half of the type volume specified in Rule 28.1(e)(2)(A).

(3) Certificate of Compliance. A brief submitted under Rule 28.1(e)(2) must comply with Rule 32(a)(7)(C).

[Text of subdivision (e) effective December 1, 2016, absent contrary Congressional action.]

(e) Length.

(1) Page Limitation. Unless it complies with Rule 28.1(e)(2), the appellant's principal brief must not exceed 30 pages; the appellee's principal and response brief, 35 pages; the appellant's response and reply brief, 30 pages; and the appellee's reply brief, 15 pages.

(2) Type-Volume Limitation.

(A) The appellant's principal brief or the appellant's response and reply brief is acceptable if it:

(i) contains no more than 13,000 words; or

(ii) uses a monospaced face and contains no more than 1,300 lines of text.

(B) The appellee's principal and response brief is acceptable if it:

(i) contains no more than 15,300 words; or

(ii) uses a monospaced face and contains no more than 1,500 lines of text.

(C) The appellee's reply brief is acceptable if it contains no more than half of the type volume specified in Rule 28.1(e)(2)(A).

(f) Time to Serve and File a Brief. Briefs must be served and filed as follows:

(1) the appellant's principal brief, within 40 days after the record is filed;

(2) the appellee's principal and response brief, within 30 days after the appellant's principal brief is served;

(3) the appellant's response and reply brief, within 30 days after the appellee's principal and response brief is served; and

(4) the appellee's reply brief, within 14 days after the appellant's response and reply brief is served, but at least 7 days before argument unless the court, for good cause, allows a later filing.

(As added April 25, 2005, eff. Dec. 1, 2005; amended Mar. 26, 2009, eff. Dec. 1, 2009; Apr. 16, 2013, eff. Dec. 1, 2013; Apr. 28, 2016, eff. Dec. 1, 2016, absent contrary Congressional action.)

RULE 29. BRIEF OF AN AMICUS CURIAE

[Text of Rule 29 effective until December 1, 2016, absent contrary Congressional action.]

(a) When Permitted. The United States or its officer or agency or a state may file an amicus-curiae brief without the consent of the parties or leave of court. Any other amicus curiae may file a brief only by leave of court or if the brief states that all parties have consented to its filing.

(b) Motion for Leave to File. The motion must be accompanied by the proposed brief and state:

(1) the movant's interest; and

(2) the reason why an amicus brief is desirable and why the matters asserted are relevant to the disposition of the case.

(c) Contents and Form. An amicus brief must comply with Rule 32. In addition to the requirements of Rule 32, the cover must identify the party or parties supported and indicate whether the brief supports affirmance or reversal. An amicus brief need

not comply with Rule 28, but must include the following:

(1) if the amicus curiae is a corporation, a disclosure statement like that required of parties by Rule 26.1;

(2) a table of contents, with page references;

(3) a table of authorities—cases (alphabetically arranged), statutes, and other authorities—with references to the pages of the brief where they are cited;

(4) a concise statement of the identity of the amicus curiae, its interest in the case, and the source of its authority to file;

(5) unless the amicus curiae is one listed in the first sentence of Rule 29(a), a statement that indicates whether:

(A) a party's counsel authored the brief in whole or in part;

(B) a party or a party's counsel contributed money that was intended to fund preparing or submitting the brief; and

(C) a person—other than the amicus curiae, its members, or its counsel—contributed money that was intended to fund preparing or submitting the brief and, if so, identifies each such person;

(6) an argument, which may be preceded by a summary and which need not include a statement of the applicable standard of review; and

(7) a certificate of compliance, if required by Rule 32(a)(7).

(d) Length. Except by the court's permission, an amicus brief may be no more than one-half the maximum length authorized by these rules for a party's principal brief. If the court grants a party permission to file a longer brief, that extension does not affect the length of an amicus brief.

(e) Time for Filing. An amicus curiae must file its brief, accompanied by a motion for filing when necessary, no later than 7 days after the principal brief of the party being supported is filed. An amicus curiae that does not support either party must file its brief no later than 7 days after the appellant's or petitioner's principal brief is filed. A court may grant leave for later filing, specifying the time within which an opposing party may answer.

(f) Reply Brief. Except by the court's permission, an amicus curiae may not file a reply brief.

(g) Oral Argument. An amicus curiae may participate in oral argument only with the court's permission.

[Text of Rule 29 effective December 1, 2016, absent contrary Congressional action.]

(a) During Initial Consideration of a Case on the Merits.

(1) Applicability. This Rule 29(a) governs amicus filings during a court's initial consideration of a case on the merits.

(2) When Permitted. The United States or its officer or agency or a state may file an amicus-curiae brief without the consent of the parties or leave of court. Any other amicus curiae may file a brief only by leave of court or if the brief states that all parties have consented to its filing.

(3) Motion for Leave to File. The motion must be accompanied by the proposed brief and state:

(A) the movant's interest; and

(B) the reason why an amicus brief is desirable and why the matters asserted are relevant to the disposition of the case.

(4) Contents and Form. An amicus brief must comply with Rule 32. In addition to the requirements of Rule 32, the cover must identify the party or parties supported and indicate whether the brief supports affirmance or reversal. An amicus brief need not comply with Rule 28, but must include the following:

(A) if the amicus curiae is a corporation, a disclosure statement like that required of parties by Rule 26.1;

(B) a table of contents, with page references;

(C) a table of authorities—cases (alphabetically arranged), statutes, and other authorities— with references to the pages of the brief where they are cited;

(D) a concise statement of the identity of the amicus curiae, its interest in the case, and the source of its authority to file;

(E) unless the amicus curiae is one listed in the first sentence of Rule 29(a)(2), a statement that indicates whether:

(i) a party's counsel authored the brief in whole or in part;

(ii) a party or a party's counsel contributed money that was intended to fund preparing or submitting the brief; and

(iii) a person—other than the amicus curiae, its members, or its counsel— contributed money that was intended to fund preparing or submitting the brief and, if so, identifies each such person;

(F) an argument, which may be preceded by a summary and which need not include a statement of the applicable standard of review; and

(G) a certificate of compliance under Rule 32(g)(1), if length is computed using a word or line limit.

(5) Length. Except by the court's permission, an amicus brief may be no more than one-half the maximum length authorized by these rules for a party's principal brief. If the court grants a party permission to file a longer brief, that extension does not affect the length of an amicus brief.

(6) Time for Filing. An amicus curiae must file its brief, accompanied by a motion for filing when necessary, no later than 7 days after the principal brief of the party being supported is filed. An amicus curiae that does not support either party must file its brief no later than 7 days after the appellant's or petitioner's principal brief is filed. A court may grant leave for later filing, specifying the time within which an opposing party may answer.

(7) Reply Brief. Except by the court's permission, an amicus curiae may not file a reply brief.

(8) Oral Argument. An amicus curiae may participate in oral argument only with the court's permission.

(b) During Consideration of Whether to Grant Rehearing.

(1) Applicability. This Rule 29(b) governs amicus filings during a court's consideration of whether to grant panel rehearing or rehearing en banc, unless a local rule or order in a case provides otherwise.

(2) When Permitted. The United States or its officer or agency or a state may file an amicus-curiae brief without the consent of the parties or leave of court. Any other amicus curiae may file a brief only by leave of court.

(3) Motion for Leave to File. Rule 29(a)(3) applies to a motion for leave.

(4) Contents, Form, and Length. Rule 29(a)(4) applies to the amicus brief. The brief must not exceed 2,600 words.

(5) Time for Filing. An amicus curiae supporting the petition for rehearing or supporting neither party must file its brief, accompanied by a motion for filing when necessary, no later than 7 days after the petition is filed. An amicus curiae opposing the petition must file its brief, accompanied by a motion for filing when necessary, no later than the date set by the court for the response.

(As amended Apr. 24, 1998, eff. Dec. 1, 1998; Apr. 28, 2010, eff. Dec. 1, 2010; Apr. 28, 2016, eff. Dec. 1, 2016, absent contrary Congressional action.)

RULE 30. APPENDIX TO THE BRIEFS

(a) Appellant's Responsibility.

(1) Contents of the Appendix. The appellant must prepare and file an appendix to the briefs containing:

   (A) the relevant docket entries in the proceeding below;

   (B) the relevant portions of the pleadings, charge, findings, or opinion;

   (C) the judgment, order, or decision in question; and

   (D) other parts of the record to which the parties wish to direct the court's attention.

(2) Excluded Material. Memoranda of law in the district court should not be included in the appendix unless they have independent relevance. Parts of the record may be relied on by the court or the parties even though not included in the appendix.

(3) Time to File; Number of Copies. Unless filing is deferred under Rule 30(c), the appellant must file 10 copies of the appendix with the brief and must serve one copy on counsel for each party separately represented. An unrepresented party proceeding in forma pauperis must file 4 legible copies with the clerk, and one copy must be served on counsel for each separately represented party. The court may by local rule or by order in a particular case require the filing or service of a different number.

(b) All Parties' Responsibilities.

(1) Determining the Contents of the Appendix. The parties are encouraged to agree on the contents of the appendix. In the absence of an agreement, the appellant must, within 14 days after the record is filed, serve on the appellee a designation of the parts of the record the appellant intends to include in the appendix and a statement of the issues the appellant intends to present for review. The appellee may, within 14 days after receiving the designation, serve on the appellant a designation of additional parts to which it wishes to direct the court's attention. The appellant must include the designated parts in the appendix. The parties must not engage in unnecessary designation of parts of the record, because the entire record is available to the court. This paragraph applies also to a cross-appellant and a cross-appellee.

(2) Costs of Appendix. Unless the parties agree otherwise, the appellant must pay the cost of the appendix. If the appellant considers parts of the record designated by the appellee to be unnecessary, the appellant may advise the appellee, who must then advance the cost of including those parts. The cost of the appendix is a taxable cost. But if any party causes unnecessary parts of the record to be included in the appendix, the court may impose the cost of those parts on that party. Each circuit must, by local rule, provide for sanctions against attorneys who unreasonably and vexatiously increase litigation costs by including unnecessary material in the appendix.

(c) Deferred Appendix.

(1) Deferral Until After Briefs Are Filed. The court may provide by rule for classes of cases or by order in a particular case that preparation of the appendix may be deferred until after the briefs have been filed and that the appendix may be filed 21 days after the appellee's brief is served. Even though the filing of the appendix may be deferred, Rule 30(b) applies; except that a party must designate the parts of the record it wants included in the appendix when it serves its brief, and need not include a statement of the issues presented.

(2) References to the Record.

   (A) If the deferred appendix is used, the parties may cite in their briefs the pertinent pages of the record. When the appendix is prepared, the record pages cited in the briefs must be indicated by inserting record page numbers, in brackets, at places in the appendix where those pages of the record appear.

   (B) A party who wants to refer directly to pages of the appendix may serve and file copies of the brief within the time required by Rule 31(a), containing appropriate references to pertinent pages of the record. In that event, within 14 days after the appendix is filed, the party must serve and file copies of the brief, containing references to the pages of the appendix in place of or in addition to the references to the pertinent pages of the record. Except for the correction of typographical errors, no other changes may be made to the brief.

(d) Format of the Appendix. The appendix must begin with a table of contents identifying the page at which each part begins. The relevant docket entries must follow the table of contents. Other parts of the record must follow chronologically. When pages from the transcript of proceedings are placed in the appendix, the transcript page numbers must be shown in brackets immediately before the included pages. Omissions in the text of papers or of the transcript must be indicated by asterisks. Immaterial formal matters (captions, subscriptions, acknowledgments, etc.) should be omitted.

(e) Reproduction of Exhibits. Exhibits designated for inclusion in the appendix may be reproduced in a separate volume, or volumes, suitably indexed. Four copies must be filed with the appendix, and one copy must be served on counsel for each separately represented party. If a transcript of a proceeding before an administrative agency, board, commission, or officer was used in a district-court action and has been designated for inclusion in the appendix, the transcript must be placed in the appendix as an exhibit.

(f) Appeal on the Original Record Without an Appendix. The court may, either by rule for all cases or classes of cases or by order in a particular case, dispense with the appendix and permit an appeal to proceed on the original record with any copies of the record, or relevant parts, that the court may order the parties to file.

(As amended Mar. 30, 1970, eff. July 1, 1970; Mar. 10, 1986, eff. July 1, 1986; Apr. 30, 1991, eff. Dec. 1, 1991; Apr. 29, 1994, eff. Dec. 1, 1994; Apr. 24, 1998, eff. Dec. 1, 1998; Mar. 26, 2009, eff. Dec. 1, 2009.)

RULE 31.   SERVING AND FILING BRIEFS

(a) Time to Serve and File a Brief.

(1) The appellant must serve and file a brief within 40 days after the record is filed. The appellee must serve and file a brief within 30 days after the appellant's brief is served. The appellant may serve and file a reply brief within 14 days after service of the appellee's brief but a reply brief must be filed at least 7 days before argument, unless the court, for good cause, allows a later filing.

(2) A court of appeals that routinely considers cases on the merits promptly after the briefs are filed may shorten the time to serve and file briefs, either by local rule or by order in a particular case.

(b) Number of Copies. Twenty-five copies of each brief must be filed with the clerk and 2 copies must be served on each unrepresented party and on counsel for each separately represented party. An unrepresented party proceeding in forma pauperis must file 4 legible copies with the clerk, and one copy must be served on each unrepresented party and on counsel for each separately represented party. The court may by local rule or by order in a particular case require the filing or service of a different number.

(c) Consequence of Failure to File. If an appellant fails to file a brief within the time provided by this rule, or within an extended time, an appellee may move to dismiss the appeal. An appellee who fails to file a brief will not be heard at oral argument unless the court grants permission.

(As amended Mar. 30, 1970, eff. July 1, 1970; Mar. 10, 1986, eff. July 1, 1986; Apr. 29, 1994, eff. Dec. 1, 1994; Apr. 24, 1998, eff. Dec. 1, 1998; Apr. 29, 2002, eff. Dec. 1, 2002; Mar. 26, 2009, eff. Dec. 1, 2009.)

RULE 32.   FORM OF BRIEFS, APPENDICES, AND OTHER PAPERS

[Text of subdivision (a) effective until December 1, 2016, absent contrary Congressional action.]

(a) Form of a Brief.

(1) Reproduction.

(A) A brief may be reproduced by any process that yields a clear black image on light paper. The paper must be opaque and unglazed. Only one side of the paper may be used.

(B) Text must be reproduced with a clarity that equals or exceeds the output of a laser printer.

(C) Photographs, illustrations, and tables may be reproduced by any method that results in a good copy of the original; a glossy finish is acceptable if the original is glossy.

(2) Cover. Except for filings by unrepresented parties, the cover of the appellant's brief must be blue; the appellee's, red; an intervenor's or amicus curiae's, green; any reply brief, gray; and any supplemental brief, tan. The front cover of a brief must contain:

(A) the number of the case centered at the top;

(B) the name of the court;

(C) the title of the case (see Rule 12(a));

(D) the nature of the proceeding (e.g., Appeal, Petition for Review) and the name of the court, agency, or board below;

(E) the title of the brief, identifying the party or parties for whom the brief is filed; and

(F) the name, office address, and telephone number of counsel representing the party for whom the brief is filed.

(3) Binding. The brief must be bound in any manner that is secure, does not obscure the text, and permits the brief to lie reasonably flat when open.

(4) Paper Size, Line Spacing, and Margins. The brief must be on 8½ by 11 inch paper. The text must be double-spaced, but quotations more than two lines long may be indented and single-spaced. Headings and footnotes may be single-spaced. Margins must be at least one inch on all four sides. Page numbers may be placed in the margins, but no text may appear there.

(5) Typeface. Either a proportionally spaced or a monospaced face may be used.

(A) A proportionally spaced face must include serifs, but sans-serif type may be used in headings and captions. A proportionally spaced face must be 14–point or larger.

(B) A monospaced face may not contain more than 10½ characters per inch.

(6) Type Styles. A brief must be set in a plain, roman style, although italics or boldface may be used for emphasis. Case names must be italicized or underlined.

(7) Length.

(A) Page limitation. A principal brief may not exceed 30 pages, or a reply brief 15 pages, unless it complies with Rule 32(a)(7)(B) and (C).

(B) Type-volume limitation.

(i) A principal brief is acceptable if:

- it contains no more than 14,000 words; or

- it uses a monospaced face and contains no more than 1,300 lines of text.

(ii) A reply brief is acceptable if it contains no more than half of the type volume specified in Rule 32(a)(7)(B)(i).

(iii) Headings, footnotes, and quotations count toward the word and line limitations. The corporate disclosure statement, table of contents, table of citations, statement with respect to oral argument, any addendum containing statutes, rules or regulations, and any certificates of counsel do not count toward the limitation.

(C) Certificate of compliance.

(i) A brief submitted under Rules 28.1(e)(2) or 32(a)(7)(B) must include a certificate by the attorney, or an unrepresented party, that the brief complies with the type-volume limitation. The person preparing the certificate may rely on the word or line count of the word-processing system used to prepare the brief. The certificate must state either:

- the number of words in the brief; or

- the number of lines of monospaced type in the brief.

(ii) Form 6 in the Appendix of Forms is a suggested form of a certificate of compliance. Use of Form 6 must be regarded as sufficient to meet the requirements of Rules 28.1(e)(3) and 32(a)(7)(C)(i).

[Text of subdivision (a) effective December 1, 2016, absent contrary Congressional action.]

(a) Form of a Brief.

(1) Reproduction.

(A) A brief may be reproduced by any process that yields a clear black image on light paper. The paper must be opaque and unglazed. Only one side of the paper may be used.

(B) Text must be reproduced with a clarity that equals or exceeds the output of a laser printer.

(C) Photographs, illustrations, and tables may be reproduced by any method that results in a good copy of the original; a glossy finish is acceptable if the original is glossy.

(2) Cover. Except for filings by unrepresented parties, the cover of the appellant's brief must be blue; the appellee's, red; an intervenor's or amicus curiae's, green; any reply brief, gray; and any supplemental brief, tan. The front cover of a brief must contain:

(A) the number of the case centered at the top;

(B) the name of the court;

(C) the title of the case (see Rule 12(a));

(D) the nature of the proceeding (e.g., Appeal, Petition for Review) and the name of the court, agency, or board below;

(E) the title of the brief, identifying the party or parties for whom the brief is filed; and

(F) the name, office address, and telephone number of counsel representing the party for whom the brief is filed.

(3) Binding. The brief must be bound in any manner that is secure, does not obscure the text, and permits the brief to lie reasonably flat when open.

(4) Paper Size, Line Spacing, and Margins. The brief must be on 8½ by 11 inch paper. The text must be double-spaced, but quotations more than two lines long may be indented and single-spaced. Headings and footnotes may be single-spaced. Margins must be at least one inch on all four sides. Page numbers may be placed in the margins, but no text may appear there.

(5) Typeface. Either a proportionally spaced or a monospaced face may be used.

(A) A proportionally spaced face must include serifs, but sans-serif type may be used in headings and captions. A proportionally spaced face must be 14–point or larger.

(B) A monospaced face may not contain more than 10½ characters per inch.

(6) Type Styles. A brief must be set in a plain, roman style, although italics or boldface may be used for emphasis. Case names must be italicized or underlined.

(7) Length.

(A) Page Limitation. A principal brief may not exceed 30 pages, or a reply brief 15 pages, unless it complies with Rule 32(a)(7)(B).

(B) Type-Volume Limitation.

(i) A principal brief is acceptable if it:

- contains no more than 13,000 words; or

- uses a monospaced face and contains no more than 1,300 lines of text.

(ii) A reply brief is acceptable if it contains no more than half of the type volume specified in Rule 32(a)(7)(B)(i).

(b) Form of an Appendix. An appendix must comply with Rule 32(a)(1), (2), (3), and (4), with the following exceptions:

(1) The cover of a separately bound appendix must be white.

(2) An appendix may include a legible photocopy of any document found in the record or of a printed judicial or agency decision.

(3) When necessary to facilitate inclusion of odd-sized documents such as technical drawings, an appendix may be a size other than 8½ by 11 inches, and need not lie reasonably flat when opened.

(c) Form of Other Papers.

(1) Motion. The form of a motion is governed by Rule 27(d).

(2) Other Papers. Any other paper, including a petition for panel rehearing and a petition for hearing or rehearing en banc, and any response to such a petition, must be reproduced in the manner prescribed by Rule 32(a), with the following exceptions:

(A) A cover is not necessary if the caption and signature page of the paper together contain the information required by Rule 32(a)(2). If a cover is used, it must be white.

(B) Rule 32(a)(7) does not apply.

(d) Signature. Every brief, motion, or other paper filed with the court must be signed by the party filing the paper or, if the party is represented, by one of the party's attorneys.

[Text of subdivision (e) effective until December 1, 2016, absent contrary Congressional action.]

(e) Local Variation. Every court of appeals must accept documents that comply with the form requirements of this rule. By local rule or order in a particular case a court of appeals may accept documents that do not meet all of the form requirements of this rule.

[Text of subdivision (e) effective December 1, 2016, absent contrary Congressional action.]

(e) Local Variation. Every court of appeals must accept documents that comply with the form requirements of this rule and the length limits set by these rules. By local rule or order in a particular case, a court of appeals may accept documents that do not meet all the form requirements of this rule or the length limits set by these rules.

[Text of subdivision (f) effective December 1, 2016, absent contrary Congressional action.]

(f) Items Excluded from Length. In computing any length limit, headings, footnotes, and quotations count toward the limit but the following items do not:

- the cover page;
- a corporate disclosure statement;
- a table of contents;
- a table of citations;
- a statement regarding oral argument;
- an addendum containing statutes, rules, or regulations;
- certificates of counsel;
- the signature block;
- the proof of service; and
- any item specifically excluded by these rules or by local rule.

[Text of subdivision (g) effective December 1, 2016, absent contrary Congressional action.]

(g) Certificate of Compliance.

(1) Briefs and Papers That Require a Certificate. A brief submitted under Rules 28.1(e)(2), 29(b)(4), or 32(a)(7)(B)—and a paper submitted under Rules 5(c)(1), 21(d)(1), 27(d)(2)(A), 27(d)(2)(C), 35(b)(2)(A), or 40(b)(1)—must include a certificate by the attorney, or an unrepresented party, that the document complies with the type-volume limitation. The person preparing the certificate may rely on the word or line count of the word-processing system used to prepare the document. The certificate must state the number of words—or the number of lines of monospaced type—in the document.

(2) Acceptable Form. Form 6 in the Appendix of Forms meets the requirements for a certificate of compliance.

(As amended Apr. 24, 1998, eff. Dec. 1, 1998; Apr. 29, 2002, eff. Dec. 1, 2002; Apr. 25, 2005, eff. Dec. 1, 2005; Apr. 28, 2016, eff. Dec. 1, 2016, absent contrary Congressional action.)

RULE 32.1 CITING JUDICIAL DISPOSITIONS

(a) Citation Permitted. A court may not prohibit or restrict the citation of federal judicial opinions, orders, judgments, or other written dispositions that have been:

(i) designated as "unpublished," "not for publication," "non-precedential," "not precedent," or the like; and

(ii) issued on or after January 1, 2007.

(b) Copies Required. If a party cites a federal judicial opinion, order, judgment, or other written disposition that is not available in a publicly accessible electronic database, the party must file and serve a copy of that opinion, order, judgment, or disposition with the brief or other paper in which it is cited.

(Added Apr. 12, 2006, eff. Dec. 1, 2006.)

RULE 33. APPEAL CONFERENCES

The court may direct the attorneys—and, when appropriate, the parties—to participate in one or more conferences to address any matter that may aid in disposing of the proceedings, including simplifying the issues and discussing settlement. A judge or other person designated by the court may preside over the conference, which may be conducted in person or by telephone. Before a settlement conference, the attorneys must consult with their clients and obtain as much authority as feasible to settle the case. The court may, as a result of the conference, enter an order controlling the course of the proceedings or implementing any settlement agreement.

(As amended Apr. 29, 1994, eff. Dec. 1, 1994; Apr. 24, 1998, eff. Dec. 1, 1998.)

RULE 34. ORAL ARGUMENT

(a) In General.

(1) Party's Statement. Any party may file, or a court may require by local rule, a statement explaining why oral argument should, or need not, be permitted.

(2) Standards. Oral argument must be allowed in every case unless a panel of three judges who have examined the briefs and record unanimously agrees that oral argument is unnecessary for any of the following reasons:

(A) the appeal is frivolous;

(B) the dispositive issue or issues have been authoritatively decided; or

(C) the facts and legal arguments are adequately presented in the briefs and record, and the decisional process would not be significantly aided by oral argument.

(b) Notice of Argument; Postponement. The clerk must advise all parties whether oral argument will be scheduled, and, if so, the date, time, and place for it, and the time allowed for each side. A motion to postpone the argument or to allow longer argument must be filed reasonably in advance of the hearing date.

(c) Order and Contents of Argument. The appellant opens and concludes the argument. Counsel must not read at length from briefs, records, or authorities.

(d) Cross-Appeals and Separate Appeals. If there is a cross-appeal, Rule 28.1(b) determines which party is the appellant and which is the appellee for purposes of oral argument. Unless the court directs otherwise, a cross-appeal or separate appeal must be argued when the initial appeal is argued. Separate parties should avoid duplicative argument.

(e) Nonappearance of a Party. If the appellee fails to appear for argument, the court must hear appellant's argument. If the appellant fails to appear for argument, the court may hear the appellee's argument. If neither party appears, the case will be decided on the briefs, unless the court orders otherwise.

(f) Submission on Briefs. The parties may agree to submit a case for decision on the briefs, but the court may direct that the case be argued.

(g) Use of Physical Exhibits at Argument; Removal. Counsel intending to use physical exhibits other than documents at the argument must arrange to place them in the courtroom on the day of the argument before the court convenes. After the argument, counsel must remove the exhibits from the courtroom, unless the court directs otherwise. The clerk may destroy or dispose of the exhibits if counsel does not reclaim them within a reasonable time after the clerk gives notice to remove them.

(As amended Apr. 30, 1979, eff. Aug. 1, 1979; Mar. 10, 1986, eff. July 1, 1986; Apr. 30, 1991, eff. Dec. 1, 1991; Apr. 22, 1993, eff. Dec. 1, 1993; Apr. 24, 1998, eff. Dec. 1, 1998; Apr. 25, 2005, eff. Dec. 1, 2005.)

RULE 35. EN BANC DETERMINATION

(a) When Hearing or Rehearing En Banc May Be Ordered. A majority of the circuit judges who are in regular active service and who are not disqualified may order that an appeal or other proceeding be heard or reheard by the court of appeals en banc. An en banc hearing or rehearing is not favored and ordinarily will not be ordered unless:

(1) en banc consideration is necessary to secure or maintain uniformity of the court's decisions; or

(2) the proceeding involves a question of exceptional importance.

[Text of subdivision (b) effective until December 1, 2016, absent contrary Congressional action.]

(b) Petition for Hearing or Rehearing En Banc. A party may petition for a hearing or rehearing en banc.

(1) The petition must begin with a statement that either:

(A) the panel decision conflicts with a decision of the United States Supreme Court or of the court to which the petition is addressed (with citation to the conflicting case or cases) and consideration by the full court is therefore necessary to secure and maintain uniformity of the court's decisions; or

(B) the proceeding involves one or more questions of exceptional importance, each of which must be concisely stated; for example, a petition may assert that a proceeding presents a question of exceptional importance if it involves an issue on which the panel decision conflicts with the authoritative decisions of other United States Courts of Appeals that have addressed the issue.

(2) Except by the court's permission, a petition for an en banc hearing or rehearing must not exceed 15 pages, excluding material not counted under Rule 32.

(3) For purposes of the page limit in Rule 35(b)(2), if a party files both a petition for panel rehearing and a petition for rehearing en banc, they are considered a single document even if they are filed separately, unless separate filing is required by local rule.

[Text of subdivision (b) effective December 1, 2016, absent contrary Congressional action.]

(b) Petition for Hearing or Rehearing En Banc. A party may petition for a hearing or rehearing en banc.

(1) The petition must begin with a statement that either:

(A) the panel decision conflicts with a decision of the United States Supreme Court or of the court to which the petition is addressed (with citation to the conflicting case or cases) and consideration by the full court is therefore necessary to secure and maintain uniformity of the court's decisions; or

(B) the proceeding involves one or more questions of exceptional importance, each of which must be concisely stated; for example, a petition may assert that a proceeding presents a question of exceptional importance if it involves an issue on which the panel decision conflicts with the authoritative decisions of other United States Courts of Appeals that have addressed the issue.

(2) Except by the court's permission:

(A) a petition for an en banc hearing or rehearing produced using a computer must not exceed 3,900 words; and

(B) a handwritten or typewritten petition for an en banc hearing or rehearing must not exceed 15 pages.

(3) For purposes of the limits in Rule 35(b)(2), if a party files both a petition for panel rehearing and a petition for rehearing en banc, they are considered a single document even if they are filed separately, unless separate filing is required by local rule.

(c) Time for Petition for Hearing or Rehearing En Banc. A petition that an appeal be heard initially en banc must be filed by the date when the appellee's brief is due. A petition for a rehearing en banc must be filed within the time prescribed by Rule 40 for filing a petition for rehearing.

(d) Number of Copies. The number of copies to be filed must be prescribed by local rule and may be altered by order in a particular case.

(e) Response. No response may be filed to a petition for an en banc consideration unless the court orders a response.

(f) Call for a Vote. A vote need not be taken to determine whether the case will be heard or reheard en banc unless a judge calls for a vote.

(As amended Apr. 30, 1979, eff. Aug. 1, 1979; Apr. 29, 1994, eff. Dec. 1, 1994; Apr. 24, 1998, eff. Dec. 1, 1998; Apr. 25, 2005, eff. Dec. 1, 2005; Apr. 28, 2016, eff. Dec. 1, 2016, absent contrary Congressional action.)

RULE 36. ENTRY OF JUDGMENT; NOTICE

(a) Entry. A judgment is entered when it is noted on the docket. The clerk must prepare, sign, and enter the judgment:

(1) after receiving the court's opinion—but if settlement of the judgment's form is required, after final settlement; or

(2) if a judgment is rendered without an opinion, as the court instructs.

(b) Notice. On the date when judgment is entered, the clerk must serve on all parties a copy of the opinion—or the judgment, if no opinion was written—and a notice of the date when the judgment was entered.

(As amended Apr. 24, 1998, eff. Dec. 1, 1998; Apr. 29, 2002, eff. Dec. 1, 2002.)

RULE 37. INTEREST ON JUDGMENT

(a) When the Court Affirms. Unless the law provides otherwise, if a money judgment in a civil case is affirmed, whatever interest is allowed by law is payable from the date when the district court's judgment was entered.

(b) When the Court Reverses. If the court modifies or reverses a judgment with a direction that a money judgment be entered in the district court, the mandate must contain instructions about the allowance of interest.

(As amended Apr. 24, 1998, eff. Dec. 1, 1998.)

RULE 38. FRIVOLOUS APPEAL— DAMAGES AND COSTS

If a court of appeals determines that an appeal is frivolous, it may, after a separately filed motion or notice from the court and reasonable opportunity to respond, award just damages and single or double costs to the appellee.

(As amended Apr. 29, 1994, eff. Dec. 1, 1994; Apr. 24, 1998, eff. Dec. 1, 1998.)

RULE 39. COSTS

(a) Against Whom Assessed. The following rules apply unless the law provides or the court orders otherwise:

 (1) if an appeal is dismissed, costs are taxed against the appellant, unless the parties agree otherwise;

 (2) if a judgment is affirmed, costs are taxed against the appellant;

 (3) if a judgment is reversed, costs are taxed against the appellee;

 (4) if a judgment is affirmed in part, reversed in part, modified, or vacated, costs are taxed only as the court orders.

(b) Costs For and Against the United States. Costs for or against the United States, its agency, or officer will be assessed under Rule 39(a) only if authorized by law.

(c) Costs of Copies. Each court of appeals must, by local rule, fix the maximum rate for taxing the cost of producing necessary copies of a brief or appendix, or copies of records authorized by Rule 30(f). The rate must not exceed that generally charged for such work in the area where the clerk's office is located and should encourage economical methods of copying.

(d) Bill of Costs: Objections; Insertion in Mandate.

 (1) A party who wants costs taxed must—within 14 days after entry of judgment—file with the circuit clerk, with proof of service, an itemized and verified bill of costs.

 (2) Objections must be filed within 14 days after service of the bill of costs, unless the court extends the time.

 (3) The clerk must prepare and certify an itemized statement of costs for insertion in the mandate, but issuance of the mandate must not be delayed for taxing costs. If the mandate issues before costs are finally determined, the district clerk must—upon the circuit clerk's request—add the statement of costs, or any amendment of it, to the mandate.

(e) Costs on Appeal Taxable in the District Court. The following costs on appeal are taxable in the district court for the benefit of the party entitled to costs under this rule:

 (1) the preparation and transmission of the record;

 (2) the reporter's transcript, if needed to determine the appeal;

 (3) premiums paid for a supersedeas bond or other bond to preserve rights pending appeal; and

 (4) the fee for filing the notice of appeal.

(As amended Apr. 30, 1979, eff. Aug. 1, 1979; Mar. 10, 1986, eff. July 1, 1986; Apr. 24, 1998, eff. Dec. 1, 1998; Mar. 26, 2009, eff. Dec. 1, 2009.)

RULE 40. PETITION FOR PANEL REHEARING

(a) Time to File; Contents; Answer; Action by the Court if Granted.

 (1) Time. Unless the time is shortened or extended by order or local rule, a petition for panel rehearing may be filed within 14 days after entry of judgment. But in a civil case, unless an order shortens or extends the time, the petition may be filed by any party within 45 days after entry of judgment if one of the parties is:

  (A) the United States;

  (B) a United States agency;

  (C) a United States officer or employee sued in an official capacity; or

  (D) a current or former United States officer or employee sued in an individual capacity for an act or omission occurring in connection with duties performed on the United States' behalf—including all instances in which the United States represents that person when the court of appeals' judgment is entered or files the petition for that person.

 (2) Contents. The petition must state with particularity each point of law or fact that the petitioner believes the court has overlooked or misapprehended and must argue in support of the petition. Oral argument is not permitted.

 (3) Answer. Unless the court requests, no answer to a petition for panel rehearing is permitted. But ordinarily rehearing will not be granted in the absence of such a request.

 (4) Action by the Court. If a petition for panel rehearing is granted, the court may do any of the following:

  (A) make a final disposition of the case without reargument;

  (B) restore the case to the calendar for reargument or resubmission; or

  (C) issue any other appropriate order.

[Text of subdivision (b) effective until December 1, 2016, absent contrary Congressional action.]

(b) Form of Petition; Length. The petition must comply in form with Rule 32. Copies must be served and filed as Rule 31 prescribes. Unless the court permits or a local rule provides otherwise, a petition for panel rehearing must not exceed 15 pages.

[Text of subdivision (b) effective December 1, 2016, absent contrary Congressional action.]

(b) Form of Petition; Length. The petition must comply in form with Rule 32. Copies must be served and filed as Rule 31 prescribes. Except by the court's permission:

(1) a petition for panel rehearing produced using a computer must not exceed 3,900 words; and

(2) a handwritten or typewritten petition for panel rehearing must not exceed 15 pages.

(As amended Apr. 30, 1979, eff. Aug. 1, 1979; Apr. 29, 1994, eff. Dec. 1, 1994; Apr. 24, 1998, eff. Dec. 1, 1998; Apr. 26, 2011, eff. Dec. 1, 2011; Apr. 28, 2016, eff. Dec. 1, 2016, absent contrary Congressional action.)

RULE 41. MANDATE: CONTENTS; ISSUANCE AND EFFECTIVE DATE; STAY

(a) Contents. Unless the court directs that a formal mandate issue, the mandate consists of a certified copy of the judgment, a copy of the court's opinion, if any, and any direction about costs.

(b) When Issued. The court's mandate must issue 7 days after the time to file a petition for rehearing expires, or 7 days after entry of an order denying a timely petition for panel rehearing, petition for rehearing en banc, or motion for stay of mandate, whichever is later. The court may shorten or extend the time.

(c) Effective Date. The mandate is effective when issued.

(d) Staying the Mandate.

(1) On Petition for Rehearing or Motion. The timely filing of a petition for panel rehearing, petition for rehearing en banc, or motion for stay of mandate, stays the mandate until disposition of the petition or motion, unless the court orders otherwise.

(2) Pending Petition for Certiorari.

(A) A party may move to stay the mandate pending the filing of a petition for a writ of certiorari in the Supreme Court. The motion must be served on all parties and must show that the certiorari petition would present a substantial question and that there is good cause for a stay.

(B) The stay must not exceed 90 days, unless the period is extended for good cause or unless the party who obtained the stay files a petition for the writ and so notifies the circuit clerk in writing within the period of the stay. In that case, the stay continues until the Supreme Court's final disposition.

(C) The court may require a bond or other security as a condition to granting or continuing a stay of the mandate.

(D) The court of appeals must issue the mandate immediately when a copy of a Supreme Court order denying the petition for writ of certiorari is filed.

(As amended Apr. 29, 1994, eff. Dec. 1, 1994; Apr. 24, 1998, eff. Dec. 1, 1998; Apr. 29, 2002, eff. Dec. 1, 2002; Mar. 26, 2009, eff. Dec. 1, 2009.)

RULE 42. VOLUNTARY DISMISSAL

(a) Dismissal in the District Court. Before an appeal has been docketed by the circuit clerk, the district court may dismiss the appeal on the filing of a stipulation signed by all parties or on the appellant's motion with notice to all parties.

(b) Dismissal in the Court of Appeals. The circuit clerk may dismiss a docketed appeal if the parties file a signed dismissal agreement specifying how costs are to be paid and pay any fees that are due. But no mandate or other process may issue without a court order. An appeal may be dismissed on the appellant's motion on terms agreed to by the parties or fixed by the court.

(As amended Apr. 24, 1998, eff. Dec. 1, 1998.)

RULE 43. SUBSTITUTION OF PARTIES

(a) Death of a Party.

(1) After Notice of Appeal Is Filed. If a party dies after a notice of appeal has been filed or while a proceeding is pending in the court of appeals, the decedent's personal representative may be substituted as a party on motion filed with the circuit clerk by the representative or by any party. A party's motion must be served on the representative in accordance with Rule 25. If the decedent has no representative, any party may suggest the death on the record, and the court of appeals may then direct appropriate proceedings.

(2) Before Notice of Appeal Is Filed—Potential Appellant. If a party entitled to appeal dies before filing a notice of appeal, the decedent's personal representative—or, if there is no personal representative, the decedent's attorney of record— may file a notice of appeal within the time prescribed by these rules. After the notice of appeal is filed, substitution must be in accordance with Rule 43(a)(1).

(3) Before Notice of Appeal Is Filed—Potential Appellee. If a party against whom an appeal may be taken dies after entry of a judgment or order in the district court, but before a notice of appeal is filed, an appellant may proceed as if the death had not occurred. After the notice of appeal is filed, substitution must be in accordance with Rule 43(a)(1).

(b) Substitution for a Reason Other Than Death. If a party needs to be substituted for any reason other than death, the procedure prescribed in Rule 43(a) applies.

(c) Public Officer: Identification; Substitution.

(1) Identification of Party. A public officer who is a party to an appeal or other proceeding in an official capacity may be described as a party by the public officer's official title rather than by name. But the court may require the public officer's name to be added.

(2) Automatic Substitution of Officeholder. When a public officer who is a party to an appeal or other proceeding in an official capacity dies, resigns, or otherwise ceases to hold office, the action does not abate. The public officer's successor is automatically substituted as a party. Proceedings following the substitution are to be in the name of the substituted party, but any misnomer that does not affect the substantial rights of the parties may be disregarded. An order of substitution may be entered at any time, but failure to enter an order does not affect the substitution.

(As amended Mar. 10, 1986, eff. July 1, 1986; Apr. 24, 1998, eff. Dec. 1, 1998.)

RULE 44. CASE INVOLVING A CONSTITUTIONAL QUESTION WHEN THE UNITED STATES OR THE RELEVANT STATE IS NOT A PARTY

(a) Constitutional Challenge to Federal Statute. If a party questions the constitutionality of an Act of Congress in a proceeding in which the United States or its agency, officer, or employee is not a party in an official capacity, the questioning party must give written notice to the circuit clerk immediately upon the filing of the record or as soon as the question is raised in the court of appeals. The clerk must then certify that fact to the Attorney General.

(b) Constitutional Challenge to State Statute. If a party questions the constitutionality of a statute of a State in a proceeding in which that State or its agency, officer, or employee is not a party in an official capacity, the questioning party must give written notice to the circuit clerk immediately upon the filing of the record or as soon as the question is raised in the court of appeals. The clerk must then certify that fact to the attorney general of the State.

(As amended Apr. 24, 1998, eff. Dec. 1, 1998; Apr. 29, 2002, eff. Dec. 1, 2002.)

RULE 45. CLERK'S DUTIES

(a) General Provisions.

(1) Qualifications. The circuit clerk must take the oath and post any bond required by law. Neither the clerk nor any deputy clerk may practice as an attorney or counselor in any court while in office.

(2) When Court Is Open. The court of appeals is always open for filing any paper, issuing and returning process, making a motion, and entering an order. The clerk's office with the clerk or a deputy in attendance must be open during business hours on all days except Saturdays, Sundays, and legal holidays. A court may provide by local rule or by order that the clerk's office be open for specified hours on Saturdays or on legal holidays other than New Year's Day, Martin Luther King, Jr.'s Birthday, Washington's Birthday, Memorial Day, Independence Day, Labor Day, Columbus Day, Veterans' Day, Thanksgiving Day, and Christmas Day.

(b) Records.

(1) The Docket. The circuit clerk must maintain a docket and an index of all docketed cases in the manner prescribed by the Director of the Administrative Office of the United States Courts. The clerk must record all papers filed with the clerk and all process, orders, and judgments.

(2) Calendar. Under the court's direction, the clerk must prepare a calendar of cases awaiting argument. In placing cases on the calendar for argument, the clerk must give preference to appeals in criminal cases and to other proceedings and appeals entitled to preference by law.

(3) Other Records. The clerk must keep other books and records required by the Director of the Administrative Office of the United States Courts, with the approval of the Judicial Conference of the United States, or by the court.

(c) Notice of an Order or Judgment. Upon the entry of an order or judgment, the circuit clerk must immediately serve a notice of entry on each party, with a copy of any opinion, and must note the date of service on the docket. Service on a party represented by counsel must be made on counsel.

(d) Custody of Records and Papers. The circuit clerk has custody of the court's records and papers. Unless the court orders or instructs otherwise, the clerk must not permit an original record or paper to be taken from the clerk's office. Upon disposition of the case, original papers constituting the record on appeal or review must be returned to the court or agency from which they were received. The clerk must preserve a copy of any brief, appendix, or other paper that has been filed.

(As amended Mar. 1, 1971, eff. July 1, 1971; Mar. 10, 1986, eff. July 1, 1986; Apr. 24, 1998, eff. Dec. 1, 1998; Apr. 29, 2002, eff. Dec. 1, 2002; Apr. 25, 2005, eff. Dec. 1, 2005.)

RULE 46. ATTORNEYS

(a) Admission to the Bar.

(1) Eligibility. An attorney is eligible for admission to the bar of a court of appeals if that attorney is of good moral and professional character and is admitted to practice before the Supreme Court of the United States, the highest court of a state, another United States court of appeals, or a United States district court (including the district courts for Guam, the Northern Mariana Islands, and the Virgin Islands).

(2) Application. An applicant must file an application for admission, on a form approved by the court that contains the applicant's personal statement showing eligibility for membership. The applicant must subscribe to the following oath or affirmation:

"I, _____, do solemnly swear [or affirm] that I will conduct myself as an attorney and counselor of this court, uprightly and according to law; and that I will support the Constitution of the United States."

(3) Admission Procedures. On written or oral motion of a member of the court's bar, the court will act on the application. An applicant may be admitted by oral motion in open court. But, unless the court orders otherwise, an applicant need not appear before the court to be admitted. Upon admission, an applicant must pay the clerk the fee prescribed by local rule or court order.

(b) Suspension or Disbarment.

(1) Standard. A member of the court's bar is subject to suspension or disbarment by the court if the member:

(A) has been suspended or disbarred from practice in any other court; or

(B) is guilty of conduct unbecoming a member of the court's bar.

(2) Procedure. The member must be given an opportunity to show good cause, within the time prescribed by the court, why the member should not be suspended or disbarred.

(3) Order. The court must enter an appropriate order after the member responds and a hearing is held, if requested, or after the time prescribed for a response expires, if no response is made.

(c) Discipline. A court of appeals may discipline an attorney who practices before it for conduct unbe-

coming a member of the bar or for failure to comply with any court rule. First, however, the court must afford the attorney reasonable notice, an opportunity to show cause to the contrary, and, if requested, a hearing.

(As amended Mar. 10, 1986, eff. July 1, 1986; Apr. 24, 1998, eff. Dec. 1, 1998.)

RULE 47. LOCAL RULES BY COURTS OF APPEALS

(a) Local Rules.

(1) Each court of appeals acting by a majority of its judges in regular active service may, after giving appropriate public notice and opportunity for comment, make and amend rules governing its practice. A generally applicable direction to parties or lawyers regarding practice before a court must be in a local rule rather than an internal operating procedure or standing order. A local rule must be consistent with—but not duplicative of—Acts of Congress and rules adopted under 28 U.S.C. § 2072 and must conform to any uniform numbering system prescribed by the Judicial Conference of the United States. Each circuit clerk must send the Administrative Office of the United States Courts a copy of each local rule and internal operating procedure when it is promulgated or amended.

(2) A local rule imposing a requirement of form must not be enforced in a manner that causes a party to lose rights because of a nonwillful failure to comply with the requirement.

(b) Procedure When There Is No Controlling Law. A court of appeals may regulate practice in a particular case in any manner consistent with federal law, these rules, and local rules of the circuit. No sanction or other disadvantage may be imposed for noncompliance with any requirement not in federal law, federal rules, or the local circuit rules unless the alleged violator has been furnished in the particular case with actual notice of the requirement.

(As amended Apr. 27, 1995, eff. Dec. 1, 1995; Apr. 24, 1998, eff. Dec. 1, 1998.)

RULE 48. MASTERS

(a) Appointment; Powers. A court of appeals may appoint a special master to hold hearings, if necessary, and to recommend factual findings and disposition in matters ancillary to proceedings in the court. Unless the order referring a matter to a master specifies or limits the master's powers, those powers include, but are not limited to, the following:

(1) regulating all aspects of a hearing;

(2) taking all appropriate action for the efficient performance of the master's duties under the order;

(3) requiring the production of evidence on all matters embraced in the reference; and

(4) administering oaths and examining witnesses and parties.

(b) Compensation. If the master is not a judge or court employee, the court must determine the master's compensation and whether the cost is to be charged to any party.

(As amended Apr. 29, 1994, eff. Dec. 1, 1994; Apr. 24, 1998, eff. Dec. 1, 1998.)

APPENDIX OF FORMS

FORM 1. NOTICE OF APPEAL TO A COURT OF APPEALS FROM A JUDGMENT OR ORDER OF A DISTRICT COURT

[Text of Form 1 effective until December 1, 2016, absent contrary Congressional action.]

United States District Court for the _____
District of _____
File Number _____

A.B., Plaintiff	)	
	)	
v.	)	Notice of Appeal
	)	
C.D., Defendant	)	

Notice is hereby given that [____ (here name all parties taking the appeal) ____, (plaintiffs) (defendants) in the above named case,*] hereby appeal to the United States Court of Appeals for the _____ Circuit (from the final judgment) (from an order (describing it)) entered in this action on the _____ day of _____, 20___.

(s) _____

Attorney for [_____]

[Address:_____]

* See Rule 3(c) for permissible ways of identifying appellants.

FORM 1. NOTICE OF APPEAL TO A COURT OF APPEALS FROM A JUDGMENT OR ORDER OF A DISTRICT COURT

[Text of Form 1 effective December 1, 2016, absent contrary Congressional action.]

United States District Court for the _____
District of _____
File Number _____

A.B., Plaintiff	)	
	)	
v.	)	*Notice of Appeal*
	)	
C.D., Defendant	)	

Notice is hereby given that [___ (here name all parties taking the appeal) ___, (plaintiffs) (defendants) in the above named case,*] hereby appeal to the United States Court of Appeals for the _____ Circuit (from the final judgment) (from an order (describing it)) entered in this action on the _____ day of _____, 20___.

(s) _____
Attorney for [_____]
[Address:_____]

[Note to inmate filers: If you are an inmate confined in an institution and you seek the timing benefit of Fed. R. App. P. 4(c)(1), complete Form 7 (Declaration of Inmate Filing) and file that declaration along with this Notice of Appeal.]

* See Rule 3(c) for permissible ways of identifying appellants.

(As amended Apr. 22, 1993, eff. Dec. 1, 1993; Mar. 27, 2003, eff. Dec. 1, 2003; Apr. 28, 2016, eff. Dec. 1, 2016, absent contrary Congressional action.)

FORM 2. NOTICE OF APPEAL TO A COURT OF APPEALS FROM A DECISION OF THE UNITED STATES TAX COURT

UNITED STATES TAX COURT

Washington, D.C.

A.B., *Petitioner*	)
	)
v.	) Docket No. _____
	)
Commissioner of Internal	)
Revenue, Respondent	)

Notice of Appeal

Notice is hereby given that [____ here name all parties taking the appeal [1] ____], hereby appeals to the United States Court of Appeals for the _____ Circuit from (that part of) the decision of this court entered in the above captioned proceeding on the _____ day of _____, 20__ (relating to _____).

(s) _____

Counsel for [_____]

[Address:_____]

(As amended Apr. 22, 1993, eff. Dec. 1, 1993; Mar. 27, 2003, eff. Dec. 1, 2003.)

[1] See Rule 3(c) for permissible ways of identifying appellants.

FORM 3. PETITION FOR REVIEW OF ORDER OF AN AGENCY, BOARD, COMMISSION OR OFFICER

United States Court of Appeals for the _____ Circuit

A.B., Petitioner　　　　　　　　)
　　　　　　　　　　　　　　　)
　　　　　　　v.　　　　　　　)　　Petition for Review
XYZ Commission, Respondent　　)

[___(here name all parties bringing the petition[1])___] hereby petitions the court for review of the Order of the XYZ Commission (describe the order) entered on _____, 20___.

　　　　　　　　　　　　　　　[(s)] _____
　　　　　　　　　　　　　　　　　Attorney for Petitioners
　　　　　　　　　　　　　　　　　Address:_____

(As amended Apr. 22, 1993, eff. Dec. 1, 1993; Mar. 27, 2003, eff. Dec. 1, 2003.)

1 See Rule 15.

164

FORM 4. AFFIDAVIT ACCOMPANYING MOTION FOR PERMISSION TO APPEAL IN FORMA PAUPERIS

UNITED STATES DISTRICT COURT
for the
< _____ > DISTRICT OF < _____ >

<Name(s) of plaintiff(s)>,	)
	)
Plaintiff(s)	)
	)
v.	)
	)
	) Case No. <Number>
<Name(s) of defendant(s)>,	)
	)
Defendant(s)	)
	)

Affidavit in Support of Motion

I swear or affirm under penalty of perjury that, because of my poverty, I cannot prepay the docket fees of my appeal or post a bond for them. I believe I am entitled to redress. I swear or affirm under penalty of perjury under United States laws that my answers on this form are true and correct. (28 U.S.C. § 1746; 18 U.S.C. § 1621.)

Signed: _____

Instructions

Complete all questions in this application and then sign it. Do not leave any blanks: if the answer to a question is "0," "none," or "not applicable (N/A)," write in that response. If you need more space to answer a question or to explain your answer, attach a separate sheet of paper identified with your name, your case's docket number, and the question number.

Date: _____

My issues on appeal are:

1. *For both you and your spouse estimate the average amount of money received from each of the following sources during the past 12 months. Adjust any amount that was received weekly, biweekly, quarterly, semiannually, or annually to show the monthly rate. Use gross amounts, that is, amounts before any deductions for taxes or otherwise.*

Income source	Average monthly amount during the past 12 months		Amount expected next month	
	You	Spouse	You	Spouse
Employment	$_____	$_____	$_____	$_____
Self-employment	$_____	$_____	$_____	$_____
Income from real property (such as rental income)	$_____	$_____	$_____	$_____
Interest and dividends	$_____	$_____	$_____	$_____
Gifts	$_____	$_____	$_____	$_____
Alimony	$_____	$_____	$_____	$_____
Child support	$_____	$_____	$_____	$_____
Retirement (such as social security, pensions, annuities, insurance)	$_____	$_____	$_____	$_____
Disability (such as social security, insurance payments)	$_____	$_____	$_____	$_____
Unemployment payments	$_____	$_____	$_____	$_____
Public-assistance (such as welfare)	$_____	$_____	$_____	$_____
Other (specify): _____	$_____	$_____	$_____	$_____

Total monthly
income: $_____ $_____ $_____ $_____

2. *List your employment history for the past two years, most recent employer first. (Gross monthly pay is before taxes or other deductions.)*

Employer	Address	Dates of employment	Gross monthly pay
_____	_____	_____	_____
_____	_____	_____	_____

3. *List your spouse's employment history for the past two years, most recent employer first. (Gross monthly pay is before taxes or other deductions.)*

Employer	Address	Dates of employment	Gross monthly pay
_____	_____	_____	_____
_____	_____	_____	_____

4. *How much cash do you and your spouse have? $_____*
Below, state any money you or your spouse have in bank accounts or in any other financial institution.

Financial institution	Type of account	Amount you have	Amount your spouse has
_____	_____	$_____	$_____
_____	_____	$_____	$_____
_____	_____	$_____	$_____

If you are a prisoner seeking to appeal a judgment in a civil action or proceeding, you must attach a statement certified by the appropriate institutional officer showing all receipts, expenditures, and balances during the last six months in your institutional accounts. If you have multiple accounts, perhaps because you have been in multiple institutions, attach one certified statement of each account.

5. *List the assets, and their values, which you own or your spouse owns. Do not list clothing and ordinary household furnishings.*

Home	(Value)	Other real estate	(Value)	Motor vehicle #1	(Value)
_____		_____		Make & year: _____	
_____		_____		Model:	
				Registration #: _____	

Motor vehicle #2	(Value)	Other assets	(Value)	Other assets	(Value)
Make & year: _____		_____		_____	
Model: _____		_____		_____	
Registration #: _____		_____		_____	

6. *State every person, business, or organization owing you or your spouse money, and the amount owed.*

Person owing you or your spouse money	Amount owed to you	Amount owed to your spouse
_____	_____	_____
_____	_____	_____

7. *State the persons who rely on you or your spouse for support.*

Name [or, if under 18, initials only]	Relationship	Age
_____	_____	_____
_____	_____	_____

8. *Estimate the average monthly expenses of you and your family. Show separately the amounts paid by your spouse. Adjust any payments that are made weekly, biweekly, quarterly, semiannually, or annually to show the monthly rate.*

	You	Your Spouse
Rent or home-mortgage payment (include lot rented for mobile home)	$_____	$_____
Are real-estate taxes included? ☐ Yes ☐ No		
Is property insurance included? ☐ Yes ☐ No		
Utilities (electricity, heating fuel, water, sewer, and Telephone)	$_____	$_____
Home maintenance (repairs and upkeep)	$_____	$_____
Food	$_____	$_____
Clothing	$_____	$_____
Laundry and dry-cleaning	$_____	$_____
Medical and dental expenses	$_____	$_____
Transportation (not including motor vehicle payments)	$_____	$_____
Recreation, entertainment, newspapers, magazines, etc.	$_____	$_____
Insurance (not deducted from wages or included in mortgage payments)		
Homeowner's or renter's:	$_____	$_____
Life:	$_____	$_____
Health:	$_____	$_____
Motor Vehicle:	$_____	$_____
Other: _____	$_____	$_____
Taxes (not deducted from wages or included in mortgage payments) (specify): __	$_____	$_____
Installment payments		
Motor Vehicle:	$_____	$_____
Credit card (name): _____	$_____	$_____
Department store (name): _____	$_____	$_____
Other: _____	$_____	$_____
Alimony, maintenance, and support paid to others	$_____	$_____
Regular expenses for operation of business, profession, or farm (attach detailed statement)	$_____	$_____
Other (specify): _____	$_____	$_____
Total monthly expenses:	$_____	$_____

9. *Do you expect any major changes to your monthly income or expenses or in your assets or liabilities during the next 12 months?*
☐ Yes ☐ No   If yes, describe on an attached sheet.

10. *Have you spent—or will you be spending—any money for expenses or attorney fees in connection with this lawsuit?* ☐ Yes ☐ No
If yes, how much? $_____

11. *Provide any other information that will help explain why you cannot pay the docket fees for your appeal.*

12.   *State the city and state of your legal residence.*

Your daytime phone number: (___) _____
Your age: _____ *Your years of schooling:* _____
Last four digits of your social-security number: _____

(As amended Apr. 24, 1998, eff. Dec. 1, 1998; Apr. 28, 2010, eff. Dec. 1, 2010; Apr. 16, 2013, eff. Dec. 1, 2013.)

FORM 5. NOTICE OF APPEAL TO A COURT OF APPEALS FROM A JUDGMENT OR ORDER OF A DISTRICT COURT OR A BANKRUPTCY APPELLATE PANEL

[Text of Form 5 effective until December 1, 2016, absent contrary Congressional action.]

United States District Court for the ....

District of ....

In re   )
)
.....................................,)
    Debtor   )
)   File No...........
.....................................,)
    Plaintiff   )
)
    v.   )
)
.....................................,)
    Defendant   )

Notice of Appeal to
United States Court of Appeals
for the .... Circuit

........................., the plaintiff [or defendant or other party] appeals to the United States Court of Appeals for the .... Circuit from the final judgment [or order or decree] of the district court for the district of .... [or bankruptcy appellate panel of the .... circuit], entered in this case on ...., 20.... [here describe the judgment, order, or decree] ....

The parties to the judgment [or order or decree] appealed from and the names and addresses of their respective attorneys are as follows:

Dated ....

Signed ....

Attorney for Appellant

Address: ....

....

FORM 5. NOTICE OF APPEAL TO A COURT OF APPEALS FROM A JUDGMENT OR ORDER OF A DISTRICT COURT OR A BANKRUPTCY APPELLATE PANEL

[Text of Form 5 effective December 1, 2016, absent contrary Congressional action.]

United States District Court for the . . . .

District of . . . .

In re   )

)

. . . . ,   )

           Debtor   )

)   File No.. . . . .

. . . . ,   )

          Plaintiff   )

)

             v.   )

)

. . . . ,   )

         Defendant   )

Notice of Appeal to
United States Court of Appeals
for the . . . . Circuit

. . . . , the plaintiff [or defendant or other party] appeals to the United States Court of Appeals for the . . . . Circuit from the final judgment [or order or decree] of the district court for the district of . . . . [or bankruptcy appellate panel of the . . . . circuit], entered in this case on . . . . , 20. . . . [here describe the judgment, order, or decree] . . . .

The parties to the judgment [or order or decree] appealed from and the names and addresses of their respective attorneys are as follows:

                              Dated   . . . .

                              Signed   . . . .

                                         Attorney for Appellant

                              Address: . . . .

                                  . . . .

*[**Note to inmate filers:** If you are an inmate confined in an institution and you seek the timing benefit of Fed. R. App. P. 4(c)(1), complete Form 7 (Declaration of Inmate Filing) and file that declaration along with this Notice of Appeal.]*

(Added Apr. 25, 1989, eff. Dec. 1, 1989; amended Mar. 27, 2003, eff. Dec. 1, 2003; Apr. 28, 2016, eff. Dec. 1, 2016, absent contrary Congressional action.)

FORM 6.　CERTIFICATE OF COMPLIANCE WITH RULE 32(A)

[Text of Form 6 effective until December 1, 2016, absent contrary Congressional action.]

Certificate of Compliance With Type-Volume Limitation, Typeface Requirements, and Type Style Requirements

1.　This brief complies with the type-volume limitation of Fed. R. App. P. 32(a)(7)(B) because:

☐ this brief contains [*state the number of*] words, excluding the parts of the brief exempted by Fed. R. App. P. 32(a)(7)(B)(iii), *or*

☐ this brief uses a monospaced typeface and contains [*state the number of*] lines of text, excluding the parts of the brief exempted by Fed. R. App. P. 32(a)(7)(B)(iii).

2.　This brief complies with the typeface requirements of Fed. R. App. P. 32(a)(5) and the type style requirements of Fed. R. App. P. 32(a)(6) because:

☐ this brief has been prepared in a proportionally spaced typeface using [*state name and version of word processing program*] in [*state font size and name of type style*], *or*

☐ this brief has been prepared in a monospaced typeface using [*state name and version of word processing program*] with [*state number of characters per inch and name of type style*].

(s)_____

Attorney for _____

Dated: _____

FORM 6. CERTIFICATE OF COMPLIANCE WITH TYPE–VOLUME LIMIT

[Text of Form 6 effective December 1, 2016, absent contrary Congressional action.]

Certificate of Compliance With Type-Volume Limit, Typeface Requirements, and Type-Style Requirements

1. This document complies with [the type-volume limit of Fed. R. App. P. [*insert Rule citation; e.g., 32(a)(7)(B)*]] [the word limit of Fed. R. App. P. [*insert Rule citation; e.g., 5(c)(1)*]] because, excluding the parts of the document exempted by Fed. R. App. P. 32(f) [and [*insert applicable Rule citation, if any*]]:

☐ this document contains [*state the number of*] words, **or**

☐ this brief uses a monospaced typeface and contains [*state the number of*] lines of text.).

2. This document complies with the typeface requirements of Fed. R. App. P. 32(a)(5) and the type-style requirements of Fed. R. App. P. 32(a)(6) because:

☐ this document has been prepared in a proportionally spaced typeface using [*state name and version of word processing program*] in [*state font size and name of type style*], **or**

☐ this document has been prepared in a monospaced typeface using [*state name and version of word-processing program*] with [*state number of characters per inch and name of type*].

(s)_____

Attorney for _____

Dated: _____

(Added Apr. 29, 2002, eff. Dec. 1, 2002; amended Apr. 28, 2016, eff. Dec. 1, 2016, absent contrary Congressional action.)

FORM 7.   DECLARATION OF INMATE FILING

[Text of Form 7 effective December 1, 2016, absent contrary Congressional action.]

[insert name of court; for example,
United States District Court for the District of Minnesota]

A.B., *Plaintiff*	)	
	)	
v.	)	*Case No.*
	)	
C.D., *Defendant*	)	

I am an inmate confined in an institution. Today, _____ *[insert date]*, I am depositing the _____ *[insert title of document; for example, "notice of appeal"]* in this case in the institution's internal mail system. First-class postage is being prepaid either by me or by the institution on my behalf.

I declare under penalty of perjury that the foregoing is true and correct (see 28 U.S.C. § 1746; 18 U.S.C. § 1621).

Sign your name here _____

Signed on _____ *[insert date]*

[Note to inmate filers: If your institution has a system designed for legal mail, you must use that system in order to receive the timing benefit of Fed. R. App. P. 4(c)(1) or Fed. R. App. P. 25(a)(2)(C).]

(Added Apr. 28, 2016, eff. Dec. 1, 2016, absent contrary Congressional action.)

APPENDIX

[Text of Appendix effective December 1, 2016, absent contrary Congressional action.]

This chart summarizes the length limits stated in the Federal Rules of Appellate Procedure. Please refer to the rules for precise requirements, and bear in mind the following:

- In computing these limits, you can exclude the items listed in Rule 32(f).
- If you use a word limit or a line limit (other than the word limit in Rule 28(j)), you must file the certificate required by Rule 32(g).
- For the limits in Rules 5, 21, 27, 35, and 40:

  - You must use the word limit if you produce your document on a computer; and

  - You must use the page limit if you handwrite your document or type it on a typewriter.

- For the limits in Rules 28.1, 29(a)(5), and 32:

  - You may use the word limit or page limit, regardless of how you produce the document; or

  - You may use the line limit if you type or print your document with a monospaced typeface. A typeface is monospaced when each character occupies the same amount of horizontal space.

	Rule	Document type	Word limit	Page limit	Line limit
Permission to appeal	5(c)	• Petition for permission to appeal • Answer in opposition • Cross–petition	5,200	20	Not applicable
Extraordinary writs	21(d)	• Petition for writ of mandamus or prohibition or other extraordinary writ • Answer	7,800	30	Not applicable
Motions	27(d)(2)	• Motion • Response to a motion	5,200	20	Not applicable
	27(d)(2)	• Reply to a response to a motion	2,600	10	Not applicable
Parties' briefs (where no cross–appeal)	32(a)(7)	• Principal brief	13,000	30	1,300
	32(a)(7)	• Reply brief	6,500	15	650
Parties' briefs (where cross–appeal)	28.1(e)	• Appellant's principal brief • Appellant's response and reply brief	13,000	30	1,300
	28.1(e)	• Appellee's principal and response brief	15,300	35	1,500
	28.1(e)	• Appellee's reply brief	6,500	15	650
Party's supplemental letter	28(j)	• Letter citing supplemental authorities	350	Not applicable	Not applicable

	Rule	Document type	Word limit	Page limit	Line limit
Amicus briefs	29(a)(5)	• Amicus brief during initial consideration of case on merits	One–half the length set by the Appellate Rules for a party's principal brief	One–half the length set by the Appellate Rules for a party's principal brief	One–half the length set by the Appellate Rules for a party's principal brief
	29(b)(4)	• Amicus brief during consideration of whether to grant rehearing	2,600	Not applicable	Not applicable
Rehearing and en banc filings	35(b)(2) & 40(b)	• Petition for hearing en banc • Petition for panel rehearing; petition for rehearing en banc	3,900	15	Not applicable

(Added Apr. 28, 2016, eff. Dec. 1, 2016, absent contrary Congressional action.)

INDEX TO
FEDERAL RULES OF APPELLATE PROCEDURE

UNITED STATES COURT OF APPEALS
FOR THE
THIRD CIRCUIT

Including Amendments Received Through
June 1, 2016

THIRD CIRCUIT LOCAL APPELLATE RULES

THIRD CIRCUIT LOCAL APPELLATE RULES

RULE 1.0   SCOPE AND TITLE OF RULES

1.1   Scope and Organization of Rules

The following Local Appellate Rules (L.A.R.) are adopted by the United States Court of Appeals for the Third Circuit as supplementary to the Federal Rules of Appellate Procedure (FRAP) and apply to procedure in this court. The numbering of the Local Appellate Rules has been organized to follow the numbering system of the Federal Rules of Appellate Procedure in order to increase public accessibility to the Rules. Where a local rule has no counterpart in the Federal Rules of Appellate Procedure it is classified as a Miscellaneous Rule. The Miscellaneous Local Appellate Rules begin with Rule 101.0.

Source: 1988 Court Rule 1.1

Cross-References: 28 U.S.C. § 2072; FRAP 1, 47

Committee Comments: The Local Appellate Rules bind all litigants in this court. Each Local Appellate Rule is numbered to correspond to its counterpart in the Federal Rules, *e.g.*, Local Appellate Rule 1.0 corresponds to Federal Rule of Appellate Procedure 1. Cross-references are provided for convenience and are not intended to be exhaustive. Committee Comments are provided by the court's Rules Committee and are intended to guide, but not bind, litigants in this court. The 1988 Local Rules were substantially revised in 1995. Unless otherwise noted, a rule was enacted in 1995. Substantive amendments made after 1995 and new rules adopted after 1995 are noted in the Committee Comments.

1.2   Title; Citation Form

These rules are to be known as the Third Circuit Local Appellate Rules, and cited as 3d Cir. L.A.R. ____. ____ (2008).

Source: None

Cross-Reference: FRAP 1

Committee Comments: The Local Rules Project of the Judicial Conference Committee on Rules and Practice recommends that all courts of appeals follow a uniform numbering and citation system, for ease of reference and indexing of local rules. This court follows the recommendation of the Local Rules Project.

[Effective December 15, 2008.]

RULE 3.0   APPEAL AS OF RIGHT—HOW TAKEN

3.1   Notice to Trial Judge; Opinion in Support of Order

No later than 30 days after the docketing of a notice of appeal, the trial judge may file and transmit to the parties a written opinion or a written amplification of a prior written or oral recorded ruling or opinion. Failure to give notice of the appeal to the trial judge will not affect the jurisdiction of this court.

Source: 1988 Court Rules 8.4

Cross–References: FRAP 3, 24, Form 1, Form 3

Committee Comments: A district court may properly prepare an opinion or memorandum explaining a decision after an appeal is taken. The rule is not intended to inhibit or discourage district courts from preparing opinions as they presently do. To the contrary, the rule was designed to provide more flexibility. Prior Court Rule 8.4 was amended in 1995 to apply to all appellants, not simply pro se habeas corpus petitioners. Otherwise, no substantive change from prior Court Rule 8.4 was intended. This rule does not authorize a trial judge to change a prior ruling except as provided by F.R.C.P. 59(e). For procedures under F.R.C.P. 60(b) when a case is on appeal, see *Venen v. Sweet*, 758 F.2d 117, 120 (3d Cir. 1985). The rule was amended in 2008 to change the time from 15 to 30 days. A requirement to notify the district court judge of the filing of a notice of appeal was deleted in 2008 because the district court's automated docketing system (CM/ECF) will do so.

3.2   Joint Notice of Appeal

When parties have filed a joint notice of appeal, only one appeal will be docketed and only one docketing fee paid. Parties filing a joint notice of appeal must file a single consolidated brief and appendix.

Source: None

Cross–References: FRAP 3(b), 28(i), 31

Committee Comments: New provision in 1995.

3.3   Payment of Fees

(a) If a proceeding is docketed without prepayment of the applicable docketing fee, the appellant must pay the fee within 14 days after docketing. If the appellant fails to do so, the clerk is authorized to dismiss the appeal.

(b) If an action has been dismissed by the district court pursuant to 28 U.S.C. § 1915 as frivolous or malicious, or if the district court certifies pursuant to § 1915(a) and FRAP 24(a) that an appeal is not taken in good faith, the appellant may either pay the applicable docketing fee or file a motion to proceed in forma pauperis within 14 days after docketing the appeal. If appellant fails to either pay the applicable docketing fee or file the motion to proceed in forma pauperis and any required supporting documents, the clerk is authorized to dismiss the appeal 30 days after docketing of the appeal.

Source: 1988 Court Rule 28.1

Cross–References: 28 U.S.C. § 1915; FRAP 3(a), 24(a); 3d Cir. L.A.R. 24.1, 39.2, Misc. 107.2(a)

Committee Comments: Subsection (b) was added in 1995 to codify existing practice. Subsection (b) is not intended to preclude a litigant who did not seek leave to proceed in forma pauperis in the district court from requesting leave to proceed in forma pauperis in the court of appeals.

3.4   Notice of Appeal in Pro Se Cases

The court will deem a document filed by a pro se litigant after the decision of the district court in a civil, criminal, or habeas corpus case to be a notice of appeal despite informality in its form or title, if it evidences an intention to appeal. The court will deem an application for leave to appeal in forma pauperis or an application for a certificate of appealability to be a notice of appeal if no formal notice has been filed.

The grant or denial of a certificate of appealability by the district court will not be treated as a notice of appeal.

Source: 1988 Court Rules 8.1, 8.3

Cross–References: 28 U.S.C. § 2253; FRAP 3, 4(d), & 22(b), 24, Form 1, Form 3

Committee Comments: This rule is designed to emphasize that the jurisdictional requirement of a notice of appeal is met in a pro se case by the filing of an informal document, a request for certificate of appealability, or a motion for in forma pauperis status in this court, but not by the mere granting or denial by the district court of a certificate of appealability. The portions of prior Court Rule 8 that were repetitive of FRAP 3 and 4 have been deleted; otherwise no substantive change from prior Court Rule 8 is intended. Technical changes were made in 1997 to conform to the Antiterrorism and Effective Death Penalty Act. The phrase "in this court" was deleted in 2008 to clarify that a request for a certificate of appealability made to a district court when the district court has already ruled on the issue should be construed as a notice of appeal.

[Effective December 15, 2008. Amended effective March 8, 2010.]

RULE 4.0   APPEAL AS OF RIGHT—WHEN TAKEN

4.1   Motions to Expedite

A party who seeks to expedite a case must file a motion within 14 days after the opening of the case setting forth the exceptional reason that warrants expedition. If a reason for expedition arises thereafter, the moving party must file a motion within 14 days of the occurrence that is the basis of the motion. Motions seeking to expedite a case must include a proposed briefing schedule that has been agreed upon by the parties, if possible, but if they cannot agree, they should submit their own proposal with reasons in the motion or response. The non-moving party may agree to a proposed briefing schedule without conceding that expedition is necessary. A response to the motion, if any, must be filed within 7 days after service of the motion and any reply within 3 days after service of the response unless otherwise directed by the court or clerk. The court or clerk may direct that service be made in the manner provided by L.A.R. 27.7.

Source: None

Cross-Reference: FRAP 4

Committee Comments: This rule was added in 1995 to emphasize that a request for an expedited appeal must be made promptly. See L.A.R. 27.7 requiring notification to the clerk of expedited or urgent matters. The rule was amended in 2008 to clarify that the rule applies to all types of cases.

[Effective December 15, 2008. Amended effective March 8, 2010.]

RULE 5.0 APPEALS BY PERMISSION UNDER 28 U.S.C. § 1292(b) [ABROGATED]

5.1 Petition for Permission to Appeal [Abrogated]

Reason for elimination of L.A.R. 5.1:

FRAP 5(b), which sets forth the contents of a petition for permission to appeal, requires that the petition include "the question itself." This requirement makes L.A.R. 5.1 unnecessary.

[Effective December 15, 2008.]

RULE 8.0 STAY OR INJUNCTION PENDING APPEAL

8.1 Motion for Stay in Court of Appeals

A motion for a stay of a judgment or order of a district court or a decision of the United States Tax Court pending appeal, or for an order suspending, modifying, restoring or granting an injunction during the pendency of an appeal must include a copy of any relevant judgment, decision, or order of the district court or the decision of the United States Tax Court and any accompanying opinion. Failure to do so is a ground for dismissal of the motion.

Source: 1988 Court Rules 11.2, 11.4

Cross-References: FRAP 8, 18, 27; 3d Cir. L.A.R. 18.0, 27.0

Committee Comments: This rule was revised in 1995 to apply to decisions of the United States Tax Court as well as the judgments and orders of the United States district court. Otherwise, no substantive change from prior Court Rules 11.2 or 11.4 is intended. The rule was amended to delete references to a supersedeas bond, because approval of a supersedeas bond must be sought in the district court under FRAP 8 (a)(1)(B).

8.2 Expedited Consideration

If the court or clerk determines that a motion under L.A.R. 8.1 requires expedited treatment, proceedings in regard to the motion will be in accordance with L.A.R. 27.7.

Source: New provision in 2002

Cross-References: None

Committee Comments: Section 8.2 was added to clarify procedures in expedited cases. See L.A.R. 27.7 requiring notification to the clerk of expedited or urgent matters.

8.3 Death Penalty Cases

Except as provided in 28 U.S.C. § 2262, the provisions of 3d Cir. L.A.R. Misc. 111.0 govern all stay proceedings in death penalty cases, including appeals from the grant or denial of a petition under 28 U.S.C. §§ 2254 or 2255, applications to file a second or successive petition under 28 U.S.C. § 2244 and/or § 2255, and in original habeas corpus actions challenging a conviction in which a sentence of death has been imposed.

In a direct appeal of conviction or sentence in a criminal case in which the district court has imposed a sentence of death, an order will be entered staying the sentence.

Source: None

Cross-References: FRAP 8, 22; Fed. R. Crim. Pro. 38(a); 3d Cir. L. A. R. Misc. 111.0

Committee Comments: New provision in 1995. To the extent consistent with FRAP and applicable statutes, all local procedure in death penalty proceedings are governed by 3d Cir. L.A.R. Misc. 111.0. Technical changes were made in 1997 to conform to the Antiterrorism and Effective Death Penalty Act.

[Effective December 15, 2008.]

RULE 9.0 RELEASE IN CRIMINAL CASES

9.1 Appeals of Orders Relating to Release or Detention; Release Before Judgment of Conviction

(a) An appeal from an order granting or denying release from custody with or without bail or for detention of a defendant prior to judgment of conviction must be by motion filed either concurrently with or promptly after filing a notice of appeal. The movant must set forth in the body of the motion the applicable facts and law and attach a copy of the reasons given by the district court for its order. The opposing party may file a response within 5 days after service of the motion, unless the court directs that the time be shortened or extended.

(b) Requests for release from custody or for detention of a defendant after judgment of conviction must be by motion filed expeditiously. The time periods and form requirements set forth in 3d Cir. L.A.R. 9.1(a) are applicable to such motions.

Source: 1988 Court Rules 11.3, 11.4

Cross-References: FRAP 9, 27; 3d Cir. L.A.R. 27.0

Committee Comments: Renumbered by the 1995 rules revision; no substantive change is intended from prior Court Rule 11.3. Response time changed to 5 days in 2010.

[Effective December 15, 2008. Amended effective March 8, 2010.]

RULE 11.0 TRANSMISSION OF THE RECORD

11.1 Duty of Appellant

Within 14 days after filing a notice of appeal, the appellant must deposit with the court reporter the estimated cost of the transcript of all or the necessary part of the notes of testimony taken at trial. Where an appellant cannot afford the cost of transcripts, counsel for appellant, or the appellant pro se, must make application to the district court within 14 days of the notice of appeal for the provision of such transcript pursuant to 28 U.S.C. § 753(f). If the district court denies the application, appellant must, within 14 days of the order denying the application, either deposit with the court reporter the fees for such transcript or apply to the court of appeals for the transcript at government expense. Failure to comply with this rule constitutes grounds for dismissal of the appeal.

Source: 1988 Court Rule 15.1

Cross-References: 28 U.S.C. § 753(f); FRAP 10(b), 11(a); 3d Cir. L.A.R. 10.1(b), Misc. 107.1(b)

Committee Comments: No substantive change from prior Court Rule 15.1 is intended. The rule codifies current practice. Time changed to 14 days in 2010 to conform to amendments in FRAP.

11.2   Retention of the Record in the District Court

A certified copy of the docket entries in the district court must be transmitted to the clerk of this court in lieu of the entire record in all counseled appeals. In all pro se cases, all documents, including briefs filed in support of dispositive motions, that are not available in electronic form on PACER, must be certified and transmitted to the clerk of this court. The clerk of the district court must transmit in any state habeas case or habeas case emanating from any territorial court or motions to vacate sentence under 28 U.S.C. § 2255, whether counseled or pro se, all documents that are not available in electronic form on PACER. In such cases, the clerk of the district court must transmit to the court of appeals any state or territorial records or any documents from the prior criminal trial lodged with the district court during its determination of the habeas case.

Source: 1988 Court Rule 14.1

Cross-References: FRAP 11(e); 22(b)

Committee Comments: Changes were made in 2008 to reflect practices for electronic records. The grant of a motion to proceed on the original record exempts a litigant from filing an appendix. Transmission of the record by the district court to the court of appeals is not a prerequisite to the granting of such motion. The fact that the district court clerk has transmitted the record to the court of appeals does not dictate the granting of the motion.

[Effective December 15, 2008. Amended effective March 8, 2010.]

RULE 15.0   REVIEW OR ENFORCEMENT OF AGENCY ORDERS—HOW OBTAINED; INTERVENTION

15.1   Brief and Argument in Enforcement and Review Proceedings

In any enforcement or review proceeding with respect to an order or action of a federal agency or board, each party adverse to the agency or board is considered to be the petitioner(s) and the federal agency or board to be the respondent, solely for the procedural purposes of briefing and oral argument, unless the court orders otherwise. Nothing in this rule has the effect of changing or modifying the burden of the agency or board of establishing its right to enforcement.

Source: 1988 Court Rule 26.1

Cross-Reference: FRAP 15

Committee Comments: The portions of prior Court Rule 26.1 that were repetitive of FRAP 15 have been deleted. This rule has been designed to expand the procedure which FRAP 15.1 limits to a single agency, the National Labor Relations Board, to encompass all federal administrative agencies.

[Effective December 15, 2008.]

RULE 18.0   STAY PENDING REVIEW

18.1   Stay of an Order or Decision of an Agency

An application to this court for stay of the judgment or order of an agency pending review, for approval of a supersedeas bond, or for an order suspending, modifying, restoring, or granting an injunction during the pendency of an appeal must include a copy of the relevant judgment, decision, or order of the agency and any accompanying opinion. In cases challenging a decision of the Board of Immigration Appeals, the opinion of the IJ (immigration judge) must be included. Failure to do so is a ground for dismissal of the motion.

Source: 1988 Court Rules 11.2, 11.4

Cross-References: FRAP 8, 18, 27; 3d Cir. L.A.R. 27.0

Committee Comments: No substantive change from prior Court Rules 1.2 or 11.4 is intended. See L.A.R. 27.7 requiring notification to the clerk of expedited or urgent matters.

[Effective December 15, 2008.]

RULE 21.0   MANDAMUS PETITIONS IN CRIME VICTIMS RIGHTS CASES

21.1   Petitions for Writ of Mandamus Pursuant to 18 U.S.C. § 3771(d)(3)

(a) A petition for writ of mandamus filed pursuant to 18 U.S.C. § 3771(d)(3), the Crime Victims' Rights Act, must bear the caption "PETITION FOR WRIT OF MANDAMUS PURSUANT TO 18 U.S.C. § 3771(d)(3), CRIME VICTIMS' RIGHTS ACT." Before filing such a petition, the petitioner's counsel, or the petitioner if appearing pro se, must notify by telephone the clerk's office of the Court of Appeals that such a petition will be filed, and must make arrangements for filing in this court and immediate service of the petition on the relevant parties.

(b) The clerk will notify the U.S. Attorney when a petition is received. The government must file a response to the petition within twenty-four hours of notification by the clerk unless the clerk directs otherwise. The government is responsible for notifying those additional victims of whom it is aware of the proceedings. Any additional victims wishing to join in the action, must file their petitions within twenty-four hours of case opening.

(c) A failure to provide advance notice of such petition, in accordance with subsection (a) of this rule, will be deemed consent to the five day continuance permitted in 18 U.S.C. § 3771(d)(3) and may be construed as a waiver of the time limits prescribed by the statute.

Source: 18 U.S.C. § 3771(d)(3)

Cross-References: FRAP 8, L.A.R. 8.0

Committee Comments: This Rule was added in 2008 to assist the court in complying with the time limits the Act places on decisions. The government is responsible for notifying crime victims of the proceedings. 18 U.S.C. § 3771(c)(1).

[Effective December 15, 2008.]

RULE 22.0 HABEAS CORPUS PROCEEDINGS

22.1 Necessity of Certificate of Appealability

(a) When a certificate of appealability is required, a formal application must be filed with the court of appeals, but the court may deem a document filed by a habeas corpus petitioner that discloses the intent to obtain appellate review to be an application for a certificate of appealability, regardless of its title or form. If an application is not filed with the notice of appeal, the appellant may file and serve an application within 21 days of either the docketing of the appeal in the court of appeals or of the entry of the order of the district court denying a certificate, whichever is later. The appellees may, but need not unless directed by the court, file a memorandum in opposition to the granting of a certificate, within 14 days of service of the application. The appellant may, but need not, file a reply within 10 days of service of the response. The length and form of any application, response, or reply must conform to the requirements of FRAP 27 governing motions.

(b) If the district court grants a certificate of appealability as to only some issues, the court of appeals will not consider uncertified issues unless appellant first seeks, and the court of appeals grants, certification of additional issues. Appellant desiring certification of additional issues must file, in the court of appeals, a separate motion for additional certification, along with a statement of the reasons why a certificate should be granted as to any issue(s) within 21 days of the docketing of the appeal in the court of appeals.

Appellees may file a memorandum in opposition within 14 days of service of the application. Appellant's reply, if any, must be filed within 10 days of the service of the response. The length and form of any application, response, or reply, must conform to the requirements of Rule 27, FRAP governing motions. If granted, the order must be included in volume one of the appendix, which may be attached to the appellant's brief. If the motions panel denies the motion to certify additional issues, the parties should brief only the issues certified unless the merits panel directs briefing of any additional issues. Notwithstanding the above, the merits panel may expand the certificate of appealability as required in the circumstances of a particular case.

(c) In a multi-issue case if the district court grants a certificate of appealability, but does not specify on which issues the certificate is granted as required by 28 U.S.C. § 2253(c)(3), the clerk will remand the case for specification of the issues.

(d) A certificate of appealability is required if a petitioner files a cross-appeal. The petitioner should apply to the district court for a certificate in the first instance.

Source: 1988 Court Rule 13.1

Cross-References: 28 U.S.C. § 2253; FRAP 3, 22; 3d Cir. L.A.R. 3.4

Committee Comments: The portions of prior Court Rule 13 that were repetitive of FRAP 22 were deleted in 1995; otherwise no substantive change from prior Court Rule 13.1 is intended. Technical changes were made to conform to FRAP 27 in 1997. The response time was lengthened to permit litigants sufficient time to file an application or response.

22.2 Statement of Reasons for Certificate of Appealability

At the time a final order denying a petition under 28 U.S.C. § 2254 or § 2255 is issued, the district judge will make a determination as to whether a certificate of appealability should issue. If the district judge issues a certificate, the judge must state the specific issue or issues that satisfy the criteria of 28 U.S.C. § 2253. If an order denying a petition under § 2254 or § 2255 is accompanied by an opinion or a magistrate judge's report, it is sufficient if the order denying the certificate references the opinion or report. If the district judge has not made a determination as to whether to issue a certificate of appealability by the time of the docketing of the appeal, the clerk will enter an order remanding the case to the district court for a prompt determination as to whether a certificate should issue.

Source: FRAP 22

Cross-References: 28 U.S.C. §§ 2253, 2254, 2255; FRAP 22

Committee Comments: Technical changes were made in 1997 to conform to the Antiterrorism and Effective Death Penalty Act.

22.3 Review of Application for Certificate of Appealability

An application for a certificate of appealability will be referred to a panel of three judges. If all the judges on the panel conclude that the certificate should not issue, the certificate will be denied, but if any judge of the panel is of the opinion that the applicant has made the showing required by 28 U.S.C. § 2253, the certificate will issue.

Source: FRAP 22

Cross-References: 28 U.S.C. § 2253; FRAP 22

Committee Comments: Technical changes were made in 1997 to conform to the Antiterrorism and Effective Death Penalty Act.

22.4 Death Penalty Cases

The provisions of 3d Cir. L.A.R. Misc. 111.0 govern all appeals from the grant or denial of a petition for writ of habeas corpus or original habeas corpus proceedings challenging a conviction in which a sentence of death has been imposed.

Source: None

Cross-References: FRAP 8, 22; 3d Cir. L.A.R. 8.0, Misc. 111.0

Committee Comments: New provision in 1997. To the extent consistent with FRAP and applicable, local procedure in all death penalty proceedings will be governed by 3d Cir. L.A.R. Misc. 111.0.

22.5 Application for Authorization to File a Second or Successive Petition Under 28 U.S.C. § 2254 or § 2255

(a) Forms for filing an application to file a second or successive petition under 28 U.S.C. § 2254 or § 2255 are available from the clerk. If the form application is not used, the application must contain the information requested in the form. The application must be accompanied by:

(1) the proposed new § 2254 or § 2255 petition;

(2) copies of all prior § 2254 or § 2255 petitions;

(3) copies of the docket entries in all prior § 2254 or § 2255 proceedings;

(4) copies of all magistrate judge's reports, district court opinions and orders disposing of the prior petitions; and

(5) any other relevant documents.

(b) The application may be accompanied by a memorandum, not exceeding 20 pages, clearly stating how the standards of § 2244(b) and/or § 2255 are satisfied.

(c) The movant must serve a copy of the application for authorization to file a second or successive petition and all accompanying attachments on the appropriate respondent.

(d) Any response to the application must be filed within 7 days of the filing of the application with the clerk.

(e) If the court determines that the motion and accompanying materials are not sufficiently complete to assess the motion, the court may deny the motion with or without prejudice to refiling or may in its discretion treat the motion as lodged, the filing being deemed complete when the deficiency is remedied.

(f) The clerk will transmit a copy of any order granting authorization to file a second or successive petition to the appropriate district court together with a copy of the petition.

(g) No filing fee is required for an application to file a second or successive petition. If the application is granted, the filing of the petition in the district court will be subject to the requirements of 28 U.S.C. § 1915(a).

(h) If the district court enters an order transferring to the court of appeals an application to file a second or successive petition or a § 2254 or § 2255 petition that the district court deems to be a second or successive petition requiring authorization, the clerk of the district court must promptly certify the record to the court of appeals as provided in L.A.R. 11.2. The record must include the documents listed in part (a)(1) through (5) of this rule. The clerk of the district court must transmit copies of its order of transfer and any necessary documents to the appropriate respondent.

(i) If a case transferred by the district court does not contain a statement by the applicant as to how the standards of § 2244(b) or § 2255 are satisfied, the clerk may direct the applicant to file a memorandum clearly stating how the statutory standards are met. Failure to file a memorandum as directed will result in the dismissal of the case by the clerk without further notice. If the applicant files a memorandum as directed, the time prescribed in § 2244(b)(3)(D) for deciding the application will run from the date the memorandum is filed.

(j) If an appeal is taken in a case in which the district court issued an order denying a petition under § 2254 or § 2255 on the grounds that it is a second or successive petition that requires authorization under § 2244, the record on appeal certified to this court must include the documents listed in part (a)(1) through (5) of this rule.

Source: FRAP 22

Cross-References: 28 U.S.C. §§ 2244, 2253, 2254, 2255; FRAP 22

Committee Comments: Technical changes were made in 1997 to conform to the Antiterrorism and Effective Death

Penalty Act. Revisions were made in 2008 to accommodate electronic records.

[Effective December 15, 2008. Amended effective March 8, 2010.]

RULE 24.0 PROCEEDINGS IN FORMA PAUPERIS

24.1 Documents Required With Application

(a) In civil cases in which 28 U.S.C. § 1915(b) applies, prisoners seeking to proceed on appeal in forma pauperis must file the following documents in the court of appeals:

(1) an affidavit of poverty that includes the amount in the prisoner's prison account;

(2) a certified copy of the prison account statement(s) (or institutional equivalent) for the 6 month period immediately preceding the filing of the notice of appeal; and

(3) a signed form authorizing prison officials to assess and deduct the filing fees in accordance with 28 U.S.C. § 1915(b).

(b) After the filing of the documents required in subsection (a) in civil cases in which 28 U.S.C. § 1915(b) applies, the clerk will issue an order directing the warden of the prison to assess and deduct the filing fees in accordance with 28 U.S.C. § 1915(b).

(c) In cases filed in which 28 U.S.C. § 1915(b) does not apply, prisoners seeking to proceed on appeal in forma pauperis must file an affidavit of poverty in the form prescribed by the Federal Rules of Appellate Procedure accompanied by a certified statement of the prison account statement(s) (or institutional equivalent) for the 6 month period preceding the filing of the notice of appeal or petition for extraordinary writ. No assessment order will be entered unless the court determines that the case is subject to the requirements of § 1915(b) and directs that assessments be made.

Source: None

Cross-References: 28 U.S.C. § 1915

Committee Comments: Technical changes were made in 1997 to conform to the Prison Litigation Reform Act.

24.2 Failure to File

Failure to file any of the documents specified in Rule 24.1 will result in the dismissal of the appeal by the clerk under L.A.R. 3.3 and L.A.R. Misc. 107.1(a).

Source: None

Cross-References: L.A.R. 3.3 and L.A.R. Misc. 107.1(a)

Committee Comments: None

24.3 Issuance of Order

If the affidavit in support of a motion to proceed in forma pauperis demonstrates that the appellant quali-

fies for in forma pauperis status and the appellant is not precluded from proceeding in forma pauperis under 28 U.S.C. § 1915(g), the clerk will issue an order granting in forma pauperis status. If 28 U.S.C. § 1915(b) applies, the order will direct prison officials to assess and deduct the filing fees in accordance with the statute and transmit such fees to the appropriate district court. The clerk must send a copy of the order to the prisoner, the warden of the prison where appellant is incarcerated, and the appropriate district court.

Source: None

Cross-References: 28 U.S.C. § 1915

Committee Comments: Technical changes were made in 1997 to conform to the Prison Litigation Reform Act.

[Effective December 15, 2008.]

RULE 25.0 FILING AND SERVICE

25.1 Electronic Filing and Service

(a) Except for original petitions such as a petition for writ of mandamus or petition for review of an agency order, counsel must file all documents electronically in accordance with the procedures of L.A.R. Misc. 113. In addition to electronically filing on CM/ECF, ten paper copies of briefs and four paper copies of the appendices must be filed with the clerk for the convenience of the court. No paper copies of motions or petitions for rehearing need be filed unless directed by the clerk.

(b) Service of electronically filed documents is governed by L.A.R. Misc. 113.4. If the opposing party has not consented to electronic service, the filer must use an alternate method of service prescribed FRAP 25(c). The method of service, whether electronic through the court's docketing system or by alternate means, must be specified in the certificate of service.

(c) Litigants proceeding pro se may, but are not required, to file documents electronically.

25.2 Facsimile Filing

Documents may not be filed by facsimile without prior authorization by the clerk. Authorization may be secured only in situations determined by the clerk to be of an emergency nature or other compelling circumstance. In such cases, the original signed document must be filed promptly thereafter.

25.3 Personal Identifiers

Certain personal identifiers must be excluded or redacted from all documents filed with the court as specified in L.A.R. Misc. 113.12 and Judicial Conference Policy.

Source: None

Cross-Reference: 3d Cir. L.A.R. Misc. 113

Committee Comments: New provision in 1995. Amendments made in 2008 regarding electronic filings. The notice of docket activity generated by CM/ECF notes whether notice has been sent to opposing parties by the court's electronic docketing system. This does not substitute for a certificate of service.

[Effective December 15, 2008.]

RULE 26.1.0   CORPORATE DISCLOSURE STATEMENT

26.1.1   Disclosure of Corporate Affiliations and Financial Interest

(a) Promptly after the notice of appeal is filed, each corporation that is a party to an appeal, whether in a civil, bankruptcy, or criminal case, must file a corporate affiliate/financial interest disclosure statement on a form provided by the clerk that identifies every publicly owned corporation with which it is affiliated but which is not named in the appeal. The form must be completed whether or not the corporation has anything to report.

(b) Every party to an appeal must identify on the disclosure statement required by FRAP 26.1 every publicly owned corporation not a party to the appeal, if any, that has a financial interest in the outcome of the litigation and the nature of that interest. The form must be completed only if a party has something to report under this section.

(c) In all bankruptcy appeals, counsel for the debtor or trustee of the bankruptcy estate must promptly file with the clerk a list identifying (1) the debtor, if not named in the caption, (2) the members of the creditors' committees or the top 20 unsecured creditors, and (3) any entity not named in the caption which is an active participant in the proceeding. If the debtor or trustee of the bankruptcy estate is not a party, the appellant must file this list with the clerk.

(d) In criminal appeals, the government must file a disclosure statement if an organization is a victim of the crime. If the organizational victim is a corporation, the statement must also identify any parent corporation and any publicly held corporation that owns 10% or more of its stock to the extent it can be obtained through due diligence. The government may seek to be relieved from the requirements of this rule by filing a motion demonstrating that compliance is impossible.

Source: 1988 Court Rule 25

Cross-References: 28 U.S.C. § 455; FRAP 26.1

Committee Comments: The rule was revised and subsection (c) was added in 1995. Prior Court Rule 25 imposed an obligation upon all parties to civil or bankruptcy cases and all corporate defendants in criminal cases to file a corporate affiliate/financial interest disclosure statement. 3d Cir. L.A.R. 26.1.1(a) limits that obligation to corporate parties only. The rule also provides that the statement must be filed promptly after the notice of appeal is filed, and must be made on a form provided by the clerk. 3d Cir. L.A.R. 26.1.1(b) retains the requirement that every party to an appeal disclose the identity of every publicly owned corporation, not a party to an appeal, that has a financial interest in the outcome of the litigation. The rule also specifies that, under these circumstances, a negative report need not be filed. "In writing" was deleted in 2008 to provide for electronic filing of the notices. Subsection d was added in 2011 to adopt similar provisions of Federal Rule of Criminal Procedure 12.4.

26.1.2   Notice of Possible Judicial Disqualification

(a) If any judge of this court participated at any stage of the case, in the trial court or in related state court proceedings, appellant, promptly after filing the notice of appeal, must separately file with the clerk a notice of the name of the judge and the other action, and must send a copy of such notice to appellee's counsel. Appellee has a corresponding responsibility to so notify the clerk if, for any reason, appellant fails to comply with this rule fully and accurately.

(b) A party seeking disqualification of a judge for any other reason must file a motion, which must comply with FRAP 27 and L.A.R. 27.

Source: 1988 Court Rule 19.1

Cross-References: 28 U.S.C. §§ 144, 455; FRAP 26.1

Committee Comments: Prior Court Rule 19.1 required appellant to notify the clerk of a possible judicial disqualification when filing the opening brief. 3d Cir. L.A.R. 26.1.2 now requires appellant to notify the clerk of such disqualification promptly after filing the notice of appeal. 3d Cir. L.A.R. 26.1.2, which was adopted in 1995, adds a requirement that appellee notify the clerk of any possible disqualification if appellant fails to do so. "In writing" was deleted in 2008 to provide for electronic filing of the notices.

[Effective December 15, 2008. Amended effective August 1, 2011.]

RULE 27.0   MOTIONS*

27.1   No Oral Argument Except When Ordered

Motions are considered and decided by the court upon the motion papers and briefs without oral argument unless ordered by the court or a judge thereof. Counsel may assume there will not be oral argument unless advised by the clerk to appear at a time and place fixed by the court.

Source: 1988 Court Rule 11.1

Cross-References: FRAP 8, 9, 18, 21, 27, 34, 40; 3d Cir. L.A.R. 8.1, 9.0, 18.0

Committee Comments: This rule was renumbered by the 1995 revision of the rules; no substantive change from prior Court Rule 11.1 is intended.

27.2   Service

(a) Counsel must file electronically all motions, responses to motions, and replies to such responses in accordance with the procedures of L.A.R. Misc. 113.

No paper copies of motions need be filed unless directed by the clerk.

(b) Service of electronically filed documents is governed by L.A.R. Misc. 113.4. If the opposing party has not consented to electronic service, the filer must use an alternate method of service prescribed FRAP 25(c). The method of service, whether electronic through the court's docketing system or by alternate means, must be specified in the certificate of service. Motions must ordinarily be served on other parties by means equally expeditious to those used to file the motion with the court. When time does not permit actual service on other parties, or the moving party has reason to believe that another party may not receive the motion in sufficient time to respond before the court acts (as in certain emergency motions), the moving party should notify such other parties by telephone, e-mail, or facsimile of the filing of the motion.

(c) Certain personal identifiers must be excluded or redacted from all documents filed with the court as specified in L.A.R. Misc. 113.12 and Judicial Conference Policy.

Source: None

Cross-References: FRAP 8, 9, 18, 25, 27, 41; 3d Cir. L.A.R. 8.1, 9.0, 18.0 and L.A.R. Misc. 113.4

Committee Comments: New provision in 1995. The period for filing a response provided by FRAP 27(a) runs from the time of service. If service is not effectuated promptly, the disposition of the motion may be delayed or parties opposing the motion may not have an opportunity to respond before the court rules on the motion. Amendments made in 2008 regarding electronic filing. The notice of docket activity generated by CM/ECF notes whether notice has been sent to opposing parties by the court's electronic docketing system. This does not substitute for a certificate of service.

27.3 Uncontested Motions

Each uncontested motion must be certified as uncontested by counsel. In the absence of a timely response, the court may treat a motion without such certification as uncontested.

Source: None

Cross-References: FRAP 8, 9, 18, 27, 41; 3d Cir. L.A.R. 8.1, 9.0, 18.0

Committee Comments: New provision in 1995. The period for filing a response provided by FRAP 27(a) is unnecessary where a motion is uncontested. A certification to that effect will aid in the speedy disposition of the motion. The rule was amended in 2008 to clarify that an uncontested motion is not automatically granted.

27.4 Motions for Summary Action

(a) A party may move for summary action affirming, enforcing, vacating, remanding, modifying, setting aside or reversing a judgment, decree or order, alleging that no substantial question is presented or that subsequent precedent or a change in circumstances warrants such action. In addition, the court may sua sponte list a case for summary action.

(b) Except for a change in circumstances or a change in law, motions for summary action or dismissal should be filed before appellant's brief is due. The court or the clerk may at any time refer a motion for summary action to a merits panel and direct that briefs be filed.

Source: Third Circuit Internal Operating Procedures 10.6 (1990)

Cross-References: 28 U.S.C. § 2106; FRAP 27; Third Circuit Internal Operating Procedure 10.6 (1994)

Committee Comments: No substantive change from current practice or IOP 10.6 is intended. The filing of a motion for summary action does not stay the regular briefing schedule set forth in FRAP 31(a).

27.5 Powers of Single Judge

A single judge of the court may not grant or deny a motion that the court has ordered to be acted on by the court or a panel thereof, and ordinarily a single judge will not entertain and grant or deny a motion for release or for modification of the conditions of release pending review in a criminal case, a motion for leave to intervene, or a motion to postpone the oral argument in a case which has been included by the clerk in the argument list for a particular weekly session of the court. The action of a single judge may be reviewed by a panel of the court.

Source: 1988 Court Rule 2.4

Cross-References: FRAP 27(c); Third Circuit Internal Operating Procedure 10.5 (1994)

Committee Comments: Prior Court Rule 2.4 provided that a single judge could not entertain a motion for leave to file a brief as amicus curiae or a motion that a party requests be heard orally by the Court. 3d Cir. L.A.R. 27.5 removes these restrictions and permits a single judge to entertain such motions.

27.6 Motions Decided by the Clerk

The clerk may entertain and dispose of any motion that can ordinarily be disposed of by a single judge of this court under the provisions of FRAP 27(c) and 3d Cir. L.A.R. 27.5, provided the subject of the motion is ministerial, relates to the preparation or printing of the appendix and briefs on appeal, or relates to calendar control. If application is promptly made, the action of the clerk may be reviewed in the first instance by a single judge or by a panel of the court.

Source: 1988 Court Rule 11.5

Cross-References: FRAP 27

Committee Comments: This rule was renumbered by the 1995 revision of the rules; no substantive change from prior Court Rule 11.5 is intended.

27.7 Motions in Which Expedited Consideration Is Requested

If the court or clerk determines that a motion requires expedited consideration, the court or the clerk will direct that a response in opposition, if any, must be filed within 7 days after service of the motion and any reply within 3 days after service of the response unless a shorter time is directed by the court or clerk. Service of documents filed under this rule, including the initial motion must be in accordance with L.A.R. 27.2 and 113.4 unless the court or clerk directs that a more expeditious method of service be used. To the fullest extent possible, the clerk must be given advance notice by telephone that a motion requiring expedited or urgent consideration may be filed.

Source: New Provision added in 2002.

Cross-References: L.A.R. 8.0

Committee Comments: Section 27.7 was added in 2002 to clarify procedures for expedited motions.

27.8 Supplemental Pro Se Motions Prohibited

Except in cases in which counsel has filed a motion to withdraw under *Anders v. California*, 386 U.S. 738 (1967), parties represented by counsel may not file a motion or other document pro se. If a party represented by counsel sends a pro se motion or other document to the court, the clerk will forward the motion to the party's attorney of record, with notice to the pro se party, for whatever action counsel deems appropriate. A party may file pro se a motion for the appointment of new counsel or a motion to proceed pro se. The party may file no other motion or document pro se unless and until the motion for new counsel or to proceed pro se is decided.

Source: None

Cross-References: L.A.R. 31.3 (pro se briefs)

Committee Comments: Rule 27.8, adopted in 2008, is intended to establish a uniform policy of dealing with pro se motions from parties who are represented by counsel. See *Martinez v. Court of Appeal of Cal.*, 528 U.S. 152 (2000) (no right to self representation on appeal).

[Effective December 15, 2008. Amended effective March 8, 2010.]

* [**Publisher's Note:** On or about November 24, 2014, the Court made available the following notice:

THIRD CIRCUIT MOTIONS PRACTICE

"When filing motions with the United States Court of Appeals for the Third Circuit, counsel's attention is drawn to Rule 27(a)(2)(A), Fed. R. App. Pro., which requires that the motion state "with particularity the grounds for the motion, the relief sought, and the legal argument necessary to support it." A "notice of motion" is not sufficient and will not be docketed. Rule 27(a)(2)(C)(ii). The form of the papers, page limits, number of copies and service, are governed by Rule 27(d). It is emphasized that these procedures apply to motions requesting a stay of removal in immigration cases. The opinions of the Immigration Judge and the BIA should accompany any motion requesting a stay of removal order. Rule 27(a)(2)(B).

"Emergency Motions. LAR 27.7 provides, 'To the fullest extent possible, the clerk must be given advance notice by telephone that a motion requiring expedited or urgent consideration may be filed.' Counsel should call the Clerk's Office at 215-597-2995 during regular business hours as soon as they are aware that an emergency motion may be filed.

"Click here http://www.ca3.uscourts.gov/allforms for information regarding electronic filing of emergency motions."

RULE 28.0 BRIEFS

28.1 Brief of the Appellant

(a) The brief of appellant/petitioner must include, in addition to the sections enumerated in FRAP 28, the following:

(1) in the statement of the issues presented for review required by FRAP 28(a)(5), a designation by reference to specific pages of the appendix or place in the proceedings at which each issue on appeal was raised, objected to, and ruled upon;

(2) after the statement of issues for review, a statement of related cases and proceedings, stating whether this case or proceeding has been before this court previously, and whether the party is aware of any other case or proceeding that is in any way related, completed, pending or about to be presented before this court or any other court or agency, state or federal. If the party is aware of any previous or pending appeals before this court arising out of the same case or proceeding, the statement should identify each such case; and

(b) The following statements should appear under a separate heading placed before the discussion of the issue: the statement of the standard or scope of review for each issue on appeal, *i.e.*, whether the trial court abused its discretion; whether its fact findings are clearly erroneous; whether it erred in formulating or applying a legal precept, in which case review is plenary; whether, on appeal or petition for review of an agency action, there is substantial evidence in the record as a whole to support the order or decision, or whether the agency's action, findings and conclusions should be held unlawful and set aside for the reasons set forth in 5 U.S.C. § 706(2).

(c) It is preferred that the documents listed in L.A.R. 32.2(c) be attached to the paper brief. The documents may be filed electronically in a document separate from the brief.

(d) The court expects counsel to exercise appropriate professional behavior in all briefs and to refrain from making ad hominem attacks on opposing counsel or parties.

Source: 1988 Court Rule 21.1

Cross-References: FRAP 28–32, 39; 3d Cir. L.A.R. 29–32, 39

Committee Comments: 3d Cir. L.A.R. 28.1, added in 1995, contains a requirement that the appellant must designate where in the proceedings each issue was preserved for appeal. Appellant should cite to the appendix, but if the germane portion of the record is not included in the appendix, the appellant must cite to the original record. If the matter has not been filed of record in the district court, appellant may cite to the original document. 3d Cir. L.A.R.

28.1 no longer requires parties to file a separate statement with the Clerk's Office identifying any previous or pending appeals because such matters must be identified in the briefs. 3d Cir. L.A.R. 28.1 also makes explicit for the first time the court's expectation that counsel will write briefs in a professional manner and refrain from making ad hominem attacks on the opposing side. The portions of prior Court Rule 21.1 that were repetitive of FRAP 28 have been deleted. See L.A.R. 32.2(c) for permissible attachments to the brief.

28.2 Brief of the Appellee

The brief of the appellee or respondent must conform to the requirements of FRAP 28(b) and 3d Cir. L.A.R. 28.1 (a)(2), (b) and (c). If the appellee is also a cross-appellant, the appellee's brief must also comply with rules 28.1(a)(1) and (a)(3). The brief of an appellee who has been permitted to file one brief in consolidated appeals must contain an appropriate cross reference index which clearly identifies and relates appellee's answering contentions to the specific contentions of the various appellants. The index must contain an appropriate reference by appellee to the question raised and the page in the brief of each appellant.

Source: 1988 Court Rule 21.1

Cross-References: FRAP 28–32; 3d Cir. L.A.R. 29–32

Committee Comments: The portions of prior Court Rule 21.1 that were repetitive of FRAP 28 were deleted in 1995. Otherwise no substantive change from prior Court Rule 21.1 is.

28.3 Citation Form; Certification

(a) In the argument section of the brief required by FRAP 28(a)(9), citations to federal opinions that have been reported must be to the United States Reports, the Federal Reporter, the Federal Supplement or the Federal Rules Decisions, and must identify the judicial circuit or district, and year of decision. Citations to the United States Supreme Court opinions that have not yet appeared in the official reports may be to the Supreme Court Reporter, the Lawyer's Edition or United States Law Week in that order of preference. Citations to United States Law Week must include the month, day and year of the decision. Citations to federal decisions that have not been formally reported must identify the court, docket number and date, and refer to the electronically transmitted decision. Citations to services and topical reports, whether permanent or looseleaf, and to electronic citation systems, must not be used if the text of the case cited has been reported in the United States Reports, the Federal Reporter, the Federal Supplement, or the Federal Rules Decisions. Citations to state court decisions should include the West Reporter system whenever possible, with an identification of the state court. Hyperlinks to decisions may be used, but are not required, as provided in L.A.R. Misc. 113.13. If hyperlinks are used, citation to a reporter, looseleaf service, or other paper document must be included, if available. If a hyperlink to a paper document is not available, the internet address of the document cited must be included.

(b) For each legal proposition supported by citations in the argument, counsel must cite to any opposing authority if such authority is binding on this court, e.g., U.S. Supreme Court decisions, published decisions of this court, or, in diversity cases, decisions of the highest state court.

(c) All assertions of fact in briefs must be supported by a specific reference to the record. All references to portions of the record contained in the appendix must be supported by a citation to the appendix, followed by a parenthetical description of the document referred to, unless otherwise apparent from context. Hyperlinks to the electronic appendix may be added to the brief. If hyperlinks are used, the brief must also contain immediately preceding the hyperlink a reference to the paper appendix page. Hyperlinks to testimony must be to a transcript. A motion must be filed and granted seeking permission to hyperlink to an audio or video file before such links may be included in the brief or appendix. Hyperlinks may not be used to link to sealed or restricted documents.

(d) Except as otherwise authorized by law, each party must include a certification in the initial brief filed by that party with the court that at least one of the attorneys whose names appear on the brief is a member of the bar of this court, or has filed an application for admission pursuant to 3d Cir. L.A.R. 46.1.

Source: 1988 Court Rule 21.1

Cross-References: 28 U.S.C. §§ 515, 517, 518; Third Circuit Internal Operating Procedure 9.1 (1994); L.A.R. Misc. 113.13

Committee Comments: Subsection (b) was adopted in 1995. It imposes upon each party the obligation to cite to authority that is binding on this court, whether that authority supports or opposes the party's propositions. Otherwise, no substantive change from prior Court Rule 21.1 is intended, including the court's longstanding practice of not requiring attorneys representing the United States, or any agency thereof, to be a member of the bar of this court. The rule was amended in 2008 to permit the use of hyperlinks.

28.4 Signing the Brief

All briefs must be signed in accordance with the provision of L.A.R. 46.4. Electronic briefs may be signed with either an electronically generated signature or "s/ typed name" in the signature location. Counsel's state Bar number, if any, and address and phone number must be included with the signature.

Source: Fed. R. Civ. P. 11

Cross-References: L.A.R. 46.4; L.A.R. Misc. 113.4

Committee Comments: This rule is derived from Fed. R. Civ. P. 11 which requires signatures on all papers. The signing of documents is important because it constitutes a certificate by the attorney or party that he or she has read the pleading or brief to ensure that it complies with all federal and local rules. The requirement is interpreted broadly and the attorney of record may designate another person to sign the brief. If a party is represented by multiple counsel, the signature from only one attorney of record is required.

28.5 Page Limitations in Cross Appeals (Abrogated in 2008 as duplicative of F.R.A.P. 28.1)

[Effective December 15, 2008.]

RULE 29.0 AMICI CURIAE BRIEFS

29.1 Time for Filing Amici Curiae Briefs on Rehearing

(a) In a case ordered for rehearing before the court en banc or before the original panel, if the court permits the parties to file additional briefs, any amicus curiae must file its brief in accordance with Rule 29(e) of the Federal Rules of Appellate Procedure. In a case ordered for rehearing in which no additional briefing is directed, unless the court directs otherwise, any new amicus must file a brief within 28 days after the date of the order granting rehearing, and any party may file a response to such an amicus brief within 21 days after the amicus brief is served. Before completing the preparation of an amicus brief, counsel for an amicus curiae must attempt to ascertain the arguments that will be made in the brief of any party whose position the amicus is supporting, with a view to avoiding any unnecessary repetition or restatement of those arguments in the amicus brief.

(b) The statement required by FRAP 29(c)(4) does not count toward the word limitations of FRAP 32(a)(7)

Source: None

Cross-Reference: FRAP 29(e)

Committee Comments: New provision in 2000. Subsection (b) was added in 2008.

[Effective December 15, 2008.]

RULE 30.0 APPENDIX TO THE BRIEFS

30.1 Number to Be Filed

(a) Counsel must electronically file the appendix in accordance with L.A.R. Misc. 113.

(b) In addition to the electronic appendix, four paper copies of the appendix must be filed for the convenience of the court, unless otherwise ordered.

(c) In addition to an electronic and paper appendix, hyperlinks to the appendix may be added to the brief. If hyperlinks are used, the brief must also contain immediately preceding the hyperlink a reference to the paper appendix page. Hyperlinks to testimony must be to a transcript. A motion must be filed and granted seeking permission to hyperlink to an audio or video file before such links may be included in the brief or appendix. Hyperlinks may not be used to link to sealed or restricted documents.

(d)* In Virgin Island cases only, one additional copy of the appendix must be filed with the clerk of the district court in the location from which the appeal is taken (St. Thomas or St. Croix).

(e) When hearing or rehearing by the court en banc is ordered, the parties will be directed to file additional paper copies for the court's use.

* [**Publisher's Note:** On October 15, 2012, the Court entered the following order: "L.A.R. 30.1(d) and 31.1(a), which require counsel in Virgin Islands cases to file one additional paper copy of the briefs and appendices with the Clerk of the District Court of the Virgin Islands, are hereby suspended until further notice. Counsel need not file copies of the briefs and appendices with the Clerk of the District Court of the Virgin Islands unless specifically directed to do so by the Court of Appeals. Counsel must continue to file ten paper copies of the briefs and four paper copies of the appendices with the Court of Appeals Clerk's Office in Philadelphia."]

Source: 1988 Court Rule 10.1

Cross-References: FRAP 30(a); 3d Cir. L.A.R. 31.1 and L.A.R. Misc. 113.

Committee Comments: The portions of prior Court Rule 10.1 that were repetitive of FRAP 30(a) were deleted in 1995. The rule now clarifies that upon the grant of a petition for rehearing, additional copies of the appendix as well as the briefs will be ordered. Otherwise no substantive change from prior Court Rule 10.1 is intended. The requirement of electronic filing was added in 2008. **See addendum to these rules** for alternative to electronic filing.**

** [**Publisher's Note:** See "Options for Filing the Appendix" following L.A.R. 113.14, *post.*]

30.2 Hearing on Original Papers

In cases involving applications for a writ of habeas corpus under 28 U.S.C. §§ 2241, 2254 or 2255, or when permission has been granted for the appellant to proceed in forma pauperis, the appeal will be heard on the original record. Appellants in such cases must strictly comply with the requirements of 3d Cir. L.A.R. 32.2(c) with respect to inclusion of the trial court's opinion or order in the brief, and must also include copies of the docket entries in the proceedings below and the notice of appeal and any order granting a certificate of appealability. These documents must be included in both the electronic and paper brief. In any other case, this court, upon motion, may dispense with the requirement of an appendix and permit an appeal or petition to be heard on the original record, with such copies of the record, or relevant parts thereof, as the court may require.

Source: 1988 Court Rule 10.2

Cross-References: FRAP 30(f); 3d Cir. L.A.R. Misc. 113

Committee Comments: The requirement of prior Court Rule 10.2 that habeas corpus petitioners or appellants proceeding in forma pauperis attach to their briefs copies of the district court opinion or order appealed from were deleted in 1995 as repetitious of 3d Cir. L.A.R. 32.2(c). 3d Cir. L.A.R. 30.2 cautions such appellants of the importance of complying with 3d Cir. L.A.R. 32.2(c), and further requires them to attach copies of the docket entries below and notice of appeal to the opening brief. The requirement of attaching a copy of the order granting a certificate of appealability was added in 2002. The requirement of electronic filing was added in 2008.

30.3 Contents of Appendix

(a) Relevant portions of a trial transcript, exhibit, or other parts of the record referred to in the briefs must be included in the appendix at such length as may be necessary to preserve context. Relevant portions of the district court briefs may be included in the appendix only if necessary to show whether an issue was raised or an argument was made in the district court or in the proceeding being reviewed. Transcript portions are not considered relevant under this rule merely because they are referred to in the Statement of the Case or Statement of Facts, if they are not otherwise necessary for an understanding of the issues presented for decision. Whenever an appeal challenges the sufficiency of the evidence to support a verdict or other determination (including an argument that a finding is clearly erroneous), the appendix must provide all the evidence of record which supports the challenged determination. In all appeals in this court, the appendix must contain, in addition to the requirements of FRAP 30(a), a table of contents with page references, a copy of the notice of appeal, the relevant opinions of the trial court or bankruptcy court, or the opinion or report and recommendation of the magistrate judge, or the decision of the administrative agency, and a copy of any order granting a certificate of appealability.

(b) Records sealed in the district court and not unsealed by order of the court must be not be included in the paper appendix. Paper copies of sealed documents must be filed in a separate sealed envelope. When filed electronically, sealed documents must be filed as a separate docket entry as a sealed volume.

(c) In an appeal challenging a criminal sentence, the appellant must file, at the time of filing the appendix, four copies of the Presentence Investigation Report and the statement of reasons for the sentence, in four sealed envelopes appropriately labeled. Grand jury materials protected by Fed. R. Crim. P. 6(c), presentence reports, statements of reasons for the sentence and any other similar material in a criminal case or a case collaterally attacking a conviction (cases under 28 U.S.C. §§ 2241, 2254, 2255) must be filed electronically and in paper as separate sealed volumes.

(e)* The documents listed in L.A.R. 32.2(c) that must be included in volume one of the appendix may be attached to the paper brief.

(f) Litigants proceeding pro se may, but are not required to, file an electronic appendix.

Source: 1988 Court Rule 10.3

Cross-References: FRAP 30(a), (b) and (f); 3d Cir. L.A.R. 32.0, Misc. 106.1(c) and L.A.R. Misc. 113

Committee Comments: The portions of prior Court Rule 10.3 that were repetitive of FRAP 30 were deleted in 1995. The portion of prior Court Rule 10.3 addressed to those cases in which the court by order has dispensed with the requirement of an appendix has also been deleted from this rule. Such cases are now addressed by 3d Cir. L.A.R. 30.2. Briefs submitted to the trial court or agency should not be included in the appendix unless the brief serves as evidence that an issue has been preserved or specifically waived. Trial exhibits which are important to the court's understanding of the issues should be reproduced either in the appendix or as exhibits to the brief. The rule was amended in 2008 to provide for electronic filing. **See addendum to these rules** for alternative to electronic filing.

* So in original.

** [**Publisher's Note:** *See* "Options for Filing the Appendix" following Rule 113.14, *post.*]

30.4 Deferred Appendix

The use of a deferred appendix pursuant to FRAP 30(c) is not favored.

Source: 1988 Court Rule 10.4

Cross-References: FRAP 30, 32; 3d Cir. L.A.R. 32.0

Committee Comments: This rule was renumbered by the 1995 revision of the rules; no substantive change from prior Court Rule 10.4 is intended.

30.5 Sanctions Pursuant to FRAP 30(b)(2)

(a) The court, sua sponte by Rule to Show Cause or on the motion of any party, may impose sanctions in the form of denial of all or some of the costs of the appeal upon finding that any party has unreasonably and vexatiously caused the inclusion of materials in an appendix that are unnecessary for the determination of the issues presented on appeal.

(b) A party filing such a motion must do so not later than 10 days after a bill of costs has been served. The movant must submit with the motion an itemized statement specifically setting forth, by name and appendix page number, the item or items that the movant asserts were unnecessarily included in the appendix.

(c) Any party against whom sanctions are requested may file an answer to the motion or Rule to Show Cause, which must be filed within 10 days after service of the motion or Rule to Show Cause.

Source: 1988 Court Rule 20.4

Cross-References: FRAP 30(b), 39; 3d Cir. L.A.R. Misc. 107.4

Committee Comments: Renumbered by the 1995 revision of the rules; no substantive change from prior Court Rule 20.4 is intended.

[Effective December 15, 2008. Amended effective March 8, 2010.]

RULE 31.0   FILING AND SERVICE OF BRIEFS

31.1   Number of Copies to Be Filed and Served

(a) Unless otherwise required by this court, each party must file ten (10) paper copies (*i.e.*, an original and nine copies) of each brief* with the clerk for the convenience of the court and, unless counsel has consented to electronic service, serve one (1) paper copy on counsel for each party separately represented. If volume one of the appendix is attached to the electronic brief, one paper copy of volume one must be served on opposing counsel. In Virgin Islands cases only, one additional paper copy of the briefs must be filed with the clerk of the district court in the location from which the appeal is taken (St. Thomas or St. Croix).** When hearing or rehearing by the court en banc is ordered, the parties will be directed to file additional paper copies for the court's use.

(b) In addition to the paper briefs, counsel for any party or amicus curiae must file with the court the same brief in electronic form.

(1) Filing must be done on the court's electronic filing system as provided in L.A.R. Misc. 113 or such other method as the court specifies.

(2) The brief must be in PDF format. The Clerk may prescribe additional requirements to aid in transmission.

(3) The date of filing the brief is the date the electronic version of the brief is received by the Clerk, provided that ten paper copies are mailed as provided in Rule 25(a)(2)(B), FRAP on the same day as electronic transmission.

(4) The electronic version of the brief is the official record copy of the brief; if corrections are required to be made to the paper brief, a corrected copy of the electronic brief must be provided.

(5) Litigants proceeding pro se need not file an electronic brief.

(c) In addition to the certification of type-volume limitations required by Rule 32(a)(7)(C), and in the same document, counsel must certify that the text of the electronic brief is identical to the text in the paper copies. Counsel must also certify that a virus detection program has been run on the file and that no virus was detected. The certification must specify the version of the virus detection program used. Sanctions may be imposed if a filing contains a computer virus or worm.

(d) A party who is a Filing User as provided in L.A.R. Misc. 113.4 consents to electronic service of the brief through the court's electronic docketing system (CM/ECF). Service by alternate means must be made on all parties who are not Filing Users. The certificate of service must note what method of service was used for each party served.

Source: 1988 Court Rule 21.2

Cross-References: FRAP 28–32; 3d Cir. L.A.R. 28–32 and L.A.R. Misc. 113.4

Committee Comments: The rule was amended in 2002 to require electronic filing of briefs. Instructions on electronic filing can be found on the court's web site at www.ca3.uscourts.gov. A party proceeding pro se need not file electronically, but if the party wishes to file electronically, this rule must be followed. PDF format makes a document more stable when electronically transmitted. This format also insures that pagination remains the same regardless of what printer is used to print the document. The PDF document should be created by converting a word processing document, not by scanning. Scanned documents that are converted to PDF are more difficult to transport and store and often are not searchable. Although the notice of docket activity issued by CM/ECF lists those parties who were served by the court's electronic docketing system, this is not a substitute for a certificate of service.

* [Publisher's Note: On April 29, 2013, the Court entered the following order:

"ORDER—REDUCED NUMBER OF COPIES OF BRIEFS REQUIRED

"L.A.R. 31.1 currently requires parties to file ten (10) paper copies (an original and 9 copies) of each brief. It is hereby ordered that for briefs filed May 1, 2013 and after, unless the Clerk directs otherwise, parties need file only 7 paper copies, (an original and 6 copies) of each brief. When a party is entitled to costs under Fed. R. App. P. 39, costs will be taxed on the number of copies actually filed, not the number required when the bill of costs is filed."]

** [Publisher's Note: On October 15, 2012, the Court entered the following order: "L.A.R. 30.1(d) and 31.1(a), which require counsel in Virgin Islands cases to file one additional paper copy of the briefs and appendices with the Clerk of the District Court of the Virgin Islands, are hereby suspended until further notice. Counsel need not file copies of the briefs and appendices with the Clerk of the District Court of the Virgin Islands unless specifically directed to do so by the Court of Appeals. Counsel must continue to file ten paper copies of the briefs and four paper copies of the appendices with the Court of Appeals Clerk's Office in Philadelphia."]

31.2   Appellee's Brief

A local, state or federal entity or agency, which was served in the district court and which is the appellee, must file a brief in all cases in which a briefing schedule is issued unless the court has granted a motion seeking permission to be excused from filing a brief. This rule does not apply to entities or agencies that are respondents to a petition for review unless the entity or agency is the sole respondent or to entities or agencies which acted solely as an adjudicatory tribunal.

Source: None

Cross-References: FRAP 28–32; 3d Cir. L.A.R. 28–32

Committee Comments: Rule 31.2 was added in 2000 and is intended to change the practice of some agencies who choose not to file briefs when they are named as appellee. Amended in 2008 to provide for electronic filing.

31.3 Supplemental Pro Se Briefs Prohibited

Except in cases in which counsel has filed a motion under L.A.R. 109.2 to withdraw under *Anders v. California*, 386 U.S. 738 (1967), parties represented by counsel may not file a brief pro se. If a party sends a pro se brief to the court, the clerk will forward the brief to the party's attorney of record, with notice to the pro se party. Counsel may choose to include the arguments in his or her brief or may in the unusual case file a motion to file a supplemental brief, if appropriate.

Source: None

Cross-References: Pro se motions and other documents are governed by L.A.R. 27.8

Committee Comments: Rule 31.3 was added in 2002 and is intended to establish a uniform policy of dealing with pro se briefs from parties who are represented by counsel. <u>See</u> *Martinez v. Court of Appeal of Cal.*, 528 U.S. 152 (2000) (no right to self representation on appeal).

31.4 Motions for Extension of Time to File a Brief***

A party's first request for an extension of time to file a brief must set forth good cause. Generalities, such as that the purpose of the motion is not for delay or that counsel is too busy, are not sufficient. A first request for an extension of 14 days or less may be made by telephone or in writing. Counsel should endeavor to notify opposing counsel in advance that such a request is being made. The grant or denial by the clerk of the extension must be entered on the court docket. If a request for extension of time is made and granted orally, Filing Users are notified by the notice of docket activity generated by the court's electronic docketing system; counsel must send a confirming letter to parties who are not Filing Users within 7 days. A first request for an extension of time should be made at least 3 days in advance of the due date for filing the brief. A motion filed less than 3 days in advance of the due date must be in writing and must demonstrate that the good cause on which the motion is based did not exist earlier or could not with due diligence have been known or communicated to the court earlier. Subsequent requests for an extension of time must be made in writing and will be granted only upon a showing of good cause that was not foreseeable at the time the first request was made. Only one motion for extension of time to file a reply brief may be granted.

Source: None

Cross-References: None

Committee Comments: The rule was adopted in 2002 to permit the oral granting of a short extension of time. The rule was amended in 2011 to modify the requirement of filing a confirming letter.

*** [**Publisher's Note:** See "Notice to Counsel—Motions for Extension of Time Disfavored" under "Selected Orders and Notices", *post.*]

[Effective December 15, 2008. Amended effective March 8, 2010; August 1, 2011; October 15, 2012; May 1, 2013.]

RULE 32.0 FORM OF BRIEFS, THE APPENDIX AND OTHER DOCUMENTS

32.1 Forms of Briefs, Appendices, Motions, and Other Papers documents

All briefs, appendices, motions and other documents (collectively "documents") must conform to the following requirements, unless otherwise provided by the FRAP:

(a) All documents filed in paper form must be firmly bound at the left margin, and any metal fasteners or staples must be covered. All fasteners must have smooth edges. Use of backbones or spines without stapling is prohibited. Forms of binding such as velo binding and spiral binding are acceptable forms of binding.

(b) All documents must have margins on both sides of each page that are no less than one (1) inch wide, and margins on the top and bottom of each page that are no less than three-quarters (3/4) of an inch wide.

(c) Typeface. Briefs must comply with the provisions of FRAP 32(a)(5) and (6).

(d) Electronic briefs must be in PDF format; the entire brief must be contained in one electronic file.

(e) Certain personal identifiers must be excluded or redacted from all documents filed with the court as specified in L.A.R. Misc. 113.12 and Judicial Conference policy.

Source: 1988 Court Rules 21.2(B), 22 and 22.1

Cross-References: FRAP 27, 32, 40; 3d Cir. L.A.R. 27.0, 35.1 and 35.2 and L.A.R. Misc. 113

Committee Comments: The portions of prior Court Rules 21.2(B) and 22.1 that were repetitive of FRAP 32 were deleted in 1995. The rule was amended to require electronic filing of the brief. The rule was amended in 2008 to require all documents to be filed electronically and to require redaction.

32.2 Form of Briefs and Appendices

(a) Excessive footnotes in briefs are discouraged. Footnotes must be printed in the same size type utilized in the text.

(b) Where a transparent cover is utilized, the underlying cover sheet of the brief or appendix must nevertheless conform to the color requirements of FRAP 32(a)(2) and 32(b)(1).

(c) Volume one of the appendix must consist only of (1) a copy of the notice of appeal, (2) the order or judgment from which the appeal is taken, and any other order or orders of the trial court which pertain to the issues raised on appeal (3) the relevant opinions of the district court or bankruptcy court, or the opinion or report and recommendation of the magistrate judge, or the decision of the administrative agency, if any and (4) any order granting a certificate of appealability. Volume one of the appendix may be bound in the paper brief and will not be counted toward the page or type volume limitations on the brief. All other volumes of the appendix must be separately bound.

(d) Where there is a multi-volume appendix, counsel should specify on the cover of each volume the pages contained therein, *e.g.*, Vol. 2, pp. 358–722. Costs to the party entitled to them will be allowed for documents appended to the brief.

(e) Certain personal identifiers must be excluded or redacted from all documents filed with the court as specified in L.A.R. Misc. 113.12 and Judicial Conference policy.

Source: 1988 Court Rule 21.2

Cross-References: FRAP 28–32; 3d Cir. L.A.R. 28–32 and L.A.R. Misc. 113

Committee Comments: The portions of prior Court Rule 21.2A that were repetitive of FRAP 32(a) were in 1995. Subsection (a) has been added to curtail the use of footnotes as a means to circumvent the page limitations set forth in FRAP. The Rule has been amended to require that additional relevant opinions be bound in the brief. Subsection (e) was added in 2008 to require redaction.

32.3 Form of Motions and Other Documents Only

(a) Briefs and memoranda in support of or in opposition to motions need not comply with the color requirements of FRAP 32(a).

(b) Petitions for rehearing en banc in which petitioner is represented by counsel must contain the "Statement of Counsel" required by 3d Cir. L.A.R. 35.1. As required in L.A.R. 35.2 and 40.1 all petitions seeking either panel rehearing or rehearing en banc must include as an exhibit a copy of the panel's judgment, order, and opinion, if any, as to which rehearing is sought.

(c) Certain personal identifiers must be excluded or redacted from all documents filed with the court as specified in L.A.R. Misc. 113.12 and Judicial Conference policy.

Source: 1988 Court Rules 21.2(B), 22 and 22.1

Cross-References: FRAP 27, 32, 40; 3d Cir. L.A.R. 27.0, 35.1 and 35.2 and L.A.R. Misc. 113

Committee Comments: The portions of prior Court Rules 21.2(B) and 22.1 that were repetitive of FRAP 32 were deleted in 1995. Otherwise no substantive change from prior Court Rules 21.2(B) and 22.1 is intended. Subsection (c) was added in 2008 to require redaction.

[Effective December 15, 2008.]

RULE 33.0   APPELLATE MEDIATION PROGRAM

33.1 Appellate Mediation Program

Appeals in civil cases and petitions for review or for enforcement of administrative action are referred to the Appellate Mediation Program to facilitate settlement or otherwise to assist in the expeditious handling of the appeal or petition. A special master will serve as the Chief Circuit Mediator and, in cooperation with the clerk, will manage the Appellate Mediation Program. Mediations will be conducted by a senior judge of the court of appeals, a senior judge of a district court, the Chief Circuit Mediator, or other person designated pursuant to Rule 48, FRAP Parties may confidentially request mediation by telephone or by letter directed to the Chief Circuit Mediator. In all cases, however, the special master will determine which cases are appropriate for mediation and will assign the matter to a mediator.

33.2 Eligibility for Appellate Mediation Program

All civil appeals and petitions for review or for enforcement of agency action are eligible for referral to the Appellate Mediation Program except: (1) original proceedings (such as petitions for writ of mandamus); (2) appeals or petitions in social security, immigration or deportation, or black lung cases; (3) prisoner petitions; (4) habeas corpus petitions or motions filed pursuant to 28 U.S.C. Sec. 2255; (5) petitions for leave to file second or successive habeas petitions; and (6) pro se cases. In all cases eligible for appellate mediation, the appellant or petitioner must file with the clerk, within 10 days of the docketing of the appeal with service on all parties, a Civil Appeals Information Statement and a Concise Summary of the Case, which is available on the court's website. Appellant must attach to the Concise Summary of the Case copies of the order(s) being appealed and any accompanying opinion or memorandum of the district court or agency. In the event the order(s) being appealed or any accompanying opinion or memorandum adopt, affirm, or otherwise refer to the report and recommendation of a magistrate judge or the decision of a bankruptcy judge, the report and recommendation or decision must also be attached. In addition, any judge or panel of the court may refer to the Chief Circuit Mediator any appeal, petition, motion or other procedural matter for review and possible amicable resolution.

33.3 Initial Screening and Deferral of Briefing for Cases Selected for Mediation

The Clerk will provide the Chief Circuit Mediator with a copy of the judgment or order on appeal, any opinion or memorandum issued by the district court or agency, appellant's Civil Appeal Information Statement and Concise Summary of the Case and any relevant motions. Following review of these materials, the Chief Circuit Mediator may refer an appeal or petition to a senior judge, himself or herself, or such other person designated pursuant to Rule 48, FRAP for mediation. The Chief Circuit Mediator will advise the parties, the chosen mediator, and the clerk of the referral.

If a case is referred to mediation, a briefing schedule will be deferred during the pendency of mediation unless the court or Chief Circuit Mediator determines otherwise. A referral to mediation will not, however, defer or extend the time for ordering any necessary transcripts.

If a case is not accepted for mediation, or if accepted but is not resolved through mediation, it will proceed in the appellate process as if mediation had not been considered or initiated.

33.4 Referral of Matters to Mediation by a Judge or Panel of the Court

At any time during the pendency of an appeal or petition, any judge or panel of the court may refer the appeal or petition to a senior judge of the court of appeals, a senior judge of a district court, the Chief Circuit Mediator, or other person designated pursuant to Rule 48, F.R.A.P. for mediation or any other purpose consistent with this rule. In addition, any judge or panel of the court may refer any appeal, petition, motion or other procedural matters for review and possible amicable resolution. The procedures set forth in L.A.R. 33.5 are applicable to matters referred for mediation pursuant to L.A.R. 33.4 unless otherwise directed by the Chief Circuit Mediator. Documents, including but not limited to, those specified in L.A.R. 33.5(a) may be required.

33.5 Proceedings After Selection for the Program

(a) **Submission of Position Papers and Documents.** Within 15 days of the case's selection for mediation by the Chief Circuit Mediator, each counsel must prepare and submit to the mediator a confidential position paper of no more than 10 pages, stating counsel's views on the key facts and legal issues in the case, as well as on key factors relating to settlement. The position paper will include a statement of motions filed in the court of appeals and their status. Copies of position papers submitted by the parties directly to the mediator should not be served upon opposing counsel. Documents prepared for mediation sessions are not to be filed with the Clerk's Office and are not to be of record in the case.

(b) **Mediation Sessions.** The mediator will notify the parties of the time, date, and place of the mediation session and whether it will be conducted in person or telephonically. Unless the mediator directs otherwise, mediation sessions must be attended by the senior lawyer for each party responsible for the appeal and by the person or persons with actual authority to negotiate a settlement of the case. If settlement

is not reached at the initial mediation session, but the mediator believes further mediation sessions or discussions would be productive, the mediator may conduct additional mediation sessions in person or telephonically.

(c) **Confidentiality of Mediation Proceedings.** The mediator will not disclose to anyone statements made or information developed during the mediation process. The attorneys and other persons attending the mediation are likewise prohibited from disclosing statements made or information developed during the mediation process to anyone other than clients, principals or co-counsel, and then, only upon receiving due assurances that the recipients will honor the confidentiality of the information. Similarly, the parties are prohibited from using any information obtained as a result of the mediation process as a basis for any motion or argument to any court. The mediation proceedings are considered compromise negotiations under Rule 408 of the Federal Rules of Evidence. Notwithstanding the foregoing, the bare fact that a settlement has been reached as a result of mediation will not be considered confidential.

(d) **Settlement.** No party will be bound by statements or actions at a mediation session unless a settlement is reached. If a settlement is reached, the agreement must be reduced to writing and will be binding upon all parties to the agreement, and counsel must file a stipulation of dismissal of the appeal pursuant to Rule 42(b), FRAP. Such a stipulation must be filed within 30 days after settlement is reached unless an extension thereof is granted by the Chief Circuit Mediator.

33.6 Mediation in Pro Se Cases

In appropriate cases, the Chief Circuit Mediator may request counsel to represent pro se litigants for purposes of mediation only. Counsel must agree to take the case on a pro bono basis, except that if an applicable statute authorizes the award of attorneys' fees, counsel may enter into a written agreement with the client assigning to the attorney any amounts designated as attorneys' fees. The case will be treated as any other case subject to mediation and all provisions of L.A.R. 33 will apply. If mediation is unsuccessful, counsel may discontinue his or her representation; however, counsel may continue to represent the litigant through the rest of the appeal if counsel wishes and the party agrees. The Chief Circuit Mediator may adopt and implement specific procedures in furtherance of this rule.

Source: New rule in 2000

Cross-References: None

Committee Comments: The rule was amended in 2011 to reflect a change in the title of the circuit mediator and to accommodate electronic filing.

[Effective December 15, 2008. Amended effective March 8, 2010; August 1, 2011.]

RULE 34.0   ORAL ARGUMENT

34.1   In General

(a) The court will allow oral argument in all cases unless the panel, after examination of the briefs and records or appendices, is unanimously of the opinion that oral argument is not needed.

(b) Any party to the appeal has the right to file a statement with the court setting forth the reasons why, in the party's opinion, oral argument should be heard. Such statement must be filed with the clerk within 7 days after the filing of appellee's or respondent's brief. The request must set forth the amount of argument time sought.

(c) In certain appeals, the clerk will inform the parties by letter of a particular issue(s) that the panel wishes the parties to address.

(d) The court will grant a motion requesting rescheduling of the argument only where the moving party shows extraordinary circumstances.

(e) A party may request oral argument by video-conference. Such a request may be made by calling the clerk's office. Counsel must notify all opposing sides that a request for video-conference has been made. Generally, a request for oral argument by video-conference should be made when the party is notified of the calendaring of the case. In any case, a request for oral argument by video must be made as soon as possible after counsel knows that a video-conference is needed. Granting of the request is at the Court's discretion.

Source: 1988 Court Rule 12.6

Cross-References: FRAP 21(b), 34; 3d Cir. L.A.R. 27.1; Third Circuit Internal Operating Procedures, Chapter 2 (1994)

Committee Comments: Because the panels are constituted in advance for a specific sitting, rescheduling of an argument may result in a second panel being assigned an appeal when one panel has already performed the necessary study of the briefs and appendix. Alternatively, it may result in members of the panel having to travel to Philadelphia at additional government expense, disrupting previously established schedules. Such needless waste of judicial resources underlies this court's precedent of declining to reschedule except upon a showing of extraordinary circumstances. Subsection (c), adopted in 1995, contains a provision that counsel in certain cases will be notified prior to the oral argument of a particular issue, if any, that is of concern to the court. The portions of prior Court Rule 12.6 that were repetitive of FRAP were deleted in 1995. Otherwise no substantive change from prior Court Rule 12.6 is intended. The rule was revised and simplified in 2000 and 2008.

34.2   Continuance

For good cause the court may pass a case listed for oral argument or order its continuance. No stipulation to pass or continue a case will be recognized as binding upon the court.

Source: 1988 Court Rule 12.5

Cross-References: FRAP 34; 3d Cir. L.A.R. 34.1

Committee Comments: This rule was renumbered by the 1995 revision of the rules; no substantive change from prior Court Rule 12.5 is intended.

34.3   No Oral Argument on Motions Except When Ordered

The court will consider and decide motions upon the motion papers and briefs, and will not hear oral argument unless ordered by the court or a judge thereof. Counsel may assume there will not be oral argument unless advised by the clerk to appear at a time and place fixed by the court.

Source: 1988 Court Rule 11.1

Cross-References: FRAP 8, 9, 18, 27, 34, 40, 41; 3d Cir. L.A.R. 27.1

Committee Comments: This rule is identical to 3d Cir. L.A.R. 27.1. No substantive change from prior Court Rule 11.1 is intended.

[Effective December 15, 2008. Amended effective March 8, 2010.]

RULE 35.0   DETERMINATION OF CAUSES BY THE COURT EN BANC

35.1   Required Statement for Rehearing En Banc

Where the party seeking rehearing en banc is represented by counsel, the petition must contain, so far as is pertinent, the following statement of counsel:

"I express a belief, based on a reasoned and studied professional judgment, that the panel decision is contrary to decisions of the United States Court of Appeals for the Third Circuit or the Supreme Court of the United States, and that consideration by the full court is necessary to secure and maintain uniformity of decisions in this court, i.e., the panel's decision is contrary to the decision of this court or the Supreme Court in [citing specifically the case or cases], OR, that this appeal involves a question of exceptional importance, i.e., [set forth in one sentence]."

Source: 1988 Court Rule 22

Cross-References: FRAP 32(b), 35, 40; 3d Cir. L.A.R. 32.3; Third Circuit Internal Operating Procedures, Chapter 9 (1994)

Committee Comments: This rule was renumbered by the 1995 revision of the rules; no substantive change from prior Court Rule 22 is intended.

35.2   Form, Filing, and Required Attachments to Petition for Rehearing En Banc

(a) A petition seeking rehearing en banc must be filed electronically as provided in L.A.R. Misc. 113. Paper copies need not be filed unless directed by the clerk. Petitions must include as an exhibit a copy of the panel's judgment, order, and opinion, if any, as to which rehearing is sought.

(b) Certain personal identifiers must be excluded or redacted from all documents filed with the court as specified in L.A.R. Misc. 113.12 and Judicial Conference policy.

Source: 1988 Court Rule 22.1

Cross-References: FRAP 32(b)(c), 35, 40; 3d Cir. L.A.R. 32.3 and L.A.R. Misc. 113

Committee Comments: The requirements of electronic filing and redaction was added in 2008. Former subsection (b) was deleted in 2008 because of electronic filing.

35.3 Composition of En Banc Quorum

For purposes of determining the majority number necessary to grant a petition for rehearing, all circuit judges currently in regular active service who are not disqualified will be counted.

Source: None

Cross-References: FRAP 35; 3d Cir. L.A.R. Misc. 101.0

Committee Comments: Changes were made in 2002 to conform the rule to Internal Operating Procedure Chapter 9. The last sentence of the 2002 rule was deleted in 2008 to conform to amendments to FRAP 35.

35.4 Caution

As noted in FRAP 35, en banc hearing or rehearing of appeals is not favored. Counsel have a duty to the court commensurate with that owed their clients to read with attention and observe with restraint the required statement for rehearing en banc set forth in 3d Cir. L.A.R. 35.1. Counsel are reminded that in every case the duty of counsel is fully discharged without filing a petition for rehearing en banc unless the case meets the rigorous requirements of FRAP 35 and 3d Cir. L.A.R. 35.1.

Source: None

Cross-References: 28 U.S.C. § 1927; FRAP 35, 38; 3d Cir. L.A.R. 35.1; Third Circuit Internal Operating Procedures, Chapter 9 (1994)

Committee Comments: New provision in 1995. This rule is modeled after U.S.Ct. of App. 5th Cir. Rule 35 (1991). The purpose of the rule is to emphasize that the court does not favor requests for hearing or rehearing en banc, and to discourage inappropriate requests from being made.

35.5 Death Penalty Cases

The provisions of 3d Cir. L.A.R. Misc. 111.7 govern all petitions seeking hearing or rehearing by the court en banc in all actions challenging a conviction in which a sentence of death has been imposed.

Source: 3d Cir. L.A.R. 8.2, 22.2

Cross References: FRAP 35, 3d Cir. L.A.R. Misc. 111.7

Committee Comments: New provision in 1995. To the extent consistent with FRAP and applicable, local procedure in

all death penalty proceedings will be governed by 3d Cir. L.A.R. Misc. 111.0.

[Effective December 15, 2008.]

RULE 36.0   ENTRY OF JUDGMENT

36.1 Opinions

All written opinions of the court and of the panels thereof will be filed with and preserved by the clerk. All opinions will be posted on the court's internet web site under the supervision of the clerk. Printed opinions need not be copied into the minutes; when posted on the court's internet web site they will be deemed to have been recorded.

Source: 1988 Court Rule 16

Cross-Reference: FRAP 36

Committee Comments: Amended in 2008 to conform to current practice of electronic posting of opinions. No substantive change from prior Court Rule 16 is intended.

36.2 Copies of Printed Opinions (Abrogated in 2008)

[Effective December 15, 2008.]

RULE 39.0   COSTS

39.1 Certification or Certiorari to Supreme Court

In all cases certified to the Supreme Court or removed thereto by certiorari, the fees of the clerk of this court must be paid before a transcript of the record is transmitted to the Supreme Court.

Source: 1988 Court Rule 17.1

Cross-References: 28 U.S.C. §§ 1254, 1913, 1920; FRAP 39

Committee Comments: This rule was renumbered by the 1995 revision of the rules; no substantive change from prior Court Rule 17.1 is intended.

39.2 Schedule of Fees and Costs

Pursuant to 28 U.S.C. § 1913, a uniform schedule of fees and costs is prescribed from time to time by the Judicial Conference of the United States. An up-to-date schedule can be found as an annotation to 28 U.S.C. § 1913 in the United States Code, the United States Code Annotated, and West's Federal Civil Judicial Procedure and Rules manual.

Source: 1988 Court Rule 17.2

Cross-References: 28 U.S.C. § 1913; FRAP 39

Committee Comments: The provisions of prior Court Rule 17.2 that were repetitive of 28 U.S.C. § 1913 and FRAP 3(b) and 24(a) have been deleted. The provisions of prior Court Rule 17.2 regarding the costs of printed opinions have been moved to 3d Cir. L.A.R. 36.2.

39.3 Taxation of Reproduction Costs

The cost of printing or otherwise producing necessary copies of briefs and appendices are taxable as follows:

(a) Number of Briefs. Costs will be allowed for ten (10) copies of each brief required to be filed with the court, two copies for the prevailing party, and one (1) copy for each party separately represented, unless the court directs a greater number of briefs to be filed. If costs are claimed for providing paper copies to parties who have consented to electronic service, and the certificate of service does not state that paper copies were provided, the clerk may require proof that paper copies were actually supplied.

(b) Number of Appendices. Costs will be allowed for four (4) copies of the appendix required to be filed with the court plus one (1) copy for each party separately represented, unless the court directs a greater number of appendices to be filed. If costs are claimed for providing paper copies to parties who have consented to electronic service and the certificate of service does not state that paper copies were provided, the clerk may require proof that paper copies were actually supplied.

(c) Costs of Reproduction of Briefs and Appendices. In taxing costs for printed or photocopied briefs and appendices, the clerk will tax costs at the following rates, or at the actual cost, whichever is less, depending upon the manner of reproduction or photocopying:

(1) Reproduction (whether by offset or typography):

Reproduction per page (for 20 copies or less)	$ 4.00
Covers (for 20 copies or less)	$ 50.00
Binding per copy	$ 4.00
Sales Tax	Applicable Rate

(2) Photocopying (whether in house or commercial):

Reproduction per page per copy	$ .10
Binding per copy	$ 4.00
Covers (for 20 copies or less)	$ 40.00
Sales Tax	Applicable Rate

(3) In the event a party subsequently corrects deficiencies in either a brief or appendix pursuant to 3d Cir. L.A.R. Misc. 107.3 and that party prevails on appeal, costs which were incurred in order to bring the brief or appendix into compliance may not be allowed.

(d) Other Costs. No other costs associated with briefs and appendices, including the costs of typing, word processing, preparation of tables and footnotes, and electronic filing will be allowed for purposes of taxation of costs.

Source: 1988 Court Rule 20.1

Cross-References: 28 U.S.C. § 1920; FRAP 39

Committee Comments: Sales tax will be included in the costs only when actually paid to a commercial photocopying service. No substantive change from prior Court Rule 20.1 is intended. Amended in 2011 to conform to L.A.R. 31 regarding copies to be served on opposing counsel and to clarify that costs for reproduction of paper briefs for opposing parties are recoverable only if paper briefs are actually provided.

39.4 Filing Date; Support for Bill of Costs

(a) The court will deny untimely bills of cost unless a motion showing good cause is filed with the bill.

(b) Parties must submit the itemized and verified bill of costs on a standard form to be provided by the clerk.

(c) An answer to objections to a bill of costs may be filed within 14 days of service of the objections.

Source: 1988 Court Rules 20.2, 20.3

Cross-Reference: FRAP 39

Committee Comments: The portions of prior Court Rules 20.2 and 20.3 that were repetitive of FRAP 39 were deleted in 1995. The rule now specifically allows for an answer to objections, a codification of existing practice. Otherwise, no substantive change from prior Court Rules 20.2 and 20.3 is intended. Time changed to 14 days in 2010 to conform to amendments in FRAP.

[Effective December 15, 2008. Amended effective March 8, 2010; August 1, 2011.]

RULE 40.0 PETITION FOR PANEL REHEARING

40.1 Form, Filing, and Required Attachments to Petition for Panel Rehearing

(a) A petition seeking rehearing must be filed electronically as provided in L.A.R. Misc. 113. Paper copies need not be filed unless directed by the clerk. Petitions must include as an exhibit a copy of the panel's judgment, order, and opinion, if any, as to which rehearing is sought.

(b) Certain personal identifiers must be excluded or redacted from all documents filed with the court as specified in L.A.R. Misc. 113.12 and Judicial Conference policy.

Source: New provision in 2000.

Cross-References: FRAP 35, 40; 3d Cir. L.A.R. Misc. 113

Committee Comments: This provision is designed to create parallel provisions for petitions for panel rehearing and rehearing en banc. It is not intended to alter the provisions of IOP 9.5.1 which provide that an unlabeled petition will be construed as requesting both panel rehearing and rehearing en banc. The requirements of electronic filing and redaction was added in 2008.

[Effective December 15, 2008.]

RULE 45.0 DUTIES OF CLERKS

45.1 Office—Where Kept

The Clerk's Office will be kept in the United States Courthouse in the city of Philadelphia.

Source: 1988 Court Rule 5.1

Cross-References: FRAP 45

Committee Comments: This rule was renumbered by the 1995 revision of the rules; no substantive change from prior Court Rule 5.1 is intended.

45.2 Daily Listing of Cases

The clerk must prepare, under the direction of the court, a list for each session of the court, on which so far as practicable each case will be listed for argument or submission on a day certain during the week.

Source: 1988 Court Rule 12.2

Cross-References: FRAP 34, 45; 3d Cir. L.A.R. 34.1

Committee Comments: Language describing the clerk's method of preparing the argument lists was deleted in 1995. Otherwise, no substantive change from prior Court Rule 12.2 is intended.

[Effective December 15, 2008.]

RULE 46.0 ATTORNEYS

46.1 Admission

(a) Except as the court otherwise directs, practice before the court is limited to the members of the bar of this court. Admission to the bar of this court is governed by the provisions of FRAP 46 and such other requirements as the court may adopt from time to time, provided, however, that (i) the applicant must be familiar with the contents of the Federal Rules of Civil Procedure, Criminal Procedure, and Appellate Procedure, as well as with the Local Appellate Rules and Internal Operating Procedures of this court, and (ii) the applicant has read and understood those provisions of the above documents dealing with briefs, motions and appendices. The fee for admission is determined by order of the court and is payable to the clerk as trustee. All funds received from such applications must be deposited in the appropriate accounts of the court designated for this purpose.

(b) Unless the court otherwise directs, an attorney must apply for admission to the bar of this court when the attorney enters an appearance, or at such time as a motion, brief, or other document is filed in this court. An attorney who will argue the appeal, if not previously admitted to the bar of this court, may apply for admission on or before the date of oral argument. Forms prescribed by the court for purpose of admission may be obtained from the clerk of this court.

(c) Any applicant for admission to the bar of this court may be admitted in open court on oral motion, on motion before a single judge of this court, or as the court may otherwise from time to time determine. However, qualified applicants to the bar of this court not previously admitted and who will argue the appeal must be admitted in open court on oral motion.

(d) An applicant for admission to the bar of this court may be admitted on written or oral motion of a member of the bar of this court or a circuit or district judge of this circuit.

(e) The initial brief filed by each party with the court must contain a certification that at least one of the attorneys whose names appear on the brief is a member of the bar of this court, or has filed an application for admission pursuant to this rule.

Source: 1988 Court Rule 9.1

Cross-References: FRAP 46; 3d Cir. L.A.R. 28.3(a) and L.A.R. Misc. 113; Third Circuit Attorney Disciplinary Rules.

Committee Comments: This rule was renumbered by the 1995 revision of the rules; no substantive change from prior Court Rule 9.1 is intended. It is not intended that current practice permitted by law be changed. See L.A.R. Misc. 113.2 for requirements for registration for electronic filing. Technical changes were made in 2008 to conform to new Judicial Conference policies regarding the deposit of funds.

46.2 Entry of Appearance

Within 14 days of notification of the docketing of a case, counsel for the appellant or petitioner must file an entry of appearance which must include an address where notices and papers may be mailed to or served upon him or her. Counsel must include an e-mail address. The entry of appearance form must be served on all parties. Not later than 14 days after the docketing of the appeal, counsel for all parties in the trial court or agency below and any other persons entitled to participate in the proceedings as appellees or respondents and desiring to do so, must file similar appearances. Any such party or other person on whose behalf counsel fails to file an entry of appearance within the time fixed by this rule will not be entitled to receive notices or copies of briefs and appendices until an entry of appearance has been entered for such party. Counsel or a party proceeding pro se who is not registered as a Filing User must be served directly with copies of notices, motions, and briefs.

Source: 1988 Court Rule 9.2

Cross-References: FRAP 46

Committee Comments: This rule was renumbered by the 1995 revision of the rules; no substantive change from prior Court Rule 9.2 is intended. The requirement of an e-mail address was added in 2008. Time changed to 14 days in 2010 to conform to amendments in FRAP.

46.3 Entry of Appearance by Eligible Law Students

(a) Eligibility.

(1) An eligible law student who represented an indigent litigant in the district court in a civil matter

or before an administrative agency may enter an appearance in this court provided that the person on whose behalf the student is appearing indicates in writing his or her consent to that appearance and a supervising lawyer also indicates in writing his or her approval of that appearance.

(2) The court may appoint, either in response to a motion for appointment of counsel or sua sponte, a law student who is participating in a law school clinic or pro bono program to represent an indigent pro se litigant. If the court appoints a law student sua sponte, the person on whose behalf the student is appearing must indicate in writing his or her consent to that appearance. Students appointed by the court must enter an appearance in accordance with this rule.

(3) In each case the written consent and approval of the person the law student represents must be filed in the record of the case and must be brought to the attention of the court.

(4) An eligible law student may engage in other activities under the general supervision of a member of the bar of this court outside the personal presence of that lawyer for the purpose of preparation of briefs, abstracts, and other documents to be filed in this court, but such documents must be signed by the supervising lawyer.

(5) An eligible law student may participate in oral argument in this court but only in the presence of the supervising lawyer, who must be prepared to supplement any written or oral statement made by the student. Students should recognize that argument may be scheduled during school breaks.

(b) Requirements and Limitations. In order to make an appearance pursuant to this rule, the law student must:

(1) Be duly enrolled in a law school approved by the American Bar Association.

(2) Have completed legal studies amounting to at least four semesters, or the equivalent if the school is on some basis other than a semester basis, or be enrolled in a law school clinic or pro bono program.

(3) If not enrolled in a law school clinic or pro bono program, be certified by the dean of his or her law school as being of good character and competent legal ability, and as being adequately trained to perform as an eligible law student under this rule.

(4) Neither ask for nor receive any compensation or remuneration of any kind from the person on whose behalf the law student renders service, but this will not prevent a lawyer, legal aid bureau, law school, public defender agency, or the government from paying compensation to the eligible law student, nor will it prevent any agency from making such charges for its services as it may otherwise properly require.

(5) Submit with the appearance form a certification in writing that the law student has read and is familiar with the rules of professional conduct governing attorneys practicing in the jurisdiction of the supervising attorney.

(6) Submit with the appearance form the following signed and notarized oath or affirmation:

"I, [name], do swear (or affirm) that I will support the Constitution of the United States, and that, in practicing as an eligible law student under 3d Cir. L.A.R. 46.3 I will conduct myself strictly in accordance with the terms of that rule and according to law."

(c) Certification.

(1) The certification of a student by the law school dean must be filed with the clerk of court and, unless it is sooner withdrawn, will remain in effect until the expiration of eighteen (18) months after it is filed, or until the announcement of the results of the first bar examination of the state where the student's law school is located following the student's graduation, whichever is earlier. For any student who passes that examination or who is admitted to the bar without taking an examination, the certification will continue in effect until the date the student is admitted to the bar. The student is responsible for advising the clerk in writing of any change in status or event affecting the student's certification.

(2) The certification may be withdrawn by the dean at any time by sending a notice to that effect to the clerk of the court. It is not necessary that the notice state the cause for withdrawal.

(3) The certification may be terminated by this court at any time without notice or hearing and without any showing of cause.

(d) Supervision. The member of the bar under whose supervision an eligible law student does any of the things permitted by this rule must:

(1) Be a lawyer in good standing of the bar of this court and enter an appearance in the case.

(2) Assume personal professional responsibility for the student's guidance in any work undertaken and for supervising the quality of the student's work.

(3) Assist the student to the extent the supervising lawyer considers it necessary.

(4) Assure that briefing schedules are met regardless of semester breaks, exams, and vacations.

(5) Be prepared to appear and argue if the student is unavailable when the case is scheduled for oral argument.

Source: 1988 Court Rule 9.3

Cross-References: FRAP 46; Third Circuit Attorney Disciplinary Rules

Committee Comments: The Model Rules of Professional Responsibility replace the Canons of Professional Ethics. No substantive change from prior Court Rule 9.3 is intended. Revised in 2011.

46.4 Signing Documents

All documents, motions and briefs must be signed by an attorney or by a party appearing pro se. Electronically filed documents must be signed with either an electronic signature or "s/typed name."

Source: Fed. R. Civ. P. 11

Cross-References: L.A.R. 28.4; L.A.R. Misc. 113.9

Committee Comments: This rule is derived from Fed. R. Civ. P. 11 which requires signatures on all papers. The signing of documents is important because it constitutes a certificate by the attorney or party that he or she has read the pleading or brief to ensure that it complies with all federal and local rules. The requirement is interpreted broadly and the attorney of record may designate another person to sign the brief. If a party is represented by multiple counsel, the signature from only one attorney of record is required. The rule was amended in 2008 to permit electronic signatures.

[Effective December 15, 2008. Amended effective March 8, 2010; August 1, 2011.]

RULE 47.0 RULES BY COURTS OF APPEALS

47.1 Advisory Committee

Any proposed change in the Third Circuit Local Appellate Rules will be forwarded for comment to the Lawyers Advisory Committee, which constitutes the advisory committee for the study of the rules of practice as required by 28 U.S.C. § 2077(b).

Source: None

Cross-References: 28 U.S.C. § 2077(b)

Committee Comments: The 1988 amendments to the Judicial Code provide for the appointment of an advisory committee to study, inter alia, local rules of practice. 3d Cir. L.A.R. 47.1 specifies the Lawyers Advisory Committee (LAC) as the statutorily-required review committee, and specifies that any proposed changes in these rules be studied by the LAC before they are adopted.

[Effective December 15, 2008.]

RULE 48.0 SPECIAL MASTERS

48.1 Special Masters

The court may appoint a master to hold hearings, if necessary, and make recommendations as to any auxiliary matter requiring a factual determination in the court of appeals. If the master is not a court officer, the compensation to be allowed to the master will be fixed by the court, and will be charged upon such of the parties as the court may direct.

Source: None

Cross-Reference: FRAP 48

Committee Comments: New provision in 1997. This rule is intended to formalize by rule the court's practice of appointing special masters to resolve factual questions where appropriate and needed by the court.

[Effective December 15, 2008.]

MISCELLANEOUS—THIRD CIRCUIT LOCAL APPELLATE RULES

RULE 101.0 CONSTITUTION OF THE COURT—PANELS—QUORUM

101.1 The Court—Judges Who Constitute It

The court consists of the circuit judges in regular active service. The circuit justice and other justices and judges so designated or assigned by the chief judge are eligible to sit as judges of the court.

Source: 1988 Court Rule 2.1

Cross-References: None

Committee Comments: Prior Court Rule 2.1 has no counterpart in FRAP and is therefore classified as Miscellaneous. No substantive change from prior Court Rule 2.1 is intended.

101.2 Quorum—Adjournment in Absence of—By Whom Adjourned

A majority of the number of judges authorized to constitute the court or a panel thereof constitutes a quorum. When necessary, a judge may attend via audio or video conference. If a quorum does not attend on any day appointed for holding a session of the court or a panel thereof, any judge who does attend may adjourn the court or panel, or, in the absence of any judges, the clerk may adjourn the court or panel.

Source: 1988 Court Rule 2.5

Cross-Reference: 28 U.S.C. § 46(d)

Committee Comments: Prior Court Rule 2.5 has no counterpart in FRAP and is therefore classified as Miscellaneous. All references in the prior rule to "divisions" of this court have been changed to "panels." Otherwise, no substantive change from prior Court Rule 2.5 is intended. The rule was amended in 2008 to clarify that judges may attend by audio or video conference.

[Effective December 15, 2008.]

RULE 102.0 SESSIONS

102.1 Sessions—When and Where Held

(a) Stated sessions of the court or of its panels will be held at Philadelphia or at another place within the circuit commencing on such dates each month as the court designates, and in the Virgin Islands commencing at such dates as the court designates. Pursuant to request of the parties or order of the court, a Virgin Islands case may be heard at another place in the circuit. The stated sessions of the court in the Virgin Islands will be held in Charlotte Amalie in even-numbered years and in Christiansted in odd-numbered years unless the court directs otherwise.

(b) Special sessions may be held at any time or place within the circuit when so ordered by the court.

Source: 1988 Court Rules 3.2 and 3.3

Cross-References: None

Committee Comments: Prior Court Rules 3.2 and 3.3 have no counterpart in FRAP and are therefore classified as Miscellaneous. The rule has been revised to give the court the option to schedule its Virgin Islands sessions in months other than April and December. A reference to the "divisions" of this court has been changed to "panels." Otherwise, no substantive change from prior Court Rules 3.2 and 3.3 is intended. The rule has been revised so that the court may sit at other places within the circuit and may, in appropriate circumstances, reverse the place or alter the timing of the Virgin Islands sitting.

[Effective December 15, 2008.]

RULE 103.0 MARSHAL, CRIER, AND OTHER OFFICERS

103.1 Who Shall Attend Court

A crier and, if requested, the marshal of the district in which the sessions of the court are held will be in attendance during the sessions of the court.

Source: 1988 Court Rule 6.1

Cross-References: None

Committee Comments: Prior Court Rule 6.1 has no counterpart in FRAP and is therefore classified as Miscellaneous. No substantive change from prior Court Rule 6.1 is intended.

[Effective December 15, 2008.]

RULE 104.0 COURT LIBRARIES

104.1 Regulations Governing Use of Libraries

The law libraries will be open during such hours as are reasonable to satisfy the needs of the court, and will be governed by such regulations as the librarian, with the approval of the court's library committee, may from time to time make effective.

Source: 1988 Court Rule 7.3

Cross-References: None

Committee Comments: Prior Court Rule 7.3 has no counterpart in FRAP and is therefore classified as Miscellaneous. No substantive change from prior Court Rule 7.3 is intended.

[Effective December 15, 2008.]

RULE 105.0 JUDICIAL CONFERENCE OF THE THIRD CIRCUIT

105.1 Attendance at Invitations to the Conference

In addition to judicial participants, attendance at the Judicial Conference of the Third Circuit may be open at the discretion of the chief judge to any member of the bar of any court within the circuit interested in the work of the courts and the administration of justice in the circuit.

Source: 1988 Court Rule 18.2

Cross-Reference: 28 U.S.C. § 333

Committee Comments: Prior Court Rule 18.2 has no counterpart in FRAP and is therefore classified as Miscellaneous. The rule has been revised to reflect the court's open invitation policy.

[Effective December 15, 2008.]

RULE 106.0 FILING OF DOCUMENTS UNDER SEAL

106.1 Necessity; Grand Jury Matters; Previously Impounded Records; Unsealing

(a) Generally. With the exception of matters relating to grand jury investigations, filing of documents under seal without prior court approval is discouraged. If a party believes a portion of a brief or other document merits treatment under seal, the party must file a motion setting forth with particularity the reasons why sealing is deemed necessary. Any other party may file objections, if any, within 7 days.

A motion to seal must explain the basis for sealing and specify the desired duration of the sealing order. If discussion of confidential material is necessary to support the motion to seal, the motion may be filed provisionally under seal. Rather than automatically requesting the sealing of an entire brief, motion, or other filing, litigants should consider whether argument relating to sealed materials may be contained in a separate sealed supplemental brief, motion or filings. Sealed documents must not be included in a regular appendix, but may be submitted in a separate, sealed volume of the appendix. In addressing material under seal (except for the presentencing report) in an unsealed brief or motion or oral argument counsel are expected not to disclose the nature of the sealed material and to apprise the court that the material is sealed.

(b) Grand Jury Matters. In matters relating to grand jury investigations, when there is inadequate time for a party to file a motion requesting permission to file documents under seal, the party may file briefs and other documents using initials or a John or Jane Doe designation to avoid disclosure of the identity of the applicant or the subject matter of the grand jury investigation. Promptly thereafter, the party must file a motion requesting permission to use such a designation. All responsive briefs and other documents must follow the same format until further order of the court.

(c) Records Impounded in the District Court.

(1) *Criminal Cases and Cases Collaterally Attacking Convictions.* Grand jury materials protected by Fed. R. Crim. P. 6(c), presentence reports, statements of reasons for the sentence and any other similar material in a criminal case or a case collaterally attacking a conviction (cases under 28 U.S.C. §§ 2241, 2254, 2255), which were filed with the district court under seal pursuant to statute, rule or an order of impoundment, and which constitute part of the record transmitted to this court, remain subject to the district court's impoundment order and will be placed under seal by the clerk of this court until further order of this court. In cases in which impounded documents other than grand jury materials, presentence reports, statements of reasons for the sentence, or other documents required to be sealed by statute or rule, are included in the record transmitted to this court under L.A.R. 11.2, the party seeking to have the document sealed must file a motion within 21 days of receiving notice of the docketing of the appeal in this court, explaining the basis for sealing and specifying the desired duration of the sealing order. If discussion of confidential material is necessary to support the motion to seal, the motion may be filed provisionally under seal.

(2) *Civil Cases.* When the district court impounds part or all of the documents in a civil case, they will remain under seal in this court for 30 days after the filing of the notice of appeal to give counsel an opportunity to file a motion to continue the impoundment, setting forth the reasons therefor. A motion to continue impoundment must explain the basis for sealing and specify the desired duration of the sealing order. If the motion does not specify a date, the documents will be unsealed, without notice to the parties, five years after conclusion of the case. If discussion of confidential material is necessary to support the motion to seal, the motion may be filed provisionally under seal. If a motion to continue impoundment is filed, the documents will remain sealed until further order of this court.

Source: 1988 Court Rule 21.3

Cross-References: 3d Cir. L.A.R. 30.3

Committee Comments: Prior Court Rule 21.3 has no counterpart in FRAP and is therefore classified as Miscellaneous. The rule has been revised to place an affirmative obligation to file a motion on the party in a civil matter who wishes to

continue the sealing of documents on appeal. The archiving center will not accept sealed documents, which presents storage problems for the court. The rule has been amended to require the parties to specify how long documents must be kept under seal after the case is closed. The rule was amended in 2008 to provide that unless otherwise specified, documents in civil cases would remain sealed only for five years.

[Effective December 15, 2008. Amended effective March 8, 2010.]

RULE 107.0 SANCTIONS

107.1 Dismissal of Appeal for Failure to Pay Certain Fees

(a) The clerk is authorized to dismiss the appeal if the appellant does not pay the docketing fee within 14 days after the case is opened in the court of appeals, as prescribed by 3d Cir. L.A.R. 3.3.

(b) The appellant's failure to comply with 3d Cir. L.A.R. 11.1 regarding transcription fees is grounds for dismissal of the appeal.

Source: 1988 Court Rules 15.1, 28.1

Cross-References: FRAP 3(a), 11; 3d Cir. L.A.R. 3.3

Committee Comments: For the convenience of counsel, all rules relating to sanctions are included in 3d Cir. L.A.R. Misc. 107.0. Where these rules have some counterpart in FRAP, they are included in both the corresponding 3d Cir. L.A.R. and Misc. 107.0. Where they have no counterpart in FRAP, they are included in 3d Cir. L.A.R. Misc. 107.0 only. Only the parts of prior Court Rules 15.1 and 28.1 setting forth sanctions have been included here. No substantive change from prior Court Rules 15.1 and 28.1 is intended. The rule was amended in 2008 to clarify when the time for payment of fees begins to run.

107.2 Dismissal for Failure to Prosecute

(a) When an appellant fails to comply with the Federal Rules of Appellate Procedure or the Local Appellate Rules of this court, the clerk will issue written notice to counsel or to the appellant who appears pro se that upon the expiration of 14 days from the date of the notice, the appeal may be dismissed for want of prosecution unless appellant remedies the deficiency within that time. If the deficiency is not remedied within this period, the clerk is authorized to dismiss the appeal for want of prosecution and issue a certified copy thereof to the clerk of the district court as the mandate. The appellant is not entitled to remedy the deficiency after the appeal is dismissed except by order of the court. A motion to set aside such an order must be justified by the showing of good cause and must be filed within 10 days of the date of dismissal. If the appeal is one taken from the District Court of the Virgin Islands, an additional 10 days will be added to the time limits specified in this paragraph.

(b) Notwithstanding subsection (a), if an appellant fails to comply with the Federal Rules of Appellate

Procedure and the Local Appellate Rules with respect to the timely filing of a brief and appendix, at any time after the seventh day following the due date, the clerk is authorized to dismiss the appeal for want of timely prosecution. The procedure to be followed in requesting an order to set aside dismissal of the appeal is the same as that set forth in subsection (a).

Source: 1988 Court Rule 28.2

Cross-Reference: FRAP 3(a)

Committee Comments: Prior Court Rule 28.2 had no counterpart in FRAP and is therefore classified as Miscellaneous. No substantive change from prior Court Rule 28.2 is intended.

107.3   Non–Conforming Motion, Brief or Appendix

If a motion, brief, or appendix submitted for filing does not comply with FRAP 27–32 or 3d Cir. L.A.R. 27.0–32.0, the clerk will file the document, but notify the party of the need to promptly correct the deficiency. The clerk will also cite this rule and indicate to the defaulting party how he or she failed to comply. In the event a party subsequently corrects the deficiencies in either a brief or appendix pursuant to this rule and that party prevails on appeal, costs which were incurred in order to bring the brief or appendix into compliance may not be allowed. If the party fails or declines to correct the deficiency, the clerk must refer the defaulting document, any motion or answer by the party, and pertinent correspondence to a judge of this court for review. If the court finds that the party continues not to be in compliance with the rules despite the notice by the clerk, the court may, in its discretion, impose sanctions as it may deem appropriate, including but not limited to the dismissal of the appeal, striking of the document, imposition of costs or disciplinary sanctions upon counsel.

Source: 1988 Court Rule 21.4

Cross-References: FRAP 3(a), 30(b)(2), 38; 3d Cir. L.A.R. 27.0–32.0

Committee Comments: Prior Court Rule 21.4 had no counterpart in FRAP and is therefore classified as Miscellaneous. No substantive change from prior Court Rule 21.4 is intended.

107.4   Sanctions Pursuant to FRAP 30(b)(2)

(a) The court, sua sponte by Rule to Show Cause or on the motion of any party, may impose sanctions in the form of denial of all or some of the costs of the appeal upon finding that any party has unreasonably and vexatiously caused the inclusion of materials in an appendix that are unnecessary for the determination of the issues presented on appeal.

(b) A party filing such a motion must do so not later than 10 days after a bill of costs has been served. The movant must submit with the motion an itemized statement specifically setting forth, by name and appendix page number, the item or items that the mov-

ant asserts were unnecessarily included in the appendix.

(c) Any party against whom sanctions are requested may file an answer to the motion or Rule to Show Cause, which must be filed within 10 days after service of the motion or Rule to Show Cause.

Source: 1988 Court Rule 20.4

Cross-References: FRAP 30(b)(2); 3d Cir. L.A.R. 30.5

Committee Comments: This Miscellaneous Rule is identical to 3d Cir. L.A.R. 30.5. No substantive change from prior Court Rule 20.4 is intended.

[Effective December 15, 2008. Amended effective March 8, 2010.]

RULE 108.0   APPLICATIONS FOR ATTORNEY'S FEES AND EXPENSES

108.1   Application for Fees

(a) Except as otherwise provided by statute, all applications for an award of attorney's fees and other expenses relating to a case filed in this court, regardless of the source of authority for assessment, must be filed within 30 days after the entry of this court's judgment, unless a timely petition for panel rehearing or rehearing en banc has been filed, in which case a request for attorney's fees must be filed within 14 days after the court's disposition of such petition. Such application must be filed with the clerk in the time set forth above whether or not the parties seek further action in the case or further review from any court.

(b) The court will strictly adhere to the time set forth above and grant exceptions only in extraordinary circumstances.

(c) The application must include a short statement of the authority pursuant to which the party seeks the award. The application must also show the nature and extent of services rendered and the amount sought, including an itemized statement in affidavit form from the attorney stating the actual time expended and the rate at which fees are computed, together with a statement of expenses for which reimbursement is sought.

Source: 1988 Court Rule 27.1

Cross-References: None

Committee Comments: Prior Court Rule 27.1 has no counterpart in FRAP and is therefore classified as Miscellaneous. No substantive change from prior Court Rule 27.1 is intended. L.A.R. Misc. 108.3 addresses claims for attorney's fees and expenses under the Criminal Justice Act, 18 U.S.C. § 3006A. Petition for rehearing en banc was substituted for "suggestion for rehearing en banc" in 2008 to conform to changes in FRAP.

108.2   Objections to Applications for Fees

Written objections to an allowance of attorney's fees, setting forth specifically the basis for objection, must be filed within 10 days after service of the application. Thereafter, the court may, when appropriate, either refer the application to the district court or agency where the case originated or refer the application to a master.

Source: 1988 Court Rule 27.2

Cross-References: FRAP 48; 3d Cir. L.A.R. 48.0

Committee Comments: Prior Court Rule 27.2 has no counterpart in FRAP and is therefore classified as Miscellaneous. No substantive change from prior Court Rule 27.2 is intended.

108.3 Fee Applications Under 18 U.S.C. § 3006A

All claims for attorney's fees and reimbursement for expenses reasonably incurred by counsel in representing a defendant under the Criminal Justice Act, 18 U.S.C. § 3006A, be must filed with the clerk no later than 45 days after the conclusion of the attorney's representation. Such claims must be itemized and prepared on prescribed forms.

Source: 1988 Court Rule 30.1

Cross-References: 18 U.S.C. § 3006A; Third Circuit Criminal Justice Act Plan, Chapter 4(2) (1991)

Committee Comments: Prior Court Rule 30.1 has no counterpart in FRAP and is therefore classified as Miscellaneous. No substantive change from prior Court Rule 30.1 is intended.

[Effective December 15, 2008. Amended effective March 8, 2010.]

RULE 109.0 COUNSEL IN DIRECT CRIMINAL APPEALS

109.1 Trial Counsel to Continue Representation on Appeal

Trial counsel in criminal cases, whether retained or appointed, are expected to continue on appeal absent extraordinary circumstances. After the entry of an order of judgment, counsel will not be permitted to withdraw from a direct criminal appeal without specific leave of this court. Trial counsel not members of the bar of this court must promptly move for admission pursuant to 3d Cir. L.A.R. 46.1.

Source: None

Cross-References: None

Committee Comments: 3d Cir. L.A.R. Misc. 109.1 is designed to remind trial counsel in criminal cases that they are expected to continue the representation of their clients through appeal. "Trial counsel" includes counsel who have represented a client at pretrial, plea or sentencing proceedings.

109.2 Motions by Trial Counsel to Withdraw Representation

(a) Where, upon review of the district court record, counsel is persuaded that the appeal presents no issue of even arguable merit, counsel may file a motion to withdraw and supporting brief pursuant to *Anders v. California*, 386 U.S. 738 (1967), which must be served upon the appellant and the United States. The United States must file a brief in response. Appellant may also file a brief in response pro se. After all briefs have been filed, the clerk will refer the case to a merits panel. If the panel agrees that the appeal is without merit, it will grant counsel's Anders motion, and dispose of the appeal without appointing new counsel. If the panel finds arguable merit to the appeal, or that the Anders brief is inadequate to assist the court in its review, it will appoint substitute counsel, order supplemental briefing and restore the case to the calendar. The panel will also determine whether to continue the appointment of current counsel or to direct the clerk to discharge current counsel and appoint new counsel.

(b) In cases in which a motion to withdraw filed by counsel appointed under the Criminal Justice Act has been granted after the filing of a brief pursuant to *Anders v. California*, 386 U.S. 738 (1967), the court in its decision determining the case may state that the issues presented in the appeal lack legal merit for purposes of counsel filing a petition for writ of certiorari in the Supreme Court. In such a case counsel is under no obligation to file a petition. In all other cases in which counsel appointed under the Criminal Justice Act is of the opinion, in his or her professional judgment, that no issues are present which warrant the filing of a petition for writ of certiorari in the Supreme Court, counsel must promptly file with the court of appeals a motion stating that opinion with particularity and requesting leave to withdraw. *See Austin v. United States*, 513 U.S. 5 (1994). Any such motion must be served on the appellant and the United States.

(c) If the court is of the opinion in a case in which counsel has been appointed under the Criminal Justice Act that there are no issues present which warrant the filing of a petition for writ of certiorari, the court may include a statement to that effect in its decision and counsel may thereafter file the appropriate motion to withdraw. Any such motion must be served on the appellant and the United States. The absence of a statement by the court with respect to the merit of issues which might be presented to the Supreme Court must not be construed as an indication of the opinion of the court of appeals of merit or lack of merit of any issue.

Source: None

Cross-References: Third Circuit Criminal Justice Act Plan, Chapter 3

Committee Comments: New provision in 1995. 3d Cir. L.A.R. Misc. 109.2 sets out for the first time the procedure by which trial counsel may withdraw from a non-meritorious criminal appeal pursuant to *Anders v. California*, 386 U.S. 738 (1967). Addition of sections (b) and (c) was made in response to *Austin v. United States*, 513 U.S. 5 (1994). Subsection (a) was revised in 2008 to conform with *United States v. Marvin*, 211 F.3d 778, 782 n.4 (3d Cir. 2000).

[Effective December 15, 2008.]

RULE 110.0   CERTIFICATION OF QUESTIONS OF STATE LAW

110.1   Certification of Questions of State Law*

When the procedures of the highest court of a state provide for certification to that court by a federal court of questions arising under the laws of that state which will control the outcome of a case pending in the federal court, this court, sua sponte or on motion of a party, may certify such a question to the state court in accordance with the procedures of that court, and will stay the case in this court to await the state court's decision whether to accept the question certified. The certification will be made after the briefs are filed in this court. A motion for certification must be included in the moving party's brief.

*[Publisher's Note: On October 15, 2012, the Court issued a Notice to Counsel that included the following: "Clarification of Requirements of Rule 110 (Certification of Questions of State Law). L.A.R. 110 states that a motion for certification of a question of state law must be included in the moving party's brief. The motion should also be separately filed on CM/ECF. Separately filing the motion allows the court and parties to better track pending motions."]

[Effective December 15, 2008.]

RULE 111.0   DEATH PENALTY CASES

111.1   Scope

This rule, in conjunction with all other applicable rules, governs all cases in which this court is required to rule on the imposition of the death penalty. The rule is applicable to direct criminal appeals, appeals from the grant or denial of a motion to vacate sentence or a petition for writ of habeas corpus, appeals from the grant or denial of requests for stay or injunctive relief, applications under 28 U.S.C. § 2244 and/or § 2255, and original petitions for writ of habeas corpus.

Source: 1988 Court Rule 29 (Introductory Paragraph)

Cross-References: 18 U.S.C. § 3731, 28 U.S.C. §§ 2254, 2255; Federal Rules of Appellate Procedure; 3d Cir. L.A.R.; 3d Cir. Internal Operating Procedures

Committee Comments: Prior Court Rule 29 (Introductory Paragraph) has no counterpart in FRAP and is therefore classified as Miscellaneous. 3d Cir. L.A.R. Misc. 111.1 broadens the scope of the prior rule to provide for review of death sentences imposed on federal as well as state prisoners. Where applicable, 3d Cir. L.A.R. Misc. 111.2–111.7 are

similarly amended to reflect the broadened scope of 3d Cir. Misc. 111.0.

111.2   Preliminary Requirements

(a) In aid of this court's potential jurisdiction, each party in any proceeding filed in any district court in this circuit challenging the imposition of a sentence of death pursuant to a federal or state court judgment must file a "Certificate of Death Penalty Case" with any initial pleading filed in the district court. A certificate must also be filed by the U.S. Attorney upon return of a verdict of death in a federal criminal case. The certificate will include the following information: names, addresses, and telephone numbers of parties and counsel; if set, the proposed date of execution of sentence; and the emergency nature of the proceedings. Upon docketing, the clerk of the district court will transmit a copy of the certificate, together with a copy of the petition, to the clerk of this court.

(b) Upon entry of an appealable order in the district court, the clerk of the district court and appellant's counsel will prepare the record for appeal. The record will be transmitted to this court within 5 days after the filing of a notice of appeal from the entry of an appealable order under 18 U.S.C. § 3731, 28 U.S.C. § 1291, or 28 U.S.C. § 1292(a)(1), unless the appealable order is entered within 14 days of the date of a scheduled execution, in which case the record must be transmitted immediately by expedited delivery.

(c) Upon the entry of a warrant or order setting an execution date in any case within the geographical boundaries of this circuit, and in aid of this court's potential jurisdiction, the clerk is directed to monitor the status of the execution and any pending litigation and to establish communications with all parties and relevant state and/or federal courts. Without further order of this court, the clerk may direct parties to lodge with this court up to five copies of (1) relevant portions of previous state and/or federal court records, or the entire record, and (2) pleadings, briefs, and transcripts of any ongoing proceedings.

Source: 1988 Court Rule 29.1

Cross-References: 18 U.S.C. § 3731, 28 U.S.C. §§ 1291, 1292

Committee Comments: Prior Court Rule 29.1 has no counterpart in FRAP and is therefore classified as Miscellaneous. The prior rule's general reference to a "certificate providing specific information" has been changed to the more specific "Certificate of Death Penalty Case" to reflect current practice. Subsection (c) directs the clerk to establish lines of communication with the sentencing court and other concerned parties and to authorize the filing of documents and court records in advance of the court's jurisdiction. This section has been added because some parties in recent cases have challenged the clerk's authority to request information in the absence of a docketed appeal. Because early warning is critical, the court expressly delegates this authority to the clerk pursuant to this local rule.

111.3 Review of Direct Criminal Appeals, Petitions for Writs of Habeas Corpus and Motions to Vacate Sentence

(a) In all such cases, the district court must articulate the reasons for its disposition of the case in a written opinion, which must be expeditiously prepared and filed, or by an oral opinion from the bench, which must be promptly transcribed.

(b) The district court must state whether a certificate of appealability is granted or denied at the time a final decision is entered on the merits of a claim seeking relief under 28 U.S.C. § 2254 or 2255. If the district court grants the certificate of appealability, it must state the issues that merit the granting of the certificate and it must also grant a stay pending disposition of the appeal except as provided in 28 U.S.C. § 2262.

(c) The denial of a certificate of appealability by the district court will not delay consideration by this court of a motion for stay or review of the merits. If the court grants a certificate of appealability, it may thereafter affirm, reverse or remand without further briefing under I.O.P. 10.6 or may direct full briefing and oral argument.

Source: 1988 Court Rule 29.2

Cross-Reference: 28 U.S.C. § 2254

Committee Comments: Subsection (c) is intended to clarify this court's practice with respect to certificates of appealability in death penalty cases. In accordance with *Barefoot v. Estelle*, 463 U.S. 880 (1982), the court of appeals may consider, in addition to whether there has been a substantial showing of the denial of a constitutional right, the severity of the sentence in determining whether a certificate of appealability should be issued. Technical changes were made in 1997 to conform to the Antiterrorism and Effective Death Penalty Act.

111.4 Motion for Stay of Execution of a Federal or State Court Judgment and Motions to Vacate Orders Granting a Stay

(a) Except as provided in 28 U.S.C. § 2262, motions for stay of execution and motions to vacate stay orders may be filed in docketed requests for certificate of appealability, applications to file a second or successive petition, or appeals from the denial of injunctive relief. No such motion may be entertained unless a case has been docketed in this court. If a stay application is submitted to this court before a district court decision is entered, the clerk must transmit the motion to the panel designated to hear and dispose of the case.

(b) **Documents Required.** The movant must file the original and three (3) copies of a motion and serve all parties. Legible copies of the documents listed in 1–10 below must be attached to the motion. If time does not permit, the motion may be filed without attachments, but the movant must file the necessary copies as soon as possible.

(1) The complaint or petition to the district court;

(2) Each brief or memorandum of authorities filed by both parties in the district court;

(3) The opinion giving the reasons advanced by the district court for granting or denying relief;

(4) The district court judgment granting or denying relief;

(5) The application to the district court for a stay;

(6) The district court order granting or denying a stay, and the statement of reasons for its action;

(7) The certificate of appealability or, if there is none, the order denying a certificate of appealability;

(8) A copy of each state or federal court opinion or judgment in cases in which appellant was a party involving any issue presented to this court or, if the ruling was not made in a written opinion or judgment, a copy of the relevant portions of the transcripts;

(9) A copy of the docket entries of the district court; and

(10) Notice of appeal.

(c) **Emergency Motions.** Emergency motions or applications, whether addressed to the court or to an individual judge, must ordinarily be filed with the clerk rather than an individual circuit judge. If time does not permit the filing of a motion or application in person, by mail, or electronically, counsel may communicate with the clerk or a single judge of this court and thereafter must file the motion with the clerk in writing as promptly as possible. The motion, application, or oral communication must contain a brief account of the prior actions of this court or judge to which the motion or application, or a substantially similar or related petition for relief, has been submitted.

Source: 1988 Court Rule 29.3

Cross-References: 28 U.S.C. § 2251; FRAP 8

Committee Comments: Prior Court Rule 29.3 has no counterpart in FRAP and is therefore classified as Miscellaneous. Except where necessary to reflect the expansion of this rule to reach federal prisoners, no substantive change from prior Court Rule 29.3 is intended.

111.5 Statement of the Case; Exhaustion; Issues Presented

In addition to requirements set forth in 3d Cir. L.A.R. 28 with respect to the contents of motions and briefs, any application, motion, or brief that may result in either a disposition on the merits or the grant or denial of a stay of execution must include:

(a) A statement of the case delineating precisely the procedural history of the case;

(b) With respect to state habeas corpus petitions brought pursuant to 28 U.S.C. § 2254, a statement of exhaustion with respect to each issue presented to the district court indicating whether it has been exhausted and if not, what circumstances exist that may justify an exception to the exhaustion requirement.

(c) The parties must fully address every issue presented to this court. Supplemental briefing will be permitted only by order of this court.

Source: 1988 Court Rule 29.4

Cross-References: None

Committee Comments: Prior Court Rule 29.4 has no counterpart in FRAP and is therefore classified as Miscellaneous. Except where necessary to reflect the expansion of this rule to reach federal prisoners, no substantive change from prior Court Rule 29.4 is intended.

111.6 Consideration of Merits

The panel to which an appeal has been assigned must consider and expressly rule on the merits before vacating or denying a stay of execution.

Source: 1988 Court Rule 29.5

Cross-References: None

Committee Comments: None

111.7 Determination of Causes by the Court En Banc

(a) Filing. The filing of petitions seeking hearing or rehearing by the court en banc is governed by FRAP 35 and 3d Cir. L.A.R. 35. However, because of the difficulty of delivering petitions seeking hearing or rehearing by the court en banc to the judges of the court, the parties are hereby notified that due to these logistical considerations any such petition filed within 48 hours of a scheduled execution may not be delivered to the judges of the court in sufficient time for adjudication prior to the time of the scheduled execution. Petitions for rehearing by the court en banc filed within 48 hours of a scheduled execution will be processed and distributed by the normal means of delivery used by the court unless the panel handling the case has entered an order for expedited voting in accordance to subsection (b) of this rule.

(b) Consideration. Consideration of a petition seeking hearing or rehearing by the court en banc will be in accordance with the procedures specified in the court's Internal Operating Procedures except that if an execution is scheduled, the original panel which has determined the matter may, upon a majority vote, direct that the time normally allowed for voting to request answers or to grant the petition may be reduced to a time specified by the panel. Upon the entry of an order by the panel reducing the time for voting, the clerk must immediately transmit the petition and the order to the court by the most expedient means available.

(c) Stays. Generally the court will not enter a stay of execution solely to allow additional time for counsel to prepare, or for the court to consider, a petition for rehearing or for rehearing by the court en banc except as follows:

(1) A stay may be granted in order to allow time for counsel to prepare, or for the court to consider, a petition for rehearing upon majority vote of the original panel. Such a vote will be based upon a determination that there is a reasonable possibility that a majority of the active members of the court would vote to grant rehearing by the court en banc and whether there is a substantial possibility of reversal of its decision, in addition to a likelihood that irreparable harm will result if the decision is not stayed.

(2) In the event that four judges vote to direct the filing of answers to a petition seeking rehearing by the court en banc, the presiding judge of the merits panel will enter a stay.

(3) A stay entered in accordance with 3d Cir. L.A.R. 8.2 in a direct appeal of a conviction or sentence in a criminal case in which the district court has imposed a sentence of death will remain in effect until the court's mandate issues. The mandate will ordinarily not issue until such time that the time for filing a petition for rehearing has expired, or if such a petition has been filed, until the petition has been determined.

(d) No petition for rehearing may be filed from the denial of a petition seeking authorization under 28 U.S.C. § 2244 or § 2255 to file a second or successive habeas corpus petition under § 2254 or motion to vacate sentence under § 2255.

Source: 6th Cir. Rule 28(k), 11th Cir. IOP 35–11.8 [L.A.R. Misc. 111.7(a)]; 4th Cir. IOP 22.3(b) [L.A.R. Misc. 111.7(c)]; 5th Cir. IOP 8.11 [L.A.R. Misc. 111.7(c)(1)]

Cross-References: FRAP 35 and 40; 3d Cir. L.A.R. 35; Third Circuit Internal Operating Procedures, Chapter 9 (1994)

Committee Comments: New Provision in 1995. Although the extraordinary nature of death penalty cases is recognized, this section must be read in conjunction with 3d Cir. L.A.R. 35.4 in which it is emphasized that the court does not favor requests for hearing or rehearing en banc. Because 28 U.S.C. § 2244(b)(3)(D) prohibits the filing of a petition for rehearing from the denial of an application seeking permission to file a second or successive § 2254 or § 2255 petition, there is no conflict with Rule 25(a), FRAP, which states that the clerk may not reject a document "solely because it is not presented in proper form." The rejection of such a petition for rehearing is not for form, but is required by statute.

111.8 Post–Judgment Motions

(a) Mandate. The panel may order that the mandate of the court issue forthwith or after such time as it may fix.

(b) Stays of Execution. In ruling on a motion for stay to permit the filing and consideration of a petition for writ of certiorari, the panel must determine whether there is a reasonable probability that the United

States Supreme Court would consider the underlying issues sufficiently meritorious to grant the petition.

Source: 1988 Court Rule 29.6

Cross-References: None

Committee Comments: No substantive change from prior Court Rule 29.6 is intended.

111.9 Second or Successive Petitions

The procedures of L.A.R. 22.5 apply to the filing of a petition seeking authorization under 28 U.S.C. § 2244 or 2255 to file a second or successive habeas corpus petition under § 2254 or motion to vacate sentence under § 2255 in a death penalty case.

Source: L.A.R. 22.5

Cross-References: 28 U.S.C. §§ 2244, 2254, and 2255

Committee Comments: This rule makes clear that the procedures for filing a second or successive petition under 28 U.S.C. § 2244 set forth in L.A.R. 22.5 also apply in death penalty cases and insures that the court will have the documents necessary to decide such petitions.

[Effective December 15, 2008. Amended effective March 8, 2010.]

RULE 112.0 PETITIONS FOR WRIT OF CERTIORARI TO THE SUPREME COURT OF THE VIRGIN ISLANDS

112.1 Considerations Governing Review on Certiorari

(a) Review on writ of certiorari is not a matter of right, but of judicial discretion, and will be granted only when there are special and important reasons therefor. The following, while neither controlling nor limiting the court's discretion, indicate the character of reasons that will be considered.

(1) The Supreme Court of the Virgin Islands has decided a question in a way that conflicts with applicable decisions of this court, other appellate courts, or the United States Supreme Court.

(2) The Supreme Court of the Virgin Islands has so far departed from the accepted and usual course of judicial proceedings, or so far sanctioned such a departure by a lower court, as to call for an exercise of this court's powers of review.

(3) The Supreme Court of the Virgin Islands has decided an important question of federal or territorial law that has not been, but should be, decided by this court.

(4) The Supreme Court of the Virgin Islands was without jurisdiction of the case, or where, because of disqualifications or other reason, the decision of the Supreme Court of the Virgin Islands lacks the concurrence of the required majority of qualified non-recused judges.

(b) A petition for a writ of certiorari will rarely be granted when the asserted error consists of erroneous findings of fact or the misapplication of a properly stated rule of law. A petition for writ of certiorari that raises any issue or relies on any material fact that was omitted from or misstated in the opinion of the Supreme Court of the Virgin Islands will normally not be considered, unless the omission or misstatement was called to the attention of the Supreme Court of the Virgin Islands in a petition for rehearing. All other issues and facts may be presented in the petition for a writ of certiorari without the necessity of filing a petition for rehearing.

Source: 48 U.S.C. § 1613

Cross-References: None

Committee Comments: L.A.R. 112.1–112.14 were enacted in 2007. The rules were amended in 2008 to provide for electronic filing.

112.2 Petition for Writ of Certiorari—How Sought

(a) In both civil and criminal cases, review of a final decision of the Supreme Court of the Virgin Islands may be sought pursuant to 48 U.S.C. § 1613 by filing a petition for a writ of certiorari with the Clerk of the United States Court of Appeals for the Third Circuit within 60 days from the entry of judgment sought to be reviewed on the docket of the Supreme Court of the Virgin Islands. A petition filed by an incarcerated person will be deemed filed when placed in the prison mail system; the petition must be accompanied by a statement under penalty of perjury stating the date the petition was placed in the prison mail system and stating that first-class postage has been pre-paid. In all other cases, the petition must be received by the Clerk in Philadelphia by the sixtieth day.

(b) Petitioner must file, with proof of service, an original and three copies of the petition for writ of certiorari. Petitioner must serve one copy of the petition for writ of certiorari on each of the parties to the proceedings in the Supreme Court of the Virgin Islands. When filing the petition, petitioner must pay the docketing fee, which shall be the same as the fees charged for an original proceeding such as a petition for writ of mandamus or petition for review of an agency order, in the Court of Appeals. Counsel for the petitioner must enter an appearance within 14 days of filing a petition. Once the case has been opened on the court's electronic docketing system, all documents must be filed electronically in accordance with L.A.R. Misc. 113.

(c) Parties interested jointly may file a joint petition. A petitioner not shown on the petition at the time of filing may not later join in that petition.

(d) If a petition for rehearing of the final decision of the Supreme Court of the Virgin Islands is timely filed pursuant to the Rules of the Supreme Court of the Virgin Islands or if that court sua sponte considers rehearing, the time for filing the petition for writ of certiorari shall run from entry of the order denying the petition or, if rehearing is granted, from entry of the order on rehearing.

Source: 48 U.S.C. § 1613

Cross-References: None

Committee Comments: L.A.R. 112.1–112.14 were enacted in 2007. The rules were amended in 2008 to provide for electronic filing. Time changed to 14 days in 2010 to conform to amendments in FRAP.

112.3   Cross–Petitions for Certiorari

(a) Unless a rule specifies a different procedure for a cross-petition for certiorari, the rules for a petition for certiorari apply to cross-petitions.

(b) A cross-petition for a writ of certiorari may be filed within 21 days after the first petition was filed. When filing the cross-petition, cross-petitioner must pay the docketing fee. The cross-petitioner must serve one copy of the petition on each of the parties to the proceedings in the Supreme Court of the Virgin Islands.

(c) a cross-petitioner need not duplicate the appendix filed by petitioner

Source: 48 U.S.C. § 1613

Cross-References: None

Committee Comments: L.A.R. 112.1–112.14 were enacted in 2007. The rules were amended in 2008 to provide for electronic filing.

112.4   Extension of Time to File Petitions

(a) A circuit judge, for good cause shown, may extend the time for filing a petition for writ of certiorari or cross-petition for a period not exceeding 30 days. Any application for extension of time within which to file a petition for writ of certiorari must set out the grounds on which the jurisdiction of this court is invoked, must identify the judgment sought to be reviewed and have appended thereto a copy of the opinion, and must set forth with specificity the reasons justifying an extension. An untimely petition for writ of certiorari must be accompanied by a motion for extension of time. However, an application for extension of time to file a petition for certiorari ordinarily will not be granted, if filed less than 5 days before the expiration of the time to file a petition.

Source: 48 U.S.C. § 1613

Cross-References: None

Committee Comments: L.A.R. 112.1–112.14 were enacted in 2007. The rules were amended in 2008 to provide for electronic filing.

112.5   Denominating Parties

(a) The party filing the first petition for the writ of certiorari shall be denominated the petitioner; petitioner's denomination in the appeal or other proceeding before the Supreme Court and the Superior Court of the Virgin Islands must be included in the first paragraph of the statement of the case.

(b) Parties to the proceeding in the court whose judgment is sought to be reviewed are deemed parties in this court and shall be denominated respondents, unless the petitioner notifies the clerk of this court in writing of petitioner's belief that one or more of the parties below has no interest in the outcome of the petition. A copy of such notice must be served on all parties to the proceeding in the Supreme Court of the Virgin Islands. A party noted as no longer interested may remain a party by notifying the clerk in writing within 14 days from the date of service of petitioner's notice, with service on all other parties, that the party has an interest in the petition. Each respondent's denomination in the proceedings before the Supreme Court and the Superior Court of the Virgin Islands must be included in the petition for writ of certiorari in the first paragraph of the statement of the case. Any respondent who supports the position of a petitioner must meet the time schedule for filing responsive document.

(c) a party who files a cross-petition for certiorari is denominated as respondent/cross-petitioner.

Source: 48 U.S.C. § 1613

Cross-References: None

Committee Comments: L.A.R. 112.1–112.14 were enacted in 2007. The rules were amended in 2008 to provide for electronic filing.

112.6   The Petition for Writ of Certiorari

(a) The petition for writ of certiorari must contain, in the following order:

(1) a table of contents;

(2) a table of authorities, including citations to the relevant constitutional provisions, treaties, statutes, ordinances, and regulations;

(3) a concise statement of the ground on which the jurisdiction of this court is invoked, with citations to applicable statutes and stating relevant facts establishing the finality of the order. The jurisdictional statement must also include the date of entry of the judgment sought to be reviewed, the date of any orders respecting rehearing, and, in the case of a cross-petition for a writ of certiorari, the date of the filing of the petition for a writ of certiorari;

(4) a concise statement, with citations to appropriate statutes, of the basis of jurisdiction of the Supreme Court of the Virgin Islands and of the Superior Court of the Virgin Islands.

(5) the questions presented for review, expressed concisely in relation to the circumstances of the case. The statement of the questions should not be argumentative or repetitious. The statement of a question presented will be deemed to comprise every subsid-

iary question fairly included therein. Only the questions set forth in the petition or fairly included therein will be considered by the court;

(6) A concise statement of the case containing the facts material to the consideration of the questions presented. The first paragraph of the statement of the case must specify the denomination of each of the parties as they appeared in the Supreme Court of the Virgin Islands and the Superior Court of the Virgin Islands. The statement of the case must specify, with appropriate citation to the record, the stage in the proceedings, both in the Superior Court and the Supreme Court of the Virgin Islands, at which the questions sought to be reviewed were raised and the ruling thereon;

(7) a direct and concise argument amplifying the reasons why the questions for review are important enough to warrant issuance of the writ;

(8) a short conclusion, which must include a statement of the specific relief requested if the writ of certiorari is granted.

(b) All contentions in support of a petition for writ of certiorari must be set forth in the body of the petition, as provided by this rule. No separate brief in support of a petition for a writ of certiorari will be received, and the clerk will refuse to file any petition for a writ of certiorari to which is annexed or appended any supporting brief.

(c) Any reason for expedited treatment or request for interim relief must be made by separate motion. The requirement in Rule 8, FRAP, that a request for stay or injunction pending appeal must first be made to the court below will be strictly enforced. Any motion for stay or injunction must attach the order of the Supreme Court of the Virgin Islands disposing of the motion for stay or injunction made to it in the first instance.

Source: 48 U.S.C. § 1613

Cross-References: None

Committee Comments: L.A.R. 112.1–112.14 were enacted in 2007. The rules were amended in 2008 to provide for electronic filing.

112.7 Appendix

(a) In addition to electronically filing the appendix, an original and three paper copies of an appendix must be filed for the convenience of the court. The appendix must contain in the following order:

(1) copies of all docket entries, opinions, orders, findings of fact, and conclusions of law, whether written or oral (if recorded and transcribed), delivered upon the rendering of the judgment or decree by the Supreme Court of the Virgin Islands; and

(2) copies of any applicable local statutes, ordinances, and regulations the above documents may be

bound with the petition provided they do not exceed 75 pages.

(b) the above documents in subparagraphs (1) and (2) may be bound with the petition provided they do not exceed 75 pages.

(c) Cross-petitioners need not duplicate materials filed by the petitioner.

(d) Respondents wishing to file materials in addition to those filed by petitioner must file a motion for permission to file a supplemental appendix.

Source: 48 U.S.C. § 1613

Cross-References: None

Committee Comments: L.A.R. 112.1–112.14 were enacted in 2007. The rules were amended in 2008 to provide for electronic filing.

112.8 Brief in Opposition—In Support—Reply— Supplemental Briefs

(a) Within 30 days of receipt of a petition for writ of certiorari, a respondent may file electronically a brief in opposition. An original and three paper copies, with certificate of service, of the opposing brief must be filed for the court's convenience. In addition to the merits of the questions presented, the brief should address whether the issues identified by the petitioner are suitable for review. The respondent may agree that the petition for certiorari should be granted because the case presents an important question, yet argue that the decision of the Supreme Court of the Virgin Islands is correct.

(b) A respondent supporting the position of the petitioner must file a response supporting the petition with 20 days of the opening of the case. Parties who file no document will not qualify for any relief from the court.

(c) If no response is received within the time prescribed, it will be assumed that the party does not wish to participate and will no longer receive notices from the clerk or be entitled to service of documents from the other parties. The clerk may direct a party to file a response. Ordinarily, a petition for certiorari will not be granted unless a response has been filed or requested.

(d) No motion by a respondent to dismiss a petition for writ of certiorari will be received. Objections to the jurisdiction of the court to grant the writ of certiorari may be included in the brief in opposition.

(e) Petitioner may file electronically a reply brief addressed to arguments first raised in the brief in opposition within 14 days of receipt of respondent's brief. An original and three paper copies, with certificate of service, of the reply brief must be filed for the court's convenience.

(f) Motions for extensions of time to file a brief are governed by Third Circuit L.A.R. 31.4.

(g) No supplemental filings may be made by any party except as provided in Rule 28(j), FRAP.

Source: 48 U.S.C. § 1613

Cross-References: None

Committee Comments: L.A.R. 112.1–112.14 were enacted in 2007. The rules were amended in 2008 to provide for electronic filing.

112.9   Format and Length

(a) The typeface, page size, margins, line spacing, binding, and text style of a petition for writ of certiorari and responses must be in compliance with Rule 32(a), FRAP and Third Circuit Local Rule 32.1 The cover of a petition for writ of certiorari must be blue; the cover of respondent's brief must be red; the cover of a reply brief must be gray.

(b) A proportionately spaced petition for a writ of certiorari and response must not exceed 5,600 words, exclusive of the table of contents and table of authorities. A reply brief must not exceed 2,300 words.

Source: 48 U.S.C. § 1613

Cross-References: None

Committee Comments: L.A.R. 112.1–112.14 were enacted in 2007. The rules were amended in 2008 to provide for electronic filing.

112.10   Disposition of a Petition for Writ of Certiorari

(a) The petition and any responses shall be referred to a motions panel for disposition. If a petition for writ of certiorari is granted, the clerk will issue a briefing schedule and the case shall proceed as other appeals in accordance with the Federal Rules of Appellate Procedure and Local Appellate Rules but with review limited to the questions on which the writ of certiorari was granted.

Source: 48 U.S.C. § 1613

Cross-References: None

Committee Comments: L.A.R. 112.1–112.14 were enacted in 2007. The rules were amended in 2008 to provide for electronic filing.

112.11   Record on Review

(a) The record on review shall consist of the record presented to the Supreme Court of the Virgin Islands.

(b) Within 30 days of an order granting a writ of certiorari, the Clerk of the Supreme Court of the Virgin Islands must file a certified copy of the docket entries in lieu of the record with the Clerk of the Court of Appeals. The filing of the certified docket entries with the Court of Appeals constitutes the filing of the record.

Source: 48 U.S.C. § 1613

Cross-References: None

Committee Comments: L.A.R. 112.1–112.14 were enacted in 2007. The rules were amended in 2008 to provide for electronic filing.

112.12   Rehearings

(a) Rules 35 and 40, FRAP, govern petitions for rehearing an order denying a petition for writ of certiorari.

(b) The grounds for a petition for rehearing of an order denying a petition for writ of certiorari are limited to intervening circumstances of substantial or controlling effect or to other substantial grounds. A petitioner must certify that the petition is restricted to the grounds specified in this paragraph and that it is presented in good faith and not for delay. This certification is in lieu of that required by Third Circuit L.A.R. 35.1.

(c) No response to a petition for rehearing will be received unless requested by the court, but no petition will be granted without an opportunity to submit a response.

(d) Consecutive petitions for rehearings will not be received.

Source: 48 U.S.C. § 1613

Cross-References: None

Committee Comments: L.A.R. 112.1–112.14 were enacted in 2007. The rules were amended in 2008 to provide for electronic filing.

112.13   Costs

(a) Each party shall bear its own costs in a proceeding seeking a writ of certiorari, unless the court either sua sponte or following a motion directs that costs be taxed under Rule 38, FRAP, for a vexatious or frivolous petition. If the writ is granted and the case proceeds to briefing and decision, costs may be taxed as in Rule 39, FRAP

Source: 48 U.S.C. § 1613

Cross-References: None

Committee Comments: L.A.R. 112.1–112.14 were enacted in 2007. The rules were amended in 2008 to provide for electronic filing.

112.14   Applicability of the Federal Rules of Appellate Procedure

(a) The Federal Rules of Appellate Procedure, to the extent that they are not inconsistent with any statutory provisions or these rules, may be applied to a proceeding seeking a writ of certiorari.

Source: 48 U.S.C. § 1613

Cross-References: None

Committee Comments: L.A.R. 112.1–112.14 were enacted in 2007. The rules were amended in 2008 to provide for electronic filing.

[Effective December 15, 2008. Amended effective March 8, 2010.]

RULE 113.0 ELECTRONIC FILING

113.1 Scope of Electronic Filing

(a) Except as otherwise prescribed by local rule or order, all cases will be assigned to the court's electronic filing system. Case-initiating documents in original proceedings in the court of appeals must be filed in paper format. Except as otherwise prescribed by local rule or court order, all briefs, motions, petitions for rehearing, and other documents subsequently filed in any case with the court by a Filing User registered as set forth under Rule 113.2 must be filed electronically using the electronic filing system.

(b) Ten paper copies of briefs and four paper copies of the appendices must be filed within 5 days as provided in L.A.R. 31.1. The clerk may direct a party to provide the court with paper copies of other documents electronically filed.

(c) Upon the court's request, a Filing User must promptly provide the clerk, in a format designated by the court, an identical electronic version of any paper document previously filed in the same case by that Filing User.

(d) By local rule or order of the court or clerk, electronic access to entire case files or portions thereof may be restricted to the parties and the court. Public documents, except those filed under seal, may be viewed at the clerk's office.

(e) Upon motion and a showing of good cause, the court may exempt a Filing User from the provisions of this Rule and authorize filing by means other than use of the electronic filing system.

Source: Model Local Rules

Cross-References: FRAP 31; L.A.R. 31.1

Committee Comments: Rules on electronic filing were added in 2008. This Local Appellate Rule is not intended to supplant the requirements of FRAP 31(b) or any local rule or procedure requiring counsel to provide additional paper copies of filings to the court. Time for filing paper copies changed to 5 days in 2010.

113.2 Eligibility, Registration, Passwords

(a) Attorneys who intend to practice in this court, including attorneys authorized to represent the United States without being admitted to the bar of this court, must register as Filing Users of the court's electronic filing system. Registration requirements will be defined by the court and may include training as a prerequisite to registration as a CM/ECF Filing User.

(b) A party to a pending civil case who is not represented by an attorney may, but is not required to, register as a Filing User in the electronic filing system solely for purposes of that case. Filing User status will be terminated upon termination of the case.

If a pro se party retains an attorney, the attorney must advise the clerk.

(c) Registration as a Filing User constitutes consent to electronic service of all documents as provided in these rules and with the Federal Rules of Appellate Procedure.

(d) Filing Users agree to protect the security of their passwords and immediately notify the PACER Service Center and the clerk if they learn that their password has been compromised. Filing Users may be sanctioned for failure to comply with this provision. The clerk may terminate without notice the electronic filing privileges of any Filing User who abuses the system by excessive filings, either in terms of quantity or length. The clerk may order that overlength or repetitive filings will not be available electronically.

(e) Upon motion showing extraordinary circumstances, the clerk may grant an exemption from electronic filing.

Source: Model Local Rules

Cross-References: L.A.R. 46

Committee Comments: Rules on electronic filing were added in 2008.

113.3 Consequences of Electronic Filing

(a) Electronic transmission of a document to the electronic filing system consistent with these rules, together with the transmission of a Notice of Docket Activity from the court, constitutes filing of the document under the Federal Rules of Appellate Procedure and the local rules of this court, and constitutes entry of the document on the docket kept by the clerk under FRAP 36 and 45(b). If the court requires a party to file a motion for leave to file a document, both the motion and document at issue should be submitted electronically; the underlying document will be filed if the court so directs.

(b) Before filing a document with the court, a Filing User must verify its legibility and completeness. Documents created by the filer and filed electronically must be in PDF text format. When a document has been filed electronically, the official record is the electronic document stored by the court, and the filing party is bound by the document as filed. Except in the case of documents first filed in paper form and subsequently submitted electronically under Rule 113.1, a document filed electronically is deemed filed at the date and time stated on the Notice of Docket Activity from the court.

(c) Filing must be completed by midnight on the last day Eastern Time to be considered timely filed that day.

Source: Model Local Rules

Cross-References: L.A.R. 27–32, 35, 40

Committee Comments: Rules on electronic filing were added in 2008. Time changed to midnight in 2010 to conform to amendments to FRAP.

113.4   Service of Documents by Electronic Means

(a) The Notice of Docket Activity that is generated by the court's electronic filing system constitutes service of the filed document on all Filing Users. Parties who are not Filing Users must be served with a copy of any document filed electronically in accordance with the Federal Rules of Appellate Procedure and the local rules.

(b) If the document is not filed and served electronically through the court's CM/ECF system, the filer must use an alternative method of service prescribed by FRAP 25(c).

(c) The Notice of Docket Activity generated by the court's electronic filing system does not replace the certificate of service required by FRAP 25. The certificate of service must state either that the other party is a Filing User and is served electronically by the Notice of Docket Activity or that the other party will be served with paper documents pursuant to FRAP 25(c).

Source: Model Local Rules

Cross-References: L.A.R. 27.2 and 31.1

Committee Comments: The electronic filing system generates a Notice of Docket Activity at the time a document is filed with the system. The Notice indicates the time of filing, the name of the party and attorney filing the document, the type of document, and the text of the docket entry. It also contains an electronic link (hyperlink) to the filed document, if one was attached to the filing, allowing anyone receiving the notice by e-mail to retrieve the document automatically. The system sends this Notice to all case participants registered as Filing Users of the electronic filing system. Under the amendments to FRAP 25, a court may, by local rule, provide that the court's automatically generated Notice of Docket Activity constitutes service of the document on all Filing Users in the case.

Parties who are not Filing Users have not consented to electronic service via the Notice of Docket Activity. They must be served in some other way authorized by FRAP 25.

If the document is not filed electronically through the court's CM/ECF system, the filer must use an alternative method of service prescribed by FRAP 25(c).

FRAP 26 provides that the three additional days to respond to service by mail will apply to electronic service as well. This provision is intended to account for technical problems that can arise during electronic service and to encourage parties to consent to electronic service.

113.5   Entry of Court–Issued Documents

(a) Except as otherwise provided by local rule or court order, all orders, decrees, judgments, and proceedings of the court relating to cases filed and maintained in the CM/ECF system will be filed in accordance with these rules, which will constitute entry on the docket kept by the clerk under FRAP 36 and

45(b). Court orders, decrees, judgments, and other documents filed by the court will contain an electronic signature. Any order or other court issued document filed electronically without a hand-written signature of a judge or authorized court personnel has the same force and effect as if the judge or clerk had signed a paper copy of the order.

(b) Orders also may be entered as "text-only" entries on the docket, without an attached document. Such orders are official and binding.

Source: Model Local Rules

Cross-References: FRAP 45

Committee Comments: Rules on electronic filing were added in 2008.

113.6   Attachments and Exhibits to Motions and Original Proceedings

(a) Filing Users must submit in electronic form all documents referenced as exhibits or attachments. A Filing User must submit as exhibits or attachments only those excerpts of the referenced documents that are directly germane to the matter under consideration by the court. Excerpted material must be clearly and prominently identified as such. The court may require parties to file additional excerpts or the complete document.

Source: Model Local Rules

Cross-References: FRAP 27; L.A.R. 27

Committee Comments: Rules on electronic filing were added in 2008. In many instances, only a small portion of a much larger document might be relevant to a matter before the court, therefore only an excerpt of the larger, original document should be submitted. The court retains the authority to require the filer to provide additional portions or the complete document, and other parties may supplement the filed excerpts or provide the entire document in support of their responsive pleadings.

113.7   Sealed Documents

(a) A motion to file documents under seal may be filed electronically unless prohibited by law, local rule, or court order.

(b) If the court grants the motion, the order of the court authorizing the filing of documents under seal may be filed electronically unless prohibited by law.

(c) With permission of the clerk, documents ordered placed under seal may be filed in paper form only. A paper copy of the authorizing order must be attached to the documents under seal and delivered to the clerk.

(d) Ex parte motions, *e.g.*, to file a document under seal, must be filed in paper form only.

Source: Model Local Rules

Cross-References: L.A.R. Misc. 106

Committee Comments: The court's electronic filing system is capable of accepting sealed documents electronically from filing users, either directly into a sealed case in which the attorney is a participant or as a sealed filing in an otherwise unsealed case. See L.A.R. Misc. 113.4, which addresses service of sealed documents filed electronically. See L.A.R. Misc. 113.12 for other provisions addressing privacy concerns arising from electronic filing. Attorneys must not include private and/or confidential information in their motions to file a document under seal and must fulfill their obligations under L.A.R. Misc. 113.12.

113.8   Retention Requirements

Documents that are electronically filed and require original signatures other than that of the Filing User must be maintained in paper form by the Filing User until 2 years after the issuance of the mandate or order closing the case, whichever is later. If counsel withdraws and a new attorney enters an appearance, documents that require original signatures must be transferred to the new attorney of record. On request of the court, the Filing User must provide original documents for review.

Source: Model Local Rules

Cross-References: None

Committee Comments: Because electronically filed documents do not include original, handwritten signatures, it is necessary to provide for retention of certain signed documents in paper form in case they are needed as evidence in the future. The Rule addresses the retention requirement for "verified documents" (in which a person verifies, certifies, affirms, or swears under oath or penalty of perjury, *e.g.*, affidavits, stipulations or the Criminal Justice Act forms) bearing original signatures of persons other than the person who files the document electronically.

113.9   Signatures

(a) The user log-in and password required to submit documents to the electronic filing system serve as the Filing User's signature on all electronic documents filed with the court. They also serve as a signature for purposes of the Federal Rules of Appellate Procedure, the local rules of court, and any other purpose for which a signature is required in connection with proceedings before the court.

(b) The name of the Filing User under whose log-in and password the document is submitted must be preceded by an "s/" and typed in the space where the signature would otherwise appear. Alternatively, an electronic signature may be used.

(c) No Filing User or other person may knowingly permit or cause to permit a Filing User's log-in and password to be used by anyone other than an authorized agent of the Filing User. Documents requiring signatures of more than one party must be electronically filed either by:

(1) submitting a scanned document containing all necessary signatures;

(2) submitting a statement representing the consent of the other parties on the document;

(3) identifying on the document the parties whose signatures are required and submitting a notice of endorsement by the other parties no later than three business days after filing; or

(4) in any other manner approved by the court. Electronically represented signatures of all parties and Filing Users as described above are presumed to be valid signatures. If any party, counsel of record, or Filing User objects to the representation of his or her signature on an electronic document as described above, he or she must, within 10 days, file a notice setting forth the basis of the objection.

Source: Model Local Rules

Cross-References: L.A.R. 28 and 46

Committee Comments: An electronic signature or the "s/" preceding a typed name indicates that the electronically filed document was endorsed by that party or Filing User. This Rule does not require a Filing User to personally file his or her own documents. The task of electronic filing may be delegated to an authorized agent, who may use the log-in and password to make the filing. Use of the log-in and password to make the filing constitutes a signature by the Filing User under the Rule, even though the Filing User does not perform the physical act of filing. Issues arise when documents being electronically filed have been signed by persons other than the filer, *e.g.*, stipulations and affidavits. For documents signed by individuals without logins and passwords (non-Filing Users), the Rule provides that the signature must appear as "s/" or as a scanned image. Under L.A.R. Misc. 113.8 above, the Filing User must retain a paper copy with the original signature of any such document filed by the Filing User.

113.10   Notice of Court Orders and Judgments

Immediately upon the entry of an order or judgment in a case assigned to the electronic filing system, the clerk will electronically transmit a Notice of Docket Activity to Filing Users in the case. Electronic transmission of the Notice of Docket Activity constitutes the notice and service of the opinion required by FRAP 36(b) and 45(c). The clerk must give notice in paper form to a person who has not consented to electronic service.

Source: Model Local Rules

Cross-References: FRAP 45

Committee Comments: Rules on electronic filing were added in 2008.

113.11   Technical Failures

A Filing User whose filing is untimely as the result of a technical failure may seek appropriate relief from the court.

Court personnel are not responsible for assisting Filing Users in the remedying of technical problems.

Source: Model Local Rules

Cross-References: L.A.R. 27 (motions)

Committee Comments: Rules on electronic filing were added in 2008.

113.12 Public Access

(a) Parties, counsel, or other persons filing any document, whether electronically or in paper, must refrain from including, or must partially redact where inclusion is necessary, the following personal data identifiers from all documents filed with the court, including exhibits thereto, whether filed electronically or in paper, unless otherwise ordered by the court:

(1) *Social Security Numbers.* If an individual's Social Security number must be included, only the last four digits of that number should be used.

(2) *Names of Minor Children.* If the involvement of a minor child must be mentioned, only the initials of that child should be used.

(3) *Dates of Birth.* If an individual's date of birth must be included, only the year should be used.

(4) *Financial Account Numbers.* If financial account numbers are relevant, only the last four digits of these numbers should be used.

(5) *Home Addresses.* In criminal cases, if a home address must be included, only the city and state should be listed.

(b) In compliance with the E–Government Act of 2002, a party wishing to file a document containing the personal data identifiers listed above may:

(1) File an un-redacted version of the document under seal, or

(2) File a reference list under seal. The reference list must contain the complete personal data identifier(s) and the redacted identifier(s) used in its(their) place in the filing. All references in the case to the redacted identifiers included in the reference list will be construed to refer to the corresponding complete personal data identifier. The reference list must be filed under seal, and may be amended as of right.

(c) The un-redacted version of the document or the reference list must be retained by the court as part of the record. The court may, however, still require the party to file a redacted copy for the public file.

(d) The responsibility for redacting these personal identifiers rests solely with the party, counsel, or other person filing the document. The clerk will not review each pleading for compliance with this rule.

Source: Model Local Rules

Cross-Reference: Judicial Conference Policy on Privacy and Public Access to Electronic Case Files

Committee Comments: It is each filer's responsibility to redact information from documents submitted by the filer. Documents containing prohibited personal identifiers must be redacted by the parties so as not to include un-redacted Social Security numbers, financial account numbers, names of minor children, or dates of birth. In criminal cases, home addresses also must be redacted. Information should be provided in shortened form, rather than completely omitted, with Social Security numbers represented as XXX–XX–1234, financial account numbers reduced to the last four digits, names of minor children represented as initials, dates of birth represented by year, and home addresses listed only by city and state.

Parties should consult the "Guidance for Implementation of the Judicial Conference Policy on Privacy and Public Access to Electronic Criminal Case Files." This Guidance explains the policy permitting remote public access to electronic criminal case file documents and sets forth redaction and sealing requirements for documents that are filed. The Guidance also lists documents for which public access should not be provided. A copy of the Guidance is available at the court's website. For further information on privacy issues, see the Judicial Conference policies on privacy and public access to documents filed in civil, criminal, and bankruptcy cases, as well as section 205(c) of the E–Government Act of 2002, Pub. L. No. 107–347, 116 Stat. 2899, 2914, as amended by Pub. L. No. 108–281, 118 Stat. 889 (2004).

113.13 Hyperlinks

(a) Electronically filed documents may contain the following types of hyperlinks:

(1) Hyperlinks to other portions of the same document; and

(2) Hyperlinks to a location on the Internet or PACER, *e.g.*, the appendix, that contains a source document for a citation. If hyperlinks are used in the brief, counsel must also include immediately preceding the hyperlink a reference to the paper appendix page. Hyperlinks to testimony must be to a transcript. A motion must be filed and granted seeking permission to hyperlink to an audio or video file before such links may be included in the brief or appendix. Hyperlinks may not be used to link to sealed or restricted documents.

(b) Hyperlinks to cited authority or documents may not replace standard citation format. Complete citations to paper documents if available must be included in the text of the filed document. If a cited reference is available on the internet only, a complete citation to the internet site must be included in addition to the hyperlink. A hyperlink, or any site to which it refers, will not be considered part of the record. Hyperlinks are simply convenient mechanisms for accessing material cited in a filed document. The court accepts no responsibility for, and does not endorse, any product, organization, or content at any hyperlinked site, or at any site to which that site might be linked. The court accepts no responsibility for the availability or functionality of any hyperlink.

(c) Hyperlinks do not replace paper copies of the appendix. Four paper copies of the appendix must be filed in accordance with L.A.R. 30.1.

Source: Model Local Rules

Cross-References: L.A.R. 28 and 30

Committee Comments: Hyperlinks are a connection from one point of electronic data to another. Because hyperlinks might be to sites outside the control of the court, the court cannot take responsibility for the viability of those links, nor does it take responsibility for the content of any linked site. Because hyperlinks are not considered part of the record, the fact that a hyperlink ceases to work or directs the user to some other site does not affect the content of the filed document.

Hyperlinks are a convenient means of accessing material cited in electronic documents. Any electronically filed document that contains a hyperlink must also contain the standard citation to the same material. This requirement ensures that anyone working with a printed version of the document has the necessary citation, and that subsequent failure of a hyperlink will not preclude finding the cited material.

Just as the complete text of a document cited in a brief or other filing in support of a legal proposition, unless specifical-ly quoted, is not considered part of the brief, the hyperlink and the site to which it refers are not considered part of the brief. Thus, they will not be considered part of the court's record.

113.14 Changes

The clerk may make changes to the procedures for electronic filing to adapt to changes in technology or to facilitate electronic filing. Any changes to procedures will be posted on the court's internet website.

Source: None

Cross-References: None

Committee Comments: None

[**Publisher's Note**: On March 19, 2009, the Clerk entered the following order:

OPTIONS FOR FILING THE APPENDIX

This order is issued pursuant to L.A.R. Misc. 113.14: "The clerk may make changes to the procedures for electronic filing to adapt to changes in technology or to facilitate electronic filing. Any changes to procedures will be posted on the court's internet website."

Counsel must file an appendix to the brief. The appendix consists of the docket entries, relevant portions of the pleadings, charge, findings or opinion, and any "other parts of the record to which the parties wish to direct the court's attention." F.R.A.P. 30(a)(1). Pursuant to L.A.R. Misc. 113 counsel must file all documents electronically. In order to facilitate electronic filing, counsel may choose one of the following options when filing the appendix with the court.

OPTION A

File all volumes of the appendix in electronic form. Counsel must also send four paper copies of the appendix to the court. Service on filing users (those registered with PACER and using electronic filing) is by the notice of docket activity sent by CM/ECF. Counsel must serve non-filing users with paper copies of the appendix. Counsel must attach a certifi-cate of service even if all opposing parties are served via CM/ECF.

OPTION B

Counsel may file four paper copies of the appendix without also filing an electronic version if

(1) when citing a document in the brief, counsel cites to the appendix page and provides parallel citations to the district court document number. (For example: District Court opinion, App. p. 27; DDE # 57 at p. 5)[1]

and

(2) counsel serves a paper copy of all volumes of the appendix on all opposing parties and includes a certificate of service.

Counsel choosing option B may file a brief that exceeds the word limit in Rule 32, F.R.A.P. by no more than 75 words without filing a motion to exceed the page limit.

Dated: March 17, 2009

[1] In agency cases, parallel citations are only required if the agency record is available in electronic form.]

APPENDIX I. INTERNAL OPERATING PROCEDURES

Effective April 29, 2015

INTRODUCTION

A. Objectives. These "Internal Operating Procedures" (I.O.P.S) cover the essential processes of this court from the distribution of the briefs to the final termination of the appeal and are designed:

(1) To insure that appeals are processed as expeditiously as possible consistent with the careful discharge of appellate responsibilities;

(2) To insure decisional stability and avoid intra-circuit conflict of decisions by providing a means for the panel system to operate efficiently and at the same time provide that a holding of a precedential opinion of the court may not be overruled without the approval of a majority of the en banc court;

(3) To insure the opportunity for contributions by every active judge to every decision of precedential or institutional significance; and

(4) To maintain the highest degree of collegiality among the judges.

B. Implementation. These I.O.P.S implement:

(1) Statutory mandates;

(2) The Federal Rules of Appellate Procedure;

(3) The Third Circuit Local Appellate Rules (L.A.R.); and

(4) The customs and traditions of this court.

C. Citation Form. These rules may be known as the Third Circuit Internal Operating Procedures and cited as 3d Cir. I.O.P. _____ (2015).

D. Computing Time. Unless otherwise specified, days means calendar days. Counting time for voting on circulating opinions and rehearing petitions begins the day after the opinion or petition is circulated. Opinions and orders may be filed after close of business on the last day for voting. In addition to the procedure for extending time to vote set forth in Chapter 9, the time for voting may be extended by consent of the court to accommodate periods when large numbers of opinions are being circulated.

[Effective April 29, 2015.]

CHAPTER 1. BRIEFS AND PREPARATION

IOP 1.1 PRIOR TO PANEL SITTING

Briefs and appendices are distributed sufficiently in advance to afford at least four (4) full weeks' study in chambers prior to the panel sitting. In special circumstances, such as expedited cases, the panel may unanimously agree to a shorter reading period. Except where typewritten briefs have been permitted, two sets of briefs and one appendix, two if available, are furnished to each chambers. At the termination of the case, the briefs and appendices need not be returned to the clerk. Generally, fully briefed cases are randomly assigned by the clerk to a three-judge panel.

[Effective April 29, 2015.]

IOP 1.2 RESPONSIBILITY OF PANEL PRIOR TO SCHEDULED SITTING

This court has the tradition of carefully reading briefs and reviewing appendices prior to oral argument or conference. Inherent in Local Appellate Rule 34.1 is the understanding that each judge will read the briefs and review the appendices a minimum of 11 calendar days before the first day of the panel sitting.

[Effective April 29, 2015.]

CHAPTER 2. ORAL ARGUMENT

IOP 2.1 DETERMINATION IN PANEL CASES

The panel determines whether there will be oral argument and the amount of time allocated. There is oral argument if it is requested by at least one judge. Each judge communicates his or her views to the other panel members. No later than 11 calendar days before the first day of the panel sitting, the presiding judge furnishes the clerk with the panel's determinations in accordance with the maximum request, up to 20 minutes per side, of any single judge. Usually, 15 minutes per side is allotted. A request for oral argument beyond 20 minutes a side is determined by a majority of the panel.

[Effective April 29, 2015.]

IOP 2.2 DETERMINATION IN CASES EN BANC

There is oral argument in an en banc case if it is requested by at least one judge of the en banc court. No later than 11 calendar days before the en banc sitting, the chief judge or, in his or her absence, the presiding judge, furnishes the clerk with the court's determination in accordance with the maximum request, up to 30 minutes per side, of any judge. A request for oral argument beyond 30 minutes a side is determined by a majority of the en banc court. Ordinarily, 30 minutes per side will be allocated and an amicus will not argue unless at least 4 members of the en banc court vote otherwise.

[Effective April 29, 2015.]

IOP 2.3 FAILURE TO NOTIFY PRESIDING JUDGE

Should a judge fail to notify other panelists orally or in writing of his or her views prior to noon of the eleventh day before the panel sitting, the presiding judge assumes that the non-notifying judge agrees to be bound by the determinations of the other two judges or of the presiding judge, as the case may be.

[Effective April 29, 2015.]

IOP 2.4 SUGGESTED CRITERIA FOR ORAL ARGUMENT

2.4.1 Experience discloses that judges usually find oral argument unnecessary when:

(a) The issue is tightly constrained, not novel, and the briefs adequately cover the arguments;

(b) The outcome of the appeal is clearly controlled by a decision of the Supreme Court or this court; or

(c) The state of the record will determine the outcome and the sole issue is either sufficiency of the evidence, the adequacy of jury instructions, or rulings as to admissibility of evidence, and the briefs adequately refer to the record.

2.4.2 Experience discloses that judges usually vote for oral argument when:

(a) The appeal presents a substantial and novel legal issue;

(b) The resolution of an issue presented by the appeal will be of institutional or precedential value;

(c) A judge has questions to ask counsel to clarify an important legal, factual, or procedural point;

(d) A decision, legislation, or an event subsequent to the filing of the last brief may significantly bear on the case;

(e) An important public interest may be affected.

2.4.3 The foregoing criteria shall not be construed to limit any judge's discretion in voting for oral argument.

[Effective April 29, 2015.]

IOP 2.5 NOTICE TO COUNSEL

No later than 10 calendar days prior to the first day of the panel sitting, the clerk communicates to counsel in each case listed the names of the members of the panel and whether the case is to be orally argued.

[Effective April 29, 2015.]

CHAPTER 3. COMPOSITION OF PANELS AND ORDER OF PRECEDENCE

IOP 3.1 COMPOSITION OF PANEL

Unless there is a judicial emergency, each panel includes either two active judges of this court or one active judge and one senior judge of this court. Composition of a panel is determined at the time cases are assigned to a panel. If an active judge assumes senior status after cases have been assigned to a panel, the panel need not be reconstituted.

[Effective April 29, 2015.]

IOP 3.2 PRESIDING JUDGE

The chief judge is the presiding judge. In the absence of the chief judge, the presiding judge is that judge of this court in active service next in precedence. See 28 U.S.C. 45(b). Other active circuit judges sit in order of precedence based on the seniority of their commissions, followed by senior circuit judges and visiting judges.

[Effective April 29, 2015.]

IOP 3.3 ENTERING COURT

The panel assembles in the robing room approximately 5 minutes prior to the opening of court. The judges enter the courtroom from the robing room in the reverse order of precedence. The next ranking judge is stationed to the right of the presiding judge facing the courtroom from the bench. All remain standing until the presiding judge sits.

[Effective April 29, 2015.]

CHAPTER 4. PANEL CONFERENCE PROCEDURE

IOP 4.1 TENTATIVE VIEWS

After a case has been argued or submitted to a panel of the court, a conference is held to exchange tentative views as to the decision. The judges express views and tentative votes in reverse order of precedence. By unanimous agreement of the panel, conferences in submitted cases may be held by telephone or views may be exchanged by electronic mail prior to the submission date.

[Effective April 29, 2015.]

IOP 4.2 OPINION ASSIGNMENT

Following discussion and tentative votes, the presiding judge assigns those cases in which opinions of the court are to be drafted to the judges of the panel for preparation of the opinion of the court. If the panel is divided in its views and the presiding judge does not concur in the decision of the majority, the assignment is made by that member of the majority who is the ranking judge of this court.

[Effective April 29, 2015.]

CHAPTER 5.   OPINIONS

IOP 5.1   FORMS OF OPINIONS

There are two forms of opinions: precedential and not precedential. A majority of the panel determines whether an opinion is designated as precedential or not precedential, unless a majority of the active judges of the court decides otherwise. The face of an opinion states whether it is precedential or not precedential.

[Effective April 29, 2015.]

IOP 5.2   PRECEDENTIAL OPINIONS

An opinion, whether signed or per curiam, is designated as precedential when it has precedential or institutional value. Precedential opinions are posted on the court's internet website.

[Effective April 29, 2015.]

IOP 5.3   NOT PRECEDENTIAL OPINIONS

An opinion, whether signed or per curiam, that appears to have value only to the trial court or the parties is designated as not precedential and unless otherwise provided by the court, it is posted on the court's internet website. A not precedential opinion may be issued without regard to whether the panel's decision is unanimous and without regard to whether the panel affirms, reverses, or grants other relief. The first page of a not precedential opinion contains a footnote stating: "This disposition is not an opinion of the full Court and pursuant to I.O.P. 5.7 does not constitute binding precedent."

[Effective April 29, 2015.]

IOP 5.4   LISTING OF COUNSEL AND JUDGE

Counsel are listed on all precedential opinions and on not precedential opinions if the case was argued. The name of the district judge or magistrate judge is listed on all opinions.

[Effective April 29, 2015.]

IOP 5.5   PREPARATION AND CIRCULATION OF OPINIONS

5.5.1   By Author. The authoring judge prepares a draft opinion in accordance with the decision of the panel at conference, but the author may express any different views reached after subsequent study of the case. The opinion will set forth the reasons supporting the court's decision.

5.5.2   Circulation Within Panel. After the draft opinion has been prepared, the authoring judge circulates it to the other two members of the panel with a request for approval or suggestions they may desire to make with respect to the draft opinion. Answering this request is given the highest priority by the other two judges, who shall communicate in writing their approval or disapproval within 8 calendar days of receipt of the opinion. This time is extended to 10 days during the month of August. Absent a request for additional time, failure to respond within that time period shall be deemed an approval of the opinion as drafted. Because it is the opinion of the court, other members of the panel are free to make any suggestions relating to the modification of, addition to, or subtraction from the proposed text. Where a textual revision or addition is suggested, the suggesting judge submits his or her modification in specific language capable of being inserted into the opinion. When one of the other two judges approves, it becomes the proposed opinion of the court. Should the other panel members disagree with the author's draft, the opinion is reassigned by either the presiding judge or the ranking judge who is a member of the panel's majority.

5.5.3   Time Schedule for Panel Drafting and Circulating Opinions; Reassignments.

(a) *60–day period for draft opinion writing.* It is the aspirational goal of the court that, except in complex cases, the authoring judge transmit to the panel a draft opinion within 60 days after assignment or after close of any supplemental briefing or other factors suspending the drafting process.

(b) *45–day period to file concurring or dissenting opinion.* If, after a second panel member approves the draft opinion, the third panel member desires to separately concur or dissent, the judge not joining in the opinion notifies the author promptly and transmits his or her separate opinion to the panel within 45 days after the second judge's approval is received. Panel opinions are not considered to be completed until each member has an opportunity to revise his or her opinion in response to those of other panel members.

5.5.4   To Non-panel Active Judges. Drafts of unanimous not precedential opinions do not circulate to non-panel judges. Drafts of not precedential opinions that contain a dissent circulate to non-panel judges. Drafts of not precedential opinions that contain a concurrence circulate to non-panel judges if a member of the panel requests that the opinion be circulated to all judges. Drafts of precedential opinions and not precedential opinions that are not unanimous are circulated to all active judges of the court after the draft opinion has been approved by all three panel members, concurring or dissenting opinions have been transmitted, or all members of the panel have had the time set forth in I.O.P. 5.5.3 to write separate opinions. Absent a request for additional time, if the third judge has not timely responded, the draft opinion is circulated to the active judges of the court with the notation added to the opinion that the third judge has not joined in the opinion. Non-panel active judges must notify the authoring judge within 8 calendar days if they desire en banc consideration. This time is extended to 10 days during the month of August. The circulation to non-panel active judges contains a request for notification if there is a desire for en banc consideration. Although senior judges do not have a vote en banc, senior judges may choose to receive circulating opinions.

5.5.5 En banc Cases. The time schedule set forth in I.O.P. 5.5.2 and 5.5.3 is also followed in en banc cases, except that judges will give preparation of en banc opinions priority over preparation of panel opinions.

[Effective April 29, 2015.]

IOP 5.6 FILING OF OPINIONS

If, 8 calendar days (10 days in August) after the opinion is transmitted for circulation, insufficient votes for rehearing are received, and the authoring judge transmits the original typescript to the Clerk for filing and notifies the author of any separate opinion to do likewise. The failure of a panel member to concur or dissent or to file a timely opinion does not delay the filing of the majority opinion or the entry of the judgment of this court.

[Effective April 29, 2015.]

IOP 5.7 CITATIONS

The court by tradition does not cite to its not precedential opinions as authority. Such opinions are not regarded as precedents that bind the court because they do not circulate to the full court before filing.

[Effective April 29, 2015.]

CHAPTER 6. JUDGMENT ORDERS

IOP 6.1 PANEL UNANIMITY

A case may be terminated in this court by a judgment order upon the unanimous decision of the panel.

[Effective April 29, 2015.]

IOP 6.2 CRITERIA

6.2.1 A judgment order is filed when the panel unanimously determines to affirm the judgment or order of the district court or decision of the Tax Court, enforce or deny review of a decision or order of an administrative agency, or dismiss the appeal or petition for review for lack of jurisdiction or otherwise, and determines that a written opinion will have no precedential or institutional value.

6.2.2 A judgment order may be used when:

(a) The judgment of the district court is based on findings of fact which are not clearly erroneous;

(b) Sufficient evidence supports a jury verdict;

(c) Substantial evidence on the record as a whole supports a decision or order of an administrative agency;

(d) No error of law appears;

(e) The district court did not abuse its discretion on matters addressed thereto; or

(f) The court has no jurisdiction.

[Effective April 29, 2015.]

IOP 6.3 FORM OF ORDER

6.3.1 A judgment order affirming the district court in a direct criminal appeal includes a statement of those issues raised by appellant and considered by the panel.

6.3.2 A judgment order may state that the case is affirmed by reference to the opinion of the district court or decision of the administrative agency and may contain one or more references to cases or other authorities.

[Effective April 29, 2015.]

IOP 6.4 PROCEDURE

6.4.1 At conference the panel decides whether the case requires an opinion or a judgment order. If the latter, the judge assigned to prepare the order furnishes other members of the panel with copies of the proposed order. The panel members indicate their approval either on a copy which is provided by the order writer or by signifying approval in writing by electronic mail or otherwise.

6.4.2 The order writer promptly arranges for filing the original with the clerk.

[Effective April 29, 2015.]

CHAPTER 7. ORDERS REVERSING OR REMANDING

IOP 7.1 RETENTION OF JURISDICTION

When a panel deems it appropriate for this court to retain jurisdiction without disposing of the case and to remand to the district court or agency, such as for correction or modification of the record pursuant to Fed.R.App.P. 10(e) or for consideration of a settlement reached on appeal, the panel may do so and hold the appeal in abeyance. In such an instance, the panel has discretion to retain assignment of the case or return it to the clerk for reassignment upon its return.

[Effective April 29, 2015.]

IOP 7.2 ASSIGNMENT FOLLOWING REMAND

When an appeal or petition for review is filed in a case which has previously been remanded, the clerk will assign the appeal to a panel in the regular course unless the original panel retained assignment.

[Effective April 29, 2015.]

IOP 7.3 REVERSAL OR REMAND

In some instances when a panel reverses or remands a case to the district court or agency and it is not feasible to write an opinion, usually because the matter requires immediate attention, the court enters a dispositive order setting forth briefly the reasons for its action. Such an order does not circulate to the non-panel judges.

[Effective April 29, 2015.]

CHAPTER 8. PANEL REHEARING

IOP 8.1 PETITION

A petition for panel rehearing is sent to the members of the panel, including senior judges or visiting judges, with the request that they notify the authoring judge within 10 calendar days of the date of the clerk's letter forwarding the petition whether they vote to grant the petition or desire that an answer be filed. A judge who does not desire panel rehearing or the filing of an answer is not expected to respond.

[Effective April 29, 2015.]

IOP 8.2 REQUEST FOR ANSWER

If any member of the majority timely notifies the other members of the panel that an answer is desired, the author, if an active or senior judge of this court, enters an order directing the filing of an answer within 14 calendar days. The clerk forwards the answer to the panel members with the request that they notify the authoring judge within 10 calendar days if they vote to grant the petition. A judge who does not desire panel rehearing is not expected to respond.

[Effective April 29, 2015.]

IOP 8.3 DISPOSITION

8.3.1 The author, if an active or senior judge of this court, enters an order granting panel rehearing if two members of the panel vote for panel rehearing, and vacates the panel's opinion and the judgment entered thereon. Otherwise, the author enters the order denying panel rehearing. If the author is a visiting judge or justice, the ranking active judge of this court on the panel majority receives responses to the petition, communicates with the clerk, signs the necessary orders, and has all the administrative responsibility set forth in this I.O.P. A senior judge of this court who was the authoring judge handles all administrative responsibility on matters on which that judge has a vote but may choose to request the ranking active judge on the panel majority to undertake such administrative responsibility.

8.3.2 Any member of the panel may file an opinion sur denial of the petition for panel rehearing and direct its publication. When the panel grants a petition for rehearing and a petition for rehearing en banc is also pending, the judge who entered the order following panel rehearing notifies the active judges of the disposition, and whether the petition for rehearing is moot or if any further vote is required.

[Effective April 29, 2015.]

CHAPTER 9. EN BANC CONSIDERATION

IOP 9.1 POLICY OF AVOIDING INTRA-CIRCUIT CONFLICT OF PRECEDENT

It is the tradition of this court that the holding of a panel in a precedential opinion is binding on subsequent panels. Thus, no subsequent panel overrules the holding in a precedential opinion of a previous panel. Court en banc consideration is required to do so.

[Effective April 29, 2015.]

IOP 9.2 HEARING EN BANC

Initial en banc hearing is extraordinary; it is ordered only when a majority of the active judges who are not disqualified, determines that the case is controlled by a prior decision of the court which should be reconsidered and the case is of such immediate importance that exigent circumstances require initial consideration by the full court.

[Effective April 29, 2015.]

IOP 9.3 CRITERIA FOR REHEARING EN BANC

9.3.1 This court strictly follows the precept of Fed. R.App.P. 35(a) and Local Appellate Rule 35.4 that rehearing en banc is not favored and will not be ordered unless consideration by the full court is necessary to secure or maintain uniformity of its decisions or the proceeding involves a question of exceptional importance.

9.3.2 This court does not ordinarily grant rehearing en banc when the panel's statement of the law is correct and the controverted issue is solely the application of the law to the circumstances of the case.

9.3.3 Rehearing en banc is ordinarily not granted when the only issue presented is one of state law.

[Effective April 29, 2015.]

IOP 9.4 COURT ORIGINATED REHEARING EN BANC

9.4.1 If, during the circulation of draft opinions pursuant to I.O.P. 5.5.2 and 5.6, a majority of the active judges who are not disqualified, votes that the case be considered en banc, the chief judge enters an order for rehearing en banc.

9.4.2 If, during the period for circulation of draft opinions, one judge has timely voted for rehearing, another judge may obtain an extension of time to consider en banc rehearing by circulating a letter asking that the time for voting be extended for a period not to exceed 5 working days beyond the 8 day (10 day in August) time period. This request results in an automatic extension. Irrespective of the number of such requests, the voting time automatically is extended this one period only, unless the chief judge, upon application, grants a further extension of time. In death penalty cases, the times set forth herein may be reduced pursuant to Local Appellate Rule Misc. 111.7(b).

9.4.3 During the circulation of draft opinions, a judge who does not desire rehearing or who has no comment is not expected to respond. The active judge who has written a dissenting opinion is presumed to have voted for rehearing en banc absent a notification in writing to the contrary.

[Effective April 29, 2015.]

IOP 9.5 REHEARING EN BANC ON PETITION BY PARTY

9.5.1 It is presumed that a petition for rehearing before the panel or suggestion for en banc rehearing filed by a party as provided by Fed.R.App.P. 40(a) or 35(b) requests both panel rehearing and rehearing en banc, unless the petition for panel rehearing under Rule 40(a) states explicitly that it does not request en banc rehearing under Rule 35(b).

9.5.2 When a petition for rehearing is filed, a copy of the petition is transmitted by the clerk to each member of the panel which heard and decided the case and to the other active judges of the court with a request that they respond to the authoring judge if they desire rehearing or an answer. When the author is not a member of the court, the clerk requests that responses be directed to the ranking judge of the majority. Any member of the panel majority may direct the clerk to request an answer.

9.5.3 Pursuant to 28 U.S.C. § 46(c), only active judges of this court may vote for rehearing en banc. Therefore, rehearing en banc shall be ordered only upon the affirmative votes of a majority of the judges of this court in regular active service who are not disqualified.

9.5.4 An active judge who does not communicate with the authoring judge concerning rehearing within 10 calendar days after the date of the clerk's letter transmitting the petition for rehearing is presumed not to desire rehearing en banc or that an answer be filed. In death penalty cases, the times set forth herein may be reduced pursuant to Local Appellate Rule Misc. 111.7(b).

9.5.5 If, during the 10 day period for circulation of petitions for rehearing, one judge has timely voted for rehearing, another judge may obtain an extension of time to consider en banc rehearing by circulating a letter asking that the time for voting be extended for a period not to exceed 5 working days beyond the 10 day time period. This request results in an automatic extension. Irrespective of the number of such requests, the voting time automatically is extended this one period only, unless the chief judge, upon application, grants a further extension of time. In death penalty cases, the times set forth herein may be reduced pursuant to Local Appellate Rule Misc. 111.7(b).

9.5.6 If four active judges vote to request an answer to the petition or if there are a total of four votes for an answer or for rehearing, provided that there is at least one vote for an answer, the authoring judge enters an order directing such an answer within 14 calendar days from the date of the order. The clerk forwards the answer to the active judges with the request that they notify the authoring judge within 10 calendar days if they vote to grant the petition. A judge who does not desire rehearing is not expected to respond. Copies of the answer are sent as a courtesy to any senior judge or visiting judge who was a member of the panel which heard and decided the case. In death penalty cases, the times set forth herein may be reduced pursuant to Local Appellate Rule Misc. 111.7(b).

9.5.7 The authoring judge enters an order denying rehearing before the panel, and denying rehearing en banc if a majority of the active judges who are not disqualified, does not vote for rehearing. Separate orders may be entered if appropriate. When the panel grants a petition for rehearing and a petition for rehearing en banc is also pending, the judge who enters the order granting panel rehearing notifies the active judges of the vacatur of the panel opinion, and all action on the petition for rehearing en banc is suspended. Following panel rehearing, the authoring judge notifies the active judges of the disposition and whether any further vote on the petition for rehearing en banc is required.

9.5.8 If there is a dissent from the denial of rehearing and no dissenting opinion is filed, a notation will be added to the dispositive order, at the affirmative request of the dissenting judge, that "Judge ___ would grant rehearing by the court en banc." Any active judge may file an opinion sur denial of the petition and direct its publication.

9.5.9 If a majority of the active judges of the court who are not disqualified votes for rehearing en banc, the chief judge enters an order which grants rehearing as to one or more of the issues, vacates the panel's opinion in full or in part and the judgment entered thereon, and assigns the case to the calendar for rehearing en banc.

[Effective April 29, 2015.]

IOP 9.6   PROCEDURE

9.6.1 If the author is a visiting judge, justice, or a senior circuit judge, the ranking active or senior judge of this court on the panel majority receives responses to the petition, communicates with the clerk, signs the necessary orders, and has all the administrative responsibility set forth in this I.O.P.

9.6.2 An en banc hearing is held only at a regularly scheduled en banc session of the court, unless a majority of the active judges who are not disqualified, votes to expedite.

9.6.3 The chief judge, when requested by a majority of the en banc court, directs the clerk to advise counsel to submit supplemental briefs on specific issues or to be prepared to discuss at oral argument any other relevant issues.

9.6.4 A senior judge of this court may elect, pursuant to 28 U.S.C. § 46(c), to participate as a member of the en banc court reviewing a decision of a panel on which the senior judge was a member. That election may be made by letter to the clerk, with copies to all active judges, covering all cases on which the senior judge may thereafter sit, or may be made on a case by case basis. Any judge participating in an en banc poll, hearing, or rehearing while in regular active service who subsequently takes senior status may elect to continue participating in the final resolution of the case.

[Effective April 29, 2015.]

CHAPTER 10.   MOTION PRACTICE

IOP 10.1   MOTION PANELS

A panel is available to receive motions at all times. The chief judge, with the consent of the court, designates standing motions panels (SMPs) to receive from the clerk motions in cases which have not been sent to merits panels.

[Effective April 29, 2015.]

IOP 10.2   DISTRIBUTION

10.2.1 Insofar as possible, the clerk equalizes the number of motions and emergency motions sent to each SMP.

10.2.2 When an emergency motion is filed, the movant may be directed by the clerk to deliver by hand or by electronic transmission copies of the moving papers that day to each member of the SMP designated by the clerk at the chambers where the judge is stationed or at such other place as may be designated.

10.2.3 Motions on non-emergency matters are distributed to the SMPs as they are complete; i.e., when responses have been filed and any necessary briefing completed.

[Effective April 29, 2015.]

IOP 10.3 PROCEDURE

10.3.1 Each standing motions panel sets its own procedures for conference and disposition. The presiding judge of each standing motions panel enters the order, generally on the motion form supplied by the clerk, or requests another judge to do so. The order notes a dissenting vote on request of the dissenting judge.

10.3.2 When a certificate of appealability is granted on behalf of an indigent appellant pursuant to 28 U.S.C. § 2254 or § 2255, the clerk appoints counsel for the appellant unless the court instructs otherwise.

10.3.3 A motion for reconsideration or rehearing of any standing motions panel or merits panel decision on a motion, other than a case-dispositive ruling, is referred only to that standing motions panel or merits panel and not to the court en banc. A petition for rehearing of a case-dispositive ruling is referred to the court en banc according to the procedures for petitions for rehearing. Non–case–dispositive rulings by either the merits panel or standing motion panel are referred to the court en banc only if the panel so orders.

10.3.4 The standing motions panel determines whether there shall be oral argument on a motion in the same manner as for an appeal.

10.3.5 A motion panel may grant a motion to dismiss an appeal. If the motion seeks dismissal for lack of jurisdiction or for untimeliness, and the panel votes not to grant the motion, the motion is referred by order, without decision and without prejudice, to the merits panel.

10.3.6 A certification under 28 U.S.C. § 1292(b), or other similar statute or rule, by a motions panel does not in any manner bind or restrict the merits panel.

[Effective April 29, 2015.]

IOP 10.4 MOTIONS REFERRED TO CLERK

The court may refer to the clerk for disposition any category of motion other than those which are case-dispositive or which by statute or rule must be decided by judges.

[Effective April 29, 2015.]

IOP 10.5 SINGLE JUDGE MOTIONS

10.5.1 A single judge may entertain and may grant or deny any request for relief which, under the Federal Rules for Appellate Procedure or an applicable statute, may properly be sought by motion, except that a single judge may not dismiss or otherwise determine an appeal or other proceeding. The action of a single judge may be reviewed by a three judge panel of the court.

10.5.2 Without limiting I.O.P. 10.5.1, this court as a matter of practice refers to a single judge, the following motions:

(a) stay pending appeal or mandamus (generally only in emergency situations);

(b) motion for appointment of counsel whether pursuant to § 1915 or under the Criminal Justice Act;

(c) approval of transcripts at government expense in criminal and civil cases;

(d) motions to withdraw;

(e) motions to expedite;

(f) motions to intervene;

(g) motions to compel the ordering of transcripts; and

(h) motions to unseal or seal.

[Effective April 29, 2015.]

IOP 10.6 SUMMARY ACTION

The court, *sua sponte* or upon motion by a party, may take summary action affirming, reversing, vacating, modifying, setting aside, or remanding the judgment, decree, or order appealed from; granting or denying a petition for review; or granting or refusing enforcement of the order of an administrative agency if it clearly appears that no substantial question is presented or that subsequent precedent or a change in circumstances warrants such action. Before taking summary action, the court will afford the parties an opportunity to submit argument in support of or in opposition to such disposition if briefs on the merits have not already been filed. Summary action may be taken only by unanimous vote of the panel. If a motion panel determines that summary action is not appropriate at that time, it may, in lieu of denial, refer the matter to the merits panel without decision and without prejudice.

[Effective April 29, 2015.]

IOP 10.7 MOTIONS RELATED TO CASES ASSIGNED TO MERITS PANELS

10.7.1 Motions related to cases assigned to merits panels are generally granted or denied by the presiding judge if they are merely administrative and unrelated to the disposition, unless the presider believes reference to the entire panel is appropriate.

10.7.2 Motions related to scheduling cases for argument are always referred to the entire panel.

[Effective April 29, 2015.]

IOP 10.8 POST–DECISION MOTIONS

10.8.1 Unless the clerk has been designated to act thereon, a motion for extension of time for filing a petition for rehearing or for leave to file out of time is referred to the author, who has authority to grant an extension of time. If the authoring judge votes to deny, the motion is referred to the entire panel for disposition.

10.8.2 Inasmuch as a stay of mandate is ordinarily not a requirement for filing a petition for a writ of certiorari, it is the practice of this court not to grant a motion for stay of the mandate or to recall the mandate unless the failure to grant a stay affects a substantive right of the applicant.

10.8.3 A motion to amend the judgment of the court is referred to the panel.

10.8.4 A motion to extend time to file a bill of costs is determined by the clerk. An appeal from the clerk's ruling is referred to the authoring judge, unless the author was a visiting judge, in which case it is referred to the ranking active judge who voted with the majority.

10.8.5 A motion for the approval of a fee under the Criminal Justice Act is referred to the authoring judge.

10.8.6 If the author is a visiting judge, the ranking active judge of this court on the panel majority receives responses to the motion, communicates with the clerk, signs the necessary orders, and has all the administrative responsibility set forth in this I.O.P. Senior judges on this court may choose to request the ranking active judge on the panel majority to undertake the above administrative responsibilities.

10.8.7 A remand from the Supreme Court is referred to the panel which decided the matter or to the court en banc, as the case may be.

[Effective April 29, 2015.]

IOP 10.9 CERTIFICATION OF QUESTIONS OF STATE LAW

When a panel has certified a question of state law under L.A.R. Misc. 110.0, the presider shall promptly notify all the other judges of the court by sending a copy of the question certified, and shall circulate the response received.

[Effective April 29, 2015.]

CHAPTER 11. RECUSAL OR DISQUALIFICATION OF JUDGES

IOP 11.1 PROCEDURE

11.1.1 Before cases are sent to a panel, the clerk transmits copies of the docket sheets and disclosure statements to each judge who responds promptly informing the clerk of those cases in which the judge is recused.

11.1.2 Each judge may submit to the clerk in writing those circumstances which would generally require a recusal, including names of businesses in which the judge or family members have a financial interest, names of lawyer relatives whose names may appear as counsel in the appeals, and names of law firms on whose cases the judge does not sit.

[Effective April 29, 2015.]

IOP 11.2 CIRCUMSTANCES

11.2.1 The provisions of 28 U.S.C. § 455 and 28 U.S.C. § 144 re recusal are fully incorporated here.

11.2.2 (a) With respect to "financial interest" as used in 28 U.S.C. § 455, ownership of a small percentage of the outstanding shares of a publicly traded corporation which is a member of a trade association that is a party to the lawsuit is not a "financial interest" in the subject matter in controversy or in a party to the proceeding unless the owner has an interest that can be substantially affected by the outcome of the proceeding.

(b) Ownership of a small percentage of the outstanding shares of a publicly traded corporation that is listed as a creditor of the bankrupt who is a party to the lawsuit is not a "financial interest" in the subject matter in controversy or in a party to the proceeding unless the owner has an interest that can be substantially affected by the outcome of the proceeding.

(c) An insurance policy issued to a judge or a member of his or her family is not a "financial interest" in the insurance company.

[Effective April 29, 2015.]

CHAPTER 12.   PROCEDURES WHEN JUDGES BECOME UNAVAILABLE

IOP 12.1   [UNTITLED]

If a judge assigned to a panel becomes unavailable for any reason, the chief judge in his or her discretion will decide whether to reconstitute the panel by naming a substitute. Unavailability includes, but is not limited to, necessity to recuse, disability, resignation, or death. If the chief judge is recused, the active judge next in precedence will act. A written order is not necessary for the reconstitution of any panel. Generally, the chief judge will exercise his or her discretion in the following manner:

(a) If after distribution of the briefs, but before the disposition date, a member of a panel becomes unavailable, the judge, or one of the remaining panel members, informs the chief judge. The chief judge will usually name a substitute and reconstitute the panel. The substituted judge on any panel is open to opinion assignments on the same basis as original panel members.

(b) If a member of a panel becomes unavailable after the disposition date but before the opinion is filed with the clerk, the two remaining judges will inform the chief judge of the status of the case, e.g. whether the remaining members of the panel agree on the disposition of the case, and whether an opinion has been drafted. The chief judge in his or her discretion will decide whether to reconstitute the panel by naming a substitute. A case may be decided without naming a substitute judge if the remaining judges agree as to disposition.

(c) If the author of an opinion becomes unavailable while the opinion is circulating to the panel or to the full court, ordinarily the opinion will be reassigned to one of the remaining panel members if they are in agreement. If the remaining panel members are not in agreement, the chief judge will name a substitute judge and reconstitute the panel.

(d) If the author of an opinion or member of the panel becomes unavailable after transmission of the opinion to the clerk, but before the opinion is filed, the chief judge may direct that the opinion be filed listing the unavailable judge on the coram, provided neither of the remaining judges has authored a concurrence or dissent. Ordinarily the opinion will be filed as a per curiam opinion but the chief judge may in his or her discretion direct that the opinion be filed with the unavailable judge listed as author. The clerk will note on the opinion that it was received in the clerk's office before the panel member became unavailable.

[Effective April 29, 2015.]

IOP 12.2   [UNTITLED]

Judges who leave the court should endeavor to insure that opinions they have authored are circulated, approved, and filed before their departure.

[Effective April 29, 2015.]

CHAPTER 13.   VISITING JUDGES

The circuit executive is charged with the responsibility of assisting the visiting judges and arranges for chambers, provides advance notification of these Internal Operating Procedures, arranges for a secretary, if necessary, and in general tends to the visitor's other needs.

[Effective April 29, 2015.]

CHAPTER 14.   STAFF ATTORNEYS

Staff attorneys based in Philadelphia work under the supervision of the clerk and chief deputy for the Legal Division. They provide legal research and assistance to the court as directed.

[Effective April 29, 2015.]

CHAPTER 15.   SENIOR JUDGE LAW CLERK VOLUNTEERS

Senior judges may volunteer use of their law clerks to assist active judges, especially in matters which can be carried out in a senior judge's chambers. Senior judges may also volunteer use of their law clerks to assist the Staff Attorneys Office in carrying out its responsibilities. A senior judge who takes an extended absence from chambers usually notifies the active judges that his or her law clerks are available, unless the law clerks will be fully occupied with court work during that period.

[Effective April 29, 2015.]

CHAPTER 16. DEATH PENALTY CASES

IOP 16.1 DOCKETING AND BRIEFING

Upon receipt of the required statement pursuant to Local Appellate Rule Misc. 111.2 (a), the clerk of this court shall establish a file and monitor the progress of any such case through the district court. At an appropriate time, the clerk may tentatively assign the case to a special panel. If no appeal is filed, the tentatively assigned panel will be returned to the pool of unassigned death penalty panel combinations. Upon the filing of any notice of appeal, request for certificate of appealability, 28 U.S.C. § 2253(c)(1) and/or for stay, the clerk may establish, at the direction of the panel to which the case is assigned, a schedule for briefing and disposition on the merits.

[Effective April 29, 2015.]

IOP 16.2 PANEL ASSIGNMENTS

The clerk will use a computer program to randomly select a panel from a pool of all possible three-judge combinations consisting of circuit judges in active service and those judges who have taken senior status and have indicated their willingness to hear death penalty cases. The computer program will be designed to use all possible three-judge combinations and to minimize the possibility of assignment of any judge to successive panels. The clerk will be responsible for maintaining the program and for making any adjustments necessitated by vacancies and appointments. Ordinarily, a case will be assigned to a single panel for all proceedings to final order. Separate appeals concerning the same petitioner that are filed in close proximity may be assigned to the same panel. In the event of the unavailability or disqualification of a member of a special panel, a new member will be randomly selected. Any unused panel will be returned to the pool for future reassignment. The chief judge periodically may address any imbalance in the caseload.

[Effective April 29, 2015.]

IOP 16.3 STAYS, TENTATIVE ASSIGNMENTS

If a stay application is filed in this court before a district court decision has been entered, the clerk shall forward the motion to a special panel. Whether or not a stay application has been filed, if no ruling has been made 10 calendar days before the time scheduled for execution of the judgment, the case shall tentatively be assigned to a panel, which will be kept advised of the status of the case, the name of the district judge before whom it is pending, and the scheduled time of execution of the judgment.

[Effective April 29, 2015.]

IOP 16.4 HEARINGS OR REHEARING EN BANC

Where the court has voted to grant hearing or rehearing en banc, the chief judge may specifically order briefing or schedule oral argument as necessary.

[Effective April 29, 2015.]

IOP 16.5 NOTICE TO SUPREME COURT

The clerk shall notify the clerk of the Supreme Court when a case involving the suspension or stay of execution of the judgment of a state or federal court is filed, and shall thereafter maintain communication with both the district court and the Supreme Court.

[Effective April 29, 2015.]

CHAPTER 17. SAMPLE FORMS

IOP 17.1 JUDGMENT ORDER— CIVIL CASES

JUDGMENT ORDER

After consideration of all contentions raised by appellant, it is

ADJUDGED AND ORDERED that the judgment of the district court be and is hereby affirmed. Costs taxed against appellant.

By the Court,

....
Chief Judge/Circuit Judge

Attest:

....
Clerk

Dated:

[Effective April 29, 2015.]

IOP 17.2 JUDGMENT ORDER— CRIMINAL CASES

JUDGMENT ORDER

After considering the contentions raised by appellant, to-wit, that the court erred: (1) in refusing to charge on the testimony of an accomplice as requested by appellant; (2) in admitting hearsay testimony of a witness; and (3) in refusing to grant a motion of acquittal on the theory of insufficiency of evidence, it is

ADJUDGED AND ORDERED that the judgment of the district court be and is hereby affirmed.

[Effective April 29, 2015.]

IOP 17.3 DISMISSAL FOR LACK OF JURISDICTION

ORDER OR JUDGMENT ORDER

After consideration of all contentions raised by the appellant and concluding that this court has no jurisdiction because the appeal is premature, see *Griggs v. Provident Consumer Discount Co.*, 459 U.S. 56 (1982), it is

ADJUDGED AND ORDERED that the appeal be and is hereby dismissed without prejudice to the filing of a timely appeal.

Costs taxed against appellant.

[Effective April 29, 2015.]

IOP 17.4 DISMISSAL FOR LACK OF CERTIFICATION UNDER FED.R.CIV.P. 54(b)

When the appeal is dismissed because of lack of certification under Fed.R.Civ.P. 54(b), an order of dismissal ordinarily contains language similar in form to:

The appeal will be dismissed without prejudice to the right of appellant to apply to the district court for a determination and direction under Fed.R.Civ.P. 54(b). However, we express no opinion as to whether the determination and direction should be made, this being a matter within the discretion of the district court. If the determination and direction are made within 30 days, a new appeal may come before us on the present briefs and record supplemented to show subsequent proceedings.

[Effective April 29, 2015.]

APPENDIX II. RULES OF ATTORNEY DISCIPLINARY ENFORCEMENT

Effective July 1, 2015

RULE 1. DEFINITIONS

1. "The Court" means the United States Court of Appeals for the Third Circuit.

2. "Another Court" means any court of the United States, the District of Columbia, or any state, territory, or commonwealth of the United States.

3. "Serious Crime" includes all felonies as well as any lesser crime involving false swearing, misrepresentation, fraud, willful failure to file income tax returns, deceit, bribery, extortion, misappropriation, theft, or an attempt or a conspiracy or solicitation of another to commit such a lesser crime.

4. "Standing Committee" means this Court's Standing Committee on Attorney Discipline.

5. "Reciprocal Discipline" means discipline imposed as a result of another court's suspension or disbarment of an attorney.

[Effective July 1, 2015.]

RULE 2. GROUNDS FOR DISCIPLINE

1. A member of the bar of this Court may be disciplined by this Court as a result of the following misconduct:

(a) conviction in another court of a serious crime;

(b) discipline, including disbarment or suspension, by another court, whether or not with the attorney's consent, or the resignation from the bar of another court while an investigation into allegations of misconduct is pending;

(c) conduct with respect to this Court which violates the Federal Rules of Appellate Procedure, the Rules or Internal Operating Procedures of this Court, or orders or other instructions of the Court;

(d) conduct that violates the Rules of conduct of any court of the United States, the District of Columbia, or any state, territory, or commonwealth of the United States to which the respondent is subject; or

(e) any other conduct unbecoming a member of the bar of this Court.

2. Administrative suspension or its equivalent by another court, including, but not limited to, suspension for failure to pay annual fees or to complete continuing legal education requirements, is not grounds for disciplinary action or similar administrative action in this Court, but may be grounds for marking an attorney inactive on the rolls of this Court.

[Effective July 1, 2015.]

RULE 3. DISCIPLINARY SANCTIONS; ASSESSMENTS UNDER 28 U.S.C. § 1927 AND FED. R. APP. P. 38

1. Discipline may consist of disbarment, suspension from practice before this Court, monetary sanction, removal from the roster of attorneys eligible for appointment as Court-appointed counsel, reprimand, or any other sanction that the Court or a panel thereof may deem appropriate.

2. Disbarment is the presumed discipline for conviction of a serious crime. Disbarment is also the presumed discipline when an attorney has resigned from the bar of another court while an investigation into allegations of misconduct is pending.

3. Except as provided in Rule 2.2, the identical discipline imposed by another court is presumed appropriate for discipline imposed by this Court as a result of that other court's suspension or disbarment of an attorney.

4. A monetary sanction imposed on disciplinary grounds is the personal responsibility of the attorney disciplined, and may not be reimbursed by a client directly or indirectly. Notice to that effect will be sent to the client by the Clerk whenever a monetary sanction is imposed.

5. Assessments of damages, costs, expenses, or attorneys' fees under 28 U.S.C. § 1927 or Fed. R. App. P. 38 are not disciplinary sanctions within the meaning of these Rules such that proceedings with respect thereto are not governed by these Rules unless the panel gives notice under Rule 4.

[Effective July 1, 2015.]

RULE 4. DISCIPLINE WHICH MAY BE IMPOSED BY A PANEL OF THE COURT AND BY THE STANDING COMMITTEE ON ATTORNEY DISCIPLINE

1. A motions, merits or other panel of the Court may impose any sanction other than suspension or disbarment. Before imposing any disciplinary sanction, a panel will notify the attorney of the alleged conduct which may justify the imposition of discipline and afford the attorney an opportunity to be heard, in writing or in person at the option of the panel. If an attorney who has been afforded an opportunity to be heard in writing files within 10 days of the date of the notice that a panel is considering disciplinary action an application requesting to appear before the panel in person, the panel will schedule a hearing. For good cause shown, the Chair of the Committee or the Clerk may on written application made within eight days of the notice extend the time to answer.

2. Any matter of attorney discipline in which suspension or disbarment may be considered as an appropriate sanction will be referred to the Court's Standing Committee or, in the case of an uncontested matter, to its Chair. The matter then proceeds under Rules 6 to 12.

3. The Standing Committee consists of three circuit judges, at least two of whom are active judges, who are appointed by the Chief Judge for three-year, staggered terms. If at the end of a three-year staggered term there has been no reappointment of a member of the Standing Committee or no appointment of a successor, the term of the member will continue until the Chief Judge reappoints the member or appoints a successor. If a reappointment or appointment is made after the prior three-year term would have expired without the extension that this Rule provides, the period of the term of the reappointed member or the successor will be for three years commencing at the end of the prior three-year term without the extension of the member being reappointed or being replaced on the Standing Committee, as the case may be. The Chief Judge will designate one of the three to serve as Chair. If any member of the Standing Committee is unable to hear a particular matter, the Chief Judge will designate another circuit judge as a member of the committee to hear that matter provided, however, that not less than two active judges will hear a particular matter.

[Effective July 1, 2015.]

RULE 5. RESPONSIBILITY OF ATTORNEY TO NOTIFY COURT OF CONVICTION OR DISCIPLINE IMPOSED BY ANOTHER COURT

1. A member of the bar of this Court must notify the Clerk within 10 days if he or she is convicted of a serious crime, if he or she is disbarred or suspended by another court, or if he or she resigns or is disbarred by consent from the bar of another court while an investigation into allegations of misconduct is pending. Administrative suspensions described in Rule 2.2 need not be reported.

2. The Clerk will refer to the Standing Committee all information received by him or her concerning disbarments, suspensions, resignations during the pendency of misconduct investigations, and other con-

duct sufficient to cast doubt upon the continuing qualification of a member of the bar of this Court to practice before it.

[Effective July 1, 2015.]

RULE 6. INITIATION OF DISCIPLINARY PROCEEDINGS

1. **Reciprocal Discipline.** When an active member of the bar of this Court is suspended or disbarred by another court for misconduct, or has resigned from the bar of another court during the pendency of a misconduct investigation, the Clerk of this Court will issue an order for the attorney to show cause why this Court should not impose upon the attorney an order disbarring or suspending the attorney, as the case may be, subject to terms or conditions comparable to those set forth by the other court. This provision requiring the Clerk to issue an order to show cause, however, does not apply in circumstances in which this Court already has initiated disciplinary proceedings against the attorney for the same conduct underlying the suspension, disbarment, or resignation in the other court either as an original disciplinary proceeding in this Court or as a reciprocal proceeding to a proceeding in another court.

2. **Original Discipline.**

(a) Upon receipt of a certified copy of a judgment or other court record demonstrating that a member, whether active or inactive, of the bar of this Court has been convicted of a serious crime, unless a proceeding has been instituted as provided in Rule 6.1, the Clerk will issue an order to show cause why the Court should not impose upon the attorney the presumed discipline described in Rule 3.2.

(b) When the Standing Committee determines that cause may exist for the suspension or disbarment of an attorney pursuant to Rule 2, one of its members or the Clerk will issue an order to show cause why such discipline should not be imposed by this Court.

3. When a disciplinary proceeding is already pending in this Court, upon notification of a separate basis for discipline, the Clerk of this Court rather than issuing an order to show cause will refer the matter to the Standing Committee for it to take such action, if any, as it deems appropriate, including the initiation of another disciplinary proceeding in this Court by a direction to the Clerk to issue an order to the attorney to show cause why this Court should not impose discipline on the attorney.

4. The Clerk will send an order to show cause issued pursuant to this Rule by email and certified mail or the equivalent to the attorney's address on file with the Clerk's Office. In reciprocal discipline cases, the Clerk will include a copy of the order of the other court on which the order to show cause is based. The

mailing of an order to the attorney's address on file is deemed proper service.

5. An order to show cause issued pursuant to this Rule will require the attorney to respond within 30 days. The Clerk, however, may shorten the response period if the Clerk deems it advisable to do so by reason of the urgency of the disposition of the matter involving the attorney or if the Standing Committee or its Chair directs the Clerk to do so. The Chair of the Committee or the Clerk may for good cause shown grant a written request for an extension of time received within 25 days of the date of the show cause order.

6. An order to show cause issued pursuant to this Rule will provide that the attorney, upon receipt of the order, must serve forthwith by mail or otherwise a copy of the order to show cause and a copy of the order of the other court on which it is based to any litigant for whom the attorney has entered an appearance in any matter pending in this Court. If an attorney later enters an appearance in this Court on behalf of a litigant during the pendency of a disciplinary action, the attorney must provide a copy of the order to show cause to the litigant.

7. Once an order to show cause has been issued pursuant to paragraph (1), (2) or (3) of this Rule, the Standing Committee may decline to accept a resignation, or a request to assume inactive status, from the lawyer and continue the proceeding in accordance with these Rules.

[Effective July 1, 2015.]

RULE 7. SUSPENSION DURING PENDENCY OF A DISCIPLINARY PROCEEDING

1. Upon receiving a certified copy of a judgment of conviction of a member, whether active or inactive, of the bar of this Court of a serious crime or upon receiving a notice from such an attorney that he or she has been convicted of such a crime, the Standing Committee may summarily issue an order suspending the attorney's privilege to practice before this Court pending the determination of appropriate discipline.

2. If an attorney fails to comply with Rule 6.6's requirement that the attorney send a copy of a show cause order to any litigant for whom he or she has entered an appearance or the Standing Committee determines that an attorney's conduct is so egregious that the attorney's client's interest, the interests of the public, or the Court may be harmed, the Standing Committee, after notice and an opportunity to be heard in writing, may suspend an attorney's privilege to practice before this Court during the course of any disciplinary investigation and proceeding. Ordinarily, no oral argument is held on suspension pending disciplinary proceedings. An attorney may request rein-

statement pending decision in any response filed under Rule 8 or at any hearing held under Rule 10.

[Effective July 1, 2015.]

RULE 8. RESPONSE TO AN ORDER TO SHOW CAUSE

1. Any response to an order to show cause issued under Rule 6 must be filed within 30 days of the date of the order. The response may:

(a) object to the entry of an order in this Court imposing the same discipline as imposed in the other court on the grounds that the attorney has been misidentified;

(b) object to the entry of an order in this Court imposing the same discipline as imposed in the other court on the grounds that the discipline imposed by the other court is administrative in nature;

(c) contest the imposition of the same discipline as imposed in the other court on the grounds:

(1) that the procedure was so lacking in notice or opportunity to be heard as to constitute a deprivation of due process;

(2) that there was such an infirmity of proof establishing the misconduct as to give rise to the clear conviction that this Court could not, consistent with its duty, accept as final the conclusion on that subject; or

(3) that the imposition of the same discipline by this Court would result in grave injustice;

(d) present evidence in mitigation with respect to the discipline imposed by the other court; or

(e) contest the imposition of original discipline by this Court.

2. An attorney responding to an order to show cause must include a certification that the attorney has complied with the requirement in Rule 6.6 that he or she serve a copy of the order to show cause and a copy of the order of the other court on which it is based to any litigant for whom the attorney has entered an appearance in any matter pending in this Court. This certification must include a list of all the litigants so notified and their addresses. An attorney must file an amended list if he or she enters an appearance during the pendency of a disciplinary action.

[Effective July 1, 2015.]

RULE 9. UNCONTESTED PROCEEDINGS

1. If the attorney fails to timely respond to the order to show cause in a case in which a presumptive discipline is specified in Rule 3 or if an attorney consents to imposition of the presumptive discipline, the matter will be deemed uncontested and the Clerk

will notify the Chair of the Standing Committee, who will enter an order imposing the presumptive discipline.

2. If the attorney fails to timely respond to an order to show cause issued pursuant to Rule 6.2 (original discipline), the matter will be deemed uncontested and the Chair of the Standing Committee will enter an order imposing appropriate discipline.

3. Any member of the bar of this Court who is the subject of an investigation by this Court into allegations of misconduct may consent to disbarment by filing with the Clerk an affidavit stating that the attorney desires to consent to disbarment and that:

(a) the attorney's consent is freely and voluntarily rendered; the attorney is not being subjected to coercion or duress; the attorney is fully aware of the implications of so consenting;

(b) the attorney is aware that there is a presently pending proceeding involving allegations that there exist grounds for the attorney's discipline the nature of which the attorney must specifically set forth; and

(c) the attorney acknowledges that he or she cannot successfully defend in the pending proceeding.

[Effective July 1, 2015.]

RULE 10.   CONTESTED PROCEEDINGS

1. If the response to an order to show cause contests the imposition of discipline in this Court, the matter will be treated as a contested proceeding unless the response does not contest the entry of an order in this Court imposing the same discipline as imposed in the other court, in which event the matter is treated as an uncontested proceeding under Rule 9.

2. In a proceeding under Rule 6.1 (reciprocal discipline) the Standing Committee may grant an attorney's timely request to be heard in person in defense or in mitigation. To be timely, a request for a hearing must be made in a timely filed response to an order to show cause. Generally, a hearing is not necessary if the ground for objection is misidentification or if the discipline imposed by the other court is administrative in nature.

3. Except for discipline imposed because of a criminal conviction, a hearing will be held in proceedings under Rule 6.2 (original discipline) if requested in the answer to the order to show cause.

4. The attorney will be given at least 30 days notice of the time, date, and place of the hearing. Prior to the hearing, the attorney will be afforded the opportunity to inspect any documents which the Standing Committee has obtained in its investigation that are relevant to the imposition of the proposed discipline. A member of the bar of this Court to whom an order to show cause is issued pursuant to

Rule 6 has the right to have counsel at all stages of the proceeding.

5. The Standing Committee may compel by subpoena the attendance of witnesses, including the attorney whose conduct is the subject of the proceeding, and the production of pertinent documents. If a hearing is held, the Standing Committee will compel by subpoena the attendance of any witness and the production of any document reasonably designated by the attorney as relevant to his or her defense.

6. At the hearing, the Standing Committee will enter upon the record the order to show cause, the response, and such evidence as it considers relevant to the issues posed for resolution. The attorney will be afforded the opportunity to cross-examine any witnesses called by the Standing Committee and to introduce evidence in defense or mitigation. The hearing will be transcribed.

7. The Standing Committee may take judicial notice of the record developed in disciplinary or criminal proceedings held by another court on a similar matter.

8. A certified copy of a judgment of conviction of any crime is conclusive evidence of the commission of that crime in any disciplinary proceeding instituted against an attorney based upon the conviction. If the conviction is subsequently reversed or vacated, any discipline imposed on the basis thereof will be promptly reviewed by the Standing Committee and the Court upon submission of a certified copy of the relevant mandate.

9. A certified copy of a judgment or order demonstrating that a member of the bar of this Court has been disbarred or suspended by another court is accepted as establishing that the conduct for which the discipline was imposed in fact occurred and that the discipline imposed was appropriate, unless it appears:[1]

(a) that the procedure was so lacking in notice or opportunity to be heard as to constitute a deprivation of due process;

(b) that there was such an infirmity of proof establishing the misconduct as to give rise to the clear conviction that this Court could not, consistent with its duty, accept as final the conclusion on that subject;

(c) that the imposition of the same discipline by this Court would result in grave injustice; or

(d) that the misconduct established is deemed by this Court to warrant substantially different discipline.

[Effective July 1, 2015.]

[1]Standards set forth in *Selling v. Radford*, 243 U.S. 46, 51 (1917).

RULE 11.   DISPOSITION

1. If an attorney's response to an order to show cause does not specifically request to be heard in person, the Standing Committee will prepare a record

consisting of the order to show cause, the response, the relevant documents, and a summary of the other relevant information obtained by the Standing Committee in its investigation. If the record so prepared contains any information not reflected in the order to show cause and the response, the attorney will be afforded the opportunity to inspect the record and to file an additional response within 10 days of the date of the notice of his or her opportunity to inspect.

2. If the Chair or the Clerk determines that the attorney has been misidentified, the case will be closed. If the Standing Committee determines that the discipline imposed by the other court is the equivalent of an administrative action such that no reciprocal discipline should be imposed or that reciprocal discipline is not appropriate, the Committee may in its discretion proceed as in part 3 of this Rule or direct the Clerk to close the case.

3. Based on the record created pursuant to Rule 10.6 or Rule 11.1, the Standing Committee will prepare a Report and Recommendation setting forth its findings of fact and recommending whether, and if so what, discipline should be imposed. A copy of the Report and Recommendation will be promptly sent to the attorney who will be afforded the opportunity to file exceptions within 21 days. The Report and Recommendation, any exceptions thereto, and the record will be submitted to the active members of the Court who will make a final decision by a majority vote based solely on those documents.

[Effective July 1, 2015.]

RULE 12.   NOTIFICATION OF DISCIPLINE IMPOSED

Unless directed otherwise, within 10 days of the imposition of discipline by this Court or a panel thereof upon a member of its bar, the Clerk will notify the attorney and all other courts before whom the attorney is admitted to practice and the National Disciplinary Data Bank, enclosing a certified copy of the order imposing discipline.

[Effective July 1, 2015.]

RULE 13.   REINSTATEMENT AFTER DISCIPLINARY ACTION

1. An attorney suspended for six (6) months or less is automatically reinstated at the end of the period of suspension upon the filing of an affidavit of compliance with the provisions of the order. An attorney suspended for more than six (6) months or disbarred may not resume practice until reinstated by order of the Court.

2. An attorney who has been disbarred may not apply for reinstatement until the expiration of 5 years from the effective date of the disbarment.

3. No petition for reinstatement may be filed within 1 year following an adverse determination on the attorney's petition for reinstatement.

4. The Clerk will refer petitions for reinstatement to the Standing Committee. If the Standing Committee is satisfied that reinstatement is appropriate based upon the findings of another court or otherwise, it may recommend to the Court that the petition be granted. If the Standing Committee is not so satisfied or if the matter is returned to it by the Court, the Standing Committee will schedule a prompt hearing on the petition. At the hearing, the petitioner has the burden of demonstrating by clear and convincing evidence that he or she has the moral qualifications, competency, and learning in the law required for admission to practice before this Court and that his or her resumption of the practice of law will not be detrimental to the integrity and standing of the bar or to the administration of justice, or subversive of the public interest. The Standing Committee will submit its Report and Recommendation, together with any exception thereto filed within 21 days of the issuance thereof, to all active members of the Court who act upon the petition by a majority vote.

5. A reinstatement may be on such terms and conditions as the Court directs. If the attorney has been disbarred or suspended for 5 years or more, this may include certification by the bar examiners of a state or other jurisdiction of the attorney's successful completion of an examination for admission to practice.

[Effective July 1, 2015.]

RULE 14.   APPOINTMENT OF COUNSEL

The Standing Committee may at any time appoint counsel to investigate or prosecute a disciplinary matter or to represent an indigent attorney ordered to show cause. The Court prefers to appoint as prosecuting counsel the disciplinary agency of the highest court of the state in which the attorney maintains his or her principal office. However, if the state disciplinary agency declines appointment, or the Court deems other counsel appropriate, it may appoint any other member of the bar as prosecuting counsel. Counsel appointed either for prosecution or defense will be compensated for his or her services as the Standing Committee directs.

[Effective July 1, 2015.]

RULE 15.   ACCESS TO DISCIPLINARY INFORMATION

1. A disciplinary proceeding before a panel conducted pursuant to Rule 4.1 is public except:

(a) for deliberations of the panel; and

(b) to the extent otherwise ordered by the panel.

2. Prior to the imposition of a suspension or disbarment or the decision by the Court on a Report and Recommendation of the Standing Committee, the proceeding is confidential, except that the pendency, subject matter, and status of an investigation may be disclosed by the Court or the Standing Committee if:

(a) the respondent has waived confidentiality;

(b) the proceeding is based upon allegations which include the conviction of a serious crime;

(c) the proceeding is based upon allegations that have become generally known to the public; or

(d) there is a need to notify another person or organization in order to protect the public, the administration of justice, or the legal profession.

3. Upon the imposition of a suspension or disbarment, the decision by the Court on a Report and Recommendation of the Standing Committee recommending a sanction other than a private reprimand, or the filing of a petition for reinstatement, the proceeding is public, except for:

(a) deliberations of the Standing Committee or the Court; and

(b) information with respect to which a protective order has been entered under paragraph (5) of this Rule.

4. When a proceeding becomes public under this Rule, any order to show cause why discipline should not be imposed, any record created by the Standing Committee pursuant to Rule 10.6 or Rule 11.1, and any Report and Recommendation of the Standing Committee will be docketed in the Clerk's Office and will be accessible to the public in the same manner as other records of the Court. Other documents previously created by or in the possession of the Standing Committee or prosecuting counsel do not become public records and are not accessible to the public.

5. In order to protect the interests of a complainant, witness, third party, or the attorney, a panel or the Standing Committee may, upon application and for good cause shown, issue a protective order prohibiting the disclosure of specific information and direct that the proceedings be conducted so as to implement the order.

6. A request for nonpublic information other than that authorized for disclosure under paragraph (2) of this Rule will be denied unless the request is from one of the following agencies:

(a) an agency authorized to investigate qualifications for admission to practice;

(b) an agency authorized to investigate qualifications for government employment, including a committee or similar group authorized to investigate qualifications for judicial position;

(c) a lawyer disciplinary enforcement agency; or

(d) a law enforcement agency.

7. If a panel or the Standing Committee decides to provide the nonpublic information requested, and if the attorney has not signed a waiver permitting the requesting agency to obtain nonpublic information, the attorney will be notified in writing at his or her address on file with the Clerk's Office that the information has been requested and by whom, together with a copy of the information proposed to be released to the requesting agency. The panel or the Standing Committee will release the information to the requesting agency 7 days after the mailing of the notice unless the attorney has satisfied the panel or the Standing Committee that there is good cause to withhold the requested information.

8. If an otherwise authorized requesting agency has not obtained a waiver from the attorney to obtain nonpublic information, and requests that the information be released without giving notice to the attorney, the requesting agency must certify that:

(a) the request is made in furtherance of an ongoing investigation;

(b) the information is essential to that investigation; and

(c) disclosure of the existence of the investigation to the lawyer would seriously prejudice that investigation.

9. Except with respect to the content of his or her own testimony, each participant in a proceeding under these Rules must maintain the confidentiality mandated by this Rule.

[Effective July 1, 2015.]

RULE 16. DISABILITY INACTIVE STATUS

1. There is hereby created a disability inactive status for an attorney whose mental or physical condition prevents the attorney from competently representing the interest of the attorney's clients.

2. An attorney is immediately and automatically transferred to disability inactive status upon proof being received by the Court that:

(a) the attorney has been declared incompetent in a judicial proceeding;

(b) the attorney has been involuntarily committed because of incapacity or disability;

(c) during a disciplinary or criminal proceeding the attorney alleges an incapability to assist in the defense due to mental or physical incapability; or

(d) the attorney has been placed on a disability inactive or equivalent status by another court.

3. If an attorney is immediately and automatically transferred to disability inactive status but desires to

contest the transfer, the attorney may institute rein- statement proceedings which are conducted as though instituted under Rule 13 by an attorney suspended for more than six (6) months. By bringing such a pro- ceeding, the attorney waives the doctor-patient privi- lege (and other similar privileges) regarding the dis- ability.

4. If the Standing Committee determines that cause may exist to place an attorney on disability inactive status and the attorney is not immediately and automatically transferred to such status under paragraph (2) of this Rule, the Standing Committee will institute proceedings which will be conducted as though instituted under Rule 6. In these proceedings Rule 15 will apply.

5. An attorney on disability inactive status may file a petition for reinstatement on the basis that the disability has been removed and the attorney is fit to resume the practice of law. The filing of a petition for reinstatement waives the doctor-patient privilege (and other similar privileges) regarding the disability. The attorney must provide in the petition the name and address of each physician, psychologist, and/or psychi- atrist who has examined or treated the attorney and any hospital or other institution in which the attorney has been examined or treated since the attorney's transfer to disability inactive status, as well as the attorney's current status in all bars to which the attorney was or is admitted. A petition for reinstate- ment is treated in the same manner as a petition for reinstatement filed under Rule 13 by an attorney suspended for more than six (6) months.

6. An attorney raising the defense of current men- tal or physical disability in a disciplinary proceeding waives the doctor-patient privilege (and other similar privileges) regarding the disability. Furthermore, if the defense of current mental or physical disability is raised, the court may order an examination of the attorney by a court-appointed physician.

[Effective July 1, 2015.]

RULE 17.   INACTIVE STATUS

1. Attorneys must advise the Clerk when their contact information changes. In order to assure that information in the Court of Appeals' attorney rolls is current, the Court establishes a renewal process and an inactive status. An attorney is marked inactive if the attorney:

(a) has not entered an appearance in a case in this Court for 5 years or has not filed the form required by part 2 of this rule updating contact information;

(b) has requested the Clerk mark him or her inac- tive except as provided in Rule 6.7;

(c) has notified the Clerk that he or she wishes to retire from the bar of this Court; or

(d) can not be contacted at the phone number on file and mail or email is returned as undeliverable.

2. On or before January 15, 2016, the Clerk will send a notice to the email address on file with the Clerk's Office to attorneys who have not entered an appearance in the last 5 years requiring them to file a form available on the Court's website updating their contact information. Every year thereafter, the Clerk will send a notice to the email address on file with the Clerk's Office to attorneys who have not entered an appearance or filed the update form in the last five years requiring them to file the form updating their contact information. No fee will be imposed. Thirty days after the notice to file the form updating contact information, attorneys who have not entered an ap- pearance within 5 years or who have not filed the form updating their contact information will be marked inactive without further notice. For ease of adminis- tration, the 5 year period runs from the last date of an entry of appearance, not from the date a case was closed. At any time, the Clerk may mark an attorney inactive if mail or email is returned as undeliverable and the attorney can not be contacted at the phone number on file.

3. Attorneys who have been marked inactive on the attorney rolls of this Court must file the return to active service form required under part 6 of this Rule and pay the applicable fee before filing an entry of appearance or any documents in this Court. If an attorney who has been marked inactive on the attor- ney rolls of this Court files an entry of appearance before filing the return to active service form, the Clerk will notify the attorney and give him or her 14 days to file the form and pay any applicable fees. In an emergency situation, the Clerk may waive or post- pone the filing of the return to active service form. Counsel are reminded that L.A.R. 27.7 provides, "To the fullest extent possible, the clerk must be given advance notice by telephone that a motion requiring expedited or urgent consideration may be filed." If an attorney fails to comply with a direction to file a return to active service form and pay applicable fees, the case will be dismissed pursuant to L.A.R. Misc. 107, or, in the case of co-counsel or appellee's counsel, the attorney's appearance will be struck and the attor- ney will not be entitled to receive notices or service of documents under L.A.R. 46.2.

4. Placement on inactive status in this Court is considered an administrative action, not a disciplinary action.

5. Law clerks and attorneys employed by the court of appeals remain in active status during their employment and for 5 years thereafter.

6. **Returning to Active Status.** An attorney may return to active status by filing the form provided by the Clerk, which contains a statement under penalty of perjury that to the best of his or her knowledge the

attorney is not currently subject to any criminal conviction or disciplinary sanction by any state or federal bar of which the attorney is a member. Counsel will be required to pay any applicable fee. An attorney will be returned to active status unless the Clerk determines that the attorney has been convicted of a crime or is under an order of disciplinary suspension or disbarment by another court. If the Clerk finds that the attorney has been convicted of a crime or is under an order of disciplinary suspension or disbarment by another court, the Clerk will refer the matter to the Standing Committee under Rule 6.

7. An attorney who has retired from the bar of this Court may be returned to active status in the same manner as prescribed in part 6 of this Rule.

8. Attorneys must inform the Clerk if they retire from a state or federal bar of which they are a member. Retirement from a state or federal bar will not result in the attorney being marked inactive in this Court.

9. Attorneys are responsible for monitoring their status as "active" or "inactive" on the rolls of the Court. Attorneys must assure themselves that they are in active status and in good standing before appearing in any matter before this Court.
[Effective July 1, 2015.]

RULE 18. MISCELLANEOUS

1. Attorneys must file all responses and documents in disciplinary proceedings using the Court's electronic docketing system unless the Clerk grants an exemption for good cause shown.

2. The formatting and page limit requirements of Rule 27, Fed. R. App. P. apply to documents filed under these Rules.

3. Computation of time under these Rules is governed by Rule 26, Fed. R. App. P.

4. The Clerk may close a disciplinary case or proceeding that is opened in error.
[Effective July 1, 2015.]

APPENDIX III. RULES FOR JUDICIAL–CONDUCT AND JUDICIAL–DISABILITY PROCEEDINGS

PREFACE

These Rules were promulgated by the Judicial Conference of the United States, after public comment, pursuant to 28 U.S.C. §§ 331 and 358, to establish standards and procedures for addressing complaints filed by complainants or identified by chief judges under the Judicial Conduct and Disability Act, 28 U.S.C. §§ 351–364.

ARTICLE I. GENERAL PROVISIONS

RULE 1. SCOPE

These Rules govern proceedings under the Judicial Conduct and Disability Act (the Act), 28 U.S.C. §§ 351–364, to determine whether a covered judge has engaged in conduct prejudicial to the effective and expeditious administration of the business of the courts or is unable to discharge the duties of office because of mental or physical disability.

[Adopted March 11, 2008, effective April 10, 2008. Amended effective September 17, 2015.]

Commentary on Rule 1

In September 2006, the Judicial Conduct and Disability Act Study Committee ("Breyer Committee"), appointed in 2004 by Chief Justice Rehnquist, presented a report ("Breyer Committee Report"), 239 F.R.D. 116 (Sept. 2006), to Chief Justice Roberts that evaluated implementation of the Judicial Conduct and Disability Act of 1980, 28 U.S.C. §§ 351–364. The Breyer Committee had been formed in response to criticism from the public and Congress regarding the effectiveness of the Act's implementation. The Executive Committee of the Judicial Conference directed its Committee on Judicial Conduct and Disability to consider the Breyer Committee's recommendations and to report on their implementation to the Conference.

The Breyer Committee found that it could not evaluate implementation of the Act without establishing interpretive standards, Breyer Committee Report, 239 F.R.D. at 132, and that a major problem faced by chief judges in implementing the Act was the lack of authoritative interpretive standards. Id. at 212–15. The Breyer Committee then established standards to guide its evaluation, some of which were new formulations and some of which were taken from the "Illustrative Rules Governing Complaints of Judicial Misconduct and Disability," discussed below. The principal standards used by the Breyer Committee are in Appendix E of its Report. Id. at 238.

Based on the Breyer Committee's findings, the Committee on Judicial Conduct and Disability concluded that there was a need for the Judicial Conference to exercise its power under Section 358 of the Act to fashion standards guiding the various officers and bodies that must exercise responsibility under the Act. To that end, the Committee on Judicial Conduct and Disability proposed rules that were based largely on Appendix E of the Breyer Committee Report and the Illustrative Rules.

The Illustrative Rules were originally prepared in 1986 by the Special Committee of the Conference of Chief Judges of the United States Courts of Appeals, and were subsequently revised and amended, most recently in 2000, by the predecessor to the Committee on Judicial Conduct and Disability. The Illustrative Rules were adopted, with minor variations, by circuit judicial councils, to govern complaints under the Judicial Conduct and Disability Act.

After being submitted for public comment pursuant to 28 U.S.C. § 358(c), the Judicial Conference promulgated the present Rules on March 11, 2008. They were amended on September 17, 2015.

RULE 2.   EFFECT AND CONSTRUCTION

(a) **Generally.** These Rules are mandatory; they supersede any conflicting judicial-council rules. Judicial councils may promulgate additional rules to implement the Act as long as those rules do not conflict with these Rules.

(b) **Exception.** A Rule will not apply if, when performing duties authorized by the Act, a chief judge, a special committee, a judicial council, the Committee on Judicial Conduct and Disability, or the Judicial Conference expressly finds that exceptional circumstances render application of that Rule in a particular proceeding manifestly unjust or contrary to the purposes of the Act or these Rules.

[Adopted March 11, 2008, effective April 10, 2008. Amended effective September 17, 2015.]

Commentary on Rule 2

Unlike the Illustrative Rules, these Rules provide mandatory and nationally uniform provisions governing the substantive and procedural aspects of misconduct and disability proceedings under the Act. The mandatory nature of these Rules is authorized by 28 U.S.C. §§ 358(a) and (c). Judicial councils retain the power to promulgate rules consistent with these Rules. For example, a local rule may authorize the electronic distribution of materials pursuant to Rule 8(b).

Rule 2(b) recognizes that unforeseen and exceptional circumstances may call for a different approach in particular cases.

RULE 3.   DEFINITIONS

(a) **Chief Judge.** "Chief judge" means the chief judge of a United States court of appeals, of the United States Court of International Trade, or of the United States Court of Federal Claims.

(b) **Circuit Clerk.** "Circuit clerk" means a clerk of a United States court of appeals, the clerk of the United States Court of International Trade, the clerk of the United States Court of Federal Claims, or the circuit executive of the United States Court of Appeals for the Federal Circuit.

(c) **Complaint.** A complaint is:

(1) a document that, in accordance with Rule 6, is filed by any person in his or her individual capacity or on behalf of a professional organization; or

(2) information from any source, other than a document described in (c)(1), that gives a chief judge probable cause to believe that a covered judge, as defined in Rule 4, has engaged in misconduct or may have a disability, whether or not the information is framed as or is intended to be an allegation of misconduct or disability.

(d) **Court of Appeals, District Court, and District Judge.** "Court of appeals," "district court," and "district judge," where appropriate, include the United States Court of Federal Claims, the United States Court of International Trade, and the judges thereof.

(e) **Disability.** "Disability" is a temporary or permanent impairment, physical or mental, rendering a judge unable to discharge the duties of the particular judicial office. Examples of disability include substance abuse, the inability to stay awake during court proceedings, or impairment of cognitive abilities that renders the judge unable to function effectively.

(f) **Judicial Council and Circuit.** "Judicial council" and "circuit," where appropriate, include any courts designated in 28 U.S.C. § 363.

(g) **Magistrate Judge.** "Magistrate judge," where appropriate, includes a special master appointed by the Court of Federal Claims under 42 U.S.C. § 300aa–12(c).

(h) **Misconduct.** Cognizable misconduct:

(1) is conduct prejudicial to the effective and expeditious administration of the business of the courts. Misconduct includes, but is not limited to:

(A) using the judge's office to obtain special treatment for friends or relatives;

(B) accepting bribes, gifts, or other personal favors related to the judicial office;

(C) having improper discussions with parties or counsel for one side in a case;

(D) treating litigants, attorneys, or others in a demonstrably egregious and hostile manner;

(E) engaging in partisan political activity or making inappropriately partisan statements;

(F) soliciting funds for organizations;

(G) retaliating against complainants, witnesses, or others for their participation in this complaint process;

(H) refusing, without good cause shown, to cooperate in the investigation of a complaint under these Rules; or

(I) violating other specific, mandatory standards of judicial conduct, such as those pertaining to restrictions on outside income and requirements for financial disclosure.

(2) is conduct occurring outside the performance of official duties if the conduct might have a prejudicial

effect on the administration of the business of the courts, including a substantial and widespread lowering of public confidence in the courts among reasonable people.

(3) does not include:

(A) an allegation that is directly related to the merits of a decision or procedural ruling. An allegation that calls into question the correctness of a judge's ruling, including a failure to recuse, without more, is merits-related. If the decision or ruling is alleged to be the result of an improper motive, *e.g.*, a bribe, ex parte contact, racial or ethnic bias, or improper conduct in rendering a decision or ruling, such as personally derogatory remarks irrelevant to the issues, the complaint is not cognizable to the extent that it attacks the merits.

(B) an allegation about delay in rendering a decision or ruling, unless the allegation concerns an improper motive in delaying a particular decision or habitual delay in a significant number of unrelated cases.

(i) Subject Judge. "Subject judge" means any judge described in Rule 4 who is the subject of a complaint.

[Adopted March 11, 2008, effective April 10, 2008. Amended effective September 17, 2015.]

Commentary on Rule 3

Rule 3 is derived and adapted from the Breyer Committee Report and the Illustrative Rules.

Unless otherwise specified or the context otherwise indicates, the term "complaint" is used in these Rules to refer both to complaints identified by a chief judge under Rule 5 and to complaints filed by a complainant under Rule 6.

Under the Act, a "complaint" may be filed by "any person" or "identified" by a chief judge. *See* 28 U.S.C. §§ 351(a), (b). Under Rule 3(c)(1), complaints may be submitted by a person, in his or her individual capacity, or by a professional organization. Generally, the word "complaint" brings to mind the commencement of an adversary proceeding in which the contending parties are left to present the evidence and legal arguments, and judges play the role of an essentially passive arbiter. The Act, however, establishes an administrative, inquisitorial process. For example, even absent a complaint under Rule 6, chief judges are expected in some circumstances to trigger the process—"identify a complaint," *see* 28 U.S.C. § 351(b) and Rule 5—and conduct an investigation without becoming a party. *See* 28 U.S.C. § 352(a); Breyer Committee Report, 239 F.R.D. at 214; Illustrative Rule 2(j). Even when a complaint is filed by someone other than the chief judge, the complainant lacks many rights that a litigant would have, and the chief judge, instead of being limited to the "four corners of the complaint," must, under Rule 11, proceed as though misconduct or disability has been alleged where the complainant reveals information of misconduct or disability but does not claim it as such. *See* Breyer Committee Report, 239 F.R.D. at 183–84.

An allegation of misconduct or disability filed under Rule 6 is a "complaint," and the Rule so provides in subsection (c)(1). However, both the nature of the process and the use of the term "identify" suggest that the word "complaint" covers more than a document formally triggering the process. The process relies on chief judges considering known information and triggering the process when appropriate. "Identifying" a "complaint," therefore, is best understood as the chief judge's concluding that information known to the judge constitutes probable cause to believe that misconduct occurred or a disability exists, whether or not the information is framed as, or intended to be, an accusation. This definition is codified in subsection (c)(2).

Rule 3(e) relates to disability and provides only the most general definition, recognizing that a fact-specific approach is the only one available. A mental disability could involve cognitive impairment or any psychiatric or psychological condition that renders the judge unable to discharge the duties of office. Such duties may include those that are administrative. If, for example, the judge is a chief judge, the judicial council, fulfilling its obligation under 28 U.S.C. § 332(d)(1) to make "necessary and appropriate orders for the effective and expeditious administration of justice," may find, under 28 U.S.C. § 45(d) or § 136(e), that the judge is "temporarily unable to perform" his or her chief-judge duties. In that event, an appropriate remedy could involve, under Rule 20(b)(1)(D)(vii), temporary reassignment of chief-judge duties to the next judge statutorily eligible to perform them.

The phrase "prejudicial to the effective and expeditious administration of the business of the courts" is not subject to precise definition, and subsection (h)(1) therefore provides some specific examples. Although the Code of Conduct for United States Judges may be informative, its main precepts are highly general; the Code is in many potential applications aspirational rather than a set of disciplinary rules. Ultimately, the responsibility for determining what constitutes misconduct under the statute is the province of the judicial council of the circuit, subject to such review and limitations as are ordained by the statute and by these Rules.

Even where specific, mandatory rules exist—for example, governing the receipt of gifts by judges, outside earned income, and financial disclosure obligations—the distinction between the misconduct statute and these specific, mandatory rules must be borne in mind. For example, an inadvertent, minor violation of any one of these rules, promptly remedied when called to the attention of the judge, might still be a violation but might not rise to the level of misconduct under the statute. By contrast, a pattern of such violations of the Code might well rise to the level of misconduct.

Under Rule 3(h)(1)(G), a judge's efforts to retaliate against any person for his or her involvement in the complaint process may constitute cognizable misconduct. The Rule makes this explicit in the interest of public confidence in the complaint process.

Rule 3(h)(1)(H) provides that a judge's refusal, without good cause shown, to cooperate in the investigation of a complaint under these Rules may constitute cognizable misconduct. While the exercise of rights under the Fifth Amendment to the Constitution would constitute good cause under Rule 3(h)(1)(H), given the fact-specific nature of the inquiry, it is not possible to otherwise anticipate all circumstances that might also constitute good cause. The Commentary on Rule 13 provides additional discussion regarding Rule 3(h)(1)(H). The Rules contemplate that judicial councils will not consider commencing proceedings under Rule

3(h)(1)(H) except as necessary after other means to acquire the information have been tried or have proven futile.

Rule 3(h)(2) reflects that an allegation can meet the statutory standard even though the judge's alleged conduct did not occur in the course of the performance of official duties. And some conduct in the categories listed under subsection (h)(1), or in categories not listed, might, depending on the circumstances, amount to "misconduct" under subsection (h)(2), or under both subsection (h)(1) and subsection (h)(2). Also, the Code of Conduct for United States Judges expressly covers a wide range of extra-official activities, and some of these activities may constitute misconduct. For example, allegations that a judge solicited funds for a charity or participated in a partisan political event are cognizable under the Act.

On the other hand, judges are entitled to some leeway in extra-official activities. For example, misconduct may not include a judge being repeatedly and publicly discourteous to a spouse (not including physical abuse) even though this might cause some reasonable people to have diminished confidence in the courts. Rule 3(h)(2) states that conduct of this sort is covered, for example, when it might lead to a "substantial and widespread" lowering of such confidence.

Rule 3(h)(3)(A) tracks the Act, 28 U.S.C. § 352(b)(1)(A)(ii), in excluding from the definition of misconduct allegations "[d]irectly related to the merits of a decision or procedural ruling." This exclusion preserves the independence of judges in the exercise of judicial power by ensuring that the complaint procedure is not used to collaterally attack the substance of a judge's ruling. Any allegation that calls into question the correctness of an official action of a judge—without more—is merits-related. The phrase "decision or procedural ruling" is not limited to rulings issued in deciding Article III cases or controversies. Thus, a complaint challenging the correctness of a chief judge's determination to dismiss a prior misconduct complaint would be properly dismissed as merits-related—in other words, as challenging the substance of the judge's administrative determination to dismiss the complaint—even though it does not concern the judge's rulings in Article III litigation. Similarly, an allegation that a judge had incorrectly declined to approve a Criminal Justice Act voucher is merits-related under this standard.

Conversely, an allegation—however unsupported—that a judge conspired with a prosecutor to make a particular ruling is not merits-related, even though it "relates" to a ruling in a colloquial sense. Such an allegation attacks the propriety of conspiring with the prosecutor and goes beyond a challenge to the correctness—"the merits"—of the ruling itself. An allegation that a judge ruled against the complainant because the complainant is a member of a particular racial or ethnic group, or because the judge dislikes the complainant personally, is also not merits-related. Such an allegation attacks the propriety of arriving at rulings with an illicit or improper motive. Similarly, an allegation that a judge used an inappropriate term to refer to a class of people is not merits-related even if the judge used it on the bench or in an opinion; the correctness of the judge's rulings is not at stake. An allegation that a judge treated litigants, attorneys, or others in a demonstrably egregious and hostile manner while on the bench is also not merits-related.

The existence of an appellate remedy is usually irrelevant to whether an allegation is merits-related. The merits-related ground for dismissal exists to protect judges' independence in making rulings, not to protect or promote the appellate process. A complaint alleging an incorrect ruling is merits-related even though the complainant has no recourse from that ruling. By the same token, an allegation that is otherwise cognizable under the Act should not be dismissed merely because an appellate remedy appears to exist (for example, vacating a ruling that resulted from an improper *ex parte* communication). However, there may be occasions when appellate and misconduct proceedings overlap, and consideration and disposition of a complaint under these Rules may be properly deferred by the chief judge until the appellate proceedings are concluded in order to avoid inconsistent decisions, among other things.

Because of the special need to protect judges' independence in deciding what to say in an opinion or ruling, a somewhat different standard applies to determine the merits-relatedness of a non-frivolous allegation that a judge's language in a ruling reflected an improper motive. If the judge's language was relevant to the case at hand—for example, a statement that a claim is legally or factually "frivolous"—then the judge's choice of language is presumptively merits-related and excluded, absent evidence apart from the ruling itself suggesting an improper motive. If, on the other hand, the challenged language does not seem relevant on its face, then an additional inquiry under Rule 11 is necessary.

With regard to Rule 3(h)(3)(B), a complaint of delay in a single case is excluded as merits-related. Such an allegation may be said to challenge the correctness of an official action of the judge—in other words, assigning a low priority to deciding the particular case. But, by the same token, an allegation of a habitual pattern of delay in a significant number of unrelated cases, or an allegation of deliberate delay in a single case arising out of an illicit motive, is not merits-related.

The remaining subsections of Rule 3 provide technical definitions clarifying the application of the Rules to the various kinds of courts covered.

RULE 4. COVERED JUDGES

A complaint under these Rules may concern the actions or capacity only of judges of United States courts of appeals, judges of United States district courts, judges of United States bankruptcy courts, United States magistrate judges, and judges of the courts specified in 28 U.S.C. § 363.

[Adopted March 11, 2008, effective April 10, 2008.]

Commentary on Rule 4

This Rule tracks the Act. Rule 8(c) and (d) contain provisions as to the handling of complaints against persons not covered by the Act, such as other court personnel, or against both covered judges and noncovered persons.

ARTICLE II.   INITIATION OF COMPLAINT

RULE 5.   IDENTIFICATION OF COMPLAINT

(a) Identification. When a chief judge has information constituting reasonable grounds for inquiry into whether a covered judge has engaged in misconduct or has a disability, the chief judge may conduct an inquiry, as he or she deems appropriate, into the accuracy of the information even if no related complaint has been filed. A chief judge who finds probable cause to believe that misconduct has occurred or that a disability exists may seek an informal resolution that he or she finds satisfactory. If no informal resolution is achieved or is feasible, the chief judge may identify a complaint and, by written order stating the reasons, begin the review provided in Rule 11. If the evidence of misconduct is clear and convincing and no informal resolution is achieved or is feasible, the chief judge must identify a complaint. A chief judge must not decline to identify a complaint merely because the person making the allegation has not filed a complaint under Rule 6. This Rule is subject to Rule 7.

(b) Submission Not Fully Complying with Rule 6. A legible submission in substantial but not full compliance with Rule 6 must be considered as possible grounds for the identification of a complaint under Rule 5(a).

[Adopted March 11, 2008, effective April 10, 2008. Amended effective September 17, 2015.]

Commentary on Rule 5

This Rule is adapted from the Breyer Committee Report, 239 F.R.D. at 245–46.

The Act authorizes a chief judge, by written order stating reasons, to identify a complaint and thereby dispense with the filing of a written complaint. *See* 28 U.S.C. § 351(b). Under Rule 5, when a chief judge becomes aware of information constituting reasonable grounds to inquire into possible misconduct or disability on the part of a covered judge, and no formal complaint has been filed, the chief judge has the power in his or her discretion to begin an appropriate inquiry. A chief judge's decision whether to informally seek a resolution and/or to identify a complaint is guided by the results of that inquiry. If the chief judge concludes that there is probable cause to believe that misconduct has occurred or a disability exists, the chief judge may seek an informal resolution, if feasible, and if failing in that, may identify a complaint. Discretion is accorded largely for the reasons police officers and prosecutors have discretion in making arrests or bringing charges. The matter may be trivial and isolated, based on marginal evidence, or otherwise highly unlikely to lead to a misconduct or disability finding. On the other hand, if the inquiry leads the chief judge to conclude that there is clear and convincing evidence of misconduct or a disability, and no satisfactory informal resolution has been achieved or is feasible, the chief judge is required to identify a complaint.

An informal resolution is one agreed to by the subject judge and found satisfactory by the chief judge. Because an informal resolution under Rule 5 reached before a complaint is filed under Rule 6 will generally cause a subsequent Rule 6 complaint alleging the identical matter to be concluded, *see* Rule 11(d), the chief judge must be sure that the resolution is fully appropriate before endorsing it. In doing so, the chief judge must balance the seriousness of the matter against the particular judge's alacrity in addressing the issue. The availability of this procedure should encourage attempts at swift remedial action before a formal complaint is filed.

When a chief judge identifies a complaint, a written order stating the reasons for the identification must be provided; this begins the process articulated in Rule 11. Rule 11 provides that once a chief judge has identified a complaint, the chief judge, subject to the disqualification provisions of Rule 25, will perform, with respect to that complaint, all functions assigned to the chief judge for the determination of complaints filed by a complainant.

In high-visibility situations, it may be desirable for a chief judge to identify a complaint without first seeking an informal resolution (and then, if the circumstances warrant, dismiss or conclude the identified complaint without appointment of a special committee) in order to assure the public that the allegations have not been ignored.

A chief judge's decision not to identify a complaint under Rule 5 is not appealable and is subject to Rule 3(h)(3)(A), which excludes merits-related complaints from the definition of misconduct.

A chief judge may not decline to identify a complaint solely on the basis that the unfiled allegations could be raised by one or more persons in a filed complaint, but none of these persons has opted to do so.

Subsection (a) concludes by stating that this Rule is "subject to Rule 7." This is intended to establish that only (i) the chief judge of the home circuit of a potential subject judge, or (ii) the chief judge of a circuit in which misconduct is alleged to have occurred in the course of official business while the potential subject judge was sitting by designation, shall have the power or a duty under this Rule to identify a complaint.

Subsection (b) provides that submissions that do not comply with the requirements of Rule 6(d) must be considered under Rule 5(a). For instance, if a complaint has been filed but the form submitted is unsigned, or the truth of the statements therein are not verified in writing under penalty of perjury, then a chief judge must nevertheless consider the allegations as known information and as a possible basis for the identification of a complaint under the process described in Rule 5(a).

RULE 6.   FILING OF COMPLAINT

(a) Form. A complainant may use the form reproduced in the appendix to these Rules or a form designated by the rules of the judicial council in the circuit in which the complaint is filed. A complaint form is also available on each court of appeals' website or may be obtained from the circuit clerk or any district court or bankruptcy court within the circuit.

A form is not necessary to file a complaint, but the complaint must be written and must include the information described in (b).

(b) Brief Statement of Facts. A complaint must contain a concise statement that details the specific facts on which the claim of misconduct or disability is based. The statement of facts should include a description of:

(1) what happened;

(2) when and where the relevant events happened;

(3) any information that would help an investigator check the facts; and

(4) for an allegation of disability, any additional facts that form the basis of that allegation.

(c) Legibility. A complaint should be typewritten if possible. If not typewritten, it must be legible. An illegible complaint will be returned to the complainant with a request to resubmit it in legible form. If a resubmitted complaint is still illegible, it will not be accepted for filing.

(d) Complainant's Address and Signature; Verification. The complainant must provide a contact address and sign the complaint. The truth of the statements made in the complaint must be verified in writing under penalty of perjury. If any of these requirements are not met, the submission will be accepted, but it will be reviewed under only Rule 5(b).

(e) Number of Copies; Envelope Marking. The complainant shall provide the number of copies of the complaint required by local rule. Each copy should be in an envelope marked "Complaint of Misconduct" or "Complaint of Disability." The envelope must not show the name of any subject judge.

[Adopted March 11, 2008, effective April 10, 2008. Amended effective September 17, 2015.]

Commentary on Rule 6

The Rule is adapted from the Illustrative Rules and is self-explanatory.

RULE 7.   WHERE TO INITIATE COMPLAINT

(a) Where to File. Except as provided in (b),

(1) a complaint against a judge of a United States court of appeals, a United States district court, a United States bankruptcy court, or a United States magistrate judge must be filed with the circuit clerk in the jurisdiction in which the subject judge holds office.

(2) a complaint against a judge of the United States Court of International Trade or the United States Court of Federal Claims must be filed with the respective clerk of that court.

(3) a complaint against a judge of the United States Court of Appeals for the Federal Circuit must be filed with the circuit executive of that court.

(b) Misconduct in Another Circuit; Transfer. If a complaint alleges misconduct in the course of official business while the subject judge was sitting on a court by designation under 28 U.S.C. §§ 291–293 and 294(d), the complaint may be filed or identified with the circuit clerk of that circuit or of the subject judge's home circuit. The proceeding will continue in the circuit of the first-filed or first-identified complaint. The judicial council of the circuit where the complaint was first filed or first identified may transfer the complaint to the subject judge's home circuit or to the circuit where the alleged misconduct occurred, as the case may be.

[Adopted March 11, 2008, effective April 10, 2008. Amended effective September 17, 2015.]

Commentary on Rule 7

Title 28 U.S.C. § 351 states that complaints are to be filed with "the clerk of the court of appeals for the circuit." However, in many circuits, this role is filled by circuit executives. Accordingly, the term "circuit clerk," as defined in Rule 3(b) and used throughout these Rules, applies to circuit executives.

Section 351 uses the term "the circuit" in a way that suggests that either the home circuit of the subject judge or the circuit in which misconduct is alleged to have occurred is the proper venue for complaints. With an exception for judges sitting by designation, the Rule requires the filing or identification of a misconduct or disability complaint in the circuit in which the judge holds office, largely based on the administrative perspective of the Act. Given the Act's emphasis on the future conduct of the business of the courts, the circuit in which the judge holds office is the appropriate forum because that circuit is likely best able to influence a judge's future behavior in constructive ways.

However, when judges sit by designation, the non-home circuit has a strong interest in redressing misconduct in the course of official business, and where allegations also involve a member of the bar—*ex parte* contact between an attorney and a judge, for example—it may often be desirable to have the judicial and bar misconduct proceedings take place in the same venue. Rule 7(b), therefore, allows transfer to, or filing or identification of a complaint in, the non-home circuit. The proceeding may be transferred by the judicial council of the filing or identified circuit to the other circuit.

RULE 8.   ACTION BY CIRCUIT CLERK

(a) Receipt of Complaint. Upon receiving a complaint against a judge filed under Rule 6 or identified under Rule 5, the circuit clerk must open a file, assign a docket number according to a uniform numbering scheme promulgated by the Committee on Judicial Conduct and Disability, and acknowledge the complaint's receipt.

(b) Distribution of Copies. The circuit clerk must promptly send copies of a complaint filed under Rule 6 to the chief judge or the judge authorized to act as chief judge under Rule 25(f), and copies of complaints filed under Rule 6 or identified under Rule 5 to each subject judge. The circuit clerk must retain the original complaint. Any further distribution should be as provided by local rule.

(c) Complaint Against Noncovered Person. If the circuit clerk receives a complaint about a person not holding an office described in Rule 4, the clerk must not accept the complaint under these Rules.

(d) Complaint Against Judge and Another Noncovered Person. If the circuit clerk receives a complaint about a judge described in Rule 4 and a person not holding an office described in Rule 4, the clerk must accept the complaint under these Rules only with regard to the judge and must so inform the complainant.

[Adopted March 11, 2008, effective April 10, 2008. Amended effective September 17, 2015.]

Commentary on Rule 8

This Rule is adapted from the Illustrative Rules and is largely self-explanatory.

The uniform docketing scheme described in subsection (a) should take into account potential problems associated with a complaint that names multiple judges. One solution may be to provide separate docket numbers for each subject judge. Separate docket numbers would help avoid difficulties in tracking cases, particularly if a complaint is dismissed with respect to some, but not all of the named judges.

Complaints against noncovered persons are not to be accepted for processing under these Rules but may, of course, be accepted under other circuit rules or procedures for grievances.

RULE 9. TIME FOR FILING OR IDENTIFYING COMPLAINT

A complaint may be filed or identified at any time. If the passage of time has made an accurate and fair investigation of a complaint impracticable, the complaint must be dismissed under Rule 11(c)(1)(E).

[Adopted March 11, 2008, effective April 10, 2008. Amended effective September 17, 2015.]

Commentary on Rule 9

This Rule is adapted from the Act, 28 U.S.C. §§ 351, 352(b)(1)(A)(iii), and the Illustrative Rules.

RULE 10. ABUSE OF COMPLAINT PROCEDURE

(a) Abusive Complaints. A complainant who has filed repetitive, harassing, or frivolous complaints, or has otherwise abused the complaint procedure, may be restricted from filing further complaints. After giving the complainant an opportunity to show cause in writing why his or her right to file further complaints should not be limited, the judicial council may prohibit, restrict, or impose conditions on the complainant's use of the complaint procedure. Upon written request of the complainant, the judicial council may revise or withdraw any prohibition, restriction, or condition previously imposed.

(b) Orchestrated Complaints. When many essentially identical complaints from different complainants are received and appear to be part of an orchestrated campaign, the chief judge may recommend that the judicial council issue a written order instructing the circuit clerk to accept only a certain number of such complaints for filing and to refuse to accept additional complaints. The circuit clerk must send a copy of any such order to anyone whose complaint was not accepted.

[Adopted March 11, 2008, effective April 10, 2008. Amended effective September 17, 2015.]

Commentary on Rule 10

This Rule is adapted from the Illustrative Rules.

Rule 10(a) provides a mechanism for a judicial council to restrict the filing of further complaints by a single complainant who has abused the complaint procedure. In some instances, however, the complaint procedure may be abused in a manner for which the remedy provided in Rule 10(a) may not be appropriate. For example, some circuits have been inundated with submissions of dozens or hundreds of essentially identical complaints against the same judge or judges, all submitted by different complainants. In many of these instances, persons with grievances against a particular judge or judges used the Internet or other technology to orchestrate mass complaint-filing campaigns against them. If each complaint submitted as part of such a campaign were accepted for filing and processed according to these Rules, there would be a serious drain on court resources without any benefit to the adjudication of the underlying merits.

A judicial council may, therefore, respond to such mass filings under Rule 10(b) by declining to accept repetitive complaints for filing, regardless of the fact that the complaints are nominally submitted by different complainants. When the first complaint or complaints have been dismissed on the merits, and when further, essentially identical submissions follow, the judicial council may issue a second order noting that these are identical or repetitive complaints, directing the circuit clerk not to accept these complaints or any further such complaints for filing, and directing the clerk to send each putative complainant copies of both orders.

ARTICLE III. REVIEW OF COMPLAINT BY CHIEF JUDGE

RULE 11. CHIEF JUDGE'S REVIEW

(a) Purpose of Chief Judge's Review. When a complaint is identified by the chief judge or is filed, the chief judge must review it unless the chief judge is disqualified under Rule 25. If a complaint contains information constituting evidence of misconduct or disability, but the complainant does not claim it as such, the chief judge must treat the complaint as if it did allege misconduct or disability and give notice to the subject judge. After reviewing a complaint, the chief judge must determine whether it should be:

(1) dismissed;

(2) concluded on the ground that voluntary corrective action has been taken;

(3) concluded because intervening events have made action on the complaint no longer necessary; or

(4) referred to a special committee.

(b) Chief Judge's Inquiry. In determining what action to take under Rule 11(a), the chief judge may conduct a limited inquiry. The chief judge, or a designee, may communicate orally or in writing with the complainant, the subject judge, and any others who may have knowledge of the matter, and may obtain and review transcripts and other relevant documents. In conducting the inquiry, the chief judge must not determine any reasonably disputed issue. Any such determination must be left to a special committee appointed under Rule 11(f) and to the judicial council that considers the special committee's report.

(c) Dismissal.

(1) *Permissible Grounds.* A complaint must be dismissed in whole or in part to the extent that the chief judge concludes that the complaint:

(A) alleges conduct that, even if true, is not prejudicial to the effective and expeditious administration of the business of the courts and does not indicate a mental or physical disability resulting in the inability to discharge the duties of judicial office;

(B) is directly related to the merits of a decision or procedural ruling;

(C) is frivolous;

(D) is based on allegations lacking sufficient evidence to raise an inference that misconduct has occurred or that a disability exists;

(E) is based on allegations that are incapable of being established through investigation;

(F) has been filed in the wrong circuit under Rule 7; or

(G) is otherwise not appropriate for consideration under the Act.

(2) *Impermissible Grounds.* A complaint must not be dismissed solely because it repeats allegations of a previously dismissed complaint if it also contains material information not previously considered and does not constitute harassment of the subject judge.

(d) Corrective Action. The chief judge may conclude a complaint proceeding in whole or in part if:

(1) an informal resolution under Rule 5 satisfactory to the chief judge was reached before the complaint was filed under Rule 6; or

(2) the chief judge determines that the subject judge has taken appropriate voluntary corrective action that acknowledges and remedies the problems raised by the complaint.

(e) Intervening Events. The chief judge may conclude a complaint proceeding in whole or in part upon determining that intervening events render some or all of the allegations moot or make remedial action impossible.

(f) Appointment of Special Committee. If some or all of a complaint is not dismissed or concluded, the chief judge must promptly appoint a special committee to investigate the complaint or any relevant portion of it and to make recommendations to the judicial council. Before appointing a special committee, the chief judge must invite the subject judge to respond to the complaint either orally or in writing if the judge was not given an opportunity during the limited inquiry. In the chief judge's discretion, separate complaints may be joined and assigned to a single special committee. Similarly, a single complaint about more than one judge may be severed and more than one special committee appointed.

(g) Notice of Chief Judge's Action; Petition for Review.

(1) *When Chief Judge Appoints Special Committee.* If the chief judge appoints a special committee, the chief judge must notify the complainant and the subject judge that the matter has been referred to a committee, notify the complainant of a complainant's rights under Rule 16, and identify the members of the committee. A copy of the order appointing the special committee must be sent to the Committee on Judicial Conduct and Disability.

(2) *When Chief Judge Disposes of Complaint Without Appointing Special Committee.* If the chief judge disposes of a complaint under Rule 11(c), (d), or (e), the chief judge must prepare a supporting memorandum that sets forth the reasons for the disposition. If the complaint was initiated by identification under Rule 5, the memorandum must so indicate. Except as authorized by 28 U.S.C. § 360, the memorandum must not include the name of the complainant or of the subject judge. The order and memoranda incorporated by reference in the order must be promptly sent to the complainant, the subject judge, and the Committee on Judicial Conduct and Disability.

(3) *Right to Petition for Review.* If the chief judge disposes of a complaint under Rule 11(c), (d), or (e), the complainant and the subject judge must be notified of the right to petition the judicial council for review of the disposition, as provided in Rule 18. If the chief judge so disposes of a complaint that was

identified under Rule 5 or filed by its subject judge, the chief judge must transmit the order and memoranda incorporated by reference in the order to the judicial council for review in accordance with Rule 19. In the event of such a transmission, the subject judge may make a written submission to the judicial council but will have no further right of review except as allowed under Rule 21(b)(1)(B). When a disposition is to be reviewed by the judicial council, the chief judge must promptly transmit all materials obtained in connection with the inquiry under Rule 11(b) to the circuit clerk for transmittal to the council.

(h) Public Availability of Chief Judge's Decision. The chief judge's decision must be made public to the extent, at the time, and in the manner provided in Rule 24.

[Adopted March 11, 2008, effective April 10, 2008. Amended effective September 17, 2015.]

Commentary on Rule 11

This Rule describes complaint-review actions available either to a chief judge or, where that judge is the subject judge or is otherwise disqualified under Rule 25, to the judge designated under Rule 25(f) to perform the chief judge's duties under these Rules. Subsection (a) of this Rule provides that where a complaint has been filed under Rule 6, the ordinary doctrines of waiver do not apply. The chief judge must identify as a complaint any misconduct or disability issues raised by the factual allegations of the complaint even if the complainant makes no such claim with regard to those issues. For example, an allegation limited to misconduct in fact-finding that mentions periods during a trial when the judge was asleep must be treated as a complaint regarding disability. Some formal order giving notice of the expanded scope of the proceeding must be given to the subject judge.

Subsection (b) describes the nature of the chief judge's inquiry. It is based largely on the Breyer Committee Report, 239 F.R.D. at 243–45. The Act states that dismissal is appropriate "when a limited inquiry ... demonstrates that the allegations in the complaint lack any factual foundation or are conclusively refuted by objective evidence." 28 U.S.C. § 352(b)(1)(B). At the same time, however, Section 352(a) states that "[t]he chief judge shall not undertake to make findings of fact about any matter that is reasonably in dispute." These two statutory standards should be read together, so that a matter is not "reasonably" in dispute if a limited inquiry shows that the allegations do not constitute misconduct or disability, that they lack any reliable factual foundation, or that they are conclusively refuted by objective evidence.

In conducting a limited inquiry under subsection (b), the chief judge must avoid determinations of reasonably disputed issues, including reasonably disputed issues as to whether the facts alleged constitute misconduct or disability, which are ordinarily left to the judicial council and its special committee. An allegation of fact is ordinarily not "refuted" simply because the subject judge denies it. The limited inquiry must reveal something more in the way of refutation before it is appropriate to dismiss a complaint that is otherwise cognizable. If it is the complainant's word against the subject judge's—in other words, there is simply no other significant evidence of what happened or of the complainant's

unreliability—then there must be a special-committee investigation. Such a credibility issue is a matter "reasonably in dispute" within the meaning of the Act.

However, dismissal following a limited inquiry may occur when a complaint refers to transcripts or to witnesses and the chief judge determines that the transcripts and witnesses all support the subject judge. Breyer Committee Report, 239 F.R.D. at 243. For example, consider a complaint alleging that the subject judge said X, and the complaint mentions, or it is independently clear, that five people may have heard what the judge said. *Id.* The chief judge is told by the subject judge and one witness that the judge did not say X, and the chief judge dismisses the complaint without questioning the other four possible witnesses. *Id.* In this example, the matter remains reasonably in dispute. If all five witnesses say the subject judge did not say X, dismissal is appropriate, but if potential witnesses who are reasonably accessible have not been questioned, then the matter remains reasonably in dispute. *Id.*

Similarly, under subsection (c)(1)(A), if it is clear that the conduct or disability alleged, even if true, is not cognizable under these Rules, the complaint should be dismissed. If that issue is reasonably in dispute, however, dismissal under subsection (c)(1)(A) is inappropriate.

Essentially, the standard articulated in subsection (b) is that used to decide motions for summary judgment pursuant to Fed. R. Civ. P. 56. Genuine issues of material fact are not resolved at the summary judgment stage. A material fact is one that "might affect the outcome of the suit under the governing law," and a dispute is "genuine" if "the evidence is such that a reasonable jury could return a verdict for the nonmoving party." *Anderson v. Liberty Lobby*, 477 U.S. 242, 248 (1986). Similarly, the chief judge may not resolve a genuine issue concerning a material fact or the existence of misconduct or a disability when conducting a limited inquiry pursuant to subsection (b).

Subsection (c) describes the grounds on which a complaint may be dismissed. These are adapted from the Act, 28 U.S.C. § 352(b), and the Breyer Committee Report, 239 F.R.D. at 239–45. Subsection (c)(1)(A) permits dismissal of an allegation that, even if true, does not constitute misconduct or disability under the statutory standard. The proper standards are set out in Rule 3 and discussed in the Commentary on that Rule. Subsection (c)(1)(B) permits dismissal of complaints related to the merits of a decision by a subject judge; this standard is also governed by Rule 3 and its accompanying Commentary.

Subsections (c)(1)(C)–(E) implement the statute by allowing dismissal of complaints that are "frivolous, lacking sufficient evidence to raise an inference that misconduct has occurred, or containing allegations which are incapable of being established through investigation." 28 U.S.C. § 352(b)(1)(A)(iii).

Dismissal of a complaint as "frivolous" under Rule 11(c)(1)(C) will generally occur without any inquiry beyond the face of the complaint. For instance, when the allegations are facially incredible or so lacking in indicia of reliability that no further inquiry is warranted, dismissal under this subsection is appropriate.

A complaint warranting dismissal under Rule 11(c)(1)(D) is illustrated by the following example. Consider a complainant who alleges an impropriety and asserts that he knows of it because it was observed and reported to him by a person who is identified. The subject judge denies that the event occurred. When contacted, the source also denies it. In such a case, the chief judge's proper course of action may turn on whether the source had any role in the allegedly improper conduct. If the complaint was based on a lawyer's statement that he or she had an improper *ex parte* contact with a judge, the lawyer's denial of the impropriety might not be taken as wholly persuasive, and it would be appropriate to conclude that a real factual issue is raised. On the other hand, if the complaint quoted a disinterested third party and that disinterested party denied that the statement had been made, there would be no value in opening a formal investigation. In such a case, it would be appropriate to dismiss the complaint under Rule 11(c)(1)(D).

Rule 11(c)(1)(E) is intended, among other things, to cover situations when no evidence is offered or identified, or when the only identified source is unavailable. Breyer Committee Report, 239 F.R.D. at 243. For example, a complaint alleges that an unnamed attorney told the complainant that the subject judge did X. *Id.* The subject judge denies it. The chief judge requests that the complainant (who does not purport to have observed the subject judge do X) identify the unnamed witness, or that the unnamed witness come forward so that the chief judge can learn the unnamed witness's account. *Id.* The complainant responds that he has spoken with the unnamed witness, that the unnamed witness is an attorney who practices in federal court, and that the unnamed witness is unwilling to be identified or to come forward. *Id.* at 243–44. The allegation is then properly dismissed as containing allegations that are incapable of being established through investigation. *Id.*

If, however, the situation involves a reasonable dispute over credibility, the matter should proceed. For example, the complainant alleges an impropriety and alleges that he or she observed it and that there were no other witnesses; the subject judge denies that the event occurred. Unless the complainant's allegations are facially incredible or so lacking indicia of reliability as to warrant dismissal under Rule 11(c)(1)(C), a special committee must be appointed because there is a material factual question that is reasonably in dispute.

Dismissal is also appropriate when a complaint is filed so long after an alleged event that memory loss, death, or changes to unknown residences prevent a proper investigation.

Subsection (c)(2) indicates that the investigative nature of the process prevents the application of claim preclusion principles where new and material evidence becomes available. However, it also recognizes that at some point a renewed investigation may constitute harassment of the subject judge and should not be undertaken, depending of course on the seriousness of the issues and the weight of the new evidence.

Rule 11(d) implements the Act's provision for dismissal if voluntary appropriate corrective action has been taken. It is largely adapted from the Breyer Committee Report, 239 F.R.D. at 244–45. The Act authorizes the chief judge to conclude the complaint proceedings if "appropriate corrective action has been taken." 28 U.S.C. § 352(b)(2). Under the Rule, action taken after a complaint is filed is "appropriate" when it acknowledges and remedies the problem raised by the complaint. Breyer Committee Report, 239 F.R.D. at 244. Because the Act deals with the conduct of judges, the emphasis is on correction of the judicial conduct that was the

subject of the complaint. *Id.* Terminating a complaint based on corrective action is premised on the implicit understanding that voluntary self-correction or redress of misconduct or a disability is preferable to sanctions. *Id.* The chief judge may facilitate this process by giving the subject judge an objective view of the appearance of the judicial conduct in question and by suggesting appropriate corrective measures. *Id.* Moreover, when corrective action is taken under Rule 5 satisfactory to the chief judge before a complaint is filed, that informal resolution will be sufficient to conclude a subsequent complaint based on identical conduct.

"Corrective action" must be voluntary action taken by the subject judge. Breyer Committee Report, 239 F.R.D. at 244. A remedial action directed by the chief judge or by an appellate court without the participation of the subject judge in formulating the directive or without the subject judge's subsequent agreement to such action does not constitute the requisite voluntary corrective action. *Id.* Neither the chief judge nor an appellate court has authority under the Act to impose a formal remedy or sanction; only the judicial council can impose a formal remedy or sanction under 28 U.S.C. § 354(a)(2). *Id.* Compliance with a previous judicial-council order may serve as corrective action allowing conclusion of a later complaint about the same behavior. *Id.*

Where a subject judge's conduct has resulted in identifiable, particularized harm to the complainant or another individual, appropriate corrective action should include steps taken by that judge to acknowledge and redress the harm, if possible, such as by an apology, recusal from a case, or a pledge to refrain from similar conduct in the future. *Id.* While the Act is generally forward-looking, any corrective action should, to the extent possible, serve to correct a specific harm to an individual, if such harm can reasonably be remedied. *Id.* In some cases, corrective action may not be "appropriate" to justify conclusion of a complaint unless the complainant or other individual harmed is meaningfully apprised of the nature of the corrective action in the chief judge's order, in a direct communication from the subject judge, or otherwise. *Id.*

Voluntary corrective action should be proportionate to any plausible allegations of misconduct in a complaint. The form of corrective action should also be proportionate to any sanctions that the judicial council might impose under Rule 20(b), such as a private or public reprimand or a change in case assignments. Breyer Committee Report, 239 F.R.D at 244–45. In other words, minor corrective action will not suffice to dispose of a serious matter. *Id.*

Rule 11(e) implements Section 352(b)(2) of the Act, which permits the chief judge to "conclude the proceeding" if "action on the complaint is no longer necessary because of intervening events," such as a resignation from judicial office. Ordinarily, however, stepping down from an administrative post such as chief judge, judicial-council member, or court-committee chair does not constitute an event rendering unnecessary any further action on a complaint alleging judicial misconduct. Breyer Committee Report, 239 F.R.D. at 245. As long as the subject of a complaint performs judicial duties, a complaint alleging judicial misconduct must be addressed. *Id.*

If a complaint is not disposed of pursuant to Rule 11(c), (d), or (e), a special committee must be appointed. Rule 11(f) states that a subject judge must be invited to respond to the complaint before a special committee is appointed, if no earlier response was invited.

Subject judges, of course, receive copies of complaints at the same time that they are referred to the chief judge, and they are free to volunteer responses to them. Under Rule 11(b), the chief judge may request a response if it is thought necessary. However, many complaints are clear candidates for dismissal even if their allegations are accepted as true, and there is no need for the subject judge to devote time to a defense.

The Act requires that the order dismissing a complaint or concluding a proceeding contain a statement of reasons and that a copy of the order be sent to the complainant. 28 U.S.C. § 352(b). Rule 24, dealing with availability of information to the public, contemplates that the order will be made public, usually without disclosing the names of the complainant or the subject judge. If desired for administrative purposes, more identifying information can be included in a non-public version of the order.

When a complaint is disposed of by the chief judge, the statutory purposes are best served by providing the complainant with a full, particularized, but concise explanation, giving reasons for the conclusions reached. *See also* Commentary on Rule 24 (dealing with public availability).

Rule 11(g) provides that the complainant and the subject judge must be notified, in the case of a disposition by the chief judge, of the right to petition the judicial council for review. Because an identified complaint has no "complainant" to petition for review, the chief judge's dispositive order on such a complaint will be transmitted to the judicial council for review. The same will apply where a complaint was filed by its subject judge. A copy of the chief judge's order, and memoranda incorporated by reference in the order, disposing of a complaint must be sent by the circuit clerk to the Committee on Judicial Conduct and Disability.

ARTICLE IV. INVESTIGATION AND REPORT BY SPECIAL COMMITTEE

RULE 12. SPECIAL COMMITTEE'S COMPOSITION

(a) Membership. Except as provided in (e), a special committee appointed under Rule 11(f) must consist of the chief judge and equal numbers of circuit and district judges. These judges may include senior judges. If the complaint is about a district judge, bankruptcy judge, or magistrate judge, then, when possible, the district-judge members of the special committee must be from districts other than the district of the subject judge. For the courts named in 28 U.S.C. § 363, the special committee must be selected from the judges serving on the subject judge's court.

(b) Presiding Officer. When appointing the special committee, the chief judge may serve as the presiding officer or else must designate a committee member as the presiding officer.

(c) Bankruptcy Judge or Magistrate Judge as Adviser. If the subject judge is a bankruptcy judge or magistrate judge, he or she may, within 14 days after being notified of the special committee's appointment, ask the chief judge to designate as a committee adviser another bankruptcy judge or magistrate judge, as the case may be. The chief judge must grant such a request but may otherwise use discretion in naming the adviser. Unless the adviser is a Court of Federal Claims special master appointed under 42 U.S.C. § 300aa–12(c), the adviser must be from a district other than the district of the subject bankruptcy judge or subject magistrate judge. The adviser cannot vote but has the other privileges of a special-committee member.

(d) Provision of Documents. The chief judge must certify to each other member of the special committee and to any adviser copies of the complaint and statement of facts, in whole or relevant part, and any other relevant documents on file.

(e) Continuing Qualification of Special–Committee Member. A member of a special committee may continue to serve on the committee even though the member relinquishes the position of chief judge, active circuit judge, or active district judge, as the case may be, but only if the member continues to hold office under Article III, Section 1, of the Constitution of the United States, or under 28 U.S.C. § 171.

(f) Inability of Special–Committee Member to Complete Service. If a member of a special committee can no longer serve because of death, disability, disqualification, resignation, retirement from office, or other reason, the chief judge must decide whether to appoint a replacement member, either a circuit or district judge as needed under (a). No special committee appointed under these Rules may function with only a single member, and the votes of a two-member committee must be unanimous.

(g) Voting. All actions by a special committee must be by vote of a majority of all members of the committee.

[Adopted March 11, 2008, effective April 10, 2008. Amended effective September 17, 2015.]

Commentary on Rule 12

This Rule is adapted from the Act and the Illustrative Rules.

Rule 12 leaves the size of a special committee flexible, to be determined on a case-by-case basis. The question of the size of a special committee is one that should be weighed with care in view of the potential for consuming the members' time; a large committee should be appointed only if there is a special reason to do so. Rule 12(a) acknowledges the common practice of including senior judges in the membership of a special committee.

Although the Act requires that the chief judge be a member of each special committee, 28 U.S.C. § 353(a)(1), it does not require that the chief judge preside. Accordingly,

Rule 12(b) provides that if the chief judge does not preside, he or she must designate another member of the special committee as the presiding officer.

Rule 12(c) provides that the chief judge must appoint a bankruptcy judge or magistrate judge as an adviser to a special committee at the request of a bankruptcy or magistrate subject judge. Subsection (c) also provides that the adviser will have all the privileges of a member of the special committee except a vote. The adviser, therefore, may participate in all deliberations of the special committee, question witnesses at hearings, and write a separate statement to accompany the committee's report to the judicial council.

Rule 12(e) provides that a member of a special committee who remains an Article III judge may continue to serve on the committee even though the member's status otherwise changes. Thus, a special committee that originally consisted of the chief judge and an equal number of circuit and district judges, as required by the law, may continue to function even though changes of status alter that composition. This provision reflects the belief that stability of membership will contribute to the quality of the work of such committees.

Stability of membership is also the principal concern animating Rule 12(f), which deals with the case in which a special committee loses a member before its work is complete. The Rule permits the chief judge to determine whether a replacement member should be appointed. Generally, appointment of a replacement member is desirable in these situations unless the special committee has conducted evidentiary hearings before the vacancy occurs. However, cases may arise in which a special committee is in the late stages of its work, and in which it would be difficult for a new member to play a meaningful role. The Rule also preserves the collegial character of the special-committee process by prohibiting a single surviving member from serving as a committee and by providing that a committee of two surviving members will, in essence, operate under a unanimity rule.

Rule 12(g) provides that actions of a special committee must be by vote of a majority of all the members. All the members of a special committee should participate in committee decisions. In that circumstance, it seems reasonable to require that special-committee decisions be made by a majority of the membership, rather than a majority of some smaller quorum.

RULE 13. CONDUCT OF SPECIAL-COMMITTEE INVESTIGATION

(a) Extent and Methods of Special-Committee Investigation. A special committee should determine the appropriate extent and methods of its investigation in light of the allegations of the complaint and its preliminary inquiry. The investigation may include use of appropriate experts or other professionals. If, in the course of the investigation, the special committee has cause to believe that the subject judge may have engaged in misconduct or has a disability that is beyond the scope of the complaint, the committee must refer the new matter to the chief judge for a determination of whether action under Rule 5 or Rule 11 is necessary before the committee's investigation is expanded to include the new matter.

(b) Criminal Conduct. If the special committee's investigation concerns conduct that may be a crime, the committee must consult with the appropriate prosecutorial authorities to the extent permitted by the Act to avoid compromising any criminal investigation. The special committee has final authority over the timing and extent of its investigation and the formulation of its recommendations.

(c) Staff. The special committee may arrange for staff assistance to conduct the investigation. It may use existing staff of the Judiciary or may hire special staff through the Director of the Administrative Office of the United States Courts.

(d) Delegation of Subpoena Power; Contempt. The chief judge may delegate the authority to exercise the subpoena powers of the special committee. The judicial council or special committee may institute a contempt proceeding under 28 U.S.C. § 332(d) against anyone who fails to comply with a subpoena.

[Adopted March 11, 2008, effective April 10, 2008. Amended effective September 17, 2015.]

Commentary on Rule 13

This Rule is adapted from the Illustrative Rules.

Rule 13, as well as Rules 14, 15, and 16, are concerned with the way in which the special committee carries out its mission. They reflect the view that the special committee has two roles that are separated in ordinary litigation. First, the special committee has an investigative role of the kind that is characteristically left to executive branch agencies or discovery by civil litigants. 28 U.S.C. § 353(c). Second, it has a formalized fact-finding and recommendation-of-disposition role that is characteristically left to juries, judges, or arbitrators. *Id.* Rule 13 generally governs the investigative stage. Even though the same body has responsibility for both roles under the Act, it is important to distinguish between them in order to ensure that appropriate rights are afforded at appropriate times to the subject judge.

Rule 13(a) includes a provision making clear that a special committee may choose to consult appropriate experts or other professionals if it determines that such a consultation is warranted. If, for example, the special committee has cause to believe that the subject judge may be unable to discharge all of the duties of office by reason of mental or physical disability, the committee could ask the subject judge to respond to inquiries and, if necessary, request the judge to undergo a medical or psychological examination. In advance of any such examination, the special committee may enter into an agreement with the subject judge as to the scope and use that may be made of the examination results. In addition or in the alternative, the special committee may ask to review existing records, including medical records.

The extent of the subject judge's cooperation in the investigation may be taken into account in the consideration of the underlying complaint. If, for example, the subject judge impedes reasonable efforts to confirm or disconfirm the presence of a disability, the special committee may still consider whether the conduct alleged in the complaint and confirmed in the investigation constitutes disability. The same would be true of a complaint alleging misconduct.

The special committee may also consider whether such a judge might be in violation of his or her duty to cooperate in an investigation under these Rules, a duty rooted not only in the Act's definition of misconduct but also in the Code of Conduct for United States Judges, which emphasizes the need to maintain public confidence in the Judiciary, *see* Canon 2(A) and Canon 1 cmt., and requires judges to "facilitate the performance of the administrative responsibilities of other judges and court personnel," Canon 3(B)(1). If the special committee finds a breach of the duty to cooperate and believes that the breach may amount to misconduct under Rule 3(h)(1)(H), it should determine, under the final sentence of Rule 13(a), whether that possibility should be referred to the chief judge for consideration of action under Rule 5 or Rule 11. *See also* Commentary on Rule 3.

One of the difficult questions that can arise is the relationship between proceedings under the Act and criminal investigations. Rule 13(b) assigns responsibility for coordination to the special committee in cases in which criminal conduct is suspected, but gives the committee the authority to determine the appropriate pace of its activity in light of any criminal investigation.

Title 28 U.S.C. § 356(a) provides that a special committee will have full subpoena powers as provided in 28 U.S.C. § 332(d). Section 332(d)(1) provides that subpoenas will be issued on behalf of a judicial council by the circuit clerk "at the direction of the chief judge of the circuit or his designee." Rule 13(d) contemplates that, where the chief judge designates someone else as presiding officer of the special committee, the presiding officer also be delegated the authority to direct the circuit clerk to issue subpoenas related to committee proceedings. That is not intended to imply, however, that the decision to use the subpoena power is exercisable by the presiding officer alone. *See* Rule 12(g).

RULE 14. CONDUCT OF SPECIAL–COMMITTEE HEARINGS

(a) Purpose of Hearings. The special committee may hold hearings to take testimony and receive other evidence, to hear argument, or both. If the special committee is investigating allegations against more than one judge, it may hold joint or separate hearings.

(b) Special–Committee Evidence. Subject to Rule 15, the special committee must obtain material, nonredundant evidence in the form it considers appropriate. In the special committee's discretion, evidence may be obtained by committee members, staff, or both. Witnesses offering testimonial evidence may include the complainant and the subject judge.

(c) Counsel for Witnesses. The subject judge has the right to counsel. The special committee has discretion to decide whether other witnesses may have counsel present when they testify.

(d) Witness Fees. Witness fees must be paid as provided in 28 U.S.C. § 1821.

(e) Oath. All testimony taken at a hearing must be given under oath or affirmation.

(f) Rules of Evidence. The Federal Rules of Evidence do not apply to special-committee hearings.

(g) Record and Transcript. A record and transcript must be made of all hearings.

[Adopted March 11, 2008, effective April 10, 2008. Amended effective September 17, 2015.]

Commentary on Rule 14

This Rule is adapted from the Act, 28 U.S.C. § 353, and the Illustrative Rules.

Rule 14 is concerned with the conduct of fact-finding hearings. Special-committee hearings will normally be held only after the investigative work has been completed and the committee has concluded that there is sufficient evidence to warrant a formal fact-finding proceeding. Special-committee proceedings are primarily inquisitorial rather than adversarial. Accordingly, the Federal Rules of Evidence do not apply to such hearings. Inevitably, a hearing will have something of an adversary character. Nevertheless, that tendency should be moderated to the extent possible. Even though a proceeding will commonly have investigative and hearing stages, special-committee members should not regard themselves as prosecutors one day and judges the next. Their duty—and that of their staff—is at all times to be impartial seekers of the truth.

Rule 14(b) contemplates that material evidence will be obtained by the special committee and presented in the form of affidavits, live testimony, etc. Staff or others who are organizing the hearings should regard it as their role to present evidence representing the entire picture. With respect to testimonial evidence, the subject judge should normally be called as a special-committee witness. Cases may arise in which the subject judge will not testify voluntarily. In such cases, subpoena powers are available, subject to the normal testimonial privileges. Although Rule 15(c) recognizes the subject judge's statutory right to call witnesses on his or her own behalf, exercise of this right should not usually be necessary.

RULE 15. SUBJECT JUDGE'S RIGHTS

(a) Notice.

(1) *Generally.* The subject judge must receive written notice of:

(A) the appointment of a special committee under Rule 11(f);

(B) the expansion of the scope of an investigation under Rule 13(a);

(C) any hearing under Rule 14, including its purposes, the names of any witnesses the special committee intends to call, and the text of any statements that have been taken from those witnesses.

(2) *Suggestion of Additional Witnesses.* The subject judge may suggest additional witnesses to the special committee.

(b) Special–Committee Report. The subject judge must be sent a copy of the special committee's report when it is filed with the judicial council.

(c) Presentation of Evidence. At any hearing held under Rule 14, the subject judge has the right to present evidence, to compel the attendance of witnesses, and to compel the production of documents. At the request of the subject judge, the chief judge or the judge's designee must direct the circuit clerk to issue a subpoena to a witness under 28 U.S.C. § 332(d)(1). The subject judge must be given the opportunity to cross-examine special-committee witnesses, in person or by counsel.

(d) Presentation of Argument. The subject judge may submit written argument to the special committee and must be given a reasonable opportunity to present oral argument at an appropriate stage of the investigation.

(e) Attendance at Hearings. The subject judge has the right to attend any hearing held under Rule 14 and to receive copies of the transcript, of any documents introduced, and of any written arguments submitted by the complainant to the special committee.

(f) Representation by Counsel. The subject judge may choose to be represented by counsel in the exercise of any right enumerated in this Rule. As provided in Rule 20(e), the United States may bear the costs of the representation.

[Adopted March 11, 2008, effective April 10, 2008. Amended effective September 17, 2015.]

Commentary on Rule 15

This Rule is adapted from the Act and the Illustrative Rules.

The Act states that these Rules must contain provisions requiring that "the judge whose conduct is the subject of a complaint ... be afforded an opportunity to appear (in person or by counsel) at proceedings conducted by the investigating panel, to present oral and documentary evidence, to compel the attendance of witnesses or the production of documents, to cross-examine witnesses, and to present argument orally or in writing." 28 U.S.C. § 358(b)(2). To implement this provision, Rule 15(e) gives the subject judge the right to attend any hearing held for the purpose of receiving evidence of record or hearing argument under Rule 14.

The Act does not require that the subject judge be permitted to attend all proceedings of the special committee. Accordingly, the Rules do not give a right to attend other proceedings—for example, meetings at which the special committee is engaged in investigative activity, such as interviewing persons to learn whether they ought to be called as witnesses or examining for relevance purposes documents delivered pursuant to a subpoena duces tecum, or meetings in which the committee is deliberating on the evidence or its recommendations.

RULE 16. COMPLAINANT'S RIGHTS IN INVESTIGATION

(a) Notice. The complainant must receive written notice of the investigation as provided in Rule 11(g)(1). When the special committee's report to the judicial council is filed, the complainant must be notified of the

filing. The judicial council may, in its discretion, provide a copy of the report of a special committee to the complainant.

(b) Opportunity to Provide Evidence. If the complainant knows of relevant evidence not already before the special committee, the complainant may briefly explain in writing the basis of that knowledge and the nature of that evidence. If the special committee determines that the complainant has information not already known to the committee that would assist in the committee's investigation, a representative of the committee must interview the complainant.

(c) Presentation of Argument. The complainant may submit written argument to the special committee. In its discretion, the special committee may permit the complainant to offer oral argument.

(d) Representation by Counsel. A complainant may submit written argument through counsel and, if permitted to offer oral argument, may do so through counsel.

(e) Cooperation. In exercising its discretion under this Rule, the special committee may take into account the degree of the complainant's cooperation in preserving the confidentiality of the proceedings, including the identity of the subject judge.

[Adopted March 11, 2008, effective April 10, 2008. Amended effective September 17, 2015.]

Commentary on Rule 16

This Rule is adapted from the Act and the Illustrative Rules.

In accordance with the view of the process as fundamentally administrative and inquisitorial, these Rules do not give the complainant the rights of a party to litigation and leave the complainant's role largely to the discretion of the special committee. However, Rule 16(b) gives the complainant the prerogative to make a brief written submission showing that he or she is aware of relevant evidence not already known to the special committee. (Such a submission may precede any written or oral argument the complainant provides under Rule 16(c), or it may accompany that argument.) If the special committee determines, independently or from the complainant's submission, that the complainant has information that would assist the committee in its investigation, the complainant must be interviewed by a representative of the committee. Such an interview may be in person or by telephone, and the representative of the special committee may be either a member or staff.

Rule 16 does not contemplate that the complainant will ordinarily be permitted to attend proceedings of the special committee except when testifying or presenting oral argument. A special committee may exercise its discretion to permit the complainant to be present at its proceedings, or to permit the complainant, individually or through counsel, to participate in the examination or cross-examination of witnesses.

The Act authorizes an exception to the normal confidentiality provisions where the judicial council in its discretion provides a copy of the report of the special committee to the complainant and to the subject judge. 28 U.S.C. § 360(a)(1). However, the Rules do not entitle the complainant to a copy of the special committee's report.

In exercising their discretion regarding the role of the complainant, the special committee and the judicial council should protect the confidentiality of the complaint process. As a consequence, subsection (e) provides that the special committee may consider the degree to which a complainant has cooperated in preserving the confidentiality of the proceedings in determining what role beyond the minimum required by these Rules should be given to that complainant.

RULE 17. SPECIAL–COMMITTEE REPORT

The special committee must file with the judicial council a comprehensive report of its investigation, including findings and recommendations for council action. The report must be accompanied by a state-ment of the vote by which it was adopted, any separate or dissenting statements of special-committee members, and the record of any hearings held under Rule 14. In addition to being sent to the subject judge under Rule 15(b), a copy of the report and any accompanying statements and documents must be sent to the Committee on Judicial Conduct and Disability.

[Adopted March 11, 2008, effective April 10, 2008. Amended effective September 17, 2015.]

Commentary on Rule 17

This Rule is adapted from the Illustrative Rules and is self-explanatory. The provision for sending a copy of the special-committee report and accompanying statements and documents to the Committee on Judicial Conduct and Disability is new.

ARTICLE V. REVIEW BY JUDICIAL COUNCIL

RULE 18. PETITION FOR REVIEW OF CHIEF–JUDGE DISPOSITION UNDER RULE 11(c), (d), OR (e)

(a) Petition for Review. After the chief judge issues an order under Rule 11(c), (d), or (e), the complainant or the subject judge may petition the judicial council of the circuit to review the order. By rules promulgated under 28 U.S.C. § 358, the judicial council may refer a petition for review filed under this Rule to a panel of no fewer than five members of the council, at least two of whom must be district judges.

(b) When to File; Form; Where to File. A petition for review must be filed in the office of the circuit clerk within 42 days after the date of the chief judge's order. The petition for review should be in letter form, addressed to the circuit clerk, and in an envelope marked "Misconduct Petition" or "Disability Petition." The name of the subject judge must not be shown on the envelope. The petition for review should be typewritten or otherwise legible. It should begin with "I hereby petition the judicial council for review of . . ." and state the reasons why the petition should be granted. It must be signed.

(c) Receipt and Distribution of Petition. A circuit clerk who receives a petition for review filed in accordance with this Rule must:

(1) acknowledge its receipt and send a copy to the complainant or subject judge, as the case may be;

(2) promptly distribute to each member of the judicial council, or its relevant panel, except for any member disqualified under Rule 25, or make available in the manner provided by local rule, the following materials:

(A) copies of the complaint;

(B) all materials obtained by the chief judge in connection with the inquiry;

(C) the chief judge's order disposing of the complaint;

(D) any memorandum in support of the chief judge's order;

(E) the petition for review; and

(F) an appropriate ballot; and

(3) send the petition for review to the Committee on Judicial Conduct and Disability. Unless the Committee on Judicial Conduct and Disability requests them, the circuit clerk will not send copies of the materials obtained by the chief judge.

(d) Untimely Petition. The circuit clerk must refuse to accept a petition that is received after the time allowed in (b).

(e) Timely Petition Not in Proper Form. When the circuit clerk receives a petition for review filed within the time allowed but in a form that is improper to a degree that would substantially impair its consideration by the judicial council—such as a document that is ambiguous about whether it is intended to be a petition for review—the circuit clerk must acknowledge its receipt, call the filer's attention to the deficiencies, and give the filer the opportunity to correct the deficiencies within the original time allowed for filing the petition or within 21 days after the date on which a notice of the deficiencies was sent to the complainant, whichever is later. If the deficiencies are corrected within the time allowed, the circuit clerk will proceed according to paragraphs (a) and (c) of this Rule. If the deficiencies are not corrected, the circuit clerk must reject the petition.

[Adopted March 11, 2008, effective April 10, 2008. Amended effective September 17, 2015.]

Commentary on Rule 18

Rule 18 is adapted largely from the Illustrative Rules.

Subsection (a) permits the subject judge, as well as the complainant, to petition for review of the chief judge's order dismissing a complaint under Rule 11(c), or concluding that appropriate corrective action or intervening events have remedied or mooted the problems raised by the complaint pursuant to Rule 11(d) or (e). Although the subject judge may ostensibly be vindicated by the dismissal or conclusion of a complaint, the chief judge's order may include language disagreeable to the subject judge. For example, an order may dismiss a complaint, but state that the subject judge did in fact engage in misconduct. Accordingly, a subject judge may wish to object to the content of the order and is given the opportunity to petition the judicial council of the circuit for review.

Subsection (b) contains a time limit of 42 days to file a petition for review. It is important to establish a time limit on petitions for review of chief judges' dispositions in order to provide finality to the process. If the complaint requires an investigation, the investigation should proceed; if it does not, the subject judge should know that the matter is closed.

The standards for timely filing under the Federal Rules of Appellate Procedure should be applied to petitions for review. *See* Fed. R. App. P. 25(a)(2)(A), (C).

Rule 18(e) provides for an automatic extension of the time limit imposed under subsection (b) if a person files a petition that is rejected for failure to comply with formal requirements.

RULE 19. JUDICIAL–COUNCIL DISPOSITION OF PETITION FOR REVIEW

(a) Rights of Subject Judge. At any time after a complainant files a petition for review, the subject judge may file a written response with the circuit clerk. The circuit clerk must promptly distribute copies of the response to each member of the judicial council or of the relevant panel, unless that member is disqualified under Rule 25. Copies must also be distributed to the chief judge, to the complainant, and to the Committee on Judicial Conduct and Disability. The subject judge must not otherwise communicate with individual judicial-council members about the matter. The subject judge must be given copies of any communications to the judicial council from the complainant.

(b) Judicial–Council Action. After considering a petition for review and the materials before it, the judicial council may:

(1) affirm the chief judge's disposition by denying the petition;

(2) return the matter to the chief judge with directions to conduct a further inquiry under Rule 11(b) or to identify a complaint under Rule 5;

(3) return the matter to the chief judge with directions to appoint a special committee under Rule 11(f); or

(4) in exceptional circumstances, take other appropriate action.

(c) Notice of Judicial–Council Decision. Copies of the judicial council's order, together with memoranda incorporated by reference in the order and separate concurring or dissenting statements, must be given to the complainant, the subject judge, and the Committee on Judicial Conduct and Disability.

(d) Memorandum of Judicial–Council Decision. If the judicial council's order affirms the chief judge's disposition, a supporting memorandum must be prepared only if the council concludes that there is a need to supplement the chief judge's explanation. A memorandum supporting a judicial-council order must not include the name of the complainant or the subject judge.

(e) Review of Judicial–Council Decision. If the judicial council's decision is adverse to the petitioner, and if no member of the council dissented, the complainant must be notified that he or she has no right to seek review of the decision. If there was a dissent, the petitioner must be informed that he or she can file a petition for review under Rule 21(b).

(f) Public Availability of Judicial–Council Decision. Materials related to the judicial council's decision must be made public to the extent, at the time, and in the manner set forth in Rule 24.

[Adopted March 11, 2008, effective April 10, 2008. Amended effective September 17, 2015.]

Commentary on Rule 19

This Rule is adapted largely from the Act and is self-explanatory.

The judicial council should ordinarily review the decision of the chief judge on the merits, treating the petition for review for all practical purposes as an appeal. The judicial council may respond to a petition for review by affirming the chief judge's order, remanding the matter, or, in exceptional cases, taking other appropriate action. A petition for review of a judicial council's decision may be filed under Rule 21(b) in any matter in which one or more members of the council dissented from the order.

RULE 20. JUDICIAL–COUNCIL ACTION FOLLOWING APPOINTMENT OF SPECIAL COMMITTEE

(a) Subject Judge's Rights. Within 21 days after the filing of the report of a special committee, the subject judge may send a written response to the members of the judicial council. The subject judge must also be given an opportunity to present argument, personally or through counsel, written or oral, as determined by the judicial council. The subject judge must not otherwise communicate with judicial-council members about the matter.

(b) Judicial–Council Action.

(1) *Discretionary Actions.* Subject to the subject judge's rights set forth in subsection (a), the judicial council may:

(A) dismiss the complaint because:

(i) even if the claim is true, the claimed conduct is not conduct prejudicial to the effective and expeditious administration of the business of the courts and does not indicate a mental or physical disability resulting in inability to discharge the duties of office;

(ii) the complaint is directly related to the merits of a decision or procedural ruling;

(iii) the facts on which the complaint is based have not been established; or

(iv) the complaint is otherwise not appropriate for consideration under 28 U.S.C. §§ 351–364.

(B) conclude the proceeding because appropriate corrective action has been taken or intervening events have made the proceeding unnecessary.

(C) refer the complaint to the Judicial Conference with the judicial council's recommendations for action.

(D) take remedial action to ensure the effective and expeditious administration of the business of the courts, including:

(i) censuring or reprimanding the subject judge, either by private communication or by public announcement;

(ii) ordering that no new cases be assigned to the subject judge for a limited, fixed period;

(iii) in the case of a magistrate judge, ordering the chief judge of the district court to take action specified by the council, including the initiation of removal proceedings under 28 U.S.C. § 631(i) or 42 U.S.C. § 300aa–12(c)(2);

(iv) in the case of a bankruptcy judge, removing the judge from office under 28 U.S.C. § 152(e);

(v) in the case of a circuit or district judge, requesting the judge to retire voluntarily with the provision (if necessary) that ordinary length-of-service requirements be waived;

(vi) in the case of a circuit or district judge who is eligible to retire but does not do so, certifying the disability of the judge under 28 U.S.C. § 372(b) so that an additional judge may be appointed; and

(vii) in the case of a circuit chief judge or district chief judge, finding that the judge is temporarily unable to perform chief-judge duties, with the result that those duties devolve to the next eligible judge in accordance with 28 U.S.C. § 45(d) or § 136(e).

(E) take any combination of actions described in (b)(1)(A)–(D) of this Rule that is within its power.

(2) *Mandatory Actions.* A judicial council must refer a complaint to the Judicial Conference if the council determines that a circuit judge or district judge may have engaged in conduct that:

(A) might constitute ground for impeachment; or

(B) in the interest of justice, is not amenable to resolution by the judicial council.

(c) Inadequate Basis for Decision. If the judicial council finds that a special committee's report, recommendations, and record provide an inadequate basis for decision, it may return the matter to the committee for further investigation and a new report, or it may conduct further investigation. If the judicial council decides to conduct further investigation, the subject judge must be given adequate prior notice in writing of that decision and of the general scope and purpose of the additional investigation. The judicial council's conduct of the additional investigation must generally accord with the procedures and powers set forth in Rules 13 through 16 for the conduct of an investigation by a special committee.

(d) Judicial–Council Vote. Judicial-council action must be taken by a majority of those members of the council who are not disqualified. A decision to remove a bankruptcy judge from office requires a majority vote of all the members of the judicial council.

(e) Recommendation for Fee Reimbursement. If the complaint has been finally dismissed or concluded under (b)(1)(A) or (B) of this Rule, and if the subject judge so requests, the judicial council may recommend that the Director of the Administrative Office use funds appropriated to the Judiciary to reimburse the judge for reasonable expenses incurred during the investigation, when those expenses would not have been incurred but for the requirements of the Act and these Rules. Reasonable expenses include attorneys' fees and expenses related to a successful defense or prosecution of a proceeding under Rule 21(a) or (b).

(f) Judicial–Council Order. Judicial-council action must be by written order. Unless the judicial council finds that extraordinary reasons would make it contrary to the interests of justice, the order must be accompanied by a memorandum setting forth the factual determinations on which it is based and the reasons for the council action. Such a memorandum may incorporate all or part of any underlying special-committee report. If the complaint was initiated by identification under Rule 5, the memorandum must so indicate. The order and memoranda incorporated by reference in the order must be provided to the complainant, the subject judge, and the Committee on Judicial Conduct and Disability. The complainant and the subject judge must be notified of any right to review of the judicial council's decision as provided in Rule 21(b). If the complaint was identified under Rule 5 or filed by its subject judge, the judicial council must transmit the order and memoranda incorporated by reference in the order to the Committee on Judicial Conduct and Disability for review in accordance with Rule 21. In the event of such a transmission, the subject judge may make a written submission to the Committee on Judicial Conduct and Disability but will have no further right of review.

[Adopted March 11, 2008, effective April 10, 2008. Amended effective September 17, 2015.]

Commentary on Rule 20

This Rule is largely adapted from the Illustrative Rules.

Rule 20(a) provides that within 21 days after the filing of the report of a special committee, the subject judge may address a written response to all of the members of the judicial council. The subject judge must also be given an opportunity to present argument to the judicial council, personally or through counsel, or both, at the direction of the council. Whether that argument is written or oral would be for the judicial council to determine. The subject judge may not otherwise communicate with judicial-council members about the matter.

Rule 20(b)(1)(D) recites the remedial actions enumerated in 28 U.S.C. § 354(a)(2) while making clear that this list is not exhaustive. A judicial council may consider lesser remedies. Some remedies may be unique to senior judges, whose caseloads can be modified by agreement or through statutory designation and certification processes.

Under 28 U.S.C. §§ 45(d) and 136(e), which provide for succession where "a chief judge is temporarily unable to perform his duties as such," the determination whether such an inability exists is not expressly reserved to the chief judge. Nor, indeed, is it assigned to any particular judge or court-governance body. Clearly, however, a chief judge's inability to function as chief could implicate "the effective and expeditious administration of justice," which the judicial council of the circuit must, under 28 U.S.C. § 332(d)(1), "make all necessary and appropriate orders" to secure. For this reason, such reassignment is among a judicial council's remedial options, as subsection (b)(1)(D)(vii) makes clear. Consistent with 28 U.S.C. §§ 45(d) and 136(e), however, any reassignment of chief-judge duties must not outlast the subject judge's inability to perform them. Nor can such reassignment result in any extension of the subject judge's term as chief judge.

Rule 20(c) provides that if the judicial council decides to conduct an additional investigation, the subject judge must be given adequate prior notice in writing of that decision and of the general scope and purpose of the additional investigation. The conduct of the investigation will be generally in accordance with the procedures set forth in Rules 13 through 16 for the conduct of an investigation by a special committee. However, if hearings are held, the judicial council may limit testimony or the presentation of evidence to avoid unnecessary repetition of testimony and evidence before the special committee.

Rule 20(d) provides that judicial-council action must be taken by a majority of those members of the council who are not disqualified, except that a decision to remove a bankruptcy judge from office requires a majority of all the members of the council as required by 28 U.S.C. § 152(e). However, it is inappropriate to apply a similar rule to the less severe actions that a judicial council may take under the Act. If some members of the judicial council are disqualified in the matter, their disqualification should not be given the effect of a vote against council action.

With regard to Rule 20(e), the judicial council, on the request of the subject judge, may recommend to the Director of the Administrative Office that the subject judge be reimbursed for reasonable expenses incurred, including attorneys' fees. The judicial council has the authority to recommend such reimbursement where, after investigation by a special committee, the complaint has been finally dismissed or concluded under subsection (b)(1)(A) or (B) of this Rule. It is contemplated that such reimbursement may be provided for the successful prosecution or defense of a proceeding under Rule 21(a) or (b), in other words, one that results in a Rule 20(b)(1)(A) or (B) dismissal or conclusion.

Rule 20(f) requires that judicial-council action be by order and, normally, that it be supported with a memorandum of factual determinations and reasons. Notice of the action must be given to the complainant and the subject judge, and must include notice of any right to petition for review of the judicial council's decision under Rule 21(b). Because an identified complaint has no "complainant" to petition for review, a judicial council's dispositive order on an identified complaint on which a special committee has been appointed must be transmitted to the Committee on Judicial Conduct and Disability for review. The same will apply where a complaint was filed by its subject judge.

ARTICLE VI. REVIEW BY COMMITTEE ON JUDICIAL CONDUCT AND DISABILITY

RULE 21. COMMITTEE ON JUDICIAL CONDUCT AND DISABILITY

(a) Committee Review. The Committee on Judicial Conduct and Disability, consisting of seven members, considers and disposes of all petitions for review under (b) of this Rule, in conformity with the Committee's jurisdictional statement. Its review of judicial-council orders is for errors of law, clear errors of fact, or abuse of discretion. Its disposition of petitions for review is ordinarily final. The Judicial Conference may, in its sole discretion, review any such Committee

decision, but a complainant or subject judge does not have a right to this review.

(b) Reviewable Matters.

(1) *Upon Petition.* A complainant or subject judge may petition the Committee for review of a judicial-council order entered in accordance with:

(A) Rule 20(b)(1)(A), (B), (D), or (E); or

(B) Rule 19(b)(1) or (4) if one or more members of the judicial council dissented from the order.

(2) *Upon Committee's Initiative.* At its initiative and in its sole discretion, the Committee may review any judicial-council order entered under Rule 19(b)(1) or (4), but only to determine whether a special committee should be appointed. Before undertaking the review, the Committee must invite that judicial council to explain why it believes the appointment of a special committee is unnecessary, unless the reasons are clearly stated in the council's order denying the petition for review. If the Committee believes that it would benefit from a submission by the subject judge, it may issue an appropriate request. If the Committee determines that a special committee should be appointed, the Committee must issue a written decision giving its reasons.

(c) **Committee Vote.** Any member of the Committee from the same circuit as the subject judge is disqualified from considering or voting on a petition for review related to that subject judge. Committee decisions under (b) of this Rule must be by majority vote of the qualified Committee members. Those members hearing the petition for review should serve in that capacity until final disposition of the petition, whether or not their term of Committee membership has ended. If only six members are qualified to consider a petition for review, the Chief Justice shall select an additional judge to join the qualified members to consider the petition. If four or fewer members are qualified to consider a petition for review, the Chief Justice shall select a panel of five judges, including the qualified Committee members, to consider it.

(d) **Additional Investigation.** Except in extraordinary circumstances, the Committee will not conduct an additional investigation. The Committee may return the matter to the judicial council with directions to undertake an additional investigation. If the Committee conducts an additional investigation, it will exercise the powers of the Judicial Conference under 28 U.S.C. § 331.

(e) **Oral Argument; Personal Appearance.** There is ordinarily no oral argument or personal appearance before the Committee. In its discretion, the Committee may permit written submissions.

(f) **Committee Decision.** A Committee decision under this Rule must be transmitted promptly to the Judicial Conference. Other distribution will be by the Administrative Office at the direction of the Committee chair.

(g) **Finality.** All orders of the Judicial Conference or of the Committee (when the Conference does not exercise its power of review) are final.

[Adopted March 11, 2008, effective April 10, 2008. Amended effective September 17, 2015.]

Commentary on Rule 21

This Rule is largely self-explanatory.

Rule 21(a) is intended to clarify that the delegation of power to the Committee on Judicial Conduct and Disability to dispose of petitions for review does not preclude review of such dispositions by the Judicial Conference. However, there is no right to such review in any party.

Rules 21(b)(1)(B) and (b)(2) are intended to fill a jurisdictional gap as to review of a dismissal or a conclusion of a complaint under Rule 19(b)(1) or (4). Where one or more members of a judicial council reviewing a petition have dissented, the complainant or the subject judge has the right to petition for review by the Committee. Under Rule 21(b)(2), the Committee may review such a dismissal or conclusion in its sole discretion, whether or not a dissent occurred, and only as to the appointment of a special committee. Any review under Rule 21(b)(2) will be conducted as soon as practicable after the dismissal or conclusion at issue. No party has a right to such review, and such review will be rare.

Rule 21(c) provides for review only by Committee members from circuits other than that of the subject judge. The Rule provides that every petition for review must be considered and voted on by at least five, and if possible by seven, qualified Committee members to avoid the possibility of tie votes. If six, or four or fewer, members are qualified, the Chief Justice shall appoint other judges to join the qualified members to consider the petition for review. To the extent possible, the judges whom the Chief Justice selects to join the qualified members should be drawn from among former members of the Committee.

Under this Rule, all Committee decisions are final in that they are unreviewable unless the Judicial Conference, in its discretion, decides to review a decision. Committee decisions, however, do not necessarily constitute final action on a complaint for purposes of Rule 24.

RULE 22. PROCEDURES FOR REVIEW

(a) **Filing Petition for Review.** A petition for review of a judicial-council decision on a complaint referred to a special committee may be filed by sending a brief written statement to the Committee on Judicial Conduct and Disability at JCD_Petitionfor Review@ao.uscourts.gov or to:

> Judicial Conference Committee on Judicial Conduct and Disability
> Attn: Office of General Counsel
> Administrative Office of the United States Courts
> One Columbus Circle, NE
> Washington, D.C. 20544

The Administrative Office will send a copy of the petition for review to the complainant or subject judge, as the case may be.

(b) **Form and Contents of Petition.** No particular form is required. The petition for review must contain a short statement of the basic facts underlying the complaint, the history of its consideration before the appropriate judicial council, a copy of the council's decision, and the grounds on which the petitioner seeks review. The petition for review must specify the date and docket number of the judicial council order for which review is sought. The petitioner may attach any documents or correspondence arising in the course of the proceeding before the judicial council or its special committee. A petition for review should not normally exceed 20 pages plus necessary attachments. A petition for review must be signed by the petitioner or his or her attorney.

(c) Time. A petition for review must be submitted within 42 days after the date of the order for which review is sought.

(d) Action on Receipt of Petition. When a petition for review of a judicial-council decision on a complaint referred to a special committee is submitted in accordance with this Rule, the Administrative Office shall acknowledge its receipt, notify the chair of the Committee on Judicial Conduct and Disability, and distribute the petition to the members of the Committee for their deliberation.

[Adopted March 11, 2008, effective April 10, 2008. Amended effective September 17, 2015.]

Commentary on Rule 22

Rule 22 is self-explanatory.

ARTICLE VII. MISCELLANEOUS RULES

RULE 23. CONFIDENTIALITY

(a) General Rule. The consideration of a complaint by a chief judge, a special committee, a judicial council, or the Committee on Judicial Conduct and Disability is confidential. Information about this consideration must not be disclosed by any judge or employee of the Judiciary or by any person who records or transcribes testimony except as allowed by these Rules. A chief judge may disclose the existence of a proceeding under these Rules when necessary or appropriate to maintain public confidence in the Judiciary's ability to redress misconduct or disability.

(b) Files. All files related to a complaint must be separately maintained with appropriate security precautions to ensure confidentiality.

(c) Disclosure in Decisions. Except as otherwise provided in Rule 24, written decisions of a chief judge, a judicial council, or the Committee on Judicial Conduct and Disability, and dissenting opinions or separate statements of members of a council or the Committee may contain information and exhibits that the authors consider appropriate for inclusion, and the information and exhibits may be made public.

(d) Availability to Judicial Conference. On request of the Judicial Conference or its Committee on Judicial Conduct and Disability, the circuit clerk must furnish any requested records related to a complaint. For auditing purposes, the circuit clerk must provide access to the Committee on Judicial Conduct and Disability to records of proceedings under the Act at the site where the records are kept.

(e) Availability to District Court. If the judicial council directs the initiation of proceedings for removal of a magistrate judge under Rule 20(b)(1)(D)(iii), the circuit clerk must provide to the chief judge of the district court copies of the report of the special committee and any other documents and records that were before the council at the time of its decision. On request of the chief judge of the district court, the judicial council may authorize release to that chief judge of any other records relating to the investigation.

(f) Impeachment Proceedings. If the Judicial Conference determines that consideration of impeachment may be warranted, it must transmit the record of all relevant proceedings to the Speaker of the House of Representatives.

(g) Subject Judge's Consent. If both the subject judge and the chief judge consent in writing, any materials from the files may be disclosed to any person. In any such disclosure, the chief judge may require that the identity of the complainant, or of witnesses in an investigation conducted under these Rules, not be revealed.

(h) Disclosure in Special Circumstances. The Judicial Conference, its Committee on Judicial Conduct and Disability, or a judicial council may authorize disclosure of information about the consideration of a complaint, including the papers, documents, and transcripts relating to the investigation, to the extent that disclosure is justified by special circumstances and is not prohibited by the Act. Disclosure may be made to judicial researchers engaged in the study or evaluation of experience under the Act and related modes of judicial discipline, but only where the study or evaluation has been specifically approved by the Judicial Conference or by the Committee on Judicial Conduct and Disability. Appropriate steps must be taken to protect the identities of the subject judge, the complainant, and witnesses from public disclosure. Other appropriate safeguards to protect against the dissemination of confidential information may be imposed.

(i) Disclosure of Identity by Subject Judge. Nothing in this Rule precludes the subject judge from acknowledging that he or she is the judge referred to in documents made public under Rule 24.

(j) Assistance and Consultation. Nothing in this Rule prohibits a chief judge, a special committee, a judicial council, or the Judicial Conference or its Committee on Judicial Conduct and Disability, in the performance of any function authorized under the Act or these Rules, from seeking the help of qualified staff or experts or from consulting other judges who may be helpful regarding the performance of that function.

[Adopted March 11, 2008, effective April 10, 2008. Amended effective September 17, 2015.]

Commentary on Rule 23

Rule 23 was adapted from the Illustrative Rules.

The Act applies a rule of confidentiality to "papers, documents, and records of proceedings related to investigations conducted under this chapter" and states that they may not be disclosed "by any person in any proceeding," with enumerated exceptions. 28 U.S.C. § 360(a). Three questions arise: Who is bound by the confidentiality rule, what proceedings are subject to the rule, and who is within the circle of people who may have access to information without breaching the rule?

With regard to the first question, Rule 23(a) provides that judges, employees of the Judiciary, and those persons involved in recording proceedings and preparing transcripts are obliged to respect the confidentiality requirement. This of course includes subject judges who do not consent to identification under Rule 23(i).

With regard to the second question, Rule 23(a) applies the rule of confidentiality broadly to consideration of a complaint at any stage.

With regard to the third question, there is no barrier of confidentiality among a chief judge, a judicial council, the Judicial Conference, and the Committee on Judicial Conduct and Disability. Each may have access to any of the confidential records for use in their consideration of a referred matter, a petition for review, or monitoring the administration of the Act. A district court may have similar access if the judicial council orders the district court to initiate proceedings to remove a magistrate judge from office, and Rule 23(e) so provides.

In extraordinary circumstances, a chief judge may disclose the existence of a proceeding under these Rules. The disclosure of such information in high-visibility or controversial cases is to reassure the public that the Judiciary is capable of redressing judicial misconduct or disability. Moreover, the confidentiality requirement does not prevent the chief judge from "communicat[ing] orally or in writing with . . . [persons] who may have knowledge of the matter" as part of a limited inquiry conducted by the chief judge under Rule 11(b).

Rule 23 recognizes that there must be some exceptions to the Act's confidentiality requirement. For example, the Act requires that certain orders and the reasons for them must be made public. 28 U.S.C. § 360(b). Rule 23(c) makes it explicit that written decisions, as well as dissenting opinions and separate statements, may contain references to information that would otherwise be confidential and that such information may be made public. However, subsection (c) is subject to Rule 24(a), which provides the general rule regarding the public availability of decisions. For example, the name of a subject judge cannot be made public in a decision if disclosure of the name is prohibited by that Rule.

The Act makes clear that there is a barrier of confidentiality between the judicial branch and the legislative branch. It provides that material may be disclosed to Congress only if it is believed necessary to an impeachment investigation or trial of a judge. 28 U.S.C. § 360(a)(2). Accordingly, Section 355(b) of the Act requires the Judicial Conference to transmit the record of a proceeding to the House of Representatives if the Conference believes that impeachment of a subject judge may be appropriate. Rule 23(f) implements this requirement.

The Act provides that confidential materials may be disclosed if authorized in writing by the subject judge and by the chief judge. 28 U.S.C. § 360(a)(3). Rule 23(g) implements this requirement. Once the subject judge has consented to the disclosure of confidential materials related to a complaint, the chief judge ordinarily will refuse consent only to the extent necessary to protect the confidentiality interests of the complainant or of witnesses who have testified in investigatory proceedings or who have provided information in response to a limited inquiry undertaken pursuant to Rule 11. It will generally be necessary, therefore, for the chief judge to require that the identities of the complainant or of such witnesses, as well as any identifying information, be shielded in any materials disclosed, except insofar as the chief judge has secured the consent of the complainant or of a particular witness to disclosure, or there is a demonstrated need for disclosure of the information that, in the judgment of the chief judge, outweighs the confidentiality interest of the complainant or of a particular witness (as may be the case where the complainant is delusional or where the complainant or a particular witness has already demonstrated a lack of concern about maintaining the confidentiality of the proceedings).

Rule 23(h) permits disclosure of additional information in circumstances not enumerated. For example, disclosure may be appropriate to permit a prosecution for perjury based on testimony given before a special committee. Another example might involve evidence of criminal conduct by a judge discovered by a special committee.

Subsection (h) also permits the authorization of disclosure of information about the consideration of a complaint, including the papers, documents, and transcripts relating to the investigation, to judicial researchers engaged in the study or evaluation of experience under the Act and related modes of judicial discipline. The Rule envisions disclosure of information from the official record of a complaint proceeding to a limited category of persons for appropriately authorized research purposes only, and with appropriate safeguards to protect individual identities in any published research results. In authorizing disclosure, a judicial council may refuse to release particular materials when such release would be contrary to the interests of justice, or when those materials constitute purely internal communications. The Rule does not envision disclosure of purely internal communications between judges and their colleagues and staff.

Under Rule 23(j), any of the specified judges or entities performing a function authorized under these Rules may seek expert or staff assistance or may consult with other judges who may be helpful regarding performance of that function; the confidentiality requirement does not preclude this. A chief judge, for example, may properly seek the advice and assistance of another judge who the chief judge deems to be in the best position to communicate with the subject judge in an attempt to bring about corrective action. As another example, a new chief judge may wish to confer with a predecessor to learn how similar complaints have been handled. In consulting with other judges, of course, a chief judge should disclose information regarding the complaint only to the extent the chief judge deems necessary under the circumstances.

RULE 24. PUBLIC AVAILABILITY OF DECISIONS

(a) General Rule; Specific Cases. When final action has been taken on a complaint and it is no longer subject to review, all orders entered by the chief judge and judicial council, including memoranda incorporated by reference in those orders and any dissenting opinions or separate statements by members of the judicial council, but excluding any orders under Rule 5 or 11(f), must be made public, with the following exceptions:

(1) if the complaint is finally dismissed under Rule 11(c) without the appointment of a special committee, or if it is concluded under Rule 11(d) because of voluntary corrective action, the publicly available materials must not disclose the name of the subject judge without his or her consent.

(2) if the complaint is concluded because of intervening events, or dismissed at any time after a special committee is appointed, the judicial council must determine whether the name of the subject judge should be disclosed.

(3) if the complaint is finally disposed of by a privately communicated censure or reprimand, the publicly available materials must not disclose either the name of the subject judge or the text of the reprimand.

(4) if the complaint is finally disposed of under Rule 20(b)(1)(D) by any action other than private censure or reprimand, the text of the dispositive order must be included in the materials made public, and the name of the subject judge must be disclosed.

(5) the name of the complainant must not be disclosed in materials made public under this Rule unless the chief judge orders disclosure.

(b) Manner of Making Public. The orders described in (a) must be made public by placing them in a publicly accessible file in the office of the circuit clerk and by placing the orders on the court's public website. If the orders appear to have precedential value, the chief judge may cause them to be published. In addition, the Committee on Judicial Conduct and Disability will make available on the Judiciary's website, www.uscourts.gov, selected illustrative orders described in paragraph (a), appropriately redacted, to provide additional information to the public on how complaints are addressed under the Act.

(c) Orders of Committee on Judicial Conduct and Disability. Orders of the Committee on Judicial Conduct and Disability constituting final action in a complaint proceeding arising from a particular circuit will be made available to the public in the office of the circuit clerk of the relevant court of appeals. The Committee on Judicial Conduct and Disability will also

make such orders available on the Judiciary's website, www.uscourts.gov. When authorized by the Committee on Judicial Conduct and Disability, other orders related to complaint proceedings will similarly be made available.

(d) Complaint Referred to Judicial Conference. If a complaint is referred to the Judicial Conference under Rule 20(b)(1)(C) or 20(b)(2), materials relating to the complaint will be made public only if ordered by the Judicial Conference.

[Adopted March 11, 2008, effective April 10, 2008. Amended effective September 17, 2015.]

Commentary on Rule 24

Rule 24 is adapted from the Illustrative Rules and the recommendations of the Breyer Committee.

The Act requires the circuits to make available only written orders of a judicial council or the Judicial Conference imposing some form of sanction. 28 U.S.C. § 360(b). The Judicial Conference, however, has long recognized the desirability of public availability of a broader range of orders and other materials. In 1994, the Judicial Conference "urge[d] all circuits and courts covered by the Act to submit to the West Publishing Company, for publication in Federal Reporter 3d, and to Lexis all orders issued pursuant to [the Act] that are deemed by the issuing circuit or court to have significant precedential value to other circuits and courts covered by the Act." Report of the Proceedings of the Judicial Conference of the United States, Mar. 1994, at 28. Following this recommendation, the 2000 revision of the Illustrative Rules contained a public availability provision very similar to Rule 24. In 2002, the Judicial Conference again voted to encourage the circuits "to submit non-routine public orders disposing of complaints of judicial misconduct or disability for publication by on-line and print services." Report of the Proceedings of the Judicial Conference of the United States, Sept. 2002, at 58. The Breyer Committee Report further emphasized that "[p]osting such orders on the judicial branch's public website would not only benefit judges directly, it would also encourage scholarly commentary and analysis of the orders." Breyer Committee Report, 239 F.R.D. at 216. With these considerations in mind, Rule 24 provides for public availability of a wide range of materials.

Rule 24 provides for public availability of orders of a chief judge, a judicial council, and the Committee on Judicial Conduct and Disability, as well as the texts of memoranda incorporated by reference in those orders, together with any dissenting opinions or separate statements by members of the judicial council. No memoranda other than those incorporated by reference in those orders shall be disclosed. However, these orders and memoranda are to be made public only when final action on the complaint has been taken and any right of review has been exhausted. The provision that decisions will be made public only after final action has been taken is designed in part to avoid public disclosure of the existence of pending proceedings. Whether the name of the subject judge is disclosed will then depend on the nature of the final action. If the final action is an order predicated on a finding of misconduct or disability (other than a privately communicated censure or reprimand) the name of the subject judge must be made public. If the final action is dismissal of the complaint, the name of the subject judge must not be disclosed. Rule 24(a)(1) provides that where a proceeding is concluded under Rule 11(d) by the chief judge on the basis of voluntary corrective action, the name of the subject judge must not be disclosed. Shielding the name of the subject judge in this circumstance should encourage informal disposition.

If a complaint is dismissed as moot, or because intervening events have made action on the complaint unnecessary, after appointment of a special committee, Rule 24(a)(2) allows the judicial council to determine whether the subject judge will be identified. In such a case, no final decision has been rendered on the merits, but it may be in the public interest—particularly if a judicial officer resigns in the course of an investigation—to make the identity of the subject judge known.

Once a special committee has been appointed, and a proceeding is concluded by the full judicial council on the basis of a remedial order of the council, Rule 24(a)(4) provides for disclosure of the name of the subject judge.

Rule 24(a)(5) provides that the identity of the complainant will be disclosed only if the chief judge so orders. Identifying the complainant when the subject judge is not identified would increase the likelihood that the identity of the subject judge would become publicly known, thus circumventing the policy of nondisclosure. It may not always be practicable to shield the complainant's identity while making public disclosure of the judicial council's order and supporting memoranda; in some circumstances, moreover, the complainant may consent to public identification.

Rule 24(b) makes clear that circuits must post on their external websites all orders required to be made public under Rule 24(a).

Matters involving orders issued following a special-committee investigation often involve highly sensitive situations, and it is important that judicial councils have every opportunity to reach a correct and just outcome. This would include the ability to reach informal resolution before a subject judge's identity must be released. But there must also come a point of procedural finality. The date of finality—and thus the time at which other safeguards and rules such as the publication requirement are triggered—is the date on which the judicial council issues a Final Order. *See In re Complaint of Judicial Misconduct*, 751 F.3d 611, 617 (2014) (requiring publication of a judicial-council order "[e]ven though the period for review had not yet elapsed" and concluding that "the order was a final decision because the Council had adjudicated the matter on the merits after having received a report from a special investigating committee"). As determined in the cited case, modifications of this kind to a final order are subject to review by the Committee on Judicial Conduct and Disability.

RULE 25. DISQUALIFICATION

(a) General Rule. Any judge is disqualified from participating in any proceeding under these Rules if the judge, in his or her discretion, concludes that circumstances warrant disqualification. If a complaint is filed by a judge, that judge is disqualified from participating in any consideration of the complaint except to the extent that these Rules provide for a complainant's participation. A chief judge who has identified a complaint under Rule 5 is not automatically disqualified from considering the complaint.

(b) Subject Judge. A subject judge is disqualified from considering a complaint except to the extent that these Rules provide for participation by a subject judge.

(c) Chief Judge Disqualified From Considering Petition for Review of Chief Judge's Order. If a petition for review of the chief judge's order entered under Rule 11(c), (d), or (e) is filed with the judicial council in accordance with Rule 18, the chief judge is disqualified from participating in the council's consideration of the petition.

(d) Member of Special Committee Not Disqualified. A member of the judicial council who serves on a special committee, including the chief judge, is not disqualified from participating in council consideration of the committee's report.

(e) Subject Judge's Disqualification After Appointment of Special Committee. Upon appointment of a special committee, the subject judge is disqualified from participating in the identification or consideration of any complaint, related or unrelated to the pending matter, under the Act or these Rules. The disqualification continues until all proceedings on the complaint against the subject judge are finally terminated with no further right of review.

(f) Substitute for Disqualified Chief Judge. If the chief judge is disqualified from performing duties that the Act and these Rules assign to a chief judge, those duties must be assigned to the most-senior active circuit judge not disqualified. If all circuit judges in regular active service are disqualified, the judicial council may determine whether to request a transfer under Rule 26, or, in the interest of sound judicial administration, to permit the chief judge to dispose of the complaint on the merits. Members of the judicial council who are named in the complaint may participate in this determination if necessary to obtain a quorum of the council.

(g) Judicial–Council Action When Multiple Judges Disqualified. Notwithstanding any other provision in these Rules to the contrary,

(1) a member of the judicial council who is a subject judge may participate in its disposition if:

(A) participation by one or more subject judges is necessary to obtain a quorum of the judicial council;

(B) the judicial council finds that the lack of a quorum is due to the naming of one or more judges in the complaint for the purpose of disqualifying that judge or those judges, or to the naming of one or more judges based on their participation in a decision excluded from the definition of misconduct under Rule 3(h)(3); and

(C) the judicial council votes that it is necessary, appropriate, and in the interest of sound judicial administration that one or more subject judges be eligible to act.

(2) otherwise disqualified members may participate in votes taken under (g)(1)(B) and (g)(1)(C).

(h) Disqualification of Members of Committee on Judicial Conduct and Disability. No member of the Committee on Judicial Conduct and Disability is disqualified from participating in any proceeding under the Act or these Rules because of consultations with a chief judge, a member of a special committee, or a member of a judicial council about the interpretation or application of the Act or these Rules, unless the member believes that the consultation would prevent fair-minded participation.

[Adopted March 11, 2008, effective April 10, 2008. Amended effective September 17, 2015.]

Commentary on Rule 25

Rule 25 is adapted from the Illustrative Rules.

Subsection (a) provides the general rule for disqualification. Of course, a judge is not disqualified simply because the subject judge is on the same court. However, this subsection recognizes that there may be cases in which an appearance of bias or prejudice is created by circumstances other than an association with the subject judge as a colleague. For example, a judge may have a familial relationship with a complainant or subject judge. When such circumstances exist, a judge may, in his or her discretion, conclude that disqualification is warranted.

Subsection (e) makes it clear that the disqualification of the subject judge relates only to the subject judge's participation in any proceeding arising under the Act or these Rules. For example, the subject judge cannot initiate complaints by identification, conduct limited inquiries, or choose between dismissal and special-committee investigation as the threshold disposition of a complaint. Likewise, the subject judge cannot participate in any proceeding arising under the Act or these Rules as a member of any special committee, the judicial council of the circuit, the Judicial Conference, or the Committee on Judicial Conduct and Disability. The Illustrative Rule, based on Section 359(a) of the Act, is ambiguous and could be read to disqualify a subject judge from service of any kind on each of the bodies mentioned. This is undoubtedly not the intent of the Act; such a disqualification would be anomalous in light of the Act's allowing a subject judge to continue to decide cases and to continue to exercise the powers of chief circuit or district judge. It would also create a substantial deterrence to the appointment of special committees, particularly where a special committee is needed solely because the chief judge may not decide matters of credibility in his or her review under Rule 11.

While a subject judge is barred by Rule 25(b) from participating in the disposition of the complaint in which he or she is named, Rule 25(e) recognizes that participation in proceedings arising under the Act or these Rules by a judge who is the subject of a special committee investigation may lead to an appearance of self-interest in creating substantive and procedural precedents governing such proceedings. Rule 25(e) bars such participation.

Under the Act, a complaint against the chief judge is to be handled by "that circuit judge in regular active service next senior in date of commission." 28 U.S.C. § 351(c). The Rules do not purport to prescribe who is to preside over meetings of the judicial council. Consequently, where the presiding member of the judicial council is disqualified from participating under these Rules, the order of precedence prescribed by Rule 25(f) for performing "the duties and responsibilities of the chief circuit judge under these Rules" does not apply to determine the acting presiding member of the council. That is a matter left to the internal rules or operating practices of each judicial council. In most cases the most senior active circuit judge who is a member of the judicial council and who is not disqualified will preside.

Sometimes a single complaint is filed against a large group of judges. If the normal disqualification rules are observed in such a case, no court of appeals judge can serve as acting chief judge of the circuit, and the judicial council will be without appellate members. Where the complaint is against all circuit and district judges, under normal rules no member of the judicial council can perform the duties assigned to the council under the statute.

A similar problem is created by successive complaints arising out of the same underlying grievance. For example, a complainant files a complaint against a district judge based on alleged misconduct, and the complaint is dismissed by the chief judge under the statute. The complainant may then file a complaint against the chief judge for dismissing the first complaint, and when that complaint is dismissed by the next senior judge, still a third complaint may be filed. The threat is that the complainant will bump down the seniority ladder until, once again, there is no member of the court of appeals who can serve as acting chief judge for the purpose of the next complaint. Similarly, complaints involving the merits of litigation may involve a series of decisions in which many judges participated or in which a rehearing en banc was denied by the court of appeals, and the complaint may name a majority of the judicial council as subject judges.

In recognition that these multiple-judge complaints are virtually always meritless, the judicial council is given discretion to determine: (1) whether it is necessary, appropriate, and in the interest of sound judicial administration to permit the chief judge to dispose of a complaint where it would otherwise be impossible for any active circuit judge in the circuit to act, and (2) whether it is necessary, appropriate, and in the interest of sound judicial administration, after appropriate findings as to need and justification are made, to permit subject judges of the judicial council to participate in the disposition of a petition for review where it would otherwise be impossible to obtain a quorum.

Applying a rule of necessity in these situations is consistent with the appearance of justice. *See, e.g., In re Complaint of Doe,* 2 F.3d 308 (8th Cir. Jud. Council 1993) (invoking the rule of necessity); *In re Complaint of Judicial Misconduct,* No. 91–80464 (9th Cir. Jud. Council 1992) (same). There is no unfairness in permitting the chief judge to dispose of a patently insubstantial complaint that names all active circuit judges in the circuit.

Similarly, there is no unfairness in permitting subject judges, in these circumstances, to participate in the review of the chief judge's dismissal of an insubstantial complaint. The remaining option is to assign the matter to another body. Among other alternatives, the judicial council may request a transfer of the petition under Rule 26. Given the administrative inconvenience and delay involved in these alternatives, it is desirable to request a transfer only if the judicial council determines that the petition for review is substantial enough to warrant such action.

In the unlikely event that a quorum of the judicial council cannot be obtained to consider the report of a special committee, it would normally be necessary to request a transfer under Rule 26.

Rule 25(h) recognizes that the jurisdictional statement of the Committee on Judicial Conduct and Disability contemplates consultation between members of the Committee and judicial participants in proceedings under the Act and these Rules. Such consultation should not automatically preclude participation by a member in that proceeding.

RULE 26. TRANSFER TO ANOTHER JUDICIAL COUNCIL

In exceptional circumstances, the chief judge or the judicial council may ask the Chief Justice to transfer a proceeding based on a complaint identified under Rule 5 or filed under Rule 6 to the judicial council of another circuit. The request for a transfer may be made at any stage of the proceeding before a reference to the Judicial Conference under Rule 20(b)(1)(C) or 20(b)(2) or a petition for review is filed under Rule 22. Upon receiving such a request, the Chief Justice may refuse the request or select the transferee judicial council, which may then exercise the powers of a judicial council under these Rules.

[Adopted March 11, 2008, effective April 10, 2008. Amended effective September 17, 2015.]

Commentary on Rule 26

Rule 26 is new; it implements the Breyer Committee's recommended use of transfers. Breyer Committee Report, 239 F.R.D. at 214–15.

Rule 26 authorizes the transfer of a complaint proceeding to another judicial council selected by the Chief Justice. Such transfers may be appropriate, for example, in the case of a serious complaint where there are multiple disqualifications among the original judicial council, where the issues are highly visible and a local disposition may weaken public confidence in the process, where internal tensions arising in the council as a result of the complaint render disposition by a less involved council appropriate, or where a complaint calls into question policies or governance of the home court of appeals. The power to effect a transfer is lodged in the Chief Justice to avoid disputes in a judicial council over where to transfer a sensitive matter and to ensure that the transferee council accepts the matter.

Upon receipt of a transferred proceeding, the transferee judicial council shall determine the proper stage at which to begin consideration of the complaint—for example, reference to the transferee chief judge, appointment of a special committee, etc.

RULE 27. WITHDRAWAL OF COMPLAINT OR PETITION FOR REVIEW

(a) Complaint Pending Before Chief Judge. With the chief judge's consent, the complainant may withdraw a complaint that is before the chief judge for a decision under Rule 11. The withdrawal of a complaint will not prevent the chief judge from identifying or having to identify a complaint under Rule 5 based on the withdrawn complaint.

(b) Complaint Pending Before Special Committee or Judicial Council. After a complaint has been referred to the special committee for investigation and before the committee files its report, the complainant may withdraw the complaint only with the consent of both the subject judge and either the special committee or the judicial council.

(c) Petition for Review. A petition for review addressed to the judicial council under Rule 18, or the Committee on Judicial Conduct and Disability under Rule 22, may be withdrawn if no action on the petition has been taken.

[Adopted March 11, 2008, effective April 10, 2008. Amended effective September 17, 2015.]

Commentary on Rule 27

Rule 27 is adapted from the Illustrative Rules and treats the complaint proceeding, once begun, as a matter of public business rather than as the property of the complainant. Accordingly, the chief judge or the judicial council remains responsible for addressing any complaint under the Act, even a complaint that has been formally withdrawn by the complainant.

Under subsection (a), a complaint pending before the chief judge may be withdrawn if the chief judge consents. Where the complaint clearly lacked merit, the chief judge may accordingly be saved the burden of preparing a formal order and supporting memorandum. However, the chief judge may, or be obligated under Rule 5, to identify a complaint based on allegations in a withdrawn complaint.

If the chief judge appoints a special committee, Rule 27(b) provides that the complaint may be withdrawn only with the consent of both the body before which it is pending (the special committee or the judicial council) and the subject judge. Once a complaint has reached the stage of appointment of a special committee, a resolution of the issues may be necessary to preserve public confidence. Moreover, the subject judge is given the right to insist that the matter be resolved on the merits, thereby eliminating any ambiguity that might remain if the proceeding were terminated by withdrawal of the complaint.

With regard to all petitions for review, Rule 27(c) grants the petitioner unrestricted authority to withdraw the petition. It is thought that the public's interest in the proceeding is adequately protected, because there will necessarily have been a decision by the chief judge and often by the judicial council as well in such a case.

RULE 28. AVAILABILITY OF RULES AND FORMS

These Rules and copies of the complaint form as provided in Rule 6(a) must be available without charge in the office of the circuit clerk of each court of appeals, district court, bankruptcy court, or other federal court whose judges are subject to the Act. Each court must also make these Rules, the complaint form, and complaint-filing instructions available on the court's website, or provide an Internet link to these items on the appropriate court of appeals website or on www.uscourts.gov.

[Adopted March 11, 2008, effective April 10, 2008. Amended effective September 17, 2015.]

RULE 29.   EFFECTIVE DATE

These Rules will become effective 30 days after promulgation by the Judicial Conference of the United States.

[Adopted March 11, 2008, effective April 10, 2008.]

APPENDIX

Complaint Form

Judicial Council of the _____ Circuit

COMPLAINT OF JUDICIAL MISCONDUCT OR DISABILITY

To begin the complaint process, complete this form and prepare the brief statement of facts described in item 4 (below). The Rules for Judicial–Conduct and Judicial–Disability Proceedings, adopted by the Judicial Conference of the United States, contain information on what to include in a complaint (Rule 6), where to file a complaint (Rule 7), and other important matters. The Rules are available in federal court clerks' offices, on individual federal courts' websites, and on www.uscourts.gov.

Your complaint (this form and the statement of facts) should be typewritten and must be legible. For the number of copies to file, consult the local rules or clerk's office of the court in which your complaint is required to be filed. Enclose each copy of the complaint in an envelope marked "COMPLAINT OF MISCONDUCT" or "COMPLAINT OF DISABILITY" and submit it to the appropriate clerk of court. **Do not put the name of any judge on the envelope.**

1.   Name of Complainant: _____
       Contact Address: _____
       _____
       Daytime telephone: (_____) _____

2.   Name(s) of Judge(s): _____
       Court: _____

3.   Does this complaint concern the behavior of the judge(s) in a particular lawsuit or lawsuits?
       [ ] Yes   [ ] No
       If "yes," give the following information about each lawsuit:
       Court: _____
       Case Number: _____
       Docket number of any appeal to the _____ Circuit: _____
       Are (were) you a party or lawyer in the lawsuit?
       [ ] Party   [ ] Lawyer   [ ] Neither
       If you are (were) a party and have (had) a lawyer, give the lawyer's name, address, and telephone number:
       _____
       _____
       _____

4.   **Brief Statement of Facts.** Attach a brief statement of the specific facts on which the claim of judicial misconduct or disability is based. Include what happened, when and where it happened, and any information that would help an investigator check the facts. If the complaint alleges judicial disability, also include any additional facts that form the basis of that allegation.

5.   **Declaration and signature:**
       I declare under penalty of perjury that the statements made in this complaint are true and correct to the best of my knowledge.

(Signature)_____ (Date)_____

[Adopted March 11, 2008, effective April 10, 2008. Amended effective September 17, 2015.]

SELECTED ORDERS AND NOTICES

STANDING ORDER REGARDING MOTIONS TO EXCEED THE PAGE LIMITATIONS OF THE FEDERAL RULES OF APPELLATE PROCEDURE

Effective Immediately

PRESENT: McKEE, **Chief Judge**, and SLOVITER, SCIRICA, RENDELL, AMBRO, FUENTES, SMITH, FISHER, CHAGARES, JORDAN, HARDIMAN, GREENAWAY, JR, VANASKIE, ALDISERT, WEIS, GARTH, STAPLETON, GREENBERG, COWEN, NYGAARD, ROTH, BARRY, and VAN ANTWERPEN, **Circuit Judges**

AND NOW, it being noted that motions to exceed the page/word limitations for briefs are filed in approximately twenty-five percent of cases on appeal, and that seventy-one percent of those motions seek to exceed the page/word limitations by more than twenty percent;

Notice is hereby given that motions to exceed the page or word limitations for briefs are strongly disfavored and will be granted only upon demonstration of extraordinary circumstances. Such circumstances may include multi-appellant consolidated appeals in which the appellee seeks to file a single responsive brief or complex/consolidated proceedings in which the parties are seeking to file jointly or the subject matter clearly requires expansion of the page or word limitations.

Accordingly, it is **ORDERED** that a three-judge Standing Motions Panel is hereby appointed to rule on all motions to exceed the page/word limitations for briefs since the page/word limitations, prescribed by Fed. R. App. P. 32(a)(7), should be sufficient to address all issues in an appeal.

It is further **ORDERED** that Counsel are advised to seek advance approval of requests to exceed the page/word limitations whenever possible or run the risk of rewriting and refiling a compliant brief. Any request to exceed page/word limitations submitted in the absence of such an advance request shall include an explanation of why counsel could not have foreseen any difficulty in complying with the limitations in time to seek advance approval from the panel.

This order shall not apply to capital habeas cases.

[Dated: January 9, 2012.]

Per Curiam,

/s/ Theodore A. McKee
Chief Judge

NOTICE TO COUNSEL—MOTIONS FOR EXTENSION OF TIME DISFAVORED

Due to greater efficiencies in processing, the Clerk's Office is able to schedule cases before a merits panel shortly after the close of briefing. Counsel are expected to comply with deadlines set forth in the rules or in scheduling orders. Motions for extension of time to file a brief or to otherwise comply with the rules are disfavored. Motions seeking lengthy extensions and repeated motions for extensions of time may be denied.

[Dated: October 15, 2012.]

INDEX TO UNITED STATES COURT OF APPEALS
FOR THE THIRD CIRCUIT

UNITED STATES DISTRICT COURT FOR THE EASTERN DISTRICT OF PENNSYLVANIA

Including Amendments Received Through
June 1, 2016

---

14. Discovery Costs.
15. Trial Depositions.

LOCAL RULES OF CIVIL PROCEDURE

RULE 1.1 EFFECTIVE DATE; REVOCATION OF PRIOR RULES

The Rules of Civil Procedure of the United States District Court for the Eastern District of Pennsylvania are adopted this 22nd day of May, 1995, and shall become effective on the 1st day of July, 1995, as amended January 21, 1997, March 3, 1997, August 3, 1998, October 24, 2003, June 2, 2004, February 15, 2005, April 2, 2007 and December 1, 2009.

[Effective July 1, 1995. Amended effective April 2, 2007; December 1, 2009.]

RULE 1.1.1 STANDING ORDERS; EFFECT UPON

The following Standing Orders are in effect and copies may be obtained from the Office of the Clerk of Court:

(a) Court Approval of Reporters Required for Taking Depositions, dated June 30, 1959;

(b) Calendar Control, dated January 1, 1970;

(c) Civil Suspense Docket, dated June 24, 1975;

(d) Bankruptcy Administration Orders dated July 25, 1984, November 8, 1990, and June 29, 1992;

(e) Assignment Procedure for Habeas Corpus and Social Security Cases for United States Magistrates dated May 29, 1990;

(f) Order Adopting Civil Justice Expense and Delay Reduction Plan dated October 25, 1991;

(g) Approval of Pre-Judgment Notice of 28 U.S.C. § 3101(d), dated May 7, 1992;

(h) Standing Order re: 1993 Amendments to Federal Rules of Civil Procedure, dated December 1, 1993; and

(i) Presentence Investigations and Time Limits, dated June 13, 1994.

[Effective July 1, 1995.]

RULE 3.2 TRANSFERS UNDER SECTION 1404(a)

Whenever a transfer of an action is ordered from this district to another district, pursuant to 28 U.S.C.

§ 1404(a), all action to carry out the transfer shall automatically be stayed for a period of twenty-one (21) days, unless the court in ordering the transfer shall expressly direct otherwise.

[Effective July 1, 1995. Amended effective December 1, 2009.]

RULE 4.1 SPECIAL APPOINTMENT FOR SERVICE OF PROCESS

When a party files a written motion with the Clerk for special appointment of a named person, other than the United States Marshal or the Marshal's deputy, to serve process pursuant to Fed.R.Civ.P. 4(c), accompanied by the representation of counsel that:

(1) the named individual is or would be competent and not less than eighteen (18) years of age;

(2) the named individual is not and will not be a party to the action;

the Clerk shall grant such motion specially appointing the named individual to serve process.

[Effective July 1, 1995.]

RULE 4.1.1 LIS PENDENS

Whenever any proceeding involving title to real property shall be commenced in this Court, and a party desires to give notice thereof by way of lis pendens, counsel for said party, at any time after commencement of said proceedings, shall file with the Clerk a written order directing him to enter said proceedings upon the judgment index, which order shall designate the persons against whom said proceeding is to be indexed. The Clerk shall note on said index the names of the persons indicated in said order, the number of said action, and the date when the entry is made. Counsel ordering the notation shall forthwith send written notice thereof to the parties designated.

[Effective July 1, 1995.]

RULE 4.1.2 SUMMONS ENFORCEMENT PROCEEDINGS PURSUANT TO 28 U.S.C. 7402(b) AND 7604(a)

(a) The Federal Rules of Civil Procedure shall be applicable in summons enforcement proceedings initiated pursuant to 26 U.S.C. 7402(b) and 7604(a) (hereinafter enforcement proceedings), except to the extent modified, limited or abrogated by this rule or by order of the Court entered during such proceedings.

(b) Each enforcement proceeding shall be initiated by complaint filed by the Secretary of the Treasury (hereinafter the Secretary) or the Secretary's delegate, which shall separately allege:

(1) that an investigation by the Internal Revenue Service is contemplated or in process, that such investigation has a legitimate purpose, and that the inquiry which is the subject of the enforcement proceeding may be relevant to that purpose.

(2) that the books, papers, records, data or testimony sought are not already in the possession of the Internal Revenue Service; and

(3) that the Secretary or the Secretary's delegate has complied with all administrative procedures required by the Internal Revenue Code of 1954, as amended. Attached to the complaint shall be an affidavit of the Secretary or the Secretary's delegate in support of each of the allegations required by this rule.

(c) Process upon such complaint shall be in the form of an order signed by the court and served upon the person summoned, directing that such person appear at a date and time certain (not less than fourteen (14) days from the date of service of the order) and show cause why an order should not be entered enforcing the administrative summons. The order to show cause shall:

(1) set a date for the filing of an answer, motion or other responsive pleading by the person summoned, together with an affidavit in support thereof, and

(2) notify the person summoned that only those issues raised in the pleadings or motions and supported by affidavit will be considered by the court on the return date, and that any uncontested allegation in the complaint will be taken as admitted for the purpose of the enforcement proceeding.

(d) At the hearing upon the order to show cause, the Secretary or Secretary's delegate shall be prepared to prove the material allegations of the complaint. The person summoned may rebut the evidence offered by the Secretary or the Secretary's delegate, and shall have the burden of proof with respect to any affirmative defenses raised in the motions or responsive pleading. If the interests of justice so require, the court may direct further proceedings in the matter, and may order such discovery as permitted by law. At the conclusion of the enforcement proceedings, the court shall make findings of fact and conclusions of law in conformity with Rule 52(a) of the Federal Rules of Civil Procedure.

[Effective July 1, 1995. Amended effective December 1, 2009; December 16, 2013.]

RULE 5.1 APPEARANCES

(a) The filing of a pleading, motion or stipulation shall be deemed an entry of appearance. Other appearances of counsel shall be by praecipe filed with the Clerk.

(b) Any party who appears pro se shall file with the party's appearance or with the party's initial pleading, an address where notices and papers can be served. Said party shall notify the Clerk within fourteen (14) days of any change of address.

(c) An attorney's appearance may not be withdrawn except by leave of court, unless another attorney of this court shall at the same time enter an appearance for the same party.

[Effective July 1, 1995. Amended January 12, 2001; December 1, 2009.]

RULE 5.1.1 PLEADING CLAIM FOR UNLIQUIDATED DAMAGES

No pleading asserting a claim for unliquidated damages shall contain any allegations as to the specific dollar amount claimed, but such pleadings shall contain allegations sufficient to establish the jurisdiction of the Court, to reveal whether the case is or is not subject to arbitration under Local Rule 53.2, and to specify the nature of the damages claimed, e.g., "compensatory," "punitive," or both.

[Effective July 1, 1995.]

RULE 5.1.2 ELECTRONIC CASE FILING

All cases and documents filed in this court are required to be filed on the Electronic Case Filing ("ECF") System in accordance with provisions of the *Electronic Case Filing ("ECF") Procedures*, as set forth below unless excepted under these procedures.

Rule 5.1.2 Electronic Case Filing
("ECF") Procedures

1. Definitions.

(a) "ECF Filing User" means those who have Court-issued log-ins and passwords to file documents electronically.

(b) "Notice of Electronic Case Filing" means the notice generated by the ECF system when a document has been filed electronically, stating that the document has been filed.

(c) "Judge" means the District Judge assigned to the case, or the Magistrate Judge to whom all or any part of a case has been referred pursuant to 28 U.S.C. § 636.

(d) "Court" shall mean the United States District Court for the Eastern District of Pennsylvania.

2. Scope of Electronic Case Filing.

(a) All civil and criminal cases filed in this court are required to be entered into the court's Electronic Case Filing ("ECF") System in accordance with these Electronic Case Filing ("ECF") Procedures. Unless an attorney is excused from ECF registration under Section 3 of these ECF Procedures or except as expressly provided in Section 16 and other sections of these ECF Procedures, or as ordered by the judge, all pleadings, documents, motions, memoranda of law, petitions, certificates of service and other documents required to be filed with the clerk of court in connection with a case must be electronically filed.

(b) The filing of all initial papers in civil cases, such as the complaint and the issuance and service of the summons, and, in criminal cases, the indictment or information, warrant for arrest or summons, will be accomplished by paper copy filed in the traditional manner rather than electronically. Parties must concurrently provide the clerk of court with a computer disk, in PDF format containing a copy of all documents provided in paper form at the time of filing. All subsequent documents and pleadings must be filed electronically, except as provided in these ECF Procedures or as ordered by the judge. Under this paragraph, all attorneys are required to complete the ECF Validation of Signature form, as described in Section 3(c) below.

(c) Once registered, an ECF Filing User may request to withdraw from participation in the ECF System by providing the clerk of court with written notice of the request which shall be forwarded to the Chief Judge for approval.

(d) Nothing in these ECF Procedures shall be construed to nullify or contradict the provisions set forth in Rule 26.1 of the Local Rules of Civil Procedure, *Discovery*, directing that interrogatories, requests for production and inspection and requests for admission under Fed. R.Civ.P. 33, 34 and 36 that answers, responses and objections to interrogatories and to Rules 34 and 36, and that requests, notices of depositions and depositions under Fed.R.Civ.P. 30 and 31 shall not be filed with the court.

(e) Nothing in these ECF Procedures shall be construed to nullify or contradict the provisions set forth in Rule 39.3 of the Local Rules of Civil Procedure, *Records, Files and Exhibits*, directing that the clerk of court maintain custody of all records, files and exhibits in all cases filed in this court until such time as the case is finally resolved, dismissed or abandoned, as set forth in paragraph (e) of Rule 39.3.

(f) All cases filed in the ECF System in which a notice of appeal is filed shall be governed by Rule 10 of the Federal Rules of Appellate Procedure and relevant Local Rules and internal operating procedures of the United States Court of Appeals for the Third Circuit, with any differences about whether the record truly discloses what occurred in the district court to be submitted to and settled by the judge. Cases in which there is a right of direct appeal to the United States Supreme Court shall be governed by the rules of the United States Supreme Court.

3. Excuse From Registration; Format of Documents in Electronic Form.
An attorney who believes he or she should be excused from registering as an ECF Filing User may apply for an exception to this rule by detailed letter to the clerk of court, who shall forward the letter to the chief judge for decision. Thereafter, attorneys and others who are excused from registering as ECF Filing Users in accordance with this section are required to comply with the procedures set forth below.

(a) All complaints must be submitted on disk in portable document format (PDF) at the time of filing, so that the complaint may be entered into the District Court's ECF system, and must be accompanied by a courtesy copy of the complaint in paper format for use by the court; under this paragraph, all attorneys are required to complete the ECF Validation of Signature form, as described in Paragraph (c) below.

(b) All documents filed by an attorney who has been excused from registering as an ECF Filing User, as defined under this rule, must be submitted on disk in PDF, so that the filings may be entered into the District Court's ECF system, and must be accompanied by a courtesy copy of the document in paper format for use by the court; under this paragraph, all attorneys are required to complete the ECF Validation of Signature form, as described in Paragraph (c) below.

(c) Attorneys who complete the ECF Validation of Signature form will receive a signature code which must be used by the attorney on the signature line of all courtesy copies submitted with a disk for purposes of signature validation pursuant to Rule 11 of the Federal Rules of Civil Procedure; the document as submitted under Section 3 of this rule will constitute the original document, except for those documents which are excluded from the provisions of rule as set forth in Section 16 of the rule; attorneys are required to have submitted a completed ECF Validation of Signature form just once in order to file all complaints and documents in all subsequent cases in this court.

(d) Service of process will continue to be made in accordance with those provisions set forth in Rule 5 of the Federal Rules of Civil Procedure.

(e) For convenience of attorneys who do not have access to compatible hardware or software, a computer with PDF conversion capability is available in the Clerk's Offices at Philadelphia and Allentown, with assistance for PDF conversion provided by Clerk's Office staff as needed; attorneys who have reason for not providing this material on disk are required to notice the Clerk's Office in writing attached to the document, explaining the reason for not providing this material on disk.

(f) Attorneys who have been excused under this section from registering as ECF Filing Users are requested to register and participate in the court's Program for Facsimile Service of Notice to Counsel or Litigants in Civil and Criminal Cases (the "Fax Noticing Program").

(g) Those documents and categories of cases which are now excluded from the provisions of this section consistent with the policy of the Judicial Conference of the United States, as may be amended from time to time, are set forth in Section 16 of this rule.

4. Eligibility, Registration and Password.

(a) Unless otherwise excused, attorneys admitted to the bar of this court, including those admitted pro hac vice, are required to register as ECF Filing Users of the court's ECF system. Registration is in a form prescribed by the clerk of court and requires the Filing User's name, address, telephone number, Internet e-mail address and a declaration that the attorney is admitted to the bar of this court and is a member in good standing.

(b) Upon the approval of the judge, a party to a case who is not represented by an attorney may register as an ECF Filing User in the ECF System solely for purposes of the action. Registration is in a form prescribed by the clerk of court and requires identification of the case as well as the name, address, telephone number and Internet e-mail address of the party. If, during the course of the case, the party retains an attorney who appears on the party's behalf, the attorney must advise the clerk of court to terminate the party's registration as a Filing User upon the attorney's appearance.

(c) Registration as an ECF Filing User constitutes agreement to receive and consent to make electronic service of all documents as provided in these ECF Procedures in accordance with Rule 5(b)(2)(D) of the Federal Rules of Civil Procedure and the Federal Rules of Criminal Procedure, as referenced in Rule 49(b) of the Federal Rules of Criminal Procedure. This agreement and consent is applicable to all future cases until revoked by the ECF Filing User.

(d) Once registration is completed, the ECF Filing User will receive notification of the user log-in and password. ECF Filing Users agree to protect the security of their passwords and immediately notify the clerk of court by telephone, with said notification confirmed immediately thereafter in writing delivered

by e-mail, facsimile or hand-delivery to the attention of the clerk of court, if they learn that their password has been compromised. Users may be subject to sanctions by the judge for failure to comply with this provision. For security reasons, the court recommends that ECF Filing Users periodically change their passwords, which shall be done by notifying the clerk of the court who shall implement the change.

5. Consequences of Electronic Filing.

(a) Electronic transmission of a document to the ECF System consistent with these ECF Procedures, together with the transmission of a notice of electronic case filing from the court, constitutes filing of the document for all purposes of the Federal Rules of Civil Procedure, the Federal Rules of Criminal Procedure and the Local Rules of this court, and constitutes entry of the document on the docket maintained by the clerk of court pursuant to Rules 58 and 79 of the Federal Rules of Civil Procedure and Rules 49 and 55 of the Federal Rules of Criminal Procedure.

(b) A document that has been filed electronically is the official record of the document, and the filing party is bound by the document as filed. Except in the case of documents first filed in paper form and subsequently submitted electronically under Section 2 above, a document filed electronically is deemed filed at the time and date stated on the notice of electronic case filing from the court.

(c) Filing a document electronically does not change any filing deadline set by the Federal Rules of Civil Procedure, the Federal Rules of Criminal Procedure, the Local Rules of the court, or an order of the judge.

(d) All pleadings and documents filed electronically must be transmitted in the form prescribed by Rule 10(a) of the Federal Rules of Civil Procedure. All transmissions for electronic case filings of pleadings and documents to the ECF system shall be titled in accordance with the approved directory of civil and criminal events of the ECF system.

6. Attachments and Exhibits. ECF Filing Users may submit all documents identified as exhibits or attachments in either paper copy filed in the traditional manner or electronic form. If using electronic form, an ECF Filing User must submit as exhibits or attachments only those excerpts of the identified documents that are relevant to the matter under consideration by the court. Excerpted material must be clearly and prominently identified as such. ECF Filing Users who file excerpts of documents as exhibits or attachments electronically pursuant to these ECF Procedures do so without prejudice to their right to file timely additional excerpts or the complete document, provided however, that the total number of pages of attachments and exhibits electronically filed shall not exceed 50 without prior approval of the judge. Pages of attachments and exhibits in excess of

50 may be filed in paper copy filed in the traditional manner. Responding parties who choose to file exhibits and attachments electronically may also timely file additional excerpts or the complete document, subject to the same page limitations as set forth above.

7. Sealed Documents. Documents ordered to be placed under seal must be filed in paper copy filed in the traditional manner and not electronically. A motion to file documents under seal may be filed electronically unless prohibited by law. The order of the court authorizing the filing of documents under seal may be filed electronically unless prohibited by law. A paper copy of the order must be attached to the documents under seal and be delivered to the clerk of court.

8. Service of Documents by Electronic Means.

(a) When an ECF Filing User electronically files a pleading or other document using the ECF system, a Notice of Electronic Case Filing shall automatically be generated by the system, and shall be sent automatically to all parties entitled to service under the Federal Rules of Civil Procedure, the Federal Rules of Criminal Procedure and the Local Rules of the Eastern District of Pennsylvania who have consented to electronic service. Electronic service of the Notice of Electronic Case Filing constitutes service of the filed document to all such parties and shall be deemed to satisfy the requirements of Rule 5(b)(2)(D) of the Federal Rules of Civil Procedure and Rule 49 of the Federal Rules of Criminal Procedure.

(b) All documents filed using the ECF system shall contain a Certificate of Service stating that the document has been filed electronically and is available for viewing and downloading from the ECF system. The Certificate of Service must identify the manner in which service on each party was accomplished, including any party who has not consented to electronic service.

(c) Parties who have not consented to electronic service are entitled to receive a paper copy of any electronically filed pleading or other document. Service of such paper copy must be made according to the Federal Rules of Civil Procedure, the Federal Rules of Criminal Procedure and the Local Rules of the Eastern District of Pennsylvania.

(d) As set forth in Section 4 of these ECF Procedures, registration as an ECF Filing User constitutes agreement to receive and consent to make electronic service of all documents as provided in these ECF Procedures in accordance with Rule 5(b)(2)(D) of the Federal Rules of Civil Procedure and Rule 49 of the Federal Rules of Criminal Procedure. This agreement and consent is applicable to all pending and future actions assigned to the ECF System until revoked by the ECF Filing User.

(e) In accordance with Rule 6(d) of the Federal Rules of Civil Procedure, service by electronic means is treated the same as service by mail for the purpose of adding three (3) days to the prescribed period to respond.

(f) In accordance with Rule 77(d) of the Federal Rules of Civil Procedure, the court may serve notice of entry of orders or judgments by electronic means as provided in Rule 5(b) and Section 4 of this Procedural Order.

(g) In civil cases, the provisions of this Section 8 apply to service of documents covered by Rule 5(a) of the Federal Rules of Civil Procedure. Service of Original Process under Rule 4 of the Federal Rules of Civil Procedure is not authorized under these ECF Procedures to be accomplished electronically. This Section 8 does not apply to service of an arrest warrant, summons or subpoena in criminal cases.

9. Signature.

(a) The user log-in and password required to submit documents to the ECF System serve as the ECF Filing User's signature on all electronic documents filed with the court. They also serve as a signature for purposes of Rule 11(a) of the Federal Rules of Civil Procedure, the Local Rules of this court, and any other purpose for which a signature is required in connection with proceedings before the court. Each document filed electronically must, if possible, indicate that it has been electronically filed. Electronically filed documents must include a signature block and must set forth the name, address, telephone number and the attorney's state bar identification number, if applicable. In addition, the name of the ECF Filing User under whose log-in and password the document is submitted must be preceded by an "s/" and typed in the space where the signature would otherwise appear.

(b) No ECF Filing User or other person may knowingly permit or cause to permit a Filing User's password to be used by anyone other than an authorized agent of the Filing User.

(c) Documents requiring signatures of more than one party must be electronically filed either by: (1) submitting a scanned document containing all necessary signatures; (2) representing the consent of the other parties on the document; (3) identifying on the document the parties whose signatures are required and by the submission of a notice of endorsement by the other parties no later than seven (7) days after filing; or (4) any other manner approved by the court.

10. Submission of Stipulations and Proposed Orders. An ECF Filing User electronically submitting stipulations or proposed orders which may require a judge's signature must promptly deliver on computer disk or e-mail the stipulation or proposed order to the clerk of court for delivery to the judge unless the judge orders otherwise. An ECF Filing User who electronically submits a stipulation or proposed order is bound by all signature requirements set forth in Section 9 of these ECF Procedures and Rule 11(a) of the Federal Rules of Civil Procedure.

11. Retention Requirements. Documents that are electronically filed and require original signatures other than that of the Filing User must be maintained in paper form by the ECF Filing User until three (3) years after the time period for appeal expires. The ECF Filing User must provide original documents for review upon request of the judge.

12. Public Access.

(a) Any person or organization, other than one registered as an ECF Filing User under Section 4 of these rules, may access the ECF Filing System at the court's Internet site, www.paed.uscourts.gov, by obtaining a PACER log-in and password. Those who have PACER access but who are not Filing Users may retrieve docket sheets and those documents which the court makes available on the Internet for the fee normally charged for this service as set by the fee schedule authorized by the Administrative Office of United States Courts, but they may not file documents.

(b) Documents should be made available electronically to the same extent that they are available for personal inspection in the office of the clerk of court at the U.S. Courthouse. Social Security numbers, dates of birth, financial account numbers and names of minor children should be modified or partially redacted in electronically filed documents.

(c) In connection with the electronic filing of any material, any person may apply by motion for an order limiting electronic access to, or prohibiting the electronic filing of, certain specifically identified materials on the grounds that such material is subject to privacy interests and that electronic access or electronic filing in the action is likely to prejudice those privacy interests. In further protection of privacy, reference is made to the provisions of Rule 5.1.3 of the Local Rules of Civil Procedure, *Excluded Personal Identifiers,* mandating the modification or redaction of such personal identifiers as Social Security numbers, dates of birth, financial account numbers and names of minor children in all documents filed either in traditional paper form or electronically.

13. Entry of Court Order. All orders, decrees, judgments and proceedings of the court will be filed in accordance with these rules which will constitute entry on the docket maintained by the clerk of court pursuant to Fed.R.Civ.P. 58 and 79, and Rules 49 and 55 of the Federal Rules of Criminal Procedure. All signed orders will be filed electronically by the clerk of court. Any order filed electronically without the original signature of a judge has the same force and effect as if the judge had affixed the judge's signature to a paper copy of the order and it had been entered on the docket in paper copy filed in the traditional manner.

14. Notice of Court Order and Judgment. Immediately upon the entry of an order or judgment, the clerk of court will transmit to ECF Filing Users in the case, in electronic form, a notice of electronic filing. Electronic transmission of the Notice of Electronic Case Filing constitutes the notice required by Rule 77(d) of the Federal Rules of Civil Procedure and Rule 49(c) of the Federal Rules of Criminal Procedure. In accordance with the Federal Rules of Civil Procedure, the clerk of court must give notice in paper form to a person who has been excused under Section 3 of Local Rule 5.1.2 from registering as ECF Filing User.

15. Technical Failure. An ECF Filing User whose filing is determined to be untimely as the result of a technical failure may seek appropriate relief from the judge, provided that the User immediately notifies the clerk of court of the technical failure by telephone, with said notification confirmed immediately thereafter in writing delivered by e-mail, facsimile or by hand to the attention of the clerk of court. The clerk of the court shall forthwith notify the chambers of the judge.

16. Categories of Cases and Types of Documents in Civil and Criminal Cases Excluded from Electronic Case Filing. As provided in Section 2(b) above, all initial papers in civil and criminal cases, including the complaint, amended complaint, third-party complaint, notice of removal, the issuance and service of the summons, and the indictment and information in criminal cases, cannot be electronically filed on the court's CM/ECF system, but must be filed on paper accompanied by a copy of the document on disk in PDF format. Additionally, the following types of documents and categories of cases, as may be amended from time to time, can neither be electronically filed on the court's CM/ECF system nor submitted on disk in PDF format by an attorney excused from participation from ECF pursuant to Section 3 of these procedures, but must be filed in paper copy filed in the traditional manner, consistent with the policy of the Judicial Conference of the United States:

A. EXCLUDED CASES

    1. Grand jury matters.

    2. Qui tam cases.

    3. Sealed cases.

B. EXCLUDED DOCUMENTS
CIVIL CASES

    1. Administrative records.

    2. All documents filed by prisoners and pro se litigants, including the initial complaint and initial habeas corpus petitions, and death penalty habeas corpus petitions.

3. Bankruptcy appeal records.

4. Sealed documents.

5. State court records.

6. Transcript of civil proceedings shall be placed on CM/ECF or PACER, unless the presiding judge otherwise directs.

7. Discovery material, as set forth in Rule 26.1 of the Local Rules of Civil Procedure, *Discovery*, including:

(a) interrogatories, requests for production and inspection and requests for admission under Rules 33, 34 and 36 of the Federal Rules of Civil Procedure;

(b) answers, responses and objections to interrogatories and to Rules 34 and 36 of the Federal Rules of Civil Procedure;

(c) requests, notices of depositions and depositions under Rules 30 and 31 of the Federal Rules of Civil Procedure.

8. Praecipe for Writ of Execution.

9. Applications for Writ of Continuing Garnishment.

10. Praecipe to Issue Writ of Revival.

11. Praecipe for Writ of Seizure.

12. Praecipe for Writ to Restore.

13. Civil Jury Verdict Sheets.

14. Civil Minute Sheets.

15. Ex Parte Motions.

CRIMINAL CASES

1. Sealed documents.

2. Transcript of criminal proceedings shall not be placed on CM/ECF or PACER, unless the presiding judge otherwise directs after giving the prosecution and defense counsel an opportunity to be heard.

3. All documents requiring the signature of a defendant in a criminal or magistrate proceeding, such as waiver of indictment, waiver of presentence report, waiver of a jury trial, plea agreement, appearance bond, affidavit, and financial affidavit.

4. Criminal Jury Verdict Sheets.

5. Presentence Reports and any objections or other documents filed related to the Presentence Reports.

6. Criminal Minute Sheets.

7. Judgment and Commitment Orders.

8. Ex parte Motions.

[Effective May 16, 2002. Amended effective April 2, 2007; June 2, 2008; December 1, 2009; December 20, 2010.]

RULE 5.1.3 MODIFICATION OR REDACTION OF PERSONAL IDENTIFIERS

As documents in civil cases may be made available for personal inspection in the office of the clerk of court at the United States Courthouse, or, if filed electronically, may be made available on the court's Electronic Case Filing system, such personal identifiers as Social Security numbers, dates of birth, financial account numbers and names of minor children should be modified or partially redacted in all documents filed either in traditional paper form or electronically.

[Effective July 1, 2002.]

RULE 5.1.5 DOCUMENTS FILED UNDER SEAL

(a) A document in a civil action may be filed under seal only if:

(1) the civil action is brought pursuant to a federal statute that prescribes the sealing of the record or of certain specific documents; or

(2) the Court orders the document sealed.

(b)(1) Where a document is sealed pursuant to § 5.1.5(a)(1), the continued status of the document under seal shall be governed by the relevant federal statute. If no federal statute governs, §§ 5.1.5(b)(2) and (c) shall apply.

(2) When a document is sealed pursuant to § 5.1.5(a)(2), the document, if it remains in the custody of the Court, shall not be unsealed for two years after the conclusion of the civil action including all appeals, unless the Court orders otherwise.

(c) If a document is still sealed at the conclusion of the two-year period and the Court has not entered an order continuing its sealed status beyond that time, the Clerk of Court shall notify the attorney for the party having submitted the sealed document at the attorney's address on the docket that the document will be unsealed unless the attorney or the submitting party advises the Clerk within sixty (60) days that said attorney or submitting party objects. If the attorney or submitting party objects to the unsealing of the document or if the Clerk's notification is returned unclaimed, the Court will make a determination, on a case-by-case basis, whether to maintain the document under seal, to unseal it, or to require further notification.

[Effective March 1, 2005.]

RULE 7.1 MOTION PRACTICE

(a) Every motion shall be accompanied by a form of order which, if approved by the court, would grant the relief sought by the motion. Every response in opposition to a motion shall be accompanied by a form of order, which, if approved by the court, will deny or amend the relief sought by the motion.

(b) Every uncontested motion shall be accompanied by a certificate of counsel that such motion is uncontested.

(c) Every motion not certified as uncontested, or not governed by Local Civil Rule 26.1(g), shall be accompanied by a brief containing a concise statement of the legal contentions and authorities relied upon in support of the motion. Unless the Court directs otherwise, any party opposing the motion shall serve a brief in opposition together with such answer or other response that may be appropriate, within fourteen (14) days after service of the motion and supporting brief. In the absence of timely response, the motion may be granted as uncontested except as provided under Fed. R.Civ.P 56. The Court may require or permit briefs or submissions if the Court deems them necessary.

(d) Every motion not certified as uncontested shall be accompanied by a written statement as to the date and manner of service of the motion and supporting brief.

(e) Within fourteen (14) days after filing any post-trial motion, the movant shall either (a) order a transcript of the trial by a writing delivered to the Court Reporter Supervisor, or (b) file a verified motion showing good cause to be excused from this requirement. Unless a transcript is thus ordered, or the movant excused from ordering a transcript, the post-trial motion may be dismissed for lack of prosecution.

(f) Any interested party may request oral argument on a motion. The court may require oral argument, whether or not requested by a party. The court may dispose of a motion without oral argument.

(g) Motions for reconsideration or reargument shall be served and filed within fourteen (14) days after the entry of the order concerned, other than those governed by Federal Rule of Civil Procedure 59(e).

[Effective July 1, 1995. Amended effective December 1, 2009; May 17, 2010; February 27, 2012; June 10, 2014.]

RULE 7.4 NOTICES; STIPULATIONS

(a) All notices by parties or counsel shall be in writing.

(b) **Stipulations of Counsel.**

(1) Stipulations of counsel relating to the business of the court, except such stipulations at bar as are noted by the Clerk upon the minutes or by the court reporter's notes, shall be written and signed by counsel of record. Upon receipt of a stipulation, the Clerk shall stamp the date it is received and forward it to the Court for consideration.

(2) In accordance with Fed. R. Civ. P.6(b), no stipulation between the parties relating to extension of time shall be effective until approved by the Court.

[Effective July 1, 1995. Amended effective February 27, 2012.]

RULE 9.3 PETITIONS FOR WRITS OF HABEAS CORPUS AND 2255 MOTIONS

(a) All petitions for writs of habeas corpus and all motions pursuant to 28 U.S.C. 2255 shall be filed on forms provided by the Court and shall contain the information called for by such forms. The required information shall be set concisely and legibly. Ordinarily, the Court will consider only those matters which are set forth on the forms provided by the Court. Any attempt to circumvent this requirement by purporting to incorporate by reference other documents which do not comply with this Rule may result in dismissal of the petition.

(b) Any petition filed under 28 U.S.C. 2254 or motion filed under 28 U.S.C. 2255 which does not substantially comply with Rules 2 and 3 of the Rules governing petitions and motions filed under those sections may be returned by the Clerk of the Court to the petitioner, if a judge of the Court so directs, together with a statement of the reason for its return. A copy of any petition or motion returned for failure to comply shall be retained by the Clerk.

[Effective July 1, 1995.]

RULE 9.4 PETITIONS UNDER 28 U.S.C. § 2254 AND MOTIONS TO VACATE SENTENCE UNDER 28 U.S.C. § 2255 IN DEATH PENALTY CASES

1. All petitions for a writ of habeas corpus under 28 U.S.C. § 2254 and motions to vacate sentence under 28 U.S.C. § 2255 must be accompanied by a cover sheet that lists:

a. petitioner's full name and prisoner number; if prosecuted under a different name or alias that name must be indicated

b. name of person having custody of petitioner (warden, superintendent, etc.)

c. petitioner's address

d. name of trial judge

e. court term and bill of information or indictment number

f. charges of which petitioner was convicted

g.   sentence for each of the charges

h.   plea entered

i.   whether trial was by jury or to the bench

j.   date of filing, docket numbers, dates of decision and results of direct appeal of the conviction

k.   date of filing, docket numbers, dates of decision and results of any state collateral attack on a state conviction including appeals

l.   date of filing, docket numbers, dates of decision of any prior federal habeas corpus or § 2255 proceedings, including appeals

m.   name and address of each attorney who represented petitioner, identifying the stage at which the attorney represented the litigant

2.   A petition for writ of habeas corpus under 28 U.S.C. § 2254 or motion to vacate sentence under 28 U.S.C. § 2255 in a death penalty case

a.   must list every ground on which the petitioner claims to be entitled to relief under 28 U.S.C. § 2254 (or § 2255 for federal prisoners) followed by a concise statement of the material facts supporting the claims;

b.   must identify at what stage of the proceedings each claim was exhausted in state court if the petition seeks relief from a state court judgment;

c.   must contain a table of contents if the petition is more than 25 pages;

d.   must contain citation to legal authority that forms the basis of the claim.

3.   Petitioner must file, not later than sixty (60) days after the date of the filing of the petition under § 2254 or motion to vacate sentence under § 2255, a memorandum of law in support. The memorandum of law must

a.   contains a statement of the case;

b.   contains a table of contents if it is more than 25 pages.

4.   The petition/motion and memorandum together must not exceed 150 pages.

5.   All documents filed must be succinct and must avoid repetition.

6.   Respondent need not file a response until the memorandum of law is filed.

a.   The response must not exceed 150 pages;

b.   The response must contain a table of contents if it is more than 25 pages;

c.   The response must be filed within sixty (60) days of the filing of the memorandum of law.

7.   Any reply to the response must be filed within twenty-one (21) days of the filing of the response and may not exceed thirty (30) pages.

8.   Upon motion and for good cause shown, the judge may extend the page limits for any document.

9.   Upon motion and for good cause shown, the judge may extend the time for filing any document.

10.   The petitioner must file with the Clerk of the District Court a copy of the "Certificate of Death Penalty Case" required by Third Circuit L.A.R. Misc. 111.2(a). Upon docketing, the Clerk of the District Court will transmit a copy of the certificate, together with a copy of the petition to the Clerk of the Court of Appeals as required by Third Circuit L.A.R. Misc. 111.2(a).

11.   Upon the entry of a warrant or order setting an execution date in any case within the geographical boundaries of this district, and in aid of this court's potential jurisdiction, the clerk is directed to monitor the status of the execution and any pending litigation and to establish communications with all parties and relevant state and/or federal courts. Without further order of this court, the clerk may, prior to the filing of a petition, direct parties to lodge with this court (1) relevant portions of previous state and/or federal court records, or the entire record, and (2) pleadings, briefs, and transcripts of any ongoing proceedings. To prevent delay, the case may be assigned to a judge, by the same selection process as for other cases, up to fourteen (14) days prior to the execution date. The identity of the judge assigned shall not be disclosed until a petition is actually docketed.

12.   In accordance with Third Circuit L.A.R. Misc. 111.3(b), at the time a final decision is entered, the court shall state whether a certificate of appealability is granted or denied. If a certificate of appealability is granted, the court must state the issues that merit the granting of a certificate and must also grant a stay pending disposition of the appeal, except as provided in 28 U.S.C. § 2262.

[Adopted effective March 1, 2000.]

RULE 14.1   TIME OF MOTION TO JOIN THIRD PARTY

(a)   Applications pursuant to Fed.R.Civ.P. 14 for leave to join additional parties after the expiration of the time limits specified in that rule will ordinarily be denied as untimely unless filed not more than ninety (90) days after the service of the moving party's answer. If it is made to appear, to the satisfaction of the Court, that the identity of the party sought to be joined, or the basis for joinder, could not, with reasonable diligence, have been ascertained within said time period, a brief further extension of time may be granted by the Court in the interests of justice.

(b)   In cases subject to compulsory arbitration pursuant to Local Civil Rule 53.2, unless otherwise ordered by the Court for cause shown, all applications for leave to join additional parties shall be deemed untimely unless filed before the entry appointing arbitrators.

[Effective July 1, 1995.]

RULE 16.1   PRETRIAL PROCEDURE

(a) Introductory Comments. Variations from the pretrial procedures established by this Rule may be ordered by the assigned judge to fit the circumstances of a particular case. In the absence of such specific order, however, the procedures outlined herein will be followed in all civil proceedings in this court except those exempt by Local Civil Rule 16.2. In addition, the assigned judge or magistrate will issue a scheduling order in compliance with Federal Rule of Civil Procedure 16(b) in all civil cases, except those expressly exempt by Local Rule 16.2.

It is contemplated that each civil case will proceed through the following pretrial steps:

(1) A scheduling conference, as provided in section (b) of this Rule.

(2) Submission of pretrial memoranda, as provided in section (c) of this rule.

(3) Such interim status calls, status reports, or interim conferences as the judge may direct.

(4) Completion of discovery.

(5) Submission of a Final Pretrial Order, if required (see section (d)(2), below).

(6) A final pretrial conference, as provided in section (d)(3) of this Rule.

(b) Scheduling Conference. In all cases except those exempt by Local Civil Rule 16.2, a scheduling conference will ordinarily be held by the assigned judge or magistrate within one hundred twenty (120) days after the filing of the complaint. Such conference may be by telephone, mail or other suitable means. The following matters, in addition to those set forth in Federal Rule of Civil Procedure 16, will be considered at the conference:

(1) Jurisdictional defects, if any.

(2) Prospects of amicable settlement.

(3) Setting a date for trial.

(4) Establishing schedules for remaining pretrial proceedings (discovery deadlines, pretrial memoranda filings, exchange of exhibits, exchange of experts' reports, etc.).

(5) Any other pertinent matters.

In all civil cases, except those exempt by Rule 16.2, a scheduling order will be issued as soon as *practical, but in no event more than one hundred twenty (120) days after filing of the complaint.*

(c) Pretrial Memoranda. Pretrial memoranda shall be filed and served at such time as the court shall direct in the scheduling order or by any other express order.

Unless the order otherwise directs, the pretrial memorandum of each party shall contain the following:

(1) A brief statement of the nature of the action and the basis on which the jurisdiction of the court is invoked.

(2) Plaintiff's pretrial memorandum shall contain a brief statement of the facts of the case. Defendant's pretrial memorandum shall contain such counterstatements of the facts as may be necessary to reflect any disagreement with plaintiff's statement. All parties omit pejorative characterizations, hyperbole, and conclusory generalizations.

(3) A list of every item of monetary damages claimed, including (as appropriate) computations of lost earnings and loss of future earning capacity, medical expenses (itemized), property damages, etc. If relief other than monetary damages is sought, information adequate for framing an order granting the relief sought shall be furnished.

(4) A list showing the names and addresses of all witnesses the party submitting the memorandum intends to call at trial. Liability and damages witnesses shall be designated separately.

(5) A schedule of all exhibits to be offered at trial by the party submitting the memorandum.

(6) An estimate of the number of days required for trial.

(7) Special comments regarding legal issues, stipulations, amendments of pleadings, or other appropriate matters.

(d) Final Preparation for Trial.

1. *Minimum Requirements.* In every case, counsel shall, before the commencement of trial:

(a) Mark and exchange all exhibits to be offered in evidence during case in chief. Authenticity of all exhibits will be deemed established unless written objection is filed (either in a pretrial memorandum or by motion) at least seven (7) days before trial.

(b) Exchange lists of witnesses. No witness not listed may be called during case in chief. Requests during trial for offers of proof will not ordinarily be entertained with respect to listed witnesses; counsel are expected to clarify any uncertainties concerning the substance of proposed testimony in advance of trial, by conferring with opposing counsel.

2. *Final Pretrial Order.* If the case is unusually complex, or if the pretrial memoranda are inadequate, or if the judge determines that the circumstances of the litigation make it desirable to do so, the judge may require the parties to prepare and submit for approval

a Final Pretrial Order. When a Final Pretrial Order is required, the following provisions shall apply:

(a) Instructions for Preparation of Proposed Final Pretrial Order. The proposed pretrial order shall consist of one document signed by all counsel, reflecting the efforts of all counsel. It is the obligation of plaintiff's counsel to initiate the procedures for its preparation, and to assemble, and to submit the proposed pretrial order to the judge.

Counsel may find it advantageous to prepare the proposed pretrial order jointly in one conference, or each attorney may prepare his or her section which will then be circulated with other counsel for review and approval. No explicit directions covering the mechanics of preparation are included in these instructions. However, after each counsel has submitted suggestions to other counsel, all counsel must have a conference to attempt to reconcile any matters on which there is disagreement. Counsel are expected to make a diligent effort to prepare a proposed pretrial order in which will be noted all of the issues on which the parties are in agreement and all of those issues on which they disagree. The proposed pretrial order shall be submitted by counsel for the plaintiff at chambers at least seven (7) days prior to the scheduled final pretrial conference, unless another date is specified by the judge.

The proposed pretrial order, if accepted by the judge, will become a final pretrial order and shall govern the conduct of the trial and shall supersede all prior pleadings in the case. Amendments will be allowed only in exceptional circumstances to prevent manifest injustice.

After the proposed pretrial order has been designated as the final pretrial order, the case will be considered ready for trial.

(b) Form of Proposed Pretrial Order. The proposed pretrial order shall be in the following form:

(CAPTION)

(1) Jurisdiction. A statement as to the nature of the action and the basis on which the jurisdiction of the court is invoked.

(2) Facts. A comprehensive written stipulation of all uncontested facts in such form that it can be read to the jury as the first evidence at trial.

(A) These facts should include all matters capable of ascertainment, such as ownership, agency, dimensions, physical characteristics, weather conditions, road surfaces, etc. Approximations and estimates which are satisfactory to counsel will be accepted by the judge.

(B) No facts should be denied unless opposing counsel expects to present contrary evidence on the point of trial, or genuinely challenges the fact on credibility grounds.

(C) The facts relating to liability and to damages are to be separately stated.

(D) The parties shall reach agreement on uncontested facts even though relevancy is disputed, if such facts are ruled admissible, they need not be proved.

(E) the parties shall also set forth their respective statements as to the facts which are in dispute, separating those referring to liability from those referring to damages.

(3) Damages or Other Relief. A statement of damages claimed or relief sought.

(A) A party seeking damages shall list each item claimed under a separate descriptive heading (personal injury, wrongful death, survival, loss of profits, loss of wages, deprivation of civil rights, false imprisonment, libel, slander, property damage, pain, suffering, past and future medical expense, balance due under a contract, performance due under a contract, interest, etc.), shall provide a detailed description of each item, and state the amount of damages claimed.

(B) A party seeking relief other than damages shall list under separate paragraphs the exact form of relief sought with precise designations of the persons, parties, places and things expected to be included in any order providing relief.

(4) Legal Issues. In separate paragraphs, each disputed legal issue that must be decided and the principal constitutional, statutory, regulatory, and decisional authorities relied upon.

(5) Witnesses. Under separate headings, and under separate headings for liability and damages, the names and addresses of all witnesses whom the plaintiff, defendant, and third parties actually intend to call at trial, during their respective case in chief.

(A) Witnesses shall be listed in the order they will be called. Each witness shall be identified and there shall be a brief statement of the evidence which the witness will give.

(B) A detailed summary of the qualifications of each expert witness shall be submitted. This summary shall be in such form that it can be read to the jury when the expert takes the stand to testify.

(C) Only those witnesses listed will be permitted to testify at trial, except to prevent manifest injustice.

(6) Exhibits. A schedule of all exhibits to be offered in evidence at trial, together with a statement of those agreed to be admissible and the grounds for objection to any not so agreed upon.

(A) The exhibits shall be serially numbered, and be physically marked before trial in accordance with the schedule.

(B) Where testimony is expected to be offered as to geographical location, building, structure, waterway, highway, road, walkway, or parcel of real estate, plaintiff shall furnish an exhibit in such form that it can be used in the courtroom as an aid to oral testimony.

(i) Except in those cases where the issues require the use of exact scale, the exhibit may be a simple single-line hand-drawn sketch.

(ii) In most instances, it will not be necessary that the exhibit be to scale or contain other than reasonably accurate features of the geographical characteristics involved.

(iii) If of adequate size and clarity, this exhibit may be an existing drawing, plan or blueprint.

(C) Except for unusual circumstances, it is expected that the authenticity or genuineness of all exhibits, including non-documentary items, documents, photographs and data from business records from sources other than parties to the litigation, will routinely be stipulated to and will be received in evidence if relevant. Counsel likewise are expected to agree upon the use of accurate extracts from or summaries of such records. Life expectancy tables, actuarial tables, and other similar statistical and tabular data routinely used in litigation in the Federal Courts should also normally be stipulated.

(D) At trial, counsel shall furnish a copy of each exhibit to the judge, if the judge so requests.

(7) Legal Issues and Pleadings. Special comments regarding the legal issues or any amendments to the legal pleadings not otherwise set forth.

(8) Trial Time. An estimate of the number of trial days required separately stated for liability and damages.

(9) Discovery Evidence and Trial Depositions. Each discovery item and trial deposition to be offered into evidence.

(A) Where the videotape or deposition of a witness is to be offered in evidence, counsel shall review it so that there can be eliminated irrelevancies, side comments, resolved objections, and other matters not necessary for consideration by the trier of fact. Counsel shall designate by page the specific portions of deposition testimony and by number the interrogatories which shall be offered in evidence at the trial.

(B) Depositions and interrogatories to be used for cross-examination or impeachment need not be listed or purged. (When a final order is required, the judge may nevertheless permit appropriate modification of the above form.)

3. *Final Pretrial Conference.* A final pretrial conference will ordinarily be held shortly before trial. It shall be attended by trial counsel, who must be either authorized or empowered to make binding decisions concerning settlement, or able to obtain such authority by telephone in the course of the conference. In addition to exploring the final positions of the parties regarding settlement, the court will consider at the conference some or all of the following:

The simplification of the issues, the necessity or desirability of amendments to the pleadings, the separation of issues, the desirability of an impartial medical examination, the limitation of the number of expert witnesses, the probable length of the trial, the desirability of trial briefs, evidentiary questions, the submission of points for charge, and such other matters as may aid in the trial or other disposition of the action.

4. *Miscellaneous Provisions Relating to Trial and Preparation for Trial.*

(a) Requests for Jury Instructions. Requests for jury instructions are not required with respect to familiar points of law not in dispute between the parties. As to such matters, counsel should consider simply listing the subject desired to be covered in the charge (e.g., negligence, proximate cause, assumption of risk, burden of proof, credibility, etc.), unless specific phraseology is deemed important in the particular case. With respect to non-routine legal issues, requests for instructions should be accompanied by appropriate citations of legal authorities. All requests for instructions shall be submitted in writing, in duplicate, at chambers; unless the judge orders otherwise, such requests shall be filed at or before commencement of the trial, but amendments or supplements may be submitted at the close of the evidence.

(b) Special Interrogatories. Proposals concerning the form of special interrogatories to the jury shall be submitted at such time as may be specified by the judge; in the absence of specific direction, such proposals shall be submitted at the earliest convenient time, and not later than the close of the evidence.

(c) Requests for Findings in Non–Jury Cases. In non-jury cases, requests for findings of fact and conclusions of law shall be submitted in duplicate at chambers at the start of the trial, or as the judge may otherwise direct.

(d) Special Arrangements. Any counsel desiring special equipment, devices, personnel, or courtroom arrangements will be responsible for assuring that such items are available as needed. Court personnel should not be expected or depended upon to provide such service for any party or counsel, unless so ordered by the judge. Arrangements for daily copy shall be made at least two weeks in advance of trial, with the assigned Court Reporter Coordinator.

(e) Continuances. Trial will not ordinarily be continued because of the unavailability of a witness, particularly an expert witness. If a witness's availability for trial is doubtful, counsel will be expected to arrange for a written or videotaped trial deposition.

[Effective July 1, 1995. Amended effective December 1, 2009.]

RULE 16.2 CIVIL CASES EXEMPT FROM ISSUANCE OF A SCHEDULING ORDER

The following categories of civil cases shall, unless the assigned judge directs otherwise, be exempt, as inappropriate, from the provision of Federal Rule of Civil Procedure 16(b) that mandate the issuance of a scheduling order, and from the requirements of Local Rule 16.1.

1. Appeals from the final determination of the Secretary of Health and Human Services, 42 U.S.C. 405(g) (Social Security Appeals).

2. Habeas Corpus petitions and actions pursuant to 28 U.S.C. 2254 and 2255.

3. Actions eligible for or referred to arbitration pursuant to Local Rule 53.2.

4. Actions for review of administrative agency actions pursuant to 5 U.S.C. 702 (Administrative Procedure Act).

5. Actions by the United States for repayment of loans in default.

6. Actions to enforce rights under an employee welfare benefit plan pursuant to 29 U.S.C. 1132 (ERISA).

7. Internal Revenue Service Proceedings to enforce civil summons pursuant to 26 U.S.C. 7402.

8. Bankruptcy Appeals.

9. Pro se prisoner civil rights actions.

10. Actions in which no pleading or appearance has been filed on behalf of any party defendant within one hundred twenty (120) days from the filing of the complaint.

11. [Rescinded].

[Effective July 1, 1995.]

RULE 23.1 CLASS ACTIONS

In any case sought to be maintained as a class action:

(a) The complaint shall bear next to its caption the legend, "Complaint—Class Action."

(b) The complaint shall contain under a separate heading, styled "Class Action Allegations":

(1) A reference to the portion or portions of Fed. R.Civ.P. 23 under which it is claimed that the suit is properly maintainable as a class action.

(2) Appropriate allegations thought to justify such claim, including, but not necessarily limited to:

A. the size (or approximate size) and definition of the alleged class,

B. the basis upon which the plaintiff (or plaintiffs) claims,

(i) to be an adequate representative of the class, or

(ii) if the class is comprised of defendants that those named as parties are adequate representatives of the class.

C. the alleged questions of law and fact claimed to be common to the class, and

D. In actions claimed to be maintainable as class actions under subdivision (b)(3) of Fed.R.Civ.P. 23, allegations thought to support the findings required by that subdivision.

(c) As early as practicable, and after considering the views of counsel, the Court shall issue an order scheduling all proceedings relating to the filing of the motion for class certification including, but not limited to, class and related merits fact discovery, expert witness discovery, the filing of the motion for class certification and responses, and, if warranted, the convening of any hearing on the class certification motion.

(d) The foregoing provisions shall apply, with appropriate adaptations, to any counterclaim or cross-claim alleged to be brought for or against a class.

[Effective July 1, 1995. Amended effective December 16, 2013.]

RULE 26.1 DISCOVERY

(a) Interrogatories, requests for production and inspection and requests for admission under Fed. R.Civ.P. 33, 34 and 36, answers, responses, and objections to interrogatories and to Rules 34 and 36 requests, notices of deposition and depositions under Fed.R.Civ.P. 30 and 31 shall not be filed with the Court. The party serving the discovery material or taking the deposition shall retain the original and be the custodian of it.

(b) Every motion pursuant to the Federal Rules of Civil Procedure governing discovery shall identify and set forth, verbatim, the relevant parts of the interrogatory, request, answer, response, objection, notice, subpoena, or depositions. Any party responding to the motion shall set forth, verbatim, in that party's memorandum any other part that the party believes necessary to the Court's consideration of the motion.

(c) If material in interrogatories, requests, answers, responses, or depositions is used as evidence in connection with any motion, the relevant parts shall be set forth, verbatim, in the moving papers or in responding memoranda. If it is used as evidence at trial, the party offering it shall read it into the record or, if directed to do so by the Court, offer it as an exhibit.

(d) The Court shall resolve any dispute that may arise about the accuracy of any quotation or discovery material used as provided in (b) and (c) and may require production of the original paper or transcript.

(e) The Court, on its own motion, on motion by any party or on application by a non-party, may require the filing of the original of any discovery paper or deposition transcript. The parties may provide for such filing by stipulation.

(f) No motion or other application pursuant to the Federal Rules of Civil Procedure governing discovery or pursuant to this rule shall be made unless it contains a certification of counsel that the parties, after reasonable effort, are unable to resolve the dispute.

(g) A routine motion to compel answers to interrogatories or to compel compliance with a request for production under Fed.R.Civ.P. 34, wherein it is averred that no response or objection has been timely served, need have no accompanying brief, and need have no copy of the interrogatories or Rule 34 request attached. The Court may summarily grant or deny such motion without waiting for a response.

[Effective July 1, 1995.]

RULE 39.1 SUMMATIONS BY ATTORNEY

(a) Unless the trial judge shall otherwise grant leave, only one attorney may sum up for any party.

(b) In actions which involve no third-party action, if evidence has been admitted on offer by both sides, plaintiff's attorney shall first sum up, stating explicitly upon what the plaintiff relies. Defendant's attorney shall next sum up as the nature of defendant's defense may require. Plaintiff's attorney may then reply, restricting himself or herself to rebuttal without assertion of any new ground on plaintiff's behalf.

In like actions, if no evidence has been admitted on offer of any defendant, the same order of summation shall prevail, except that plaintiff's attorney shall not reply.

(c) In actions which involve a third-party claim, if evidence has been admitted on offer by each party, the plaintiff's attorney shall first sum up as provided in section (b) of this rule. Defendant's attorney shall next sum up for defendant as in section (b) of this rule and for defendant as third-party plaintiff shall state explicitly upon what defendant relies against the third-party defendant. The attorney for the third-party defendant shall next sum up as the nature of third-party defendant's defense may require. The attorney for third-party plaintiff may then reply in rebuttal and thereafter the attorney for the original plaintiff may reply in rebuttal only of original defendant.

(d) In multi-party actions and in actions which involve third-party actions, if one or more of the parties offers no evidence, the order of summation shall be determined by the trial judge.

(e) In actions involving more than one plaintiff, defendant or third-party defendant, if the attorneys are unable to agree, the trial judge shall determine the order of speaking, inter se, of attorneys for plaintiffs, defendants and third-party defendants.

[Effective July 1, 1995.]

RULE 39.3 RECORDS, FILES AND EXHIBITS

(a) No record or paper belonging to the files of the Court shall be taken from the office or custody of the Clerk except by the order of the Court.

(b) The Clerk shall not be required to enter upon the records of this Court any written paper which does not set forth the number of the original suit.

(c) If the papers in a case are mislaid or lost and cannot be found when the case is called for trial, they may be supplied by copies.

(d) All exhibits received in evidence, or offered and rejected, upon the hearing of any cause or motion shall be delivered to the Clerk, who shall keep the same in custody, unless otherwise ordered by the Court, except that the Clerk may, without special order, permit an Official Court Reporter to retain custody pending preparation of the transcript.

(e) All exhibits referred to in section (d) shall be taken from the Clerk's custody by the party by whom they were produced or offered within sixty (60) days after the dismissal of the case by the parties or pursuant to Local Civil Rule 41.1 or the entry of final judgment by this Court, or, in the event of an appeal, within ninety (90) days after the receipt and filing of a mandate or other process or certificate showing the disposition of the case by the appellate court; otherwise, such exhibits shall be deemed abandoned and shall be destroyed or otherwise disposed of by the Clerk.

[Effective July 1, 1995.]

RULE 39.3.1   VIDEO TAPES

(a) One hundred eighty (180) days after the time for appeal has expired following final judgment or one hundred eighty (180) days after a cause is settled of record, each video tape filed of record shall be returned to the party who caused it to be filed.

(b) Nothing in this rule shall prevent this Court, for special reasons, from making such other order with respect to any video tapes as it may deem advisable.

[Effective July 1, 1995. Amended effective December 1, 2009.]

RULE 40.1   ASSIGNMENT OF COURT BUSINESS

(a) All civil litigation in this Court shall be divided into the following categories:

(1) Federal Question Cases:

A. Indemnity contract, marine contract and all other contracts.

B. FELA.

C. Jones Act—Personal Injury.

D. Antitrust.

E. Patent.

F. Labor–Management Relations.

G. Civil Rights.

H. Habeas Corpus.

I. Securities Act(s) Cases.

J. All other federal question cases.

(2) Diversity Jurisdiction Cases:

A. Insurance Contract and other Contracts.

B. Airplane Personal Injury.

C. Assault, Defamation.

D. Marine Personal Injury.

E. Motor Vehicle Personal Injury.

F. Other Personal Injury.

G. Products Liability.

H. All Other Diversity Cases.

(b) Where it appears from the designation form filed by counsel, or from the complaint, petition, motion, answer, response or other pleading in a civil case, that a plaintiff or defendant resides in or that the accident, incident or transaction occurred in the counties of Berks, Lancaster, Lehigh or Northampton, said cases shall be assigned or reassigned for trial and pretrial procedures to a Judge stationed in Reading, Allentown or Easton, who shall be given appropriate credit by category for any case so assigned, reassigned or transferred and, unless otherwise directed by the court, all trial and pretrial procedures with respect thereto shall be held in Reading, Allentown or Easton. All other cases, unless otherwise directed by the court, shall be tried in Philadelphia and as each case is filed, it shall be assigned to a judge, who shall thereafter have charge of the case for all purposes. The assignment shall take place in the following manner:

(1) There shall be a separate block of assignment cards for each category of civil cases. In each block of assignment cards for civil categories in the name of each active judge shall appear an equal number of times in a nonsequential manner except that the name of the Chief Judge shall appear one-half the number of times of each of the other active judges. The sequence of judges' names within each block shall be kept secret and no person shall directly or indirectly ascertain or divulge or attempt to ascertain or divulge the name of the judge to whom any case may be assigned before the assignment. The case number shall be stamped on the assignment card at the time of filing and assignment, and all assignment cards shall be preserved.

(2) The assignment clerk shall stamp on the complaint, petition or other initial paper of every case filed, and on the file jacket, the number of the case and the initials (or other designation) of the judge to whom it is assigned. The numbering and assignment of each case shall be completed before processing of the next case is begun.

(3) *Related Cases.* At the time of filing any civil action or proceeding, counsel shall indicate on the appropriate form whether the case is related to any other pending or within one (1) year previously terminated action of this court.

A. Civil cases are deemed related when a case filed relates to property included in another suit, or involves the same issue of fact or grows out of the same transaction as another suit, or involve the validity or infringement of a patent involved in another suit.

B. All habeas corpus petitions, pro se civil rights actions and social security appeals filed by the same individual shall be deemed related to a prior case filed in the same category of federal question cases.

(c) Assignment of Related Cases.

(1) If the fact of relationship is indicated on the appropriate form at the time of filing, the assignment clerk shall assign the case to the same judge to whom the earlier numbered related case is assigned, and shall note such assignment by means of a separate block of cards on which the clerk shall place the case number and the category and the name of the judge. If the judge receiving the later case is of the opinion that the relationship does not exist, the judge shall refer the case to the assignment clerk for reassignment by random selection in the same manner as if it were a newly filed case.

(2) If the fact of relationship does not become known until after the case is assigned, the judge receiving the later case may refer the case to the Chief Judge for reassignment to the judge to whom the earlier related case is assigned. If the Chief Judge determines that the cases are related, the Chief Judge shall transfer the later case to the judge to whom the earlier case is assigned; otherwise, the Chief Judge shall send the later case back to the judge to whom it was originally assigned.

(3) Whenever related cases require handling in such a way as to amount to substantially separate treatment of each case, and one or more of these related cases remain to be tried after disposition or trial of the other related case, the judge in question may call the matter to the attention of the Chief Judge and request leave to reassign a case of like category and approximately similar age. If the Chief Judge determines that such reassignment is desirable in promoting the substantially equal distribution of the work load, the Chief Judge shall reassign such equivalent case, either to the judge who originally transferred a later related case, or to a judge selected by lot (by reference to the assignment clerk), as the case may be.

(4) If a pending civil action or proceeding and a pending criminal action are related, the Chief Judge, at the request of any party or judge, may reassign the civil action or proceeding, in the interest of justice, to the judge to whom the criminal action is assigned.

[Effective July 1, 1995. Amended effective March 3, 1997. Amended April 5, 1999, effective April 19, 1999. Amended effective May 13, 2008.]

Note

In addition to the requirements of Local Rule 3, and in order to conform to the request of the Judicial Conference of the United States, the court, on December 19, 1974, effective January 1, 1975, ordered as follows:

1. The Clerk is authorized and directed to require a completed and executed AO Form JS44(c),* Civil Cover Sheet, which shall accompany each civil case to be filed.

2. The Clerk is directed to reject the filing of a civil case which is not accompanied by a completed and executed Civil Cover Sheet.

3. At the time of filing a civil case, those persons who are in the Custody of the City, State or Federal Institutions, and persons filing civil cases pro se, are exempt from the foregoing requirements.

* Forms and instructions are available in the Clerk's Office.

RULE 40.1.1 EMERGENCY JUDGE

The judge who is designated as "Emergency Judge" shall have the following duties:

(1) Acting in lieu of the judge to whom a case is assigned, whenever the assigned judge is absent from the Court House and cannot feasibly return prior to the expiration of the time within which judicial action is required.

A. Where the Emergency Judge is required to hold an extensive hearing or otherwise perform a substantial amount of work, the Chief Judge may, at the Emergency Judge's request, assign the case to the Emergency Judge for all purposes, and permit him to transfer an equivalent case to the judge originally assigned.

B. Orders entered by the Emergency Judge may be modified, prospectively, by the assigned judge upon the assigned judge's return.

(2) Ceremonial Functions.

[Effective July 1, 1995.]

RULE 40.3 CALENDAR CONTROL; OPERATING PROCEDURES

Calendar control and other matters affecting the conduct of the business of the Court shall be governed by written statements of policy on file in the Office of the Clerk, as such policies may from time to time be adopted or modified by the Court in the implementation of these Rules (but not in derogation thereof), and also in the implementation of such operating agreements as may be in effect from time to time between this Court and certain other courts concerning conflicting engagements of counsel, recognition of busyslips, and the like.

[Effective July 1, 1995.]

RULE 40.3.1 CALENDAR REVIEW

The Chief Judge (or, in case of the absence or disability of the Chief Judge, the next most senior active judge) shall serve as Calendar Judge, and as such shall have the following duties and responsibilities:

(1) The duties and responsibilities set forth in Rule 40.1 of these Rules.

(2) The Chief Judge may recommend to the judges of this Court the reassignment of substantial numbers of cases whenever a judge falls appreciably farther behind in the judge's trial work than the other members of the Court, and in the interests of justice to litigants and fairness to the Court as a whole, such reassignments are deemed appropriate. No such reassignment of substantial numbers of cases shall take place without the approval of a majority of the judges of this Court.

(3) Where particular counsel or law firms are unable to keep reasonably current with their trial assignments, the Chief Judge may confer with counsel in an attempt to rectify the situation through voluntary action on the part of counsel. In extreme cases, the

Chief Judge may recommend to the judges of this Court the adoption of a policy requiring reassignment of cases in excess of a certain number per lawyer beyond a certain age; or for the non-recognition of busy slips for cases in excess of a certain age, etc. No such mandatory reassignment or change in policy shall be effective unless approved by a majority vote of the judges of this Court.

[Effective July 1, 1995.]

RULE 41.1   DISMISSAL AND ABANDONMENT OF ACTIONS

(a) Whenever in any civil action the Clerk shall ascertain that no proceeding has been docketed therein for a period of more than one year immediately preceding such ascertainment, the Clerk shall send notice to counsel of record, or, if none, to the parties that the action shall be dismissed, unless the court upon written application filed within thirty (30) days from the date of such notice and upon good cause shown, shall otherwise order. In the absence of such application to or order by the court, the Clerk shall, without special order, enter upon the record "dismissed, with prejudice under Rule 41.1," and shall, upon application by defendant, tax the costs against the plaintiffs.

(b) Whenever in any civil action counsel shall notify the Clerk or the judge to whom the action is assigned that the issues between the parties have been settled, the Clerk shall, upon order of the judge to whom the case is assigned, enter an order dismissing the action with prejudice, without costs, pursuant to the agreement of counsel. Any such order of dismissal may be vacated, modified, or stricken from the record, for cause shown, upon the application of any party served within ninety (90) days of the entry of such order of dismissal, provided the application of the ninety-day time limitation is consistent with Federal Rule of Civil Procedure 60(c).

[Effective July 1, 1995. Amended effective April 5, 2004; June 10, 2014.]

RULE 41.2   MINORS, INCAPACITATED PERSONS, AND DECEDENTS' ESTATES

(a) No claim of a minor or incapacitated person or of a decedent's estate in which a minor or incapacitated person has an interest shall be compromised, settled, or dismissed unless approved by the court.

(b) No distribution of proceeds shall be made out of any fund obtained for a minor, incapacitated person or such decedent's estate as a result of a compromise, settlement, dismissal or judgment unless approved by the court.

(c) No counsel fee, costs or expenses shall be paid out of any fund obtained for a minor, incapacitated person or such decedent's estate as a result of a compromise, settlement, dismissal or judgment unless approved by the court.

[Adopted effective July 1, 1999.]

RULE 43.1   CONDUCT OF TRIALS

(a) On the trial of an issue of fact, only one attorney for any party shall examine or cross-examine any witness, unless otherwise permitted by the Court.

(b) It is the right and duty of attorneys in a case to be present in the courtroom at all times the Court may be in session in that case. Any attorney who voluntarily is absent during such times or during the deliberation of the jury, waives the right, and that of the client, to be present and consents to such proceedings as may occur in the courtroom during such absence.

[Effective July 1, 1995.]

RULE 43.1.1   ATTACHMENTS FOR WITNESSES

No action, when called for trial, shall be passed or delayed on account of an attachment for witnesses unless application therefore shall have been made within an hour after the opening of Court on the day on which the case is called for trial, or it is shown that the witness or witnesses were in attendance at the time and departed without leave.

[Effective July 1, 1995.]

RULE 45.1   SUBPOENAS FOR TRIAL

No trial shall be continued on account of the absence of any witness unless a subpoena for the attendance of such witness has been served at least seven (7) days prior to the date set for trial. This rule shall not dispense with the obligation to take the deposition of any witness where the party requiring his/her attendance, or counsel, knows that such witness intends to be absent from the district at the time of the trial, or where such witness is not subject to subpoena within this jurisdiction.

[Effective July 1, 1995. Amended effective December 1, 2009.]

RULE 45.1.1   APPEARANCE OF JUDICIAL OFFICER OF THIS COURT AS CHARACTER WITNESS

(a) No subpoena to compel a judge of this court, U.S. Magistrate or Bankruptcy Judge to testify as a character witness shall be issued served, or enforced unless the issuance of the subpoena shall have been specially allowed pursuant to this Rule.

(b) Petitions for allowance of a subpoena shall be filed in the Office of the Clerk of this court, shall be verified and shall set forth:

(1) The caption and criminal docket number of the proceeding in which the witness is to appear together with a brief description of the nature of the proceedings;

(2) the name and judicial office of the witness;

(3) facts demonstrating that the character testimony to be given by the witness will not be merely cumulative and that the rights of petitioner shall be unduly prejudiced by the application of the general order prohibiting the appearance of judicial officer of this court as character witness in this court;

(4) a copy of the desired form of subpoena; and

(5) a certificate of service showing service of the petition upon the witness and upon all parties to the proceeding.

(c) Within seven (7) days after service of the petition, the witness or any party to the proceedings below may file in the office of the clerk of this court a verified answer setting forth, if desired, a counter statement of the facts and any arguments in support of or in opposition to the petition.

(d) Petitions for allowance of a subpoena acted upon by a committee consisting of the Chief Judge of this court and two other judges of this court designated by the Chief Judge. The Committee may act upon petitions under this order with or without a hearing.

(e) No petition for allowance of a subpoena shall be considered unless it has been filed at least twenty-one (21) days prior to the date on which the case in which the witness is to appear has been listed for trial.

(f) No judge of this court, U.S. Magistrate or Bankruptcy Judge shall testify as a character witness except pursuant to a subpoena specially allowed pursuant to this Rule.

[Effective July 1, 1995. Amended effective December 1, 2009.]

RULE 48.1 JURY

(a) Challenge to Array. Every challenge to the array of jurors shall be made at least fourteen (14) days before the first day of the trial period for which the jurors have been summoned.

(b) Number of Jurors, Civil Trials.

(1) Except as provided in subparagraph (2) below, juries in civil cases shall consist, initially, of eight members. Trials in such cases shall continue so long as at least six jurors remain in service. If the number of jurors falls below six, a mistrial shall be declared upon prompt application therefor by any party then on the record, unless the parties stipulate that the

verdict may be taken from the number of jurors then remaining.

(2) Whenever it appears likely that the trial will be unusually protracted, or whenever the court in its discretion determines that the interests of justice so require, the jury may be enlarged to include as many as twelve (12) members, and any number of alternates may be used, as the court may determine; but not more than twelve (12) persons shall participate in the deliberations of the jury, nor may any verdict be rendered by a jury consisting of more than twelve (12) persons, or fewer than six (6) persons.

[Effective July 1, 1995. Amended effective December 1, 2009.]

RULE 53.1 MARSHAL'S SALES

(a) In cases wherein the proceeds of any Marshal's sale shall be before the Court for distribution and the claims upon such proceeds shall be referred to a Master, the procedure prescribed by Fed.R.Civ.P. 53 shall be followed.

(b) Before the acknowledgment of any deed executed by the Marshal for any interest in real estate sold by the Marshal by virtue of any process from this court shall be taken, the process under which such sale shall have been made shall be duly returned and filed with the Clerk.

(c) Notice of any sale by the Marshal which requires confirmation by the court shall contain, as well, notice of the time of application for confirmation. A motion for confirmation of such sale and acknowledgment of such deeds may be heard on any motion day at least fourteen (14) days after the filing of the return of process. Notice of sale, including the notice of time and place of application for confirmation, shall be given to all interested parties in advance of the sale.

(d) Whenever any such sale shall be postponed by the Marshal or by order of court, notice of the postponed time and place of the sale and of the postponed time and place of application for confirmation shall, if then known, be given by public announcement at the time and place originally fixed for such sale and, if not known, shall thereafter be given to all interested parties and, in either event, shall be published at least once in the official legal publication of the county in which the sale is to be held at least seven (7) days prior to the date of the proposed sale.

[Effective July 1, 1995. Amended effective December 1, 2009.]

RULE 53.2 ARBITRATION—THE SPEEDY CIVIL TRIAL

1. Certification of Arbitrators.

A. The Chief Judge shall certify as many arbitrators as the Chief Judge determines to be necessary under this rule.

B. Any individual may be certified to serve as an arbitrator if: (1) he or she has been for at least five years a member of the bar of the highest court of a state or the District of Columbia, (2) he or she is admitted to practice before this court, and (3) he or she is determined by the Chief Judge to be competent to perform the duties of an arbitrator.

C. Any member of the bar possessing the qualifications set forth in subsection B., desiring to become an arbitrator, shall complete the application form obtainable in the office of the Clerk and when completed shall file it with the Clerk of Court who shall forward it to the Chief Judge of the Court for the Chief Judge's determination as to whether the applicant should be certified.

D. Each individual certified as an arbitrator shall take the oath or affirmation prescribed by Title 28 U.S.C. 453 before serving as an arbitrator.

E. A list of all persons certified as arbitrators shall be maintained in the office of the Clerk.

F. Any member of the Bar certified as an arbitrator may be removed from the list of certified arbitrators for cause by a majority of the judges of this court.

2. Compensation and Expenses of Arbitrators. The arbitrators shall be compensated $150.00 each for services in each case assigned for arbitration. Whenever the parties agree to have the arbitration conducted before a single arbitrator, the single arbitrator shall be compensated $150.00 for services. In the event that the arbitration hearing is protracted, the court will entertain a petition for additional compensation. The fees shall be paid by or pursuant to the order of the director of the Administrative Office of the United States Courts.

Arbitrators shall not be reimbursed for actual expenses incurred by them in the performance of their duties under this rule.

3. Cases Eligible for Compulsory Arbitration.

A. The Clerk of Court shall, as to all cases filed on or after September 13, 1999, designate and process for compulsory arbitration all civil cases (including adversary proceedings in bankruptcy, excluding, however, (1) social security cases, (2) cases in which a prisoner is a party, (3) cases alleging a violation of a right secured by the U.S. Constitution, and (4) actions in which jurisdiction is based in whole or in part on 28 U.S.C. § 1343) wherein money damages only are being sought in an amount not in excess of $150,000.00 exclusive of interest and costs. All cases filed prior to September 13, 1999 which were designated by Clerk of Court for compulsory arbitration shall continue to be processed pursuant to this Rule.

B. The parties may by written stipulation agree that the Clerk of Court shall designate and process for arbitration pursuant to this rule any civil case eligible for arbitration pursuant to Section 3.A. of this local civil rule (including adversary proceedings in bankruptcy) wherein money damages only are being sought in an amount in excess of $150,000.00, exclusive of interest and costs.

C. For purposes of this rule only, damages shall be presumed to be not in excess of $150,000.00, exclusive of interest and costs, unless:

(1) Counsel for plaintiff, at the time of filing the complaint, or in the event of the removal of a case from state court or transfer of a case from another district to this court, within fourteen (14) days of the docketing of the case in this district filed a certification that the damages sought exceed $150,000.00, exclusive of interest and costs; or

(2) Counsel for a defendant, at the time of filing a counterclaim or cross-claim filed a certification with the court that the damages sought by the counterclaim or cross claim exceed $150,000.00, exclusive of interest and costs.

(3) The judge to whom the case has been assigned may "sua sponte" or upon motion filed by a party prior to the appointment of the arbitrators to hear the case pursuant to section 4(C), order the case exempted from arbitration upon a finding that the objectives of an arbitration trial (i.e., providing litigants with a speedier and less expensive alternative to the traditional courtroom trial) would not be realized because (a) the case involves complex legal issues, (b) legal issues predominate over factual issues, or (c) for other good cause.

4. Scheduling Arbitration Trial.

A. After an answer is filed in a case determined eligible for arbitration, the arbitration clerk shall send a notice to counsel setting forth the date and time for the arbitration trial. The date of the arbitration trial set forth in the notice shall be a date about one hundred twenty (120) days (one hundred fifty (150) days for cases filed prior to May 18, 1989) from the date the answer was filed. The notice shall also advise counsel that they may agree to an earlier date for the arbitration trial provided the arbitration clerk is notified within thirty (30) days of the date of the notice. The notice shall also advise counsel that they have ninety (90) days (one hundred twenty (120) days for cases filed prior to May 18, 1989) from the date the answer was filed to complete discovery unless the judge to whom the case has been assigned orders a shorter or longer period for discovery. In the event a third party has been brought into the action, this notice shall not be sent until an answer has been filed by the third party.

B. The arbitration trial shall be held before a panel of three arbitrators, one of whom shall be designated as chairperson of the panel, unless the parties agree to have the hearing before a single arbitrator. The arbitration panel shall be chosen through a random selection process by the clerk of the court from among the lawyers who have been certified as arbitrators. The arbitration clerk shall endeavor to assure insofar as reasonably practicable that each panel of three arbitrators shall consist of one arbitrator whose practice is primarily representing plaintiffs, one whose practice is primarily representing defendants, and a third panel member whose practice does not fit either category. The arbitration panel shall be scheduled to hear not more than four (4) cases on a date or dates several months in advance.

C. The judge to whom the case has been assigned shall at least thirty (30) days prior to the date scheduled for the arbitration trial sign an order setting forth the date and time of the arbitration trial and the names of the arbitrators designated to hear the case. In the event that a party has filed a motion to dismiss the complaint, a motion for summary judgment, a motion for judgment on the pleadings, or a motion to join necessary parties, the judge shall not sign the order until the court has ruled on the motion, but the filing of such a motion on or after the date of said order shall not stay the arbitration unless the judge so orders.

D. Upon entry of the order designating the arbitrators, the arbitration clerk shall send to each arbitrator a copy of all the pleadings, including the order designating the arbitrators, and the guidelines for arbitrators.

E. Persons selected to be arbitrators shall be disqualified for bias or prejudice as provided in Title 28, U.S.C. 144, and shall disqualify themselves in any action in which they would be required under Title 28, U.S.C. 455 to disqualify themselves if they were a justice, judge or magistrate.

F. The arbitrators designated to hear the case shall not discuss settlement with the parties or their counsel, or participate in any settlement discussions concerning the case which has been assigned to them.

5. The Arbitration Trial.

A. The trial before the arbitrators shall take place on the date and at the time set forth in the order of the Court. The trial shall take place in the United States Courthouse in a room assigned by the arbitration clerk. The arbitrators are authorized to change the date and time of the trial provided the trial is commenced within thirty (30) days of the trial date set forth in the Court's order. Any continuance beyond this thirty (30) day period must be approved by the judge to whom the case has been assigned. The arbitration clerk must be notified immediately of any continuance.

B. Counsel for the parties shall report settlement of the case to the arbitration clerk and all members of the arbitration panel assigned to the case.

C. The trial before the arbitrators may proceed in the absence of any party who, after notice, fails to be present. In the event, however, that a party fails to participate in the trial in a meaningful manner, the Court may impose appropriate sanctions, including, but not limited to the striking of any demand for a trial de novo filed by that party.

D. Rule 45 of the Federal Rules of Civil Procedure shall apply to subpoenas for attendance of witnesses and the production of documentary evidence at the trial before the arbitrators. Testimony at the trial shall be under oath or affirmation.

E. The Federal Rules of Evidence shall be used as guides to the admissibility of evidence. Copies or photographs of all exhibits, except exhibits intended solely for impeachment, must be marked for identification and delivered to adverse parties at least fourteen (14) days prior to the trial and the arbitrators shall receive such exhibits into evidence without formal proof unless counsel has been notified at least seven (7) days prior to the trial that the adverse party intends to raise an issue concerning the authenticity of the exhibit. The arbitrators may refuse to receive into evidence any exhibit, a copy or photograph of which has not been delivered prior to trial to the adverse party, as provided herein.

F. A party may have a recording and transcript made of the arbitration hearing at the party's expense.

6. Arbitration Award and Judgment.

The arbitration award shall be filed with the court promptly after the trial is concluded and shall be entered as the judgment of the court after the thirty (30) day time period for requesting a trial de novo has expired, unless a party has demanded a trial de novo, as hereinafter provided. The judgment so entered shall be subject to the same provisions of law, and shall have the same force and effect as a judgment of the court in a civil action, except that it shall not be the subject of appeal. In a case involving multiple claims and parties, any segregable part of an arbitration award concerning which a trial de novo has not been demanded by the aggrieved party before the expiration of the thirty (30) day time period provided for filing a demand for trial de novo shall become part of the final judgment with the same force and effect as a judgment of the court in a civil action, except that it shall not be the subject of appeal.

7. Trial De Novo.

A. Within thirty (30) days after the arbitration award is entered on the docket, any party may demand a trial de novo in the district court. Written notification of such a demand shall be served by the moving party upon all counsel of record or other parties. Withdrawal of a demand for a trial de novo shall not reinstate the arbitrators' award and the case shall proceed as if it had not been arbitrated.

B. Upon demand for a trial de novo, the action shall be placed on the trial calendar of the Court and treated for all purposes as if it had not been referred to arbitration. In the event it appears to the judge to whom the case was assigned that the case will not be reached for trial de novo within ninety (90) days of the filing of the demand for trial de novo, the judge shall request the Chief Judge to reassign the case to a judge whose trial calendar will make it possible for the case to be tried de novo within ninety (90) days of the filing of the demand for trial de novo. Any right of trial by jury which a party would otherwise have shall be preserved inviolate.

C. At the trial de novo, the court shall not admit evidence that there had been an arbitration trial, the nature or amount of the award, or any other matter concerning the conduct of the arbitration proceeding unless the evidence would otherwise be admissible in the Court under the Federal Rules of Evidence.

D. To make certain that the arbitrators' award is not considered by the Court or jury either before, during or after the trial de novo, the arbitration clerk shall, upon the filing of the arbitration award, enter onto the docket only the date and "arbitration award filed" and nothing more, and shall retain the arbitrators' award in a separate file in the Clerk's office. In the event no demand for trial de novo is filed within the designated time period, the arbitration clerk shall enter the award on the docket and place it in the case file.

[Effective July 1, 1995. Amended effective September 13, 1999; April 5, 2004; December 1, 2009.]

RULE 53.3   ALTERNATIVE DISPUTE RESOLUTION

1. Litigants in all civil actions, exempting only social security appeals, pro se prisoner civil rights actions, and petitions for habeas corpus, shall be required to consider the use of an alternative dispute resolution process (the "ADR process") at an appropriate stage in the litigation.

2. ADR processes may include mediation and settlement conferences and such other ADR processes as the judge to whom the case is assigned (the "assigned judge") may designate.

3. All ADR processes subject to this Rule shall be confidential, and disclosure by any person of confidential dispute resolution communications is prohibited unless confidentiality has been waived by all participants in the ADR process, or disclosure is ordered by the assigned judge for good cause shown.

4. Nothing in the Rule shall be construed to limit the assigned judge from (a) conducting settlement conferences or referring a matter to a magistrate judge for a settlement conference, or (b) ordering the litigants to participate in an ADR process, or (c) approving or disapproving of an ADR process selected by the litigants.

5. The Alternative Dispute Resolution ("ADR") Committee of the court shall administer, oversee, and evaluate the court's ADR program in accordance with the Alternative Dispute Resolution Act of 1998. The Clerk of Court, or such other person as may be designated from time to time by the Chief Judge, shall serve as the ADR coordinator. Under the direction of the ADR committee, the coordinator shall administer a program for recruitment, screening and training of attorneys to serve as neutrals.

6. The Rule is intended to be flexible so as to permit the court to adopt, from time to time, guidelines and policies for the administration of the ADR program. The procedures promulgated by the court for the implementation of the ADR program shall be maintained on file in the office of the Clerk.

7. Nothing in the Rule shall be construed to amend or modify the provisions of Local Civil Rule 53.2 (compulsory and voluntary arbitration with right of trial de novo). Local Civil Rule 53.2.1 (compulsory mediation) is repealed by separate order.

[Effective July 1, 2003.]

COURT-ANNEXED MEDIATION PROTOCOL UNDER LOCAL CIVIL RULE 53.3

In accordance with the Alternative Dispute Resolution Act of 1998 and Local Rule of Civil Procedure 53.3, the Court adopts the following protocol (the "Protocol") which shall guide the administration of the Court–Annexed mediation program. Mediation is a facilitated negotiation process. The role of mediation is to bring the parties to, or closer to, a negotiated settlement.

A. Selection and Training of Mediators

1. Any attorney who has been admitted to practice in any federal court for at least ten years and who is a member in good standing of the bar of the Court is eligible to apply for approval as a mediator.

2. In order to obtain approval as a mediator the applicant must:

a. be knowledgeable about civil litigation in federal court; and,

b. complete at least four hours of training as a mediator approved by the Court.

3. Any attorney eligible to serve as a mediator may apply to become an approved mediator by filing an application, in a form authorized by the Alternative Dispute Resolution ("ADR") Committee of the Court, which fully discloses all the relevant personal and professional information requested.

4. Any attorney eligible for approval as a mediator under ¶1 above and who meets the criteria established in ¶2 above shall be approved by the Chief Judge to act as a mediator.

5. The ADR Coordinator shall maintain a list (the "Mediators' List") of all attorneys who have been approved by the Chief Judge.

6. The ADR Coordinator under the direction of the ADR Committee shall establish and administer a mediation training program of at least four hours in conjunction with a recognized professional training organization.

7. Any attorney who has been approved by the Chief Judge to serve as a mediator will be removed from the Mediators' List:

a. Upon his/her request in writing to the ADR Coordinator; or,

b. Upon good cause shown at the discretion of the Chief Judge.

B. Assignment of Cases to a Mediator

8. The parties shall include in their report submitted to the Court under F.R.C.P. 26(f) a statement regarding their position(s) on mediation or other forms of alternative dispute resolution.

9. Cases may be assigned to mediation:

a. By the assigned judge at or before a pretrial conference under F.R.C.P. 16; and,

b. By agreement of the parties before or after the pretrial conference under F.R.C.P. 16 with the approval of the assigned judge.

10. Promptly after a case has been assigned to mediation, the ADR Coordinator shall designate a mediator from the Mediators' List to conduct mediation in the case.

11. The designation of a mediator from the Mediators' List shall be made on a rotating basis unless (a) a specific mediator on the list is requested by the parties and approved by the assigned judge or (b) a specific mediator is designated to serve in a case by the assigned judge. Designation under (a) or (b) shall only be made after consultation with the ADR Coordinator in order to avoid overburdening any mediator.

12. Persons acting as mediators under this rule are assisting the Court in performing its judicial function. They shall be disqualified for bias or prejudice as provided by 28 U.S.C. 144 and shall disqualify themselves in any action in which they would be required under 28 U.S.C. 455 to disqualify themselves if they were a justice, judge or magistrate judge.

13. If any time after being designated to serve on a case, the designated mediator shall be unable or unwilling to serve, the ADR Coordinator shall designate a new mediator in accordance with the procedures set forth in ¶11 for designation of mediators.

14. Once a mediator has been designated (See ¶10) and has accepted the designation, the ADR Coordinator shall notify the assigned judge and counsel of the designation, fix a date and time for the mediation and assign a room in the courthouse or in such other facility as the ADR Coordinator deems appropriate to conduct the mediation.

15. If the time fixed for any conference is not convenient, the mediator is authorized to change it, provided the conference takes place within 15 days of the date fixed and the ADR Coordinator gives notice of the change at the request of the mediator. Any postponement of more than 15 days after that date must be submitted to the ADR Coordinator for approval by the assigned judge.

C. The Mediation Process

16. a. The mediator shall preside at the mediation and shall establish ground rules by which the mediation will proceed consistent with the rules of the Court and this Protocol.

b. As promptly as possible during the mediation, the mediator should identify the issues and discuss them with the parties to focus on achieving a negotiated settlement. The mediator should consider using a procedure by which he or she speaks to counsel for each party separately and confidentially in an effort to determine each party's "real position." During such process, the mediator should also maintain the confidentiality of the statements made by each party unless that party specifically authorizes the mediator to disclose information divulged during such a private session.

c. In some cases, the mediator may consider suggesting specific settlement terms. Such action is not required, or even appropriate, in every case, and should generally be employed only if the parties request it and the mediator concludes it will aid the parties and their counsel in reaching a settlement. Any such settlement recommendation should be based on the mediator's experience or other knowledge concerning jury verdicts and settlement value.

17. Not later than three (3) days before the mediation, each party shall deliver, fax, or e-mail to

the mediator a memorandum summarizing, in concise fashion, the nature of the case and the party's positions on (1) the major factual and legal issues affecting liability, (2) the relief sought by each party, and (3) settlement. The memorandum submitted to the mediator is solely for use in mediation and shall not be served on opposing parties or the assigned judge or filed with the Clerk of Court.

18. Counsel primarily responsible for the case shall attend the mediation. At the mediation, the parties shall be prepared to discuss: (1) all liability issues; (2) all damages and other relief issues; and (3) the positions of the parties on settlement. Counsel shall make arrangements for the client, or a representative of the client with full decision-making authority, to be present at the mediation for the purpose of discussing settlement unless the parties agree that the client or authorized representative may be available by telephone, and the agreement is approved by the mediator.

19. If, during the course of the mediation, the parties reach an agreement settling their dispute, the parties shall reduce the agreement to writing at the conference and the mediator shall adjourn the mediation and promptly notify the ADR Coordinator and the assigned judge that the case has been settled.

20. Whenever the mediator determines that settlement of the case is not likely to result from the mediation process, the mediator shall adjourn the mediation and promptly notify the ADR Coordinator and the assigned judge of the termination of the mediation.

21. Whenever the mediator determines that an additional mediation session is likely to result in settlement of the case, the mediator, with the consent of the parties, may schedule an additional mediation within thirty (30) days. The mediator shall promptly notify the ADR Coordinator who shall fix a date, time, and place for the additional mediation session and, in turn, will notify counsel and the assigned judge.

D. General Rules

22. Once the mediator completes and forwards to the ADR Coordinator a report of the outcome of the mediation, (See ¶¶ 19–20) and unless an additional session has been scheduled (See ¶ 21), the mediator's services are completed in the case.

23. No recording or transcript of any part of the mediation, including conversations between the mediator and counsel or the parties, shall be made.

24. The mediator shall serve in a pro bono capacity without compensation.

25. The mediation process shall be subject to the case management authority of the assigned

judge including, but not limited to, the authority to impose sanctions.

26. The mediator shall not communicate with the assigned judge during the mediation.

[Effective July 1, 2003.]

RULE 54.1   COSTS: SECURITY FOR, TAXATION, PAYMENT

(a) In every action in which the plaintiff was not a resident of the Eastern District of Pennsylvania at the time suit was brought, or having been so afterwards removed from this District, an order for security for costs may be entered, upon application therefor within a reasonable time and upon notice. In default of the entry of such security at the time fixed by the court, judgment of dismissal shall be entered on motion.

(b) All bills of costs requiring taxation shall be taxed by the Clerk, subject to an appeal to the court. Any party appellant shall, within seven (7) days of such taxation, file a written specification of the items objected to and the grounds of objection. A copy of the specifications of objections shall be served on the opposite party or his attorney within seven (7) days. An appeal shall be dismissed for non-compliance with the appeal requirements.

(c) Any party requesting taxation of costs by the Clerk shall give the Clerk and all other parties fourteen (14) days' written notice of such request. The Clerk shall fix the time for taxation and notify the parties or their counsel.

(d) The Clerk shall not enter an order of dismissal or of satisfaction of judgment until the Clerk's and Marshal's costs have been paid. The Clerk, in cases settled by parties without payment of costs, may have an order on one or more of the parties to pay the costs. Upon failure to pay the costs within fourteen (14) days, or at such time as the court may otherwise direct, the Clerk may issue execution for recovery of costs.

[Effective July 1, 1995. Amended February 5, 2001; December 1, 2009; May 21, 2010.]

RULE 56.1   JUDGMENTS PURSUANT TO A WARRANT OF ATTORNEY

No judgment shall be entered on any warrant of attorney more than ten (10) years old but less than twenty (20) years old without leave of Court. If the warrant is more than ten (10) but less than twenty (20) years old, the motion for leave shall be accompanied by an affidavit of one having knowledge of the facts, stating the due execution of the warrant, non-payment and that the obligor is alive. If the warrant is twenty (20) or more years old, a petition shall be filed for a rule to show cause why leave should not be granted and service of the petition and rule shall be made on the obligor, if he is within this district.

[Effective July 1, 1995.]

RULE 67.1 BAIL, SURETIES AND SECURITY

(a) No attorney or officer of this Court shall be acceptable as surety, bail or security of any kind in any proceeding in this Court.

(b) Exceptions to bail or surety shall be in writing, filed with the Clerk and notice thereof in writing shall be given by the expectant to the opposing party or his attorney and to the Marshal within forty-eight (48) hours days from the filing thereof.

[Effective July 1, 1995.]

RULE 67.2 DEPOSITS IN COURT

(a) Payments into Court shall unless otherwise determined by the Clerk, be in cash, money order, certified or cashier's check.

(b) When funds on deposit with the Clerk are disbursed, payment shall be made by clerk payable to the party entitled thereto and the resident attorney of record, if any, representing such party and the check shall be delivered to such attorney unless otherwise ordered by the Court.

[Effective July 1, 1995.]

RULE 72.1 UNITED STATES MAGISTRATE JUDGES

I. Authority of United States Magistrates Judges in Civil Matters.

(a) **Duties Under 28 U.S.C. 636.** Each United States magistrate judge of this district is authorized to exercise the powers and perform the duties prescribed by 28 U.S.C. 636(a).

(b) **Prisoner Cases Under 28 U.S.C. 2254 and 2255.** A magistrate judge may perform any or all of the duties imposed upon a judge by the rules governing proceedings in the United States District Courts under 28 U.S.C. 2254 and 2255, except signing CJA vouchers for compensation to be paid unless representation is furnished exclusively before a magistrate judge. In so doing, a magistrate judge may issue any preliminary orders and conduct any necessary evidentiary hearing or other appropriate proceeding and shall submit to a judge a report containing proposed findings of fact and recommendation for disposition of the petition by the judge. Any order disposing of the petition may be made only by a judge.

(c) **Prisoner Cases Under 42 U.S.C. 1983.** A magistrate judge may issue any preliminary orders and conduct any necessary evidentiary hearing or other appropriate proceeding and shall submit to a judge a report containing proposed findings of fact and recommendations for the disposition of complaints filed by prisoners challenging the conditions of their confinement.

(d) **Special Master References.** A magistrate judge may be designated by a judge to serve as a special master in appropriate civil cases in accordance with U.S.C. 636(b)(2) and Fed.R.Civ.P. 53. Upon the consent of the parties, a magistrate judge may be designated by a judge to serve as a special master in any civil case.

(e) **Other Duties.** A magistrate judge is also authorized to:

(1) Exercise general supervision of civil calendars, conduct calendar and status calls and determine motions to expedite or postpone the trial of cases for the judges;

(2) Conduct pretrial conferences, settlement conferences, omnibus hearings, and related pretrial proceedings in civil cases;

(3) Conduct voir dire and select petit juries;

(4) Accept petit jury verdicts in civil cases in the absence of a judge;

(5) Issue subpoenas, writs of habeas corpus ad testificandum or habeas corpus ad prosequendum, or other orders necessary to obtain the presence of parties, witnesses or evidence needed for Court proceedings;

(6) Order the exoneration or forfeiture of bonds;

(7) Conduct proceedings for the collection of civil penalties of not more than $200 assessed under the Federal Boat Safety Act of 1971, in accordance with 46 U.S.C. 4311(d) and 12309(c);

(8) Conduct examinations of judgment debtors in accordance with Fed.R.Civ. P. 69;

(9) Conduct proceedings for initial commitment of narcotics addicts under Title III of the Narcotic Addict Rehabilitation Act, with the final determination and order of commitment to be made by the district judge assigned to the case; and

(10) Perform any additional duty that is not inconsistent with the Constitution and laws of the United States.

II. Assignment of Matters to Magistrate Judges in Civil Matters.

(a) **In General.** In accordance with procedures adopted by the Board of Judges, each district judge shall have an assigned magistrate judge. The assignment list shall be posted in the office of the Clerk. Matters shall be referred to magistrate judges at the direction of the district judge to whom the case is assigned.

III.   Procedures Before the Magistrate Judge in Civil Matters.

(a) In General.   In performing duties for the Court, a magistrate judge shall conform to all applicable provisions of federal statutes and rules, to the general procedural rules of this Court, and to the requirements specified in any order of reference from a judge.

(b) Special Provisions for the Disposition of Civil Cases by a Magistrate Judge on Consent of the Parties—28 U.S.C. 636(c).

(1) *Notice.*   The Clerk of Court shall notify the parties in all civil cases that they may consent to have a magistrate judge conduct any or all proceedings in the case and order the entry of a final judgment. Such notice shall be handed or mailed to the plaintiff or the plaintiff's representative at the time an action is filed and to other parties as attachments to copies of the complaint and summons, when served. Additional notices may be furnished to the parties at later stages of the proceedings, and may be included with pretrial notices and instructions.

(2) *Execution of Consent.*   The plaintiff shall be responsible for securing the execution of consent forms by the parties and for filing such forms with the Clerk of Court. Unless otherwise ordered by the district judge to whom the case is assigned, consent forms may be filed at any time prior to trial. No consent form will be made available nor will its contents be made known to any judge or magistrate judge, unless all parties have consented to the reference to a magistrate judge.

(3) *Reference.*   After consent forms have been executed and filed, the clerk shall transmit them to the judge to whom the case has been assigned for approval and possible referral of the case to a magistrate judge.

IV.   Reconsideration and Appeal in Civil Matters.

(a) Reconsideration of Non–Dispositive Matters—28 U.S.C. 636(b)(1)(A).   Any party may object to a magistrate judge's order determining a motion or matter under 28 U.S.C. 636(b)(1)(A), within fourteen (14) days after issuance of the magistrate judge's order, unless a different time is prescribed by the magistrate judge or a judge. Such party shall file with the Clerk of Court, and serve on the magistrate judge and all parties, a written statement of objections which shall specifically designate the order, or part thereof, subject to the objections and the basis for such objection.

(b) Review of Case–Dispositive Motions and Prisoner Litigation—28 U.S.C. 636(b)(1)(B).   Any party may object to a magistrate judge's proposed findings, recommendations or report under 28 U.S.C. 636(b)(1)(B), and subsections 1(c) and (d) of this Rule within fourteen (14) days after being served with a copy thereof. Such party shall file with the Clerk of Court, and serve on the magistrate judge and all parties, written objections which shall specifically identify the portions of the proposed findings, recommendations or report to which objection is made and the basis for such objections. Any party may respond to another party's objections within fourteen (14) days after being served with a copy thereof.

(c) All issues and evidence shall be presented to the magistrate judges, and unless the interest of justice requires it, new issues and evidence shall not be raised after the filing of the Magistrate Judge's Report and Recommendation if they could have been presented to the magistrate judge.

[Effective July 1, 1995. Amended effective January 1, 1999; June 3, 2002; December 1, 2009.]

RULE 83.3   BROADCASTING, FILMING AND RECORDING IN COURTROOMS AND APPURTENANT AREAS

(a) No judicial proceedings may be broadcast by radio or television, or filmed by still or motion-picture camera, except that investitive, naturalization or other ceremonial proceedings may be broadcast, or filmed, subject to the supervision of the Clerk, and pursuant to regulations formulated by the Clerk, with the approval of the Chief Judge, which regulations are calculated to insure that the solemnity of such proceedings is not jeopardized.

(b) No cameras, broadcasting mechanisms, or related apparatus may be brought into, or retained or operated within, any District Court courtroom or any hall on the same floor as such courtroom, except when no non-ceremonial judicial proceedings are in session on such floor of the Courthouse. The bringing of cameras, broadcasting mechanisms, or related apparatus into any vacant courtroom or its appurtenant hallways, and the retention or operation of such apparatus therein, are subject to the supervision of the Clerk, pursuant to regulations formulated by the Clerk with approval of the Chief Judge.

(c) No person not employed in such office may bring any cameras, broadcasting mechanisms, or related apparatus into the Clerk's Office, the Marshal's Office, the Probation Office, the Office of Pre-trial Services, or any other office which is an administrative component of the District Court, except as permitted and supervised by the chief of that office or an authorized designee thereof.

(d) No cameras, broadcasting mechanisms, or related apparatus may be operated within 50 feet of the elevator bay on the ground floor of the Courthouse.

[Effective July 1, 1995.]

RULE 83.5   ADMISSION TO PRACTICE

(a) Any attorney who is a member in good standing of the bar of the Supreme Court of Pennsylvania may, by a verified application and upon motion of a member of the bar of this Court, make application to be admitted generally as an attorney of the Court. A fee established by this court shall be assessed for all such admissions. No admission shall be effective until such time as the fee has been paid.

(b) The petition for admission shall aver, under oath, all pertinent facts. The Court may admit the petitioner upon such petition and motion or may require that the petitioner offer satisfactory evidence of present good moral and professional character.

(c) Upon admission the petitioner shall take and subscribe to the following oath or affirmation:

"I do swear (or affirm) that I will demean myself as an attorney of this Court uprightly and accordingly to law and that I will support and defend the Constitution of the United States."

(d) Upon appropriate motion and the taking of the oath prescribed in subparagraph (c), any attorney admitted to the limited practice provided by Subchapter C of the Pennsylvania Bar Admission Rules may be admitted to a similar limited practice before this court as to all causes in which the defender association or legal services program with which that attorney is affiliated acts as counsel.

1. The right to practice under this rule shall terminate upon termination of admission to practice under Subchapter C of the Pennsylvania Bar Admission Rules.

2. The roll of attorneys maintained by the Clerk of this Court shall be specially noted to show those admitted under the provisions of this subparagraph.

(e) Any attorney who is a member in good standing of the bar of the highest court of any state, territory, or the District of Columbia may, without being admitted generally as an attorney of this Court, act as an attorney in this Court on behalf of the United States Government or any of its departments or agencies.

(f) An attorney applying for first-time admission to the bar of this court must simultaneously inform the court of any previous public discipline by any other court of the United States or the District of Columbia, or by a court of any state, territory, commonwealth or possession of the United States and of any conviction for a "serious crime" as defined in these rules.

Petitions for first-time admission filed by an attorney who has previously been publicly disciplined by another court or convicted of a serious crime shall be filed with the Chief Judge of this court. Upon receipt of the petition, the Chief Judge shall assign the matter for prompt hearing before one or more judges of this court appointed by the Chief Judge. The judge or judges assigned to the matter shall thereafter schedule a hearing at which the petitioner shall have the burden of demonstrating, by clear and convincing evidence, that the petitioner has the moral qualifications, competency and learning in the law required for admission to practice law before this court, and that the petitioner's admission shall not be detrimental to the integrity and standing of the bar or to the administration of justice, or subversive of the public interest.

In all the above-described proceedings, the attorney applying for first-time admission shall have the right to counsel. All such petitions shall be accompanied by an advance cost deposit in an amount to be set by the court, from time to time, to cover anticipated costs of the proceeding.

(g) The judge or judges to whom a matter is assigned under Local Rule 83.5(f) shall make a report and recommendation to the court after a hearing. The court shall decide the matter.

[Effective July 1, 1995. Amended effective February 1, 1997; March 3, 1997; March 1, 2000; October 1, 2002.]

RULE 83.5.1   STUDENT PRACTICE RULE

A. Purpose. The following Student Practice Rule is designed to encourage law schools to provide clinical instruction in litigation of varying kinds, and thereby enhance the competence of lawyers in practice before the United States courts.

B. Student Requirements. An eligible student must:

1. Be duly enrolled in a law school;

2. have completed at least three semesters of legal studies, or the equivalent;

3. be enrolled for credit in a law school clinical program which has been certified by this court;

4. be certified by the Dean of the law school, or the Dean's designee, as being of good character and sufficient legal ability, in accordance with subparagraphs 1–3 above, to fulfill the student's responsibilities as a legal intern to both the student's client and this Court;

5. be certified by this court to practice pursuant to this Rule;

6. not accept personal compensation for legal services the student performs from a client or other source.

C. Program Requirements.

1. must be a law school clinical practice program for credit, in which a law student obtains academic and practice advocacy training, utilizing law school faculty or adjunct faculty for practice supervision, including federal government attorneys or private practitioners;

2. must be certified by this court;

3. must be conducted in such a manner as not to conflict with normal court schedules;

4. may accept compensation other than from a client;

5. must maintain malpractice insurance for its activities.

D. Supervisor Requirements. A supervisor must:

1. have faculty or adjunct faculty status at the responsible law school and be certified by the Dean of the law school as being of good character and sufficient legal ability and as being adequately trained to fulfill a supervisor's responsibilities.

2. be admitted to practice in this court;

3. be present with the student at all times in court, and at other proceedings, including depositions, in which testimony is taken;

4. co-sign all pleadings or other documents filed with the court;

5. assume full personal professional responsibility for the student's guidance in any work undertaken and for the quality of a student's work, and be available for consultation with represented clients;

6. assist and counsel the student in activities mentioned in this rule, and review such activities with the student, to the extent required for the proper practical training of the student and the protection of the client;

7. be responsible to supplement oral or written work of the student as necessary to ensure proper representation of the client.

E. Certification of Student, Program and Supervisor.

1. *Students:*

a. Certification by the law school Dean and approval by this court shall be filed with the Clerk of Court, and unless it is sooner withdrawn, shall remain in effect until expiration of 18 months;

b. Certification of a program may be withdrawn by this court at any time, in the discretion of the court, and without any showing of cause.

2. *Program:*

a. Certification of a program by this court shall be filed with the Clerk of Court and shall remain in effect indefinitely unless withdrawn by the court;

b. Certification of a program may be withdrawn by this court at any time.

3. *Supervisor:*

a. Certification of a supervisor must be filed with the Clerk of the Court, and shall remain in effect indefinitely unless withdrawn by this court;

b. Certification of a supervisor may be withdrawn by this court at any time;

c. Certification of a supervisor may be withdrawn by the Dean by mailing the notice to that effect to the Clerk of Court.

F. Activities. A certified student, under the personal supervision of the student's supervisor, as set forth in Part D of this Rule, may:

1. represent any client including federal, state or local government bodies, in any civil or administrative matter, if the client on whose behalf the student is appearing has indicated consent in writing to that appearance and the supervising lawyer has also indicated in writing the supervisor's approval of that appearance;

2. engage in all activities on behalf of the student's client that a licensed attorney may engage in.

G. Limitation of Activities. The court retains the power to limit a student's participation in any particular case to such activities as the court deems consistent with the appropriate administration of justice.

[Effective July 1, 1995. Amended effective December 16, 2013.]

RULE 83.5.2 ASSOCIATE COUNSEL

(a) Except for attorneys appearing on behalf of the United States Government or a department or agency thereof pursuant to Rule 83.5(e), any attorney who is not a member of the bar of this court shall, in each proceeding in which that attorney desires to appear, have as associate counsel of record a member of the bar of this court upon whom all pleadings, motions, notices and other papers can be served conformably to the Federal Rules of Civil Procedure and rules of this court.

(b) An attorney who is not a member of the bar of this Court shall not actively participate in the conduct of any trial or pre-trial or post-trial proceeding before this Court unless, upon motion of a member of the bar of this Court containing a verified application, leave to do so shall have been granted. A fee established by this court shall be assessed for all such applications. No admission shall be effective until such time as the fee has been paid, *except that any counsel appearing in a case transferred pursuant to an Order of the*

Judicial Panel on Multidistrict Litigation need not pay such a fee.

[Effective July 1, 1995. Amended October 1, 2002; September 6, 2013; December 16, 2013.]

RULE 83.6 RULES OF ATTORNEY CONDUCT

Table of Contents

The United States District Court for the Eastern District of Pennsylvania, in furtherance of its inherent power and responsibility to supervise the conduct of attorneys who are admitted to practice before it, promulgates the following Rules of Disciplinary Enforcement superseding all of its other Rules pertaining to disciplinary enforcement heretofore promulgated.

[Effective July 1, 1995. Amended effective March 3, 1997; March 1, 2000; February 4, 2002.]

Rule I. Attorneys Convicted of Crimes

A. An attorney admitted to practice in this court shall promptly notify the Clerk of this court whenever he or she has been convicted in any court of the United States, or the District of Columbia, or of any state, territory, commonwealth or possession of the United States of a serious crime as hereinafter defined. Upon such notification or upon the filing with this court of a certified copy of the judgment of conviction, the court shall enter an order immediately suspending that attorney, whether the conviction resulted from plea of guilty or nolo contendere or from a verdict after trial or otherwise, and regardless of the pendency of any appeal, until final disposition of a disciplinary proceeding to be commenced upon such conviction. A copy of such order shall immediately be served upon the attorney. Upon good cause shown, the court may set aside such order when it appears in the interest of justice to do so.

B. The term "serious crime" shall include any felony and any lesser crime a necessary element of which, as determined by the statutory or common law definition of such crime in the jurisdiction where the judgment was entered, involves false swearing, misrepresentation, fraud, willful failure to file income tax returns, deceit, bribery, extortion, misappropriation, theft, or an attempt or a conspiracy or solicitation of another to commit a "serious crime".

C. A certified copy of a judgment of conviction of an attorney for any crime shall be conclusive evidence of the commission of that crime in any disciplinary proceeding instituted against that attorney based upon the conviction.

D. Upon the filing of a certified copy of a judgment of conviction of an attorney for a serious crime, the court shall in addition to suspending that attorney in accordance with the provisions of this Rule, also refer the matter to counsel for the institution of a disciplinary proceeding before the court in which the sole issue to be determined shall be the extent of the final discipline to be imposed as a result of the conduct resulting in the conviction, provided that a disciplinary proceeding so instituted will not be brought to final hearing until all appeals from the conviction are concluded.

E. Upon the filing of a certified copy of a judgment of conviction of an attorney for a crime not constituting a "serious crime," the court may refer the matter to counsel for whatever action counsel may deem warranted, including the institution of a disciplinary proceeding before the court; provided, however, that the court may in its discretion make no reference with respect to convictions for minor offenses.

F. An attorney suspended under the provisions of this Rule will be reinstated immediately upon the filing of a certificate demonstrating that the underlying conviction of a serious crime has been reversed but the reinstatement will not terminate any disciplinary proceeding then pending against the attorney, the disposition of which shall be determined by the court on the basis of all available evidence pertaining to both guilt and the extent of discipline to be imposed.

Rule II. Discipline or Prohibitions Imposed By Other Courts or Authorities

A. Any attorney admitted to practice before this court, upon being subjected to public discipline by any other court of the United States or the District of Columbia, or by a court of any state, territory, commonwealth or possession of the United States, or upon being prohibited from the practice of law for failure to fulfill any continuing legal education requirement, for voluntarily entering into inactive status, or for any other reason, shall promptly notify the Clerk of this court of such action. Placement on inactive status or other action taken for failure to maintain a bona fide office in another jurisdiction shall not be grounds for discipline or other action by this court so long as the attorney maintains a bona fide office in another jurisdiction.

B. Upon notification as required under paragraph A or the filing of a certified or exemplified copy of a judgment or order demonstrating that an attorney admitted to practice before this court has been disciplined by another court or otherwise has been prohibited from the practice of law, the Chief Judge of this court, if he or she deems it appropriate, shall forthwith issue a notice directed to the attorney containing:

1. a copy of the judgment or order from the other court or authority; and

2. an order to show cause directing that the attorney inform this court within thirty 30 days after service of that order upon the attorney, personally or by mail, of any claim by the attorney predicated upon the grounds set forth in (D.) hereof that the imposition of the identical discipline or prohibition by the court would be unwarranted and the reasons therefor.

C. In the event the discipline or prohibition imposed in the other jurisdiction has been stayed there, any reciprocal action imposed in this court shall be deferred until such stay expires.

D. Upon the expiration of thirty (30) days from service of the notice issued pursuant to the provisions of (B) above and after an opportunity for any attorney contesting the imposition of the identical discipline or prohibition to be heard by one or more judges designated by the Chief Judge, this court shall impose the identical discipline or prohibition unless the respondent-attorney demonstrates, or this court finds, that upon the face of the record upon which the discipline or prohibition in another jurisdiction is predicated it clearly appears:

1. that the procedure was so lacking in notice or opportunity to be heard as to constitute a deprivation of due process; or

2. that there was such an infirmity of proof as to give rise to the clear conviction that this court could not, consistent with its duty, accept as final the conclusion on that subject; or

3. that the imposition of the same discipline or prohibition by this court would result in grave injustice; or

4. that the misconduct or other basis established for the discipline or prohibition is deemed by this court to warrant substantially different action.

Where this court determines that any of said elements exist, it shall enter such other order as it deems appropriate.

E. In all other respects, a final adjudication in another court or authority that an attorney has been guilty of misconduct or otherwise should be prohibited from the practice of law shall establish conclusively the facts for purposes of a proceeding under this Rule in the court of the United States.

F. This court may at any stage appoint counsel to investigate and/or prosecute the proceeding under this Rule.

G. The judge or judges to whom any proceeding under this Rule is assigned shall make a report and recommendations to the court after the parties have been heard, which will be filed under seal and served on the parties. A party shall serve and file under seal any objections within fourteen (14) days thereafter. Further submissions by any party shall be served and filed under seal within seven (7) days after service of any objections. The court shall then decide the matter; after decision the report and recommendation, any objections, and any submissions shall be unsealed unless otherwise ordered by the court.

H. Any attorney who is disciplined or otherwise prohibited from the practice of law by a state court or authority may continue to practice in this court if this court decides, in accordance with this Rule, that no discipline or prohibition should be imposed. However, continuance of practice in this court does not authorize an attorney to practice in any other jurisdiction, and no attorney shall hold out himself or herself as authorized to practice law in any jurisdiction in which the attorney is not admitted.

Rule III. Disbarment on Consent or Resignation in other Courts

A. Any attorney admitted to practice before this court who shall be disbarred on consent or resign from the bar of any other court of the United States or the District of Columbia, or from the bar of any state, territory, commonwealth or possession of the United States while an investigation into allegations of misconduct is pending, shall, upon the filing with this court of a certified or exemplified copy of the judgment or order accepting such disbarment on consent or resignation, cease to be permitted to practice before this court and be stricken from the roll of attorneys admitted to practice before this court.

B. Any attorney admitted to practice before this court shall, upon being disbarred on consent or resigning from the bar of any other court of the United States or the District of Columbia, or from the Bar of any state, territory, commonwealth or possession of the United States while an investigation into allegations of misconduct is pending, promptly inform the Clerk of this court of such disbarment on consent or resignation.

Rule IV. Standards for Professional Conduct

A. For misconduct defined in these Rules, and for good cause shown, and after notice and opportunity to be heard, any attorney admitted to practice before this court may be disbarred, suspended from practice before this court, reprimanded or subjected to such other disciplinary action as the circumstances may warrant.

B. Acts or omissions by an attorney admitted to practice before this court, individually or in concert with any other person or persons, which violate the Rules of Professional Conduct adopted by this Court shall constitute misconduct and shall be grounds for discipline, whether or not the act or omission occurred in the course of any attorney-client relationship.

The Rules of Professional Conduct adopted by this court are the Rules of Professional Conduct adopted by the Supreme Court of Pennsylvania, as amended from time to time by that state court, except as otherwise provided by specific Rule of this Court after consideration of comments by representatives of bar associations within the state, except that prior court approval as a condition to the issuance of a subpoena addressed to an attorney in any criminal proceeding, including a grand jury, shall not be required. The propriety of such a subpoena may be considered on a motion to quash.

A. When the misconduct or other basis for action against an attorney (other than as set forth in Rule II) or allegations of the same which, if substantiated, would warrant discipline or other action against an attorney admitted to practice before this court shall come to the attention of a Judge of this court, whether by complaint or otherwise, and the applicable procedure is not otherwise mandated by these Rules, the judge shall refer the matter to the Chief Judge who shall issue an order to show cause.

B. Upon the respondent-attorney's answer to the order to show cause, if any issue of fact is raised or the respondent-attorney wishes to be heard in mitigation the Chief Judge shall set the matter for prompt hearing before one or more judges of this court, provided however that if the proceeding is predicated upon the complaint of a judge of this court the hearing shall be conducted before a panel of three other judges of this court appointed by the Chief Judge.

C. This court may at any stage appoint counsel to investigate and/or prosecute the proceeding under this Rule.

D. This court may refer any matter under this Rule to the appropriate state disciplinary or other authority for investigation and decision before taking any action. The attorney who is the subject of the referral shall promptly notify this court of the decision of any state court or authority and shall take whatever steps are necessary to waive any confidentiality requirement so that this court may receive the record of that referral.

E. The judge or judges to whom any proceeding under this Rule is assigned shall make a report and recommendations to the court after the parties have been heard, which will be filed under seal and served on the parties. A party shall serve and file under seal any objections within fourteen (14) days thereafter. Further submissions by any party shall be served and filed under seal within seven (7) days after service of any objections. The court shall then decide the matter; after decision the report and recommendation, any objections, and any submissions shall be unsealed unless otherwise ordered by the court.

Rule V. Disciplinary or Other Proceedings Against Attorneys

A. When the misconduct or other basis for action against an attorney (other than as set forth in Rule II) or allegations of the same which, if substantiated, would warrant discipline or other action against an attorney admitted to practice before this court shall come to the attention of a Judge of this court, whether by complaint or otherwise, and the applicable procedure is not otherwise mandated by these Rules, the judge shall refer the matter to the Chief Judge who shall issue an order to show cause.

B. Upon the respondent-attorney's answer to the order to show cause, if any issue of fact is raised or the respondent-attorney wishes to be heard in mitigation the Chief Judge shall set the matter for prompt hearing before one or more judges of this court, provided however that if the proceeding is predicated upon the complaint of a judge of this court the hearing shall be conducted before a panel of three other judges of this court appointed by the Chief Judge.

C. This court may at any stage appoint counsel to investigate and/or prosecute the proceeding under this Rule.

D. This court may refer any matter under this Rule to the appropriate state disciplinary or other authority for investigation and decision before taking any action. The attorney who is the subject of the referral shall promptly notify this court of the decision of any state court or authority and shall take whatever steps are necessary to waive any confidentiality requirement so that this court may receive the record of that referral.

E. The judge or judges to whom any proceeding under this Rule is assigned shall make a report and recommendation to the court after the parties have been heard, which will be filed under seal and served on the parties. A party shall serve and file under seal any objections within fourteen (14) days thereafter. Further submissions by any party shall be served and filed under seal within seven (7) days after service of any objections. The court shall then decide the matter; after decision the report and recommendation, any objections, and any submissions shall be unsealed unless otherwise ordered by the court.

Rule VI.   Disbarment on Consent While Under Disciplinary Investigation or Prosecution

A. Any attorney admitted to practice before this court who is the subject of an investigation into, or a pending proceeding involving, allegations of misconduct may consent to disbarment, but only by delivering to this court an affidavit stating that the attorney desires to consent to disbarment and that:

1. the attorney's consent is freely and voluntarily rendered; the attorney is not being subjected to coercion or duress; the attorney is fully aware of the implications of so consenting;

2. the attorney is aware that there is a presently pending investigation or proceeding involving allegations that there exist grounds for the attorney's discipline the nature of which the attorney shall specifically set forth;

3. the attorney acknowledges that the material facts so alleged are true; and

4. the attorney so consents because the attorney knows that if charges were predicated upon the matters under investigation, or if the proceeding were prosecuted, the attorney could not successfully defend himself or herself.

B. Upon receipt of the required affidavit, this court shall enter an order disbarring the attorney.

C. The order disbarring the attorney on consent shall be a matter of public record. However, the affidavit required under the provisions of this Rule shall not be publicly disclosed or made available for use in any other proceeding except upon the order of this court.

Rule VII.   Reinstatement

A. After Disbarment or Suspension. An attorney suspended for three months or less shall be automatically reinstated at the end of the period of suspension upon the filing with the court of an affidavit of compliance with the provisions of the order. An attorney suspended for more than three months or disbarred may not resume practice until reinstated by order of this court.

B. Time of Applications Following Disbarment. A person who has been disbarred after hearing or by consent may not apply for reinstatement until the expiration of at least five years from the effective date of the disbarment.

C. Hearing on Application. Petitions for reinstatement under this rule by an attorney who has been disbarred, suspended or otherwise prohibited from the practice of law shall be filed with the Clerk of this court. Upon the filing of the petition, the Chief Judge shall assign the matter for prompt hearing before one or more judges of this court, provided however that if the proceeding was predicated upon the complaint of a judge of this court the hearing shall be conducted before a panel of three other judges of this court appointed by the Chief Judge. The judge or judges assigned to the matter shall promptly schedule a hearing at which the petitioner shall have the burden of demonstrating by clear and convincing evidence that the petitioner has the moral qualifications, competency and learning in the law required for admission to practice law before this court and that the petitioner's resumption of the practice of law will not be detrimental to the integrity and standing of the bar or to the administration of justice, or subversive of the public interest. In the case where this court has imposed discipline or otherwise taken adverse action identical to that imposed or taken by a state court or authority, any petition for reinstatement in this court shall be held in abeyance until a petition for reinstatement to practice in the state court has been filed and finally decided. Nonetheless, if the petition for reinstatement to practice in the state curt remains pending before the state court or authority for more than a year without a final decision, this court may proceed to consider and decide the petition pending before it. Whenever the state court renders a final decision, the attorney shall promptly file with this court a copy of said decision including any findings of fact and conclusions of law. After review of the state court decision, this court may reconsider its action upon notice and an opportunity to be heard. This court shall not hold the reinstatement petition in abeyance where the state disciplining or taking other action against the attorney does not provide for reinstatement under the circumstances. If the discipline imposed or other action taken by this court was different from that imposed or taken by the state court or authority, this court will proceed to consider the petition for reinstatement upon receipt.

D. The court may at any stage appoint counsel in opposition to a petition for reinstatement.

E. Deposit for Costs of Proceeding. Petitions for reinstatement under this Rule shall be accompanied by an advance cost deposit in an amount to be set from time to time by the court to cover anticipated costs of the reinstatement proceeding.

F. Conditions of Reinstatement. If the petitioner is found unfit to resume the practice of law, the petition shall be dismissed. If the petitioner is found fit to resume the practice of law, the judgment shall reinstate the petitioner, provided that the judgment may make reinstatement conditional upon the payment of all or part of the costs of the proceedings, and upon the making of partial or complete restitution to parties harmed by petitioner whose conduct led to the suspension or disbarment. Provided further, that if the petitioner has been suspended or disbarred for five years or more, reinstatement may be conditioned, in the discretion of the judge or judges before whom the matter is heard, upon the furnishing of proof of competency and learning in the law, which proof may include certification by the bar examiners of a state or other jurisdiction of the attorney's successful completion of an examination for admission to practice subsequent to the date of suspension or disbarment.

G. Successive Petitions. No petition for reinstatement under this Rule shall be filed within one year following an adverse judgment upon a petition for reinstatement filed by or on behalf of the same person.

H. The judge or judges to whom any proceeding under this Rule is assigned shall make a report and recommendation to the court after the parties have been heard, which will be filed under seal and served on the parties. A party shall serve and file under seal any objections within fourteen (14) days thereafter. Further submissions by any party shall be served and filed under seal within seven (7) days after service of any objections. The court shall then decide the matter; after decision the report and recommendation, any objections, and any submissions shall be unsealed unless otherwise ordered by the court.

I. Any attorney who is reinstated may practice before this court notwithstanding the refusal or failure of any state court to reinstate said attorney to practice. However, reinstatement to practice before this court does not authorize an attorney to practice in any other jurisdiction, and no attorney shall hold out himself or herself as authorized to practice law in any jurisdiction in which the attorney is not admitted.

Rule VIII. Attorneys Specially Admitted

Whenever an attorney applies to be admitted or is admitted to this court for purposes of a particular proceeding, the attorney shall be deemed thereby to have conferred disciplinary jurisdiction upon this court for any alleged misconduct of that attorney arising in the course of or in the preparation for such proceeding.

Rule IX. Service of Papers and Other Notices

Service of an order to show cause instituting a formal disciplinary proceeding shall be made by personal service or by registered or certified mail addressed to the respondent-attorney at the address shown in the roll of attorneys of this court or the most recent edition of the Legal Directory. Service of any other papers or notices required by these Rules shall be deemed to have been made if such paper or notice is addressed to the respondent-attorney at the address shown on the roll of attorneys of this court or the most recent edition of the Legal Directory; or the respondent's attorney at the address indicated in the most recent pleading or other document filed by them in the course of any proceeding.

Rule X. Appointment of Counsel

Whenever counsel is to be appointed pursuant to these Rules to investigate allegations of misconduct or prosecute disciplinary proceedings or in conjunction with a reinstatement petition filed by a disciplined attorney this court shall appoint as counsel the disciplinary agency of the Supreme Court of Pennsylvania, or other disciplinary agency having jurisdiction. If no such disciplinary agency exists or such disciplinary agency declines appointment, or such appointment is clearly inappropriate, this court shall appoint as counsel one or more members of the Bar of this court to investigate allegations of misconduct or to prosecute disciplinary proceedings under these rules, provided, however, that the respondent-attorney may move to disqualify an attorney so appointed who is or has been engaged as an adversary of the respondent-attorney in any matter. Counsel, once appointed, may not resign unless permission to do so is given by this court.

Rule XI. Duties of the Clerk

A. Upon being informed that an attorney admitted to practice before this court has been convicted of any crime, the Clerk of this court shall determine whether the clerk of the court in which such conviction occurred has forwarded a certificate of such conviction to this court. If a certificate has not been forwarded, the Clerk of this court shall promptly obtain a certificate and file it with this court.

B. Upon being informed that an attorney admitted to practice before this court has been subjected to discipline by another court, the Clerk of this court shall determine whether a certified or exemplified copy of the disciplinary judgment or order has been filed with this court, and if not, the Clerk shall promptly obtain a certified or exemplified copy of the disciplinary judgment or order and file it with this court.

C. Whenever it appears that any person convicted of any crime or disbarred or suspended or censured or disbarred on consent by this court is admitted to practice law in any other jurisdiction or before any other court, the Clerk of this court shall, within ten (10) days of that conviction, disbarment, suspension, censure, or disbarment on consent, transmit to the disciplinary authority in such other jurisdiction, or for such other court, a certificate of the conviction or a certified exemplified copy of the judgment or order of disbarment, suspension, censure, or disbarment on consent, as well as the last known office and residence addresses of the defendant or respondent.

D. The Clerk of this court shall, likewise, promptly notify the National Discipline Data Bank operated by the American Bar Association of any order imposing public discipline upon any attorney admitted to practice before this court.

Rule XII. Jurisdiction

Nothing contained in these Rules shall be construed to deny to this court such powers as are necessary for the court to maintain control over proceedings conducted before it, such as proceedings for contempt under Title 18 of the United States Code or under Rule 42 of the Federal Rules of Criminal Procedure.

Rule XIII. Effective Date

These rules shall become effective on August 1, 1980, provided that any formal disciplinary proceeding then pending before this court shall be concluded under the procedure existing prior to the effective date of these Rules.

Background of the Proposed Model Federal Rules of Disciplinary Enforcement and Recommendation of the Judicial Conference Committee on Court Administration.

For some years there has been a demonstrated concern by federal judges and the lawyers who practice in the federal courts over the lack of uniform rules of disciplinary enforcement in the federal courts. The American Bar Association through its Standing Committee on Professional Discipline (and its two predecessor committees) has provided the various state courts with a model plan of state court coordinated rules of disciplinary enforcement for their consideration and use. A vast majority of the states have adopted substantially the A.B.A. model plan.

On the federal court side, in 1970 as a result of a previous study, a report of an American Bar Association Committee on Evaluation of Disciplinary Enforcement, headed by the late Justice Tom C. Clark was issued, and was unanimously approved by the American Bar Association. Following that report, in 1973 the Standing Committee on Professional Discipline of the American Bar Association was created to continue the work in view of the conclusion earlier reached by the Clark Committee that effective disciplinary enforcement in the federal courts requires that professional discipline for the entire federal system be coordinated among the courts which constitute that system and also coordinated with existing state disciplinary agencies within all federal court jurisdictions. The Clark Report highlighted the existing problem of inadequate provision for reciprocal action when an attorney disciplined in one jurisdiction is admitted to practice in another jurisdiction, as well as the problem of discipline of attorneys in federal courts based on prior state court discipline.

On April 17, 1975, as work on a proposed draft of uniform disciplinary rules of procedure progressed under the guidance of the A.B.A. Standing Committee,

the Director of the Administrative Office of the United States Courts, the Director of the Federal Judicial Center and others met with the Standing Committee in furtherance of the ongoing study. On July 31, 1975, the Standing Committee forwarded to the Administrative Office of the United States Courts a proposed set of Uniform Guidelines (rules) of Disciplinary Enforcement with the request that they be studied by the Judicial Conference of the United States.

At the direction of the Chief Justice the Committee on Court Administration of the Judicial Conference on April 11, 1976, accepted the responsibility of studying the Proposed Uniform Rules of Disciplinary Enforcement and the making of appropriate comments and recommendations to the Judicial Conference.

On April 12, 1976, the Committee on Court Administration, through its Subcommittee on Judicial Improvements, sent the Proposed Draft of the Uniform Rules to all federal judges requesting that they study the proposed draft and make such comments, criticisms, and recommendations as they thought appropriate A substantial number of federal judges responded, many with constructive comments and suggestions which are carefully studied by the Subcommittee on Judicial Improvements and sent to the A.B.A. Standing Committee for its study. Thereafter, the Subcommittee met with representatives of the A.B.A. Standing Committee. There resulted a revised proposed draft written in the light of the earlier comments and suggestions. This revised draft was submitted through the committee on Court Administration to the Judicial Conference at its September 23–24, 1976 Session with the recommendation that the judges of the federal courts should have further opportunity to comment on the revised draft and to submit their views.

The Judicial Conference accepted the recommendation of the Committee on Court Administration, broadened it to include all state bar presidents, and directed dissemination of the revised draft to all federal judges and state bar presidents for their study, views and comments. Again, a substantial number of federal judges as well as State bar presidents and state bar associations responded with comments and suggestions. All of these comments and suggestions were fully considered by the Subcommittee on Judicial Improvements and after consultation with the A.B.A. Standing Committee some additional revisions in the Proposed Uniform Rules were made in the light of those suggestions and comments.

On February 14, 1978, at the midyear meeting of the American Bar Association in New Orleans the Standing Committee presented the currently Revised Proposed Uniform Rules to the House of Delegates of the American Bar Association for its consideration and action. On that same date the House of Delegates approved the Proposed Uniform Rules of Disciplinary Enforcement with several minor suggestions.

At its June, 1978 meeting the Subcommittee on Judicial Improvements reviewed the suggestions made by the A.B.A. House of Delegates, accepted them as strengthening and clarifying the Proposed Uniform Rules and unanimously approved a revised draft incorporating those recommendations.

It is the expressed hope of the Committee and Subcommittee members who have actively participated in the study that the various courts of the United States will choose to adopt these Proposed Rules so as to assure uniformity of procedure in the federal court system on a coordinated basis with the various state systems, as well as to assure an effective and reasonable procedure for needed discipline within the federal system.

Recommendation

The subcommittee on Judicial Improvements unanimously recommends to the Committee on Court Administration that it approve these Revised Proposed Model Federal Rules of Disciplinary Enforcement and in turn recommended to the Judicial Conference of the United States that it approve these Proposed Model Rules and recommend their adoption by the various courts of the United States on an optional basis.

RULE 83.6.1 EXPEDITION OF COURT BUSINESS

(a) Attorneys shall promptly advise the Clerk of the settlement or other final disposition of a case.

(b) No attorney shall, with* just cause, fail to appear when that attorney's case is before the Court on a call, motion, pretrial or trial, or shall present to the Court vexatious motions or vexatious opposition to motions or shall fail to prepare for presentation to the Court, or shall otherwise so multiply the proceedings in a case as to increase unreasonably and vexatiously the costs thereof.

(c) Any attorney who fails to comply with (a) or (b) may be disciplined as the Court shall deem just.

[Effective July 1, 1995.]

* [**Publisher's Note:** So in original. Probably should read "without."]

CORRELATION TABLE
LOCAL RULES OF CIVIL PROCEDURE TO FEDERAL RULES OF CIVIL PROCEDURE

The Local Rules of Civil Procedure for the Eastern District of Pennsylvania have been renumbered to create nationwide uniformity. Below are listed the Local Rules in the order of their previously assigned number with the newly assigned number.

Local Rule 1 Effective Date; Revocation of Prior Rules.
Renumbered: 1.1

Local Rule 2 Standing Orders; Effect Upon.
Renumbered: 1.1.1

Local Rule 3 Assignment of Court Business.
Renumbered: 40.1

Local Rule 4 Emergency Judge.
Renumbered: 40.1.1

Local Rule 5 Calendar Control; Operating Procedures.
Renumbered: 40.3

Local Rule 6 Calendar Review.
Renumbered: 40.3.1

Local Rule 7 United States Magistrate.
Renumbered: 72.1

Local Rule 8 Arbitration—The Speedy Civil Trial.
Renumbered: 53.2

Local Rule 9 Appearance of Judicial Officer of This Court as Character Witness.
Renumbered: 45.1.1

Local Rule 10 Broadcasting, Filming and Recording in Courtrooms and Appurtenant Areas.
Renumbered: 83.3

Local Rule 11 Admission to Practice.
Renumbered: 83.5

Local Rule 12 Student Practice Rule.
Renumbered: 83.5.1

Local Rule 13 Associate Counsel.
Renumbered: 83.5.2

Local Rule 14 Rules of Disciplinary Enforcement.
Renumbered: 83.6

Local Rule 15 Court–Annexed Mediation (Early Settlement Conference).
Renumbered: RESCINDED

Local–Rule 16 Reserved.

Local Rule 17 Notices; Stipulations.
Renumbered: 7.4

Local Rule I8 Appearances.

Renumbered:	5.1		**Local Rule 32**	Lis Pendens.
			Renumbered:	4.1.1
Local Rule 19	Expedition of Court Business.			
Renumbered:	83.6.1		**Local Rule 33**	Letters Rogatory.
			Renumbered:	RESCINDED
Local Rule 20	Motion Practice.			
Renumbered:	7.1		**Local Rule 34**	Jury.
			Renumbered:	48.1
Local Rule 21	Pretrial Procedure.			
Renumbered:	16.1		**Local Rule 35**	Subpoenas for Trial.
			Renumbered:	45.1
Local Rule 22	Time of Motion to Join Third Party.			
			Local Rule 36	Attachments for Witnesses.
Renumbered:	14.1		Renumbered:	43.1.1
Local Rule 23	Dismissal and Abandonment of Actions.		**Local Rule 37**	Conduct of Trials.
			Renumbered:	43.1
Renumbered:	41.1			
			Local Rule 38	Summations by Attorney.
Local Rule 24	Discovery.		Renumbered:	39.1
Renumbered:	26.1			
			Local Rule 39	Records, Files and Exhibits.
Local Rule 25	Impartial Medical Examination.		Renumbered:	39.3
Renumbered:	RESCINDED		**Local Rule 40**	Video Tapes.
			Renumbered:	39.3.1
Local Rule 26	Mandatory Exchange of Medical Reports in Personal Injury Cases.		**Local Rule 41**	Deposits in Court.
			Renumbered:	67.2
Renumbered:	RESCINDED			
			Local Rule 42	Costs: Security for, Taxation, Payment.
Local Rule 27	Class Actions.			
Renumbered:	23.1		Renumbered:	54.1
Local Rule 28	Summons Enforcement Proceedings Pursuant to 26 U.S.C. § 7402(b) and 7604(a).		**Local Rule 43**	Marshal's Sales.
			Renumbered:	53.1
Renumbered:	4.1.2		**Local Rule 44**	Petitions for Writs of Habeas Corpus and 2255 Motions.
Local Rule 29	Special Appointment for Service of Process.		Renumbered:	9.3
Renumbered:	4.1		**Local Rule 45**	Judgments Pursuant to Warrant of Attorney.
Local Rule 30	Pleading Claim for Unliquidated Damages.		Renumbered:	56.1
Renumbered:	5.1.1		**Local Rule 46**	Bail, Sureties and Security.
			Renumbered:	67.1
Local Rule 31	Transfers Under Section 1404(a).		**Local Rule 47**	Civil Cases Exempt From Issuance of a Scheduling Order.
Renumbered:	3.2		Renumbered:	16.2

LOCAL CRIMINAL RULES

RULE 1.1 ADOPTION OF RULES: EFFECTIVE DATE

(a) Pursuant to Rule 57 of the Federal Rules of Criminal Procedure, the following criminal rules of the United States District Court for the Eastern District of Pennsylvania are adopted this 29th day of February, 1972[1] and shall become effective the 1st day of March, 1972. These rules shall apply to all cases pending on that date to the extent feasible.

(b) These Rules may be cited and referred to as "Local Criminal Rules" or abbreviated as "L.C.R."

(c) Unless otherwise indicated, reference to these rules to the Judge shall mean the Judge to whom the case is assigned, (or in his or her absence the Emergency Judge) and to the Magistrate Judge shall mean the United States Magistrate Judge to whom the case is assigned.

(d) Unless otherwise indicated, reference in these Rules to the United States Attorney shall also mean the Assistant United States Attorney, Assistant Attorneys General or Special Government Attorneys assigned to a case.

(e) In cases where defendants proceed pro se, reference to defendant's attorney applies to defendant.

[Effective January 1, 1998.]

[1] Note: Except as otherwise noted.

RULE 1.2 APPLICABILITY AND EFFECT OF LOCAL RULES

The following Local Civil Rules shall be fully applicable in all criminal proceedings: Rule 5.1, Appearances; Rule 5.1.2, Electronic Case Filing; Rule 7.1(g), Motions for Reconsideration or Reargument; Rule 7.4, Notices, Stipulations; Rule 40.1.1, Emergency Judge; Rule 40.3, Calendar Control, Operating Procedures; Rule 40.3.1, Calendar Review; Rule 43.1.1, Attachments for Witnesses; Rule 45.1, Subpoenas for Trial; Rule 45.1.1, Appearance of a Judicial Office of this Court as a Character Witness; Rule 48.1(a), Challenges to Array; Rule 67.1, Bail, Sureties and Security; Rule 72.1, United States Magistrate Judges; Rule 83.3, Broadcasting, Filming and Recording in Courtroom and Appurtenant Areas; Rule 83.5, Admissions to Practice; Rule 83.5.2, Associate Counsel; Rule 83.6, Rules of Disciplinary Enforcement; and Rule 83.6.1, Expedition of Court Business.

[Effective January 1, 1998. Amended effective May 16, 2002; January 1, 2004; May 17, 2004.]

RULE 6.1 THE GRAND JURY

(a) **Empaneling of Grand Jury.** The emergency judge shall empanel and charge each grand jury at the commencement of its terms, and provide whatever services it may require including a convenient place for its deliberations.

(b) **Assignment of Legal Proceedings Arising Out of Grand Jury Matters.** At the time of issuance of the initial affidavit, notice, motion, or grand jury subpoena, the United States Attorney shall designate in the initial document the matter to which it relates. This designation shall be accomplished by an endorsement of the subpoena as follows:

In Re: Grand Jury Matter (Calendar Year); (Numerical designation of the matter);

Sample

In Re: Grand Jury Matter 80–1

The subpoena shall note that any affidavit, motion or other document filed of record with the clerk of court concerning a grand jury matter shall bear that numerical designation in the caption of the grand jury matter and that papers filed by any person with respect to any grand jury matter are subject to the secrecy requirements of Rule 6.1(c). At the time of the filing of the initial affidavit, motion, notice, or other document arising out of a grand jury matter, the clerk of court shall assign at random from the block of assignment cards said initial affidavit, notice, motion or other document to the calendar of a judge of this court. All grand jury matters arising out of an investigation of the same criminal transaction or series of transactions are deemed related. The assignment of grand jury numerical designations by the United States Attorney shall be in accordance with the written statement of policy of the United States Attorney on file in the office of the clerk of court. Each document filed after the initial document relating to the same grand jury matter shall be deemed related and assigned to the calendar of the judge to whom the initial document was assigned. The relationship shall be determined by the clerk on the basis of the numerical designation which shall be set forth in the caption of grand jury matter.

In order to assure that each particular witness or party before the grand jury has secrecy in respect to the witness's own matters, the grand jury docket shall identify, as stated above, each matter only by calendar year and numerical designation of the investigation; but in respect to each separate witness or party whose matter comes before the court, all of the affidavits, notices, motions, orders or other documents relating to that witness or party shall be assigned a separate sequential case number by the clerk of court.

For Example:

80–4–1 (This is the 4th grand jury matter for 1980. Witness John Smith has been given the designation "1" in regard to all matters concerning him before this particular grand jury. Only he and his attorney and the United States Attorney will receive copies of documents pertaining to his matters so designated.)

80–4–2 (Same as above except that these matters concern a different witness or party, designated by the clerk as "2").

80–4 (This is a general designation for any matters in respect to grand jury #4 that do not particularly apply only to a separate witness or party.)

(c) Grand Jury Secrecy. In legal proceedings relating to grand jury investigations, including, but not limited to, motions to quash, limit, modify or enforce a grand jury subpoena or for a protective order with respect thereto, motions to furnish identifying characteristics to the grand jury or its agent, or to compel testimony before the grand jury, and motions for an order of immunity:

1. The United States (whether acting as a party or as counsel for the grand jury) shall not disclose the identity of any grand jury witness, person under investigation or specific grand jury investigative subject area in any affidavit, motion or other paper filed in the public record, nor in the caption thereof, except in camera, under seal, or where the paper is already subject to an order of impoundment; provided, however, that the United States may disclose in such affidavit, motion or other paper, the identity of a grand jury witness or person under investigation who, pursuant to leave of court, has previously disclosed his, her or its own identity in relation to the same proceedings in any publicly filed paper, or where such disclosure has been expressly authorized by an order of this Court; and provided further that this rule shall not prohibit attorneys for the government from the use of such matters as are necessary for the performance of their duties in accordance with Federal Criminal Rule 6(e).

2. No person shall disclose in any affidavit, motion or other paper filed in the public record, nor in the caption thereof, the identity of any grand jury witness, or person under investigation or specific grand jury investigative subject area, other than that of himself, herself, or itself unless in camera, under seal, or where the paper is already subject to an order of impoundment, except where the grand jury witness or person under investigation has, pursuant to leave of court, disclosed his, her or its own identity in relation to the same proceedings in any publicly filed paper, or where such disclosure has been expressly authorized by an order of this Court.

3. In order to facilitate implementation of this rule, any motion, affidavit or other paper relating to

matters or proceedings before the grand jury may be filed anonymously or pseudonymously, with the name or information thus protected provided to the Court in camera and under seal.

4. In order to facilitate implementation of this rule, and to avoid inadvertent disclosures of the identity of any grand jury witness, person under investigation, or specific grand jury investigation subject area, all motions, affidavits or other papers relative to legal proceedings relating to grand jury investigations shall be automatically impounded, i.e., filed under seal, by the Clerk of Court. The Clerk of Court shall thereupon forthwith transmit the motions, affidavits, or other papers to the assigned judge. Any grand jury witness or person under investigation who desires to have his, her or its name disclosed upon the public record shall file with the assigned judge a motion for authorization to make such disclosure. Leave to disclose shall be freely given, subject to appropriate provision protecting grand jury secrecy as to other persons and matters.

(d) Deputy Clerk to Assist Grand Jury. The Clerk of Court shall designate a deputy to serve as Clerk to the Grand Jury. Such Deputy Clerk shall keep a docket and appropriate records relating to grand jury proceedings and assist in providing whatever services the Grand Jury may require.

(e) Return of Grand Jury Indictments. Grand Jury returns shall be made to the duty magistrate judge and in his or her absence, to the emergency judge.

[Effective January 1, 1998.]

RULE 10.1   ARRAIGNMENT AND PLEA

Arraignments shall be conducted before a Magistrate Judge or Judge. The United States Attorney shall furnish the Courtroom Deputy of the Judge with a copy of the indictment for each defendant and the name of the defendant's attorney if known. The Courtroom Deputy shall thereupon send a copy of the indictment or information to the defendant and said attorney together with notice of the time and place of the arraignment, unless the United States Attorney has reason to believe that defendant will become a fugitive, in which event a copy shall be served upon the defendant within a reasonable time after his or her arrest and prior to his or her arraignment before a Magistrate Judge or a Judge.

When, at the arraignment before a Magistrate Judge, a defendant expresses a desire to plead guilty, the Magistrate Judge shall refer this matter immediately to the Judge, or in his or her absence to the Emergency Judge for the purpose of accepting the plea only.

314

At any preliminary hearing before a Magistrate Judge, the defendant shall be given a copy of the complaint.

[Effective January 1, 1998.]

RULE 12.1 PRETRIAL MOTION PRACTICE

Motions required under Fed.R.Crim.P. 12 to be raised prior to trial shall be filed within fourteen (14) days after arraignment, unless otherwise provided by the Court. All motions shall be filed with the Clerk of Court, copies being sent to the Deputy Clerk of the Judge, and shall be accompanied by a brief or memorandum of law containing a concise statement of the legal contentions and authorities relied upon in support of said motion. A copy of each such motion and memorandum or brief shall be filed of record and served upon the opposing party. Within seven (7) days after the receipt of such motion, any party desiring to oppose such motion shall file and serve on the opposing party in the aforementioned manner an answer and a legal memorandum in opposition thereto. If the Court determines that oral argument is necessary, it shall advise counsel of the date and time that such argument is to be provided.

[Effective January 1, 1998. Amended effective December 1, 2009.]

RULE 16.1 PRETRIAL DISCOVERY AND INSPECTION

(a) Pretrial Conference. Within seven (7) days after the arraignment, or within such other period as the Court may set, counsel for the Government and for the defendant shall confer; and at such conference ("counsel's conference"), upon request of the defendant, the Government shall comply, or if compliance is then impossible, agree to comply as soon as possible with the requirements of Fed.R.Crim.P. 16(a)(1)(A–D).

(b) Disclosure of Evidence by the Defendant. If at the counsel's conference the defendant requests disclosure under subparagraph (a)(1)(C) or (D) of Fed.R.Crim.P. 16, upon compliance with such request by the Government, the defendant, upon request of the Government, shall comply with Fed.R.Crim.P. 16(b)(1)(A) and (B).

(c) Regulation of Discovery.

(1) If, in the judgment of the attorney for either party, the requested discovery is beyond the scope of Rule 16 or if the attorney has reasonable grounds to believe that a protective order should be entered regarding such a discovery request, disclosure may be declined. A declination of any requested disclosure shall be in writing, directed to opposing counsel, and shall specify the types of disclosure that are declined and the reasons therefor.

(2) If the defendant or the Government desires to contest such declination or seeks additional discovery not specified in these rules, its attorney shall promptly confer with opposing counsel with a view to satisfying these requests in a cooperative atmosphere without recourse to the Court.

(3) In the event that the conference prescribed by subparagraph (c)(2) does not resolve the dispute concerning discovery of items not specifically mentioned in Rule 16, the party seeking disclosure may file a motion for such additional discovery on or before the date set for filing of pretrial motions under Fed. R.Crim.P. 12 and Local Rule 12.1. If the requested discovery materials are specifically mandated by Rule 16, then the declining party must move for a protective order on or before the date set for filing of pretrial motions under Fed.R.Crim.P. 12 and Local Rule 12.1. The motion papers for additional discovery or a protective order shall contain:

(A) the statement that the prescribed counsel's conference was held;

(B) the date of said conference;

(C) the name of opposing counsel with whom the conference was held;

(D) the statement that agreement could not be reached concerning the discovery or inspection that is the subject of the motion; and

(E) a request for a hearing to resolve the dispute, or a waiver of argument and a suggestion that the Court rule by reference to the motion papers alone, or a request that the party be permitted to make its showing, in whole or in part, in the form of a written statement to be inspected by the Judge alone. The answer to any motion under this subparagraph may contain a request for a hearing, or a statement of that party's opposition to any request for an ex parte showing.

(d) Failure to Comply. The failure of a party to comply with this Rule or with Fed.R.Crim.P. 16 may be brought to the attention of the Court at any time, whereupon the Court may take such action as is prescribed by Fed.R.Crim.P. 16(d), or such other action that the Court deems proper under the circumstances.

[Effective January 1, 1998. Amended effective December 1, 2009.]

RULE 17.1.1 STATUS CALLS AND PRETRIAL CONFERENCES: COMPLEX CASES

Each Judge may schedule status reports and pretrial conferences as he or she deems appropriate. Attendance at such reports and conferences shall be mandatory and failure to attend without just cause shall subject counsel to disciplinary proceedings.

If at any time, it appears to the Judge that the case is a complex one, the Judge may, with the consent of the parties, adapt to the needs of the case pretrial techniques aimed at simplifying the issues and reducing trial time, including but not limited to the taking of depositions of expert or other witnesses, the filing of pretrial memoranda, and pretrial identification and marking of all exhibits.

[Effective January 1, 1998.]

RULE 24.1 CONTACT WITH JURORS

(a) Before the trial of a case, no attorney, party or witness shall communicate or cause another to communicate with anyone the lawyer, party or witness knows to be a member of the venire from which the jury will be selected for the trial of the case.

(b) During the trial of a case, no attorney, party or witness shall communicate with or cause another to communicate with any member of the jury.

(c) After the conclusion of a trial no attorney, party or witness shall communicate with or cause another to communicate with any member of the jury without first receiving permission of the Court.

[Effective January 1, 1998.]

RULE 32.1 LOAN OF PRESENTENCE IN-VESTIGATION REPORT TO U.S. PA-ROLE COMMISSION AND U.S. BU-REAU OF PRISONS

Any copy of a presentence report which the court makes available to the United States Parole Commission or the Bureau of Prisons constitutes a confidential court document and shall be presumed to remain under the continuing control of the court during the time it is in the temporary custody of these agencies. Such copy shall be loaned to the Parole Commission and the Bureau of Prisons only for the purpose of enabling those agents to carry out their official functions and shall be returned to the court immediately after such use.

[Effective January 1, 1998.]

Note:

This rule is enacted in order to place a presentence report outside the "agency record" definition set forth in *United States v. Carson*, 631 F.2d 1088 (D.C.Cir.1980).

RULE 32.2 SENTENCE LIEN ON BAIL DEPOSIT

Whenever a defendant has been sentenced to pay a fine or a fine and costs, the sentence shall constitute a lien in favor of the United States on the bail deposit, if any, which can be removed only by the Judge.

[Effective January 1, 1998.]

RULE 32.3 PRESENTENCE INVESTIGATIONS AND TIME LIMITS

It is hereby ORDERED that the following standing order is adopted for use in criminal cases in which sentences are imposed under the Sentencing Reform Act of 1984:

1. Sentencing will occur without unnecessary delay and not less than eighty (80) days following the date on which a defendant pleads guilty, nolo contendere, or is found guilty, unless an individual judge directs that the sentence be imposed on an earlier or later date.

2. At the time the presentence investigation and report are ordered, a sentencing hearing date will be fixed by the sentencing judge; and, the attorney for the Government will make available to the probation officer all investigative and file material relevant to the case. The sentencing hearing date may be continued if necessary.

3. Not less than thirty-five (35) days before the sentencing hearing, the probation officer must furnish the presentence report to the defendant, the defendant's counsel, and the attorney for the Government. The probation officer's recommendation for the sentence will not be disclosed unless directed by an individual judge.

4. Within fourteen (14) days after receiving the presentence report, the parties shall deliver in writing to the probation officer, and to each other, any objections to any material information, sentencing classifications, sentencing guideline ranges, and policy statements contained in or omitted from the presentence report. If no objections will be filed, the probation officer shall be so notified in writing within the aforesaid time limits. Any objection not filed will be deemed waived unless the Court finds good cause for allowing it to be raised.

5. Should the attorney for the Government intend to file a motion for a downward departure under the United States Sentencing Guidelines Section 5K1.1, or under a statutory mandatory minimum, the probation officer will be notified in writing on or before the submission date set for the filing of objections, and be provided with whatever information supports the motion.

6. Not later than seven (7) days before the sentencing hearing, the probation officer must submit the presentence report to the Court, together with an addendum setting forth any unresolved objections, the grounds for these objections, and the probation officer's comments on the objections. At the same time, the probation officer must furnish the revisions of the presentence report and the addendum to the defendant, the defendant's counsel, and the attorney for the government.

This rule takes into account the amendments to Rule 32 of the Federal Rules of Criminal Procedure which have an effective date of December 1, 1994.

[Effective January 1, 1998. Amended effective December 1, 2009.]

RULE 40.1 PROCEEDINGS IN REMOVAL CASES

In cases where a defendant has been brought before the Magistrate Judge on a warrant originating in another federal jurisdiction and the defendant has been ordered held to this Court for removal to the originating jurisdiction pursuant to Rule 40, Federal Rules of Criminal Procedure, the petition for removal by the United States Attorney shall be presented to the Magistrate Judge who shall be authorized to issue a warrant or removal. The petition and any order or warrant of removal by the Magistrate Judge may be by minute order. In case of a defendant not in custody, the defendant shall be given a copy of the order of removal, which copy shall specify the place of his or her required appearance in the prosecuting jurisdiction.

[Effective January 1, 1998.]

RULE 41.1 WIRE INTERCEPTION AND INTERCEPTION OF ORAL COMMUNICATIONS

In addition to the procedural requirements of 18 U.S.C. § 2510 et seq., the following procedures shall be followed in all criminal cases in which the Government has secured or wishes to secure evidence pursuant to that statute:

(a) Filing and Docketing of Orders. Applications made, orders, and inventories pursuant to 18 U.S.C. § 2518(8)(b) shall be filed with and docketed by the Clerk of Court. The applications, orders and all inventories filed pursuant thereto and the dockets relating thereto shall be retained by the Clerk of Court in a separate file which shall be impounded and shall not be available for inspection except by order of Court. Disclosure of any fact relating to such application, order or inventory to any person not authorized by the statute or these rules to have access to them shall be a violation of these rules and shall be punishable by contempt in accordance with 18 U.S.C. § 2518(8)(c).

(b) Assignment of Applications; Motions to Suppress. All applications for wire interceptions shall be assigned on a random basis to each Judge of the Court, or in his or her absence the Emergency Judge, in accordance with the provisions of Local Civil Rule 40.1. Any motion by an aggrieved party, as defined in 18 U.S.C. § 2510(11), attacking the validity or sufficiency of an order authorizing or approving the interception of a wire or oral communication issued by a Judge of this Court shall be heard by the Judge. Any other motion attacking such interception shall be heard by the Judge to whom the case is assigned.

(c) Transcription of Intercepted Communications. In any case involving the interception of oral or wire communications, the Judge may by appropriate pretrial order require the following:

(1) Disclosure to defense counsel within a reasonable time before trial of the original recordings of such oral or wire communications together with transcripts identifying the names of the persons who are speaking.

(2) As to any such oral or wire communication which the Government proposes to use in court, the preparation by the Government of a detailed exhibit consisting of an accurate transcript of any recording believed to be relevant, identifying so far as is reasonably possible the names of the persons who are speaking. Within a reasonable time before trial, the Court may rule preliminarily upon the admissibility of such evidence, whereupon all communications to be admitted may, as the Court directs, be recorded on a single tape together with a sufficient number of transcripts for the Court, counsel and each member of the jury. If only part of a conversation is offered in evidence by the Government, the Court may require the introduction of all of it which is relevant to the part proposed to be introduced, if in its discretion fairness so requires, and the defense may introduce any other parts.

[Effective January 1, 1998.]

RULE 44.1 FILING APPEARANCES OF ATTORNEYS

An attorney representing a defendant in any criminal proceedings pending in this Court shall file an appearance which shall include the attorney's name, local address, city (including zip code) and local telephone number. A copy of the appearance shall be served on the United States Attorney.

The appearance must be filed prior to or simultaneously with the initial Court appearance or the filing of any motion, brief or other document with this Court, whichever occurs first. This appearance shall constitute a representation to the Court that counsel so appearing shall represent the defendant until final disposition of the case in this Court. No appearances may be withdrawn except by leave of Court.

[Effective January 1, 1998.]

RULE 47.1 MOTIONS FOR JUDGMENT OF ACQUITTAL, NEW TRIAL AND ARREST OF JUDGMENT

Post-trial motions for a judgment of acquittal, new trial or an arrest of judgment pursuant to Rules 29, 33 and 34, Federal Rules of Criminal Procedure shall be supported by memoranda filed within the time provided by such rules, or such additional time as the Court shall allow.

[Effective January 1, 1998.]

RULE 50.1 ASSIGNMENT OF CRIMINAL BUSINESS

(a) All criminal cases in this jurisdiction shall be divided into the following categories:

(1) Antitrust.

(2) Income Tax and other Tax Prosecutions.

(3) Commercial Mail Fraud.

(4) Controlled Substances.

(5) Violations of 18 U.S.C. Chapters 95 and 96 (Sections 1951-55 and 1961-68) and Mail Fraud other than commercial.

(6) General Criminal.

(b) All grand jury litigation shall be designated as follows:

(1) Grand Jury Matters.

(c) Except for the assignment of grand jury matters, where it appears from the designation form filed by counsel, or from the indictment, information or other pleading in a criminal case, that a defendant resides in or that events which are the subject matter of the indictment occurred in the counties of Berks, Lancaster, Lehigh or Northampton, said case shall be assigned or reassigned for trial and pretrial procedures to a judge stationed in Reading, Lancaster, Easton or Allentown, who shall be given appropriate credit by category for any case so assigned, reassigned or transferred and, unless otherwise directed by the court, all trial and pre-trial procedures with respect thereto shall be held in Reading, Lancaster, Easton or Allentown. All other cases, unless otherwise directed by the court, shall be tried in Philadelphia. As each case is filed, it shall be assigned to a judge, who shall thereafter have charge of the case for all purposes. In respect to grand jury matters, the assignment of the judge shall not in any way be dependent upon the location of the residence of anyone, or the location of any incident or a transaction which is the subject of the grand jury investigation.

(d) The assignment shall take place in the following manner:

(1) There shall be a separate block of assignment cards for each category of criminal cases and for grand jury matters. In each block of assignment cards, the name of each active judge shall appear an equal number of times in a non-sequential manner except that the name of the chief judge shall appear one-half the number of times of each of the other active judges. The sequences of judges' names within each block shall be kept secret and no person shall directly or indirectly ascertain or divulge or attempt to ascertain or divulge the name of the judge to whom any case may be assigned before the assignment. The case number shall be stamped on the assignment card at the time of filing and assignment, and all assignment cards shall be preserved.

(2) The assignment clerk shall stamp on the indictment information, complaint, petition, or other initial paper of every case filed, and on the file jacket, the number of the case and the initials (or other designation) of the judge to whom it is assigned. The numbering and assignment of each case shall be completed before processing of the next case is begun.

(3) At the time of filing any criminal indictment or information, counsel for the government shall indicate whether a case is related to any other prior or pending action in this court. Criminal cases are deemed related if a defendant or defendants are alleged to have participated in the same action or transaction, or in the same series of acts or transactions, constituting an offense or offenses.

(4) If the fact of relationship is indicated on the appropriate form at the time of filing, the assignment clerk shall assign the case to the same judge to whom the earlier numbered related case is assigned. If the judge receiving the later case determines that the relationship does not exist, the judge shall refer the case to the assignment clerk for reassignment by random selection in the same manner as if it were a newly filed case.

(5) If the relationship does not become known until after the case is assigned, the judge receiving the later case may refer it to the Chief Judge for reassignment to the judge to whom the earlier related case is assigned. If the Chief Judge determines that the cases are related, the Chief Judge shall transfer the later case to the judge to whom the earlier case is assigned. Otherwise, the Chief Judge shall return the later case to the judge to whom it was originally assigned.

[Effective January 1, 1998. Amended April 5, 1999, effective April 19, 1999. Amended effective February 1, 2010.]

RULE 50.2 UNITED STATES MAGISTRATE JUDGES

I. In criminal matters, each United States magistrate judge of this district is authorized to exercise all powers and perform all duties conferred or imposed upon them or United States commissioners by law, by the Federal Rules of Criminal Procedure, by the Local Criminal Rules, or by orders or decisions of the United States Supreme Court, Third Circuit Court of Appeals, or the United States District Court for the Eastern District of Pennsylvania. These shall include, but are not limited to, all powers and duties conferred or imposed upon them under:

(a) *The following statutes:* 18 U.S.C. § 3041, **Powers of Courts and Magistrates;** 18 U.S.C. § 3060, **Preliminary Examination;** 18 U.S.C. §§ 3121–3127, **Pen Registers and Trap and Trace Devices;** 18 U.S.C. §§ 3141–3156, **Release and Detention Pending Judicial Proceedings;** 18 U.S.C. §§ 3181–3196, **Extradition;** 18 U.S.C. §§ 3401–3402, **Trial by United States Magistrates;** 18 U.S.C. §§ 4100–4115, **Transfer to or From Foreign Countries;** 28 U.S.C. § 636, **Jurisdiction, Powers, and Temporary Assignment.**

(b) *The following Federal Rules of Criminal Procedure:* Fed. R. Crim. P.3, **The Complaint;** Fed. R. Crim. P. 4, **Arrest Warrant or Summons Upon Complaint;** Fed. R. Crim. P. 5, **Initial Appearance Before the Magistrate Judge;** Fed. R. Crim. P. 5.1, **Preliminary Examination;** Fed. R. Crim. P. 6, **The Grand Jury;** Fed. R. Crim. P. 9, **Warrant or Summons Upon Indictment or Information;** Fed. R. Crim. P. 17, **Subpoena;** Fed. R. Crim. P. 32.1, **Revocation or Modification of Probation or Supervised Release;** Fed. R. Crim. P. 40, **Commitment to Another District;** Fed. R. Crim. P. 41, **Search and Seizure;** Fed. R. Crim. P. 54, **Application and Exception;** Fed. R. Crim. P.58, **Procedure for Misdemeanors and Other Petty Offenses.**

(c) *The following Local Rules of Criminal Procedure:* L.R.Crim.P. 6.1, **The Grand Jury;** L.R.Crim.P. 10.1, **Arraignment and Plea;** L.R.Crim.P. 58.1, **Forfeiture of Collateral in Lieu of Appearance and Mandatory Court Appearance.**

II. In a criminal matter, each United States magistrate judge of this district is authorized to exercise the following powers and duties when requested by the district judge assigned to the criminal matter:

(a) Supervise the criminal calendar, conduct status calls, conferences, and hear and determine any pretrial motion or matter permitted by 28 U.S.C. § 636(b)(1)(A).

(b) Hear and submit proposed findings of fact and recommendations for any motion permitted by 28 U.S.C. § 636(b)(1)(B).

(c) Select a petit jury with the express voluntary consent and waiver of all counsel, the government, and the defendant.

(d) Perform such additional duties as are legally proper.

III. Criminal matters shall be assigned to the United States magistrate judge of this district under the following procedures:

(a) *(Felony Cases)* Upon the return of an indictment, or the filing of an information, all felony cases shall be assigned by the Clerk to a duty magistrate judge for the purpose of conducting an arraignment unless the district judge assigned to that case otherwise directs.

(b) *(Misdemeanor cases)* Upon the filing of an information, complaint, violation notice, or return of an indictment, all misdemeanor cases shall be assigned by the Clerk to a particular magistrate judge who shall proceed in accordance with the provisions of 18 U.S.C. § 3401 and the applicable Rules of Criminal Procedure.

IV. Reconsideration and Appeal in Criminal Matters.

(a) *Reconsideration of pretrial matters—28 U.S.C. § 636(b)(1)(A).* A defendant or the government may object to a magistrate judge's order determining a motion or matter under 28 U.S.C. § 636(b)(1)(A) within fourteen (14) days after issuance of the magistrate judge's order, unless a different time is prescribed by the magistrate judge or a judge. The party objecting shall file with the Clerk of Court, and serve on the magistrate judge and all parties, a brief, along with a written statement of objections which shall specifically designate the order, or part thereof, subject to the objections and the basis for such objections. The District Court may upon the filing of objections or *sua sponte* reconsider, affirm, reject, modify, or recommit any pretrial motion or matter handled by a magistrate judge.

(b) *Review of Proposed Findings and Recommendations—28 U.S.C. § 636(b)(1)(B).* A defendant or the government may object to a magistrate judge's proposed findings, recommendations or report under 28 U.S.C. § 636(b)(1)(B) within fourteen (14) days after being served with a copy thereof by following the procedure set forth in 28 U.S.C. § 636(b)(1)(C). The party objecting shall file with the Clerk of Court and serve on the magistrate judge and all parties, a brief, along with written objections which shall specifically identify the portions of the proposed findings, recommendations or report to which objections are made and the basis for such objections.

(c) *Appeal of Misdemeanor Convictions—18 U.S.C. § 3402.* A defendant may appeal from a magistrate judge's judgment of conviction of a misdemeanor under 18 U.S.C. § 3402 within fourteen (14) days after the entry of judgment. The party appealing shall file with the Clerk of Court, and serve on the magistrate judge and all parties, a brief, along with a notice of appeal which shall set forth the basis for such appeal. The scope of appeal shall be the same as in an appeal from the District Court to the Court of Appeals.

[Effective January 1, 1999. Amended effective December 1, 2009.]

RULE 53.1 RELEASE OF INFORMATION BY ATTORNEYS AND COURT HOUSE PERSONNEL IN CRIMINAL CASES

(a) The Duty of Attorneys.

(1) It is the duty of the lawyer not to release or authorize the release of information or opinion for dissemination by any means of public communication, in connection with pending or imminent criminal litigation with which the lawyer is associated, if there is a reasonable likelihood that such dissemination will interfere with a fair trial or otherwise prejudice the due administration of justice.

(2) With respect to a grand jury or other pending investigation of any criminal matter, a lawyer participating in the investigation shall refrain from making any extrajudicial statement for dissemination by any means of public communication, that goes beyond the public record or that is not necessary to inform the public that the investigation is underway, to describe the general scope of the investigation, to obtain assistance in the apprehension of a suspect, to warn the public of any dangers, or otherwise to aid in the investigation.

(3) From the time of arrest, issuance of an arrest warrant or the filing of a complaint, information, or indictment in any criminal matter until the commencement of trial or disposition without trial, a lawyer associated with the prosecution or defense shall not release or authorize the release of any extrajudicial statement for dissemination by any means of public communication, relating to that matter and concerning:

A. The prior criminal record (including arrests, indictments, or other charges of crime), or the character or reputation of the accused, except that the lawyer may make a factual statement of the accused's name, age, residence, occupation, and family status, and if the accused has not been apprehended, a lawyer associated with the prosecution may release any information necessary to aid in his or her apprehension or to warn the public of any dangers the accused may present;

B. The existence of contents of any confession, admission, or statement given by the accused, or the refusal or failure of the accused to make any statement;

C. The performance of any examinations or tests or the accused's refusal or failure to submit to an examination or test;

D. The identity, testimony, or credibility of prospective witnesses, except that the lawyer may announce the identity of the victim if the announcement is not otherwise prohibited by law;

E. The possibility of a plea of guilty to the offense charged or a lesser offense;

F. Any opinion as to the accused's guilt or innocence or as to the merits of the case or the evidence in the case.

The foregoing shall not be construed to preclude the lawyer during this period, in the proper discharge of the lawyer's official or professional obligations, from announcing the fact and circumstances of arrest (including time and place of arrest, resistance, pursuit, and use of weapons), the identity of the investigation and arresting officer or agency, and length of the investigation; from making an announcement at the time of seizure of any physical evidence other than a confession, admission or statement, which is limited to a description of the evidence seized; from disclosing the nature, substance, or text of the charge, including a brief description of the offense charged; from quoting or referring without comment to public records of the court in the case; from announcing the scheduling or result of any stage in the judicial process; from requesting assistance in obtaining evidence; or from announcing without further comment that the accused denies the charges made against him, her or it.

(4) During the trial of any criminal matter, including the period of selection of the jury, no lawyer associated with the prosecution or defense shall give or authorize any extrajudicial statement or interview, relating to the trial or the parties or issues in the trial for dissemination by any means of public communication, except that the lawyer may quote from or refer without comment to public records of the court in the case.

(5) After the completion of a trial or disposition without trial of any criminal matter, and prior to the imposition of sentence, a lawyer associated with the prosecution or defense shall refrain from making or authorizing any extrajudicial statement for dissemination by any means of public communication if there is a reasonable likelihood that such dissemination will affect the imposition of sentence.

(6) Nothing in this rule is intended to preclude the formulation or application of more restrictive rules relating to the release of information about juvenile or other offenders, to preclude the holding of a hearing or the lawful issuance of reports by legislative, administrative, or investigative bodies, or to preclude any lawyer from replying to charges of misconduct that are publicly made against him or her.

(b) The Duty of Courthouse Personnel.

All courthouse personnel, including among others, marshals, deputy marshals, court clerks, law clerks, bailiffs, court reporters, and secretaries are prohibited from disclosing any information relating to a pending criminal case that is not part of the public records, unless authorized by the court. The rule precludes disclosure of any information whether acquired at a formal or informal proceeding.

[Effective January 1, 1998.]

RULE 53.2 ELECTRONIC CASE FILE PRIVACY

In compliance with the policy of the Judicial Conference of the United States, and the E-Government Act of 2002, and in order to promote electronic access to documents in the criminal case files while also protecting personal privacy and other legitimate interests, parties shall refrain from including, or shall partially redact where inclusion is necessary, the following personal data identifiers from all documents filed with the court, including exhibits thereto, whether filed electronically or in paper, unless otherwise ordered by the court:

(a) **Social Security Numbers.** If an individual's Social Security number must be included, only the last four digits of that number should be used.

(b) **Names of Minor Children.** If the involvement of a minor child must be mentioned, only the initials of the child should be used.

(c) **Dates of Birth.** If an individual's date of birth must be included, only the year should be used.

(d) **Financial Account Numbers.** If financial account numbers are relevant, only the last four digits of the number should be used.

(e) **Home Addresses.** If a home address must be included, only the city and state should be listed.

In compliance with the E-Government Act of 2002, a party wishing to file a document containing the personal data identifiers listed above may file an unredacted document under seal. This document shall be retained by the court as part of the record. The court may, however, still require the party to file a redacted copy for the public file. Trial exhibits may be safeguarded by means other than redaction, and the court may modify this rule to fit the requirements of particular cases.

The responsibility for redacting these personal identifiers rests solely with counsel and the parties. The Clerk need not review filings for compliance with this rule.

[Effective October 1, 2004.]

RULE 58.1 FORFEITURE OF COLLATERAL IN LIEU OF APPEARANCE AND MANDATORY COURT APPEARANCE

(A) For petty offenses listed in the general or special schedules discussed below, whether originating under the applicable state statute by virtue of the Assimilated Crimes Act (18 U.S.C. § 13) occurring within the territorial jurisdiction of the United States Magistrate Judge, including areas within the boundaries of the United States military installations, bases, hospitals and outposts, it is hereby ordered that collateral may be posted in lieu of the appearance of the offender. Upon the failure of the person charged with an offense or offenses to appear before the designated United States Magistrate Judge for trial of the offenses listed below (except those offenses designated by an asterisk (*) which require the mandatory appearance of the person charged) the collateral in the amount listed in the general or special schedules shall be forfeited to the United States and the posting of said collateral shall signify that the offender does not contest the charge nor request a hearing before the designated United States Magistrate Judge. Either the Clerk or Magistrate Judge shall certify the record of any conviction of a traffic violation as required by the applicable state statute to the proper state authority.

Where an asterisk (*) is inserted next to the listed violation, no forfeiture will be permitted and the person charged must appear before the designated United States Magistrate Judge. No forfeiture will be permitted on violations contributing to an accident with personal injury, or property damage in excess of $100.00. No forfeiture of collateral will be permitted for a subsequent offense or offenses not arising out of the same facts or sequence of events resulting in the original offense or offenses.

All offenses which occur in Hopewell Village National Historic Site, Elverson, Pa., and in the Blue Marsh Lake Recreation Area which require a mandatory court appearance shall be presented to the United States Magistrate Judge at Reading, Pa.

(B) General Schedule.* The general schedule which has been approved by the court specifies the collateral which may be posted for designated petty offenses in violation of laws of the United States (including the Assimilated Crimes Act, where applicable). Section 1 (specified Federal Statutes) applies to all property within the Eastern District of Pennsylvania. Section 2 (Assimilated Crimes Act offenses under specified Pennsylvania statutes) applies to all property within the special maritime and territorial jurisdiction of the United States (see 18 U.S.C. § 7) located in the Eastern District of Pennsylvania. Copies of this schedule shall be available for public inspection at the office of the Clerk of Court, and may be made available for public inspection at the headquarters of each agency issuing violation notices pursuant to this Rule at each site or property upon which such violation notices are issued.

(C) Special Schedules. The below listed agencies have filed special schedules of offenses pursuant to Federal regulations enacted by them, and listing the collateral which may be posted for each offense. These agencies are: Army Corps of Engineers, the National Park Service, the General Services Administration, the Veterans Administration and the United States Fish and Wildlife Services. Each of these special schedules has been approved by the court and applies to all property within the Eastern District of Pennsylvania under the charge and control of the filing agency. Additional agencies may from time to time after the adoption of this amendment apply to the court for approval of a special schedule which, if approved by the court, will become effective as set forth in paragraph (D) below. Copies of all special schedules shall be available for public inspection at the office of the Clerk of Court. Copies of each special schedule may also be available for public inspection at the headquarters of the filing agency within the East-ern District of Pennsylvania and at each site or property upon which it applies.

(D) Effective Date. The effective date of the General Schedule or any special schedule or any amendments thereto, shall become effective upon the approval of the court, and the filing of the same with the Clerk of Court, unless otherwise set forth by the court in its order approving the same.

[Effective January 1, 1998.]

* [**Publisher's Note:** For the current General Schedule, please contact the Clerk's Office.]

LOCAL RULES OF ADMIRALTY

RULE 1. APPLICABILITY

These rules apply to the procedure in claims governed by the Supplemental Rules for Certain Admiralty and Maritime Claims of the Federal Rules of Civil Procedure (hereafter "Admiralty Supplemental Rules"), and to Rule 9(h) admiralty and maritime actions generally. The Local Rules of this Court shall also apply to admiralty cases. In the event of a conflict between the Local Rules and Admiralty Local Rules, the Admiralty Local Rules shall control in admiralty cases.

[Effective July 1, 1986.]

RULE 2. DEPOSIT OF FEES WITH MARSHAL

No process in rem in an action provided for in the Admiralty Supplemental Rules shall be served, except on behalf of the United States, or on special order of the Court, unless the party seeking the same shall deposit with the Marshal for this district such sums as may be required by the Marshal as an advance against attachment and custodial costs. This rule does not apply if seizure is effected pursuant to an order of Court appointing a custodian of the property seized, in which case no deposit shall be required. Further, the party seizing the property may be required by the Marshal, to give him a full release and agreement to indemnify the Marshal for any liability which he may incur as a result of arresting the vessel or other property.

[Effective July 1, 1986.]

RULE 3. [RESERVED]

[Revoked effective July 1, 1986.]

RULE 4. SERVICE OF PROCESS

(A) Process issued pursuant to Supplemental Rule B may be served by a person specially appointed to serve process in accordance with Federal Rule 4(c) and Local Rule 29.

(B) If the court has appointed a substitute custodian, the Warrant for Arrest, issued pursuant to Supplemental Rule C, may be served by a person specially appointed in accordance with Federal Rule 4(c) and Local Rule 29.

[Effective July 1, 1986.]

RULE 5. POST–SEIZURE HEARING

Where property is arrested or attached, any person claiming an interest in the property arrested or attached may upon a showing of any improper practice or manifest want of equity on the part of the plaintiff, be entitled to an order requiring the plaintiff to show cause forthwith why the arrest or attachment should not be vacated or other relief granted consistent with these rules. A hearing shall be held on the order to show cause within forty-eight (48) hours of service of the order upon counsel for the plaintiff. The hearing shall be held before the judge to whom the matter is assigned, or, if unavailable, before the emergency judge. This rule shall have no application to suits for seamen's wages when process is issued upon a certificate of sufficient cause filed pursuant to section 4546 of the Revised Statutes (Title 46, U.S. Code, Sections 603 and 604).

[Effective July 1, 1986.]

RULE 6. ADVERTISEMENT OF SEIZURE [REPEALED]

[Effective July 1, 1986; repealed effective June 3, 2002.]

RULE 7. INTERVENTION AND EXPENSES OF JUSTICE

(A) Whenever a vessel or other property is seized, attached or arrested and is in the custody of the Court, anyone asserting a maritime lien or a writ of foreign attachment against the vessel or property may upon motion to the court, with notice to counsel of record, be permitted to intervene.

(B) Intervenors under this rule shall be liable for advancing expenses of justice together with the party originally effecting seizure on any reasonable basis determined by the Court. Intervenors may be required by the Marshal to advance their share of expenses accrued to the date of intervention and expected future expenses of justice giving due regard to the respective amounts of the various claims. Relief from such assessment may be granted by the Court upon motion.

(C) Release of seizure or dismissal by the party originally effecting seizure shall not quash the seizure if there remains pending any claim by intervenors, unless by unanimous consent of intervenors or order of Court.

[Effective July 1, 1986.]

RULE 8. NOTICE OF SALE

Notice must be given by the Marshal of the sale of property by order of this Court. Such notice shall be by advertisement in a newspaper of general circulation within the District in which the sale will take place, unless otherwise ordered by the Court. Such notice shall be published three times a week for two consecutive weeks with the last date of publication not more than twenty-one (21) nor less than seven (7) days immediately preceding the sale. In addition thereto, publication shall be made elsewhere in at least one specialized trade publication of national circulation.

[Effective July 1, 1986. Amended effective December 1, 2009.]

RULE 9. JUDICIAL SALE, RETURN OF MARSHAL

Upon the payment of the proceeds of sale of property into the registry of the court, the Marshal shall send written notice within seven (7) days to all persons known to him or by the substitute custodian to have claims for charges incurred while the vessel or property was in the custody of the court, and shall notify such persons of the necessity of filing claims within fourteen (14) days of the mailing of such notice.

[Effective July 1, 1986. Amended effective December 1, 2009.]

RULE 10. CONFIRMATION OF SALE

In all sales by the Marshal pursuant to orders of sale under the Admiralty Supplemental Rules, the Marshal shall report to the Court the fact of sale, the price brought, and the name of the buyer. If, within seven (7) days after the sale, computed in accordance with F.R.C.P. 6(a), no written objection is filed, the sale shall automatically stand confirmed if the buyer has performed the terms of his purchase.

[Effective July 1, 1986. Amended effective December 1, 2009.]

RULE 11. JOINDER

(A) Except as otherwise provided by the Admiralty Supplemental Rules, parties may sue and parties (including a vessel or other res) may be sued either jointly, severally or alternatively in one suit, and persons having separate causes of action may join in one suit if the causes of action involve substantially the same questions and arise out of the same transactions.

(B) Persons who, under the preceding paragraph of this rule, might have joined as co-plaintiffs, and, in suits for wages, any other seamen claiming wages for the same voyage, not made parties in the original complaint, may, upon motion, be joined to prosecute as co-plaintiffs upon such terms as the court may deem reasonable.

[Effective July 1, 1986.]

RULE 12. CONSOLIDATION

When various suits are pending, all resting upon the same matter of right or defense, although there be no common interest between the parties, the Court may consolidate or compel said suits to be tried together, and enter a single decree or decrees in each case.

[Effective July 1, 1986.]

RULE 13. TRIAL OF LIMITATION OF LIABILITY CASES

Where the vessel interests seeking limitation pursuant to 46 U.S.C. § 181, et seq., have raised the statutory defense by way of answer or complaint, the plaintiff in the former or the damage claimant in the latter shall proceed with its proof first, as is normal at civil trials.

[Effective July 1, 1986.]

RULE 14. DISCOVERY COSTS

When discovery is requested which requires counsel for the parties to travel outside the district, the parties will each advance their own travel costs. The award of these costs following trial shall be in accordance with established law.

[Effective July 1, 1986.]

RULE 15. TRIAL DEPOSITIONS

(A) Once a deposition of a witness is noticed, if a party wishes to take the deposition to preserve testimony for trial, that party may, at his option, proceed with his examination first; upon completion of the direct examination, the cross-examination of the witness by the other parties shall proceed as if on discovery or on such other terms as the parties may agree. Any party shall have the right to preserve such testimony by means of a videotape deposition.

(B) In order to enable the Court to control the trial calendar, and recognizing the difficulty in obtaining the attendance of witnesses in some admiralty cases, the Court may, in appropriate cases order that a video deposition be taken for use at trial.

[Effective July 1, 1986.]

ELECTRONIC CASE FILING PROCEDURES

*[**Publisher's Note:** For procedures on Electronic Case Filing, see Local Rule 5.1.2. See, also, Clerk's Office Procedural Handbook and appendices thereto.]*

INDEX TO UNITED STATES DISTRICT COURT
FOR THE EASTERN DISTRICT OF PENNSYLVANIA

CLERK'S OFFICE PROCEDURAL HANDBOOK
U.S. DISTRICT COURT FOR THE EASTERN
DISTRICT OF PENNSYLVANIA

Clerk's Office Procedural Handbook.

APPENDICES

A. ECF Procedures.
B. PDF File Information.
C. Validation of Signature Form, Local Rule 5.1.2.
D. ECF Registration and Notification Forms.
E. ECF Training Application Form.
F. Designation Form.
G. Disclosure Statement Form.
H. Civil Cover Sheet.
I. Civil Case Management Track Designation Form.
J. [Omitted].
K. Consent to Facsimile Transmission of Notices of Orders.
L. Mail Information Form.
M. Judges' Room Numbers and ZIP Code + 4-Digit Extension Numbers.
N. Summons in a Civil Action.
O. Writ of Execution.

P. Transcript Purchase Order.
Q. Consent, and Reference of a Civil Action to a Magistrate Judge.
R. Bill of Costs.
S. Special Listing Agreement.
T. Busy Slip.
U. Standing Order re: Sentencing Reform Act of 1984.
V. Credit Card Collection Network Procedures.
W. Bail Bond Secured by Property or Real Estate.
X. Attorney Admissions Application (Pro Hac Vice).
Y. Transcript Order Form.
Z. Tape Order Form.
AA. Notice of Electronic Availability of Transcripts in Case Management/Electronic Case Files (CM/ECF) and Transcript Redaction.
BB. Audio File Electronic Access Program.
CC. [Omitted].
DD. Directory of Court-Automated Services.
EE. Electronic Case Filing (ECF) Electronic Filing of Complaints.

CLERK'S OFFICE PROCEDURAL HANDBOOK

This handbook has been prepared as a supplement to the Local Rules of the United States District Court for the Eastern District of Pennsylvania. It is intended to provide administrative information and act as a guide for specific procedural areas. However, if there is a conflict between this supplemental guide and the Local or Federal Rules of Procedure, the Rules govern.

I greatly acknowledge Kevin Dunleavy and Lucy Chin of my staff for their efforts in the production of this handbook.

We welcome any comments or suggestions for improving this handbook. Please forward your comments to: The Office of the Clerk of Court, United States District Court, Eastern District of Pennsylvania, 2609 United States Courthouse, Philadelphia, PA 19106–1797 or fax them to: 215–597–6390.

Michael E. Kunz
Clerk of Court

http://www.paed.uscourts.gov

ELECTRONIC CASE FILING SYSTEM

The United States District Court for the Eastern District of Pennsylvania utilizes an automated civil docketing system, Case Management/Electronic Case Filing ("CM/ECF").

Effective May 27, 2003, dockets for all civil cases filed since July 1, 1990 and dockets for all criminal cases filed since July 1, 1992 will be available for viewing and printing from the CM/ECF system.

All new civil cases filed in this court are entered into this court's Electronic Case Filing ("ECF") system in accordance with provisions of the Electronic Case Filing

Procedures *(Appendix A)*. CM/ECF provides a new, easy-to-use electronic case filing feature that will allow users to file and view court documents over the Internet. Documents are automatically docketed as part of the filing process and are immediately available electronically. CM/ECF also offers the following benefits:

- 24–hour access to filed documents over the Internet;
- automatic e-mail notice of case activity to attorneys of record and judges;
- ability to download and print documents directly from the court system;
- concurrent access to case files by multiple parties; and
- secure storage of documents.

A. Rule 5.1.2—Electronic Case Filing Procedures. All cases and documents filed in this court are required to be filed on the Electronic Case Filing ("ECF") System in accordance with provisions of the *Electronic Case Filing ("ECF") Procedures*, as set forth below unless excepted under these procedures.

Rule 5.1.2   Electronic Case Filing ("ECF") Procedures

1. *Definitions.*

(a) "ECF Filing User" means those who have Court-issued log-ins and passwords to file documents electronically.

(b) "Notice of Electronic Case Filing" means the notice generated by the ECF system when a document has been filed electronically, stating that the document has been filed.

(c) "Judge" means the District Judge assigned to the case, or the Magistrate Judge to whom all or any part of a case has been referred pursuant to 28 U.S.C. § 636.

(d) "Court" shall mean the United States District Court for the Eastern District of Pennsylvania.

2. *Scope of Electronic Case Filing.*

(a) All civil and criminal cases filed in this court are required to be entered into the court's Electronic Case Filing ("ECF") System in accordance with these Electronic Case Filing ("ECF") Procedures. Unless an attorney is excused from ECF registration under Section 3 of these ECF Procedures or except as expressly provided in Section 16 and other sections of these ECF Procedures, or as ordered by the judge, all pleadings, documents, motions, memoranda of law, petitions, certificates of service and other documents required to be filed with the Clerk of Court in connection with a case must be electronically filed.

(b) The filing of all initial papers in civil cases, such as the complaint and the issuance and service of the summons, and, in criminal cases, the indictment or information, warrant for arrest or summons, will be accomplished by paper copy filed in the traditional manner rather than electronically. Parties must concurrently provide the Clerk of Court with a computer disk, in PDF format *(Appendix B)* containing a copy of all documents provided in paper form at the time of filing. All subsequent documents and pleadings must be filed electronically, except as provided in these ECF Procedures or as ordered by the judge. Under this paragraph, all attorneys are required to complete the ECF Validation of Signature form *(Appendix C)*, as described in Section 3(c) below.

(c) Once registered, an ECF Filing User may request to withdraw from participation in the ECF System by providing the Clerk of Court with written notice of the request which shall be forwarded to the Chief Judge for approval.

(d) Nothing in these ECF Procedures shall be construed to nullify or contradict the provisions set forth in Rule 26.1 of the Local Rules of Civil Procedure, *Discovery*, directing that interrogatories, requests for production and inspection and requests for admission under Fed. R.Civ.P. 33, 34 and 36 that answers, responses and objections to interrogatories and to Rules 34 and 36, and that requests, notices of depositions and depositions under Fed.R.Civ.P. 30 and 31, shall not be filed with the court.

(e) Nothing in these ECF Procedures shall be construed to nullify or contradict the provisions set forth in Rule 39.3 of the Local Rules of Civil Procedure, *Records, Files and Exhibits,* directing that the Clerk of Court maintain custody of all records, files and exhibits in all cases filed in this court until such time as the case is finally resolved, dismissed or abandoned, as set forth in paragraph (e) of Rule 39.3.

(f) All cases filed in the ECF System in which a notice of appeal is filed shall be governed by Rule 10 of the Federal Rules of Appellate Procedure and relevant Local Rules and internal operating procedures of the United States Court of Appeals for the Third Circuit, with any differences about whether the record truly discloses what occurred in the district court to be submitted to and settled by the judge. Cases in which there is a right of direct appeal to the United States Supreme Court shall be governed by the rules of the United States Supreme Court.

3. *Excuse From Registration; Format of Documents in Electronic Form.* An attorney who believes he or she should be excused from registering as an ECF Filing User may apply for an exception to this rule by detailed letter to the Clerk of Court, who shall forward the letter to the chief judge for decision. Thereafter, attorneys and others who are excused from registering as ECF Filing Users in accordance with this section are required to comply with the procedures set forth below.

(a) All complaints must be submitted on disk in portable document format (PDF) at the time of filing, so that the complaint may be entered into the District Court's ECF system, and must be accompanied by a courtesy copy of the complaint in paper format for use by the court; under this paragraph, all attorneys are required to complete the ECF Validation of Signature form *(Appendix C)*, as described in Paragraph (c) below.

(b) All documents filed by an attorney who has been excused from registering as an ECF Filing User, as defined under this rule, must be submitted on disk in PDF, so that the filings may be entered into the District Court's ECF system, and must be accompanied by a courtesy copy of the document in paper format for use by the court; under this paragraph, all attorneys are required to complete the ECF Validation of Signature form, as described in Paragraph (c) below.

(c) Attorneys who complete the ECF Validation of Signature form will receive a signature code which must be used by the attorney on the signature line of all courtesy copies submitted with a disk for purposes of signature validation pursuant to Rule 11 of the Federal Rules of Civil Procedure; the document as submitted under Section 3 of this rule will constitute the original document, except for those documents which are excluded from the provisions of rule as set forth in Section 16 of the rule; attorneys are required to have submitted a completed ECF Validation of Signature form just once in order to file all complaints and documents in all subsequent cases in this court.

(d) Service of process will continue to be made in accordance with those provisions set forth in Rule 5 of the Federal Rules of Civil Procedure.

(e) For convenience of attorneys who do not have access to compatible hardware or software, a computer with PDF conversion capability is available in the Clerk's Offices at Philadelphia and Allentown, with assistance for PDF conversion provided by Clerk's Office staff as needed; attorneys who have reason for not providing this material on disk are required to notice the Clerk's Office in writing attached to the document, explaining the reason for not providing this material on disk.

(f) Attorneys who have been excused under this section from registering as ECF Filing Users are requested to register and participate in the court's

Program for Facsimile Service of Notice to Counsel or Litigants in Civil and Criminal Cases (the "Fax Noticing Program").

(g) Those documents and categories of cases which are now excluded from the provisions of this section consistent with the policy of the Judicial Conference of the United States, as may be amended from time to time, are set forth in Section 16 of this rule *(Appendix A, Section 16)*.

4. *Eligibility, Registration and Password.*

(a) Unless otherwise excused, attorneys admitted to the bar of this court, including those admitted pro hac vice, are required to register as ECF Filing Users of the court's ECF system. Registration is in a form prescribed by the Clerk of Court *(Appendix D)* and requires the Filing User's name, address, telephone number, Internet e-mail address and a declaration that the attorney is admitted to the bar of this court and is a member in good standing.

(b) Upon the approval of the judge, a party to a case who is not represented by an attorney may register as an ECF Filing User in the ECF System solely for purposes of the action. Registration is in a form prescribed by the Clerk of Court and requires identification of the case as well as the name, address, telephone number and Internet e-mail address of the party. If, during the course of the case, the party retains an attorney who appears on the party's behalf, the attorney must advise the Clerk of Court to terminate the party's registration as a Filing User upon the attorney's appearance.

(c) Registration as an ECF Filing User constitutes agreement to receive and consent to make electronic service of all documents as provided in these ECF Procedures in accordance with Rule 5(b)(2)(D) of the Federal Rules of Civil Procedure and the Federal Rules of Criminal Procedure, as referenced in Rule 49(b) of the Federal Rules of Criminal Procedure. This agreement and consent is applicable to all future cases until revoked by the ECF Filing User.

(d) Once registration is completed, the ECF Filing User will receive notification of the user log-in and password. ECF Filing Users agree to protect the security of their passwords and immediately notify the Clerk of Court by telephone, with said notification confirmed immediately thereafter in writing delivered by e-mail, facsimile or hand-delivery to the attention of the Clerk of Court, if they learn that their password has been compromised. Users may be subject to sanctions by the judge for failure to comply with this provision. For security reasons, the court recommends that ECF Filing Users periodically change their passwords which shall be done by notifying the clerk of the court who shall implement the change.

5. *Consequences of Electronic Filing.*

(a) Electronic transmission of a document to the ECF System consistent with these ECF Procedures, together with the transmission of a notice of electronic case filing from the court, constitutes filing of the document for all purposes of the Federal Rules of Civil Procedure, the Federal Rules of Criminal Procedure and the Local Rules of this court, and constitutes entry of the document on the docket maintained by the Clerk of Court pursuant to Rules 58 and 79 of the Federal Rules of Civil Procedure and Rules 49 and 55 of the Federal Rules of Criminal Procedure.

(b) A document that has been filed electronically is the official record of the document, and the filing party is bound by the document as filed. Except in the case of documents first filed in paper form and subsequently submitted electronically under Section 2 above, a document filed electronically is deemed filed at the time and date stated on the notice of electronic case filing from the court.

(c) Filing a document electronically does not change any filing deadline set by the Federal Rules of Civil Procedure, the Federal Rules of Criminal Procedure, the Local Rules of the court, or an order of the judge.

(d) All pleadings and documents filed electronically must be transmitted in the form prescribed by Rule 10(a) of the Federal Rules of Civil Procedure. All transmissions for electronic case filings of pleadings and documents to the ECF system shall be titled in accordance with the approved directory of civil and criminal events of the ECF system.

6. *Attachments and Exhibits.* ECF Filing Users may submit all documents identified as exhibits or attachments in either paper copy filed in the traditional manner or electronic form. If using electronic form, an ECF Filing User must submit as exhibits or attachments only those excerpts of the identified documents that are relevant to the matter under consideration by the court. Excerpted material must be clearly and prominently identified as such. ECF Filing Users who file excerpts of documents as exhibits or attachments electronically pursuant to these ECF Procedures do so without prejudice to their right to file timely additional excerpts or the complete document, provided however, that the total number of pages of attachments and exhibits electronically filed shall not exceed 50 without prior approval of the judge. Pages of attachments and exhibits in excess of 50 may be filed in paper copy filed in the traditional manner. Responding parties who choose to file exhibits and attachments electronically may also timely file additional excerpts or the complete document, subject to the same page limitations as set forth above.

7. *Sealed Documents.* Documents ordered to be placed under seal must be filed in paper copy filed in the traditional manner and not electronically. A motion to file documents under seal may be filed electronically unless prohibited by law. The order of the court authorizing the filing of documents under seal may be filed electronically unless prohibited by law. A paper copy of the order must be attached to the documents under seal and be delivered to the Clerk of Court.

8. *Service of Documents by Electronic Means.*

(a) When an ECF Filing User electronically files a pleading or other document using the ECF system, a Notice of Electronic Case Filing shall automatically be generated by the system, and shall be sent automatically to all parties entitled to service under the Federal Rules of Civil Procedure, the Federal Rules of Criminal Procedure and the Local Rules of the Eastern District of Pennsylvania who have consented to electronic service. Electronic service of the Notice of Electronic Case Filing constitutes service of the filed document to all such parties and shall be deemed to satisfy the requirements of Rule 5(b)(2)(D) of the Federal Rules of Civil Procedure and Rule 49 of the Federal Rules of Criminal Procedure.

(b) All documents filed using the ECF system shall contain a Certificate of Service stating that the document has been filed electronically and is available for viewing and downloading from the ECF system. The Certificate of Service must identify the manner in which service on each party was accomplished, including any party who has not consented to electronic service.

(c) Parties who have not consented to electronic service are entitled to receive a paper copy of any electronically filed pleading or other document. Service of such paper copy must be made according to the Federal Rules of Civil Procedure, the Federal Rules of Criminal Procedure and the Local Rules of the Eastern District of Pennsylvania.

(d) As set forth in Section 4 of these ECF Procedures, registration as an ECF Filing User constitutes agreement to receive and consent to make electronic service of all documents as provided in these ECF Procedures in accordance with Rule 5(b)(2)(D) of the Federal Rules of Civil Procedure and Rule 49 of the Federal Rules of Criminal Procedure. This agreement and consent is applicable to all pending and future actions assigned to the ECF System until revoked by the ECF Filing User.

(e) In accordance with Rule 6(d) of the Federal Rules of Civil Procedure, service by electronic means is treated the same as service by mail for the purpose of adding three (3) days to the prescribed period to respond.

(f) In accordance with Rule 77(d) of the Federal Rules of Civil Procedure, the court may serve notice of entry of orders or judgments by electronic means as provided in Rule 5(b) and Section 4 of this Procedural Order.

(g) In civil cases, the provisions of this Section 8 apply to service of documents covered by Rule 5(a) of the Federal Rules of Civil Procedure. Service of Original Process under Rule 4 of the Federal Rules of Civil Procedure is not authorized under these ECF Procedures to be accomplished electronically. This Section 8 does not apply to service of an arrest warrant, summons or subpoena in criminal cases.

9. *Signature.*

(a) The user log-in and password required to submit documents to the ECF System serve as the ECF Filing User's signature on all electronic documents filed with the court. They also serve as a signature for purposes of Rule 11(a) of the Federal Rules of Civil Procedure, the Local Rules of this court, and any other purpose for which a signature is required in connection with proceedings before the court. Each document filed electronically must, if possible, indicate that it has been electronically filed. Electronically filed documents must include a signature block and must set forth the name, address, telephone number and the attorney's state bar identification number, if applicable. In addition, the name of the ECF Filing User under whose log-in and password the document is submitted must be preceded by an "s/" and typed in the space where the signature would otherwise appear.

(b) No ECF Filing User or other person may knowingly permit or cause to permit a Filing User's password to be used by anyone other than an authorized agent of the Filing User.

(c) Documents requiring signatures of more than one party must be electronically filed either by: (1) submitting a scanned document containing all necessary signatures; (2) representing the consent of the other parties on the document; (3) identifying on the document the parties whose signatures are required and by the submission of a notice of endorsement by the other parties no later than seven (7) days after filing; or (4) any other manner approved by the court.

10. *Submission of Stipulations and Proposed Orders.* An ECF Filing User electronically submitting stipulations or proposed orders which may require a judge's signature must promptly deliver on computer disk or e-mail the stipulation or proposed order to the Clerk of Court at ECF_clerksoffice@paed.uscourts.gov for delivery to the judge unless the judge orders otherwise. An ECF Filing User who electronically submits a stipulation or proposed order is bound by all signature requirements set forth in Section 9 of these ECF Procedures and Rule 11(a) of the Federal Rules of Civil Procedure.

11. *Retention Requirements.* Documents that are electronically filed and require original signatures other than that of the Filing User must be maintained in paper form by the ECF Filing User until three (3) years after the time period for appeal expires. The ECF Filing User must provide original documents for review upon request of the judge.

12. *Public Access.*

(a) Any person or organization, other than one registered as an ECF Filing User under Section 4 of these rules, may access the ECF Filing System at the court's Internet site, www.paed.uscourts.gov by obtaining a PACER log-in and password. Those who have PACER access but who are not Filing Users may retrieve docket sheets and those documents which the court makes available on the Internet for the fee normally charged for this service as set by the fee schedule authorized by the Administrative Office of United States Courts, but they may not file documents.

(b) Documents should be made available electronically to the same extent that they are available for personal inspection in the office of the Clerk of Court at the

U.S. Courthouse. Social Security numbers, dates of birth, financial account numbers and names of minor children should be modified or partially redacted in electronically filed documents.

(c) In connection with the electronic filing of any material, any person may apply by motion for an order limiting electronic access to, or prohibiting the electronic filing of, certain specifically identified materials on the grounds that such material is subject to privacy interests and that electronic access or electronic filing in the action is likely to prejudice those privacy interests. In further protection of privacy, reference is made to the provisions of Rule 5.1.3 of the Local Rules of Civil Procedure, *Excluded Personal Identifiers*, mandating the modification or redaction of such personal identifiers as Social Security numbers, dates of birth, financial account numbers and names of minor children in all documents filed either in traditional paper form or electronically.

13. *Entry of Court Order.* All orders, decrees, judgments and proceedings of the court will be filed in accordance with these rules which will constitute entry on the docket maintained by the Clerk of Court pursuant to Fed.R.Civ.P. 58 and 79, and Rules 49 and 55 of the Federal Rules of Criminal Procedure. All signed orders will be filed electronically by the Clerk of Court. Any order filed electronically without the original signature of a judge has the same force and effect as if the judge had affixed the judge's signature to a paper copy of the order and it had been entered on the docket in paper copy filed in the traditional manner.

14. *Notice of Court Order and Judgment.* Immediately upon the entry of an order or judgment, the Clerk of Court will transmit to ECF Filing Users in the case, in electronic form, a notice of electronic filing. Electronic transmission of the Notice of Electronic Case Filing constitutes the notice required by Rule 77(d) of the Federal Rules of Civil Procedure and Rule 49(c) of the Federal Rules of Criminal Procedure. In accordance with the Federal Rules of Civil Procedure, the Clerk of Court must give notice in paper form to a person who has been excused under Section 3 of Local Rule 5.1.2 from registering as an ECF Filing User.

15. *Technical Failure.* An ECF Filing User whose filing is determined to be untimely as the result of a technical failure may seek appropriate relief from the judge, provided that the User immediately notifies the Clerk of Court of the technical failure by telephone, with said notification confirmed immediately thereafter in writing delivered by e-mail, facsimile or by hand to the attention of the Clerk of Court. The clerk of the court shall forthwith notify the chambers of the judge.

16. *Categories of Cases and Types of Documents in Civil and Criminal Cases Excluded from Electronic Case Filing.* As provided in Section 2(b) above, all initial papers in civil and criminal cases, including the complaint, amended complaint, third-party complaint, notice of removal, the issuance and service of the summons, and the indictment and information in criminal cases, cannot be electronically filed on the court's CM/ECF system, but must be filed on paper accompanied by a copy of the document on disk in PDF format. Additionally, the following types of documents and categories of cases, as may be amended from time to time *(Appendix A, Section 16)*, can neither be electronically filed on the court's CM/ECF system nor submitted on disk in PDF format by an attorney excused from participation from ECF pursuant to Section 3 of these procedures, but must be filed in paper copy, filed in the traditional manner, consistent with the policy of the Judicial Conference of the United States:

A. Excluded Cases.

   1. Grand jury matters.

   2. Qui tam cases.

   3. Sealed cases.

B. Excluded Documents.

CIVIL CASES

1.   Administrative records.

2.   All documents filed by prisoners and pro se litigants, including the initial complaint and initial habeas corpus petitions, and death penalty habeas corpus petitions.

3.   Bankruptcy appeal records.

4.   Sealed documents.

5.   State court records.

6.   Transcript of civil proceedings shall be placed on CM/ECF or PACER, unless the presiding judge otherwise directs.

7.   Discovery material, as set forth in Rule 26.1 of the Local Rules of Civil Procedure, *Discovery*, including:

a) interrogatories, requests for production and inspection and requests for admission under Rules 33, 34 and 36 of the Federal Rules of Civil Procedure;

b) answers, responses and objections to interrogatories and to Rules 34 and 36 of the Federal Rules of Civil Procedure;

c) requests, notices of depositions and depositions under Rules 30 and 31 of the Federal Rules of Civil Procedure.

8.   Praecipe for Writ of Execution.

9.   Applications for Writ of Continuing Garnishment.

10.   Praecipe to Issue Writ of Revival.

11.   Praecipe for Writ of Seizure.

12.   Praecipe for Writ to Restore.

13.   Civil Jury Verdict Sheets.

14.   Civil Minute Sheets.

15.   Ex Parte Motions.

CRIMINAL CASES

1.   Sealed documents.

2.   Transcript of criminal proceedings shall not be placed on CM/ECF or PACER, unless the presiding judge otherwise directs after giving the prosecution and defense counsel an opportunity to be heard.

3.   All documents requiring the signature of a defendant in a criminal or magistrate proceeding, such as waiver of indictment, waiver of presentence report, waiver of a jury trial, plea agreement, appearance bond, affidavit, and financial affidavit.

4.   Criminal Jury Verdict Sheets.

5.   Presentence Reports and any objections or other documents filed related to the Presentence Reports.

6.   Criminal Minute Sheets.

7.   Judgment and Commitment Orders.

8.   Ex parte Motions.

17.   *Training Seminars.*   ECF training is available to members of the bar, paralegals, secretaries and automation support staff.   For information regarding participation in the court's CM/ECF system, see *Appendix E*.

FILING A CIVIL ACTION

The filing of all initial papers in civil case, such as the complaint and the issuance and service of the summons, and, in criminal case, the indictment information, and warrant for arrest or summons, will be accomplished by paper copy filed in the traditional manner, rather than electronically. Parties must concurrently provide the Clerk of Court with a computer disk containing a PDF format copy of all documents provided in paper form at the time of filing. All subsequent documents and pleadings must be filed electronically, except as provided in ECF Procedures or as ordered by the judge. Under this paragraph, all attorneys are required to complete the ECF Validation of Signature form, as described in Section 3(c) of the ECF Procedures.

All new civil actions are to be filed on 8 ½" × 11" paper in the Clerk's Office, Room 2609, second floor of the Federal Courthouse, or in the divisional office in Allentown, Pennsylvania, between the hours of 8:30 a.m. and 5:00 p.m. Filings are accepted by mail, as well as in person. The addresses are:

United States District Court
Eastern District of Pennsylvania
U.S. Courthouse
601 Market Street, Room 2609
Philadelphia, PA 19106–1797
(215) 597–7704

or

United States District Court
U.S. Courthouse and Federal Building
504 West Hamilton Street, Suite 1601
Allentown, PA 18101–1500
(610) 434–3896

Parties are invited to participate in a pilot filing complaints electronically on the CM/ECF system. If you are interested in this program, please complete an information form *(Appendix EE)* and you will be contacted by the Clerk's Office for training.

The cost for filing a civil action is $400.00 (a $350 filing fee established by 28 U.S.C. § 1914(A), plus a $50 administrative fee established by The Judicial Conference. The $50 administrative fee shall not be charged to petitioners in civil actions seeking Habeas Corpus relief pursuant to 28 U.S.C. §§ 2241–2266). Payment may be made in three forms: cash, credit card, or checks made payable to: *"Clerk, U.S. District Court"*.

All subsequent filings, motions, pleadings and other papers are to be filed electronically by the ECF system or on disk in PDF format accompanied by a courtesy copy, by mail or, in person in Room 2609 at the courthouse in Philadelphia or Suite 1601 at the divisional office in Allentown.

Counsel should include the following in the drafting of the complaint or petition:

(a) name of court;

(b) name and address of both parties, in caption form;

(c) title of action;

(d) a short and plain statement of the grounds upon which the court's jurisdiction depends;

(e) a short and plain statement of the claim showing that the pleader is entitled to relief;

(f) a demand for judgment for the relief to which the plaintiff deems himself entitled;

(g) jury demand; and

(h) name, address, Pennsylvania attorney identification number and signature of plaintiff's attorney.

A. Civil Justice Expense and Delay Reduction Plan. In response to a mandate by the Civil Justice Reform Act of 1990 and, in an effort to reduce the cost and delay of civil litigation in the federal courts, this district adopted The Civil Justice Expense and Delay Reduction Plan with an effective date of December 31, 1991. A copy of the plan can be obtained by contacting Aida Ayala at (267) 299–7099. This district was selected as a pilot district and was required to implement a plan by December 31, 1991. An Advisory Group was appointed in April, 1991 to prepare a report and recommendation on the status of the Eastern District of Pennsylvania. Based on this report, the judges adopted the expense and delay reduction plan.

B. Designation Form. The designation form *(Appendix F)* is to be used by counsel to designate the category of the cause of action for the purpose of assignment to the appropriate calendar. It is to be completed by plaintiff's counsel and submitted at the time of filing.

The court requires two (2) copies of the designation form. Additional forms are not required for additional defendants, nor are additional forms required when the United States Government or an officer or agency thereof is involved.

INSTRUCTIONS FOR COMPLETING THE DESIGNATION FORM

1. *Address of Plaintiff and Defendant.* House or apartment address, street, city, county and zip codes are required in this section.

2. *Place of Accident.* The place of the accident, incident, or transaction; house or apartment address, street, city, county and zip code are required in this section. NOTE: Counsel should continue on reverse side if additional space is needed to fully explain this matter.

3. *Disclosure Statement.* In accordance with Federal Rule of Civil Procedure 7.1(a), *Disclosure Statement*, a non-governmental corporate party to an action or proceeding in a district court must file copies of a statement that identifies any parent corporation and any publicly held corporation that owns 10% or more of its stock or state that there is no such corporation *(Appendix G)*.

A party must file the Rule 7.1(a) statement with its first appearance, pleading, petition, motion, response, or other request addressed to the court, and promptly file a supplemental statement upon any change in the information that the statement requires.

4. *Related Cases.* This refers to pending cases or cases disposed of in the United States District Court for the Eastern District of Pennsylvania within a one-year period.

If the case is related, counsel must indicate the case number, the presiding judge, and the date terminated.

5. *Civil Category Checklist.* Counsel is required to determine whether the action arises under: (a) federal question, Title 28 U.S.C. § 1331; or (b) diversity, Title 28 U.S.C. § 1332. Counsel must check off the **one** specific category within the appropriate classification to which that case pertains. This is for the purpose of proper case assignment by classification.

6. *Arbitration Certification.* The arbitration certification is used to determine whether or not the case exceeds the damages threshold of $150,000, which is the maximum amount for any arbitration proceeding. Counsel is advised to refer to Local Civil Rule 53.2, Section 3, Paragraph C, which states that damages will be presumed to be less than $150,000 and thus, eligible for arbitration unless counsel, at the time of filing, states that the damages exceed that amount. The effect of this

certification is to remove the case from eligibility for arbitration. Date and signature must be included in this section.

7. *Date and Signature.* The date of filing and signature of counsel is required in this section.

C. Civil Cover Sheet (Form JS44). The Civil Cover Sheet *(Appendix H)* is required by the Clerk of Court for the purpose of initiating the civil docket sheet. It is completed by plaintiff's counsel and submitted at the time of filing. Only one civil cover sheet is required by the court to accompany the complaint, regardless of whether or not the United States of America, or an officer of any agency thereof, is a party.

INSTRUCTIONS FOR COMPLETING A CIVIL COVER SHEET

1. *Parties.* The complete name(s), and address(es) of plaintiff(s) and defendant(s) are required in this section.

2. *Attorneys.* Plaintiff's Attorney: Firm name, address, Pennsylvania Bar identification number and telephone number are required.

Defendant's Attorney: Firm name, address, Pennsylvania Bar identification number and telephone number, if known, are required.

3. *Jurisdiction.* Counsel should place an "X" in the appropriate box corresponding to the jurisdictional basis of the action.

The following order of priority should be utilized in cases where more than one basis of jurisdiction is set out in the complaint.

(a) United States Plaintiff. Jurisdiction is based on 28 U.S.C. §§ 1345 and 1348. Suits by agencies and officers of the United States are in this category.

(b) United States Defendant. Jurisdiction is based on 28 U.S.C. § 1346 and includes suits against agencies and officers of the United States.

(c) Federal Question. Various statutes give the district court jurisdiction to hear and determine controversies where federal rights between parties are covered by statute or Constitution.

(d) Diversity of Citizenship. This refers to suits under 28 U.S.C. § 1332. In this situation, parties are residents of different states.

<u>Note</u>: If diversity is checked, it must be further categorized in the box to the right.

4. *Nature of Suit.* Counsel must indicate the general description of the suit by placing an "X" in the appropriate box. If more than one possible category applies, select the most explicit and specific classification.

<u>Note</u>: Only one check mark is to be made in this area.

Explanatory Information for Social Security. In the section for Social Security, six (6) possible types of claims or actions are listed.

SUIT CODE NUMBER	ABBREVIATION FOR CAUSE OF ACTION	SUBSTANTIVE STATEMENT EXPLAINING TYPE
861	HIA	All claims for health insurance benefits (Medicare) under Title XVIII, Part A, of the Social Security Act, as amended. Also includes claims by hospitals, skilled nursing facilities, etc. for certification as providers of services under

SUIT CODE NUMBER	ABBREVIATION FOR CAUSE OF ACTION	SUBSTANTIVE STATEMENT EXPLAINING TYPE
		the program. (42 U.S.C. § 395f(b)).
862	BL	All claims for "black lung" benefits under Title IV, Part B, of the Federal Coal Mine Health and Safety Act of 1969 (30 U.S.C. § 923).
863	DIWC	All claims filed by insured workers for disability insurance benefits under Title II of the Social Security Act, as amended; plus all claims filed for child's insurance benefits based on disability (42 U.S.C. § 405(g)).
863	DIWW	All claims filed for widows' or widowers' insurance benefits based on disability under Title XVI of the Social Security Act, as amended (42 U.S.C. § 405(g)).
864	SSID	All claims for supplemental security income payments based upon disability filed under Title XVI of the Social Security Act, as amended.
865	RSI	All claims for retirement (old age) and survivors' benefits under Title II of the Social Security Act, as amended. (42 U.S.C. § 405(g)).

5. *Origin.* Counsel is required to indicate which one of the seven possible categories is applicable to the case being filed. The following explanatory guidelines should be consulted in this matter.

(a) Original Proceeding. This category will be the appropriate one for most cases.

(b) Removed from State Court. Proceedings initiated in the State Courts may be removed to the District Court under Title 28 U.S.C. § 1441.

(c) Remanded from Appellate Court. Use the date of remand as the filing date.

(d) Reinstated or Reopened. Use the reopening date as the filing date.

(e) Transferred from Another District. Self–Explanatory.

(f) Multidistrict Litigation. Use when a multidistrict case is transferred into this district (Title 28 U.S.C. § 1407).

6. *Cause of Action.* In this section, a citation must be used for the U.S. civil statute under which the filing is made. In addition, a brief statement of the cause of action must also be included by counsel.

7. *Class Action.* This item should be checked if the case is alleged to be a class action under Fed. R. Civ. P. 23.

Demand: The dollar amount which is sought in the case should be inserted in this space.

Jury Demand: Counsel should check "yes" in this section only if a jury trial is demanded in the complaint.

8. *Related Case(s), if any.* This section is used to reference relating pending cases, if any. If there are related pending cases or cases disposed of within a one-year period, insert the docket numbers and the corresponding judges' names for such cases.

9. *Date and Signature.* The date of filing and the signature should be the final insertion on the Civil Cover Sheet.

D. Case Management Track Designation Form. Each civil case will be assigned to one of the following tracks *(Appendix I)*:

1. *Habeas Corpus.* Cases brought under 28 U.S.C. § 2241 through § 2255.

2. *Social Security.* Cases requesting review of a decision made by the Secretary of Health and Human Services that denied the plaintiff Social Security benefits.

3. *Arbitration.* Cases designated for arbitration under Local Civil Rule 53.2.

4. *Asbestos.* Cases involving claims for personal injury or property damage from exposure to asbestos.

5. *Special Management.* Cases that do not fall into tracks 1 through 4 or that need special or intense management by the court do to one or more of the following factors:

    (a) large number of parties;

    (b) large number of claims;

    (c) complex factual issues;

    (d) large volume of evidence;

    (e) problems locating or preserving evidence;

    (f) extensive discovery;

    (g) exceptionally long time needed to prepare for disposition;

    (h) decision needed within an exceptionally short time; or

    (i) need to decide preliminary issues before final disposition.

6. *Standard Management.* Cases that do not fall into any of the other tracks.

E. Verifications. Verifications or affidavits are not required to be filed with a complaint, except:

(a) where the complaint seeks entry of a temporary restraining order [Federal Rule of Civil Procedure 65(b)]; and

(b) in shareholder derivative actions [Federal Rule of Civil Procedure 23.1].

In lieu of a verification or an affidavit, it is appropriate to submit an unsworn declaration in the form set forth in 28 U.S.C. § 1746.

F. Filing an Amended Complaint. A party may amend its pleading once as a matter of course within: (a) 21 days after serving it; or (b) if the pleading is one to which a responsive pleading is required, 21 days after service of a responsive pleading, or 21 days after service of a motion under Rule 12(b), (e) or (f), whichever is earlier.

G. Class Action Complaints—Local Rule 23.1. Class action complaints must bear next to their caption, the legend, "Complaint—Class Action." In addition, they must set forth certain "Class Action Allegations" which are described in Local Civil Rule 23.1.

H.   Copies of Complaints.   It is not necessary to deliver multiple copies of the complaint and amended complaint to the Clerk's Office to be served on the defendants.   It is only necessary to deliver an original complaint or an original amended complaint for filing.   The Clerk's Office will process all completed summonses and return them to counsel for service on the opposing party.

I.   Service of Process.   Defendants have 21 days after the service of the summons and complaint to file an answer to the complaint unless otherwise ordered by the court.

The U.S. Attorney has 60 days after service to file an answer to the complaint in actions against the United States of America, an office or agency thereof.

J.   Waiver of Service of Summons.   Rule 4 of the Federal Rules of Civil Procedure requires certain parties to cooperate in saving cost of the service of summons and complaint.   A defendant who, after being notified of an action and asked to waive service of summons, fails to do so, will be required to bear the cost of such service unless good cause is shown for its failure to sign and return the waiver.

It is not good cause for a failure to waive service that a party believes that the complaint is unfounded, or that the action has been brought in an improper place or in a court that lacks jurisdiction over the subject matter of the action or over its person or property.   A party who waives service of the summons retains all defenses and objections (except relating to the summons or to the service of the summons), and may later object to the jurisdiction of the court or to the place where the action has been brought.

A defendant who waives service must, within the time specified on the waiver form, serve on the plaintiff's attorney (or unrepresented party) a response to the complaint and must also file a signed copy of the response with the court.   If the answer or motion is not served within this time, a default judgment may be taken against the defendant.   By waiving service, a defendant is allowed more time to answer than if the summons had been actually served when the request for waiver of service was received.

If you need additional information on filing complaints contact Rick Sabol, Operations Manager, at (267) 299–7011.

DOCUMENTS

The original docket sheets, record files, and indices to all cases are available for inspection in the Clerk's Office, Room 2609, in Philadelphia or in Suite 1601 of the divisional office in Allentown.   The civil dockets are divided among ten (10) clerks and the *last* digit of each case number determines the docket clerk to whom the case is assigned for processing.

The following personnel perform case processing duties in the civil section in the Philadelphia Clerk's Office:

(#1)	Rob Fehrle	(267) 299–7001
(#2)	Vincent Alia	(267) 299–7002
(#3)	Kristin Pepin	(267) 299–7003
(#4)	Tashia Irving	(267) 299–7004
(#5)	Kimberly Williams	(267) 299–7005
(#6)	Michele Helmer	(267) 299–7006
(#7)	Joseph Lavin	(267) 299–7007
(#8)	Ashley Mastrangelo	(267) 299–7008
(#9)	Steve Gill	(267) 299–7009
(#10)	Frank DelCampo	(267) 299–7010

At the divisional office in Allentown, Pennsylvania, contact:

Evelyn Renner	(610) 434–3896

Matthew A. Sheetz . . . .   (610) 776–6116
Kris Yerry . . . .   (610) 776–6115
Lauren Wentz . . . .   (610) 776–6121

Criminal case processing is divided among clerks:
   (#1–3) Kirk Kopacz . . . .   (267) 299–7035
   (#4–6) Tom Giambrone . . . .   (267) 299–7024
   (#7–8) Mark Ciamaichelo . . . .   (267) 299–7145
   (#9–0) Angela Burge . . . .   (267) 299–7160

Carlos Cardona at (267) 299–7023, reviews overall compliance with the Speedy Trial Act. The Magistrate Judges' Docket Clerk is Mark Ciamaichelo at (267) 299–7145.

Rule 11 of the Federal Rules of Civil Procedure requires that every pleading, motion and other paper of a party represented by an attorney be signed by the attorney. Please be sure to date the pleadings, attach a certificate of service, and include the address and phone number of counsel. It is not necessary to send a cover letter when filing routine pleadings. However, if you are filing a pleading which requires special attention, please include a cover letter.

The user log-in and password required to submit documents to the ECF system serves as the ECF Filing User's signature on all electronic documents filed with the court. They also serve as a signature for purposes of Rule 11(a) of the Federal Rules of Civil Procedure, the Local Rules of this court, and any other purpose for which a signature is required in connection with proceedings before the court. Each document filed electronically must, if possible, indicate that it has been electronically filed.

Electronically filed documents must include a signature block and must set forth the name, address, telephone number and the attorney's state bar identification number, if applicable. In addition, the name of the ECF Filing User under whose log-in and password the document is submitted must be preceded by an "s/" and typed in the space where the signature would otherwise appear. Documents requiring signatures of more than one party must be electronically filed either by:

(1) submitting a scanned document containing all necessary signatures;

(2) representing the consent of the other parties on the document;

(3) identifying on the document the parties whose signatures are required and by the submission of a notice of endorsement by the other parties no later than three (3) business days after filing; or

(4) any other manner approved by the court.

A. Copies of Paper Documents. Paper documents must be accompanied by a copy of the document on disk in PDF format. We suggest you do not combine pleadings, but file a separate pleading for each action in which a resolution is sought. When filing individual pleadings, it is easier and more efficient for the judge to have the option to sign an order ruling on the individual pleading rather than have to prepare an order.

It is important that pleadings be assembled with all documents in support thereof attached in sets. This ensures proper filing and also enables the judge to have complete sets.

Note: **The Clerk's Office does not date-stamp copies of pleadings unless accompanied by self-addressed, stamped envelopes. The document will be date-stamped and returned by mail.**

B. Certificate of Service. When filing pleadings, it is necessary to attach a *Certificate of Service* indicating the names of all counsel and/or parties you have served.

When an ECF Filing User electronically files a pleading or other document using the ECF system, a Notice of Electronic Case Filing shall automatically be generated by the system, and shall be sent automatically to all parties entitled to service under the Federal Rules of Civil Procedure, the Federal Rules of Criminal Procedure and the Local Rules of the Eastern District of Pennsylvania who have consented to electronic service. Electronic service of the Notice of Electronic Case Filing constitutes service of the filed document to all such parties and shall be deemed to satisfy the requirements of Rule 5(b)(2)(D) of the Federal Rules of Civil Procedure and Rule 49 of the Federal Rules of Criminal Procedure.

All documents filed using the ECF system shall contain a Certificate of Service stating the document has been filed electronically and is available for viewing and downloading from the ECF system. The Certificate of Service must identify the manner in which service on each party was accomplished, including any party who has not consented to electronic service.

C. Third–Party Complaint. Leave of court is not necessary to file a third-party complaint if it is filed by the defendant within 14 days after service of the original answer to the complaint. However, leave of court is necessary if the defendant files the third-party complaint after the expiration of 14 days of the service of the answer. Counsel must file a *Motion for Leave to File a Third–Party Complaint*, together with a memorandum, proposed order and the proposed third-party complaint. When the judge signs the order, the clerk will process the complaint. *(See Rule 14, Federal Rules of Civil Procedure.)*

D. Excluded Personal Identifiers—Local Rule of Civil Procedure 5.1.3. As documents in civil cases may be available for personal inspection in the office of the clerk at the United States Courthouse, or, if filed electronically, may be made available on the court's Electronic Case Filing system, such personal identifiers as Social Security numbers, dates of birth, financial account numbers and names of minor children should be modified or partially redacted in all documents filed either in traditional form or electronically. *(Appendix J)*.

E. Electronic Case File Privacy—Local Rule of Criminal Procedure 53.2. In compliance with the policy of the Judicial Conference of the United States and the E–Government Act of 2002, and in order to promote electronic access to documents in the criminal case files while also protecting personal privacy and other legitimate interests, parties shall refrain from including, or shall partially redact where inclusion is necessary, the following personal data identifiers from all documents filed with the court, including exhibits thereto, whether filed electronically or in paper format, unless otherwise ordered by the court:

(1) *Social Security Numbers.* If an individual's Social Security number must be included, only the last four digits of that number should be used.

(2) *Names of Minor Children.* If the involvement of a minor child must be mentioned, only the initials of the child should be used.

(3) *Dates of Birth.* If an individual's date of birth must be included, only the year should be used.

(4) *Financial Account Numbers.* If financial account numbers are relevant, only the last four digits of the number should be used.

(5) *Home Addresses.* If a home address must be included, only the city and state should be listed.

In compliance with the E–Government Act of 2002, a party wishing to file a document containing the personal data identifiers listed above may file an unredacted document under seal. This document shall be retained by the court as part of the record. The court may, however, still require the party to file a redacted copy for the public file. Trial exhibits may be safeguarded by means other than redaction, and the court may modify this rule to fit the requirements of particular cases.

The responsibility for redacting these personal identifiers rests solely with counsel and the parties. The Clerk need not review filings for compliance with this rule.

F. Sealed Pleadings. Sealed cases and documents ordered to be placed under seal are excluded from the provisions of the ECF Procedures *(Appendix A)* and must be filed in paper format, filed in the traditional manner, and not electronically. A motion to file documents under seal may be filed electronically unless prohibited by law. A paper copy of the order must be attached to the documents under seal to be delivered to the Clerk of Court. Include a cover letter identifying the contents of the envelope and information pertaining to the sealing of the document and/or case. The envelope containing the sealed pleading should reflect the caption and case number and should also identify the type of pleading contained in the envelope. If a document is being filed and sealed pursuant to a protective order or other order, refer to the sealed document in your cover letter. Please include the word "SEALED" near the top margin of the letter to alert the person opening the mail to exercise caution in processing the envelope.

Local Rule of Civil Procedure 5.1.5 provides that a document in a civil action may be filed under seal only if:

(1) the civil action is brought pursuant to a federal statute that prescribes the sealing of the record or of certain specific documents; or

(2) the Court orders the documents sealed.

Where a document is sealed pursuant to § 5.1.5(a)(1), the continued status of the document under seal shall be governed by the relevant federal statute. If no federal statute governs, §§ 5.1.5(b)(2) and (c) shall apply.

When a document is sealed pursuant to § 5.1.5(a)(2), the document, if it remains in the custody of the Court, shall not be unsealed for two years after the conclusion of the civil action, including all appeals, unless the Court orders otherwise.

If a document is still sealed at the conclusion of the two-year period and the Court has not entered an order continuing its sealed status beyond that time, the Clerk of Court shall notify the attorney for the party having submitted the sealed document at the attorney's address on the docket that the document will be unsealed unless the attorney or the submitting party advises the Clerk within sixty (60) days that said attorney or submitting party objects. If the attorney or submitting party objects to the unsealing of the document, or if the Clerk's notification is returned unclaimed, the Court will make a determination on a case-by-case basis, whether to maintain the document under seal, to unseal it, or to require further notification.

G. False Claims Act Cases. All False Claims Act cases are filed *under seal*. The Complaint is docketed and no summons is issued. The Complaint is impounded and sent to the assigned judge.

The Government may file a number of motions for an extension of the seal on the False Claims Act cases. If the Government files a Notice of Election to Decline Intervention or Election to Intervene, it is docketed and forwarded to the Court. If there is a complaint or an amended complaint attached to the notice, it is also docketed and forwarded to the Court. A summons is never issued unless directed by the Court.

Only upon Court order is the complaint unsealed. At this point, the Court will issue an order directing the Clerk's Office and the U.S. Attorney's Office how to proceed.

H. Pleadings that are *NOT* Filed. The following pleadings are not filed pursuant to Local Civil Rule 26.1—Discovery:

● Requests for Production of Documents;

● Requests for Admissions;

● Interrogatories;

● Answers to Interrogatories;

● Notices of Deposition; and

● Depositions.

I. Facsimile Transmission of Notice of Orders in Civil and Criminal Cases. Attorneys who do not register to participate in the ECF program are requested to register and participate in the Court's Program for Facsimile service of Notice to Counsel or Litigants in Civil and Criminal Cases (the "Fax Noticing Program"). This program allows attorneys and pro se litigants to waive the provisions of Federal Rule of Civil Procedure 77(d) or Federal Rule of Criminal Procedure 49(c), which requires service of Notice of Orders and Judgments by means of mail, and instead consent to receive Notice of Orders and Judgments by means of facsimile transmission.

Forms of Consent to Receive Notice of Orders and Judgments by means of Facsimile Transmission and Waiver of the Provisions of Fed.R.Civ.P. 77(d) or Fed.R.Crim.P. 49(c), providing for said Notice by means of mail are available through the Clerk's Office *(Appendix K)*. Execution of the Facsimile Transmission Authorization form authorizes the Clerk of Court to serve notice of the entry of Orders and Judgments pursuant to Fed.R.Civ.P. 77(d) or Fed.R.Crim.P. 49(c) by facsimile in lieu of notice by means of mail. The Facsimile Transmission Authorization form also serves as Notice to and Authorization for the Clerk of Court to keep your name and the relevant information on file so that the Facsimile Transmission Authorization form will apply to all pending and future civil and criminal cases in which the attorney or pro se litigant is, or will be, either counsel or a party to litigation.

The waiver of the provisions providing for notice of the entry of Orders or Judgments by mail will include all pending civil and criminal cases in the Eastern District of Pennsylvania for the pro se litigant and all pending civil and criminal cases in the Eastern District of Pennsylvania in which the attorney either represents a party or is a party to the litigation, except for grand jury proceedings and impounded cases.

The Clerk of Court will make three attempts to transmit the Notice of Entry of Orders and Judgments by means of Facsimile. If after three attempts facsimile transmission is unsuccessful, Notice shall be made by means of mail pursuant to Fed.R.Civ.P. 77(d) or Fed.R.Crim.P. 49(c).

J. Mail. The court, in its ongoing commitment to provide more timely notice and enhance the level of service to members of the bar, litigants and the public, has joined efforts with the U.S. Postal Service to implement procedures to streamline and facilitate the delivery and processing of mail directed to and from the U.S. Courthouse.

MAIL SENT TO COUNSEL

In order to expedite delivery of notices from judicial officers and the Clerk of Court, members of the bar are requested to furnish the following information by completing an Information Form *(Appendix L)*: Name; Bar I.D. Number; Firm; Address; City; State; Zip Code and *4-digit extension number*; and Facsimile Number. Please return the completed form to the Clerk of Court at:

Michael E. Kunz, Clerk of Court
United States District Court
For The Eastern District of Pennsylvania
U.S. Courthouse
601 Market Street, Room 2609
Philadelphia, PA 19106–1797

or, by facsimile to: (215) 597–6390, (267) 299–7135 or (610) 434–6174.

MAIL SENT TO THE COURT

In order to take full advantage of these procedures, all mail sent to the United States District Court for the Eastern District of Pennsylvania at 601 Market Street, Philadelphia, PA and divisional office locations should include both the *zip code and 4–digit extension number*. Accordingly, all mail submitted to a judicial officer should be addressed as follows:

(*Name of Judicial Officer*)	Michael E. Kunz, Clerk of Court
United States District Court	United States District Court
Eastern District of Pennsylvania	Eastern District of Pennsylvania
U.S. Courthouse	U.S. Courthouse
601 Market Street, Room ___	601 Market Street, Room 2609
Philadelphia, PA 19106–1797	Philadelphia, PA 19106–1797

The use of bar coding technology that is currently available in word processing software packages for addressing envelopes is encouraged. A listing of the room numbers and Zip Code and 4–digit extension numbers of the judicial officers is available in the Clerk's Office. (*Appendix M*).

MOTIONS

An application to the court for an order (unless made during a hearing or trial) shall be made in writing stating with particularity the grounds therefor, and shall set forth the relief sought. [See Federal Rule of Civil Procedure 7(b)(1) and Local Civil Rule 7.1(a).]

All motions shall contain a caption setting forth the name of the court, the title of the action, the file number, and a Rule 7(a) designation. [See Federal Rule of Civil Procedure 10(a).]

Every motion not certified as uncontested must be accompanied by a brief containing a concise statement of the legal contentions and authorities relied upon in support of the motion. Every motion shall be accompanied by a form of order which, if approved by the court, would grant the relief sought by the motion. Uncontested motions must be accompanied by a written statement as to the date and manner of service of the motion and supporting brief.

Every motion of a party represented by an attorney shall be signed by at least one attorney of record in the attorney's individual name, whose address shall be stated. A party who is not represented by an attorney shall sign each motion and state their correct address as indicated.

A brief in opposition to the motion, together with such answer or other response as may be appropriate, is required if the served party opposes the motion.

The response to the motion must be made within fourteen (14) days after service of the motion and supporting brief: [See Local Rule 7.1(c)]

SUMMONS

Summonses shall be prepared by counsel (*Appendix N*). At the time of the filing of a complaint, all summonses shall be submitted to the Clerk of Court's Office for signature and seal. Each defendant's name, as it appears on the complaint (without its address), is to be typed on a summons and submitted to the deputy clerk. The original and sufficient copies for each defendant will be returned to counsel. To issue a second summons, file a Praecipe to Issue Alias Summons, naming the defendants.

JURISDICTION

The Eastern District of Pennsylvania includes the counties of Berks, Bucks, Chester, Delaware, Lancaster, Lehigh, Montgomery, Northampton and Philadelphia. Please take note that effective April 19, 1999, jurisdiction of the county of Schuylkill was transferred to the U.S.D.C. for the Middle District of Pennsylvania.

Court for the Eastern District is held at Philadelphia, Reading, Allentown and Easton. When it appears from the designation form filed by counsel, or from the complaint, petition, motion, answer, response, indictment, information or other pleading in a civil or criminal case, that a plaintiff or defendant resides in or that the accident, incident or transaction occurred in the counties of Berks, Lancaster, Lehigh or Northampton, said case shall be assigned for trial and pretrial procedures to a judge assigned to hear cases from Reading, Allentown or Easton.

All other cases, unless otherwise directed by the court, shall be tried in Philadelphia, and as each case is filed, assigned to a judge, who shall thereafter have charge of the case for all purposes. [See Local Civil Rule 40.1]

The Office of the Clerk of Court maintains two Clerks' Offices and accepts all filings in Philadelphia and Allentown, Pennsylvania at the following addresses:

United States District Court **Eastern District of Pennsylvania**	**United States District Court** **Edward N. Cahn United States** **Courthouse**
United States Courthouse **601 Market Street, Room 2609**	**& Federal Building** **504 West Hamilton Street, Suite** **1601**
Philadelphia, PA 19106–1797	**Allentown, PA 18101–1500**
(215) 597–7704	**(610) 434–3896**

SUBPOENAS

(Rule 45, Federal Rules of Civil Procedure as amended December, 1991 and Rule 17, Federal Rules of Criminal Procedure)

A. Civil. Under Rule 45 of the Federal Rules of Civil Procedure, attorneys are authorized to issue subpoenas in the name of any court in which they are authorized to practice, and in the case of a deposition or a production of documents taking place in another district, in the name of the court where the deposition or the production is to take place. Attorneys issuing subpoenas must comply with the appropriate Federal Rules and Local Rules.

Although it is no longer necessary that subpoenas be issued by the Clerk, the Clerk still has the authority to do so. In those instances in which counsel elects to have the Clerk of Court issue the subpoena, an original and one copy is needed for each witness to be served. The requirement that a subpoena be issued under seal has been abolished.

For a foreign deposition (deposition being taken in a state other than Pennsylvania), subpoenas are issued in blank by the Clerk's office, completed and served by counsel. They are not signed by the court where the original notice to take the deposition is filed.

All subpoenas may be served by a person who is not a party and is not less than 18 years of age. There is no provision in the rules for subpoenas to be served by mail.

Pursuant to F.R.C.P. 45(b)(2), a subpoena may be served anywhere within the district. However, subpoenas may only be served outside the district if they are within 100 miles of the place designated in the subpoena for the deposition, trial, production of documents, hearing, or inspection. The federal rules also permit the service of a subpoena that is outside of the district, but within the state if certain conditions are met. See, F.R.C.P. 45(b)(2). All subpoenas must be accompanied by a check made payable to the witness for the witness fee ($40 per day) and mileage (57.5 cents per mile, round trip).

A copy of the subpoena is left with the witness and the original subpoena is returned to counsel.

B. Criminal. Under Rule 17 of the Federal Rules of Criminal Procedure, the Clerk of Court or the Magistrate Judge hearing the matter shall issue subpoenas. An original and one copy are needed for each witness to be served. All subpoenas issued by the Clerk are: (1) completed by counsel; (2) signed by the Clerk of Court; and (3) have the seal of the court placed over the name of the Clerk of Court before being served on the witness.

All subpoenas may be served by a person who is not a party and is not less than 18 years of age. There is no provision in the rules for subpoenas to be served by mail.

All subpoenas must be accompanies by a check made payable to the witness for the witness fee ($40.00 per day) and mileage (57.5 cents per mile, round trip), unless the subpoena was issued on behalf of the United States or the court has determined upon an ex parte motion that the defendant is financially unable to pay.

A criminal subpoena requiring the attendance of a witness at a hearing or trial may be served at any place within the United States. Subpoenas which are directed at witnesses in a foreign country shall be issued in accordance with 28 U.S.C. § 1783.

For more detailed information on criminal subpoenas, refer to Federal Rule of Criminal Procedure 17.

FOREIGN SUBPOENAS

(Rule 45, Federal Rules of Civil Procedure)

A foreign subpoena is one issued out of a court other than where the original case is pending. For example, a case is pending in California, but counsel would like to take the deposition of someone in the Eastern District of Pennsylvania.

A. Filing Procedure in Out-of-State Court. Counsel should complete the subpoena forms, attach a check for the witness fee and mileage in the sum of $40.00 per day, plus 57.5 cents per mile, round trip, and send them, together with the stamped copy of the notice to take the deposition, to the United States District Court nearest where the deponent resides. The referred court, where the deposition shall issue will stamp the name of the clerk, have the form signed by a deputy and affix the seal of its court over the signature.

B. Service. Service of the deposition subpoena must be by process server. There is no provision for service by mail. The subpoena is left with the witness, together with the witness fee. Counsel should make arrangements with a special process server for serving the subpoena.

C. To Contest. To contest a foreign (deposition) subpoena, file a motion to quash the deposition subpoena in the district where the subpoena was issued. File an original motion with the court. The case is filed as a miscellaneous case, with an associated filing fee of $46.00.

D. Attendance. A person to whom a civil subpoena for the taking of a deposition is directed may be required to attend at any place within 100 miles from the place where the person resides, is employed or transacts business in person, is served, or at such other convenient place is fixed by an order of the court.

DISCOVERY

In accordance with Local Civil Rule 26.1, discovery material is not filed with the court. The party serving the discovery material or taking the deposition shall retain the original and be the custodian of it. Every motion governing discovery shall identify and set forth, verbatim, the relevant parts of the interrogatory, request, answer, response, objection, notice, subpoena or deposition. Any party responding to the motion shall set forth, verbatim, in that party's memorandum, any other part that the party believes necessary to the court's consideration of the motion.

TEMPORARY RESTRAINING ORDER (T.R.O.)

The assigned judge will set a time (usually the same day you file the T.R.O.) to meet with you and opposing counsel, if any. File the case in the Clerk's Office and give the clerk sufficient time to assemble the case for the judge and prepare the docket. If the judge grants the temporary restraining order, it is the responsibility of counsel for plaintiff to make service of the T.R.O. on the defendant.

We suggest you call Rick Sabol, the Operations Manager, at (267) 299–7011 with any questions.

WRITS OF GARNISHMENT, ATTACHMENT AND EXECUTION

Writs of Garnishment and Attachment are prepared by counsel, filed with the Clerk's Office for processing and served by the U.S. Marshal. Counsel is responsible for notice to opposing counsel. Notice must be given to all owners of the property. *(Appendix O)*.

You must wait 14 days before you can execute on a judgment, unless a Motion to Vacate, Motion to Stay, Motion for Reconsideration, or Motion for a New Trial is pending. If counsel requests, we will process the Praecipe for a Writ of Garnishment or Execution immediately, referring the matter to the assigned judge, if available, or to the judge's chambers for guidance. (See, Rule 62, Federal Rules of Civil Procedure).

FILING A JUDGMENT BY DEFAULT

A. Rule 55(a), Federal Rules of Civil Procedure. You must file a request with the Clerk for the entry of a default for want of answer or other defense. Set forth the following information: (1) defendant was properly served on a particular date; (2) the time for defendant to file an answer to the complaint has expired; (3) that as of the date of the filing of the request for entry of the default, no answer (or motion to dismiss or motion for summary judgment) has been filed; and (4) instruct the Clerk to enter a default against the defendant (name the defendant if more than one in a case) for want of answer or other defense.

If the defendant is an individual, be sure that the defendant was served a copy of the complaint by either special process server, or waiver of service provisions of the Federal Rules of Civil Procedure, Rule 4(d) or otherwise in accordance with Federal Rules of Civil Procedure, Rule 4.

B. Rule 55(b), Federal Rules of Civil Procedure. To file a request for judgment by default for an individual, file an affidavit indicating the individual is (1) not an infant; (2) not incompetent; (3) not in the military; (4) amount due and owing; and (5) form of judgment.

To file a request for judgment by default for a corporation, file only an affidavit of amount due. If the amount requested in the complaint differs from that requested in the proposed judgment, the affidavit of amount due should explain the discrepancy.

MULTIDISTRICT LITIGATION

Due to the volume of litigants and the complexity of procedural requirements, those cases that are classified as being multidistrict litigation are governed by a separate and unique set of procedural rules. These rules are contained in the *Procedural Manual for Multidistrict Litigation*. Counsel may review this manual in the Clerk's Office, Room 2609, or may purchase copies from the Multidistrict Litigation Panel in Washington, D.C. Specific requests for information and related inquiries should be directed to Jeffrey N. Luthi, Clerk of the Panel, Multidistrict Litigation Panel, One Columbus Circle, N.E., Suite G–255, North Lobby, Washington, D.C. 20002–8004 or at (202) 502–2800.

On July 29, 1991, the Judicial Panel on Multidistrict Litigation entered an opinion and order transferring all asbestos cases that were not on trial and were pending outside the Eastern District of Pennsylvania to this Court and assigned them to the late Honorable Charles R. Weiner for coordinated or consolidated pretrial proceedings pursuant to 28 U.S.C. § 1407, MDL 875, In Re: Asbestos Products Liability Litigation. MDL 875 has been reassigned to the Honorable Eduardo C. Robreno. The deputy clerk with general responsibility for local involvement in multidistrict litigation matters is Eric Sobieski, at (267) 299–7018.

ARBITRATION

Our arbitration program provides litigants with a more prompt and less expensive alternative to the traditional courtroom trial. It has been in operation since 1978 and includes all civil cases (except social security cases, cases in which a prisoner is a party, cases alleging a violation of a constitutional right and cases where jurisdiction is based on 28 U.S.C. § 1343) where money damages only are sought in an amount not exceeding $150,000. Counsel is advised to refer to Local Civil Rule 53.2 for the specific types and categories of cases that are considered to be eligible for arbitration.

A. Procedure for Cases Eligible for Arbitration. When a complaint is filed, our local civil rule provides that damages are presumed to be not in excess of $150,000 unless counsel certifies that the damages exceed that amount. Immediately after the answer is filed, the attorneys receive a letter from the Clerk's Office advising them of the date for the arbitration hearing and also notifying them that discovery must be completed within 90 days. The clerk schedules the arbitration hearing for a specific day, usually a date about four months after an answer has been filed. In the event a party files a motion for judgment on the pleadings, summary judgment, or similar relief, our local rule provides that the case may not be heard until the court has ruled on the motion. However, the filing of a motion after the judge designates the arbitrators who will hear the case (usually about 30 days prior to the arbitration hearing) shall not stay the arbitration unless the judge so orders.

B. Trial Procedure. Although the Federal Rules of Evidence are designated as guides for the admissibility of evidence at the arbitration hearing, copies of photographs of exhibits must be marked for identification and delivered to the adverse party at least ten (10) days prior to arbitration. The arbitrators shall receive such exhibits in evidence without formal proof, unless counsel has been notified at least five (5) days prior to the hearing that their opponent intends to raise an issue concerning the authenticity of the exhibit. The arbitration hearing is not recorded unless a party, at their own expense, arranges for a recording. The arbitrators are authorized to change the date of the arbitration hearing, provided it takes place within thirty (30) days of the date originally scheduled.

C. Arbitrators. We currently have over 1500 lawyers certified as arbitrators. In order to qualify for certification, the lawyer must be admitted to practice before our court, be a member of the bar for at least five (5) years, and be determined by our Chief Judge to be competent to perform the duties of an arbitrator. An arbitrator receives $150 for each case arbitrated. Three arbitrators are appointed for each case. They are randomly selected by the Clerk and each panel of three arbitrators is composed of one whose practice is primarily representing plaintiffs, one whose practice is primarily representing defendants, and one whose practice does not fit either category. The arbitrators are scheduled for hearing dates several months in advance. However, it is not until the judge signs the order designating the arbitrators who will hear the case (approximately 30 days prior to the arbitration hearing) that counsel learn the identity of the arbitrators and the arbitrators become aware of the a case assigned to them.

D. Arbitrator's Award. Immediately after the hearing, the arbitrators make a simple award, e.g., "Award in favor of defendant" or "Award in favor of plaintiff" in the amount of $ XXX against (naming one or more defendants). The arbitrators are instructed that they should not file findings of fact, conclusions of law, nor opinions of any kind. The arbitrator's award shall be entered as the final judgment of the Court, unless within 30 days of the filing of the award a party demands a trial de novo.

E. Demands for Trial De Novo. Upon the filing of a demand for trial de novo, the case proceeds as if it had never been heard by the arbitrators.

APPEALS

A. Civil. In civil cases, you have 30 days to file an appeal, unless the government is a party, in which case you have 60 days. The time commences from the date the order or judgment is entered on the docket (calendar days, not working days). A cross appeal should be filed 14 days from the filing of the first appeal.

All cases filed in the ECF System in which a notice of appeal is filed shall be governed by Rule 10 of the Federal Rules of Appellate Procedure and relevant Local Rules and internal operating procedures of the United States Court of Appeals for the Third Circuit, with any differences about whether the record truly discloses what occurred in the district court to be submitted to and settled by the judge. Cases in which there is a right of direct appeal to the United States Supreme Court shall be governed by the rules of the United States Supreme Court.

B. Criminal. In criminal cases you have 14 days to file an appeal. Cross appeals should also be filed within 14 days.

If the attorney is court-appointed, pursuant to the provisions of the Criminal Justice Act, a filing fee is not required.

C. Report and Recommendation of U.S. Magistrate Judge. A party has 14 days to file objections. An original and one copy are required.

D. Bankruptcy. A party has 14 days to file a bankruptcy appeal to the District Court. This appeal is filed in the Bankruptcy Court. An original and copies for all counsel of record are required. Counsel must file designation of record on appeal (Bankruptcy's Rule 8006).

E. Patent, "Little Tucker Act" and Claims Court Transfer Cases. Appeals in patent and "Little Tucker Act" cases [28 U.S.C. §§ 1295(a)(1)–(2)] from certain interlocutory orders in these cases [28 U.S.C. § 1295(c)], and from orders transferring or refusing to transfer cases to the United States Claims Court [28 U.S.C. § 1292(d)(4)(B)], go to the United States Court of Appeals for the Federal Circuit. Federal Circuit Rules, practice notes, and appendix of forms are found in the Rules of Practice Before the United States Court of Appeals for the Federal Circuit, available from the Clerk of that Court upon request. Call (202) 633–6550 or write to: 717 Madison Place, N.W., Washington, DC 20439.

F. Service. Appellate Rule 25(c) outlines the procedures for service of the notice of appeal.

The Clerk of Court is responsible for serving a copy of the notice of appeal by mail/e-mail to counsel of record other than the appellant. The date the notice of appeal was filed is noted on each copy served. A notation is made on the docket by the clerk of the names of the parties to whom copies are mailed and the date of mailing.

G. Filing Fee. The $5 filing fee for the notice of appeal and the $500 docket fee for the Court of Appeals are tendered to the Clerk of Court at the time of filing the notice of appeal. If the fee is not paid within 14 days after the docketing, the clerk is authorized to dismiss the appeal.

H. Preparation of the Record on Appeal. Rule 11 of the Federal Rules of Appellate Procedure provide for certification and transmittal of the original district court records file and exhibits to the Court of Appeals. However, the United States Court of Appeals for the Third Circuit has initiated an experimental program for retention of records in the district courts. In order to monitor record and case management, the district courts have been directed to retain the court records and to certify to the Court of Appeals that the record is available on ECF.

However, Rule 11 of the Third Circuit Rules provides that all reinstated parts of the record are to be transmitted if any party or the court requests such at any time during the pendency of the proceeding.

Rule 11 requires the appellant within 14 days after filing of the notice of appeal, to order from the court reporter, a transcript of the proceedings not already on file that the appellant deems necessary for inclusion in the record (*Appendix P*). Rule 11 of the Third Circuit Rules also requires that a deposit be made with the court reporter of the estimated cost of transcript.

Any questions you may have concerning appeals should be directed to a supervisor in the Civil or Criminal section.

CERTIFICATION OF JUDGEMENT (AO 451)

Check Appellate Rule 4(a)(4) before issuing an AO 451. Also check the docket sheet for any post-judgment motions which may have the effect of "staying" the execution on the judgment.

The clerk does not have the authority to issue an AO 451 if a Motion to Vacate the Judgment, Motion for Reconsideration or Motion to Stay is pending or unless the "appeal time" has expired, except when ordered by the court that entered the judgment for good cause shown. (28 U.S.C. § 1963, as amended). The appeal time commences to run from the date the judgment is entered on the docket, unless otherwise ordered by the Court. The clerk is not authorized to issue an AO 451 before the expiration of the appeal time because the case may be "reversed" on appeal and result in substantial loss to plaintiff because of the executions on the property of the defendant.

Normally, all civil cases may be appealed within 30 days from the date of entry of the final judgment on the docket. The United States always has 60 days within which to file an appeal. Be sure to attach a certified copy of the judgment to the AO 451 form.

REFERRAL TO UNITED STATES MAGISTRATE JUDGE

In accordance with the provisions of 28 U.S.C. § 636(c) and Local Civil Rule 72.1, U.S. Magistrate Judges may conduct, upon consent of all the parties in a civil case, any or all proceedings, including a jury or non-jury trial, and order the entry of a final judgment.

Your decision to consent, or not to consent, to the referral of your case to a U.S. Magistrate Judge for disposition is entirely voluntary and should be communicated solely to the Clerk of Court. Appropriate consent forms for this purpose are available from the Clerk's Office *(Appendix Q)*.

Only if all the parties in the case consent to the referral to a magistrate judge will either the district court judge or the magistrate judge be informed of your decision. The judge will then decide whether or not to refer the case to a magistrate judge for disposition, but no action eligible for arbitration will be referred by consent of the parties until the arbitration has been concluded and trial de novo demanded pursuant to Local Civil Rule 53.2. The court may, for good cause shown on its motion, or under extraordinary circumstances shown by any party, vacate a referral of a civil matter to a magistrate judge.

When a case is referred to a magistrate judge for all further proceedings, including the entry of final judgment, the final judgment may be appealed directly to the Court of Appeals for the Third Circuit, unless the parties elect to have the case reviewed by the appropriate district judge (in which event any further appeal to the Court of Appeals would only be by petition for leave to appeal). (See Local Civil Rule 721.).

POST JUDGMENT INTEREST RATE

In accordance with 28 U.S.C. § 1961 and 40 U.S.C. § 258, interest shall be allowed on any money judgment in a civil case recovered in a district court. Execution therefor may be levied by the marshal, in any case where, by the law of the State in which such court is held, execution may be levied for interest on judgments recovered in the courts of the State. Such interest shall be calculated from the date of the entry of the judgment, at a rate equal to the weekly average 1–year constant maturity Treasury yield, as published by the Board of Governors of the Federal Reserve System, for the calendar week preceding the date of the judgment. Requests for the current rate and any questions should be directed to Richard Sabol, Operations Manager, at (267) 299–7011 or Terry Milano, Assistant Operations Manager, at (267) 299–7013. Current rates are available through a link to the Federal Reserve from our website: http://www.paed.uscourts.gov.

TAXATION OF COSTS
BY THE
CLERK OF THE UNITED STATES DISTRICT COURT
FOR THE
EASTERN DISTRICT OF PENNSYLVANIA

AUGUST 7, 2012

TABLE OF CONTENTS:

A. Normally Allowable District Court Costs in General. It is well-established that district court costs may not be imposed in federal district courts except where they are authorized by either a statute or a rule of court.[1] Excluding from the discussion those district court costs taxable pursuant to Federal Rule of Civil Procedure 68 (which will be discussed in Section F of this manual), and certain narrowly-defined appellate court costs which are taxable by the district court (which will be discussed in Section G of this manual), federal district court costs are governed by Federal Rule of Civil Procedure 54(d).[2] The text of Federal Rule of Civil Procedure 54(d) is divided into two sections:

● Federal Rule of Civil Procedure 54(d) (2), which by its own terms governs *"Attorney's Fees;"* and

● Federal Rule of Civil Procedure 54(d) (1), which by its own terms governs *"(District Court) Costs Other Than Attorney's Fees."*

All of those "(District Court) Costs Other Than Attorney's Fees" made taxable by Federal Rule of Civil Procedure 54(d)(1) are listed in 28 U.S.C. § 1920,[3] and the Clerk[4] has authority to tax those types of district court costs which are listed in 28 U.S.C. § 1920 in favor of the prevailing party or parties, and against the non-prevailing party or parties.[5] (Federal Rule of Civil Procedure 54(d)(1) costs may be assessed by the Clerk even when attorney fees pursuant to Federal Rule of Civil Procedure 54(d)(2) are disallowed by the presiding judge).[6]

Those items of district court costs taxable in the first instance by the Clerk, as listed in 28 U.S.C. § 1920, are:

"(1) Fees of the clerk or marshal;

(2) Fees for printed or electronically recorded transcripts necessarily obtained for use in the case;

(3) Fees and disbursements for printing and witnesses;

(4) Fees for exemplification and the cost of making copies of any materials where the copies are necessarily obtained for use in the case;

(5) Docket fees under (28 U.S.C. § 1923); and

(6) Compensation of court appointed experts, compensation of interpreters, and salaries, fees, expenses, and costs of special interpretation services under (28 U.S.C. § 1828)."

The prevailing party, having had judgment entered in its favor, may file a bill of costs seeking any of the items authorized by 28 U.S.C. § 1920.

A bill of costs must be supported by an affidavit pursuant to 28 U.S.C. § 1924, stating that the costs sought were both actually incurred and necessarily incurred.[7]

It is generally advisable for the prevailing party to not file a bill of costs until after any appeals are decided, or until after any period for filing appeals, or for filing post-trial motions, expires, so that if any additional costs are incurred, the bill of costs will not have to be amended. [8]

The bill of costs will then be forwarded to the deputy clerk responsible for taxation of costs.

The section of Federal Rule of Civil Procedure 54(d)(1) requiring fourteen days' notice simply means that *at least fourteen days* must elapse between the filing of the bill of costs and the taxing of costs; as a practical matter, it is usually necessary in the Eastern District of Pennsylvania for much more than fourteen days to process a taxation of costs request pursuant to § 1920 and these procedures. Costs will not be taxed until the underlying litigation is completed, and until after any period in which an appeal may be raised has lapsed; this is based on the simple principle that until the underlying litigation is over, the issue of who is the ultimately "prevailing party" has not yet been determined.[9] Once the issue of who is the ultimately prevailing party has been finally determined, the clerk shall send letters to both parties (or their counsel) asking for objections in writing from the non-prevailing party within fourteen (14) days, with the prevailing party then having fourteen (14) days to respond in writing. Local Rule of Civil Procedure 5.1(b) requires all counsel and any pro se litigants to provide the Clerk with an address for purposes of notices and service; the aforesaid letter will therefore be mailed to counsel (or to a pro se litigant) at their last known addresses, which constitutes proper and valid service upon them (pursuant to Federal Rule of Civil Procedure 5(b)(2)(C)) (it is for this reason that in the event that any of these letters are returned to the Clerk by the Postal Service as undeliverable, that the Clerk will not conduct any further investigation to find a current address for any of these persons).

All of the aforesaid objections and all of the aforesaid responses to the objections must be made by means of a court filing (letters shall not suffice).

In order to avoid the possibility of the Clerk entering a taxation opinion which may possibly have to be vacated at a later point in time, the Clerk will delay the taxing of costs until after all appeals have been exhausted[10] (or, until after the time period for filing an appeal has lapsed).[11]

The Clerk will make a determination based on the bill of costs itself, and the arguments made in writing (if any); in addition, any relevant statutes, rules of court, and/or case law may play a role in the Clerk's determination of whether district court costs should be taxed and, if warranted, in what amount.

After making his determination, the Clerk will thereafter enter a written taxation of costs opinion, accompanied, if warranted, by a judgment. A true and correct copy of the taxation opinion and any attached judgment shall be forwarded to all parties of record, or their counsel. Costs are effective as of the date the Clerk's judgment is entered on the docket. Either party can appeal the Clerk's taxation opinion and/or judgment to the presiding Article III judicial officer within seven (7) days, pursuant to F.R.C.P. 54(d)(1) (this seven day period is not jurisdictional, and the court has discretion to consider any untimely appeal of Clerk's taxation opinion and/or judgment in the event of "excusable neglect" on the part of the appealing party).[12]

B. Normally Unallowable District Court Costs in General. Normally, the Clerk will tailor his taxation of costs opinion around the items requested and the actual objections raised by the losing party or parties, and will not raise issues sua sponte; however, as stated previously, since the Clerk's power is strictly limited by 28 U.S.C. § 1920, a necessary corollary is that if a requested item is never authorized by 28 U.S.C. § 1920 under any circumstances, the Clerk may not tax that item as a 28 U.S.C. § 1920 cost, even where the losing party or parties have not raised any objections to the item or items in question.[13]

Congress has provided for the assessment of attorney fees by means of Federal Rule of Civil Procedure 54(d)(2); as they are not specifically listed in 28 U.S.C. § 1920, attorney fees are clearly not taxable pursuant to Federal Rule of Civil Procedure 54(d)(1).[14] Pursuant to the language of Federal Rule of Civil Procedure 54(d) itself, attorney fees are only recoverable from the presiding judge pursuant to Federal Rule of Civil Procedure 54(d)(2), and not from the Clerk pursuant to Federal Rule of Civil Procedure 54(d)(1). An Award or disallowance of attorney fees pursuant to Federal Rule of Civil Procedure 54(d)(2) is totally separate and distinct from an award of statutory costs pursuant to Federal Rule of Civil Procedure 54(d)(1).[15] The rationale supporting this standard is that unlike attorney fees, an assessment of 28 U.S.C. § 1920 costs is considered to be purely ministerial, and is not considered to be punitive toward the non-prevailing party, but merely as reimbursement to the prevailing party for their costs in bringing a successful civil action[16] (whereas an assessment of attorney fees is considered to be punitive).[17]

In addition, those litigation costs which are more closely associated with the routine overhead of practicing law than with the types of district court costs listed in 28 U.S.C. § 1920 are not taxable pursuant to Federal Rule of Civil Procedure 54(d)(1), as they are seen as analogous to attorney fees.[18] (The fact that counsel did not perform the actual work leading to an unallowable item of cost, but was charged with it by an "evidence" provider as a condition of obtaining evidence, or by a stenographer, as a condition of obtaining a transcript, does not change the fact that the item is not listed in 28 U.S.C. § 1920 and is therefore unallowable).[19]

By this standard, costs which are not, even arguably among those types of district court costs listed in 28 U.S.C. § 1920, include:

(1) the costs of attorney work product, such as pleadings, motions, memoranda and briefs, as well as case-related correspondence.[20] (Although costs related to the production of exact copies[21] of original documentary evidence[22] such as records[23] as taxable under 28 U.S.C. § 1920, we repeat once again that costs of attorney work product are not taxable under that statute; therefore, the prevailing party must be able to explain what types of documents were copied when requesting the taxing of these types of costs);[24]

(2) the costs of attorney court-admission fees (including court fees for admission "pro hac vice.")[25] "Mediation fees" are also not taxable pursuant to 28 U.S.C. § 1920;[26]

(3) The costs of law firm rent, the costs of law firm utilities and costs for any and all non-attorney law firm staffing,[27] such as the costs of paralegals[28] and the costs of secretarial services[29] (including the costs of typing[30] and the costs of word processing);[31]

(4) attorney travel expenses[32] (including attorney airfare,[33] attorney meals,[34] attorney lodging,[35] attorney parking[36] and attorney car rentals).[37] Accordingly, these costs are prohibited in a Clerk's Taxation of Costs. (Travel expenses for a witness, unlike travel expenses for an attorney, are, at least arguably, taxable by the Clerk pursuant to 28 U.S.C. § 1920(3)).[38]

(5) costs related to legal research;[39]

(6) telephone expenses[40] (including both long distance and local telephone calls);[41]

(7) costs related to the use of the facsimile machines;[42]

(8) costs of courier, local delivery and/or messenger services.[43] (We hasten to point out that this standard does not apply to costs for governmental service of process or private service of process, which may be taxed pursuant to 28 U.S.C. § 1920(1);[44]

(9) postage costs;[45]

(10) costs of shipping and handling (including shipping and handling by means of the "United Parcel Service" or by means of "Federal Express.");[46]

(11) fees paid to a special master;[47]

(12) the costs of investigative services;[48]

(13) costs related to the preparation of an expert's testimony or report,[49] including costs related to an Independent Medical Examination.[50] (Although expert witness fees may be allowable in some situations pursuant to 28 U.S.C. § 1920(3) and/or 28 U.S.C. § 1920(6));

(14) case-related work performed by accounting professionals;[51]

(15) the cost of telegrams;[52]

(16) unexplained requests for "miscellaneous" costs;[53]

C. Burden of Proof Regarding Normally Allowable District Court Costs. Federal Rule of Civil Procedure 54(d)(1) directs that "(district court) costs—other than attorney fees" (i.e. those costs authorized by 28 U.S.C. § 1920[54] "*should* be allowed to the prevailing party (emphasis added)." This language is evidence of "specific intent"[55] on the part of Congress that there should be a heavy presumption[56] that "the 'prevailing party' *automatically* is entitled to costs"[57] as a matter of course, once it has been shown that the costs sought are, at least arguably, of those types of costs listed in 28 U.S.C. § 1920,[58] provided that those costs were both *actually incurred* (as evidenced by a sworn affidavit)[59] and *necessarily incurred* ("necessarily" meaning that the costs were reasonably incurred for the prevailing party's effective preparation, judged in light of the situation existing when the costs in question were actually incurred, without regard to whether the costs relate to items which were actually used).[60]

The rationale supporting this heavy presumption is that unlike attorney fees, an assessment of 28 U.S.C. § 1920 costs is considered to be purely ministerial, and is not considered to be punitive toward the non-prevailing party or parties, but merely as reimbursement to the prevailing party or parties for their costs in bringing or pursuing a successful civil action[61] (whereas an assessment of attorney fees _is_ considered to be punitive).[62] A consequence of this heavy presumption is that the non-prevailing party or parties bear the burden of proof, and must overcome the aforesaid heavy presumption in favor of the taxing of district court costs against that non-prevailing party or parties.[63] Because of this heavy presumption, it is considered punitive towards the prevailing party or parties to deny to that prevailing party or parties district court costs which are ordinarily automatically taxed under 28 U.S.C. § 1920,[64] and it is not necessary for the prevailing party or parties to argue that the non-prevailing party or parties did something that was wrong or inappropriate.[65]

As a further result of the aforesaid heavy presumption, in the event taxable district court costs are denied to the prevailing party or parties, the Clerk must specifically state what defect, bad act or impropriety on the part of that prevailing party or parties leads the Clerk to deny to that prevailing party or parties otherwise allowable costs.[66]

As the United States Court of Appeals for the Third Circuit appropriately noted in 2010, it is for precisely these reasons that counsel should always advise each client, before commencing the litigation process, that in the event that their litigation is unsuccessful, that there is a risk of taxation of district court costs against that client pursuant to 28 U.S.C. § 1920.[67]

D. General Objections to Normally Allowable District Court Costs in Their Entirety.

(1) _Alleged Pretrial Stipulation._ It is well-settled law that if the parties to a civil action have stipulated prior to the final judgment in the underlying lawsuit as to how district court costs will be apportioned or taxed, that stipulation is controlling, if a bill of costs is ultimately filed.[68] In situations where the parties disagree on this issue, it is important to recall that the Clerk has no fact-finding mechanism; accordingly, the Clerk must not address this general objection, and will proceed to tax costs as if there was no pre-judgment stipulation between the parties as to how these costs would be apportioned; if any party is not satisfied with this result, they can appeal the Taxation Opinion and the accompanying Judgment to the trial judge.[69] (A Clerk's Taxation of Costs proceeding is not a forum for re-examining the underlying facts of the lawsuit or for re-litigating the underlying lawsuit).[70]

(2) _Alleged Economic Disparity Between the Parties._ According to a 2010 decision of the United States Court of Appeals for the Third Circuit, economic disparity between the parties is an objection that this clerk and/or this court "**_may not consider_**."[71]

To go into further detail, we not that Federal Rule of Civil Procedure 54(d)(1) directs that "costs—other than attorney fees" (i.e. those costs authorized by 28 U.S.C. § 1920) "**_should_** be allowed to the prevailing party (emphasis added)." This language is evidence of "specific intent"[72] on the part of Congress that there should be a heavy presumption[73] that "the 'prevailing' party automatically is entitled to costs[74] as a matter of course, once it has been shown that the costs sought are, at least arguably, of those types of costs listed in 28 U.S.C. § 1920.[75] We are therefore of the view that the Clerk has no discretion to disallow otherwise allowable costs based on an argument rooted in economics; economic disparity between the parties is not a basis for disallowing costs, and a very strong presumption exists that consideration of the equities does not favor a disallowance of costs by the court.[76]

The Clerk may tax costs not only where the losing party is less affluent than the prevailing party, but also where the losing party is actually indigent.[77] Even complete and utter inability to pay is not grounds for a disallowance of costs.[78] Likewise, even the granting of in forma pauperis status to the losing party does not rebut this heavy presumption.[79]

(3) *Bankruptcy.*

i. Bills of costs filed against a debtor in bankruptcy. Judicial proceedings relating to a claim against a debtor who has filed for bankruptcy are void **ab initio** absent relief from the automatic stay.[80] As a result of the automatic stay, all formal and informal actions taken against a debtor in bankruptcy are stayed.[81] Accordingly, costs may not be taxed against a debtor in bankruptcy because of the automatic stay provision of the Bankruptcy Code.[82]

ii. Bills of costs filed by, or on behalf of, a debtor in bankruptcy. "Within one action, claims *against a debtor* will be suspended by the automatic stay, even though closely related claims asserted *by the debtor* may continue."[83] Accordingly, a debtor in bankruptcy, or the debtor's estate in bankruptcy, may have 28 U.S.C. § 1920 costs taxed in his, or her or its favor.

(4) *Alleged Chilling Effect.* According to a 2010 decision of the United States Court of Appeals for the Third Circuit, the objection that awarding costs would have a "chilling effect" on litigation which is allegedly socially important is always "*unpersuasive*,"[84] since "(t)he fact that a prevailing party prosecutes its rights under the Federal Rules of Civil Procedure to an award of costs *cannot* be seen as chilling the flow of litigation.[85]

To go into further detail, a Clerk's Taxation of Costs proceeding is not a forum for re-examining the facts of the underlying lawsuit;[86] therefore, as stated previously, there is a *heavy presumption*[87] in favor of "*automatically*"[88] taxing those types of costs which are listed in 28 U.S.C. § 1920[89] which the prevailing party both *actually incurred* (as evidenced by a sworn affidavit)[90] and *necessarily incurred* ("necessarily" meaning that the costs were reasonably incurred for the prevailing party's effective preparation, judged in light of the situation existing when the costs in question were actually incurred, without regard to whether the costs relate to items which were actually used).[91]

(5) *Alleged Good Faith by Non–Prevailing Party.* According to a 2010 decision of the United States Court of Appeals for the Third Circuit, the alleged good faith of the non-prevailing party is an objection that the Clerk and/or the Court "*may not consider*."[92]

To go into further detail, the bare allegation that an action was brought in good faith and was neither frivolous, unreasonable nor without foundation is not sufficient to overcome the presumption inherent in Fed. R. Civ. P. 54 (d) that "costs ... *should* be allowed to the prevailing party (emphasis added)."[93] As the court explained in *Popeil Brothers v. Schick Electric*, 516 F.2d 772 (7th Cir. 1975), "(i)f the awarding of costs could be thwarted every time the unsuccessful party is a normal, average party and not a knave, Rule 54(d) would have little substance remaining." 516 F.2d at 776. Hence, "good faith litigation does not absolve a party from imposition of costs."[94] If costs were only taxable in those situations where the losing party acted in bad faith, 28 U.S.C. § 1920 would have very little meaning.[95] A Clerk's Taxation of Costs proceeding is simply not a forum for re-examining, or for re-litigating, the underlying facts of the lawsuit.[96] Therefore, it is not a valid objection that the issues in the underlying case were closely contested and that the final judgment allegedly could have, or allegedly should have, gone in the other direction; the alleged complexity or closeness of the issues litigated is not relevant to the taxing of costs by the Court or Clerk.[97]

There is a *heavy presumption*[98] in favor of "*automatically*"[99] taxing those types of costs listed in 28 U.S.C. § 1920[100] which the prevailing party both *actually incurred* (as evidenced by a sworn affidavit)[101] and *necessarily incurred* ("necessarily" meaning that the costs were reasonably incurred for the prevailing party's effective preparation, judged in light of the situation existing when the costs in question were actually incurred, without regard to whether the cots relate to items which were actually used).[102]

(6) *The Issues in the Underlying Case were Allegedly Close.*   The general objection that the facts and/or issues in this case were closely contested and allegedly could have, or should have, gone in the other direction and resulted in a victory for the non-prevailing party is an objection that this clerk and/or this court *"may not consider."*[103]

A Clerk's Taxation of Costs proceeding is simply not a forum for re-examining, or for re-litigating, the underlying facts of the lawsuit.[104]   Therefore, it is not a valid objection that the issues in the underlying case were closely contested and that the final judgment allegedly could have, or allegedly should have, gone in the other direction; the complexity or closeness of the issues litigated is not relevant to the taxing of costs by the Court or Clerk.[105]

There is a *heavy presumption*[106] in favor of *"automatically"*[107] taxing those types of costs which are listed in 28 U.S.C. § 1920[108] which the prevailing party both *actually incurred* (as evidenced by a sworn affidavit)[109] and *necessarily incurred* ("necessarily" meaning that the costs were reasonably incurred for the prevailing party's effective preparation, judged in light of the situation existing when the costs in question were actually incurred, without regard to whether the costs relate to items which were actually used).[110]

(7) *Allegedly Untimely Filing of the Bill of Costs.*   The Eastern District of Pennsylvania is one of very few districts in the federal system that has no local rule governing the time for filing a bill of costs.   In the absence of any local rule, courts have held that bills of cost must be filed within a "reasonable" time after the conclusion of the litigation.[111]   It is generally advisable for the prevailing party to not file a bill of costs until after any appeals are decided, or until after any period for filing appeals expires, so that if any additional costs are incurred, that bill of costs will not have to be amended.[112]

To avoid the possibility of the Clerk entering a taxation opinion which may possibly have to be vacated at a later point in time, the Clerk will delay the taxing of costs until after all appeals have been exhausted[113] (or, until after the time period for filing an appeal has lapsed).[114]

(8) *Alleged Misconduct.*

   A.   Alleged Misconduct by the Prevailing Party.   Often a general objection to the bill of costs in its entirety is made, which alleges that costs were allegedly incurred as a result of bad faith on the part of the prevailing party and/or their counsel during the underlying litigation.

   A request for taxation of 28 U.S.C. § 1920 costs may be disallowed where there has been misconduct by the prevailing party during the litigation process which led to excessive costs;   however, there is a strong presumption in taxation situations that the prevailing party *did not* act in bad faith,[115] and the heavy burden of proving such bad faith rests with the non-prevailing party.[116]

   For purposes of taxation of district courts costs, allegedly bad conduct must be analyzed in the light of the situation as it appeared to exist at the time the said allegedly bad act was undertaken (and not in the light of the situation as it appears with the benefit of hindsight).[117]

   The Third Circuit has stated a lawyer's act of making an argument which could be construed as "well-intentioned zeal" on their client's behalf cannot be construed as evidence of such bad faith,[118] even where the prevailing party did not win regarding every argument made in the underlying litigation.[119]   The fact that the prevailing party may have incurred some costs relating to a line of argument in the underlying litigation that was ultimately unsuccessful is irrelevant in a taxation matter,[120] as is the relative degree of complexity of the various issues in the underlying litigation.[121]

The determination of whether such misconduct has occurred must be made by the presiding judicial officer, as the Clerk has no fact-finding procedure, and as a Clerk's Taxation of Costs proceeding is not a forum for re-examining the underlying facts of the lawsuit or for relitigating the underlying lawsuit.[122]　Therefore, the Clerk may not consider this general objection; if there is an appeal of the taxation opinion by any party, the court may consider this argument pursuant to Federal Rule of Civil Procedure 54(d)(1).

B. Alleged Misconduct by the Non-prevailing Party.　The prevailing party may allege that the non-prevailing parties acted in bad faith during the litigation process.　We note that it is considered to be punitive towards a prevailing party to deny to that prevailing party district court costs which are ordinarily automatically[123] taxed under 28 U.S.C. § 1920,[124] and it is not necessary for the prevailing party to argue that the non-prevailing party did something that was wrong or inappropriate;[125] however, although it is not necessary, a finding of bad faith on the part of the non-prevailing party would be grounds for **_not_** reducing costs and/or grounds for **_not_** disallowing costs.[126]　This determination must be made by the presiding judicial officer, as the Clerk has no fact-finding procedure, and a Clerk's Taxation of Costs proceeding is not a forum for re-examining the underlying facts of the lawsuit or for re-litigating the underlying lawsuit.[127]　If there is an appeal of the taxation opinion by any party, the court may consider this argument pursuant to Federal Rule of Civil Procedure 54(d)(1).

C. Alleged Malice on the Part of the Prevailing Party.　Often a non-prevailing party will argue that filing of the bill of costs against it was allegedly motivated by malice on the part of the prevailing party.　We note that the prevailing party's state of mind is irrelevant to the taxing of costs.

(9) *Prevailing Party in the Underlying Lawsuit.*　A general objection to the bill of costs is often made stating that the prevailing party allegedly prevailed on some issues at the trial, even though judgment was entered in favor of his opponent.　The relevant rule of court, Federal Rule of Civil Procedure 54(d)(1), directs the taxing of costs in favor of "the prevailing party."　In order to determine the issue of which party, or parties, prevailed, "the court must (first) identify the relief plaintiff sought,"[128] then, after that, the court must read the text of the final entry of judgment in the underlying lawsuit,[129] and then, after that, the court must ask itself "whether the plaintiff achieved 'some of the benefit sought' by the party bringing the suit."[130]　Applying this standard, it is clear that although it is not necessary for a plaintiff to receive **_all_** of the relief sought, the plaintiff must still receive at least **_some_** of the relief sought in order to be considered a prevailing party.[131]　The plaintiff is considered the prevailing party and the defendants are considered the non-prevailing parties in those situations where a favorable judgment is entered for plaintiff on any of the claims plaintiff asserted, even if plaintiff is only successful on a fraction of the claims asserted and even if plaintiff obtains only a fraction of the relief sought.[132]

Likewise, the law is clear that where a reading of the text of the judgment indicates that plaintiff had not prevailed on any of its claims or obtained any relief, defendant is considered to be the prevailing party.[133]　This rule applies and a defendant is considered to be the prevailing party, even where the defendant does not prevail on its counterclaims.[134]　The law is also clear that costs incurred by a defendant may be taxed against a plaintiff who ultimately withdraws an action, even where the withdrawal was voluntary.[135]

If a situation is presented to the Clerk in which plaintiff is either wholly or partially successful on its claims, and defendant is also either wholly or partially successful on its counterclaims, the issue of who is the prevailing party must be decided by the court on a case-by-case basis, and not by the Clerk of Court,[136] since it requires consideration of the unique facts of the underlying lawsuit and since the Clerk of Court has no fact-finding mechanism for re-examining the underlying facts of the lawsuit or for re-litigating the underlying lawsuit.[137]

It is irrelevant to the taxing of costs that the matter was disposed of by means of summary judgment and no trial took place.[138]   It is irrelevant to the taxing of costs that this matter was disposed of by means of a directed verdict.[139]   It is also irrelevant to the taxing of costs that this matter was disposed of by means of a judgment NOV.[140]

It also merits comment that the party who has prevailed at the final stage a lawsuit reaches is considered the prevailing party for the entire lawsuit and may recover costs related to all stages of the lawsuit; this includes earlier stages at which the ultimately prevailing party did not prevail.[141]

(10) *Itemization.*   A general objection to the bill of costs in its entirety is often raised which claims that the costs sought are allegedly not sufficiently explained. Provided that the bill of costs is neat and legible, there is no need for counsel to use the court's official bill of costs form;[142] there is likewise, no requirement for the prevailing party to supply receipts[143] (even in a situation where receipts or a more detailed itemization would be useful to the court and/or opposing counsel),[144] rather, caselaw holds that the standard is that costs must be sufficiently explained to the extent that opposing counsel can make informed objections and the Clerk of Court can make an informed determination of whether requested costs are allowable.[145]

The bill of costs must be accompanied by an affidavit from prevailing party or its counsel stating, under penalty of perjury, that the costs are correct and were actually and necessarily incurred; the existence of such an affidavit in a Clerk's Taxation of Costs proceeding is given very great weight with respect to the aforesaid burden of proof in favor of the taxation of those types of costs listed in the taxation statute.[146]

(11) *Alleged Failure of the Prevailing Party to Actually Pay Requested Costs.* The objection is sometimes raised of whether costs can be taxed for items which the prevailing party has not paid, which the prevailing party admits are overdue, but nevertheless claims are taxable.   Research by this Clerk has uncovered no precedential caselaw on this issue, either in this court or in any federal district or circuit court.

28 U.S.C. § 1924 establishes the standard that an amount sought in a bill of costs must be "correct" and must have been "necessarily incurred."   This manual has already addressed the subject of "correctness."   Concerning the subject of whether these costs have been "necessarily incurred," and with no caselaw on this issue, the Clerk of the Eastern District of Pennsylvania sought a solution to this issue in the *Webster's II New Riverside University Dictionary* (1984).   This dictionary defines the word "incur" as "to become liable or subject to, especially because of one's own actions."   The standard for taxing costs, therefore, is not whether costs have already been paid by the prevailing party; rather, the standard is whether the prevailing party is liable for these costs.   The word "incurred" is not synonymous with the words "already paid."

(12) *Alleged Actions of the Trial Court and Alleged Interaction with Attorney Fees.*   Where the court has expressly allowed or disallowed district court costs **pursuant to 28 U.S.C. § 1920** (that is, district court costs other than attorney fees and attorney costs) in the final order or judgment, the Clerk is bound to comply with that Order;[147] however, an award or disallowance of attorney fees and attorney costs pursuant to Federal Rule of Civil Procedure 54(d)(2) it totally separate and distinct from an award of statutory costs pursuant to Federal Rule of Civil Procedure 54(d)(1);[148] accordingly, if there is a court Order in the underlying case denying "attorney fees and costs," it does not preclude the taxing of § 1920 costs,[149] and Federal Rule 54(d)(1) costs may be assessed even when attorney fees are disallowed.[150]   (Parenthetically, statutes mentioning "attorney fees and costs" mean "attorney fees and attorney costs," and do not relate to § 1920 costs).[151]

(13) *Alleged Failure to Make Use of the Official Bill of Costs Form.*   Although there is a standard form provided by the Administrative Office of the United States Courts, use of this form is optional; where the official form is not used, district court

costs may yet be taxed where the request for costs is neat, legible and understandable.[152]

(14) *Allegedly Joint and Several Liabilities.* In a case where multiple parties on one side of the bar do not prevail, costs against those multiple losing parties are presumptively joint and several, and any losing party or parties who want costs to be taxed against them in any way other than jointly and severally bears the burden of proving that these costs should be so taxed.[153]

(15) *Cases Brought in Federal Court Pursuant to 28 U.S.C. § 1332 (Commonly known as "diversity jurisdiction").* Where an action is brought in federal court pursuant to 28 U.S.C. § 1332 and there are both state and federal cost-shifting statutes or rules of court that may possibly apply, the federal statute or rule trumps the state statute or rule, so that the state procedures may be disregarded, and district court costs may be taxed in diversity jurisdiction cases pursuant to 28 U.S.C. § 1920 and Federal Rule of Civil Procedure 54(d)(1).[154]

(16) *United States as a Party.* Title 28 U.S.C. § 2412 permits taxation against the United States or any agency or official thereof. The Federal Courts Administration Act of 1992[155] provides that the United States may recover filing fees when it prevails in a civil action.

(17) *State Government as a Party.* The Eleventh Amendment to the Constitution does not bar taxation of district court costs against state government, its agencies or officials.[156]

(18) *Costs in Admiralty Cases.* District court clerks may tax 28 U.S.C. § 1920 costs in admiralty cases.[157]

(19) *Interveners.* The prevailing practice is that interveners in agency actions are treated like any other prevailing or losing party.[158]

(20) *Language on costs in Jurisdictional Statute.* In any case brought under a specific statute, the clerk's office must check to see if that statute has provisions concerning costs; if there is a statutory provision concerning costs, that statutory rule, and not 28 U.S.C. § 1920, applies.[159] Statutes mentioning "attorney fees and costs" mean "attorney fees and attorney costs," and do not relate to § 1920 costs.[160]

E. Specific Objections to Normally Allowable District Court Costs. The following is a discussion of the manner in which the Clerk of the United States District Court for the Eastern District of Pennsylvania addresses issues regarding specific items of district court costs which are listed in 28 U.S.C. § 1920.

(1) *28 U.S.C. § 1920(1).*

i. Fees of the Clerk. The relevant statute, 28 U.S.C. § 1920(1) directs the taxing of fees of the Clerk.[161] Costs related to both fees of a state clerk and costs for removal to federal court are recoverable in federal court pursuant to 28 U.S.C. § 1920(1)[162] (The Federal Courts Administration Act of 1992 provides that when the United States is a plaintiff that prevails in a civil action, it may recover fees of the Clerk). [163]

There is a heavy presumption[164] in favor of "***automatically***"[165] taxing those types of costs listed in 28 U.S.C. § 1920[166] which the prevailing party both ***actually incurred*** (as evidenced by a sworn affidavit)[167] and ***necessarily incurred*** ("necessarily" meaning that the costs were reasonably incurred for the prevailing party's effective preparation, judged in light of the situation existing when the costs in question were actually incurred, without regard to whether the costs relate to items which were actually used).[168]

ii. Fees of the Marshal. The relevant statute, 28 U.S.C. § 1920(1), directs the taxing of fees of the Marshal, which includes the costs of service or process, including subpoena service.[169] Federal courts interpret this provision of 28 U.S.C. § 1920(1) as permitting the taxing of costs for both governmental process servers and private process servers.[170] Federal courts also interpret this provision of 28 U.S.C. § 1920(1) as permitting the taxing of costs for a process server's mileage in connection with that service.[171] It is relevant to the taxing of costs whether the non-prevailing party offered to waive service, or whether the prevailing party did or did not request a waiver of service pursuant to Federal Rule of Civil Procedure 4.[172] Costs related to the production of exact copies of an original copy of documentary evidence, including the costs of a subpoena duces tecum (also known as a records subpoena or a records deposition)[173] are seen as taxable costs pursuant to 28 U.S.C. § 1920(4), and will be discussed later in this taxation opinion.

There is a heavy presumption[174] in favor of *"__automatically__"*[175] taxing those types of costs listed in 28 U.S.C. § 1920[176] which the prevailing party both *__actually incurred__* (as evidenced by a sworn affidavit)[177] and *__necessarily incurred__* ("necessarily" meaning that the costs were reasonably incurred for the prevailing party's effective preparation, judged in light of the situation existing when the costs in question were actually incurred, without regard to whether the costs relate to items which were actually used).[178]

(2) *28 U.S.C. § 1920(2).*

i. Deposition Costs. The relevant statute, 28 U.S.C. § 1920(2), directs the taxing of costs for "transcripts necessarily obtained for use in the case." This provision governing "transcripts" applies to deposition transcripts;[179] and modern caselaw states that both stenographic depositions and videotaped depositions are considered "transcripts" for purposes of 28 U.S.C. § 1920(2);[180] by this standard, a prevailing party may also recover costs associated with the playback of video-taped depositions.[181]

The Clerk also notes that deposition costs are taxable for the depositions of both fact witnesses and expert witnesses.[182]

There is a heavy presumption[183] in favor of *"__automatically__"*[184] taxing those types of costs listed in 28 U.S.C. § 1920[185] which the prevailing party both *__actually incurred__* (as evidenced by a sworn affidavit)[186] and *__necessarily incurred__* ("necessarily" meaning that the costs were reasonably incurred for the prevailing party's effective preparation, judged in light of the situation existing when the costs in question were actually incurred, without regard to whether the costs relate to items which were actually used).[187] Examples of situations where deposition transcripts are seen as necessary for a party's effective preparation, even where they were not used, *__include, but are not limited to__*, situations involving deponents who ultimately do not testify at a trial;[188] situations involving deponents who ultimately are not permitted by the court to testify at a trial;[189] and situations where deposition transcripts were necessary to support, or to oppose, pre-trial motions[190] and/or post-trial motions[191] (including motions seeking the entry of summary judgment,[192] and/or motions seeking the entry of a default judgment[193] and/or motions seeking the entry of a judgment NOV[194]). *__Both__* stenographic copies of deposition transcripts *__and__* videotaped copies of transcripts of the exact same testimony are taxable[195] where both copies were necessary to counsel's effective preparation (judged in light of the situation existing when the costs in question were actually incurred, without regard to whether the costs related to items which were actually used.[196]

However, even if a deposition transcript is "necessarily obtained," counsel may not always recover costs incurred in having it prepared on an expedited basis. Expedited rates for deposition transcripts have been allowed where circumstances justify such a schedule, judged in light of the situation existing at the time of the taking of the testimony in question.[197]

ii. Costs of Other Types of Transcripts. The relevant statute, 28 U.S.C. § 1920(2), directs the taxing of costs for "transcripts necessarily obtained for use in the case." This provision governing "transcripts" applies to trial transcripts and allows for their taxation.[198] This provision governing "transcripts" also applies to transcripts of hearings and other pre-trial proceedings, and allows for their taxation.[199] This provision governing "transcripts" also applies to transcripts of extra-judicial, non-judicial, or other out-of-court proceedings or conferences, and allows for their taxation.[200]

There is a heavy presumption[201] in favor of "automatically"[202] taxing those types of costs listed in 28 U.S.C. § 1920[203] which the prevailing party both ***actually incurred*** (as evidenced by a sworn affidavit)[204] and ***necessarily incurred*** ("necessarily" meaning that the costs were reasonably incurred for the prevailing party's effective preparation, judged in light of the situation existing when the costs in question were actually incurred, without regard to whether the costs relate to items which were actually used).[205] Examples of situations where transcripts are seen as necessarily obtained, even where they were not used, ***include, but are not limited to***, situations where the transcripts were needed to support, or to oppose, pre-trial motions[206] and/or post-trial motions.[207]

However, even if such a transcript is "necessarily obtained," counsel may not always recover costs incurred in having it prepared on an expedited basis. Expedited rates have been allowed where circumstances justify such a schedule, judged in light of the situation existing at the time of the taking of the testimony in question.[208]

(3) *28 U.S.C. § 1920(3).*

i. Printing Costs. The relevant statute, 28 U.S.C. § 1920(3), directs the taxing of "printing" costs[209] (although typing costs are not taxable under this statute).[210]

There is a heavy presumption[211] in favor of "***automatically***"[212] taxing those types of costs listed in 28 U.S.C. § 1920[213] which the prevailing party both ***actually incurred*** (as evidenced by a sworn affidavit)[214] and ***necessarily incurred*** ("necessarily" meaning that the costs were reasonably incurred for the prevailing party's effective preparation, judged in light of the situation existing when the costs in question were actually incurred, without regard to whether the costs relate to items which were actually used).[215]

ii. Witness Attendance Fees. The relevant statute, 28 U.S.C. § 1920(3), directs the taxing of witness fees. Witness fees are capped by the witness fee statute, 28 U.S.C. § 1821.[216] The United States Supreme Court has held that the witness fee statute (28 U.S.C. § 1821 or its direct predecessor statute) is incorporated by reference into 28 U.S.C. § 1920(3) (or its direct predecessor statute).[217]

28 U.S.C. § 1821(b) limits witness attendance fees to $40.00 per witness per day. Witness attendance fees actually incurred by the prevailing party or parties are taxable for every day a witness is either present in court, or present at a deposition hearing,[218] with a reasonable "good faith" expectation on the part of the prevailing party's counsel that the witness may have to testify, even where the witness does not actually testify.[219] (Authority also permits the taxing of attendance costs pursuant to 28 U.S.C. § 1821(b) for "travel days," where reasonable.)[220]

This limit of $40.00 per witness per day of attendance applies to both fact and expert witnesses,[221] except where the expert witness in question was court-appointed pursuant to 28 U.S.C. § 1920(6).[222] Costs related to an expert's preparation, or to the creation of an expert report, are not set forth in 28 U.S.C. § 1920, and are therefore not taxable.[223]

In addition, although no witness fees are taxable for witnesses who are parties to the litigation,[224] witness fees are taxable for employees of a corporate party as long as they are not real parties in interest to the litigation.[225]

There is a heavy presumption[226] in favor of "***automatically***"[227] taxing those types of costs listed in 28 U.S.C. § 1920[228] which the prevailing party both ***actually incurred*** (as evidenced by a sworn affidavit)[229] and ***necessarily incurred*** ("necessarily" meaning that the costs were reasonably incurred for the prevailing party's effective preparation, judged in light of the situation existing when the costs in question were actually incurred, without regard to whether the costs relate to items which were actually used).[230]

iii. Witness Travel Costs Fees. The relevant statute, 28 U.S.C. § 1920(3), directs the taxing of witness fees. Witness fees are capped by the witness fee statute, 28 U.S.C. § 1821.[231] The United States Supreme Court has held that the witness fee statute (28 U.S.C. § 1821 or its direct predecessor statute) is incorporated by reference into 28 U.S.C. § 1920(3) (or its direct predecessor statute).[232]

28 U.S.C. § 1821(c) sets limits, based on reasonableness, on witness travel and mileage costs.

Travel costs are taxable pursuant to 28 U.S.C. § 1920(3) where the need to travel was reasonable, judged in light of the situation existing at the time the travel costs were incurred.[233] (Although travel costs for a witness are, at least arguably, taxable pursuant to 28 U.S.C. § 1920, we hasten to point out that travel costs for an attorney are not taxable pursuant to 28 U.S.C. § 1920).[234]

There is a heavy presumption[235] in favor of *automatically*"[236] taxing those types of costs listed in 28 U.S.C. § 1920[237] which the prevailing party both *actually incurred* (as evidenced by a sworn affidavit)[238] and *necessarily incurred* ("necessarily" meaning that the costs were reasonably incurred for the prevailing party's effective preparation, judged in light of the situation existing when the costs in question were actually incurred, without regard to whether the costs relate to items which were actually used).[239]

iv. Witness Subsistence Fee. The relevant statute, 28 U.S.C. § 1920(3), directs the taxing of witness fees. Witness fees are capped by the witness fee statute, 28 U.S.C. § 1821.[240] The United States Supreme Court has held that the witness fee statute (28 U.S.C. § 1821 or its direct predecessor statute) is incorporated by reference into 28 U.S.C. § 1920(3) (or its direct predecessor statute).[241]

28 U.S.C. § 1821(d) limits witness subsistence (meals and lodging) allowances in "high cost" areas such as the Eastern District of Pennsylvania to $328.50 per day when the traveling witness can supply *all* of his or her receipts for their requested subsistence allowance (and $219.00 per day when the witness cannot supply *all* of his or her receipts for their requested subsistence allowance); the witness can also recover a flat rate of $49.50 in subsistence for the last day of their trip.

Witness subsistence fees are taxable pursuant to 28 U.S.C. § 1920(3) where the need to travel was reasonable, judged in light of the situation existing at the time the costs were incurred.[242] (Although subsistence fees for a witness are, at least arguably, taxable pursuant to 28 U.S.C. § 1920, we hasten to point out that subsistence fees for an attorney are not taxable pursuant to 28 U.S.C. § 1920).[243]

There is a heavy presumption[244] in favor of *automatically*"[245] taxing those types of costs listed in 28 U.S.C. § 1920[246] which the prevailing party both *actually incurred* (as evidenced by a sworn affidavit)[247] and *necessarily incurred* ("necessarily" meaning that the costs were reasonably incurred for the prevailing party's effective preparation, judged in light of the situation existing when the costs in question were actually incurred, without regard to whether the costs relate to items which were actually used).[248]

(4) *28 U.S.C. § 1920(4).*

i. Documentary Evidence. The relevant statute, 28 U.S.C. § 1920(4), directs the taxing of "fees for exemplification and the cost of making copies of any materials where the copies are necessarily obtained for use in the case(.)" The United States Court of Appeals for the Third Circuit spoke on 28 U.S.C. § 1920(4) in *Race Tires America, Inc. v. Hoosier Racing Tire Corp.*, 674 F.3d 158 (3d Cir. 2012).

Citing Webster's Third International Dictionary 504 (3d edition 1993) as authority, the Race Tires America court noted that the word "copy" means "*an imitation, transcript or reproduction of an original work*."

The Race Tires America court applied this dictionary definition to conclude that for purposes of 28 U.S.C. § 1920(4), *the word "copying" means the "scanning," "conversion" or "reproduction" of an "original" item of "evidence" so as to create a "duplicate" copy of that "evidence."* The Race Tires America court also applied this dictionary definition to conclude that *the word "copying" also means the "scanning," "conversion" or "reproduction" of an "original" "transcript," so as to create a "duplicate" copy of that "transcript."*

Accordingly, a duplicate copy of original records,[249] or a duplicate copy of other original documents produced in discovery,[250] as well as the costs of a subpoena duces tecum (also known as a records subpoena or a records deposition)[251] are taxable costs pursuant to 28 U.S.C. § 1920(4).[252]

There is a heavy presumption[253] in favor of *automatically*"[254] taxing those types of costs listed in 28 U.S.C. § 1920[255] which the prevailing party both *actually incurred* (as evidenced by a sworn affidavit)[256] and *necessarily incurred* ("necessarily" meaning that the costs were reasonably incurred for the prevailing party's effective preparation, judged in light of the situation existing when the costs in question were actually incurred, without regard to whether the costs relate to items which were actually used).[257]

Situations where costs of exact duplicate copies of original evidence are seen as "necessary" pursuant to 28 U.S.C. § 1920(4) (even where the duplicate copies in question were not used) *include, but are not limited to*, situations where such exact duplicate copies of original evidence are attached to any deposition transcript,[258] and/or situations where such exact duplicate copies of original evidence are attached to any pleading[259] and/or situations where such exact duplicate copies of original evidence are attached to any motion[260] (including a motion for summary judgment).[261]

ii. Demonstrative Evidence. The relevant statute, 28 U.S.C. § 1920(4), directs the taxing of "fees for exemplification and the cost of making copies of any materials where the copies are necessarily obtained for use in the case(.)" The United States Court of Appeals for the Third Circuit spoke on 28 U.S.C. § 1920(4) in *Race Tires America, Inc. v. Hoosier Racing Tire Corp.*, 674 F.3d 158 (3d Cir. 2012). The Race Tires America court held that the word "copies" means an exact copy, or an exact duplicate, of an original piece of evidence. The Race Tires America court also found that because, in drafting 28 U.S.C. § 1920(4), Congress had specifically used two different words in the same statute ("copies" and "exemplification"), that that word "copies" and the word "exemplification" presumptively do not have the same meaning (although the Race Tires America court pointedly declined to offer a definition of the word "exemplification").

With no guidance from the Third Circuit in Race Tires America, the only *controlling* guidance in *this* jurisdiction regarding a definition of the word "exemplification" for purposes of 28 U.S.C. § 1920(4) is found in In re: Kulicke and Soffa Industries Securities Litigation, 747 F. Supp. 1136 (E.D. Pa. 1990); aff'd without comment, 944 F.2d 897 (3rd Cir. 1991), which held that the concept of "exemplification" incorporates the concept "demonstrative evidence." Federal courts in other jurisdictions have reached the same conclusion.[262] Examples of such taxable costs relating to demonstrative evidence include the costs of photos,[263] models,[264] maps,[265] blow-ups,[266] charts,[267] diagrams,[268] computer graphics,[269] and the like; however, costs related to an expert's preparation or to the creation of an expert report are a prohibited item which cannot be allowed as exemplification).[270]

There is a heavy presumption[271] in favor of *"automatically*"[272] taxing those types of costs listed in 28 U.S.C. § 1920[273] which the prevailing party both *actually incurred* (as evidenced by a sworn affidavit)[274] and *necessarily incurred* ("necessarily" meaning that the costs were reasonably incurred for the prevailing party's effective preparation, judged in light of the situation existing when the costs in question were actually incurred, without regard to whether the costs relate to items which were actually used).[275] Examples of situations where such costs are seen as necessary pursuant to 28 U.S.C. § 1920(4), even where the demonstrative evidence in question was not used, *include, but are not limited to*, situations where such demonstrative evidence is attached to any deposition transcript,[276] and/or situations where such demonstrative evidence is attached to any pleading[277] and/or situations where such demonstrative evidence is attached to any motion[278] (including a motion for summary judgment).[279]

(5) *28 U.S.C. § 1920(5).*

i. Docket Fees. The relevant statute, 28 U.S.C. § 1920(5), directs the taxing of those types of docket fees authorized by under 28 U.S.C. § 1923.[280]

There is a heavy presumption[281] in favor of "***automatically***"[282] taxing those types of costs listed in 28 U.S.C. § 1920[283] which the prevailing party both ***actually incurred*** (as evidenced by a sworn affidavit)[284] and ***necessarily incurred*** ("necessarily" meaning that the costs were reasonably incurred for the prevailing party's effective preparation, judged in light of the situation existing when the costs in question were actually incurred, without regard to whether the costs relate to items which were actually used).[285]

(6) *28 U.S.C. § 1920(6).*

i. Court Appointed Experts. The relevant statute, 28 U.S.C. § 1920(6), directs the taxing of costs of "court appointed experts." Costs related to the preparation of an expert's testimony or report are not mentioned in 28 U.S.C. § 1920 and are therefore not taxable[286] (although we note that costs incurred for an expert's preparation of an exhibit may be taxable in a situation where the prevailing party can demonstrate that these costs are strictly limited to exhibit preparation and do not involve preparation of testimony or a report.)[287] Such unallowable costs also include costs related to an Independent Medical Examination.[288]

There is a heavy presumption[289] in favor of ***automatically***"[290] taxing those types of costs listed in 28 U.S.C. § 1920[291] which the prevailing party both ***actually incurred*** (as evidenced by a sworn affidavit)[292] and ***necessarily incurred*** ("necessarily" meaning that the costs were reasonably incurred for the prevailing party's effective preparation, judged in light of the situation existing when the costs in question were actually incurred, without regard to whether the costs relate to items which were actually used).[293]

ii. Interpreters. The relevant statute, 28 U.S.C. § 1920(6), authorizes "(the) compensation of interpreters." These costs are limited to the cost of oral translation, and do not include the cost of document translation (based on the ordinary definition of the word "interpreters").[294]

In addition, the fees and the salaries, expenses, and costs of special interpretation services under 28 U.S.C. § 1818 are recoverable pursuant to 28 U.S.C. § 1920(6).

There is a heavy presumption[295] in favor of ***automatically***"[296] taxing those types of costs listed in 28 U.S.C. § 1920[297] which the prevailing party both ***actually incurred*** (as evidenced by a sworn affidavit)[298] and ***necessarily incurred*** ("necessarily" meaning that the costs were reasonably incurred for the prevailing party's effective preparation, judged in light of the situation existing when the costs in question were actually incurred, without regard to whether the costs relate to items which were actually used).[299]

F. Special Procedures for Allowance of District Court Costs in Situations Involving Federal Rule of Civil Procedure 68. As previously stated, it is well-established that costs may not be imposed in federal district courts except where they are authorized by either a statute or a rule of court.[300]

Federal Rule of Civil Procedure 68 provides that:

"(A) party defending against a claim may serve on an opposing party an offer to allow judgment on specified terms, with the costs then accrued . . . (if this offer is not accepted, and the subsequent) judgment that the offeree finally obtains is not more favorable than the unaccepted offer, the offeree must pay the costs incurred after the offer was made."

The policy supporting Rule 68 is the societal interest in encouraging settlement of cases, thereby saving the litigants and the court from unnecessary costs and effort.[301]

Rule 68 costs are taxable only by a district court judge, not the Clerk of the District Court.

Rule 68 costs may include attorney fees where the substantive statute at the heart of the case defines "costs" as including attorney fees; however, where the substantive statute at the heart of the case does not define "costs" as including attorney fees, then attorney fees are customarily not taxable pursuant to Rule 68.[302] According to this rule, where the offer does not specifically mention attorney fees as part of costs, such an offer does not necessarily exclude an allowance of attorney fees: the key factor is the language of the substantive statute at the heart of the case.[303]

Rule 68 does not apply in situations where a defendant serves upon the adverse party an offer to allow judgment to be taken against the defendant, and the final judgment is entered **in favor of the defendant, not the plaintiff.**[304]

G. Taxation of Appellate Court Costs and Supreme Court Costs by the Clerk of the District Court. It is well-established that costs may not be imposed by the clerk of the district court except where they are authorized by either a statute or a rule of court.[305] As previously stated, Federal Rule of Civil Procedure 54(d)(1) expressly makes those items of district court costs which are listed in 28 U.S.C. § 1920[306] taxable by the clerk of the district court.[307] In addition, Federal Rule of Appellate Procedure 39(e) "expressly"[308] makes certain items of appellate court costs which are listed in that rule taxable by the clerk of the district court.[309] Those items of appellate court costs made taxable by the district court clerk by Federal Rule of Appellate Procedure 39(e) are:

(1) the preparation and transmission of the record;

(2) the reporter's transcript, if needed to determine the appeal:

(3) premiums paid for a supersedeas bond, or other bond to preserve rights pending appeal; and

(4) the fee for filing the notice of appeal.

We note that those types of costs listed in F.R.A.P. 39(e) are plainly not the same types of costs listed in the taxation statute, 28 U.S.C. § 1920;[310] however, we also note that F.R.A.P. 39(e) "*expressly*"[311] states that the types of costs listed in that appellate rule of court are taxable by the clerk of the district court.[312] In resolving this apparent conflict, it must be noted that since the adoption of the procedures created by F.R.A.P. 39(e) postdates the adoption of the procedures created by 28 U.S.C. § 1920, that to the extent that there is any apparent conflict, the district court clerk must give F.R.A.P. 39(e) more weight than 28 U.S.C. § 1920 when taxing appellate court costs.[313] *Accordingly, appellate court costs which are listed in F.R.A.P. 39(e) are taxable by the clerk of the district court, "regardless of whether § 1920 authorizes an award of those (appellate court) costs.*"[314] The rationale behind this procedure directing the district court clerk, rather than the appellate court clerk, to tax appellate court costs pursuant to F.R.A.P. 39(e) is "general convenience."[315]

Once the appellate court has entered a final judgment in the underlying litigation, the clerk of the district court may tax these F.R.A.P. 39(e) costs without the need to wait for an instruction from the appellate court or from the appellate clerk directing the district clerk to tax them[316] (except where there is dispute between the parties pursuant to Federal Rule of Appellate Procedure 39(a)(4) as to who exactly is the prevailing party in the appellate court).[317] In addition, the district clerk has the discretion to tax costs even where the appellate court orders that both sides shall bear their own costs.[318]

In addition to these procedures, it bears noting that one of the most firmly established constitutional principles is the mandate principle, which hold that when a higher court issues a mandate, lower courts must obey it with regard to all issues which that higher court addressed.[319] In addition, mandate costs imposed by an appellate court leave no discretion in the hands of the district court or its Clerk; the Clerk of the district court *must* tax costs as shown on mandate of a United States Court of Appeals[320] (the rationale behind this procedure is that a federal district court is the only federal court with the authority to actually execute on a judgment).[321]

This document will now address the request for costs incurred before the United States Supreme Court.

It is well-established that costs may not be imposed in federal district courts except where they are authorized by either a statute or a rule of court.[322] Costs taxable by the United States Supreme Court are limited pursuant to Supreme Court Rule 43.3 to fees of the Clerk of the United States Supreme Court and costs of printing the joint appendix; the Clerk of the United States Supreme Court shall include these costs in the mandate; when a higher court issues a mandate; lower courts must obey it with regard to all issues which that higher court addressed.[323] Accordingly, the Clerk of the district court *must* tax costs as shown on mandate of the United States Supreme Court[324] (the rationale behind this procedure is that a federal district court is the only federal court with the authority to actually execute on a judgment).[325]

[1]*Taniguchi v. Kan Pacific Saipan, Ltd.*, 132 S.Ct. 1997 (2012); *Alyeska Pipeline Service Co. v. Wilderness Society*, 421 U.S. 240 (1975); *Fleischmann Distilling Co. v. Maier Brewing Co.*, 386 U.S. 714 (1967); *Reger v. The Nemours Foundation*, 599 F.3d 285 (3d Cir. 2010); *Abrams v. Lightolier, Inc.*, 50 F.3d 1204 (3d Cir. 1995).

[2]*Reger v. The Nemours Foundation*, 599 F.3d 285 (3d Cir. 2010); *Abrams v. Lightolier, Inc.*, 50 F.3d 1204 (3d Cir. 1995).

[3]*Taniguchi v. Kan Pacific Saipan, Ltd.*, 132 S.Ct. 1997 (2012); *Buchanan v. Stanships, Inc.*, 485 U.S. 265 (1988); *Alyeska Pipeline Service Co. v. Wilderness Society*, 421 U.S. 240 (1975); *Fleischmann Distilling Co. v. Maier Brewing Co.*, 386 U.S. 714 (1967); *Reger v. The Nemours Foundation*, 599 F.3d 285 (3d Cir. 2010); In re: Paoli Railroad Yard PCB Litigation, 221 F.3d 449 (3d Cir. 2000); *Adams v. Teamsters Local 115*, 678 F.Supp.2d 314 (E.D. Pa. 2007).

[4] *Taniguchi v. Kan Pacific Saipan, Ltd.*, 132 S.Ct. 1997 (2012); *Buchanan v. Stanships, Inc.*, 485 U.S. 265 (1988); *Reger v. The Nemours Foundation*, 599 F.3d 285 (3d Cir. 2010); *McKenna v. City of Philadelphia*, 582 F.3d 447 (3d Cir. 2009).

[5]*Greene v. Fraternal Order of Police*, 183 F.R.D. 445 (E.D. Pa. 1998); *Lacovara v. Merrill Lynch, Pierce, Fenner & Smith*, 102 F.R.D. 959 (E.D. Pa. 1984).

[6]*Buchanan v. Stanships, Inc.*, 485 U.S. 265 (1988); *Friedman v. Ganassi*, 853 F.2d 207 (3d Cir. 1988); *Adams v. Teamsters Local 115*, 678 F.Supp.2d 314 (E.D. Pa. 2007); *Greene v. Fraternal Order of Police*, 183 F.R.D. 445 (E.D. Pa. 1998).

[7]*Brazos Valley Coalition for Life, Inc. v. City of Bryan, Texas*, 421 F.3d 314 (5th Cir. 2005); *Trepel v. Roadway Express, Inc.*, 266 F.3d 418 (6th Cir. 2001); *Holmes v. Cessna Aircraft Co.*, 11 F.3d 63 (5th Cir. 1994); *Dovenmuehle v. Gilldorn Mortgage Midwest Corp.*, 871 F.2d 697 (7th Cir. 1989); *Mason v. Belieu*, 543 F.2d 215 (D.C. Cir. 1976); *Wahl v. Carrier Manufacturing Co.*, 511 F.2d 209 (7th Cir. 1975); *McInnis v. Town of Weston*, 458 F.Supp.2d 7 (D. Conn. 2006); *Sullivan v. Cheshier*, 991 F.Supp. 999 (N.D. Ill. 1998); *Hollenbeck v. Falstaff Brewing Corp.*, 605 F.Supp. 421 (E.D. Mo. 1984); *Morrissey v. County Tower Corp.*, 568 F.Supp. 980 (E.D. Mo. 1983).

[8]*Crawford Fitting Company v. J. T. Gibbons, Inc.*, 482 U.S. 437 (1987); *Reger v. The Nemours Foundation*, 599 F.3d 285 (3d Cir. 2010); In re: Paoli Railroad Yard PCB Litigation, 221 F.3d 449 (3d Cir. 2000); *Abrams v. Lightolier, Inc.*, 50 F.3d 1204 (3d Cir. 1995); *Institutionalized Juveniles v. Secretary of Public Welfare*, 758 F.2d 897 (3d Cir. 1985); *Nugget Distributors Cooperative of America v. Mr. Nugget, Inc.*, 145 F.R.D. 54 (E.D.Pa. 1992). Accord, *Perry v. Metro Suburban Bus Authority*; 236 FRD 110 (EDNY 2006); *Schmitz–Werke GMBH v. Rockland Industries*, 271 F.Supp. 2d 734 (D. Maryland 2003); *Roberts v. Interstate Distrib. Co.*, 242 F.Supp. 2d 850 (D. Oregon 2002); In Re: Glacier Bay, 746 F.Supp. 1379 (D. Alaska 1990).

[9]*Brazos Valley Coalition for Life, Inc. v. City of Bryan, Texas*, 421 F.3d 314 (5th Cir. 2005); *Trepel v. Roadway Express, Inc.*, 266 F.3d 418 (6th Cir. 2001); *Holmes v. Cessna Aircraft Co.*, 11 F.3d 63 (5th Cir. 1994); *Dovenmuehle v. Gilldorn Mortgage Midwest Corp.*, 871 F.2d 697 (7th Cir. 1989); *Mason v. Belieu*, 543 F.2d 215 (D.C. Cir. 1976); *Wahl v. Carrier Manufacturing Co.*, 511 F.2d 209 (7th Cir. 1975); *McInnis v. Town of Weston*, 458 F.Supp.2d 7 (D. Conn. 2006); *Sullivan v. Cheshier*, 991 F.Supp. 999 (N.D. Ill. 1998); *Hollenbeck v. Falstaff Brewing Corp.*, 605 F.Supp. 421 (E.D. Mo. 1984); *Morrissey v. County Tower Corp.*, 568 F.Supp. 980 (E.D. Mo. 1983).

[10]*Brown v. American Enka Corp.*, 452 F.Supp. 154 (ED Tenn. 1976).

[11]*Brown v. American Enka Corp.*, 452 F.Supp. 154 (ED Tenn. 1976).

[12]In re: Paoli Railroad Yard PCB Litigation, 221 F.3d 449 (3rd Cir. 2000). *Accord, Soberay Mach. & Equip. Co. v. MRF Ltd.*, 181 F.3d 759 (6th Cir. 1999); *Lorenz v. Valley Forge Insurance Co.*, 23 F.3d 1259 (7th Cir. 1994); *McGuigan v. Cae Link Corp.*, 155 FRD 31 (NDNY 1994); *American Key Corp. v. Cumberland Associates*, 102 FRD 496 (NDGa 1984); and *Dorothy K. Winston & Co. v. Town Heights Dev., Inc.*, 68 FRD 431 (DDC 1975).

[13]*Northbrook Excess and Surplus Insurance Co. v. Procter & Gamble Co.*, 924 F.2d 633 (7th Cir. 1991).

[14]*Alyeska Pipeline Service Co. v. Wilderness Society*, 421 U.S. 240 (1975); *Adams v. Teamsters Local 115*, 678 F.Supp.2d 314 (E.D. Pa. 2007); *Nugget Distributors Cooperative of America v. Mr. Nugget, Inc.*, 145 F.R.D. 54 (E.D.Pa. 1992). *Accord, Cook Children's Medical Center v. New England PPO Plan of Gen. Consol. Management*, 491 F.3d 266 (5th Cir. 2007); *Perry v. Metro Suburban Bus Authority*; 236 F.R.D. 110 (EDNY 2006); *Schmitz–Werke GMBH v. Rockland Industries*, 271 F.Supp. 2d 734 (D. Maryland 2003); *Roberts v. Interstate Distrib. Co.*, 242 F.Supp.2d 850 (D. Oregon 2002); *US v. Bedford Associates*, 548 F.Supp. 748 (SDNY 1982).

[15]*Buchanan v. Stanships, Inc.*, 485 U.S. 265 (1988); *Friedman v. Ganassi*, 853 F.2d 207 (3d Cir. 1988); *Adams v. Teamsters Local 115*, 678 F.Supp.2d 314 (E.D. Pa. 2007).

[16]*Abrams v. Lightolier, Inc.*, 50 F.3d 1204 (3d Cir. 1995); *Smith v. SEPTA*, 47 F.3d 97 (3d Cir. 1995); *Friedman v. Ganassi*, 853 F.2d 207 (3d Cir. 1988); *Institutionalized Juveniles v. Secretary of Public Welfare*, 758 F.2d 897 (3rd Cir. 1985); *Pearlstine v. United States*, 649 F.2d 194 (3rd Cir. 1981); *Delaney v. Capone*, 642 F.2d 57 (3d Cir. 1981); *Samuel v. University of Pittsburgh*, 538 F.2d 991 (3d Cir. 1976); *ADM Corp. v. Speedmaster Packing Corp.*, 525 F.2d 662 (3d Cir. 1975); *Greene v. Fraternal Order of Police*, 183 F.R.D. 445 (E.D.Pa. 1998). *Accord,* In Re: Air Crash Disaster at John F. Kennedy International Airport on June 24, 1975, 687 F.2d 626 (2nd Cir. 1982); In Re: Glacier Bay, 746 F.Supp. 1379 (D. Alaska 1990).

[17]*Chambers v. NASCO, Inc.*, 501 U.S. 32 (1991); *Alyeska Pipeline Service Co. v. Wilderness Society*, 421 U.S. 240 (1975); *Fleischmann Distilling Co. v. Maier Brewing Co.*, 386 U.S. 714 (1967).

[18]*Nugget Distributors Cooperative of America v. Mr. Nugget, Inc.*, 145 F.R.D. 54 (E.D.Pa. 1992). *Accord, Alyeska Pipeline Service Co. v. Wilderness Society*, 421 U.S. 240 (1975); In re: Paoli Railroad Yard PCB Litigation, 221 F.3d 449 (3d Cir. 2000); *Abrams v. Lightolier, Inc.*, 50 F.3d 1204 (3d Cir. 1995). *See, also, Harkins v. Riverboat Services*, 286 F. Supp. 2d 976 (ND Ill. 2003), *aff'd*, 385 F.3d 1099 (7th Cir. 2004); and In Re: Glacier Bay, 746 F.Supp. 1379 (D. Alaska 1990).

[19]*Race Tires America, Inc. v. Hoosier Racing Tire Corp.*, 2012 WL 887593 (3d Cir. March 16, 2012).

[20]In re: Paoli Railroad Yard PCB Litigation, 221 F.3d 449 (3d Cir. 2000); *Levin v. Parkhouse*, 484 F.Supp. 1091 (E.D. Pa. 1980). *Accord,* In Re: San Juan Dupont Plaza Hotel Fire Litigation, 994 F.2d 956 (1st Cir. 1993); *Krouse v. American Sterilizer Co.*, 928 F.Supp. 543 (W.D. Pa. 1996); In Re: Glacier Bay, 746 F.Supp. 1379 (D. Alaska 1990); *Stacy v. Williams*, 50 F.R.D. 52 (N.D. Miss. 1970); *Bourazak v. North River Insurance Co.*, 280 F.Supp. 89 (S.D. Ill. 1968).

[21]*Race Tires America, Inc. v. Hoosier Racing Tire Corp.*, 2012 WL 887593 (3d Cir. March 16, 2012).

[22]*Smith v. Tenet Healthsystems SL, Inc.*, 436 F.3d 879 (8th Cir. 2006); *Helms v. WalMart Stores, Inc.*, 808 F.Supp. 1568 (ND Ga. 1992), *aff'd* 998 F.2d 1023 (11th Cir. 1993); *Soler v. McHenry*, 771 F.Supp. 252 (ND Ill. 1991), *aff'd*, 989 F.2d 251 (7th Cir. 1993); *Haagen–Dazs Co. v. Rainbow Gourmet Ice Creams, Inc.*, 920 F.2d 587 (9th Cir. 1990); *Rodriguez–Garcia v. Davila*, 904 F.2d 90 (1st Cir. 1990); *Allen v. United States Steel Corp.*, 665 F.2d 689 (5th Cir. 1982); *McGuigan v. CAE Link Corp.*, 155 FRD 31 (NDNY 1994); *Nelson v. Darragh Co.*, 120 FRD 517 (WD Ark. 1988); *Radol v. Thomas*, 113 FRD 172 (SD Ohio 1986); *Roche v. Normandy*, 566 F.Supp. 37 (ED Mo. 1983); *Meadows v. Ford Motor Co.*, 62 FRD 98 (WD Ky. 1973); *Gillam v. A. Shyman, Inc.*, 31 FRD 271 (D. Alaska 1962).

[23]*Smith v. Tenet Healthsystems SL, Inc.*, 436 F.3d 879 (8th Cir. 2006).

[24]*Yasui v. Maui Electric Co.*, 78 F.Supp. 2d 1124 (D. Hawaii 1999); *Garonzik v. Whitman Diner*, 910 F.Supp 167 (D.N.J. 1995); *Corsair Asset Management, Inc. v. Moskovitz*, 142 FRD 347 (N.D. Ga. 1992).

[25]*Montgomery County v. Microvote Corp.*, 2004 WL 1087196 (EDPA 2004); *Sun Media Systems, Inc. v. KDSM, LLC*, 587 F.Supp. 2d 1059 (S.D. Iowa 2008).

[26]*Gary Brown and Associates v. Ashdon, Inc.*, 268 Fed.Appx. 837 (11th Cir. 2008); *Jensen v. Lawler*, 338 F.Supp. 2d 739 (SD Texas 2004).

[27]*Nugget Distributors Cooperative of America v. Mr. Nugget, Inc.*, 145 F.R.D. 54 (E.D.Pa. 1992). *Accord,* In Re: San Juan Dupont Plaza Hotel Fire Litigation, 994 F.2d 956 (1st Cir. 1993); *United States Football League v. National Football League*, 887 F.2d 408 (2nd Cir. 1989); *Wahl v. Carrier Manufacturing Co.*, 511 F.2d 209 (7th Cir. 1975); In Re: Glacier Bay, 746 F.Supp. 1379 (D. Alaska 1990); *Hollenbeck v. Falstaff Brewing Corp.*, 605 F.Supp. 421 (ED Mo. 1984).

[28]*United States Football League v. National Football League*, 887 F.2d 408 (2nd Cir. 1989); *Allen v. United States Steel Corp.*, 665 F.2d 689 (5th Cir. 1982).

[29]*Nugget Distributors Cooperative of America v. Mr. Nugget, Inc.*, 145 F.R.D. 54 (E.D.Pa. 1992). *Accord, Avirgan v. Hull*, 705 F.Supp. 1544 (SD Fla 1989), *aff'd*, 932 F.2d 1572 (11th Cir. 1991); *Wahl v. Carrier Manufacturing Co.*, 511 F.2d 209 (7th Cir. 1975); *Corsair Asset Management, Inc. v. Moskovitz*, 142 F.R.D. 347 (ND Ga 1992); In Re: Glacier Bay, 746 F.Supp. 1379 (D. Alaska 1990).

[30]*Wahl v. Carrier Manufacturing Co.*, 511 F.2d 209 (7th Cir. 1975); In Re: Glacier Bay, 746 F.Supp. 1379 (D. Alaska 1990).

[31]*Corsair Asset Management, Inc. v. Moskovitz*, 142 F.R.D. 347 (ND Ga 1992); *Litton Systems, Inc. V. American Telephone & Telegraph Co.*, 613 F.Supp. 824 (SDNY 1985).

[32]*Nugget Distributors Cooperative of America v. Mr. Nugget, Inc.*, 145 F.R.D. 54 (E.D.Pa. 1992). Accord, *Gary Brown and Associates v. Ashdon, Inc.*, 268 Fed.Appx. 837 (11th Cir. 2008);*Avirgan v. Hull*, 705 F.Supp. 1544 (SD Fla 1989), aff'd, 932 F.2d 1572 (11th Cir. 1991); *Wahl v. Carrier Manufacturing Co.*, 511 F.2d 209 (7th Cir. 1975); *Sun Media Systems, Inc. v. KDSM, LLC*, 587 F.Supp. 2d 1059 (S.D. Iowa 2008); *Yasui v. Maui Electric Co.*, 78 F.Supp.2d 1124 (D. Hawaii 1999); *Royal Palace Hotel Associates v. International Resort Classics*, 178 FRD 595 (MD Fl. 1998); *Corsair Asset Management, Inc. v. Moskovitz*, 142 FRD 347 (ND Ga 1992); In Re: Glacier Bay, 746 F.Supp. 1379 (D. Alaska 1990); *Central Delaware Branch of the NAACP v. City of Dover, Delaware*, 123 FRD 85 (D. Delaware 1988); *Hollenbeck v. Falstaff Brewing Corp.*, 605 F.Supp. 421 (ED Mo. 1984); *Evans v. Fuller*, 94 F.R.D. 311, 314 (W.D. Ark. 1982); *Neely v. General Electric Co.*, 90 F.R.D. 627, 630 (N.D. Ga. 1981); *United States v. Bexar County*, 89 F.R.D. 391, 394 (W.D. Tex. 1981).

[33]*Sun Media Systems, Inc. v. KDSM, LLC*, 587 F.Supp. 2d 1059 (S.D. Iowa 2008).

[34]*Gary Brown and Associates v. Ashdon, Inc.*, 268 Fed.Appx. 837 (11th Cir. 2008); *Sun Media Systems, Inc. v. KDSM, LLC*, 587 F.Supp. 2d 1059 (S.D. Iowa 2008); *Central Delaware Branch of the NAACP v. City of Dover, Delaware*, 123 F.R.D. 85 (D. Delaware 1988).

[35]*Sun Media Systems, Inc. v. KDSM, LLC*, 587 F.Supp. 2d 1059 (S.D. Iowa 2008); *Central Delaware Branch of the NAACP v. City of Dover, Delaware*, 123 F.R.D. 85 (D. Delaware 1988).

[36]*Sun Media Systems, Inc. v. KDSM, LLC*, 587 F.Supp. 2d 1059 (S.D. Iowa 2008); *Yasui v. Maui Electric Co.*, 78 F.Supp.2d 1124 (D. Hawaii 1999); *Cody v. Private Agencies Collaborating Together, Inc.*, 911 F.Supp. 1 (D.D.C. 1995).

[37]*Sun Media Systems, Inc. v. KDSM, LLC*, 587 F.Supp. 2d 1059 (S.D. Iowa 2008).

[38]*Central Delaware Branch of the NAACP v. City of Dover, Delaware*, 123 F.R.D. 85 (D. Delaware 1988).

[39]*Nugget Distributors Cooperative of America v. Mr. Nugget, Inc.*, 145 F.R.D. 54 (E.D.Pa. 1992); See, also, *Gary Brown and Associates v. Ashdon, Inc.*, 268 Fed.Appx. 837 (11th Cir. 2008); *Duckworth v. Whisenant*, 97 F.3d 1393 (11th Cir. 1993); *Avirgan v. Hull*, 705 F.Supp. 1544 (SD Fla 1989), aff'd, 932 F.2d 1572 (11th Cir. 1991); *Sun Media Systems, Inc. v. KDSM, LLC*, 587 F.Supp. 2d 1059 (S.D. Iowa 2008); *DiBella v. Hopkins*, 407 F.Supp.2d 537 (SDNY 2005); *Yasui v. Maui Electric Co.*, 78 F.Supp.2d 1124 (D. Hawaii 1999); *Royal Palace Hotel Associates v. International Resort Classics*, 178 FRD 595 (MD Fl. 1998); *Corsair Asset Management, Inc. v. Moskovitz*, 142 FRD 347 (ND Ga 1992); *Aloha Towers Associates v. Millenium Aloha, Inc.*, 938 F. Supp. 646 (D. Hawaii 1996); *U.S. v. Bedford Associates*, 548 F.Supp. 748, 753 (S.D.N.Y. 1982).

[40]*Nugget Distributors Cooperative of America v. Mr. Nugget, Inc.*, 145 F.R.D. 54 (E.D.Pa. 1992). Accord, In Re: San Juan Dupont Plaza Hotel Fire Litigation, 994 F.2d 956 (1st Cir. 1993); *Wahl v. Carrier Manufacturing Co.*, 511 F.2d 209 (7th Cir. 1975); *Avirgan v. Hull*, 705 F.Supp. 1544 (SD Fla 1989), aff'd, 932 F.2d 1572 (11th Cir. 1991); *Massachusetts Fair Share v. Law Enforcement Assistance Association*, 776 F.2d 1066, 1070 (D.C. Cir. 1985); *Sun Media Systems, Inc. v. KDSM, LLC*, 587 F.Supp. 2d 1059 (S.D. Iowa 2008); *Yasui v. Maui Electric Co.*, 78 F.Supp.2d 1124 (D. Hawaii 1999); *Royal Palace Hotel Associates v. International Resort Classics*, 178 FRD 595 (MD Fl. 1998); *Cody v. Private Agencies Collaborating Together, Inc.*, 911 F.Supp. 1 (D.D.C. 1995); *Corsair Asset Management, Inc. v. Moskovitz*, 142 FRD 347 (ND Ga 1992); In Re: Glacier Bay, 746 F.Supp. 1379 (D. Alaska 1990); *General Drivers and Dairy Employees, Local 563 v. Bake Rite Baking Co.*, 580 F.Supp. 426, 440 (E.D. Wisc. 1984); *Hollenbeck v. Falstaff Brewing Corp.*, 605 F.Supp. 421 (ED Mo. 1984).

[41]In Re: Glacier Bay, 746 F.Supp. 1379 (D. Alaska 1990); *Hollenbeck v. Falstaff Brewing Corp.*, 605 F.Supp. 421 (ED Mo. 1984).

[42]*Nugget Distributors Cooperative of America v. Mr. Nugget, Inc.*, 145 F.R.D. 54 (E.D.Pa. 1992). Accord, *Avirgan v. Hull*, 705 F.Supp. 1544 (SD Fla 1989), aff'd, 932 F.2d 1572 (11th Cir. 1991); *Sun Media Systems, Inc. v. KDSM, LLC*, 587 F.Supp. 2d 1059 (S.D. Iowa 2008); *Cody v. Private Agencies Collaborating Together, Inc.*, 911 F.Supp. 1 (D.D.C. 1995); *Corsair Asset Management, Inc. v. Moskovitz*, 142 F.R.D. 347 (ND Ga 1992); In Re: San Juan Dupont Plaza Hotel Fire Litigation, 142 F.R.D. 41 (D.P.R. 1992); *Hollenbeck v. Falstaff Brewing Corp.*, 605 F.Supp. 421 (ED Mo. 1984).

[43]*Nugget Distributors Cooperative of America v. Mr. Nugget, Inc.*, 145 F.R.D. 54 (E.D.Pa. 1992). Accord, *Gary Brown and Associates v. Ashdon, Inc.*, 268 Fed.Appx. 837 (11th Cir. 2008); *Avirgan v. Hull*, 705 F.Supp. 1544 (SD Fla 1989), aff'd, 932 F.2d 1572 (11th Cir. 1991); *Yasui v. Maui Electric Co.*, 78 F.Supp.2d 1124 (D. Hawaii 1999); *Corsair Asset Management, Inc. v. Moskovitz*, 142 FRD 347 (ND Ga 1992); In Re: Glacier Bay, 746 F.Supp. 1379 (D. Alaska 1990); *Hollenbeck v. Falstaff Brewing Corp.*, 605 F.Supp. 421 (ED Mo. 1984).

[44]*McGuigan v. CAE Link Corp.*, 155 FRD 31 (NDNY 1994).

[45]In the Matter of Penn Central Transportation Co., 630 F.2d 183 (3d Cir. 1980); *Nugget Distributors Cooperative of America v. Mr. Nugget, Inc.*, 145 F.R.D. 54 (E.D.Pa. 1992). Accord, *Gary Brown and Associates v. Ashdon, Inc.*, 268 Fed.Appx. 837 (11th Cir. 2008); *Duckworth v. Whisenant*, 97 F.3d 1393 (11th Cir. 1993); *Avirgan v. Hull*, 705 F.Supp. 1544 (SD Fla 1989), aff'd, 932 F.2d 1572 (11th Cir. 1991); *Wahl v. Carrier Manufacturing Co.*, 511 F.2d 209 (7th Cir. 1975); *Zeuner v. Rare Hospitality Int'l*, 386 F.Supp. 2d 635 (MDNC 2005); *Yasui v. Maui Electric Co.*, 78 F.Supp.2d 1124 (D. Hawaii 1999); *Royal Palace Hotel Associates v. International Resort Classics*, 178 FRD 595 (MD Fl. 1998); *Cody v. Private Agencies Collaborating Together, Inc.*, 911 F.Supp. 1 (D.D.C. 1995); *Corsair Asset Management, Inc. v. Moskovitz*,

142 FRD 347 (ND Ga 1992); In Re: Glacier Bay, 746 F.Supp. 1379 (D. Alaska 1990); *Hollenbeck v. Falstaff Brewing Corp.*, 605 F.Supp. 421 (ED Mo. 1984).

[46]*Wahl v. Carrier Manufacturing Co.*, 511 F.2d 209 (7th Cir. 1975); *Sun Media Systems, Inc. v. KDSM, LLC*, 587 F.Supp. 2d 1059 (S.D. Iowa 2008); In Re: Glacier Bay, 746 F.Supp. 1379 (D. Alaska 1990); *Hollenbeck v. Falstaff Brewing Corp.*, 605 F.Supp. 421 (ED Mo. 1984).

[47]*Nelson v. Darragh Co.*, 120 F.R.D. 517 (W.D. Ark. 1988); *Mallonee v. Fahey*, 117 F.Supp. 259 (S.D. Cal. 1953).

[48]*Marquez v. American Export Lines*, 41 FRD 386 (SDNY 1967).

[49]*Sierra Club v. EPA*, 769 F.2d 796 (DC Cir. 1985); In Re: Air Crash Disaster at John F. Kennedy International Airport on June 24, 1975, 687 F.2d 626 (2nd Cir. 1982); *Griffith v. Mt. Carmel Medical Center*, 157 F.R.D. 499 (D. Kansas 1994); *Radol v. Thomas*, 113 FRD 172 (SD Ohio 1986); *Marquez v. American Export Lines*, 41 FRD 386 (SDNY 1967).

[50]*Jensen v. Lawler*, 338 F.Supp. 2d 739 (SD Texas 2004).

[51]In Re: San Juan Dupont Plaza Hotel Fire Litigation, 142 F.R.D. 41 (D.P.R. 1992); *Parts & Electric Motors, Inc. v. Sterling Electric*, 123 FRD 584 (ND Ill. 1988).

[52]*Corsair Asset Management, Inc. v. Moskovitz*, 142 FRD 347 (ND Ga 1992)

[53]*Wahl v. Carrier Manufacturing Co.*, 511 F.2d 209 (7th Cir. 1975); *Hollenbeck v. Falstaff Brewing Corp.*, 605 F.Supp. 421 (ED Mo. 1984).

[54]*Buchanan v. Stanships, Inc.*, 485 U.S. 265 (1988); *Reger v. The Nemours Foundation*, 599 F.3d 285 (3d Cir. 2010); In re: Paoli Railroad Yard PCB Litigation, 221 F.3d 449 (3d Cir. 2000).

[55]*Delta Air Lines, Inc. v. August*, 450 U.S. 346, 353 (1981).

[56]*Reger v. The Nemours Foundation*, 599 F.3d 285 (3d Cir. 2010); In re: Paoli Railroad Yard PCB Litigation, 221 F.3d 449 (3d Cir. 2000); *Abrams v. Lightolier, Inc.*, 50 F.3d 1204 (3d Cir. 1995); *Smith v. SEPTA*, 47 F.3d 97 (3d Cir. 1995); *Friedman v. Ganassi*, 853 F.2d 207 (3d Cir. 1988); *Institutionalized Juveniles v. Secretary of Public Welfare*, 758 F.2d 897 (3d Cir. 1985); *Pearlstine v. United States*, 649 F.2d 194 (3rd Cir. 1981); *Delaney v. Capone*, 642 F.2d 57 (3d Cir. 1981); *Samuel v. University of Pittsburgh*, 538 F.2d 991 (3d Cir. 1976); *ADM Corp. v. Speedmaster Packing Corp.*, 525 F.2d 662 (3d Cir. 1975); *City of Rome, Italy v. Glanton*, 184 F.R.D. 547 (E.D. Pa. 1999); *Greene v. Fraternal Order of Police*, 183 F.R.D. 445 (E.D. Pa. 1998); *Action Alliance for Senior Citizens of Greater Philadelphia v. Shapp*, 74 F.R.D. 617 (E.D. Pa. 1977).

[57]*Buchanan v. Stanships, Inc.*, 485 U.S. 265, 268 (1988)(emphasis added). Accord, *Delta Air Lines, Inc. v. August*, 450 U.S. 346 (1981). See, also, *Reger v. The Nemours Foundation*, 599 F.3d 285 (3d Cir. 2010); In re: Paoli Railroad Yard PCB Litigation, 221 F.3d 449 (3d Cir. 2000); *Abrams v. Lightolier, Inc.*, 50 F.3d 1204 (3d Cir. 1995); *Smith v. SEPTA*, 47 F.3d 97 (3d Cir. 1995); *Friedman v. Ganassi*, 853 F.2d 207 (3d Cir. 1988); *Institutionalized Juveniles v. Secretary of Public Welfare*, 758 F.2d 897 (3d Cir. 1985); *Pearlstine v. United States*, 649 F.2d 194 (3rd Cir. 1981); *Delaney v. Capone*, 642 F. 2d 57 (3d Cir. 1981); *Samuel v. University of Pittsburgh*, 538 F.2d 991 (3d Cir. 1976); *ADM Corp. v. Speedmaster Packing Corp.*, 525 F.2d 662 (3d Cir. 1975); *City of Rome, Italy v. Glanton*, 184 F.R.D. 547 (E.D. Pa. 1999); *Greene v. Fraternal Order of Police*, 183 F.R.D. 445 (E.D. Pa. 1998); *Action Alliance for Senior Citizens of Greater Philadelphia v. Shapp*, 74 F.R.D. 617 (E.D. Pa. 1977).

[58]*Buchanan v. Stanships, Inc.*, 485 U.S. 265 (1988); *Delta Air Lines, Inc. v. August*, 450 U.S. 346 (1981). Accord, *Reger v. The Nemours Foundation*, 599 F.3d 285 (3d Cir. 2010); In re: Paoli Railroad Yard PCB Litigation, 221 F.3d 449 (3d Cir. 2000); *Abrams v. Lightolier, Inc.*, 50 F.3d 1204 (3d Cir. 1995); *Smith v. SEPTA*, 47 F.3d 97 (3d Cir. 1995); *Friedman v. Ganassi*, 853 F.2d 207 (3d Cir. 1988); *Institutionalized Juveniles v. Secretary of Public Welfare*, 758 F.2d 897 (3d Cir. 1985); *Pearlstine v. United States*, 649 F.2d 194 (3rd Cir. 1981); *Delaney v. Capone*, 642 F.2d 57 (3d Cir. 1981); *Samuel v. University of Pittsburgh*, 538 F.2d 991 (3d Cir. 1976); *ADM Corp. v. Speedmaster Packing Corp.*, 525 F.2d 662 (3d Cir. 1975); *City of Rome, Italy v. Glanton*, 184 F.R.D. 547 (E.D. Pa. 1999); *Greene v. Fraternal Order of Police*, 183 F.R.D. 445 (E.D. Pa. 1998); *Action Alliance for Senior Citizens of Greater Philadelphia v. Shapp*, 74 F.R.D. 617 (E.D. Pa. 1977).

[59]*Brazos Valley Coalition for Life, Inc. v. City of Bryan, Texas*, 421 F.3d 314 (5th Cir. 2005); *Trepel v. Roadway Express, Inc.*, 266 F.3d 418 (6th Cir. 2001); *Holmes v. Cessna Aircraft Co.*, 11 F.3d 63 (5th Cir. 1994); *Dovenmuehle v. Gilldorn Mortgage Midwest Corp.*, 871 F.2d 697 (7th Cir. 1989); *Mason v. Belieu*, 543 F.2d 215 (D.C. Cir. 1976); *Wahl v. Carrier Manufacturing Co.*, 511 F.2d 209 (7th Cir. 1975); *McInnis v. Town of Weston*, 458 F.Supp.2d 7 (D. Conn. 2006); *Sullivan v. Cheshier*, 991 F.Supp. 999 (N.D. Ill. 1998); *Hollenbeck v. Falstaff Brewing Corp.*, 605 F.Supp. 421 (E.D. Mo. 1984); *Morrisey v. County Tower Corp.*, 568 F.Supp. 980 (E.D. Mo. 1983).

[60]In Re: Kulicke & Soffa Industries Inc. Securities Litigation, 747 F.Supp. 1136 (E.D.Pa. 1990), aff'd, 944 F.2d 897 (3rd Cir. 1991); *ADM Corp. v. Speedmaster Packing Corp.*, 525 F.2d 662 (3d Cir. 1975); *Nugget Distributors Cooperative of America v. Mr. Nugget, Inc.*, 145 F.R. D. 54 (E.D.Pa. 1992). Accord, *Charter Medical Corp v. Cardin*, 127 F. R.D. 111 (D. Maryland 1989); *Women's Federal Savings and Loan Association of Cleveland v. Nevada National Bank*, 108 F.R.D. 396 (D. Nevada 1985); *International Wood Processors v. Power Dry, Inc.*, 598 F. Supp. 299 (D.S. C. 1984); *Morrissey v. County Tower Corp.*, 568 F.Supp. 178 (ED Mo. 1983).

[61]*Delta Air Lines, Inc. v. August*, 450 U.S. 346 (1981); *Reger v. The Nemours Foundation*, 599 F.3d 285 (3d Cir. 2010); *Abrams v. Lightolier, Inc.*, 50 F.3d 1204 (3d Cir. 1995); *Smith v. SEPTA*, 47 F.3d 97 (3d Cir.

1995); *Friedman v. Ganassi*, 853 F.2d 207 (3d Cir. 1988); *Institutionalized Juveniles v. Secretary of Public Welfare*, 758 F.2d 897 (3rd Cir. 1985); *Pearlstine v. United States*, 649 F.2d 194 (3rd Cir. 1981); *Delaney v. Capone*, 642 F.2d 57 (3d Cir. 1981); *Samuel v. University of Pittsburgh*, 538 F.2d 991 (3d Cir. 1976); *ADM Corp. v. Speedmaster Packing Corp.*, 525 F.2d 662 (3d Cir. 1975); *Greene v. Fraternal Order of Police*, 183 F.R.D. 445 (E.D.Pa. 1998). Accord, In Re: Air Crash Disaster at John F. Kennedy International Airport on June 24, 1975, 687 F.2d 626 (2nd Cir. 1982); In Re: Glacier Bay, 746 F.Supp. 1379 (D. Alaska 1990).

62*Chambers v. NASCO, Inc.*, 501 U.S. 32 (1991); *Alyeska Pipeline Service Co. v. Wilderness Society*, 421 U.S. 240 (1975).

63*Reger v. The Nemours Foundation*, 599 F.3d 285 (3d Cir. 2010); In re: Paoli Railroad Yard PCB Litigation, 221 F.3d 449 (3d Cir. 2000); *Friedman v. Ganassi*, 853 F.2d 207 (3d Cir. 1988); *Adams v. Teamsters Local 115*, 678 F.Supp.2d 314 (E.D. Pa. 2007); *Montgomery County v. Microvote Corp.*, 2004 WL 1087196 (EDPA 2004); *Greene v. Fraternal Order of Police*, 183 F.R.D. 445 (E.D.Pa. 1998). Accord, *McGuigan v. CAE Link Corp.*, 155 F.R.D. 31 (NDNY 1994).

64*Reger v. The Nemours Foundation*, 599 F.3d 285 (3d Cir. 2010); *Smith v. SEPTA*, 47 F.3d 97 (3d Cir. 1995); *Friedman v. Ganassi*, 853 F.2d 207 (3d Cir. 1988); *Institutionalized Juveniles v. Secretary of Public Welfare*, 758 F.2d 897, 926 (3rd Cir. 1985); *Pearlstine v. United States*, 649 F.2d 194 (3rd Cir. 1981); *Delaney v. Capone*, 642 F.2d 57 (3d Cir. 1981); *Samuel v. University of Pittsburgh*, 538 F.2d 991 (3d Cir. 1976); *ADM Corp. v. Speedmaster Packing Corp.*, 525 F.2d 662 (3d Cir. 1975); *Adams v. Teamsters Local 115*, 678 F.Supp.2d 314 (E.D. Pa. 2007).

65*Reger v. The Nemours Foundation*, 599 F.3d 285 (3d Cir. 2010).

66*Reger v. The Nemours Foundation*, 599 F.3d 285 (3d Cir. 2010); *Friedman v. Ganassi*, 853 F.2d 207 (3d Cir. 1988); *Pearlstine v. United States*, 649 F.2d 194 (3rd Cir. 1981); *ADM Corp. v. Speedmaster Packaging Corp.*, 525 F.2d 662, (3rd Cir. 1975); *Adams v. Teamsters Local 115*, 678 F.Supp.2d 314 (E.D. Pa. 2007). Accord, In Re Olympia Brewing Co. Securities Litigation, 613 F.Supp. 1286, 1302 (N.D.Ill. 1985).

67*Reger v. The Nemours Foundation*, 599 F.3d 285 (3d Cir. 2010).

68*Thomas v. Duralite Co., Inc.*, 524 F.2d 577 (3rd Cir. 1975). Accord, *Dail v. George A. Arab, Inc.*, 391 F.Supp. 2d 1142 (M.D. Fla 2005); *DiCecco v. The Dillard House, Inc.*, 149 F.R.D. 239 (N.D.Ga. 1993); *Frigiquip Corp. v. Parker–Hannifin Corp.*, 75 F.R.D. 605 (W.D. Okla. 1977).

69See, Federal Rule of Civil Procedure 54(d)(1).

70*Buchanan v. Stanships, Inc.*, 485 U.S. 265 (1988); *Samaad v. City of Dallas*, 922 F.2d 216 (5th Cir. 1991).

71*Reger v. The Nemours Foundation*, 599 F.3d 285, 289 Footnote 3 (3d Cir. 2010) (emphasis added).

72*Delta Air Lines, Inc. v. August*, 450 U.S. 346, 353 (1981).

73*Reger v. The Nemours Foundation*, 599 F.3d 285 (3d Cir. 2010); In re: Paoli Railroad Yard PCB Litigation, 221 F.3d 449 (3d Cir. 2000); *Abrams v. Lightolier, Inc.*, 50 F.3d 1204 (3d Cir. 1995); *Smith v. SEPTA*, 47 F.3d 97 (3d Cir. 1995); *Friedman v. Ganassi*, 853 F.2d 207 (3d Cir. 1988); *Institutionalized Juveniles v. Secretary of Public Welfare*, 758 F.2d 897 (3d Cir. 1985); *Pearlstine v. United States*, 649 F.2d 194 (3rd Cir. 1981); *Delaney v. Capone*, 642 F.2d 57 (3d Cir. 1981); *Samuel v. University of Pittsburgh*, 538 F.2d 991 (3d Cir. 1976); *ADM Corp. v. Speedmaster Packing Corp.*, 525 F.2d 662 (3d Cir. 1975); *City of Rome, Italy v. Glanton*, 184 F.R.D. 547 (E.D. Pa. 1999); *Greene v. Fraternal Order of Police*, 183 F.R.D. 445 (E.D. Pa. 1998); *Action Alliance for Senior Citizens of Greater Philadelphia v. Shapp*, 74 F.R.D. 617 (E.D. Pa. 1977).

74*Buchanan v. Stanships, Inc.*, 485 U.S. 265, 268 (1988)(emphasis added). Accord, *Delta Air Lines, Inc. v. August*, 450 U.S. 346 (1981).

75*Buchanan v. Stanships, Inc.*, 485 U.S. 265 (1988); *Delta Air Lines, Inc. v. August*, 450 U.S. 346 (1981); *Reger v. The Nemours Foundation*, 599 F.3d 285 (3d Cir. 2010); In re: Paoli Railroad Yard PCB Litigation, 221 F.3d 449 (3d Cir. 2000); *Abrams v. Lightolier, Inc.*, 50 F.3d 1204 (3d Cir. 1995); *Smith v. SEPTA*, 47 F.3d 97 (3d Cir. 1995); *Friedman v. Ganassi*, 853 F.2d 207 (3d Cir. 1988); *Institutionalized Juveniles v. Secretary of Public Welfare*, 758 F.2d 897 (3d Cir. 1985); *Pearlstine v. United States*, 649 F.2d 194 (3rd Cir. 1981); *Delaney v. Capone*, 642 F.2d 57 (3d Cir. 1981); *Samuel v. University of Pittsburgh*, 538 F.2d 991 (3d Cir. 1976); *ADM Corp. v. Speedmaster Packing Corp.*, 525 F.2d 662 (3d Cir. 1975); *City of Rome, Italy v. Glanton*, 184 F.R.D. 547 (E.D. Pa. 1999); *Greene v. Fraternal Order of Police*, 183 F.R.D. 445 (E.D. Pa. 1998); *Action Alliance for Senior Citizens of Greater Philadelphia v. Shapp*, 74 F.R.D. 617 (E.D. Pa. 1977).

76*Reger v. The Nemours Foundation*, 599 F.3d 285 (3d Cir. 2010); In re: Paoli Railroad Yard PCB Litigation, 221 F.3d 449 (3d Cir. 2000); *Smith v. SEPTA*, 47 F.3d 97 (3d Cir. 1995); *Friedman v. Ganassi*, 853 F.2d 207 (3d Cir. 1988); *Adams v. Teamsters Local 115*, 678 F.Supp.2d 314 (E.D. Pa. 2007); *Action Alliance for Senior Citizens of Greater Philadelphia v. Shapp*, 74 F.R.D. 617 (ED Pa. 1977). Accord, *Matthew v. Crosby*, 480 F.3d 1265 (11th Cir. 2007); *Weaver v. Toombs*, 948 F.2d 1004 (6th Cir. 1991); *Perry v. Metro Suburban Bus Authority*, 236 FRD 110 (EDNY 2006).

77*Reger v. The Nemours Foundation*, 599 F.3d 285 (3d Cir. 2010); *Adams v. Teamsters Local 115*, 678 F.Supp.2d 314 (E.D. Pa. 2007); *Action Alliance for Senior Citizens of Greater Philadelphia v. Shapp*, 74 F.R.D. 617 (ED Pa. 1977).

78*Reger v. The Nemours Foundation*, 599 F.3d 285 (3d Cir. 2010); In re: Paoli Railroad Yard PCB Litigation, 221 F.3d 449 (3d Cir. 2000); *Adams v. Teamsters Local 115*, 678 F.Supp.2d 314 (E.D. Pa. 2007); *Greene v. Fraternal Order of Police*, 183 F.R.D. 445 (ED Pa. 1998).

[79]*Adams v. Teamsters Local 115*, 678 F.Supp.2d 314 (E.D. Pa. 2007). <u>Accord,</u> *Washington v. Patlis*, 916 F.2d 1036 (5th Cir. 1990); *Chevrette v. Marks*, 558 F.Supp. 1133 (M.D. Pa. 1983).

[80]*Constitution Bank v. Tubbs*, 68 F.3d 685 (3rd Cir. 1995).

[81]*Association of St. Croix Condominium Owners v. St. Croix Hotel Corp.*, 682 F.2d 446 (3rd Cir 1982).

[82]*Franklin Savings Association v. Office of Thrift Supervision*, 31 F.3d 1020 (10th Cir. 1994); *Aerotech Resources Inc. v. Dodson Aviation, Inc.*, 237 F.R.D. 659 (D. Kansas 2005).

[83]*Maritime Electric Co. v. United Jersey Bank*, 959 F.2d 1194, 1205 (3rd Cir. 1991) (emphasis added). <u>See, also,</u> *Jefferson Ward Stores, Inc. v. Doody Co.*, 48 BR 276 (ED Pa 1985). <u>Accord,</u> *Farley v. Henson*, 2 F.3d 273 (8th Cir. 1993); *Martin–Trigona v. Champion Federal Savings and Loan Association*, 892 F.2d 575 (7th Cir. 1989); *Carley Capital Group v. Fireman's Fund Insurance Co.*, 889 F.2d 1126 (DC Cir 1989).

[84]*Reger v. The Nemours Foundation*, 599 F.3d 285, 289 (3d Cir. 2010)(emphasis added).

[85]*Reger v. The Nemours Foundation*, 599 F.3d 285 (3d Cir. 2010)(emphasis added).

[86]*Buchanan v. Stanships, Inc.*, 485 U.S. 265 (1988). <u>Accord,</u> *Samaad v. City of Dallas*, 922 F.2d 216 (5th Cir. 1991).

[87]*Reger v. The Nemours Foundation*, 599 F.3d 285 (3d Cir. 2010); <u>In re: Paoli Railroad Yard PCB Litigation,</u> 221 F.3d 449 (3d Cir. 2000); *Abrams v. Lightolier, Inc.*, 50 F.3d 1204 (3d Cir. 1995); *Smith v. SEPTA*, 47 F.3d 97 (3d Cir. 1995); *Friedman v. Ganassi*, 853 F.2d 207 (3d Cir. 1988); *Institutionalized Juveniles v. Secretary of Public Welfare*, 758 F.2d 897 (3d Cir. 1985); *Pearlstine v. United States*, 649 F.2d 194 (3rd Cir. 1981); *Delaney v. Capone*, 642 F.2d 57 (3d Cir. 1981); *Samuel v. University of Pittsburgh*, 538 F.2d 991 (3d Cir. 1976); *ADM Corp. v. Speedmaster Packing Corp.*, 525 F.2d 662 (3d Cir. 1975); *Adams v. Teamsters Local 115*, 678 F.Supp.2d 314 (E.D. Pa. 2007); *City of Rome, Italy v. Glanton*, 184 F.R.D. 547 (E.D. Pa. 1999); *Greene v. Fraternal Order of Police*, 183 F.R.D. 445 (E.D. Pa. 1998); *Action Alliance for Senior Citizens of Greater Philadelphia v. Shapp*, 74 F.R.D. 617 (E.D. Pa. 1977).

[88]*Buchanan v. Stanships, Inc.*, 485 U.S. 265, 268 (1988)(emphasis added). <u>Accord,</u> *Delta Air Lines, Inc. v. August*, 450 U.S. 346 (1981). <u>See, also,</u> *Reger v. The Nemours Foundation*, 599 F.3d 285 (3d Cir. 2010); <u>In re: Paoli Railroad Yard PCB Litigation,</u> 221 F.3d 449 (3d Cir. 2000); *Abrams v. Lightolier, Inc.*, 50 F.3d 1204 (3d Cir. 1995); *Smith v. SEPTA*, 47 F.3d 97 (3d Cir. 1995); *Friedman v. Ganassi*, 853 F.2d 207 (3d Cir. 1988); *Institutionalized Juveniles v. Secretary of Public Welfare*, 758 F.2d 897 (3d Cir. 1985); *Pearlstine v. United States*, 649 F.2d 194 (3rd Cir. 1981); *Delaney v. Capone*, 642 F. 2d 57 (3d Cir. 1981); *Samuel v. University of Pittsburgh*, 538 F.2d 991 (3d Cir. 1976); *ADM Corp. v. Speedmaster Packing Corp.*, 525 F.2d 662 (3d Cir. 1975); *City of Rome, Italy v. Glanton*, 184 F.R.D. 547 (E.D. Pa. 1999); *Greene v. Fraternal Order of Police*, 183 F.R.D. 445 (E.D. Pa. 1998); *Action Alliance for Senior Citizens of Greater Philadelphia v. Shapp*, 74 F.R.D. 617 (E.D. Pa. 1977).

[89]*Buchanan v. Stanships, Inc.*, 485 U.S. 265 (1988); *Delta Air Lines, Inc. v. August*, 450 U.S. 346 (1981). <u>Accord,</u> *Reger v. The Nemours Foundation*, 599 F.3d 285 (3d Cir. 2010); <u>In re: Paoli Railroad Yard PCB Litigation,</u> 221 F.3d 449 (3d Cir. 2000); *Abrams v. Lightolier, Inc.*, 50 F.3d 1204 (3d Cir. 1995); *Smith v. SEPTA*, 47 F.3d 97 (3d Cir. 1995); *Friedman v. Ganassi*, 853 F.2d 207 (3d Cir. 1988); *Institutionalized Juveniles v. Secretary of Public Welfare*, 758 F.2d 897 (3d Cir. 1985); *Pearlstine v. United States*, 649 F.2d 194 (3rd Cir. 1981); *Delaney v. Capone*, 642 F.2d 57 (3d Cir. 1981); *Samuel v. University of Pittsburgh*, 538 F.2d 991 (3d Cir. 1976); *ADM Corp. v. Speedmaster Packing Corp.*, 525 F.2d 662 (3d Cir. 1975); *City of Rome, Italy v. Glanton*, 184 F.R.D. 547 (E.D. Pa. 1999); *Greene v. Fraternal Order of Police*, 183 F.R.D. 445 (E.D. Pa. 1998); *Action Alliance for Senior Citizens of Greater Philadelphia v. Shapp*, 74 F.R.D. 617 (E.D. Pa. 1977).

[90]*Brazos Valley Coalition for Life, Inc. v. City of Bryan, Texas*, 421 F.3d 314 (5th Cir. 2005); *Trepel v. Roadway Express, Inc.*, 266 F.3d 418 (6th Cir. 2001); *Holmes v. Cessna Aircraft Co.*, 11 F.3d 63 (5th Cir. 1994); *Dovenmuehle v. Gilldorn Mortgage Midwest Corp.*, 871 F.2d 697 (7th Cir. 1989); *Mason v. Belieu*, 543 F.2d 215 (D.C. Cir. 1976); *Wahl v. Carrier Manufacturing Co.*, 511 F.2d 209 (7th Cir. 1975); *McInnis v. Town of Weston*, 458 F.Supp.2d 7 (D. Conn. 2006); *Sullivan v. Cheshier*, 991 F.Supp. 999 (N.D. Ill. 1998); *Hollenbeck v. Falstaff Brewing Corp.*, 605 F.Supp. 421 (E.D. Mo. 1984); *Morrissey v. County Tower Corp.*, 568 F.Supp. 980 (E.D. Mo. 1983).

[91]<u>In Re: Kulicke & Soffa Industries Inc. Securities Litigation</u>, 747 F.Supp. 1136 (E.D.Pa. 1990), aff'd, 944 F.2d 897 (3rd Cir. 1991); *ADM Corp. v. Speedmaster Packing Corp.*, 525 F.2d 662 (3d Cir. 1975); *Nugget Distributors Cooperative of America v. Mr. Nugget, Inc.*, 145 F. R. D. 54 (E.D.Pa. 1992). <u>Accord,</u> *Charter Medical Corp v. Cardin*, 127 F. R.D. 111 (D. Maryland 1989); *Women's Federal Savings and Loan Association of Cleveland v. Nevada National Bank*, 108 F.R.D. 396 (D. Nevada 1985); *International Wood Processors v. Power Dry, Inc.*, 598 F. Supp. 299 (D.S. C. 1984); *Morrissey v. County Tower Corp.*, 568 F.Supp. 178 (ED Mo. 1983).

[92]*Reger v. The Nemours Foundation*, 599 F.3d 285, 289 Footnote 3 (3d Cir. 2010) (emphasis added).

[93]*Reger v. The Nemours Foundation*, 599 F.3d 285 (3d Cir. 2010); *Friedman v. Ganassi*, 853 F.2d 207 (3d Cir. 1988). <u>Accord,</u> *McGuigan v. CAE Link Corp.*, 155 F.R.D. 31 (NDNY 1994).

[94]*Maldonado v. Parasole*, 66 F.R.D. 388,390 (EDNY 1975). <u>Accord,</u> *Buchanan v. Stanships, Inc.*, 485 U.S. 265 (1988); *Reger v. The Nemours Foundation*, 599 F.3d 285 (3d Cir. 2010); <u>In re: Paoli Railroad Yard PCB Litigation,</u> 221 F.3d 449 (3d Cir. 2000); *Smith v. SEPTA*, 47 F.3d 97 (3d Cir. 1995); *Friedman v. Ganassi*, 853 F.2d 207 (3d Cir. 1988); *Greene v. Fraternal Order of Police*, 183 F.R.D. 445 (ED Pa. 1998). <u>See, also,</u> *McGuigan v. Cae Lank Corp.*, 155 F.R.D. 31 (NDNY 1994); *Phillips v. Cameron Tool Corp.*, 131 F.R.D. 151 (SD Ind. 1990).

[95]*Friedman v. Ganassi*, 853 F.2d 207 (3d Cir. 1988). See, also, *Popeil Brothers v. Schick Electric*, 516 F.2d 772 (7th Cir. 1975); *McGuigan v. Cae Lank Corp.*, 155 F.R.D. 31 (NDNY 1994); *Phillips v. Cameron Tool Corp.*, 131 F.R.D. 151 (S D. Ind. 1990); *Maldonado v. Parasole*, 66 F.R.D. 388,390 (EDNY 1975).

[96]*Buchanan v. Stanships, Inc.*, 485 U.S. 265 (1988); *Reger v. The Nemours Foundation*, 599 F.3d 285 (3d Cir. 2010). Accord, *Samaad v. City of Dallas*, 922 F.2d 216 (5th Cir. 1991).

[97]*Buchanan v. Stanships, Inc.*, 485 U.S. 265 (1988); *Reger v. The Nemours Foundation*, 599 F.3d 285 (3d Cir. 2010); In re: Paoli Railroad Yard PCB Litigation, 221 F.3d 449 (3d Cir. 2000); *Smith v. SEPTA*, 47 F.3d 97 (3d Cir. 1995); *Friedman v. Ganassi*, 853 F.2d 207 (3d Cir. 1988); *Greene v. Fraternal Order of Police*, 183 F.R.D. 445 (ED Pa. 1998). Accord, *McGuigan v. Cae Lank Corp.*, 155 F.R.D. 31 (NDNY 1994); *Phillips v. Cameron Tool Corp.*, 131 F.R.D. 151 (S.D. Ind. 1990); *Maldonado v. Parasole*, 66 F.R.D. 388,390 (EDNY 1975).

[98]*Reger v. The Nemours Foundation*, 599 F.3d 285 (3d Cir. 2010); In re: Paoli Railroad Yard PCB Litigation, 221 F.3d 449 (3d Cir. 2000); *Abrams v. Lightolier, Inc.*, 50 F.3d 1204 (3d Cir. 1995); *Smith v. SEPTA*, 47 F.3d 97 (3d Cir. 1995); *Friedman v. Ganassi*, 853 F.2d 207 (3d Cir. 1988); *Institutionalized Juveniles v. Secretary of Public Welfare*, 758 F.2d 897 (3d Cir. 1985); *Pearlstine v. United States*, 649 F.2d 194 (3rd Cir. 1981); *Delaney v. Capone*, 642 F.2d 57 (3d Cir. 1981); *Samuel v. University of Pittsburgh*, 538 F.2d 991 (3d Cir. 1976); *ADM Corp. v. Speedmaster Packing Corp.*, 525 F.2d 662 (3d Cir. 1975); *Adams v. Teamsters Local 115*, 678 F.Supp.2d 314 (E.D. Pa. 2007); *City of Rome, Italy v. Glanton*, 184 F.R.D. 547 (E.D. Pa. 1999); *Greene v. Fraternal Order of Police*, 183 F.R.D. 445 (E.D. Pa. 1998); *Action Alliance for Senior Citizens of Greater Philadelphia v. Shapp*, 74 F.R.D. 617 (E.D. Pa. 1977).

[99]*Buchanan v. Stanships, Inc.*, 485 U.S. 265, 268 (1988)(emphasis added). Accord, *Delta Air Lines, Inc. v. August*, 450 U.S. 346 (1981). See, also, *Reger v. The Nemours Foundation*, 599 F.3d 285 (3d Cir. 2010); In re: Paoli Railroad Yard PCB Litigation, 221 F.3d 449 (3d Cir. 2000); *Abrams v. Lightolier, Inc.*, 50 F.3d 1204 (3d Cir. 1995); *Smith v. SEPTA*, 47 F.3d 97 (3d Cir. 1995); *Friedman v. Ganassi*, 853 F.2d 207 (3d Cir. 1988); *Institutionalized Juveniles v. Secretary of Public Welfare*, 758 F.2d 897 (3d Cir. 1985); *Pearlstine v. United States*, 649 F.2d 194 (3rd Cir. 1981); *Delaney v. Capone*, 642 F. 2d 57 (3d Cir. 1981); *Samuel v. University of Pittsburgh*, 538 F.2d 991 (3d Cir. 1976); *ADM Corp. v. Speedmaster Packing Corp.*, 525 F.2d 662 (3d Cir. 1975); *City of Rome, Italy v. Glanton*, 184 F.R.D. 547 (E.D. Pa. 1999); *Greene v. Fraternal Order of Police*, 183 F.R.D. 445 (E.D. Pa. 1998); *Action Alliance for Senior Citizens of Greater Philadelphia v. Shapp*, 74 F.R.D. 617 (E.D. Pa. 1977).

[100]*Buchanan v. Stanships, Inc.*, 485 U.S. 265 (1988); *Delta Air Lines, Inc. v. August*, 450 U.S. 346 (1981). Accord, *Reger v. The Nemours Foundation*, 599 F.3d 285 (3d Cir. 2010); In re: Paoli Railroad Yard PCB Litigation, 221 F.3d 449 (3d Cir. 2000); *Abrams v. Lightolier, Inc.*, 50 F.3d 1204 (3d Cir. 1995); *Smith v. SEPTA*, 47 F.3d 97 (3d Cir. 1995); *Friedman v. Ganassi*, 853 F.2d 207 (3d Cir. 1988); *Institutionalized Juveniles v. Secretary of Public Welfare*, 758 F.2d 897 (3d Cir. 1985); *Pearlstine v. United States*, 649 F.2d 194 (3rd Cir. 1981); *Delaney v. Capone*, 642 F.2d 57 (3d Cir. 1981); *Samuel v. University of Pittsburgh*, 538 F.2d 991 (3d Cir. 1976); *ADM Corp. v. Speedmaster Packing Corp.*, 525 F.2d 662 (3d Cir. 1975); *City of Rome, Italy v. Glanton*, 184 F.R.D. 547 (E.D. Pa. 1999); *Greene v. Fraternal Order of Police*, 183 F.R.D. 445 (E.D. Pa. 1998); *Action Alliance for Senior Citizens of Greater Philadelphia v. Shapp*, 74 F.R.D. 617 (E.D. Pa. 1977).

[101]*Brazos Valley Coalition for Life, Inc. v. City of Bryan, Texas*, 421 F.3d 314 (5th Cir. 2005); *Trepel v. Roadway Express, Inc.*, 266 F.3d 418 (6th Cir. 2001); *Holmes v. Cessna Aircraft Co.*, 11 F.3d 63 (5th Cir. 1994); *Dovenmuehle v. Gilldorn Mortgage Midwest Corp.*, 871 F.2d 697 (7th Cir. 1989); *Mason v. Belieu*, 543 F.2d 215 (D.C. Cir. 1976); *Wahl v. Carrier Manufacturing Co.*, 511 F.2d 209 (7th Cir. 1975); *McInnis v. Town of Weston*, 458 F.Supp.2d 7 (D. Conn. 2006); *Sullivan v. Cheshier*, 991 F.Supp. 999 (N.D. Ill. 1998); *Hollenbeck v. Falstaff Brewing Corp.*, 605 F.Supp. 421 (E.D. Mo. 1984); *Morrissey v. County Tower Corp.*, 568 F.Supp. 980 (E.D. Mo. 1983).

[102]In Re: Kulicke & Soffa Industries Inc. Securities Litigation, 747 F.Supp. 1136 (E.D.Pa. 1990), aff'd, 944 F.2d 897 (3rd Cir. 1991); *ADM Corp. v. Speedmaster Packing Corp.*, 525 F.2d 662 (3d Cir. 1975); *Nugget Distributors Cooperative of America v. Mr. Nugget, Inc.*, 145 F.R. D. 54 (E.D.Pa. 1992). Accord, *Charter Medical Corp v. Cardin*, 127 F. R.D. 111 (D. Maryland 1989); *Women's Federal Savings and Loan Association of Cleveland v. Nevada National Bank*, 108 F.R.D. 396 (D. Nevada 1985); *International Wood Processors v. Power Dry, Inc.*, 598 F. Supp. 299 (D.S. C. 1984); *Morrissey v. County Tower Corp.*, 568 F.Supp. 178 (ED Mo. 1983).

[103]*Reger v. The Nemours Foundation*, 599 F.3d 285, 289 Footnote 3 (3d Cir. 2010) (emphasis added).

[104]*Buchanan v. Stanships, Inc.*, 485 U.S. 265 (1988); *Reger v. The Nemours Foundation*, 599 F.3d 285 (3d Cir. 2010). Accord, *Samaad v. City of Dallas*, 922 F.2d 216 (5th Cir. 1991).

[105]*Buchanan v. Stanships, Inc.*, 485 U.S. 265 (1988); *Reger v. The Nemours Foundation*, 599 F.3d 285 (3d Cir. 2010); In re: Paoli Railroad Yard PCB Litigation, 221 F.3d 449 (3d Cir. 2000); *Smith v. SEPTA*, 47 F.3d 97 (3d Cir. 1995); *Friedman v. Ganassi*, 853 F.2d 207 (3d Cir. 1988); *Greene v. Fraternal Order of Police*, 183 F.R.D. 445 (ED Pa. 1998). Accord, *McGuigan v. Cae Lank Corp.*, 155 F.R.D. 31 (NDNY 1994); *Phillips v. Cameron Tool Corp.*, 131 F.R.D. 151 (S D. Ind. 1990); *Maldonado v. Parasole*, 66 F.R.D. 388,390 (EDNY 1975).

[106]*Reger v. The Nemours Foundation*, 599 F.3d 285 (3d Cir. 2010); In re: Paoli Railroad Yard PCB Litigation, 221 F.3d 449 (3d Cir. 2000); *Abrams v. Lightolier, Inc.*, 50 F.3d 1204 (3d Cir. 1995); *Smith v. SEPTA*, 47 F.3d 97 (3d Cir. 1995); *Friedman v. Ganassi*, 853 F.2d 207 (3d Cir. 1988); *Institutionalized Juveniles v. Secretary of Public Welfare*, 758 F.2d 897 (3d Cir. 1985); *Pearlstine v. United States*, 649 F.2d 194 (3rd Cir. 1981); *Delaney v. Capone*, 642 F.2d 57 (3d Cir. 1981); *Samuel v. University of Pittsburgh*, 538

F.2d 991 (3d Cir. 1976); *ADM Corp. v. Speedmaster Packing Corp.*, 525 F.2d 662 (3d Cir. 1975); *Adams v. Teamsters Local 115*, 678 F.Supp.2d 314 (E.D. Pa. 2007); *City of Rome, Italy v. Glanton*, 184 F.R.D. 547 (E.D. Pa. 1999); *Greene v. Fraternal Order of Police*, 183 F.R.D. 445 (E.D. Pa. 1998); *Action Alliance for Senior Citizens of Greater Philadelphia v. Shapp*, 74 F.R.D. 617 (E.D. Pa. 1977).

[107]*Buchanan v. Stanships, Inc.*, 485 U.S. 265, 268 (1988)(emphasis added). Accord, *Delta Air Lines, Inc. v. August*, 450 U.S. 346 (1981). See, also, *Reger v. The Nemours Foundation*, 599 F.3d 285 (3d Cir. 2010); In re: Paoli Railroad Yard PCB Litigation, 221 F.3d 449 (3d Cir. 2000); *Abrams v. Lightolier, Inc.*, 50 F.3d 1204 (3d Cir. 1995); *Smith v. SEPTA*, 47 F.3d 97 (3d Cir. 1995); *Friedman v. Ganassi*, 853 F.2d 207 (3d Cir. 1988); *Institutionalized Juveniles v. Secretary of Public Welfare*, 758 F.2d 897 (3d Cir. 1985); *Pearlstine v. United States*, 649 F.2d 194 (3rd Cir. 1981); *Delaney v. Capone*, 642 F. 2d 57 (3d Cir. 1981); *Samuel v. University of Pittsburgh*, 538 F.2d 991 (3d Cir. 1976); *ADM Corp. v. Speedmaster Packing Corp.*, 525 F.2d 662 (3d Cir. 1975); *City of Rome, Italy v. Glanton*, 184 F.R.D. 547 (E.D. Pa. 1999); *Greene v. Fraternal Order of Police*, 183 F.R.D. 445 (E.D. Pa. 1998); *Action Alliance for Senior Citizens of Greater Philadelphia v. Shapp*, 74 F.R.D. 617 (E.D. Pa. 1977).

[108]*Buchanan v. Stanships, Inc.*, 485 U.S. 265 (1988); *Delta Air Lines, Inc. v. August*, 450 U.S. 346 (1981). Accord, *Reger v. The Nemours Foundation*, 599 F.3d 285 (3d Cir. 2010); In re: Paoli Railroad Yard PCB Litigation, 221 F.3d 449 (3d Cir. 2000); *Abrams v. Lightolier, Inc.*, 50 F.3d 1204 (3d Cir. 1995); *Smith v. SEPTA*, 47 F.2d 97 (3d Cir. 1995); *Friedman v. Ganassi*, 853 F.2d 207 (3d Cir. 1988); *Institutionalized Juveniles v. Secretary of Public Welfare*, 758 F.2d 897 (3d Cir. 1985); *Pearlstine v. United States*, 649 F.2d 194 (3rd Cir. 1981); *Delaney v. Capone*, 642 F.2d 57 (3d Cir. 1981); *Samuel v. University of Pittsburgh*, 538 F.2d 991 (3d Cir. 1976); *ADM Corp. v. Speedmaster Packing Corp.*, 525 F.2d 662 (3d Cir. 1975); *City of Rome, Italy v. Glanton*, 184 F.R.D. 547 (E.D. Pa. 1999); *Greene v. Fraternal Order of Police*, 183 F.R.D. 445 (E.D. Pa. 1998); *Action Alliance for Senior Citizens of Greater Philadelphia v. Shapp*, 74 F.R.D. 617 (E.D. Pa. 1977).

[109]*Brazos Valley Coalition for Life, Inc. v. City of Bryan, Texas*, 421 F.3d 314 (5th Cir. 2005); *Trepel v. Roadway Express, Inc.*, 266 F.3d 418 (6th Cir. 2001); *Holmes v. Cessna Aircraft Co.*, 11 F.3d 63 (5th Cir. 1994); *Dovenmuehle v. Gilldorn Mortgage Midwest Corp.*, 871 F.2d 697 (7th Cir. 1989); *Mason v. Belieu*, 543 F.2d 215 (D.C. Cir. 1976); *Wahl v. Carrier Manufacturing Co.*, 511 F.2d 209 (7th Cir. 1975); *McInnis v. Town of Weston*, 458 F.Supp.2d 7 (D. Conn. 2006); *Sullivan v. Cheshier*, 991 F.Supp. 999 (N.D. Ill. 1998); *Hollenbeck v. Falstaff Brewing Corp.*, 605 F.Supp. 421 (E.D. Mo. 1984); *Morrissey v. County Tower Corp.*, 568 F.Supp. 980 (E.D. Mo. 1983).

[110]In Re: Kulicke & Soffa Industries Inc. Securities Litigation, 747 F.Supp. 1136 (E.D.Pa. 1990), aff'd, 944 F.2d 897 (3rd Cir. 1991); *ADM Corp. v. Speedmaster Packing Corp.*, 525 F.2d 662 (3d Cir. 1975); *Nugget Distributors Cooperative of America v. Mr. Nugget, Inc.*, 145 F.R.D. 54 (E.D.Pa. 1992). Accord, *Charter Medical Corp v. Cardin*, 127 F. R.D. 111 (D. Maryland 1989); *Women's Federal Savings and Loan Association of Cleveland v. Nevada National Bank*, 108 F.R.D. 396 (D. Nevada 1985); *International Wood Processors v. Power Dry, Inc.*, 598 F. Supp. 299 (D.S. C. 1984); *Morrissey v. County Tower Corp.*, 568 F.Supp. 178 (ED Mo. 1983).

[111]*United States v. Hoffa*, 497 F.2d 294 (7th Cir. 1974); *Radol v. Thomas*, 113 F.R.D. 172 (SD Ohio 1986).

[112]*Radol v. Thomas*, 113 F.R.D. 172 (SD Ohio 1986).

[113]*Brown v. American Enka Corp.*, 452 F.Supp. 154 (ED Tenn. 1976).

[114]*Brown v. American Enka Corp.*, 452 F.Supp. 154 (ED Tenn. 1976).

[115]In re: Paoli Railroad Yard PCB Litigation, 221 F.3d 449 (3d Cir. 2000); *Institutionalized Juveniles v. Secretary of Public Welfare*, 758 F.2d 897, 926 (3rd Cir. 1985).

[116]In re: Paoli Railroad Yard PCB Litigation, 221 F.3d 449 (3d Cir. 2000); *Institutionalized Juveniles v. Secretary of Public Welfare*, 758 F.2d 897, 926 (3rd Cir. 1985).

[117]*ADM. Corp. v. Speedmaster Packaging Corp.*, 525 F.2d 662, 664 (3rd Cir. 1975).

[118]*Race Tires America, Inc. v. Hoosier Racing Tire Corp.*, 2012 WL 887593 (3d Cir. March 16, 2012).

[119]*Institutionalized Juveniles v. Secretary of Public Welfare*, 758 F.2d 897, 926 (3rd Cir. 1985).

[120]In re: Paoli Railroad Yard PCB Litigation, 221 F.3d 449 (3d Cir. 2000); *Institutionalized Juveniles v. Secretary of Public Welfare*, 758 F.2d 897, 926 (3rd Cir. 1985); *Montgomery County v. Microvote Corp.*, 2004 WL 1087196 (EDPA 2004); *Lacovara v. Merrill Lynch*, 102 F.R.D. 959 (ED Pa. 1984). Accord, *Zackaroff v. Koch Transfer Co.*, 862 F.2d 1263 (6th Cir. 1988); *First Community Traders, Inc. v. Heinold Commodities, Inc.*, 766 F.2d 1007 (7th Cir. 1985); *Friends for All Children v. Lockheed Aircraft Corp.*, 725 F.2d 1392 (DC Cir. 1984); *Superturf, Inc. v. Monsanto Co.*, 660 F.2d 1275 (8th Cir. 1981); *Jones v. Diamond*, 594 F.2d 997 (4th Cir. 1979); *U.S. v. Mitchell*, 580 F.2d 789 (5th Cir. 1978); *K–2 Ski Co. v. Head Ski Co.*, 506 F.2d 47 (9th Cir. 1974); *Garonzik v. Whitman Diner*, 910 F.Supp. 167 (D.N.J. 1995); *Weseloh–Hurtig v. Hepker*, 152 F.R.D. 198 (D. Kansas 1993); *Bruno v. Western Electric Co.*, 618 F.Supp. 398 (D. Colorado 1985); *Seber v. Daniels Transfer Co.*, 618 F.Supp. 1311 (W.D. Pa. 1985); *Wade v. Mississippi Cooperative Extension Service*, 64 F.R.D. 102 (N.D.Miss. 1974); *Sperry Rand Corp. v. A–T–O, Inc.*, 58 F.R.D. 132 (E.D.Va. 1973).

[121]In re: Paoli Railroad Yard PCB Litigation, 221 F.3d 449 (3d Cir. 2000); *Institutionalized Juveniles v. Secretary of Public Welfare*, 758 F.2d 897, 926 (3rd Cir. 1985).

[122]*Buchanan v. Stanships, Inc.*, 485 U.S. 265 (1988); *Samaad v. City of Dallas*, 922 F.2d 216 (5th Cir. 1991).

[123]*Buchanan v. Stanships, Inc.*, 485 U.S. 265, 268 (1988)(emphasis added). <u>Accord</u>, *Delta Air Lines, Inc. v. August*, 450 U.S. 346 (1981). <u>See, also</u>, *Reger v. The Nemours Foundation*, 599 F.3d 285 (3d Cir. 2010); In re: Paoli Railroad Yard PCB Litigation, 221 F.3d 449 (3d Cir. 2000); *Abrams v. Lightolier, Inc.*, 50 F.3d 1204 (3d Cir. 1995); *Smith v. SEPTA*, 47 F.3d 97 (3d Cir. 1995); *Friedman v. Ganassi*, 853 F.2d 207 (3d Cir. 1988); *Institutionalized Juveniles v. Secretary of Public Welfare*, 758 F.2d 897 (3d Cir. 1985); *Pearlstine v. United States*, 649 F.2d 194 (3rd Cir. 1981); *Delaney v. Capone*, 642 F. 2d 57 (3d Cir. 1981); *Samuel v. University of Pittsburgh*, 538 F.2d 991 (3d Cir. 1976); *ADM Corp. v. Speedmaster Packing Corp.*, 525 F.2d 662 (3d Cir. 1975); *City of Rome, Italy v. Glanton*, 184 F.R.D. 547 (E.D. Pa. 1999); *Greene v. Fraternal Order of Police*, 183 F.R.D. 445 (E.D. Pa. 1998); *Action Alliance for Senior Citizens of Greater Philadelphia v. Shapp*, 74 F.R.D. 617 (E.D. Pa. 1977).

[124]*Reger v. The Nemours Foundation*, 599 F.3d 285 (3d Cir. 2010); *Smith v. SEPTA*, 47 F.3d 97 (3d Cir. 1995); *Friedman v. Ganassi*, 853 F.2d 207 (3d Cir. 1988); *Institutionalized Juveniles v. Secretary of Public Welfare*, 758 F.2d 897, 926 (3rd Cir. 1985); *Pearlstine v. United States*, 649 F.2d 194 (3rd Cir. 1981); *Delaney v. Capone*, 642 F.2d 57 (3d Cir. 1981); *Samuel v. University of Pittsburgh*, 538 F.2d 991 (3d Cir. 1976); *ADM Corp. v. Speedmaster Packing Corp.*, 525 F.2d 662 (3d Cir. 1975).

[125]*Reger v. The Nemours Foundation*, 599 F.3d 285 (3d Cir. 2010).

[126]*Reger v. The Nemours Foundation*, 599 F.3d 285 (3d Cir. 2010).

[127]*Buchanan v. Stanships, Inc.*, 485 U.S. 265 (1988); *Samaad v. City of Dallas*, 922 F.2d 216 (5th Cir. 1991).

[128]*Institutionalized Juveniles v. Secretary of Public Welfare*, 758 F.2d 897, 911 (3rd Cir. 1985). The Third Circuit in Institutionalized Juveniles first applied this standard to attorney fees, and then held that it also applies to 28 U.S.C. § 1920 costs. <u>Accord</u>, *Montgomery County v. Microvote Corp.*, 2004 WL 1087196 (E.D.Pa. 2004).

[129]*Montgomery County v. Microvote Corp.*, 2004 WL 1087196 (E.D.Pa. 2004); *Greene v. Fraternal Order of Police*, 183 F.R.D. 445 (E.D. Pa. 1998); *Lacovara v. Merrill Lynch, Pierce, Fenner & Smith*, 102 F.R.D. 959 (E.D. Pa. 1984). <u>See, also</u>, *Hines v. Perez*, 242 F.2d 459 (9th Cir. 1957); *Garonzik v. Whitman Diner*, 910 F.Supp. 167 (D.N.J. 1995); *Sperry Rand Corp. v. A–T–O, Inc.*, 58 F.R.D. 132 (E.D.Va. 1973).

[130]*Institutionalized Juveniles v. Secretary of Public Welfare*, 758 F.2d 897, 910 (3rd Cir. 1985). The Third Circuit in Institutionalized Juveniles first applied this standard to attorney fees, and then held that it also applies to 28 U.S.C. § 1920 costs. <u>Accord</u>, *Montgomery County v. Microvote Corp.*, 2004 WL 1087196 (E.D.Pa. 2004).

[131]*Institutionalized Juveniles v. Secretary of Public Welfare*, 758 F.2d 897 (3rd Cir. 1985); *Montgomery County v. Microvote Corp.*, 2004 WL 1087196 (EDPA 2004); *Greene v. Fraternal Order of Police*, 183 F.R.D. 445 (ED Pa. 1998). <u>Accord</u>, *Roberts v. Interstate Distrib. Co.*, 242 F.Supp. 2d 850 (D. Oregon 2002); *Garonzik v. Whitman Diner*, 910 F.Supp. 167 (D.N.J. 1995); *Green Construction Co. v. Kansas Power and Light Co.*, 153 F.R.D. 670 (D. Kansas 1994); *Weseloh–Hurtig v. Hepker*, 152 F.R.D. 198 (D. Kansas 1993).

[132]*Institutionalized Juveniles v. Secretary of Public Welfare*, 758 F.2d 897 (3d Cir. 1985); *Montgomery County v. Microvote Corp.*, 2004 WL 1087196 (EDPA 2004). <u>Accord</u>, *Zackaroff v. Koch Transfer Co.*, 862 F.2d 1263 (6th Cir. 1988); *First Community Traders, Inc. v. Heinold Commodities, Inc.*, 766 F.2d 1007 (7th Cir. 1985); *Friends for All Children v. Lockheed Aircraft Corp.*, 725 F.2d 1392 (DC Cir. 1984); *Superturf, Inc. v. Monsanto Co.*, 660 F.2d 1275 (8th Cir. 1981); *Jones v. Diamond*, 594 F.2d 997 (4th Cir. 1979); *U.S. v. Mitchell*, 580 F.2d 789 (5th Cir. 1978); *K–2 Ski Co. v. Head Ski Co.*, 506 F.2d 47 (9th Cir. 1974); *Garonzik v. Whitman Diner*, 910 F.Supp. 167 (D.N.J. 1995); *Weseloh–Hurtig v. Hepker*, 152 F.R.D. 198 (D. Kansas 1993); *Bruno v. Western Electric Co.*, 618 F.Supp. 398 (D. Colorado 1985); *Seber v. Daniels Transfer Co.*, 618 F.Supp. 1311 (W.D. Pa. 1985); *Wade v. Mississippi Cooperative Extension Service*, 64 F.R.D. 102 (N.D.Miss. 1974); *Sperry Rand Corp. v. A–T–O, Inc.*, 58 F.R.D. 132 (E.D.Va. 1973).

[133]*Greene v. Fraternal Order of Police*, 183 F.R.D. 445 (ED Pa. 1998); *Lacovara v. Merrill Lynch*, 102 F.R.D. 959 (ED Pa. 1984). <u>Accord</u>, *Scientific Holding Co. v. Plessey*, 510 F.2d 15 (2nd Cir. 1974).

[134]*Lacovara v. Merrill Lynch*, 102 F.R.D. 959 (ED Pa. 1984). <u>Accord</u>, *Scientific Holding Co. v. Plessey*, 510 F.2d 15 (2nd Cir. 1974).

[135]*Brandt v. Schal Associates*, 854 F.2d 948 (7th Cir. 1988); *Bishop v. West American Insurance Co.*, 95 F.R.D. 494 (N.D.Ga. 1982).

[136]*City of Rome, Italy v. Glanton*, 184 F.R.D. 547 (ED Pa. 1999); *Lacovara v. Merrill Lynch*, 102 F.R.D. 959 (ED Pa. 1984).

[137]*Buchanan v. Stanships, Inc.*, 485 U.S. 265 (1988); *Samaad v. City of Dallas*, 922 F.2d 216 (5th Cir. 1991).

[138]*Mitchell v. City of Moore, Oklahoma*, 218 F.3d 1190 (10th Cir. 2000); *Stearns Airport Equipment Co., Inc. v. FMC Corporation*, 170 F.3d 518 (5th Cir. 1999); *Cengr v. Fusibond Piping Systems, Inc.*, 135 F.3d 445 (7th Cir. 1998); *Johnson v. Henderson*, 67 F.3d 299 (6th Cir. 1995); *Sevenson Environmental Services, Inc. v. Shaw Environmental, Inc.*, 246 F.R.D. 154 (WDNY 2007); *Yasui v. Maui Electric Company*, 78 F.Supp.2d 1124 (D. Hawaii 1999); *Woolfson v. Doyle*, 180 F.Supp. 86 (SDNY 1960).

[139]*LaVay Corporation v. Dominion Federal Savings and Loan*, 830 F.2d 522 (4th Cir. 1987).

[140]*Neumann v. Reinforced Earth Company*, 109 FRD 698 (DDC 1986).

[141]*Furman v. Cirrito*, 782 F.2d 353 (2d Cir. 1986); *Knox v. Schweiker*, 567 F.Supp. 959 (D.Del. 1983).

142*Women's Federal Savings and Loan Association of Cleveland v. Nevada National Bank*, 108 F.R.D. 396 (D. Nevada 1985).

143*McInnis v. Town of Weston*, 458 F.Supp.2d 7 (D. Conn 2006); *Sullivan v. Cheshier*, 991 F.Supp. (ND Ill. 1998); *McGuigan v. CAE Link Corp.*, 155 F.R.D. 31 (NDNY 1994).

144*McInnis v. Town of Weston*, 458 F.Supp.2d 7 (D. Conn 2006).

145*Harkins v. Riverboat Services*, 286 F.Supp. 2d 976 (ND Ill. 2003), aff'd, 385 F.3d 1099 (7th Cir. 2004); *McGuigan v. CAE Link Corp.*, 155 F.R.D. 31 (N.D.N.Y. 1994); *Morrissey v. County Tower Corp.*, 568 F. Supp. 980 (E.D. Mo. 1983); *Harceg v. Brown*, 536 F.Supp. 125 (N.D. Ill. 1982). Accord, *Seidman v. American Mobile Systems*, 965 F.Supp. 612 (E.D. Pa. 1997).

146*Brazos Valley Coalition for Life, Inc. v. City of Bryan, Texas*, 421 F.3d 314 (5th Cir. 2005); *Trepel v. Roadway Express, Inc.*, 266 F.3d 418 (6th Cir. 2001); *Holmes v. Cessna Aircraft Co.*, 11 F.3d 63 (5th Cir. 1994); *Dovenmuehle v. Gilldorn Mortgage Midwest Corp.*, 871 F.2d 697 (7th Cir. 1989); *Mason v. Belieu*, 543 F.2d 215 (D.C. Cir. 1976); *Wahl v. Carrier Manufacturing Co.*, 511 F.2d 209 (7th Cir. 1975); *McInnis v. Town of Weston*, 458 F.Supp.2d 7 (D. Conn. 2006); *Sullivan v. Cheshier*, 991 F.Supp. 999 (N.D. Ill. 1998); *Hollenbeck v. Falstaff Brewing Corp.*, 605 F.Supp. 421 (E.D. Mo. 1984); *Morrissey v. County Tower Corp.*, 568 F.Supp. 980 (E.D. Mo. 1983).

147*Friedman v. Ganassi*, 853 F.2d 207 (3d Cir. 1988).

148*Buchanan v. Stanships, Inc.*, 485 U.S. 265 (1988); *Friedman v. Ganassi*, 853 F.2d 207 (3d Cir. 1988); *Adams v. Teamsters Local 115*, 678 F.Supp.2d 314 (E.D.Pa, 2007).

149*Friedman v. Ganassi*, 853 F.2d 207 (3d Cir. 1988); *Dr. Bernard Heller Foundation v. Lee*, 847 F.2d 83 (3rd Cir. 1988); *Dominic v. Hess Oil V.I. Corp.*, 841 F.2d 513 (3rd Cir. 1988).

150*Buchanan v. Stanships, Inc.*, 485 U.S. 265 (1988); *Abrams v. Lightolier, Inc.*, 50 F.3d 1204 (3d Cir. 1995); *Friedman v. Ganassi*, 853 F.2d 207 (3d Cir. 1988); *Adams v. Teamsters Local 115*, 678 F.Supp.2d 314 (E.D.Pa, 2007); *Greene v. Fraternal Order of Police*, 183 F.R.D. 445 (E.D. Pa. 1998).

151*Friedman v. Ganassi*, 853 F.2d 207 (3d Cir. 1988); *Dr. Bernard Heller Foundation v. Lee*, 847 F.2d 83 (3rd Cir. 1988); *Dominic v. Hess Oil V.I. Corp.*, 841 F.2d 513 (3rd Cir. 1988).

152*Women's Federal Savings and Loan Association of Cleveland v. Nevada National Bank*, 108 F.R.D. 396 (D. Nevada 1985).

153In re: *Paoli Railroad Yard PCB Litigation*, 221 F.3d 449 (3d Cir. 2000). Accord, *Tubbs v. Sacramento County Jail*, 258 F.R.D. 657 (E.D. Cal. 2009); *Electronic Specialty Co. v. International Controls Corp.*, 47 F.R.D. 158 (SDNY 1969).

154*Abrams v. Lightolier, Inc.*, 50 F.3d 1204 (3d Cir. 1995).

155P.L. 102–572.

156*Samuel v. University of Pittsburgh*, 538 F.2d 991 (3rd Cir. 1976); *Halderman v. Pennhurst State School and Hospital*, 533 F.Supp. 631, 639 (E.D. Pa. 1981). See, also, *Gay Students Services v. Texas A&M University*, 612 F.2d 160, 165 (5th Cir. 1980); *Gary W. v. Louisiana*, 601 F.2d 240 (5th Cir. 1979); *Kovats v. Rutgers*, 633 F.Supp. 1469, 1475 (D.N.J. 1986).

157*Copperweld Steel Co. v. DeMag–Mannesmann–Bohler*, 624 F.2d 7 (3rd Cir. 1980).

158*American Truck Assoc., Inc. v. I.C.C.*, 666 F.2d 167, 169 (5th Cir. 1982); *American Railway Supervisors Association v. United States*, 582 F.2d 1066, 1067 (7th Cir. 1978); *Delta Airlines, Inc. v. Civil Aeronautics Board*, 505 F.2d 386 (D.C. Cir.1974); *Smith v. Board of School Commissioners of Mobile County*, 119 F.R.D. 440, 443 (S.D. Ala. 1988); *Monroe v. United Air Lines, Inc.*, 565 F.Supp. 274 (N.D.Ill 1983).

159*Buchanan v. Stanships, Inc.*, 485 U.S. 265 (1988); *Friedman v. Ganassi*, 853 F.2d 207 (3d Cir. 1988).

160*Friedman v. Ganassi*, 853 F.2d 207 (3d Cir. 1988); *Dr. Bernard Heller Foundation v. Lee*, 847 F.2d 83 (3rd Cir. 1988); *Dominic v. Hess Oil V.I. Corp.*, 841 F.2d 513 (3rd Cir. 1988).

161*Proffitt v. Municipal Authority of Borough of Morrisville*, 716 F.Supp. 845 (E.D. Pa. 1989), aff'd, 897 F.2d 523 (3d Cir. 1990); *Nugget Distributors Cooperative of America v. Mr. Nugget, Inc.*, 145 F.R. D. 54 (E.D.Pa. 1992). Accord, *East v. Barnhart*, 377 F.Supp. 2d 1170 (MD Alabama 2003); *United States v. Orenic*, 110 F.R.D. 584 (W.D. Va. 1986); *Bishop v. West American Insurance Co.*, 95 F.R.D. 494 (N.D.Ga. 1982).

162*McGuigan v. CAE Link Corp.*, 155 F.R.D. 31 (N.D.N.Y. 1994); *Bishop v. West American Insurance Co.*, 95 F.R.D. 494 (N.D.Ga. 1982).

163United States Public Law 102–572.

164*Reger v. The Nemours Foundation*, 599 F.3d 285 (3d Cir. 2010); In re: Paoli Railroad Yard PCB Litigation, 221 F.3d 449 (3d Cir. 2000); *Abrams v. Lightolier, Inc.*, 50 F.3d 1204 (3d Cir. 1995); *Smith v. SEPTA*, 47 F.3d 97 (3d Cir. 1995); *Friedman v. Ganassi*, 853 F.2d 207 (3d Cir. 1988); *Institutionalized Juveniles v. Secretary of Public Welfare*, 758 F.2d 897 (3d Cir. 1985); *Pearlstine v. United States*, 649 F.2d 194 (3rd Cir. 1981); *Delaney v. Capone*, 642 F.2d 57 (3d Cir. 1981); *Samuel v. University of Pittsburgh*, 538 F.2d 991 (3d Cir. 1976); *ADM Corp. v. Speedmaster Packing Corp.*, 525 F.2d 662 (3d Cir. 1975); *City of Rome, Italy v. Glanton*, 184 F.R.D. 547 (E.D. Pa. 1999); *Greene v. Fraternal Order of Police*, 183 F.R.D. 445 (E.D. Pa. 1998); *Action Alliance for Senior Citizens of Greater Philadelphia v. Shapp*, 74 F.R.D. 617 (E.D. Pa. 1977).

165Buchanan v. Stanships, Inc., 485 U.S. 265, 268 (1988)(emphasis added). Accord, Delta Air Lines, Inc. v. August, 450 U.S. 346 (1981). See, also, Reger v. The Nemours Foundation, 599 F.3d 285 (3d Cir. 2010); In re: Paoli Railroad Yard PCB Litigation, 221 F.3d 449 (3d Cir. 2000); Abrams v. Lightolier, Inc., 50 F.3d 1204 (3d Cir. 1995); Smith v. SEPTA, 47 F.3d 97 (3d Cir. 1995); Friedman v. Ganassi, 853 F.2d 207 (3d Cir. 1988); Institutionalized Juveniles v. Secretary of Public Welfare, 758 F.2d 897 (3d Cir. 1985); Pearlstine v. United States, 649 F.2d 194 (3rd Cir. 1981); Delaney v. Capone, 642 F. 2d 57 (3d Cir. 1981); Samuel v. University of Pittsburgh, 538 F.2d 991 (3d Cir. 1976); ADM Corp. v. Speedmaster Packing Corp., 525 F.2d 662 (3d Cir. 1975); City of Rome, Italy v. Glanton, 184 F.R.D. 547 (E.D. Pa. 1999); Greene v. Fraternal Order of Police, 183 F.R.D. 445 (E.D. Pa. 1998); Action Alliance for Senior Citizens of Greater Philadelphia v. Shapp, 74 F.R.D. 617 (E.D. Pa. 1977).

166Buchanan v. Stanships, Inc., 485 U.S. 265 (1988); Delta Air Lines, Inc. v. August, 450 U.S. 346 (1981). Accord, Reger v. The Nemours Foundation, 599 F.3d 285 (3d Cir. 2010); In re: Paoli Railroad Yard PCB Litigation, 221 F.3d 449 (3d Cir. 2000); Abrams v. Lightolier, Inc., 50 F.3d 1204 (3d Cir. 1995); Smith v. SEPTA, 47 F.3d 97 (3d Cir. 1995); Friedman v. Ganassi, 853 F.2d 207 (3d Cir. 1988); Institutionalized Juveniles v. Secretary of Public Welfare, 758 F.2d 897 (3d Cir. 1985); Pearlstine v. United States, 649 F.2d 194 (3rd Cir. 1981); Delaney v. Capone, 642 F.2d 57 (3d Cir. 1981); Samuel v. University of Pittsburgh, 538 F.2d 991 (3d Cir. 1976); ADM Corp. v. Speedmaster Packing Corp., 525 F.2d 662 (3d Cir. 1975); City of Rome, Italy v. Glanton, 184 F.R.D. 547 (E.D. Pa. 1999); Greene v. Fraternal Order of Police, 183 F.R.D. 445 (E.D. Pa. 1998); Action Alliance for Senior Citizens of Greater Philadelphia v. Shapp, 74 F.R.D. 617 (E.D. Pa. 1977).

167Brazos Valley Coalition for Life, Inc. v. City of Bryan, Texas, 421 F.3d 314 (5th Cir. 2005); Trepel v. Roadway Express, Inc., 266 F.3d 418 (6th Cir. 2001); Holmes v. Cessna Aircraft Co., 11 F.3d 63 (5th Cir. 1994); Dovenmuehle v. Gilldorn Mortgage Midwest Corp., 871 F.2d 697 (7th Cir. 1989); Mason v. Belieu, 543 F.2d 215 (D.C. Cir. 1976); Wahl v. Carrier Manufacturing Co., 511 F.2d 209 (7th Cir. 1975); McInnis v. Town of Weston, 458 F.Supp.2d 7 (D. Conn. 2006); Sullivan v. Cheshier, 991 F.Supp. 999 (N.D. Ill. 1998); Hollenbeck v. Falstaff Brewing Corp., 605 F.Supp. 421 (E.D. Mo. 1984); Morrissey v. County Tower Corp., 568 F.Supp. 980 (E.D. Mo. 1983).

168In Re: Kulicke & Soffa Industries Inc. Securities Litigation, 747 F.Supp. 1136 (E.D.Pa. 1990), aff'd, 944 F.2d 897 (3rd Cir. 1991); ADM Corp. v. Speedmaster Packing Corp., 525 F.2d 662 (3d Cir. 1975); Nugget Distributors Cooperative of America v. Mr. Nugget, Inc., 145 F.R. D. 54 (E.D.Pa. 1992). Accord, Charter Medical Corp v. Cardin, 127 F. R.D. 111 (D. Maryland 1989); Women's Federal Savings and Loan Association of Cleveland v. Nevada National Bank, 108 F.R.D. 396 (D. Nevada 1985); International Wood Processors v. Power Dry, Inc., 598 F. Supp. 299 (D.S. C. 1984); Morrissey v. County Tower Corp., 568 F.Supp. 178 (ED Mo. 1983).

169Proffitt v. Municipal Authority of Borough of Morrisville, 716 F.Supp. 845 (ED Pa. 1989), aff'd, 897 F.2d 523 (3d Cir. 1990); Montgomery County v. Microvote Corp., 2004 WL 1087196 (EDPA 2004). Accord, Long v. Howard University, 561 F.Supp.2d 85 (D.D.C. 2008); Shared Medical System v. Ashford Presbyterian Community Hospital, 212 F. R.D. 50 (D.P.R. 2002); McGuigan v. CAE Link Corp., 155 F.R.D. 31 (NDNY 1994).

170Montgomery County v. Microvote Corp., 2004 WL 1087196 (EDPA 2004). Accord, Shared Medical System v. Ashford Presbyterian Community Hospital, 212 F.R.D. 50 (D.P.R. 2002); Griffith v. Mt. Carmel Medical Center, 157 F.R.D. 499 (D. Kansas 1994); McGuigan v. CAE Link Corp., 155 F.R.D. 31 (NDNY 1994).

171Movitz v. First National Bank of Chicago, 982 F.Supp. 571 (ND Ill 1997).

172Montgomery County v. Microvote Corp., 2004 WL 1087196 (EDPA 2004).

173Montgomery County v. Microvote Corp., 2004 WL 1087196 (EDPA 2004); McGuigan v. CAE Link Corp., 155 FRD 31 (NDNY 1994).

174Reger v. The Nemours Foundation, 599 F.3d 285 (3d Cir. 2010); In re: Paoli Railroad Yard PCB Litigation, 221 F.3d 449 (3d Cir. 2000); Abrams v. Lightolier, Inc., 50 F.3d 1204 (3d Cir. 1995); Smith v. SEPTA, 47 F.3d 97 (3d Cir. 1995); Friedman v. Ganassi, 853 F.2d 207 (3d Cir. 1988); Institutionalized Juveniles v. Secretary of Public Welfare, 758 F.2d 897 (3d Cir. 1985); Pearlstine v. United States, 649 F.2d 194 (3rd Cir. 1981); Delaney v. Capone, 642 F.2d 57 (3d Cir. 1981); Samuel v. University of Pittsburgh, 538 F.2d 991 (3d Cir. 1976); ADM Corp. v. Speedmaster Packing Corp., 525 F.2d 662 (3d Cir. 1975); City of Rome, Italy v. Glanton, 184 F.R.D. 547 (E.D. Pa. 1999); Greene v. Fraternal Order of Police, 183 F.R.D. 445 (E.D. Pa. 1998); Action Alliance for Senior Citizens of Greater Philadelphia v. Shapp, 74 F.R.D. 617 (E.D. Pa. 1977).

175Buchanan v. Stanships, Inc., 485 U.S. 265, 268 (1988)(emphasis added). Accord, Delta Air Lines, Inc. v. August, 450 U.S. 346 (1981). See, also, Reger v. The Nemours Foundation, 599 F.3d 285 (3d Cir. 2010); In re: Paoli Railroad Yard PCB Litigation, 221 F.3d 449 (3d Cir. 2000); Abrams v. Lightolier, Inc., 50 F.3d 1204 (3d Cir. 1995); Smith v. SEPTA, 47 F.3d 97 (3d Cir. 1995); Friedman v. Ganassi, 853 F.2d 207 (3d Cir. 1988); Institutionalized Juveniles v. Secretary of Public Welfare, 758 F.2d 897 (3d Cir. 1985); Pearlstine v. United States, 649 F.2d 194 (3rd Cir. 1981); Delaney v. Capone, 642 F. 2d 57 (3d Cir. 1981); Samuel v. University of Pittsburgh, 538 F.2d 991 (3d Cir. 1976); ADM Corp. v. Speedmaster Packing Corp., 525 F.2d 662 (3d Cir. 1975); City of Rome, Italy v. Glanton, 184 F.R.D. 547 (E.D. Pa. 1999); Greene v. Fraternal Order of Police, 183 F.R.D. 445 (E.D. Pa. 1998); Action Alliance for Senior Citizens of Greater Philadelphia v. Shapp, 74 F.R.D. 617 (E.D. Pa. 1977).

176Buchanan v. Stanships, Inc., 485 U.S. 265 (1988); Delta Air Lines, Inc. v. August, 450 U.S. 346 (1981). Accord, Reger v. The Nemours Foundation, 599 F.3d 285 (3d Cir. 2010); In re: Paoli Railroad Yard PCB

<u>Litigation</u>, 221 F.3d 449 (3d Cir. 2000); *Abrams v. Lightolier, Inc.*, 50 F.3d 1204 (3d Cir. 1995); *Smith v. SEPTA*, 47 F.3d 97 (3d Cir. 1995); *Friedman v. Ganassi*, 853 F.2d 207 (3d Cir. 1988); *Institutionalized Juveniles v. Secretary of Public Welfare*, 758 F.2d 897 (3d Cir. 1985); *Pearlstine v. United States*, 649 F.2d 194 (3rd Cir. 1981); *Delaney v. Capone*, 642 F.2d 57 (3d Cir. 1981); *Samuel v. University of Pittsburgh*, 538 F.2d 991 (3d Cir. 1976); *ADM Corp. v. Speedmaster Packing Corp.*, 525 F.2d 662 (3d Cir. 1975); *City of Rome, Italy v. Glanton*, 184 F.R.D. 547 (E.D. Pa. 1999); *Greene v. Fraternal Order of Police*, 183 F.R.D. 445 (E.D. Pa. 1998); *Action Alliance for Senior Citizens of Greater Philadelphia v. Shapp*, 74 F.R.D. 617 (E.D. Pa. 1977).

177*Brazos Valley Coalition for Life, Inc. v. City of Bryan, Texas*, 421 F.3d 314 (5th Cir. 2005); *Trepel v. Roadway Express, Inc.*, 266 F.3d 418 (6th Cir. 2001); *Holmes v. Cessna Aircraft Co.*, 11 F.3d 63 (5th Cir. 1994); *Dovenmuehle v. Gilldorn Mortgage Midwest Corp.*, 871 F.2d 697 (7th Cir. 1989); *Mason v. Belieu*, 543 F.2d 215 (D.C. Cir. 1976); *Wahl v. Carrier Manufacturing Co.*, 511 F.2d 209 (7th Cir. 1975); *McInnis v. Town of Weston*, 458 F.Supp.2d 7 (D. Conn. 2006); *Sullivan v. Cheshier*, 991 F.Supp. 999 (N.D. Ill. 1998); *Hollenbeck v. Falstaff Brewing Corp.*, 605 F.Supp. 421 (E.D. Mo. 1984); *Morrissey v. County Tower Corp.*, 568 F.Supp. 980 (E.D. Mo. 1983).

178<u>In Re: Kulicke & Soffa Industries Inc. Securities Litigation</u>, 747 F.Supp. 1136 (E.D.Pa. 1990), aff'd, 944 F.2d 897 (3rd Cir. 1991); *ADM Corp. v. Speedmaster Packing Corp.*, 525 F.2d 662 (3d Cir. 1975); *Nugget Distributors Cooperative of America v. Mr. Nugget, Inc.*, 145 F.R. D. 54 (E.D.Pa. 1992). <u>Accord</u>, *Charter Medical Corp v. Cardin*, 127 F. R.D. 111 (D. Maryland 1989); *Women's Federal Savings and Loan Association of Cleveland v. Nevada National Bank*, 108 F.R.D. 396 (D. Nevada 1985); *International Wood Processors v. Power Dry, Inc.*, 598 F. Supp. 299 (D.S. C. 1984); *Morrissey v. County Tower Corp.*, 568 F.Supp. 178 (ED Mo. 1983).

179*In Re: Kulicke & Soffa Industries, Inc. Securities Litigation*, 747 F.Supp. 1136 (ED Pa. 1990) aff'd 944 F.2d 897 (3rd Cir. 1991); *Montgomery County v. Microvote Corp.*, 2004 WL 1087196 (EDPA 2004); *Nugget Distributors Cooperative v. Mr. Nugget, Inc.*, 145 F.R.D. 54 (ED Pa. 1992). <u>Accord</u>, *McGuigan v. CAE Link Corp.*, 155 F.R.D. 31 (NDNY 1994).

180*BDT Products, Inc. v. Lexmark International, Inc.*, 405 F.3d 415 (6th Cir. 2005); *Tilton v. Capital Cities/ABC Inc.*, 115 F.3d 1471 (10th Cir. 1997); *Morrison v. Reichhold Chems.*, 97 F.3d 460 (11th Cir. 1996); *Commercial Credit Equipment Corp. v. Stamps*, 920 F.2d 1361 (7th Cir. 1990); *Rio Props v. Stewart Annoyances, Ltd.*, 420 F.Supp. 2d 1127 (D. Nevada 2006); *United International Holdings v. Wharf, Ltd.*, 174 F.R. D. 479 (D. Colo. 1997); *Garonzik v. Whitman Diner*, 910 F.Supp 167 (D.N.J. 1995); *McGuigan v. CAE Link Corp.*, 155 F.R.D. 31 (NDNY 1994); *Weseloh–Hurtig v. Hepker*, 152 F.R.D. 198 (D. Kansas 1993); *Deaton v. Dreis & Krump Mfg. Co.* (ND Ohio 1991).

181*Garonzik v. Whitman Diner*, 910 F.Supp. 167 (D.N.J. 1995).

182Although 28 U.S.C. § 1920 does limit the payment of fees to an expert witness, 28 U.S.C. § 1920 does not contain a limit on the payment of fees to a court reporter in connection to the testimony of an expert witness.

183*Reger v. The Nemours Foundation*, 599 F.3d 285 (3d Cir. 2010); <u>In re: Paoli Railroad Yard PCB Litigation</u>, 221 F.3d 449 (3d Cir. 2000); *Abrams· v. Lightolier, Inc.*, 50 F.3d 1204 (3d Cir. 1995); *Smith v. SEPTA*, 47 F.2d 97 (3d Cir. 1995); *Friedman v. Ganassi*, 853 F.2d 207 (3d Cir. 1988); *Institutionalized Juveniles v. Secretary of Public Welfare*, 758 F.2d 897 (3d Cir. 1985); *Pearlstine v. United States*, 649 F.2d 194 (3rd Cir. 1981); *Delaney v. Capone*, 642 F.2d 57 (3d Cir. 1981); *Samuel v. University of Pittsburgh*, 538 F.2d 991 (3d Cir. 1976); *ADM Corp. v. Speedmaster Packing Corp.*, 525 F.2d 662 (3d Cir. 1975); *City of Rome, Italy v. Glanton*, 184 F.R.D. 547 (E.D. Pa. 1999); *Greene v. Fraternal Order of Police*, 183 F.R.D. 445 (E.D. Pa. 1998); *Action Alliance for Senior Citizens of Greater Philadelphia v. Shapp*, 74 F.R.D. 617 (E.D. Pa. 1977).

184*Buchanan v. Stanships, Inc.*, 485 U.S. 265, 268 (1988)(emphasis added). <u>Accord</u>, *Delta Air Lines, Inc. v. August*, 450 U.S. 346 (1981). <u>See</u>, <u>also</u>, *Reger v. The Nemours Foundation*, 599 F.3d 285 (3d Cir. 2010); <u>In re: Paoli Railroad Yard PCB Litigation</u>, 221 F.3d 449 (3d Cir. 2000); *Abrams v. Lightolier, Inc.*, 50 F.3d 1204 (3d Cir. 1995); *Smith v. SEPTA*, 47 F.3d 97 (3d Cir. 1995); *Friedman v. Ganassi*, 853 F.2d 207 (3d Cir. 1988); *Institutionalized Juveniles v. Secretary of Public Welfare*, 758 F.2d 897 (3d Cir. 1985); *Pearlstine v. United States*, 649 F.2d 194 (3rd Cir. 1981); *Delaney v. Capone*, 642 F. 2d 57 (3d Cir. 1981); *Samuel v. University of Pittsburgh*, 538 F.2d 991 (3d Cir. 1976); *ADM Corp. v. Speedmaster Packing Corp.*, 525 F.2d 662 (3d Cir. 1975); *City of Rome, Italy v. Glanton*, 184 F.R.D. 547 (E.D. Pa. 1999); *Greene v. Fraternal Order of Police*, 183 F.R.D. 445 (E.D. Pa. 1998); *Action Alliance for Senior Citizens of Greater Philadelphia v. Shapp*, 74 F.R.D. 617 (E.D. Pa. 1977).

185*Buchanan v. Stanships, Inc.*, 485 U.S. 265 (1988); *Delta Air Lines, Inc. v. August*, 450 U.S. 346 (1981). <u>Accord</u>, *Reger v. The Nemours Foundation*, 599 F.3d 285 (3d Cir. 2010); <u>In re: Paoli Railroad Yard PCB Litigation</u>, 221 F.3d 449 (3d Cir. 2000); *Abrams v. Lightolier, Inc.*, 50 F.3d 97 (3d Cir. 1995); *Smith v. SEPTA*, 47 F.3d 97 (3d Cir. 1995); *Friedman v. Ganassi*, 853 F.2d 207 (3d Cir. 1988); *Institutionalized Juveniles v. Secretary of Public Welfare*, 758 F.2d 897 (3d Cir. 1985); *Pearlstine v. United States*, 649 F.2d 194 (3rd Cir. 1981); *Delaney v. Capone*, 642 F.2d 57 (3d Cir. 1981); *Samuel v. University of Pittsburgh*, 538 F.2d 991 (3d Cir. 1976); *ADM Corp. v. Speedmaster Packing Corp.*, 525 F.2d 662 (3d Cir. 1975); *City of Rome, Italy v. Glanton*, 184 F.R.D. 547 (E.D. Pa. 1999); *Greene v. Fraternal Order of Police*, 183 F.R.D. 445 (E.D. Pa. 1998); *Action Alliance for Senior Citizens of Greater Philadelphia v. Shapp*, 74 F.R.D. 617 (E.D. Pa. 1977).

186*Brazos Valley Coalition for Life, Inc. v. City of Bryan, Texas*, 421 F.3d 314 (5th Cir. 2005); *Trepel v. Roadway Express, Inc.*, 266 F.3d 418 (6th Cir. 2001); *Holmes v. Cessna Aircraft Co.*, 11 F.3d 63 (5th Cir. 1994); *Dovenmuehle v. Gilldorn Mortgage Midwest Corp.*, 871 F.2d 697 (7th Cir. 1989); *Mason v. Belieu*, 543

F.2d 215 (D.C. Cir. 1976); *Wahl v. Carrier Manufacturing Co.*, 511 F.2d 209 (7th Cir. 1975); *McInnis v. Town of Weston*, 458 F.Supp.2d 7 (D. Conn. 2006); *Sullivan v. Cheshier*, 991 F.Supp. 999 (N.D. Ill. 1998); *Hollenbeck v. Falstaff Brewing Corp.*, 605 F.Supp. 421 (E.D. Mo. 1984); *Morrissey v. County Tower Corp.*, 568 F.Supp. 980 (E.D. Mo. 1983).

187In Re: Kulicke & Soffa Industries Inc. Securities Litigation, 747 F.Supp. 1136 (E.D.Pa. 1990), aff'd, 944 F.2d 897 (3rd Cir. 1991); *ADM Corp. v. Speedmaster Packing Corp.*, 525 F.2d 662 (3d Cir. 1975); *Nugget Distributors Cooperative of America v. Mr. Nugget, Inc.*, 145 F.R. D. 54 (E.D.Pa. 1992). Accord, *Charter Medical Corp v. Cardin*, 127 F. R.D. 111 (D. Maryland 1989); *Women's Federal Savings and Loan Association of Cleveland v. Nevada National Bank*, 108 F.R.D. 396 (D. Nevada 1985); *International Wood Processors v. Power Dry, Inc.*, 598 F. Supp. 299 (D.S.C. 1984); *Morrissey v. County Tower Corp.*, 568 F.Supp. 178 (ED Mo. 1983).

188*In Re: Kulicke & Soffa Industries, Inc. Securities Litigation*, 747 F.Supp. 1136 (E.D. Pa. 1990) aff'd 944 F.2d 897 (3rd Cir. 1991).

189*Sullivan v. Cheshire*, 991 F.Supp. 999 (ND Ill. 1998).

190In Re: Kulicke & Soffa Industries Inc. Securities Litigation, 747 F.Supp. 1136 (E.D.Pa. 1990), aff'd, 944 F.2d 897 (3rd Cir. 1991).

191In Re: Kulicke & Soffa Industries Inc. Securities Litigation, 747 F.Supp. 1136 (E.D.Pa. 1990), aff'd, 944 F.2d 897 (3rd Cir. 1991).

192*Mitchell v. City of Moore, Oklahoma*, 218 F.3d 1190 (10th Cir. 2000); *Stearns Airport Equipment Co., Inc. v. FMC Corporation*, 170 F.3d 518 (5th Cir. 1999); *Cengr v. Fusibond Piping Systems, Inc.*, 135 F.3d 445 (7th Cir. 1998); *Sevenson Environmental Services, Inc. v. Shaw Environmental, Inc.*, 246 F.R.D. 154 (WDNY 2007); *Yasui v. Maui Electric Company*, 78 F.Supp.2d 1124 (D. Hawaii 1999).

193*LaVay Corporation v. Dominion Federal Savings and Loan*, 830 F.2d 522 (4th Cir. 1987).

194*Neumann v. Reinforced Earth Company*, 109 FRD 698 (DDC 1986).

195*BDT Products, Inc. v. Lexmark International, Inc.*, 405 F.3d 415 (6th Cir. 2005); *Tilton v. Capital Cities/ABC, Inc.*, 115 F.3d 1471 (10th Cir. 1997); *Garonzik v. Whitman Diner*, 910 F.Supp. 167 (D.N.J. 1995).

196In re: Paoli Railroad Yard PCB Litigation, 221 F.3d 449 (3rd Cir. 2000); In Re: Kulicke & Soffa Industries Inc. Securities Litigation, 747 F.Supp. 1136 (E.D.Pa. 1990), aff'd, 944 F.2d 897 (3rd Cir. 1991); *ADM Corp. v. Speedmaster Packing Corp.*, 525 F.2d 662 (3d Cir. 1975); *Nugget Distributors Cooperative of America v. Mr. Nugget, Inc.* , 145 F.R.D. 54 (E.D.Pa. 1992). Accord, *Charter Medical Corp v. Cardin*, 127 F.R.D. 111 (D. Maryland 1989); *Women's Federal Savings and Loan Association of Cleveland v. Nevada National Bank*, 108 FRD 396 (D. Nevada 1985); *International Wood Processors v. Power Dry, Inc.*, 598 F. Supp. 299 (D.S.C. 1984); *Morrissey v. County Tower Corp.*, 568 F.Supp. 178 (ED Mo. 1983).

197*McGuigan v. CAE Link Corp.*, 155 F.R.D. 31 (NDNY 1994).

198In Re: Kulicke & Soffa Industries Inc. Securities Litigation, 747 F.Supp. 1136 (E.D.Pa. 1990), aff'd, 944 F.2d 897 (3rd Cir. 1991); *Montgomery County v. Microvote Corp.*, 2004 WL 1087196 (E.D.Pa 2004). Accord, *Holmes v. Cessna Aircraft Co.*, 11 F.3d 63 (5th Cir. 1994).

199*Montgomery County v. Microvote Corp.*, 2004 WL 1087196 (E.D.Pa. 2004). Accord, *Weeks v. Samsung Heavy Industries*, 126 F.3d 1997); *Karsian v. Inter Regional Financial Group, Inc.*, 13 F.Supp.2d 1085 (D. Colorado 1998); *Movitz v. First National Bank of Chicago*, 982 F.Supp. 571 (ND Ill. 1997); *Marcoin, Inc. v. Edwin K. Williams & Co., Inc.*, 88 FRD 588 (E.D.Va. 1980); *Electronic Specialty Co. v. International Controls Corp.*, 47 FRD 158 (SDNY 1969).

200*Morrissey v. County Tower Corp.*, 568 F.Supp. 980 (ED Mo. 1983).

201*Reger v. The Nemours Foundation*, 599 F.3d 285 (3d Cir. 2010); In re: Paoli Railroad Yard PCB Litigation, 221 F.3d 449 (3d Cir. 2000); *Abrams v. Lightolier, Inc.*, 50 F.3d 1204 (3d Cir. 1995); *Smith v. SEPTA*, 47 F.3d 97 (3d Cir. 1995); *Friedman v. Ganassi*, 853 F.2d 207 (3d Cir. 1988); *Institutionalized Juveniles v. Secretary of Public Welfare*, 758 F.2d 897 (3d Cir. 1985); *Pearlstine v. United States*, 649 F.2d 194 (3rd Cir. 1981); *Delaney v. Capone*, 642 F.2d 57 (3d Cir. 1981); *Samuel v. University of Pittsburgh*, 538 F.2d 991 (3d Cir. 1976); *ADM Corp. v. Speedmaster Packing Corp.*, 525 F.2d 662 (3d Cir. 1975); *City of Rome, Italy v. Glanton*, 184 F.R.D. 547 (E.D. Pa. 1999); *Greene v. Fraternal Order of Police*, 183 F.R.D. 445 (E.D. Pa. 1998); *Action Alliance for Senior Citizens of Greater Philadelphia v. Shapp*, 74 F.R.D. 617 (E.D. Pa. 1977).

202*Buchanan v. Stanships, Inc.*, 485 U.S. 265, 268 (1988)(emphasis added). Accord, *Delta Air Lines, Inc. v. August*, 450 U.S. 346 (1981). See, also, *Reger v. The Nemours Foundation*, 599 F.3d 285 (3d Cir. 2010); In re: Paoli Railroad Yard PCB Litigation, 221 F.3d 449 (3d Cir. 2000); *Abrams v. Lightolier, Inc.*, 50 F.3d 1204 (3d Cir. 1995); *Smith v. SEPTA*, 47 F.3d 97 (3d Cir. 1995); *Friedman v. Ganassi*, 853 F.2d 207 (3d Cir. 1988); *Institutionalized Juveniles v. Secretary of Public Welfare*, 758 F.2d 897 (3d Cir. 1985); *Pearlstine v. United States*, 649 F. 2d 194 (3rd Cir. 1981); *Delaney v. Capone*, 642 F. 2d 57 (3d Cir. 1981); *Samuel v. University of Pittsburgh*, 538 F.2d 991 (3d Cir. 1976); *ADM Corp. v. Speedmaster Packing Corp.*, 525 F.2d 662 (3d Cir. 1975); *City of Rome, Italy v. Glanton*, 184 F.R.D. 547 (E.D. Pa. 1999); *Greene v. Fraternal Order of Police*, 183 F.R.D. 445 (E.D. Pa. 1998); *Action Alliance for Senior Citizens of Greater Philadelphia v. Shapp*, 74 F.R.D. 617 (E.D. Pa. 1977).

203*Buchanan v. Stanships, Inc.*, 485 U.S. 265 (1988); *Delta Air Lines, Inc. v. August*, 450 U.S. 346 (1981). Accord, *Reger v. The Nemours Foundation*, 599 F.3d 285 (3d Cir. 2010); In re: Paoli Railroad Yard PCB

Litigation, 221 F.3d 449 (3d Cir. 2000); *Abrams v. Lightolier, Inc.*, 50 F.3d 1204 (3d Cir. 1995); *Smith v. SEPTA*, 47 F.3d 97 (3d Cir. 1995); *Friedman v. Ganassi*, 853 F.2d 207 (3d Cir. 1988); *Institutionalized Juveniles v. Secretary of Public Welfare*, 758 F.2d 897 (3d Cir. 1985); *Pearlstine v. United States*, 649 F.2d 194 (3rd Cir. 1981); *Delaney v. Capone*, 642 F.2d 57 (3d Cir. 1981); *Samuel v. University of Pittsburgh*, 538 F.2d 991 (3d Cir. 1976); *ADM Corp. v. Speedmaster Packing Corp.*, 525 F.2d 662 (3d Cir. 1975); *City of Rome, Italy v. Glanton*, 184 F.R.D. 547 (E.D. Pa. 1999); *Greene v. Fraternal Order of Police*, 183 F.R.D. 445 (E.D. Pa. 1998); *Action Alliance for Senior Citizens of Greater Philadelphia v. Shapp*, 74 F.R.D. 617 (E.D. Pa. 1977).

204*Brazos Valley Coalition for Life, Inc. v. City of Bryan, Texas*, 421 F.3d 314 (5th Cir. 2005); *Trepel v. Roadway Express, Inc.*, 266 F.3d 418 (6th Cir. 2001); *Holmes v. Cessna Aircraft Co.*, 11 F.3d 63 (5th Cir. 1994); *Dovenmuehle v. Gilldorn Mortgage Midwest Corp.*, 871 F.2d 697 (7th Cir. 1989); *Mason v. Belieu*, 543 F.2d 215 (D.C. Cir. 1976); *Wahl v. Carrier Manufacturing Co.*, 511 F.2d 209 (7th Cir. 1975); *McInnis v. Town of Weston*, 458 F.Supp.2d 7 (D. Conn. 2006); *Sullivan v. Cheshier*, 991 F.Supp. 999 (N.D. Ill. 1998); *Hollenbeck v. Falstaff Brewing Corp.*, 605 F.Supp. 421 (E.D. Mo. 1984); *Morrissey v. County Tower Corp.*, 568 F.Supp. 980 (E.D. Mo. 1983).

205In Re: Kulicke & Soffa Industries Inc. Securities Litigation, 747 F.Supp. 1136 (E.D.Pa. 1990), aff'd, 944 F.2d 897 (3rd Cir. 1991); *ADM Corp. v. Speedmaster Packing Corp.*, 525 F.2d 662 (3d Cir. 1975); *Nugget Distributors Cooperative of America v. Mr. Nugget, Inc.*, 145 F.R. D. 54 (E.D.Pa. 1992). Accord, *Charter Medical Corp v. Cardin*, 127 F. R.D. 111 (D. Maryland 1989); *Women's Federal Savings and Loan Association of Cleveland v. Nevada National Bank*, 108 F.R.D. 396 (D. Nevada 1985); *International Wood Processors v. Power Dry, Inc.*, 598 F. Supp. 299 (D.S. C. 1984); *Morrissey v. County Tower Corp.*, 568 F.Supp. 178 (ED Mo. 1983).

206In Re: Kulicke & Soffa Industries Inc. Securities Litigation, 747 F.Supp. 1136 (E.D.Pa. 1990), aff'd, 944 F.2d 897 (3rd Cir. 1991).

207In Re: Kulicke & Soffa Industries Inc. Securities Litigation, 747 F.Supp. 1136 (E.D.Pa. 1990), aff'd, 944 F.2d 897 (3rd Cir. 1991).

208In re: Paoli Railroad Yard PCB Litigation, 221 F.3d 449 (3d Cir. 2000); *Montgomery County v. Microvote Corp.*, 2004 WL 1087196 (EDPA 2004); *Tracy v. Goldberg*, 203 F.Supp. 188 (E.D. Pa. 1962). See, also, *Charter Medical Corp. v. Cardin*, 127 F.R.D. 111 (D. Maryland 1989); *Harrisburg Coalition Against Ruining the Environment v. Volpe*, 65 F.R.D. 608 (M.D. Pa. 1974).

209*Proffitt v. Municipal Authority of Borough of Morrisville*, 716 F.Supp. 845 (E.D. Pa. 1989), aff'd, 897 F.2d 523 (3d Cir. 1990); *Shannon v. United States Department of Housing and Urban Development*, 433 F.Supp. 249 (E.D. Pa. 1977).

210In Re: Glacier Bay, 746 F.Supp. 1379 (D. Alaska 1990).

211*Reger v. The Nemours Foundation*, 599 F.3d 285 (3d Cir. 2010); In re: Paoli Railroad Yard PCB Litigation, 221 F.3d 449 (3d Cir. 2000); *Abrams v. Lightolier, Inc.*, 50 F.3d 1204 (3d Cir. 1995); *Smith v. SEPTA*, 47 F.3d 97 (3d Cir. 1995); *Friedman v. Ganassi*, 853 F.2d 207 (3d Cir. 1988); *Institutionalized Juveniles v. Secretary of Public Welfare*, 758 F.2d 897 (3d Cir. 1985); *Pearlstine v. United States*, 649 F.2d 194 (3rd Cir. 1981); *Delaney v. Capone*, 642 F.2d 57 (3d Cir. 1981); *Samuel v. University of Pittsburgh*, 538 F.2d 991 (3d Cir. 1976); *ADM Corp. v. Speedmaster Packing Corp.*, 525 F.2d 662 (3d Cir. 1975); *City of Rome, Italy v. Glanton*, 184 F.R.D. 547 (E.D. Pa. 1999); *Greene v. Fraternal Order of Police*, 183 F.R.D. 445 (E.D. Pa. 1998); *Action Alliance for Senior Citizens of Greater Philadelphia v. Shapp*, 74 F.R.D. 617 (E.D. Pa. 1977).

212*Buchanan v. Stanships, Inc.*, 485 U.S. 265, 268 (1988)(emphasis added). Accord, *Delta Air Lines, Inc. v. August*, 450 U.S. 346 (1981). See, also, *Reger v. The Nemours Foundation*, 599 F.3d 285 (3d Cir. 2010); In re: Paoli Railroad Yard PCB Litigation, 221 F.3d 449 (3d Cir. 2000); *Abrams v. Lightolier, Inc.*, 50 F.3d 1204 (3d Cir. 1995); *Smith v. SEPTA*, 47 F.3d 97 (3d Cir. 1995); *Friedman v. Ganassi*, 853 F.2d 207 (3d Cir. 1988); *Institutionalized Juveniles v. Secretary of Public Welfare*, 758 F.2d 897 (3d Cir. 1985); *Pearlstine v. United States*, 649 F.2d 194 (3rd Cir. 1981); *Delaney v. Capone*, 642 F. 2d 57 (3d Cir. 1981); *Samuel v. University of Pittsburgh*, 538 F.2d 991 (3d Cir. 1976); *ADM Corp. v. Speedmaster Packing Corp.*, 525 F.2d 662 (3d Cir. 1975); *City of Rome, Italy v. Glanton*, 184 F.R.D. 547 (E.D. Pa. 1999); *Greene v. Fraternal Order of Police*, 183 F.R.D. 445 (E.D. Pa. 1998); *Action Alliance for Senior Citizens of Greater Philadelphia v. Shapp*, 74 F.R.D. 617 (E.D. Pa. 1977).

213*Buchanan v. Stanships, Inc.*, 485 U.S. 265 (1988); *Delta Air Lines, Inc. v. August*, 450 U.S. 346 (1981). Accord, *Reger v. The Nemours Foundation*, 599 F.3d 285 (3d Cir. 2010); *In re: Paoli Railroad Yard PCB Litigation*, 221 F.3d 449 (3d Cir. 2000); *Abrams v. Lightolier, Inc.*, 50 F.3d 1204 (3d Cir. 1995); *Smith v. SEPTA*, 47 F.3d 97 (3d Cir. 1995); *Friedman v. Ganassi*, 853 F.2d 207 (3d Cir. 1988); *Institutionalized Juveniles v. Secretary of Public Welfare*, 758 F.2d 897 (3d Cir. 1985); *Pearlstine v. United States*, 649 F.2d 194 (3rd Cir. 1981); *Delaney v. Capone*, 642 F.2d 57 (3d Cir. 1981); *Samuel v. University of Pittsburgh*, 538 F.2d 991 (3d Cir. 1976); *ADM Corp. v. Speedmaster Packing Corp.*, 525 F.2d 662 (3d Cir. 1975); *City of Rome, Italy v. Glanton*, 184 F.R.D. 547 (E.D. Pa. 1999); *Greene v. Fraternal Order of Police*, 183 F.R.D. 445 (E.D. Pa. 1998); *Action Alliance for Senior Citizens of Greater Philadelphia v. Shapp*, 74 F.R.D. 617 (E.D. Pa. 1977).

214*Brazos Valley Coalition for Life, Inc. v. City of Bryan, Texas*, 421 F.3d 314 (5th Cir. 2005); *Trepel v. Roadway Express, Inc.*, 266 F.3d 418 (6th Cir. 2001); *Holmes v. Cessna Aircraft Co.*, 11 F.3d 63 (5th Cir. 1994); *Dovenmuehle v. Gilldorn Mortgage Midwest Corp.*, 871 F.2d 697 (7th Cir. 1989); *Mason v. Belieu*, 543 F.2d 215 (D.C. Cir. 1976); *Wahl v. Carrier Manufacturing Co.*, 511 F.2d 209 (7th Cir. 1975); *McInnis v. Town of Weston*, 458 F.Supp.2d 7 (D. Conn. 2006); *Sullivan v. Cheshier*, 991 F.Supp. 999 (N.D. Ill. 1998);

Hollenbeck v. Falstaff Brewing Corp., 605 F.Supp. 421 (E.D. Mo. 1984); *Morrissey v. County Tower Corp.*, 568 F.Supp. 980 (E.D. Mo. 1983).

215In Re: Kulicke & Soffa Industries Inc. Securities Litigation, 747 F.Supp. 1136 (E.D.Pa. 1990), aff'd, 944 F.2d 897 (3rd Cir. 1991); *ADM Corp. v. Speedmaster Packing Corp.*, 525 F.2d 662 (3d Cir. 1975); *Nugget Distributors Cooperative of America v. Mr Nugget, Inc.*, 145 F. R. D. 54 (E.D.Pa. 1992). Accord, *Charter Medical Corp v. Cardin*, 127 FRD 111 (D. Maryland 1989); *Women's Federal Savings and Loan Association of Cleveland v. Nevada National Bank*, 108 FRD 396 (D. Nevada 1985); *International Wood Processors v. Power Dry, Inc.*, 598 F. Supp. 299 (D.S. C. 1984); *Morrissey v. County Tower Corp.*, 568 F.Supp. 178 (ED Mo. 1983).

216*Kansas v. Colorado*, 129 S.Ct. 1294 (2009).

217*Crawford Fitting Company v. J. T. Gibbons, Inc.*, 482 U.S. 437 (1987); *Henkel v. Chicago, St. Paul, Minneapolis and Omaha Railroad Company*, 284 U.S. 444 (1932).

218*Griffith v. Mt. Carmel Medical Center*, 157 F.R.D. 499 (D. Kansas 1994).

219*Brazos Valley Coalition for Life, Inc. v. City of Bryan, Texas*, 421 F.3d 314 (5th Cir. 2005); *Trepel v. Montgomery County v. Microvote Corp.*, 2004 WL 1087196 (EDPA 2004); *Greene v. Fraternal Order of Police*, 183 F.R.D. 445 (E.D. Pa. 1998). Accord, *Nissho–Iwai Co. v. Occidental Crude Sales*, 729 F.2d 1530 (5th Cir. 1984); *Quy v. Air America, Inc.*, 667 F.2d 1059 (D.C. Cir. 1981); *Karsian v. Inter Regional Financial Group, Inc.*, 13 F.Supp.2d 1085 (D. Colorado 1998); *Marino v. Town of Kirkland*, 146 F.R.D. 49 (N.D.N.Y. 1993); *Morrissey v. County Tower Corp.*, 568 F. Supp. 980 (E.D. Mo. 1983); *Independence Tube Corp. v. Copperweld Corp.*, 543 F.Supp. 706 (N.D.Ill. 1982); *Christian v. Tackett*, 86 F.R.D. 220 (N.D. Miss. 1979); *Gillam v. A. Shyman, Inc.*, 31 F.R.D. 271 (D. Alaska 1962).

220*Dr. Bernard Heller Foundation v. Lee*, 847 F.2d 83 (3rd Cir. 1988); *Greene v. Fraternal Order of Police*, 183 F.R.D. 445 (E.D. Pa. 1998). See, also, *Louisiana Power and Light Co. v. Kellstrom*, 50 F.3d 319 (5th Cir. 1995); *McGuigan v. CAE Link Corp.*, 155 F.R.D. 31 (NDNY 1994).

221*Kansas v. Colorado*, 129 S.Ct. 1294 (2009); *Crawford Fitting Company v. J. T. Gibbons, Inc.*, 482 U.S. 437 (1987); *In re Philadelphia Mortgage Trust*, 930 F.2d 306 (3rd Cir. 1990); *Friedman v. Ganassi*, 853 F.2d 207 (3rd Cir. 1988); *Dr. Bernard Heller Foundation v. Lee*, 847 F.2d 83 (3rd Cir. 1988); *Dominic v. Hess Oil V.I. Corp.*, 841 F.2d 513 (3rd Cir. 1988).

222*Crawford Fitting Company v. J. T. Gibbons, Inc.*, 482 U.S. 437 (1987); In re Philadelphia Mortgage Trust, 930 F.2d 306 (3rd Cir. 1990); *Friedman v. Ganassi*, 853 F.2d 207 (3rd Cir. 1988); *Dr. Bernard Heller Foundation v. Lee*, 847 F.2d 83 (3rd Cir. 1988); *Dominic v. Hess Oil V.I. Corp.*, 841 F.2d 513 (3rd Cir. 1988).

223*Sierra Club v. EPA*, 769 F.2d 796 (DC Cir. 1985); In Re: Air Crash Disaster at John F. Kennedy International Airport on June 24, 1975, 687 F.2d 626 (2nd Cir. 1982); *Griffith v. Mt. Carmel Medical Center*, 157 F.R.D. 499 (D. Kansas 1994); *Radol v. Thomas*, 113 F.R.D. 172 (SD Ohio 1986); *Marquez v. American Export Lines*, 41 F.R.D. 386 (SDNY 1967).

224*Greene v. Fraternal Order of Police*, 183 F.R.D. 445 (E.D. Pa. 1998). See, also, *Bee v. Greaves*, 910 F.2d 686 (10th Cir. 1990); *Jensen v. Lawler*, 338 F.Supp. 2d 739 (SD Texas 2004); *Heverly v. Lewis*, 99 F.R.D. 135, 136 (D.Nev. 1983); *Gillam v. Shyman, Inc.*, 31 F.R.D. 271 (D. Alaska 1962).

225*Greene v. Fraternal Order of Police*, 183 F.R.D. 445 (E.D. Pa. 1998). See, also, *Griffith v. Mt. Carmel Medical Center*, 157 F.R.D. 499 (D. Kansas 1994); *Todd Shipyards Corp. v. Turbine Services, Inc.*, 592 F.Supp. 380 (E.D. La. 1984); *Morrison v. Alleluia Cushion Co.*, 73 F.R.D. 70, 71 (N.D. Miss. 1976); *Sperry Rand Corp. v. A–T–O Co.*, 58 F.R.D. 132 (E.D. Va. 1973).

226*Reger v. The Nemours Foundation*, 599 F.3d 285 (3d Cir. 2010); In re: Paoli Railroad Yard PCB Litigation, 221 F.3d 449 (3d Cir. 2000); *Abrams v. Lightolier, Inc.*, 50 F.3d 1204 (3d Cir. 1995); *Smith v. SEPTA*, 47 F.3d 97 (3d Cir. 1995); *Friedman v. Ganassi*, 853 F.2d 207 (3d Cir. 1988); *Institutionalized Juveniles v. Secretary of Public Welfare*, 758 F.2d 897 (3d Cir. 1985); *Pearlstine v. United States*, 649 F.2d 194 (3rd Cir. 1981); *Delaney v. Capone*, 642 F.2d 57 (3d Cir. 1981); *Samuel v. University of Pittsburgh*, 538 F.2d 991 (3d Cir. 1976); *ADM Corp. v. Speedmaster Packing Corp.*, 525 F.2d 662 (3d Cir. 1975); *City of Rome, Italy v. Glanton*, 184 F.R.D. 547 (E.D. Pa. 1999); *Greene v. Fraternal Order of Police*, 183 F.R.D. 445 (E.D. Pa. 1998); *Action Alliance for Senior Citizens of Greater Philadelphia v. Shapp*, 74 F.R.D. 617 (E.D. Pa. 1977).

227*Buchanan v. Stanships, Inc.*, 485 U.S. 265, 268 (1988)(emphasis added). Accord, *Delta Air Lines, Inc. v. August*, 450 U.S. 346 (1981). See, also, *Reger v. The Nemours Foundation*, 599 F.3d 285 (3d Cir. 2010); In re: Paoli Railroad Yard PCB Litigation, 221 F.3d 449 (3d Cir. 2000); *Abrams v. Lightolier, Inc.*, 50 F.3d 1204 (3d Cir. 1995); *Smith v. SEPTA*, 47 F.3d 97 (3d Cir. 1995); *Friedman v. Ganassi*, 853 F.2d 207 (3d Cir. 1988); *Institutionalized Juveniles v. Secretary of Public Welfare*, 758 F.2d 897 (3d Cir. 1985); *Pearlstine v. United States*, 649 F.2d 194 (3rd Cir. 1981); *Delaney v. Capone*, 642 F. 2d 57 (3d Cir. 1981); *Samuel v. University of Pittsburgh*, 538 F.2d 991 (3d Cir. 1976); *ADM Corp. v. Speedmaster Packing Corp.*, 525 F.2d 662 (3d Cir. 1975); *City of Rome, Italy v. Glanton*, 184 F.R.D. 547 (E.D. Pa. 1999); *Greene v. Fraternal Order of Police*, 183 F.R.D. 445 (E.D. Pa. 1998); *Action Alliance for Senior Citizens of Greater Philadelphia v. Shapp*, 74 F.R.D. 617 (E.D. Pa. 1977).

228*Buchanan v. Stanships, Inc.*, 485 U.S. 265 (1988); *Delta Air Lines, Inc. v. August*, 450 U.S. 346 (1981). Accord, *Reger v. The Nemours Foundation*, 599 F.3d 285 (3d Cir. 2010); *In re: Paoli Railroad Yard PCB Litigation*, 221 F.3d 449 (3d Cir. 2000); *Abrams v. Lightolier, Inc.*, 50 F.3d 1204 (3d Cir. 1995); *Smith v. SEPTA*, 47 F.3d 97 (3d Cir. 1995); *Friedman v. Ganassi*, 853 F.2d 207 (3d Cir. 1988); *Institutionalized Juveniles v. Secretary of Public Welfare*, 758 F.2d 897 (3d Cir. 1985); *Pearlstine v. United States*, 649 F.2d 194 (3rd Cir. 1981); *Delaney v. Capone*, 642 F.2d 57 (3d Cir. 1981); *Samuel v. University of Pittsburgh*, 538

F.2d 991 (3d Cir. 1976); *ADM Corp. v. Speedmaster Packing Corp.*, 525 F.2d 662 (3d Cir. 1975); *City of Rome, Italy v. Glanton*, 184 F.R.D. 547 (E.D. Pa. 1999); *Greene v. Fraternal Order of Police*, 183 F.R.D. 445 (E.D. Pa. 1998); *Action Alliance for Senior Citizens of Greater Philadelphia v. Shapp*, 74 F.R.D. 617 (E.D. Pa. 1977).

229*Brazos Valley Coalition for Life, Inc. v. City of Bryan, Texas*, 421 F.3d 314 (5th Cir. 2005); *Trepel v. Roadway Express, Inc.*, 266 F.3d 418 (6th Cir. 2001); *Holmes v. Cessna Aircraft Co.*, 11 F.3d 63 (5th Cir. 1994); *Dovenmuehle v. Gilldorn Mortgage Midwest Corp.*, 871 F.2d 697 (7th Cir. 1989); *Mason v. Belieu*, 543 F.2d 215 (D.C. Cir. 1976); *Wahl v. Carrier Manufacturing Co.*, 511 F.2d 209 (7th Cir. 1975); *McInnis v. Town of Weston*, 458 F.Supp.2d 7 (D. Conn. 2006); *Sullivan v. Cheshier*, 991 F.Supp. 999 (N.D. Ill. 1998); *Hollenbeck v. Falstaff Brewing Corp.*, 605 F.Supp. 421 (E.D. Mo. 1984); *Morrissey v. County Tower Corp.*, 568 F.Supp. 980 (E.D. Mo. 1983).

230In Re: Kulicke & Soffa Industries Inc. Securities Litigation, 747 F.Supp. 1136 (E.D.Pa. 1990), aff'd, 944 F.2d 897 (3rd Cir. 1991); *ADM Corp. v. Speedmaster Packing Corp.*, 525 F.2d 662 (3d Cir. 1975); *Nugget Distributors Cooperative of America v. Mr. Nugget, Inc.*, 145 F.R. D. 54 (E.D.Pa. 1992). Accord, *Charter Medical Corp v. Cardin*, 127 FRD 111 (D. Maryland 1989); *Women's Federal Savings and Loan Association of Cleveland v. Nevada National Bank*, 108 FRD 396 (D. Nevada 1985); *International Wood Processors v. Power Dry, Inc.*, 598 F. Supp. 299 (D.S. C. 1984); *Morrissey v. County Tower Corp.*, 568 F.Supp. 178 (ED Mo. 1983).

231*Kansas v. Colorado*, 129 S.Ct. 1294 (2009).

232*Crawford Fitting Company v. J. T. Gibbons, Inc.*, 482 U.S. 437 (1987); *Henkel v. Chicago, St. Paul, Minneapolis and Omaha Railroad Company*, 284 U.S. 444 (1932).

233*Greene v. Fraternal Order of Police*, 183 F.R.D. 445 (E.D. Pa. 1998); *Raio v. American Airlines*, 102 F.R.D. 608 (E.D. Pa. 1984). See, also, *Women's Federal Savings and Loan Association of Cleveland v. Nevada National Bank*, 108 F.R.D. 396 (D. Nevada 1985).

234*Central Delaware Branch of the NAACP v. City of Dover, Delaware*, 123 FRD 85 (D. Delaware 1988).

235*Reger v. The Nemours Foundation*, 599 F.3d 285 (3d Cir. 2010); In re: Paoli Railroad Yard PCB Litigation, 221 F.3d 449 (3d Cir. 2000); *Abrams v. Lightolier, Inc.*, 50 F.3d 1204 (3d Cir. 1995); *Smith v. SEPTA*, 47 F.3d 97 (3d Cir. 1995); *Friedman v. Ganassi*, 853 F.2d 207 (3d Cir. 1988); *Institutionalized Juveniles v. Secretary of Public Welfare*, 758 F.2d 897 (3d Cir. 1985); *Pearlstine v. United States*, 649 F.2d 194 (3rd Cir. 1981); *Delaney v. Capone*, 642 F.2d 57 (3d Cir. 1981); *Samuel v. University of Pittsburgh*, 538 F.2d 991 (3d Cir. 1976); *ADM Corp. v. Speedmaster Packing Corp.*, 525 F.2d 662 (3d Cir. 1975); *City of Rome, Italy v. Glanton*, 184 F.R.D. 547 (E.D. Pa. 1999); *Greene v. Fraternal Order of Police*, 183 F.R.D. 445 (E.D. Pa. 1998); *Action Alliance for Senior Citizens of Greater Philadelphia v. Shapp*, 74 F.R.D. 617 (E.D. Pa. 1977).

236*Buchanan v. Stanships, Inc.*, 485 U.S. 265, 268 (1988)(emphasis added). Accord, *Delta Air Lines, Inc. v. August*, 450 U.S. 346 (1981). See, also, *Reger v. The Nemours Foundation*, 599 F.3d 285 (3d Cir. 2010); In re: Paoli Railroad Yard PCB Litigation, 221 F.3d 449 (3d Cir. 2000); *Abrams v. Lightolier, Inc.*, 50 F.3d 1204 (3d Cir. 1995); *Smith v. SEPTA*, 47 F.3d 97 (3d Cir. 1995); *Friedman v. Ganassi*, 853 F.2d 207 (3d Cir. 1988); *Institutionalized Juveniles v. Secretary of Public Welfare*, 758 F.2d 897 (3d Cir. 1985); *Pearlstine v. United States*, 649 F.2d 194 (3rd Cir. 1981); *Delaney v. Capone*, 642 F. 2d 57 (3d Cir. 1981); *Samuel v. University of Pittsburgh*, 538 F.2d 991 (3d Cir. 1976); *ADM Corp. v. Speedmaster Packing Corp.*, 525 F.2d 662 (3d Cir. 1975); *City of Rome, Italy v. Glanton*, 184 F.R.D. 547 (E.D. Pa. 1999); *Greene v. Fraternal Order of Police*, 183 F.R.D. 445 (E.D. Pa. 1998); *Action Alliance for Senior Citizens of Greater Philadelphia v. Shapp*, 74 F.R.D. 617 (E.D. Pa. 1977).

237*Buchanan v. Stanships, Inc.*, 485 U.S. 265 (1988); *Delta Air Lines, Inc. v. August*, 450 U.S. 346 (1981). Accord, *Reger v. The Nemours Foundation*, 599 F.3d 285 (3d Cir. 2010); In re: Paoli Railroad Yard PCB Litigation, 221 F.3d 449 (3d Cir. 2000); *Abrams v. Lightolier, Inc.*, 50 F.3d 1204 (3d Cir. 1995); *Smith v. SEPTA*, 47 F.3d 97 (3d Cir. 1995); *Friedman v. Ganassi*, 853 F.2d 207 (3d Cir. 1988); *Institutionalized Juveniles v. Secretary of Public Welfare*, 758 F.2d 897 (3d Cir. 1985); *Pearlstine v. United States*, 649 F.2d 194 (3rd Cir. 1981); *Delaney v. Capone*, 642 F.2d 57 (3d Cir. 1981); *Samuel v. University of Pittsburgh*, 538 F.2d 991 (3d Cir. 1976); *ADM Corp. v. Speedmaster Packing Corp.*, 525 F.2d 662 (3d Cir. 1975); *City of Rome, Italy v. Glanton*, 184 F.R.D. 547 (E.D. Pa. 1999); *Greene v. Fraternal Order of Police*, 183 F.R.D. 445 (E.D. Pa. 1998); *Action Alliance for Senior Citizens of Greater Philadelphia v. Shapp*, 74 F.R.D. 617 (E.D. Pa. 1977).

238*Brazos Valley Coalition for Life, Inc. v. City of Bryan, Texas*, 421 F.3d 314 (5th Cir. 2005); *Trepel v. Roadway Express, Inc.*, 266 F.3d 418 (6th Cir. 2001); *Holmes v. Cessna Aircraft Co.*, 11 F.3d 63 (5th Cir. 1994); *Dovenmuehle v. Gilldorn Mortgage Midwest Corp.*, 871 F.2d 697 (7th Cir. 1989); *Mason v. Belieu*, 543 F.2d 215 (D.C. Cir. 1976); *Wahl v. Carrier Manufacturing Co.*, 511 F.2d 209 (7th Cir. 1975); *McInnis v. Town of Weston*, 458 F.Supp.2d 7 (D. Conn. 2006); *Sullivan v. Cheshier*, 991 F.Supp. 999 (N.D. Ill. 1998); *Hollenbeck v. Falstaff Brewing Corp.*, 605 F.Supp. 421 (E.D. Mo. 1984); *Morrissey v. County Tower Corp.*, 568 F.Supp. 980 (E.D. Mo. 1983).

239In Re: Kulicke & Soffa Industries Inc. Securities Litigation, 747 F.Supp. 1136 (E.D.Pa. 1990), aff'd, 944 F.2d 897 (3rd Cir. 1991); *ADM Corp. v. Speedmaster Packing Corp.*, 525 F.2d 662 (3d Cir. 1975); *Nugget Distributors Cooperative of America v. Mr. Nugget, Inc.*, 145 F.R. D. 54 (E.D.Pa. 1992). Accord, *Charter Medical Corp v. Cardin*, 127 F. R.D. 111 (D. Maryland 1989); *Women's Federal Savings and Loan Association of Cleveland v. Nevada National Bank*, 108 F.R.D. 396 (D. Nevada 1985); *International Wood Processors v. Power Dry, Inc.*, 598 F. Supp. 299 (D.S. C. 1984); *Morrissey v. County Tower Corp.*, 568 F.Supp. 178 (ED Mo. 1983).

[240]*Kansas v. Colorado*, 129 S.Ct. 1294 (2009).

[241]*Crawford Fitting Company v. J. T. Gibbons, Inc.*, 482 U.S. 437 (1987); *Henkel v. Chicago, St. Paul, Minneapolis and Omaha Railroad Company*, 284 U.S. 444 (1932).

[242]*Greene v. Fraternal Order of Police*, 183 F.R.D. 445 (E.D. Pa. 1998); *Raio v. American Airlines*, 102 F.R.D. 608 (E.D. Pa. 1984). See, also, *Women's Federal Savings and Loan Association of Cleveland v. Nevada National Bank*, 108 F.R.D. 396 (D. Nevada 1985).

[243]*Central Delaware Branch of the NAACP v. City of Dover, Delaware*, 123 FRD 85 (D. Delaware 1988).

[244]*Reger v. The Nemours Foundation*, 599 F.3d 285 (3d Cir. 2010); In re: Paoli Railroad Yard PCB Litigation, 221 F.3d 449 (3d Cir. 2000); *Abrams v. Lightolier, Inc.*, 50 F.3d 1204 (3d Cir. 1995); *Smith v. SEPTA*, 47 F.3d 97 (3d Cir. 1995); *Friedman v. Ganassi*, 853 F.2d 207 (3d Cir. 1988); *Institutionalized Juveniles v. Secretary of Public Welfare*, 758 F.2d 897 (3d Cir. 1985); *Pearlstine v. United States*, 649 F.2d 194 (3rd Cir. 1981); *Delaney v. Capone*, 642 F.2d 57 (3d Cir. 1981); *Samuel v. University of Pittsburgh*, 538 F.2d 991 (3d Cir. 1976); *ADM Corp. v. Speedmaster Packing Corp.*, 525 F.2d 662 (3d Cir. 1975); *City of Rome, Italy v. Glanton*, 184 F.R.D. 547 (E.D. Pa. 1999); *Greene v. Fraternal Order of Police*, 183 F.R.D. 445 (E.D. Pa. 1998); *Action Alliance for Senior Citizens of Greater Philadelphia v. Shapp*, 74 F.R.D. 617 (E.D. Pa. 1977).

[245]*Buchanan v. Stanships, Inc.*, 485 U.S. 265, 268 (1988)(emphasis added). Accord, *Delta Air Lines, Inc. v. August*, 450 U.S. 346 (1981). See, also, *Reger v. The Nemours Foundation*, 599 F.3d 285 (3d Cir. 2010); In re: Paoli Railroad Yard PCB Litigation, 221 F.3d 449 (3d Cir. 2000); *Abrams v. Lightolier, Inc.*, 50 F.3d 1204 (3d Cir. 1995); *Smith v. SEPTA*, 47 F.3d 97 (3d Cir. 1995); *Friedman v. Ganassi*, 853 F.2d 207 (3d Cir. 1988); *Institutionalized Juveniles v. Secretary of Public Welfare*, 758 F.2d 897 (3d Cir. 1985); *Pearlstine v. United States*, 649 F.2d 194 (3rd Cir. 1981); *Delaney v. Capone*, 642 F. 2d 57 (3d Cir. 1981); *Samuel v. University of Pittsburgh*, 538 F.2d 991 (3d Cir. 1976); *ADM Corp. v. Speedmaster Packing Corp.*, 525 F.2d 662 (3d Cir. 1975); *City of Rome, Italy v. Glanton*, 184 F.R.D. 547 (E.D. Pa. 1999); *Greene v. Fraternal Order of Police*, 183 F.R.D. 445 (E.D. Pa. 1998); *Action Alliance for Senior Citizens of Greater Philadelphia v. Shapp*, 74 F.R.D. 617 (E.D. Pa. 1977).

[246]*Buchanan v. Stanships, Inc.*, 485 U.S. 265 (1988); *Delta Air Lines, Inc. v. August*, 450 U.S. 346 (1981). Accord, *Reger v. The Nemours Foundation*, 599 F.3d 285 (3d Cir. 2010); In re: Paoli Railroad Yard PCB Litigation, 221 F.3d 449 (3d Cir. 2000); *Abrams v. Lightolier, Inc.*, 50 F.3d 1204 (3d Cir. 1995); *Smith v. SEPTA*, 47 F.3d 97 (3d Cir. 1995); *Friedman v. Ganassi*, 853 F.2d 207 (3d Cir. 1988); *Institutionalized Juveniles v. Secretary of Public Welfare*, 758 F.2d 897 (3d Cir. 1985); *Pearlstine v. United States*, 649 F.2d 194 (3rd Cir. 1981); *Delaney v. Capone*, 642 F.2d 57 (3d Cir. 1981); *Samuel v. University of Pittsburgh*, 538 F.2d 991 (3d Cir. 1976); *ADM Corp. v. Speedmaster Packing Corp.*, 525 F.2d 662 (3d Cir. 1975); *City of Rome, Italy v. Glanton*, 184 F.R.D. 547 (E.D. Pa. 1999); *Greene v. Fraternal Order of Police*, 183 F.R.D. 445 (E.D. Pa. 1998); *Action Alliance for Senior Citizens of Greater Philadelphia v. Shapp*, 74 F.R.D. 617 (E.D. Pa. 1977).

[247]*Brazos Valley Coalition for Life, Inc. v. City of Bryan, Texas*, 421 F.3d 314 (5th Cir. 2005); *Trepel v. Roadway Express, Inc.*, 266 F.3d 418 (6th Cir. 2001); *Holmes v. Cessna Aircraft Co.*, 11 F.3d 63 (5th Cir. 1994); *Dovenmuehle v. Gilldorn Mortgage Midwest Corp.*, 871 F.2d 697 (7th Cir. 1989); *Mason v. Belieu*, 543 F.2d 215 (D.C. Cir. 1976); *Wahl v. Carrier Manufacturing Co.*, 511 F.2d 209 (7th Cir. 1975); *McInnis v. Town of Weston*, 458 F.Supp.2d 7 (D. Conn. 2006); *Sullivan v. Cheshier*, 991 F.Supp. 999 (N.D. Ill. 1998); *Hollenbeck v. Falstaff Brewing Corp.*, 605 F.Supp. 421 (E.D. Mo. 1984); *Morrissey v. County Tower Corp.*, 568 F.Supp. 980 (E.D. Mo. 1983).

[248]In Re: Kulicke & Soffa Industries Inc. Securities Litigation, 747 F.Supp. 1136 (E.D.Pa. 1990), aff'd, 944 F.2d 897 (3rd Cir. 1991); *ADM Corp. v. Speedmaster Packing Corp.*, 525 F.2d 662 (3d Cir. 1975); *Nugget Distributors Cooperative of America v. Mr. Nugget, Inc.*, 145 F.R. D. 54 (E.D.Pa. 1992). Accord, *Charter Medical Corp v. Cardin*, 127 FRD 111 (D. Maryland 1989); *Women's Federal Savings and Loan Association of Cleveland v. Nevada National Bank*, 108 FRD 396 (D. Nevada 1985); *International Wood Processors v. Power Dry, Inc.*, 598 F. Supp. 299 (D.S. C. 1984); *Morrissey v. County Tower Corp.*, 568 F.Supp. 178 (ED Mo. 1983).

[249]*Smith v. Tenet Healthsystems SL, Inc.*, 436 F.3d 879 (8th Cir. 2006).

[250]*Helms v. WalMart Stores, Inc.*, 808 F.Supp. 1568 (ND Ga. 1992), aff'd 998 F.2d 1023 (11th Cir. 1993); *Haagen–Dazs Co. v. Rainbow Gourmet Ice Creams, Inc.*, 920 F.2d 587 (9th Cir. 1990); *Rodriguez–Garcia v. Davila*, 904 F.2d 90 (1st Cir. 1990); *Allen v. United States Steel Corp.*, 665 F.2d 689 (5th Cir. 1982); *McGuigan v. CAE Link Corp.*, 155 FRD 31 (NDNY 1994); *Nelson v. Darragh Co.*, 120 FRD 517 (WD Ark. 1988); *Meadows v. Ford Motor Co.*, 62 FRD 98 (WD Ky. 1973); *Gillam v. A. Shyman*, Inc., 31 FRD 271 (D. Alaska 1962).

[251]*Montgomery County v. Microvote Corp.*, 2004 WL 1087196 (EDPA 2004); *McGuigan v. CAE Link Corp.*, 155 FRD 31 (NDNY 1994).

[252]*Race Tires America, Inc. v. Hoosier Racing Tire Corp.*, 674 F.3d 158 (3d Cir. 2012).

[253]*Reger v. The Nemours Foundation*, 599 F.3d 285 (3d Cir. 2010); In re: Paoli Railroad Yard PCB Litigation, 221 F.3d 449 (3d Cir. 2000); *Abrams v. Lightolier, Inc.*, 50 F.3d 1204 (3d Cir. 1995); *Smith v. SEPTA*, 47 F.3d 97 (3d Cir. 1995); *Friedman v. Ganassi*, 853 F.2d 207 (3d Cir. 1988); *Institutionalized Juveniles v. Secretary of Public Welfare*, 758 F.2d 897 (3d Cir. 1985); *Pearlstine v. United States*, 649 F.2d 194 (3rd Cir. 1981); *Delaney v. Capone*, 642 F.2d 57 (3d Cir. 1981); *Samuel v. University of Pittsburgh*, 538 F.2d 991 (3d Cir. 1976); *ADM Corp. v. Speedmaster Packing Corp.*, 525 F.2d 662 (3d Cir. 1975); *City of Rome, Italy v. Glanton*, 184 F.R.D. 547 (E.D. Pa. 1999); *Greene v. Fraternal Order of Police*, 183 F.R.D. 445

(E.D. Pa. 1998); *Action Alliance for Senior Citizens of Greater Philadelphia v. Shapp*, 74 F.R.D. 617 (E.D. Pa. 1977).

254*Buchanan v. Stanships, Inc.*, 485 U.S. 265, 268 (1988)(emphasis added). Accord, *Delta Air Lines, Inc. v. August*, 450 U.S. 346 (1981). See, also, *Reger v. The Nemours Foundation*, 599 F.3d 285 (3d Cir. 2010); In re: Paoli Railroad Yard PCB Litigation, 221 F.3d 449 (3d Cir. 2000); *Abrams v. Lightolier, Inc.*, 50 F.3d 1204 (3d Cir. 1995); *Smith v. SEPTA*, 47 F.3d 97 (3d Cir. 1995); *Friedman v. Ganassi*, 853 F.2d 207 (3d Cir. 1988); *Institutionalized Juveniles v. Secretary of Public Welfare*, 758 F.2d 897 (3d Cir. 1985); *Pearlstine v. United States*, 649 F.2d 194 (3rd Cir. 1981); *Delaney v. Capone*, 642 F. 2d 57 (3d Cir. 1981); *Samuel v. University of Pittsburgh*, 538 F.2d 991 (3d Cir. 1976); *ADM Corp. v. Speedmaster Packing Corp.*, 525 F.2d 662 (3d Cir. 1975); *City of Rome, Italy v. Glanton*, 184 F.R.D. 547 (E.D. Pa. 1999); *Greene v. Fraternal Order of Police*, 183 F.R.D. 445 (E.D. Pa. 1998); *Action Alliance for Senior Citizens of Greater Philadelphia v. Shapp*, 74 F.R.D. 617 (E.D. Pa. 1977).

255*Buchanan v. Stanships, Inc.*, 485 U.S. 265 (1988); *Delta Air Lines, Inc. v. August*, 450 U.S. 346 (1981). Accord, *Reger v. The Nemours Foundation*, 599 F.3d 285 (3d Cir. 2010); In re: Paoli Railroad Yard PCB Litigation, 221 F.3d 449 (3d Cir. 2000); *Abrams v. Lightolier, Inc.*, 50 F.3d 1204 (3d Cir. 1995); *Smith v. SEPTA*, 47 F.3d 97 (3d Cir. 1995); *Friedman v. Ganassi*, 853 F.2d 207 (3d Cir. 1988); *Institutionalized Juveniles v. Secretary of Public Welfare*, 758 F.2d 897 (3d Cir. 1985); *Pearlstine v. United States*, 649 F.2d 194 (3rd Cir. 1981); *Delaney v. Capone*, 642 F.2d 57 (3d Cir. 1981); *Samuel v. University of Pittsburgh*, 538 F.2d 991 (3d Cir. 1976); *ADM Corp. v. Speedmaster Packing Corp.*, 525 F.2d 662 (3d Cir. 1975); *City of Rome, Italy v. Glanton*, 184 F.R.D. 547 (E.D. Pa. 1999); *Greene v. Fraternal Order of Police*, 183 F.R.D. 445 (E.D. Pa. 1998); *Action Alliance for Senior Citizens of Greater Philadelphia v. Shapp*, 74 F.R.D. 617 (E.D. Pa. 1977).

256*Brazos Valley Coalition for Life, Inc. v. City of Bryan, Texas*, 421 F.3d 314 (5th Cir. 2005); *Trepel v. Roadway Express, Inc.*, 266 F.3d 418 (6th Cir. 2001); *Holmes v. Cessna Aircraft Co.*, 11 F.3d 63 (5th Cir. 1994); *Dovenmuehle v. Gilldorn Mortgage Midwest Corp.*, 871 F.2d 697 (7th Cir. 1989); *Mason v. Belieu*, 543 F.2d 215 (D.C. Cir. 1976); *Wahl v. Carrier Manufacturing Co.*, 511 F.2d 209 (7th Cir. 1975); *McInnis v. Town of Weston*, 458 F.Supp.2d 7 (D. Conn. 2006); *Sullivan v. Cheshier*, 991 F.Supp. 999 (N.D. Ill. 1998); *Hollenbeck v. Falstaff Brewing Corp.*, 605 F.Supp. 421 (E.D. Mo. 1984); *Morrissey v. County Tower Corp.*, 568 F.Supp. 980 (E.D. Mo. 1983).

257In Re: Kulicke & Soffa Industries Inc. Securities Litigation, 747 F.Supp. 1136 (E.D.Pa. 1990), aff'd, 944 F.2d 897 (3rd Cir. 1991); *ADM Corp. v. Speedmaster Packing Corp.*, 525 F.2d 662 (3d Cir. 1975); *Nugget Distributors Cooperative of America v. Mr. Nugget, Inc.*, 145 F.R. D. 54 (E.D.Pa. 1992). Accord, *Charter Medical Corp v. Cardin*, 127 F. R.D. 111 (D. Maryland 1989); *Women's Federal Savings and Loan Association of Cleveland v. Nevada National Bank*, 108 F.R.D. 396 (D. Nevada 1985); *International Wood Processors v. Power Dry, Inc.*, 598 F. Supp. 299 (D.S. C. 1984); *Morrissey v. County Tower Corp.*, 568 F.Supp. 178 (ED Mo. 1983).

258*Johnson v. Holway*, 522 F.Supp. 2d 12 (DDC 2007).

259*Johnson v. Holway*, 522 F.Supp. 2d 12 (DDC 2007).

260*Johnson v. Holway*, 522 F.Supp. 2d 12 (DDC 2007).

261*Haroco, Inc. v. American National Bank and Trust Company of Chicago*, 38 F.3d 1429 (7th Cir. 1994); *Johnson v. Holway*, 522 F.Supp. 2d 12 (DDC 2007).

262Accord, *Soler v. McHenry*, 771 F.Supp. 252 (ND Ill. 1991), aff'd, 989 F.2d 251 (7th Cir. 1993); *Maxwell v. Hapag–Lloyd Aktiengesellschaft*, 862 F.2d 767 (9th Cir. 1988); *Nissho–Iwai Co. v. Occidental Crude Sales, Ltd.*, 729 F.2d 1530 (5th Cir. 1984); *DiBella v. Hopkins*, 407 F.Supp. 2d 537 (SDNY 2005); *Jensen v. Lawler*, 338 F.Supp. 2d 739 (SD Texas 2004); *United Intern. Holdings, Inc. v. Wharf (Holdings) Ltd.*, 174 FRD 479 (D. Colo. 1997); *Phillips v. Cameron Tool Corp.*, 131 F.R.D. 151 (SD Ind. 1990).

263*Soler v. McHenry*, 771 F.Supp. 252 (ND Ill. 1991), aff'd, 989 F.2d 251 (7th Cir. 1993); *Maxwell v. Hapag–Lloyd Aktiengesellschaft*, 862 F.2d 767 (9th Cir. 1988); *In Re: Air Crash Disaster at John F. Kennedy International Airport on June 24, 1975*, 687 F.2d 626 (2nd Cir. 1982); *Jensen v. Lawler*, 338 F.Supp. 2d 739 (SD Texas 2004); *United Intern. Holdings, Inc. v. Wharf (Holdings) Ltd.*, 174 FRD 479 (D. Colo. 1997).

264*Jensen v. Lawler*, 338 F.Supp. 2d 739 (SD Texas 2004).

265In Re: Air Crash Disaster at John F. Kennedy International Airport on June 24, 1975, 687 F.2d 626 (2nd Cir. 1982).

266*Soler v. McHenry*, 771 F.Supp. 252 (ND Ill. 1991); aff'd, 989 F.2d 251 (7th Cir. 1993); *Nissho–Iwai Co. v. Occidental Crude Sales, Ltd.*, 729 F.2d 1530 (5th Cir. 1984); *DiBella v. Hopkins*, 407 F.Supp. 2d 537 (SDNY 2005); *Jensen v. Lawler*, 338 F.Supp. 2d 739 (SD Texas 2004).

267In Re: Air Crash Disaster at John F. Kennedy International Airport on June 24, 1975, 687 F.2d 626 (2nd Cir. 1982); *DiBella v. Hopkins*, 407 F.Supp.2d 537 (SDNY 2005); *United Intern. Holdings, Inc. v. Wharf (Holdings) Ltd.*, 174 F.R.D. 479 (D. Colo. 1997).

268*Phillips v. Cameron Tool Corp.*, 131 F.R.D. 151 (SD Ind. 1990).

269*DiBella v. Hopkins*, 407 F.Supp.2d 537 (SDNY 2005).

270*Sierra Club v. EPA*, 769 F.2d 796 (DC Cir. 1985); In Re: Air Crash Disaster at John F. Kennedy International Airport on June 24, 1975, 687 F.2d 626 (2nd Cir. 1982); *Griffith v. Mt. Carmel Medical Center*,

157 F.R.D. 499 (D. Kansas 1994); *Radol v. Thomas*, 113 F.R.D. 172 (SD Ohio 1986); *Marquez v. American Export Lines*, 41 F.R.D. 386 (SDNY 1967).

271*Reger v. The Nemours Foundation*, 599 F.3d 285 (3d Cir. 2010); In re: Paoli Railroad Yard PCB Litigation, 221 F.3d 449 (3d Cir. 2000); *Abrams v. Lightolier, Inc.*, 50 F.3d 1204 (3d Cir. 1995); *Smith v. SEPTA*, 47 F.3d 97 (3d Cir. 1995); *Friedman v. Ganassi*, 853 F.2d 207 (3d Cir. 1988); *Institutionalized Juveniles v. Secretary of Public Welfare*, 758 F.2d 897 (3d Cir. 1985); *Pearlstine v. United States*, 649 F.2d 194 (3rd Cir. 1981); *Delaney v. Capone*, 642 F.2d 57 (3d Cir. 1981); *Samuel v. University of Pittsburgh*, 538 F.2d 991 (3d Cir. 1976); *ADM Corp. v. Speedmaster Packing Corp.*, 525 F.2d 662 (3d Cir. 1975); *City of Rome, Italy v. Glanton*, 184 F.R.D. 547 (E.D. Pa. 1999); *Greene v. Fraternal Order of Police*, 183 F.R.D. 445 (E.D. Pa. 1998); *Action Alliance for Senior Citizens of Greater Philadelphia v. Shapp*, 74 F.R.D. 617 (E.D. Pa. 1977).

272*Buchanan v. Stanships, Inc.*, 485 U.S. 265, 268 (1988)(emphasis added). Accord, *Delta Air Lines, Inc. v. August*, 450 U.S. 346 (1981). See, also, *Reger v. The Nemours Foundation*, 599 F.3d 285 (3d Cir. 2010); In re: Paoli Railroad Yard PCB Litigation, 221 F.3d 449 (3d Cir. 2000); *Abrams v. Lightolier, Inc.*, 50 F.3d 1204 (3d Cir. 1995); *Smith v. SEPTA*, 47 F.3d 97 (3d Cir. 1995); *Friedman v. Ganassi*, 853 F.2d 207 (3d Cir. 1988); *Institutionalized Juveniles v. Secretary of Public Welfare*, 758 F.2d 897 (3d Cir. 1985); *Pearlstine v. United States*, 649 F.2d 194 (3rd Cir. 1981); *Delaney v. Capone*, 642 F. 2d 57 (3d Cir. 1981); *Samuel v. University of Pittsburgh*, 538 F.2d 991 (3d Cir. 1976); *ADM Corp. v. Speedmaster Packing Corp.*, 525 F.2d 662 (3d Cir. 1975); *City of Rome, Italy v. Glanton*, 184 F.R.D. 547 (E.D. Pa. 1999); *Greene v. Fraternal Order of Police*, 183 F.R.D. 445 (E.D. Pa. 1998); *Action Alliance for Senior Citizens of Greater Philadelphia v. Shapp*, 74 F.R.D. 617 (E.D. Pa. 1977).

273*Buchanan v. Stanships, Inc.*, 485 U.S. 265 (1988); *Delta Air Lines, Inc. v. August*, 450 U.S. 346 (1981). Accord, *Reger v. The Nemours Foundation*, 599 F.3d 285 (3d Cir. 2010); In re: Paoli Railroad Yard PCB Litigation, 221 F.3d 449 (3d Cir. 2000); *Abrams v. Lightolier, Inc.*, 50 F.3d 1204 (3d Cir. 1995); *Smith v. SEPTA*, 47 F.3d 97 (3d Cir. 1995); *Friedman v. Ganassi*, 853 F.2d 207 (3d Cir. 1988); *Institutionalized Juveniles v. Secretary of Public Welfare*, 758 F.2d 897 (3d Cir. 1985); *Pearlstine v. United States*, 649 F.2d 194 (3rd Cir. 1981); *Delaney v. Capone*, 642 F.2d 57 (3d Cir. 1981); *Samuel v. University of Pittsburgh*, 538 F.2d 991 (3d Cir. 1976); *ADM Corp. v. Speedmaster Packing Corp.*, 525 F.2d 662 (3d Cir. 1975); *City of Rome, Italy v. Glanton*, 184 F.R.D. 547 (E.D. Pa. 1999); *Greene v. Fraternal Order of Police*, 183 F.R.D. 445 (E.D. Pa. 1998); *Action Alliance for Senior Citizens of Greater Philadelphia v. Shapp*, 74 F.R.D. 617 (E.D. Pa. 1977).

274*Brazos Valley Coalition for Life, Inc. v. City of Bryan, Texas*, 421 F.3d 314 (5th Cir. 2005); *Trepel v. Roadway Express, Inc.*, 266 F.3d 418 (6th Cir. 2001); *Holmes v. Cessna Aircraft Co.*, 11 F.3d 63 (5th Cir. 1994); *Dovenmuehle v. Gilldorn Mortgage Midwest Corp.*, 871 F.2d 697 (7th Cir. 1989); *Mason v. Belieu*, 543 F.2d 215 (D.C. Cir. 1976); *Wahl v. Carrier Manufacturing Co.*, 511 F.2d 209 (7th Cir. 1975); *McInnis v. Town of Weston*, 458 F.Supp.2d 7 (D. Conn. 2006); *Sullivan v. Cheshier*, 991 F.Supp. 999 (N.D. Ill. 1998); *Hollenbeck v. Falstaff Brewing Corp.*, 605 F.Supp. 421 (E.D. Mo. 1984); *Morrissey v. County Tower Corp.*, 568 F.Supp. 980 (E.D. Mo. 1983).

275In Re: Kulicke & Soffa Industries Inc. Securities Litigation, 747 F.Supp. 1136 (E.D.Pa. 1990), aff'd, 944 F.2d 897 (3rd Cir. 1991); *ADM Corp. v. Speedmaster Packing Corp.*, 525 F.2d 662 (3d Cir. 1975); *Nugget Distributors Cooperative of America v. Mr. Nugget, Inc.*, 145 F. R. D. 54 (E.D.Pa. 1992). Accord, *Charter Medical Corp v. Cardin*, 127 FRD 111 (D. Maryland 1989); *Women's Federal Savings and Loan Association of Cleveland v. Nevada National Bank*, 108 FRD 396 (D. Nevada 1985); *International Wood Processors v. Power Dry, Inc.*, 598 F. Supp. 299 (D.S. C. 1984); *Morrissey v. County Tower Corp.*, 568 F.Supp. 178 (ED Mo. 1983).

276*Johnson v. Holway*, 522 F.Supp. 2d 12 (DDC 2007).

277*Johnson v. Holway*, 522 F.Supp. 2d 12 (DDC 2007).

278*Johnson v. Holway*, 522 F.Supp. 2d 12 (DDC 2007).

279*Haroco, Inc. v. American National Bank and Trust Company of Chicago*, 38 F.3d 1429 (7th Cir. 1994); *Johnson v. Holway*, 522 F.Supp. 2d 12 (DDC 2007).

280*Winniczek v. Nagelberg*, 400 F.3d 503 (7th Cir. 2005).

281*Reger v. The Nemours Foundation*, 599 F.3d 285 (3d Cir. 2010); In re: Paoli Railroad Yard PCB Litigation, 221 F.3d 449 (3d Cir. 2000); *Abrams v. Lightolier, Inc.*, 50 F.3d 1204 (3d Cir. 1995); *Smith v. SEPTA*, 47 F.3d 97 (3d Cir. 1995); *Friedman v. Ganassi*, 853 F.2d 207 (3d Cir. 1988); *Institutionalized Juveniles v. Secretary of Public Welfare*, 758 F.2d 897 (3d Cir. 1985); *Pearlstine v. United States*, 649 F.2d 194 (3rd Cir. 1981); *Delaney v. Capone*, 642 F.2d 57 (3d Cir. 1981); *Samuel v. University of Pittsburgh*, 538 F.2d 991 (3d Cir. 1976); *ADM Corp. v. Speedmaster Packing Corp.*, 525 F.2d 662 (3d Cir. 1975); *City of Rome, Italy v. Glanton*, 184 F.R.D. 547 (E.D. Pa. 1999); *Greene v. Fraternal Order of Police*, 183 F.R.D. 445 (E.D. Pa. 1998); *Action Alliance for Senior Citizens of Greater Philadelphia v. Shapp*, 74 F.R.D. 617 (E.D. Pa. 1977).

282*Buchanan v. Stanships, Inc.*, 485 U.S. 265, 268 (1988)(emphasis added). Accord, *Delta Air Lines, Inc. v. August*, 450 U.S. 346 (1981). See, also, *Reger v. The Nemours Foundation*, 599 F.3d 285 (3d Cir. 2010); In re: Paoli Railroad Yard PCB Litigation, 221 F.3d 449 (3d Cir. 2000); *Abrams v. Lightolier, Inc.*, 50 F.3d 1204 (3d Cir. 1995); *Smith v. SEPTA*, 47 F.3d 97 (3d Cir. 1995); *Friedman v. Ganassi*, 853 F.2d 207 (3d Cir. 1988); *Institutionalized Juveniles v. Secretary of Public Welfare*, 758 F.2d 897 (3d Cir. 1985); *Pearlstine v. United States*, 649 F.2d 194 (3rd Cir. 1981); *Delaney v. Capone*, 642 F. 2d 57 (3d Cir. 1981); *Samuel v. University of Pittsburgh*, 538 F.2d 991 (3d Cir. 1976); *ADM Corp. v. Speedmaster Packing Corp.*, 525 F.2d 662 (3d Cir. 1975); *City of Rome, Italy v. Glanton*, 184 F.R.D. 547 (E.D. Pa. 1999); *Greene v. Fraternal*

Order of Police, 183 F.R.D. 445 (E.D. Pa. 1998); *Action Alliance for Senior Citizens of Greater Philadelphia v. Shapp*, 74 F.R.D. 617 (E.D. Pa. 1977).

283*Buchanan v. Stanships, Inc.*, 485 U.S. 265 (1988); *Delta Air Lines, Inc. v. August*, 450 U.S. 346 (1981). Accord, *Reger v. The Nemours Foundation*, 599 F.3d 285 (3d Cir. 2010); In re: Paoli Railroad Yard PCB Litigation, 221 F.3d 449 (3d Cir. 2000); *Abrams v. Lightolier, Inc.*, 50 F.3d 1204 (3d Cir. 1995); *Smith v. SEPTA*, 47 F.3d 97 (3d Cir. 1995); *Friedman v. Ganassi*, 853 F.2d 207 (3d Cir. 1988); *Institutionalized Juveniles v. Secretary of Public Welfare*, 758 F.2d 897 (3d Cir. 1985); *Pearlstine v. United States*, 649 F.2d 194 (3rd Cir. 1981); *Delaney v. Capone*, 642 F.2d 57 (3d Cir. 1981); *Samuel v. University of Pittsburgh*, 538 F.2d 991 (3d Cir. 1976); *ADM Corp. v. Speedmaster Packing Corp.*, 525 F.2d 662 (3d Cir. 1975); *City of Rome, Italy v. Glanton*, 184 F.R.D. 547 (E.D. Pa. 1999); *Greene v. Fraternal Order of Police*, 183 F.R.D. 445 (E.D. Pa. 1998); *Action Alliance for Senior Citizens of Greater Philadelphia v. Shapp*, 74 F.R.D. 617 (E.D. Pa. 1977).

284*Brazos Valley Coalition for Life, Inc. v. City of Bryan, Texas*, 421 F.3d 314 (5th Cir. 2005); *Trepel v. Roadway Express, Inc.*, 266 F.3d 418 (6th Cir. 2001); *Holmes v. Cessna Aircraft Co.*, 11 F.3d 63 (5th Cir. 1994); *Dovenmuehle v. Gilldorn Mortgage Midwest Corp.*, 871 F.2d 697 (7th Cir. 1989); *Mason v. Belieu*, 543 F.2d 215 (D.C. Cir. 1976); *Wahl v. Carrier Manufacturing Co.*, 511 F.2d 209 (7th Cir. 1975); *McInnis v. Town of Weston*, 458 F.Supp.2d 7 (D. Conn. 2006); *Sullivan v. Cheshier*, 991 F.Supp. 999 (N.D. Ill. 1998); *Hollenbeck v. Falstaff Brewing Corp.*, 605 F.Supp. 421 (E.D. Mo. 1984); *Morrissey v. County Tower Corp.*, 568 F.Supp. 980 (E.D. Mo. 1983).

285In Re: Kulicke & Soffa Industries Inc. Securities Litigation, 747 F.Supp. 1136 (E.D.Pa. 1990), aff'd, 944 F.2d 897 (3rd Cir. 1991); *ADM Corp. v. Speedmaster Packing Corp.*, 525 F.2d 662 (3d Cir. 1975); *Nugget Distributors Cooperative of America v. Mr. Nugget, Inc.*, 145 F.R. D. 54 (E.D.Pa. 1992). Accord, *Charter Medical Corp v. Cardin*, 127 FRD 111 (D. Maryland 1989); *Women's Federal Savings and Loan Association of Cleveland v. Nevada National Bank*, 108 F.R.D. 396 (D. Nevada 1985); *International Wood Processors v. Power Dry, Inc.*, 598 F. Supp. 299 (D.S. C. 1984); *Morrissey v. County Tower Corp.*, 568 F.Supp. 178 (ED Mo. 1983).

286*Sierra Club v. EPA*, 769 F.2d 796 (DC Cir. 1985); In Re: Air Crash Disaster at John F. Kennedy International Airport on June 24, 1975, 687 F.2d 626 (2nd Cir. 1982); *Griffith v. Mt. Carmel Medical Center*, 157 F.R.D. 499 (D. Kansas 1994); *Radol v. Thomas*, 113 F.R.D. 172 (SD Ohio 1986); *Marquez v. American Export Lines*, 41 F.R.D. 386 (SDNY 1967).

287In Re: Air Crash Disaster at John F. Kennedy International Airport on June 24, 1975, 687 F.2d 626 (2nd Cir. 1982).

288*Jensen v. Lawler*, 338 F.Supp. 2d 739 (SD Texas 2004).

289*Reger v. The Nemours Foundation*, 599 F.3d 285 (3d Cir. 2010); In re: Paoli Railroad Yard PCB Litigation, 221 F.3d 449 (3d Cir. 2000); *Abrams v. Lightolier, Inc.*, 50 F.3d 1204 (3d Cir. 1995); *Smith v. SEPTA*, 47 F.3d 97 (3d Cir. 1995); *Friedman v. Ganassi*, 853 F.2d 207 (3d Cir. 1988); *Institutionalized Juveniles v. Secretary of Public Welfare*, 758 F.2d 897 (3d Cir. 1985); *Pearlstine v. United States*, 649 F.2d 194 (3rd Cir. 1981); *Delaney v. Capone*, 642 F.2d 57 (3d Cir. 1981); *Samuel v. University of Pittsburgh*, 538 F.2d 991 (3d Cir. 1976); *ADM Corp. v. Speedmaster Packing Corp.*, 525 F.2d 662 (3d Cir. 1975); *City of Rome, Italy v. Glanton*, 184 F.R.D. 547 (E.D. Pa. 1999); *Greene v. Fraternal Order of Police*, 183 F.R.D. 445 (E.D. Pa. 1998); *Action Alliance for Senior Citizens of Greater Philadelphia v. Shapp*, 74 F.R.D. 617 (E.D. Pa. 1977).

290*Buchanan v. Stanships, Inc.*, 485 U.S. 265, 268 (1988)(emphasis added). Accord, *Delta Air Lines, Inc. v. August*, 450 U.S. 346 (1981). See, also, *Reger v. The Nemours Foundation*, 599 F.3d 285 (3d Cir. 2010); In re: Paoli Railroad Yard PCB Litigation, 221 F.3d 449 (3d Cir. 2000); *Abrams v. Lightolier, Inc.*, 50 F.3d 1204 (3d Cir. 1995); *Smith v. SEPTA*, 47 F.3d 97 (3d Cir. 1995); *Friedman v. Ganassi*, 853 F.2d 207 (3d Cir. 1988); *Institutionalized Juveniles v. Secretary of Public Welfare*, 758 F.2d 897 (3d Cir. 1985); *Pearlstine v. United States*, 649 F.2d 194 (3rd Cir. 1981); *Delaney v. Capone*, 642 F. 2d 57 (3d Cir. 1981); *Samuel v. University of Pittsburgh*, 538 F.2d 991 (3d Cir. 1976); *ADM Corp. v. Speedmaster Packing Corp.*, 525 F.2d 662 (3d Cir. 1975); *City of Rome, Italy v. Glanton*, 184 F.R.D. 547 (E.D. Pa. 1999); *Greene v. Fraternal Order of Police*, 183 F.R.D. 445 (E.D. Pa. 1998); *Action Alliance for Senior Citizens of Greater Philadelphia v. Shapp*, 74 F.R.D. 617 (E.D. Pa. 1977).

291*Buchanan v. Stanships, Inc.*, 485 U.S. 265 (1988); *Delta Air Lines, Inc. v. August*, 450 U.S. 346 (1981). Accord, *Reger v. The Nemours Foundation*, 599 F.3d 285 (3d Cir. 2010); In re: Paoli Railroad Yard PCB Litigation, 221 F.3d 449 (3d Cir. 2000); *Abrams v. Lightolier, Inc.*, 50 F.3d 1204 (3d Cir. 1995); *Smith v. SEPTA*, 47 F.3d 97 (3d Cir. 1995); *Friedman v. Ganassi*, 853 F.2d 207 (3d Cir. 1988); *Institutionalized Juveniles v. Secretary of Public Welfare*, 758 F.2d 897 (3d Cir. 1985); *Pearlstine v. United States*, 649 F.2d 194 (3rd Cir. 1981); *Delaney v. Capone*, 642 F.2d 57 (3d Cir. 1981); *Samuel v. University of Pittsburgh*, 538 F.2d 991 (3d Cir. 1976); *ADM Corp. v. Speedmaster Packing Corp.*, 525 F.2d 662 (3d Cir. 1975); *City of Rome, Italy v. Glanton*, 184 F.R.D. 547 (E.D. Pa. 1999); *Greene v. Fraternal Order of Police*, 183 F.R.D. 445 (E.D. Pa. 1998); *Action Alliance for Senior Citizens of Greater Philadelphia v. Shapp*, 74 F.R.D. 617 (E.D. Pa. 1977).

292*Brazos Valley Coalition for Life, Inc. v. City of Bryan, Texas*, 421 F.3d 314 (5th Cir. 2005); *Trepel v. Roadway Express, Inc.*, 266 F.3d 418 (6th Cir. 2001); *Holmes v. Cessna Aircraft Co.*, 11 F.3d 63 (5th Cir. 1994); *Dovenmuehle v. Gilldorn Mortgage Midwest Corp.*, 871 F.2d 697 (7th Cir. 1989); *Mason v. Belieu*, 543 F.2d 215 (D.C. Cir. 1976); *Wahl v. Carrier Manufacturing Co.*, 511 F.2d 209 (7th Cir. 1975); *McInnis v. Town of Weston*, 458 F.Supp.2d 7 (D. Conn. 2006); *Sullivan v. Cheshier*, 991 F.Supp. 999 (N.D. Ill. 1998); *Hollenbeck v. Falstaff Brewing Corp.*, 605 F.Supp. 421 (E.D. Mo. 1984); *Morrissey v. County Tower Corp.*, 568 F.Supp. 980 (E.D. Mo. 1983).

293In Re: Kulicke & Soffa Industries Inc. Securities Litigation, 747 F.Supp. 1136 (E.D.Pa. 1990), aff'd, 944 F.2d 897 (3rd Cir. 1991); *ADM Corp. v. Speedmaster Packing Corp.*, 525 F.2d 662 (3d Cir. 1975); *Nugget Distributors Cooperative of America v. Mr. Nugget, Inc.*, 145 F.R. D. 54 (E.D.Pa. 1992). Accord, *Charter Medical Corp v. Cardin*, 127 FRD 111 (D. Maryland 1989); *Women's Federal Savings and Loan Association of Cleveland v. Nevada National Bank*, 108 F.R.D. 396 (D. Nevada 1985); *International Wood Processors v. Power Dry, Inc.*, 598 F. Supp. 299 (D.S. C. 1984); *Morrissey v. County Tower Corp.*, 568 F.Supp. 178 (ED Mo. 1983).

294*Taniguchi v. Kan Pacific Saipan, Ltd.*, 132 S.Ct. 1997 (2012).

295*Reger v. The Nemours Foundation*, 599 F.3d 285 (3d Cir. 2010); In re: Paoli Railroad Yard PCB Litigation, 221 F.3d 449 (3d Cir. 2000); *Abrams v. Lightolier, Inc.*, 50 F.3d 1204 (3d Cir. 1995); *Smith v. SEPTA*, 47 F.3d 97 (3d Cir. 1995); *Friedman v. Ganassi*, 853 F.2d 207 (3d Cir. 1988); *Institutionalized Juveniles v. Secretary of Public Welfare*, 758 F.2d 897 (3d Cir. 1985); *Pearlstine v. United States*, 649 F.2d 194 (3rd Cir. 1981); *Delaney v. Capone*, 642 F.2d 57 (3d Cir. 1981); *Samuel v. University of Pittsburgh*, 538 F.2d 991 (3d Cir. 1976); *ADM Corp. v. Speedmaster Packing Corp.*, 525 F.2d 662 (3d Cir. 1975); *City of Rome, Italy v. Glanton*, 184 F.R.D. 547 (E.D. Pa. 1999); *Greene v. Fraternal Order of Police*, 183 F.R.D. 445 (E.D. Pa. 1998); *Action Alliance for Senior Citizens of Greater Philadelphia v. Shapp*, 74 F.R.D. 617 (E.D. Pa. 1977).

296*Buchanan v. Stanships, Inc.*, 485 U.S. 265, 268 (1988)(emphasis added). Accord, *Delta Air Lines, Inc. v. August*, 450 U.S. 346 (1981). See, also, *Reger v. The Nemours Foundation*, 599 F.3d 285 (3d Cir. 2010); In re: Paoli Railroad Yard PCB Litigation, 221 F.3d 449 (3d Cir. 2000); *Abrams v. Lightolier, Inc.*, 50 F.3d 1204 (3d Cir. 1995); *Smith v. SEPTA*, 47 F.3d 97 (3d Cir. 1995); *Friedman v. Ganassi*, 853 F.2d 207 (3d Cir. 1988); *Institutionalized Juveniles v. Secretary of Public Welfare*, 758 F.2d 897 (3d Cir. 1985); *Pearlstine v. United States*, 649 F.2d 194 (3rd Cir. 1981); *Delaney v. Capone*, 642 F. 2d 57 (3d Cir. 1981); *Samuel v. University of Pittsburgh*, 538 F.2d 991 (3d Cir. 1976); *ADM Corp. v. Speedmaster Packing Corp.*, 525 F.2d 662 (3d Cir. 1975); *City of Rome, Italy v. Glanton*, 184 F.R.D. 547 (E.D. Pa. 1999); *Greene v. Fraternal Order of Police*, 183 F.R.D. 445 (E.D. Pa. 1998); *Action Alliance for Senior Citizens of Greater Philadelphia v. Shapp*, 74 F.R.D. 617 (E.D. Pa. 1977).

297*Buchanan v. Stanships, Inc.*, 485 U.S. 265 (1988); *Delta Air Lines, Inc. v. August*, 450 U.S. 346 (1981). Accord, *Reger v. The Nemours Foundation*, 599 F.3d 285 (3d Cir. 2010); In re: Paoli Railroad Yard PCB Litigation, 221 F.3d 449 (3d Cir. 2000); *Abrams v. Lightolier, Inc.*, 50 F.3d 1204 (3d Cir. 1995); *Smith v. SEPTA*, 47 F.3d 97 (3d Cir. 1995); *Friedman v. Ganassi*, 853 F.2d 207 (3d Cir. 1988); *Institutionalized Juveniles v. Secretary of Public Welfare*, 758 F.2d 897 (3d Cir. 1985); *Pearlstine v. United States*, 649 F.2d 194 (3rd Cir. 1981); *Delaney v. Capone*, 642 F.2d 57 (3d Cir. 1981); *Samuel v. University of Pittsburgh*, 538 F.2d 991 (3d Cir. 1976); *ADM Corp. v. Speedmaster Packing Corp.*, 525 F.2d 662 (3d Cir. 1975); *City of Rome, Italy v. Glanton*, 184 F.R.D. 547 (E.D. Pa. 1999); *Greene v. Fraternal Order of Police*, 183 F.R.D. 445 (E.D. Pa. 1998); *Action Alliance for Senior Citizens of Greater Philadelphia v. Shapp*, 74 F.R.D. 617 (E.D. Pa. 1977).

298*Brazos Valley Coalition for Life, Inc. v. City of Bryan, Texas*, 421 F.3d 314 (5th Cir. 2005); *Trepel v. Roadway Express, Inc.*, 266 F.3d 418 (6th Cir. 2001); *Holmes v. Cessna Aircraft Co.*, 11 F.3d 63 (5th Cir. 1994); *Dovenmuehle v. Gilldorn Mortgage Midwest Corp.*, 871 F.2d 697 (7th Cir. 1989); *Mason v. Belieu*, 543 F.2d 215 (D.C. Cir. 1976); *Wahl v. Carrier Manufacturing Co.*, 511 F.2d 209 (7th Cir. 1975); *McInnis v. Town of Weston*, 458 F.Supp.2d 7 (D. Conn. 2006); *Sullivan v. Cheshier*, 991 F.Supp. 999 (N.D. Ill. 1998); *Hollenbeck v. Falstaff Brewing Corp.*, 605 F.Supp. 421 (E.D. Mo. 1984); *Morrissey v. County Tower Corp.*, 568 F.Supp. 980 (E.D. Mo. 1983).

299In Re: Kulicke & Soffa Industries Inc. Securities Litigation, 747 F.Supp. 1136 (E.D.Pa. 1990), aff'd, 944 F.2d 897 (3rd Cir. 1991); *ADM Corp. v. Speedmaster Packing Corp.*, 525 F.2d 662 (3d Cir. 1975); *Nugget Distributors Cooperative of America v. Mr. Nugget, Inc.*, 145 F.R. D. 54 (E.D.Pa. 1992). Accord, *Charter Medical Corp v. Cardin*, 127 FRD 111 (D. Maryland 1989); *Women's Federal Savings and Loan Association of Cleveland v. Nevada National Bank*, 108 FRD 396 (D. Nevada 1985); *International Wood Processors v. Power Dry, Inc.*, 598 F. Supp. 299 (D.S. C. 1984); *Morrissey v. County Tower Corp.*, 568 F.Supp. 178 (ED Mo. 1983).

300*Reger v. The Nemours Foundation*, 599 F.3d 285 (3d Cir. 2010); *Abrams v. Lightolier, Inc.*, 50 F.3d 1204 (3d Cir. 1995).

301*Delta Air Lines, Inc. v. August*, 450 U.S. 346 (1981).

302*Sea Coast Foods, Inc. v. Lu–Mar Lobster & Shrimp*, 260 F.3d 1054 (9th Cir. 2001).

303*Sea Coast Foods, Inc. v. Lu–Mar Lobster & Shrimp*, 260 F.3d 1054 (9th Cir. 2001).

304*Delta Air Lines, Inc. v. August*, 450 U.S. 346 (1981).

305*Abrams v. Lightolier, Inc.*, 50 F.3d 1204 (3d Cir. 1995).

306*Buchanan v. Stanships, Inc.*, 485 U.S. 265 (1988); *Alyeska Pipeline Service Co. v. Wilderness Society*, 421 U.S. 240 (1975); *Fleischmann Distilling Co. v. Maier Brewing Co.*, 386 U.S. 714 (1967); *Reger v. The Nemours Foundation*, 599 F.3d 285 (3d Cir. 2010); In re: Paoli Railroad Yard PCB Litigation, 221 F.3d 449 (3d Cir. 2000); *Adams v. Teamsters Local 115*, 678 F.Supp.2d 314 (E.D. Pa. 2007).

307*Buchanan v. Stanships, Inc.*, 485 U.S. 265 (1988); *Reger v. The Nemours Foundation*, 599 F.3d 285 (3d Cir. 2010); *McKenna v. City of Philadelphia*, 582 F.3d 447 (3d Cir. 2009).

308*Buchanan v. Stanships, Inc.*, 485 U.S. 265 (1988); *Reger v. The Nemours Foundation*, 599 F.3d 285 (3d Cir. 2010); *McKenna v. City of Philadelphia*, 582 F.3d 447 (3d Cir. 2009).

309*SNA, Inc. v. Array*, 173 F.Supp.2d 347 (E.D.Pa. 2001). <u>Accord</u>, *L–3 Communications Corp. v. OSI Systems, Inc.*, 607 F.3d 24, 30 (2d Cir. 2010); *Republic Tobacco Co. v. North Atlantic Trading Co.*, 481 F.3d 442 (7th Cir. 2007); *Emmenegger v. Bull Moose Tube Co.*, 324 F.3d 616 (8th Cir. 2003); *Berthelsen v. Kane*, 907 F.2d 617 (6th Cir. 1990); *Choice Hotels International, Inc. v. Kaushik*, 203 F.Supp.2d 1281 (M.D. Ala. 2002).

310*Republic Tobacco Co. v. North Atlantic Trading Co.*, 481 F.3d 442 (7th Cir. 2007).

311*Republic Tobacco Co. v. North Atlantic Trading Co.*, 481 F.3d 442, 448 (7th Cir. 2007)(emphasis added).

312*Republic Tobacco Co. v. North Atlantic Trading Co.*, 481 F.3d 442 (7th Cir. 2007).

313*Republic Tobacco Co. v. North Atlantic Trading Co.*, 481 F.3d 442 (7th Cir. 2007).

314*Republic Tobacco Co. v. North Atlantic Trading Co.*, 481 F.3d 442, 448 (7th Cir. 2007)(emphasis added).

315Advisory Committee Notes on the 1967 adoption of Federal Rule of Appellate Procedure 39(e).

316*L–3 Communications Corp. v. OSI Systems, Inc.*, 607 F.3d 24 (2d Cir. 2010).

317*L–3 Communications Corp. v. OSI Systems, Inc.*, 607 F.3d 24 (2d Cir. 2010).

318*Republic Tobacco Co. v. North Atlantic Trading Co.*, 481 F.3d 442 (7th Cir. 2007).

319*Casey v. Planned Parenthood of Southeastern Pennsylvania*, 14 F. 3d 848 (3rd Cir. 1994).

320*Briggs v. Pennsylvania Railroad Co.*, 334 U.S. 304 (1948). Although it is over sixty years old, the United States Supreme Court's decision in <u>Briggs</u> has never been reversed and remains vital law to this date. <u>Accord</u>, *Casey v. Planned Parenthood of Southeastern Pennsylvania*, 14 F.3d 848 (3rd Cir. 1994).

321*Pease v. Rathbun–Jones Engineering Co.*, 243 U.S. 273 (1917).

322*Abrams v. Lightolier, Inc.*, 50 F.3d 1204 (3d Cir. 1995).

323*Casey v. Planned Parenthood of Southeastern Pennsylvania*, 14 F. 3d 848 (3rd Cir. 1994).

324*Briggs v. Pennsylvania Railroad Co.*, 334 U.S. 304 (1948). Although it is over sixty years old, the United States Supreme Court's decision in <u>Briggs</u> has never been reversed and remains vital law to this date. <u>Accord</u>, *Casey v. Planned Parenthood of Southeastern Pennsylvania*, 14 F.3d 848 (3rd Cir. 1994).

325*Pease v. Rathbun–Jones Engineering Co.*, 243 U.S. 273 (1917).

COURTROOM DEPUTY CLERKS

Each judge is assigned a courtroom deputy clerk who is responsible for scheduling and monitoring cases on the judge's calendar. The courtroom deputy clerk acts as a liaison between the judge and counsel, scheduling dates and times for hearings or motions, pretrial hearings and trials, and conferring with attorneys on any special trial procedures.

A. New Case Procedures. The Eastern District of Pennsylvania operates on an individual calendar system, as opposed to a master calendar system, which means that the assigned judge is responsible for all cases assigned, from filing to disposition.

After a case is filed, the courtroom deputy clerk checks the docket for timely service of process and the filing of an answer. If service has not been made within 90 days, a letter will be sent by the courtroom deputy clerk asking that service be made by the 120th day. If service has been made, but the complaint has not been answered, again a letter will be sent by the courtroom deputy requesting counsel to motion for judgment by default. Please do not ignore these notices. If you do, it could result in dismissal of the case for lack of prosecution. [See Federal Rule of Civil Procedure 4m and 12A].

Counsel may receive a status request form by contacting the courtroom deputy to the judge to whom the case is assigned. This form contains questions relating to the scheduling of the case, such as, length of time needed for discovery and estimated length of time for trial.

B. Pretrial Practices. After a complaint is filed, service has been made, and an answer is filed, an order is prepared which sets forth a discovery schedule. The order will specify a date by which all discovery must be completed and schedules a final pretrial conference, generally four to six weeks after the discovery deadline. Usually the case is put in the civil pool for trial in one month. However, not all judges follow the same pretrial practices. If you have questions, call the courtroom deputy clerk of the judge to whom the case is assigned, or check the court's website at http://www.paed.uscourts.gov for judges' policies and procedures.

C. Scheduling Cases. When discovery has been completed and pretrial conferences have been held, there are three ways in which a case can be scheduled for trial:

1. *Civil Trial Pool.* Most judges have the majority of cases in this pool.

2. *Date Certain.* This is a target date set weeks or months in advance and depends on the judge's calendar and availability of attorneys for the date to be met.

3. *Special Listing.* An agreement exists between the District Court judges and the State Court judges in the nine county area of Bucks, Chester, Delaware, Montgomery, Philadelphia, Berks, Lancaster, Lehigh and Northampton. (***Appendix S***).

These special listings take precedence over all other trial engagements provided the following requirements are met:

- the listing is established 30 days in advance by notice to counsel involved and all active judges;

- all district court judges and the judges in the 9–county area are notified at least 30 days in advance of counsel involved and of probable duration of trial:

- that not more than one such special listing shall be granted by the same judge to one lawyer in a six-month period, except for good cause.

The notice which is sent to district court judges and to court administrators in other courts must contain the name of the case, the date the case is scheduled, name of counsel, and the approximate amount of time required for trial.

D. Trial List. Each judge maintains a trial list of cases generally ready for trial. The federal trial list is published in the Legal Intelligencer from Monday through Friday. Below is a sample listing:

J. Curtis Joyner, C.J.
Courtroom 17A
Deputy Clerk: Sharon Carter
Phone: 267–299–7419

Mon., March 5, 2007
On Trial
Civil Jury Trial
10:00 a.m.
2006–8995 J. Smith
Becker v. ABC Company
M. Doe; J.P. Stewart

Trial Pool
2005–7213 p.p.
Jones v. Friedman
D. Wood

The following notice is published each day in the Legal Intelligencer and explains the policy of the Judges of the United States District Court for listing cases in the Eastern District of Pennsylvania.

1. Counsel shall promptly notify the deputy clerk to each judge before whom he/she has a case listed upon becoming attached for trial in another court. To be accorded recognition, a busy slip, using the designated form, ***MUST*** be filed in Room 2609 before 1:00 p.m. on the day after counsel becomes attached.

2. Cases in the trial pools do not necessarily appear in the order in which they will be called. Counsel should therefore be ready to begin trial upon receiving telephone call notice, subject to the following:

(a) Counsel whose cases are in the pools will be given 48 hours' notice, if feasible, but not less than 24 hours' notice to be ready for trial with witnesses.

(b) It is counsel's responsibility to check with each judge's deputy clerk on the status and movement of criminal and civil cases in that judge's pool.

(c) Counsel will not be required to commence trial less than 24 hours after completing trial of another case.

E. Judicial Schedule of Trials—Automated System Inquiry (JUST-ASK). The Judicial Schedule of Trials—Automated System Inquiry (JUST-ASK) system provides up-to-date information on the status of trials scheduled in the United States District Court seven days a week, twenty-four hours a day. JUST-ASK is offered free of charge and is accessible to any individual office with a PC and internet access.

Events, such as verdicts, settlements, and continuances constantly change the status of cases on the Court's trial list. JUST-ASK immediately reflects the daily status of listings as the information becomes available to the Clerk of Court.

All cases scheduled for trial, presently on trial, in the trial pool and special notices from the Court are included on the system. JUST-ASK also provides the capability of viewing a report on the disposition of cases previously listed on the system. For user convenience, all information contained in this system is available by judge, date, case number, party name and/or attorney name. The user may choose the option which is most convenient to view listings. For example, JUST-ASK allows the user to retrieve a list of cases in which a specified attorney is involved, then the information can be printed at the user's computer. If you have any questions on scheduling, please contact the courtroom deputy.

The JUST-ASK system can be accessed through the District Court's website at http://www.paed.uscourts.gov.

F. Lobby Kiosk Information System. An automated informational kiosk system, located in the U.S. Courthouse lobby, includes current information on district court and court of appeals hearings, as well as a directory of judges and court clerks, location of other government agencies and general information. The kiosk provides touch screen technology, as well as mapping techniques to guide visitors to their destinations.

G. Busy Slips. It is important that busy slips (*Appendix T*) be filed promptly so that cases can be properly scheduled. Busy slips can be obtained at the front counter of the Clerk's Office, Room 2609, and should be filed in the Clerk's Office by 1:00 p.m. the day after counsel becomes attached. If a conflict arises before a particular judge, priority is given to the oldest case by date of filing. Please advise the courtroom deputy when the attorney is again available, or if the case was settled.

H. Attachments for Trial. Attorneys can only be attached three business days prior to a date of trial and can only be held for attachment for three business days.

I. Continuances—Criminal Cases. The Speedy Trial Act requires that defendants be brought to trial within a 70–day period after indictment or initial appearance before a judicial officer. This 70–day period can be extended only by a judge for specific reasons set forth in the Speedy Trial Act Plan which is on file and available for inspection in the Clerk's Office.

J. Motions. When filing a motion, please include a proposed order for the judge's signature. Since courtroom deputies are responsible for tracking motions, it is important that a certificate of service be attached to the motion so that they can calculate the date a response is due. If the parties have reached an agreement, notify us by stipulation. If a motion has been filed and the parties have settled their dispute, let the courtroom deputy know as soon as possible.

K. Exhibits. At the completion of trial, either the courtroom deputy clerk will keep exhibits or the Court will have counsel maintain custody until all appeals are exhausted or the appeal time has expired. If the courtroom deputy clerk has custody, the exhibits will be returned to counsel. If the exhibits are too large or too bulky to mail, the courtroom deputy will send a letter to the attorney requesting that the exhibits be picked up. If the exhibits are not picked up, they will be deemed abandoned and will then be destroyed (see Local Civil Rule 39).

L. Other Duties. Some additional duties performed by courtroom deputy clerks are:

- noting the appearance of counsel in matters before the court;
- impaneling the jury and administering oaths to jurors; providing liaison with the jury clerk as to ordering and canceling or juries; and keeping required records on other jury matters;
- administering oaths to witnesses, interpreters, attorneys on admission, and oaths of allegiance to applicants for citizenship;
- recording proceedings and rulings for minutes of the court; filing, marking, storing, and returning exhibits; and composing minute orders to carry out expressed intention of the judge;
- preparing verdict forms and judgments;
- advising the financial section of the Clerk's Office on matters affecting that section, particularly the imposition of fines and orders or restitution by the judge in criminal cases.

The following charts list the courtroom deputy clerks according to their assigned judge, along with their telephone numbers.

DISTRICT COURT JUDGES	COURTROOM DEPUTY	PHONE NUMBER
Petrese B. Tucker, Chief Judge	Michael Owens	267–299–7619
Legrome D. Davis	Donna Croce	267–299–7659
Cynthia M. Rufe	Velma White (Civil) Erica Pratt (Criminal)	267–299–7491 267–299–7499
Timothy J. Savage	Harry Grace	267–299–7489
James Knoll Gardner	Christine Stein (Civil) Jennifer Fitzko (Criminal)	610–434–3457 610–391–7019
Gene E.K. Pratter	Michael Coyle	267–299–7359
Lawrence F. Stengel	Patricia Cardella (Civil) Laura Buenzle (Criminal)	267–299–7761 267–299–7769
Paul S. Diamond	Lenora Kashner Wittje	267–299–7739
Juan R. Sanchez	Nancy DeLisle	267–299–7789
Joel H. Slomsky	Margaret Gallagher	267–299–7349
C. Darnell Jones II	A'ishah El–Shabazz	267–299–7759
Mitchell S. Goldberg	Steve Sonnie	267–299–7509
Nitza I. Quinones Alejandro	Carey Doris Widman (Civil) Rosalind Burton–Hoop (Criminal)	267–299–7461 267–299–7467
L. Felipe Restrepo	Maryellen Fox (Civil) Nelson Malave (Criminal)	267–299–7741 267–299–7691
Jeffrey L. Schmehl	Barbara A. Crossley	267–299–7560 610–320–5099
Gerald A. McHugh	Patricia K. Clark (Civil) Christian Henry (Criminal)	267–299–7302 267–299–7307
Edward G. Smith	Shana Restucci (Civil) Jaime M. Kulick (Criminal)	610–333–1836 610–333–1837
Wendy Beetlestone	Aaris M. Wilson (Civil) Michael Mani (Criminal)	267–299–7451 267–299–7459
Mark A. Kearney	Ulrike Hevener	267–299–7688
Gerald J. Pappert	Jeff Lucini	267–299–7537
Joseph F. Leeson, Jr.	Diane J. Abeles (Civil) Justin F. Wood (Criminal)	610–391–7020 610–776–6118

SENIOR JUDGES	COURTROOM DEPUTY	PHONE NUMBER
J. William Ditter, Jr.		267–299–7211
Norma L. Shapiro	Madeline Ward	267–299–7549
Thomas N. O'Neill, Jr.	Charles Ervin	267–299–7559
Robert F. Kelly	Mark Rafferty	267–299–7319
Jan E. DuBois	Milahn Hull	267–299–7339
Ronald L. Buckwalter	Matthew Higgins	267–299–7369
William H. Yohn, Jr.	Thomas McCann	267–299–7379
Harvey Bartle III	Kristin Makely	267–299–7389
Stewart Dalzell	Eileen Adler	267–299–7399
John R. Padova	Patricia Feldman (Civil) Michael Beck (Criminal)	215–597–1178 267–299–7409
J. Curtis Joyner	Sharon Carter	267–299–7419
Eduardo C. Robreno	Ronald Vance	267–299–7429
Anita B. Brody	James Scheidt	267–299–7439
Berle M. Schiller	Jean Pennie (Civil) Christopher Campoli (Criminal)	267–299–7621 267–299–7629
Mary A. McLaughlin	Dennis Hartman	267–299–7609
R. Barclay Surrick	Donna Marley (Civil) Christina Franzese (Criminal)	267–299–7631 267–299–7639
Michael M. Baylson	JoAnne Bryson (Civil) Janice Lutz (Criminal)	267–299–7571 267–299–7291

MAGISTRATE JUDGES	COURTROOM DEPUTY	PHONE NUMBER
Carol Sandra Moore Wells, Chief Magistrate Judge	Edward Andrews	215–597–7833
Thomas J. Rueter	Lisa Tipping	215–597–0048
Linda K. Caracappa	Ian Broderick	267–299–7640
Timothy R. Rice	Chavela Settles	267–299–7660
David R. Strawbridge	Lorraine DiSanti	267–299–7790
Henry S. Perkin	Helen Nicholas	610–434–3823
Elizabeth T. Hey	Lara Karlson	267–299–7670
Lynne A. Sitarski	Regina Zarnowski	267–299–7810
M. Faith Angell	Shelli MacElderry	215–597–6079
Jacob P. Hart	Deborah Stevenson	215–597–2733

STANDING ORDER RE: SENTENCING REFORM ACT OF 1984

In accordance with the resolution approved by the Judges of this Court on January 19, 1988, a standing order (*Appendix U*) was adopted for use in criminal cases in which sentences are imposed under the Sentencing Reform Act of 1984 (Chapter II of the Comprehensive Crime Control Act, Public Law No. 98473, 98 Stat. 1837, 1976 (enacted October 12, 1984)).

AFTER–HOURS CONTACT FOR EMERGENCY MATTERS

A deputy clerk is on duty in the Clerk's Office each week day from 8:30 a.m. to 5:30 p.m. Attorneys who wish to contact the United States District Court for the Eastern District of Pennsylvania during the evenings after 5:30 p.m. or on weekends may do so by calling (215) 597–0374 or toll-free at (800) 525–5726 or (877) 437–7411. These numbers connect with the Court Security Office and Federal Protective Service which is staffed 24 hours a day, 7 days a week. Attorneys who call these numbers will be referred to the Clerk or a deputy clerk on duty. This service is available for attorneys who have to file an injunction, ship attachment, or other emergency business during non-business hours.

AFTER–HOURS FILING DEPOSITORY

An After–Hours Filing Depository is provided in the lobby of the courthouse past the metal detectors and is able to receive documents for filing after 5:00 p.m. A time recorder is affixed to the depository which enables the person submitting documents for filing to note the time and date the documents are placed in the depository. If the documents are submitted after the doors are locked, access to the building may be gained by activating the buzzer adjacent to the main entrance on Market Street.

OPINION / CORRESPONDENCE CLERK

Margaret Stipa and Matthew Cocci are responsible for answering general corre-spondence inquiries. Margaret can be reached at (267) 299–7047; Matthew can be reached at (267) 299–7094.

We maintain civil case files for calendar years 2012 to the present year and criminal case files from 2011 to the present, in addition to all open cases, in the Clerk's Office. Files for previous years are stored at the Federal Records Center. Send a letter to the attention of the correspondence clerks specifying the case number of the file you need and the documents in which you are interested. They will obtain the file and send you a copy of the papers that you need at a cost of 50¢ per page. There is an additional fee of $11 for a certified copy. The cost of retrieving a file from the Federal Records Center is $64 for the first box and $39 for each additional box.

Any inquiries to search the index for case numbers, judgment, decrees, etc., will be handled by the correspondence clerks. The fee is $30 per name searched.

Judicial opinions filed in the Eastern District since June 1, 1997, as well as opinions filed in Civil Action Number 96–963, A.C.L.U., et al. v. Janet Reno, Attorney General of the U.S., in Civil Action Number 96–1458, American Library, et al. v. U.S. Department of Justice, in Civil Action Number 96–2486, Cyber Pro-motions, Inc. v. American Online, Inc., and in Civil Action Number 96–5213, America Online, Inc. v. Cyber Promotions, Inc., may be obtained through the opinion section on the Eastern District of Pennsylvania's Internet website at http://www.paed. uscourts.gov.

HOW TO FIND A CASE NUMBER

Cases are indexed using the microfiche system, public access computers and **PACER** (see section on **PACER**). At the computers located in the Clerk's Office, you will find printed explanations on the procedure to locate a case number in order to find the docket sheet for that case. Every microfiche index is labeled with the filing time frames for each category. Information on cases filed prior to the specified time frames may be obtained from the Records Room.

CLERK'S INDEX FILE BY NATURE OF SUIT

The Clerk's Office makes this service available at no cost. It is an Index to Civil Actions by Subject prior to March 21, 1994, and is arranged under these main topics: Persons, Property, Contracts, Torts & Other Statutes. Subject headings are exactly the same as those specified on the Civil Cover Sheet.

Refer to the Table of Contents under the appropriate main heading and find the page number on which reference is made to civil actions on the desired subject. Copy down the case number(s) shown and draw the case file jackets or docket sheets to see if the cases listed are helpful.

COPY WORK

Adjacent to Room 2609 is the Reproduction Room. To have copies made, you must complete a request form and prepay the cost, either in person or by mail.

It is possible to obtain copy work the same day. However, it depends on the quantity of work and the time constraints of the photocopy operator.

RECORDS ROOM

Adjacent to the Reproduction Room is the Records Room where all open case files for civil and criminal cases are maintained. In addition to all open case files, all civil files from 2012 to the present year, and all criminal cases from 2011 to the present year, are located in the file room. Individual files and papers may be inspected in this area by the general public. Files are available from the Federal Records Center through our office. The fee for this service is $64 for the first box and $39 for each additional box retrieved. If you have questions, you may contact the records room at (267) 299–7082.

CREDIT CARD COLLECTION NETWORK

In September of 1987, the Department of Treasury established a government credit card collection network to enable federal agencies to accept credit cards (Visa, MasterCard, American Express, Discovery and Diners Club) for the collection of receipts due the government.

Credit cards are accepted as payment at the counter for the following transactions in the Clerk's office:

- filing fees;
- copy work (docket sheets, opinions, etc.);
- copies of ESR–taped proceedings;
- attorney admission fees;
- searches and certifications;
- retrieval fees for case files maintained at the Federal Records Center.

For counter transactions, submit the charge card for recording, validating, and imprinting onto a bank charge slip. The amount of the charge, transaction code, date and time appear on the bank charge slip and cash register receipt. The original cash register receipt and bank charge slip are given to the customer, and the copies are kept on file in the Clerk's Office.

For those law firms that are concerned with the safekeeping of the actual credit card, the Clerk's Office will maintain the firm's credit card number, expiration date and signature of one of the firm's partners after completion of an authorization form (*Appendix V*). The courier will reference the authorization form and the transaction will be processed. On the bank charge slip, *"AUTHORIZATION ON FILE"* would appear in the signature block.

Credit Cards are *not* accepted as payment for mail or telephone requests.

REQUIRED CHECK CONVERSION DISCLOSURE

When you provide a check as payment, you authorize us either to use information from your check to make a one-time electronic fund transfer from your account or to process the payment as a check transaction. When we use information from your check to make an electronic fund transfer, funds may be withdrawn from your account as soon as the same day we receive your payment, and you will not receive your check back from your financial institution. For inquiries, please call (267) 299–7107.

If the electronic fund transfer cannot be completed because there are insufficient funds in your account, we may impose a one-time fee of $53.00 against your account, which we will also collect by electronic fund transfer.

A Privacy Act Statement required by 5 U.S.C. § 552a(e)(3) stating our authority for soliciting and collecting the information from your check, and explaining the purposes and routine uses which will be made of your check information, is available from our internet site at www.paed.uscourts.gov or by calling toll free at (866) 945–7920 to obtain a copy by mail. Furnishing the check information is voluntary, but a decision not to do so may require you to make payment by some other method.

DEPOSITING / WITHDRAWING MONIES

The Fiscal Department is responsible for coordinating all financial transactions involving the district court. All court-related fees are paid and disbursements are made through this department. In order to deposit or withdraw monies from the registry, you must submit a proposed order. Please call Lucy Chin, the Financial Manager at (267) 299–7112 with any questions on this procedure.

A. Deposits. All checks should be made payable to "*Clerk, U.S. District Court*." It is recommended that all deposits made into the registry of the court for subsequent disbursement be accomplished by a treasurer's check or a certified check.

B. Registry Fund, Deposit Fund, Interest–Bearing Accounts. Disbursements are made from the registry fund upon order of the court only. The case docket is reviewed to determine if disbursement is appropriate, then the financial ledger amount is compared with the court order amount. A voucher is prepared by the financial deputy and a check is drawn and mailed to the payee.

As a result of appropriation authority approved by the Judicial Conference, a fee in the amount of 10% of the annual interest has been established to cover the costs to the Judiciary for handling registry funds placed in interest-bearing accounts. The fee shall apply to all money and property held in the Court's registry and invested in interest-bearing accounts, except unclaimed monies held in accounts for individuals or persons whose whereabouts are unknown. Assessment of this fee will commence on all case payments (withdrawals) from the registry of the Court made on or after December 1, 1988. However, fees will be assessed only for the holding of funds after September 30, 1988. As to previously existing accounts, September 30 will be considered the original date of deposit with respect to the starting case balance and the number of days held. The fee will be computed at the time of withdrawal from the date of receipt into the registry through the date of withdrawal based on the average daily balance in the account. Payment of the fee will be deducted from the balance on deposit at the time of distribution.

Disbursements from the deposit fund, i.e., court-appointed counsel fees, are accomplished by preparing a voucher and forwarding it to the certifying officer. When the certified voucher is returned, a check is drawn on the voucher and mailed to the payee.

Upon order of the court, an interest-bearing account is closed with the local bank and deposited into the registry fund as a bank transfer. A U.S. Treasury check is drawn and handled the same as a registry disbursement.

CRIMINAL DEBT
(SPECIAL ASSESSMENT, RESTITUTION AND FINES)

Criminal debt payments to be paid in person or received through the mail are sent to the Fiscal Department. A payment is checked against the court's financial accounting system to ascertain that the amount received is proper and not an overpayment. After the payment is verified as correct, the cashier accepts and processes the payment. A receipt is issued if the debt is paid in person; if a special request accompanies a mailed check, a receipt will be issued. The money is deposited into the U.S. Treasury (General or Special Fund). Restitution payments are disbursed to victims on a monthly basis.

Criminal debt that is recovered through the Probation Office is hand-delivered by Probation personnel to the cashier.

CENTRAL VIOLATIONS BUREAU (CVB)

In the district courts, the CVB provides a case management system for petty offenses (and some misdemeanors) which originate with the filing of a violation notice sent by the issuing government agency directly to the CVB. If collateral is forfeited to the CVB within the specified time, the date and amount is entered and the case is closed. In cases which are not disposed of through forfeiture of collateral, the CVB schedules a hearing before a Magistrate Judge, notifies the defendant, and records the Magistrate Judge's disposition of the case.

BAIL BONDS

Bail is generally set by the court from one of the following categories:

1. **Own Recognizance.** In this instance, the defendant signs an Appearance Bond in the amount fixed by the court without posting any security.

2. **In an Amount Equal to 10% of the Total Amount of the Bond.** In this instance, the defendant or someone on their behalf deposits 10% of the amount of the bond. If it is the defendant's cash, only the defendant signs the appearance bond. If it is the surety's cash, then both must sign. Local Civil Rule 67.1(a) states that "no attorney, or officer of this court shall be acceptable as surety bail, or security of any kind in any proceeding in this court."

3. **In an Amount with Good Security.** In this instance, both the defendant and the surety must sign the appearance bond with acceptable security being posted. Security may be one of the following:

- **Cash**—only cash, certified or cashier's check, or money order are acceptable:
- **Corporate Surety**—with power of attorney;
- **Individual Sureties—Real Estate**—explained on sample form "Bail Bond Secured by Property or Real Estate Bail" (*Appendix W*);
- **Securities**—only negotiable securities are acceptable.

ATTORNEY ADMISSIONS

Applications for admission to the bar of our court for those attorneys who are currently members in good standing of the bar of the Supreme Court of Pennsylvania pursuant to Local Rule of Civil Procedure 83.5(a) may be obtained at the front counter of the Clerk's Office. Admission ceremonies are held once a week. The fee for attorney admission is $201.00. There is an $18.00 fee for a duplicate certificate of admission or certificate of good standing. For further information on attorney admissions, call Aida Ayala, the attorney admissions clerk at (267) 299-7099.

Pursuant to Local Rule of Civil Procedure 83.5(b), attorneys who are not currently admitted to either the bar of this court or the bar of the Supreme Court of Pennsylvania shall not actively participate in the conduct of any trial or pre-trial or post-trial proceeding before this court unless, upon motion of a member of the bar of this court containing a verified application, leave to do so is granted (*Appendix X*). A $40 fee is assessed for such admissions.

COURT REPORTING / RECORDING SERVICES

Orders for transcripts produced by court reporters can be accomplished through the Court Reporter Supervisor, Joan Carr at (267) 299–7104, by means of a Transcript Order Form (*Appendix Y*).

Orders for transcripts produced by electronic sound recording can be accomplished through the Transcript Coordinator, David Hayes at (267) 299–7041 or Connie Flores at (267) 299–7041, by means of a Transcript Order Form (*Appendix Y*). Orders for tapes or CDs produced by ESR can be accomplished by means of the Tape Order Form (*Appendix Z*).

ELECTRONIC TRANSCRIPTS OF COURT PROCEEDINGS

With the exception of sealed transcripts which are excluded from electronic filing, effective June 2, 2008, electronic transcripts of court proceedings in the United States District Court, Eastern District of Pennsylvania, will be made available to the public as follows:

- Transcripts of civil court proceedings will be placed on CM/ECF or PACER with the approval of the presiding judge.
- Transcripts of criminal court proceedings will not be placed on CM/ECF or PACER unless approved by the presiding judge.

If electronic transcripts are to be made available to the public upon approval of the assigned judge:

- A transcript provided to the court reporter or transcriber will be available at the office of the Clerk for inspection for a period of 90 days after it is delivered to the Clerk.
- During the 90–day period a copy of the transcript may also be obtained by purchase from the court reporter or transcriber through the office of the Clerk. An attorney who obtains the transcript from the office of the Clerk will be allowed remote access to the transcript through the court's CM/ECF system.
- After the 90–day period has expired, the filed transcript will be available for inspection and copying in the Clerk's office. With the approval of the presiding judge, the transcript may also be available for download from the court's CM/ECF system through the PACER system.

In addition, amendments to the Federal Civil and Criminal Rules of Procedure (Civil Rule 5.2 and Criminal Rule 49.1) require that personal identification information be redacted from documents filed with the court, including Social Security numbers, names of minor children, financial account numbers, dates of birth, and in criminal cases, home addresses.

For more information on electronic transcripts, please contact Joan Carr, Supervisor of Court Reporters, at (267) 299–7104 or Michael Hearn, Electronic Sound Recording Coordinator, at (267) 299–7039. (See *Appendix AA*).

DIGITAL AUDIO FILE ELECTRONIC ACCESS

Digital audio recordings of courtroom proceedings will be publicly available on PACER upon the approval of the presiding judge. The project enables PACER users to download, in MP3 format, court proceedings that have been recorded using electronic sound recording technology. (See *Appendix BB*).

For more information, contact Michael Hearn, Electronic Sound Recording Coordinator, at (267) 299–7039.

VIDEO RECORDING SERVICES

The Clerk's Office has video recording facilities for the taking of depositions of witnesses. These services are provided at the discretion of the assigned judge. To request video recording of witnesses, contact Edward Morrissy at (267) 299–7044. There is no charge for the use of the video recording service, but counsel is required to supply the necessary DVDs.

Counsel is required to give notice to the opposing party as to their intention to utilize the video recording procedure.

VIDEO TELECONFERENCING

On June 1, 1995, the Eastern District of Pennsylvania started a video teleconferencing pilot program sponsored by the United States Marshal Service and the Federal Bureau of Prisons. This program establishes a closed-circuit television link between the United States District Court in Philadelphia and the Federal Correctional Institute at Fairton, New Jersey. In May 1988, this program was expanded to include links between the District Court and State Correctional Institutions, including Graterford, Greene and Camp Hill. The program allows criminal defendants incarcerated at these institutions to fully participate in court appearances, interviews and conferences. The equipment and facilities are also available to the Office of Pretrial Services, the United States Probation Office, the Federal Defender, the United States Attorney, and the defense bar when not in use by the Court. All requests to use the VTC equipment for conferences are to be submitted to the VTC Coordinator, who can be reached at (267) 299–7039.

The VTC Program has not been limited to only cases in which defendants are incarcerated. For visiting judge cases in which judges of this court sit by designation in Middle or Western District Court cases, this program has been successfully utilized to conduct conferences between this court and counsel from outside districts which are similarly equipped with VTC equipment. For further information on this service, please contact the VTC coordinator.

COURTROOM TECHNOLOGY

Several courtrooms provide an array of technical components that support evidence presentation, remote site interactions, language interpreting and audio enhancement. The state-of-the-art technologies include assisted listening systems, integrated court interpreting systems, video teleconferencing systems, document/video presentation systems, evidence trolleys, annotation pads, document cameras, as well as connectivity at counsel tables for use with court-or-attorney-provided PCs. The court welcomes the bar to make use of these technologies and training is available at the courthouse. For further information, contact Michael Hearn at (267) 299–7039 or Edward Morrissy at (267) 299–7044.

INTERPRETERS' SERVICES

Effective September 1, 1997, the Clerk's Office became responsible for scheduling interpreters for all criminal proceedings and for all civil cases initiated by the Government. The interpreter coordinator, Larry Bowman, (267) 299–7029, will schedule all interpreters required for court appearances.

Once the need for an interpreter has been established, the courtroom deputy to the assigned judge will be responsible for notifying the interpreter coordinator of all court proceedings requiring the use of an interpreter.

JURY SELECTION

The jury section is responsible for selecting and maintaining a pool of citizens qualified to serve as grand and petit jurors in this district and summoning these individuals for jury service. Jurors are selected pursuant to the *Plan for the Random Selection of Grand and Petit Jurors for the Eastern District of Pennsylvania, amended December 4, 2009*. A copy of this plan is available for inspection in the Office of the Clerk of Court. The jury section is also responsible for preparation of vouchers and documentation required to reimburse jurors for their service.

A. Term of Jury Service. If selected for a trial, jurors are required to serve until the completion of the trial.

B. Excuse from Jury Service on Request. In addition to members of groups and occupational classes subject to excuse from jury service pursuant to 28 U.S.C. §§ 1863(b)(5) and (7), any person summoned for jury service may, on request, be excused temporarily by a judge of this court. The person must show undue hardship or extreme inconvenience by reason of great distance, either in miles or travel time, from the place of holding court, grave illness in the family or any other emergency which outweighs in urgency the obligation to serve as a juror when summoned, or any other factor which the court determines to constitute an undue hardship or to create an extreme inconvenience to the juror. Additionally, in situations where it is anticipated that a trial or grand jury proceeding may require more than thirty days of service, the court may consider, as a further basis for temporary excuse, severe economic hardship to an employer which would result from the absence of a key employee during the period of such service.

The period for which such prospective jurors may be excused shall be the period of time which the judge deems necessary under the circumstances, which shall be fixed in the order granting the excuse. At the expiration of the period so fixed, such persons shall be summoned again for jury service within a reasonable time.

C. Payment. Jurors receive $40 for each day in attendance, plus .575 cents* per mile (eff. 1/1/2015) as measured from their residence to the courthouse (roundtrip). The court calculates the computation of this fee. If a juror lives more than 50 miles from the courthouse and remains overnight, the juror will be reimbursed for room and living expenses. Subsistence allowance is:

LOCATION	DATE	AMOUNT
PHILADELPHIA	7/1/15 – 8/31/15	$208
PHILADELPHIA	9/1/15 – 11/30/15	$232
PHILADELPHIA	12/1/15 – 2/28/16	$205
PHILADELPHIA	3/1/16 – 6/30/16	$237
READING	Through 9/30/15	$150
ALLENTOWN	Through 9/30/15	$139
EASTON	Through 9/30/15	$139

INCLEMENT WEATHER

In the event of inclement or otherwise extreme weather conditions, the public is urged to call the court's Coda–A–Phone line for a special announcement on whether the courthouse will be closed or if trials have been cancelled for that day. A recorded message on the toll-free number (1–800) 829–0189 will be accessible from about 5:30 a.m. Attorneys and jurors are requested to call this number before leaving their office or residence to attend court. It is also suggested that the public tune into radio and television news stations, which will also broadcast announcements if jury trials have been adjourned or if the courthouse will be closed for that day. If no announcement is made by 6:00 a.m. and there is no special message on the recording, it should be assumed that court will be in session and jurors are to report for jury duty as scheduled.

PACER—PUBLIC ACCESS TO COURT ELECTRONIC RECORDS

The **PACER** system provides improved access to court records for attorneys and other members of the public. This electronic access system allows any member of the public to access information contained in the court's civil/criminal docket database via internet access. The user is able to access a search of information either through a case name or a case number and can request docket reports. The information is either saved on the user's PC or the report is printed during online access.

All civil cases filed since July 1, 1990 and all criminal cases filed since July, 1992 are contained on the **PACER** system. In addition, the **PACER** system will allow an end-user to check recent activity. If there has been no recent activity, the **PACER** system will confirm that fact in seconds.

The **PACER** system is available 24 hours a day, 7 days a week. Electronic case filings and updates to the docket are available for immediate view.

The Eastern District of Pennsylvania's **PACER** system is administered by the **PACER** Service Center. The center provides all support services as well as billing services for **PACER** access.

Many Eastern District of Pennsylvania **PACER** users are already registered with the **PACER** Service Center for access to the **PACER** systems throughout the federal court system. If you are currently registered with the **PACER** Service Center, please call the center at (1–800) 676–6856 to add the Eastern District of Pennsylvania to your account.

If you are not registered with the center, complete a **PACER** registration form (*Appendix CC*) available on the court's website at http://www.paed.uscourts.gov and forward it to the **PACER** Service Center, P.O. Box 780549, San Antonio, TX 78278–0549, or fax it to: (201) 301–6441, or a completed application may be submitted via e-mail. The address for **PACER** is http://www.pacer.gov. Users may access **PACER** by using their **PACER** login and password. The fee for accessing **PACER** is 10¢ per page.

Should you have any questions concerning **PACER** service or registration, please contact the center at (1–800) 676–6856.

INTERNET WEBSITE

Information on multiple services and all judicial opinions filed since June 1, 1997 in the United States District Court for the Eastern District of Pennsylvania, as well as e-mail capabilities are available on the internet at http://www.paed.uscourts.gov. The site contains the following:

- Judicial opinions filed since June 1, 1997, including a *Recent Opinions* section;
- E-mail capabilities with the Office of the Clerk of Court;
- Directory of automated services (*Appendix DD*);
- Local civil, criminal and Bankruptcy rules:
- Court notices;

- Electronic Case Filing;
- Forms:
- Report of cases specially listed for U.S. District Court and surrounding county courts;
- Multidistrict litigation information;
- Criminal documents;
- Frequently asked questions;
- Clerk's Office Procedural Handbook containing information on: filing civil actions / documents, general motion practice and pretrial procedures, fees, judicial chambers information (phone numbers, addresses, staff), forms (appendices), Clerk's Office directory, appeals, bill of costs and after hours filing;
- Telephone directory and address information;
- Judicial Schedule of Trials—Automated System Inquiry (JUST–ASK);
- Search capabilities;
- Link to **PACER**;
- Judicial policies and procedures;
- Juror information;
- Federal holidays; and
- Arbitrator and mediator applications.

LOCAL RULES

The local rules of court-civil, criminal, admiralty and bankruptcy are available from the Clerk's office and also on the internet at http://www.paed.uscourts.gov. Inquiries should be directed to Aida Ayala at (267) 299–7099, in room 2625.

PORTABLE ELECTRONIC DEVICES AND PUBLIC TELEPHONES

Visitors to the U.S. Courthouse are permitted to carry portable electronic devices, such as cell phones and laptops into the courthouse, but all equipment will be subject to x-ray and visual inspection by the Court Security Officers at the security screening station. All equipment must be turned off before entering courtrooms and chambers, unless otherwise authorized by the presiding judge. Failure to follow this restriction may result in sanctions by the judge.

While cell phones are permitted in the courthouse, pay telephones available for use by the public are located in the first floor lobby hallway, adjacent to the public elevators.

DIRECTORY OF PUBLIC TELEPHONE LOCATIONS

U.S. COURTHOUSE

PHILADELPHIA, PA

FLOOR	TELEPHONE NUMBER	LOCATION OF TELEPHONE
Lobby	215–922–8886	Hallway adjacent to public elevators
Lobby	215–922–8668	Hallway adjacent to public elevators
Lobby	215–922–8673	Hallway adjacent to public elevators
Lobby	215–922–8683	Hallway adjacent to public elevators
Lobby	215–922–8682	Hallway adjacent to public elevators

FLOOR	TELEPHONE NUMBER	LOCATION OF TELEPHONE
Lobby	215–922–8671	Hallway adjacent to public elevators

August 3, 2015

UNITED STATES DISTRICT COURT
EASTERN DISTRICT OF PENNSYLVANIA

CLERK'S OFFICE EMPLOYEE LIST

[**Publisher's Note**: For contact and other information concerning staff, please contact the Clerk's Office.]

APPENDIX EE ....   ELECTRONIC CASE FILING—ELECTRONIC
FILING OF COMPLAINTS INFORMATION
FORM

[Amended effective February 1, 2011; November 2011; April 17, 2012; September 2012; June 2013; January 2014; August 2015.]

* [**Publisher's Note:** So in original. Probably should be "57.5 cents."]

APPENDICES
APPENDIX A. ECF PROCEDURES

Local Civil Rule 5.1.2 Electronic Case Filing. All cases and documents filed in this court are required to be filed on the Electronic Case Filing ("ECF") System in accordance with provisions of the *Electronic Case Filing ("ECF") Procedures*, as set forth below, unless excepted under these procedures.

Rule 5.1.2 Electronic Case Filing ("ECF") Procedures*

* **[Publisher's Note:** The text of Local Civil Rule 5.1.2 is reproduced, *ante.*]

APPENDIX B.   PDF FILE INFORMATION

What is a PDF file?

Portable Document Format (PDF) is a universal file format that preserves all fonts, formats, graphics and other typesetting attributes of a source (original) document, regardless of what application was used to create the source document. PDF files are most easily viewed using Adobe Acrobat Reader®, which is a free download available from www.adobe.com.

Why Convert Word and WordPerfect Documents to a PDF File?

PDF files are compact and are easily and quickly transmitted via the Web or through electronic mail. Although PDF files can be shared, viewed, navigated and printed, PDF files cannot be edited or altered by the recipient, thus preserving the integrity of the source document.

You must convert all of your documents to PDF format before submitting the documents to the District Clerk's Office through the Electronic Case Filing (ECF) system.

How Do You Convert a Word Processing Document to a PDF File?

1.   WordPerfect 9 or later versions:

WordPerfect 9 and later versions have a built-in capability to convert any document to a PDF file:

1.   Open the source document in WordPerfect.

2.   While the source document is on the screen, choose **FILE** from the menu bar.

3.   From the drop-down **FILE** menu, select **PUBLISH TO PDF**.

4.   To save the source document as a PDF file, type the document name where prompted in the PDF window. To save the PDF file to a floppy disk, place floppy disk in appropriate hardware slot, and type *A:\[document name]* in the "Publish To PDF" pop-up window. Press "**OK**".

The source document is now saved in PDF format either on the hard drive or on a floppy disk.

2.   All other WordPerfect versions, MS Word, or other Applications:

To convert a source document from an application other than WordPerfect 9, Adobe Acrobat 5.0® (which contains a "writer" function) must be installed on your computer. Adobe Acrobat 5.0® is available for purchase from www.adobe.com.

1.   Open the source document.

2.   From the menu bar, select **PRINT**.

3.   In the "Printer" window, select **CURRENT PRINTER**.

4.   At the drop-down menu in the **CURRENT PRINTER** window, select **ACRO-BAT DISTILLER**.

5.   Press "OK" to print the file to your hard drive or floppy disk, instead of to the printer.

6.   After you press "OK", verify that the SAVED FILE TYPE is **PDF**, and press the **SAVE** button.

APPENDIX C. VALIDATION OF SIGNATURE FORM, LOCAL RULE 5.1.2

UNITED STATES DISTRICT COURT
EASTERN DISTRICT OF PENNSYLVANIA

OFFICE OF THE CLERK OF COURT

**Rule 5.1.2 of the Local Rules of Civil Procedure
Electronic Case Filing**

Validation of Signature Form

Pursuant to Rule 5.1.2, *Electronic Case Filing*, all attorneys who have been excused from registering as an ECF Filing User, as defined in the ECF Procedures set forth in Rule 5.1.2, are required to complete this *Validation of Signature* form validating his or her signature for submission of filings on disk in portable document format (PDF), so that the filings may be entered into the District Court's ECF system. The document on disk must be accompanied by a courtesy copy of the document in paper format for use by the court. Attorneys who complete this form will receive a signature code which must be used by the attorney on the signature line of all courtesy copies submitted with a disk. The document as submitted on the disk will constitute the original document under Section 3 of Local Civil Rule 5.1.2.

(Please Print or Type)

First Name: _____ Middle Initial/Name: _____

Last Name: _____ Generation (i.e., Sr., Jr.) _____

Firm: _____ Bar ID No. and State: _____

Address: _____

Address: _____

City: _____ State: _____ Zip Code _____

Telephone No: (___)_____ FAX No: (___) _____

E-mail Address: _____

Are you admitted to practice in the Eastern District of Pennsylvania?

Yes   No

If yes, are you a member in good standing?

Yes   No

Are you admitted to practice pro hac vice in the Eastern District of Pennsylvania?

Yes   No

Are you registered as an ECF Filing User in the Eastern District of Pennsylvania?

Yes   No

If no, would you like to also register as an ECF Filing User in the Eastern District of Pennsylvania?

Yes   No

By submitting this registration form, the undersigned agrees/consents to the following:

1. I have read and understood the provisions of Rule 5.1.2 of the Local Rules of Civil Procedure, *Electronic Case Filing*, and the court's *ECF Procedures* set forth in Rule 5.1.2, and I agree to abide by all provisions set forth therein.

2. I agree that this form constitutes my signature for filings which must be submitted on disk in portable document format (PDF), as required by Section 3 of Rule 5.1.2, *Electronic Case Filing*. I understand that I will be provided

with a signature code which I must use on the signature line of all courtesy copies submitted with a disk I have read and understood the provisions of Rule 11 of the Federal Rules of Civil Procedure, and I agree that my signature code used on the signature line of all courtesy copies submitted with a disk will serve as my signature for purposes of Rule 11. I further understand that the document as submitted on the disk will constitute the original document under Section 3 of Local Civil Rule 5.1.2.

3. I understand and agree that service of process will be made in accordance with those provisions set forth in Rule 5 of the Federal Rules of Civil Procedure.

I hereby certify that the above information is true and correct and I am a member in good standing of the United States District Court for the Eastern District of Pennsylvania.

_____	_____
Signature	Date

Please return completed form by U.S. Mail to: Michael E. Kunz
U.S. District Court
2609 U.S. Courthouse
601 Market Street
Philadelphia, PA 19106–1797

[Effective May 17, 2004; revised April 2007.]

APPENDIX D. ECF REGISTRATION AND NOTIFICATION FORMS
OFFICE OF THE CLERK OF COURT

ELECTRONIC CASE FILING (ECF)
ACCOUNT REGISTRATION FORM

This Electronic Case Filing (ECF) Account Registration Form shall be used to register for an account with the U.S.D.C. for the Eastern District of Pennsylvania's Electronic Case Filing (ECF) system. ECF Registered attorneys will have privileges to electronically submit documents in accordance with Local Civil Rule 5.1.2 and Local Criminal Rule 1.2.

(Please Print or Type)

First Name: _____ Middle Initial/Name: _____

Last Name: _____ Generation (i.e., Sr., Jr.): _____

Firm: _____ Bar Id No. and State: _____

Address: _____

Address: _____

City: _____ State: _____ Zip Code: _____

Telephone No: _____ FAX No: _____

E-mail Address: _____

Last 4 digits of your Social Security number (to be used for the log-in code): ____

       Are you admitted to practice in the Eastern District of Pennsylvania?
       ☐ Yes   ☐ No

       If yes, are you a member in good standing?
       ☐ Yes   ☐ No

       Are you admitted to practice pro hac vice in the Eastern District of Pennsylvania?
       ☐ Yes   ☐ No

       Are you a registered ECF Filer in another U.S. District or Bankruptcy Court?
       ☐ Yes   ☐ No

If yes, please provide the district in which you are a registered ECF User and the log-in and password if you would like to have the same log-in and password. (Passwords must be at least eight characters long, include both upper and lower case and at least one digit or special character.)

District: _____ Log–in: _____ Password: _____

By submitting this account registration form, the undersigned agrees/consents to the following:

1. I have read and understood the provisions of Rule 5.1.2 of the Local Rules of Civil Procedure, "Electronic Case Filing," amended Rule 1.2 of the Local Rules of Criminal Procedure, "Applicability and Effect of Local Rules," and the court's ECF Procedures set forth in Rule 5.1.2, and I agree to abide by all provisions set forth therein.

2. I agree that the combination of the user log-in and password will serve as my signature for purposes of the Federal Rules of Civil and Criminal Procedure. I further agree to protect the security of my password and to immediately notify the clerk of court by telephone, with said notification confirmed immediately thereafter in writing delivered by e-mail, facsimile or hand-delivery to the attention of the clerk of court, as soon as I learn that my password may have been compromised.

3. In accordance with the provisions of Rule 5(b)(2)(D) of the Federal Rules of Civil Procedure and Section 8 of the ECF Procedures, I agree that service may be given to me by electronic transmission and I consent to make electronic service of all documents.

4. I have read and understood the provisions of Rule 11 of the Federal Rules of Civil Procedure, particularly as referenced in Sections 9 and 10 of the ECF Procedures, and I agree to abide by the provisions set forth therein.

5. I agree to waive the provisions of Rule 77(d) of the Federal Rules of Civil Procedure and Rule 49(c) of the Federal Rules of Criminal Procedure, providing for service of notice by mail, and I consent that such notice may be served by electronic transmission in accordance with Section 14 of the ECF Procedures.

6. All transmissions for electronic case filings of pleadings and documents to the ECF system shall be titled in accordance with the approved directory of civil and criminal events of the ECF system in a case in which an attorney is counsel of record or on any document which is construed as an entry of appearance in accordance with Local Civil Rule 5.1.

I hereby certify that the above information is true and correct and I am a member in good standing of the United States District Court for the Eastern District of Pennsylvania.

_____	_____
Signature	Date

Please return completed form by U.S. Mail to:	Michael E. Kunz U.S. District Court 2609 U.S. Courthouse 601 Market Street Philadelphia, PA 19106–1797 Attn: ECF

You will be notified of your user log-in and password by electronic mail. If you have any questions on the ECF registration process or the use of the electronic filing system, you may contact the Electronic Filing Information Center toll-free at 1–866–ECF–4ECF.

**UNITED STATES DISTRICT COURT
EASTERN DISTRICT OF PENNSYLVANIA**

Electronic Case Filing (ECF)

Notification of Case Activity Request Form

As a registered Electronic Case Filing User, I am requesting that the following e-mail address(es) receive electronic notification of case activity on any case in which I have entered my appearance. I understand that the e-mail address(es) listed below will receive the electronic notification of case activity, in addition to the e-mail address that I listed on my ECF Registration Form.

(Please print or type the e-mail address(es))

E-Mail Address(es)

Maximum of 3

_____

_____

_____

_____   _____
Attorney Name (Printed)   Attorney Signature

_____   _____
Telephone No.   Date

If there are any future changes to the information listed above, an amended *Notification of Case Activity Request Form* must be submitted. If more than 3 e-mail addresses are required, please submit a request to the Clerk of Court.

Please return this completed form to: Michael E. Kunz, Clerk of Court, 601 Market Street, Room 2609, Philadelphia, PA 19106–1797, ATTN: ECF or FAX (215) 597–6390.

[Revised March 9, 2016.]

APPENDIX E.   ECF TRAINING APPLICATION FORM
NOTICE

I am pleased to announce that the Clerk's Office for the United States District Court for the Eastern District of Pennsylvania will be conducting hands-on training sessions for Civil and Criminal on the Electronic Case Filing System (ECF). This training will be held at the United States Courthouse, 601 Market Street, Philadelphia, PA and is available to members of the bar, paralegals, secretaries and automation support staff.

CM/ECF will allow attorneys to file and view documents from their office, home or anywhere they have access to the Internet, 24 hours a day. Documents are automatically docketed as part of the filing process and are immediately available electronically. CM/ECF also provides the following benefits:

- 24-hour access to filed documents over the Internet
- Automatic e-mail notice of case activity
- The ability to download and print documents directly from the court system
- Concurrent access to case files by multiple parties
- Secure storage of documents

If you are interested in attending a training session, please complete the attached registration form indicating three date preferences. The training sessions are held every Tuesday and Thursday at 10:30 a.m. The training sessions will last approximately two hours. You will be notified of the date you are scheduled for training.

Thank you for your interest in the ECF system and if you have any questions on the ECF system, please call the toll-free number 1-866-ECF-4ECF (1-866-323-4323).

Michael E. Kunz
Clerk of Court

UNITED STATES DISTRICT COURT
EASTERN DISTRICT OF PENNSYLVANIA

Office of the Clerk of Court

ECF Training Registration

Name: _____ Title: _____

Firm: _____

Address: _____

Address: _____

City: _____ State: _____ Zip Code: _____

Telephone: _____ Fax: _____

E–Mail Address: _____

1st Date Preference: _____ 10:30 am

2nd Date Preference: _____ 10:30 am

3rd Date Preference: _____ 10:30 am

Please FAX the completed form to (215) 597–6390

–or by e–mail to–

PAED_clerksoffice@paed.uscourts.gov

–or by mail to–

Office of the Clerk of Court
2609 United States Courthouse
601 Market Street
Philadelphia, PA 19106
Attn: ECF Training Registration Form

APPENDIX F. DESIGNATION FORM

UNITED STATES DISTRICT COURT

FOR THE EASTERN DISTRICT OF PENNSYLVANIA—DESIGNATION FORM to be used by counsel to indicate the category of the case for the purpose of assignment to appropriate calendar.

Address of Plaintiff: _____

Address of Defendant: _____

Place of Accident, Incident or Transaction: _____

(Use Reverse Side For Additional Space)

Does this civil action involve a nongovernmental corporate party with any parent corporation and any publicly held corporation owning 10% or more of its stock?

  (Attach two copies of the Disclosure Statement Form in accordance with Fed.R.Civ.P. 7.1(a))   Yes☐   No☐

Does this case involve multidistrict litigation possibilities?   Yes☐   No☐

RELATED CASE, IF ANY:

Case Number: _____ Judge _____ Date Terminated: _____

Civil cases are deemed related when yes is answered to any of the following questions:

1. Is this case related to property included in an earlier numbered suit pending or within one year previously terminated action in this court?   Yes☐   No☐

2. Does this case involve the same issue of fact or grow out of the same transaction as a prior suit pending or within one year previously terminated action in this court?   Yes☐   No☐

3. Does this case involve the validity or infringement of a patent already in suit or any earlier numbered case pending or within one year previously terminated action in this court?   Yes☐   No☐

4. Is this case a second or successive habeas corpus, social security appeal, or pro se civil rights case filed by the same individual?   Yes☐   No☐

CIVIL: (Place √ in ONE CATEGORY ONLY)

A. *Federal Question Cases:*

1. ☐ Indemnity Contract, Marine Contract, and All Other Contracts
2. ☐ FELA
3. ☐ Jones Act–Personal Injury
4. ☐ Antitrust
5. ☐ Patent
6. ☐ Labor–Management Relations
7. ☐ Civil Rights
8. ☐ Habeas Corpus
9. ☐ Securities Act(s) Cases
10. ☐ Social Security Review Cases
11. ☐ All other Federal Question Cases (Please specify) _____

B. *Diversity Jurisdiction Cases:*

1. ☐ Insurance Contract and Other Contracts
2. ☐ Airplane Personal Injury
3. ☐ Assault, Defamation
4. ☐ Marine Personal Injury
5. ☐ Motor Vehicle Personal Injury
6. ☐ Other Personal Injury (Please specify)
7. ☐ Products Liability
8. ☐ Products Liability—Asbestos
9. ☐ All other Diversity Cases (Please specify) _____

ARBITRATION CERTIFICATION
(Check Appropriate Category)

I, _____, counsel of record do hereby certify:

☐ Pursuant to Local Civil Rule 53.2, Section 3(c)(2), that to the best of my knowledge and belief, the damages recoverable in this civil action case exceed the sum of $150,000.00 exclusive of interest and costs;

☐ Relief other than monetary damages is sought.

DATE: _____   _____   _____
                                              Attorney-at-Law   Attorney I.D.#

NOTE: A trial de novo will be a trial by jury only if there has been compliance with F.R.C.P. 38.

I certify that, to my knowledge, the within case is not related to any case now pending or within one year previously terminated action in this court except as noted above.

DATE: _____   _____   _____
                                              Attorney-at-Law   Attorney I.D.#

CIV. 609 (5/2012)

[Revised effective May 2012.]

APPENDIX G.   DISCLOSURE STATEMENT FORM

UNITED STATES DISTRICT COURT
EASTERN DISTRICT OF PENNSYLVANIA

```
                              :
                              :
        V.                    :     Civil Action
                              :     No: _____
                              :
```

DISCLOSURE STATEMENT FORM

Please check one box:

☐   The nongovernmental corporate party, _____, in the above listed civil action does not have any parent corporation and publicly held corporation that owns 10% or more of its stock.

☐   The nongovernmental corporate party, _____, in the above listed civil action has the following parent corporation(s) and publicly held corporation(s) that owns 10% or more of its stock:

_____
_____
_____
_____
_____

_____   _____
          Date   Signature

Counsel for: _____

Federal Rule of Civil Procedure 7.1 Disclosure Statement

(a) WHO MUST FILE; CONTENTS. A nongovernmental corporate party must file two copies of a disclosure statement that:

   (1) identifies any parent corporation and any publicly held corporation owning 10% or more of its stock; or

   (2) states that there is no such corporation.

(b) TIME TO FILE; SUPPLEMENTAL FILING. A party must:

   (1) file the disclosure statement with its first appearance, pleading, petition, motion, response, or other request addressed to the court; and

   (2) promptly file a supplemental statement if any required information changes.

UNITED STATE DISTRICT COURT
EASTERN DISTRICT OF PENNSYLVANIA

USA   :   Criminal Action
                                       :
v.   :
                                       :
                                       :
                                       :   No.

DISCLOSURE STATEMENT FORM

Please check one box:

☐   The nongovernmental corporate party, _____, in the
    above listed criminal action does not have any parent corporation and
    publicly held corporation that owns 10% or more of its stock.

☐   The nongovernmental corporate party, _____, in the
    above listed criminal action has the following parent corporation(s) and
    publicly held corporation(s) that owns 10% or more of its stock:

_____

_____

_____

_____

_____

_____   _____
Date   Signature

                    Counsel for: _____

Federal Rule of Criminal Procedure 12.4 Disclosure Statement

   (a) WHO MUST FILE.

      (1) NONGOVERNMENTAL CORPORATE PARTY. Any nongovernmental
         corporate party to a proceeding in a district court must file a statement that
         identifies any parent corporation and any publicly held corporation that
         owns 10% or more of its stock or states that there is no such corporation.

      (2) ORGANIZATIONAL VICTIM. If an organization is a victim of the alleged
         criminal activity, the government must file a statement identifying the
         victim. If the organizational victim is a corporation, the statement must
         also disclose the information required by Rule 12.4(a)(1) to the extent that it
         can be obtained through due diligence.

   (b) TIME FOR FILING; SUPPLEMENTAL FILING. A party must:

      (1) file the Rule 12.4(a) statement upon the defendant's initial appearance; and

      (2) promptly file a supplemental statement upon any change in the information
         that the statement requires.

[Revised April 28, 2009.]

APPENDIX H.   CIVIL COVER SHEET

CIVIL COVER SHEET

JS 44 (Rev. 12/12)

The JS 44 civil cover sheet and the information contained herein neither replace nor supplement the filing and service of pleadings or other papers as required by law, except as provided by local rules of court. This form, approved by the Judicial Conference of the United States in September 1974, is required for the use of the Clerk of Court for the purpose of initiating the civil docket sheet. *(SEE INSTRUCTIONS ON NEXT PAGE OF THIS FORM.)*

I. (a) PLAINTIFFS

DEFENDANTS

(b) County of Residence of First Listed Plaintiff _____
(EXCEPT IN U.S. PLAINTIFF CASES)

County of Residence of First Listed Defendant _____
(IN U.S. PLAINTIFF CASES ONLY)

NOTE: IN LAND CONDEMNATION CASES, USE THE LOCATION OF THE TRACT OF LAND INVOLVED.

(c) Attorneys *(Firm Name, Address, and Telephone Number)*

Attorneys *(If Known)*

II. BASIS OF JURISDICTION *(Place an "X" in One Box Only)*

- ☐ 1 U.S. Government Plaintiff
- ☐ 2 U.S. Government Defendant
- ☐ 3 Federal Question *(U.S. Government Not a Party)*
- ☐ 4 Diversity *(Indicate Citizenship of Parties in Item III)*

III. CITIZENSHIP OF PRINCIPAL PARTIES *(Place an "X" in One Box for Plaintiff and One Box for Defendant)* *(For Diversity Cases Only)*

	PTF	DEF		PTF	DEF
Citizen of This State	☐ 1	☐ 1	Incorporated or Principal Place of Business In This State	☐ 4	☐ 4
Citizen of Another State	☐ 2	☐ 2	Incorporated and Principal Place of Business In Another State	☐ 5	☐ 5
Citizen or Subject of a Foreign Country	☐ 3	☐ 3	Foreign Nation	☐ 6	☐ 6

IV. NATURE OF SUIT *(Place an "X" in One Box Only)*

CONTRACT	TORTS		FORFEITURE/PENALTY	BANKRUPTCY	OTHER STATUTES
☐ 110 Insurance ☐ 120 Marine ☐ 130 Miller Act ☐ 140 Negotiable Instrument ☐ 150 Recovery of Overpayment & Enforcement of Judgment ☐ 151 Medicare Act ☐ 152 Recovery of Defaulted Student Loans (Excludes Veterans) ☐ 153 Recovery of Overpayment of Veteran's Benefits ☐ 160 Stockholders' Suits ☐ 190 Other Contract ☐ 195 Contract Product Liability ☐ 196 Franchise	**PERSONAL INJURY** ☐ 310 Airplane ☐ 315 Airplane Product Liability ☐ 320 Assault, Libel & Slander ☐ 330 Federal Employers' Liability ☐ 340 Marine ☐ 345 Marine Product Liability ☐ 350 Motor Vehicle ☐ 355 Motor Vehicle Product Liability ☐ 360 Other Personal Injury ☐ 362 Personal Injury - Medical Malpractice	**PERSONAL INJURY** ☐ 365 Personal Injury - Product Liability ☐ 367 Health Care/ Pharmaceutical Personal Injury Product Liability ☐ 368 Asbestos Personal Injury Product Liability **PERSONAL PROPERTY** ☐ 370 Other Fraud ☐ 371 Truth in Lending ☐ 380 Other Personal Property Damage ☐ 385 Property Damage Product Liability	☐ 625 Drug Related Seizure of Property 21 USC 881 ☐ 690 Other	☐ 422 Appeal 28 USC 158 ☐ 423 Withdrawal 28 USC 157 **PROPERTY RIGHTS** ☐ 820 Copyrights ☐ 830 Patent ☐ 840 Trademark	☐ 375 False Claims Act ☐ 400 State Reapportionment ☐ 410 Antitrust ☐ 430 Banks and Banking ☐ 450 Commerce ☐ 460 Deportation ☐ 470 Racketeer Influenced and Corrupt Organizations ☐ 480 Consumer Credit ☐ 490 Cable/Sat TV
REAL PROPERTY	**CIVIL RIGHTS**	**PRISONER PETITIONS**	**LABOR**	**SOCIAL SECURITY**	☐ 850 Securities/Commodities/ Exchange ☐ 890 Other Statutory Actions ☐ 891 Agricultural Acts ☐ 893 Environmental Matters ☐ 895 Freedom of Information Act ☐ 896 Arbitration
☐ 210 Land Condemnation ☐ 220 Foreclosure ☐ 230 Rent Lease & Ejectment ☐ 240 Torts to Land ☐ 245 Tort Product Liability ☐ 290 All Other Real Property	☐ 440 Other Civil Rights ☐ 441 Voting ☐ 442 Employment ☐ 443 Housing/ Accommodations ☐ 445 Amer. w/Disabilities - Employment ☐ 446 Amer. w/Disabilities - Other ☐ 448 Education	**Habeas Corpus:** ☐ 463 Alien Detainee ☐ 510 Motions to Vacate Sentence ☐ 530 General ☐ 535 Death Penalty **Other:** ☐ 540 Mandamus & Other ☐ 550 Civil Rights ☐ 555 Prison Condition ☐ 560 Civil Detainee - Conditions of Confinement	☐ 710 Fair Labor Standards Act ☐ 720 Labor/Management Relations ☐ 740 Railway Labor Act ☐ 751 Family and Medical Leave Act ☐ 790 Other Labor Litigation ☐ 791 Employee Retirement Income Security Act	☐ 861 HIA (1395ff) ☐ 862 Black Lung (923) ☐ 863 DIWC/DIWW (405(g)) ☐ 864 SSID Title XVI ☐ 865 RSI (405(g)) **FEDERAL TAX SUITS** ☐ 870 Taxes (U.S. Plaintiff or Defendant) ☐ 871 IRS - Third Party 26 USC 7609	☐ 899 Administrative Procedure Act/Review or Appeal of Agency Decision ☐ 950 Constitutionality of State Statutes
		IMMIGRATION ☐ 462 Naturalization Application ☐ 465 Other Immigration Actions			

V. ORIGIN *(Place an "X" in One Box Only)*

- ☐ 1 Original Proceeding
- ☐ 2 Removed from State Court
- ☐ 3 Remanded from Appellate Court
- ☐ 4 Reinstated or Reopened
- ☐ 5 Transferred from Another District *(specify)*
- ☐ 6 Multidistrict Litigation

VI. CAUSE OF ACTION

Cite the U.S. Civil Statute under which you are filing *(Do not cite jurisdictional statutes unless diversity):*

Brief description of cause:

VII. REQUESTED IN COMPLAINT:
☐ CHECK IF THIS IS A CLASS ACTION UNDER RULE 23, F.R.Cv.P.

DEMAND $ _____

CHECK YES only if demanded in complaint:

JURY DEMAND: ☐ Yes ☐ No

VIII. RELATED CASE(S) IF ANY *(See instructions):*

JUDGE _____   DOCKET NUMBER _____

DATE _____   SIGNATURE OF ATTORNEY OF RECORD _____

FOR OFFICE USE ONLY

RECEIPT # _____ AMOUNT _____ APPLYING IFP _____ JUDGE _____ MAG. JUDGE _____

JS 44 Reverse (Rev. 12/12)

INSTRUCTIONS FOR ATTORNEYS COMPLETING CIVIL COVER SHEET FORM JS 44

Authority For Civil Cover Sheet

The JS 44 civil cover sheet and the information contained herein neither replaces nor supplements the filings and service of pleading or other papers as required by law, except as provided by local rules of court. This form, approved by the Judicial Conference of the United States in September 1974, is required for the use of the Clerk of Court for the purpose of initiating the civil docket sheet. Consequently, a civil cover sheet is submitted to the Clerk of Court for each civil complaint filed. The attorney filing a case should complete the form as follows:

I.(a) **Plaintiffs-Defendants.** Enter names (last, first, middle initial) of plaintiff and defendant. If the plaintiff or defendant is a government agency, use only the full name or standard abbreviations. If the plaintiff or defendant is an official within a government agency, identify first the agency and then the official, giving both name and title.

(b) **County of Residence.** For each civil case filed, except U.S. plaintiff cases, enter the name of the county where the first listed plaintiff resides at the time of filing. In U.S. plaintiff cases, enter the name of the county in which the first listed defendant resides at the time of filing. (NOTE: In land condemnation cases, the county of residence of the "defendant" is the location of the tract of land involved.)

(c) **Attorneys.** Enter the firm name, address, telephone number, and attorney of record. If there are several attorneys, list them on an attachment, noting in this section "(see attachment)".

II. **Jurisdiction.** The basis of jurisdiction is set forth under Rule 8(a), F.R.Cv.P., which requires that jurisdictions be shown in pleadings. Place an "X" in one of the boxes. If there is more than one basis of jurisdiction, precedence is given in the order shown below.
United States plaintiff. (1) Jurisdiction based on 28 U.S.C. 1345 and 1348. Suits by agencies and officers of the United States are included here.
United States defendant. (2) When the plaintiff is suing the United States, its officers or agencies, place an "X" in this box.
Federal question. (3) This refers to suits under 28 U.S.C. 1331, where jurisdiction arises under the Constitution of the United States, an amendment to the Constitution, an act of Congress or a treaty of the United States. In cases where the U.S. is a party, the U.S. plaintiff or defendant code takes precedence, and box 1 or 2 should be marked.
Diversity of citizenship. (4) This refers to suits under 28 U.S.C. 1332, where parties are citizens of different states. When Box 4 is checked, the citizenship of the different parties must be checked. (See Section III below; **NOTE: federal question actions take precedence over diversity cases.**)

III. **Residence (citizenship) of Principal Parties.** This section of the JS 44 is to be completed if diversity of citizenship was indicated above. Mark this section for each principal party.

IV. **Nature of Suit.** Place an "X" in the appropriate box. If the nature of suit cannot be determined, be sure the cause of action, in Section VI below, is sufficient to enable the deputy clerk or the statistical clerk(s) in the Administrative Office to determine the nature of suit. If the cause fits more than one nature of suit, select the most definitive.

V. **Origin.** Place an "X" in one of the six boxes.
Original Proceedings. (1) Cases which originate in the United States district courts.
Removed from State Court. (2) Proceedings initiated in state courts may be removed to the district courts under Title 28 U.S.C., Section 1441. When the petition for removal is granted, check this box.
Remanded from Appellate Court. (3) Check this box for cases remanded to the district court for further action. Use the date of remand as the filing date.
Reinstated or Reopened. (4) Check this box for cases reinstated or reopened in the district court. Use the reopening date as the filing date.
Transferred from Another District. (5) For cases transferred under Title 28 U.S.C. Section 1404(a). Do not use this for within district transfers or multidistrict litigation transfers.
Multidistrict Litigation. (6) Check this box when a multidistrict case is transferred into the district under authority of Title 28 U.S.C. Section 1407. When this box is checked, do not check (5) above.

VI. **Cause of Action.** Report the civil statute directly related to the cause of action and give a brief description of the cause. **Do not cite jurisdictional statutes unless diversity.** Example: U.S. Civil Statute: 47 USC 553 Brief Description: Unauthorized reception of cable service

VII. **Requested in Complaint.** Class Action. Place an "X" in this box if you are filing a class action under Rule 23, F.R.Cv.P.
Demand. In this space enter the actual dollar amount being demanded or indicate other demand, such as a preliminary injunction.
Jury Demand. Check the appropriate box to indicate whether or not a jury is being demanded.

VIII. **Related Cases.** This section of the JS 44 is used to reference related pending cases, if any. If there are related pending cases, insert the docket numbers and the corresponding judge names for such cases.

Date and Attorney Signature. Date and sign the civil cover sheet.

[Revised December 2012.]

APPENDIX I. CIVIL CASE MANAGEMENT
TRACK DESIGNATION FORM

IN THE UNITED STATES DISTRICT COURT
FOR THE EASTERN DISTRICT OF
PENNSYLVANIA

CASE MANAGEMENT TRACK DESIGNATION FORM

                   :   CIVIL ACTION
                   :
v.   :
                   :
                   :   NO.

In accordance with the Civil Justice Expense and Delay Reduction Plan of this court, counsel for plaintiff shall complete a Case Management Track Designation Form in all civil cases at the time of filing the complaint and serve a copy on all defendants. (See § 1:03 of the plan set forth on the reverse side of this form.) In the event that a defendant does not agree with the plaintiff regarding said designation, that defendant shall, with its first appearance, submit to the clerk of court and serve on the plaintiff and all other parties, a case management track designation form specifying the track to which that defendant believes the case should be assigned.

SELECT ONE OF THE FOLLOWING CASE MANAGEMENT TRACKS:

(a) Habeas Corpus—Cases brought under 28 U.S.C. § 2241 through § 2255.   ( )

(b) Social Security—Cases requesting review of a decision of the Secretary of Health and Human Services denying plaintiff Social Security Benefits.   ( )

(c) Arbitration—Cases required to be designated for arbitration under Local Civil Rule 53.2.   ( )

(d) Asbestos—Cases involving claims for personal injury or property damage from exposure to asbestos.   ( )

(e) Special Management—Cases that do not fall into tracks (a) through (d) that are commonly referred to as complex and that need special or intense management by the court. (See reverse side of this form for a detailed explanation of special management cases.)   ( )

(f) Standard Management—Cases that do not fall into any one of the other tracks.   ( )

_____   _____   _____
Date   Attorney-at-law   Attorney for

_____   _____   _____
Telephone   FAX Number   E-mail Address

Civ. 660 (10/02)

Civil Justice Expense and Delay Reduction Plan
Section 1:03—Assignment to a Management Track

(a) The clerk of court will assign cases to tracks (a) through (d) based on the initial pleading.

(b) In all cases not appropriate for assignment by the clerk of court to tracks (a) through (d), the plaintiff shall submit to the clerk of court and serve with the complaint on all defendants a case management track designation form specifying that the plaintiff believes the case requires Standard Management or Special Management. In the event that a defendant does not agree with the plaintiff regarding said designation, that defendant shall, with its first appearance, submit to the clerk of court and serve on the plaintiff and all other parties, a case management track designation form specifying the track to which that defendant believes the case should be assigned.

(c) The court may, on its own initiative or upon the request of any party, change the track assignment of any case at any time.

(d) Nothing in this Plan is intended to abrogate or limit a judicial officer's authority in any case pending before that judicial officer, to direct pretrial and trial proceedings that are more stringent than those of the Plan and that are designed to accomplish cost and delay reduction.

(e) Nothing in this Plan is intended to supersede Local Civil Rules 40.1 and 72.1, or the procedure for random assignment of Habeas Corpus and Social Security cases referred to magistrate judges of the court.

SPECIAL MANAGEMENT CASE ASSIGNMENTS
(See § 1.02(e) Management Track Definitions
of the Civil Justice Expense and Delay
Reduction Plan)

Special Management cases will usually include that class of cases commonly referred to as "complex litigation" as that term has been used in the Manuals for Complex Litigation. The first manual was prepared in 1969 and the Manual for Complex Litigation Second, MCL 2d was prepared in 1985. This term is intended to include cases that present unusual problems and require extraordinary treatment. See § 0.1 of the first manual. Cases may require special or intense management by the court due to one or more of the following factors: (1) large number of parties; (2) large number of claims or defenses; (3) complex factual issues; (4) large volume of evidence; (5) problems locating or preserving evidence; (6) extensive discovery; (7) exceptionally long time needed to prepare for disposition; (8) decision needed within an exceptionally short time; and (9) need to decide preliminary issues before final disposition. It may include two or more related cases. Complex litigation typically includes such cases as antitrust cases; cases involving a large number of parties or an unincorporated association of large membership; cases involving requests for injunctive relief affecting the operation of large business entities; patent cases; copyright and trademark cases; common disaster cases such as those arising from aircraft crashes or marine disasters; actions brought by individual stockholders; stockholder's derivative and stockholder's representative actions; class actions or potential class actions; and other civil (and criminal) cases involving unusual multiplicity or complexity of factual issues. See § 0.22 of the first Manual for Complex Litigation and Manual for Complex Litigation Second, Chapter 33.

APPENDIX J. [OMITTED]

[*Publisher's Note*: Omitted; see Local Rule 5.1.3, *ante*].

APPENDIX K. CONSENT TO FACSIMILE TRANSMISSION OF NOTICES OF ORDERS

NOTICE

PROGRAM FOR FACSIMILE SERVICE OF NOTICE TO
COUNSEL OR LITIGANTS IN CIVIL AND CRIMINAL CASES

The Court has authorized the Clerk of Court to implement a pilot program in civil and criminal cases to allow attorneys and pro se litigants to waive the provisions of Federal Rule of Civil Procedure 77(d) or Federal Rule of Criminal Procedure 49(c), which requires service of Notice of Orders and Judgments by means of mail, and instead consent to receive Notice of Orders and Judgments by means of facsimile transmission.

This notice is being sent to you because you either represent a party or are a party to litigation currently pending in this district. Enclosed please find a form of Consent to Receive Notice of Orders and Judgments by means of Facsimile Transmission and Waiver of the Provisions of Fed.R.Civ.P. 77(d) or Fed.R.Crim.P. 49(c) Providing for said Notice by means of Mail. Execution of this enclosed Facsimile Transmission Authorization form authorizes the Clerk of Court to serve notice of the entry of Orders or Judgments pursuant to Fed.R.Civ.P. 77(d) or Fed.R.Crim.P. 49(c) by facsimile in lieu of notice by means of mail. Please be advised that this enclosed Facsimile Transmission Authorization form also serves as Notice to and Authorization for the Clerk of Court to keep your name and the relevant information on file so that the Facsimile Transmission Authorization form will apply to all pending and future civil and criminal cases in which you are, or will be, either counsel or a party to litigation.

You are requested to complete the enclosed Facsimile Transmission Authorization form and return it to this office. Please be advised that waiver of the provisions providing for notice of the entry of Orders or Judgments by mail will include all pending civil and criminal cases in the Eastern District of Pennsylvania in which you either represent a party or are a party to the litigation, except for grand jury proceedings and impounded cases.

Please also be advised that the Clerk of Court shall make no more than three attempts to transmit the Notice of Entry of Orders and Judgments by means of facsimile. If after three attempts facsimile transmission is unsuccessful, Notice shall be made by means of mail pursuant to Fed.R.Civ.P. 77(d) or Fed.R.Crim.P. 49(c).

Thank you for your willingness to consider participating in this program. Should you have any questions concerning this notice, please contact Susan Matlack at (267) 299–7051.

Michael E. Kunz

Clerk of Court

UNITED STATES DISTRICT COURT
EASTERN DISTRICT OF PENNSYLVANIA

CONSENT TO RECEIVE NOTICE OF ORDERS AND JUDGMENTS IN CIVIL AND CRIMINAL CASES BY MEANS OF FACSIMILE TRANSMISSION AND WAIVER OF PROVISIONS OF FED.R.CIV.P. 77(d) OR FED.R. CRIM.P. 49(c) PROVIDING FOR SAID NOTICE BY MEANS OF MAIL

TO THE CLERK OF COURT:

I hereby waive the provisions of Fed.R.Civ.P. 77(d) or Fed.R.Crim.P. 49(c) providing for notice of the entry of Orders or Judgments by mail in the manner provided by Fed.R.Civ.P. 5 or Fed.R.Crim.P. 49(c), and consent that notice may be given to me, in all pending and future civil or criminal cases in which I enter my appearance, by the Clerk of Court by facsimile in lieu of notice by means of mail. I understand that this form, when executed, will serve as Notice to and Authorization for the Clerk of Court to keep this information on file for all pending and future civil or criminal cases in which I enter my appearance.

I hereby confirm, by execution of this form, that I understand that it is my responsibility to notify the Clerk of Court, in writing, of my current address and facsimile number.

_____   _____
Name (Printed)   Bar ID Number

_____   _____
Address (Printed)   Telephone Number

_____   _____
Address (Printed)   FAX Number

_____   _____
Signature   Date

APPENDIX L.   MAIL INFORMATION FORM
UNITED STATES DISTRICT COURT
EASTERN DISTRICT OF PENNSYLVANIA
INFORMATION FORM

Name: _____   Bar ID No.: _____

Firm: _____

Address: _____

_____

_____

City: _____   State: ____   Zip Code*: _____-_____

Facsimile No: _____

Please return completed form to:

Michael E. Kunz
Clerk of Court
United States District Court
for the Eastern District of Pennsylvania
U.S. Courthouse
601 Market Street, Room 2609
Philadelphia, PA 19106–1797

—or—

FAX to:

(215) 597–6390
(267) 299–7135
(610) 434–6174

* Please include zip code and 4–digit extension number

☐ Indicate here if you would like to receive information on the Pilot Fax Notice Program

☐ Indicate here if you would like to receive a Directory of Automated Services

[June 2003.]

APPENDIX M. JUDGES' ROOM NUMBERS AND ZIP CODE + 4-DIGIT EXTENSION NUMBERS

US District Court
601 Market St 19106

Philadelphia			
District Court Judges	**Room #**	**Zip Code**	**plus 4**
Judge J. Curtis Joyner	17614	19106	1761
Judge John R. Padova	17613	19106	1759
Judge Harvey Bartle III	16614	19106	1772
Judge Petrese B. Tucker	16613	19106	1709
Judge Eduardo C. Robreno	15614	19106	1705
Judge Stewart Dalzell	15613	19106	1773
Judge Ronald L. Buckwalter	14614	19106	1724
Judge Lawrence F. Stengel	14613	19106	1753
Judge Joel H. Slomsky	13614	19106	1748
Judge Berle M. Schiller	13613	19106	1747
Judge Cynthia M. Rufe	12614	19106	1714
Judge Jan E DuBois	12613	19106	1766
Judge Juan R. Sanchez	11614	19106	1711
Judge Robert F. Kelly	11613	19106	1765
Judge Norma L. Shapiro	10614	19106	1774
Judge Gene E.K. Pratter	10613	19106	1723
Judge Timothy J. Savage	9614	19106	1718
Judge Gerald A. McHugh	9613	19106	1742
Judge R. Barclay Surrick	8614	19106	1716
Judge L. Felipe Restrepo	8613	19106	1740

Philadelphia			
District Court Judges	**Room #**	**Zip Code**	**plus 4**
Judge Mitchell S. Goldberg	7614	19106	1741
Judge Anita B. Brody	7613	19106	1717
Judge Legrome D. Davis	6614	19106	1708
Judge Paul S. Diamond	6613	19106	1743
Vacant	5918	19106	1744
Judge Gerald J. Pappert	5614	19106	1745
Judge C. Darnell Jones II	5613	19106	1726
Judge Mark A. Kearney	5118	19106	1775
Judge Thomas N. O'Neill, Jr.	4007	19106	1749
Visiting Judges	4006	19106	1750
Judge Marilyn Heffley	4001	19106	1752

Judge Nitza I. Quinones Alejandro	4000	19106	1754
Judge Michael M. Baylson	3810	19106	1751
Judge Wendy Beetlestone	3809	19106	1725
Judge Linda K. Caracappa	3042	19106	1789
Visiting Judges	3041	19106	1738
Judge Donald W. VanArtsdalen	3040	19106	1755
Judge J. William Ditter, Jr.	3040	19106	1755
Judge Elizabeth T. Hey	3038	19106	1727
JudgeDavid R. Strawbridge	3030	19106	1756
Judge Timothy R. Rice	3029	19106	1757
Judge Carol Sandra Moore Wells	3016	19106	1730
Judge Lynne A. Sitarski	3015	19106	1758
Judge Jacob P. Hart	3006	19106	1762
Judge Thomas J. Rueter	3000	19106	1739

Divisional Office Locations

Philadelphia

Judge Richard A. Lloret
Rm 219
The Robert N. C. Nix Building
900 Market St.
Philadelphia, PA 19107-4237

Judge M. Faith Angell
Rm 211
The Robert N. C. Nix Building
900 Market St.
Philadelphia, PA 19107-4237

Allentown

Judge Joseph F. Leeson
504 Hamilton St.
Room 3401
Allentown, PA 18101-1514

Judge James Knoll Gardner
504 Hamilton St.
Room 4701
Allentown, PA 18101-1514

Judge Henry S. Perkin
504 Hamilton St.
Room 4401
Allentown, PA 18101-1533

Reading

Judge Juan R. Sanchez
Rm 201
The Madison Building
400 Washington St
Reading, PA 19601-3933

Judge Lawerence F. Stengel
Rm 201
The Madison Building
400 Washington St
Reading, PA 19601-3933

Judge Jeffery L. Schmehl
Rm 401
The Madison Building
400 Washington St
Reading, PA 19601-3956

Easton

Judge Edward G. Smith
Room 400
Larry Holmes Building
101 Larry Holmes Blvd.
Easton, PA 18042-7722

[Effective June 2008. Revised May 1, 2009; February 2011; November 2011; April 2012; September 2012; October 1, 2014; November 3, 2015.]

APPENDIX N.   SUMMONS IN A CIVIL ACTION

UNITED STATES DISTRICT COURT
for the

	)
	)
	)
_____	)
Plaintiff(s)	)
v.	) Civil Action No.
	)
	)
	)
	)
_____	)
Defendant(s)	)

SUMMONS IN A CIVIL ACTION

To: *(Defendant's name and address)*

A lawsuit has been filed against you.

Within 21 days after service of this summons on you (not counting the day you received it) — or 60 days if you are the United States or a United States agency, or an officer or employee of the United States described in Fed. R. Civ. P. 12 (a)(2) or (3) — you must serve on the plaintiff an answer to the attached complaint or a motion under Rule 12 of the Federal Rules of Civil Procedure. The answer or motion must be served on the plaintiff or plaintiff's attorney, whose name and address are:

If you fail to respond, judgment by default will be entered against you for the relief demanded in the complaint. You also must file your answer or motion with the court.

CLERK OF COURT

Date: _____   _____
                                      Signature of Clerk or Deputy Clerk

PROOF OF SERVICE

***(This section should not be filed with the court
unless required by Fed. R. Civ. P. 4(l))***

This summons for *(name of individual and title, if any)* _____ was received by me on *(date)* _____.

☐ I personally served the summons on the individual at *(place)* _____ on *(date)* _____; or

☐ I left the summons at the individual's residence or usual place of abode with *(name)* _____, a person of suitable age and discretion who resides there, on *(date)* _____, and mailed a copy to the individual's last known address; or

☐ I served the summons on *(name of individual)* _____, who is designated by law to accept service of process on behalf of *(name of organization)* _____ on *(date)* _____; or

☐ I returned the summons unexecuted because _____; or

☐ Other *(specify):*

My fees are $ ___ for travel and $ ___ for services, for a total of $ <u>0.00</u>.

I declare under penalty of perjury that this information is true.

Date: _____   _____

                                              Server's signature

                                 _____

                                       Printed name and title

                                 _____

                                           Server's address

Additional information regarding attempted service, etc.:

[June 2003. Revised February 2009; December 2009; June 2012.]

APPENDIX O.   WRIT OF EXECUTION

IN THE UNITED STATES DISTRICT COURT
FOR THE EASTERN DISTRICT OF PENNSYLVANIA

:	**CIVIL ACTION**
:	
:	
:	
:	
:	**NO.**

PRAECIPE FOR WRIT OF EXECUTION

TO THE CLERK:

ISSUE WRIT OF EXECUTION in the above matter, directed to the United States Marshal for the Eastern District of Pennsylvania, and against _____ and against _____ (Name and Address of Garnishee) garnishee, and index this writ against* _____ and against _____ as garnishee, as a lis pendens against real property of the judgment debtor in the name of the garnishee, as follows:

_____

_____

Amount Due $ _____
Interest From _____ $ _____

_____
Attorney for

Date: _____

*Applicable to real estate only [Rule 3104(c) Pa.R.C.P.]

Civ637 (7/00)

IN THE UNITED STATES DISTRICT COURT
FOR THE EASTERN DISTRICT OF PENNSYLVANIA

:	**CIVIL ACTION**
:	
:	
:	
:	**NO.**

WRIT OF EXECUTION

TO THE UNITED STATES MARSHAL FOR THE EASTERN DISTRICT OF PENNSYLVANIA:

To satisfy judgment, interest, and costs against _____ (Name of Defendant), defendant

(1) You are directed to levy upon the property of the defendant and to sell his interest therein:

(2) You are also directed to attach the property of the defendant not levied upon in the possession of _____ (Name of Garnishee), as garnishee.

_____ (Specifically Describe Property) and to notify the garnishee that

(a) an attachment has been issued;

(b) the garnishee is enjoined from paying any debt to or for the account of the defendant and from delivering any property of the defendant or otherwise disposing thereof;

(3) if property of the defendant not levied upon and subject to attachment is found in the possession of anyone other than a named garnishee, you are directed to notify him that he has been added as a garnishee and is enjoined as above stated.

Amount Due   _____ $ _____
Interest From   _____ $ _____
(Cost to be Added) $ _____

MICHAEL E. KUNZ
(Clerk of Court)

Seal of the Court

BY: _____
(Deputy Clerk)

MAJOR EXEMPTIONS UNDER PENNSYLVANIA AND FEDERAL LAW

1. $300 statutory exemption

2. Bibles, school books, sewing machines, uniforms, and equipment

3. Most wages and unemployment compensation

4. Social Security benefits

5. Certain retirement funds and accounts

6. Certain veteran and armed forces benefits

7. Certain insurance proceeds

8. Such other exemptions as may be provided by law

Civ 638 (7/00)

IN THE UNITED STATES DISTRICT COURT
FOR THE EASTERN DISTRICT OF PENNSYLVANIA

:   CIVIL ACTION
:
:
:
:   NO.

WRIT OF EXECUTION NOTICE

This paper is a Writ of Execution. It has been issued because there is a judgment against you. It may cause your property to be held or taken to pay the judgment. You may have legal rights to prevent your property from being taken. A lawyer can advise you more specifically of these rights. If you wish to exercise your rights, you must act promptly.

The law provides that certain property cannot be taken. Such property is said to be exempt. There is a debtor's exemption of $300. There are other exemptions which may be applicable to you. Attached is a summary of some of the major exemptions. You may have other exemptions or rights.

If you have an exemption, you should do the following promptly: (1) Fill out the attached claim form and demand for a prompt hearing. (2) Deliver the form or mail it to the United States Marshal's office at the address noted.

You should come to court ready to explain your exemption. If you do not come to court and prove your exemption, you may lose some of your property.

YOU SHOULD TAKE THIS PAPER TO YOUR LAWYER AT ONCE. IF YOU DO NOT HAVE A LAWYER OR CANNOT AFFORD ONE, GO TO OR TELEPHONE THE OFFICE SET FORTH BELOW TO FIND OUT WHERE YOU CAN GET LEGAL HELP.

LAWYER REFERENCE SERVICE

(Name)

ONE READING CENTER
11th FLOOR

PHILADELPHIA, PA 19107

(Address)

(215) 238–1701

(Telephone Number)

Civ 639 (7/00)

IN THE UNITED STATES DISTRICT COURT
FOR THE EASTERN DISTRICT OF PENNSYLVANIA

                                            :   **CIVIL ACTION**
                                            :
                                            :
                                            :
                                            :   **NO.**

CLAIM FOR EXEMPTION

To the U.S. Marshal:

I, the above named defendant, claim exemption of property from levy or attachment:

(1) From my personal property in my possession which has been levied upon.

    (a) I desire that my $300 statutory exemption be

        (i) set aside in kind (specify property to be set aside in kind): _____

        (ii) paid in cash following the sale of the property levied upon; or

    (b) I claim the following exemption (specify property and basis of exemption):

_____

(2) From my property which is in the possession of a third party, I claim the following exemptions:

        (a) My $300 statutory exemption: in cash   in kind
(specify property): _____
        (b) Social security benefits on deposit in the amount of $ _____
        (c) Other (specify amount and basis of exemption): _____
_____

I request a prompt court hearing to determine the exemption. Notice of the hearing should be given to me at _____

_____   _____
(Address)   (Telephone Number)

I declare under penalty of perjury that the foregoing statements made in this claim for exemption are true and correct.

Date: _____

_____
(Signature of Defendant)

THIS CLAIM TO BE FILED WITH THE OFFICE OF THE U.S. MARSHAL FOR THE EASTERN DISTRICT OF PENNSYLVANIA:

2110 United States Courthouse
601 Market Street
Philadelphia, PA 19106

(Address)

(215) 597–7272

(Telephone Number)

Note: Under paragraphs (1) and (2) of the writ, a description of specific property to be levied upon or attached may be set forth in the writ or included in a separate direction to the United States Marshal.

Under paragraph (2) of the writ, if the attachment of a named garnishee is desired, his name should be set forth in the space provided.

Under paragraph (3) of the writ, the United States Marshal may, as under prior practice, add as a garnishee any person not named in this writ who may be found in possession of property of the defendant. See Rule 3111(a). For limitations on the power to attach tangible personal property, see Rule 3108 (a).

Each court shall by local rule designate the officer, organization, or person to be named in the notice.

Civ 640 (7/00)

IN THE UNITED STATES DISTRICT COURT
FOR THE EASTERN DISTRICT OF PENNSYLVANIA

UNITED STATES OF AMERICA	:	**CIVIL ACTION**
Plaintiff	:	
V.	:	
_____	:	**NO.**
Defendant	:	
_____	:	
Garnishee	:	

TO: _____

_____

_____

Date of Notice: _____

IMPORTANT NOTICE

You are in default because you failed to take action required of you in this case. Unless you act within ten days from the date of this Notice, a judgment may be entered against you without a hearing, and you may lose your property or other important rights. You should take this Notice to a lawyer at once. If you do not have a lawyer or cannot afford one, go to or telephone the following office to find out where you can get legal help.

Lawyer Reference Service One

Reading Center

11th Floor

Philadelphia, PA 19107

(215) 238–1701

_____

Attorney for

Civ 641 (7/00)

APPENDIX P. TRANSCRIPT PURCHASE ORDER

TRANSCRIPT PURCHASE ORDER
For Third Circuit Court of Appeals

District Court	Court of Appeals Docket No.
	District Court Docket No.

Short Case Title _____

Date Notice of Appeal Filed by Clerk of District Court _____

Part I. (To be completed by party responsible for ordering transcript)   NOTE: A SEPARATE FORM IS TO BE TYPED FOR
A. Check one of the following and serve ALL COPIES: EACH COURT REPORTER IN THIS CASE.

TRANSCRIPT:

___ None   ___ Unnecessary for appeal purposes.

___ Already on file in the District Court Clerk's office.

___ This is to order a transcript of the proceedings heard on the date listed below from _____ (Court Reporter)

(Specify on lines below exact date of proceedings to be transcribed). If requesting only partial transcript of the proceedings, specify exactly what portion or what witness testimony is desired.

_____

_____

If proceeding to be transcribed was a trial, also check any appropriate box below for special requests; otherwise, this material will NOT be included in the trial transcripts.

___ Voir dire   ___ Opening Statement of Plaintiff   ___ Opening Statement of Defendant

___ Closing Argument of Plaintiff   ___ Closing Argument of Defendant

___ Jury Instructions   ___ Sentencing Hearings

FAILURE TO SPECIFY IN ADEQUATE DETAIL THOSE PROCEEDINGS TO BE TRANSCRIBED OR FAILURE TO MAKE PROMPT SATISFACTORY FINANCIAL ARRANGEMENTS FOR TRANSCRIPT ARE GROUNDS FOR DISMISSAL OF THE APPEAL OR IMPOSITION OF SANCTIONS.

B. This is to certify that satisfactory financial arrangements have been completed with the court reporter for payment of the cost of the transcript. The method of payment will be:

___ CJA Form submitted to District Court Judge   ___ Motion for Transcript has been submitted to District Court

___ CJA Form submitted to Court of Appeals   ___ Private Funds

Signature _____   Date _____

Print Name _____   Counsel for _____

Address _____   Telephone _____

Part II. COURT REPORTER ACKNOWLEDGEMENT (To be completed by the Court Reporter and forwarded to the Court of Appeals on the same day transcript order is received.)

Date transcript order received	Estimated completion date; if not within 30 days of date financial arrangements made, motion for extension to be made to Court of Appeals	Estimated number of pages

___ Arrangements for payment were made on _____

___ Arrangements for payment have not been made pursuant to FRAP 10(b)

_____   _____   _____
Date   Name of Court Reporter   Telephone

Part III. NOTIFICATION THAT TRANSCRIPT HAS BEEN FILED IN THE DISTRICT COURT (To be completed by court reporter on date of filing transcript in District Court.   Notification must be forwarded to Court of Appeals on the same date.)
This is to certify that the transcript has been completed and filed with the District Court today.

Actual Number of Pages _____   Actual Number of Volumes _____

_____   _____
Date   Signature of Court Reporter

[June 2003.]

446

APPENDIX Q. CONSENT, AND REFERENCE OF A CIVIL ACTION TO A MAGISTRATE JUDGE

UNITED STATES DISTRICT COURT
FOR THE EASTERN DISTRICT OF PENNSYLVANIA

_____)	
Plaintiff)	
)	
v.)	*Civil Action No.*
_____)	
Defendant)	

CONSENT, AND REFERENCE OF A CIVIL ACTION TO A MAGISTRATE JUDGE

The following parties consent (subject to approval by the assigned Article III judicial officer) to have a United States magistrate judge conduct all proceedings in this case including trial, the entry of final judgment, and all post-trial proceedings.

Parties' Printed Names: Signatures of Parties or Attorneys: Dates:

_____   _____   _____

_____   _____   _____

_____   _____   _____

_____   _____   _____

Reference Order

IT IS ORDERED: This case is referred to a United States magistrate judge _____ to conduct all proceedings and order the entry of a final judgment in accordance with 28 U.S.C. § 636(c) and Fed. R. Civ. P. 73.

_____
District Judge's signature

Date: _____   _____
(Printed Name and Title)

Note: Return this form to the clerk of court only if you are consenting to the exercise of jurisdiction by a United States magistrate judge.

Do not return this form to a judge.

(05/2013)

United States District Court
Eastern District of Pennsylvania

NOTICE OF PROCEDURE TO CONSENT TO REFERENCE OF
CIVIL ACTION OR PROCEEDING TO MAGISTRATE JUDGE

1.   When authorized under 28 U.S.C. § 636(c), a magistrate judge may, if all parties consent, and if it is approved by the district judge to whom the case is assigned, conduct a civil action or proceeding, including a jury or non-jury trial or proceeding [Fed. R. Civ. P. 73(a); Local R. Civ. P. 72.1 III.(b)].

2.   A party is free to withhold consent to referral to a magistrate judge without adverse substantive consequences [Fed. R. Civ. P. 73(b)(2)].

3.   A party's decision to consent, or not to consent, will not be made known to the assigned judge or magistrate judge unless the parties have consented to the reference to the magistrate judge [Fed. R. Civ. P. 73(b)(1); Local R. Civ. P. 72.1 III.(b)(2)].

4.   No action eligible for arbitration will be referred to a magistrate judge until the arbitration has been concluded and trial de novo demanded [Local R. Civ. P. 53.2.7.].

5.   The Court may, for good cause shown, on its own motion, or under extraordinary circumstances shown by any party, vacate a reference of a civil matter or proceeding to a magistrate judge [Fed. R. Civ. P. 73(b)(3)].

6.   When a case is referred to a magistrate judge to conduct a civil action or proceeding, including the entry of final judgment, the final judgment may be taken to the court of appeals in the same manner as an appeal from any other judgment of a district court [Fed. R. Civ. P. 73(c)].

PETRESE B. TUCKER
CHIEF JUDGE

MICHAEL E. KUNZ
CLERK OF COURT

*This Notice is being given pursuant to 28 U.S.C. § 636(c), Fed. R. Civ. P. 73 and Local R.Civ. P. 72.1, 53.2.

[June 2011.   Revised effective March 2013;   May 2013.]

APPENDIX R.   BILL OF COSTS

AO 133 (Rev. 12/09) Bill of Costs

UNITED STATES DISTRICT COURT
for the

)
)
     v.   )   Case No.:
)
)

Bill of Costs

Judgment having been entered in the above entitled action on _____ against _____,
                                                Date
the Clerk is requested to tax the following as costs:

Fees of the Clerk . . . . $_____

Fees for service of summons and subpoena . . . .   _____

Fees for printed or electronically recorded transcripts necessarily
obtained for use in the case . . . .   _____

Fees and disbursements for printing . . . .   _____

Fees for witnesses *(itemize on page two)* . . . .   _____ 0.00

Fees for exemplification and the costs of making copies of any materials where the copies are necessarily obtained for use
in the case . . . .   _____

Docket fees under 28 U.S.C. 1923 . . . .   _____

Costs as shown on Mandate of Court of Appeals . . . .   _____

Compensation of court-appointed experts . . . .   _____

Compensation of interpreters and costs of special interpretation ser-
vices under 28 U.S.C. 1828 . . . .   _____

Other costs *(please itemize)* . . . .   _____

                                                 TOTAL $_____ 0.00

SPECIAL NOTE: Attach to your bill an itemization and documentation for requested costs in
all categories.

Declaration

I declare under penalty of perjury that the foregoing costs are correct and were necessarily
incurred in this action and that the services for which fees have been charged were actually and
necessarily performed. A copy of this bill has been served on all parties in the following
manner:

     ☐   Electronic service.

     ☐   First class mail, postage prepaid

     ☐   Other

s/ Attorney: _____

Name of Attorney: _____

For: _____   Date: _____
        Name of Claiming Party

Taxation of Costs

Costs are taxed in the amount of _____ and included in the judgment.

_____   By: _____   _____
    Clerk of Court   *Deputy Clerk*   *Date*

UNITED STATES DISTRICT COURT

NAME, CITY AND STATE OF RESIDENCE	ATTENDANCE		SUBSISTENCE		MILEAGE		Total Cost Each Witness
	Days	Total Cost	Days	Total Cost	Miles	Total Cost	
							$0.00
							$0.00
							$0.00
							$0.00
							$0.00
							$0.00
							TOTAL $0.00

Witness Fees (computation, cf. 28 U.S.C. 1821 for statutory fees)

NOTICE

Section 1924, Title 28, U.S. Code (effective September 1, 1948) provides:
"Sec. 1924. Verification of bill of costs."
"Before any bill of costs is taxed, the party claiming any item of cost or disbursement shall attach thereto an affidavit, made by himself or by his duly authorized attorney or agent having knowledge of the facts, that such item is correct and has been necessarily incurred in the case and that the services for which fees have been charged were actually and necessarily performed."

See also Section 1920 of Title 28, which reads in part as follows:
"A bill of costs shall be filed in the case and, upon allowance, included in the judgment or decree."

The Federal Rules of Civil Procedure contain the following provisions:
RULE 54(d)(1)

Costs Other than Attorneys' Fees.
Unless a federal statute, these rules, or a court order provides otherwise, costs—other than attorney's fees — should be allowed to the prevailing party. But costs against the United States, its officers, and its agencies may be imposed only to the extent allowed by law. The clerk may tax costs on 14 day's notice. On motion served within the next 7 days, the court may review the clerk's action.

RULE 6

(d) Additional Time After Certain Kinds of Service.

When a party may or must act within a specified time after service and service is made under Rule 5(b)(2)(C), (D), (E), or (F), 3 days are added after the period would otherwise expire under Rule 6(a).

RULE 58(e)

Cost or Fee Awards:

Ordinarily, the entry of judgment may not be delayed, nor the time for appeal extended, in order to tax costs or award fees. But if a timely motion for attorney's fees is made under Rule 54(d)(2), the court may act before a notice of appeal has been filed and become effective to order that the motion have the same effect under Federal Rule of Appellate Procedure 4(a)(4) as a timely motion under Rule 59.

[Revised November 2008; December 2009.]

APPENDIX S. SPECIAL LISTING AGREEMENT

GENERAL COURT REGULATION NO. 73–2 COURT OF COMMON PLEAS

D.* Conflicts in the Engagement of Counsel.

(1) *Common Pleas Court.* Common Pleas Court will recognize as engaged all counsel appearing of record in any case actually on trial before a Judge in the United States District Court in Philadelphia and one back-up case as published in the Legal Intelligencer. The engagement in the case actually on trial shall be effective until the trial terminates by verdict or otherwise and in the back-up case for a period of three (3) days including the day said case is first published.

(2) *United States District Court in Philadelphia.* The District Court will recognize as engaged all counsel of record in any case actually on trial before a Common Pleas Court Judge and in cases appearing in the first 20 cases on the Major Case List and in the first 15 cases published on the General Jury Trial List. The engagement in the case actually on trial shall be effective until the trial terminates by verdict or otherwise and the case appearing in the first 20 or 15 for a period of three (3) days after said case reaches that position on the respective list.

(3) Both the Common Pleas Court and the United States District Court will observe the procedure of alternating assignments, i.e., counsel assigned to trial in the Common Pleas Court must upon completion be available for assignment in the United States District Court before accepting another assignment in the Common Pleas Court and vice versa.

No Counsel shall try successive cases in either court except by agreement between the respective judges involved as set forth in Paragraph 3 of Section "D" (4) hereof.

(4) *General.*

Counsel Must Report Case Terminations to Appropriate Clerks. Counsel must immediately report the termination of all trials (by verdict or settlement conference) to the appropriate Clerk of the United States District Court or the Common Pleas Court. Failure to do so will result in the imposition of appropriate sanctions.

Engagement of Counsel in Non-Jury and Arbitration Cases. The United States District Court will not recognize engagements of counsel on the Non–Jury List of the Common Pleas Court or in Arbitration Cases, and conflicts encountered by counsel in this type of case shall be handled on an ad hoc basis as heretofore.

Problems of a Particular Case to be Taken Up With Appropriate Judge. Problems not otherwise covered in this regulation regarding the listing or assignment of a case for trial shall be taken up in the United States District Court with the Judge on whose individual calendar the case appears and in the Common Pleas Court with the Calendar Judge.

* [**Publisher's Note:** So in original.]

APPENDIX T.   BUSY SLIP

IN THE UNITED STATES DISTRICT COURT
FOR THE EASTERN DISTRICT OF
PENNSYLVANIA

BUSY SLIP

I, _____

of _____,

(Address)

_____,   do   hereby   certify   that   I

(Telephone Number)

am   engaged   in   trial   or   appellate   argument   before

_____,   in

(Name of Judge or Judges)

_____,   _____,

(Title or Name of Court of Record)   (Room Number)

in the case of _____

vs. _____,

_____. The   case   is   expected   to

(Court Term & No.)

take approximately _____ trial days.

    My case is number _____ on Judge _____

list in the U.S. District Court.   Caption and number is as follows:

_____

I will notify that Judge's respective court clerk immediately upon the conclusion of this engagement.

Busy slips must be filed in Room 2609 on the designated form no later than 1:00 p.m. on the day after the day counsel becomes attached. If counsel is listed in the Legal Intelligencer on any Judge's trial list, counsel shall call that Judge's respective court clerk promptly so the attachment may be noted before the filing of a busy slip. It will be the duty of counsel to notify the Judge's respective court clerk immediately upon the conclusion of his engagement.

Failure to comply, including failure to use the designated form, will result in non-recognition of counsel's engagement.

_____

Attorney for (name of party)

Date Filed:

Date Withdrawn:

cc: All Counsel

Civ. 17 (8/80)

APPENDIX U.   STANDING ORDER RE: SENTENCING REFORM ACT OF 1984

IN THE UNITED STATES DISTRICT COURT
FOR THE EASTERN DISTRICT OF
PENNSYLVANIA

STANDING ORDER
RE: SENTENCING REFORM ACT OF 1984

STAGE 1. Unless otherwise ordered by an individual judge, sentencing will occur without unnecessary delay not less than eighty (80) days after a defendant pleads guilty, nolo contendere, or is found guilty.

STAGE 2. Not less than thirty-five (35) days before the sentencing hearing, the probation officer must furnish the presentence report to the defendant, the defendant's counsel, and the attorney for the Government. The probation officer's recommendation for sentence will not be disclosed unless directed by an individual judge.

STAGE 3. Within fourteen (14) days after receiving the presentence report, the parties shall deliver in writing to the probation officer, and to each other, any objections to any material information, sentencing classifications, sentencing guideline ranges, and policy statements contained in or omitted from the presentence report. If no objections will be filed, the probation officer shall be so notified in writing within the aforesaid time limits. Any objection not filed will be deemed waived unless the Court finds good cause for allowing it to be raised.

STAGE 4. Should the attorney for the Government intend to file a motion for a downward departure under United States Sentencing Guideline Section 5K1.1, or from a statutory mandatory minimum, the probation officer will be notified in writing on or before the submission date set for the filing of objections, and be provided with whatever information supports the motion.

STAGE 5. Not later than seven (7) days before the sentencing hearing, the probation officer must submit the presentence report to the Court, together with an addendum setting forth any unresolved objections, the grounds for those objections, and the probation officer's comments on the objections. At the same time, the probation officer must furnish the revisions of the presentence report and the addendum to the defendant, the defendant's counsel, and the attorney for the Government.

STAGE 6. The presentence report is a confidential document. Rule 32(b)(3)(A) provides that copies of the presentence report are provided to prosecution and the defense attorneys for the purpose of the sentencing hearing. The attorneys may retain these copies. The attorney for the Government may also retain the presentence report for use in collecting financial penalties. 18 U.S.C. § 3552(d).

Defendant: _____ Criminal No. _____

Date of Plea:

_____

Date of Sentencing:

_____

Time of Sentencing: o'clock   .m.

_____

(To be distributed to each defendant and each counsel at time presentence report is ordered)

cc: **Pretrial Services (via FAX)**
Cr. 37 (2/96)

APPENDIX V. CREDIT CARD COLLECTION
NETWORK PROCEDURES

In September of 1987, the Department of Treasury through its Financial Management Service (FMS), established a government credit card collection network to enable federal agencies to accept two types of credit cards (Visa and MasterCard) for the collection of receipts due the government. Now, most other major credit cards, including American Express, Discover and Diners Club are accepted for financial transactions by the Office of the Clerk of Court.

As a follow-up to the request of the Clerk of Court for the Eastern District of Pennsylvania in August of 1986, the Administrative Office of the United States Courts approved it as the pilot district for implementation of the credit card network within the Judiciary. Subsequently, the Administrative Office on behalf of the United States Courts, entered into a contract with a bank which provides clerks' offices with processing services for credit card transactions.

To implement the program in the Clerk's Office, we first identified potential transactions which we felt were conducive to the use of credit cards, as follows:

- filing fees
- copywork (including docket sheets, documents, judicial opinions)
- copies of ESR-taped proceedings
- fines and restitution
- bail
- attorney admission fees
- searches and certifications
- retrieval fees for records maintained at FRC, and
- CVB payments

Next, we selected 25 law firms and 10 sole practitioners in the Philadelphia and surrounding areas to participate in a pilot program, prior to announcing this service to the general bar and public. We conducted a one-day seminar for members of those law firms and outlined the program to them with a series of presentations from members of the Clerk's Office staff and bank representatives.

We believe the use of credit cards by members of the bar and the public facilitates the processing of financial transactions at the district court. From the government's perspective, the use of credit cards provides next-day availability of funds, reduces the amount of cash handled each day by cashiers, thereby minimizing the possibility of error, and facilitates the bookkeeping process for both the Clerk's Office and participating customers. Conservative estimates place the volume of charges of government transactions at $3 to $10 billion annually. By providing next-day availability of funds to the government, savings of at least $2 million a year will be realized.

From the law firms' perspective, the benefits are even greater. Using a credit card for payment of transactions in the Clerk's Office means that legal couriers no longer are required to carry cash to pay filing or copy fees; blank checks are no longer drawn because amounts are unknown; and the billing procedures fit easily into any internal accounting method used.

For those law firms concerned with the safekeeping of an actual credit card, after completion of an authorization form (Attachment 1), the Clerk's Office will maintain the firm's credit card number and expiration date in a secured drawer. The law firm's courier will reference the authorization form and the transaction will be processed. On the bank charge slip, "AUTHORIZATION ON FILE" would appear in the signature block.

Credit card transactions are handled in the same manner as transactions paid for by check or cash.

For counter transactions, the charge card is obtained from the customer for recording, validating, and imprinting onto a bank charge slip. The customers card is then "swiped" through the terminal and the amount of sale is entered on the keyboard. The bank is contacted electronically through the terminal and an authorization number is obtained.

Once authorization is received, the slip is given to the payor for signature. The amount of the charge is entered into the register and it records the sale and payment data on the receipt in the slip printer. The bank charge slip is then inserted into the register printer and this action records the transaction code, date, time, charge, and amount onto the bank charge slip and matches the data recorded on the cash register receipt.

The original cash register receipt and bank charge slip are given to the customer and the copies are kept on file in the Clerks Office.

Attachment 1

UNITED STATES DISTRICT COURT
EASTERN DISTRICT OF PENNSYLVANIA

CREDIT CARD COLLECTION NETWORK
AUTHORIZATION FORM

_____

(Name of Company/Firm)

hereby authorizes the United States District Court for the Eastern District of Pennsylvania to charge the following bank credit card number for payment of filing fees and other court-related expenses.

PLEASE PRINT:

Visa No.: _____ Exp. Date: _____

MasterCard No.: _____ Exp. Date: _____

American Express: _____ Exp. Date: _____

Other: _____ Exp. Date: _____

Name: _____

Address: _____

City: _____ State: _____ Zip Code: _____

Phone No.: _____ Fax No.: _____

This information shall remain in effect until specifically revoked in writing. It is the responsibility of the firm/company named herein to notify the Clerk's Office of the new expiration date when a credit card has been renewed, or if a credit card has been canceled or revoked.

Signature (Firms Partner): _____ Date: _____

[Effective June 2003. Amended effective April 1, 2012; September 2012; March 13, 2015.]

APPENDIX W. BAIL BOND SECURED
BY PROPERTY OR REAL ESTATE

IN THE UNITED STATES DISTRICT COURT
FOR THE EASTERN DISTRICT OF
PENNSYLVANIA

BAIL BOND SECURED BY PROPERTY OR REAL ESTATE BAIL

1. The deed to the property must be presented and all titled owners must sign the bail bond and affidavit of surety.

2. Proof of equity is required and if the real estate or property is located in Philadelphia a bail certificate issued by the City Controller's Office must be presented. If real estate or property located outside the City of Philadelphia is posted as security the following are required unless otherwise ordered by the Court:

(a) An appraisal by a qualified real estate appraiser located in the area.

(b) A copy of the settlement sheet evidencing the assessed valuation of the premises, if the property has been purchased within three years.

(c) A lien search statement by a title company.

(d) The latest receipt for taxes paid.

3. The justification of surety affidavit attached to the bail bond must be completed.

4. The deed is returned to surety unless special circumstances require that it be held by the Clerk during the pendency of the case.

5. A bail bond secured by real estate or property is entered as an outstanding encumbrance against the real estate or property posted as security in the judgment index of the Clerk of the United States District Court for the Eastern District of Pennsylvania.

6. Counsel for defendant or surety is required to file a certified copy of the bail bond with the Recorder of Deeds and the Prothonotary of the Court of Common Pleas or Court of general jurisdiction of the county wherein the real estate or property which is posted as security is located. The filing of a certified copy of the bail bond with the Prothonotary enters judgment by confession and records the bail bond as an outstanding encumbrance against the real estate or property during the pendency of the case or until exoneration of surety by the United States District Court.
Within ten (10) business days counsel for the defendant or surety is required to return to the Clerk's office time-stamped copies of the local filings together with a verification that this requirement has been satisfied. A copy of the verification is to be served upon the Assistant U.S. Attorney assigned to the case.

7. The certified copy of the bail bond filed with the Prothonotary must be accompanied by a form of notice to defendant of entry of judgment and properly stamped envelopes addressed to the defendant and Clerk of the United States District Court for the Eastern District of Pennsylvania.

8. Upon termination of proceedings or upon entry of an Order exonerating surety in the United States District Court counsel for defendant or surety is required to file a certified copy of the judgment of the United States District Court or a certified copy of an Order exonerating surety with the Recorder of Deeds and the Prothonotary of the Court of the county where the bail bond is recorded as an outstanding encumbrance against the property posted as security.

Civ. 611 (10/00)

JUSTIFICATION OF SURETY REAL ESTATE OR PROPERTY BAIL

AFFIDAVIT

The undersigned, about to become Surety in the case cited herein, being duly sworn (or affirmed) deposes and says:

1. (I/We) reside at _____ .

2. (I/We) have no undisposed of criminal cases against me (us) pending in any Court, except as follows: _____
_____
_____ .

3. (I am/We are) free from any trust,

____ the sole owner(s) of   )
____ joint tenant(s) in   )
____ tenant(s) by the entirety in   ) _____,

(address of
property)

real estate situated in the said County of _____ ,
as follows, viz.: a parcel of ground in size _____
_____ , situated at _____
_____ , in the _____ Ward,
in the ___ Boro., ___ Twp., ___ City of _____ ,
which is improved with the following buildings: _____
_____
_____

(All other joint tenants or tenants by the entirety must co-sign this bond and state their addresses on the last page of this form or on an attachment hereto.)

4. The said property was obtained by _____ Deed _____ Will.

5. The _____ Deed _____ Will is dated _____ , and is recorded in the office of the _____ Recorder of Deeds _____ Register of Wills, of _____ County, _____ Deed _____ Will Book, Vol. ___ , Page _____ , and the title is in _____ my name _____ and my spouse's name.

   Also, a parcel of ground, in size _____ ,
   situated at _____ ,
   in the ____ Ward, in the ____ Boro., _____ Twp., _____ City of
   _____ ,
   which is improved with the following buildings: _____
   _____
   _____ .

   The said property was obtained by me by _____ Deed _____ Will. The _____ Deed _____ Will is dated _____ and is recorded in _____ Deed _____ Will Book, Vol. _____ , Page _____ of _____ County, and is in _____ my name _____ and my spouse's name.

6. I am not Surety on any kind except as follows:

Date	Amount	Defendant

7. (I am/We are) not surety, guarantor, nor indorser for anyone, except as follows: _____

_____

_____ .

8. There are no mortgages, or other liens or encumbrances of any kind or description, upon the said premises, and there are no judgments against me, except as follows: _____

_____

_____

Mortgages as set forth in the Recorder of Deeds on first property

_____

Mortgages as set forth in the Recorder of Deeds on second property

_____

Judgments and Liens _____
Real estate taxes have been paid except: _____

_____

9. The assessed valuation of said premises is _____ .

10. No judgment has been entered or action instituted against me upon a forfeited recognizance except: _____ .

11. There are no negotiations pending for the sale of any part of the said real estate or property; that there are no foreclosure proceedings now pending against me or the real estate or property herein described; that I have not acquired, taken, or received, the title to the said real estate or property, or any part thereof, with any design or intention to make any false, fraudulent, or deceptive showing of my sufficiency as surety in this behalf or otherwise than in good faith, but with the intention of holding and using the said real estate and property as my own.

12. I (We) promise not to transfer or encumber said property until final disposition of this case and exoneration of the subject bond.

13. I (We) further state that I (we) have read the bond of the defendant named above to which this affidavit is attached and made a part of, and I (we) acknowledge that I (we) and my (our) personal representatives are bound, jointly and severally with the defendant and any other sureties, to pay to the United States of America the bond amount specified in the event the bond is forfeited.

14. And further in accordance with law, we do hereby empower any attorney of any court of record within the United States District Court for the Eastern District of Pennsylvania or elsewhere to appear for us at any time, and with or without declarations filed, and whether or not the said obligation be in default, to confess judgment against us, and in favor of the United States of America for use of the aforesaid government, for the above sum and costs, with release of all errors, without stay of execution, and inquisition on and extension upon any levy or real estate is hereby waived, and condemnation agreed to, and the exemption of personal property from levy and sale on any execution hereon is also hereby expressly waived, and no benefit of exemption is claimed under and by virtue of any exemption law now in force or which may be passed hereafter. And for so doing this shall be sufficient warrant. A copy of this bond and warrant being filed in said action, it shall not be necessary to file the original as a warrant of attorney, any law or rule of the Court to the contrary, notwithstanding.

15. I (We) agree to pay the fees and costs of the Prothonotary of the Common Pleas Court or the Court of general jurisdiction wherein the real estate or property posted as security is located for recording the lien, notifying the Clerk of the United States District Court for the Eastern District of

Pennsylvania of the entry of the lien, and for recording of the satisfaction after proceedings have been terminated or surety is otherwise exonerated by the United States District Court.

16.   I (We) have read carefully the foregoing affidavit and know that it is true and correct.

_____ (SEAL) _____
(Surety)   Address
_____ (SEAL) _____
(Surety)   Address
_____ (SEAL) _____
(Co–Surety*)   Address

Sworn (affirmed) and subscribed before me this _____ day of _____, ____.

_____

* Co-Surety, if any, co-joint tenant or co-tenant by the entirety.

[June 2003.]

APPENDIX X.   ATTORNEY ADMISSIONS
APPLICATION (PRO HAC VICE)

IN THE UNITED STATES DISTRICT COURT
FOR THE EASTERN DISTRICT OF PENNSYLVANIA

	:	CIVIL ACTION
	:	
v.	:	
	:	
	:	NO.

ORDER

AND NOW, this _____ Day of _____, 20___, it is hereby

ORDERED that the application of _____, Esquire, to practice in this court pursuant to Local Rule of Civil Procedure 83.5.2(b) is

☐ GRANTED.

☐ DENIED.

_____
J.

IN THE UNITED STATES DISTRICT COURT
FOR THE EASTERN DISTRICT OF PENNSYLVANIA

Civil Action No#

_____

APPLICATION FORM FOR THOSE ATTORNEYS SEEKING TO PRACTICE IN THIS COURT PURSUANT TO LOCAL RULE OF CIVIL PROCEDURE 83.5.2(b)

I.   APPLICANT'S STATEMENT

I, _____ the undersigned, am an attorney who is not currently admitted to either the bar of this court or the bar of the Supreme Court of Pennsylvania, and I hereby apply for admission to practice in this court pursuant to Local Rule of Civil Procedure 83.5.2(b), and am submitting a check, number _____, for the $40.00 admission fee.

A. I state that I am currently admitted to practice in the following state jurisdictions:

_____ _____ _____
(State where admitted) (Admission date) (Attorney Identification Number)

_____ _____ _____
(State where admitted) (Admission date) (Attorney Identification Number)

_____ _____ _____
(State where admitted) (Admission date) (Attorney Identification Number)

B. I state that I am currently admitted to practice in the following federal jurisdictions:

(Court where admitted)	(Admission date)	(Attorney Identification Number)

(Court where admitted)	(Admission date)	(Attorney Identification Number)

(Court where admitted)	(Admission date)	(Attorney Identification Number)

C. I state that I am at present a member of the aforesaid bars in good standing, and that I will demean myself as an attorney of this court uprightly and according to law, and that I will support and defend the Constitution of the United States.

I am entering my appearance for _____

_____
(Applicant's Signature)

_____
(Date)

APPLICANT'S OFFICE ADDRESS AND TELEPHONE NUMBER:
_____
_____
_____

Sworn and subscribed before me this

___Day _____ of, 200___

_____
Notary Public

II. SPONSOR'S STATEMENT, MOTION AND CERTIFICATE OF SERVICE

The undersigned member of the bar of the United States District Court for the Eastern District of Pennsylvania hereby moves for the admission of _____ to practice in said court pursuant to Local Rule of Civil Procedure 83.5.2(b), and certify that I know (or after reasonable inquiry believe) that the applicant is a member in good standing of the above- referenced state and federal courts and that the applicant's private and personal character is good. I certify that this application form was on this date mailed, with postage prepaid, to all interested counsel.

Sponsor's Name	Sponsor's Signature	Admission date	Attorney Identification No.

SPONSOR'S OFFICE ADDRESS AND TELEPHONE NUMBER:
_____
_____
_____

Sworn and subscribed before me this

___ Day _____ of, 200___

_____
Notary Public

IN THE UNITED STATES DISTRICT COURT
FOR THE EASTERN DISTRICT OF PENNSYLVANIA

:   CIVIL ACTION
:
v.   :
:
:   NO.

CERTIFICATE OF SERVICE

I declare under penalty of perjury that a copy of the application of _____ Esquire, to practice in this court pursuant to Local Rule of Civil Procedure 83.5.2(b) and the relevant proposed Order which, if granted, would permit such practice in this court was mailed today with postage prepaid to:

_____

_____

_____

                             _____
                             Signature of Attorney

                             _____
                             Name of Attorney

                             _____
                             Name of Moving Party

                             _____
                             Date

APPENDIX Y.   TRANSCRIPT ORDER FORM

AO 435 (Rev. 03/08) *Please Read Instructions:*	Administrative Office of the United States Courts **TRANSCRIPT ORDER**		FOR COURT USE ONLY DUE DATE:

1. NAME	2. PHONE NUMBER	3. DATE

4. MAILING ADDRESS	5. CITY	6. STATE	7. ZIP CODE

8. CASE NUMBER	9. JUDGE	DATES OF PROCEEDINGS	
		10. FROM	11. TO
12. CASE NAME		LOCATION OF PROCEEDINGS	
		13. CITY	14. STATE

15. ORDER FOR

☐ APPEAL	☐ CRIMINAL	☐ CRIMINAL JUSTICE ACT	☐ BANKRUPTCY
☐ NON-APPEAL	☐ CIVIL	☐ IN FORMA PAUPERIS	☐ OTHER *(Specify)*

16. TRANSCRIPT REQUESTED (Specify portion(s) and date(s) of proceeding(s) for which transcript is requested)

PORTIONS	DATE(S)	PORTION(S)	DATE(S)
☐ VOIR DIRE		☐ TESTIMONY (Specify Witness)	
☐ OPENING STATEMENT (Plaintiff)			
☐ OPENING STATEMENT (Defendant)			
☐ CLOSING ARGUMENT (Plaintiff)		☐ PRE-TRIAL PROCEEDING (Spcy)	
☐ CLOSING ARGUMENT (Defendant)			
☐ OPINION OF COURT			
☐ JURY INSTRUCTIONS		☐ OTHER (Specify)	
☐ SENTENCING			
☐ BAIL HEARING			

17. ORDER

CATEGORY	ORIGINAL (Includes Certified Copy to Clerk for Records of the Court)	FIRST COPY	ADDITIONAL COPIES	NO. OF PAGES ESTIMATE	COSTS
ORDINARY	☐	☐	NO. OF COPIES		
EXPEDITED	☐	☐	NO. OF COPIES		
DAILY	☐	☐	NO. OF COPIES		
HOURLY	☐	☐	NO. OF COPIES		
REALTIME	☐	☐			

CERTIFICATION (18. & 19.) By signing below, I certify that I will pay all charges (deposit plus additional).	ESTIMATE TOTAL	$ 0.00
18. SIGNATURE	PROCESSED BY	
19. DATE	PHONE NUMBER	
TRANSCRIPT TO BE PREPARED BY	COURT ADDRESS	

	DATE	BY			
ORDER RECEIVED					
DEPOSIT PAID			DEPOSIT PAID		
TRANSCRIPT ORDERED			TOTAL CHARGES	$	0.00
TRANSCRIPT RECEIVED			LESS DEPOSIT	$	0.00
ORDERING PARTY NOTIFIED TO PICK UP TRANSCRIPT			TOTAL REFUNDED		
PARTY RECEIVED TRANSCRIPT			TOTAL DUE	$	0.00

DISTRIBUTION: COURT COPY   TRANSCRIPTION COPY   ORDER RECEIPT   ORDER COPY

AO435
(Rev. 03/08)

INSTRUCTIONS

GENERAL

Use. Use this form to order the transcription of proceedings. Complete a separate order form for each case number for which transcripts are ordered.

Completion. Complete Items 1–19. Do *not* complete shaded areas which are reserved for the court's use.

Order Copy. Keep a copy for your records.

Mailing or Delivering to the Court. Mail or deliver the original, and two copies of this form to the Clerk of Court.

Deposit Fee. The court will notify you of the amount of the required deposit fee which may be mailed or delivered to the court. Upon receipt of the deposit, the court will process the order.

Deliver Time. Delivery time is computed from the date of receipt of the deposit fee or for transcripts ordered by the federal government from the date of receipt of the signed order form.

Completion of Order. The court will notify you when the transcript is completed.

Balance Due. If the deposit fee was insufficient to cover all charges, the court will notify you of the balance due which must be paid prior to receiving the completed order.

SPECIFIC

Items 1–19.	These items should always be completed.
Item 8.	Only one case number may be listed per order.
Item 15.	Place an "X" in each box that applies.
Item 16.	Place an "X" in the box for each portion requested. List specific date(s) of the proceedings for which transcript is requested. Be sure that the description is clearly written to facilitate processing. Orders may be placed for as few pages of transcript as are needed.
Item 17.	*Categories.* There are five (5) categories of transcripts which may be ordered. These are:

Ordinary. A transcript to be delivered within thirty (30) calendar days after receipt of an order. (Order is received upon receipt of the deposit.)

Expedited. A transcript to be delivered within seven (7) calendar days after receipt of an order.

Daily. A transcript to be delivered following adjournment and prior to the normal opening hour of the court on the following morning whether or not it actually is a court day.

Hourly. A transcript of proceedings ordered under unusual circumstances to be delivered within two (2) hours.

Realtime. A draft unedited transcript produced by a certified realtime reporter as a byproduct of realtime to be delivered electronically during proceedings or immediately following adjournment.

NOTE: Full price may be charged only if the transcript is delivered within the required time frame. For example, if an order for expedited transcript is not completed and delivered within seven (7) calendar days, payment would be at the *ordinary* delivery rate.

Ordering. Place an "X" in each box that applies. Indicate the number of additional copies ordered.

Original. Original typing of the transcript. An original must be ordered and prepared prior to the availability of copies. The original fee is charged only once. The fee for the original includes the copy for the records of the court.

First Copy. First copy of the transcript after the original has been prepared. All parties ordering copies must pay this rate for the first copy ordered.

Additional Copies. All other copies of the transcript ordered by the same party.

Item 18.	Sign in this space to certify that you will pay all charges. (This includes the deposit plus any additional charges.)
Item 19.	Enter the date of signing.

Shaded Area. Reserved for the court's use.

APPENDIX Z. TAPE ORDER FORM

AO 436 (Rev. 12/04)	Administrative Office of the United States Courts	

Read Instructions on Next Page.

CD/TAPE ORDER

1. NAME	2. PHONE NUMBER	3. DATE	
4. MAILING ADDRESS	5. CITY	6. STATE	7. ZIP CODE

8. CASE NUMBER	9. CASE NAME	DATES OF PROCEEDINGS	
		10. FROM	11. TO
12. PRESIDING JUDGE		LOCATION OF PROCEEDINGS	
		13. CITY	14. STATE

15. ORDER FOR

☐ APPEAL ☐ CRIMINAL ☐ CRIMINAL JUSTICE ACT ☐ BANKRUPTCY
☐ NON-APPEAL ☐ CIVIL ☐ IN FORMA PAUPERIS ☐ OTHER (Specify)

16. TAPE REQUESTED (Specify portion(s) and date(s) of proceeding(s) for which duplicate cd/tape(s) are requested.)

PORTION(S)	DATE(S)	PORTION(S)	DATE(S)
☐ VOIR DIRE		☐ TESTIMONY (Specify Witness)	
☐ OPENING STATEMENT (Plaintiff)			
☐ OPENING STATEMENT (Defendant)			
☐ CLOSING ARGUMENT (Plaintiff)		☐ PRE-TRIAL PROCEEDING (Spcy)	
☐ CLOSING ARGUMENT (Defendant)			
☐ OPINION OF COURT			
☐ JURY INSTRUCTIONS		☐ OTHER (Specify)	
☐ SENTENCING			
☐ BAIL HEARING			

17. ORDER

	NO. OF COPIES REQUESTED	COSTS
☐ REFORMATTED DUPLICATE TAPE(S) FOR PLAYBACK ON A STANDARD CASSETTE RECORDER AT 1-7/8 INCHES PER SECOND		
☐ UNREFORMATTED DUPLICATE TAPE(S) FOR PLAYBACK ON A 4-TRACK CASSETTE RECORDER AT 1-7/8 INCHES PER SECOND		
☐ UNREFORMATTED DUPLICATE TAPE(S) FOR PLAYBACK ON A 4-TRACK CASSETTE RECORDER AT 15/16 INCHES PER SECOND		
☐ RECORDABLE COMPACT DISC - CD		

CERTIFICATION (18. & 19.) By signing below, I certify that I will pay all charges (deposit plus additional) upon completion of the order.	ESTIMATE TOTAL	0.00
18. SIGNATURE	19. DATE	
PROCESSED BY	PHONE NUMBER	

	DATE	BY		
ORDER RECEIVED			DEPOSIT PAID	
DEPOSIT PAID			TOTAL CHARGES	0.00
TAPE / CD DUPLICATED			LESS DEPOSIT	0.00
ORDERING PARTY NOTIFIED TO PICK UP TAPE			TOTAL REFUNDED	
PARTY RECEIVED TAPE / CD			TOTAL DUE	0.00

DISTRIBUTION: COURT COPY ORDER RECEIPT ORDER COPY

AO436
(Rev. 12/04)

INSTRUCTIONS

GENERAL

Use. Use this form to order duplicate CD's/tapes of proceedings. Complete a separate order form for each case number for which tapes are ordered.

Completion. Complete Items 1–19. Do not complete shaded areas which are reserved for the court's use.

Order Copy. Keep a copy for your records.

Mailing or Delivering to the Court. Mail or deliver two copies to the Office of the Clerk of Court.

Deposit Fee. For orders of 20 or more CD's/tapes, the court will notify you of the amount of the required deposit fee which may be mailed or delivered to the court. Upon receipt of the deposit, the court will process the order.

Delivery Time. Delivery time is computed from the date of receipt of the deposit fee (if requested, otherwise computed from the court's receipt date).

Completion of Order. The court will notify you when the CD's/tapes are completed.

Balance Due. If the deposit fee was insufficient to cover all charges, the court will notify you of the balance due which must be paid prior to receiving the completed order.

SPECIFIC

Items 1–19.	These items should always be completed.
Item 8.	Only one case number may be listed per order.
Item 15.	Place an "X" in each box that applies.
Item 16.	Check specific portion(s) and list specific date(s) of the proceedings for which a copy is requested.
Item 17.	Place an "X" in each box that applies. Indicate the number of additional copies ordered.
Item 18.	Sign in this space to certify that you will pay all charges upon completion of the order. (This includes the deposit plus any additional charges.)
Item 19.	Enter the date of signing.

Shaded Area. Reserved for the court's use.

APPENDIX AA. NOTICE OF ELECTRONIC AVAILABILITY OF TRANSCRIPTS IN CASE MANAGEMENT/ELECTRONIC CASE FILES (CM/ECF) AND TRANSCRIPT REDACTION

At its September 2007 session, the Judicial Conference of the United States approved a new policy to make electronic transcripts of court proceedings available to the public. **Effective immediately**, this new policy will be implemented in the Office of the Clerk, United States District Court, Eastern District of Pennsylvania, as follows:

- Transcripts of civil court proceedings will be placed on CM/ECF or **PACER** unless the presiding judge otherwise directs.

- Transcripts of criminal court proceedings will not be placed on CM/ECF or **PACER** unless the presiding judge otherwise directs after giving the prosecution and defense counsel an opportunity to be heard.

If electronic transcripts are to be made available to the public upon approval of the assigned judge:

- A transcript provided to the court by a court reporter or transcriber will be available at the office of the clerk for inspection for a period of 90 days after it is delivered to the clerk.

- During the 90–day period a copy of the transcript may also be obtained by purchase from the court reporter or transcriber through the office of the clerk. An attorney who obtains the transcript from the office of the clerk will be allowed remote electronic access to the transcript through the court's CM/ECF system.

- After the 90–day period has expired, the filed transcript will be available for inspection and copying in the clerk's office and for download from the court's CM/ECF system through the **PACER** system.

In addition, amendments to the Federal Civil and Criminal Rules of Procedure (Civil Rule 5.2 and Criminal Rule 49.1) require that personal identification information be redacted from documents filed with the court, including Social Security numbers, names of minor children, financial account numbers, dates of birth, and in criminal cases, home addresses. Under the new transcripts access policy, procedures for applying redaction requirements to transcripts of court proceedings are outlined in the attachment to this Notice. It is important to note that it is *not* the responsibility of the court reporter nor transcriber to identify material in the transcript that should be redacted. The Judicial Conference policy imposes that responsibility on counsel.

Should you require clarification or additional information on this new policy, please contact Joan Carr, Supervisor of Court Reporters (267–299–7104) or Michael Hearn, Electronic Sound Recording Coordinator (267–299–7039).

Attachment

United States District Court for the Eastern District of Pennsylvania
Electronic Availability of Transcripts and Transcript Redaction Procedures

- The requirement of the court reporter and transcriber to provide a certified copy of a transcript to the clerk for the records of the court has not changed, i.e. when a transcript is originally produced, a certified copy must be promptly delivered to the clerk. The Guide to Judiciary Policies and Procedures states that the transcript copy should be delivered to the clerk concurrently with—but not later than three working days after—delivery to the requesting party. Sealed transcripts are excluded from electronic filing.

- Transcripts of civil court proceedings will be placed on CM/ECF or **PACER** unless the presiding judge otherwise directs.

- Transcripts of criminal court proceedings will not be placed on CM/ECF or **PACER** unless the presiding judge otherwise directs after giving the prosecution and defense counsel an opportunity to be heard.

- If electronic transcripts are to be made available, a certified transcript provided to the court by a court reporter or transcriber will be available for review and inspection at the court's public terminal in the office of the clerk for a period of 90 days after it is delivered to the clerk.

- If electronic transcripts are to be made available, during the 90–day period a copy of the transcript may also be obtained by purchase from the court reporter or transcriber through the office of the clerk. An attorney who obtains the transcript from the office of the clerk will be allowed remote electronic access to the transcript through the court's CM/ECF system. Counsel of record in a case who have not purchased a copy of the transcript will not have access to the transcript through CM/ECF until they purchase it from the court reporter or transcriber through the office of the clerk or until the 90–day period has expired.

- If electronic transcripts are to be made available, after the 90–day period has expired, the filed transcript will be available for inspection and copying in the clerk's office and for download from the court's CM/ECF system through the **PACER** system.

- If electronic transcripts are to be made available, members of the public, including the news media, who purchase a transcript from the court reporter or transcriber through the clerk's office within the 90–day period, will not be granted remote electronic access during the restriction period. At the end of the restriction period, the public will be provided remote electronic access through **PACER** to the transcript originally submitted, or, if redaction was made, to the redacted transcript, unless it is under seal.

- The redaction of transcripts will be requested by counsel to a case. Even if the court reporter or transcriber notices that redactions will be necessary as he/she is preparing a transcript, he/she does not have the responsibility to redact information unless there is a redaction request made by the parties to the case. Court reporters and transcribers also do not have a responsibility to notify the parties of material that should be redacted. The Judicial Conference policy imposes the responsibility on counsel to identify material in the transcript that should be redacted.

- **Personal identifiers that a party may request be redacted:** Social Security numbers (or taxpayer identification numbers) to the last four digits, financial account numbers to the last four digits, dates of birth, individuals known to be minor children to the initials, and in criminal cases, any home addresses stated in court to the city and state. Information other than these specified identifiers may be redacted only if the moving party receives a ruling of the court to do so.

- The portion of a transcript that includes the voir dire or other juror information will not be made available thorough electronic access.

- Unless otherwise ordered by the court, the attorney must review the following portions of the transcripts:

  (a) opening and closing statements made on the party's behalf;

  (b) statements of the party;

  (c) the testimony of any witness called by the party;

  (d) sentencing proceedings; and

  (e) any other portion of the transcript as ordered by the court.

- Counsel is to file a Notice of Intent to Request Redaction with the clerk within seven business days of the transcript being delivered to the clerk (or filing in CM/ECF). Counsel is then to follow-up, within 21 calendar days of initial delivery of the transcript to the clerk, with a specific request for redaction noting the page numbers and line numbers where redaction is required.

- If an attorney files a Notice of Intent to Request Redaction or a motion for extension of time to file this notice, and then does not submit a Redaction Request, the court may take action, either to have the attorney withdraw the Notice of Intent to Request Redaction or to issue a show cause order as to why the attorney has not met the redaction requirements.

- Once a court reporter or transcriber receives the list of redactions (Redaction Requests) from the clerk's office, he/she has ten days after the deadline for receipt of the attorneys' redaction request to redact the transcript and file the redacted transcript with the clerk. The original unredacted electronic transcript will be retained by the clerk of court as a restricted document.

- The court reporter or transcriber does not have the obligation to notify the parties that the certified copy of the transcript has been filed, nor is the court reporter or transcriber required to send a copy of the redacted transcript to the parties who originally ordered the transcript. The Clerk of Court notifies the parties that the transcript has been filed so that the parties are aware that the 7–day period within which to request redaction has begun.

- Statements of redaction (Redaction Requests) are to be filed by attorneys with the clerk. The statement should be worded in such a way that the personal information at issue is not repeated (i.e., Redact the Social Security number on page 12, line 9 to read xxx-xx–6789.) since the document is publicly available. There is no requirement that the redaction statements should be served on opposing counsel or parties.

[June 2008. Amended effective January 30, 2012.]

APPENDIX BB.   AUDIO FILE ELECTRONIC ACCESS PROGRAM
NOTICE

The United States District Court for the Eastern District of Pennsylvania participated in a national Digital Audio File Electronic Access Pilot Program. The pilot program was authorized by the Judicial Conference of the United States and provided digital audio files of court proceedings through the Public Access to Court Electronic Records (PACER) system. The Judicial Conference of the United States Committee on Court Administration and Case Management selected five pilot courts. The Eastern District of Pennsylvania and the District of Nebraska were the district courts selected to participate in the project. The Eastern District of North Carolina, the Northern District of Alabama and the District of Maine are the bankruptcy courts that were selected to participate in this project.

During the pilot project digital audio recordings of courtroom proceedings were publicly available on PACER upon the approval of the presiding judge. The project enables PACER users to download, in MP3 format, court proceedings that have been recorded using electronic sound recording technology. During the pilot program, access to the digital audio files cost 16 cents; 8 cents for accessing the docket sheet and another 8 cents for selecting the audio file. More than 840,000 subscribers already use PACER to access docket and case information from federal appellate, district and bankruptcy courts.

Digital audio recording has been an authorized method of making an official record of court proceedings since 1999, when it was approved by the Judicial Conference of the United States. Digital audio recording is used in district and bankruptcy courts in the federal court system. A majority of Eastern District of Pennsylvania district court judges and all magistrate judges use digital audio recordings of court proceedings.

At its March 2010 meeting, the Judicial Conference of the United States voted to allow courts, at the discretion of the presiding judge, to make digital audio recordings of court hearings available online to the public through PACER, for $2.40 per audio file Should you have any questions concerning the program, please contact Michael Hearn, Electronic Sound Recording Coordinator, at 267–299–7039.

Michael E. Kunz

Clerk of Court

[Amended effective February 6, 2012.]

APPENDIX CC. [OMITTED]

[**Publisher's Note:** Omitted; the online registration form is available at https://pacer.psc. uscourts.gov/regform.html]

APPENDIX DD. DIRECTORY OF COURT-AUTOMATED SERVICES

DIRECTORY OF COURT–AUTOMATED SERVICES

DISTRICT COURT

Internet Web Site—<http://www.paed.uscourts.gov>

Case Management/Electronic Case Filing (CM/ECF). The Eastern District of Pennsylvania has been selected by the Administrative Office of the United States Courts (AO) from among several court applicants to be an alpha court site for implementation in and testing in of the Case Management/Electronic Case Files (CM/ECF) initiative currently under development by the AO. The system was implemented for civil cases on May 1, 2002 and for criminal cases on May 27, 2003. Through Internet technology attorneys can file documents from their offices via a Web browser and have immediate access to other documents filed electronically. CM/ECF provides the capability to view filings after normal court business hours and file documents 24 hours a day. Information and training is available by calling toll-free 1–866–ECF–4ECF.

Courtroom Technology. Several courtrooms provide a wide array of technical components that support evidence presentation, remote site interactions, language interpreting and audio enhancement. The state-of-the-art technologies include assisted listening systems, integrated court interpreting systems, video conferencing systems, document/video presentation systems, evidence trolleys, annotation pads, document cameras, as well as connectivity at counsel tables for use with court or attorney provided PCs. The court welcomes the bar to make use of these technologies and training is available at the courthouse. For further information, contact Michael Hearn or Ed Morrissy at (267) 299–7039.

Public Access to Court Electronic Records (PACER). The PACER system allows any member of the bar or the public who has access to a computer to obtain civil and criminal docket records and documents. The user can obtain the complete electronic history of all civil cases filed since July 1, 1990, and all pending civil cases as of July 1, 1990, except asbestos and prisoner cases, filed prior to July 1, 1990, and all criminal cases filed since July 1, 1992. Also available on the PACER system are civil documents filed in electronic form since May 1, 2002 and criminal documents filed in electronic form since May 27, 2003. To register for the PACER system call (800) 676–6856 or the form may be completed on-line at <http://pacer.psc.uscourts. gov>. The PACER system is available through the Internet at <https://ecf.paed. uscourts.gov>. The fee for accessing PACER on the Internet is $.10 per page with the charge capped at the cost for 30 pages for accessing any single document. Internet PACER provides access to an unlimited number of users.

Lobby Kiosk Information System. The redesign of the US. Courthouse lobby was completed in December 2001. The district and circuit courts included in the redesign the installation of an automated informational kiosk and the development of a liaison relationship with the new Constitution Center on Independence Mall. The kiosk system includes a daily information on district court and court of appeals hearings, as well as a directory of judges and court clerks, a directory of other government agencies, and general information. The kiosk includes touch screen technology, as well as mapping techniques to guide visitors to their destinations.

Internet—Web Site. Information on available services and judicial opinions filed since June 1, 1997 in the United States District Court for the Eastern District of

Pennsylvania, as well as court notices, local rules, multidistrict litigation information, Clerk's Office Procedure Handbook, Frequently Asked Questions, Judicial Procedures, e-mail capabilities and more are available on the Internet <http://www.paed.uscourts.gov>.

Pilot Program for Facsimile Service of Notice of Orders and Judgments. The court has authorized the Clerk of Court to implement a pilot program in civil and criminal cases to allow attorneys and pro se litigants to waive the provisions of Federal Rule of Civil Procedure 77(d) or Federal Rule of Criminal Procedure 49(c), which requires service of Notice of Orders and Judgments by means of mail, and instead consent to receive Notice of Orders and Judgments by means of facsimile transmission.

FAX Ordering of Docket/Document Copies and/or Searches. Any member of a law firm, legal agency, or the public can FAX a request to obtain the following: (1) copies of dockets; (2) copies of documents; (3) name searches performed on records.

Judicial Schedule of Trials—Automated System Inquiry (JUST–ASK). JUST–ASK provides up-to-date information on the status of trials scheduled in the U.S. District Court seven days a week, twenty-four hours a day. All cases scheduled for trial, presently on trial, in the trial pool and special notices are included on the system. All information in JUST–ASK is available by judge, case number, party, attorney or entire listing. Events, such as verdicts, settlements, and continuances constantly change the status of cases on the court's trial list. JUST–ASK immediately reflects the daily status of listings as the information becomes available to the Clerk of Court.

Credit Card Collection Network. Any law firm, legal agency, company or individual can arrange to use a Visa, MasterCard, Discover, American Express or Diners Club when making payment for filing fees and other district-court-related expenses.

Credit card payment provides for an alternative to cash/checks that easily accommodates any internal accounting procedure. The network supports in-person, telephone, and mail requests.

Telephone Access for the Hearing and/or Speech Impaired. A hearing and/or speech impaired individual equipped with a Telecommunications Device for the Deaf (TDD) can contact the Office of the Clerk of Court by calling the General Service Administration's (GSA's) Federal Information Relay Service (FIRS) at (800) 877–8339.

Mail Directed To and From the U.S. Courthouse. In order to expedite delivery of notices from judicial officers and the clerk of court, members of the bar are requested to furnish their zip code and 4–digit extension number. In order to take full advantage of these procedures, all mail sent to the courthouse should include the zip code and 4–digit extension number. Forms for supplying the full zip code and listings of the full zip codes for all judicial officers are available in the Office of the Clerk of Court or on the internet.

Video Teleconferencing Pilot Program (VTC). Video Teleconferencing is available between the U.S. District Court in Philadelphia and FCI Fairton, as well as several state correctional institutions. The program was initiated in 1995 with FCI Fairton for the video teleconferencing of criminal proceedings and expanded in 1998 to state correctional institutions primarily for use in prisoner civil rights pretrial proceedings. The system is available for court proceedings and for use by counsel when available. All requests to use the VTC system are to be directed to the VTC Coordinators at (267) 299–7039.

BANKRUPTCY COURT

Public Access to Court Electronic Records (PACER). The PACER system allows any member of the bar or the public who has access to a computer to obtain bankruptcy docket records. The fee for accessing PACER on the Internet is $.08 per page with the charge capped at the cost for 30 pages for accessing any single document. Internet PACER provides access to an unlimited number of users.

Voice Case Information System (VCIS). The VCIS system allows the general public to obtain voice BANCAP information from any standard touch-tone telephone.

Access VCIS by dialing (215) 597–2244.

For More Information . . .
Please check the appropriate service(s) listed below and
provide the indicated address information:

District Court
☐ Case Management/Electronic Case Filing (CM/ECF)
☐ Courtroom Technology
☐ PACER (Civil/Criminal)
☐ Kiosk Information System
☐ Internet—Web Site
☐ Pilot FAX Program for Service of Orders and Judgments
☐ FAX Ordering
☐ JUST–ASK
☐ Credit Card Collection Network
☐ Telephone Access for Hearing/Speech–Impaired
☐ Mail Delivered to and From the Courthouse

Bankruptcy Court
☐ PACER (Bankruptcy)
☐ Voice Case Information System

☐ ALL OF THE ABOVE

ADDRESS INFORMATION

NAME _____

FIRM _____

ADDRESS _____

CITY _____ STATE _____ ZIP _____

PHONE( ) _____ FAX( ) _____

E–MAIL ADDRESS _____

Send this completed form to . . .
MICHAEL E. KUNZ, CLERK OF COURT
United States District Court
2609 U.S. Courthouse
601 Market Street
Philadelphia, PA 19106–1797
Fax: (215) 597–6390
or
<http://www.paed.uscourts.gov>

[June 2004. Amended effective March 26, 2012.]

APPENDIX EE.   ELECTRONIC CASE FILING (ECF)
ELECTRONIC FILING OF COMPLAINTS
NOTICE

The United States District Court for the Eastern District of Pennsylvania has authorized a program to file complaints electronically on the CM/ECF system. If you are interested in filing complaints electronically, please complete the information below and you will be contacted to arrange a mutually convenient time for training.

If you have any questions on filing complaints electronically on the CM/ECF system, please do not hesitate to contact this office at 1–866–ECF–4ECF.

Michael E. Kunz

Clerk of Court

Name: _____   Phone: _____

Address: _____

Email: _____   FAX: _____

Please return the completed form to the Clerk of Court by fax to 215–597–6390 or 267–299–7135

[Amended effective August 21, 2013.]

UNITED STATES BANKRUPTCY COURT FOR THE EASTERN DISTRICT OF PENNSYLVANIA

Including Amendments Received Through
June 1, 2016

NOTES ON ORGANIZATION AND SOURCES

1. The current compilation is an update of the Local Rules compendium last published in booklet form following the amendments that were effective on November 25, 2008.

2. The Local Bankruptcy Rules have been numbered as required by the directive of the Judicial Conference of the United States that "a numbering system for local rules . . . [must] correspond to" the F.R.B.P. In addition, the organization, content, and numbering of the Local Bankruptcy Rules conforms substantially to the Uniform Numbering System for Local Bankruptcy Rules, which has been recommended to the district courts by the Advisory Committee on Bankruptcy Rules.

3. With the exception of the 2006, 2008 and 2009 Explanatory Notes, all of the "Source" materials and Explanatory Notes included in this compilation were drafted by the Local Rules Advisory Committee of the Eastern District of Pennsylvania Bankruptcy Conference in connection with the advisory role that organization played in the rules adoption process. The 2006, 2008 and 2009 Explanatory Notes were drafted by the Board of Bankruptcy Judges.

LOCAL RULE 1001–1. LOCAL RULES—GENERAL

(a) **Scope.** The Local Bankruptcy Rules and Local Bankruptcy Forms are adopted to govern the practice and procedure before the United States Bankruptcy Court for the Eastern District of Pennsylvania.

(b) **Short Title.** These rules shall be cited and referred to herein as the Local Bankruptcy Rules (or "L.B.R.") and the forms as the Local Bankruptcy Form (or "L.B.F.").

(c) **Construction.** These rules and forms shall be construed in a manner consistent with the Federal Rules of Bankruptcy Procedure, referred to herein as "F.R.B.P.," and Official Bankruptcy Forms.

(d) **Effective Date.** The L.B.R. and L.B.F. shall become effective on the thirtieth day following promulgation and shall govern the practice and procedure before the United States Bankruptcy Court for the Eastern District of Pennsylvania for all pending and future cases.

(e) **Rescission.** On the effective date of the L.B.R. and L.B.F., all previously enacted local rules and local forms are rescinded.

[Effective February 1, 1999.]

SOURCE

Subdivisions (a)-(c). 97 L.B.R. 1001.1.

Subdivisions (d) and (e). 97 L.B.R. 1001.2.

LOCAL RULE 1002–1. PETITION— GENERAL

(a) **Number of Copies.** An original petition filed with the clerk shall be accompanied by the following number of copies of the petition:

(1) three copies of a petition requesting relief under chapter 7, 12, or 13;

(2) four copies of a petition requesting relief under chapter 9 or 11, other than a petition of a railroad under subchapter IV of chapter 11; or

(3) nine copies of a petition of a railroad under subchapter IV of chapter 11.

(b) Evidence of Authority to File. If the debtor is other than an individual, evidence of authority to initiate the case shall be filed with the petition.

[Effective February 1, 1999.]

SOURCE

Subdivision (a). 97 L.B.R. 1002.1(a) and (b).

Subdivision (b). 97 L.B.R. 1002.2(c).

LOCAL RULE 1002–2. COMPLEX CHAPTER 11 CASES: GENERAL

(a) Complex Chapter 11 Case. A complex chapter 11 case is a chapter 11 case in which the total debt in the case is $10 million or more and either

(1) the debtor's debt or equity securities are publicly traded, or

(2) there are 100 or more parties in interest in the case.

(b) Statement of Qualification for Complex Chapter 11 Case Status: Administration. A chapter 11 debtor may file with the petition a Statement of Qualification for Complex Chapter 11 Case Status, substantially in the form of L.B.F. 1002–2A, that sets forth the reasons why the debtor's chapter 11 case qualifies under subdivision (a) as a complex chapter 11 case. If a Statement of Qualification is filed with the petition, the case shall be administered as a complex chapter 11 case, unless the court orders otherwise on the court's own motion, or in response to an objection made under subdivision (e), or a later motion. A Motion for the Scheduling of an Expedited Hearing may be combined with the Statement of Qualification.

(c) Expedited Hearing. If the debtor, within 10 days of filing the chapter 11 case that is being administered as a complex chapter 11 case, files a motion for the Scheduling of an Expedited Hearing, the judge who is assigned the chapter 11 case shall use the judge's best efforts to schedule an expedited hearing as soon as appropriate under the circumstances of the case but not more than 3 business days after the filing of the Motion for the Scheduling of an Expedited Hearing, unless the debtor requests a later date. If the assigned judge is unavailable, the Emergency Judge serving pursuant to L.B.R. 5001–1(a) shall use the judge's best efforts to arrange for an expedited hearing within the three (3) day period. The courtroom deputy shall promptly inform the debtor of the date and time of the expedited hearing and what motions and applications will be heard (the Expedited Hearing Agenda).

(d) Notice of Expedited Hearing: Service of Motions and Applications.

(1) *Service.* The debtor shall serve a Notice of Expedited Hearing substantially in the form of L.B.F. 1002–2B, copies of the motions and applications that will be heard at the Expedited Hearing, and the proposed order that accompanies each motion and application on the following parties, or, if represented, their counsel:

(i) the United States trustee;

(ii) the Commonwealth of Pennsylvania, Department of Labor and Industry;

(iii) the Commonwealth of Pennsylvania, Department of Revenue;

(iv) any prepetition committee of unsecured creditors;

(v) any official committee and the 20 largest unsecured creditors of the debtor;

(vi) the Internal Revenue Service and the City of Philadelphia at the address shown on the list maintained by the Clerk in accord with F.R. Bank. P. 5003 (c); and

(vii) any entity whose interest would be directly, materially, and adversely affected if the relief requested in the motion were granted and whose interests are not adequately represented by persons on whom service is otherwise required.

On the day the debtor is notified by the court of the date of the Expedited Hearing, the debtor, if feasible, shall make service under this subdivision. If service is not made on the day the debtor is notified by the court of the date of the Expedited Hearing, service shall be made no later than the next day.

(2) *Supplemental Notice.* On the day the debtor is notified of the date of the Expedited Hearing, the debtor shall give notice by telephone, fax, or email of the date, time, and place of the Expedited Hearing and the Expedited Hearing Agenda to any of the parties required to be served under subdivision (d)(1) who will not be served until the next day.

(3) *Certificate of Service and Notice.* The debtor shall file a certificate of service and notice prepared as required by L.B.R. 9014–4 before the Expedited Hearing or with the court at the Expedited Hearing.

(4) *Adequacy of Service or Notice.* If the court determines that for any motion or application on the Expedited Hearing Agenda the service or notice completed in advance of the Expedited Hearing is inadequate, the court may deny some or all of the relief requested or continue the hearing.

(e) Objection to Statement of Qualification: Response to Motion or Application. L.B.R. 9013–1(e) and L.B.R. 9014–3(i), which require that any written objection to an application or a written answer or objection to a motion be filed within a specified period, do not apply to an application or motion that is scheduled to be heard at the Expedited Hearing. An objection to the debtor's Statement of Qualification and an objection or answer to an application or motion scheduled to be heard at an Expedited Hearing may be filed before the Expedited Hearing or with the court at the Expedited Hearing or made orally at the Expedited Hearing.

(f) Advance Notice to and Service on the United States Trustee.

(1) *Notice to United States Trustee.* Counsel for the debtor, with or without naming the debtor or including information that identifies the debtor, shall, if feasible, advise the United States Trustee of a debtor's intent to file a complex chapter 11 case and of the motions and applications the debtor intends to request be heard at an Expedited Hearing. Counsel shall give this notice to the United States Trustee as soon as practical, which ordinarily should be at least 48 hours before the chapter 11 case is filed.

(2) *Service on United States Trustee.* The debtor shall hand deliver, if feasible, the applications and motions (in substantially final form) that the debtor intends to request be heard at an Expedited Hearing to the United States Trustee at least 24 hours before the filing of the chapter 11 case.

(3) *Certificate of Service and Notice.* The debtor shall file a certificate of service and notice prepared as required by L.B.R. 9014–4 before the Expedited Hearing or with the court at the Expedited Hearing.

(g) Notice of Entry of Orders. On the day the debtor is notified of the entry of the order disposing of a matter heard at the Expedited Hearing, the debtor, if feasible, shall serve a copy of the order on the parties required to be served under subdivision (d)(1). If service is not made on the day the debtor is notified of entry of the order, service shall be made no later than the next day.

[Effective May 16, 2005. Amended effective December 1, 2009.]

Committee's Explanatory Note

Subdivision (a) identifies the criteria to be used in determining whether a chapter 11 case qualifies for complex chapter 11 case status. A court on the motion of a debtor may order that even though the chapter 11 case is not a complex chapter 11 case under subdivision (a) the case shall be administered as a complex chapter 11 case.

Subdivisions (b) and (c). Time is important at the beginning of a complex chapter 11 case. Preservation of the business and the likelihood of a successful reorganization may depend, in part, on the debtor being able to have certain matters heard and determined by the court shortly after the complex chapter 11 case is filed. Under the ordinary practice, motions are not heard very quickly. L.B.R. 9014–3(h) allows 15 days for the filing of an answer to a motion. Thus a hearing on a motion is after the 15–day period expires. Moreover, L.B.R. 5070–1(a) provides that a hearing on a motion will be scheduled on the presiding judge's next available list.

A debtor may attempt to obtain an earlier hearing date by filing a motion for expedited consideration under L.B.R. 5070–1(f) that demonstrates "with particularity the reasons supporting the need for expedited consideration." How long it will take for the court to rule on the motion and, if the motion is granted, when the hearing will be held are uncertain. In addition, it is necessary for the court in each case to enter an order governing service, notice, and other procedural matters that must be addressed when a motion is heard on an expedited basis.

The criteria in subdivision (a) are designed to identify as a complex chapter 11 cases those cases where there is a high probability that there is ample reason why expedited consideration is needed and, therefore, appropriate. Subdivisions (b) and (c) create a simplified process for obtaining an expedited hearing at the very beginning of a complex chapter 11 case and other subdivisions of this rule address service, notice, and other procedural matters.

L.B.R. 5070–1(f) permits the filing of a motion for the Scheduling of an Expedited Hearing at any time. Subdivision (c) provides that if the debtor in a case being administered as a complex chapter 11 case files a motion for the Scheduling of an Expedited Hearing within 10 days of the filing of the chapter 11 case, the court will, if possible, schedule an expedited hearing within three business days of the filing of the motion.

Under subdivision (b), a case will be administered as a complex chapter 11 case if the debtor files with the petition a Statement of Qualification for Complex Chapter 11 Case Status. The court, however, may on its own motion in an appropriate case determine that even though a Statement of Qualification has been filed, the case should not be administered as a complex chapter 11 case. Moreover, subdivision (e) specifically authorizes a party in interest to orally object to the debtor's Statement of Qualification at the Expedited Hearing or to file an objection with the clerk before the Expedited Hearing or with the court at the Expedited Hearing. A Motion to Terminate Complex Chapter 11 Case Status may be filed at any time after the Expedited Hearing.

Subdivision (d) imposes additional service obligations on a debtor who obtains an expedited hearing under this rule.

Subdivision (d)(1) requires service on the same entities that are required to be served under L.B.R. 9014–3(f), which governs general motion practice, and also follows L.B.R. 9014–3(f) by requiring that service be completed, if feasible, on the day the court informs the debtor of the Expedited Hearing date or, at the latest, the next day. If service cannot be completed on the day the court informs the debtor of the date of the hearing, the debtor is required by subdivision (d)(2) to give supplemental notice of both the hearing date and the hearing agenda by telephone, fax, or e-mail. The supplemental notice must be given on the day the court informs the debtor of the Expedited Hearing date. F.R.B.P. 9014(b) and 7004 and F.R.Civ.P. 4 specify how service of a motion is made. Because of the short time available, the debtor will either have to deliver the motion to the parties that must be served or use one of the overnight carriers to complete service.

Even if the debtor completes the service required by this rule, the court may find that the service and notice required by this rule are not adequate for a particular motion or application, or for a particular party. In addition, the debtor may fail to complete service and notice as required by this rule. Subdivision (d)(4) takes account of these and other possibilities by stating that a motion or application may have to be denied in whole or in part or a motion or application may have to be continued to a later hearing date if the service or notice is inadequate.

Subdivision (e) specifically makes L.B.R. 9013–1(e) and L.B.R. 9014–3(h), which require the filing of a written response to an application or a motion, inapplicable to a response to an application or a motion that is scheduled to be heard at an Expedited Hearing. Because of the short time period between service of the notice of the Expedited Hearing and the Expedited Hearing, the subdivision authorizes an oral response at the Expedited Hearing as well as the filing of a written response before the Expedited Hearing or with the court at the Expedited Hearing.

Subdivision (f)(1) requires counsel for a debtor to notify the United States Trustee before the chapter 11 case is filed that a debtor will be filing a complex chapter 11 case. Copies of the substantive motions and applications that the debtor will request be heard at the expedited hearing are to be delivered to the United States Trustee at least 24 hours before the complex chapter 11 case is filed.

Subdivision (g) requires the debtor to serve copies of orders entered on matters heard at the Expedited Hearing on the parties listed in subdivision (d)(1) who were served with the motion and applications. Rule 5(b), F.R.Civ.P. prescribes the manner of service.

L.B.F. 1002–2A. STATEMENT OF QUALIFICATIONS AS COMPLEX CHAPTER 11 CASE

In re: :   Chapter 11

                :

Debtor   :   Bankruptcy No.

STATEMENT OF QUALIFICATION AS COMPLEX CHAPTER 11 CASE

This chapter 11 case was filed on _____, 20 ___. The undersigned attorney for the debtor believes that this case qualifies under Local Bankruptcy Rule 1002–2 as a complex chapter 11 case because the debtor's total debt exceeds the minimum requirement under Local Bankruptcy Rule 1002–2 of total debt in the amount of $10 million, and

___ the debtor's debt securities are publicly traded

___ the debtor's equity securities are publicly traded, and/or

___ there are 100 or more parties in interest in the case.

Date: _____ 20 ___

Signed: _____

Attorney for the Debtor

[Attorney's name] ...., Esq.

[Firm Name] ....

[Address] ....

[Phone No] ....

[Fax No.] ....

The Statement may also be signed by a chapter 11 individual debtor, or by an authorized person if the chapter 11 debtor is a corporation, limited liability company, partnership, or other business entity. The form should be adapted to properly reflect the status of the person signing the Statement.

[Effective May 16, 2005.]

L.B.F. 1002–2B. NOTICE OF DATE OF EXPEDITED HEARING, MATTERS THAT WILL BE HEARD AT THE EXPEDITED HEARING, AND HOW TO RESPOND

UNITED STATES BANKRUPTCY COURT FOR THE EASTERN DISTRICT OF PENNSYLVANIA

In re: :   Chapter

                :

Debtor   :   Bankruptcy No.

* * * * *

NOTICE OF DATE OF EXPEDITED HEARING, MATTERS THAT WILL BE HEARD AT THE EXPEDITED HEARING, AND HOW TO RESPOND

(Name of debtor) has filed a chapter 11 case, a Statement of Qualification for Complex Chapter 11 Case Status, and a motion for Scheduling an Expedited Hearing.

The chapter 11 case is being administered under L.B.R. 1001–(2) as a Complex Chapter 11 case.

An Expedited Hearing is scheduled to be held before the Honorable (name of bankruptcy judge) on XX/XX/XX, at _____ in Courtroom ___, United States Bankruptcy Court, (address of Bankruptcy Court). At the Expedited Hearing, the court will consider the Debtor's motion(s) and application(s) that are listed below:

_____

Your rights may be affected. You should read these papers carefully and discuss them with your attorney, if you have one in this bankruptcy case. (If you do not have an attorney, you may wish to consult an attorney.)

1.　If you do not want the court to grant the relief sought in a motion or an application, or if you to object to the Debtor's chapter 11 case being administered as a Complex Chapter 11 case, or if you want the court to consider your views on a motion or an application, then you or your attorney must

(a) file an answer or objection explaining your position at (*address of bankruptcy clerk's office*) before the start of the Expedited Hearing on XX/XX/XX; or

(b) come to the Expedited Hearing on XX/XX/XX and either

　(i) file an answer or objection explaining your position by delivering it to the court, or

　(ii) orally present an answer or objection explaining your position.

If you mail your answer to the bankruptcy clerk's office for filing, you must mail it early enough so that it will be received on or before the start of the Expedited Hearing on XX/XX/XX.

2.　If you file an answer or objection with the bankruptcy clerk's office or with the court at the Expedited Hearing, you must also provide a copy of your answer or objection to the Debtor's attorney. You may have it delivered by mail or other means of delivery to the Debtor's attorney at the address shown below before the date of the Expedited Hearing or you may deliver it to the Debtor's attorney at the Expedited hearing.

[Attorney's name] ....

[Firm name] ....

[Address] ....

[Phone No.] ....

[Fax No.] ....

　　　　[If applicable, name and address
　　　　　　of others to be served.]

3.　If you or your attorney do not take the steps described in paragraphs 1 and 2 above, the court may enter an order granting the relief requested in a motion or an application.

4.　Copies of motion(s) and applications that will be heard at the Expedited Hearing are enclosed. [or will be delivered separately].

5.　Unless the court orders otherwise, the hearing will be an evidentiary hearing at which witnesses may testify with respect to disputed material factual issues in the manner directed by Fed. R. Bankr. P. 9014(d).

Date ...., ...

[Effective May 16, 2005.]

LOCAL RULE 1002–3. COMPLEX CHAPTER 11 CASES: SELECTION OF MOTIONS AND APPLICATIONS FOR EXPEDITED HEARING

(a) Criteria. A motion or application will be scheduled for an Expedited Hearing held pursuant to L.B.R. 1002–2 only if it appears that an expedited ruling will either (i) materially enhance the possibility that the debtor will be able to continue to operate the business, (ii) contribute to the preservation of the assets of the estate, or (iii) facilitate the orderly and efficient administration of the case.

(b) Typical Motions. The following are examples of motions or applications that ordinarily will be scheduled for an Expedited Hearing if the debtor requests:

Administrative Matters

1.　Motion for Joint Administration of Related Chapter 11 Cases;

2.　Motion for Approval of Debtor Serving Notice of the Section 341 Creditors' Meeting;

3.　Motion for Approval of Notice Procedures;

4.　Motion for Approval of Claims Agent or Notice Agent;

5.　Motion under L.B.R. 2090–1 for Admission of an Attorney *Pro Hac Vice*; and

6.　Motion for Order Scheduling Omnibus Hearing Dates.

Financing

7.　Motion for Interim Authorization of Use of Cash Collateral;

8.　Motion for Interim Authorization of Post–Petition Borrowing;

9.　Motion for Approval of Debtor's Continuing Use of Existing Bank Accounts, Business Forms, and Cash Management System, or Related Relief; and

10.　Motion for Approval of Interim Modified Section 345 Investment Procedures and for Scheduling of Hearing on Permanent Modified Section 345 Investment Procedures;

Operation of the Debtor's Business

11.　Motion for Approval to Pay Pre–Petition Employee Wage Claims, Benefits, and Related Taxes to all Employees, Independent Contractors, and Tax Authorities;

12. Motion for Approval to Pay Pre–Petition Trust Fund and/or Priority Taxes;

13. Motion for Approval to Pay or Honor Obligations to Customers;

14. Motion for Approval to Pay Other Pre–Petition Claims;

15. Motion for Order Authorizing and Directing Banks to Honor Certain Pre–Petition Checks; and

16. Motion for Interim Relief and for Scheduling of Hearing on Determination of Adequate Assurance to Utilities.

(c) Other Motions. A debtor's motion for an Expedited Hearing may request that motions or applications that are not listed in subdivision (b) be heard at the Expedited Hearing.

[Effective May 16, 2005.]

Committee's Explanatory Note

Subdivision (a) sets forth three criteria for determining whether a motion or application should be scheduled to be heard at an Expedited Hearing.

Subdivision (b) lists motions that will ordinarily be scheduled for an Expedited Hearing because these motions will satisfy one or more of the subdivision (a) criteria. It is important to note that a motion seeking the court's approval of the use of cash collateral, post-petition borrowing, or adoption of modified Section 345 investment procedures will be scheduled for the expedited hearing only if the motion requests interim authorization of the proposed relief. The debtor may combine in one motion a request for interim authorization and a request for final relief, for example, interim authorization to borrow under a post-petition line of credit and a request for final approval of the line of credit.

Subdivision (c) makes it clear that even if a motion or application is not listed in subdivision (b), the debtor may request that the motion or application be scheduled to be heard at the expedited hearing.

LOCAL RULE 1002–4. COMPLEX CHAPTER 11 CASES: INTERIM CASH COLLATERAL AND BORROWING MOTIONS

A motion for Interim Authorization to Use Cash Collateral or Interim Authorization of Post–Petition Borrowing shall have a separate section at the beginning of the motion that lists in bold face type any of the following terms that are included in either the proposed order that accompanies the motion or in the loan agreement that will be entered into by the debtor if the borrowing motion is granted:

1. Cross-collateralization clauses that provide that pre-petition debt is secured by post-petition assets that the secured party would not otherwise have a

security interest in by virtue of its pre-petition security agreement.

2. Provisions or findings of fact which relate to the validity, perfection, or amount of the secured party's lien or the amount of outstanding debt and are binding on parties in interest, other than the debtor or signatories to any agreement for which court approval is requested.

3. Provisions or findings of fact which relate to the relative priorities of a secured party's lien and the liens held by persons who are not parties to the loan transaction, for example, an order providing that the secured party's lien is a first priority lie, and are binding on parties in interest, other than the debtor or signatories to any agreement for which court approval is requested.

4. Waivers of rights under Section 506(c).

5. Provisions that operate, as a practical matter, to divest the debtor in possession of any discretion in the formulation of a plan or administration of the estate or limit the debtor's right of access to the court to seek relief under the Code or other applicable law.

6. Releases of liability for the creditor's alleged pre-petition torts or breaches of contract.

7. Waivers of avoidance actions arising under the Code or other applicable law.

8. Automatic termination or modification of the Section 362 stay on default, conversion to chapter 7, or appointment of a trustee.

9. Waivers of the procedural requirements of applicable non-bankruptcy law governing foreclosure.

10. Adequate protection provisions that create liens or claims for relief arising under Sections 506(c), 544, 545, 547, 548, and 549.

11. Waivers of the debtor's right to request bankruptcy court approval under Section 363(c)(2)(B) of the debtor's use of cash collateral without the secured party's consent that are triggered by default or expiration of a prior cash collateral order.

12. Findings of fact on matters extraneous to the court's approval of the motion. (For example, if the debtor seeks to borrow on a secured basis, a finding that the debtor cannot obtain unsecured credit is appropriate but a "finding," binding on all parties, that the lender acted in good faith in declaring the pre-petition loan in default is not appropriate.)

13. Granting of a lien to a post-petition lender that is given priority over a pre-petition lien on the same collateral.

[Effective May 16, 2005.]

Committee's Explanatory Note

Motions for interim authorization to use cash collateral and to borrow post-petition present particularly sensitive issues.

This rule requires the debtor to disclose at the beginning of these motions whether any of the terms listed in the rule are included in the proposed order or loan agreement. This calls the attention of the court and the parties to the particularly noteworthy aspects of the proposed order or loan agreement.

LOCAL RULE 1002–5. COMPLEX CHAPTER 11 CASES: AUTOMATIC RECONSIDERATION

(a) Automatic Reconsideration. The court shall reconsider an order entered on a matter heard at an Expedited Hearing held pursuant to L.B.R. 1002–2, other than an order entered pursuant to 11 U.S.C. Sections 363 and 364 relating to the use of cash collateral or approval of post-petition financing, if a timely motion for reconsideration of the order is filed. A motion for reconsideration is timely filed if it is filed within 30 days of entry of the order, or, if F.R.B.P. 9023 applies to the motion, the motion is filed within the time prescribed by Rule 59(e).

(b) Expedited Schedule. If requested by the movant for reconsideration, the reconsideration shall be on an expedited basis

(c) Burden of Proof. The party who had the burden of proof on the motion or application that resulted in the entry of the order being reconsidered also has the burden of proof on reconsideration of the order.

[Effective May 16, 2005. Amended effective December 1, 2009.]

Committee's Explanatory Note

Subdivision (a) provides that if a timely motion for reconsideration of an order disposing of a matter heard at the expedited hearing is filed, the court will automatically reconsider the motion. A motion for reconsideration is timely filed under subdivision (a) if it is filed within 30 days of entry of the order, unless the order is subject to F.R.Civ. P. 59, which requires that the motion be filed within 10 days. Under F.R.B.P. 9023, F.R.Civ. P. 59, which governs new trials and motions to alter or amend a judgment, applies to appealable orders that are entered in cases under the Code. See F.R.B.P. 9001(7).

Once the motion for reconsideration is filed, the movant must obtain a date for the reconsideration hearing and then make service and otherwise comply with L.B.R. 9014–3.

While scheduling an expedited hearing almost immediately after a complex chapter 11 case is filed increases the likelihood the debtor will be able to preserve the business and confirm a plan of reorganization, at that very early stage of the case creditors and other parties in interest may not yet understand the debtor's financial condition or business prospects or be able to evaluate the legal issues raised by the matters heard at the Expedited Hearing. In addition, some parties may find it difficult for a variety of reasons to fully participate at the Expedited Hearing. Automatic reconsideration of orders entered on the matters heard at the Expedited Hearing, as provided by this rule, assures parties in interest that there will no procedural impediments to their presenting

to the court their reasons why the order being reconsidered should not have been entered.

Subdivision (b). If the movant requests, a motion for reconsideration will be scheduled on an expedited basis

Subdivision (c). Whoever had the burden of proof when a motion or application was originally heard, also has the burden of proof on the motion for reconsideration.

LOCAL RULE 1007–1. LISTS, SCHEDULES, STATEMENTS, AFFIDAVIT, AND NOTICE: NUMBER OF COPIES

(a) Chapter 11 and 12 Cases.

(1) *Additional Lists.* In a chapter 11 and chapter 12 case, in addition to the documents required by F.R.B.P. 1007, the debtor shall file with the petition in a voluntary case and within 14 days after entry of the order for relief in an involuntary case:

    (b) a list of the name and address (including zip code) of each creditor who the debtor knows is a member of any committee organized by creditors before the commencement of the case; and

    (c) a list of the name and address (including zip code) of each creditor who the debtor knows claims a security interest in cash collateral, as defined by § 363(a) of the Code; or

    (d) if the debtor is unable to file either of the lists, the debtor, a partner of a partnership debtor, or a responsible officer of a corporate debtor shall file an affidavit setting forth with particularity the reason it is unable to file a list or lists.

(2) *Extension to File Additional Lists.* If an affidavit permitted under subdivision (a)(1)(c) is filed by the debtor or on behalf of the debtor and the debtor is engaged in business, the debtor shall file the lists required by subdivision (a)(1) within 14 days after the filing of the petition in a voluntary case or within 30 days after entry of an order for relief in an involuntary case.

(b) Statement of Operations. In a chapter 11 case, if the debtor is engaged in business, and in a chapter 12 case the debtor shall file within 14 days after the filing of the petition in a voluntary case, or within 14 days after entry of an order for relief in an involuntary case, if prepared and available, a statement of operations listing receipts and disbursements by category for the most recent month or quarter and for the most recent fiscal year prior to the commencement of the case.

(c) Cash Collateral. In a chapter 11 case, the debtor shall notify each creditor known to the debtor to claim a security interest in cash collateral, as defined by § 363(a) of the Code, of the filing of the petition in a voluntary case or of the entry of an order for relief in an involuntary case within 1 day of the filing of the petition or the entry of the order for relief. The debtor shall promptly file a certificate of notice.

(d) Number of Copies. The number of copies of the schedules, statements and lists required to be filed under F.R.B.P. 1007 and this rule shall correspond to the number of copies of the petition required by L.B.R. 1002–1.

[Effective February 1, 1999. Amended effective December 1, 2009.]

SOURCE

Subdivisions (a)-(c) are substantially the same as 97 L.B.R. 1007.1.

Subdivision (d) is the same as 97 L.B.R. 1002.1(c).

LOCAL RULE 1007–2. MATRIX LIST OF CREDITORS

(a) Matrix List of Creditors. A matrix list of creditors is a centered single column list of the name and complete address of each creditor.

(b) Voluntary Case. In a voluntary case, the debtor shall file a Matrix List of Creditors with the petition.

(c) Involuntary Case. In an involuntary case, the debtor shall file a Matrix List of Creditors within 14 days of the entry of the order for relief.

(d) Chapter 13 Case: Copies. In a chapter 13 case the debtor shall file an additional copy of the Matrix List of Creditors and any supplement.

(e) Supplement to Matrix List of Creditors. The Matrix List of Creditors is supplemented by filing a separate page or pages prepared in accord with subdivision (a) of this rule. Each page of the filing shall contain the following legend at the bottom right side of the page:

Supplement to Matrix List of Creditors

Dated: [date supplement filed]

Page No. ___ of ___ page(s)

The originally filed Matrix List of Creditors and any supplement shall constitute the Matrix List of Creditors for the purpose of these rules.

(f) No Duty to Supplement. A debtor does not have to file a supplement to include a party who has filed a request for notices under F.R.B.P. 2002(j).

(g) List of Creditors. A copy of the Matrix List of Creditors prepared pursuant to L.B.R. 1007–2 may be filed by the debtor as the list of creditors required under F.R.B.P. 1007(a)(1) or 1007(a)(2).

[Effective February 1, 1999. Amended effective December 1, 2009.]

SOURCE

This rule is derived from 97 L.B.R. 1007.2. Subdivisions (a) and (f) set forth the format for the Matrix List of Creditors and for a supplement to the Matrix which adds creditors. The Matrix must be filed with the petition in all voluntary cases in order to facilitate prompt administration of the case and the noticing of the meeting of creditors.

Subdivision (g) is new.

LOCAL RULE 1007–3. SUBMISSION OF PAYMENT ADVICES OR OTHER EVIDENCE OF PAYMENT RECEIVED WITHIN 60 DAYS BEFORE THE DATE OF THE FILING OF THE PETITION

(a) In lieu of filing with the court the documents required by § 521(a)(1)(B)(iv), a debtor may submit to the trustee and the United States Trustee in electronic format by e-mail either

(1) the required documents, or

(2) the documents available to the debtor accompanied by a statement that sets forth the reason why some payment documents have not been submitted and the debtor's estimate of and other evidence, if any, of the payments received within the 60 day time period.

(b) If the trustee has not been appointed on the day the schedules are filed, the submission shall be transmitted to the trustee promptly after the trustee is appointed.

(c) Upon the request of any creditor, the debtor shall promptly provide a copy of the submission to the creditor.

[Effective November 25, 2008.]

SOURCE

This rule is new.

LOCAL RULE 1009–1. AMENDMENTS TO VOLUNTARY PETITION AND SCHEDULE: ADDING A CREDITOR

(a) Amendment of Voluntary Petition or Schedule. An amendment to a voluntary petition or schedule shall be served on the trustee, any official committee, the United States trustee, and all parties affected by the amendment. The amendment shall be accompanied by a certification of service. If there are no parties affected by the amendment, the certification of service shall so state.

(b) Addition of Creditor.

(1) An amendment adding a creditor to the debtor's schedule shall be served on that creditor. If the creditor is added after the notice of the § 341 meeting has been mailed, a copy of the notice of the § 341 meeting and any other notices which have been served on all

creditors in the case shall be served by the debtor's counsel with the amendment.

(2) An amendment adding a creditor shall be accompanied by the fee prescribed by the Administrative Office of the United States Court or by an application under L.B.R. 5080–1 to waive that fee due to the debtor's inability to pay the fee.

(c) Supplement to Matrix List of Creditors. An amendment filed by the debtor adding a creditor to the schedule or a request by the debtor to add an interested party shall be accompanied by a Supplement to the Matrix List of Creditors prepared in accord with L.B.R. 1007–2(e) which lists the added creditors.

[Effective February 1, 1999.]

SOURCE

This rule is the same as 97 L.B.R. 1009.1.

LOCAL RULE 1017–1. CONVERSION OF CASE

(a) Debtor's Notice of Conversion. On the day a notice of conversion under §§ 1208(a) or 1307(a) is filed, the debtor shall serve a copy of the notice on the trustee.

(b) Certain Motions of Debtor to Convert. A motion of a debtor to convert a case to a case under another chapter under §§ 706(a) or 1112(a) of the Code is governed by L.B.R. 9014–2 (Motions Determined Without Hearing).

(c) Other Motions to Convert. Except as provided in subdivision (b), a motion to convert a case to a case under another chapter is governed by L.B.R. 9014–3. The notice of the motion, hearing date, and the time to file an answer required to be given under L.B.R. 9014–3(h) shall be given to those on the Matrix List of Creditors instead of to those on the Clerk's Service List.

(d) Notice of Conversion. If a case is converted from one chapter to another, the clerk shall provide timely notice of the conversion of the case to those on the Matrix List of Creditors and the Clerk's Service List, the United States trustee, and the trustee.

[Effective February 1, 1999.]

SOURCE

Subdivision (a) is new. Under F.R.B.P. 1017(d), a debtor who files a notice of conversion of a case with the court pursuant to §§ 1208(a) or 1307(a) does not have to notify anyone that the case has been converted. Subdivision (a) requires that notice of conversion of the case be given to the trustee.

Subdivision (b) is similar to 97 L.B.R. 1017.3(a), except that a motion must be filed rather than an application.

Subdivision (c) is similar to 97 L.B.R. 1017.3(b), but this rule also applies to motions filed by a person other than the debtor.

Subdivision (d) is the same as 97 L.B.R. 1019.1.

LOCAL RULE 1017–2. DISMISSAL OF CASE

(a) Certain Motions of Debtor to Dismiss. A motion of a debtor to voluntarily dismiss a case under §§ 1208(b) or 1307(b) of the Code is governed by L.B.R. 9014–2 (Motions Determined Without Hearing). The motion shall be served on the trustee and the United States trustee.

(b) Other Motions to Dismiss. Except as provided in subdivision (a), a motion to dismiss a case is governed by L.B.R. 9014–3. L.B.R. 9014–3(h) does not apply to motions to dismiss under either § 707(a)(3) or § 707(b). The notice of motion, hearing date, and time to file an answer required to be given under L.B.R. 9014–3(h) shall be given to those on the Matrix List of Creditors instead of to those on the Clerk's Service List.

(c) Notice of Dismissal. If a case is dismissed, the clerk shall provide timely notice of the dismissal of the case to those on the Matrix List of Creditors and the Clerk's Service List, the United States trustee, and the trustee.

(d) Debtor's Address. If the case is dismissed, the debtor shall advise the trustee within 10 days of entry of the order of dismissal of the address to which any refund of money paid to the trustee may be made.

[Effective February 1, 1999. Amended effective March 1, 2000.]

SOURCE

Subdivision (a) is the same as 97 L.B.R. 1017.1(a) except that the debtor must file a motion rather than an application.

Subdivision (b). Amended pursuant to the February 28, 2000, Order of the U.S. District Court for the Eastern District of Pennsylvania and effective March 1, 2000.

Subdivisions (c) and (d) are derived from 97 L.B.R. 1017.1(c) and (d).

LOCAL RULE 1019–1. CONVERSION: FILINGS FOLLOWING

(a) Conversion to Chapter 7. Within 14 days after entry of an order converting a case under another chapter to a chapter 7 case, the debtor shall file

(1) the original and three copies of the schedule of post petition debts, if any, which arose subsequent to the filing of the petition but prior to the conversion to chapter 7; and

(2) if appropriate, a supplement to the Matrix List of Creditors prepared in accord with L.B.R. 1007–2(e).

(b) Conversion to Chapter 13. Within 14 days after entry of an order converting a case under another chapter to a chapter 13 case, the debtor shall file

(1) the original and three copies of the schedule of post petition debts, if any, which arose subsequent to the filing of the petition but prior to the conversion to chapter 13, and

(2) if appropriate, a supplement to the Matrix List of Creditors prepared in accord with L.B.R. 1007–2(e).

[Effective February 1, 1999. Amended effective December 1, 2009.]

SOURCE

Subdivision (a) is the same as 97 L.B.R. 1019.2.

Subdivision (b) is the same as 97 L.B.R. 1019.3.

LOCAL RULE 2002–1. NOTICE TO CREDITORS

(a) Notice of Order for Relief in Consumer Cases. The notice required to be mailed by F.R.B.P. 2002(*o*) shall be combined with the notice required to be sent by F.R.B.P. 2002(a)(1) and mailed by the clerk within 21 days after the filing of the petition.

(b) Notice of Hearing on Application for Compensation. Notice of the filing of an application for compensation or reimbursement of expenses, when required by F.R.B.P. 2002(a)(6), shall be mailed by the applicant and the applicant shall file with the court a certification of notice. Notice of the filing of an application by counsel for the debtor for compensation must be provided under F.R.B.P. 2002(a)(6) only if the statement required by § 329 of the Code and L.B.R. 2016–4 indicates that the post-petition compensation plus the amount of the reimbursement for expenses exceeds the amount specified in F.R.B.P. 2002(a)(6).

(c) Clerk's Service List. The clerk shall maintain a Clerk's Service List which lists the name, address, phone number, and fax number of the debtor, counsel for the debtor, the trustee, counsel for any committee and the members of the committee, and all creditors and equity security holders who have filed requests that all notices be mailed to them under F.R.B.P. 2002(I).

[Effective February 1, 1999. Amended effective December 11, 2000; December 1 2009.]

SOURCE

Subdivision (a). 97 L.B.R. 2002.1.

Subdivision (b) is derived from 97 L.B.R. 2002.2(a), which was first modified to make it clear that the monetary trigger for notice to all creditors is based only on the amount of the fee and expenses incurred for postpetition services. A second modification, effective December 11, 2000, revised the "trigger" to track the sum specified in F.R.B.P. 2002(a)(6).

Subdivision (c) is derived from 97 L.B.R. 2002.5.

Under L.B.R. 9014–3, which governs motion practice, a movant must give notice of the filing of the motion and the hearing date to those on the Clerk's Service List; however, the movant is no longer required to provide a copy of the motion to those on the Clerk's Service List. A copy of the motion must be provided by the movant only to persons on the Clerk's Service List who request a copy of the motion.

LOCAL RULE 2004–1. DEPOSITIONS AND EXAMINATIONS

Before filing a motion for an examination under F.R.B.P. 2004, counsel for the moving party shall, except in extraordinary circumstances, give 3 days notice to counsel for the party to be examined or, if the party is not represented, to the party that a motion for examination will be filed, and counsel for the moving party shall attempt, before filing the motion, to arrange a mutually convenient time and date for the examination.

[Effective February 1, 1999.]

SOURCE

This rule is the same as 97 L.B.R. 2004.1 with the exception that this rule refers to a motion, rather than an application, for an examination.

LOCAL RULE 2010–1. TRUSTEES: MANAGEMENT AND DISBURSEMENT OF ESTATE'S FUNDS

If trustee is serving in a chapter 7 or 11 case, the trustee shall be the sole person with signatory or other authority to control or disburse funds or other property of the estate.

[Effective February 1, 1999.]

SOURCE

This rule is the same as 97 L.B.R. 2010.1.

LOCAL RULE 2014–1. EMPLOYMENT OF PROFESSIONALS

(a) Application. Requests to employ attorneys, accountants, appraisers, auctioneers, agents, or other professionals shall be made by application under the procedure set forth in L.B.R. 9013–1(d) or (e), whichever is applicable.

(b) Service.

(1) An application of the trustee, debtor-in-possession, or any official creditors' committee to employ bankruptcy counsel must be served on the United States trustee and, if appropriate, counsel for the debtor, and any trustee.

(2) All other applications to employ must be served on the United States trustee, counsel for the debtor,

counsel for any official creditors' committee, and those on the Clerk's Service List.

[Effective February 1, 1999.]

SOURCE

This rule is substantially the same as 97 L.B.R. 2014.1.

LOCAL RULE 2014–2. ATTORNEY'S CONTROL OF FUNDS OF THE ESTATE PROHIBITED

An attorney whose employment is approved under § 327 of the Code, except (i) when also serving as the trustee, or (ii) when serving as an escrow agent, shall not establish or exercise any signatory or other authority to control or disburse funds or other property of the estate.

[Effective February 1, 1999.]

SOURCE

This rule is similar to 97 L.B.R. 2014.2. Added to the "except" clause is a reference to the trustee who is also serving as an attorney.

LOCAL RULE 2015–1. TRUSTEES AND DEBTORS IN POSSESSION: OPERATING REPORTS

A trustee or debtor-in-possession who submits an operating report to the United States trustee shall file a copy of the report on the same day and shall serve a copy of the report on counsel for any official creditors' committee within 3 days of filing the report.

[Effective February 1, 1999.]

SOURCE

This rule is derived from L.B.R. 2015.1.

LOCAL RULE 2016–1. COMPENSATION OF PROFESSIONALS: SERVICE, NOTICE, AND DISPOSITION OF APPLICATION

(a) Service: Courtesy Copy. A copy of the application for compensation and reimbursement for expenses shall be served by the applicant on any trustee or interim trustee, the trustee's counsel, the United States trustee, the debtor, the debtor's counsel, and counsel for any official committee. The applicant shall file a certification of service. An applicant shall furnish a copy of an application to any party in interest who requests a copy of the application and who agrees to reimburse the applicant for the actual cost of producing and delivering the copy of the application.

(b) Notice. Before or on the date an application for compensation and reimbursement of expenses is filed, the applicant shall, if notice of a hearing on the application is required under F.R.B.P. 2002(a)(6), give to those on the Matrix List of Creditors or, if there is an official committee serving in the case to those on the Clerk's Service List, notice of the identity of the applicant, and the amounts requested, and the requirement that any objection to the application must be filed and served on the applicant or, if the applicant is represented, counsel for the applicant within 21 days of the date on which the application is filed.

(c) Certification of Notice and Whether Any Objection Has Been Filed. After the expiration of the 21 day period to file an objection, the applicant shall file a certification of notice, which also certifies whether any timely objection has been filed. The applicant may include in the certification a request that a hearing be held.

(d) Disposition of Application. After the filing of a Certification of Notice under subdivision (c), the court may either rule on the application or set a hearing date.

(e) Notice of Hearing. If the court sets a hearing date for an application for compensation and reimbursement of expenses, the clerk or, if the court directs, the applicant shall give notice of the hearing to the applicant, the objector, those required to be served or to be given notice under subdivisions (a) or (b), and any other person the court directs.

(f) Disposition Without Hearing: Reduced Award. If the court, without holding a hearing, awards an applicant less than the requested amount of compensation and reimbursement of expenses, an applicant's motion under Rule 9023 of the F.R.B.P. to alter or amend the order may include a request for a hearing on the application or be accompanied by a brief in support of the application. Such a motion to alter or amend is governed by L.B.R. 9014–2, Motions Determined Without a Hearing, except that the court shall hold a hearing if an applicant requests a hearing.

[Effective February 1, 1999. Amended effective December 1, 2009.]

SOURCE

This rule is derived from 97 L.B.R. 2002.2(b)-(d).

Subdivision (a). The last sentence of subdivision (a) requires an applicant to provide a copy of the application to any party who requests a copy of the application and pays the cost of copying and delivering a copy of the application.

Subdivision (f). If the court rules on a fee application without holding a hearing, an applicant may file a motion under F.R.B.P. 9023 to alter or amend the order. This subdivision provides that if a Rule 9023 motion contains a request for a hearing, the court must hold a hearing before ruling on the Rule 9023 motion. If the Rule 9023 motion does not contain a request for a hearing, the court may dispose of the motion under L.B.R. 9014–2 without a hearing.

LOCAL RULE 2016–2. COMPENSATION OF DEBTOR'S COUNSEL IN CHAPTER 13 CASE.

(a) Application for Compensation for Services Rendered Before Confirmation.

(1) *Short Form Application.* Counsel for a chapter 13 debtor may file a short form application that conforms substantially to L.B.F. 2016–2A if the services were rendered:

(A) for a chapter 13 debtor with above-median income (the amount on line 15 of Form B22C is not less than the amount on line 16) and counsel will receive total compensation of $3,500 or less for all services rendered before confirmation, or

(B) for a chapter 13 debtor with below-median income (the amount on line 15 of Form B22C is less than the amount on line 16) and counsel will receive total compensation of $3,000 or less for all services rendered before confirmation.

(2) *Long Form Application.* If counsel for a chapter 13 debtor is not authorized under subdivision (a)(1) to file a short form application for services rendered before confirmation, counsel shall file a long form application that conforms substantially to L.B.F. 2016–2B.

(b) Application for Compensation for Services Rendered After Confirmation: Supplemental Application. If counsel for a chapter 13 debtor renders services after confirmation and seeks compensation payable by the chapter 13 trustee, counsel shall file a supplemental application that conforms substantially to L.B.F. 2016–2C.

[Effective February 1, 1999. Amended effective February 26, 2008.]

EXPLANATORY NOTE (2005)

Subdivision (a), which applies only to applications of counsel for the debtor in chapter 13 cases, is designed to simplify the fee applications filed therein. The services performed must be described but time records need not accompany the application. This amendment is mandated by *Lamie v. United States Trustee*, 124 S.Ct. 1023 (2004), holding that 11 U.S.C. § 330(a)(1) does not authorize compensation awards to debtors' attorneys from estate funds, unless they are employed by the chapter 7 trustee as authorized by 11 U.S.C. § 327. Therefore, all applications by professionals, other than an attorney representing a chapter 13 debtor, shall be governed by F.R.B.P. 2016(a) and L.B.R. 2016–1, 2016–3 and L.B.F. 2016–3.

EXPLANATORY NOTE (2008)

The rule has been amended in order to: (1) modify the maximum amount of counsel fees that may be requested under the simplified procedure and (2) reference new forms developed for use in connection with applications for compensation in chapter 13 cases.

L.B.F. 2016–2A. "SHORT FORM" APPLICATION OF COUNSEL FOR DEBTOR FOR COMPENSATION AND REIMBURSEMENT OF EXPENSES IN CHAPTER 13 CASE PURSUANT TO L.B.R. 2016–2(A)

UNITED STATES BANKRUPTCY COURT FOR THE EASTERN DISTRICT OF PENNSYLVANIA

In re:)   Chapter 13
)
   Debtor(s))
)   Bky. No.
)

APPLICATION FOR COMPENSATION AND REIMBURSEMENT OF EXPENSES

Name of applicant applies under § 330 of the Bankruptcy Code for an award of compensation and reimbursement of actual, necessary expenses and represents:

1. Applicant is counsel for the debtor.
2. The debtor filed a petition under chapter 13 of the Bankruptcy Code on *(date)*.
3. The debtor's annualized current monthly income as set forth on Form B22C is:

___ above median (the amount on line 15 is not less than the amount on line 16)

___ below median (the amount on line 15 is less than the amount on line 16).

4. All services rendered and expenses incurred for which compensation or reimbursement is requested were performed or incurred for or on behalf of the debtor, the services and expenses were actual and necessary, and the compensation requested for those services is reasonable.
5. Applicant requests an award of compensation of $_____ for ___ hours expended in providing the following services: *(Description of Services)*.
6. Applicant requests reimbursement of expenses in the amount of $___ for the following expenses: *(Description of Expenses)*.
7. The debtor paid Applicant $_____ prior to the filing of the petition.
8. A copy of the Applicant's disclosure of compensation pursuant to Fed. R. Bankr. P. 2016(b) is attached hereto as Exhibit "A."
9. None of the compensation paid to applicant will be shared with any person other than a member

or regular associate of applicant's law firm unless 11 U.S.C. § 504(c) applies.

WHEREFORE, Applicant requests an award of $_____ in compensation and of $_____ in reimbursement of actual, necessary expenses.

Dated: _____, 20___

Signed: _____

Applicant

By: _____

Name: _____

Address: _____

Phone No.: (___) _____

Fax No.: (___) _____

[Effective February 1, 1999. Amended effective February 23, 2004; May 16, 2005; February 26, 2008.]

L.B.F. 2016–2B. "LONG FORM" APPLICATION OF COUNSEL FOR DEBTOR FOR COMPENSATION AND REIMBURSEMENT OF EXPENSES IN CHAPTER 13 CASE

UNITED STATES BANKRUPTCY COURT FOR THE EASTERN DISTRICT OF PENNSYLVANIA

In re:)   Chapter 13
)
Debtor(s)   )
)   Bky. No.
)

APPLICATION FOR COMPENSATION AND REIMBURSEMENT OF EXPENSES

Name of applicant applies under § 330 of the Bankruptcy Code for an award of compensation and reimbursement of actual, necessary expenses and represents:

1. Applicant is counsel for the debtor.

2. The debtor filed a petition under chapter 13 of the Bankruptcy Code on *(date)*.

3. The debtor's annualized current monthly income as set forth on Form B22C is:

___ above median (the amount on line 15 is not less than the amount on line 16)

___ below median (the amount on line 15 is less than the amount on line 16).

4. All services rendered and expenses incurred for which compensation or reimbursement is requested were performed or incurred for or on behalf of the debtor, the services and expenses were actual and necessary, and the compensation requested for those services is reasonable.

5. Applicant requests an award of compensation of $_____ for ___ hours expended on the initial consultation with client(s) and in providing before confirmation (i) the customary services of counseling and representing the chapter 13 debtor(s) in connection with the analysis of the financial situation; preparation, review and filing with the court of all required documents; correspondence, telephone conversations and miscellaneous contact with creditors, the trustee, attorneys and other parties in interest; preparation for and attendance at 341(a) meeting, and (ii) in representing the debtor(s) in connection with *[check applicable item(s)]*:

___ cure of a residential mortgage default or other treatment of residential real property claims

___ ownership and claims relating to other real property *(specify the number of properties and describe the issues)*

___ motor vehicle loans or leases

___ state or federal tax claims

___ domestic support obligations

___ student loans

___ an operating business

___ 20 or more creditors listed in Schedule F

___ automatic stay litigation

___ other litigation *(describe)*

6. *[Optional. Applicant may supplement paragraph five with a description of those matters, whether or not they are listed in paragraph 5, that took an unusual amount of time to complete or involved complex legal or factual issues.]*

7. Applicant requests that compensation be awarded at the following hourly rate(s): *(Specify the hourly rate for each person who provided services).*

8. Applicant requests reimbursement of expenses in the amount of $_____ for the following expenses: *(Description of Services).*

9. The debtor paid Applicant $_____ prior to the filing of the petition.

10. A copy of the Applicant's disclosure of compensation pursuant to Fed. R. Bankr. P. 2016(b) is attached hereto as Exhibit "A."

11. None of the compensation paid to applicant will be shared with any person other than a member or regular associate of applicant's law firm unless 11 U.S.C. § 504(c) applies.

12. Attached as Exhibit "B" is a copy of Applicant's time records setting forth the dates and amount of time expended for the services performed on behalf of the debtor.

WHEREFORE, Applicant requests an award of $_____ in compensation and of $_____ in reimbursement of actual, necessary expenses.

Dated: _____, 20___

Signed: _____

Applicant

By:

_____

Name:

_____

Address:

_____

Phone No.: (___) _____

Fax No.: (___) _____

[Effective February 26, 2008.]

L.B.F. 2016–2C. "SUPPLEMENTAL" APPLICATION OF COUNSEL FOR DEBTOR FOR COMPENSATION AND REIMBURSEMENT OF EXPENSES FOR POST CONFIRMATION SERVICES PAYABLE BY THE CHAPTER 13 TRUSTEE

UNITED STATES BANKRUPTCY COURT
FOR THE EASTERN DISTRICT OF
PENNSYLVANIA

In re:)
)   Chapter
)
)
Debtor   )   Bankruptcy No.

SUPPLEMENTAL APPLICATION FOR COMPENSATION AND REIMBURSEMENT OF EXPENSES FOR SERVICES PERFORMED AFTER CONFIRMATION OF CHAPTER 13 PLAN

. . . .

Name of applicant

applies under § 330 of the Code for an order directing the chapter 13 trustee to pay an award of compensation and reimbursement of actual, necessary expenses for services performed after confirmation of the debtor's chapter 13 plan and represents:

1. Applicant is counsel for the debtor.

2. The debtor filed a petition under chapter 13 of the Bankruptcy Code on (*date*)

3. The debtor's chapter 13 plan was confirmed by the court on (*date*).

4. The debtor paid the applicant $_____ prior to the filing of the chapter 13 petition.

5. Applicant's prior applications:

First Application Period

xx/xx/xx to xx/xx/xx Date of Order xx/xx/xx

	Requested	Allowed	Paid	Due
Fees	$ _____	$ _____	$ _____	$ _____
Expenses	$ _____	$ _____	$ _____	$ _____

Second Application Period

xx/xx/xx to xx/xx/xx Date of Order xx/xx/xx

	Requested	Allowed	Paid	Due
Fees	$ _____	$ _____	$ _____	$ _____
Expenses	$ _____	$ _____	$ _____	$ _____
Grand Totals	$ _____	$ _____	$ _____	$ _____

6. Applicant requests an award of supplemental compensation of $_____ for _____ hours expended in providing the following services: (*Description of Services*).

7. Applicant requests that compensation be awarded at the following hourly rate(s): (*Specify the hourly rate for each person who provided services*).

8. Applicant requests reimbursement of expenses in the amount of $ _____ for the following expenses (*Description of expenses*).

9. A copy of the applicant's disclosure of compensation pursuant to F.R.B.P. 2016(b) is attached as Exhibit "A".

10. Attached as Exhibit B is a copy of the applicant's time records setting forth the dates and amount of time expended for the services performed on behalf of the debtor after confirmation of debtor's chapter 13 plan.

11. All services rendered and expenses incurred for which compensation or reimbursement is requested

   a. were performed or incurred for or on behalf of the debtor, the services and expenses were actual and necessary, and the compensation requested for those services is reasonable; and

   b. are not duplicative of services and expenses for which compensation or reimbursement was previously requested.

12. If this supplemental application is granted, the debtor's confirmed chapter 13 plan (check whichever is applicable)

___ is adequately funded.

___ is not adequately funded.

13. None of the compensation paid to applicant will be shared with any person other than a member or regular associate of applicant's law firm unless 11 U.S.C. § 504(c) applies.

WHEREFORE, Applicant requests an award of $_____ in compensation and of $_____ in reimbursement of actual, necessary expenses.

Dated: _____, 20XX

Signed: _____

Applicant

By: _____

Name: _____

Address: _____

Phone No.: (___) _____

Fax No.: (___) _____

[Effective February 26, 2008.]

LOCAL RULE 2016–3. COMPENSATION OF PROFESSIONALS: DETAILED FORM OF APPLICATION

(a) **Content of Application.** An application for compensation or reimbursement of expenses required by F.R.B.P. 2016(a) shall, unless the application is governed by L.B.R. 2016–2, include the following:

(1) a description of the services performed that identifies each service separately in sufficient detail to allow evaluation of the benefit derived from the service, the date each service was performed, and the time expended for each service.

(2) the professional time expended shall be set forth either

(A) by each professional or paraprofessional in chronological order, or

(B) by day in chronological order showing all professionals or paraprofessionals that expended time on each day; and

(3) a list by type of the expenses for which reimbursement is sought that includes for each type of expense either

(A) a statement that the amount of the expense is calculated using the applicant's actual in-house cost or the actual amount billed by a third party provider, or

(B) an explanation of how the amount of the expense is calculated.

(b) **Form of Application.** An application for compensation or reimbursement of expenses that conforms substantially to L.B.F. 2016–3, satisfies the requirements of subdivision (a).

(c) **Categories of Service.** An application for compensation that requests professional fees in excess of $50,000 shall set forth separately, to the extent applicable, the professional time expended under the following categories of service.

(1) Asset Analysis and Recovery (identification and review of potential assets including causes of action and non-litigation recoveries).

(2) Asset Disposition (sales, leases [§ 365 matters], abandonment and related transaction work).

(3) Business Operations (issues related to debtor-in-possession operating in chapter 11 such as employee, vendor, tenant issues and other similar problems).

(4) Case Administration (coordination and compliance activities, including preparation of statement of financial affairs; schedules; list of contracts; United States Trustee interim statements and operating reports; contacts with the United States Trustee; general creditor inquiries).

(5) Claims Administration and Objections (specific claim inquiries; bar date motions; analyses, objections and allowances of claims.)

(6) Employee Benefits/Pensions (review issues such as severance, retention, 401K coverage and continuance of pension plan).

(7) Fee/Employment Applications (preparations of employment and fee applications for self or others; motions to establish interim procedures).

(8) Fee/Employment Objections (review of and objections to the employment and fee applications of others).

(9) Financing (matters under §§ 361, 363, and 364 including cash collateral and secured claims; loan document analysis).

(10) Litigation (there should be a separate category established for each major matter).

(11) Meetings of Creditors (preparing for and attending the conference of creditors, the § 341(a) meeting and other creditors' committee meetings).

(12) Plan and Disclosure Statement (formulation, presentation and confirmation; compliance with the plan confirmation order, related orders and rules; disbursement and case closing activities, except those related to the allowance and objections to allowance of claims).

(13) Relief from Stay Proceedings (matters relating to termination or continuation of automatic stay under § 362).

(14) Accounting/Auditing (activities related to maintaining and auditing books of account, preparation of financial statements and account analysis).

(15) Business Analysis (preparation and review of company business plan; development and review of strategies; preparation and review of cash flow forecasts and feasibility studies).

(16) Corporate Finance (review financial aspects of potential mergers, acquisitions and disposition of company or subsidiaries).

(17) Data Analysis (management information systems review, installation and analysis, construction, maintenance and reporting of significant case financial data, lease rejection, claims, etc.).

(18) Litigation Consulting (providing consulting and expert witness services relating to various bankruptcy matters such as insolvency, feasibility, avoiding actions; forensic accounting, etc.).

(19) Reconstruction Accounting (reconstructing books and records from past transactions and bringing accounting current).

(20) Tax Issues (analysis of tax issues and preparation of state and federal tax returns).

(21) Valuation (appraise or review appraisals of assets).

An applicant may use additional categories of service.

(d) **Court Ordered Categories of Service.** On its own motion or on the motion of a party in interest, the court may order that different categories be used for services performed after a date certain that is a reasonable period of time after the entry of the order.

[Effective February 1, 1999.]

SOURCE

Subdivisions (a) and (c) are similar to 97 L.B.R. 2002(a). The categories in subdivision (c) are the categories in the fee application regulation published by the Office of United States Trustee. Counsel need only use the categories that cover services rendered during the application period.

Subdivision (d) authorizes the court to specify that other categories must be used.

Subdivision (b) authorizes the use of a standard form of fee application. The form is derived in part from the fee application regulation published by the Office of United States Trustee.

L.B.F. 2016–3. APPLICATION FOR COMPENSATION OR REIMBURSEMENT OF EXPENSES

UNITED STATES BANKRUPTCY COURT FOR THE EASTERN DISTRICT OF PENNSYLVANIA

In re:) Chapter
)
)
)
      Debtor) Bankruptcy No.

_____ APPLICATION FOR
first, second, etc. as applicable

COMPENSATION AND REIMBURSEMENT
OF EXPENSES

Of _____
name of applicant, professional capacity

For _____
entity represented or engaged by

For THE PERIOD _____ THROUGH _____
_____ in accordance
*Name of applicant, professional
capacity, and entity represented
or engaged by*

with F.R.B.P. 2016 applies under § 330 of the Code for an award of compensation and reimbursement of actual, necessary expenses and represents:

Part A Preliminary Statement

1. Applicant is [professional capacity] for [entity represented or engaged by].

2. All services rendered and expenses incurred for which compensation or reimbursement is requested were performed or incurred for or on behalf of [entity represented or engaged by].

3. The services described in this Application are actual, necessary services and the compensation requested for those services is reasonable.

4. The expenses described in this Application are actual, necessary expenses.

[Additional numbered paragraphs may be used by the Applicant to set forth other statements or information.]

Part B General Information

1. Period xx/xx/xx to xx/xx/xx

Final Application _____

Interim Application _____

                        Requested

    Fees $_____

2. General Information

    a. Date case filed: xx/xx/xx

    b. Date application to approve employment filed: xx/xx/xx

    c. Date employment approved: xx/xx/xx

    d. First date services rendered in the case: xx/xx/xx

    e. Compensation request is under § 330: _____Yes _____No

    If other statutory basis, specify: § _____

    f. Any fees awarded will be paid from the estate:

       _____ Yes _____ No

    If no, state the source of payment of any fee that is awarded. _____

g. This application is for a period less than 120 days after the filing of the case or less than 120 days after the end of the period of the last application.

_____ Yes _____ No

If yes, state date and terms of court order allowing filing at shortened intervals.

Order date: xx/xx/xx

Terms, if any _____

_____

3. Prior Applications

First Application Period

xx/xx/xx to xx/xx/xx Date of Order xx/xx/xx

	Requested	Allowed	Paid	Due
Fees	$	$	$	$
Expenses	$	$	$	$

Second Application Period   Date of Order xx/xx/xx

xx/xx/xx to xx/xx/xx

	Requested	Allowed	Paid	Due
Fees	$	$	$	$
Expenses	$	$	$	$
Grand Totals	$	$	$	$

4. Attorneys' Billing for Current Period

Name	Admitted	Hours	Billing Rate	Total
				$
etc.	etc.	etc.	etc.	etc.
Grand Total				$

5. Paralegals Billing for Current Period

Name	Hours	Billing Rate	Total
Grand Totals			$

6. Billing Rates

a. Are any of the billing rates different than the billing rates set forth in your last application? _____ Yes _____ No

b. If yes, indicate whose billings rates are different and explain why?_____

_____

_____

Part C Billing Summary

1. **Description of Services.** Provide adequate detail appropriate for the amount of time billed and the nature and variety of the services rendered.

2. **Detail of Hours Expended.** Set forth in list form or attach a list that shows the name of the professional or paraprofessional, date, activity, and time expended. The list may be organized in either of two ways.

(a) By each professional or paraprofessional in chronological order for the application period; or

(b) By day in chronological order showing all professionals or paraprofessionals that billed time on a particular day during the application period.

* * * * *

Category Reporting. If category reporting of time expended is required under L.B.R. 2016-3(c), only categories for which services were rendered during the period covered by the application should be included. A separate Description of Services and Detail of Hours Expended shall be provided for each category.

Part D Expense Summary

Set forth in list form or attach a list that shows the type of expenses for which reimbursement is sought. For each type of expense either

(a) state the amount of the expense that is calculated using the applicant's in-house actual cost or the actual amount billed by a third party provider, or

(b) explain how the amount of the expense is calculated.

WHEREFORE, Applicant requests an award of $_____ in compensation and of $_____ in reimbursement of actual, necessary expenses.

Dated: _____ Signed: _____

                                Applicant

                By: _____

                Name
                Address
                Phone No. (___) _____
                Fax No. (___) _____

[Effective February 1, 1999.]

LOCAL RULE 2016–4. DISCLOSURE BY DEBTOR'S COUNSEL AND PRO SE DEBTOR

(a) Disclosure by Attorney. The statement of counsel for the debtor required by § 329 of the Code and F.R.B.P. 2016(b) shall list separately (i) the total amount of the compensation and the total amount of reimbursement of expenses, (ii) the amount of each total attributable to services rendered before the filing of the petition, and (iii) the amount of each total attributable to services rendered or to be rendered after the filing of the petition.

(b) Disclosure of Payments by Debtor. In all pro se cases, at the time the petition is filed, the clerk shall require the debtor to complete a statement on L.B.F. 2016–4 setting forth all persons or business entities from whom the debtor received assistance or to whom the debtor paid or agreed to pay money in connection with the case.

[Effective February 1, 1999.]

Subdivisions (a) and (b) are the same as 97 L.B.R. 2016.1(a) and (c). There is added to subdivision (a) the requirement that the disclosure statement separately list fees and expenses for pre- and post-petition services. The amount of compensation requested for post-petition services and the amount of reimbursement sought for post-petition expenses determines whether notice must be sent to all creditors. See L.B.R. 2002–1(b). The 2000 amendment to F.R.B.P. 2002(a)(6), effective December 1, 2000, raised the amount that triggers the duty to give notice from "exceeds $500," which is referred to above, to "exceeds $1000."

L.B.F. 2016–4. STATEMENT OF PRO SE DEBTOR(S)

Debtor's Name _____   Case No. _____
Address _____   Chapter of Case _____
Telephone Number (home) _____   Date Case Filed _____
Telephone Number (work) _____   Date this Form Submitted _____

1.   List the name, address, and telephone number of any person or business assisting you in filing or preparing papers for this case:

_____

_____

_____

2.   State how you were referred to the person or business named above or the source of advertisement you responded to.

_____

3.   a.   Total fee charged by person or business named above $_____

b.   Amount of fee paid as of the date you filed bankruptcy $_____

c.   Did the preparer tell you the amount of court costs that must be paid to file your case?

YES   NO   (circle one)

4.   Were various chapters or types of bankruptcy explained to you?

YES   NO   (circle one)

Other Comments_____

5.   Did the preparer explain to you that you have the right to claim certain property as exempt?

YES   NO   (circle one)

6.   Did the preparer give you a copy of the papers he prepared for you?

YES   NO   (circle one)

_____

Signature of Debtor(s)

[Effective February 1, 1999.]

This form is a revised version of L.B.F. 2016.1.

LOCAL RULE 2016–5. PAYMENT ON ACCOUNT TO PROFESSIONALS IN COMPLEX CHAPTER 11 CASE

(a) **Applicability.** This rule applies to any case being administered as a complex chapter 11 case. An application under this rule for payment on account is governed by this rule and L.B.R. 9013–1(a) and (b).

(b) **Payment on Account.** Unless otherwise ordered by the court and subject to subdivision (c), a professional employed under Sections 327 or 1103, who has rendered services for a period of at least one month but not yet filed an application for compensation and reimbursement of expenses under L.B.R. 2016–3 covering that period, may file an application for payment on account toward the compensation and reimbursement that will later be requested in an application filed in accordance with L.B.R. 2016–3.

(c) **Limitation on Period Covered by Application.** A professional who has rendered services for a period but not yet filed an application for compensation under L.B.R. 2016–3 covering that period may only request payment on account for a total of four months. Once an application under L.B.R. 2016–3 is filed covering a period, a professional may resume filing applications for payment on account for up to a total of four months for services rendered after the period covered by the L.B.R. 2016–3 application.

(d) **Content of Application.** An application for payment on account shall include (1) a list by name of each professional or paraprofessional, their billing rate, number of hours billed, and the total amount requested for the period; (2) a general description of the service rendered during the period by the applicant in the categories of service listed in L.B.R. 2016–3 (c), and (3) a list of the type and amount of expenses for which reimbursement is requested.

(e) **Service of Application and Notice.** On the day an application for payment on account is filed, the applicant shall serve

(1) A copy of the application, and

(2) A notice of the filing of the application and the requirement that any objection to the application must be filed and served on the applicant, or if the applicant is represented, counsel for the applicant, within 21 days of the date on which the application is filed, on the following, or, if represented, their counsel of record,

(i) the debtor;

(ii) the United States trustee;

(iii) any trustee;

(iv) any official committee or, if no committee has been appointed in a chapter 11 case, the 20 largest unsecured creditors of the debtor; and

(v) those on the Clerk's Service List.

(f) Form of Objection. An objection to an application for payment on account shall identify the objector, state the basis of the objection, and identify the amount of the requested payment that is objected to and the amount that is not objected to.

(g) Certification Relating to Objection. After the expiration of the 21 day period to file an objection, the applicant shall file a certification, prepared as required by L.B.R. 9014–4, of notice and service which also states whether any timely objection has been filed and, if a timely objection has been filed, the specific amount of the total payment requested that is objected to. The applicant shall serve a copy of the certification on the debtor.

(h) Payment on Account. If the debtor receives a certification under subdivision (g) that indicates that no timely objection has been filed or that there was no objection to a portion of the payment requested in the application, the debtor shall pay the professional 80% of the fees and 100% of the expenses described in the application that are not objected to.

(i) Hearing Date on Objection and Notice of Hearing. An applicant, but not an objector, may under L.B.R. 5070–1(a) obtain a hearing date for consideration of objections that have been timely filed to one or more applications for payment on account. The clerk shall give notice of the hearing to the objector, those that must be served under subdivision (e), and any other entity the court directs.

(j) No Binding Effect. The right of a professional or a party in interest to request, object to, or otherwise dispute any issue relating to an application for compensation and reimbursement filed under L.B.R. 2016–3 is not affected by the fact the party in interest did not file any objection to the application for payment on account, the professional received payment on account, or that an application for payment on account was either objected to or denied by the court.

(k) Return of Payment on Account. If the amount paid on account to a professional exceeds the amount of final compensation awarded by the court, the professional shall repay the excess amount to the debtor within 14 days of entry of the order allowing final compensation, unless the court fixes another date for the repayment.

(*l*) Content of Application for Compensation or Reimbursement of Expenses. An application for compensation and reimbursement of expenses that covers a period for which a professional has received payment on account pursuant to this rule shall, in addition to conforming to L.B.R. 2016–3, include the following:

(1) a list of the applications for payment on account that were filed during the period showing for each application whether (i) any objections were filed, (ii) a hearing on the objection has been held or scheduled to be held, and (iii) the amount, if any, paid on account;

(2) a tabulation that shows the difference, if any, between the amounts requested in the applications for payment on account and the application for compensation and reimbursement filed under L.B.R. 2016–3; and

(3) an explanation of the differences in the amounts requested.

[Effective May 16, 2005. Amended effective December 1, 2009.]

Committee's Explanatory Note

This rule was originally noticed as proposed L.B.R. 2016–4. It has been renumbered consistent with existing local rules.

Subdivision (a) This rule applies to cases being administered as complex chapter 11 cases under L.B.R. 1002–2. In general, the rule permits professionals to submit monthly applications for payment of fees on account. If there is no objection, the debtor pays 80% of the fees and 100% of the expenses. If a portion of the fee is objected to, only 80% of the unobjected to portion may be paid.

A maximum of four months in fees may be requested by applications for payment on account. Once a long form fee application under L.B.R. 2016–3 is filed that covers the period for which applications for payment on account have been filed, the professional may resume requesting payment on account.

Subdivision (b) establishes one month as the shortest period that may be covered by an application for payment on account.

Subdivision (c) establishes four months as the maximum period that may be covered by applications for payment on account. The four-month period begins anew once the professional files a fee application under L.B.R. 2016–3.

Subdivision (d) requires less detail concerning what matters each professional worked on than is required under L.B.R. 2016–3. The information that is required by this rule will be ample for parties to determine whether an objection should be filed. Under subdivision (j), a failure to object to an application for payment on account does not preclude a party from objecting to a fee application under L.B.R. 2016–3.

Subdivision (e) requires service of an application for payment on account on the same persons who have to be served with fee applications under L.B.R. 2016–1(a). There is no requirement that a separate notice of the filing of the application on account be given to those on this matrix list of creditors. See L.B.R. 2016–1(b).

Subdivision (f) requires an objection to specifically state how much of the requested fee is objected to.

Subdivision (g) is similar to L.B.R. 2016–1(c).

Subdivision (h) requires the debtor on receipt of a certificate from the applicant to pay 80% of the unobjected to fees and 100% of the unobjected to expenses. No obligation to pay on account arises if the debtor or another party objects to the application. If, when the debtor receives the certification, the debtor has a basis for not paying the professional, the debtor may file a motion seeking authority to withhold payment.

Subdivision (i) The filing of an objection to an application for payment on account automatically prevents payment of the amount objected to. Thus, there is no reason to hold a hearing on the objection unless the applicant disputes the objection. Only the applicant may have a hearing on an objection scheduled.

Subdivision (j) provides that the rights of all parties are preserved and may be asserted when a fee application under L.B.R. 2011–3 is filed.

Subdivision (k) states the obligation of a professional to return fees paid on account when the final fee allowance is less than the amount paid on account.

Subdivision (l) requires an applicant to include in a L.B.R. 2016–3 fee application information relating to amounts paid on account.

LOCAL RULE 2082–1. CHAPTER 12—GENERAL

(a) Form of Plan Payment. Payments to the chapter 12 trustee under § 1226(a) of the Code or under a confirmed plan shall be made by certified check or money order. Each payment shall be legibly marked with the bankruptcy number of the case and with the name of the debtor as that name appears in the caption of the case.

(b) Duration of Payments. Payments to the trustee under a confirmed plan shall continue until an order is entered dismissing the case, the debtor has completed all payments required by the plan, the debtor files a motion for discharge or dismissal, or the debtor files a notice of conversion under § 1208(a).

(c) Effect of Wage Order. The debtor shall continue to make the payments required under subdivision (b) even if the debtor files a motion for a wage order or a wage order is entered, unless the debtor's employer or other entity subject to the wage order makes the payment to the trustee.

(d) Transmission of Copy of Local Rule. The chapter 12 trustee shall mail a copy or summary of this local rule to the debtor and counsel for the debtor.

(e) Standing Trustee's Fee. If a chapter 12 case is dismissed or converted prior to the entry of a discharge, whether or not a plan has been confirmed, the standing trustee shall be entitled to retain (i) from any payments from the debtor the amount of $35.00 or the amount of the percentage fee authorized under 28 U.S.C. § 586(e)(1), whichever amount is greater, and (ii) the interest earned on any payments from the debtor.

(f) Monthly Disbursements. The trustee shall make post-confirmation disbursements to creditors on a monthly basis.

(g) Final Account. On the termination of a chapter 12 case, the trustee shall file with the clerk a final account of all monies receive and disbursed, and shall mail a copy of the final account to the debtor and counsel for the debtor.

(h) Notice of Dismissal. The clerk shall provide timely notice of the dismissal of a chapter 12 case to all creditors on the Matrix List of Creditors and to the trustee.

[Effective February 1, 1999.]

SOURCE

This rule is the same as 97 L.B.R. 1017.2 with the exceptions that subdivision (d) of 97 L.B.R. 1017.2 is omitted because a chapter 12 debtor does not have to make pre-confirmation payments and subdivision (f) is omitted as unnecessary. Also subdivision (e) of this rule applies only if a chapter 12 standing trustee is serving as the trustee in the chapter 12 case.

Subdivision (f) of this rule is new.

LOCAL RULE 2083–1. CHAPTER 13—GENERAL

(a) Form of Plan Payment. Payments to the chapter 13 trustee under § 1326(a) of the Code or under a confirmed plan shall be made by certified check or money order. Each payment shall be legibly marked with the bankruptcy number of the case and with the name of the debtor as that name appears in the caption of the case.

(b) Duration of Payments. Payments to the trustee under § 1326(a) of the Code or under a confirmed plan shall continue until an order is entered dismissing or converting the case, the debtor completes all payments required by the plan, the debtor files a motion for discharge or dismissal, or the debtor files a notice of conversion under § 1307(a).

(c) Effect of Wage Order. The debtor shall continue to make the payments required under subdivision (b) even if the debtor files a motion for a wage order or a wage order is entered, unless the debtor's employer or other entity subject to the wage order makes the payment to the trustee.

(d) Transmission of Copy of Local Rule. The chapter 13 trustee shall mail a copy or a summary of this rule to the debtor and counsel for the debtor.

(e) Standing Trustee's Fee. If a chapter 13 case is dismissed or converted prior to the entry of a discharge, whether or not a plan has been confirmed, the standing trustee shall be entitled to retain (i) from any payments made from the debtor the amount of $35.00 or the amount of the percentage fee authorized under 28 U.S.C. § 586(e)(1), whichever amount is greater, and (ii) the interest earned on any payments from the debtor.

(f) Monthly Disbursements. The trustee shall make post-confirmation disbursements to creditors on a monthly basis.

(g) Final Account. On the termination of a chapter 13 case, the trustee shall file with the clerk a final account of all monies receive and disbursed, and shall mail a copy of the final account to the debtor and counsel for the debtor.

(h) Notice of Dismissal. The clerk shall provide timely notice of the dismissal of a chapter 13 case to all creditors on the Matrix List of Creditors and to the trustee.

[Effective February 1, 1999.]

SOURCE

This rule is the same as 97 L.B.R. 1017.2 with the exception that subdivisions (d) and (f) of 97 L.B.R. 1017.2 have been omitted as unnecessary.

Subdivision (f) is new.

LOCAL RULE 2090–1. ATTORNEYS— ADMISSION TO PRACTICE

(a) Attorney Practice Before the Court. Only an attorney who either is (i) admitted to practice in the United States District Court for the Eastern District of Pennsylvania and presently in good standing before the district court; (ii) representing the United States and authorized to practice before the district court under Local Civil Rule 83.5(e); or (iii) admitted to practice pro hac vice under subdivision (c) may practice before the court.

(b) General Admission. An attorney who is admitted to practice in the United States District Court for the Eastern District of Pennsylvania and presently in good standing before the district court is automatically admitted to practice before this court and is a member of the bar of this court.

(c) Admission Pro Hac Vice. An attorney who is a member in good standing of the bar of any United States District Court or the highest court of any state or of the District of Columbia may be admitted to practice before this court in a particular case.

(1) *Adversary Proceedings.* A request for admission pro hac vice to appear in an adversary proceeding shall be made by verified application and upon motion of a member of the bar of this court and shall be accompanied by an admission fee[2] established by the district court. The motion may be granted without hearing under L.B.R. 9014–2; however, no such admission shall be effective until such time as the fee has been paid.

(2) *Non-Adversary Proceedings.* A request for admission pro hac vice to appear in any matter other than an adversary proceeding shall be made as set forth in subparagraph (c)(1) above, except that:

the court, in its discretion, may waive the requirement of a written application and motion, and in lieu thereof may permit same to be made on the record by a member of the bar of this court; however, no such admission shall be effective until such time as the admission fee established by the district court has been paid.

(d) Student Practice.

(1) *Generally.* A law student may appear before the court in any case or matter on behalf of any person if the person on whose behalf the law student is appearing has indicated in writing consent to that appearance and the approved supervising attorney, who must be counsel of record for the person on whose behalf the law student is appearing, has also indicated in writing his approval of that appearance.

(2) *Eligibility Requirements.* In order to be eligible to appear before the court, the law student must:

(i) be duly enrolled in a law school approved by the American Bar Association;

(ii) have completed legal studies amounting to at least three semesters, or the equivalent if the school is on a basis other than a semester basis;

(iii) be introduced to the court in which the law student is appearing for the first time by an attorney admitted to practice before the court;

(iv) announce to the court each time that the law student appears that the student is a law student appearing pursuant to this rule;

(v) neither ask for nor receive any compensation or remuneration of any kind for services from the person on whose behalf he renders services; and

(vi) have read and be familiar with the Rules of Professional Conduct adopted by the Supreme Court of Pennsylvania, as amended from time to time, and any Rule of professional conduct adopted, from time to time, by the United States District Court for the Eastern District of Pennsylvania, the F.R.Evid., the F.R.Civ.P., the F.R.B.P., the Code, and L.B.R. and the L.B.F.

(3) *Compensation.* An eligible law student may be paid by an attorney, legal services agency, law school, public defender agency, or the United States government.

(4) *Termination of Eligibility.* The eligibility of a law student to appear before the court or perform other services in a bankruptcy case or proceeding may be terminated by any judge within this district after notice and hearing.

(5) *Supervising Attorney.* Any member of the bar of this court who chooses to supervise an eligible law student:

(i) shall be an attorney who has previously received from the Board of Bankruptcy Judges approval to supervise eligible law students, such approval having been given after the filing of an application;

(ii) shall assume personal professional responsibility for the quality of the services performed by the law student; and

(iii) shall assist the law student in his preparation to the extent necessary to make the product of the law student's efforts indistinguishable from those of a licensed member of the bar.

(6) *Role of Students.* The clerk shall maintain a roll of all approved supervising attorneys and law students.

(7) *Miscellaneous.* Nothing contained in this rule shall affect the right of any person who is not admitted to practice law to perform any act he might lawfully perform prior to the adoption of this rule.

[Effective February 1, 1999. Amended effective February 1, 2003; April 5, 2004.]

2 The fee for admissions of attorneys pro hac vice in the Bankruptcy Court, effective February 1, 2003, will be set at $40 per attorney per case. Any payment by means of check or money order is to be payable to "Clerk, United States District Court".

SOURCE

Subdivision (a) is derived from 97 L.B.R. 9010.4(a) and (b).

Subdivision (b) is derived from 97 L.B.R. 9010.4(a).

Subdivision (c) is the same as 97 L.B.R. 9010.4(b).

Subdivision (d) is derived from 97 L.B.R. 9010.3. Under subdivision(d)(2)(ii), a law student who has completed three semesters may qualify to appear under the student practice rule.

LOCAL RULE 2090–2. ATTORNEYS— DISCIPLINE AND DISBARMENT

(a) **Standards of Professional Conduct.** The standards of professional conduct adopted by the United States District Court for the Eastern District of Pennsylvania and applicable to attorneys practicing before the district court are applicable to attorneys practicing before the bankruptcy court. The bankruptcy court may govern and control the conduct of attorneys practicing before the bankruptcy court.

(b) **Discipline by District Court and Bankruptcy Court.** The bankruptcy court may discipline attorneys practicing before the bankruptcy court, except that the bankruptcy court may not suspend or disbar an attorney. If a judge of the bankruptcy court has good cause to believe that an attorney should be suspended or disbarred, the judge shall notify the Chief Judge of the district court who shall proceed with the matter in accordance with Local Rules of Disciplinary Enforcement of the United States District Court for the Eastern District of Pennsylvania.

(c) **Expedition of the Court's Business.** An attorney engaged in practice before the bankruptcy court.

(1) shall promptly advise the clerk of the settlement or other final disposition of any matter scheduled before the court, and

(2) shall not, without just cause, fail to appear when any matter is scheduled before the court, fail to prepare for presentation to the court, present to the court vexatious motions or vexatious opposition to the motion, or multiply the proceedings to increase unreasonably and vexatiously the costs of the case or any other matter before the court.

An attorney who does not comply with this subdivision may be disciplined as permitted under subdivision (b).

[Effective February 1, 1999.]

SOURCE

Subdivision (a). The first sentence of this subdivision is new. Under Rule IV of the District Court's Local Rules of Disciplinary Enforcement (Local Rule of Civil Procedure 83.6), the Rules of Professional Conduct adopted by the Supreme Court of Pennsylvania are the rules of professional conduct for attorneys practicing before the Eastern District of Pennsylvania. The second sentence of this subdivision is derived from 97 L.B.R. 9010.4(c).

Subdivision (b) is derived from 97 L.B.R. 9010.4(c). Suspension or disbarment of an attorney from practice before the bankruptcy court may only be imposed by the district court in accord with the procedures of Local Rule of Civil Procedure 83.6.

Subdivision (c) is derived from 97 L.B.R. 9011.1.

LOCAL RULE 2091–1. ATTORNEYS— WITHDRAWAL

An attorney may not withdraw his or her appearance except by order of the court unless another attorney eligible to appear before the court enters his or her appearance simultaneously with the request for withdrawal of appearance. A motion for withdrawal of counsel shall specify the basis for withdrawal.

[Effective February 1, 1999.]

SOURCE

The rule is derived from 97 L.B.R. 9010.1(d).

LOCAL RULE 3001–1. PROOFS OF CLAIM IN CHAPTER 12 AND CHAPTER 13 CASES

(a) **Service.** A creditor who files a secured or priority claim in a chapter 12 or chapter 13 case shall serve a copy of the proof of claim on the debtor or, if the debtor is represented, counsel for the debtor, and shall file a certification of service.

(b) **Secured Claims.** If the last payment due from the debtor will be after the date of the final payment under the chapter 12 or 13 plan, a creditor who files a secured claim in a chapter 12 or 13 case shall attach to the proof of claim an itemized statement which includes the following:

(1) the balance of principal due on the debt;

(2) the total amount of all payments due but not paid prior to the date the petition was filed ("prepetition arrearage"); and

(3) all interest, late charges, or other fees.

(c) Notice. The order and notice of the § 341(a) meeting of creditors shall include a summary of the requirements set forth in subdivisions (a) and (b).

[Effective February 1, 1999.]

SOURCE

This rule is derived from 97 L.B.R.3001.1.

LOCAL RULE 3007–1. OBJECTIONS TO CLAIMS

(a) Form of Objection. An objection to a proof of claim shall identify the objector, the number of the proof of claim objected to, the name of claimant, the amount claimed, and the basis of the objection. An objection shall state in bold type on the right hand side adjacent to the caption the date, time and place set for the hearing.

(b) Scheduling of Hearing. Prior to the filing of an objection, the objector shall obtain a hearing date in the manner provided in L.B.R. 5070–1.

(c) Papers to Accompany an Objection. The following papers shall accompany an objection:

(1) A copy of the claim to which objection is made without exhibits or attachments;

(2) A proposed form of order which, if entered by the court, would grant the relief sought by the objection. Each proposed form of order shall list in the lower left-hand corner of the signature page or on the left-hand side of an attached page(s), the name and address of the debtor, the claimant, the objecting party and the trustee to whom copies of the order, if entered, should be sent;

(3) A certification of notice to the parties identified in paragraph (d).

(d) Notice of the Hearing on Objection to Claims. A notice of hearing substantially in the form of L.B.F. 3007–1 shall be mailed or delivered with a copy of the objection to the debtor, the claimant, and the trustee at least 30 days prior to the date set for a hearing.

(e) No Response Required: Hearing. No response is required to an objection to a claim. There shall be a hearing on an objection to a claim.

[Effective February 1, 1999.]

SOURCE

Subdivisions (a), (c) and (d) of this rule are derived from 97 L.B.R.3007.1.

Subdivisions (b) and (e) are new.

L.B.F. 3007–1. NOTICE OF OBJECTION TO CLAIM AND HEARING DATE

UNITED STATES BANKRUPTCY COURT
FOR THE EASTERN DISTRICT
OF PENNSYLVANIA

In re   : Chapter
                               :
                               :
                               :
         Debtor : Bankruptcy No.

* * * * *

NOTICE OF OBJECTION TO CLAIM
AND HEARING DATE

_____ **has filed an objection to the proof of claim you filed in this bankruptcy case.**

Your claim may be reduced, modified, or eliminated. You should read theses papers carefully and discuss them with your attorney, if you have one.

If you do not want the court to eliminate or change your claim, you or your lawyer must attend the hearing on the objection, scheduled to be held before the Honorable (*name of bankruptcy judge*) on xx/xx/xx, at _____, in Courtroom ___, United States Bankruptcy Court (*address of Bankruptcy Court*). If you or your attorney do not attend the hearing on the objection, the court may decide that you do not oppose the objection to your claim.

Date: _____, _____   Attorney for Objector

[Effective February 1, 1999.]

LOCAL RULE 3015–1. CHAPTER 12 AND CHAPTER 13 PLANS

(a) Summary of Plan. A notice of the meeting of creditors under § 341 of the Code may include a summary of a chapter 12 or chapter 13 plan or of a portion of a plan applicable to a class of creditors.

(b) Service. The debtor shall serve a copy of the initial chapter 12 or chapter 13 plan on all priority and secured creditors and the trustee. The debtor shall file a certification of service within 7 days after the plan is filed.

(c) Objection to Confirmation. An objection to confirmation of a debtor's chapter 12 or chapter 13 plan or modified chapter 12 or chapter 13 plan shall be filed and served on the debtor, the debtor's counsel, the trustee, and the United States trustee no later than 7 days before the date of the hearing on confirmation of the plan or modified plan, unless the court otherwise permits.

[Effective February 1, 1999. Amended effective December 1, 2009.]

SOURCE

Subdivision (a) is new. A copy or a summary of a chapter 12 or 13 plan must accompany the notice of the hearing on confirmation of the plan. F.R.B.P. 3015(d). Notice of the confirmation hearing is commonly given as part of the Notice of the Meeting of Creditors. Subdivision (a) makes it clear that a summary of the plan may be included with the notice.

Subdivision (b) is the same as 97 L.B.R. 3015.1

Subdivision (c) is derived from 97 L.B.R. 3020.1, except the time for filing and service of an objection is 5 days before the date of the confirmation hearing.

LOCAL RULE 3015–2. CHAPTER 12 OR CHAPTER 13 PLANS: MODIFICATION

(a) Modification Before Confirmation.

(1) *Service of Modified Plan.* If a modified chapter 12 or chapter 13 plan is filed before the scheduled hearing on confirmation, the debtor shall serve the modified plan on all priority and secured creditors, the trustee, the United States trustee, and on all other creditors who are adversely affected by the changes to the original plan. Service shall be made on the day the modified plan is filed and the debtor shall file a certification of service.

(2) *Delinquencies in Plan Payments.* If a modified plan, which is filed and served as required by subdivision (a)(1), provides for the reduction, abatement, or suspension of original plan payments that are delinquent, a separate motion to reduce, abate, or suspend the delinquent payment need not be filed.

(3) *Confirmation of Modified Plan.* If a modified chapter 12 or chapter 13 plan is served less than (i) 21 days before the date of a chapter 12 confirmation hearing date, or (ii) 28 days before the date of a chapter 13 confirmation hearing date, the debtor shall advise the courtroom deputy for the judge to whom the case is assigned on or before the date of service that the confirmation hearing must be rescheduled.

(b) Modification of a Confirmed Plan.

(1) *Motion.* A confirmed chapter 12 or chapter 13 plan may be modified after confirmation under Code §§ 1229 or 1329 only on motion.

(2) *Delinquencies in Plan Payment.* If a motion to modify a confirmed plan is duly filed and served, a separate motion to reduce, abate, or suspend delinquent plan payments need not be filed.

[Effective February 1, 1999. Amended effective December 1, 2009.]

SOURCE

Subdivisions (a)(1) and (a)(2) are derived from 97 L.B.R. 3019.1(a) and (b). Subdivision (a)(3) is a reformulation of 97 L.B.R. 3019.1(c).

Subdivision (b) is derived from 97 L.B.R. 3019.1(d). A motion under subdivision (b) is subject to the general motion practice of L.B.R. 9014–3. An objection to the motion must be filed within 20 days. F.R.B.P. 3015(g).

LOCAL RULE 3016–1. CHAPTER 11 PLANS: DISCLOSURE STATEMENT APPROVAL REQUIRED

(a) **Applicability.** This rule applies when a chapter 11 plan proponent is required by § 1125 to obtain approval of a disclosure statement before soliciting acceptance or rejection of a plan.

(b) **Filing of Disclosure Statement, Voting Procedures, and Disbursing Agent Proposal.** Unless the court orders otherwise, the proponent of a plan in a chapter 11 case shall file with the plan (1) the disclosure statement required by § 1125; (2) a motion for approval of the disclosure statement and for approval of plan voting procedures; and (3) if the plan provides for the liquidation of a material portion of the property of the estate and the distribution of the proceeds to creditors, a disbursing agent proposal conforming to subdivision (e).

(c) **When Considered by Court.** The court shall consider the motion for approval of voting procedures at the hearing on the disclosure statement. The court may consider the disbursing agent proposal at the hearing on the disclosure statement or at the hearing on confirmation of the plan.

(d) **Motion for Approval of Disclosure Statement and Voting Procedures.** The motion for approval of a disclosure statement and voting procedures shall set forth the procedures for transmission of the voting materials and casting of ballots and be accompanied by a proposed order approving the voting procedures and fixing the dates for (1) mailing the voting materials; (2) casting ballots; (3) filing the report of voting; and (4) the confirmation hearing.

(e) **Disbursing Agent Proposal.** The disbursing agent proposal shall include (1) the name of a person competent and willing to serve as disbursing agent; (2) the duties to be performed by the disbursing agent; (3) the amount and costs of a bond or reasons why a bond should not be required, and (4) the method and source of payment of the disbursing agent.

(f) Service of Documents. The documents required to be filed under sub-divisions (b)(2) and (3) of this rule shall accompany the plan and disclosure statement that are mailed under F.R.B.P. 3017(a) to the debtor; the trustee, if one has been appointed; the committee; the Securities and Exchange Commission; any party in interest who requests in writing copies of the disclosure statement or plan; and the U.S. trustee.

(g) Objections. No later than 7 days before the hearing on the disclosure statement, an objection to a motion for approval of a disclosure statement or to the documents required to be filed under subdivisions (b)(2) shall be filed and served on the parties specified in subdivision (f), unless the court orders otherwise.

(h) Small Business Cases. In a small business case governed by F.R.B.P. 3017.1, subdivisions (b)–(e) and (g) apply except that a reference to a motion for approval of the disclosure statement and voting procedures shall be read as a reference to an application for conditional approval of the disclosure statement and approval of the voting procedures. The disbursing agent proposal required to be filed under subdivision (b)(3) shall be served with the application in accordance with L.B.R. 9013–1(e).

[Effective February 1, 1999. Amended effective December 1, 2009.]

SOURCE

Subdivision (a) makes it clear that this rule only applies if a disclosure statement must be approved by the court prior to postpetition solicitation of acceptance or rejection of a plan. L.B.R. 3016–2 governs chapter 11 cases in which voting on a plan has been completed prepetition.

Subdivisions (b)-(e) are derived from 97 L.B.R. 3016–1.

Subdivision (g) is new. It establishes the time for filing an objection to a disclosure statement and related documents. The court by order may fix a different time to file an objection.

Subdivision (h). On December 1, 1997 new F.R.B.P. 3017.1, which governs small business cases, became effective. This subdivision adapts L.B.R. 3016–1 to the small business case in which an application for conditional approval of the disclosure statement is filed.

LOCAL RULE 3016–2. CHAPTER 11 PLANS: COMPLIANCE OF PREPETITION SOLICITATION WITH § 1126(b)

If a plan proponent submits with a chapter 11 plan evidence that there was prepetition solicitation of acceptance or rejection of the plan in compliance with § 1126(b), the court shall determine at the plan confirmation hearing whether the prepetition solicitation complied with § 1126(b).

[Effective February 1, 1999.]

SOURCE

This rule is new.

LOCAL RULE 3021–1. REPORTS ON POST–CONFIRMATION DISTRIBUTION

(a) Plan Implementation Reports. Unless otherwise provided in the confirmation order, an order closing the case, or a separate order the debtor, trustee, disbursing agent, or other person designated in a chapter 11 plan to make distributions to creditors after confirmation of a chapter 11 plan shall (1) prepare, file, and serve the interim and cumulative plan implementation reports required by this rule, and (2) request and give notice of the hearing to consider the cumulative plan implementation report.

(b) Reporting Periods. An interim plan implementation report shall be prepared for the following reporting periods: from the date of entry of the confirmation order through the last day of the calendar month, and for each of the next six full calendar months. If the confirmation order is entered less than 14 days before the end of the calendar month, the report for that initial period may be made as part of the report for the first full calendar month.

(c) Cumulative Report. A cumulative plan implementation report shall be prepared for either the reporting period from the date of entry of the confirmation order through the last day of the sixth full calendar month after the date of the entry of the confirmation order, or, if the plan distributions are completed before the end of the sixth full calendar month, the reporting period from the date of entry of the confirmation order through the last day of the full calendar month in which plan distributions are complete.

(d) Contents of Report. A plan implementation report shall include for the reporting period

(i) the amount available for distribution at the beginning of the period;

(ii) the source and amount of all funds received;

(iii) the name of the institution where funds are deposited, the account number and name of the account, and the person who has signatory authority over the account;

(iv) if funds are invested in instruments, the type, amount, and maturity date of the instruments; and

(v) the names of the persons to whom distributions have been made and the amount of each distribution.

(e) Time to File. Plan implementation reports shall be filed on or before the 14th day after the end of the reporting period.

(f) Service. All plan implementation reports shall be served on the debtor and counsel for the debtor;

members of any official committee and counsel to any committee, unless the committee's service terminated on confirmation of the plan or counsel is no longer retained by the committee; the United States trustee; and those on the Clerk's Service List. Unless the court otherwise directs, the cumulative plan implementation report shall also be served on all creditors.

(g) Hearing on Cumulative Plan Implementation Report. The court shall hold a hearing to consider the cumulative plan implementation report, whether the case should remain open, and whether additional plan implementation reports should be filed and such other matters as are brought before the court. Notice of that hearing shall be given to all persons who are served with a copy of the cumulative plan implementation report.

[Effective February 1, 1999. Amended effective December 1, 2009.]

SOURCE

This rule is the same 97 L.B.R. 3021.1, except that in subdivision (a) reference is made to the possibility that the court may order that this rule does not apply.

LOCAL RULE 4002–1. DEBTOR—DUTIES: AUTHORITY TO COMPENSATE

(a) Authority to Compensate. Subject to subdivision (b), the debtor may pay compensation for services to the debtor, if an individual, or to the members of a partnership, or to an officer of a corporation at a rate equal to or less than the annual rate of compensation paid to the person as of the 90th day before the filing of the petition or such other amount as the court orders for cause shown.

(b) Termination of Authority to Compensate. The debtor's authority to pay compensation under subdivision (a) terminates on the 45th day after the filing of the petition in a voluntary case or on the 45th day after the entry of an order for relief in an involuntary case unless the debtor gives notice as required by subdivision (c) and files the certification of notice by the last day of the applicable 45 day period.

(c) Notice. Within 45 days of the filing of a petition in a voluntary case or 45 days after the entry of an order for relief in an involuntary case, the debtor shall give the notice described in subdivision (d) by mail to (I) the members of any official committee and counsel for the committee or, if no committee has been appointed, the creditors holding the 20 largest unsecured claims, (ii) creditors holding secured claims, and (iii) the United States trustee. A certification of notice shall be filed.

(d) Content of Notice. The notice shall contain

(i) the name of the person receiving compensation from the debtor under subdivision (a);

(ii) a description of the position, title and duties of the person; and

(iii) the rate of compensation paid to the person on the 90th day before the filing of the petition and the rate being paid by the debtor under subdivision (a).

(e) Objections.

(1) *Form of Objection.* An objection to the debtor's retention of a person or the amount of compensation paid to a person listed in the debtor's notice shall identify the objector and the basis of the objection. An objection shall state in bold type on the right hand side adjacent to the caption the date, time and place set for the hearing.

(2) *Scheduling of Hearing.* Prior to the filing of an objection, the objector shall obtain a hearing date in the manner provided in L.B.R. 5070–1.

(3) *Papers to Accompany an Objection.* The following papers shall accompany an objection:

(i) a copy of the debtor's notice to which objection is made;

(ii) a proposed form of order which, if entered by the court, would grant the relief sought by the objection. Each proposed form of order shall list in the lower left-hand corner of the signature page or on the left-hand side of an attached page(s), the name and address of the debtor, the claimant, the objecting party and the trustee to whom copies of the order, if entered, should be sent;

(iii) a certification of notice to the parties required under subdivision (e)(4).

(4) *Notice of the Hearing on Objection.* A notice of hearing on the objection shall be mailed or delivered with a copy of the objection to the debtor and the parties referred to in subdivision (c) of this rule at least 21 days before the date of the hearing.

(f) No Response Required: Hearing. No response is required to an objection filed under subdivision (e) of this rule. There shall be a hearing on the objection.

[Effective February 1, 1999. Amended effective December 1, 2009.]

SOURCE

This rule is derived from 95 L.B.R. 4002.1. If a party objects to the debtor continuing to pay compensation as provided in subdivision (a), the objector obtains a hearing date and gives notice of the hearing date.

LOCAL RULE 4003–1. OBJECTIONS TO EXEMPTIONS

(a) Form of Objection. An objection to an exemption filed under F.R.B.P. 4003(b) shall identify the objector and the basis for the objection. An objection shall state in bold type on the right-hand side adjacent to the caption the date, time and place set for the hearing on the objection.

(b) Scheduling of Hearing. Prior to filing an objection, the objector shall obtain a hearing date in the manner provided in L.B.R. 5070–1.

(c) Papers to Accompany Objections. The following papers shall accompany an objection:

(1) A proposed form of order which, if entered by the court, would grant the relief sought by the motion. Each proposed form of order shall list, in the lower left-hand corner of the signature page or on the left-hand side of an attached page(s), the names and addresses of all interested persons to whom it is suggested that copies of the order, if entered, should be sent.

(2) A certification of notice to the parties identified in paragraph (d).

(d) Notice of Hearing on Objection to Exemption. A notice of hearing substantially in the form of L.B.F. 4003–1 shall be mailed or delivered with a copy of the objection to the trustee, the debtor or other person who claimed the exemption, and the attorney for the debtor or other person who claimed the exemption at least 28 days before the date of the hearing.

(e) No Response Required: Hearing. No response is required to an objection to an exemption. There shall be a hearing on an objection to an exemption.

[Effective February 1, 1999. Amended effective December 1, 2009.]

SOURCE

This rule is new. The time within which to object to a claim of exemption is fixed by F.R.B.P. 4003(b) which requires that an objection must be filed "within 30 days after the conclusion of the meeting of creditors... or the filing of any amendment" to the list of exemptions.

L.B.F. 4003–1. NOTICE OF OBJECTION TO CLAIM OF EXEMPTION AND HEARING DATE

UNITED STATES BANKRUPTCY COURT
FOR THE EASTERN DISTRICT
OF PENNSYLVANIA

In re: :   Chapter
                :
                :
                :
      Debtor :   Bankruptcy No.

* * * * *

NOTICE OF OBJECTION TO CLAIM OF EXEMPTION AND HEARING DATE

_____ has filed an objection to your claim of exemption in this bankruptcy case.

Your claim of exemption may be eliminated or changed by the court because an objection has been filed. You should read these papers carefully and discuss them with your attorney, if you have one in this bankruptcy case. (If you do not have an attorney, you may wish to consult an attorney.)

If you do not want the court to eliminate or change your claim of exemption, or if you want the court to consider your views, you or your lawyer must attend the hearing on the objection, scheduled to be held before the Honorable (_name of bankruptcy judge_) on xx/xx/xx, at _____, in Courtroom ___, United States Bankruptcy Court (_address of Bankruptcy Court_).

Date: _____, _____   Attorney for Objector

[Effective February 1, 1999.]

LOCAL RULE 4004–1. DISCHARGE: DISCHARGE HEARINGS

(a) Chapter 7 Debtor's Motion to Defer Entry of Discharge Order. A motion of a chapter 7 debtor under F.R.B.P. 4004(c) to defer entry of a discharge order is governed by L.B.R. 9014–2 (Motions Determined Without Hearing).

(b) Chapter 7 Case.

(1) A discharge order will be entered unless a motion for approval of a reaffirmation agreement is pending or the debtor has requested that a discharge hearing be held.

(2) If a motion for approval of a reaffirmation agreement is pending, the debtor has requested that a discharge hearing be held, or the court directs, the clerk shall schedule a discharge hearing and give notice of the hearing to the debtor, debtor's counsel, and the trustee.

(c) Chapter 12 or Chapter 13 Case.

(1) On completion of the payments under a confirmed chapter 12 or chapter 13 plan, the trustee shall promptly file a final report.

(2) The clerk shall promptly give notice to the debtor, debtor's counsel, and all creditors provided for in the plan that

     i.   the final report has been filed; and

     ii.   any objection to the final report must be filed within 21 days from the date of the notice and served on the debtor and the debtor's counsel.

(3) A discharge order will be entered unless an objection to the trustee's final report is filed, a motion for approval of a reaffirmation agreement is pending or subsections (f), (g) or (h) of § 1328 of the Code are applicable.

(4) If a motion for approval of a reaffirmation agreement is pending, an objection to the trustee's final report is timely filed, or the court directs, the clerk shall schedule a discharge hearing and give notice of the hearing to the debtor, debtor's counsel, the trustee, and to any objector.

[Effective February 1, 1999. Amended effective February 26, 2008; December 1, 2009.]

SOURCE

Subdivision (a) is new. A request to defer entry of a discharge order under F.R.B.P. 4004(c) is made by motion and determined by the court without hearing.

Subdivisions (b) and (c) are derived from 97 L.B.R. 4008.1, and 4008. 2.

EXPLANATORY NOTE (2009)

This amendment to L.B.R. 4004–1(c)(3) and (3) corrects a technical error by eliminating a reference to a "debtor's statement," a document that is not otherwise referenced in the local rules. The amendment also implements the 2005 amendments to § 1328 of the Code, which impose certain requirements that must be satisfied before a chapter 13 discharge order may be entered.

EXPLANATORY NOTE (2008)

This amendment eliminated the requirement previously set forth in L.B.R. 4004(b) that the trustee provide a chapter 7 debtor with a "Discharge Information Sheet," L.B.F. 4004–1. This amendment also eliminated the requirement previously set forth in L.B.R. 4004(c) that the Clerk provide chapter 12 and chapter 13 debtors with a "Discharge Information Sheet," L.B.F. 4004–2. Both L.B.F. 4004–1 and L.B.F. 4004–2 have been stricken.

LOCAL RULE 5001–1. COURT ADMINISTRATION

(a) Emergency Judge.

(1) The judge who is designated as "Emergency Judge" shall act instead of the judge to whom a case is assigned whenever the assigned judge is absent from the Courthouse and cannot feasibly return prior to the expiration of the time within which judicial action is required.

(2) Whenever counsel requests immediate judicial action, the clerk shall contact the assigned judge and in the event that the judge cannot be reached or the judge consents to action by the Emergency Judge, the Emergency Judge shall act in accordance with paragraph (1) of this subdivision.

(3) If the Emergency Judge is required to hold an extensive hearing or otherwise perform a substantial amount of work, the clerk may, at the request of the Emergency Judge and with the consent of the assigned judge, reassign the case to the Emergency Judge for all purposes.

(4) All inquiries concerning the Emergency Judge should be referred to the clerk who shall obtain complete information concerning the nature of the emergency, the name of the case, the names and telephone numbers of counsel and shall provide this information to the Emergency Judge who shall determine what action, if any, is required of the Emergency Judge.

(b) Division of Court. Where it appears from the petition that the debtor's domicile, residence, principal place of business or principal assets were located for the 180 days immediately preceding the commencement of the case (or for a longer portion of such 180-day period than they were located elsewhere) in Bucks County, Chester County, Delaware County, Lancaster County, Montgomery County, or Philadelphia County, the case shall be assigned to the Philadelphia Division. All other cases shall be assigned to a judge of the Reading Division.

(c) Assignment of Cases.

(1) Each case in the Philadelphia Division shall be assigned as soon as possible by a blind lottery method to a judge of the Philadelphia Division.

(2) If the filed papers indicate a later case is related to an earlier filed case, the clerk shall assign the later case to the same judge to whom the earlier case is assigned and notify the judge of that assignment. If the judge receiving the later case is of the opinion that a relationship does not exist, the receiving judge may refer the case to the clerk for assignment by the blind lottery method in the same manner as if it were a newly filed case.

(3) Whether the relationship between the later case and the earlier case is or is not indicated on the filed papers, (A) any interested party may file a motion requesting the judge to whom a case is assigned to reassign the case to another judge, and (B) the judge to whom a case is assigned may determine that a case is related to another numbered case or is more appropriately heard by another judge and may, with the consent of the receiving judge, refer the case to the receiving judge.

[Effective February 1, 1999.]

SOURCE

Subdivision (a) is derived from 97 L.B.R. 5001.1.

Subdivision (b) is derived from 95 L.B.R. 5001.2(a).

Subdivision (c) is derived from 97 L.B.R. 5001.2(b)-(e).

EXPLANATORY NOTE (2006)

The District Court Order of December 13, 2006 designated the amended rule as an interim amended rule subject to reevaluation, with any further proposed amendments to be subject to the requirements of notice and publication.

LOCAL RULE 5003–1. DOCUMENTS FILED UNDER SEAL

(a) A document may be filed under seal only if:

(1) the action is brought pursuant to a federal statute that prescribes the sealing of the record or of certain specific documents; or

(2) the Court orders the document sealed.

(b)(1) Where a document is sealed pursuant to L.B.R. 5003–1(a)(1), the continued status of the document under seal shall be governed by the relevant federal statute. If no federal statute governs, L.B.R. 5003–1(b)(2) and (3) shall apply.

(2) When a document is sealed pursuant to L.B.R. 5003–1(a)(2), the document, if it remains in the custody of the Court, shall not be unsealed for two years after the conclusion of the action including all appeals, unless the Court orders otherwise.

(3) If a document is still sealed at the conclusion of the two-year period and the Court has not entered an order continuing its sealed status beyond that time, the Clerk of Court shall notify the attorney for the party having submitted the sealed document at the attorney's address on the docket that the document will be unsealed unless the attorney or the submitting party advises the Clerk within sixty (60) days that said attorney or the submitting party objects. If the attorney or submitting party objects to the unsealing of the document or if the Clerk's notification is returned unclaimed, the Court will make a determination, on a case-by-case basis, whether to maintain the document under seal, to unseal it, or to require further notification.

[Effective February 26, 2008.]

EXPLANATORY NOTE (2008)

This rule is new. It is based on the local rule of the district court addressing the same subject matter.

LOCAL RULE 5005. FILING BY ELECTRONIC MEANS

Documents may be filed, signed and verified by electronic means in accordance with the procedures set forth in the Standing Order re: Electronic Case Filing, dated April 1, 2003, as it may be amended from time to time by the court. A document filed pursuant to this rule constitutes a written paper for the purpose of these Local Bankruptcy Rules, the Federal Rules of Bankruptcy Procedure, the Federal Rules of Civil Procedure and § 107 of the Bankruptcy Code.

[Effective April 1, 2003.]

LOCAL RULE 5009–1. CLOSING OF CHAPTER 11 CASES

(a) Notice. No later than 180 days after the confirmation of a chapter 11 plan, the clerk shall give notice to counsel for the debtor or former debtor and to counsel to any official creditors' committee of subdivision (b) of this rule.

(b) Final Decree. Within the later of 180 days after confirmation of a chapter 11 plan or the conclusion of the hearing to consider the cumulative plan implementation report held under L.B.R. 3021–1, the court shall enter a Final Decree closing the case, unless a motion to keep the case open for cause is filed within the 180 day period.

[Effective February 1, 1999.]

SOURCE

Subdivision (a) is new.

Subdivision (b) is the same as 97 L.B.R. 3022.1.

LOCAL RULE 5011–1. WITHDRAWAL OF REFERENCE

(a) Motion and Brief. A motion for withdrawal of a case or proceeding under 28 U.S.C. § 157(d) shall be accompanied by a form of order which, if approved by the court, would grant the relief sought by the movant and a brief containing a concise statement of the legal contentions and authorities relied on in support of the motion.

(b) Caption. The caption of a motion for withdrawal shall conform substantially to L.B.F. 5011–1.

(c) Filing. An original of the motion, proposed order, and brief shall be filed with the clerk of the bankruptcy court and a copy of each shall be filed on the same day with the clerk of the district court.

(d) Docketing in District Court. The clerk of the district court shall promptly docket the motion for withdrawal as a miscellaneous matter.

(e) Service. The movant shall serve the motion, proposed order, and brief on

1. the parties in interest listed in L.B.R. 9014–3(g), if the motion is to withdraw the case, or

2. the parties to an adversary proceeding, if the motion is to withdraw an adversary proceeding.

(f) Opposition. Unless the district court directs otherwise, any party opposing the motion shall file with the district court and serve on the movant and the parties referred to in paragraphs (e)(1) or (e)(2) of this rule, whichever is appropriate, a brief in opposition, together with such answer or other response which may be appropriate, within 14 days after service of the motion and supporting brief.

(g) Further Proceedings in District Court. Rule 7.1 of the Local Rules of Civil Procedure governs all proceedings in the district court relating to the motion for withdrawal.

[Effective February 1, 1999. Amended effective April 5, 2004.]

SOURCE

This rule is new and is designed to facilitate the district court's consideration of a motion to withdraw the reference.

L.B.F. 5011–1. CAPTION OF MOTION FOR WITHDRAWAL

UNITED STATES DISTRICT COURT
FOR THE EASTERN DISTRICT
OF PENNSYLVANIA

Miscellaneous Matter No. _____

In re: :   Chapter _____
                  :
                  :
                  :
       Debtor   :   Bankruptcy Court No. _____

MOTION OF _____
     FOR WITHDRAWAL OF REFERENCE

[Effective February 1, 1999.]

LOCAL RULE 5070–1. CALENDARS AND SCHEDULING

(a) Hearing Dates. A person who files a motion, application, objection, or notice for which a hearing is required under a F.R.B.P. or for which these rules require the scheduling of a hearing shall, before filing the paper, consult with the courtroom deputy for the judge to whom the case is assigned to obtain a hearing date on the judge's calendar. The hearing date shall allow for adequate time for the movant or objector to complete any service or notice required by the F.R.B.P. or these rules.

(b) Completion of Hearing. If a hearing is called on the day scheduled but not completed, the court may continue the hearing to a date certain without further written notice.

(c) Rescheduling by Court. If the Court, on its own initiative, reschedules a hearing date or cancels a scheduled hearing, the courtroom deputy, unless the court directs otherwise, shall notify all interested parties of the new hearing date or the cancellation.

(d) Party-Initiated Informal Request to Reschedule. A party who desires to reschedule a matter scheduled before the court shall consult with all other interested counsel to attempt to reach an agreement to reschedule the matter to a date certain. If the interested parties agree to reschedule the matter to a date certain, the party who initiated the proposed rescheduling shall, under subdivision (a) of this rule, consult with the courtroom deputy for the judge to whom the case is assigned to request rescheduling of the hearing. Approval of a new hearing date is at the discretion of the court. If a new hearing date is assigned, the party who initiated the rescheduling shall give notice promptly to the interested parties of the new hearing date.

(e) Motion to Reschedule. If any of the interested parties do not agree to reschedule a matter, if the interested parties are unable to agree on a proposed new date, or if an informal request to reschedule is not granted, the party requesting the rescheduling must proceed by motion under L.B.R. 9014–3, by oral motion in open court made at the scheduled hearing, or during a telephone conference convened under L.B.R. 9076–1.

(f) Expedited Consideration.

(1) *Consultation.* A party who desires to obtain a hearing date earlier than the hearing date that would ordinarily be assigned under subdivision (a) of this rule or other expedited consideration, shall, to the extent practicable, consult with all other interested parties to attempt to reach an agreement that an expedited hearing is appropriate and on the suggested hearing date or dates.

(2) *Content of Motion.* A motion for expedited consideration shall set forth

     (i) with particularity the reasons supporting the need for expedited consideration;

     (ii) who was provided a copy of the motion or given notice of the motion for expedited consideration before the motion was filed, when and how the notice was given, and with whom the movant consulted in accord with subdivision (f)(1); and

     (iii) what agreement, if any, resulted from the consultation with other interested parties.

(3) *Combined Motion.* A motion for expedited consideration may be stated as part of the underlying motion or application for which expedited consideration is requested. The title of the underlying motion or application shall indicate the motion or application also includes a motion for an expedited hearing date or other expedited consideration.

(4) *Papers to Accompany Motion.* The motion for expedited consideration shall be accompanied by

     (i) a proposed order that grants expedited consideration by fixing an early hearing date or other expedited consideration and provides for a method of prompt service of the order as well as the underlying motion or application, and

     (ii) unless a combined motion under paragraph (f)(3) is filed, a copy of the underlying motion or application for which expedited consideration is requested.

(5) *Disposition.* A motion for expedited consideration may be determined without a hearing under L.B.R. 9014–2. If the Court grants an expedited hearing, the court may fix the hearing for the date requested or some other date.

[Effective February 1, 1999.]

SOURCE

Subdivision (a) is new.

Subdivision (b), which is derived from 97 L.B.R. 1017.2(f), is expanded to apply to all scheduled hearings.

Subdivision (c) is a revised version of 97 L.B.R. 9013.2(b).

Subdivisions (d) and (e) are based on 97 L.B.R. 9013.2(a) and (c) respectively. Because time may be an important factor, subdivision (e) authorizes a party seeking rescheduling to request a telephone conference with the court.

Subdivision (f) is a revision of 97 L.B.R. 9014.2. A motion for expedited consideration may be determined without a hearing.

LOCAL RULE 5080–1. FEES— GENERALLY

If a document, other than a petition, for which there is a filing fee is accompanied by an application to waive the filing fee (i) the clerk shall accept the document for filing, and (ii) the document is deemed filed on the day it is delivered to the clerk unless the application is denied and the filing fee is not paid within 14 days of entry of the order denying the application. The application may be determined without hearing.

[Effective February 1, 1999. Amended effective December 1, 2009.]

SOURCE

97 L.B.R. 9004.1(c)

LOCAL RULE 5081–1. FEES— FORM OF PAYMENT

The Clerk shall accept cash, money orders, certified checks, or checks drawn on attorney's accounts made payable to the "Clerk, United States Bankruptcy Court" and the Clerk may also accept major credit cards.

[Effective February 1, 1999.]

SOURCE

This rule is derived from 97 L.B.R. 1002.2(b). Whether a fee may be paid by use of a major credit card is matter within the discretion of the Clerk.

LOCAL RULE 6004–1. MOTION TO SELL FREE AND CLEAR OF LIENS OR OTHER INTERESTS

A motion to sell free and clear of liens or other interests under F.R.B.P. 6004(c) is governed by L.B.R. 9014.3 except that an objection rather than an answer shall be filed and served on the movant or, if the movant is represented, counsel for the movant no later than 14 days after the date on which the movant serves the motion.

[Effective February 1, 1999. Amended effective December 1, 2009.]

SOURCE

This rule is new. Rule 6004(c) requires that if a sale is to be free and clear of liens a motion must be filed. When a motion to sell free and clear is filed the notice of the intent to sell which must be given to all creditors under Rule 6004(a) must include the date of the hearing and the time to file an objection. This rule fixes the time to file an objection to a motion to sell free and clear at 15 days after the date of service. This period is the same as the 15 day period to answer other motions under L.B.R. 9014–3.

LOCAL RULE 6007–1. OBJECTIONS TO ABANDONMENT

(a) Form of Objection. An objection to a proposed abandonment or disposition of property shall identify the objector and state the basis of the objection. An objection shall state in bold type on the right hand side adjacent to the caption the date, time, and place of the hearing on the objection.

(a)* Scheduling of Hearing. Prior to the filing of an objection, the objector shall obtain a hearing date in the manner provided in L.B.R. 5070–1.

(c) Papers to Accompany an Objection. The following papers shall accompany an objection:

(1) A copy of the notice to which objection is made;

(2) A proposed form of order which, if entered by the court, would grant the relief sought by the objection. Each proposed form of order shall list in the lower left-hand corner of the signature page or on the left-hand side of an attached page(s), the names and addresses of interested parties to whom it is suggested copies of the order, if entered, should be sent;

(3) A certification of notice prepared as required by L.B.R. 9014–4.

(d) Notice of the Hearing on Objection. On the day the objection is filed, the objector shall give notice of the date, time, and place of hearing on the objection to the debtor or trustee who gave notice of the proposed abandonment, the United States trustee, and those on the Clerk's Service List. The notice to the debtor or trustee who gave the notice of the proposed abandonment and to the United State trustee shall be accompanied by a copy of the objection.

(c)** No Response Required: Hearing. No response is required to an objection. There shall be a hearing on an objection.

[Effective February 1, 1999.]

* [**Publisher's Note:** So in original. Probably should read "(b)".]

** [**Publisher's Note:** So in original. Probably should read "(e)".]

SOURCE

This rule is new. F.R.B.P. 6007(a) requires that a debtor or trustee give notice of his intent to abandon property of the estate and permits an objection to be filed within 15 days.

LOCAL RULE 7003–1. ADVERSARY PROCEEDING COVER SHEET

Any complaint filed under Part VII of the F.R.B.P. shall be accompanied by an Adversary Proceeding Cover Sheet which shall be provided by the clerk.

[Effective February 1, 1999.]

LOCAL RULE 7005–1. MOTIONS IN ADVERSARY PROCEEDINGS

(a) Incorporation of General Motion Practice. The following L.B.R. apply to motions filed in adversary proceedings:

L.B.R. 9014–3(b)	Form
L.B.R. 9014–3(c)	Scheduling of Hearing
L.B.R. 9014–3(d)	Filing
L.B.R. 9014–3(f)(1)-(3)	Papers to Accompany Motion
L.B.R. 9014–3(i)	Answer to Motion
L.B.R. 9014–3(j)	Determination Without Hearing

(b) Summary Judgment Motions. A summary judgment motion to which no timely answer is filed under L.B.R. 9014–3(i) is governed by Fed.R.Civ.P. 56(c).

(c) Discovery Motions. A motion relating to discovery is governed by L.B.R. 7026–1. A routine motion to compel discovery may be ruled on by the court before the time to answer under L.B.R. 9014–3(i) expires.

[Effective February 1, 1999.]

SOURCE

This rule incorporates most of the general motion practice provisions of L.B.R. 9014–3. Service is made on the parties to the adversary proceeding.

LOCAL RULE 7016–1. PRETRIAL STATEMENT

(a) If the court orders a pretrial statement but does not specify the form and content of the pretrial statement, counsel shall jointly prepare the pretrial statement in the manner described in District Court Local Civil Rule 16.1(d)2.(a) and address the following:

1. Basis of jurisdiction, and also state whether the matter is core or non-core. If the matter is non-core, the parties shall state whether they have consented in their pleadings to the court's entry of a final order under 28 U.S.C. § 157(c)(2) and, if they have not consented in their pleadings, the parties shall state whether they now consent to the court's entry of a final order under 28 U.S.C. § 157(c)(2).

2. Statement of uncontested facts.

3. Statement of facts which are in dispute.

4. *Damages or Other Relief.* A statement of damages claimed or relief sought. A party seeking damages shall list each item claimed under a separate descriptive hearing, shall provide a detailed description of each item and state the amount of damages claimed. A party seeking relief other than damages shall list the exact form of relief sought with precise designations of persons, parties, places and things expected to be included in any order providing relief.

5. Legal issues presented set forth in separate paragraphs and the constitutional, statutory, regulatory and decisional authorities relied on. (Counsel should include a brief statement regarding which party has the burden of proof on each legal issue.)

6. Witnesses' names and addresses listed separately for liability and damages in the order they will be called along with a brief statement of the evidence the witnesses will give. Expert witnesses shall be identified as experts and a summary of the experts' qualifications shall be attached.

7. A list of all exhibits to be offered into evidence which shall be serially numbered and physically marked before trial in accordance with the schedule.

8. A list of each discovery item and trial deposition to be offered into evidence. (Counsel shall designate by page the portion of deposition testimony and by number the interrogatories which shall be offered in evidence at trial.)

9. Estimated trial time.

10. A certification that the parties have attempted good faith settlement discussions without success.

[Effective February 1, 1999. Amended December 11, 2000.]

SOURCE

This rule was initially a revision of 97 L.B.R. 7016.1. It was further modified, effective December 11, 2000, to delete former subdivision (a) as inconsistent with F.R.Civ.P. 26, which became effective on December 1, 2000. Current subdivision (a) is former subdivision (b).

LOCAL RULE 7023–1. CLASS ACTIONS

Rule 23.1 of Local Rules of Civil Procedure of the United States District Court for the Eastern District of Pennsylvania, set forth as follows, shall apply in all adversary proceedings:

Rule 23.1 Class Actions

In any case sought to be maintained as a class action:

(a) The Complaint shall bear next to its caption the legend, "Complaint—Class Action."

(b) The Complaint shall contain under a separate heading, styled "Class Action Allegations."

(1) A reference to the portion or portions of Rule 23, Fed.R.Civ. P., under which it is claimed that the suit is properly maintainable as a class action.

(2) Appropriate allegations thought to justify such claim, including, but not necessarily limited to:

A. The size (or approximate size) and definition of the alleged class,

B. The basis on which the plaintiff (or plaintiffs) claims

(i) to be an adequate representative of the class, or

(ii) if the class is comprised of defendants, that those named as parties are adequate representatives of the class.

C. The alleged questions of law and fact claimed to be common to the class, and

D. In actions claimed to be maintainable as class actions under subdivision (b)(3) of Fed. R.Civ.P. 23, allegations thought to support the findings required by that subdivision.

(c) Within ninety (90) days after the filing of a complaint in a class action, unless this period is extended on motion of good cause appearing, the plaintiff shall move for a determination under subdivision (c)(1) of Fed.R.Civ.P. 23, as to whether the case is to be maintained as a class action. In ruling on a motion, the Court may allow the action to be so maintained, may disallow and strike the class action allegations, or may order postponement of the determination pending discovery of such other preliminary procedures as appear to be appropriate and necessary in the circumstances. Whenever possible, where it is held that the determination should be postponed, a date will be fixed by the Court for renewal of the motion.

(d) The foregoing provisions shall apply, with appropriate adaption, to any counterclaim or cross-claim alleged to be brought for or against a class.

[Effective February 1, 1999.]

SOURCE
97 L.B.R. 7023.1.

LOCAL RULE 7026–1. DISCOVERY

(a) General. Rule 26.1(a)-(f) of the Local Rules of Civil Procedure of the United States District Court for the Eastern District of Pennsylvania, set forth as follows, shall apply in all proceedings:

Rule 26.1 Discovery

(a) Interrogatories, requests for production and inspection and requests for admission under Fed. R.Civ.P. 33, 34 and 36, answers, responses, and objections to interrogatories and to requests under Fed.R.Civ.P. Rules 34 and 36, and notices of deposition and depositions under Fed.R.Civ.P. 30 and 31 shall not be filed with the court. The party serving the discovery material or taking the deposition shall retain the original and be the custodian of it.

(b) Every motion under the Federal Rules of Civil Procedure governing discovery shall identify and set forth, verbatim, the relevant parts of the interrogatory, request, answer, response, objection, notice, or subpoena, or dispositions. Any party responding to the motion shall set forth, verbatim, in that party's memorandum any other part that the party believes necessary to the Court's consideration of the motion.

(c) If material in interrogatories, requests, answers, responses, or depositions is used as evidence in connection with any motion, the relevant parts shall be set forth, verbatim, in the moving papers or in responding memoranda. If it is used as evidence at trial, the party offering it shall read it into the record, or if directed to do so by the Court, offer it as an exhibit.

(d) The Court shall resolve any dispute that may arise about the accuracy of any quotation or discovery material used as provided in sections (b) and (c) and may require production of the original paper or transcript.

(e) The Court, on its own motion, on motion by any party or an application by a non-party, may require the filing of the original of any discovery paper or deposition transcript. The parties may provide for such filing by stipulation.

(f) No motion or other application under the Federal Rules of Civil Procedure governing discovery or under this rule shall be made unless it contains a certification of counsel that the parties, after reasonable effort, are unable to resolve the dispute.

(b) Motions to Compel. A routine motion to compel answers to interrogatories or to compel compliance with a request for production under Fed.R.Civ.P. 34, because no response or objection has been timely served, shall be accompanied by a copy of the interrogatories or Rule 34 request but a brief need not be filed. The court may summarily grant or deny such motion without waiting for a response.

[Effective February 1, 1999. Amended December 11, 2000.]

SOURCE
Former subdivision (a) was deleted, effective December 11, 2000, as inconsistent with F.R.Civ.P. 26, which became effective December 1, 2000. Current subdivision (a) is former subdivision (b) and is the same as 97 L.B.R. 7037.1. The

reference to the Local Civil Rule is now to Local Civil Rule 26 to conform to the 1995 amendments to Local Civil Rules. Current subdivision (b) is former subdivision (c) and is a revised version of Local Civil Rule 26.1(g).

Subdivision (b) is the same as 97 L.B.R. 7037.1. The reference to the Local Civil Rule is now to Local Civil Rule 26 to conform to the 1995 amendments to Local Civil Rules.

Subdivision (c) is a revised version of Local Civil Rule 26.1(g).

LOCAL RULE 7041–1. NOTICE OF DISMISSAL OF ADVERSARY PROCEEDING

Before any adversary proceeding shall be involuntarily dismissed as to a debtor or other party who is the plaintiff in any adversary proceeding, notice shall be given by the clerk to the debtor or the party and to their counsel.

[Effective February 1, 1999.]

SOURCE

97 L.B.R. 7041.1.

LOCAL RULE 7041–2. SETTLEMENT OF ADVERSARY PROCEEDINGS AND CONTESTED MATTERS

Whenever, in an adversary proceeding or contested matter, counsel notifies the courtroom deputy for the judge to whom the adversary proceeding or contested matter is assigned that the issues between the parties have been settled, the parties shall file any necessary stipulation and any requisite motion to compromise or settle within 30 days, or the adversary proceeding or contested matter may be dismissed at the discretion of the court. A motion to extend the time, for cause shown, may be filed within the 30 day period.

[Effective February 1, 1999.]

SOURCE

This rule is a revised version of 97 L.B.R. 7041.2.

LOCAL RULE 8001–1. TRANSMITTAL OF NOTICE OF APPEAL TO BANKRUPTCY JUDGE: OPINION IN SUPPORT OF ORDER

(a) **Transmittal of Notice of Appeal to Bankruptcy Judge.** On the day a notice of appeal is filed, an appellant shall mail or deliver a copy of the notice of appeal to the bankruptcy judge whose order is the subject of the appeal. The failure of an appellant to provide a copy of the notice of appeal to the bankruptcy judge shall not affect the jurisdiction of the district court to hear the appeal.

(b) **Opinion in Support of Order.** The bankruptcy judge whose order is the subject of an appeal may,

within 14 days of the filing of the notice of appeal, file a written opinion in support of the order or a written supplemental opinion that amplifies any earlier written opinion or recorded oral bench ruling or opinion.

[Effective February 1, 1999. Amended effective December 1, 2009.]

SOURCE

This rule is derived from L.A.R. 3.1 of the Third Circuit's Local Rules. Under subdivision (b) of this rule, a bankruptcy judge has the same opportunity as a district judge to file an opinion after an appeal has been taken.

LOCAL RULE 8001–2. MOTIONS FILED IN CONNECTION WITH AN APPEAL

(a) **General.**

(1) This rule applies to motions relating to an appeal that may be determined by a bankruptcy judge, including a motion under F.R.B.P 8001(c)(1) to withdraw an appeal before the appeal is docketed; under F.R.B.P 8002(c) for an extension of the time to appeal, if the motion is filed after the expiration of the time to appeal; and under F.R.B.P 8005 for a stay of the judgment, order, or decree appealed from.

(2) A motion under F.R.B.P. 8002(c) for an extension of the time to appeal, if the motion is filed before the expiration of the time to appeal, is governed by Rule 9014–3, Motions Determined Without Hearing.

(b) **Incorporation of General Motion Practice.** The following L.B.R. apply to a motion relating to an appeal that may be determined by a bankruptcy judge:

L.B.R. 9014–3(b)	Form
L.B.R. 9014–3(c)	Scheduling of Hearing
L.B.R. 9014–3(d)	Filing
L.B.R. 9014–3(f)(1)-(3)	Papers to Accompany Motion
L.B.R. 9014–3(i)	Answer to Motion
L.B.R. 9014–3(j)	Determination Without Hearing

(c) **Service of Motion.** On the day the motion is filed, the movant shall, in accordance with F.R.B.P. 8008(b), serve a Notice of Motion and Hearing Date substantially in the form of L.B.F. 9014–3, the proposed order, and a copy of the motion (assembled in that order) on the parties to the appeal, or, if represented, their counsel of record.

[Effective February 1, 1999.]

SOURCE

The three motions listed in subdivision (a)(1) require disposition by the bankruptcy judge. The motion practice for these motions is the same as the general motion practice under L.B.R. 9014–3 except that under subdivision (c) of this rule service is made only on the parties to the appeal. Notice does not have to be provided to those on the Clerk's Service List.

A motion for leave to appeal under 28 U.S.C. § 158(a), which is governed by F.R.B.P. 8003, is not subject to L.B.R. 8001–1. Although this motion and an answer to the motion are filed with the clerk of the bankruptcy court, the district court rules on the motion.

LOCAL RULE 9004–1. PAPERS

(a) General. All papers submitted to the clerk for filing shall measure 8½ x 11 inches and shall be stapled or fastened at the top.

(b) Date Stamped Copies of Filed Papers.

(1) The clerk shall, if requested at the time of filing, date-stamp one copy of any paper that is filed.

(2) If a paper that is filed by mail is accompanied by a copy of the paper and a self-addressed, stamped envelope, the clerk shall date-stamp the copy and mail the copy to the person who filed the paper.

[Effective February 1, 1999.]

SOURCE

This rule is a revision of 97 L.B.R. 9004.1(a)-(c).

LOCAL RULE 9004–2. CAPTION

All pleadings, motions, applications, objections, and any other papers filed with the clerk shall contain a caption in a form described as follows:

(i) appearing at the top of the first page and centered thereon shall be:

UNITED STATES BANKRUPTCY COURT
FOR THE EASTERN DISTRICT
OF PENNSYLVANIA

(ii) appearing below the name of the court and to the left of center shall be the name of the debtor who shall be identified as such. In an adversary proceeding only, the name of the plaintiff and the defendant in that order shall be shown below that of the debtor;

(iii) appearing below the name of the court and to the right of center shall be the chapter of the case in which the pleading is being filed;

(iv) appearing below the chapter of the case shall be the bankruptcy number of the case and, if applicable, any adversary number; and

(v) appearing below that which is specified in (i) through (iv) of this rule, and centered shall be the full title of the pleading, motion, application, objection, or other paper which includes the name of the proponent and describes the relief requested.

[Effective February 1, 1999.]

SOURCE

This rule is the same as 97 L.B.R. 9004.2 except for the addition of the phrase "describes the relief requested" at the end of the last paragraph of the rule. This addition is intended to make it clear that the title of a motion, applica-tion, or other paper should effectively communicate what relief is sought from the court. A title adequately describes the relief requested if it is plain from the title what the motion, application, or other paper is about and what specific relief is sought. For example, if the motion is for relief from the automatic stay to permit foreclosure of a lien on real property, the title of the motion should state as follows: "Motion of Bank of Philadelphia for Relief from the Automat-ic Stay to Permit the Bank of Philadelphia to Foreclose on 333 Main Street, Philadelphia, PA."

LOCAL RULE 9008–1. PUBLICATION OF NOTICES

(a) General. Whenever a notice is to be given by publication, unless the court orders otherwise, the notice shall be published one time in a newspaper of general circulation in the county of the debtor's last known address and one time in the legal periodical, if any, that serves that county.

(b) Official Newspaper. The Legal Intelligencer of Philadelphia, Pennsylvania, is hereby designated as the official newspaper of the United States Bankrupt-cy Court for the Eastern District of Pennsylvania for the publication of notices of petitions filed, discharges granted or denied, opinions entered, trial lists, dis-missals, the official rules and any other announcement concerning court administration.

[Effective February 1, 1999.]

SOURCE

This rule is a revision of 97 L.B.R. 9008.1.

LOCAL RULE 9010–1. ATTORNEYS— APPEARANCE

(a) Notice of Appearance. A notice of appearance filed under F.R.B.P. 9010(b) shall also include the fax number of the attorney filing the appearance.

(b) Filing Petition as Appearance for Debtor. The filing of a petition in bankruptcy by an attorney on behalf of a debtor shall constitute an entry of appearance in any and all matters arising during the administration of the case including, but not limited to, all applications, motions, and adversary proceed-ings.

(c) Filing Paper as Appearance. An attorney who files any application, motion, stipulation, or other pa-per with the clerk shall be deemed to have entered an appearance for the party on whose behalf the paper is filed.

(d) Change of Address: Filing. Any attorney who has entered an appearance shall advise the clerk of any change of address of the attorney's office, or a change of address of the entity on whose behalf the attorney has made an entry of appearance, by filing with the clerk a Request to Note Change of Address which shall request that the clerk note the change of address on the bankruptcy court docket and the Clerk's Service List.

(e) Change of Address: Notice. An attorney who files a request under subdivision (d) shall mail a copy of the request to any trustee in the case and to any attorney who has entered an appearance in an adversary proceeding or contested matter which is pending at the time the above request is filed with the clerk.

[Effective February 1, 1999.]

SOURCE

Subdivision (a) is new.

Subdivision (b) is the same as 97 L.B.R. 9010.2.

Subdivisions (c)-(e) are the same as subdivisions (c)-(e) respectively of 97 L.B.R. 9010.1.

LOCAL RULE 9011–1. INFORMATION ACCOMPANYING SIGNATURE

Any document filed in the case shall include the name, address, telephone number and the fax number of the person signing the document.

[Effective February 1, 1999.]

SOURCE

This rule is new.

LOCAL RULE 9013–1. APPLICATIONS

(a) Form. An application shall identify the applicant, the nature of the relief sought, and the basis for the relief sought.

(b) Papers to Accompany Applications. The following papers shall accompany each application:

(1) a proposed form of order which, if entered by the court, would grant the relief sought by the application. Each proposed form of order shall list, in the lower left-hand corner of the signature page or on the left-hand side of an attached page(s), the names and addresses of all interested persons to whom it is suggested that copies of the order, if entered, should be sent, and

(2) if the court imposes a general requirement that applications be accompanied by a cover sheet, a cover sheet substantially conforming to the form of cover sheet that accompanies the court's order.

(c) Applications for Compensation of a Professional. L.B.R. 2016 governs the giving of notice and the service as well as the time to object to an application for compensation of a professional.

(d) Applications Considered Without a Hearing. The court may consider without a hearing an application

(1) under F.R.B.P. 1006(b) for payment of filing fees in installments;

(2) under F.R.B.P. 2007.1(c) for approval of the appointment of an elected or appointed trustee or an examiner;

(3) under F.R.B.P. 2014(a) for approval of the employment of bankruptcy counsel to represent a trustee, debtor in possession, or a creditors' committee; or

(4) under L.B.R. 5080–1 for waiver of a filing fee.

(e) Accelerated Procedure. An application which is permitted under F.R.B.P., but is not governed by subdivisions (c) or (d), is governed by this subdivision. This subdivision applies to an application under F.R.B.P. 2014(a) for approval of the employment of a professional who will serve in a case as other than bankruptcy counsel and under F.R.B.P. 3017.1 and L.B.R. 3016–(g)* for conditional approval of a disclosure statement.

(1) *Notice.* On the day an application is filed, the applicant shall give notice of the filing of the application and of the requirement that any objection to the application must be filed and served on the applicant, or if the applicant is represented, counsel for the applicant within 7 days of the date on which the application is filed to the

(i) the debtor;

(ii) the United States trustee;

(iii) any trustee or interim trustee; and

(iv) any official committee or, if no committee has been appointed in a chapter 11 case, 20 largest unsecured creditors of the debtor;

(2) *Certification of Notice and Whether any Objection Has Been Filed.* After the expiration of the 7 day period to file an objection, the applicant shall file a certification of notice, prepared as required by L.B.R. 9014–4, which also certifies whether any timely objection has been filed.

(3) *Disposition of Application.* After the filing of a Certification of Notice under subdivision (e)(3),

(i) if the applicant certifies no timely objection has been filed, the court shall rule on the motion, or

(ii) if the applicant certifies a timely objection has been filed, the court may either rule on the motion or set a hearing date.

(4) *Notice of Hearing.* If the court sets a hearing date for an application, the clerk shall give notice of the hearing to the applicant, the objector, and any other person the court directs.

(f) Service of Application to Employ a Professional. On the day an application to employ a professional is filed, the applicant shall serve a copy of the application on those specified in L.B.R. 2014–1(b).

[Effective February 1, 1999. Amended effective December 1, 2009.]

* [**Publishers Note:** So in original. Probably should be "L.B.R. 3016–1(g)".]

SOURCE

This rule is derived from 97 L.B.R. 9013–3. Only requests for relief which are authorized to be made by application under the F.R.B.P. are subject to this rule. Under subdivision (b)(2) a cover sheet does not have to be filed with an application; however, the court may in the future order that a cover sheet be filed. The period within which to object to an application governed by L.B.R. 9013–1(e) has been changed from five to eight days because amended F.R.B.P. 9006(a) now provides that weekends and legal holidays are excluded from the computation of the time to act if the period to act is less than eight days.

LOCAL RULE 9014–1. MOTIONS

(a) **Motions for Withdrawal.** A motion for withdrawal of a case or proceeding is governed by L.B.R. 5011–1.

(b) **Motions Filed in an Adversary Proceeding.** A motion filed in adversary proceeding is governed by L.B.R. 7005–1.

(c) **Motions Filed in Connection With an Appeal.** A motion filed in connection with an appeal is governed by L.B.R. 8001–1.

(d) **Other Motions Filed in a Case.** A motion filed in a case means a motion that is not subject to subdivisions (a)-(c) or this rule. A motion filed in a case is governed by either L.B.R. 9014–2, Motions Determined Without Hearing, or L.B.R. 9014–3, General Motion Practice.

[Effective February 1, 1999.]

SOURCE

This rule is new. All requests for relief, except where the F.R.B.P. provide for use of an application, are made by motion. F.R.B.P. 9013.

Subdivision (a). L.B.R. 5011–1 establishes a procedure for a movant who files a motion for withdrawal to also file a copy of the motion in the district court and thereby trigger a specific procedure for obtaining a resolution of the motion by the district court.

Subdivisions (b) and (c). Separate rules for motion practice in adversary proceedings and appeals are set forth respectively in L.B.R. 7005–1 and 8001–1 because there is no need to provide service or notice to anyone other than the parties in the adversary proceeding or to the appeal. The motion practice under these two rules is otherwise the same as the general motion practice under L.B.R. 9014–3.

Subdivision (d). The general motion practice under L.B.R. 9014–3 is derived from 97 L.B.R. 9014.1. An order directing any answer is no longer necessary. L.B.R. 9014–3(i) provides that an answer must be filed within 15 days. In addition, it is no longer necessary to provide a copy of a motion to those on the Clerk's Service List. Instead, those on the Clerk's Service List are provided with notice of the motion and may request a copy of the motion from the movant. The movant obtains a hearing date prior to filing the motion.

L.B.R. 9014–2, Motions Determined Without Hearing, provides that for certain motions no notice need be given and service need only be made on the trustee or debtor in possession and, in a chapter 11 case, the committee. No answer is required and a hearing is not scheduled. Rather, the court determines whether the motion will be granted or denied based on the motion. The court may, however, elect to require an answer or to set a hearing.

LOCAL RULE 9014–2. MOTIONS DETERMINED WITHOUT HEARING

(a) **Applicability.** This rule applies to a motion

(1) under § 362(j) for entry of an order under § 362(c) confirming that the automatic stay has been terminated;

(2) under §§ 1225(c) or 1325(c) for entry of a wage order;

(3) under F.R.B.P. 1007(a)(4) or 1007(c) or (e) for an extension of time;

(4) under L.B.R. 1017–1(a) or 1017–2(a) to convert or dismiss a case;

(5) under F.R.B.P. 2002(h) or (i) to limit notice;

(6) under L.B.R. 2090–1(c)(2) to appear pro hac vice;

(7) under F.R.B.P. 3003(c) to fix the time within which proofs of claim or interest may be filed;

(8) under F.R.B.P. 4004(c) and L.B.R. 4004–1(a) to defer entry of a discharge order;

(9) under L.B.R. 5070–1(f) for expedited consideration;

(10) under F.R.B.P. 9006(b)(1) for enlargement of the time to act made before the time to act expired;

(11) under F.R.B.P. 9006(c)(1) for reduction of the time to act;

(12) under F.R.B.P. 9023, if the motion does not include a request for a hearing, to alter or amend an order awarding an applicant less than the requested amount of compensation and reimbursement of expenses; and

(13) to limit service of papers or notice otherwise prescribed by these rules.

(b) **Form, Accompanying Order, and Cover Sheet.** A motion shall identify the movant, the nature of the relief sought, and the basis for the relief sought and be accompanied by (i) a proposed form of order which, if entered by the court would grant the relief requested; (ii) a certification of service as required under subdivision (c); and (iii) if the court imposes a general requirement that motions be accompanied by a cover sheet, a cover sheet substantially conforming to the form of cover sheet that accompanies the court's order.

(c) Service. On the day a motion is filed, a movant shall make service on the trustee and the debtor and, in a chapter 11 case, on the official committee and the United States trustee.

(d) Disposition. The court may rule on a motion without a hearing.

[Effective February 1, 1999. Amended effective February 26, 2008.]

SOURCE

The rule is derived from 97 L.B.R. 9013–3(b), which governed *ex parte* applications.

This rule provides that for the motions listed in subdivision (b) no notice need be given and service need only be made on the trustee or debtor in possession, and in a chapter 11 case, the committee. No answer is required and a hearing is not scheduled. Rather, the court determines whether the motion will be granted or denied based on the motion. The court may, however, elect to require an answer or to set a hearing.

EXPLANATORY NOTE (2008)

The new subsections are L.B.R. 9014–2(a)(1) and 9014–2(a)(7). The other subsections have been renumbered appropriately.

LOCAL RULE 9014–3. GENERAL MOTION PRACTICE

(a) Applicability. This rule applies to a motion in a case that is not governed by L.B.R. 9014–2, *Motions Determined Without Hearing.*

(b) Form. A motion shall identify the movant, the nature of the relief sought, and the basis for the relief sought. A motion shall state in bold type on the right-hand side adjacent to the caption the date, time and place set for the hearing scheduled under subdivision (c) of this rule.

(c) Scheduling of Hearing. Prior to filing a motion, the movant shall obtain a hearing date in the manner provided in L.B.R. 5070–1.

(d) Filing. The movant shall file a motion no later than 2 days after the day on which the hearing date is assigned.

(e) Discovery. Rule 7026 is applicable to contested matters but the following provisions of F.R.C.P. 26 do not apply to contested matters:

(1) the disclosure requirements of Rule 26(a)(1)–(3);

(2) the prohibition on discovery until the discovery conference under Rule 26(d); and

(3) the requirements for a discovery conference and the submission of a discovery plan under Rule 26(f).

(f) Papers to Accompany Motion. The following papers shall accompany each motion:

(1) a proposed form of order which, if entered by the court, would grant the relief sought by the motion. Each proposed form of order shall list, in the lower left-hand corner of the signature page or on the left-hand side of an attached page(s), the names and addresses of all interested persons to whom it is suggested that copies of the order, if entered, should be sent;

(2) a certification of service and notice prepared as required by L.B.R. 9014–4; and

(3) if the court imposes a general requirement that motions be accompanied by a cover sheet, a cover sheet that conforms substantially to the cover sheet that accompanies the court's order.

(g) Service of Motion.

(1) *General.* On the day the motion is filed, the movant shall serve a Notice of Motion and Hearing Date substantially in the form of L.B.F. 9014–3, the proposed order, and a copy of the motion (assembled in that order) on the following parties, or, if represented, their counsel of record:

(i) the debtor and counsel to the debtor;

(ii) the United States trustee;

(iii) any trustee or interim trustee;

(iv) any official committee or, if no committee has been appointed in a chapter 11 case, the 20 largest unsecured creditors of the debtor;

(v) any person whose interest would be directly, materially and adversely affected if the relief requested in the motion were granted and whose interests are not adequately represented by persons on whom service is otherwise required.

(2) *Expedited Service.* If a courtesy copy of the motion is delivered to chambers by expedited delivery, service under this subdivision shall also be made by expedited delivery.

(h) Notice.

(1) On the day the motion is filed, a movant shall give notice substantially in the form of L.B.F. 9014–3 of the filing of the motion, the relief sought, the hearing date, and, either (i) the time to file an answer within the time prescribed by subdivision (h), or (ii) the time to file an objection within the time prescribed by F.R.B.P. 3015(g) (to a motion to modify a confirmed chapter 12 or 13 plan); L.B.R. 3016–1(e) (to a motion for approval of a disclosure statement); F.R.B.P. 4001(d)(2) (to a motion for approval of an agreement); or L.B.R. 6004–1 (to a motion to sell free and clear of liens or other interests).

(2) The notice shall be given to those on the Clerk's Service List who are not required to be served under subdivision (f). A movant, at the movant's expense, shall promptly furnish a copy of the motion and proposed order to anyone on the Clerk's Service List who requests a copy of the particular motion. A movant may make service in the manner provided in

subdivision (f) instead of giving notice under this subdivision.

(i) Answer or Objection to Motion. Unless the court grants a motion for expedited consideration or otherwise fixes a different time, an answer to a motion shall be filed and served on the movant, or if the movant is represented, counsel for the movant no later than 14 days after the date on which the movant serves the motion. An objection to a motion shall be filed and served in the manner and within the time provided under F.R.B.P. 3015(g), L.B.R. 3016–1(e), F.R.B.P. 4001(d)(2), or L.B.R. 6004–1.

(j) Determination Without Hearing if No Answer or Objection Timely Filed. If an answer or objection is required to be filed and no timely answer or objection is filed, the movant may file a certification of no opposition with the court and, unless a hearing is required under the F.R.B.P., may request that the court grant the relief requested in the motion without a hearing. The courtroom deputy for the judge to whom the case is assigned may be contacted to ascertain whether the hearing has been canceled.

(k) Stipulated Disposition of a Disputed Motion. L.B.R. 7041–2 applies if after an answer is filed or a hearing is convened and the movant and the parties who have opposed the motion agree to a stipulated disposition of the motion.

(*l*) Supplemental Requirements of the F.R.B.P. In addition to the service and notice required under subdivisions (f) and (g) of this rule, a movant also shall serve any party on whom service must be made under the F.R.B.P. and give notice to any party who must be given notice under the F.R.B.P. If the F.R.B.P. requires that the court conduct a hearing, a movant's certification of no timely filing of an answer or objection shall not include a request that the motion be determined without a hearing.

[Effective February 1, 1999. Amended effective December 11, 2000; December 1, 2009.]

SOURCE

This rule, which is derived from 97 L.B.R. 9014.1, changes general motion practice in some important ways. An order directing an answer is no longer necessary. L.B.R. 9014–3(i) provides that an answer must be filed within 15 days. It is no longer necessary to provide a copy of a motion to those on the Clerk's Service List. Instead, those on the Clerk's Service List are provided with notice of the motion and may request a copy of the motion from the movant. The movant obtains a hearing date prior to filing the motion. A cover sheet does not have to be filed with the motion.

The F.R.B.P have two rules which refer to motion practice. Rule 9013 requires that a request for relief be made by motion unless the F.R.B.P. authorize the filing of an application. A movant must file a motion, Rule 5005(a)(1), and must serve it "on the trustee or debtor in possession." Rule 9013.

L.B.R. 9014–3 spells out the mechanics of motion practice, including the following

—how to obtain a hearing date before filing a motion;

—what papers must be filed with a motion;

—who, in addition to the trustee or debtor in possession, must be served with the motion;

—who must be given notice of a motion and the hearing date;

—the time within which an answer must be filed; and

—the certification procedure to be followed if no answer is filed and the movant elects to request that the motion be determined without a hearing.

A motion filed in a case, other than a motion subject to L.B.R. 9014–2, is governed by L.B.R. 9014–3.

Motion practice under L.B.R. 9014–3 works in this way. A movant consults with court's courtroom deputy before the motion is filed and obtains a hearing date. The motion and the Notice of Motion and Hearing Date are served as a matter of course on the debtor, the trustee, the United States trustee, any official committee, and any person who will be materially and adversely affected if the motion is granted. Notice of the motion and the hearing date must be given to all persons on the Clerk's Service List who have not been served. If a timely answer is not filed, the movant may so certify and request that the motion be determined without a hearing.

For a small number of motions, compliance with L.B.R. 9014–3 does not fulfill the movant's obligation under the F.R.B.P. because the applicable rule of the F.R.B.P. requires either service or notice in addition to that required under L.B.R. 9014–3. Subdivision (*l*) is included in L.B.R. 9014–3 in order to call counsel's attention to the need to consult the applicable F.R.B.P.

Note:

Subdivision (e) was added, effective December 11, 2000, in order to maintain, as much as possible, the current practice in contested matters in light of the amendments to F.R.Civ.P. 26, which became effective on December 1, 2000.

L.B.F. 9014–3. NOTICE OF MOTION, RESPONSE DEADLINE AND HEARING DATE

UNITED STATES BANKRUPTCY COURT
FOR THE EASTERN DISTRICT
OF PENNSYLVANIA

In re: : Chapter
                   :
Debtor   : Bankruptcy No.

* * * * *

NOTICE OF MOTION, RESPONSE DEADLINE AND HEARING DATE

(*Name of movant*) has filed (*specify name of motion*) with the court for (*describe the relief sought in the motion*).

Your rights may be affected. You should read these papers carefully and discuss them with your

attorney, if you have one in this bankruptcy case. (If you do not have an attorney, you may wish to consult an attorney.)

1. If you do not want the court to grant the relief sought in the motion or if you want the court to consider your views on the motion, then on or before XX/XX/XX you or your attorney must do <u>all</u> of the following:

(a) file an answer explaining your position at

(*address of bankruptcy clerk's office*   )

If you mail your answer to the bankruptcy clerk's office for filing, you must mail it early enough so that it will be received on or before the date stated above; and

(b) mail a copy to the movant's attorney:

[Attorney's name]_____

[Firm name]_____

[Address]_____

[Phone No.]_____

[Fax No.]_____

[If applicable, name and address of others to be served.]

2. If you or your attorney do not take the steps described in paragraphs 1(a) and 1(b) above and attend the hearing, the court may enter an order granting the relief requested in the motion.

3. A hearing on the motion is scheduled to be held before the Honorable (*name of bankruptcy judge*) on XX/XX/XX, at _____ in Courtroom _____, United States Bankruptcy Court, (*address of Bankruptcy Court*).

4. If a copy of the motion is not enclosed, a copy of the motion will be provided to you if you request a copy from the attorney named in paragraph 1(b).

5. You may contact the Bankruptcy Clerk's office(s) in Philadelphia at 215–408–2800 or Reading at 610–208–5040 to find out whether the hearing has been canceled because no one filed an answer.

Date: _____, _____

[Effective February 1, 1999. Amended effective February 1, 2003; February 23, 2016.]

SOURCE

This form is derived from Official Form 20A.

L.B.R. 9004–2 provides in paragraph (v) that the caption of a motion shall contain "the full title of the....motion which includes the name of the .... [movant] and describes the relief requested." A title of a motion adequately describes the relief requested if it is plain from the title what the motion is about and what specific relief is sought. For example, if the motion is for relief from the automatic stay to permit foreclosure of a lien on real property, the title of the motion should state as

follows: "Motion of Bank of Philadelphia for Relief from the Automatic Stay to Permit the Bank of Philadelphia to Foreclose on 333 Main Street, Philadelphia, PA."

The first paragraph of the L.B.F. 9014–3 also requires the movant to "describe the relief sought in the motion." If the movant has properly titled the motion as required by L.B.R. 9004–2, that description of the relief requested may be used in the L.B.F. 9014–3 Notice of Motion. If there is any doubt about whether the title of the caption is adequate, the movant should substitute in the Notice of Motion a description of the relief requested that does adequately describe the relief requested.

This form may have to be adapted in some situations.

1. If an objection to the motion is the proper response, "objection" should be substituted for "answer." It should also be noted that the time for filing an objection may be established by a specific F.R.B.P. or a L.B.R. rather than the 15 day period of L.B.R. 9014–3(i). An objection to modification of a confirmed chapter 12 or 13 plan must be filed within 20 days, F.R.B.P. 3015(g), and an objection to a disclosure statement must be filed no later than five days before the hearing, L.B.R. 3016–1(e). On the other hand, objections to a motion to sell free and clear, L.B.R. 6004–1, and for approval of an agreement under F.R.B.P. 4004(d)(2) must be filed within 15 days.

2. Under L.B.R. 9014–3(h), notice of a motion must be given only to those on the Clerk's Service List, but the movant must provide a copy to anyone on the Clerk's Service List who requests a copy. Paragraph 4 is appropriate when the notice is provided only to those on the Clerk's Service List. If notice is given to all creditors, paragraph 4 should be amended to read.

If a copy of the motion is not enclosed, a copy of the motion will be provided to you if you are on the Clerk's Service List and you request a copy from the attorney named in paragraph 1(b).

LOCAL RULE 9014–4. CERTIFICATION OF SERVICE OR NOTICE

(a) **Service.** A certification of service of an application, motion, objection, or other paper filed with the court shall state the title of the paper served, the names of all persons on whom and the address where the paper has been served, the entities those persons represent, and when and how service has been made.

(b) **Notice.** A certification of notice shall include (1) the text of the notice that was given or be accompanied by a copy of the notice that was given; and (2) contain the names of all persons on whom and the address where the notice has been given, the entities those persons represent, and when and how notice has been given.

(c) **Combined Certification.** A certification of service and a certification of notice may be combined.

[Effective February 1, 1999.]

SOURCE

This rule is a revised version of 97 L.B.R. 9013.1. Subdivision (b) explicitly covers the form of certification of notice.

LOCAL RULE 9015–1. JURY TRIAL

A statement of consent to have a jury trial conducted by a bankruptcy judge specially designated to conduct a jury trial under 28 U.S.C. § 157(e) shall be filed and served (1) by a party demanding a jury trial within the time permitted under F.R.Civ.P. 38(b) to demand a jury trial, and (2) by all other parties within 14 days of the timely filing of a statement of consent by the party demanding a jury trial.

[Effective February 1, 1999. Amended effective December 1, 2009.]

SOURCE

On December 1, 1997, a new F.R.B.P. 9015 became effective. New F.R.B.P. 9015(b) leaves to local rule making the determination of when a consent to a jury trial before a bankruptcy judge specially designated to conduct a jury trial under 28 U.S.C. 157(e) must be filed.

F.R.B.P. 9015(a) makes F.R.Civ.P. 38 applicable to bankruptcy cases and proceedings. Under Rule 38(b), a demand for a jury trial must be filed and served "not later than 10 days after the service of a last pleading directed" to the issue or issues for which a jury trial is demanded. Under L.B.R. 9015–1, the party demanding a jury trial must also file and serve a statement of consent to a jury trial before the bankruptcy judge within the 10 day period of Rule 38(b). If a statement of consent is timely filed by the party demanding a jury trial, the other parties have 10 days from the filing of that consent to file their own consents. If the consents of all of the other parties are filed within the 10 day period, the bankruptcy court may conduct the jury trial.

LOCAL RULE 9019–1. SETTLEMENTS AND AGREED ORDERS

In any matter in which a proponent of a settlement or stipulation in a case or adversary proceeding seeks court approval without notice to those specified in F.R.B.P. 9019 and 2002, the proponent shall state with particularity the reasons why such notice is not necessary.

[Effective February 1, 1999.]

SOURCE

97 L.B.R. 9019.1.

LOCAL RULE 9019–2. ARBITRATION

Any adversary proceeding classified by the plaintiff's counsel as an action to recover money damages not in excess of $150,000 shall be subject to compulsory arbitration before a panel of arbitrators. The procedure for arbitration shall be that set forth in Rule 53.2 of the Local Rules of Civil Procedure of the United States District Court for the Eastern District of Pennsylvania, the procedures of which Rule are hereby adopted as part of these Rules. The trial de novo under that Rule shall be to the bankruptcy court.

[Effective February 1, 1999. Amended effective March 1, 2000.]

SOURCE

Amended pursuant to the February 28, 2000, Order of the U.S. District Court for the Eastern District of Pennsylvania and effective March 1, 2000.

LOCAL RULE 9019–3. MEDIATION

(a) Certification of Mediators. The Chief Judge shall certify as many mediators as the Chief Judge determines are necessary.

(b) Application. An application for certification as a mediator may be obtained from the clerk. A properly completed application may be submitted to the clerk.

(c) Selection Criteria.

(1) *Attorney Applicants.* An attorney admitted to the bar of this court under L.B.R. 2090–1 may be certified as a mediator if the attorney (i) has served as a mediator on a regular basis or participated in or is willing to participate in formal mediation training and (ii) has been involved actively for at least 3 years

    (A) as counsel of record in bankruptcy cases either for the debtor, debtor in possession, trustee, or creditors' committee, or for a party to adversary proceedings or contested matters; or

    (B) as an academic or practicing attorney in matters that involve legal or factual issues or business transactions that are the subject of litigation before this court.

(2) *Non–Attorney Applicants.* A person who is not an attorney may be certified as a mediator if the person (i) has served as a mediator on a regular basis or participated in or is willing to participate in formal mediation training and (ii) has been involved actively for at least three (3) years

    (A) as a professional in bankruptcy cases; or

    (B) as a participant or a professional in matters that involve legal or factual issues or business transactions that are the subject of litigation before this court.

(d) Register of Certified Mediators: Retention of Appointment Orders. The clerk shall maintain a Register of Certified Mediators and provide a copy of the Register on request. Orders appointing mediators shall be retained by the clerk and the clerk shall maintain a record of each mediator's appointments.

(e) Orders Appointing a Mediator. Any matter arising in a case, other than an adversary proceeding subject to compulsory arbitration under L.B.R. 9019–2, may be assigned for mediation. The court, on its own motion, or on the request of a party may assign a matter for mediation. If the court determines a matter will be assigned for mediation, the court, after consultation with the parties, shall appoint a mediator from the Register of Certified Mediators. The clerk shall mail promptly a copy of the order to the mediator.

(f) Compensation. A mediator who accepts an appointment volunteers the time expended to prepare for the mediation and to conduct a mediation conference or conferences lasting up to four (4) hours. After completion of four (4) hours in a mediation conference or conferences, the mediator may either (i) continue to volunteer the mediator's time or (ii) give the parties the option to agree to pay the mediator $150 per hour for additional time spent on the mediation. The parties shall each pay a pro rata share of the mediator's compensation, unless they agree to some other allocation of the obligation to pay the fee. A motion to enforce a party's obligation under this subdivision to compensate a mediator is governed by L.B.R. 9014–3.

(g) Disqualification to Serve as Mediator. Mediators shall be disqualified for bias or prejudice as provided in 28 U.S.C. § 144 and shall disqualify themselves from proceeding with any appointment when they would be required to disqualify themselves under 28 U.S.C. § 455 if they were a justice, judge, or magistrate judge. Within 7 days of receiving an order of appointment the mediator shall notify the clerk that the appointment is accepted and there is no ground for disqualification or that mediator is disqualified.

(h) Confidentiality: Service of Mediator's Law Firm. A mediator shall treat all information obtained during the mediation process as confidential. A mediator's law firm is not automatically disqualified from employment as a professional in a case or from representing a party in the case solely because of the mediator's prior service in a case. If the mediator's law firm is employed as a professional in a case or undertakes representation of a party in the case and disclosure of information obtained by the mediator in the mediation would be harmful, an appropriate screening mechanism shall be established by the mediator's law firm to insure the mediator has no connection with the law firm's discharge of its responsibilities in the case.

(i) Parties to the Mediation. On the request of the mediator or on the court's own motion, the court may direct that additional parties participate in the mediation or be invited to participate in the mediation.

(j) Scheduling Mediation Conference.

(1) *Authority of Mediator.* The mediator shall select the date, time, and, subject to subdivision (j)(2), the location of the initial mediation conference and all other mediation activities.

(2) *Location.* Promptly after the entry of an order appointing a mediator, the clerk shall advise the mediator of the dates and times mediation facilities are available at the courthouse. The initial mediation conference and any additional conferences shall be held in the courthouse unless the mediator determines that it is in the interest of the mediator and the parties to hold the conference at another location designated by the mediator.

(3) *Date.* The date of the initial mediation conference shall be no later than 30 days after the mediator is notified of the appointment.

(4) *Notice.* The clerk shall give notice to the parties of the name of the mediator and the date, time, and location of the initial mediation conference at least 14 days before the date of the initial mediation conference.

(5) *Continuance.* The mediator may continue the initial conference to a date that is no later than 60 days after the mediator is notified of the appointment if the parties consent and the mediator finds that exceptional circumstances prevent holding the initial conference on the original date or fairness to the parties justifies a continuance. If the initial conference is continued to a later date, the mediator shall notify the judge who entered the appointment order.

(6) *Additional Conferences.* The mediator, with the consent of the parties, may schedule additional mediation conferences.

(k) Mediation Procedure.

(1) *No Automatic Continuance of Matters Assigned to Mediation.* A trial or hearing will not be continued to accommodate a mediation unless the parties consent to the continuance and the court so directs.

(2) *Mediation Memorandum.* Not later than 3 days before the initial mediation conference, each party shall deliver or telecopy to the mediator and to each other party a mediation conference memorandum no longer than 2 pages, summarizing the nature of the matter and the party's positions on (1) the major factual and legal issues affecting liability, (2) the relief sought by each party and (3) settlement. Mediation memoranda are solely for use in the mediation process and shall not be filed.

(3) *Attendance of Counsel at Mediation Conference.* An attorney who is responsible for the representation of a party shall attend the initial mediation conference and any additional mediation conferences. Local counsel for an attorney attending a conference does not have to appear. Each attorney shall be prepared to discuss in good faith the following:

(i) all liability issues;

(ii) all damage issues; and

(iii) the client's position on settlement.

(4) *Attendance of Parties at Mediation Conference.* If an individual or any other entity that is a party to a mediation resides within or has its principal place of business located within the Eastern District of Pennsylvania, the individual shall attend the mediation conference in person and any other entity shall have a person with decision making authority for it attend the mediation conference. All other individuals or entities that are parties to the mediation must be available by telephone and the person available by telephone must have decision making authority. The mediator for cause may excuse attendance completely or authorize participation by telephone.

(5) *Sanctions.* Willful failure of an attorney or a party to comply with subdivisions (k)(3) or (k)(4) shall be reported to the judge who entered the appointment order and may result in imposition of appropriate sanctions.

(6) *No Recording of Mediation Conference.* A mediation conference shall not be recorded by any means.

(7) *Conclusion of Mediation.* The mediator shall file a Mediation Report on the form provided by the clerk within 14 days of the conclusion of the mediation. If the mediation results in an agreement for the resolution of the matter, the parties shall determine which of them will prepare the stipulation of settlement, have the stipulation of settlement executed, and file the requisite motion for court approval. A motion for court approval shall be filed no later than 28 days after the conclusion of the mediation.

(8) *Confidentiality of Mediation: No Use at Trial or Otherwise.* A Mediation Submission, a mediator's written settlement recommendation memorandum or any oral suggestions relating to settlement, and any statement of a party, an attorney, the mediator, or other participant is confidential and privileged and shall not be disclosed to third parties. F.R.E. 408 applies to mediation under this rule and no statement made during the mediation process or writing used during the mediation process shall be offered or admissible as evidence in any trial or hearing, made known to the court or jury, or construed for any purpose as an admission. Papers relating to the mediation, except the Mediation Report, shall not be filed or delivered to a judge of the court. This subdivision does not apply to the reporting of or processing of complaints about unlawful or unethical conduct during the mediation process.

[Effective February 1, 1999. Amended effective December 1, 2009.]

SOURCE

This rule is derived from the Standing Order of the Bankruptcy Court dated May 2, 1994 (S.O.) and Local Rule of Civil Procedure 53.2.1.

Subdivision (a) is derived from S.O. ¶ 1.1.

Subdivision (b) is derived from L.R.Civ.P. 53.2.1(1)(c).

Subdivision (c)(1) is a revision of S.O. ¶¶ 1.2(b), 1.3, and 1.4. Subdivision (c)(2), which authorizes the certification of individuals who are not attorneys as mediators, is new.

Subdivision (d) is a revision of S.O. ¶¶ 1.1, 2.2, and 3.5.

Subdivision (e) is derived from S.O. ¶¶ 3.1 and 3.2.

Subdivision (f) is new.

Subdivision (g) is derived from L.R.Civ.P. 53.2.1(4)(e).

Subdivision (h) is derived from S.O. ¶ 3.6.

Subdivision (i) is derived from S.O. ¶ 3.1.

Subdivision (j) is derived from S.O. ¶¶ 4.2 and 4.9. Subdivision (j)(2) is new. Mediation conferences are to be held in the courthouse unless the mediator determines that there is a significant reason why everyone would be better served by holding the conference at a different location.

Subdivision (k). The sources of the respective parts of this subdivision are as follows:

(1) No Automatic Continuance	¶ 3.1
(2) Mediation Memorandum	L.R.Civ.P. 53.2.1(5)(a)
(3) Attendance of Counsel	¶ 4.4
(4) Attendance of Parties	¶ 4.5
(5) Sanctions	¶ 4.6
(6) No Recording	¶ 4.7
(7) Conclusion of Mediation	¶ 5.1
(8) Confidentiality	¶¶ 4.3, 4.7, and 4.8

LOCAL RULE 9076–1. TELEPHONE AND VIDEO CONFERENCES AND HEARINGS

(a) Availability. The court, on its own motion or on the request of a party, may direct that a conference on any matter or the argument or a hearing on any motion, application, or objection be by telephone or video conference without court appearance.

(b) Scheduling and Procedures.

(1) *Contact With the Courtroom Deputy.* A party requesting a telephone or video conference or hearing shall first seek the agreement of opposing counsel and then contact the courtroom deputy for the judge to whom the case is assigned to request court permission. The requesting party shall discuss with the courtroom deputy the existence of any other procedural or technical requirements for the proceedings. Technical arrangements to use the court's video conference system shall, when practicable, be made 7 days in advance of the scheduled proceeding date in consultation with the judge's courtroom deputy.

(2) *Telephone Conference or Hearing.* The party requesting a telephone conference or hearing shall initiate the call unless otherwise directed by the court. If multiple parties will be participating, the requesting party shall arrange to join the other parties on the line. The person participating in the proceeding by telephone must be available by the telephone before

the time set and must take any steps necessary to keep the telephone lines open so that the call can be timely placed.

(3) *Record.* A verbatim record of a telephone or video hearing shall be made in all cases. A verbatim record of a telephone or video conference shall be made if directed by the court.

[Effective November 20, 2006. Amended effective December 1, 2009.]

SOURCE

This rule is new.

EXPLANATORY NOTE (2006)

The rule has been amended to provide more detailed procedures for the use of the improved technology that permits interested parties to participate in court hearings from remote locations. The District Court Order of December 13, 2006 designated the amended rule as an interim amended rule subject to reevaluation, with any further proposed amendments to be subject to the requirements of notice and publication.

ELECTRONIC CASE FILING
STANDING ORDER 03–3005. PROVISIONS
FOR ELECTRONIC CASE FILING

AND NOW, this 1st day of April, 2003, Federal Rules of Civil Procedure 5(e) and 83 and Federal Rules of Bankruptcy Procedure 5005(a), 9011 and 9029 authorize this court by local rule to permit the filing, signing and verification of documents by electronic means;

And Local Bankruptcy Rule 5005 (L.B.R. 5005) having been adopted to provide such authorization;

And to implement L.B.R. 5005 certain practices and procedures have been developed to facilitate electronic filing of documents in this court;

And the judges of this court intending that those practices and procedures be binding on parties participating in the electronic case filing system ("ECF") offered by the court;

It is hereby **ORDERED** that the document attached as Exhibit A (Procedures for Filing, Signing and Verifying Pleadings and Papers by Electronic Means dated March 27, 2003, and as amended from time to time) is hereby **APPROVED**.

EXHIBIT A

PROCEDURES FOR FILING, SIGNING AND VERIFYING PLEADINGS AND PAPERS BY ELECTRONIC MEANS:

1. Scope of Electronic Filing.

a. Effective April 1, 2003, all cases will be assigned to the Electronic Filing System. Except in exceptional circumstances preventing a person with a court-issued log-in and password ("Filing User") from filing electronically or as otherwise provided in paragraph 5 and 6 below, all petitions, motions, memoranda of law, or other pleadings and documents required to be filed with the court thereafter must be electronically filed by the Filing User. Once registered, a Filing User may withdraw from participation in the Electronic Filing System by providing the clerk's office with written notice of the withdrawal.

b. In a case assigned to the Electronic Filing System after it has been opened, documents previously filed in paper form will not be converted to electronic format unless the court orders otherwise. All documents filed subsequently must be done so electronically except as provided in these rules.

c. Notwithstanding the foregoing, attorneys and others who are not Filing Users in the Electronic Filing System are not required to electronically file pleadings and other papers in a case assigned to the System; provided, however, that any paper document presented for filing shall be accompanied by a computer disk containing a copy of the document in Portable Document Format (PDF). Attorneys who are unable to create and submit computer disks in PDF format may scan the paper document utilizing a document scanner that will be available in the Clerk's Office. Documents not accompanied by a PDF formatted disk or scanned by the attorney shall be found deficient and may, after notice to counsel with an opportunity to cure the defect, be stricken by the Court.

2. Eligibility, Registration, Passwords, Filing Fees.

a. Attorneys admitted to the bar of this court (including those admitted pro hac vice), United States trustees and their assistants, standing Chapter 13 trustees and their assistants, private trustees, and others as the court deems appropriate, may register as Filing Users of the court's Electronic Filing System. Registration is in a form prescribed by the clerk and requires the Filing User's name, address, telephone number, Internet e-mail address, and, in the case of an attorney, a declaration that the attorney is admitted to the bar of this court and is in good standing.

b. A party to a pending contested matter or adversary proceeding who is not represented by an attorney may be permitted to register as a Filing User in the Electronic Filing System as the court deems appropriate. Registration is in a form prescribed by the clerk and requires identification of the action as well as the name, address, telephone number and Internet e-mail address of the party. If, during the course of the action, the party retains an attorney who appears on the party's behalf, the attorney must advise the clerk to terminate the party's registration as a Filing User upon the attorney's appearance.

c. Provided that a Filing User has an Internet e-mail address, registration as a Filing User constitutes: (1) waiver of the right to receive notice by first class mail and consent to receive notice electronically; and (2) waiver of the right to service by personal service or first class mail and consent to electronic service, except with regard to service of a summons and complaint under Fed.R.Bankr.P. 7004. Waiver of service and notice by first class mail includes waiver of notice of the entry of an order or judgment under Fed.R.Bankr.P. 9022.

d. Non–Filing Users may also receive notice and service of electronically filed documents by registering with the clerk in a form prescribed for that purpose which requires the Non–Filing User's name, address, telephone number, and Internet e-mail address. Such registration shall constitute the waivers described in paragraph c above.

d.* Once registration is completed, the Filing User will receive notification of the user log-in and password. Filing Users agree to protect the security of their passwords and immediately notify the clerk by telephone with written confirmation if they learn that their password has been compromised. Users may be subject to sanctions for failure to comply with this provision.

e.* Filing Users eligible to pay by credit card will pay all applicable filing fees on-line in accordance with the procedures set forth in the User's Manual for Electronic Case Filing. Such fees shall be paid at the time of the filing of the document requiring a fee or, if the Filing User intends to make multiple filings in the System that day, filing fees incurred during the day may be accumulated and paid at one time but no later than the close of business on the day of the filing.

3. Consequences of Electronic Filing.

a. Electronic transmission of a document to the Electronic Filing System consistent with these rules, together with the transmission of a Notice of Electronic Filing from the court, constitutes filing of the document for all purposes of the Federal Rules of Bankruptcy Procedure and the local rules of this court, and constitutes entry of the document on the docket kept by the clerk under Fed.R.Bankr.P. 5003.

b. When a document has been filed electronically, the official record is the electronic recording of the document as stored by the court, and the filing party is bound by the document as filed. Except in the case of documents first filed in paper form and subsequently submitted electronically under Rule 1, a document filed electronically is deemed filed at the date and time stated on the Notice of Electronic Filing from the court.

c. Filing a document electronically does not alter the filing deadline for that document. Filing must be completed before midnight local time where the court is located to be considered timely filed that day.

4. Entry of Court Orders.

a. All orders, decrees, judgments, and proceedings of the court will be filed in accordance with these rules, which will constitute entry on the docket kept by the clerk under Fed.R.Bankr.P. 5003 and 9021. All signed orders will be filed electronically by the court or court personnel. Any order filed electronically without the original signature of a judge has the same force and effect as if the judge had affixed the judge's signature to a paper copy of the order and it had been entered on the docket in a conventional manner.

b. A Filing User submitting a document electronically that requires a judge's signature must also promptly deliver the document in such form as the judge requires.

5. Attachments and Exhibits. Filing Users must submit in electronic form all documents referenced as exhibits or attachments, unless the court permits conventional filing. Unless the exhibits or attachments are in digital form, a Filing User must submit as exhibits or attachments only those excerpts of the referenced documents that are directly germane to the matter under consideration by the court. Excerpted material must be clearly and prominently identified as such. Upon request, the Filing User shall within three (3) business days transmit the complete document without charge to any party that so requests. Filing Users who file excerpts of documents as exhibits or attachments under this rule do so without prejudice to their right to timely file additional excerpts or the complete document; provided, however, that the total number of pages of attachments and exhibits electronically filed shall not exceed 20 without prior approval of the judge. Pages of exhibits and attachments in excess of 20 may be filed as of right in hard copy in the traditional manner. Responding parties who choose to file attachments and exhibits electronically may timely file additional excerpts or the complete document subject to the same limitations as set forth above. At any hearing at which the exhibit or attachment is to be considered, counsel shall have a complete copy for the court and all parties.

6. Sealed Documents. Documents ordered to be placed under seal must be filed conventionally, and not electronically, unless specifically authorized by the court. A motion to file documents under seal may be filed electronically unless prohibited by law. The order of the court authorizing the filing of documents under seal may be filed electronically unless prohibited by law. A paper copy of the order must be attached to the documents under seal and be delivered to the clerk.

7. Retention Requirements. Documents that are electronically filed and require original signatures other than that of the Filing User must be maintained in paper form by the Filing User until three years after the main case is closed. On request of the court, the Filing User must provide original documents for review.

8. Signatures.

a. The user log-in and password required to submit documents to the Electronic Filing System serve as the Filing User's signature on all electronic documents filed with the court. They also serve as a signature for purposes of Fed.R.Bankr.P. 9011, the other Federal Rules of Bankruptcy Procedure, the local rules of this court, and any other purpose for which a signature is required in connection with proceedings before the court. Each document filed electronically must, if possible, indicate that it has been electronically filed. Electronically filed documents must include a signature block and must set forth the name, address, and telephone number of the Filing User. In addition, the name of the Filing User under whose log-in and password the document is submitted must be preceded by an "s/" and typed in the space where the signature would otherwise appear.

b. No Filing User or other person may knowingly permit or cause to permit a Filing User's password to be used by anyone other than an employee of the Filing User who has been trained in the use of CM/ECF.

c. All documents filed by a Filing User, including petitions, lists, schedules, statements and amendments thereto that are required to be verified under Fed. R.Bankr.P. 1008 or contain an unsworn declaration as provided in 28 U.S.C. § 1746, and all writings, affidavits or pleadings in which a person verifies, certifies, affirms or swears under oath or penalty of perjury the truth of matters set forth in that document must be filed electronically. The signature on the filed copy must be conformed to the original verified pleading by affixing the notation "s/" above the typed name of the person whose signature appears on the original. Such notation constitutes a representation by the Filing User that the fully executed original verified pleading is in his or her possession at the time of filing.

d. Documents requiring signatures of more than one party other than documents referenced in paragraph 8(c) above must be electronically filed either by: (1) submitting a scanned document containing all necessary signatures; or (2) endorsing the document with a statement that certifies that the document is filed pursuant to Paragraph 8(d) of this Order or (3) any other manner approved by the court.

e. Certification of compliance with paragraph 8(d) of the Standing Order constitutes the submitting attorney's representation that he/she has received a copy of the original document containing the signatures of all parties to the document and that such original document will be retained pursuant to the requirements of paragraph 7 of the Standing Order. The original document requirement shall not require retention of a document with original signature to the extent the parties to a stipulation have provided in the document for acceptance of facsimile signatures.

9. Service of Documents by Electronic Means. When a Filing User electronically files a pleading or other document using the Electronic Filing System, a "Notice of Electronic Filing" shall automatically be generated by the system and shall be sent automatically to parties entitled to service or notice by reason of their registration in compliance with paragraph 2(c) and (d). Electronic transmission of the "Notice of Electronic Filing" constitutes service or notice of the filed document. Parties not deemed to have consented to electronic notice or service are entitled to receive a paper copy of any electronically filed pleading or other document. Except as expressly provided in this Order, service or notice must be made according to the Federal Rules of Bankruptcy Procedure and the local rules.

10. Notice of Court Orders and Judgments. Immediately upon the entry of an order or judgment in an action assigned to the Electronic Filing System, the clerk will transmit to Filing Users in the case, in electronic form, a Notice of Electronic Filing. Electronic transmission of the Notice of Electronic Filing constitutes the notice required by Fed.R.Bankr.P. 9022. The clerk must give notice to a person who has not consented to electronic service in paper form in accordance with the Federal Rules of Bankruptcy Procedure and Local Bankruptcy Rules.

11. Technical Failures. A Filing User whose filing is made untimely as the result of a technical failure may seek appropriate relief from the court by motion pursuant to Local Rule 9014–2, provided that such User immediately notifies the Clerk in writing delivered by facsimile or hand of the technical failure. Technical failures include problems accessing the court's automated system as well as unanticipated technical failures in the Filing User's system. Any party in interest that objects to the relief being sought must file an objection within five (5) days of service of the motion.

12. Public Access.

a. Any person or organization, other than one registered as a Filing User, may access the Electronic Filing System at the court's Internet site, www.paeb.uscourts.gov by obtaining a PACER log-in and password. Those who have PACER access but who are not Filing Users may retrieve docket sheets and documents, but they may not file documents.

b. In connection with the filing of any material in an action assigned to the Electronic Filing System, any person may apply by motion for an order limiting electronic access to or prohibiting the electronic filing of certain specifically-identified materials on the grounds that such material is subject to privacy interests and that electronic access or electronic filing in the action is likely to prejudice those privacy interests. Information posted on the System must not be downloaded for uses inconsistent with the privacy concerns of any person.

[Effective April 1, 2003; as revised by Standing Order 03-3011, dated November 25, 2003; as revised by Standing Order 04-3009, dated October 19, 2004; as revised by Standing Order 04-3011, dated December 1, 2004.]

* So in original.

STANDING ORDER 04–3009. ORDER AMENDING
ECF STANDING ORDER 03-3005

AND NOW, this 19th day of October, 2004, this Court having issued Standing Order No. 03–3005 on April 1, 2003 (the "Standing Order") providing for the implementation of electronic case filing in this Court;

And that Standing Order approved Exhibit A thereto (Procedures for Filing, Signing and Verifying Pleadings and Papers by Electronic Means);

And it now becomes necessary to amend Exhibit A by reason of this Court's requirement, effective January 15, 2005, that all attorneys become "Filing Users" (i.e., hold a court-issued log-in to the Electronic Filing System and file documents only through the Electronic Filing System);

And it further becomes necessary to amend Exhibit A to clarify that Filing Users may not allow court-issued passwords to be used by third parties not under their employ;

NOW, therefore, it is hereby ORDERED, that:

1. Attorneys appearing in this Court shall file all papers electronically as of **January 15, 2005**, and shall register in the Court's CM/ECF system for that purpose by **December 15, 2004.**

2. Attorneys who will not be able to file electronically by January 15, 2004, or who are thereafter unable to do so, may apply for an extension or waiver. Such requests shall be made by letter, addressed to the Clerk, showing good cause to file and serve pleadings in the traditional manner, and setting forth why the attorney is unable to comply, what steps have been taken to comply, and how long compliance will take. Requests will be determined by the Chief Judge or her designee.

3. Unless otherwise ordered by the Court, attorneys who are granted extensions or waivers will be required to comply with paragraph c. of Amendment 1 to the Standing Order which requires paper filings to be accompanied by a disk or CD-ROM containing in portable document format (PDF) all documents filed with the Court. Attorneys who are granted extensions or waivers and are unable to create and submit computer disks in PDF format may scan the paper document utilizing a document scanner that will be available in the Clerk's Office. Documents not accompanied by a PDF formatted disk or scanned by the attorney shall be found deficient and may, after notice to counsel with an opportunity to cure the defect, be stricken by the Court.

4. Counsel appearing pro hac vice shall, within ten (10) days of the order so admitting, register for electronic filing or comply with the show cause procedure described above, unless local counsel is a Filing User and will be responsible for filing all pleadings with the Court.

5. Paragraph 8(b) of Procedures shall be amended to substitute "an employee of the Filing User who has been trained in the use of CM/ECF" for "authorized agent."

[Dated: October 19, 2004.]

AMENDED PROCEDURES RE: PRIVACY–RELATED AMENDMENTS
TO FEDERAL RULES OF BANKRUPTCY PROCEDURE

The following is an amended summary of procedures to be followed in light of the approval by the Judicial Conference of Amendments to Rules 1005, 1007, and 2002 of the Federal Rules of Bankruptcy Procedure effective December 1, 2003.

Attorneys and pro se filers, not the clerk, are responsible for redacting social security numbers (SSN) and other personal identifiers on documents that they file with the court. Official Form 1, Voluntary Petition, is amended effective December 1, 2003 to require only the last four digits of the social security number. Additionally, in compliance with the E–Government Act of 2002, a party wishing to file a document containing personal data identifiers may:

(a) file an unredacted document under seal to be retained by the court as part of the record, or

*(b) file a reference list under seal. The reference list shall contain the complete personal data identifier(s) and the redacted identifiers used in its (their) place in the filing. All references in the case to the redacted identifiers included in the reference list will be construed to refer to the corresponding complete identifier. The reference list will be construed to refer to the corresponding complete identifier. The reference list must be filed under seal, and may be amended as of right. It shall be retained by the court as part of the record.

Debtor's counsel is responsible for submitting a Form B–21, Statement of Social Security Number, when a new bankruptcy petition is filed. Form B–21 is a verified statement containing the full nine-digit social security number. If Form B–21 is not submitted at the time that the bankruptcy petition is filed, the court may, after notice and an opportunity to cure the defect, dismiss the case.

During the pendency of the bankruptcy case, if the debtor amends the full SSN, counsel or the pro se debtor will be required to submit an amended form B–21. It will be the responsibility of counsel and/or the debtor to notify all parties that the SSN was amended and to file a certificate of service along with a redacted copy of the notice.

The full social security number will appear on the recipient's copy of the 341 notice, but will not be included on the copy maintained in the court file.

When creditors are added to a bankruptcy case, Local Rule 1009–1 applies.

Counsel is responsible for entering the full nine-digit social security number when a petition is filed electronically or by the case upload module. Counsel must also submit Form B–21. An event code has been created for attorneys who are registered filing users in the CM/ECF System to docket Form B–21. It is located under: **Bankruptcy->Other>Statement of Social Security Form B–21.** The attorney must keep the signed original B–21 form in his/her possession for a period of three years from the date the case is closed.

Disk Submission:

A bankruptcy petition filed on disk must be in PDF form and must be accompanied by Form B–21 on a separate disk. The attorney must keep the signed original of Form B–21 in his/her possession for a period of three years from the date the case is closed.

Manual Submission:

A Form B–21 submitted by a pro se debtor in paper form will be maintained by the clerk outside of the public case file. The case administrator or intake clerk in the clerk's office will date-stamp the document and will be responsible for processing the form.

[Dated: November 1, 2004.]

   * In August, 2004, Section 205(c)(3) of the E–Government Act of 2002 was amended to provide this additional method of dealing with redacted documents.

NOTICE TO FILING USERS IN THE COURT'S CM/ECF SYSTEM RE: REDACTION RESPONSIBILITY

The United States Bankruptcy Court for the Eastern District of Pennsylvania has installed CM/ECF Version 3.3.2, the newest upgrade to the system, as of August 13, 2009. In keeping with the Federal Judiciary's commitment to protecting private information in publicly accessible records, as part of this upgrade, CM/ECF has been modified to display the following message at the login screen to remind filing users of their responsibility to redact certain private information from the documents that they file.

"IMPORTANT NOTICE OF REDACTION RESPONSIBILITY: All filers must redact: Social Security or taxpayer-identification numbers; dates of birth; names of minor children; and financial account numbers in compliance with Fed. R. Bankr. P. 9037. This requirement applies to all documents, including attachments.

☐ I understand that, if I file, I must comply with the redaction rules. I have read this notice."

A user will not be able to complete the login process without checking the box on the last line of the message. An additional reminder message will be displayed at the screen where the filer finalizes submission of the filed document asking "Have you redacted?" No affirming keystroke is required for this message.

Software vendors who have been identified have been alerted to this modification and should be incorporating any necessary changes into their software package.

[Dated: August 11, 2009.]

USER'S MANUAL FOR ELECTRONIC CASE FILING

INTRODUCTION

Effective April 1, 2003, all cases filed in the United States Bankruptcy Court for the Eastern District of Pennsylvania are assigned to the Electronic Case Filing System ("System"). This User's Manual has been developed to provide (1) commentary to this Court's Standing Order No. M03–3005 dated April 1, 2003, and Exhibit A thereto (Procedures for Filing, Signing and Verifying Pleadings and Papers By Electronic Means) dated March 27, 2003, as amended from time to time, and (2) details and instructions regarding certain of the procedures outlined in Exhibit A. To facilitate use of this Manual, reference to the Paragraph of Exhibit A to the Order will be provided where applicable. As issues are presented and addressed for which systemic solutions are developed, this Manual shall be updated.

I. SCOPE OF ELECTRONIC FILING (Paragraph 1)

A. The court contemplates that all persons registering to become Filing Users shall file all documents electronically absent exceptional circumstances or as otherwise allowed under the Standing Order.

B. Effective January 15, 2005, all attorneys are required to become "Filing Users" (i.e., hold a court-issued log-in to the Electronic Filing System and file documents only through the Electronic Filing System). Attorneys who will not be able to file electronically by January 15, 2005, or who are thereafter unable to do so, may apply for an extension or waiver. Such requests shall be made by letter, addressed to the Clerk, showing good cause to file and serve pleadings in the traditional manner, and setting forth why the attorney is unable to comply, what steps have been taken to comply, and how long compliance will take. Requests will be determined by the Chief Judge or designee.

Unless otherwise ordered by the Court, attorneys who are granted extensions or waivers will be required to comply with paragraph c. of Amendment 1 to the Standing Order which requires paper filings to be accompanied by a disk or CD–ROM containing in portable document format (PDF) all documents filed with the Court. Attorneys who are granted extensions or waivers and are unable to create and submit computer disks in PDF format may scan the paper document utilizing a document scanner that will be available in the Clerk's Office. Documents not accompanied by a PDF formatted disk or scanned by the attorney shall be found deficient and may, after notice to counsel with an opportunity to cure the defect, shall be stricken by the Court.

Counsel appearing pro hac vice shall, within ten (10) days of the order so admitting, register for electronic filing or comply with the show cause procedure described above, unless local counsel is a Filing User and will be responsible for filing all pleadings with the Court.

Unless as may otherwise be provided in the Standing Order, documents filed by pro se filers are not subject to these provisions.

C. While expedited motions shall be filed electronically, the Filing User shall provide contemporaneous (or if after court hours, at 8:30 a.m. the following day) telephonic notice of such filing to the deputy clerk for the judge administering the case.

D. A Filing User may withdraw from participation in the System by providing written notice of the withdrawal to the clerk of court. Upon receipt of such notice, the clerk's office will immediately cancel the participant's password and will delete the participant from any applicable electronic service list.

E. Registration as a Filing User by one member of a law firm does not require other members of the firm to file electronically. A Filing User is an individual, not a firm. While the court is hopeful that a firm will embrace ECF as a whole, the varying automation skills of its members may dictate different approaches.

II. ELIGIBILITY FOR ELECTRONIC FILING (Paragraph 2)

1. Attorneys admitted to the bar of this court (including those admitted pro hac vice) and who are in good standing, United States trustees and their assistants, Chapter 13 standing trustees and their assistants, and private trustees may presently register for the System. The Standing Order contemplates that others, including non-admitted attorneys and unrepresented persons (e.g., institutional creditors seeking to file proofs of claim), may be allowed to register in the System as the court deems appropriate. This decision shall be made on a case-by-case basis upon submission of a registration form with a letter to the Clerk requesting participation by a person not meeting the automatic eligibility criteria.

2. Filing by non-admitted attorneys shall be consistent with this court's Local Rule 2090(c) regarding pro hac vice admissions.

III. REGISTRATION FOR ELECTRONIC FILING
AND ELECTRONIC NOTICE (Paragraph 2)

1. The registration form set forth in Exhibit I shall be submitted by each person seeking to participate in the System and become a Filing User.

2. A condition to registration and issuance of a password enabling electronic filing is attendance at court-sponsored training either conducted by this court or any other bankruptcy or district court utilizing ECF.

4.* Each registrant shall be entitled to one System password to permit participation in the electronic retrieval and filing of pleadings and other papers in accordance with the System.

5. Each registrant will be required to provide an Internet e-mail address. A registered Filing User will automatically receive an e-mail notification when a document has been filed in a case in which that user is a participant by reason of having filed a pleading or a request for notices.

6. Once registration is approved, each registrant will become a Filing User and will be notified by telephone or by e-mail to come to the clerk's office in person to retrieve an envelope containing an assigned user log-in and password. Only the Filing User or a representative authorized in writing by the Filing User on the letterhead of the Filing User's firm may retrieve the envelope. The clerk will mail or e-mail the log-in and the password to the Filing User only upon written request.

7. Filing Users are encouraged to change their court-assigned passwords periodically, which they may do by accessing CM/ECF § Utilities § Maintain Your ECF Account § More User Information. Any participant having reason to believe that the security of an existing password has been compromised or that a threat to the court's computer system may exist shall immediately notify the clerk of court by telephone and confirm the notice in writing to prevent possible unauthorized access to the court's computer system. Users may be subject to court sanctions, including the disqualification from the participation in the System for failing to do so.

8. Persons who are not Filing Users may register to receive electronic notice and service of documents by submitting the request form set forth in Exhibit II to the Clerk's office.

9. A completed application for registration as a Filing User or a recipient of electronic notices constitutes written consent for the registrant to receive electronic service and notice of documents subject to the electronic case filing system pursuant to Fed. R. Bankr. P. 7005 with the exception of those documents to which the service requirements of Fed. R. Bankr. P. 7004 apply.

IV. PAYMENT OF FILING FEES WHEN FILING
ELECTRONICALLY (Paragraph 2)

1. Filing Users will pay applicable incurred filing fees in CM/ECF with a credit card on-line at the time of filing or by the close of business on the date of filing. Filing Users should be prepared to have credit card information on hand at the time of e-filing any pleading which requires a filing fee. The system does not retain the user's account information. The Court accepts the following credit cards for payment: American Express, Diner's Club, Discover, MasterCard and VISA. The Filing User may close out their account at any time by running the Internet Payment Due Report which allows the filer to review all outstanding (pending) fees and to pay those fees immediately without e-filing another pleading. The report displays each pending fee and allows the filer to Pay Now or Continue Filing. Filing Users may also access the Internet Payment History Report which allows the filer to review their completed credit payments over any specified period of time. This report may be helpful to run for reconciliation purposes.

2. If payment is not received on the day of filing, the filer will receive an e-mail the following morning indicating that the fees are outstanding and must be paid. If the filer fails to pay by 7 a.m. the following day (two days post filing), the filer will be referred to the court to show cause why filing privileges should not be terminated until the amounts are paid in full.

3. Filing Users will receive electronic notification when a receipt is entered into the system.

V. SIGNATURES (Paragraph 8)

1. The User log-in and password required to submit documents to the Electronic Filing System serve as the Filing User's signature on all electronic documents filed with the court. In lieu of the signature, the Filing User shall indicate with a "s/" that a signature is affixed to the original document. This notation shall be utilized in lieu of signature on all documents that require one or more original signatures. The "s/" indicates that when the filed document is viewed or printed, the original was in fact signed.

2. If the task of electronic filing is delegated by the Filing User to an employee of the Filing User, the use of the log-in and password to make the filing constitutes a signature by the Filing User even though the Filing User does not do the physical act of the filing.

VI. SERVICE (Paragraph 9)

1. The Notice of Electronic Filing indicates the time of filing, the name of the party and the name of the attorney filing the document, and the text of the docket entry. It also contains an electronic link (hyperlink) to the filed document, allowing anyone receiving the Notice by e mail to retrieve the document automatically. This Notice is automatically sent to all case participants registered to use the electronic filing system.

2. Upon receipt of a "Notice of Electronic Filing," the recipient will be provided with one "free look" at the document filed. Each subsequent query of the document will subject the recipient to applicable PACER charges.

3. Service of documents by electronic means does not include service of process for purposes of obtaining personal jurisdiction (i.e., Fed. R. Bankr. P. 7004—3Service).

4. Pleadings or other documents which are filed conventionally rather than electronically shall be served on the parties entitled to notice in the manner set forth

in the Federal Rules of Bankruptcy Procedure and the Local Rules of this court, except as otherwise provided by order of the court. The clerk must give notice of court orders and judgments to a person who has not consented to electronic service in paper form in accordance with the Federal Rules of Bankruptcy Procedure.

VII. TECHNICAL REQUIREMENTS

1. Hardware Requirements. A computer with an internet connection is necessary.

It is suggested that filers in the CM/ECF system utilize a flatbed scanner for documents that need to be imaged and filed with the court.

2. Software Requirements. An operating system that supports a web browser including Windows, Linux, Macintosh and others will allow access to the System. Mozilla Firefox and Microsoft's Internet Explorer are compatible for use as a web browser. A word processor such as WordPerfect or Microsoft Word is required. To convert text files to Portable Document Format (PDF), Adobe Acrobat is a standard conversion tool. Anti-virus software is not a requirement but it is strongly suggested for the security of your system and that of the court.

VIII. PUBLIC ACCESS TO THE DOCKETS AND ELECTRONICALLY FILED DOCUMENTS

1. Internet Access to Court Records through the PACER System. Any person or organization may access the Electronic Filing System at the court's internet site, http://ecf.paeb.uscourts.gov by obtaining a PACER log-in and password. Such access to the System will be provided subject to applicable PACER charges.

2. Public Access at the Court. For persons without a PACER log-in and password, the case docket and documents electronically filed in the System can be viewed via public access computer terminals at the clerk's office during regular business hours, Monday through Friday, from 8:30 a.m. through 5:00 p.m. in the Philadelphia clerk's office and from 8:00 a.m. through 4:30 p.m. in the Reading Clerk's office.

Copies of electronically filed documents may be secured from the clerk's office. Such documents may be certified in the same manner as paper documents. The fee for copying and any certification will be in accordance with 28 U.S.C. Sec. 1930.

IX. TRAINING MATERIALS

1. The clerk's office has prepared training materials, including an Electronic Filing System User's Training Manual, which may be updated from time to time. Interested parties may access the latest training materials on the court's web site.

X. HELP DESK

The Clerk's office has established a help desk to assist with technical and operational questions in connection with ECF. This assistance will be available during regular business hours in the Philadelphia Division by telephoning (215) 408–2826 or (215) 408–2827 for operational questions and (215) 408–2860 for technical questions.

In the Reading division, during regular business hours, call (610) 320–5255 ext.240.

Additionally, questions regarding the filing of a new bankruptcy petition or adversary complaint can be referred to the clerk's office intake department during regular business hours in the Philadelphia Division by telephoning (215) 408–2800, extension 2268 or in the Reading Division by telephoning (610) 320–5255, extension 225. Operational questions can be referred to the appropriate case administrator during regular business hours by telephoning the clerk's office in the Philadelphia Division at (215) 408–2800 and in the Reading Division at (610) 320–5255 and by following the appropriate directory options.

EXHIBIT I

REGISTRATION FORM FOR ELECTRONIC FILING

UNITED STATES BANKRUPTCY COURT FOR THE
EASTERN DISTRICT OF PENNSYLVANIA

CASE MANAGEMENT ELECTRONIC CASE FILES (CM/ECF) SYSTEM

PARTICIPANT REGISTRATION FORM

This form is to be used to register for FILING PRIVILEGES for filing documents via the Internet component of the Case Management/Electronic Case Files system (hereafter CM/ECF), in the United States Bankruptcy Court for the Eastern District of Pennsylvania. A registered participant will have the privilege of filing documents with the Clerk's Office via the Internet.

The following information is required for CM/ECF registration in the Live database:

Name (First, Middle, Last): _____Bar ID#: _____State of Admission: _____

Firm Name: _____

Mailing Address: _____

                              _____

Telephone Number: (_____) _____Email Address: _____

I am requesting the following privileges (select one only): _____ Attorney _____ Trustee _____
Creditor (limited log-in) _____ Other (explain on back)

I (or my authorized employee) _____ (Name
and position) have completed CM/ECF bankruptcy training at the following location _____.

I am an attorney who represents parties in the Eastern District of PA on a pro hac vice basis by order dated
_____ in case number _____

I prefer to receive notices in _____ HTML format or _____ text format.

I prefer to receive _____ separate notices for each filing or _____ daily summary report of all filings.

By signing and submitting this registration form, I agree to abide by the following requirements:

1. Pursuant to Federal Rule of Bankruptcy Procedure 9011, every pleading, motion and other paper shall be signed by at least one attorney of record and that the signatures shall be indicated by "s/" and the typed name of the person signing in the following format: "s/Jane Smith" on the signature line. My password constitutes my signature.

2. The login and password for filing via the Internet shall be used exclusively by me and by any of my employees to whom I give authorization. I will not knowingly permit my login and password to be used by anyone who is not so authorized.

3. I will immediately contact the Clerk's Office IT Dept. At 215–408–2860 to report any suspected compromise of my password.

4. I waive any right to service by personal service or by first class mail and consent to electronic service, except with regard to service of a summons and complaint under FRBP 7004. I will receive service of documents and any docket activity electronically pursuant to FRBP 9030, where service of documents is otherwise permitted by first class mail. In so doing, I agree to maintain a current and active e-mail address to receive notification in CM/ECF.

5. I will abide by all of the requirements set forth in the Standing Order of the court and the User's Manual governing electronic case filing relating to the filing,

signing, maintaining and verifying of pleadings and papers in the CM/ECF system currently in effect and any changes or additions that may be made later.

_____ I declare, under penalty of perjury, that I am currently admitted to practice before the bar of the U.S. District Court for the Eastern District of PA and that I am currently in good standing.

_____ I am a party to a pending action who is not represented by an attorney. The court has permitted me to register as a Filing User in the electronic filing system in the matter of: _____ (Caption and case no.)

_____   _____   _____
Applicant Name (Please Print)   Applicant Signature   Date

Mail or deliver this completed   U.S. Bankruptcy Court
        form to:
                                        Attn: IT Department
                                    900 Market Street, Suite 400
                                    Philadelphia, PA 19106–4299

FOR INTERNAL USE ONLY
Application process by _____   (Deputy Clerk)   _____ (Date Received)

EXHIBIT II

REGISTRATION FORM FOR ELECTRONIC NOTICE

UNITED STATES BANKRUPTCY COURT

EASTERN DISTRICT OF PENNSYLVANIA

CASE MANAGEMENT ELECTRONIC CASE FILES (CM/ECF) SYSTEM

ELECTRONIC NOTICE REGISTRATION FORM

Live System

This form is to be used to register Non–Filing Users to receive notice and service of electronically filed documents in the Case Management/Electronic Case filing system (hereafter CM/ECF), in the United States Bankruptcy Court for the Eastern District of Pennsylvania.

Name (First, Middle, Last): _____

Bar ID#: _____ State of Admission: _____

Firm Name: _____

Mailing Address: _____

Telephone Number: _____

E–Mail Address: _____

Case Number (*if applicable*) _____

By signing and submitting this registration form, I agree to abide by the following requirements:

1. Pursuant to Paragraph 2d of Standing Order No. M03–3005 this registration form shall allow Non–Filing Users to receive notice and service of electronically filed documents. Such registration shall constitute the (1) waiver of the right to receive notice by first class mail and consent to receive notice electronically, and (2) of the right to service by personal service or first class mail and consent to electronic service, except with regard to service of a summons and complaint under Fed. R. Bankr.P. 7004. Waiver of service and notice by first class mail includes notice of the entry of an order or judgment under Fed.R.Bankr.P. 9022.

2. I will receive service of documents and any docket activity electronically pursuant to FRBP 9036, where service of documents is otherwise permitted by first class mail. In so doing, I agree to maintain a current and active e-mail address to receive notification in CM/ECF.

3. I prefer to receive notices in _____ HTML format or _____ text format.

4. I prefer to receive _____ separate notice for each filing or _____ a daily summary report of all filings.

_____   _____
Applicant Name (Please Print)   Applicant Signature

_____
Last 4 Digits of SS# (for security purposes)

Mail or deliver this completed form to: U.S. Bankruptcy Court
                                              Attn: IT Department
                                              900 Market St., Suite 400
                                              Philadelphia, PA 19106–4299

FOR INTERNAL USE ONLY

Application processed by _____   _____
                              Deputy Clerk   Date Received

[Effective April 1, 2003; amended April 6, 2004; December 10, 2004; January 14, 2005; March 19, 2008.]

*[**Publisher's Note:** So in original. Probably should be "3."]

PROCEDURES FOR PAYMENT OF FILING FEES WHEN ELECTRONIC FILING IN CM/ECF (INTERNET CREDIT CARD PROCESSING)

Overview.

Internet Credit Card Processing is a new enhancement incorporated into CM/ECF, effective **December 6, 2004.** Previously, most CM/ECF registered users maintained a credit card account number on file with the Clerk's Office for payment of filing fees incurred during filing in CM/ECF. With this new enhancement, attorney filers will pay any incurred filing fees in CM/ECF with a credit card at the time of filing or by the close of business on the day of the filing. The Court will no longer charge the user's credit card account number on file with the Clerk's Office. **Attorneys and their staff should be prepared to have credit card information on hand at the time of e–filing any pleading which requires a filing fee**. The system does not retain the user's account information. The Court accepts the following credit cards for payment: American Express, Discover, Diner's Club, VISA, and MasterCard.

Benefits to the Bar.

* Ability to receive a receipt number immediately upon charging a credit card

* Ability to review internet credit card transaction payment history at any time

* Ability to review any outstanding payments due to the Court at any time

* Ability to make online payments of unpaid balances at any time

Instructions.

Effective August 28, 2005, Internet Explorer 5.5 (or higher) will be the only browser that can be used when making fee payments by Internet credit card through the Pay.gov system.

Upon completion of e-filing a pleading which requires a filing fee, a pop-up credit card payment window will appear on the screen overlaying the CM/ECF Notice of Electronic Filing. This screen will contain the new filing fee charge and any other outstanding CM/ECF filing fees. The filer must select one of the following options: "**Pay Now**" or "**Continue Filing**". If the filer chooses to "**Pay Now**", the filer will be electronically connected to the U.S. Treasury site. The filer will be requested to enter payment information including: (1) Type of Card (i.e., VISA, MasterCard, etc.); (2) Card Number; and (3) Expiration Date (year must be four digits, i.e., 2006). Once this information is entered, the filer will be requested to **Continue**. The filer will receive a Payment Summary and Authorization which confirms the information and requests the filer to authorize the transaction. Once the information is verified and authorized, the payment will be processed by clicking on the **Make Payment** button. The event is docketed to each case for which a payment is made, even if fees for multiple cases are paid with one payment transaction. If multiple fees are paid for a case, multiple docket entries are made to that case, one for each fee paid. A notice of electronic filing is not sent for this entry. The payment is reflected on the "Pleadings Requiring Fees" report.

If the credit card transaction is approved, the filer will receive a message indicating that the transaction has been completed, the amount of the transaction, and the transaction number.

If the payment is declined, the user must contact the card-issuing bank to determine why the card was declined. If the issue cannot be resolved, the intake work leader or the intake supervisor in the clerk's office should be contacted to arrange for an alternative method of payment. The telephone numbers are as follows: Philadelphia Clerk's Office: (215) 408–2800 (ext. 2268 for Intake, ext. 2272 for supervisor); Reading Clerk's Office: (610) 320–5255 (ext. 225 for Intake, ext. 226 for supervisor).

Selecting "**Continue Filing**" allows the filer to continue filing in CM/ECF and accumulate any filing fees incurred during the day. This allows the filer the option to pay all filing fees at once upon completing filing for the day. If this option is chosen, the filer will be returned to CM/ECF to continue filing.

When making an installment payment, the filer must go to "Bankruptcy" - "Other" - "Installment Payment".

Upon the completion of each additional filing, the filer will receive the pop-up credit card payment window on the screen overlaying the CM/ECF Notice of Electronic Filing. This pop-up window will contain a summary of the current charges that remain outstanding. To close the account at any time, click the "**Pay Now**" option and proceed as instructed above. **All accounts must be paid in full by the close of business on the day that the fee was incurred. If payment is not received on the day of filing, the filer will receive an e-mail the following morning indicating that their fees are outstanding and must be paid. If the filer fails to pay by 7 a.m. the following day (two days post-filing), the filer will be referred to the Court to show cause why filing privileges should not be terminated until the amounts are paid in full.**

Exemptions.

The United States and any other federal agencies or programs funded from judiciary appropriations under Title 28, U.S. Code, section 1930, are exempt from the above-mentioned procedure regarding delinquent accounts.

The filer may close out their account at any time by running the Internet Payments Due report (see the section on **Reports** for more information).

Reports.

Two new reports will be available from the [Utilities] menu in CM/ECF: Internet Payment History and Internet Payments Due.

The **Internet Payment History** report allows the filer to review their completed credit payments over any specified period of time. This report may be helpful to run for reconciliation purposes.

The **Internet Payments Due** report allows the filer to review all outstanding (pending) fees and to pay those fees immediately without e-filing another pleading. There are no selection screens or sort options offered. The report displays each pending fee and allows the filer to Pay Now or Continue Filing.

Refunds.

If the filer suspects that a payment is incorrect or a refund is due, immediately contact the Financial department at (215) 408–2800, ext. 2242 or 2239 or submit a letter to the Clerk of Court requesting a refund.

Contact Information.

If the filer has any questions regarding this procedure, contact any Case Administrator in Philadelphia at (215) 408–2800 or in Reading at (610) 320–5255. For technical problems, please contact the Court's Automation Department at (215) 408–2817.

Technical Notes.

Effective August 28, 2005, Internet Explorer 5.5 or higher will be the only browser that can be used.

Browser needs 128-bit encryption enabled to pay over the Internet.

Pop-ups need to be enabled.

The Internet History/cache needs to be cleared to get the option "Internet Payments Due" from the Utilities menu.

The Court appreciates your continued support and participation as we continue to provide enhancements to the CM/ECF program.

[Effective December 8, 2004. Revised effective July 28, 2005.]

SELECTED ORDERS
IN RE: BANKRUPTCY ADMINISTRATION [DISTRICT COURT ORDER]

This 25th day of July, 1984, pursuant to authorization provided in 28 U.S.C. § 157, as amended, and pursuant to Resolution approved by the judges of this court, it is

ORDERED that any and all cases under chapter 7, 11, 12, and 13 of Title 11 and any and all proceedings arising under Title 11 or arising in or related to a chapter 7, 11, 12, or 13 case under Title 11 are and shall be referred to the Bankruptcy Judges for the district, and it is

FURTHER ORDERED that the Bankruptcy Judges of the district are authorized to perform the duties to the full extent set forth in 28 U.S.C. § 157, as amended, and subject to the review procedures set forth in 28 U.S.C. §§ 157(c)(1) and 158. It is

FURTHER ORDERED that personal injury tort and wrongful death claims in bankruptcy cases pending in this district shall be tried in this district court or in the district court in the district in which the claim arose, as determined by a judge of this district. This Order shall not be deemed to affect the status of any case, matter or proceeding presently pending before a district judge.

[Dated: July 25, 1984. Amended November 8, 1990.]

STANDING ORDER NO. M–05–3009. IN THE MATTER OF: DEBTORS ASSERTING AN EXCEPTION TO THE LIMITATION OF THE AUTOMATIC STAY UNDER 11 U.S.C. § 362(l) AND PROCEDURE FOR RECEIVING RENT DEPOSITS

WHEREAS, the Bankruptcy Abuse Prevention and Consumer Protection Act of 2005 amended 11 U.S.C. § 101 et seq., ("Code") including the automatic stay provisions of 11 U.S.C. § 362 in regards to actions to recover possession of residential property occupied by a debtor by the enactment of 11 U.S.C. § 362(l), and

WHEREAS, the court requires uniformity in the procedure for the deposit of rent by debtors and transmittal of rent to lessors under § 362(l)(1)(B) and § 362(5)(D) of the Code, it is hereby

ORDERED that any deposit of rent made by or on behalf of a debtor pursuant to § 362(l)(1)(B) of the Code must be in the form of a certified check or money order payable to the order of the lessor, and delivered to the Clerk of Court upon filing of the petition and the certification made under § 362(l)(1)(A) of the Code, and it is

FURTHER ORDERED that the debtor must file a copy of the Judgment for Possession together with the petition, and it is

FURTHER ORDERED that upon the Clerk's receipt of a certified check or money order payable to the order of the lessor, with a copy of the Judgment for Possession, tendered by a debtor pursuant to § 362(1)(l) of the Code, the Clerk is directed to promptly transmit the certified check or money order to the lessor to the address listed on the petition.

[Dated: November 16, 2005.]

MISCELLANEOUS ORDER NO. M–08–3016. IN RE: PROCEDURE FOR REFUNDS OF FEES PAID ELECTRONICALLY

WHEREAS the Judicial Conference has a long-standing policy prohibiting the refund of filing fees, and

WHEREAS, with the implementation of the Case Management/Electronic Case Filing (CM/ECF) system, the Judicial Conference recognizes the necessity to grant limited refund authority by the courts when errors in electronic payments are made, and

WHEREAS the authority to approve a refund is a judicial determination, but may be delegated to the clerk of court under procedures clearly addressing the type of refund that a clerk can approve, it is hereby

ORDERED AS FOLLOWS:

(1) All requests for the refund of fees shall be made upon application to the court.

(2) The decision to refund fees shall be a judicial determination, except the clerk of court is delegated the specific authority to approve a refund when:

(a) a filing fee is erroneously incurred due to a technical automation error on the part of counsel when submitting a document, or

(b) a filing fee is erroneously generated due to a technical automation error in the CM/ECF or electronic credit card systems.

(3) All refunds shall be processed through the court's electronic credit card system and not by check.

(4) If the court finds that a particular attorney or law firm continues to make repeated errors when submitting fee generating documents followed by requests for refunds, the court may consider remedial action, such as the issuance of an order to show cause why further requests for refunds should be considered.

[Dated: June 26, 2008.]

MISCELLANEOUS ORDER NO. M-08-3017. STANDING ORDER IN RE: REDACTION PROCEDURES ELECTRONIC TRANSCRIPT

WHEREAS the Judicial Conference's Privacy Policy for Public Access to Electronic Case Files (The Judicial Conference Privacy Policy) seeks to protect certain personal information about parties, witnesses and others involved in a civil, criminal or bankruptcy case,[1] and

WHEREAS the Judicial Conference's Privacy Policy contains procedures for redacting certain protected personal information from transcripts of court proceedings available to the public in electronic format, it is hereby

ORDERED that the following transcript redaction procedures shall be implemented by the United States Bankruptcy Court for the Eastern District of Pennsylvania effective October 1, 2008:

1. Unless otherwise directed by the court, transcripts will be submitted by the transcribers to the clerk of court for filing. The docket entry will note that the transcript is available at the clerk's office for inspection only for 90 days after the filing. During this 90 day period, electronic access to the transcript will be limited to court staff, public terminal users in the clerk's office, attorneys or parties who have purchased the transcript from the transcriber and other parties as may be directed by the court.

2. Upon the filing of a transcript, counsel of record who have appeared at the hearing, as well as parties appearing pro se, must review the transcript and request redaction of any personal data identifiers.[2] The responsibility for redacting personal data identifiers is that of counsel and the parties. Neither the clerk of court nor the transcriber will review transcripts for redaction purposes. The scope of responsibility of an attorney or pro se party includes review of the following portions of a transcript:

● opening and closing statements made on the party's behalf;

● statements of the party;

● testimony of any witnesses called by the party; and

- any other portion of the transcript as ordered by the court.

3.   Upon the filing of a transcript, a notice of the filing (Exhibit A), setting forth deadlines related to restriction and redaction, will be issued by the clerk's office to all attorneys of record and pro se parties who attended the hearing.

4.   Within seven (7) calendar days of the filing of the transcript, each party wishing to redact must inform the court by filing a notice of the party's intention with the clerk of court.

5.   If redaction is requested, the requesting party is to submit to the transcriber, and file a copy with the court, within 21 calendar days of the filing of the transcript, or longer if the court so orders, a statement indicating where the personal data identifiers to be redacted appear in the transcript.   This procedure is limited to the redaction of the following personal identifiers:

- social security numbers to the last four digits;
- financial account numbers to the last four digits;
- dates of birth to the year; and
- names of minor children to the initials.

6.   The transcriber must, within 31 calendar days of the filing of the transcript with the clerk, or longer if the court so orders, perform the requested redactions, provide a copy of the redacted transcript to the requester and file a redacted version of the transcript with the clerk of court.

7.   During the 90–day restriction period, the transcript and any redacted versions will not be available via remote electronic access.   The transcript will be available at the court for internal use and will be available for viewing at the court's public terminals but will include the heading "AVAILABLE AT THE PUBLIC TERMI-NAL FOR VIEWING ONLY" to alert court staff that they may not copy or print the transcript for a requester during the restriction period.   An attorney who purchases the transcript from the transcriber will be given remote electronic access to the transcript and any redacted version filed via the court's CM/ECF system.

8.   At the end of the 90–day restriction period, if a redacted version of the transcript is filed, the redacted version will be made available via remote electronic access and at the clerk's office public viewing terminal for viewing and printing. The unredacted version will be retained by the clerk and remain a restricted document.   The "viewing only" header will remain on the transcript and it will not be available via remote electronic access, but will remain available for printing by clerk's office staff unless the court orders otherwise.

9.   If, at the end of the 90–day restriction period, a redacted version of the transcript is not filed, and if there are no other redaction documents or motions linked to the transcript, the transcript on file will be made available via remote electronic access at the clerk's office public viewing terminal for viewing and printing.

[Dated: September 29, 2008.]

1 This information, as described in Fed. R. Bankr. P. 9037, includes social security numbers, birth dates, the names of individuals known to be minors, and financial account numbers (a/k/a "Personal Data Identifiers").

2 This policy only applies to transcripts of proceedings held before this court.   Transcripts of depositions or proceedings of state courts or other jurisdictions are not covered by this policy.

EXHIBIT A

UNITED STATES BANKRUPTCY COURT
EASTERN DISTRICT OF PENNSYLVANIA

In re: :   Chapter

                        :   Bankruptcy No.

        Debtor   :

NOTICE OF FILING OF TRANSCRIPT
AND OF DEADLINES RELATED TO RESTRICTION AND REDACTION

A transcript of the proceeding held on _____ was filed on _____. The following deadlines apply:

The parties have until ___ _____ (7 calendar days from the date of filing of the transcript) to file with the court a *Notice of Intent to request Redaction* of this transcript. The deadline for filing a *request for redaction* is _____ (21 days from the date of filing of the transcript).

If a Request for redaction is filed, the redacted transcript is due _____ (31 days from the date of filing of the transcript).

If no such notice is filed, the transcript may be made available for remote electronic access upon expiration of the restriction period, which is _____ (90 calendar days from the date of filing of the transcript) unless extended by court order.

To review the transcript for redaction purposes, you may purchase a copy from the transcriber (contact the court for contact information) or you may view the document at the clerk's office public terminal.

FOR THE COURT

TIMOTHY B. McGRATH

CLERK

By: _____
Deputy Clerk

Date:

MISCELLANEOUS ORDER M–09–3008.   IN RE: DEPOSIT OF FUNDS RECEIVED IN THE REGISTRY OF THE COURT

AND NOW, this 24th day of March, 2009, it is hereby ORDERED that funds received in the registry of the court be deposited pursuant to Rule 7067 of the Federal Rules of Bankruptcy Procedure and Rule 67 of the Federal Rules of Civil Procedure, and it is

FURTHER ORDERED that the clerk is hereby served with an order of deposit authorizing the clerk to invest funds received in an interest-bearing account and to be invested or deposited directly into depositories in the name of and to the credit of the court, and it is

FURTHER ORDERED that separate accounts must be maintained for each case, and the case title and number should be included in the account name, and it is

FURTHER ORDERED that a variable rate fee not to exceed 10% as authorized by the Judicial Conference of the United States and set by the Director of the Administrative Office of the United States shall be deducted no less than once a year and deposited to the credit of the Treasury of the United States.

[Dated: March 24, 2009.]

MISCELLANEOUS ORDER NO. M–09–3009.   IN RE: COURTROOM SECURITY CAMERAS

Pursuant to the April 10, 2009 recommendation of the Judicial Conference of the United States Committee on Judicial Security regarding courtroom security cameras, the United States Bankruptcy Court for the Eastern District of Pennsylvania

544

prohibits the dissemination of any recorded courtroom transmissions by any means, for any purpose, by or to any person, without a court order authorizing such dissemination.

[Dated: June 2, 2009.]

NOTICE RE: ELECTRONIC DEVICE POLICY

Attorneys, court employees, jurors and the public are permitted to carry electronic devices including, but not limited to, cell phones, personal data assistants, blackberries and laptop computers into the courthouse subject to x-ray screening and visual inspection by Court Security Officers at the courthouse entrance lobby.

All electronic devices as described above may remain operable but must be rendered inaudible before entering any bankruptcy courtroom, bankruptcy judicial chambers or the office of the clerk of the bankruptcy court.

No photographic or recording features may be used while in the courthouse building at anytime without prior permission of the court.

Any disruptive or improper use of electronic devices may result in their confiscation until the end of the court day.

This notice supercedes any previous notices issued by the bankruptcy court regarding the use of electronic devices.

[Effective October 1, 2009.]

MISCELLANEOUS CASE NO. M–11–3016. IN RE: PROCEDURES FOR PRO SE INVOLUNTARY PETITIONS

AND NOW, this 5th day of October, 2011, it is hereby **ORDERED** that:

(1) The order entered on June 28, 2007, in In Re Procedures for Pro Se Involuntary Petitions, Miscellaneous No. 07–3009, is **VACATED**.

(2) The clerk shall reinstate the following procedure, as originally set forth in this court's order of July 22, 2004, at Miscellaneous Case No. 04–3006, when an involuntary petition is filed by a pro se petitioner against an alleged debtor:

(a) The clerk shall accept the involuntary petition for filing, along with the payment of all required filing fees. The petition shall be randomly assigned to a judge and a miscellaneous case number shall be assigned to the involuntary petition. The fact of the involuntary filing shall be entered on the court's Miscellaneous Docket identifying the putative debtor by initials and without entering that information into CM/ECF. The clerk shall provide a copy of the petition to the assigned judge forthwith.

(b) The clerk shall not provide the petitioner with a time-stamped copy of the involuntary petition before an Order for Relief is entered unless specifically authorized by the assigned judge.

(c) The clerk may provide the petitioner with a receipt for the payment of the filing fee that indicates that the fee was paid in connection with the filing of an involuntary petition. However, the receipt shall not indicate the name of the alleged debtor.

(d) Unless the assigned judge directs otherwise, the clerk shall issue a summons. However, the summons shall not be delivered to the petitioner. Instead, the clerk shall serve the summons on the alleged debtor by mail in accordance with Fed. R. Bankr. P. 7004.

(e) Pursuant to 11 U.S.C. § 107(b)(2), unless a specific order is entered by the assigned judge to the contrary, or until an Order for Relief is entered against the alleged debtor, the clerk shall take all steps necessary to:

(i) maintain a paper file of all pleadings and documents filed in the case;

(ii) insure that none of the pleadings or other documents filed in connection with the case were reviewed by the public, except, with the express permission of the assigned judge; and

(iii) insure that no copies of any pleadings or documents shall be available on the court's CM/ECF system unless the assigned judge directs the clerk to electronically image these documents and open a case on the court's CM/ECF system.

(f) The clerk shall deliver a copy of this order to the petitioner and direct his or her attention to paragraph (g) below.

(g) The petitioner shall not inform any third-party of the filing of the involuntary petition without the specific written authorization of the assigned judge.

[Dated: October 5, 2011.]

STANDING ORDER MISC. NO. 15–3008.   IN RE: PROCEDURES RELATING TO UNPAID FILING FEES DEBTOR

AND NOW, this 18th day of August 2015, WHEREAS:

A. Various documents filed with the court must be accompanied by a prescribed filing fee. See 28 U.S.C. § 1930.

B. The electronic filing system of the court ("CM/ECF") allows a Filing User[1] to upload and file a document without paying the filing fee immediately, with the expectation that the filing fee will be paid within twenty–four (24) hours.

C. Presently, there is no administrative enforcement mechanism for the collection of unpaid filing fees for electronically filed documents.

D. Presently the delinquency in unpaid filing fees for electronically filed documents is at a substantial level.

E. The Board of Judges has determined that the level of unpaid filing fees for electronically filed documents is sufficient to warrant some corrective administrative action by the court

It is therefore **ORDERED**, pursuant to a resolution adopted by the Board of Judges on **August 12, 2015** that:

1. If an electronically filed document requires the payment of a filing fee, such filing fee shall be paid no later than forty-eight (48) hours after the filing.

2. The Clerk's Office shall follow the procedures set forth below if a Filing User fails to pay the prescribed fee for an electronically filed document within forty-eight (48) hours after the filing:

    a. By electronic notice, the Clerk shall advise the Filing User of the delinquency, the duty to pay the filing fee forthwith and the Clerk's intention to refer the matter to the Chief Judge if the delinquency is not paid timely.

    b. If the delinquency is not paid within seven (7) days after the Clerk has given notice under Paragraph 2.a., the Clerk shall refer the matter to the Chief Judge.

    c. After referral of a filing fee delinquency under Paragraph 2.b., the Chief Judge, with or without further notice, may suspend the electronic filing privileges of the Filing User.

    d. After paying all delinquent fees, a Filing User whose electronic filing privileges have been suspended may seek reinstatement of electronic filing privileges by filing a motion. Such motion shall be determined without a hearing pursuant to L.B.R. 9014–2.

3. This Order is administrative in nature and nothing in the Order shall restrict the authority of the court, in any case, from striking a document, denying the relief requested in a motion, application or objection, or dismissing a case or adversary proceeding[2] for failure to pay the prescribed filing fee.

4. The Clerk shall serve this Order electronically on all Filing Users forthwith.

5. This Order shall be effective on **September 1, 2015**.

[Dated: August 18, 2015.]

[1] In this Order, the term Filing User has the meaning employed in the court's Standing Order M–03–3005 (April 1, 2003).

[2] Dismissal is authorized by 11 U.S.C. § 707(a)(2), 1112(b)(4)(K), 1208(c)(2) and 1307(c)(2).

UNITED STATES DISTRICT COURT FOR THE MIDDLE DISTRICT OF PENNSYLVANIA

Including Amendments Received Through
June 1, 2016

SECTION I

CHAPTER I.   SCOPE OF RULES

LR 1.1   APPLICATION OF RULES

These rules apply to all proceedings in this court whether criminal or civil unless specifically provided to the contrary or not applicable in the context.

[Effective April 15, 1997.]

LR 1.2   STANDING ORDERS

Unless revoked expressly or by necessary implication by these rules, all standing orders of court now in effect shall remain in effect.

[Effective April 15, 1997.]

LR 1.3   SUSPENSION OF RULES

The court may suspend these rules in individual cases by written order. When a judge of this court issues any order in a specific case which is not consistent with these rules, such order shall constitute a suspension of these rules for such case only and only to the extent that it is inconsistent. By way of illustration, but not of limitation, a judge of this court may issue an order in a specific case governing the practice and procedure, in whole or in part, in that case.

[Effective April 15, 1997.]

LR 1.4   DEFINITION OF TERM "PARTY" AS USED IN THESE RULES

Wherever used in these rules, the term "party", whether in the singular or plural, shall mean the party or parties appearing in the action pro se, or the attorney or attorneys of record for such party or parties, where appropriate.

[Effective April 15, 1997.]

CHAPTER II. COMMENCEMENT OF ACTION/PARTIES

LR 4.1 SERVICE OF PROCESS

Plaintiff or plaintiff's attorney shall be responsible for prompt service of the summons and a copy of the complaint as provided in Fed.R.Civ.P.4. Service shall be made by anyone who is not a party and is not less than 18 years of age. In order that a scheduling conference as required by Fed.R.Civ.P.16(b) can be arranged promptly, immediate service of process should be effected and an affidavit of such service shall be filed within fourteen (14) days thereafter. Where the plaintiff is the United States, an agent or instrumentality thereof, service shall be pursuant to 28 U.S.C. § 566(c).

[Effective April 15, 1997. Amended effective December 1, 2005; December 1, 2009.]

LR 4.2 PROOF OF SERVICE OF ALL OTHER PLEADINGS AND PAPERS

Proof of service of all other pleadings and papers required or permitted to be served, other than those for which a method of proof is prescribed in the Federal Rules of Civil Procedure, shall be by written acknowledgment of service, by affidavit of the person making service or by certification of counsel. A party who has been prejudiced by failure to receive due notice may apply to the court for appropriate relief. Proof of service of discovery material shall not be filed unless required in accordance with Local Rule 5.4.

[Effective April 15, 1997.]

LR 4.3 PAYMENT OF FEES IN ADVANCE

The clerk shall not be required to enter any civil action, file any paper or issue any process therein, nor shall the marshal be required to serve any paper or perform any service unless the fees therefor shall first be paid by the party requesting the same. This rule shall not apply in actions properly instituted or defended in forma pauperis under applicable law.

[Effective April 15, 1997.]

LR 4.4 COLLECTION OF CLERK'S AND MARSHAL'S FEES

In all civil actions prosecuted to final judgment or settled by the parties, in which the costs have not been paid or provided for, the clerk or marshal to whom they are due shall be entitled to an order requiring the party against whom such judgment is entered or in favor of whom such settlement is made, or otherwise as directed by the court, to pay these costs, in default of which execution may issue in the name of the clerk or the marshal therefor as the case may be. Where no action of any kind has been taken by any party in any civil action for two (2) years or more, the clerk or marshal to whom any costs may be due may apply to the court, and the court may enter an appropriate order that such costs be taxed and require any party to pay such costs, and in default thereof that any claim or defense of such party be dismissed. This rule shall not apply in actions properly instituted or defended in forma pauperis under applicable law.

[Effective April 15, 1997.]

LR 4.5 [RESERVED]

[Reserved effective December 1, 2007.]

LR 4.6 [RESERVED]

[Reserved effective August 16, 1999.]

LR 4.7 IN FORMA PAUPERIS PROCEEDINGS INITIATED BY PRISONERS UNDER 28 U.S.C. § 1915

(a) Civil complaints filed by prisoners seeking in forma pauperis status under 28 U.S.C. § 1915 are subject to the provisions of the Prison Litigation Reform Act ("PLRA"). In order to promote the speedy, just and efficient administration of civil rights complaints subject to the PLRA, the court has established forms to be used by prisoners for filing civil rights actions. The prisoner/plaintiff should complete and file the court-approved forms when initiating a civil complaint.

(b) The court-approved forms consist of (1) a cover sheet, (2) a complaint, (3) an application to proceed in forma pauperis, and (4) an authorization form. The authorization form, when completed by the plaintiff, directs the agency holding the plaintiff in custody to forward to the clerk of court a certified copy of the plaintiff's institutional trust fund account and to disburse from the plaintiff's account the full statutory filing fee in amounts specified by 28 U.S.C. § 1915(b). Forms may be obtained from the clerk of court.

(c) Properly completing and filing the authorization form satisfies the plaintiff's obligation under 28 U.S.C. § 1915(a)(2) to submit a certified copy of the plaintiff's trust fund account with the complaint.

[Effective April 15, 1997. Amended effective August 16, 1999.]

LR 4.8 IN FORMA PAUPERIS PROCEEDINGS IN HABEAS CORPUS ACTIONS

For local rule regarding filing in forma pauperis in a Habeas Corpus action, see LR 83.32.3.

[Effective April 15, 1997.]

CHAPTER III. SERVICE AND FILING OF PLEADINGS AND OTHER PAPERS

LR 5.1 SIZE AND OTHER PHYSICAL CHARACTERISTICS OF PAPERS AND OTHER DOCUMENTS

Papers or other documents filed in this court, except original or true copies of exhibits, shall be on paper approximating eight and one-half (8½) inches by eleven (11) inches in size. Any paper or other document filed shall be sufficient as to format and other physical characteristics if it substantially complies with the following requirements:

(a) Prepared on white paper (except for covers, dividers, and similar sheets) of good quality with typed or printed matter six and one-half (6½) inches by nine and one-half (9½) inches.

(b) The first sheet of any paper or other document that is not filed electronically shall contain a three (3) inch space from the top of the paper for all court stampings, filing notices, etc.

(c) The lettering or typeface shall be clearly legible and shall not be smaller than 14 point word processing font or, if typewritten, shall not be smaller than pica. The text must be double-spaced, but quotations more than two lines long may be indented and single-spaced. Headings and footnotes may be single-spaced. The font type and size used in footnotes shall be the same as that used in the body of the brief. Margins must be at least one inch on all four sides. Page numbers shall be placed in the margins, but no text may appear there.

(d) The lettering or typeface shall be on only one (1) side of a page.

(e) All papers and other documents filed in this court shall be securely fastened with a paper clip, binder clip or rubber band. The use of plastic strips, staples or other such fasteners is prohibited, with the exception that administrative and judicial records may be firmly bound.

(f) Exhibits to a brief or motion shall accompany the brief or motion, but shall not be attached to or bound with the brief or motion. Exhibits shall be secured separately, using either lettered or numbered separator pages to separate and identify each exhibit. Each exhibit also shall be identified by letter or number on the top right hand corner of the first page of the exhibit. Exhibits in support of a pleading or other paper shall accompany the pleading or other paper but shall not be physically bound thereto. In all instances where more than one exhibit is part of the same filing, there shall be a table of contents for the exhibits.

(g) A proposed order shall accompany each motion or other request for relief, but shall not be fastened together.

(h) Each motion and each brief shall be a separate document.

(i) Exceptions to the provisions of this rule may be made only upon motion and for good cause or in the case of papers filed by a pro se litigant.

[Effective April 15, 1997. Amended effective August 16, 1999; December 1, 2001; March 3, 2003; December 1, 2005; December 1, 2008.]

LR 5.2 DOCUMENTS TO BE FILED WITH THE CLERK

(a) As to any document required or permitted to be filed with the court in paper form, only the original shall be filed with the clerk except that parties shall file an original and one copy of any document in excess of 200 pages.

(b) Any document signed by an attorney for filing shall contain under the signature line the name, address, telephone number, fax number, e-mail address (if applicable) and Pennsylvania or other state bar identification number. When listing the bar identification number, the state's postal abbreviation shall be used as a prefix (e.g., PA 12345, NY 246810).

(c) Documents shall not be faxed to a judge without prior leave of court. Documents shall not be faxed to the clerk's office, except in the event of a technical failure with the court's Electronic Case Filing ("ECF") system. Technical Failure is defined as a malfunction of court owned/leased hardware, software, and/or telecommunications facility which results in the inability of a Filing User to submit a filing electronically. Technical failure does not include malfunctioning of a Filing User's equipment.

(d) A filed document in a case (other than a social security case) shall not contain any of the personal data identifiers listed in this rule unless permitted by an order of the court or unless redacted in conformity with this rule. The personal data identifiers covered by this rule and the required redactions are as follows:

1. *Social Security Numbers.* If an individual's Social Security Number must be included in a document, only the last four digits of that number shall be used;

2. *Names of Minor Children.* If the involvement of a minor child must be mentioned, only that child's initials shall be used;

3. *Dates of Birth.* If an individual's date of birth must be included, only the year shall be used;

4. *Financial Account Numbers.* If financial account numbers must be included, only the last four digits shall be used.

Additional personal data identifier in a criminal case document only:

5. *Home Addresses.* If a home address must be included, only the city and state shall be listed.

(e) A party wishing to file a document containing the personal data identifiers listed above may file in addition to the required redacted document:

1. a sealed and otherwise identical document containing the unredacted personal data identifiers, or

2. a reference list under seal. The reference list shall contain the complete personal data identifier(s) and the redacted identifier(s) used in its(their) place in the filing. All references in the case to the redacted identifiers included in the reference list will be construed to refer to the corresponding complete personal data identifier. The reference list must be filed under seal, and may be amended as of right.

The sealed unredacted version of the document or the sealed reference list shall be retained by the court as a part of the record.

The responsibility for redacting these personal identifiers rests solely with counsel and the parties. The clerk will not review each document for redaction.

[Effective April 15, 1997. Amended effective August 16, 1999; December 1, 2001; March 3, 2003; April 16, 2003; November 1, 2004.]

LR 5.3   ASSIGNED JUDGE'S NAME ON FIRST PAGE OF DOCUMENTS

After a case is assigned to a judge, all documents filed must include that judge's name in parenthesis directly below the case number.

[Effective April 15, 1997.]

LR 5.4   SERVICE AND FILING OF DISCOVERY MATERIAL

(a) The parties in pro se cases, Health and Human Services cases (Social Security Appeals), and U.S. Government loan cases shall not be obligated to meet and confer prior to instituting discovery. Discovery shall commence no later than thirty (30) days from the date the complaint is served upon the defendant(s).

(b) Interrogatories, requests for disclosures, requests for documents, requests for admissions, and answers and responses thereto shall be served upon other counsel and parties but shall not be filed with the court except as authorized by a provision of the Federal Rules of Civil Procedure or upon an order of the court. The party responsible for serving a discovery request shall retain and become the custodian of the original response. Proof of service or certificates of service of discovery material shall not be filed separately with the clerk. The original transcript or recording of any deposition upon oral examination shall be retained by the party who arranged for the transcript or the recording.

(c) If relief is sought under any of the Federal Rules of Civil Procedure, a copy of the discovery matters in dispute shall be filed with the court contemporaneously with any motion filed under these rules by the party seeking to invoke the court's relief.

(d) When documentation of discovery not previously in the record is needed for appeal purposes, upon an application and order of the court or by stipulation of counsel, the necessary discovery papers shall be filed with the clerk.

[Effective April 15, 1997. Amended effective December 1, 2001; March 3, 2003; December 1, 2005.]

LR 5.5   FORM OF SERVICE OF INTERROGATORIES

For local rule on form of service of interrogatories, see LR 33.1.

[Effective April 15, 1997.]

LR 5.6   FILING OF DOCUMENTS BY ELECTRONIC MEANS

Any document required or permitted to be filed shall be filed electronically and shall be signed and verified by electronic means to the extent and in the manner authorized by the court's Standing Order regarding Electronic Case Filing Policies and Procedures and the ECF User Manual, except that a pro se litigant who is not a registered user of the court's Electronic Case Filing system shall file in paper form rather than electronically. An attorney may be granted a reasonable exception from the mandatory electronic filing requirement by the Chief Judge only upon a showing of good cause. A document filed by electronic means in compliance with this Local Rule constitutes a written document for the purposes of applying these Local Rules, the Federal Rules of Civil Procedure and the Federal Rules of Criminal Procedure.

[Effective March 3, 2003. Amended effective December 1, 2007.]

LR 5.7 SERVICE OF DOCUMENTS BY ELECTRONIC MEANS

Documents may be served through the court's transmission facilities by electronic means to the extent and in the manner authorized by the Standing Order regarding Electronic Case Filing Policies and Procedures and the ECF User Manual. Transmission of the Notice of Electronic Filing constitutes service of the filed document upon each party in the case who

is registered as a Filing User. Any other party or parties shall be served documents according to these Local Rules, the Federal Rules of Civil Procedure and the Federal Rules of Criminal Procedure.

[Effective March 3, 2003.]

LR 5.8 FILING OF DOCUMENTS UNDER SEAL

Unless otherwise prescribed by federal statutes, the Federal Rules of Criminal Procedure, the Federal Rules of Civil Procedure or other provisions of these Rules, including LR 5.2(e), no document shall be filed under seal unless authorized by an order of court. The filing of documents under seal shall be in accordance with LCrR 49.

[Effective December 1, 2005.]

CHAPTER IV. PLEADINGS AND MOTIONS

LR 7.1 MOTIONS TO BE WRITTEN

A motion must be written, and shall contain a certification by counsel for the movant that he or she has sought concurrence in the motion from each party, and that it has been either given or denied. No concurrence need be sought in pro se prisoner cases. A certificate of nonconcurrence does not eliminate the need for counsel to comply with Local Rule 26.3 relating to conferences between counsel in all discovery motions directed toward a resolution of the motion. Every motion shall be accompanied by a form of order which, if entered by the court, would grant the relief sought in the motion.

[Effective April 15, 1997. Amended effective December 1, 2009.]

LR 7.2 [RESERVED]

LR 7.3 EXHIBITS AND OTHER DOCUMENTS SUBSTANTI-ATING MOTIONS

When allegations of fact are relied upon in support of a motion, all pertinent affidavits, transcripts, and other documents must be filed simultaneously with the motion and shall comply with Local Rule 5.1(f).

[Effective April 15, 1997. Amended effective December 1, 2001; December 1, 2009.]

LR 7.4 MOTIONS FOR SUMMARY JUDGMENT

For local rule regarding the filing of a motion for summary judgment, see LR 56.1. Briefing schedules under Local Rules 7.5, 7.6 and 7.7 are applicable to

any brief filed in connection with a motion for summary judgment.

[Effective April 15, 1997. Amended effective December 1, 2010.]

LR 7.5 SUBMISSION OF BRIEFS SUPPORTING MOTIONS

Within fourteen (14) days after the filing of any motion, the party filing the motion shall file a brief in support of the motion. If the motion seeks a protective order, a supporting brief shall be filed with the motion. If a supporting brief is not filed within the time provided in this rule the motion shall be deemed to be withdrawn. A brief shall not be required: (a) In support of a motion for enlargement of time if the reasons for the request are fully stated in the motion, (b) In support of any motion which has concurrence of all parties, and the reasons for the motion and the relief sought are fully stated therein, or (c) In support of a motion for appointment of counsel.

[Effective April 15, 1997. Amended effective August 16, 1999; March 3, 2003; December 1, 2005; December 1, 2009.]

LR 7.6 SUBMISSION OF BRIEFS OPPOSING MOTIONS

Any party opposing any motion, other than a motion for summary judgment, shall file a brief in opposition within fourteen (14) days after service of the movant's brief, or, if a brief in support of the motion is not required under these rules, within seven (7) days after service of the motion. Any party who fails to comply with this rule shall be deemed not to oppose such motion. Nothing in this rule shall be construed to limit the authority of the court to grant any motion before expiration of the prescribed period for filing a brief in opposition. A brief in opposition to a motion for summary judgment and LR 56.1 responsive statement, together with any transcripts, affidavits or other relevant documentation, shall be filed within twenty-one (21) days after service of the movant's brief.

[Effective April 15, 1997. Amended effective March 3, 2003; December 1, 2005; December 1, 2009; December 1, 2010.]

LR 7.7   REPLY BRIEFS

A brief in reply to matters argued in a brief in opposition may be filed by the moving party within fourteen (14) days after service of the brief in opposition. No further briefs may be filed without leave of court.

[Effective April 15, 1997. Amended effective March 3, 2003; December 1, 2009.]

LR 7.8   CONTENTS AND LENGTH OF BRIEFS

(a) Contents of Briefs. Briefs shall contain complete citations of all authorities relied upon, including whenever practicable, citations both to official and unofficial reports. No brief may incorporate by reference all or any portion of any other brief. A copy of any unpublished opinion which is cited must accompany the brief as an attachment. The brief of the moving party shall contain a procedural history of the case, a statement of facts, a statement of questions involved, and argument. The brief of the opposing party may contain a counter statement of the facts and of the questions involved and a counter history of the case. If counter statements of facts or questions involved are not filed, the statements of the moving party will be deemed adopted. The brief of each party, if more than fifteen (15) pages in length, shall contain a table of contents, with page references, and table of citations of the cases, statutes and other authorities referred to therein, with references to the pages at which they are cited. A brief may address only one motion, except in the case of cross motions for summary judgment.

(b) Length of Briefs.

(1) Unless the requirements of Local Rule 7.8(b)(2) and (3) are met, no brief shall exceed fifteen (15) pages in length.

(2) A brief may exceed fifteen (15) pages so long as it does not exceed 5,000 words. If a brief is filed in accordance with this subsection, counsel, or an unrepresented party, must include a certificate (subject to Fed. R. Civ. P. 11) that the brief complies with the word-count limit described in this subsection. The person preparing the certificate may rely on the word count feature of the word-processing system used to prepare the brief. The certificate must state the actual number of words in the brief.

(3) No brief exceeding the limits described in this rule may be filed without prior authorization. Any motion seeking such authorization shall specify the length of the brief requested and shall be filed at least two (2) working days before the brief is due.

(c) Length of Briefs in Appeals from Bankruptcy Court. Unless otherwise ordered by the court, the provisions of subparagraph (b) of this rule relating to the length of briefs shall not apply to matters on appeal to the district court from the bankruptcy court.

[Effective April 15, 1997. Amended effective December 1, 2001; March 3, 2003; December 1, 2006; December 1, 2009.]

LR 7.9   ORAL ARGUMENTS ON MOTIONS

Promptly upon the expiration of the time for filing of all briefs in support of or in opposition to a motion, the judge to whom the action has been assigned may order oral argument at such time and place as the judge shall direct, either in open court or in chambers. The judge, in his or her discretion, may grant oral argument sua sponte or at the request of either or both parties.

[Effective April 15, 1997. Amended effective December 1, 2001; December 1, 2009.]

LR 7.10   MOTIONS FOR RECONSIDERATION

Any motion for reconsideration or reargument must be accompanied by a supporting brief and filed within fourteen (14) days after the entry of the order concerned. This rule is not applicable to a motion to alter or amend a judgment under Fed. R. Civ. P. 59.

[Effective April 15, 1997. Amended effective December 1, 2008; December 1, 2009; December 1, 2010.]

LR 7.34   AFTER-DISCOVERED EVIDENCE

A motion for a new trial on the ground of after-discovered evidence shall, in addition to all other requirements, be accompanied by the affidavits of the witnesses relied upon, stating the substance of their testimony and the reasons why it could not have been introduced at trial.

[Effective April 15, 1997.]

LR 7.35   NOTICE OF APPEAL TO TRIAL JUDGE

Upon the filing of any appeal from any judgment, order or decree of this court, notice thereof shall be given promptly to the judge who entered the same.

[Effective April 15, 1997.]

LR 7.36 CITATION OF SUPPLEMENTAL AUTHORITIES

If pertinent and significant cases are decided or authorities are enacted, relating to an issue raised in a motion pending before the court, after the party's final brief has been filed—or after oral argument but before decision—the party may file a notice of supplemental authority setting forth the supplemental citations. The notice of supplemental authority shall indicate the motion to which the supplemental authority may be relevant, but it must not include any argument. The body of the notice of supplemental authority may not exceed 100 words.

[Effective March 3, 2003.]

LR 8.1 STATEMENT OF AMOUNT OF DAMAGES

The demand for judgment required in any pleading in any civil action pursuant to Fed.R.Civ.P. 8(a)(3) may set forth generally that the party claiming damages is entitled to monetary relief but shall not claim any specific sum where unliquidated damages are involved. The short plain statement of jurisdiction, required by Fed.R.Civ.P. 8(a)(1), shall set forth any amounts needed to invoke the jurisdiction of the court but no other.

[Effective April 15, 1997.]

LR 8.2 CLAIMS FOR UNLIQUIDATED DAMAGES

Whenever an amount or amounts claimed in an action has become relevant for any purpose in the action, the party making the demand shall file a statement with the court setting forth the amount or amounts of such demand or the maximum or minimum amount claimed.

[Effective April 15, 1997.]

LR 14.1 MOTION TO JOIN THIRD PARTIES UNDER FED.R.CIV.P. 14(a), TIME FOR

A motion by a defendant for leave to join a third-party defendant under Fed.R.Civ.P. 14(a) shall be made within three (3) months after an order has been entered setting the case for trial, or within six (6) months after the date of service of the moving defendant's answer to the complaint, whichever shall first occur.

[Effective April 15, 1997.]

LR 14.2 MOTION TO JOIN THIRD PARTIES UNDER FED.R.CIV.P. 14(b), TIME FOR

A motion by a plaintiff for leave to join a third-party defendant under Fed.R.Civ.P. 14(b) shall be made within three (3) months after an order has been entered setting the case for trial, or within six (6) months after the date of service of the moving plaintiff's answer to the counterclaim, whichever shall first occur.

[Effective April 15, 1997.]

LR 14.3 MOTION TO JOIN THIRD PARTIES, TIME FOR, SUSPENSION OF RULES

The provisions of this rule may be suspended upon a showing of good cause.

[Effective April 15, 1997.]

LR 15.1 AMENDED PLEADINGS

(a) **Proposed Amendment to Accompany the Motion.** When a party files a motion requesting leave to file an amended pleading, the proposed amended pleading must be retyped or reprinted so that it will be complete in itself including exhibits and shall be filed on paper as a separate document or, in the Electronic Filing System, as an attachment to the motion. If the motion is granted, the clerk shall forthwith file the amended pleading. Unless otherwise ordered, an amended pleading that does not add a new defendant shall be deemed to have been served for the purpose of determining the time for response under Fed.R.Civ.P. 15(a), on the date the Court grants leave for its filing. A party granted leave to amend its pleading, when the amended pleading would add a new defendant, shall file and effect service of the amended pleading within thirty (30) days after the date of the Order granting leave for its filing.

(b) **Highlighting of Amendments.** The party filing the motion requesting leave to file an amended pleading shall provide: (1) the proposed amended pleading as set forth in subsection (a) of this rule, and (2) a copy of the original pleading in which stricken material has been lined through and any new material has been inserted and underlined or set forth in bold-faced type.

[Effective August 16, 1999. Amended effective March 3, 2003.]

CHAPTER V. CASE MANAGEMENT AND PRETRIAL CONFERENCES

LR 16.1 REQUIREMENT OF HOLDING COURT CONFERENCES

Unless otherwise ordered by the court, there shall be a minimum of two (2) court conferences in every civil action: an initial case management conference and a final pretrial conference. Health and Human Services cases (Social Security Appeals), prisoner, pro se parties and U.S. Government loan cases are exempted from the requirement of holding said conferences unless otherwise ordered by the court.

[Effective April 15, 1997.]

LR 16.2 COURT CONFERENCES, PARTICIPANTS AT

(a) At least one attorney for each of the parties shall be present to represent the interests of the party at the initial case management conference.

(b) Lead counsel for each party shall be present to represent the interests of the party at the final pretrial conference. Each party or a person with full settlement authority for the party shall attend the final pretrial conference, unless otherwise approved by the court. Upon approval of the court the party or person with full settlement authority may be available by telephone. Parties may be required to participate at any conference at the discretion of the court. If settlement requires approval of a committee of an insurance carrier, all of the members of such committee, or a majority thereof, if such majority is empowered to act, shall be reasonably available by telephone. Counsel must notify the person, or committee with settlement authority, of the requirements of this rule, as well as the dates of each conference and trial.

[Effective April 15, 1997. Amended effective December 1, 2010.]

LR 16.3 CONFERENCES OF ATTORNEYS

(a) In each civil action, lead counsel for each party shall confer at least fourteen (14) days prior to the initial case management conference to consider the matters set forth on the court's case management form, as set forth in Appendix A to these rules, and shall thereafter file a concise joint case management statement consisting of the completed case management form. It shall be the duty of counsel for the plaintiff to take the initiative in holding such a conference and in assuring the completion and filing of the joint case management plan form. The filing of this form satisfies the requirement of a proposed discovery plan under Fed.R.Civ.P. 26(f). The joint case management form shall be filed seven (7) days prior to the case management conference. The information in the case management form will not be deemed an admission by any party.

(b) At least fourteen (14) calendar days prior to the final pretrial conference, lead counsel for each of the parties shall meet and confer for the purpose of attempting to enter into agreements with respect to the subjects referred to in Fed.R.Civ.P.16 and to discuss settlement of the action. It shall be the duty of counsel for the plaintiff to take the initiative in holding such a conference and initiating discussion concerning settlement and to report to the court at the final pretrial conference the results of efforts to arrive at settlement. At the conference all exhibits which any party intends to introduce at trial whether on the case in chief or in rebuttal shall be examined, numbered and listed. Only exhibits so listed shall be offered in evidence at the trial, except for good cause shown. Counsel shall attempt in good faith to agree as to the authenticity and admissibility of such exhibits insofar as possible and note an objection to any not so agreed upon. Counsel shall attempt in good faith to agree insofar as possible upon a comprehensive written statement of all undisputed facts which statement shall be included in plaintiff's pretrial memorandum. Lists of potential witnesses with their addresses shall be exchanged.

[Effective April 15, 1997. Amended effective August 16, 1999; December 1, 2001; December 1, 2008; December 1, 2009.]

LR 16.4 SCHEDULING CONFERENCES

The court shall issue a scheduling order within one hundred and twenty (120) days after service of the complaint after consulting with counsel and any pro se litigants by conference, telephone, mail, or any other suitable means. Inasmuch as no Health and Human Services cases (Social Security Appeals) ever reach the trial stage and relatively few prisoner and U.S. Government loan cases reach that stage, such cases are exempted from the mandatory case management conference and scheduling order requirements.

[Effective April 15, 1997.]

LR 16.5 SPECIAL PRETRIAL ORDERS

The judge to whom any action is assigned may make special pretrial orders governing such action.

[Effective April 15, 1997.]

LR 16.6 PRETRIAL MEMORANDUM

Each party to a civil action shall file a pretrial memorandum and serve a copy on all other parties, at least **seven** (7) days prior to the final pretrial conference, containing the information requested, and in the form set forth in Appendix B to these rules. The instructions contained in said official form of pretrial memorandum are a part of these rules.

[Effective April 15, 1997. Amended effective August 16, 1999; December 1, 2001; December 1, 2009.]

CHAPTER VI.   ALTERNATIVE DISPUTE RESOLUTION

LR 16.7 ALTERNATIVE DISPUTE RESOLUTION

Litigants in all civil cases shall consider the use of an alternative dispute resolution process at an appropriate stage in the litigation. A judge may in his or her discretion set a civil case for an alternative method of dispute resolution approved by the court's Civil Justice Reform Act Expense and Delay Reduction Plan: the Mediation Program, the Settlement Officer Program, or the Summary Jury Trial Program; provided, however, that he or she gives consideration to any reasons advanced by the parties as to why such particular alternative method of dispute resolution would not be in the best interests of justice.

[Effective April 15, 1997. Amended effective December 1, 2001.]

LR 16.8 COURT–ANNEXED MEDIATION PROGRAM

LR 16.8.1.   General Rule. The court adopts this rule for the purpose of implementing a court-annexed mediation program to provide litigants with an alternative method to dispose of their case. As hereinafter provided, commencing January 1, 1994 (and continuing until further action by the court) each judicial officer of this court may refer civil actions to mediation. Cases may be subject to mandatory mediation under the Mandatory Mediation Program of the court as set forth in the Standing Orders of Court, which can be found on the court's website @ www.pamd.uscourts.gov.

LR 16.8.2 Certification of Mediators.

(a) The chief judge shall certify as many mediators as determined to be necessary under this rule.

(b) An individual may be certified at the discretion of the chief judge as a mediator if: (1) he or she has been a member of the bar of the highest court of a state or the District of Columbia for a minimum of ten (10) years; (2) he or she has been admitted to practice before this court; and (3) he or she has been determined by the chief judge to be competent to perform the duties of a mediator; and (4) he or she has successfully completed the mediation training program established by the Middle District. The training requirement may be waived by the chief judge when the qualifications and experience of the applicant are deemed sufficient.

(c) The court shall solicit qualified individuals to serve as mediators.

(d) Each individual certified as a mediator shall take the oath or affirmation prescribed by 28 U.S.C. § 453 before serving as a mediator.

(e) A list of all persons certified as mediators shall be maintained in the office of the clerk.

(f) A member of the bar certified as a mediator may be removed from the list of certified mediators by the chief judge.

LR 16.8.3 Compensation and Expenses of Mediators.

(a) The mediator's preparation time and the first six hours of mediation services shall be provided pro bono. After six hours of mediation, the parties and the mediator shall agree to one of the following courses of action:

(1) to terminate the mediation; (2) to continue the mediation with the mediator providing his or her services on a pro bono basis; or (3) to continue the mediation with the mediator providing his or her services at the mediator's regular hourly rate for professional services rendered to the mediator's typical clientele or, in the absence of a standard hourly rate, at the rate of $200.00 per hour.

If the parties and the mediator are unable to agree on a course of action, the mediation shall be terminated. If the parties and the mediator select option (3), all terms and conditions of the mediator's fee agreement must be set forth in writing. The parties shall pay the mediator directly. The court assumes no responsibility for the supervision or enforcement of the parties' agreement to pay for mediation services.

(b) An individual certified as a mediator shall not be called upon more than three times in a calendar year to serve as a mediator without prior approval of the mediator.

(c) Except as provided herein, a mediator shall not accept anything of value from any source for services provided under the court-annexed mediation program.

LR 16.8.4 Cases Eligible for Mediation. Every civil action filed in the Middle District of Pennsylvania is eligible for mediation except any case which the assigned judge determines, after application by any party or by the mediator, is not suitable for mediation.

LR 16.8.5 Scheduling Mediation Conference.

(a) When the court makes a determination that referral to mediation is appropriate, it shall issue an order referring the case to mediation, appointing the mediator, directing the mediator to establish the date, time and place for the mediation session and setting forth the name, address, and telephone number of the mediator. The order will also direct the mediator to fix the date for the initial mediation session to be a date within sixty (60) days from the date of the order of referral unless otherwise extended by the court.

(b) The mediation session shall be held before a mediator selected by the assigned judge from the list of mediators certified by the chief judge.

(c) The clerk shall provide the mediator with a current docket sheet. The mediator shall advise the clerk as to which documents in the case file the mediator desires copies of for the mediation session. The clerk shall provide the mediator with all requested copies.

(d) Any continuance of the mediation session beyond the period prescribed in the referral order must be approved by the assigned judge.

(e) A person selected as a mediator shall be disqualified for bias or prejudice as provided by 28 U.S.C. § 144, and shall disqualify himself or herself in any action where disqualification would be required under 28 U.S.C. § 455 if he or she were a justice, judge, or magistrate judge. A party may assert the bias or prejudice of an assigned mediator by filing an affidavit with the assigned judge stating that the mediator has a personal bias or prejudice. The judge may in his or her discretion end alternative dispute resolution efforts, refer the case to another mediator, refer the case back to the original mediator or initiate another alternative dispute resolution mechanism.

LR 16.8.6 The Mediation Session and Confidentiality of Mediation Communications.

(a) The mediation session shall take place as directed by the court and the assigned mediator. The mediation session shall take place in a neutral setting designated by the mediator. The parties shall not contact or forward documents to the mediator except as directed by the mediator or the court.

(b) If the mediator determines that no settlement is likely to result from the mediation session, the mediator shall terminate the session and promptly thereafter file a report with the Clerk of Court stating that there has been compliance with the requirements of mediation in accordance with the local rules, but that no settlement has been reached. In the event that a settlement is achieved at the mediation session, the mediator shall file a report with the Clerk of Court

stating that a settlement has been achieved. The order of referral may direct the mediator to file the report in a specific form.

(c) Unless stipulated in writing by all parties and the mediator or except as required by law or otherwise ordered by the court, all discussions which occur during mediation shall remain strictly confidential and no communication at any mediation session (including, without limitation, any verbal, nonverbal or written communication which refers to or relates to mediation of the pending litigation) shall be disclosed to any person not involved in the mediation process, and no aspect of the mediation session shall be used by anyone for any reason.

(d) No one shall have a recording or transcript made of the mediation session, including the mediator.

(e) The mediator shall not be called to testify as to what transpired in the mediation session.

LR 16.8.7 Duties of Participants at the Mediation Session.

(a) **Parties.** All named parties and their counsel are required to attend the mediation session, participate in good faith and be prepared to discuss all liability issues, all defenses and all possible remedies, including monetary and equitable relief. Those in attendance shall possess complete settlement authority, independent of any approval process or supervision, except as set forth in subparagraphs (1) and (2) below. Unless attendance is excused under paragraph (d), willful failure to attend the mediation session will be reported by the mediator to the court and may result in the imposition of sanctions.

(1) *Corporation or Other Entity.* A party other than a natural person (e.g., a corporation or association) satisfies this attendance requirement if represented by a person (other than outside counsel) who either has authority to settle or who is knowledgeable about the facts of the case, the entity's position, and the policies and procedures under which the entity decides whether to accept proposed settlements.

(2) *Government Entity.* A unit or agency of government satisfies this attendance requirement if represented by a person who either has authority to settle or who is knowledgeable about the facts of the case, the government unit's position, and the policies and procedures under which the governmental unit decides whether to accept proposed settlements. If the action is brought by or defended by the government on behalf of one or more individuals, at least one such individual also shall attend.

(b) **Counsel.** Each party shall be accompanied at the mediation session by the attorney who will be primarily responsible for handling the trial of the matter.

(c) Insurers. Insurer representatives are required to attend in person unless excused under paragraph (d), below, if their agreement would be necessary to achieve a settlement. Insurer representatives shall possess complete settlement authority, independent of any approval process or supervision.

(d) Request to be Excused. A person who is required to attend a mediation session may be excused from attending in person only after a showing that personal attendance would impose an extraordinary or otherwise unjustifiable hardship. A person seeking to be excused must submit, no fewer than fourteen (14) days before the date set for the mediation, a written request to the mediator, simultaneously copying all counsel. The written request shall set forth all considerations that support the request and shall indicate whether the other party or parties join in or object to the request. A proposed order prepared for the signature of the Judge shall be submitted to the mediator with the request. The mediator shall promptly consider the request and shall submit the proposed order to the Judge with a recommendation that the request be granted or denied. In the absence of an order excusing attendance, the person must attend.

[Effective April 15, 1997. Amended effective August 16, 1999; December 1, 2001; March 3, 2003; December 1, 2006; December 1, 2008; December 1, 2009; December 1, 2010.]

LR 16.9   SETTLEMENT OFFICER PROGRAM

LR 16.9.1 General Rule. Any time after an action or proceeding has been filed, the action may be referred to another judicial officer, including a magistrate judge, or to a neutral evaluator for the purpose of conducting a settlement conference(s).

LR 16.9.2 Agreement of the Parties. The parties may agree, with the approval of the court, upon the selection of the settlement officer.

LR 16.9.3 Discretion of the Court. Notwithstanding any other provision of this rule, in all actions the court shall have the right to designate the settlement officer and make the referral.

LR 16.9.4 Participants and Settlement Authority.

(a) At least one attorney for each party who is a member of the bar of this court shall appear at the settlement conference, except in the case of attorneys admitted to practice in such cases under Local Rule 83.8.2.1, .2, .3, or .4. Any party appearing in a case pro se shall attend the settlement conference. At least one attorney for each party who is fully familiar with the case and has complete authority to settle the case shall appear for each party. If any attorney does not have complete settlement authority, the party or a person with full settlement authority shall accompany the attorney or shall be available by telephone. Parties may be required to attend and participate during the settlement session at the discretion of the settlement officer.

(b) No proceeding at any settlement conference authorized by this rule (including any statement made or written submissions provided by a party, attorney, or other participant) shall be disclosed to any person not involved in the settlement conference, unless otherwise stipulated in writing by all parties and the settlement officer. None of the proceedings shall be used by any adverse party for any reason in the litigation at issue.

LR 16.9.5 Fees. No fees shall be assessed to any party for the costs of the settlement officer program. If a neutral evaluator is the settlement officer, the services of the neutral evaluator shall be provided pro bono to the court unless other arrangements have been approved by all parties and the assigned judge prior to appointing the neutral evaluator to the case.

[Effective April 15, 1997. Amended effective August 16, 1999; December 1, 2001.]

CHAPTER VII.   CLASS ACTIONS

LR 23.1   CLASS ACTIONS, FORM OF DESIGNATION OF COMPLAINT

The complaint shall bear next to its caption the legend, "Complaint—Class Action."

[Effective April 15, 1997.]

LR 23.2   CLASS ACTIONS, CONTENTS OF COMPLAINTS

The complaint shall contain under a separate heading, styled "Class Action Allegations":

(a) A reference to the portion or portions of Fed. R.Civ.P.23 under which it is claimed that the suit is properly maintainable as a class action.

(b) Appropriate allegations thought to justify such claim, including, but not necessarily limited to:

(1) The size (or approximate size) and definition of the alleged class,

(2) The basis upon which the plaintiff (or plaintiffs) claims

(A) To be an adequate representative of the class, or

(B) If the class is comprised of defendants, that those named as parties are adequate representatives of the class,

(3) The alleged questions of law and fact claimed to be common to the class, and

(4) In actions claimed to be maintainable as class actions under subdivision (b)(3) of Fed.R.Civ.P.23, allegations thought to support the finding required by that subdivision.

[Effective April 15, 1997.]

LR 23.3   CLASS ACTION DETERMINATION

Within ninety (90) days after filing of a complaint in a class action, unless this period is extended on motion for good cause appearing, the plaintiff shall move for a determination under subdivision (c)(1) of Fed.R.Civ.

P.23, as to whether the case is to be maintained as a class action. In ruling upon such a motion, the court may allow the action to be so maintained, may disallow and strike the class action allegations, or may order postponement of the determination pending discovery or such other preliminary procedures as appear to be appropriate and necessary in the circumstances. Whenever possible, where it is held that the determination should be postponed, a date will be fixed by the court for renewal of the motion before the same judge.

[Effective April 15, 1997.]

CHAPTER VIII. DEPOSITIONS AND DISCOVERY

LR 26.1   DUTY TO INVESTIGATE AND DISCLOSE

(a) Prior to the conference of attorneys required by Local Rule 16.3, counsel for the parties shall inquire into the computerized information-management systems used by their clients so that they are knowledgeable about the operation of those systems, including how information is stored and how it can be retrieved. At the same time, counsel shall inform their clients of the duty to preserve electronically stored information.

(b) In making the disclosures required by Fed. R. Civ. P. 26(a)(1), the parties must disclose electronically stored information to the same extent they would be required to disclose information, files or documents stored by any other means.

(c) During the conference of attorneys required by Local Rule 16.3(a), in addition to those matters described in that rule, counsel shall discuss and seek to reach agreement on the following:

(1) *Electronically stored information in general.* Counsel shall attempt to agree on steps the parties will take to segregate and preserve electronically stored information in order to avoid accusations of spoliation.

(2) *E-mail information.* Counsel shall attempt to agree on the scope of e-mail discovery and e-mail search protocol.

(3) *Deleted information.* Counsel shall attempt to agree on whether deleted information still exists, the extent to which restoration of deleted information is needed, and who will bear the costs of restoration.

(4) *Back-up and archival data.* Counsel shall attempt to agree on whether back-up and archival data exists, the extent to which back-up and archival data is needed, and who will bear the cost of obtaining such data.

(5) *Costs.* Counsel shall discuss the anticipated scope, cost, and time required for disclosure or production of data beyond what is reasonably available to

the parties in the ordinary course of business, and shall attempt to agree on the allocation of costs.

(6) *Format and media.* Counsel shall discuss and attempt to agree on the format and media to be used in the production of electronically stored information.

(d) In the event the parties cannot agree on the matters described in subparagraph (c), counsel shall note the issue of disagreement in Section 10 ("Other Matters") of the joint case management plan so that the court may, if appropriate, address the matter during the case-management conference.

[Effective December 1, 2005. Amended effective December 1, 2008; December 1, 2009.]

LR 26.2   SERVICE AND FILING OF DISCOVERY MATERIAL

For local rule on service and filing of discovery material, see LR 5.4.

[Effective April 15, 1997.]

LR 26.3   DISCOVERY MOTIONS, STATEMENT OF CONFERENCE TO RESOLVE OBJECTIONS

Counsel for movant in a discovery motion shall file as part of the motion a statement certifying that counsel has conferred with counsel for the opposing party in a good faith effort to resolve by agreement the issues raised by the motion without the intervention of the court, together with a detailed explanation why such agreement could not be reached. If part of the issues raised by the motion have been resolved by agreement, the statement shall specify the issues so resolved and the issues remaining unresolved.

[Effective April 15, 1997. Amended effective March 3, 2003.]

LR 26.4   DISCOVERY PROCEEDINGS, CLOSING OF

In the absence of a discovery deadline set forth in a court order, each party to a civil action shall complete all discovery proceedings within six (6) months of the date of the last pleading filed by that party. The word "pleading" shall have the same meaning in this rule as in Fed.R.Civ.P.7(a). After the expiration of the discovery deadline, the parties are deemed ready for trial.

[Effective April 15, 1997.]

LR 30.1   [RESERVED]

[Effective April 15, 1997; reserved effective December 1, 2001.]

LR 30.2   VIDEOTAPE DEPOSITIONS, GENERAL AUTHORITY AND RULES GOVERNING

Any deposition to be taken upon oral deposition may be recorded by videotape. Except as otherwise provided by this rule, all other rules governing the practice and procedure in depositions and discovery shall apply.

[Effective April 15, 1997.]

LR 30.3   VIDEOTAPE DEPOSITIONS, SUBPOENA AND NOTICES OF

Every notice or subpoena for the taking of a videotape deposition shall state that it is to be videotaped, the name and address of the person whose deposition is to be taken, the name and address of the person before whom it is to be taken, and the name and address of the videotape operator and the operator's employer. The operator may be an employee of the attorney taking the deposition.

[Effective April 15, 1997.]

LR 30.4   VIDEOTAPE DEPOSITIONS, TRANSCRIPT

A stenographic transcript of the deposition shall not be required, unless, upon motion of any party, or sua sponte, the court so directs, and apportions the cost of same among the parties as appropriate. Any party may elect to provide a transcript at his or her expense, in which event copies shall be made available to all other counsel at cost.

[Effective April 15, 1997.]

LR 30.5   VIDEOTAPE DEPOSITIONS, PROCEDURE

The deposition shall begin by the operator stating on camera (1) the operator's name and address, (2) the name and address of the operator's employer, (3) the date, time and place of the deposition, (4) the caption of the case, (5) the name of the witness, and (6) the party on whose behalf the deposition is being taken.

The officer before whom the deposition is taken shall then identify himself or herself and swear the witness on camera. At the conclusion of the deposition the operator shall state on camera that the deposition is concluded. When the length of the deposition requires the use of more than one tape, the end of each and the beginning of each succeeding tape shall be announced on camera by the operator.

[Effective April 15, 1997.]

LR 30.6   VIDEOTAPE DEPOSITIONS, TIMING

The deposition shall be timed by a digital clock on camera which shall show continually each hour, minute and second of each tape of the deposition.

[Effective April 15, 1997.]

LR 30.7   VIDEOTAPE DEPOSITIONS, SIGNATURE

No signature of the witness will be required, unless the transcript is prepared pursuant to Local Rule 30.4.

[Effective April 15, 1997.]

LR 30.8   VIDEOTAPE DEPOSITIONS, CUSTODY AND COPIES

The attorney for the party taking the deposition shall take custody and be responsible for the safeguarding of the videotape and shall permit the viewing of and shall provide a copy of the videotape or the audio portion thereof upon the request and at the cost of a party.

[Effective April 15, 1997.]

LR 30.9   VIDEOTAPE DEPOSITIONS, USE

A videotape deposition may be used to the same extent and in the same manner as an oral deposition under Fed.R.Civ.P.32.

[Effective April 15, 1997.]

LR 30.10   DEPOSITIONS, CERTIFICATE OF CONFERENCE TO REMOVE OBJECTIONS

If an oral or videotape deposition is to be used at trial, counsel for the party who intends to introduce such deposition shall file a certificate with the court at the final pretrial conference stipulating that the attorney has conferred with counsel for the opposing party in an effort to eliminate irrelevancies, side comments, resolved objections, and other matters not necessary for consideration by the trier of fact. It shall be the duty of counsel to make good faith efforts to remove such portions of such depositions prior to trial. If a videotape transcript is not available, counsel shall preview the videotape in order to comply with this rule. If the court finds that any counsel failed in good faith to seek to remove such portions, the court may make such order as is just, including an order that the entire deposition be read against a party, or that the entire deposition be excluded.

[Effective April 15, 1997.]

LR 30.11 VIDEOTAPE DEPOSITIONS, TRANSCRIPTION, MARKING AS EX-HIBIT, CUSTODY AND RETURN

At a trial or hearing that part of the audio portion of a videotape deposition which is offered in evidence and admitted, or which is excluded on objection, shall be transcribed in the same manner as the testimony of other witnesses, unless a transcript is prepared pursuant to Local Rule 30.4, in which event the transcript shall be received in evidence and shall constitute the record of the testimony. The videotape shall be marked as an exhibit and shall remain in the custody of the court, and shall be returned to the party filing it within six (6) months after the case has been terminated.

[Effective April 15, 1997.]

LR 30.12 VIDEOTAPE DEPOSITIONS, EXPENSES AND COUNSEL FEES

At any oral deposition taken outside this district, including a videotape deposition, a party may apply to the court for an order requiring the party requesting the deposition to pay the opposing party reasonable expenses and counsel fees incident thereto.

[Effective April 15, 1997. Amended effective March 3, 2003.]

LR 33.1 INTERROGATORIES AND ANSWERS OR OBJECTIONS, FORM OF SERVICE

When interrogatories are served upon another party pursuant to Fed.R.Civ.P.33, the original and two (2) copies thereof shall be served upon the party who is to answer such interrogatories. Interrogatories shall be prepared in such fashion that sufficient space is provided immediately after each interrogatory or subsection thereof for insertion of the answer or objection and supporting reasons for the objection. If there is insufficient space to answer or object to an interrogatory, the remainder of the answer or objection shall follow on a supplemental sheet. The answers shall be under oath.

[Effective April 15, 1997.]

LR 33.2 INTERROGATORIES, SUPPLEMENTAL ANSWERS TO

Upon discovery by any party of information which renders that party's prior answers to interrogatories substantially inaccurate, incomplete or untrue, such party shall serve appropriate supplemental answers with reasonable promptness on all counsel or parties.

[Effective April 15, 1997.]

LR 33.3 INTERROGATORIES, NUMBER OF

Interrogatories to a party, as a matter of right, shall not exceed twenty five (25) in number. Interrogatories inquiring as to the names and locations of witnesses, or the existence, location and custodian of documents or physical evidence each shall be construed as one interrogatory. All other interrogatories, including subdivisions of one numbered interrogatory, shall be construed as separate interrogatories. If counsel for a party believes that more than twenty five (25) interrogatories are necessary, counsel shall consult with opposing counsel promptly and attempt to reach a written stipulation as to a reasonable number of additional interrogatories. Counsel are expected to comply with this requirement in good faith. In the event a written stipulation cannot be agreed upon, the party seeking to submit additional interrogatories shall file a motion with the court showing the necessity for relief.

[Effective April 15, 1997.]

LR 36.1 REQUESTS FOR ADMISSION, NUMBER OF

Requests for admissions to a party, as a matter of right, shall not exceed twenty five (25) in number. All requests for admissions, including subdivisions of one numbered request for admission, shall be construed as separate requests for admissions. If counsel for a party believes that more than twenty five (25) requests for admissions are necessary, counsel shall consult with opposing counsel promptly and attempt to reach a written stipulation as to a reasonable number of additional requests for admissions. Counsel are expected to comply with this requirement in good faith. In the event a written stipulation cannot be agreed upon, the party seeking to submit additional requests for admissions shall file a motion with the court showing the necessity for relief.

[Effective April 15, 1997.]

LR 36.2 REQUESTS FOR ADMISSIONS, FORM OF OBJECTIONS TO

Objections to requests for admissions pursuant to Fed.R.Civ.P.36 shall identify and quote verbatim each request for admission to which objection is made and the supporting reasons for the objection.

[Effective April 15, 1997.]

LR 37.1 DISCOVERY ABUSE, SANCTIONS FOR

In addition to the application of those sanctions specified in Local Rule 83.3, the court may impose upon any party or counsel such sanctions as may be just, including the payment of reasonable expenses and attorney's fees, if any party or attorney abuses the discovery process in seeking, making or resisting discovery. In an appropriate case, the court may, in addition to other remedies, notify the Attorney General of the United States in a public writing that the United States, through its officers or attorneys, has failed without good cause to cooperate in discovery or has otherwise abused the discovery process.

[Effective April 15, 1997.]

CHAPTER IX. TRIALS

LR 39.1 CIVIL TRIALS, ONE ATTORNEY FOR EACH PARTY

Unless the trial judge shall otherwise grant leave, only one attorney may open or sum up for any party.

[Effective April 15, 1997.]

LR 39.2 CIVIL TRIALS, ORDER OF ADDRESSES

Counsel for the party having the affirmative of the issue on the pleadings shall open the case and shall be immediately followed by opposing counsel, and by third parties, each of whom shall succinctly state without argument their various positions and contentions, and recite briefly the evidence intended to be introduced in support of the same.

[Effective April 15, 1997.]

LR 39.3 CIVIL TRIALS, GENERAL ORDER OF SUMMATION

At the conclusion of the evidence, counsel who opened the case shall first address the jury and be followed by counsel for the opposite party, and by third parties. Counsel making the first address shall have the right to reply, restricting the reply to rebuttal without assertion of any new grounds or repetition of arguments previously made.

[Effective April 15, 1997.]

LR 39.4 CIVIL TRIALS, ORDER OF SUMMATION IN THIRD–PARTY ACTION

In actions which involve a third-party action and if evidence has been presented by each party, the plaintiff's attorney shall first sum up as in Local Rule 39.3. Defendant's attorney shall next sum up for defendant as in Local Rule 39.3 and, for defendant as third-party plaintiff, shall state explicitly upon what he or she relies against the third-party defendant. The attorney for the third-party defendant shall next sum up as the nature of his or her third-party defense may require. The attorney for third-party plaintiff may then reply in rebuttal and thereafter the attorney for the original plaintiff may reply in rebuttal only of original defendant.

[Effective April 15, 1997.]

LR 39.5 CIVIL TRIALS, OTHER MULTI–PARTY ACTIONS

In other multi-party actions the order of summation shall be determined by the trial judge.

[Effective April 15, 1997.]

LR 39.6 CIVIL TRIALS, ORDER OF ADDRESSES IN CO–PARTY CASES

In actions involving more than one plaintiff, defendant, or third-party defendant, if the attorneys are unable to agree, the trial judge shall determine the order of speaking.

[Effective April 15, 1997.]

LR 39.7 CIVIL TRIALS, TRIAL BRIEFS

No later than three (3) days before trial, counsel shall file a trial brief and serve copies on all opposing counsel. The trial brief shall contain a succinct statement of the evidence to be presented and the position of the party filing the same with respect to anticipated legal issues, and the legal authorities relied upon to support the same. A trial brief shall conform to the requirements of Local Rule 7.8 as to content and length.

[Effective April 15, 1997. Amended effective December 1, 2001.]

LR 41.1 DISMISSAL OF ACTION

Any action may be dismissed by the court at any time no proceedings appear to have been taken for one full calendar year. At least twenty eight (28) days written notice of such intended dismissal shall be given to all parties by the judge to whom such action is assigned, or by the clerk, and the action shall thereafter be dismissed, unless for good cause it shall be shown that the action should not be dismissed. Dismissal under this rule shall be in addition to and not in lieu of action which may be taken under Fed. R.Civ.P.41.

[Effective April 15, 1997. Amended effective December 1, 2009.]

LR 42.1 CIVIL TRIALS, ORDER OF PROOF AND BIFURCATION

The court may compel the plaintiff in any action to produce all evidence upon the question of the defendant's liability before any witness is called to testify solely to the extent of the injury or damages. The defendant's attorney may then move for a judgment as a matter of law. If the motion is refused, the trial shall proceed. The court may, however, allow witnesses to be called out of order. The court may order that the issues of liability and damages be bifurcated and that separate trials be held on each issue. Separate issues of liability or damages may be further subdivided for separate trials.

[Effective April 15, 1997. Amended effective August 16, 1999.]

LR 43.1 CIVIL TRIALS, ATTORNEY AS WITNESS

If an attorney for any party becomes a witness on behalf of a client and gives evidence upon the merits of the case the attorney shall forthwith withdraw as trial counsel unless, upon motion, permitted to remain as trial counsel by the court.

[Effective April 15, 1997.]

LR 43.2 CIVIL TRIALS, NUMBER OF ATTORNEYS TO EXAMINE WITNESS

On the trial of an issue of fact, only one attorney on either side shall examine or cross-examine any witness, unless otherwise permitted by the court.

[Effective April 15, 1997.]

LR 43.3 CIVIL TRIALS, OFFERS OF PROOF

The party calling a witness, when required by the court, shall state briefly what is proposed to be proved by the testimony and the legal purpose of it.

[Effective April 15, 1997.]

LR 43.10 SPECIAL TRIAL ORDERS—WITNESSES, ATTORNEYS, PUBLIC ATTENDANCE, NUMBER AND LENGTH OF ADDRESSES

Subject to the requirements of due process of law and of the constitutional rights of the parties, a trial judge may make an order in any case covering any of the following matters:

Limitation of Witnesses. Limiting the number of witnesses whose testimony is similar or cumulative;

Limitation of Witness Interrogation. Limiting the time to be spent on the direct examination or the cross examination of a witness or of a party's overall examination and cross examination of witnesses;

Limitation of Attorneys. Limiting the number of attorneys representing the same party or the same group of parties, who may actively participate in the trial of the case or the examination of witnesses;

Number and Length of Addresses. Regulating the number and length of addresses to the jury or to the court;

Regulating and Excluding Public Attendance. Regulating or excluding the public or persons having no interest in the proceedings, whenever the court deems such order of exclusion to be in the interest of the public good, order or morals.

[Effective April 15, 1997.]

LR 43.20 CIVIL TRIALS, VIEW

A party desiring to have the jury view any premises involved in the litigation, may make application therefor either prior to the listing of the case for trial, or at the bar during the actual trial of the case. In all such cases, the allowance of the application shall be within the discretion of the court, which may impose upon the applicant such reasonable costs or expenses as may be involved in connection with such view, or may direct that any costs thereby incurred shall follow the judgment entered in such action as in other cases.

[Effective April 15, 1997.]

LR 48.1 CIVIL TRIALS, JURIES

Juries in civil cases shall consist, initially, of at least eight (8) members. Trials in such cases shall continue so long as at least six (6) jurors remain in service. If the number of jurors falls below six (6), a mistrial shall be declared upon prompt application therefor by any party then on the record unless the parties stipulate that the number of jurors may fall below six (6).

[Effective April 15, 1997.]

LR 48.2 CIVIL TRIALS, TRIAL WITHOUT A JURY

In a civil action tried without a jury, counsel shall file requests for findings of fact and conclusions of law with the pretrial memorandum. Additional requests may be made during the trial as to matters that could not have been reasonably anticipated before trial.

[Effective April 15, 1997. Amended effective December 1, 2001.]

LR 51.1 CIVIL TRIALS, REQUESTS TO INSTRUCT THE JURY

Requests to instruct the jury shall not exceed twelve (12) in number without leave of court. Each shall be a single request, on a separate numbered page, indicating the party making the request, and framed so that it can be either affirmed or denied. It shall cite the authority upon which it is based. When the authority relied upon is case law, the reference shall include the page(s) of the decision containing the point being proposed as well as the case citation. The requests shall be filed and served no later than three (3) days before trial. Such requests may be supplemented for matters arising during the trial that could not have been reasonably anticipated before trial.

[Effective April 15, 1997. Amended effective December 1, 2001; March 3, 2003.]

CHAPTER X. JUDGMENT

LR 54.1 JUDGMENT BY CONFESSION

Judgment may be entered on a confession of judgment or a warrant of attorney to confess judgment, in accordance with the practice in effect in the courts of the Commonwealth of Pennsylvania, providing the requisites of federal jurisdiction are set forth in the papers filed in connection with the entry of judgment. The caption of all papers filed in connection with confession of judgment cases subsequent to the complaint shall include the phrase "Confession of Judgment" directly below the assigned judge's name.

[Effective April 15, 1997.]

LR 54.2 SECURITY FOR COSTS

In any action in which the plaintiff was not a resident of the Middle District of Pennsylvania at the time suit was brought, or, having been so afterwards removed from this district, the court may enter an order for security for costs upon application and notice. If the party or parties fail to post security as fixed by the court, a judgment of dismissal may be entered upon motion.

[Effective April 15, 1997. Amended effective August 16, 1999.]

LR 54.3 BILLS OF COSTS

Bills of costs, unless an extension is granted, shall be filed no later than thirty (30) days after entry of final judgment. All bills of costs requiring taxation shall be taxed by the clerk, subject to an appeal to the court. Any party appellant shall, within seven (7) days of such taxation, file a written specification of the items objected to and the grounds of objection. A copy of the specifications and objections shall be served on the opposite party or that party's attorney within seven (7) days. An appeal may be dismissed for non-compliance with the appeal requirements.

[Effective April 15, 1997. Amended effective March 3, 2003; December 1, 2009.]

LR 54.4 TAXATION OF COSTS

Costs shall be taxed in conformity with the provisions of 28 U.S.C. §§ 1920–1923 and such other provisions of law as may be applicable and such directives as the court may from time to time issue. Taxable items include:

(1) **Clerk's Fees and Service Fees.** Clerk's fees (see 28 U.S.C. § 1920) and service fees are allowable by statute. Fees required to remove a case from the state court to federal court are allowed as follows: fees paid to clerk of state court; fees for services of process in state court; costs of documents attached as exhibits to documents necessarily filed in state court, and fees for witnesses attending depositions before removal.

(2) **Trial Transcripts.** The cost of an original of a trial transcript, a daily transcript and of a transcript of matters prior or subsequent to trial, furnished to the court is taxable at the rate authorized by the Judicial Conference when either requested by the court, or prepared pursuant to stipulation. Mere acceptance by the court does not constitute a request. Copies of transcripts for counsel's own use are not taxable in the absence of a special order of the court.

(3) **Deposition Costs.** The reporter's charge for the original deposition and/or a copy is taxable whether or not the same is actually received into evidence, and whether or not it is taken solely for discovery, regardless of which party took the deposition. Additional copies are not taxable. The reasonable expenses of the deposition reporter, and the notary, or other official presiding at the taking of the depositions are taxable, including travel and subsistence. Expenses incurred in taking a deposition are not taxable. Fees for the

witness at the taking of a deposition are taxable at the same rate as for attendance at trial. Fees for video-taped depositions may not be taxed without prior court approval. The witness need not be under sub-poena. A reasonable fee for a necessary interpreter at the taking of a deposition is taxable.

(4) Witness Fees, Mileage and Subsistence. The rate for witness fees, mileage and subsistence are fixed by statute (see 28 U.S.C. § 1821). Such fees are taxable even though the witness does not take the stand provided the witness necessarily attends the court. Such fees are taxable even though the witness attends voluntarily upon request and is not under subpoena. The mileage taxation is that which is trav-eled based on the most direct route. Mileage fees for travel outside the district shall not exceed 100 miles each way without prior court approval. Witness fees and subsistence are taxable only for the reasonable period during which the witness is within the district. No party shall receive witness fees for testifying in his or her own behalf but this shall not apply where a party is subpoenaed to attend court by the opposing party. Witness fees for officers of a corporation are taxable if the officers are not defendants and recovery is not sought against the officers individually. Fees for expert witnesses are not taxable in a greater amount than that statutorily allowable for ordinary witnesses. Allowance of fees for a witness on deposition shall not depend on whether or not the deposition is admitted into evidence.

(5) Exemplification and Copies of Papers. The cost of an exhibit necessarily attached to a document (or made part of a deposition transcript) required to be filed and served is taxable. The cost of copies submitted in lieu of originals because of the conven-ience of offering counsel or client are not taxable. The cost of reproducing copies of motions, pleadings, no-tices and other routine case papers is not taxable. The cost of reproducing the required number of copies of the clerk's record on appeal is allowable.

(6) Maps, Charts, Models, Photographs, Sum-maries, Computations and Statistical Summaries. The cost of maps and charts are taxable if they are admitted into evidence. The cost of photographs 8″ by 10″ in size or less, are taxable if admitted into evi-dence, or attached to documents required to be filed and served on opposing counsel. Enlargements great-er then 8″ by 10″ are not taxable except by order of the court. The cost of models is not taxable except by order of the court. The cost of compiling summaries, computations and statistical comparisons is not tax-able.

(7) Interpreter Fees. The reasonable fee of a com-petent interpreter is taxable if the fee of the witness involved is taxable. The reasonable fee of a competent translator is taxable if the document translated is necessarily filed, or admitted in evidence.

(8) Docket Fees. Docket fees and costs of briefs are taxable pursuant to 28 U.S.C. § 1923.

(9) Other items may be taxed with prior court approval.

(10) The certificate of counsel required by 28 U.S.C. § 1924 and the local rules shall be prima facie evidence of the facts recited therein. The burden is on the opposing party to establish that a claim is incor-rectly stated, unnecessary or unreasonable.

[Effective April 15, 1997. Amended effective March 3, 2003.]

LR 54.5   NOTICE OF TAXATION OF COSTS

Any party requesting taxation of costs by the clerk shall give the clerk and all other parties seven (7) days written notice of such request. The clerk shall fix the time for taxation and notify the parties or their coun-sel.

[Effective April 15, 1997. Amended effective December 1, 2009.]

LR 54.6   PAYMENT OF CLERK'S OR MARSHAL'S COSTS

The clerk shall not enter an order of dismissal or of satisfaction of judgment until the clerk's and marshal's costs have been paid. The clerk, in cases settled by parties without payment of costs, may have an order on one or more of the parties to pay the costs. Upon failure to pay costs within fourteen (14) days, or at such time as the court may otherwise direct, the clerk may issue execution for recovery of costs.

[Effective April 15, 1997. Amended effective December 1, 2009.]

LR 54.7   WITNESS FEES, COSTS, ETC.

The fees and mileage of witnesses shall be paid by the party on whose behalf the witness was subpoe-naed, and upon the filing of proof of such payment, by affidavit filed in the case, as required by 28 U.S.C. § 1924, such costs shall be taxed and form part of the judgment in the case.

[Effective April 15, 1997.]

LR 56.1   MOTIONS FOR SUMMARY JUDGMENT

A motion for summary judgment filed pursuant to Fed.R.Civ.P.56, shall be accompanied by a separate, short and concise statement of the material facts, in numbered paragraphs, as to which the moving party contends there is no genuine issue to be tried. The papers opposing a motion for summary judgment shall include a separate, short and concise statement of the material facts, responding to the numbered paragraphs set forth in the statement required in the foregoing paragraph, as to which it is contended that there exists a genuine issue to be tried. Statements of material facts in support of, or in opposition to, a motion shall include references to the parts of the record that support the statements. All material facts set forth in the statement required to be served by the moving party will be deemed to be admitted unless controverted by the statement required to be served by the opposing party.

[Effective April 15, 1997. Amended effective December 1, 2001.]

LR 58.1 MARSHAL'S DEEDS

Marshal's deeds for property sold in execution shall not be acknowledged or delivered until fourteen (14) days after the date of the execution sale, during which time any objections to any sale or to the right of the purchaser, as a lien creditor, to apply a lien in satisfaction of a bid shall be filed.

[Effective April 15, 1997. Amended effective December 1, 2009.]

CHAPTER XI.   PROVISIONAL AND FINAL REMEDIES

LR 65.1 COURT OFFICERS NOT TO BECOME BAIL OR SECURITY

No attorney, clerk, marshal, bailiff or other officer of the court shall furnish bail or security in any matter in or before the court.

[Effective April 15, 1997.]

LR 67.1   INVESTMENT OF REGISTRY FUNDS PENDING LITIGATION

(a) Investment of Funds by Clerk of Court. The Clerk of Court will invest funds under Fed. R. Civ. P. 67 as soon as the business of his or her office allows.

(b) Deposit in Court Pursuant to Fed. R. Civ. P. 67.

(1) *Receipt of Funds.*

A. No money shall be sent to the Court or its officers for deposit in the Court's registry without a court order signed by the presiding judge in the case or proceeding.

B. The party making the deposit or transferring funds to the Court's registry shall serve the order permitting the deposit or transfer on the Clerk of Court, the Chief Deputy and the Financial Administrator.

C. Unless provided for elsewhere in the Order, all monies ordered to be paid to the Court or received by its officers in any case pending or adjudicated shall be deposited with the Treasurer of the United States in the name and to the credit of this Court pursuant to 28 U.S.C. § 2041 through depositories by the Treasury to accept such deposit on its behalf.

(2) *Investment of Registry Funds.*

A. Where, by order of the Court, funds on deposit with the Court are to be placed in some form of interest-bearing account, or invested in a court-approved, interest-bearing instrument in accordance with Rule 67 of the Federal Rules of Civil Procedure, the Court Registry Investment System ("CRIS"), administered by the Administrative Office of the United States Courts under 28 U.S.C. § 2045, shall be the only investment mechanism authorized.

B. Money from each case deposited in the CRIS shall be "pooled" together with those on deposit with Treasury to the credit of other courts in the CRIS and used to purchase Government Account Series securities through the Bureau of Public Debt, which will be held at Treasury, in an account in the name and to the credit of the Director of Administrative Office of the United States Courts, hereby designated as Custodian ("Custodian") for CRIS. Funds held in the CRIS remain subject to the control and jurisdiction of the Court.

C. An account for each case will be established in the CRIS titled in the name of the case giving rise to the investment in the fund. Income generated from fund investments will be distributed to each case based on the ratio each account's principal and earnings has to the aggregate principal and income total in the fund. Reports showing the interest earned and the principal amounts contributed in each case will be prepared and distributed to each court participating in the CRIS and made available to litigants and/or their counsel upon request.

(3) *Deduction of Fees.*

A. The Custodian is authorized to deduct the investment services fee for the management of investments in the CRIS and the registry fee for maintaining accounts deposited with the Court.

B. The investment services fee is assessed from interest earnings according to the Court's Miscellaneous Fee Schedule.

C. The registry fee is assessed by the Custodian from each case's pro rata distribution of the earnings and is to be determined on the basis of the rates published by the Director of the Administrative Office of the United States Courts as approved by the Judicial Conference of the United States.

(4) *Withdrawal of a Deposit Pursuant to Fed. R. Civ. P 67.* The Court's order for disbursement of

invested registry funds must include the name and address of the payee(s) in addition to the total amount of the principal and interest (if the interest is not known, the order may read "plus interest") which will be disbursed to each payee. In order for the Clerk of Court to comply with the Internal Revenue Code and the rules thereunder, payees receiving earned interest must provide a W–9 Taxpayer Identification and Certification form to the office of the Clerk of Court prior to disbursement from the invested account. The disbursement order should be reviewed by the Clerk of Court or the Financial Supervisor prior to being signed by the Judge in order to insure that the necessary information is provided.

(c) Funds regularly deposited in the registry of the court such as bail, removal bonds and civil garnishments are placed in the Treasury of the United States and accrue no interest.

[Effective April 15, 1997. Amended effective December 1, 2007; December 1, 2009; December 1, 2010; December 1, 2014.]

CHAPTER XII. SPECIAL PROCEEDINGS

LR 71A.1 CONDEMNATION PROCEDURES

LR 71A.1.1 Formal Filing Requirements. In condemnation proceedings, all documents presented for filing shall contain in the caption a reference to the tract number or numbers, in numerical order, to which the document refers, and the name of the owner, owners, reputed owner, or reputed owners, as the case may be. All correspondence from counsel to the court or the clerk shall bear a similar notation immediately preceding the salutation.

LR 71A.1.2 Separate Files for Separate Tracts. For each tract, economic unit or ownership for which the just compensation is required to be separately determined in a total lump sum, there shall be a separate civil action file opened by the clerk, which shall be given a serial number such as is given in all other civil actions. The condemnor's counsel shall make the initial determination of each tract, economic unit or ownership for which just compensation is required to be separately determined in a lump sum, subject to review by the court after filing.

LR 71A.1.3 Master File. The file in the civil action containing the first complaint filed under a single declaration of taking shall be designated as the Master File for all the civil actions based upon the single declaration of taking. The numerical designation as the Master File shall be shown by adding as a suffix to the civil action serial number and the symbol MF_____. (In the blank shall be inserted a code number or numbers, selected by the condemnor, designating the project or projects and the number assigned the declaration of taking with which the property concerned is connected.) The single declaration of taking shall be filed in the Master File only. In all other civil actions for condemnation of property which is the subject of the declaration of taking, an appropriate reference to the Master File number in a standard form of complaint shall be deemed to incorporate in the cause the declaration of taking by reference, and shall be a sufficient filing of the declaration of taking referred to.

LR 71A.1.4 Separate Complaint in Master File. For the civil action designated as the Master File there shall be a separate complaint. At the option of the condemnor this complaint and exhibits shall (1) describe all owners, and other parties affected and all properties that are the subject of the declaration of taking, or (2) describe only the owner or owners of the first property or properties in the declaration of taking for which the issue of just compensation is separately determinable.

LR 71A.1.5 Standard Form Complaint. A standard form of complaint may be used for each civil action filed to condemn a tract, economic unit or ownership for which the issue of just compensation is required to be determined in a single lump sum. In the body of the complaint it shall not be necessary to designate the owner or owners of the property concerned, other parties affected by the civil action, or to describe the property concerned in the civil action. The names of the owners, and other parties affected, and the description of the property concerned in the civil action, may be set forth in an exhibit or exhibits incorporated by reference in the standard form of complaint and filed with the complaint.

LR 71A.1.6 Combined Notice or Process. In any notice or process required or permitted by law or by the Federal Rules of Civil Procedure (including but not limited to process under Fed.R.Civ.P.71A(d)) the condemnor, at its option, may combine in a single notice or process, notice or process in as many separate civil actions as it may choose in the interests of economy and efficiency.

LR 71A.1.7 Effect of Filing in Master File. The filing of a declaration of taking in the Master File constitutes a filing of the same in each of the actions to which it relates.

[Effective April 15, 1997. Amended effective March 3, 2003.]

CHAPTER XIII. MAGISTRATE JUDGES

LR 72.1 AUTHORITY OF MAGISTRATE JUDGES

(a) In General. Magistrate judges are judicial officers of the court. Any magistrate judge of this district may perform any duty authorized or allowed by law to be performed by a magistrate judge. Except as otherwise provided by law, rule, or order of this court, the performance of a duty by a magistrate judge shall be in accordance with such other provisions of these rules as would apply if that duty were performed by a district judge. A magistrate judge may determine any preliminary matters; require parties, attorneys, and witnesses to appear; require briefs, proofs, and argument; and conduct any hearing, conference, or other proceeding the magistrate judge deems appropriate in performing his or her duties.

(b) Special Designation to Exercise Civil Consent Authority. Any magistrate judge of this district may, upon consent of the parties, conduct any or all proceedings in a civil matter and order entry of judgment in the matter. (See 28 U.S.C. § 636(c)(1))

(c) Special Designation to Conduct Misdemeanor Trials. Any magistrate judge of this district may try persons accused of misdemeanor offenses and sentence persons convicted of misdemeanor offenses. (See 18 U.S.C. § 3401)

[Effective April 15, 1997.]

LR 72.2 APPEALS FROM NON-DISPOSITIVE ORDERS OF MAGISTRATE JUDGES

Any party may appeal from a magistrate judge's order determining a non-dispositive pretrial motion or matter in any civil or criminal case in which the magistrate judge is not the presiding judge of the case, within fourteen (14) days after issuance of the magistrate judge's order, unless a different time is prescribed by the magistrate judge or a judge. Such party shall file with the clerk of court, and serve on the magistrate judge and all parties, a written statement of appeal which shall specifically designate the order, or part thereof, appealed from and the basis for any objection thereto. At the time the appeal is filed, the appellant shall also file a brief addressed to the issue raised by the objection to the order or part appealed from. Any party opposing the appeal shall file a responsive brief within fourteen (14) days after service of the appellant's brief. A brief in reply may be filed within seven (7) days after service of the opposing party's brief. A judge of the court shall consider the appeal and shall set aside any portion of the magistrate judge's order found to be clearly erroneous or contrary to law. The judge may also reconsider sua sponte any matter determined by a magistrate judge under this rule.

[Effective April 15, 1997. Amended effective December 1, 2009.]

LR 72.3 REVIEW OF REPORTS AND RECOMMENDATIONS OF MAGISTRATE JUDGES ADDRESSING CASE DISPOSITIVE MOTIONS

Any party may object to a magistrate judge's proposed findings, recommendations or report addressing a motion or matter described in 28 U.S.C. § 636 (b)(1)(B) or making a recommendation for the disposition of a prisoner case or a habeas corpus petition within fourteen (14) days after being served with a copy thereof. Such party shall file with the clerk of court, and serve on the magistrate judge and all parties, written objections which shall specifically identify the portions of the proposed findings, recommendations or report to which objection is made and the basis for such objections. The briefing requirements set forth in Local Rule 72.2 shall apply. A judge shall make a de novo determination of those portions of the report or specified proposed findings or recommendations to which objection is made and may accept, reject, or modify, in whole or in part, the findings or recommendations made by the magistrate judge. The judge, however, need conduct a new hearing only in his or her discretion or where required by law, and may consider the record developed before the magistrate judge, making his or her own determination on the basis of that record. The judge may also receive further evidence, recall witnesses or recommit the matter to the magistrate judge with instructions.

[Effective April 15, 1997. Amended effective December 1, 2009.]

LR 72.4 MAGISTRATE JUDGES, APPEAL FROM JUDGMENTS IN MISDEMEANOR CASES—18 U.S.C. § 3402

For local rule of criminal procedure regarding Magistrate Judges, Appeal from Judgments in Misdemeanor Cases, see Section II, Chapter I, LCrR 58.1.

[Effective April 15, 1997.]

LR 72.5 MAGISTRATE JUDGES, AUTHORITY FOR FORFEITURE OF COLLATERAL

For local rules on Magistrate Judges authority and general provisions for Forfeiture of Collateral, see Section II, Chapter I, LCrR 58.2 and LCrR 58.3.

[Effective April 15, 1997.]

LR 73.1 MAGISTRATE JUDGES, SPECIAL PROVISIONS FOR THE DISPOSITION OF CIVIL CASES ON CONSENT OF THE PARTIES—28 U.S.C. § 636(c)

(a) Notice. The clerk of court shall notify the parties in all civil cases that they may consent to have a magistrate judge conduct any or all proceedings in the case and order the entry of a final judgment. Such notice shall be handed or mailed to the plaintiff or his or her representative at the time an action is filed and to other parties as attachments to copies of the complaint and summons, when served.

(b) Execution of Consent. The clerk shall not accept a consent form unless it has been signed by all parties in a case. The plaintiff shall be responsible for securing the execution of a consent form by the parties and for filing such form with the clerk of court within sixty (60) days after the filing date of the case. No consent form will be made available, nor will its contents be made known to any judge or magistrate judge, unless all parties have consented to the reference to a magistrate judge. No magistrate judge, judge, or other court official may attempt to persuade or induce any party to consent to the reference of any matter to a magistrate judge. This rule, however, shall not preclude a judge or magistrate judge from informing the parties that they may have the option of referring a case to a magistrate judge.

(c) Reference. After the consent form has been executed and filed, the clerk shall transmit it to the judge to whom the case has been assigned for approval and referral of the case to a magistrate judge. Once the case has been assigned to a magistrate judge, the magistrate judge shall have the authority to conduct any and all proceedings to which the parties have consented and to direct the clerk of court to enter a final judgment in the same manner as if a judge had presided.

(d) Cases Referred to a Magistrate Judge by Rotational Assignment. A civil case may be referred to a magistrate judge at the time of the filing of the complaint under the rotational assignment plan of the court and, at the same time, will be assigned to a district court judge. The magistrate judge, independent of the parties' consent, is authorized to exercise all the judicial authority that is provided for by law for a magistrate judge.

The magistrate judge may, despite the initial absence of consent to proceed before the magistrate judge, establish a deadline for a consent decision in the case management order. The parties shall be advised that they are free to withhold consent without adverse substantive consequences.

(e) Joint Case Management Plan. The parties in completing the joint case management plan form before the case management conference, in all civil cases, shall state whether all parties consent to have a magistrate judge conduct all proceedings including trial and the entry of a final judgment. Upon the consent of all of the parties, the assigned district court judge may direct the clerk to reassign the case to a magistrate judge. In a case that has been referred to a magistrate judge on a rotational basis, upon a statement in the joint case management plan that the parties consent to proceed before the magistrate judge, the clerk shall reassign the case to that magistrate judge.

[Effective April 15, 1997.]

CHAPTER XIV. DISTRICT COURTS AND CLERKS

LR 77.1 CLERK'S OFFICES

The clerk's office shall be at Scranton, Pennsylvania, unless otherwise directed by the court. Auxiliary clerk's offices shall be maintained at such places as designated by the court and provided by law, staffed by deputy clerks, where actions may be commenced and process issued and permanent records of the court may be maintained, with the same force and effect as if done at Scranton, Pennsylvania.

[Effective April 15, 1997.]

LR 79.1 ENTRIES IN CLERK'S RECORDS

No one other than the clerk or deputy clerks duly authorized shall make any entry in the clerk's records, unless specifically ordered to do so by the court.

[Effective April 15, 1997.]

LR 79.2 REMOVAL OF COURT RECORDS

No papers or records or things filed, entered for record or admitted into evidence in any action shall be removed from the official records of the court officers or staff except upon order of the court.

[Effective April 15, 1997.]

LR 79.3 DEPOSITS FOR COSTS

The clerk and the marshal may require reasonable deposits for anticipated cost from parties filing papers or requesting services.

[Effective April 15, 1997.]

LR 79.4 REMOVAL OR DISPOSITION OF EXHIBITS

Except for those documentary exhibits required to remain permanently with case records, attorneys are responsible, after final judgment including appeal, for removing or authorizing the clerk to dispose of document exhibits which do not fit in the regular case file. Documents of unusual bulk or weight and physical exhibits other than documents are to be removed immediately after trial and, if necessary in an appeal, attorneys must make arrangements for transport to and receipt of such exhibits at the court of appeals. If not removed or disposition authorized, upon thirty (30) days notice from the clerk, such exhibits will be destroyed or otherwise disposed of by the court.

[Effective April 15, 1997.]

LR 79.5 UNSEALING OF CIVIL CASES/DOCUMENTS

Unless good cause is shown, all civil cases and/or documents in those cases which still remain under seal after the case is terminated will be unsealed by the court no later than two (2) years after the final judgment and/or the exhaustion of all appeals.

[Effective April 15, 1997.]

CHAPTER XV.   GENERAL PROVISIONS

LR 83.1 USE OF PHOTOGRAPHY, RADIO AND TELEVISION EQUIPMENT IN THE COURTROOM AND ITS ENVIRONS

LR 83.1.1 Judicial Proceedings. The taking of photographs in the courtroom or its environs, or radio or television broadcasting from the courtroom or its environs, or taping or recording in the courtroom or its environs during the progress of and in connection with judicial proceedings, including proceedings before a United States Magistrate Judge, whether or not court is actually in session, is prohibited. Environs of the courtroom shall include the entire floor on which is located any courtroom, grand jury room, marshal's office, clerk's office, or office of the United States Attorney, or any lock-up, and the corridor or lobby on the main floor or street floor constituting an entrance area to the building in which is located any elevator door for elevators leading from such entrance areas of the building to any such floor. The court may make such orders as may be necessary in connection with any specific case to protect the rights of all parties and the public.

LR 83.1.2 Ceremonial Proceedings. In the discretion of any judge of this court, broadcasting, photographing, televising, or recording of investigative, naturalization, or ceremonial proceedings in a courtroom may be permitted under such conditions as the judge may prescribe.

[Effective April 15, 1997.]

LR 83.2 EXTRAJUDICIAL STATEMENTS IN CIVIL PROCEEDINGS

(a) A lawyer representing a party in a civil matter triable to a jury shall not make any extrajudicial statement that a reasonable person would expect to be disseminated by means of public communication if the lawyer or other person knows or reasonably should know that it will have a substantial likelihood of causing material prejudice to an adjudicative proceeding.

(b) A statement referred to in LR 83.2(a) ordinarily is likely to have such an effect when it relates to:

(1) the character, credibility, reputation or criminal record of a party or witness, the identity of a witness, or the expected testimony of a party or witness;

(2) the performance or results of any examination or test, the refusal or failure of a person to submit to an examination or test, or the identity or nature of physical evidence expected to be presented; and

(3) information the lawyer knows or reasonably should know is likely to be inadmissible as evidence in a trial and would if disclosed create a substantial risk of prejudice to an impartial trial.

(c) Notwithstanding LR 83.2(a) and (b), a lawyer involved in the litigation of a matter may state without elaboration:

(1) the general nature of a claim or defense;

(2) the information contained in a public record;

(3) the scheduling or result of any step in litigation; and

(4) a request for assistance in obtaining evidence and the information necessary thereto.

(d) Nothing in this Rule is intended to preclude either the formulation or application of more restrictive rules relating to the release of any information about parties or witnesses in an appropriate case.

(e) Nothing in this Rule is intended to apply to the holding of hearings or the lawful issuance of reports by legislative, administrative or investigative bodies, nor to a reply by any attorney to charges of misconduct publicly made against that attorney.

(f) The court's supporting personnel including, among others, the marshal, deputy marshals, the clerk, deputy clerks, court reporters and employees or subcontractors retained by the court-appointed official reporters, probation officers and their staffs, and members of the Judges' staffs, are prohibited from disclosing to any person, without authorization by the court, information relating to a proceeding that is not part of the public record of the court. The disclosure of information concerning in camera arguments and hearings held in chambers or otherwise outside the presence of the public is also forbidden.

(g) The court, on motion of any party or on its own motion, may issue a special order governing such matters as extrajudicial statements by parties and witnesses likely to interfere with the rights of a party to a fair trial by an impartial jury, the seating and conduct in the courtroom of spectators and news media representatives, the management and sequestration of jurors and witnesses, and any other matters which the court may deem appropriate for inclusion in such an order.

[Effective April 15, 1997. Amended effective December 1, 2001; December 1, 2006.]

LR 83.3 SANCTIONS

LR 83.3.1 Sanctions in the Discretion of Court. In the sound discretion of any judge of this court, after notice and an opportunity to be heard, one or more of the following sanctions may be imposed for failure to comply with any rule or order of court:

(a) *Dismissal, Default and Preclusion Orders.* Failure of counsel for any party to appear before the court at any case management conference or final pretrial conference or to complete the necessary preparations therefor in accordance with these rules or to be prepared for trial at the time of any scheduled date for trial, or otherwise to comply with any of the rules contained herein, or any order of court, may be considered an abandonment or failure to prosecute or defend diligently, and an order precluding counsel from offering specific evidence or raising certain issues, or judgment, may be entered against the defaulting party either with respect to a specific issue or on the entire case.

(b) *Imposition of Costs on Attorneys.* If counsel acts in a dilatory manner or files motions for the purpose of delay, or fails to comply with any rule or order of court, and the judge finds that the sanctions in subsection 83.3.1(a) above are inadequate or unjust to the parties in light of the facts or circumstances, the judge may, in addition to, or in lieu of, such sanctions assess reasonable costs directly against counsel whose action has obstructed the effective administration of the court's business, or suspend counsel from practicing in this court for a specified period of time not exceeding six (6) months. Any such suspension shall not be subject to Chapter XVII, Attorney Disciplinary Enforcement.

LR 83.3.2 Failure to Exercise Reasonable Diligence in Effecting Settlement of a Case. Whenever the court finds that any party or lawyer in any case before the court has acted in bad faith, or has failed to exercise reasonable diligence in effecting the settle-

ment of such case at the earliest practicable time, the court may impose upon any such party or lawyer the jury costs, including mileage and per diem, resulting therefrom. The court may, in its discretion, hold a hearing to inquire into the facts with respect thereto.

LR 83.3.3 Additional Sanctions. In addition to the sanctions set forth above, the court may impose sanctions in discovery matters as set forth in Local Rule 37.1.

[Effective April 15, 1997. Amended effective December 1, 2005.]

LR 83.4 JUROR CONTACT

No attorney or party or anyone acting on behalf of such attorney or party shall, without express permission from the court, initiate any communication with any juror pertaining to any case in which that juror may be drawn, is participating, or has participated.

[Effective April 15, 1997. Amended effective December 1, 2006.]

LR 83.5 COURTHOUSE AND COURTROOM SECURITY

Matters of policy relating to courthouse and courtroom security and the use of electronic devices are addressed in Standing Orders of Court, which can be found on the court's website at www.pamd.uscourts. gov.

[Effective December 1, 2010.]

LR 83.6 PLACE OF TRIAL

LR 83.6.1 General Rule. Every action shall be tried at the place in the district designated for the holding of court which is nearest to the residence or principal place of business of the defendant or the residence or principal place of business of the principal defendant of multiple defendants, provided that such defendant maintains a bona fide residence or place of business in this district, except that in civil actions arising out of the operation of motor vehicles or other civil actions sounding in tort, the place of trial of such cases shall be at the place for the holding of court which is nearest the scene of the principal event giving rise to the cause of action.

LR 83.6.2 Agreement of the Parties. The parties may agree, with the approval of the court, upon the place of trial of any civil action in which they are interested.

LR 83.6.3 Discretion of the Court. Notwithstanding any other provision of this rule, in all actions the court shall have the right to designate the place of trial for the convenience of the court or of all parties and witnesses.

[Effective April 15, 1997.]

LR 83.7 JUDICIAL MISCONDUCT AND DISABILITY

Copies of the Rules of the Judicial Council of this Circuit implementing the Judicial Conduct and Dis-

ability Act, 28 U.S.C. § 372, are available from the clerk of court without charge.

[Effective April 15, 1997.]

CHAPTER XVI. ATTORNEYS

LR 83.8 ADMISSION TO PRACTICE

In order to practice in this court, an attorney must be admitted to practice under these rules, except as provided in Federal Rule of Civil Procedure 45(f).

LR 83.8.1 General Admission.

LR 83.8.1.2 *Qualifications.* Any person of good, moral and professional character shall be entitled to admission as an attorney of this court, provided that the person is a member of the bar of the Supreme Court of Pennsylvania, and provided that the person is a member in good standing in every jurisdiction where the person has been admitted to practice and neither has been disbarred nor is subject to pending disciplinary proceedings.

LR 83.8.1.3 *Procedure.* A person seeking admission under this rule shall file a petition, on a form provided by the clerk, setting forth the basis for admission. The petitioner must have a sponsor who is a member in good standing of the Bar of this Court. A sponsor's certificate must be included with the petition for admission and the sponsor must be present at the swearing in ceremony to move for admission. The clerk of the court shall receive and maintain all papers submitted by persons seeking admission under this rule. The court may grant admission by oral or written order and by notifying the clerk of the court. A fee shall be charged for admission under this rule. Petition forms shall be available from the clerk.

LR 83.8.2 Special Admissions.

LR 83.8.2.1 *Pro Hac Vice Admission.* An attorney who is admitted to practice in any United States District Court and the highest court of any state, and who is a member of the bar in good standing in every jurisdiction where admitted to practice, and who is not subject to pending disciplinary proceedings in any jurisdiction, may be admitted to practice by leave granted in the discretion of the court but only for the purpose of a particular case. The name, address telephone number and bar identification number of the associate counsel required by Local Rule 83.9 shall be provided on the application at the time of filing.

LR 83.8.2.2. *Attorneys for the United States.* An attorney who is a member in good standing of the bar of the highest court of any state, territory, or the District of Columbia, and who is not subject to pending disciplinary proceedings in any jurisdiction may,

represent in this court the United States, an agency of the United States, or an officer of the United States when that officer is a party in the officer's official capacity.

LR 83.8.2.3 *Attorneys for Federal Defender Organizations.* An attorney who is employed by a federal defender organization and is a member of the bar of any United States District Court, who is a member of the bar in good standing in every jurisdiction in which the attorney has been admitted to practice, and who is not subject to pending disciplinary proceedings in any jurisdiction, shall be permitted to represent in this court individuals provided representation pursuant to the Criminal Justice Act of 1964 as amended.

LR 83.8.2.4 *Attorneys Employed by or Associated With Organized Legal Services Programs.* An attorney who is employed by or associated with an organized legal services program (which is sponsored, approved or recognized by the local county bar association or is duly authorized by Pennsylvania Legal Services Center, Inc., and which provides legal assistance to indigents in civil matters) and is a member of the bar of the highest court in any state (including territories and the District of Columbia) shall be admitted to practice before this court in all cases in which the attorney is associated with the organized legal services program. Admission to practice under this section shall cease to be effective whenever the attorney is no longer associated with such program. Within twenty one (21) days after termination of an attorney's association, a statement to that effect shall be filed with the clerk of the court by a representative of the legal services program. In no event shall admission to practice under this section remain in effect longer than two and one-half (2–1/2) years without being renewed in accordance with the applicable procedures.

LR 83.8.2.5 *Procedure.* An attorney seeking special admission under Local Rule 83.8.2.1, .2, .3 or .4 of this chapter shall file a petition with the court, setting forth the basis for admission under that section. In cases where admission under Local Rule 83.8.2.2, .3 or .4 is sought, the attorney shall submit a statement from a superior stating that the attorney performs duties which qualify him or her for admission under that section. The clerk of the court shall record and maintain all legal papers submitted by attorneys seeking admission under this rule. The court may grant special admission under this rule by oral or written order and by notifying the clerk of the court. A fee, to be established by Standing Order, shall be charged by the clerk for each Special Admission under Local Rules 83.8.2.1, but no fee shall be charged for attorneys seeking special admission under Local Rule 83.8.2.2, .3, or .4. Petition forms shall be available from the clerk.

[Effective April 15, 1997. Amended effective December 1, 2005; December 1, 2008; December 1, 2009; December 1, 2010; December 1, 2014.]

LR 83.9 ASSOCIATE COUNSEL REQUIRED

Any attorney specially admitted under Local Rule 83.8.2.1 shall, in each proceeding in which he or she appears, have associate counsel who is generally admitted under Local Rule 83.8.1 to practice in this court, whose appearance shall also be entered of record and upon whom all pleadings, motions, notices, and other papers may be served in accordance with any statute or applicable rule. The attendance of any such associate counsel upon the hearing of any motion or the taking of any testimony shall be sufficient appearance for the party or parties represented by such associate counsel. If a specially admitted attorney is unavailable for any hearings or motions, arguments, conferences and trials, associate counsel shall be fully prepared to proceed therewith.

[Former LR 83.12 effective April 15, 1997. Renumbered LR 83.9 and amended effective December 1, 2005.]

LR 83.10 CONFLICTS AND CONTINUANCES

LR 83.10.1 Observation of Dates and Times. All members of the bar of this court and those permitted to practice in a particular action shall strictly observe the dates and times fixed for hearings on motions, conferences and trials.

LR 83.10.2 [Reserved].

LR 83.10.3 Illness. Illnesses of parties and material witnesses shall be substantiated by a current medical certificate.

LR 83.10.4 Subpoena Requirement. No trial shall be continued on account of the absence of any witness unless a subpoena for the attendance of such witness has been served at least seven (7) days prior to the date set for trial. This rule shall not dispense with the obligation to take the depositions of any witness where the party or counsel requiring such attendance knows that such witness intends to be absent from the district at the time of trial, or where such witness is not subject to subpoena within this jurisdiction.

LR 83.10.5 Court Conflicts. Conflicts with dates fixed for hearings on motions, conferences and trials will be recognized only in respect to the Supreme Court of the United States, the Court of Appeals for the Third Circuit, the Pennsylvania Supreme Court, the Pennsylvania Superior Court, and, when not sitting as a trial court, the Pennsylvania Commonwealth Court. In case of all other conflicts there shall be a member of the bar of this court or any attorney specially admitted for the purpose of the case fully prepared to proceed.

[Effective April 15, 1997. Amended effective December 1, 2001; December 1, 2005; December 1, 2009.]

LR 83.11 REGISTERED ADDRESSES

LR 83.11.1 Address on File. An attorney admitted to the bar of this court under Local Rule 83.8 shall file with the clerk of this court an address in the state of Pennsylvania for the service or receipt of all pleadings, motions, notices, and other papers served or sent pursuant to any statute or applicable rule. Any changes of address shall be reported promptly. The clerk may maintain this registry, by card or other format, singularly or in conjunction with the roll of attorneys.

LR 83.11.2 Latest Address. In cases of attorneys admitted for a particular case under Local Rules 83.8.2.1, .2, .3 and .4, the registered address of each such attorney shall be the latest address appearing in that case file.

[Effective April 15, 1997. Amended effective December 1, 2005.]

LR 83.12 ROLL OF ATTORNEYS

An alphabetical roll of the attorneys admitted to practice in this court under Local Rule 83.8 shall be kept by the clerk in a format approved by the court. Said record shall contain the full name of each attorney, his or her residence, the date of admission and upon whose motion.

[Former LR 83.13 effective April 15, 1997. Renumbered LR 83.12 effective and amended December 1, 2005.]

LR 83.13 [RESERVED]

[Reserved effective December 1, 2005.]

LR 83.14 APPEARANCE

The signing of a pleading or motion shall be deemed an entry of appearance. Appearance by attorneys or parties not signing pleadings or motions shall be by praecipe filed with the clerk except as provided in Local Rule 83.9.

[Effective April 15, 1997. Amended effective December 1, 2005.]

LR 83.15 WITHDRAWAL OF APPEARANCE

Appearance of counsel shall not be withdrawn except by leave of court. The court may refuse to approve withdrawal. If counsel is superseded by new counsel, such new counsel shall enter an appearance and counsel who is superseded shall comply with this rule and apply for leave to withdraw from the action. The court may refuse to grant a motion for leave to withdraw unless substitute counsel has entered an appearance.

[Effective April 15, 1997.]

LR 83.16 WARRANT OF ATTORNEY

The court may require any attorney to file his or her warrant of attorney.

[Effective April 15, 1997.]

LR 83.17 AGREEMENTS TO BE IN WRITING

All agreements of attorneys relating to the conduct of any business before the court not made in open court shall be in writing, or otherwise they will not be enforced.

[Effective April 15, 1997.]

LR 83.18 APPEARANCE OF PARTIES NOT REPRESENTED BY COUNSEL

Whenever a party by whom or on whose behalf an initial paper is offered for filing is not represented in the action, such party shall maintain on file with the clerk a current address at which all notices and copies of pleadings, motions or papers in the action may be served upon such party. Service of any notices, copies of pleadings, motions or papers in the action at the address currently maintained on file in the clerk's office by a party shall be deemed to be effective service upon such party.

[Effective April 15, 1997.]

LR 83.19 STUDENT PRACTICE RULE

(a) **Purpose.** The following Student Practice Rule is designed to encourage law schools to provide clinical instruction in litigation of varying kinds, and thereby enhance the competence of lawyers in practice before the United States District Court.

(b) **Student Requirements.** An eligible student must:

(1) be duly enrolled in a law school;

(2) have completed at least four (4) semesters of legal studies, or the equivalent;

(3) be enrolled for credit in a law school clinical program which has been certified by this court;

(4) be certified by the Dean of the law school, or the Dean's designee, as being of good character and sufficient legal ability, in accordance with Section 13 above, to fulfill the responsibilities as a legal intern to both the client and this court;

(5) be certified by this court to practice pursuant to this rule;

(6) not accept personal compensation for legal services from a client or other source;

(7) be introduced to the judge before whom the student is to practice by the supervising attorney.

(c) **Program Requirements.** The program:

(1) must be a law school clinical practice program for credit, in which a law student obtains academic and practice advocacy training, utilizing law school faculty for practice supervision, including federal government attorneys, private practitioners, or attorneys working for public defender offices, district attorney offices, the Office of Attorney General, or legal services programs, providing all such attorneys utilized for this purpose have been admitted to practice in this court;

(2) must be certified by this court;

(3) must be conducted in such a manner as not to conflict with normal court schedules;

(4) may accept compensation other than from a client;

(5) must secure and maintain professional liability insurance for its activities and file a certificate of such insurance with the clerk of court.

(d) **Supervisor Requirements.** A supervisor must:

(1) have faculty or adjunct faculty status at the responsible law school and be certified by the Dean of the law school as being of good character and sufficient legal ability and as being adequately trained to fulfill the responsibilities as a supervisor, or in the alternative must be approved by either the court or the Dean of the law school;

(2) be admitted to practice in this court;

(3) be present with the student at all times in court, and at other proceedings, including depositions, in which testimony is taken;

(4) co-sign all pleadings or other documents filed with this court;

(5) assume full personal professional responsibility for the student's guidance in any work undertaken and for the quality of a student's work, and be available for consultation with represented clients;

(6) assist and counsel the student in activities mentioned in this rule, and review such activities with the

student, to the extent required for the proper practical training of the student and the protection of the client;

(7) be responsible to supplement oral or written work of the student as necessary to ensure proper representation of the client.

(e) Certification of Student, Program and Supervisor.

(1) *Students.*

a. Certification by the law school Dean and approval by this court shall be filed with the clerk of court, and unless it is sooner withdrawn, shall remain in effect until expiration of 18 months;

b. Certification to appear in a particular case may be withdrawn by this court at any time, in the discretion of the court, and without any showing of cause.

(2) *Program.*

a. Certification of a program by this court shall be filed with the clerk of court and shall remain in effect indefinitely unless withdrawn by the court;

b. Certification of a program may be withdrawn by this court at any time.

(3) *Supervisor.*

a. Certification of a supervisor must be filed with the clerk of court, and shall remain in effect indefinitely unless withdrawn by this court;

b. Certification of a supervisor may be withdrawn by this court at any time;

c. Certification of a supervisor may be withdrawn by the Dean by mailing the notice to that effect to the clerk of court.

(f) Activities. A certified student, under the personal supervision of the supervisor, as set forth in Part (d) of this rule, may:

(1) represent any client including federal, state or local government bodies, in any civil or administrative matter, if the client on whose behalf the student is appearing has indicated in writing their consent to that appearance and the supervising lawyer has also indicated in writing, approval of that appearance;

(2) engage in all activities on behalf of the clients that a licensed attorney may engage in.

(g) Limitation of Activities. The court retains the power to limit a student's participation in any particular case to such activities as the court deems consistent with the appropriate administration of justice.

[Effective April 15, 1997.]

CHAPTER XVII. ATTORNEY DISCIPLINARY ENFORCEMENT

LR 83.20 ATTORNEYS CONVICTED OF CRIMES

LR 83.20.1 Immediate Suspension. Upon the filing with this court of a certified copy of a judgment of conviction demonstrating that any attorney admitted to practice before this court has been convicted in any court of the United States, or the District of Columbia, or of any state, territory, commonwealth or possession of the United States, of a serious crime as hereinafter defined, the court shall enter an order immediately suspending that attorney, whether the conviction resulted from a plea of guilty or nolo contendere or from a verdict after trial or otherwise, and regardless of the pendency of any appeal, until final disposition of a disciplinary proceeding to be commenced upon such conviction. A copy of such order shall immediately be served upon the attorney. Upon good cause shown, the court may set aside such order when it appears in the interest of justice.

LR 83.20.2 Definition of Serious Crime. The term "serious crime" shall include any felony and any lesser crime a necessary element of which, as determined by the statutory or common law definition of such crime in the jurisdiction where the judgment was entered, involves false swearing, misrepresentation, fraud, willful failure to file income tax returns, deceit, bribery, extortion, misappropriation, theft, or an attempt or a conspiracy or solicitation of another to commit a "serious crime."

LR 83.20.3 Certified Copy of Conviction as Evidence. A certified copy of a judgment of conviction of an attorney for any crime shall be conclusive evidence of the commission of that crime in any disciplinary proceeding instituted against that attorney based upon the conviction.

LR 83.20.4 Mandatory Reference for Disciplinary Proceeding. Upon the filing of a certified copy of a judgment of conviction of an attorney for a serious crime, the court shall in addition to suspending that attorney in accordance with the provisions of this rule, also refer the matter to counsel for the institution of a disciplinary proceeding before the court in which the sole issue to be determined shall be the extent of the final discipline to be imposed as a result of the conduct resulting in the conviction, provided that a disciplinary proceeding so instituted will not be brought to final hearing until all appeals from the conviction are concluded.

LR 83.20.5 Discretionary Reference for Disciplinary Proceedings. Upon the filing of a certified copy of a judgment of conviction of an attorney for a crime not constituting a serious crime, the court may refer the matter to counsel for whatever action counsel may deem warranted, including the institution of a disciplinary proceeding before the court; provided, however, that the court may in its discretion make no reference with respect to convictions for minor offenses.

LR 83.20.6 Reinstatement Upon Reversal. An attorney suspended under the provisions of this rule will be reinstated immediately upon the filing of a certificate demonstrating that the underlying conviction of a serious crime has been reversed but the reinstatement will not terminate any disciplinary proceeding then pending against the attorney, the disposition of which shall be determined by the court on the basis of all available evidence pertaining to both guilt and the extent of discipline to be imposed.

[Effective April 15, 1997. Amended effective August 16, 1999.]

LR 83.21 DISCIPLINE IMPOSED BY OTHER COURTS

LR 83.21.1 Notice by Attorney of Public Discipline. Any attorney admitted to practice before this court shall, upon being subjected to public discipline by any other court of the United States or the District of Columbia, or by a court of any state, territory, commonwealth or possession of the United States, promptly inform the clerk of this court of such action.

LR 83.21.2 Proceedings After Notice of Discipline. Upon the filing of a certified or exemplified copy of a judgment or order demonstrating that an attorney admitted to practice before this court has been disciplined by another court, this court shall forthwith issue a notice directed to the attorney containing:

(a) A copy of the judgment or order from the other court and

(b) An order to show cause directing that the attorney inform this court within thirty (30) days after service of that order upon the attorney, personally or by mail, of any claim by the attorney predicated upon the grounds set forth in Local Rule 83.21.4 that the imposition of the identical discipline by the court would be unwarranted and the reasons therefor.

LR 83.21.3 Stay of Discipline in Other Jurisdiction. In the event the discipline imposed in the other jurisdiction has been stayed there, any reciprocal discipline imposed in this court shall be deferred until such stay expires.

LR 83.21.4 Reciprocal Discipline. Upon the expiration of thirty (30) days from service of the notice issued pursuant to the provisions of Local Rule 83.21.2(b) above, this court shall impose the identical discipline unless the respondent attorney demonstrates, or this court finds, that upon the face of the record upon which the discipline in another jurisdiction is predicated it clearly appears:

(a) That the procedure was so lacking in notice or opportunity to be heard as to constitute a deprivation of due process; or

(b) That there was such an infirmity of proof establishing the misconduct as to give rise to the clear conviction that this court could not, consistent with its duty, accept as final the conclusion on that subject; or

(c) That the imposition of the same discipline by this court would result in grave injustice; or

(d) That the misconduct established is deemed by this court to warrant substantially different discipline.

Where this court determines that any of said elements exist, it shall enter such other order as it deems appropriate.

LR 83.21.5 Conclusive Evidence of Final Adjudication. In all other respects, a final adjudication in another court that an attorney has been guilty of misconduct shall establish conclusively the misconduct for the purposes of a disciplinary proceeding in this court.

LR 83.21.6 Appointment of Counsel. This court may at any stage appoint counsel to prosecute the disciplinary proceedings.

[Effective April 15, 1997.]

LR 83.22 DISBARMENT ON CONSENT OR RESIGNATION IN OTHER COURTS

LR 83.22.1 Automatic Cessation of Right to Practice. Any attorney admitted to practice before this court who shall be disbarred on consent or resign from the bar of any other court of the United States or the District of Columbia, or from the bar of any state, territory, commonwealth or possession of the United States, while an investigation into allegations of misconduct is pending, shall, upon the filing with this court of a certified or exemplified copy of the judgment or order accepting such disbarment on consent or resignation, cease to be permitted to practice before this court and be stricken from the roll of attorneys admitted to practice before this court.

LR 83.22.2 Attorney to Notify Clerk of Disbarment. Any attorney admitted to practice before this court shall, upon being disbarred on consent or resigning from the bar of any other court of the United States or the District of Columbia or from the bar of any state, territory, commonwealth or possession of the United States, while an investigation into allegations of misconduct is pending, promptly inform the clerk of this court of such disbarment on consent or resignation.

[Effective April 15, 1997.]

LR 83.23 STANDARDS FOR PROFESSIONAL CONDUCT

LR 83.23.1 Sanction for Misconduct. For misconduct defined in these rules, and for good cause shown, and after notice and opportunity to be heard any attorney admitted to practice before this court may be disbarred, suspended from practice before this court, reprimanded or subjected to such other disciplinary action as the circumstances may warrant.

LR 83.23.2 Adoption of Rules of Professional Conduct. Acts or omissions by an attorney admitted to practice before this court, individually or in concert with any other person or persons, which violate the Rules of Professional Conduct adopted by this court, shall constitute misconduct and shall be grounds for discipline, whether or not the act or omission occurred in the course of an attorney-client relationship. The Rules of Professional Conduct adopted by this court are: (1) the Rules of Professional Conduct adopted by the Supreme Court of Pennsylvania, except Rule 3.10, as amended from time to time by that court, unless specifically excepted in this court's rules; and (2) the Code of Professional Conduct enacted in the Middle District of Pennsylvania's Civil Justice Reform Act Plan. See Appendix C.

[Effective April 15, 1997. Amended effective August 16, 1999.]

LR 83.24 DISCIPLINARY PROCEEDINGS

LR 83.24.1 Reference to Counsel. When misconduct or allegations of misconduct which, if substantiated, would warrant discipline on the part of an attorney admitted to practice before this court shall come to the attention of a judge of this court, whether by complaint or otherwise, and the applicable procedure is not otherwise mandated by these rules, the judge shall refer the matter to counsel for investigation and the prosecution of a formal disciplinary proceeding or the formulation of such other recommendation as may be appropriate.

LR 83.24.2 Recommendation of Counsel. Should counsel conclude after investigation and review that a formal disciplinary proceeding should not be initiated against the respondent attorney because sufficient evidence is not present, or because there is pending another proceeding against the respondent-attorney, the disposition of which in the judgment of the counsel should be awaited before further action by this court is considered or for any other valid reason, counsel shall file with this court a recommendation for disposition of the matter, whether by dismissal, admonition, deferral, or otherwise setting forth the reasons therefor.

LR 83.24.3 Order to Show Cause. To initiate formal disciplinary proceedings, counsel shall obtain an order of this court upon a showing of probable cause requiring the respondent-attorney to show cause within thirty (30) days after service of that order upon that attorney, personally or by mail, why the attorney should not be disciplined.

LR 83.24.4 Hearings. Upon the respondent-attorney's answer to the order to show cause, if any issue of fact is raised or the respondent-attorney wishes to be heard in mitigation, this court shall set the matter for prompt hearing before one or more judges of this court, provided, however, that if the disciplinary proceeding is predicated upon the complaint of a judge of this court the hearing shall be conducted before a panel of three other judges of this court appointed by the chief judge, or if there are less than three judges eligible to serve or the chief judge is the complainant, by the chief judge of the court of appeals for this circuit. Where a judge merely refers a matter and is not involved in the proceeding, the judge shall not be considered a complainant.

[Effective April 15, 1997.]

LR 83.25 DISBARMENT ON CONSENT WHILE UNDER DISCIPLINARY INVESTIGATION OR PROSECUTION

LR 83.25.1 Consent to Disbarment. Any attorney admitted to practice before this court who is the subject of an investigation into, or a pending proceeding involving, allegations of misconduct may consent to disbarment, but only by delivering to this court an affidavit stating that the attorney desires to consent to disbarment and that:

(a) The attorney's consent is freely and voluntarily rendered; the attorney is not being subjected to coercion or duress; the attorney is fully aware of the implications of so consenting;

(b) The attorney is aware that there is a presently pending investigation or proceeding involving allegations that there exist grounds for the attorney's discipline, the nature of which the attorney shall specifically set forth;

(c) The attorney acknowledges that the material facts so alleged are true; and

(d) The attorney so consents because the attorney knows that if charges were predicated upon the matters under investigation, or if the proceeding were prosecuted, the attorney could not successfully defend himself or herself.

LR 83.25.2 Consent Order. Upon receipt of the required affidavit, this court shall enter an order disbarring the attorney.

LR 83.25.3 Public Record. The order disbarring the attorney on consent shall be a matter of public record. However, the affidavit required under the provisions of this rule shall not be publicly disclosed or made available for use in any other proceeding except upon order of this court.

[Effective April 15, 1997.]

LR 83.26   REINSTATEMENT

LR 83.26.1 After Disbarment or Suspension. An attorney suspended for three (3) months or less shall be automatically reinstated at the end of the period of suspension upon the filing with the court of an affidavit of compliance with the provisions of the order. An attorney suspended for more than three (3) months or disbarred may not resume practice until reinstated by order of this court.

LR 83.26.2 Time of Application Following Disbarment. A person who has been disbarred after hearing or by consent may not apply for reinstatement until the expiration of at least five (5) years from the effective date of this disbarment.

LR 83.26.3 Petitions for Reinstatement. Petitions for reinstatement by a disbarred or suspended attorney under this rule shall be filed with the chief judge of this court.

(a) Upon receipt of the petition, the chief judge shall determine whether the attorney is entitled to reinstatement without a hearing and issue an appropriate order.

(b) If the petitioner is not entitled to reinstatement without a hearing the chief judge shall promptly refer the petition to counsel and shall assign the matter for prompt hearing before one or more judges of this court, provided, however, that if the disciplinary proceeding was predicated upon the complaint of a judge of this court, the hearing shall be conducted before a panel of three (3) other judges of this court appointed by the chief judge, or, if there are less than three (3) judges eligible to serve or the chief judge was the complainant, by the chief judge of the court of appeals for this circuit. The judge or judges assigned to the matter shall within thirty (30) days after referral schedule a hearing at which the petitioner shall have the burden of demonstrating by clear and convincing evidence that he or she has the moral qualifications, competency and learning in the law required for admission to practice law before this court and that his or her resumption of the practice of law will not be detrimental to the integrity and standing of the bar or to the administration of justice, or subversive of the public interest. Absent extraordinary circumstances, no such petition for reinstatement shall be granted unless the attorney seeking reinstatement meets the requirements for admission set forth in Local Rule 83.8.1.2. In the case where this court has imposed discipline or otherwise taken adverse action identical to that imposed or taken by a state court or authority, any petition for reinstatement in this court shall be held in abeyance until a petition for reinstatement to practice in the state court has been filed and finally decided, unless otherwise ordered by this court.

LR 83.26.4 Duty of Counsel. In all proceedings upon a petition for reinstatement, cross-examination of the witnesses of the respondent-attorney and the submission of evidence, if any, in opposition to the petition shall be conducted by counsel.

LR 83.26.5 Fees and Costs of Proceeding. Upon order of court at the conclusion of any reinstatement proceeding, costs may be assessed to the petitioner. The Clerk of Court shall account for these costs in the same manner as general attorney admissions.

LR 83.26.6 Conditions of Reinstatement. If the petitioner is found unfit to resume the practice of law, the petition shall be dismissed. If the petitioner is found fit to resume the practice of law, the judgment shall reinstate the petitioner, provided that the judgment may make reinstatement conditional upon the payment of all or part of the costs of the proceedings, and upon the making of partial or complete restitution to parties harmed by the petitioner whose conduct led to the suspension or disbarment. Provided further, that if the petitioner has been suspended or disbarred for five (5) years or more, reinstatement may be conditioned, in the discretion of the judge or judges before whom the matter is heard, upon the furnishing of proof of competency and learning in the law, which proof may include certification by the bar examiners of a state or other jurisdiction of the attorney's successful completion of an examination for admission to practice subsequent to the date of suspension or disbarment.

LR 83.26.7 Successive Petitions. No petition for reinstatement under this rule shall be filed within one (1) year following an adverse judgment upon a petition for reinstatement filed by or on behalf of the same person.

[Effective April 15, 1997. Amended effective December 1, 2001; December 1, 2014.]

LR 83.27   ADMISSION TO PRACTICE AS CONFERRING DISCIPLINARY JURISDICTION

Whenever an attorney applies to be admitted or is admitted to this court for purposes of a particular proceeding (pro hac vice), the attorney shall be deemed thereby to have conferred disciplinary jurisdiction upon this court for any alleged misconduct of that attorney arising in the course of or in the preparation for such proceeding.

[Effective April 15, 1997.]

LR 83.28 SERVICE OF PAPERS AND OTHER NOTICES

Service of an order to show cause instituting a formal disciplinary proceeding or other papers or notices required by these rules shall be made by personal service or by registered or certified mail addressed to the respondent-attorney at the address most recently registered by the attorney with the clerk. Service of any other papers or notices required by these rules shall be deemed to have been made if such paper or notice is addressed to the respondent-attorney at the address shown on the most recent registration statement filed pursuant to Local Rule 83.11.1; or to counsel or the respondent's attorney at the address indicated in the most recent pleading or other document filed by them in the course of any proceeding under these rules.

[Effective April 15, 1997.]

LR 83.29 APPOINTMENT OF COUNSEL

Whenever counsel is to be appointed pursuant to these rules to investigate allegations of misconduct or to prosecute disciplinary proceedings or in conjunction with a reinstatement petition filed by a disciplined attorney, this court in its discretion and with prior agreement of the Disciplinary Board of the Supreme Court of Pennsylvania shall appoint as counsel attorneys serving in the Office of Disciplinary Counsel of the Disciplinary Board or one or more members of the bar of this court to investigate allegations of misconduct or to prosecute disciplinary proceedings under these rules or in conjunction with such a reinstatement petition, provided, however, that the respondent-attorney may move to disqualify an attorney so appointed who is or has been engaged as an adversary of the respondent-attorney in any matter. Counsel, once appointed, may not resign unless permission to do so is given by this court.

[Effective April 15, 1997.]

LR 83.30 DUTIES OF THE CLERK

LR 83.30.1 Filing Certificate of Conviction. Upon being informed that an attorney admitted to practice before this court has been convicted of any crime, the clerk of this court shall determine whether the clerk of the court in which such conviction occurred has forwarded a certificate of such conviction to this court. If a certificate has not been so forwarded, the clerk of this court shall promptly obtain a certificate and file it with this court.

LR 83.30.2 Filing Disciplinary Judgment. Upon being informed that an attorney admitted to practice

before this court has been subjected to discipline by another court, the clerk of this court shall determine whether a certified or exemplified copy of the disciplinary judgment or order has been filed with this court, and, if not, the clerk shall promptly obtain a certified or exemplified copy of the disciplinary judgment or order and file it with this court.

LR 83.30.3 Filing Consent Order. Upon being informed that an attorney admitted to practice before this court has been disbarred on consent or resigned in another jurisdiction while an investigation into allegations of misconduct was pending, the clerk of this court shall determine whether a certified or exemplified copy of the disciplinary judgment or order striking the attorney's name from the rolls of those admitted to practice has been filed with the court, and, if not, shall promptly obtain a certified or exemplified copy of such judgment or order and file it with the court.

LR 83.30.4 Transmittal of Record to Other Courts. Whenever it appears that any person convicted of any crime or disbarred or suspended or censured or disbarred on consent by this court is admitted to practice law in any other jurisdiction or before any other court, the clerk of this court shall, within fourteen (14) days of that conviction, disbarment, suspension, censure, or disbarment on consent, transmit to the disciplinary authority in such other jurisdiction, or for such other court, a certificate of the conviction or a certified or exemplified copy of the judgment or order of disbarment, suspension, censure, or disbarment on consent, as well as the last known office and residence addresses of the defendant or respondent.

LR 83.30.5 National Discipline Data Bank. The clerk of this court shall promptly notify the National Discipline Data Bank operated by the American Bar Association of any order imposing public discipline upon any attorney admitted to practice before this court.

[Effective April 15, 1997. Amended effective December 1, 2009.]

LR 83.31 COURT DEFINED

When in this Chapter reference is made to this court it shall mean the United States District Court for the Middle District of Pennsylvania. Administration of this Chapter shall be under the authority of the Chief Judge. Actions and proceedings under this Chapter shall be taken by the Chief Judge of this court or the designee(s) of the Chief Judge.

[Effective April 15, 1997. Amended effective December 1, 2001.]

CHAPTER XVIII.   HABEAS CORPUS AND MOTIONS ATTACKING SENTENCE AND APPEALS WHERE PARTY IS INCARCERATED

LR 83.32   PETITIONS FOR WRIT OF HABEAS CORPUS AND MOTIONS PURSUANT TO 28 U.S.C. § 2255

LR 83.32.1   Form of Petitions and Motions. A petition for a writ of habeas corpus by a person who is in custody or who faces future custody pursuant to the judgment or order of a federal or state court or agency, or a motion pursuant to 28 U.S.C. § 2255 attacking a sentence imposed by this court, shall be filed according to these Rules. The petition or motion, unless prepared by counsel, shall be on the standard form supplied by the clerk of court when the petition or motion is a § 2241 or a § 2254 habeas corpus petition or a § 2255 motion. When the petition or motion is filed by counsel, the standard form need not be used, but the petition or motion shall contain the same categories of information and shall address the same matters as provided for by the standard form, and the petition or motion shall be double spaced and shall be no more than twenty (20) pages in length. The Rules Governing § 2254 Cases In The United States District Courts and the Rules Governing § 2255 Proceedings For The United States District Courts, adopted by the Supreme Court of the United States, are a part of the Rules of this District applicable to § 2254 habeas corpus cases and § 2255 motions. A petition for a writ of habeas corpus in a death penalty case shall be governed by Local Rule 83.32.2.

LR 83.32.2 Petitions Under 28 U.S.C. § 2254 and Motions to Vacate Sentence Under 28 U.S.C. § 2255 in Death Penalty Cases. In a death penalty case:

A.   A petition for a writ of habeas corpus under 28 U.S.C. § 2254 or a motion to vacate sentence under 28 U.S.C. § 2255 must be accompanied by a cover sheet that lists:

1.   petitioner's full name and prisoner number; if prosecuted under a different name or alias that name must be indicated;

2.   name of person having custody of petitioner (warden, superintendent, etc.);

3.   petitioner's address;

4.   name of trial judge;

5.   court term and bill of information or indictment number;

6.   charges of which petitioner was convicted;

7.   sentence for each of the charges;

8.   plea entered;

9.   whether trial was by jury or to the bench;

10.   date of filing, docket numbers, dates of decision and results of direct appeal of the conviction;

11.   date of filing, docket numbers, dates of decision and results of any state collateral attack on a state conviction including appeals;

12.   date of filing, docket numbers, dates of decision of any prior federal habeas corpus or § 2255 proceedings, including appeals;

13.   name and address of each attorney who represented petitioner, identifying the stage at which the attorney represented the litigant.

B.   A petition for writ of habeas corpus under 28 U.S.C. § 2254 or motion to vacate sentence under 28 U.S.C. § 2255:

1.   must list every ground on which the petitioner claims to be entitled to relief under 28 U.S.C. § 2254 (or § 2255 for federal prisoners) followed by a concise statement of the material facts supporting the claims;

2.   must identify at what stage of the proceedings each claim was exhausted in state court if the petition seeks relief from a state court judgment;

3.   must contain a table of contents if the petition is more than 25 pages;

4.   may contain citation to legal authority that form the basis of the claim.

C.   Petitioner must file and serve, not later than 60 days after the date of the filing of the petition under § 2254, or motion to vacate sentence under § 2255, a memorandum of law in support.

The memorandum of law:

1.   must contain a statement of the case;

2.   must contain a table of contents if it is more than 25 pages.

D.   The petition/motion and memorandum together must not exceed 100 pages.

E.   All documents filed must be succinct and must avoid repetition.

F.   Respondent need not file a response until the petitioner's supporting memorandum of law is served:

1.   The response must not exceed 100 pages.

2.   The response must contain a table of contents if it is more than 25 pages.

3.   The response must be filed and served within 60 days of service of the petitioner's supporting memorandum of law.

G. Any reply to the response must be filed and served within 21 days of service of the response and may not exceed 30 pages.

H. Upon motion and for good cause shown, the judge may extend the page limits for any document.

I. Upon motion and for good cause shown, the judge may extend the time for filing any document.

J. The petitioner must file with the Clerk of the District Court a copy of the "Certificate of Death Penalty Case" required by Third Circuit L.A.R. Misc. 111.2(a). Upon docketing, the clerk of the district court will transmit a copy of the certificate, together with a copy of the petition to the Clerk of the Court of Appeals as required by Third Circuit L.A.R. Misc. 111.2(a).

K. Upon the entry of a warrant or order setting an execution date in any case within the geographical boundaries of this district, and in aid of this court's potential jurisdiction, the clerk is directed to monitor the status of the execution and any pending litigation and to establish communications with all parties and relevant state and/or federal courts. Without further order of this court, the clerk may, prior to the filing of a petition, direct parties to lodge with this court (1) relevant portions of previous state and/or federal court records, or the entire record, and (2) pleadings, briefs, and transcripts of any ongoing proceedings. To prevent delay, the case may be assigned to a judge, by the same selection process as for other cases, prior to the execution date. The identity of the judge assigned shall not be disclosed until a petition is actually docketed.

L. In accordance with Third Circuit L.A.R. Misc. 111.3(b), at the time a final decision is entered, the court shall state whether a certificate of appealability is granted or denied. If a certificate of appealability is granted, the court must state the issues that merit the granting of a certificate and must also grant a stay pending disposition of the appeal, except as provided in 28 U.S.C. § 2262.

LR 83.32.3 In Forma Pauperis Proceedings.

(a) *Affidavit Required.* A petitioner or movant seeking to proceed in forma pauperis must complete the in forma pauperis affidavit or declaration attached at the back of the petition for a writ of habeas corpus and shall set forth information which establishes, pursuant to 28 U.S.C. § 1915, that he or she is unable to pay the fees and costs, or give security therefor. In the absence of exceptional circumstances, leave to proceed in forma pauperis may be denied if the value of the money and securities in the petitioner's institutional account exceeds fifty dollars ($50.00).

(b) *Warden's Certificate.* Under Rule 3 of the rules governing § 2254 cases a certificate of the warden or other appropriate officer of the institution in which the petitioner is confined is required in addition to the affidavit or declaration of poverty. Such a certificate is provided at the end of the standard form for filing § 2254 cases, and this certificate must be completed and returned with the forms. The certificate may be considered by the court in acting upon the request to proceed in forma pauperis.

LR 83.32.4 Addresses and Reference of Petitions and Motions.
Petitions and motions shall be addressed to the Clerk of the United States District Court for the Middle District of Pennsylvania. Petitioners or movants shall send to the clerk an original and a sufficient number of copies of the completed petition or motion for service on all named respondents. A petition or motion addressed to an individual judge shall be directed to the clerk of the court for processing. Whenever possible, successive petitions and motions by a person in custody shall be directed by the clerk to the judge who handled prior petitions and motions by such person.

[Effective April 15, 1997. Amended effective August 16, 1999; December 1, 2001; December 1, 2005.]

LR 83.33   TIME FOR APPEAL WHERE PARTY IS INCARCERATED

When it appears that a party who is incarcerated has delivered a notice of appeal within thirty (30) days after the entry of a civil judgment to the authorities in charge of that party's incarceration, the time for filing the notice of appeal is extended for a period not to exceed thirty (30) days in order to allow for the handling and transmission of the notice of appeal by the authorities to the clerk of the court.

[Effective April 15, 1997.]

CHAPTER XIX.   PRO BONO ATTORNEYS FOR INDIGENT LITIGANTS

LR 83.34   ADMINISTRATION OF PRO BONO PROGRAM

LR 83.34.1   Indigent Litigant Application for a Volunteer Attorney. A Pro Se indigent litigant may apply to the court to have a volunteer attorney appointed to represent the litigant in a civil case.

LR 83.34.2   Request for Volunteer Attorney. A judge may request a member of the bar of this court to enter his or her appearance for an indigent civil litigant.

LR 83.34.3   Panel of Volunteer Attorneys. The Middle District Chapter of the Federal Bar Association has assembled a panel of volunteer attorneys who will consider representing indigent civil litigants at the request of the court. The court may present a request for a volunteer attorney to the pro bono chair of the Middle District Chapter to the Federal Bar Association.

LR 83.34.4 Mechanism for Requesting Volunteer Attorney. When the court makes a determination that a request for a volunteer attorney is appropriate, it shall conditionally grant the motion for the appointment of counsel. The court shall in its order direct that a copy of the order be sent to the pro bono chair of the Middle District Chapter of the Federal Bar Association and shall direct that the court be informed in due course by the pro bono chair whether a volunteer attorney will enter his or her appearance or, in the alternative, that no volunteer attorney accepts the appointment.

LR 83.34.5 Revocation of Conditional Appointment Order. When the pro bono chair of the Middle District Chapter of the Federal Bar Association reports to the court that no volunteer attorney is willing to accept an appointment of counsel the court may revoke the conditional order for the appointment of counsel.

LR 83.34.6 Procedure for Requesting Reimbursement. At the conclusion of a case, any court-appointed pro bono attorney may request reimbursement of costs necessarily incurred, not to exceed the maximum amount established by Standing Order, pro-vided that the attorney has not received or will not receive funds sufficient to cover the costs incurred, whether by way of a monetary judgment for the client under a contingent fee arrangement, an award of attorney's fees made by the court, or other payment. A "Request for Pro Bono Reimbursement," including an accounting of the expenses claimed, shall be submitted directly to the Chief Judge. The document shall not be filed with the Clerk. The form must be typewritten and include the caption of the case, case number, presiding judge and be entitled "Request for Pro Bono Reimbursement;" the document must be signed and verified by the pro bono attorney requesting reimbursement.

LR 83.34.7 Fund to Reimburse Volunteer Attorneys. The court has established a non-appropriated fund for the purpose of reimbursing court-appointed pro bono attorneys for costs necessarily incurred while representing indigent litigants in civil cases. This fund shall be referred to as the court's "Pro Bono Fund." The special admission fee collected by the Clerk of Court pursuant to Local Rule 83.8.2.5 shall be deposited into the Pro Bono Fund, which shall be maintained by the Clerk of Court as trustee in a specially designated account. The Clerk of Court shall account for and disburse sums from the Pro Bono fund pursuant to guidelines established by the court through a Standing Order.

[Effective August 16, 1999.]

CHAPTER XX.   SOCIAL SECURITY APPEALS

LR 83.40   SOCIAL SECURITY DISABILITY CASE PROCEDURES

LR 83.40.1 Form of Review. A civil action brought to review a decision of the Social Security Administration denying a claim for social security disability benefits shall be adjudicated as an appeal pursuant to this rule.

LR 83.40.2 Summons and Complaint. The plaintiff shall cause the summons and complaint to be served upon the defendant in the manner specified by Fed.R.Civ.P.4(i) within fourteen (14) days of the date of filing the complaint with the Clerk of Court.

LR 83.40.3 Answer and Transcript. Defendant shall serve and file an answer, together with a certified copy of the transcript of the administrative record, within sixty (60) days of service of the complaint.

LR 83.40.4 Plaintiff's Brief. Plaintiff shall serve and file a brief within forty-five (45) days of service of defendant's answer that shall comply with the following requirements:

(a) Statement of the Case. This statement shall briefly outline the course of the proceedings and its disposition at the administrative level and shall set forth a brief statement of pertinent facts. This statement of facts shall include plaintiff's age, education and work experience, a summary of the physical and mental impairments alleged; and a brief outline of the pertinent factual, medical and/or vocational evidence of record. Each statement of fact shall be supported by reference to the page(s) in the record where the evidence may be located.

(b) Statement of Errors. This statement shall set forth in separate numbered paragraphs the specific errors committed at the administrative level which entitle plaintiff to relief. The court will consider only those errors specifically identified in the briefs. A general argument that the findings of the administrative law judge are not supported by substantial evidence is not sufficient.

(c) Argument. The argument shall be divided into sections separately addressing each issue and shall set forth the contentions of plaintiff with respect to each issue and the reasons therefor. Each contention must be supported by specific reference to the portion of the record relied upon and by citations to statutes, regulations and cases supporting plaintiff's position.

(d) Conclusion. The plaintiff's brief shall conclude with a short statement of the relief sought.

LR 83.40.5 Defendant's Brief. Within thirty (30) days after service of plaintiff's brief, defendant shall file and serve upon opposing counsel a brief which responds specifically to each issue raised by the plaintiff. The response shall not address matters not put at issue by the plaintiff. Defendant shall not include a "statement of the case," described above, unless plaintiff's statement is inaccurate or incomplete. In that event, defendant need only address those limited areas.

LR 83.40.6 Reply Brief. Plaintiff may file, and serve upon defendant, a brief in reply to the brief of defendant within fourteen (14) days of the filing of defendant's brief.

LR 83.40.7 Length of Briefs. The brief for the plaintiff shall not exceed fifteen (15) pages. The brief for the defendant shall not exceed fifteen (15) pages. The reply brief shall not exceed ten (10) pages.

[Effective August 16, 1999. Amended effective December 1, 2009.]

SECTION II

CHAPTER I. INDICTMENT

LCrR 7.1 SUPERSEDING INDICTMENTS

Upon the filing of a superseding indictment, the government shall file a statement indicating whether the United States has filed or will file a motion for a continuance of trial based upon the filing of the superseding indictment and indicating the changes that have been made in the superseding indictment in comparison to the preceding indictment.

[Effective December 1, 2005.]

CHAPTER II. PLEADINGS AND PRETRIAL MOTIONS

LCrR 12.1 PRETRIAL MOTIONS: DUTY TO ADDRESS SPEEDY TRIAL ACT EXCLUDABLE TIME IMPLICATIONS

(a) A motion for a continuance of trial and any other pretrial motion filed after arraignment, whether by the government or the defendant, shall include:

(1) a statement of whether or not any delay occasioned by the making, hearing or granting of that motion will constitute, in whole or in part, excludable time as defined by 18 U.S.C. § 3161(h), and, if so, a statement or estimation of the number of days to be excluded or a statement describing how excludable time should be determined by reference to a specified future event; and

(2) a proposed form of order that, if adopted, will state fully and with particularity the reasons for granting the motion and that states with particularity the proposed findings of the court as to excludable time.

(b) A party opposing a motion shall file, with the responsive brief to the substance of the motion, its agreement with or opposition to the statements or estimations of the moving party made pursuant to subsection (a).

(c) Briefs in support of and in opposition to a motion for a continuance of trial shall be filed as follows:

(1) A party filing a motion for a continuance of trial shall file a supporting brief at the time the motion is filed. A brief shall not be required in support of a motion for a continuance trial if the reasons for the request, specifically the grounds in support of a finding that the ends of justice served by the granting of a continuance outweigh the best interests of the public and the defendant in a speedy trial, are fully stated in the motion.

(2) A party opposing a motion for a continuance of trial shall file a brief in opposition to the motion within seven (7) days after service of the motion. No further briefs may be filed without leave of court.

(3) A party who does not file a brief in opposition to a motion shall be deemed not to oppose the motion.

(d) This rule shall not apply to any motion to be heard ex parte.

[Effective December 1, 2005. Amended effective December 1, 2009.]

LCrR 12.4 ORGANIZATIONAL VICTIM DISCLOSURE STATEMENT

In a case in which the government is aware that an organizational victim of the alleged criminal activity is a corporation and in which the corporation has not provided to the government the information required by Fed.R.Crim.P. 12.4(a)(1), the government shall so indicate in its Fed.R.Crim.P. 12.4(a)(2) statement. In the absence of a statement from the government identifying Fed.R.Crim.P. 12.4(a)(1) parent corporation information and stock ownership information relating to a corporate victim, the court will proceed by presuming the absence of a parent corporation and the absence of an ownership of more than 10% of the corporate victim's stock by another corporation unless the court has actual knowledge of such information. [Effective December 1, 2007.]

CHAPTER III. POST–CONVICTION PROCEDURES

LCrR 32.1 PRESENTENCE PROCEDURE

(a) Upon a verdict of guilty or the entry of a plea of guilty or nolo contendere, the court shall set a date by which the probation officer shall disclose the presentence report to the defendant, the defendant's counsel, and the attorney for the government, and shall set a sentencing date. The presentence report disclosure date shall be no later than fifty-six (56) days after a verdict of guilty or the entry of a plea of guilty or nolo contendere. The sentencing date shall be no later than ninety-eight (98) days after the verdict of guilty, or the entry of a plea of guilty or nolo contendere.

(b) The probation officer shall provide defense counsel with notice and a reasonable opportunity to attend any interview of the defendant by a probation officer in the course of a presentence investigation. Unless an interview is declined on advice of counsel, the probation officer shall interview the defendant immediately after the verdict of guilty or the entry of a plea of guilty or nolo contendere. Upon request by defense counsel, or if the probation officer's schedule so requires, the probation officer shall postpone the interview. However, any postponement greater than seven (7) days shall require approval of the presiding judge.

(c) Within seven (7) days after a verdict of guilty or the entry of a plea of guilty or nolo contendere, the attorney for the government shall provide to the probation officer and to the defendant's counsel a comprehensive Statement of Offense Conduct and supporting documentation. If a defendant is responsible for restitution, the government must within twenty-eight (28) days submit sufficient information to enable the court to determine entitlement, the name of each victim, the amount of loss for each victim, and documentary support for each amount. If liability for restitution is joint and several, the government shall itemize the restitution amount for which each defendant is responsible. The Statement of Offense Conduct shall address all Chapter Two and Chapter Three adjustments of the United States Sentencing Commission Guidelines Manual which are necessary to calculate the sentencing guidelines.

(d) The government shall provide to the defendant's counsel a copy of any documentary information provided to the probation officer to be considered in the preparation of the presentence report at the same time as it is provided to the probation officer. The defendant or the defendant's counsel may submit documentary information to the probation officer and shall provide a copy to the attorney for the government at the same time as it is provided to the probation officer.

(e) At least thirty-five (35) days before the sentencing hearing, the probation officer shall provide a copy of the presentence report to the defendant, the defendant's counsel and the attorney for the government.

(f) Within fourteen (14) days after receiving the presentence report, the parties shall communicate in writing to the probation officer, and to each other, any objections to material information, sentencing guideline ranges, and policy statements contained in or omitted from the report. The written communication shall contain detailed information regarding any disputed issues. After receiving any objections, the probation officer may require counsel for both parties as well as the defendant and/or case agent to meet with the probation officer to discuss unresolved factual and legal issues. The probation officer may also undertake further investigation and revise the presentence report as necessary.

(g) At least seven (7) days before the sentencing hearing, the probation officer shall submit the final presentence report to the court, together with an addendum setting forth any unresolved objections, the grounds for those objections, and the probation officer's comments on the objections. At the same time, the probation officer shall transmit the final presentence report and the Addendum to the defendant, the defendant's counsel, and the attorney for the government.

(h) Except for any unresolved objection under Fed. R.Crim.P. 32, the court may, at the hearing, accept the presentence report as its findings of fact. For good cause shown, the court may allow a new objection to be raised at any time before imposing sentence.

(i) The probation officer shall not disclose any sentencing recommendation unless so ordered by the court.

(j) The time limits set forth in this Rule may be modified by the court for good cause.

[Effective December 1, 2012.]

CHAPTER IV. SERVING AND FILING OF PAPERS

LCrR 49. FILING OF DOCUMENTS UNDER SEAL

(a) Authorization Required. Unless otherwise prescribed by federal statutes, the Federal Rules of Criminal Procedure, the Federal Rules of Civil Procedure or other provisions of these Rules, including LR 5.2(e), no document shall be filed under seal unless authorized by an order of court.

(b) Definitions.

(1) *Document "Filed Under Seal".* A document filed under seal is a document that is filed and docketed in the case but held by the Clerk separate from other documents and not made available for inspection by any person except as permitted by order of the court.

(2) *Document "Pending Sealing Decision".* A document pending sealing decision is a document that has been submitted to the Clerk with a motion to file the document under seal. Pending an order of the court deciding the motion to seal the document, the document is kept separate from other documents and is not made available for inspection by any person except as permitted by order of the court.

(c) Procedure.

(1) *Motion to File a Document Under Seal.* A motion to file a document under seal shall be filed on paper. The motion to file a document under seal shall contain no description or identification of the document for which the sealing order is sought or statement of reasons why the filing of the document under seal should be authorized.

(2) *The Presentation to the Clerk of the Document(s) Pending Sealing Decision.* When the motion is filed, the party filing the motion shall present to the Clerk's Office, on paper:

a. the document(s) for which the sealing order is sought,

b. a statement of the legal and factual justification for the sealing order that is being sought, and

c. a proposed form of order.

The document(s), statement and proposed order shall be presented to the Clerk in a sealed envelope marked with the case number, case caption and the descriptive label of "Documents pending sealing decision."

(3) *Document Authorized to Be Filed Under Seal by an Existing Court Order.* A document authorized to be filed under seal by an existing court order shall be filed on paper accompanied by the court order authorizing it to be filed under seal and submitted in a sealed envelope marked with the case number, case caption, and the words "sealed document."

(d) Exempt Documents. The Clerk shall in all cases, without motion, seal the following documents:

(1) A defendant's ex parte request for a subpoena, a writ of habeas corpus ad testificandum, or authorization to obtain investigative, expert or other services in accordance with subsection (e) of the Criminal Justice Act, 18 U.S.C. § 3006A(e).

(2) An ex parte request by the government for issuance of a writ of habeas corpus ad testificandum.

(3) Any writ issued in response to a request under subparagraph (1) and (2).

(4) A request in a criminal case by the defendant for substitution of appointed counsel.

(e) Motion to Unseal. It shall be the duty of the party who obtained an order to file under seal to move to unseal the document as soon as the basis for the sealing order has ended.

[Effective December 1, 2005. Revised effective December 1, 2006.]

CHAPTER V. GENERAL PROVISIONS

LCrR 57. EXTRAJUDICIAL STATEMENTS IN CRIMINAL PROCEEDINGS

(a) A lawyer representing a party with respect to a criminal matter, or any other proceeding that could result in incarceration, shall not make any extrajudicial statement that a reasonable person would expect to be disseminated by means of public communication if the lawyer or other person knows or reasonably should know that it will have a substantial likelihood of causing material prejudice to an adjudicative proceeding.

(b) A statement referred to in LCrR 57(a) ordinarily is likely to have such an effect when it relates to:

(1) the character, credibility, reputation or criminal record of a defendant, suspect in a criminal investigation or witness, the identity of a witness, or the expected testimony of a party or witness;

(2) the possibility of a plea of guilty to the offense or the existence or contents of any confession, admission or statement given by a defendant or suspect, or that person's refusal or failure to make a statement;

(3) the performance or results of any examination or test, the refusal or failure of a person to submit to an examination or test, or the identity or nature of physical evidence expected to be presented;

(4) any opinion as to the guilt or innocence of a defendant or suspect; or

(5) information the lawyer knows or reasonably should know is likely to be inadmissible as evidence in a trial and would if disclosed create a substantial risk of prejudice to an impartial trial.

(c) Notwithstanding LCrR 57(a) and (b), a lawyer involved in the investigation or prosecution of a matter may state without elaboration:

(1) the general nature of a charge or defense;

(2) the information contained in a public record;

(3) that an investigation of the matter is in progress, including the general scope of the investigation, the offense, claim or defense involved and, except when prohibited by law, the identity of the persons involved;

(4) the scheduling or result of any step in litigation;

(5) a request for assistance in obtaining evidence and the information necessary thereto;

(6) a warning of danger concerning the behavior of a person involved, when there is reason to believe that there exists the likelihood of substantial harm to an individual or to the public interest;

(7) the identity, residence, occupation and family status of the accused;

(8) if the accused has not been apprehended, information necessary to aid in apprehension of that person;

(9) the fact, time and place of arrest; and

(10) the identity of investigating and arresting officers or agencies and the length of the investigation.

(d) The prohibitions set forth in LCrR 57(a), (b) and (c) pertain to all stages of criminal proceedings, including investigation before a grand jury, the post–arrest pretrial period, jury selection, trial through verdict or disposition without trial and imposition of sentence.

(e) Nothing in this Rule is intended to preclude either the formulation or application of more restrictive rules relating to the release of any information about juvenile or other offenders.

(f) Nothing in this Rule is intended to apply to the holding of hearings or the lawful issuance of reports by legislative, administrative or investigative bodies, nor to a reply by any attorney to charges of misconduct publicly made against that attorney.

(g) The court's supporting personnel including, among others, the marshal, deputy marshals, the clerk, deputy clerks, court reporters and employees or subcontractors retained by the court–appointed official reporters, probation officers and their staffs, and members of the Judges' staffs, are prohibited from disclosing to any person, without authorization by the court, information relating to a proceeding that is not part of the public record of the court. The disclosure of information concerning in camera arguments and hearings held in chambers or otherwise outside the presence of the public is also forbidden.

(h) The court, on motion of any party or on its own motion, may issue a special order governing such matters as extrajudicial statements by parties and witnesses likely to interfere with the rights of a party to a fair trial by an impartial jury, the seating and conduct in the courtroom of spectators and news media representatives, the management and sequestration of jurors and witnesses, and any other matters which the court may deem appropriate for inclusion in such an order.

[Effective December 1, 2006.]

LCrR 58.1 MAGISTRATE JUDGES, APPEAL FROM JUDGMENTS IN MISDEMEANOR CASES—18 U.S.C. § 3402

An appeal from a judgment of conviction by a United States Magistrate Judge may be taken to a judge of the district court in accordance with Rule 58 of the Federal Rules of Criminal Procedure. The appellant shall, within fourteen (14) days of the date of filing of the appeal, serve and submit a brief. The United States Attorney shall serve and submit a brief within fourteen (14) days after receipt of a copy of the appellant's brief. The appellant may serve and submit a reply brief within seven (7) days after receipt of the appellee's brief. The appeal shall be considered and disposed of on the briefs without hearing or oral argument unless the judge to whom the appeal is assigned specifically directs otherwise upon an application for such hearing or argument by one or both of the parties. Any appellant who fails to comply with this rule shall be deemed to have withdrawn the appeal. If the United States Attorney in any such appeal fails to comply with this rule, it shall be deemed that the United States Attorney does not oppose the appeal.

[Effective April 15, 1997. Amended effective December 1, 2009.]

LCrR 58.2 PETTY OFFENSES BROUGHT BY VIOLATION NOTICE

An authorized enforcement officer may initiate a petty offense charge by a violation notice. A separate violation notice shall be used for each separate offense charged. The violation notice form shall be completed by stating the date and time of the offense, the offense charged, the place of the offense, an offense description, the defendant's name and address and other appropriate identification information, and vehicle description information when appropriate. The violation notice shall inform the defendant of the court address and of the date and time of the defendant's court appearance. The date, time and place for the defendant to appear in court shall be inserted by the issuing officer, at the time of issuing the violation notice, on the basis of instructions from the assigned United States Magistrate Judge. The violation notice shall inform the defendant whether the defendant must appear in court or may elect instead to forfeit collateral. The violation notice shall include a statement of probable cause made under penalty of perjury. The original and one copy of the violation notice(s) shall be promptly sent to the Central Violations Bureau by the issuing agency.

[Effective April 15, 1997. Amended effective March 3, 2003.]

LCrR 58.3 AUTHORITY FOR FORFEITURE OF COLLATERAL IN CERTAIN PETTY OFFENSES; FORFEITURE OF COLLATERAL CASES—PROCEDURES

(a) In the case of a petty offense listed in the court's *Standing Order Re: Forfeiture of Collateral Schedule*, the violation notice shall be completed by the issuing officer so as to contain the collateral forfeiture amount established by the *Forfeiture of Collateral Schedule*, except that if a mandatory appearance is an option under the *Forfeiture of Collateral Schedule* the issuing officer may elect not to insert a collateral forfeiture amount upon the violation notice and to therefore require the appearance of the defendant in court. The *Forfeiture of Collateral Schedule* does not create or define any offense. Offenses are created and defined by federal statutes or regulations, or assimilated state statutes. A violation notice must refer by citation to the applicable statute(s) or regulation(s).

(b) The violation notice shall contain instructions for paying the collateral to the Central Violations Bureau. The defendant shall be given a mail-in envelope addressed to the Central Violations Bureau Lock Box by the issuing officer. The violation notice shall contain a checkoff option for the defendant to state an election to forfeit collateral or to plead not guilty and to promise to appear in court. The notice shall instruct the defendant to mail the violation notice form stating the defendant's election to the Central Violations Bureau in no more than twenty-one (21) days.

(c) A collateral forfeiture amount shall not be inserted upon a violation notice for any offense not included in the *Forfeiture of Collateral Schedule*.

(d) When an "X" appears next to a listed violation in the *Forfeiture of Collateral Schedule*, the issuing officer may, in his or her discretion, elect not to insert a forfeiture of collateral amount upon the violation notice and therefore require the appearance of the defendant in court. A mandatory appearance may be chosen by the issuing officer when there is good cause for not permitting a collateral forfeiture.

(e) When the charged petty offense is not listed in the *Forfeiture of Collateral Schedule*, or when a mandatory appearance is chosen by the issuing officer for an "X" designated charged petty offense, forfeiture of collateral by the defendant will not be permitted. The appearance of the defendant in court, as provided under Rule 58 of the Federal Rules of Criminal Procedure, is required.

(f) For any petty offense in which the issuing officer does not insert a collateral amount as provided under these Rules and the *Forfeiture of Collateral Schedule*, the defendant shall be issued a violation notice containing the information required in these Rules, except that in the space provided for the amount of collateral there shall be inserted the letters "MA" (Mandatory Appearance). The violation notice shall contain a check-off box stating "You must appear in court." This box shall be checked by the issuing officer in the case of a mandatory appearance violation notice.

(g) Remittance of collateral by a defendant shall be deemed a forfeiture of collateral, unless otherwise ordered by the court. A forfeiture of collateral is taken by the court as an acknowledgment of no contest to the violation notice and as an acknowledgment of guilt. The defendant is deemed convicted of the offense for which collateral is forfeited.

(h)(1) In a case where the defendant does not forfeit collateral and does not appear in court on the date and at the time and place set forth on the violation notice, a Notice to Appear may be issued by the magistrate judge or an arrest warrant may be issued upon a showing of probable cause and of actual notice to the defendant to appear. The court may, upon issuing a Notice to Appear, afford the defendant an additional opportunity to forfeit collateral or may convert the violation notice to a mandatory appearance.

(2) If the defendant does not appear as directed by a Notice to Appear, the magistrate judge may issue an arrest warrant upon a showing of probable cause. The amount of collateral may be increased up to the amount of the maximum fine provided for by law, or collateral forfeiture may be eliminated as an option.

[Effective April 15, 1997. Amended effective March 3, 2003.]

APPENDICES
APPENDIX A. JOINT CASE MANAGEMENT PLAN

Attorneys for Plaintiff

Attorneys for Defendant

UNITED STATES DISTRICT COURT
MIDDLE DISTRICT OF PENNSYLVANIA

) CASE NO.
)
)
)
)
) JUDGE_____
)
)
)
)

JOINT CASE MANAGEMENT PLAN

Instructions: In many cases there will be more parties in the action than there are spaces provided in this form. Each party shall provide all requested information. If the space on this form is not sufficient, the form should be retyped or additional pages attached.

No party may submit a separate Case Management Plan. Disagreements among parties with respect to any of the matters below shall be set forth in the appropriate section.

Having complied with the meet and confer requirements set forth in the LOCAL RULES, or with any orders specifically modifying their application in the above-captioned matter, the parties hereby submit the following Joint Case Management Plan.

1. **Principal Issues**

1.1 Separately for each party, please give a statement summarizing this case:

By plaintiff(s):

By defendant(s):

1.2 The facts the parties <u>dispute</u> are as follows:

<u>agree</u> upon are as follows:

1.3 The legal issues the parties <u>dispute</u> are as follows:

agree upon are as follows:

1.4 Identify any unresolved issues as to service of process, personal jurisdiction, subject matter jurisdiction, or venue:

1.5 Identify any named parties that have not yet been served:

1.6 Identify any additional parties that:

   plaintiff(s) intends to join:

   defendant(s) intends to join:

1.7 Identify any additional claims that:
   plaintiff(s) intends to add:

   defendant(s) intends to add:

2.0 Disclosures

The undersigned counsel certify that they have made the initial disclosures required by Federal Rule of Civil Procedure 26(a)(1) or that they will do so within the time provided by that rule.

2.1 Separately for each party, list by name and title/position each person whose identity has been disclosed.

   Disclosed by _____:

Name	Title/Position
_____	_____
_____	_____
_____	_____
_____	_____

   Disclosed by _____:

Name	Title/Position
_____	_____
_____	_____
_____	_____
_____	_____

3.0 Early Motions

Identify any motion(s) whose early resolution would likely have a significant effect either on the scope of discovery or other aspects of the litigation:

Nature of Motion   Moving Party   Anticipated Filing Date

4.0 Discovery

4.1 Briefly describe any discovery that has been completed or is in progress:

By plaintiff(s):

By defendant(s):

4.2 Describe any discovery that all parties agree should be conducted, indicating for each discovery undertaking its purpose or what kinds of information will be developed through it (e.g., "plaintiff will depose Mr. Jones, defendant's controller, to learn what defendant's revenue recognition policies were and how they were applied to the kinds of contracts in this case"):

4.3 Describe any discovery that one or more parties want(s) to conduct but to which another party objects, indicating for each such discovery undertaking its purpose or what kinds of information would be developed through it:

4.4 Identify any subject area limitations on discovery that one or more parties would like imposed, at the first stage of or throughout the litigation:

4.5 For each of the following discovery tools, recommend the per-party or per-side limitation (specify a number) that should be fixed, subject to later modification by stipulation or court order on an appropriate showing (where the parties cannot agree, set forth separately the limits . . . . recommended by plaintiff(s) and by defendant(s)):

4.5.1 depositions (excluding experts) to be taken by:

plaintiff(s): _____   defendant(s): _____

4.5.2 interrogatories to be served by:

plaintiff(s): _____   defendant(s): _____

4.5.3 document production requests to be served by:

plaintiff(s): _____   defendant(s): _____

4.5.4 requests for admission to be served by:

plaintiff(s): _____   defendant(s): _____

4.6 Discovery of Electronically Stored Information

☐ Counsel certify that they have conferred about the matters addressed in M.D. Pa LR 26.1 and that they are in agreement about how those matters will be addressed in discovery.

☐ Counsel certify that they have conferred about the matters addressed in M.D. Pa. LR 26.1 and that they are in agreement about how those matters will be addressed in discovery with the following exceptions:

5.0 Protective Order

5.1 If entry of a protective order is sought, attach to this statement a copy of the proposed order. Include a statement justifying the propriety of such a protective order under existing Third Circuit precedent.

5.2 If there is a dispute about whether a protective order should be entered, or about certain terms of the proposed order, briefly summarize each party's position below:

6.0 Scheduling

6.1 Final date for joining additional parties:

___ Plaintiff(s)

___ Defendants(s)

6.2 Final date for amending pleadings:

___ Plaintiff(s)

___ Defendants(s)

6.3 All fact discovery commenced in time to be completed by: _____

6.4 All potentially dispositive motions should be filed by: _____

6.5 Reports from retained experts due:

from plaintiff(s) by _____

from defendant(s) by _____

6.6 Supplementations due _____

6.7 All expert discovery commenced in time to be completed by _____

6.8 This case may be appropriate for trial in approximately:

___ 240 Days from the filing of the action in this court

___ 365 Days from the filing of the action in this court

___ Days from the filing of the action in this court

6.9 Suggested Date for the final Pretrial Conference:

_____ (month/year)

6.10 Trial

6.10.1 Suggested Date for Trial:

_____ (month/year)

7.0 Certification of Settlement Authority (All Parties Shall Complete the Certification)

I hereby certify that the following individual(s) have settlement authority.

_____

Name

_____

Title

_____

_____

Address

( ) ___–___ Daytime Telephone

_____

Name

_____

Title

_____

_____

Address

( ) ___–___ Daytime Telephone

8.0 Alternative Dispute Resolution ("ADR")

8.1 Identify any ADR procedure to which this case already has been assigned or which the parties have agreed to use.

ADR procedure _____

Date ADR to be commenced _____

Date ADR to be completed _____

8.2 If the parties have been unable to agree on an ADR procedure, but one or more parties believes that the case is appropriate for such a procedure, identify the party or parties that recommend ADR and the specific ADR process recommended:

8.3 If all parties share the view that no ADR procedure should be used in this case, set forth the basis for that view:

9.0 Consent to Jurisdiction by a Magistrate Judge

Indicate whether all parties agree, pursuant to 28 U.S.C. § 636(c)(1), to have a magistrate judge preside as the judge of the case with appeal lying to the United States Court of Appeals for the Third Circuit:

All parties agree to jurisdiction by a magistrate judge of this court: ___ Y ___ N.

If parties agree to proceed before a magistrate judge, please indicate below which location is desired for the proceedings:

___ Scranton/Wilkes–Barre

___ Harrisburg

10.0 Other Matters

Make any other suggestions for the case development process, settlement, or trial that may be useful or necessary to the efficient and just resolution of the dispute.

11.0 Identification of Counsel

Counsel shall be registered users of the court's Electronic Case Files System (ECF) and shall file documents electronically in accordance with the Local Rules of Court and the Standing Order RE: Electronic Case Filing Policies and Procedures. Electronic filing is required unless good cause is shown to the Chief Judge why counsel cannot comply with this policy. Any request for waiver of electronic filing must be filed with the Clerk's Office prior to the case management conference. The Chief Judge may grant or deny such request.

Identify by name, address, and telephone number lead counsel for each party. Also please indicate ECF User status below.

Dated: _____

       Attorney(s) for Plaintiff(s)

☐ ECF User(s)

☐ Waiver requested (as separate document)

☐ Fed.R.Civ.P.7.1 (statement filed if necessary)*

Dated: _____

       Attorneys(s) for Defendant(s)

☐ ECF User(s)

☐ Waiver requested (as separate document)

☐ Fed.R.Civ.P.7.1 (statement filed if necessary)*

* Fed.R.Civ.P.7.1 requires a nongovernmental corporate party to file a statement with the initial pleading, first entry of appearance, etc., that identifies any parent corporation and any publicly held corporation that owns 10% or more of its stock, or state there is no such corporation.

[Former Appendix B effective April 15, 1997. Redesignated Appendix A effective August 16, 1999. Amended effective November 1, 2004; December 1, 2007; December 1, 2009.]

APPENDIX B.   PRETRIAL MEMORANDUM FORMAT

UNITED STATES DISTRICT COURT
FOR THE MIDDLE DISTRICT
OF PENNSYLVANIA

	:	
	:	
v.	:	CIVIL ACTION NO.
	:	
	:	

PRETRIAL MEMORANDUM

Date conference was held by counsel:

A.   A brief statement as to federal court jurisdiction.

B.   A summary statement of facts and contentions as to liability.

C.   A comprehensive statement of undisputed facts as agreed to by counsel at the conference of attorneys required by Local Rule 16.3. No facts should be denied unless opposing counsel expects to present contrary evidence or genuinely challenges the fact on credibility grounds. The parties must reach agreement on uncontested facts even though relevancy is disputed.

D.   A brief description of damages, including, where applicable:

(1) Principal injuries sustained:

(2) Hospitalization and convalescence:

(3) Present disability:

(4) Special monetary damages, loss of past earnings, medical expenses, property damages, etc.:

(5) Estimated value of pain and suffering, etc.:

(6) Special damage claims:

E.   Names and addresses of witnesses, along with the specialties and qualifications of experts to be called.

F.   Summary of testimony of each expert witness.

G.   Special comment about pleadings and discovery, including depositions and the exchange of medical reports.

H.   A summary of legal issues involved and legal authorities relied upon.

I.   Stipulations desired.

J.   Estimated number of trial days.

K.   Any other matter pertinent to the case to be tried.

L.   Pursuant to Local Rule 16.3 append to this memorandum a prenumbered schedule of exhibits, with brief identification of each, on the clerk's Exhibit Form.

M.   Append any special verdict questions which counsel desires to submit.

N.   Defense counsel must file a statement that the person or committee with settlement authority has been notified of the requirements of and possible sanctions under Local Rule 16.2.

O.   Certificate must be filed as required under Local Rule 30.10 that counsel have met and reviewed depositions and videotapes in an effort to eliminate irrelevancies, side comments, resolved objections, and other matters not necessary for consideration by the trier of fact.

P. In all trials without a jury, requests for findings of both fact and law shall be submitted with this Memorandum as required under Local Rule 48.2.

[Former Appendix C effective April 15, 1997. Redesignated Appendix B effective August 16, 1999.]

APPENDIX C. CODE OF PROFESSIONAL CONDUCT

UNITED STATES DISTRICT COURT FOR THE
MIDDLE DISTRICT OF PENNSYLVANIA

CODE OF PROFESSIONAL CONDUCT

As a member of the Bar of the United States District Court for the Middle District of Pennsylvania, I will strive for the following professional ideal:

1. The rule of law will govern my entire conduct. I will not violate the law or place myself above the law.

2. I will treat with civility and respect the lawyers, clients, opposing parties, the court and all the officials with whom I work. Professional courtesy is compatible with vigorous advocacy and zealous representation. Even though antagonism may be expected by my client, it is not part of my duty to my client.

3. I will respect other lawyers' schedules as my own, and will seek agreement on meetings, depositions, hearings, and trial dates. A reasonable request for a scheduling accommodation should never be unreasonably refused.

4. Communications are life lines. I will keep the lines open. Telephone calls and correspondence are a two-way channel; I will respond to them promptly.

5. I will be punctual in appointments, communications and in honoring scheduled appearances. Neglect and tardiness are demeaning to others and to the judicial system.

6. I will earnestly attempt to resolve differences through negotiation, expeditiously and without needless expense.

7. Procedural rules are necessary to judicial order and decorum. I will be mindful that pleadings, discovery processes and motions cost time and money. I will not use them heedlessly. If an adversary is entitled to something, I will provide it without unnecessary formalities.

8. I will not engage in conduct that brings disorder or disruption to the courtroom. I will advise my client and witnesses appearing in court of the proper conduct expected and required there and, to the best of my ability, prevent my client and witnesses from creating disorder or disruption.

9. Before dates for hearings or trials are set, or if that is not feasible immediately after such date has been set, I will attempt to verify the availability of necessary participants and witnesses so I can promptly notify the court of any likely problems.

I agree to subscribe to the above
Code of Professional Conduct:

_____
Signature

[Former Appendix D effective April 15, 1997. Redesignated Appendix C effective August 16, 1999.]

ELECTRONIC CASE FILING

ELECTRONIC CASE FILING POLICIES AND PROCEDURES

1. Definitions.

1.1 "Electronic Filing System" refers to the court's automated system that receives and stores documents filed in electronic form. The program is part of the CM/ECF (Case Management/Electronic Case Files) software which was developed for the Federal Judiciary by the Administrative Office of the United States Courts.

1.2 "Filing User" is an individual who has a court-issued login and password to file documents electronically.

1.3 "Notice of Electronic Filing" is a notice automatically generated by the Electronic Filing System at the time a document is filed with the system, setting forth the time of filing, the name of the party and attorney filing the document, the type of document, the text of the docket entry, the name of the party and/or attorney receiving the notice, and an electronic link (hyperlink) to the filed document, which allows recipients to retrieve the document automatically.

1.4 "PACER" (Public Access to Court Electronic Records) is an automated system that allows an individual to view, print and download court docket information over the internet.

1.5 "PDF" refers to Portable Document Format. A document file created with a word processor, or a paper document which has been scanned, must be converted to portable document format to be filed electronically with the court. Converted files contain the extension ".pdf".

1.6 "Proposed Order" is a draft document submitted by an attorney for a judge's signature. A proposed order shall accompany a motion or other request for relief as an electronic attachment to the document.

1.7 "Technical Failure" is defined as a malfunction of court owned/leased hardware, software, and/or telecommunications facility which results in the inability of a Filing User to submit a filing electronically. Technical failure does not include malfunctioning of a Filing User's equipment.

2. Scope of Electronic Filing.
All civil, criminal and miscellaneous cases shall be assigned to the Electronic Filing System. Except as expressly provided herein or by order of court, or in exceptional circumstances including technical failures, a Filing User shall electronically file all documents required to be filed with the court.

The filing of initial papers may be accomplished either electronically under procedures outlined in the court's ECF User Manual or traditionally on paper. In a case removed to the federal court, parties are required to provide electronic copies of all documents previously filed in the state court. Service of the summons and complaint must be made under Federal Rule of Civil Procedure 4.

An attorney who is not a Filing User must show to the chief judge good cause to file and serve pleadings and other papers in the traditional manner. A party who is not represented by counsel may file papers with the clerk in the traditional manner, but is not precluded from filing electronically.

3. Eligibility, Registration, Passwords.
An attorney admitted to the Bar of this court, including an attorney admitted pro hac vice, may register as a Filing User by completing the prescribed registration form (See Exhibit A) and submitting it to the clerk. Registration as a Filing User constitutes consent to electronic service of all documents as provided in this order in accordance with the Federal Rules of Civil Procedure and the Federal Rules of Criminal Procedure.

A person who is a party to an action who is not represented by an attorney may register as a Filing User in the Electronic Filing System solely for purposes of the action. If during the course of the action the person retains an attorney who appears on the person's behalf, the attorney must advise the clerk to terminate the person's registration as a Filing User upon the attorney's appearance.

When registering, an individual must have an established PACER account and certify that ECF training has been completed. An individual may register more than one Internet e-mail address. Once the registration is processed by the clerk, the Filing User will receive notification of the user login and password. A Filing User shall protect the security of the User's password and immediately notify the clerk if the Filing User learns that the password has been compromised.

Once registration is complete, a Filing User may not withdraw from participation in the Electronic Filing System except by leave of court.

4. Consequences of Electronic Filing. Electronic transmission of a document to the Electronic Filing System in accordance with this order, together with the transmission of a Notice of Electronic Filing from the court, constitutes filing of the document for all purposes of the Federal Rules of Civil Procedure, the Federal Rules of Criminal Procedure and the Local Rules of this court, and constitutes entry of the document on the docket kept by the clerk under Fed.R.Civ.P. 58 and 79, and Fed.R.Crim.P. 49 and 55.

When a document has been filed electronically, the official record of that document is the electronic recording as stored by the court, and the filing party is bound by the document as filed. A document filed electronically is deemed filed on the date and time stated on the Notice of Electronic Filing from the court.

The fact that a party files a document electronically does not alter the filing deadline for that document. Electronic filing must be completed before midnight Eastern time in order to be considered timely filed that day. In accordance with Fed.R.Civ.P. 6(d) and Fed.R.Crim.P. 45(c), service by electronic means is treated the same as service by mail for the purposes of adding three (3) days to the prescribed period to respond.

5. Entry of Court Orders and Related Papers. A document entered or issued by the court will be filed in accordance with this Order and such filing shall constitute entry on the docket kept by the clerk under Fed.R.Civ.P. 58 and 79, and Fed.R.Crim.P. 55.

All signed orders will be filed electronically by the court or court personnel. An order filed electronically without the original signature of a judge shall have the same force and effect as if the judge had affixed a signature to a paper copy of the order and the order had been entered on the docket in a conventional manner.

A Filing User submitting a document that requires a judge's signature shall submit the document as an electronic attachment to a motion or other request for relief in accordance with the procedure for a "Proposed Order" as outlined in the court's ECF User Manual.

6. Notice of Court Orders and Judgments. Immediately upon the entry of an order or judgment in an action, the clerk will transmit to Filing Users in the case, in electronic form, a Notice of Electronic Filing. Electronic transmission of the Notice of Electronic Filing constitutes the notice required by Fed.R.Civ.P. 77(d) and Fed.R.Crim.P. 49(c). The clerk must give notice in paper form to a person who has not consented to electronic service.

7. Attachments and Exhibits. A Filing User must submit in electronic form all documents referenced as exhibits or attachments in accordance with the court's ECF User Manual, unless otherwise ordered by the court. A Filing User shall submit as exhibits or attachments only those excerpts of the referenced documents that are directly germane to the matter under consideration by the court. Excerpted material must be clearly and prominently identified as such. Filing Users who file excerpts of documents as exhibits or attachments under this rule do so without prejudice to their right to timely file additional excerpts or the complete document. Responding parties may timely file additional excerpts or the complete document that they believe are directly germane.

8. Filing of Documents Under Seal. According to Local Rule LCrR 49, no document shall be filed under seal unless authorized by an order of court. A motion to file a document under seal shall be filed on paper and contain no description or identification of the document for which the sealing order is sought or statement of reasons why the filing of the document under seal should be authorized. The Rule sets forth the procedure for presenting the document(s) which are the subject of the motion to seal. Accordingly, the following documents are to be presented to the clerk in paper form in a sealed envelope marked with the case number, case caption and the descriptive label of "Documents pending sealing decision:"

(a) the document(s) for which the sealing order is sought,

(b) a statement of the legal and factual justification for the sealing order that is being sought, and

(c) a proposed form of order.

LCrR 49(c)(3) sets forth the following procedure for documents authorized to be filed under seal by an existing court order:

A document authorized to be filed under seal by an existing court order shall be filed on paper accompanied by the court order authorizing it to be filed under seal and submitted in a sealed envelope marked with the case number, case caption and the words "sealed document."

The order of the court authorizing the filing of documents under seal may be filed electronically, unless prohibited by law.

9. Special Filing Requirements and Exceptions.

9.1 *Special Filing Requirements.* The documents listed below shall be presented for filing on paper:

Sealed

In Camera

Confidential Agreements

Ex Parte

Qui Tam Cases

9.2 *Exceptions.*

9.2.1. Permissive Exceptions. The following documents may be excluded from the Electronic Filing System and filed solely on paper:

ANY DOCUMENT WHICH CONTAINS MORE THAN 200 PAGES.

9.2.2 Mandatory Exceptions. The following documents are excluded from the Electronic Filing System and shall be filed solely on paper:

ADMINISTRATIVE RECORDS IN SOCIAL SECURITY CASES

GRAND JURY MATTERS:

The following documents are examples of grand jury matters:

    1) Minute Sheets of Swearing in and empanelment;

    2) Grand Jury Returns;

    3) Voting Slips;

    4) Order appointing alternate juror (existing juror requests to be excused from grand jury for medical or some other reason);

    5) Motions to quash subpoenas and orders ruling on them;

    6) Motions to enforce subpoenas and orders ruling on them;

    7) Motions for immunity and orders ruling on them;

    8) Motions for appointment of counsel and orders ruling on them.

WARRANTS ISSUED:

1) Arrest Warrants;

2) Seizure Warrants;

3) Search Warrants;

4) Pen Registers (Wiretap Orders);

5) Bench Warrants

PRE–INDICTMENT/PRE–INFORMATION:

1) Affidavits (These usually accompany criminal complaints and are signed by the federal agent). Federal agents include FBI, DEA, Attorney General Task Force, IRS.

2) Warrant issued by another district for a defendant residing in our district. The Rule 5 (arraignment) hearing is held in our district and then the paperwork is sent to other district on a Rule 40 Transfer.

JURY EMPANELMENT LISTS

10. Retention Requirements. A document that is electronically filed and requires an original signature other than that of the Filing User must be maintained in paper form by counsel and/or the firm representing the party on whose behalf the document was filed until one year after all periods for appeals expire. Such papers in criminal cases shall be retained by the United States Attorney. On request of the court, said counsel must provide the original document for review.

11. Signatures. The user login and password required to submit documents to the Electronic Filing System serve as the Filing User's signature on all electronic documents filed with the court. They serve as a signature for purposes of Fed.R.Civ. P.11, all other Federal Rules of Civil Procedure, the Federal Rules of Criminal Procedure, the Local Rules of this court, and any other purpose for which a signature is required in connection with proceedings before the court.

Each document filed electronically must indicate in the caption that it has been electronically filed. An electronically filed document must include a signature block in compliance with Local Rule 5.2(b), and must set forth the name, address, telephone number, fax number, e-mail address, and the attorney's Pennsylvania or other state bar identification number, if applicable. When listing the identification number, the state's postal abbreviation shall be used as a prefix (e.g., PA12345, NY2243316). In addition, the name of the Filing User under whose login and password the document is submitted must be preceded by an "s/" and typed in the space where the signature would otherwise appear. No Filing User or other person may knowingly permit or cause to permit a Filing User's password to be used by anyone other than an authorized agent of the Filing User.

A document containing the signature of a defendant in a criminal case shall be electronically filed as a scanned document in PDF format that contains an image of the defendant's original signature. The Filing User is required to verify the readability of the scanned document before filing it electronically with the court.

A document requiring signatures of more than one party must be filed electronically either by: (1) submitting a scanned document containing all necessary signatures; (2) representing the consent of the other parties on the document; (3) identifying on the document the parties whose signatures are required and by the submission of a notice of endorsement by the other parties no later than three business days after filing; or (4) in any other manner approved by the court.

12. Service of Documents by Electronic Means.*

12.1 *Service of Process.* Fed.R.Civ.P. 5(b) and Fed.R.Crim.P. 49(b) do **not** permit electronic service of process for purposes of obtaining personal jurisdiction, i.e., Rule 4 service. Therefore, service of process must be effected in the traditional manner.

12.2 *Other Types of Service.*

12.2.1   Filing User. Upon the electronic filing of a pleading or other document, the court's ECF System will automatically generate and send a Notice of Electronic Filing to all Filing Users associated with that case. Transmission of the Notice of Electronic Filing constitutes service of the filed document.

The Notice of Electronic Filing must include the time of filing, the name of the party and attorney filing the document, the type of document, the text of the docket entry, and an electronic link (hyperlink) to the filed document, allowing anyone receiving the notice by e-mail to retrieve the document automatically. If the Filing User becomes aware that the Notice of Electronic Filing was not transmitted successfully to a party, or that the notice is deficient, i.e. the electronic link to the document is defective, the filer shall serve the electronically filed document by e-mail, hand, facsimile, or by first-class mail postage prepaid immediately upon notification of the deficiency of the Notice of Electronic Filing.

12.2.2   Individual who is not a Filing User. A Non–Filing User is entitled to receive a paper copy of any electronically filed document from the party making such filing. Service of such paper copy must be made according to the Federal Rules of Civil Procedure, the Federal Rules of Criminal Procedure and the Local Rules.

12.3   Time to Respond Under Electronic Service. In accordance with Fed. R.Civ.P. 6(d) and Fed.R.Crim.P. 45(c), service by electronic means is treated the same as service by mail for the purposes of adding three (3) days to the prescribed period to respond.

13.   Technical Failures. The clerk shall deem the court's Electronic Case Filing Web Site to be subject to a technical failure if the site is unable to accept filings continuously or intermittently for more than one hour occurring after 12:00 noon (Eastern Time) that day. If a Filing User experiences technical failure, the document may be submitted to the court that day in an alternative manner, provided that it is accompanied by an affidavit of the Filing User's failed attempts to file electronically at least two times in one hour increments after 12:00 noon. The following methods of filing are acceptable as a result of a technical failure:

13.1   via electronic mail in a PDF attachment, sent to the e-mail address for technical failures listed in the ECF User Manual;

13.2   in person, by bringing the document to the clerk's office on paper;

13.3   through facsimile transmission to the clerk's office where the presiding judicial officer is stationed. When a Filing User subject to technical failure submits a document by fax, the document shall be filed electronically on the next business day. Please refer to the fax numbers listed in the ECF User manual.

The initial point of contact for a Filing User experiencing technical difficulty filing a document electronically shall be the court's ECF Help Desk at the toll free numbers listed in the ECF User Manual.

A Filing User who suffers prejudice as a result of a technical failure may seek appropriate relief from the court.

14.   Public Access. A person may retrieve information from the Electronic Filing System at the court's Internet site by obtaining a PACER login and password. A person who has PACER access may retrieve docket sheets and documents in civil cases other than **social security cases**, in which only counsel in the case may retrieve certain documents and for most criminal cases/documents filed on or after November 1, 2004, in conjunction with Judicial Conference Policies on Privacy and Electronic Public Access. Any case or document under seal shall not be available to the public through electronic or any other means.

14.1   *Sensitive Information.* As the public may access certain case information over the Internet through the court's Electronic Filing System, sensitive information should not be included in any document filed with the court unless such inclusion is necessary and relevant to the case. In accordance with Local Rule 5.2(d), if sensitive information must be included, the following personal data identifiers must be partially redacted from the document in a civil or criminal case (except in a Social Security Case), whether it is filed traditionally or electronically: Social Security numbers to the last four digits, financial account numbers to the last four digits, dates of birth to the year and the names of minor children to the initials.[1] **Note: In criminal case documents only, home addresses also must be redacted to the city and state.**

In compliance with the E–Government Act of 2002, a party wishing to file a document containing the personal data identifiers specified above may file in addition to the required redacted document: 1) a sealed and otherwise identical document containing the unredacted personal identifiers; or 2) a reference list under seal. The reference list shall contain the complete personal data identifier(s) and the redacted identifier(s) used in its(their) place in the filing. All references in the case to the redacted identifiers included in the reference list will be construed to refer to the corresponding complete personal data identifier. The reference list must be filed under seal, and may be amended as of right.

The sealed unredacted version of the document or the sealed reference list shall be retained by the court as a part of the record.

In addition, caution must be exercised when filing documents that contain the following:

1) Personal identifying number, such as a driver's license number;

2) medical records, treatment and diagnosis;

3) employment history;

4) individual financial information; and

5) proprietary or trade secret information;

Additional items for criminal cases only:

6) information regarding an individual's cooperation with the government;

7) information regarding the victim of any criminal activity;

8) national security information; and

9) sensitive security information as described in 49 U.S.C. Section 114(s).

Counsel is strongly urged to share this information with all clients so that an informed decision about the inclusion of certain materials may be made. If a redacted document is filed, it is the sole responsibility of counsel and the parties to be sure that pleadings and other papers comply with the rules and orders of this court requiring redaction of personal identifiers. The clerk will not review each filing for redaction.

[1] Documents in social security cases are excluded from the redaction requirement as they are not electronically available to the public over the Internet, pursuant to the privacy policy of the Judicial Conference of the United States.

Exhibit A

United States District Court
For the Middle District of Pennsylvania

ECF REGISTRATION FORM

This form shall be used to register as a Filing User for the court's Electronic Case Files (ECF) system. A Filing User may file documents with the court through the court's ECF web site, and view and retrieve docket sheets and case documents electronically. Registration as a Filing User also serves as your consent to electronic service of all documents through the court's transmission facilities in accordance with the Federal Rules of Civil Procedure and the Federal Rules of Criminal Procedure. By signing this form, you shall certify that you have complet-

ed the ECF tutorial on the court's web site (www.pamd.uscourts.gov), and have a PACER account. Visit the PACER web site at http://pacer.psc.uscourts.gov to establish a PACER account.

Please complete the following information to register for ECF: (THIS FORM MUST BE TYPED)

Last Name: _____ First Name: _____ Middle Initial: ___

Firm Name: _____

Address: _____

_____

City, State: _____ Zip Code: _____

Telephone Number: (_____)_____ Fax Number: (_____)_____

PA or other State Bar ID: _____ (e.g. PA12345, NY22316)

Last Four Digits of Social Security Number: _____ (for security purposes)

E–Mail Address(es) for Electronic Service: _____

_____

If registered for ECF in another court, provide your Login Name: _____

E–Mail the form to: ecfreg@pamd.uscourts.gov

Mail to: USDC ECF Registration
      PO Box 1148
      Scranton, PA 18501–1148

Fax to: ECF Registration (570) 207–5689

_____

(Signature/Date)

Court Use Only:

Login Assigned: _____

Password Assigned: _____

* [**Publisher's Note:** On December 3, 2012, the Court issued the following Notice:

All ECF Registered Users and Counsel:

Beginning Monday, December 3, 2012 there will be a new procedure for issuing a summons in a civil case in the Middle District of PA.

We will begin using an electronic summons, which means there will no longer be a "hard" court seal on the summons form. The summons form will now contain an electronic court seal. The summons issued event will be entered on the docket and counsel will receive it electronically if they are a registered ECF user. If they are not an ECF registered user, they will receive the summons by U.S. Mail.

ECF Registered Users: You will receive the summons electronically through ECF. When you receive the Notice of Electronic Filing in your e-mail, you MUST click on the document number (not the docket/case number), and print or save the Summons. If you choose to print it, you should select how many copies you need to serve. If you do not print or save the summons and need to get it at a future date, you will need to go into PACER and you will be charged for the 2 page document.

NOTE: YOU STILL ARE REQUIRED TO SERVE THE SUMMONS AND COMPLAINT PURSUANT TO RULE 4 OF THE FEDERAL RULES OF CIVIL PROCEDURE.]

[Effective March 3, 2003. Amended effective April 16, 2003; October 4, 2004; December 1, 2005; November 18, 2009; December 3, 2012.]

STANDING ORDER NO. 04–5. IN RE: NOTICE OF ELECTRONIC AVAILABILITY OF CASE FILE INFORMATION

The Clerk of Court is hereby directed to provide the attached Notice of Electronic Availability of Civil and Criminal Case File Information to counsel and parties in accordance with the privacy policy of the Judicial Conference of the United States regarding Public Access to Electronic Case Files and the E–Government Act of 2002 as amended August 2, 2004.

Such notice shall be posted on the court's Internet web site and also disseminated through manual or electronic means. The order supersedes Standing Order 03-3 dated April 16, 2003.

Notice of Electronic Availability of Civil and Criminal Case File Information

The Office of the Clerk for the United States District Court, Middle District of Pennsylvania, is now accepting electronically filed documents and making the content of civil documents (except in Social Security cases) available to the public on the court's Internet web site via WebPACER. Effective November 1, 2004, the office also will make electronic criminal case file documents available to the public via remote access pursuant to the implementation guidelines and model local rule adopted by the Judicial Conference of the United States. Any subscriber to WebPACER will be able to read, download, store, and print the full content of electronically filed documents. The clerk's office will not make electronically available documents that have been sealed or otherwise restricted by court order.

You should not include sensitive information in any civil case document filed with the Court unless such inclusion is necessary and relevant to the case. You *shall not* include sensitive information in any *criminal* case document filed with the Court. You must remember that any personal information not otherwise protected will be made available over the Internet via WebPACER. The following personal data identifiers must be partially redacted from the document in a civil or criminal case (except a Social Security Case), whether it is filed traditionally or electronically: Social Security numbers to the last four digits; financial account numbers to the last four digits; dates of birth to the year; and the names of minor children to the initials.[1] Note: In criminal case documents only, home addresses must be redacted from the city and state.

In compliance with the E-Government Act of 2002, a party wishing to file a document containing the personal identifiers specified above may file in addition to the required redacted document:

(a) a sealed and otherwise identical document containing the unredacted personal data identifiers, or

(b) a reference list under seal. The reference list shall contain the complete personal data identifier(s) and the redacted identifier(s) used in its (their) place in the filing. All references in the case to the redacted identifiers included in the reference list will be construed to refer to the corresponding complete identifier. The reference list must be filed under seal, and may be amended as of right.

The sealed, unredacted version of the document or the sealed reference list shall be retained by the Court as part of the record.

In addition, exercise caution when filing documents that contain the following:

(1) Personal identifying number, such as driver's license number;

(2) Medical records, treatment, and diagnosis;

(3) Employment history;

(4) Individual financial information; and

(5) Proprietary or trade secret information.

Additional items for criminal cases only:

(6) Information regarding an individual's cooperation with the government;

(7) Information regarding the victim of any criminal activity;

(8) National security information; and

(9) Sensitive security information as described in 49 U.S.C. § 114(s).

Counsel is strongly urged to share this notice with all clients so that an informed decision about the inclusion of certain materials may be made. It is the sole responsibility of counsel and the parties to be sure that all documents and pleadings comply with the rules of this Court requiring redaction of personal identifiers. The clerk will not review each document for redaction.

[Dated: October 4, 2004.]

1 Documents in social security cases are excluded from the redaction requirement as they are not electronically available to the public over the Internet pursuant to the privacy policy of the Judicial Conference of the United States.

STANDING ORDER NO. 07–01. IN RE: COMPLIANCE WITH ELECTRONIC CASE FILING REGISTRATION REQUIREMENTS

WHEREAS, on March 3, 2003, the Court established by Standing Order No. 03–1 an Electronic Case Filing System and adopted Electronic Case Filing Policies and Procedures to govern the program; and

WHEREAS, Standing Order No. 03–1 requires attorneys who did not register as electronic filing users by September 3, 2003, to show cause why they should be permitted to file in the traditional manner; and

WHEREAS, on October 4, 2004, the Court issued Standing Order No. 04–7 requiring counsel of record in cases then pending in this court to register as filing users for the court's Electronic Case Filing System and file documents electronically or show cause why they should not be required to register as filing users and file documents electronically; and

WHEREAS, on February 2, 2005, the Court issued Standing Order No. 05–1 finding that the failure of numerous counsel of record to respond to Standing Order No. 04–7 or request an extension of time in which to do so was impairing the effective administration of the Court's business and demonstrating disregard for the authority of the court; and

WHEREAS, Standing Order No. 05–1 required counsel who failed to respond to Standing Order No. 04–7 to register as filing users for the Court's Electronic Case Filing System and file documents electronically or show cause to the Chief Judge in writing why they should not be required to file documents through the Court's Electronic Case Filing System; and

WHEREAS, counsel were advised that failure to comply with Standing Order 05–1 could result in commencement of contempt of court and/or disciplinary proceedings; and

WHEREAS, a review of the Court's docket has revealed numerous instances of continued noncompliance with electronic filing registration requirements; and

NOW, THIS 22nd DAY OF JANUARY 2007, IT IS HEREBY ORDERED THAT:

Within fourteen days from the date of this order, counsel of record in cases now pending in the United States District Court for the Middle District of Pennsylvania shall register as filing users for the court's Electronic Case Filing System and file documents electronically or show cause to the Chief Judge why they should not be required to register as filing users and file documents electronically.[1] Failure to comply with this Order may result in commencement of contempt of court and/or disciplinary proceedings that could result in suspension of the right to practice in this Court in accordance with Local Rule of Court 83.3.1.

[Dated: January 22, 2007.]

1 The Court's website provides substantial information regarding the Electronic Case Filing System, including information regarding registration and training in the use of the system. See www.pamd.uscourts. gov. Additional information may be obtained by contacting the Clerk of Court. The Court also notes that

waivers of the requirement that counsel must file documents through the Court's Electronic Case Filing System may still be obtained by making an appropriate showing to the Chief Judge.

JUDICIAL CONFERENCE POLICY WITH REGARD TO THE ELECTRONIC AVAILABILITY OF TRANSCRIPTS OF COURT PROCEEDINGS

Effective May 12, 2008, the U.S. District Court, Middle District of Pennsylvania, in accordance with Judicial Conference Policy and amendments to Federal Rule of Civil Procedure 5.2 and Federal Rule of Criminal Procedure 49.1, will implement the following policy regarding official court transcripts:

1. A transcript provided to the court by a court reporter or transcriber will be available at the Clerk's Office, for inspection only, for a period of 90 days after it is filed. The transcript may NOT be copied nor reproduced by the Clerk's Office for a period of 90 days.

2. During the 90–day period, a copy of the transcript may be obtained from the court reporter or transcriber at the rate established by the Judicial Conference. The transcript will be available at the public terminal at the Courthouse and electronically available only to attorneys of record who have purchased a copy from the court reporter.

3. After the 90–day period has ended, the transcript will be available for copying in the Clerk's Office and remotely through PACER to view, download or print a copy at .08 cents per page or from the Clerk's Office public terminal at a rate of .10 cents per page.

4. Contract Court Reporters shall call the Clerk's Office for instructions on how to electronically file the original transcript in the court's ECF system. A login and password will be provided to the contract court reporter.

Note: This policy applies to transcripts of events taking place in the court's courtrooms, not depositions taken outside of court or proceedings of state courts or other jurisdictions. This policy establishes a procedure for counsel to request the redaction from the transcript of specific personal data identifiers before the transcript is made electronically available to the general public.

Counsel are strongly urged to share this notice with their clients so that an informed decision about the inclusion of certain materials may be made. The responsibility for redacting rests solely with counsel and the parties. Neither the Clerk nor the Court Reporter will review transcripts for compliance with this policy.

Redaction Request: If a redaction is requested, counsel must file with the Court Reporter a Request for Redaction (form available here) within 21 days from the filing of the transcript, indicating where the personal identifiers appear in the transcript by page and line number. The Request for Redaction should not be electronically filed in the court's ECF system nor filed on paper in the Clerk's Office. The Request for Redaction must be e-mailed to the court reporter. Court Reporters' names, telephone numbers, and e-mail addresses are listed on the next page.

Note: This procedure is limited to the redaction of the specific personal data identifiers listed below:

- social security numbers to the last four digits;
- financial account numbers to the last four digits;
- dates of birth to the year;
- names of minor children to the initials; and
- home addresses to the city and state (criminal cases only).

Requests for Additional Redactions. If counsel would like to request further redactions, in addition to those personal identifiers listed above, counsel must move the Court by filing a separate Motion to Redact Additional Items from Transcript, within the 21–day Request for Redaction time period. Until the Court has ruled on any such motion, the transcript will not be electronically available, even if the 90–day restriction period has ended.

Remote Public Access to Transcripts. If a redacted transcript is filed with the Court, that redacted transcript will be electronically available through PACER after 90 calendar days from the date of filing of the original transcript and the original transcript will not be made publicly available. If the original transcript is filed without redaction, that original transcript will be electronically available through PACER after 90 calendar days.

PACER Fees. PACER fees will be applied both during and after the 90–day restriction period. Charges will not be capped at 30 pages as they are for other court documents, but will accrue for the entire transcript. The user will incur PACER charges for each time the transcript is accessed even though he/she may have purchased it from the court reporter and obtained electronic access through CM/ECF. There is no "free look" for transcripts.

Court Reporters

Name	Phone Number	Email Address
Armstrong, Wesley J.	(717)542–5569	Wesley_Armstrong@pamd.uscourts.gov
Boyanowski, Laura	(570) 332–6114	Laura_Boyanowski@pamd.uscourts.gov
Fausnaught, Lori A.	(570) 323–6704	Lori_Fausnaught@pamd.uscourts.gov
Gilbride, Diana	(570) 348–0869	Diana_Gilbride@pamd.uscourts.gov
Halko, Suzanne A.	(570) 341–6703	Suzanne_Halko@pamd.uscourts.gov
Shuey, Lori A.	(717) 215–1270	Lori_Shuey@pamd.uscourts.gov
Steinbach, Joan D.	(570) 772–5769	Joan Steinbach@pamd.uscourts.gov
Yeager, Kristin L.	(570) 344–1323	Kristin_Yeager@pamd.uscourts.gov
Yinger, Wendy C.	(717) 440–1535	Wendy_Yinger@pamd.uscourts.gov

CRIMINAL JUSTICE ACT PLAN

I. AUTHORITY

Pursuant to the provisions of the Criminal Justice Act of 1964, as amended, 18 U.S.C. 3006A, [hereinafter referred to as "CJA"] and the Guidelines for the Administration of the Criminal Justice Act, Volume VII, Guide to Judiciary Policies and Procedures (CJA Guidelines), the Judges of the United States District Court for the Middle District of Pennsylvania adopt this Plan for furnishing representation in federal court for any person financially unable to obtain adequate representation in accordance with the CJA.

II. STATEMENT OF POLICY

A. Objectives.

1. The objective of this Plan is to attain the ideal of equality before the law for all persons. Therefore, this Plan shall be administered so that those accused of crime, or otherwise eligible for services pursuant to the CJA will not be deprived, because they are financially unable to pay for adequate representation, of any element of representation necessary to an effective defense.

2. The further objective of this Plan is to particularize the requirements of the CJA, the Anti–Drug Abuse Act of 1988 (codified in part at section 848(q) of title 21, United States Code), and the CJA Guidelines in a way that meets the needs of this district.

B. Compliance.

1. The court, its clerk, the federal public defender organization, and private attorneys appointed under the CJA shall comply with the CJA Guidelines approved by the Judicial Conference of the United States and/or its Committee on Defender Services and with this Plan.

2. Each private attorney shall be provided by the federal public defender with a then-current copy of this Plan and the CJA Guidelines upon the attorney's first appointment under the CJA or designation as a member of the Panel of Private Attorneys under the Criminal Justice Act (CJA Panel).

III. DEFINITIONS

A. "Appointed attorney" includes private attorneys, the federal public defender and staff attorneys of the federal public defender organization.

B. "Judge" means United States District Judge or United States Magistrate Judge.

C. "Representation" includes counsel and investigative, expert, and other services necessary for an adequate defense.

IV. PROVISION OF REPRESENTATION

A. Circumstance.

1. *Mandatory.* Representation shall be provided for any financially eligible person who:

    a. is charged with a felony or with a Class A misdemeanor;

    b. is a juvenile alleged to have committed an act of juvenile delinquency as defined in section 5031 of title 18, United States Code;

    c. is charged with a violation of probation, or faces a change of a term or condition of probation (unless the modification sought is favorable to the probationer and the government has not objected to the proposed change);

    d. is under arrest, when such representation is required by law;

    e. is entitled to appointment of counsel in parole proceedings;

    f. is charged with a violation of supervised release or faces modification, reduction, or enlargement of a condition, or extension or revocation of a term of supervised release;

    g. is subject to a mental condition hearing under chapter 313 of title 18, United States Code;

    h. is in custody as a material witness;

    i. is seeking to set aside or vacate a death sentence under sections 2254 or 2255 of title 28, United States Code;

    j. is entitled to appointment of counsel in verification of consent proceedings pursuant to a transfer of an offender to or from the United States for the execution of a penal sentence under section 4109 of title 18, United States Code;

    k. is entitled to appointment of counsel under the Sixth Amendment to the Constitution; or

    l. faces loss of liberty in a case and federal law requires the appointment of counsel.

2. *Discretionary.* Whenever a judge determines that the interests of justice so require, representation <u>may</u> be provided for any financially eligible person who:

    a. is charged with a petty offense (Class B or C misdemeanor, or an infraction) for which a sentence to confinement is authorized;

    b. is seeking relief, other than to set aside or vacate a death sentence, under sections 2241, 2254, or 2255 of title 28, United States Code;

    c. is charged with civil or criminal contempt who faces loss of liberty;

    d. has been called as a witness before a grand jury, a court, the Congress, or a federal agency or commission which has the power to compel testimony, and there is reason to believe, either prior to or during testimony, that the witness could be subject to a criminal prosecution, a civil or criminal contempt proceeding, or face loss of liberty;

    e. is proposed by the United States attorney for processing under a pretrial diversion program;

    f. is held for international extradition under chapter 209 of title 18, United States Code.

Representation may also be furnished for financially eligible persons in ancillary matters appropriate to the proceedings pursuant to subsection (c) of the CJA.

B. When Counsel Shall Be Provided. Counsel shall be provided to eligible persons as soon as feasible after they are taken into custody, when they appear before a judge, when they are formally charged or notified of charges if formal charges are sealed, or when a judge otherwise considers appointment of counsel appropriate under the CJA, whichever occurs earliest.

In appointing counsel, the Court shall select the federal public defender organization or an attorney from the panel of private attorneys approved by the court, except in extraordinary circumstances where appointment of other qualified and experienced counsel becomes necessary.

Appointment of counsel may be <u>retroactive</u> to include representation furnished pursuant to this plan prior to appointment. The Court shall appoint separate counsel for persons having interests that cannot be represented by the same counsel or when other good cause is shown.

C. Number and Qualifications of Counsel.

1. *Number.* More than one attorney may be appointed in any case determined by the court to be extremely difficult. In a capital case, the following applies:

    a. Federal Capital Prosecutions. Pursuant to 18 U.S.C. § 3005, a person charged with a federal capital offense is <u>entitled</u> to the appointment of two attorneys, at least one of whom shall be learned in the law applicable to capital cases. Pursuant to 21 U.S.C. § 848(q)(4), if necessary for adequate representation, more than two attorneys may be appointed to represent a defendant in such a case.

b.   Habeas Corpus Proceedings.   Pursuant to 21 U.S.C. § 848(q)(4), a financially eligible person seeking to vacate or set aside a death sentence in proceedings under 28 U.S.C. § 2254 or 2255 is entitled to appointment of one or more qualified attorneys.   Due to the complex, demanding, and protracted nature of death penalty proceedings, judicial officers should consider appointing at least two counsel.

2.   *Qualifications*

a.   Appointment of Counsel.   Pursuant to 21 U.S.C. § 848(q)(5), at least one of the attorneys appointed must have been admitted to practice in this court for not less than five years, and must have had not less than three years experience in the actual trial of felony prosecutions in that court.   Pursuant to 18 U.S.C. § 3005, at least one of the attorneys appointed must be knowledgeable in the law applicable to capital cases.

Pursuant to 18 U.S.C. § 3005, in appointing counsel in federal capital prosecutions, the court shall consider the recommendation of the federal public defender.

b.   Attorney Qualification Waiver.   Pursuant to 21 U.S.C. § 848(q)(7), the presiding judicial officer, for good cause, may appoint an attorney who may not qualify under 21 U.S.C. § 848(q)(5) or (q)(6), but who has the background, knowledge, and experience necessary to represent the defendant properly in a capital case, giving due consideration to the seriousness of the possible penalty and the unique and complex nature of the litigation.

D.   Eligibility for Representation.

1.   *Fact finding.*   The determination of eligibility for representation under the CJA is a judicial function to be performed by a judge after making appropriate inquiries concerning the person's financial condition.

2.   *Disclosure of Change in Eligibility.*   If, at any time after appointment, counsel obtains information that a client is financially able to make payment, in whole or in part, for legal or other services in connection with his or her representation, and the source of the attorney's information is not protected as a privileged communication, counsel shall advise the court.

V.   FEDERAL PUBLIC DEFENDER ORGANIZATION

A.   Establishment.

1.   The federal public defender organization of the Middle District of Pennsylvania, previously established in this district pursuant to the provisions of the CJA, is hereby recognized as the federal public defender organization for this district.

2.   The federal public defender organization shall be capable of providing legal services throughout the district and shall maintain offices in Harrisburg, Scranton, and Williamsport, Pennsylvania.

B.   Supervision of Defender Organization.   The federal public defender shall be responsible for the supervision and management of the federal public defender organization.   Accordingly, the federal public defender shall be appointed in all cases assigned to that organization for subsequent assignment to staff attorneys at the discretion of the federal public defender.

C.   Management of CJA Panel.   The management of the CJA Panel is subject to the provisions of the Plan for the Composition, Administration, and Management of the Panel of Private Attorneys under the Criminal Justice Act, found at Appendix I of this CJA Plan.

VI.   PRIVATE ATTORNEYS

A. Establishment of CJA Panel. The existing, previously established panel of attorneys (CJA Panel) who are eligible and willing to be appointed to provide representation under the CJA is hereby recognized. The court shall review the recommendations of the Panel Selection and Management Committee and approve attorneys for membership on the panel who are competent to give adequate representation to parties under the Criminal Justice Act. The court has established and approved a separate panel of attorneys for the Harrisburg, Scranton/Wilkes–Barre, and Williamsport vicinages. All members of the CJA Panel shall serve at the pleasure of the Court.

B. Organization. The Plan for the Composition, Administration, and Management of the Panel of Private Attorneys under the Criminal Justice Act is found at Appendix I of this CJA Plan.

C. Ratio of Appointments. Where practical and cost effective, private attorneys from the CJA Panel shall be appointed in a substantial proportion of the cases in which the accused is determined to be financially eligible for representation under the CJA. "Substantial" shall usually be defined as approximately 25 percent of the appointments under the CJA annually throughout the district.

VII. REPRESENTATION IN DEATH PENALTY HABEAS CORPUS PROCEEDINGS

Appointment of Counsel in proceedings under 28 U.S.C. §§ 2254 and 2255.

The court shall appoint counsel to represent financially eligible persons seeking habeas corpus relief in death penalty proceedings under sections 2254 and 2255 of title 28, United States Code. The appointment of counsel shall be made from the following sources:

1. The Federal Public Defender Office for the Middle District of Pennsylvania (Capital Habeas Unit);

2. The Defender Association of Philadelphia (Capital Habeas Unit);

3. The Federal Defender Office for the Western District of Pennsylvania (Capital Habeas Unit); or

4. a member or members of the Death Penalty Panel; or

5. an other attorney who qualifies for appointment under section 848(q) of title 21, United States Code.

Before appointment of counsel in a capital habeas case the court should obtain the consent of the defender or counsel the court seeks to appoint.

VIII. DUTIES OF APPOINTED COUNSEL

A. Standards. The services to be rendered a person represented by appointed counsel shall be commensurate with those rendered if counsel were privately employed by the person.

B. Professional Conduct. Attorneys appointed pursuant to the CJA shall conform to the highest standards of professional conduct, including but not limited to the provisions of the Pennsylvania Rules of Professional Conduct.

C. No Receipt of Other Payment. Appointed counsel may not require, request, or accept any payment or promise of payment or any other valuable consideration for representation under the appointment, unless such payment is approved by order of the court.

D. Continuing Representation. Once counsel is appointed under the CJA, counsel shall continue the representation until the matter, including appeals or review by certiorari, is closed; until substitute counsel has filed a notice of appearance; until an order has been entered allowing or requiring the person represented to proceed pro se; or until the appointment is terminated by court order.

IX. DUTIES OF LAW ENFORCEMENT AND RELATED AGENCIES

A. Presentation of Accused for Appointment of Counsel. Federal law enforcement and prosecutorial agencies, probation officers, and pretrial services officers in this district, and those acting on their behalf, shall promptly ask any person who is in custody, or who otherwise may be entitled to counsel under the CJA, whether he or she is financially able to secure representation, and shall, in such cases in which the person indicates that he or she is not able, notify the federal public defender who shall discuss with the person the right to representation and right to appointed counsel, and if appointment of counsel seems likely, assist in the completion of a financial affidavit (CJA Form 23) and arrange to have the person promptly presented before a judge of this court for determination of financial eligibility and appointment of counsel.

B. Pretrial Services Interview. Appointed counsel should be furnished to financially eligible defendants prior to the defendants being interviewed by a pretrial services or probation officer. If appointed counsel is not available within 30 minutes of notification of the defendant's arrival at the federal building, the pretrial services or probation officer may interview the defendant.

C. Notice of Indictment or Criminal Information. Upon the return or unsealing of an indictment, the filing of a criminal information, or the filing of a petition to modify or revoke probation or supervised release, the United States attorney, the probation officer, or clerk's office staff as appropriate, immediately shall mail, transmit or otherwise deliver a copy of the document to appointed counsel, or to the defendant if without counsel, at the address shown on defendant's bond papers or to the jail in which the defendant is incarcerated.

X. MISCELLANEOUS

A. Forms. Standard forms, pertaining to the CJA and approved by the Judicial Conference of the United States or its Committee on Defender Services and prescribed and distributed by the Director of the Administrative Office of the United States Courts, shall be used, where applicable, in all proceedings under this Plan.

B. Claims. Claims for compensation of private attorneys providing representation under the CJA shall be submitted on the appropriate CJA form, to the office of the clerk of the court or the federal public defender. That office shall review the claim form for mathematical and technical accuracy and for conformity with the CJA Guidelines, and, if correct, shall forward the claim form for the consideration of the appropriate judge. The court will exert its best effort to avoid delays in reviewing payment vouchers and in submitting them for further processing.

C. Supersession. This Plan supersedes all prior Criminal Justice Act Plans of this court.

XI. EFFECTIVE DATE

This Plan shall become effective when approved by the Judicial Council of the Third Circuit.

APPENDIX:

1. Plan for the Composition, Administration, and Management of the Panel of Private Attorneys under the Criminal Justice Act.

THE FOREGOING PLAN IS ADOPTED BY THE JUDGES OF THE UNITED STATES DISTRICT COURT FOR THE MIDDLE DISTRICT OF PENNSYLVANIA.

[Dated: January 30, 2006; approved by the Judicial Council of the Third Circuit on November 15, 2006.]

APPENDIX I
TO THE CRIMINAL JUSTICE ACT PLAN

Plan for the Composition, Administration, and Management of the
Panel of Private Attorneys Under the Criminal Justice Act

I. INTRODUCTION

Pursuant to the Guidelines for the Administration of the Criminal Justice Act and the Middle District of Pennsylvania Criminal Justice Act Plan, the United States District Court for the Middle District of Pennsylvania has established the following "Plan for the Composition, Administration, and Management of the Panel of Private Attorneys Under the Criminal Justice Act."

II. COMPOSITION OF PANEL OF PRIVATE ATTORNEYS

A. Panels.

1. *Approval.* The Court shall establish two panels of private attorneys (hereinafter referred to as the "CJA Panel" and "Death Penalty Panel") who are eligible and willing to be appointed to provide representation under the Criminal Justice Act. The Court shall approve attorneys for membership on the panel after receiving recommendations from the "Panel Selection and Management Committee," established pursuant to paragraph II(B) of this Plan. Members of the CJA Panels serve at the pleasure of the Court. Any attorney aggrieved by the decision on his or her application may present a written grievance to the committee whose review and decision shall then be final.

2. *CJA Panel.* The CJA Panel established by the Court shall consist of a sufficient number of experienced attorneys to meet the needs of each of the three vicinages of the Middle District of Pennsylvania. Each vicinage shall have at least fifteen (15) lawyers and no more than forty-five (45) lawyers available for appointment by the court. A group within the CJA Panel interested in appellate work shall be identified and available to handle appeals should the need arise.

3. *Death Penalty Panel.* The Death Penalty Panel established by the Court shall consist of a sufficient number of qualified lawyers to meet the needs of the Middle District of Pennsylvania.

4. *Eligibility.* To be eligible to serve on the CJA Panel or Death Penalty Panel, an attorney must be admitted to practice before the United States District Court for the Middle District of Pennsylvania pursuant to the Middle District Local Rules, and must have demonstrated experience in and knowledge of the Federal Rules of Criminal Procedure, the Federal Rules of Appellate Procedure, the Federal Rules of Evidence, the Sentencing Guidelines and the Local Rules of Court for the Middle District of Pennsylvania and the Local Rules for the Third Circuit Court of Appeals.

a. Minimum Eligibility for CJA Panel. An attorney seeking initial membership in the CJA Panel must during the four years prior to the application have served for at least two years in a state or federal judicial clerkship, have served for at least two years in a state or federal public defender's or prosecutor's office, or have served for at least three years in private practice and have had a caseload of criminal cases in state and federal court making up 25% or more of the attorney's overall caseload.

An attorney seeking initial membership must also have:

    i. attended at least one two hour seminar on a federal sentencing topic within one (1) year prior to the application;

    ii. attended at least one two-hour seminar on a federal criminal defense topic within one (1) year prior to the application; and

    iii. been counsel or second chair for one federal criminal trial or guilty plea within one year prior to the application.

Preference for appointment to the panel will be afforded to attorneys who reside in the Middle District of Pennsylvania or have a principal office in this district.

b. Specific Requirements for CJA Panel Members Available for Appeals. CJA Panel attorneys available for appointments involving appellate work must have filed at least three (3) appeals to the Third Circuit Court of Appeals and had at least one (1) oral argument before the Third Circuit.

c. Specific Requirements of Death Penalty Panel. All attorneys seeking membership on the Death Penalty Panel must meet the following minimum eligibility requirements:

i. must have been admitted to practice in the United States District Court for the Middle District of Pennsylvania for not less than five (5) years; AND

ii. must have had not less than three (3) years experience in the actual trial of felony prosecutions in the Middle District Court within the five (5) years prior to the application; AND

iii. must have attended a comprehensive training program in the defense of capital cases within one (1) year of the application; AND

iv. actual trial experience in state or federal court on a first degree murder case, capital or otherwise within the five (5) years prior to the application.

Attorneys seeking membership on the Death Panel should meet qualification standards for defense counsel formulated by relevant courts, bar associations, and other entities with regard to capital representation, e.g. Guideline 5.7, ABA Guidelines for the Appointment and Performance of Defense Counsel in Death Penalty Cases; Rule 801 of the Pennsylvania Rules of Criminal Procedure.

Attorneys seeking membership on the Death Panel should meet the training and education guidelines and rules as set forth by relevant courts, bar associations, and other entities with regard to capital representation, e.g. Guideline 8.1, ABA Guidelines for the Appointment and Performance of Defense Counsel in Death Penalty Cases; Rule 801 of the Pennsylvania Rules of Criminal Procedure.

d. Second Chair—Training Procedure. At the reapplication process for the entire panel, attorneys who indicate on the application that they have had prior trial/guilty plea experience in federal court will also be asked to indicate whether they would be willing to accept a second chair. A list of attorneys expressing this willingness will be maintained by the Federal Public Defender in such manner that names can be provided on a rotating basis. The names of at least three attorneys willing to accept a second chair shall be provided to each applicant. Attorneys seeking membership on the CJA Panel who need second chair experience to meet their eligibility requirements will be responsible for calling both the Federal Public Defender and the attorney(s) with whom they wish to second chair.

All arrangements for the applicant's second chair experience shall be made between the applicant and the first chair attorney, except that: it shall be the responsibility of the first chair attorney to make the status of the second chair attorney clear to both the Court and his/her client; AND the second chair attorney shall not represent the client in any part of the trial or guilty plea unless specifically authorized in writing by the client on a form provided, a copy of said form signed by the client to be presented to the Court; AND second chair attorneys shall not be compensated in any way for the time spent as second chair.

At the completion of the second chair experience, the first chair attorney shall, if requested, provide certification in writing that the applicant second chaired the entire trial and/or guilty plea. It shall be the responsibility of the applicant to complete this requirement within the time period provided in paragraph II(A)(4)(a). Service as "second chair" does not guarantee admission of an attorney to the CJA Panel.

5. *Appointments.* Counsel furnishing representation under the plan shall be selected from the panel of attorneys designated or approved by the court or from the defender organization furnishing representation pursuant to the plan.

6. *Special Appointments.* When the judge presiding over the case, or the chief judge if a judge has not yet been assigned to the case, determines that the

appointment of an attorney, who is not a member of the CJA or Death Penalty Panels, is in the interest of justice, judicial economy or continuity of representation, or there is some other compelling circumstance warranting his or her appointment, the attorney may be admitted to the CJA or Death Penalty Panels pro hac vice and appointed to represent the defendant. Consideration for preserving the integrity of the panel selection process suggests that such appointments should be made only in exceptional circumstances. Further, the attorney, who may or may not maintain an office in the district, should possess such qualities as would qualify him or her for admission to the Middle Districts' panels in the ordinary course of panel selection.

7. *Terms.*

a. CJA Panel. An attorney appointed to serve on the CJA Panel will be appointed to serve for three years. Appointments shall be made to the panel each year. The Panel Selection and Management Committee will strive to make appointments each year to achieve a sufficient number of qualified lawyers to meet the needs of the Middle District of Pennsylvania.

b. Death Penalty Panel. There are no term limits on the death penalty panel.

8. *Removal from the CJA and Death Penalty Panels.*

a. Removal from either panel shall be automatic upon proof made to the Chief Judge that a panel attorney has been charged or convicted with any crime in either state or federal court carrying a possible maximum penalty of more than two (2) years imprisonment.

b. The possibility of removal from either panel shall be reviewed by the Panel Selection and Management Committee upon complaint received from a client, a judge or another attorney concerning the panel member's performance in court. His or her discipline shall be determined by the Disciplinary Board of the Supreme Court of Pennsylvania and his or her sanction by either the District Court or the Circuit Court. The panel member being considered for removal shall be asked to meet with the Panel Selection and Management Committee reviewing the request for removal and shall be permitted to present information in his/her own behalf to dispute the claim raised. A decision shall be rendered by the Panel Selection and Management Subcommittee after it is satisfied that all relevant information has been received and shall be communicated in writing to the panel member, with reasons stated for the decision. Appeal of the decision of the subcommittee shall be made to the full committee. The decision of the full committee shall be final. There is no presumption that because a client has alleged the ineffectiveness of his/her attorney in a collateral attack on his/her conviction, that attorney must be removed from the panel.

9. *Reappointment.* Preference may be given by the Panel Selection and Management Committee in appointments to the Panel to an attorney who has been off the panel for a year or more or an attorney who has not previously been on the panel over an attorney whose term is finishing.

Continued eligibility for membership on the CJA Panel shall be maintained by accepting at least two appointments per each three year term and by attendance at two seminars on a federal criminal defense topic per each three year term. Members interested in appeals should seek continuing legal education in appellate matters.

10. *Application.* Application forms for membership on the CJA and Death Penalty Panels shall be made available, upon request, by the Federal Public Defender and the Clerk of the Court. Completed applications shall be submitted to the Federal Public Defender Office in the most convenient vicinage. The defender office will transmit the applications to all other members of the Panel Selection and Management Committee.

11. *Equal Opportunity.* All qualified attorneys shall be encouraged to participate in the furnishing of representation in CJA cases, without regard to race, color, religion, sex, age, national origin, or disabling condition.

B.   Panel Selection and Management Committee.

1. *Membership.* A Panel Selection and Management Committee shall be established by the Court. The following groups shall be represented: the United States District Judges, United States Magistrate Judges, federal public defender staff and CJA Panel attorneys.

The full committee shall consist of one (1) district judge from Harrisburg, one (1) district judge from Scranton/Wilkes–Barre, and one (1) district judge from Williamsport, a United States magistrate judge from each of the three vicinages of the District, a federal public defender representative from each vicinage, and nine (9) private attorneys. The Chief Judge of the District, or his/her designee, shall chair the full committee.

The full committee shall consist of three (3) local subcommittees. Each subcommittee shall consist of one (1) district judge, one (1) magistrate judge, the federal public defender (or his/her representative), and three (3) private attorneys.

2. *Duties*

a.   Each vicinage's subcommittee of the Panel Selection and Management Committee shall meet at least once a year for the purposes of reviewing applications and making recommendations for membership on the CJA and Death Penalty Panels. The subcommittee shall ensure the establishment and maintenance of a sufficient panel of private attorneys who are willing and able to accept appointments for the CJA Panel. The subcommittees shall review the qualifications of applicants and recommend, for approval by the Court, those applicants best qualified to fill the vacancies.

b.   If, at any time during the course of a year, the number of vacancies due to resignation, removal, or death significantly decreases the size of the panel in a vicinage, the subcommittee shall solicit applications for the vacancies, convene a special meeting to review the qualifications of the applicants, and select prospective members for recommendation to the Court for approval. Members approved by the Court to fill mid-term vacancies shall serve until the expiration of the term that was vacated, and shall be immediately eligible for reappointment.

c.   The full Panel Selection and Management Committee shall meet at least once a year to review the operation and administration of the panel over the preceding year, and to recommend to the Court any changes deemed necessary or appropriate by the Committee regarding the appointment process and panel management. Further, the full committee is charged with the establishment and maintenance of the Death Penalty Panel.

3. *Term.* In each vicinage a private attorney will be selected each year by the Chief Judge to serve a three year term as a member of the committee. The federal public defender shall serve continuously on the full committee. Judicial representatives to the Committee and their terms shall be determined by the Chief Judge.

III.   SELECTION FOR APPOINTMENT

A. Maintenance of List and Distribution of Appointments. The Federal Public Defender and Clerk of Court shall maintain a current list of all attorneys included on the CJA and Death Penalty Panels, with current office addresses, e-mail addresses and telephone numbers, as well as a statement of qualifications and experience. The Federal Public Defender shall furnish a copy of this list to each judge and magistrate. The Federal Public Defender shall also maintain a public record of assignments to private counsel, and, when appropriate, statistical data reflecting the proration of appointments between attorneys for the Federal Public Defender office and private attorneys, according to the formula described in the CJA Plan for the Middle District.

B.   Method of Selection. Appointments from the list of private attorneys should be made on a rotational basis, subject to the Court's discretion to make exceptions due to the nature and complexity of the case, an attorney's experience, and geographical considerations. This procedure should result in a balanced distribution of appointments and compensation among the members of the CJA and Death Penalty Panels, and quality representation for each CJA defendant.

Upon the determination of a need for the appointment of counsel, the judge shall notify the Federal Public Defender of the need for counsel and the nature of the case.

The Federal Public Defender shall advise the judge as to the status of distribution of cases, where appropriate, as between the Federal Public Defender and the panel of private attorneys. If the judge decides to appoint an attorney from the panel, the Federal Public Defender shall determine the name of the next panel member on the list who is available for appointment and shall provide the name to the appointing judge.

In the event of an emergency, i.e., weekends, holidays, or other non-working hours of the Federal Public Defender and Clerk of Court offices, the presiding judge may appoint any attorney from the list. In all cases where members of the CJA Panel are appointed out of sequence, the appointing judge or magistrate shall notify the Federal Public Defender as to the name of the attorney appointed and the date of the appointment.

There are situations where the defender office should not be involved in the appointment process. The clerk's office may furnish the judicial officer the name of an available panel attorney. In such cases the defender office should merely be notified that a "Doe" appointment has been made. In such a situation there is no need to report which panel attorney received the appointment if the revelation could compromise the need for confidentiality.

IV. COMPENSATION—FILING OF VOUCHERS

Claims for compensation shall be submitted on the appropriate CJA form, to the office of the Clerk of Court or Federal Public Defender. The Clerk of the Court or Federal Public Defender shall review the claim form for mathematical and technical accuracy, and for conformity with the Guidelines for the Administration of the Criminal Justice Act (Volume VII, Guide to Judiciary Policies and Procedures) and, if correct, shall forward the claim form for the consideration and action of the presiding judge.

It is the general policy of the Middle District that vouchers shall not be reduced. However, it is acknowledged that in some cases reduction will be necessary or appropriate. In those cases, the procedure set forth in the balance of this section shall be followed.

In any case where the judicial officer intends to reduce the amount of payment requested in a trial level voucher, CJA counsel shall be notified of the amount of the intended reduction and the reasons for same, and may request an opportunity for review by the judicial officer. After review of any submission by appointed counsel, including his/her response to the judicial officer's reasons for the reduction, and the completion of any other steps deemed appropriate by the judicial officer, the judicial officer shall take action on the voucher consistent with the Plan, the CJA and the interests of justice. The Panel Management Committee shall be available to make recommendation on voucher issues.

The Third Circuit shall approve all vouchers submitted by appellate counsel.

[Dated: November 15, 2006.]

SPEEDY TRIAL PLAN
SPEEDY TRIAL PLAN FOR THE UNITED STATES DISTRICT COURT FOR THE MIDDLE DISTRICT OF PENNSYLVANIA
ARTICLE I

101. Adoption of Plan. In compliance with the Speedy Trial Act of 1974, the Speedy Trial Act Amendments Act of 1979, and specifically 18 U.S.C. §§ 3165 and 3166, the judges of the United States District Court for the Middle District of Pennsylvania hereby adopt this amended Plan for the disposition of criminal cases in this district. This revision to the District Plan was approved by the court on 29 of April, 2005, and shall become effective upon the approval of the Judicial Council of the Third Circuit and the Chief Judge of this District, in accordance with 18 U.S.C. § 3165(d).

102. Members of the Speedy Trial Act Working Group of this District.

Honorable Christopher C. Conner, U.S. District Judge
Honorable J. Andrew Smyser, U.S. Magistrate Judge
Martin Carlson, Chief Assistant U.S. Attorney
James F. Wade, Federal Public Defender
Chris Fisanick, Assistant U.S. Attorney
Mary E. D'Andrea, Clerk
Cathy Dolinish, Chief Deputy Clerk
Gary L. Hollinger, Chief Deputy Clerk
Kevin Calpin, Operations Manager

103. Location of Records. In compliance with 18 U.S.C. § 3165(f), the amended District Plan shall become a public document upon approval of the Board of Judges and upon final adoption of the amended Plan. Copies will be available as follows:

(a) *For Inspection*: At the Clerk's Offices at Scranton, Harrisburg and Williamsport and also available on the court's website at www.pamd.uscourts.gov.

(b) *For Purchasing*: At Clerk's Offices (See (a)(1) above) at the charge currently in effect for copies of documents.

ARTICLE II   STATEMENT OF TIME LIMITS AND PROCEDURES FOR IMPLEMENTING THEM

201. Pursuant to the requirements of the Speedy Trial Act of 1974 (18 U.S.C. Chapter 208), the Speedy Trial Act Amendments Act of 1979 (P.L. No. 96–43, 93 Stat. 327), and the Federal Juvenile Delinquency Act (18 U.S.C. §§ 5036 and 5037), the judges of the United States District Court for the Middle District of Pennsylvania have adopted the following time limits and procedures to minimize undue delay and to further the prompt disposition of criminal cases and certain juvenile proceedings.[1]

202. Applicability.

(a) *Offenses*. The time limits set forth herein are applicable to all criminal offenses except for petty offenses as defined in 18 U.S.C. § 19 and Rule 58(a) of the Federal Rules of Criminal Procedure. Except as specifically provided, they are not applicable to proceedings under the Federal Juvenile Delinquency Act. [18 U.S.C. §§ 5031–5042]

(b) *Time Computations*. For the purpose of sanctions as provided in § 3162 of the Act, a time limit in this Plan which ends on a Saturday, a Sunday or a legal holiday will be computed as provided for in Rule 45(a) of the Federal Rules of Criminal Procedure.

203. Priorities in Scheduling Criminal Cases.

(a) *Preference Generally.* Preference shall be given to criminal proceedings as far as practicable as required by Rule 50 of the Federal Rules of Criminal Procedure.

(b) *Preference as Between Criminal Defendants.* The trial of defendants in custody solely awaiting trial on the federal charge contained in the pertinent indictment, information, or complaint should be given preference over other criminal cases. [18 U.S.C. § 3164(a)]

204. Time Within Which an Indictment or Information must be Filed.

(a) *Time Limits.* If an individual is arrested or served with a summons and the complaint charges an offense to be prosecuted in this District, any indictment or information subsequently filed in connection with such charge shall be filed within thirty (30) days of arrest or service. [18 U.S.C. § 3161(b)]

(b) *Grand Jury Not in Session.* If the defendant is charged with a felony to be prosecuted in this District, and no grand jury in the district has been in session during the thirty (30) day period prescribed in subsection (a), such period shall be extended an additional thirty (30) days. [18 U.S.C. § 3161(b)]

(c) *Measurement of Time Periods.* If a person has not been arrested or served with a summons, an arrest will be deemed to have been made with respect to a federal charge in this District at such time as the person (i) is held in custody solely for the purpose of responding to that charge; (ii) is delivered to the custody of a federal official in connection with that charge; or (iii) appears before a judicial officer in connection with the charge.

(d) *Related Procedures.*

(1) At the time of the earliest appearance before a judicial officer of a person who has been arrested for an offense not charged in an indictment or information, the judicial officer shall establish for the record the date on which the arrest took place.

(2) In the absence of a showing to the contrary, a summons shall be considered to have been served on the date of service shown on the return thereof.

205. Time Within Which Trial Must Commence.

(a) *Time Limits.* In accordance with 18 U.S.C. § 3161(c)(1), the trial of a defendant shall commence not later than seventy (70) days after the last to occur of the following dates:

(1) The date on which an indictment or information is filed and made public;

(2) The date of the defendant's first appearance before a judicial officer of this District.

(b) *Retrial; Trial After Reinstatement of an Information or Indictment.* The retrial of a defendant shall commence within seventy (70) days from the date the order occasioning the retrial becomes final, as shall the trial of a defendant upon an indictment or information dismissed by a trial court and reinstated following an appeal. If the retrial or trial follows an appeal or collateral attack, the court may extend the period if unavailability of witnesses or other factors resulting from passage of time make trial within seventy (70) days impractical. The extended period shall not exceed one hundred eighty (180) days. [18 U.S.C. § 3161(d)(2) and (e)]

(c) *Withdrawal of Plea.* If a defendant enters a plea of guilty or nolo contendere to any or all charges in an indictment or information and is subsequently permitted to withdraw it, the time limit shall be determined for all counts as if the indictment or information were filed on the day the order permitting withdrawal of the plea became final. [18 U.S.C. § 3161(i)]

(d) *Superseding Charges.* If, after an indictment or information has been filed, a complaint, indictment or information is filed that charges the defendant with the same offense or with an offense required to be joined with that offense, the time limit applicable to the subsequent charge will be determined as follows:

(1) If the original indictment or information was dismissed on motion of the defendant before the filing of the subsequent charge, the time limit shall be determined without regard to the existence of the original charge. [18 U.S.C. § 3161(d)(1)]

(2) If the original indictment or information is pending at the time the subsequent charge is filed, the trial shall commence within the time limit for commencement of trial on the original indictment or information.

(3) If the original indictment or information was dismissed on motion of the United States Attorney before the filing of the subsequent charge, the trial shall commence within the time limit for commencement of trial on the original indictment or information, but the period during which the defendant was not under charges shall be excluded from the computations. Such period is the period between the dismissal of the original indictment or information and the date the time would have commenced to run on the subsequent charge had there been no previous charge. If the subsequent charge is contained in a complaint, the formal time limit within which an indictment or information must be obtained on the charge shall be determined without regard to the existence of the original indictment or information.

(4) In the event that the complaint, indictment, or information is filed against a defendant charged in a pending indictment or information or in an indictment or information dismissed on motion of the United States Attorney, the trial on the new charge shall commence within the time limit for commencement of trial on the original indictment or information, unless the court finds that the new charge is not for the same offense charged in the original indictment or information or an offense required to be joined therewith.

(e) *Measurement of Time Periods.* For the purpose of this section:

(1) In the event of a transfer to this District under Rule 20 of the Federal Rules of Criminal Procedure, the indictment or information shall be deemed filed in this District when the papers in the proceeding or certified copies thereof are received by the Clerk.

(2) A trial in a jury case shall be deemed to commence at the beginning of voir dire.

(3) A trial in a non-jury case shall be deemed to commence on the day the case is called, provided that some step in the trial procedure immediately follows.

(f) *Related Procedures.*

(1) At the time of the defendant's earliest appearance before a judicial officer of this District, the judicial officer will take appropriate steps to assure that the defendant is represented by counsel and shall appoint counsel where appropriate under the Criminal Justice Act, Rule 44 of the Federal Rules of Criminal Procedure and the court's Criminal Justice Act Plan.

(2) The magistrate judge or clerk shall obtain from the defendant, and place on the record, a good address and telephone number where the defendant can be reached or served by the court, and shall instruct the defendant to notify the court immediately of any change of address or phone number.

(3) In a case where it is not certain that the defendant already has retained or will retain private counsel, the Clerk and/or Federal Public Defender will arrange for the defendant to receive the financial affidavit form for appointment of counsel impressing the importance of prompt filing. The court will set a time limit within which:

a. The defendant will obtain private counsel or proceed pro se, if the defendant does not qualify for court appointed counsel.

b. If the defendant qualifies for court appointed counsel, such counsel will be appointed.

(4) At the time of arraignment or as soon thereafter as is practicable, each case will be set for trial on a day certain or listed for trial on a weekly or other short term calendar.

(5) Individual calendars shall be managed so that it will be reasonably anticipated that every criminal case set for trial will be reached during the week of original setting or will be reached as expeditiously as possible within the short term calendar list. A conflict in schedules of Assistant United States Attorneys or defense counsel will be grounds for a continuance or delayed setting only if approved by the court, and called to the court's attention at the earliest practicable time. The court shall state the reason(s) for the continuance in its order granting any continuance(s). The United States Attorney will familiarize himself or herself with the scheduling procedures of each judge and will assign or reassign cases in such manner that the government will be ready for trial.

(6) All pretrial hearings shall be conducted as soon after the arraignment as possible, consistent with the priorities of other matters on the court's criminal docket.

(7) The Chief Judge may reassign any or all of the criminal cases of one judge to other judges whenever the Chief Judge determines that because of sickness, disability, or extensive time in trial likely to be required in a criminal or civil case already started, or for other good reason, reassignment is necessary to meet the time limit for commencing trial in such cases.

206. Defendants in Custody.

(a) *Time Limits.* In accordance with 18 U.S.C. § 3164(b), notwithstanding any longer time periods that may be permitted under sections 204 and 205 of this Plan, the trial of a defendant held in custody solely for the purpose of trial on a federal charge shall commence within ninety (90) days following the beginning of continuous custody on the federal charges pending in the Middle District.

(b) *Measurement of Time Periods.* For the purposes of this section:

(1) A defendant is deemed to be in detention awaiting trial when arrested on a federal charge or otherwise held for the purpose of responding to a federal charge. Detention is deemed to be solely because the defendant is awaiting trial unless the person exercising custodial authority has an independent basis (not including a detainer) for continuing to hold the defendant.

(2) If a Middle District case is transferred pursuant to Rule 20 of the Federal Rules of Criminal Procedure and the defendant subsequently rejects disposition under Rule 20 or the court declines to accept the plea, a new period of continuous detention awaiting trial will begin at that time.

(3) A trial shall be deemed to commence as provided in section 205(e)(2) and (3).

207. Exclusion of Time from Computation.

(a) *Applicability.* In computing any time limit under sections 204, 205, or 206, periods of delay set forth in 18 U.S.C. § 3161(h) shall be excluded. Such periods of delay shall not be excluded in computing the minimum period for commencement of trial under section 208. It shall be the responsibility of any party filing a motion that seeks any form of relief that results in periods of delay that are subject to exclusion under 18 U.S.C. § 3161(h), to identify and describe fully those periods of excludable delay for the court in the party's motion, enabling the court to make a meaningful judgment regarding the Speedy Trial Act implications of the motion, and provide the court with a proposed form of order that specifically addresses any applicable Speedy Trial Act exclusions.

(b) *Records of Excludable Time.* The Clerk shall enter on the docket, in the form prescribed by the Administrative Office of the United States Courts, information with respect to excludable periods of time for each criminal defendant. With respect to proceedings prior to the filing of an indictment or information, excludable time shall be reported to the Clerk by the United States Attorney.

(c) *Pre–Indictment Procedures.*

(1) In the event that the United States Attorney anticipates that an indictment or information will not be filed within the time limit set forth in section 204, the United States Attorney may file a written motion with the court for a determination of excludable time. In the event that the United States Attorney seeks a continuance under 18 U.S.C. § 3161(h)(8), the United States Attorney shall file a written motion with the court requesting such a continuance.

(2) The motion of the United States Attorney shall state (i) the period of time proposed for exclusion, and (ii) the basis of the proposed exclusion. If the motion is for a continuance under 18 U.S.C. § 3161(h)(8), it shall also state whether or not the defendant is being held in custody on the basis of the complaint. In appropriate circumstances, the motion may include a request that some or all of the supporting material be considered ex parte and *in camera.*

208.   Minimum Period for Defense Preparation.   Unless the defendant consents in writing to the contrary, the trial shall not commence earlier than thirty (30) days from the date on which the indictment or information is filed or, if later, from the date on which counsel first enters an appearance or on which the defendant expressly waives counsel and elects to proceed pro se. In circumstances in which the seventy-day time limit for commencing trial on a charge in an indictment or information is determined by reference to an earlier indictment or information pursuant to section 205(d) the thirty-day minimum period shall also be determined by reference to the earlier indictment or information. When prosecution is resumed on an original indictment or information following a mistrial, appeal, or withdrawal of a guilty plea, a new thirty-day minimum period will not begin to run. [18 U.S.C. § 3161(c)(2)]

209.   Time Within Which Defendant Should be Sentenced.

(a) *Time Limits.*   Sentencing proceedings shall be scheduled in accordance with Local Rule of Criminal Procedure 32.1.

(b) *Related Procedures.*   Presentence investigations and reports shall be prepared in accordance with Rule 32 of the Federal Rules of Criminal Procedure and Local Rule of Criminal Procedure 32.1.

210.   Juvenile Proceedings.   Proceedings in juvenile matters shall be scheduled in accordance with 18 U.S.C. §§ 5036 and 5037.

211.   Sanctions.

(a) *Dismissal or Release from Custody.*   Failure to comply with the requirements of Title I of the Speedy Trial Act may entitle the defendant to dismissal of the charges or to release from pretrial custody. Nothing in this Plan shall be construed to require that a case be dismissed or a defendant released from custody in circumstances in which such action would not be required by 18 U.S.C. §§ 3162 and 3164.[2]

(b) *Discipline of Attorneys.*   In a case in which counsel:

(1) Knowingly allows the case to be set for trial without disclosing the fact that a necessary witness would be unavailable for trial,

(2) Files a motion solely for the purpose of delay that counsel knows is frivolous and without merit,

(3) Makes a statement for the purpose of obtaining a continuance that counsel knows to be false and that is material to the granting of the continuance, or

(4) Otherwise willfully fails to proceed to trial without justification consistent with 18 U.S.C. § 3161, the court may punish such counsel as provided in 18 U.S.C. § 3162(b) and (c).

212. Persons Serving Terms of Imprisonment. If the United States Attorney knows that a person charged with an offense is serving a term of imprisonment in any penal institution, the United States Attorney shall promptly seek to obtain the presence of the prisoner for trial, or cause a detainer to be filed, in accordance with the provisions of 18 U.S.C. § 3161(j).

ARTICLE III   DISTRICT EXPERIENCE UNDER THE ACT

301. Effect of the Prevailing Time Limits on Criminal Justice Administration.

(a) The prevailing time limits make it imperative that there be prompt and continuous communication among the persons, parties, and agencies in the criminal justice system. This will need to be stressed in the training of staff for all positions.

(b) Prosecutors and defense attorneys will have to avoid case overload. They will have to concentrate on a lesser individual case load to prepare and to respond properly to all case activities and events within the time limits.

(c) Attention to detail has become an important aspect in avoiding delay. Record keeping needs to be thorough and accurate. Record keepers must be well trained, supervised, and continuously updated. These aspects, as well as communication in (a), supra, indicates greater attention in the future to individual training, to supervision, and to selection of more qualified personnel.

(d) There are no indications to date that the time limits have had an effect on transfer of cases.

(e) Current records and statistics do not show that the time limits have had any effect on appeals. As sanctions might be imposed, there is a possibility for some appeals.

(f) General costs do not appear to be affected by Speedy Trial Act time limits. However, the time limits and additional procedural and record keeping requirements do have a greater impact, presently unmeasured, on personal time. Therefore, some cost is involved but can not be accurately determined at this time.

ARTICLE IV   CHANGES IN PROCEDURES AND INNOVATIONS THAT HAVE BEEN OR WILL BE ADOPTED BY THE COURT TO EXPEDITE THE DISPOSITION OF CRIMINAL CASES IN ACCORDANCE WITH THE SPEEDY TRIAL ACT.

401. Changes Adopted by the Court. The court intends to adopt Local Rules of Criminal Procedure addressing certain speedy trial issues. The court will consider possible modifications and additions to those rules on an ongoing basis. The court will also continue to consider modifications, additions and deletions to the Speedy Trial Plan, as deemed necessary by the Chief Judge.

This revision to the District Plan was approved by the court on 29 of April, 2005, and shall become effective upon the approval of the reviewing panel in accordance with 18 U.S.C. § 3165(d).

[Dated April 29, 2005; approved by the Judicial Council of the Third Circuit on August 30, 2006. Amended effective December 1, 2012.]

1If a defendant's presence has been obtained through the filing of a detainer with state authorities, the Interstate Agreement on Detainers, 18 U.S.C., Appendix, may require that trial commence before the deadline established by the Speedy Trial Act. *see United States v. Mauro*, 436 U.S. 340, 356–57 n. 24 (1978).

2 Dismissal may also be required in some cases under the Interstate Agreement on Detainers, 18 U.S.C. Appendix.

JURY PLAN

JUROR SELECTION PLAN
UNITED STATES DISTRICT COURT
FOR THE MIDDLE DISTRICT OF PENNSYLVANIA

Pursuant to the Jury Selection and Service Act of 1968, as amended, 28 U.S.C. § 1861 et seq., ("the Act") the following Plan is hereby adopted by this court, subject to approval by a reviewing panel and to such rules and regulations as may be adopted from time to time by the Judicial Conference of the United States. Pursuant to 28 U.S.C. § 1878(a), jurors are qualified and summoned in a single procedure, in lieu of two separate procedures otherwise provided for by the Act.

POLICIES

Section 101   Policy of inclusion

It is the policy of the court that all litigants have the right to grand and petit jurors selected at random from a fair cross section of the community in each division where the court convenes. All citizens shall have the opportunity to be considered for service on grand and petit juries in this court, and shall have an obligation to serve when summoned for that purpose.

Section 102   Policy of nondiscrimination

No citizen shall be excluded from service as a grand or petit juror on account of race, color, religion, sex, national origin or economic status.

APPLICABILITY OF PLAN

Section 201   Counties comprising the Middle District

This plan is applicable to the Middle District of Pennsylvania which consists of the counties of Adams, Bradford, Cameron, Carbon, Centre, Clinton, Columbia, Cumberland, Dauphin, Franklin, Fulton, Huntingdon, Juniata, Lackawanna, Lebanon, Luzerne, Lycoming, Mifflin, Monroe, Montour, Northumberland, Perry, Pike, Potter, Schuylkill,[1] Snyder, Sullivan, Susquehanna, Tioga, Union, Wayne, Wyoming and York.

Section 202   Divisions of the Middle District

The Middle District of Pennsylvania shall be divided into divisions for jury selection purposes, pursuant to § 1869(e) of the Act, as follows:

A. The Scranton/Wilkes–Barre Division, consisting of the counties of Carbon, Lackawanna, Luzerne, Monroe, Pike, Schuylkill, Susquehanna, Wayne, and Wyoming.

B. The Williamsport Division, consisting of the counties of Bradford, Cameron, Centre, Clinton, Columbia, Lycoming, Montour, Northumberland, Potter, Snyder, Sullivan, Tioga and Union.

C. The Harrisburg Division, consisting of the counties of Adams, Cumberland, Dauphin, Franklin, Fulton, Huntingdon, Juniata, Lebanon, Mifflin, Perry and York.

Provisions of this Plan shall apply to all divisions in the district unless otherwise indicated.

MANAGEMENT AND SUPERVISION OF THE JURY SELECTION PROCESS

Section 301   Personnel

The Clerk of Court and authorized Deputy Clerks shall manage the jury selection process under the supervision and control of the Chief Judge of the district.

RANDOM SELECTION FROM SOURCE LIST

Section 401 Voter registration lists

Voter registration lists represent a fair cross section of the community in the Middle District of Pennsylvania. Accordingly, names of grand and petit jurors serving in this court shall be selected by randomized procedure from the voter registration lists of all the counties within the relevant divisions. The voter registration lists are maintained by the Commonwealth of Pennsylvania Department of State.

Section 402 Other sources may be authorized

In accordance with 28 U.S.C. § 1863(b)(2), the court may authorize the Clerk to draw names of prospective jurors from one or more supplementary sources of names in addition to voter registration lists where necessary to foster the policy and protect the rights secured by 28 U.S.C. §§ 1861 and 1862. These sources may include the Pennsylvania Departments of Transportation, State, Revenue and Public Welfare. The selection of names from such additional lists shall be done in a manner consistent with the selection procedure described in this Plan.

Section 403 Voter registration lists defined

Voter registration lists referred to throughout this Plan shall mean the voter registration lists for a statewide primary or general election as maintained by the Commonwealth of Pennsylvania Department of State on electronic data files ("voter datafiles"). The Clerk shall also obtain from the Secretary of the Commonwealth an affidavit enumerating the total registered voters in each county in the district.

Section 404 Selection to be random and proportional

After consultation with the court, the selection of names from complete source list databases in electronic media for the master jury wheel shall be accomplished by a purely randomized process through a properly programmed electronic data processing system. Random selection of names from the source list for inclusion in the master wheel by data computer personnel must ensure that each county within the jury division is substantially proportionally represented in the master jury wheel in accordance with 28 U.S.C. § 1863(b)(3). The selections of names from the source list and the master wheel must also ensure that the mathematical odds of any single name being picked are substantially equal.

After first determining the total number of names needed for the master jury wheel, the Clerk shall proceed through the use of a properly programmed data computer system to make the initial selection of names from the list of voters of each county. The number of names drawn from each county shall be substantially in the same proportion to the total number drawn from all counties within the division as the number of names on that county's list of voters bears to the number of names on the lists of voters for all counties within the Division. For example, if there are exactly 240,000 names on the lists of voters of all counties within the Division, and there are 48,000 names on County "A's" lists (twenty percent of the total), then the number of County "A's" names initially selected should be substantially twenty percent of the total number selected from all counties within the Division.

The number taken as the total for each county shall be based upon a certified affidavit enumerating the total registered voters in each county from the Secretary of the Commonwealth Department of State.

Section 405 Method for automated selection

The court has authorized use of the Jury Management System (JMS), an electronic data processing system, to select names from the master jury wheel to fill the qualified wheels; to select names from the qualified wheels for persons to be summoned to serve as grand or petit jurors, and for the recording of names of prospective jurors and other information on any papers and records needed by the court to administer the selection and payment of jurors.

MAINTAINING THE MASTER JURY WHEEL

Section 501   Master wheels maintained in each division

The Clerk shall maintain a master jury wheel for each of the divisions within the district. The names and addresses of all persons randomly selected from the lists of voters shall be placed in the master jury wheel for that division. Pursuant to 28 U.S.C. § 1863(b)(4), the minimum number of names to be placed in the master jury wheel(s) shall be at least ½ of 1% of the total number of names on all county voter lists. The Chief Judge may order additional names to be placed in the master jury wheels from time to time, as necessary and in accordance with the formula herein above described. The master jury wheels shall be emptied and refilled biennially, or more frequently if necessary, to maintain a current database of official registered voters, between December 1st and April 30th following each general election.

Section 502   Names to be drawn

The Clerk, either at one time or at periodic intervals, shall draw at random from the master jury wheels the names of as many persons as may be required to maintain an adequate number of names in the qualified jury wheels. The number of names to be drawn shall be determined by the Clerk based upon anticipated juror demands by the court plus a margin of extra names sufficient to compensate for the estimated number that will turn out to be unavailable or ineligible.

Section 503   Disclosure of names in the master jury wheel

The Clerk may, upon order of the court, prepare an alphabetical list of the names drawn from the master jury wheel. Any list so prepared shall not be disclosed to any person except as specifically authorized by law.

Unless otherwise authorized by law, the contents of records or papers used by the Clerk in connection with the jury selection process shall not be disclosed.

Section 504   Juror qualification questionnaire and issuance of summons

The Clerk shall prepare through JMS and have mailed to every person whose name is so drawn, a juror qualification questionnaire form and summons accompanied by instructions to execute and return the questionnaire (either by mail or through the court's internet website) to the Clerk by mail within ten days, in accordance with 28 U.S.C. § 1864(a). If the person is unable to fill out the form, another shall prepare it and indicate the reason therefor. In any case in which it appears that there is an omission, ambiguity, or error in a form, the Clerk shall return the form with instructions to the person to make such additions or corrections as may be necessary and to return the corrected form to Clerk within ten days. Any person who fails to return a completed juror qualification form as instructed may be summoned by the Clerk forthwith to appear before the Clerk to fill out a juror qualification form. A person summoned to appear because of failure to return a juror qualification form as instructed and who personally appears and executes a juror qualification form before the Clerk may, at the discretion of the court, except where the person's prior failure to execute and mail such form was willful, be entitled to receive for such appearance the same fees and travel allowance paid to jurors under 28 U.S.C. § 1871. At the time of a person's appearance for jury service, any person may be required to fill out another juror qualification form in the presence of the Clerk or the court, at which time, in such cases as it appears warranted, the person may be questioned, but only with regard to the person's responses to questions contained on the form. Any information thus acquired by the Clerk may be noted on the juror qualification form and transmitted to the Chief Judge.

At the option of the Clerk, the questionnaire and summons may be mailed by the Clerk's office, by a commercial mailing service, or by delivery to the United States Marshal for direct service upon the prospective jurors.

QUALIFICATIONS FOR JURY SERVICES

Section 601   Determined by and noted on completed questionnaire

Under the supervision of the Chief Judge, the Clerk shall determine solely on the basis of information provided on the juror qualification questionnaire and other competent evidence whether a person is unqualified for, exempt from, or to be excused from jury service. The Clerk or Deputy Clerk shall enter such determination in the space provided on the juror qualification questionnaire and in JMS.

Section 602   Disqualification of potential jurors

In making such determination the Clerk, under the supervision of the Chief Judge, shall deem any person qualified to serve on grand and petit juries in the district unless the person:

A.   is not a citizen of the United States,[2] eighteen years old, or has not resided for a period of one year within the judicial district;

B.   is unable to read, write and understand the English language with a degree of proficiency sufficient to fill out satisfactorily the juror qualification questionnaire;

C.   is unable to speak the English language;

D.   is incapable, by reason of mental or physical infirmity, to render satisfactory jury service; or

E.   has a felony charge pending against the person, or the person has been convicted of, in a state or federal court, a crime punishable by imprisonment for more than one year and the person's civil rights have not been restored.

EXCUSES AND EXCLUSIONS

Section 701   Excuses automatically granted on individual request

The court hereby finds that jury service by members of the following occupational classes or groups of persons would entail undue hardship or extreme inconvenience to the members thereof, and the excusing of such members for the life of the unexpired master wheel will not be inconsistent with the Act, and shall be granted upon individual request:

1.   Persons over 70 years of age;

2.   Actively engaged members of the clergy;

3.   Persons having active care and custody, during hours of normal jury service, of a child or children under 12 years of age whose health/safety would be jeopardized by their absence for jury service, or a person who is essential to the care of the aged or infirmed persons;

4.   Actively practicing attorneys, physicians and dentists;

5.   Persons who have served as a grand or petit juror in a state or federal court within the past two years;

6.   Any person whose services are so essential to the operation of a business, commercial or agricultural enterprise that said enterprise must close if such person were required to perform jury duty;

7.   Volunteer safety personnel who serve without compensation as firefighters, members of a rescue squad or ambulance crew for a public agency. Public agency for the purpose of this plan means the United States, the Commonwealth of

Pennsylvania, or any unit of local government, department or instrumentality of any of the foregoing;

8. Teachers or students in actual attendance at a university, college, academy, or other school having a regular schedule of classes.

Section 702   Temporary excuses, exclusions (after qualification)

Requests to be excused from jury service shall be in writing. Except as otherwise provided by this Plan, no person or class of persons shall be disqualified, excluded, or exempted from service as jurors, provided that any person summoned for jury service may be (1) excused by the court or the Clerk under supervision of the court, upon a showing of undue hardship or extreme inconvenience, as defined in 28 U.S.C. § 1869(j), for such period as the court deems necessary, at the conclusion of which such person shall be summoned again for jury service, or (2) excluded by the court on the grounds that such person may be unable to render impartial jury service or that the person's service as a juror would be likely to disrupt the proceedings, or (3) excluded upon peremptory challenge as provided by law, or (4) excluded pursuant to the procedure specified by law upon a challenge by any party for good cause shown, or (5) excluded upon determination by the judge in open court that the person's service as a juror would be likely to threaten the secrecy of the proceedings, or otherwise adversely affect the integrity of jury deliberation, and that exclusion of such persons will not be inconsistent with 28 U.S.C. §§ 1861 and 1862.

Persons excluded under (1) above shall be kept on the pool list if excused for less than the life of the pool, however, if excused for a longer period of time, but not permanently, they may be added to and summoned for another pool at a later date.

Section 703   Requests for excuses to be made in advance

Jurors who do not make a request in advance to be excused, and who report for jury service and request immediate release, will not be paid by the court for their service, unless they can prove that circumstances so warranted their making the trip to the courthouse.

Section 704   Clerk to record excuses and exclusions

Whenever a person is excused or excluded from jury service, this determination shall be noted in the Jury Management System.

EXEMPTIONS FROM JURY SERVICE

Section 801   Persons considered exempt

The following persons are barred from jury service on the grounds that they are exempt:

1. Members in active service in the Armed Forces of the United States.

2. Members of the fire or police departments of the Commonwealth of Pennsylvania or any subdivision thereof.

3. Public officers in the executive, legislative or judicial branches of the Government of the United States, or the Commonwealth of Pennsylvania or subdivision thereof, who are actively engaged in the performance of official duties.

QUALIFIED JURY WHEELS

Section 901   Qualified wheels to be maintained in each division

The Clerk shall maintain separate qualified jury wheels for each division in the district, and shall place in such wheels the names of all persons drawn from the master wheels and not disqualified, exempted, or excused pursuant to this plan.

Section 902   Maintenance of qualified wheels

The Clerk shall maintain the qualified wheels through the Jury Management System.

The persons to be summoned for a particular pool will be selected by a purely randomized process through JMS.

Section 903   Qualified pools

From time to time, the court may direct the Clerk to draw at random from the qualified wheels such number of persons as may be required for grand and petit jury pools.

Section 904   Disclosure of juror names and other identifying information

Names and personal information concerning petit and grand jurors shall not be disclosed to attorneys, parties, the public, or the media, except as required by law or provided herein.

Names and personal information concerning prospective and sitting petit jurors shall not be disclosed to the public or to the media outside open court, except upon order of the court. A request for disclosure of petit jurors names and personal information must be directed to the presiding judge in writing.

The Clerk may provide names and personal information concerning prospective petit jurors to the attorneys of record one week before a case is set for trial, unless otherwise directed by the court. The names and information will be provided in written form only (hereafter "the jury list"). The attorneys may not share the jury list or information contained therein except as necessary for purposes of jury selection. Following jury selection, the attorneys must return the original jury lists and any copies to the Clerk.

The court may order juror names and personal information to be kept confidential where the interests of justice so require.

The names of grand jurors shall not be maintained in any public record or otherwise disclosed to the public except upon an order of the court issued on a showing that exceptional circumstances have created a demonstrated need for disclosure.

Section 905   Limitation on requirements to serve as jurors

In any two year period, no person shall be required to (1) serve as a petit juror for a total of more than 10 days, except when necessary to complete service in a particular case, or (2) serve on more than one grand jury, or (3) serve as both a grand and petit juror.

Section 906   Those who have not served to be drawn first

Whenever petit jurors are required for service in civil or criminal cases, the Clerk at the discretion of the Court, shall first draw a sufficient number from the petit pool from those jurors not having served and then secondly from those who have served but not yet reached the required days of service for excusal from further service. The Clerk shall notify them to appear for duty at the time and place fixed for jury selection.

Section 907   Random assignment of reporting jurors for jury selection

The names of all jurors reporting for petit jury service shall be placed in a wheel or other container from which names shall be drawn at random and assigned to cases for selection as jurors. Alternatively, the names shall be drawn at random by automated means and assigned to cases for selection as jurors. The names of jurors not selected for one case shall be available for service on other cases.

Section 908   Unused jurors returned to petit pool

The names of jurors on a panel shall be returned to the petit pool when the panel is no longer needed for the case for which it was drawn.

Section 909   Petit pools remain in effect until court directs otherwise

Panels of jurors shall be drawn from the petit pool until such time as the court directs that a new petit pool be put in effect.

Section 910   Grand jury pools

The grand jury pool shall constitute the grand jury panel. The grand jury in each division shall serve until discharged by the court. The term of service shall not exceed eighteen months unless otherwise extended by the court for up to an additional six months.

RECORDS

Section 1001   Jury selection records and material

Copies of this Jury Selection Plan shall be available for public inspection at the office of the Clerk of Court.

All records necessary to effectuate and carry out this Plan shall be maintained by the Clerk. The contents of records or papers used by the Clerk in connection with the jury selection process shall not be disclosed, unless otherwise directed by this court.

[Amended July 16, 2013. Approved by the Judicial Conference of the Third Circuit September 12, 2013. Amended October 4, 2013.]

[1] On April 19, 1999, Schuylkill County became part of the Middle District of Pennsylvania. See Pub. L. 105–277. Before then, it was within the Eastern District of Pennsylvania.

[2] Notice of persons who identify themselves as non-citizens through the juror qualification process will be provided to appropriate election officials for verifying voter registration eligibility.

SELECTED ORDERS
STANDING ORDER 98–3. [CONDITIONS OF PROBATION AND SUPERVISED RELEASE]*

This Court has adopted as the standard conditions of supervision for probationers and supervised releasees those conditions set forth on Probation Form 7A.

The Court hereby adopts as standard conditions of supervision for probationers and supervised releasees the following additional conditions:

-- The defendant shall notify the Court of any material change in the defendant's economic circumstances that might affect the defendant's ability to pay restitution, fines or special assessments;

-- The defendant shall not incur new credit charges or open additional lines of credit without the approval of the Probation Officer unless the defendant is in compliance with the installment schedule for payment of restitution, fines or special assessments;

-- The defendant shall provide the Probation Officer with access to any requested financial information.

Conditions of Probation and Supervised Release

**UNITED STATES DISTRICT COURT
FOR THE
MIDDLE DISTRICT OF PENNSYLVANIA**

Name: _____

Docket No.: _____

Address: _____

_____

Under the terms of your sentence, you have been placed on probation/supervised release (strike one) by the Honorable _____, United States District Judge for the District of _____. Your term of supervision is for a period of _____ commencing _____.

While on probation/supervised release (strike one), you shall not commit another federal, state, or local crime. You shall not illegally possess a controlled substance.

If the judgment imposed a fine or a restitution obligation, it shall be a condition of probation/supervised release that you pay any such fine or restitution that remains unpaid at the commencement of the term of supervision in accordance with any Schedule of Payments set forth in the Criminal Monetary penalties sheet of the judgment. In any case, you should cooperate with the probation officer in meeting any financial obligations.

You shall report in person to the probation office in the district to which you are released within 72 hours of release from the custody of the Bureau of Prisons (supervised release cases only).

[ ] You shall not possess a firearm as defined in 18 U.S.C. § 921. (Check, if applicable.)

For offenses committed on or after September 13, 1994:

You shall refrain from any unlawful use of a controlled substance. You shall submit to one drug test within 15 days of release from imprisonment or placement on probation and at least two periodic drug tests thereafter, as directed by the probation officer.

[ ] The above drug testing condition is suspended based on the court's determination that you pose a low risk of future substance abuse. (Check, if applicable.)

It is the order of the Court that you shall comply with the following standard conditions:

(1) You shall not leave the judicial district without the permission of the Court or probation officer;

(2) You shall report to the probation officer and shall submit a truthful and complete written report within the first five days of each month;

(3) You shall answer truthfully all inquiries by the probation officer and follow the instructions of the probation officer;

(4) You shall support your dependents and meet other family responsibilities;

(5) You shall work regularly at a lawful occupation unless excused by the probation officer for schooling, training, or other acceptable reasons;

(6) You shall notify the probation officer ten days prior to any change in residence or employment;

(7) You shall refrain from excessive use of alcohol;

(8) You shall not frequent places where controlled substances are illegally sold, used, distributed, or administered;

(9) You shall not associate with any persons engaged in criminal activity, and shall not associate with any person convicted of a felony unless granted permission to do so by the probation officer;

(10) You shall permit a probation officer to visit you at any time at home or elsewhere and shall permit confiscation of any contraband observed in plain view of the probation officer;

(11) You shall notify the probation officer within seventy-two hours of being arrested or questioned by a law enforcement officer;

(12) You shall not enter into any agreement to act as an informer or a special agent of a law enforcement agency without the permission of the Court;

(13) As directed by the probation officer, you shall notify third parties of risks that may be occasioned by your criminal record or personal history or characteristics, and shall permit the probation officer to make such notifications and to confirm your compliance with such notification requirement.

(14) You shall refrain from possessing a firearm, destructive device, or other dangerous weapon;

(15) You shall participate in a program of testing and treatment for drug abuse, as directed by the Probation Officer, until such time as you are released from the program by the Probation Officer.

The special conditions ordered by the Court are as follows:

Upon a finding of a violation of probation or supervised release, I understand that the Court may (1) revoke supervision or (2) extend the term of supervision and/or modify the conditions of supervision.

These conditions have been read to me. I fully understand the conditions, and have been provided a copy of them.

(Signed)_____
Defendant

_____
Date

_____
U.S. Probation Officer/Designated
Witness

_____
Date

* [**Publisher's Note:** Title editorially supplied.]

STANDING ORDER NO. 04–3. AUTHORIZING SYSTEMATIC RANDOM MANDATORY MEDIATION REFERRALS IN CERTAIN CASE TYPES

THE BACKGROUND OF THIS ORDER IS AS FOLLOWS:

In April, 1994, the Court created an Alternative Dispute Resolution Program under its Civil Justice Reform Act Plan. Mediation is one of three alternative procedures adopted under the ADR Program, and is the most frequently used alternative process in the district. Attorneys and litigants participating in mediation report a high level of satisfaction with the Middle District's Program. Among the advantages of mediation are the opportunity to narrow issues in controversy and streamline discovery, the preservation or mending of relationships between the parties, savings in time and money, and eliminating the risks of litigation. Despite these benefits, only a small percentage of all eligible cases are referred to mediation.

It is the general perception of the Court that its Mediation Program is an under-utilized asset. That view is shared by the Middle District's Mediation Advisory Group, which formally has recommended that the Court systematically refer approximately 180 cases to mediation per year over a two year period. The Advisory Group has concluded that a focused program of mandatory referrals, in which all judicial officers participate by having selected cases proceed to early mediation by a member of the Court's certified panel of attorney mediators, would be an effective way to promote the acceptance of mediation among the bench and bar as an effective, inexpensive, method of resolving civil disputes. At its April 30, 2004 meeting, the Board of Judges adopted the recommendations of the Mediation Advisory Group, and authorized the establishment of a program of random mandatory referral of cases to mediation by Standing Order to certified members of the district's mediation panel. The program is designed for the narrow purpose of promoting broader acceptance of mediation among the bench and bar.

In doing so, the Court emphasizes the critical importance of the federal judicial process in our nation's history and in our system of justice. Mediation is non-binding. Participation in this program will in no way diminish a party's right to seek recovery or defend against claims through the full panoply of judicial processes, including the right to public trial. To this end, the program will be administered to ensure that no mediation referral results in the impairment of any rights as a litigant or in the creation of any unfair or unreasonable economic burden.

NOW, THEREFORE, IT IS HEREBY ORDERED THAT:

1. The Clerk of Court shall implement a program of random mandatory referral of cases to mediation effective October 1, 2004, and continue the program for a period of two years unless the Court orders otherwise.

2. In each twelve-month period beginning October 1, 2004, the Clerk of Court shall randomly identify for mandatory mediation referrals a total of 180 cases from the following nature of suit categories: (a) 60 cases from nature of suit category 440 (Civil Rights Other); (b) 60 cases from nature of suit category 442 (Civil Rights Employment); and (c) 60 cases consisting of (i) all filings from nature of suit category 362 (P.I. Medical Malpractice), and (ii) the balance from cases filed in nature of suit categories 350 (P.I. Motor Vehicle) and 360 (P.I. Other).

3. The ADR Coordinator shall assign mediators to cases identified for the program, making every effort to match the mediator's areas of expertise to the subject matter of the case, and to equalize appointments among mediators.

4. The judicial officer presiding over a case designated by the Clerk of Court for mandatory mediation referral shall refer such case to the Court-annexed Mediation Program as soon as practicable after the Case Management Conference, unless for good cause shown the parties demonstrate that the matter should not be subject to mandatory mediation referral.

5. The Clerk of Court shall work with the Mediation Advisory Group as well as the Court's Alternative Dispute Resolution Committee, to monitor the progress of this initiative and make a formal report to the Board of Judges on April 1, 2005 and every six (6) months thereafter.

[Dated: July 26, 2004.]

STANDING ORDER NO. 05–03. IN RE: POSSESSION AND USE OF ELECTRONIC DEVICES IN COURTHOUSES

IT IS HEREBY ORDERED that the following Electronic Device Policy has been adopted by the Court:

(1) The term "Electronic Devices" refers to those devices (both currently available as well as future technology) that have as their primary function wireless communication, the storage and retrieval of digitized data, and computer applications.

(2) All persons granted entrance into the Federal Courthouse are permitted to possess any Electronic Device, as defined herein, including cell phones, pagers, notebook/laptop computers, handheld computers and schedulers (such as Palm Pilots and Pocket PCs), and wireless devices (such as Blackberries). However, unless otherwise permitted by court order, use of any device to take photographs anywhere inside this United States Courthouse and Federal Building is expressly forbidden.

(3) Before persons with Electronic Devices are granted entry into the Courthouse, all devices must be physically examined by Court Security Personnel. This examination includes, but is not limited to, placing the device through an X-Ray machine, evaluation with an ionic detector and any other physical assessment deemed necessary.

(4) Persons possessing an Electronic Device may use their device while in common areas of the Courthouse, such as lobbies, but, with the exception of United States Marshals Service personnel, the power to all electronic devices must be turned off upon entry to a courtroom or judicial chambers. Nor shall persons be permitted to leave electronic devices on when entering courtrooms by setting audible alarms to a non-audible mode (such as vibrate). An Electronic Device may be rendered operable in any courtroom or judicial chambers only with the express permission of the presiding judge.

(5) Jurors in possession of electronic devices will surrender these devices to court staff prior to entering the jury room to commence deliberations. Grand jurors in possession of electronic devices will surrender these devices to court staff prior to entering the Grand Jury room.

(6) This Order may be superceded on a temporary basis in the interests of security and in order to ensure fair and impartial justice in individual cases.

[Effective June 1, 2005.]

STANDING ORDER NO. 06–1.5.   IN RE: ELECTRONIC PAYMENT OF FILING FEES THROUGH PAY.GOV

WHEREAS this Court has been authorized to accept payment of fees through an electronic credit card payment system established by the United States Department of Treasury, and known as "pay.gov"; and

WHEREAS use of the pay.gov electronic payment system would enable fees to be paid without requiring submission of credit card information to the Clerk of Court by automatically re-directing registered users of the Court's Electronic Case Filing (ECF) system to pay.gov; and

WHEREAS this Court has determined that payment of fees through the pay.gov electronic credit card payment system shall be required of all registered users of the Court's ECF system because it would eliminate the need for registered users to submit and the Clerk of Court to retain credit card information, **NOW, THEREFORE, IT IS HEREBY ORDERED THAT:**

1. Effective May 1, 2006, registered users of the Court's ECF system, upon presentation of a document for filing electronically, shall be re-directed to the pay.gov site and shall pay the filing fee by use of the pay.gov internet credit card payment system.

2. All credit card information obtained by the Court from ECF Registration Forms shall be discarded. Effective May 1, 2006, the Court will no longer request credit card information on the ECF Registration Form.

[Dated: March 22, 2006.]

STANDING ORDER NO. 08–6.   IN RE: PROGRAM AUTHORIZING SYSTEMATIC RANDOM MANDATORY MEDIATION REFERRALS IN CERTAIN CASE TYPES

WHEREAS, in Standing Order No. 04–3 the court implemented a program of random mandatory referral of cases to mediation which, as amended on 10/16/06, expires on October 31, 2008; and

WHEREAS, the court approved the permanent implementation of the Mandatory Mediation Program at its Board of Judges' meeting on October 24, 2008;

THEREFORE, IT IS HEREBY ORDERED THAT the Clerk of Court shall assign appropriate cases to the Mandatory Mediation Program as directed in Standing Order 04–3.

[Dated: October 24, 2008.]

STANDING ORDER NO. 09–3.   IN RE: PROHIBITING DISSEMINATION OF RECORDED COURTROOM TRANSMISSIONS

IT IS HEREBY ORDERED THAT, the dissemination of any and all recorded courtroom transmissions by any means, for any purpose, by or to any person shall be prohibited without an Order from this court authorizing such dissemination.

[Dated: May 18, 2009.]

STANDING ORDER NO. 10–1. IN RE: FEES FOR
GENERAL ADMISSION OF ATTORNEYS

Effective February 1, 2010, the fee to be charged by the Clerk for general admission to the bar of this court shall be that amount set by the Judicial Conference of the United States (presently $150.00) which shall be deposited to the Treasury of the United States and an additional assessment of $25.00 which shall be placed in the deposit fund and monthly transferred to the Library Fund of this court.

The Library Fund shall be maintained by the Clerk of Court "as Trustee" in the depository designated by the court.

IT IS FURTHER ORDERED that the trustee shall account for and disburse from the Library Fund such sums as shall be authorized and approved by the court pursuant to the guidelines established for the fund.

[Dated: January 29, 2010.]

STANDING ORDER NO. 10–2. IN RE: FEES FOR
SPECIAL ADMISSION OF ATTORNEYS

Effective February 1, 2010, in accordance with Local Rule 83.8.2, the following fees shall be charged by the Clerk for special admissions to the bar of this court:

(a) Admission under Local Rules 83.8.2.2, .3, or .4 (Fee waived)

(b) Pro Hac Vice Admission under Local Rules 83.8.2.1 and 83.8.2.5 ($50.00 Assessment)

Such fees shall be placed in the deposit fund and transferred monthly to the Pro Bono Fund of this court.

[Dated: January 29, 2010.]

STANDING ORDER NO. 13–9. STANDING PRACTICE
ORDER IN SOCIAL SECURITY APPEALS

This order is intended to inform the parties of the briefing and other litigation responsibilities that commonly arise during the course of a social security appeal. In doing so, this order will describe the major provisions of Local Rules relating to social security appeals. The parties should consult the actual rules for a complete description of their requirements. Social Security cases filed in this district are treated as appeals. (Local Rule (LR) 83.40.1) This standing order shall be issued by the Clerk's Office upon the filing of a social security appeal accompanied by an application to proceed in forma pauperis or the filing fee and shall be binding on all parties. Failure of a party to comply will result in the sanctions specified herein.

NOW, THEREFORE, IT IS HEREBY ORDERED THAT:

1) In cases where the filing fee has been paid, the plaintiff shall cause the summons and complaint to be served upon the defendant in the manner specified by Rule 4(i) of the Federal Rules of Civil Procedure within fourteen (14) days of the date of filing of the complaint with the Clerk of Court. (LR 83.40.2)

2) In cases where an application to proceed in forma pauperis has been filed by the plaintiff, upon the approval of the application by the judge assigned the case, the Clerk of Court is directed to issue process to the United States Marshal who is directed to serve plaintiff's complaint in accordance with Fed.R.Civ.P. 4(i) within fourteen (14) days of the date of the order granting the application to proceed in forma pauperis. (LR 83.40.2)

3) The defendant shall serve and file an answer, together with a certified copy of the transcript of the administrative record, within sixty (60) days of service of the complaint. (LR 83.40.3)

4) Within forty-five (45) days after service of the defendant's answer, the plaintiff shall serve and file a brief containing the following: statement of the case, statement of errors, argument and conclusion. (LR 83.40.4) Unless otherwise allowed by Order of Court, the brief shall not exceed fifteen (15) pages. (LR 83.40.7)

5) Within thirty (30) days after service of the plaintiff's brief, the defendant shall serve and file a brief in response to the plaintiff's brief. (LR 83.40.5) The brief shall comply with LR 83.40.5. Unless otherwise allowed by Order of Court, the brief shall not exceed fifteen (15) pages. (LR 83.40.7)

6) Within fourteen (14) days after filing of the defendant's brief, the plaintiff may file a reply brief. (LR 83.40.6) Unless otherwise allowed by Order of Court, the reply brief shall not exceed ten (10) pages. (LR 83.40.7)

7) No extensions of time will be permitted without a specific order of the court. Furthermore, failure of the plaintiff to comply with paragraph 4 of this order relating to the filing of a supporting brief will result in the dismissal of the case for failure to prosecute and abide by a court order. Noncompliance of the plaintiff with paragraph 4 will result in the dismissal without any further warning from the court. Failure of the defendant to comply with paragraph 5 of this order relating to the filing of an opposition brief will result in the plaintiff's appeal being deemed unopposed.

8) The parties shall comply with LR 7.1 through 7.8 with respect to any motions filed in this case.

[Dated: December 11, 2013.]

STANDING ORDER NO. 14–1. IN RE: ORDER REGARDING DEPOSIT AND INVESTMENT OF REGISTRY FUNDS

The Court, having determined that it is necessary to amend Local Rule 67.1 to reflect the transition of accountability and administration of the Court Registry Investment System ("CRIS") from the United States District Court for the Southern District of Texas to the Administrative Office of the United States Courts, as well as ensure the continued uniformity in the deposit and investment of funds in the Court's Registry,

IT IS ORDERED that the following shall govern the receipt, deposit and investment of registry funds:

I. Receipt of Funds

A. No money shall be sent to the Court or its officers for deposit in the Court's registry without a court order signed by the presiding judge in the case or proceeding.

B. The party making the deposit or transferring funds to the Court's registry shall serve the order permitting the deposit or transfer on the Clerk of Court.

C. Unless provided for elsewhere in the Order, all monies ordered to be paid to the Court or received by its officers in any case pending or adjudicated shall be deposited with the Treasurer of the United States in the name and to the credit of this Court pursuant to 28 U.S.C. § 2041 through depositories by the Treasury to accept such deposit on its behalf.

II. Investment of Registry Funds

A. Where, by order of the Court, funds on deposit with the Court are to be placed in some form of interest-bearing account, or invested in a court-approved, interest-bearing instrument in accordance with Rule 67 of the Federal Rules of Civil Procedure, the Court Registry Investment System ("CRIS"), administered by the Administrative Office of the United States Courts under 28 U.S.C. § 2045, shall be the only investment mechanism authorized.

B. The Director of Administrative Office of the United States Courts is designated as custodian for CRIS. The Director or the Directors's designee shall perform the duties of custodian. Funds held in the CRIS remain subject to the control and jurisdiction of the Court.

C. Money from each case deposited in the CRIS shall be "pooled" together with those on deposit with Treasury to the credit of other courts in the CRIS and used to purchase Government Account Series securities through the Bureau of Public Debt, which will be held at Treasury, in an account in the name and to the credit of the Director of Administrative Office of the United States Courts. The pooled funds will be invested in accordance with the principals of the CRIS Investment Policy as approved by the Registry Monitoring Group.

D. An account for each case will be established in the CRIS titled in the name of the case giving rise to the investment in the fund. Income generated from fund investments will be distributed to each case based on the ratio each account's principal and earnings has to the aggregate principal and income total in the fund. Reports showing the interest earned and the principal amounts contributed in each case will be prepared and distributed to each court participating in the CRIS and made available to litigants and/or their counsel.

III.   Deduction of Fees

A. The custodian is authorized and directed by this Order to deduct the investment services fee for the management of investments in the CRIS and the registry fee for maintaining accounts deposited with the Court.

B. The investment services fee is assessed from interest earnings to the pool according to the Court's Miscellaneous Fee Schedule and is to be assessed before a pro rata distribution of earnings to court cases.

C. The registry fee is assessed by the custodian from each case's pro rata distribution of the earnings and is to be determined on the basis of the rates published by the Director of the Administrative Office of the United States Courts as approved by the Judicial Conference of the United States.

IV.   Transition From Former Investment Procedure

A. The Clerk of Court is further directed to develop a systematic method of redemption of all existing investments and their transfer to the CRIS.

B. Parties not wishing to transfer certain existing registry deposits into the CRIS may seek leave to transfer them to the litigants or their designees on proper motion and approval of the judge assigned to the specific case.

C. This Order supersedes and abrogates all prior orders of this Court regarding the deposit and investment of registry funds.

[Dated: February 21, 2014.]

STANDING ORDER NO. 14–2.   PRETRIAL DIVERSION PROGRAM

The Court hereby adopts the attached policy regarding the Pretrial Diversion Program which replaces Standing Order 93–7.

IN THE UNITED STATES DISTRICT COURT
FOR THE MIDDLE DISTRICT OF PENNSYLVANIA

PRETRIAL DIVERSION OPERATIONS AGREEMENT

The United States Attorney's Office and the Probation Office shall operate the Pretrial Diversion Program in accordance with the terms adopted by the U.S. District Court for the Middle District of Pennsylvania.

IN THE UNITED STATES DISTRICT COURT
FOR THE MIDDLE DISTRICT OF PENNSYLVANIA

PRETRIAL DIVERSION PROGRAM

I. Legal Authority

Pursuant to 18 U.S.C. § 3154(10), the probation office shall, to the extent provided for in an agreement between the Chief Probation Officer and the U.S. Attorney, collect, verify, and prepare reports for the U.S. Attorney's Office pertaining to the pretrial diversion of any person who is or may be charged with an offense and perform such other duties as may be required under any such agreement.

II. Definition

Pretrial diversion is an alternative to prosecution which seeks to divert certain candidates from traditional criminal justice processing into a program of community supervision administered by the probation office. The Diversion Program may begin prior to or subsequent to the formal filing of charges. In either case, prosecution is suspended. If charges have been filed, they are dismissed following successful completion of the program. A candidate's participation in the Diversion Program shall be voluntary.

III. Objectives

The objectives of the Pretrial Diversion Program are to prevent future criminal activity by certain candidates against whom prosecutable cases exist; to save prosecutive and judicial resources; and to provide, where appropriate, a vehicle for restitution to victims of crime.

IV. Eligibility Criteria

An individual may be diverted when a prosecutable case exists and if the individual meets established criteria (Exhibit A).

V. Legal Representation

Candidates for pretrial diversion shall be represented by legal counsel. If an indigent individual is being considered for diversion prior to the filing of formal charges and is without counsel, the U.S. Attorney's Office shall refer the individual to the Federal Public Defender's Office or schedule an appearance before a U.S. Magistrate Judge for consideration of eligibility for the appointment of counsel.

VI. Referrals

The U.S. Attorney's Office shall be responsible for selecting persons to be considered for the Pretrial Diversion Program. If the Probation Office identifies a potential candidate, the Chief Probation Officer (or his/her designee) may request the U.S. Attorney (or his/her designee) to consider the person for the Pretrial Diversion Program. When the U.S. Attorney's Office identifies a case for referral to the Pretrial Diversion Program, the Assistant U.S. Attorney shall provide Defense Counsel or the candidate with the Application for Pretrial Diversion Program (Exhibit B). Defense Counsel shall discuss the program with the candidate and review the waiver of rights to a speedy trial and, if applicable, the presentment to a grand jury within the statute of limitations. If the candidate wishes to participate, Defense Counsel shall notify the U.S. Attorney's Office and return the completed application. The Assistant U.S. Attorney shall then forward to the Chief Probation Officer a referral letter with a copy, if applicable, to the assigned judicial officer (Exhibit C), investigative reports, and a copy of the completed application. The Chief Probation Officer (or his/her designee) shall acknowledge the referral and identify the Probation Officer assigned to conduct the investigation (Exhibit D). No pretrial diversion investigation shall be initiated until a request is received from the U.S. Attorney's Office.

VII. Pretrial Diversion Report

The Probation Office shall conduct an investigation to assess the candidate's suitability for participation in the Pretrial Diversion Program and shall prepare a written report (Exhibit J) within 40 days after receipt of the U.S. Attorney's referral letter. The report shall include, but shall not be limited to, the following: Details of the Offense, Personal History, Prior Criminal Record, and Recommendation. The report shall also include whether the candidate accepts responsibility for the offense. Upon completion of the report, the Probation Officer shall provide a brief written summary of the case to a Judge on the Criminal Law Committee acting on behalf of the Court. If the Court does not concur with the recommendation of the Probation Officer, the Judge shall communicate with the Probation Officer within five (5) days of receipt of the written summary. If the Court interposes no objection, the Probation Officer shall provide the report and recommendation to the U.S. Attorney's Office and Defense Counsel. Defense Counsel shall return the report to the Probation Office when the candidate is accepted or rejected for the Pretrial Diversion Program. A person's admission to the Pretrial Diversion Program shall be subject to the concurrence of the U.S. Attorney's Office and the Probation Office. If, during the investigation, the Probation Office determines that the candidate is not appropriate for the pretrial diversion program, the Chief Probation Officer (or his/her designee) shall advise the Assistant U.S. Attorney, Defense Counsel, and the Judicial Officer (if applicable) in writing of the reason for the recommendation.

VIII. Pretrial Diversion Agreement

When a person is approved for admission to the Pretrial Diversion Program, the Assistant U.S. Attorney shall prepare a Pretrial Diversion Agreement within seven (7) days of receiving the report. The agreement shall contain the terms and conditions of the Pretrial Diversion Program. The length of supervision is not to exceed 18 months. Persons admitted to the Pretrial Diversion Program shall abide by the standard conditions adopted by the Court and any special conditions included in the Pretrial Diversion Agreement (Exhibit E). The Assistant U.S. Attorney or the Probation Officer shall schedule a conference with the candidate, Defense Counsel, the Assistant U.S. Attorney, and the Probation Officer. At the conference, the terms and conditions of the Pretrial Diversion Program shall be reviewed and the Agreement executed by the parties. Supervision commences upon execution of the Agreement. If charges have been filed, the U.S. Attorney's Office shall, after execution of the Agreement, submit to the supervising Judicial Officer an Order dismissing the charges without prejudice (Exhibit F). If the candidate is not admitted to the Pretrial Diversion Program, the Assistant U.S. Attorney shall so advise the Probation Officer and Defense Counsel. A candidate not admitted to the Pretrial Diversion Program is subject to prosecution.

IX. Supervision

The Probation Office shall supervise the person under the Pretrial Diversion Program in accordance with the terms and conditions of the Agreement.

A. Confidentiality. The Pretrial Diversion Agreement shall not be a public document, and the fact that a person is on pretrial diversion is confidential and shall not be disclosed, except as provided by law.

B. Third Party Risk. A determination of risk shall be made in each case. Factors to consider in making this evaluation are the facts of the case, the person's conduct, and prior criminal record. Consideration shall be given to the person's current employment and other circumstances which might present the person with an opportunity or temptation to engage in criminal or anti-social behavior related to the person's criminal background. At the onset of supervision and, thereafter, if the circumstances of the divertee change, the Probation Officer shall review the case to determine whether a reasonably foreseeable risk to a third party exists. Reasonably foreseeable risk means that the circumstances of the relationship between the divertee and the third party (e.g., employer and employee) suggest that the person may engage in a criminal or anti-social manner similar or related to past conduct. Matters related to third party risk shall be reported to the U.S. Attorney's Office. Resolution of such issues shall be subject to the concurrence of the U.S. Attorney (or his/her designee) and the Chief Probation Officer (or his/her designee). Unresolved issues shall be referred to a Judge on the Criminal Law Committee.

C. Restitution. If, after conducting an investigation, it is determined that restitution is due, Pretrial Services Form 4 (Exhibit G) shall be completed by the Probation Officer and executed by a Judge on the Criminal Law Committee. The form shall be filed under seal in the Clerk's Office. Thereafter, the Clerk's Office shall receive and disburse restitution payments in accordance with the pretrial diversion agreement and in the manner in which restitution payments are received and disbursed for criminal judgments.

D. Flash Notices. Flash Notices and Access to Law Enforcement Systems (ATLAS) Supervised Release Files (SRF) are not entered for cases supervised under pretrial diversion agreements. Therefore, as part of the ongoing supervision process, officers shall conduct record checks via ATLAS and the Administrative Office of Pennsylvania Courts (AOPC) every 90 days, to determine whether there have been any law enforcement contacts.

E. Early Discharge. A divertee who has fulfilled the terms and conditions of the Pretrial Diversion Agreement may be granted an early discharge from the Pretrial Diversion Program. Termination prior to the expiration date shall be subject to the concurrence of the Assistant U.S. Attorney and Chief Probation Officer (or his/her designee).

X. Violations

The Probation Office shall immediately notify the Assistant U.S. Attorney assigned to the case of any apparent violation of the conditions and terms of the Pretrial Diversion Agreement The U.S. Attorney's Office and the Probation Office shall confer regarding alleged violations. The Assistant U.S. Attorney, with the concurrence of the Chief Probation Officer (or his/her designee), may terminate a divertee from the Pretrial Diversion Program or may modify the conditions of the Pretrial Diversion Agreement. If the Assistant U.S. Attorney and Chief Probation Officer (or his/her designee) do not concur regarding violation issues, the matter shall be referred to a Judge on the Criminal Law Committee for resolution. The Assistant U.S. Attorney shall notify Defense Counsel and the divertee of any modification of the terms or termination of the Pretrial Diversion Agreement.

XI. Termination

Upon satisfactory completion of the Pretrial Diversion Program by the divertee, the Probation Office shall promptly provide written certification to the Assistant U.S. Attorney and, if applicable, the Judicial Officer (Exhibits H–1 and H–2). Upon receipt of that notification in cases where charges have previously been filed, the Assistant U.S. Attorney shall promptly prepare an Order for the supervising Judicial Officer dismissing the charges with prejudice (Exhibit I) and shall forward a copy of the Order of Dismissal to the divertee, Defense Counsel, and the Probation Office. If no formal charges were filed, the Assistant U.S. Attorney shall communicate to the divertee, Defense Counsel, and the Probation Office that no charges shall be filed.

Exhibit A

ELIGIBILITY CRITERIA

The U.S. Attorney's Office, acting in accordance with Department of Justice policy, may divert any individual against whom a prosecutable case exists and who is not:

1) Accused of an offense which, under existing Department of Justice guidelines, should be diverted to the state for prosecution;

2) A person with two or more prior felony convictions;

3) A public official or former public official accused of an offense arising out of an alleged violation of a public trust;

4) Accused of an offense related to national security or foreign affairs; or

5) A person who fails to accept responsibility for having committed the alleged federal offense(s).

Exhibit B

APPLICATION FOR PRE–TRIAL DIVERSION PROGRAM

All answers must be complete   Use X marks where appropriate

1.   Name _____ Phone No. ( )

Address _____
        (Street)   (City)   (State)   (Zip)

Length of Residence at Present Address _____

2.   Age _____ 3. DOB _____ 4. Place of Birth _____

5.   Sex _____ F _____ M   6. Social Security No. _____

7.   Marital Status ____ Never Married ____ Married ____ Widow/Widower
                    ____ Separated   ____ Divorced

8.   No of Dependents _____ 0 _____ 1 _____ 2 _____ 3 _____ 4 _____ 5
     _____ 6 and over

9.   Present Living Arrangements _____ Alone _____ w/Parent(s)
                                _____ w/Spouse

                                _____ w/Relatives _____ w/Friend(s)

10. Education _____ Less than 8th grade _____ Less than 12th grade

               _____ High School Graduate _____ Other

11. Vocation Training Completed _____ Yes Type _____
     _____ No;

12. Military Service _____ Yes _____ No; Branch _____

     Type of Discharge _____ Date _____
13. Nearest Contact (Person who would usually know your whereabouts)

     Name _____ Phone No. ( )

     Address _____
             (Street)   (City)   (State)   (Zip)

     Relationship to Defendant _____

14. Defense Attorney:

     Name _____ Phone No. ( )

     Address _____
             (Street)   (City)   (State)   (Zip)

15. Present Employer _____ Phone No. ( )

     Address _____
             (Street)   (City)   (State)   (Zip)

     Date Employed _____ Occupation _____ Salary _____

16. Employment History (Begin with last previous place of employment*

     Name of Employer _____ Phone No. ( )

     Address _____
             (Street)   (City)   (State)   (Zip)

     Dates Employed: From _____ to _____ Occupation _____

     Reason Left _____

Name of Employer _____ Phone No. ( )_____

Address _____
               (Street)   (City)   (State)   (Zip)

Dates Employed: From _____ to _____ Occupation _____

Reason Left _____

Name of Employer _____ Phone No. ( )_____

Address _____
               (Street)   (City)   (State)   (Zip)

Dates Employed: From _____ to _____ Occupation _____

Reason Left _____

Name of Employer _____ Phone No. ( )_____

Address _____
               (Street)   (City)   (State)   (Zip)

Dates Employed: From _____ to _____ Occupation _____

Reason Left _____

*List employment for the past six years. If you need additional space, use blank sheet of paper.

17.   Source of Income _____ Employment (self) _____ Employment (spouse)
_____ Unemployment Compensation (Amount $_____)
_____ Public Assistance (Amount _____)
_____ Parents _____ Relatives _____ Friends _____ Other

18.   Prior Offense Record _____ None _____ Juvenile _____ Adult

Detailed Criminal History (Begin with first arrest)

Date	Place	Charge(s)	Disposition

I hereby apply for status as a participant in the pretrial diversion program. I authorize the probation office to conduct an investigation to determine my suitability for this program.

A false answer to any question in this application may be grounds for recommendation against placement into this program or removal after placement in the program, in which case, the U.S. Attorney may resume prosecution on the original charge.

_____
Applicant

Date _____

_____
Attorney for Applicant

Exhibit C

Date

MEMORANDUM

To: Anthony G. Harvilla
            Chief Probation Officer

FROM: _____
            Assistant U.S. Attorney

SUBJECT: _____
            PTD Referral

I am recommending pretrial diversion for _____ who has been reported to have violated Title ___, United States Code, Section _____.

I have enclosed the investigative reports and Application for Pretrial Diversion Upon completion of the investigation, please submit a report and recommendation to the U.S. Attorney's Office.

cc: Judicial Officer (if applicable)

Exhibit D

Date

MEMORANDUM

To: _____
Assistant U.S. Attorney

FROM: Anthony C. Harvilla
Chief Probation Officer

SUBJECT: John Doe
PTD Referral

This will acknowledge receipt of your correspondence.

Our office will conduct a Pretrial Diversion Investigation. This case has been assigned to Probation Officer _____.

Exhibit E

MIDDLE DISTRICT OF PENNSYLVANIA

UNITED STATES OF AMERICA

v.

_____

AGREEMENT FOR PRETRIAL DIVERSION

It appearing that you are reported to have committed an offense against the United States on or about _____ in violation of Title ___, United States Code, Section(s) _____ in that you did: _____.

Upon accepting responsibility for your behavior and by your signature on this Agreement, it appearing, after an investigation of the offense and your background, that the interest of justice will be served by the following procedure; therefore.

On the authority of the Attorney General of the United States, by the United States Attorney for the Middle District of Pennsylvania, prosecution in this District for this offense shall be deferred for the period of ___ months from this date, provided you abide by the following conditions and requirements of this Agreement set out below.

Should you violate any condition of this Agreement, the United States Attorney (or his/her designee), with the concurrence of the Chief Probation Officer (or his/her designee), may terminate you from the Pretrial Diversion Program or may modify the conditions of the Pretrial Diversion Agreement. In no event shall the term of supervision exceed 18 months. The United States Attorney may release you from supervision at any time. The United States Attorney may at any time within the period of your supervision, initiate prosecution for this offense should you violate any condition of this Agreement. In this case, he/she will furnish you with notice specifying the condition of the Agreement which you have violated.

After successfully completing your diversion program and fulfilling all the terms and conditions of the Agreement, no prosecution for the offense set forth in this Agreement will be instituted in this District, and the charges against you, if any, will be dismissed.

Neither this Agreement no any other document filed with the United States Attorney as a result of your participation in the Pretrial Diversion Program shall be used against you, except for impeachment purposes, in connection with any prosecution for the above-described offense.

Standard Conditions

1) You shall not commit a federal, state, or local crime during the term of supervision;

2) You shall not leave the judicial district without the permission of the probation officer;

3) You shall report to the probation officer and shall submit a truthful and complete monthly supervision report;

4) You shall answer truthfully all inquiries by the probation officer and follow the instructions of the probation officer;

5) You shall support your dependents and meet other family responsibilities;

6) You shall work regularly at a lawful occupation, unless excused by the probation officer for schooling, training, or other acceptable reasons;

7) You shall notify the probation officer at least ten days prior to any change in residence or employment;

8) You shall refrain from excessive use of alcohol and shall not purchase, possess, use, distribute, or administer any controlled substance or any paraphernalia related to any controlled substances, except as prescribed by a physician;

9) You shall not frequent places where controlled substances are illegally sold, used, distributed, or administered;

10) You shall not associate with any persons engaged in criminal activity and shall not associate with any person convicted of a felony, unless granted permission to do so by the probation officer;

11) You shall permit a probation officer to visit you at any time at home or elsewhere and shall permit confiscation of any contraband observed in plain view of the probation officer;

12) You shall notify the probation officer within seventy-two hours of being arrested or questioned by a law enforcement officer;

13) You shall not enter into any agreement to act as an informer or a special agent of a law enforcement agency without the permission of the court;

14) As directed by the probation officer, you shall notify third parties of risks that may be occasioned by your criminal record or personal history or characteristics and shall permit the probation officer to make such notifications and to confirm the your compliance with such notification requirement; and

15) You shall notify the court of any material change in your economic circumstances that might affect your ability to pay restitution.

Special Conditions

(May include, but are not limited to, performance of community service, payment of restitution, participation in substance abuse or mental health treatment, and surrender of a driver's license or a professional license.)

I understand that if I violate the conditions of supervision, I may be removed from the pretrial diversion program and prosecuted by the United States Attorney.

I assert and certify that I am aware of the fact that the Sixth Amendment to the Constitution of the United States provides that in all criminal prosecutions the accused shall enjoy the right to a speeding and public trial. I also am aware that Rule 48(b) of the Federal Rules of Criminal Procedure provides that the Court may dismiss an indictment, information, or complaint for unnecessary delay in presenting a charge to the Grand Jury, filing an information or in bringing a defendant to trial. I hereby request the United States Attorney for the Middle District of Pennsylvania to defer such prosecution. I agree and consent that any delay from the date of this Agreement to the date of initiation of prosecution, as provided for in the terms expressed therein, shall be deemed to be a necessary delay at my request, and I waive any defense to such prosecution on the ground that such delay operated to deny my rights under Rule 48(b) of the Federal Rules of Criminal Procedure and the Sixth Amendment to the Constitution of the United States to a speedy trial or to bar the prosecution by reason of the running of the statute of limitations for a period of months equal to the period of this agreement.

I hereby state that the above has been read and explained to me. I understand the conditions of my pretrial diversion program and agree that I will comply with them.

_____   _____
Divertee   Date

Defense Counsel   Date

Assistant U.S. Attorney   Date

Probation Officer   Date

Exhibit F

UNITED STATES DISTRICT COURT
FOR THE MIDDLE DISTRICT OF PENNSYLVANIA

UNITED STATES OF AMERICA

V.   Dkt. No. _____

_____

ORDER FOR DISMISSAL

Pursuant to Rule 48(a) of the Federal Rules of Criminal Procedure and by leave of Court endorsed hereon, the United States Attorney for the Middle District of Pennsylvania hereby dismisses _____ (Indictment, Information, Complaint, Violation Notice) against _____. (Name of Defendant) This dismissal is without prejudice.

_____
United States Attorney

Leave of Court is granted for the filing of the foregoing dismissal.

_____
United States District Judge

Date: _____

Exhibit G

● PS 4
(3/06)

PRETRIAL DIVERSION AGREEMENT

IN THE UNITED STATES DISTRICT COURT

_____ DISTRICT _____

IN RE _____   File No. _____
        (Name of Divertee)

(Or, if case filed)

UNITED STATES OF AMERICA   Case No. _____

V.

_____
        Defendant

The court has been advised that _____ (Divertee/Defendant) has entered into a pretrial diversion agreement dated _____, with the United States Attorney's office. A copy of the agreement is attached to this order and is incorporated by reference.

The pretrial diversion agreement includes a condition that requires _____ (Divertee/Defendant) to make restitution in the amount of $ __ to _____ (Address(es)) _____ (Address(es))

It is ORDERED that the clerk of the court accept and receive restitution payments from _____ (Divertee/Defendant) and disburse them to _____ (Address(es)) _____ (Address(es)) in accordance with the pretrial diversion agreement and in the manner in which restitution payments are received and disbursed for criminal judgments.

_____   _____
Name and Title of Judge   Signature of Judge

                                   _____
                                   Date

Exhibit H–1

(No Charges Filed)

CERTIFICATION OF COMPLETION
OF PRETRIAL DIVERSION PROGRAM

Attention: _____

   Assistant U.S. Attorney

Re: _____

Dear _____:

   I hereby certify that the subject has complied with the conditions and terms set forth in the Pretrial Diversion Agreement.

Sincerely,

_____

U.S. Probation Officer

cc: _____.

   Defense Counsel

Exhibit H–2

(Charges Filed)

CERTIFICATION OF COMPLETION
OF PRETRIAL DIVERSION PROGRAM

Attention: _____

    Assistant U.S. Attorney

Re: _____

Dear _____ :

    I hereby certify that the subject has complied with the conditions and terms set forth in the Pretrial Diversion Agreement.

    Please furnish a copy of the Order of Dismissal With Prejudice.

                      Sincerely,

              _____

              U.S. Probation Officer

cc: _____

    Defense Counsel

Exhibit I

UNITED STATES DISTRICT COURT
FOR THE MIDDLE DISTRICT OF PENNSYLVANIA

UNITED STATES OF AMERICA
  v.

_____

Criminal No. _____

ORDER FOR DISMISSAL

Pursuant to Rule 48(a) of the Federal Rules of Criminal Procedure and leave of court endorsed hereon, the United States Attorney for the Middle District of Pennsylvania hereby dismisses the _____ (Indictment, Information, Complaint) against _____ (Defendant) for the reason that the defendant satisfactorily completed the Pretrial Diversion Program. This dismissal is with prejudice.

_____
Assistant United States Attorney

Leave of Court is granted for the filing of the foregoing dismissal.

_____
United States District Judge

Exhibit J

PRETRIAL DIVERSION REPORT
MIDDLE DISTRICT OF PENNSYLVANIA

Name (Last, First, Middle)					
SANCHEZ, Christian Anthony					

Mailing Address 12 Atlantic Avenue, Apt. 2 Little Silver, PA 18555	Employment Address Greater Life Securities, Inc. 222 Smith Street Breaker Bay, PA 18554	Docket Number Violation Notice 123456
		Social Security No. 150-40-8684
		Citizenship U.S.

Time at Address 4 months	Time in Community Lifelong resident		Gross Monthly Income $1,500		Time in Empl./School 3 months
Age 22	Race White	Date of Birth 3/15/90	Place of Birth Breaker Bay, PA	Sex Male	Education College graduate

Marital Status Single	Dependents Self only

Offense
Operating Under the Influence With a BAC Above .08% [36 CFR 4.23(a-2)]

Release Bond [If Applicable] 7/22/12: Released on personal recognizance	Arrest Date [If Applicable] Not arrested

Other Defendants [If Applicable]
None

Assistant United States Attorney Michael Ross P.O. Box 999 Breaker Bay, PA 18554 (717) 555-1212	Defense Counsel [Name, Address and Telephone] Bertha Robinson Assistant Federal Public Defender Breaker Bay, PA 18554 (717) 555-1122

U.S. Pretrial Services Officer Denise Hart	Date October 1, 2012

Exhibit J

Re: Christian Anthony Sanchez

OFFENSE:

On July 22, 2012, National Park Service rangers stationed at the Delaware Water Gap National Recreation Area observed a vehicle traveling north on Route 209. The vehicle swerved abruptly into the southbound lane and returned to the northbound lane. After traffic in front of the vehicle made a lefthand turn, the vehicle drove away at a high rate of speed.

The rangers stopped the vehicle and identified the operator as Christian Sanchez. The subject's girlfriend was a passenger. The rangers detected an odor of alcoholic beverages. A breathalyzer revealed a BAC of .089% (legal limit is up to .08%).

Christian Sanchez was issued a citation for Operating Under the Influence With a BAC Above .08% and was released on personal recognizance to the custody of his girlfriend.

In an interview with the probation officer, the subject indicated that he and his girlfriend were en route home from a party. He reportedly had consumed three beers.

CANDIDATE'S PERSONAL HISTORY:

Christian Anthony Sanchez was born on March 15, 1990, in Breaker Bay, Pennsylvania. He is the younger of two children born to Roger and Doris (nee Sherman) Sanchez. His father, 55, is a banker. The subject's mother, 52, is a bookkeeper. They reside in Breaker Bay. A sister, Diane, 18, is a freshman at Smith College, Green Valley, Pennsylvania. Though the subject reports a close relationship with his parents and sister, they are not aware of the pending charges.

In June 2008, Christian Sanchez graduated from Ewing High School, Breaker Bay. On May 30, 2012, he earned a Bachelor of Science degree in Business Administration from Bucknell University, Lewisburg, Pennsylvania.

Christian Sanchez has not married and has no children. Since February 2012, he has dated Felicia Gregory. Ms. Gregory, 21, attends Bucknell University. She was present when the subject was stopped by rangers on July 22, 2012. In her opinion, Christian Sanchez does not have a drinking problem and was driving erratically only because he was texting a friend. She remains supportive.

Until June 15, 2012, with the exception of when he attended Bucknell University, Christian Sanchez resided with his parents in Breaker Bay. Since June 15, 2012, he and Felicia Gregory have lived in a modestly furnished one bedroom apartment in Little Silver, Pennsylvania.

Since July 1, 2012, Christian Sanchez has been employed as an administrative assistant at Fortunato Industries, Franklin Hills, Pennsylvania. He earns $375 weekly. His employer is not aware of the pending charge.

Prior to June 2012, the subject worked seasonally as a laborer at Antonio's Pumpkin Farm, Breaker Bay. He earned minimum wage.

Christian Sanchez reports good physical health. He denies the use of illicit drugs and reportedly consumes four or five beers weekly. Although the subject describes the instant offense as "an anomaly," he is amenable to treatment. It is noted that a drug screen secured at the time of the pretrial diversion interview tested negative for illicit drugs. There is no history of psychiatric problems.

PRIOR CRIMINAL RECORD:

None

RECOMMENDATION:

Pretrial Services recommends that Christian Sanchez be placed into the Pretrial Diversion program for a period of six (6) months under the general conditions. As part of our supervision plan, the subject will be required to undergo an alcohol evaluation and possible treatment.

Respectfully submitted,

Denise Hart
U.S. Probation Officer

United States Probation Office

MIDDLE DISTRICT OF PENNSYLVANIA

Memorandum

TO:	The Honorable William J. Nealon U.S. District Judge
FROM:	Denise Hart U.S. Probation Officer
DATE:	October 1, 2012
SUBJECT:	Christian Anthony Sanchez **Pretrial Diversion Summary**

The Government alleges that on July 22, 2012, Christian Sanchez operated a motor vehicle in an erratic manner at the Delaware Water Gap Recreation Area while under the influence of alcohol. A blood alcohol test revealed a BAC of .089% (legal limit is up to .08%).

Christian Sanchez, 22, has no prior criminal record. He has not married and has no children.

On May 30, 2012, the subject earned a Bachelor of Science degree in Business Administration from Bucknell University, Lewisburg, Pennsylvania. Since June 1, 2012, Christian Sanchez has been employed as an administrative assistant at Fortunato Industries, Franklin Hills, Pennsylvania. He earns $375 weekly. His employer is not aware of the pending charge.

According to the subject, he generally consumes four or five alcoholic beverages weekly. Although he does not feel that his drinking is problematic, he is amenable to treatment if deemed necessary. There is no evidence of illicit drug use.

Our office recommends that the defendant be placed in the Pretrial Diversion Program for six (6) months under the general conditions. As part of our supervision plan, the subject will be required to undergo an alcohol evaluation and possible treatment.

If the Court interposes no objection, the report and recommendation will be provided to government counsel and defense counsel.

Approved: _____

Date: _____

[Dated: April 11, 2014.]

STANDING ORDER NO. 15–3. IN RE: WEAPONS IN THE COURTROOM

AND NOW, this 15th day of May, 2015, upon consideration of the memorandum of understanding regarding court security dated January 21, 2004, and entered by the United States Department of Homeland Security, the United States Department of Justice, and the Administrative Office of the United States Courts, delegating to the United States Marshals Service sole responsibility for provision of security services to the Federal Judiciary, including protection during court proceedings, and the court concluding that judicial security considerations compel restrictions on the presence of weapons in the courtrooms of the United States District Court for the Middle District of Pennsylvania, see 18 U.S.C. § 930(f) ("Nothing in this section limits the power of a court of the United States . . . to promulgate rules or orders regulating, restricting, or prohibiting the possession of weapons within any building housing such court . . ."), it is hereby ORDERED that permission to carry weapons in the courtrooms of the United States District Court for the Middle District of Pennsylvania is granted exclusively to Deputy United States Marshals and Court Security Officers, for the purpose of providing judicial and courtroom security. Exceptions to this order may be granted upon application to and approval by the United States Marshal for the Middle District of Pennsylvania.

[Dated: May 15, 2015.]

INDEX TO UNITED STATES DISTRICT COURT
FOR THE MIDDLE DISTRICT OF PENNSYLVANIA

UNITED STATES BANKRUPTCY COURT FOR THE MIDDLE DISTRICT OF PENNSYLVANIA

Including Amendments Received Through
June 1, 2016

LOCAL BANKRUPTCY RULES

Administrative Procedures for Filing, Signing and Verifying Pleadings and Papers by Electronic Means.

Proposed Order Guidelines.

A. Electronic Case Filing System Attorney Registration Form Please Type.

B. [Reserved].

C. Certificate of Service.

D. Request to Discontinue Service of Notices.

E. Application for Limited Use Password for Electronic Case Filing System.

SELECTED ORDERS

84–0203. In re: Referral of Bankruptcy Matters [District Court Order] [Vacated by Standing Order No. 16–3, effective March 11, 2016].

00–3. In re: Standing Order of Reference in Bankruptcy Matters [District Court Order] [Vacated by Standing Order No. 16–3, effective March 11, 2016].

In re: Amended Order Adopting Interim Federal Bankruptcy Rule 1007–I, as Amended Retroactively Effective December 18, 2015.

16–3. In re: Amended Order of Reference in Bankruptcy Matters [District Court Order].

LOCAL BANKRUPTCY RULES

PART I. COMMENCEMENT OF CASE; PROCEEDINGS RELATING TO PETITION AND ORDER FOR RELIEF

RULE 1001–1. LOCAL RULES—GENERAL

(a) **Scope.** The Local Bankruptcy Rules and Local Bankruptcy Forms are adopted to govern the practice and procedure before the United States Bankruptcy Court for the Middle District of Pennsylvania.

(b) **Short Title.** These rules may be cited and referred to as the Local Bankruptcy Rules (or "L.B.R.") and the forms as the Local Bankruptcy Forms (or "L.B.F.").

[Effective January 1, 2005.]

RULE 1002–1. PETITION—GENERAL

(a) **Unsigned Petition.** The clerk must accept for filing any petition in bankruptcy. If a petition is not signed by either the petitioner or counsel, a signed document must be filed within seven (7) days or the petition may be dismissed. The clerk will notify the party of the deficiency and the deadline by which the deficiency must be cured.

(b) **Petition Submitted by Facsimile.** A petition may not be filed by facsimile unless prior approval has been obtained from the court. The court will not approve a filing by facsimile except in an emergency, as determined by the court.

[Effective January 1, 2005. Amended effective January 1, 2008; December 1, 2009.]

RULE 1006–1. FEES—INSTALLMENT PAYMENTS AND WAIVER

(a) **Petitions.** Each petition must be accompanied by the prescribed filing fee, including the miscellaneous fee, unless the petition is accompanied by an application to pay these fees in installments, or for a waiver in accordance with F.R.B.P. 1006(c). If a petition is filed without the required fee, without an application to pay in installments, or without a request for waiver, it is considered deficient and may be dismissed if the fee is not paid within seven (7) days. The court may dismiss a case without further notice if the approved installments are not paid when due.

(b) **Other Filings.** The clerk must accept all pleadings for filing regardless of whether the fee required by the bankruptcy court fee schedule is paid. If the required fee is not paid at the time the pleading is filed, the clerk will notify the filing party that the party has seven (7) days to pay the fee or the pleading may be stricken by the court. Current information regarding fees and the number of copies required by the clerk may be found on the court's website (www.pamb.uscourts.gov).

[Effective January 1, 2005. Amended effective January 1, 2008; December 1, 2009.]

RULE 1007–1. LISTS, SCHEDULES, STATEMENTS, PLANS, AND OTHER DOCUMENTS

(a) **Motion.** A motion for an extension of time to file lists, schedules, statements, plans, or other required documents must be filed with the court within fourteen (14) days of the entry of an order for relief or before any previously granted extension expires. If the motion is untimely, the court may deny the motion and dismiss the case. The motion must state why the extension is needed and be served on the unsecured creditors' committee and any examiner, if one has been appointed.

(b) Objection to Extension. An objection to an extension of time must be filed within seven (7) days of service of the motion requesting the extension.

(c) Certification of No Payment Advices. If a debtor does not receive payment advices, he must file a certification (L.B.F. 1007–1(c)) within the time specified in F.R.B.P.1007(c). Nothing in this rule is intended to create an exception to the requirements of 11 U.S.C. § 521 or F.R.B.P. 1007.

[Effective January 1, 2005. Amended effective January 1, 2008; December 1, 2009.]

RULE 1007–2. MAILING LIST OR MATRIX

(a) Mailing Matrix Required. Unless filed electronically through the ECF system, the debtor must file with the petition a master list of creditors and other parties in interest ("mailing matrix") in the form prescribed by the clerk. Failure to file the matrix may constitute cause for dismissal of the case.

(b) Form of Paper Mailing Matrix.

(1) The mailing matrix must be filed with the petition in paper form as prescribed by the clerk.

(2) Mailing matrices must be prepared so that each address is contained within five (5) lines, with each line not exceeding forty (40) characters (including spaces).

(c) Electronically Filed Cases. Electronic filers must comply with the instructions found on the court's website (www.pamb.uscourts.gov) when entering the matrix docket event and uploading creditors into the ECF system in lieu of filing a paper matrix.

(d) Accuracy of Mailing Matrix. The debtor is responsible for the accuracy and completeness of the mailing matrix. If debtor's counsel or a pro se debtor is notified by the Bankruptcy Noticing Center (BNC) that the creditors' meeting notice was not served on a party because of an incomplete address, counsel or the pro se debtor must notify the clerk in writing of the correct address and must remail the notice to the affected party.

[Effective January 1, 2005. Amended effective January 1, 2008; December 1, 2009.]

RULE 1007–3. SUMMARY OF YOUR ASSETS AND LIABILITIES AND CERTAIN STATISTICAL INFORMATION

A debtor must timely complete and file the Summary of Your Assets and Liabilities and Certain Statistical Information (Official Form 106Sum).

[Effective October 15, 2010. Amended effective September 1, 2014; June 1, 2016.]

RULE 1009–1. AMENDMENTS TO VOLUNTARY PETITIONS, LISTS, SCHEDULES, AND STATEMENTS

(a) Notice. An amendment to a voluntary petition, schedule, or statement must be served on any official committee and any affected entity or creditor. The debtor must file a certification that service has been made on these parties.

(b) Requirements. An amendment must contain:

(1) the caption of the case;

(2) the case number; and

(3) a title including the word "AMENDED" or "AMENDMENT."

(c) Form. An amendment to a schedule or statement must be filed in a format similar to the original official form and include only the additions or deletions to the schedule or statement. The change must be prefaced by the statement: "ADD" or "DELETE." An entire set of statements and schedules should not be refiled.

(d) Electronically Filed Amendments. Debtor's counsel must comply with the instructions found on the court's website (www.pamb.uscourts.gov) regarding uploading any new creditors into the ECF system.

[Effective January 1, 2005. Amended effective January 1, 2008.]

RULE 1015–1. JOINT ADMINISTRATION/CONSOLIDATION

(a) Joint Administration.

(1) *Motion.* A request for joint administration must be made by motion. For each case subject to the motion, movant must serve the motion and notice of the answer date on:

(A) the debtor;

(B) all secured creditors;

(C) all parties in interest who have filed a request to receive copies and notices; and

(D) any creditors' committee. If there is no creditors' committee, then the motion must be served as specified in F.R.B.P. 1007(d).

(2) *Passive Notice.* Notice of the filing of a motion for joint administration must provide for a twenty-one (21) day objection period. If no objection is filed within twenty-one (21) days, the court may enter the order. A hearing will be set only upon filing of a timely objection to the motion.

(b) Substantive Consolidation. A request for substantive consolidation must be filed using the self-scheduling procedures set forth in L.B.R. 9002–1. Unless service is made electronically through the ECF system, the movant must serve the motion and hearing required notice upon all parties in interest. The notice must provide for a twenty-one (21) day objection period.

(c) Severance or Deconsolidation.

(1) A request to deconsolidate cases that have been substantively consolidated must be filed using the self-scheduling procedures set forth in L.B.R. 9002–1. Unless service is made electronically through the ECF system, the movant must serve the motion and hearing required notice upon all parties in interest.

(2) A request to sever jointly administered cases must be made by motion. Unless service is made electronically through the ECF system, the movant must serve the motion and passive notice on the debtor, all secured creditors, all parties who have specifically asked to receive copies and notices, and the creditors' committee. If there is no creditors' committee, then the motion must be served as specified in F.R.B.P. 1007(d). No hearing will be held on a motion to sever jointly administered cases unless an objection to the motion is filed within fourteen (14) days of service.

[Effective January 1, 2005. Amended effective January 1, 2008; December 1, 2009; October 15, 2010; September 1, 2014.]

COMMENTS:

L.B.R. 1015–1 was amended effective October 15, 2010, to eliminate subparagraph (c)(3). The amendment reflects the present capability of CM/ECF to dismiss a debtor from a joint case without requiring case severance.

RULE 1017–1. REINSTATEMENT OF DISMISSED CASE

(a) A motion to reinstate a dismissed case must be in writing. If the court sets a hearing on the motion, notice of the date by which objections must be filed and the hearing date must be served on the following:

(1) the debtor; and

(2) all parties previously notified of the dismissal under F.R.B.P. 2002(f)(2).

(b) Any motion to reinstate a dismissed case may be granted summarily.

[Effective January 1, 2005. Amended effective January 1, 2008; December 1, 2009; December 1, 2011. Renumbered as Rule 1017–1 effective September 1, 2014.]

RULE 1019–1. FINAL REPORTS IN CASES CONVERTED FROM CHAPTER 13 TO CHAPTER 7

Pursuant to F.R.B.P. 1019(5)(B), the chapter 13 trustee must file a final report and account within sixty (60) days after conversion of the case.

[Effective April 4, 2011. Amended effective September 1, 2014.]

RULE 1071–1. DISTRICT BOUNDARIES AND DIVISIONAL OFFICES

(a) The Middle District of Pennsylvania is comprised of the following counties as set forth in 28 U.S.C. § 118(b): Adams, Bradford, Cameron, Carbon, Centre, Clinton, Columbia, Cumberland, Dauphin, Franklin, Fulton, Huntingdon, Juniata, Lackawanna, Lebanon, Luzerne, Lycoming, Mifflin, Monroe, Montour, Northumberland, Perry, Pike, Potter, Schuylkill, Snyder, Sullivan, Susquehanna, Tioga, Union, Wayne, Wyoming, and York.

(b) For the purpose of accepting bankruptcy petitions, conducting hearings, and all other court business, the Middle District is organized under geographical divisions of Wilkes–Barre, Harrisburg, and Williamsport. Subject to court discretion, the counties listed in subsection (a) above are assigned to these divisions, with specific county assignment posted on the court's website under the "County Maps" link. (www.pamb.uscourts.gov).

[Effective December 1, 2011.]

RULE 1071–2. ASSIGNMENT OF CASES

(a) Upon filing, the clerk will assign bankruptcy cases to a bankruptcy judge within this District by random blind draw so that no party, their attorneys, or the public at large is able to make a deliberate choice of a particular judge.

(b) The provisions of L.B.R. 1071–2(a) do not apply to cases filed under chapter 9. These cases are assigned to a bankruptcy judge by the Chief Judge of the Third Circuit Court of Appeals pursuant to 11 U.S.C. § 921(b).

[Effective December 1, 2011. Amended effective September 1, 2014.]

PART II. OFFICERS AND ADMINISTRATION; NOTICES; MEETINGS; EXAMINATIONS; ELECTIONS; ATTORNEYS AND ACCOUNTANTS

RULE 2002–1. NOTICE TO CREDITORS AND OTHER INTERESTED PARTIES

(a) Passive Notice. A notice served under F.R.B.P. 2002(a)(3), (6), (7), or (8) must provide that if no objections are filed by the objection deadline, the court may grant the relief requested. No hearing date will be included in the notice unless a written request is filed.

(b) Notice to Parties in Interest. In a case filed under any chapter, a proponent must give notice to all parties in interest as required under F.R.B.P. 2002(a)(2), (4), (5), and (6). In a chapter 11 case, a proponent also must give the notice required by F.R.B.P. 2002(b) and (d).

(c) Notices by a Chapter 7, 11, 12, or 13 Trustee. Generally, the clerk will provide any notice required to be served on all parties in interest by a chapter 7, 11, 12, or 13 trustee. Notwithstanding the above, a chapter 7 trustee pursuing assets is required to provide notice to all creditors and parties in interest, under these rules or under the Federal Rules of Bankruptcy Procedure, of the following:

(1) a trustee's application for compensation;

(2) an attorney for trustee's application for compensation;

(3) any notice of sale;

(4) any notice of compromise or settlement pursuant to F.R.B.P. 9019; and

(5) notice of a trustee's final report, if the net proceeds realized exceed $1,500.00.

(d) Notice of § 341(a) Meeting.

(1) *General Rule.* The clerk must serve notice of a meeting under 11 U.S.C. § 341(a) on all parties in interest listed on the mailing matrix.

(2) *Amended Mailing Matrix.* The debtor must serve notice of a meeting under 11 U.S.C. § 341(a) on all parties in interest added to the mailing matrix after notice of the meeting has been served pursuant to L.B.R. 2002–1(d)(1).

(3) *Notice of Rescheduled Meeting.* If the meeting under 11 U.S.C. § 341(a) is rescheduled before the meeting is called to order, notice of the rescheduled meeting must be given to all parties in interest by the party requesting the rescheduled meeting. When rescheduling is caused by inclement weather, Acts of God, sudden illness, or the debtor's failure to file required documents, the clerk will provide notice of the rescheduled meeting. However, in each case for a pro se debtor, the clerk must provide notice of the rescheduled meeting to all parties in interest.

(4) *Chapter 13 Cases.* In a chapter 13 case, notice of the meeting under 11 U.S.C. § 341(a) must include instructions on filing a proof of claim under L.B.R. 3001–1.

(e) Notice to Equity Security Holders. The debtor must provide notice of the order for relief and any other notices required under F.R.B.P. 2002(d) to its equity security holders.

(f) Certificate of Service. The certificate of service showing compliance with this rule must be filed with the clerk no later than seven (7) days following the date of service.

[Effective January 1, 2005. Amended effective December 1, 2009; September 1, 2014; June 1, 2016.]

RULE 2003–1. MEETING OF CREDITORS AND EQUITY SECURITY HOLDERS

(a) Date and Place. Any request to deviate from the general requirement that a debtor personally appear at a meeting under 11 U.S.C. § 341(a) must be made first to the United States trustee, or his designee. If the United States trustee denies the request, the debtor may file a motion with the court.

(b) Attendance. Debtor's attorney should accompany debtor to a meeting under 11 U.S.C. § 341(a). If a debtor's attorney is unable to attend, he or she must arrange for a partner, member, or regular associate of his or her firm to serve as counsel or for another attorney to attend, if permitted under the Pennsylvania Rules of Professional Conduct.

(c) Adjournment/Continuance. If the meeting under 11 U.S.C. § 341(a) has been called to order by the trustee, the trustee must orally announce the new date and time to the parties in attendance at the originally scheduled meeting. The requirement, pursuant to F.R.B.P. 2003(e), that the presiding official, the trustee, file a statement specifying the date and time to which a meeting of creditors is adjourned may be satisfied by using the continued feature within the trustee interface of the ECF system.

[Effective January 1, 2005. Amended effective December 1, 2011; September 1, 2014.]

RULE 2004–1. DEPOSITIONS AND EXAMINATIONS

The court will consider a motion under F.R.B.P. 2004(a) fourteen (14) days after service on the respondent. If no objection or answer is filed within four-teen (14) days, an order may be entered by the court. The order may be entered immediately if the motion contains a certification that the respondent has agreed to submit to the examination.

[Effective January 1, 2005. Amended effective December 1, 2009.]

RULE 2014–1. EMPLOYMENT OF PROFESSIONALS

(a) Application to Employ Counsel or Other Professionals. An application to employ counsel or other professionals must be filed with the clerk along with a verified statement of disinterestedness and a proposed order.

(b) Application to Employ Persons for the Sale or Lease of Estate Property. An application for employment of an agent or broker for the sale or lease of estate property must be accompanied by a copy of the signed written contract employing the agent or broker. An application for employment of an auction-eer must be accompanied by a copy of the auctioneer's surety bond. A contract for employment must provide that it is effective only upon court approval. When an applicant seeks appointment as a real estate agent or broker, as an appraiser, or as an auctioneer, the applicant must state if he or she is seeking compensation at a flat rate or on a percentage basis. Under L.B.R. 6005–1(b), an applicant for compensation at a flat rate or on a percentage basis may request the court to approve the terms of compensation without filing a separate fee application, but if applicant later requests compensation on different terms, the court must approve compensation. An application for employment under this rule requires conformity with the notice requirements of F.R.B.P. 2002(a)(6).

(c) Objection by the United States Trustee. Any objection to an application to employ must be filed by the United States trustee within seven (7) days from the date of service of the application unless the application is filed within fourteen (14) days of the filing of the petition. If the application is filed within fourteen (14) days of the filing of the petition, any objection must be filed within twenty-one (21) days of the filing of the petition.

[Effective January 1, 2005. Amended effective January 1, 2008. Amended effective December 1, 2009.]

RULE 2016–1. COMPENSATION OF PROFESSIONALS

This rule governs the procedure for professional applications for compensation. All professional fees paid from property of the estate are subject to court approval. Compensation of attorneys for chapter 13

debtors are also subject to the provisions of L.B.R. 2016–2.

(a) Fee Applications. A fee application must include:

(1) *Cover Sheet.* A fee application must include a cover sheet that provides the court with a summary of the fee application. The cover sheet must conform substantially to L.B.F. 2016–1.

(2) the date of the order appointing the professional;

(3) a statement indicating whether the application is for final or interim compensation and expenses, the total amounts requested, and the time period for the services rendered;

(4) the date and amount of previous compensation, if any, including any retainers paid;

(5) a chronological listing of services performed. Whenever applicable, the listing should include:

(A) an identification of the subject matter of any correspondence or phone call together with the party with whom that communication occurred;

(B) an identification of the subject matter of and parties involved in any hearing or trial, if the service involved is attendance at a hearing or trial;

(C) an identification of any pleading drafted; and

(D) the date the service or expense was incurred and the time expended, in tenths of hours, for the service rendered;

(6) an itemization of the expenses for which reimbursement is requested;

(7) an allegation that the professional is a disinterested person and has not represented or held an interest adverse to the interest of the estate on the matter on which he or she was employed in compliance with 11 U.S.C. § 327(a);

(8) for applications filed on behalf of attorneys, a history of the case in narrative form. The history should include, if applicable:

(A) a description of the debtor's financial situation when the case was filed;

(B) a description of significant events that have occurred post-petition;

(C) a description of specific issues that the debtor is required to resolve before a plan can be confirmed or the case otherwise resolved (for example, liquidation of real estate or resolution of pre-petition litigation);

(D) the status of any specific issues and their resolution; and

(E) items that need to be completed before the case can be confirmed or otherwise brought to a conclusion;

(9) a certification that the entity on whose behalf the applicant is employed has been given the opportunity to review the application and whether that entity has approved the requested amount;

(10) the names and hourly rates of all applicant's professionals and paraprofessionals who billed time. This should be accompanied by an explanation of any changes in hourly rates from those previously billed; and

(11) a proposed order of the court approving the application.

(b) Categorical Listing of Services.

(1) In a case under any chapter in which the total aggregate amount requested for compensation by a professional is in excess of $100,000.00 the applicant must include a categorical listing of services. Appendix 2016–1 provides a nonexclusive list of suggested project categories.

(2) The description of each category must include the following information:

(A) a heading generally describing the services within the category;

(B) a narrative summary that:

(i) describes the project and its status, including all pending litigation for which compensation and reimbursement are requested; and

(ii) states the number of hours spent and the amount of compensation requested for each professional and paraprofessional on the project.

(c) Non–Attorney Professionals Compensated on Non–Hourly Basis. If the court has previously entered an order approving the employment of a non-attorney who is customarily paid on a non-hourly basis and whose terms of compensation the court has approved as provided in L.B.R. 2014–1(b), then no application for compensation is required for such non-attorney.

[Effective January 1, 2005. Amended effective September 1, 2014.]

RULE 2016–2. COMPENSATION OF DEBTORS' ATTORNEYS IN CHAPTER 13 CASES.

The provisions of this rule will apply to all chapter 13 cases filed on or after October 1, 2014.

(a) Rights and Responsibilities Agreement. Unless otherwise ordered by the court, in all chapter 13 cases in which a debtor is represented by an attorney, the debtor and the attorney must execute the Rights and Responsibilities Agreement as set forth in L.B.F. 2016–2(a). Counsel must retain the original Agreement in the case file and provide a fully executed copy to the debtor.

(b) General Rule. Except as provided in L.B.R. 2016–2(c), an attorney representing a debtor in a chapter 13 case must file an application for approval of compensation in order to be paid for all services rendered after the filing of the case. The fee application must comply with L.B.R. 2016–1, except the information required under (a)(1) and (a)(8) of that rule may be omitted. A model fee application form for use by attorneys representing a chapter 13 debtor is set forth in L.B.F. 2016–2(b) ("lodestar fee"). The attorney must also file a certification that a Rights and Responsibilities Agreement (L.B.F. 2016–2(a)) has been executed by the attorney and by the debtor. Filing of the certification may be accomplished by a virtual entry in the ECF system. After the petition is filed, an attorney may not receive payment of fees except through the chapter 13 plan, unless payment is otherwise approved by the court.

(c) Presumptively Reasonable Fee. When the Rights and Responsibilities Agreement provides for the payment of the presumptively reasonable fee, the attorney may receive compensation in the maximum amount of $4000.00. Further, no fee application is required to be filed where the presumptively reasonable fee is agreed to. In such case, the attorney is only required to file L.B.F. 2016–2(c)—Request for Payment of Chapter 13 Compensation and Expenses, with parts A and C completed. If the chapter 13 trustee requires the debtor to file a business report, or if the debtor holds a controlling interest in a corporation or LLC operating a business, an attorney may receive additional compensation in the maximum amount of $1000.00 without seeking approval from the court. An attorney representing a consumer debtor who proposes to make mortgage payments through a chapter 13 plan ("conduit plan") may receive additional compensation of $500.00, without seeking approval from the court. When an attorney agrees to accept a presumptively reasonable fee, all covered legal services rendered by the attorney through confirmation of the plan must be included in the fee, except as provided in paragraph (e). Approval of the allowance of a presumptively reasonable fee will be considered by the court at confirmation and any approval will be given by virtue of the entry of the confirmation order. Consideration of the allowance of a fee for the preparation, filing, and defense of a modified plan will be given by virtue of the entry of the order granting or denying the motion to modify.

(d) Indication of Type of Fee in Plan. The attorney for the debtor must indicate in section 3B of the model plan (L.B.F. 3015–1) whether the attorney seeks the presumptively reasonable fee or the lodestar fee.

(e) Additional Fees. An attorney who has agreed to accept a presumptively reasonable fee may request additional fees under L.B.R. 2016–2(b) for services rendered after confirmation of the plan or in connection with adversary proceedings. In the event that an attorney determines that services required to be rendered before confirmation of plan exceed normal and customary services in a chapter 13 case, the attorney may seek approval of additional fees under L.B.R. 2016–2(b).

(f) Post–Confirmation Modification Plans. An attorney who has agreed to payment of the presumptively reasonable fee may receive additional compensation of $500.00 for each post-confirmation plan modification which is filed, without seeking approval from the court.

(g) Payment of Fees Through Plan. An attorney who has agreed to be paid through a proposed plan must file a Request for Payment of Chapter 13 Compensation and Expenses (L.B.F. 2016–2(c) ("Request for Payment")) no later than seven (7) days before the confirmation hearing on the plan. Failure to timely file a Request for Payment may result in a delay of confirmation of the chapter 13 plan. In the event the confirmation hearing is continued, the Request for Payment is not required to be refiled, if no additional fees are requested. When additional fees are requested, a new Request for Payment must be filed no later than seven (7) days before the continued confirmation hearing.

[Effective September 1, 2014. Amended effective September 1, 2015.]

COMMENTS:

Effective September 1, 2015, former L.B.R. 2016–2(h) was repealed because it conflicted with the Supreme Court decision Harris v. Viegelahn, 135 S.Ct. 1829 (2015).

L.B.R. 2016–2 is being adopted as of September 1, 2014, to provide for specific procedures for the approval of attorneys' fees in chapter 13 cases. The new rule will apply to chapter 13 cases which are filed on or after October 1, 2014. The general rule will be applicable to attorneys who have agreed to provide services using the lodestar approach. A fee application form is adopted as L.B.F. 2016–2(b). To provide a more efficient means of approving fees in chapter 13 cases, a presumptively reasonable fee is being adopted; this will enable attorneys to obtain approval for fees in certain amounts without filing a fee application. The rule also adopts a Rights and Responsibilities Agreement form to be completed by all represented debtors and their attorneys. The Agreement specifies the services an attorney will perform, if required under the circumstances of a particular case, as well as the responsibilities of the debtor to assist in the prosecution of the case. The Agreement also will specify the compensation arrangements agreed to by the debtor and the attorney. The rule also provides for a Request for Payment of Chapter 13 Compensation and Expenses to be

filed prior to confirmation to allow the chapter 13 trustee to determine the amount of fees that will be paid through the plan. The rule also provides that when a case is converted or dismissed and the chapter 13 trustee is required to return payments made to the debtor, counsel may request the payment of outstanding attorneys' fees.

RULE 2090–1. ATTORNEYS—ADMISSION TO PRACTICE

(a) General Admission. Except as provided below, no attorney may appear on behalf of another unless first admitted to practice in the United States District Court for the Middle District of Pennsylvania.

(b) Admission Pro Hac Vice. An attorney who is admitted to practice before any United States district court and the highest court of any state or the District of Columbia, and who is a member of the bar in good standing in every jurisdiction where admitted to practice, and who is not subject to pending disciplinary proceedings in any jurisdiction, may be admitted to practice before this court, but only for the purpose of a particular case and not generally under subdivision (a). A request for admission under this subdivision must be made by written motion of a member of the bar of this court or by the attorney intending to practice before this court. The court, in its discretion, may grant an oral motion for admission made in open court.

[Effective January 1, 2005. Amended effective January 1, 2008.]

RULE 2090–2. ATTORNEYS—DISCIPLINE AND DISBARMENT

(a) Suspension or Disbarment from Practice. This court has the power and authority to govern, control, and discipline the conduct of attorneys appearing before it, including the power to suspend or disbar attorneys from practice before it.

(b) Failure to Appear. An attorney who fails to appear without just cause, either on a matter before the court or as counsel for a debtor who fails to attend the debtor's § 341(a) meeting, may be subject to discipline by the court.

(c) Failure to Prepare. An attorney who, without just cause, fails to adequately prepare for any pretrial conference, hearing, or trial may be subject to discipline by the court.

[Effective January 1, 2005. Amended effective January 1, 2008; September 1, 2014.]

PART III. CLAIMS AND DISTRIBUTION TO CREDITORS AND EQUITY INTEREST HOLDER; PLANS

RULE 3001–1. CLAIMS AND EQUITY SECURITY INTERESTS— GENERAL

(a) Proof of Claim—Contents. Any proof of claim filed must be substantially in compliance with the Proof of Claim (Official Form 410) and F.R.B.P. 3001.

(b) Proof of Claim—Service. In a chapter 7 asset case, a chapter 12 case, or a chapter 13 case, a claimant must serve a copy of its proof of claim, with all attachments, on a pro se debtor.

[Effective January 1, 2005. Amended effective January 1, 2008; December 1, 2011.]

COMMENTS:

L.B.R. 3001–1 was amended effective December 1, 2011, to avoid repetition of the provisions of F.R.B.P. 3001 and to incorporate the requirements of F.R.B.P. 3001(c) for proofs of claim filed in individual debtor cases.

RULE 3002–1. FILING PROOFS OF CLAIM IN CLOSED CASES

Unless filed electronically, any proof of claim received by the clerk in a closed case will be returned to the claimant and marked: "Not Filed, Case Closed."

[Effective January 1, 2005. Amended effective January 1, 2008.]

RULE 3002.1–1 RESPONSE TO NOTICE OF FINAL CURE PAYMENTS

In chapter 13 cases, a holder's response to a notice of final cure payment made pursuant to F.R.B.P. 3002.1(g) must be made by filing and serving the Response to Notice of Final Cure Payment (Official Form 4100R). Filing and service must be made in accordance with the provisions of F.R.B.P. 3002.1(g).

[Effective March 1, 2013. Amended effective September 1, 2014; June 1, 2016.]

COMMENTS:

L.B.R. 3002.1–1 was amended effective June 1, 2016, to provide for the use of Official Form 4100R—Response to Notice of Final Cure Payment and to eliminate L.B.F. 3002.1–1.

RULE 3003–1. FILING PROOFS OF CLAIM IN CHAPTER 11 CASES

In chapter 11 cases, notice of a deadline for proofs of claim must be given in the following manner:

(a) Party Request. A party requesting the court to set a date within which claims must be filed must provide notice of the bar date and a form of proof of claim to all creditors.

(b) Sua Sponte. If the court sua sponte sets a date within which claims must be filed, the clerk must provide notice of the bar date and a form of proof of claim to all creditors.

[Effective January 1, 2005. Amended effective January 1, 2008.]

RULE 3004–1. FILING OF PROOFS OF CLAIM BY DEBTOR OR TRUSTEE

A debtor or trustee filing a proof of claim in the name of a creditor under F.R.B.P. 3004 must file an original and serve a copy on the creditor.

[Effective January 1, 2005. Amended effective January 1, 2008.]

RULE 3005–1. FILING OF PROOFS OF CLAIM BY CO–DEBTOR

A co-debtor filing a proof of claim in the name of a creditor under F.R.B.P. 3005 must file an original and serve a copy on the creditor, any co-debtors, and the debtor.

[Effective January 1, 2005. Amended effective January 1, 2008; September 1, 2014.]

RULE 3006–1. CLAIMS—WITHDRAWAL

A request to withdraw a claim must state:

(a) whether an objection to the claim was filed;

(b) whether a complaint was filed against the claimant; and

(c) whether the claimant has accepted or rejected a plan or otherwise participated significantly in the case.

[Effective January 1, 2005.]

RULE 3007–1. CLAIMS—OBJECTION

(a) Contents. An objection to a claim must list in the caption or the pleading the claim number recorded on the claims register and state particular grounds for the objection, including, but not limited to:

(1) whether the claim should be disallowed in its entirety;

(2) whether the claim should be allowed in an amount different from that requested; or

(3) whether the classification of the claim (secured, priority unsecured, general unsecured) is incorrect.

(b) Separate Objection. A separate objection must be filed for each claim objected to, except for omnibus objections filed pursuant to F.R.B.P. 3007(d).

(c) Filing and Hearing Notice for ECF Filers. An objection to claim must be filed using the self-scheduling procedures set forth in L.B.R. 9002-1. Unless service is made electronically through the ECF system, the objector must serve the objection and notice (L.B.F. 3007-1—Notice of Objection to Claim and Hearing Date) upon the persons specified under F.R.B.P. 3007(a). The ECF filer must also file a certificate of service which complies with L.B.R. 9013-2.

(d) Filing and Hearing Notice for Non–ECF Filers. A non–ECF filer must file an objection to claim with the clerk's office. When the objection to claim is filed, the non–ECF filer must, within five (5) days, mail a copy of the objection to claim to the claimant and the trustee. The non–ECF filer must also file a certificate of service which complies with L.B.R. 9013-2. After the certificate of service is filed, the clerk will then issue and send a notice, at least thirty (30) days prior to the hearing, setting a claim objection hearing date.

(e) No Response Required: Hearing. No response is required to an objection to a claim. There will be a hearing on an objection to a claim.

[Effective January 1, 2005. Amended effective January 1, 2008; October 15, 2010; September 1, 2014; July 1, 2015.]

COMMENTS:

L.B.R. 3007-1 was amended effective July 1, 2015, it having been determined that provisions of the prior rule authorizing entry of a default judgment against a claimant on a claim objection if the claimant did not: (1) file an answer; (2) file an amended claim; or, (3) request a hearing, conflicts with provisions of 11 U.S.C. § 502(b) and F.R.B.P. 3007.

RULE 3010–1. SMALL DIVIDENDS IN CHAPTER 13 CASES

The chapter 13 trustee may make payments of amounts less than $15.00 to a creditor.

[Effective January 1, 2005.]

RULE 3015–1. CHAPTER 13—MODEL PLAN

(a) Use of Plan Form. In chapter 13 cases, the plan must be filed in substantial conformity with L.B.F. 3015-1.

COMMENTS:

L.B.R. 3015-1 was amended effective March 1, 2013, principally to eliminate repetition of, or any conflict with, the

provisions of F.R.B.P. 3002.1 and to avoid any repetition of, or any conflict with, the requirements of RESPA concerning qualified written requests concerning residential mortgages.

(b) Service. If a chapter 13 plan includes either a motion to value collateral or a motion to avoid a lien, service of the plan must be made on affected parties under F.R.B.P. 9014(b).

[Effective January 1, 2008; Amended effective February 7, 2008; March 1, 2013; September 1, 2014.]

RULE 3015–2. CHAPTER 12 OR CHAPTER 13—AMENDMENTS TO PLANS

(a) Numbering. Amended plans must be numbered sequentially beginning with "First Amended Plan."

(b) Amendments to the Chapter 12 or Chapter 13 Plan Prior to Confirmation. Once a plan has been filed, any changes to the plan proposed by the debtor must be made by filing an amended plan and not by filing a stipulation between the affected parties.

(c) Filing and Service of Chapter 12 or Chapter 13 Amended Plan—Pre Confirmation by a CM/ECF Filer. If an amended plan is filed after the clerk's office notices the initial confirmation hearing but prior to the confirmation of the plan, a CM/ECF filer may request a new confirmation hearing date by using the self-scheduling procedures as set forth in L.B.R. 9002-1. At the time the amended plan is filed, the CM/ECF filer must provide a copy of the amended plan and the notice setting confirmation objection and hearing dates for the pre confirmation amended plan to each party on the mailing matrix, either by U.S. mail or electronically through the CM/ECF system.

(d) Filing and Service of Chapter 12 or Chapter 13 Amended Plan—Pre Confirmation by a Pro Se Debtor. A chapter 12 or chapter 13 debtor who represents him or herself must file the amended plan with the clerk's office. When the amended plan is filed, the pro se debtor must, within five (5) days, mail a copy of the amended plan to each party on the mailing matrix. The pro se debtor must also file a certificate of service, which complies with L.B.R. 9013-2. After the certificate of service is filed, the clerk will then issue and send to creditors and parties in interest a notice setting confirmation objection and hearing dates for the pre confirmation amended plan.

(e) Modification of the Chapter 12 or Chapter 13 Plan After Confirmation by a CM/ECF Filer. After a plan has been confirmed, a motion may be filed to modify the confirmed plan. The proposed modified plan and a proposed order must be attached to the motion to modify.

(f) Service of Chapter 13 Amended Plan After Confirmation by a CM/ECF Filer. An amended post confirmation plan and a passive notice containing the objection date must be provided to each creditor and party in interest, either by U.S. mail or electronically through the CM/ECF system. If an amended plan is filed that alters the treatment of the claims of a limited number of creditors, the debtor may be excused from serving the motion, notice, and amended plan on all creditors by filing L.B.F. 3015–2(a), certifying that service has been made on the affected creditors. Further, if an amended plan is filed to alter funding of the plan or to make technical amendments, but does not affect the payment of any creditor's claim, the debtor may be excused from serving the motion, notice, and amended plan on all creditors by filing L.B.F. 3015–2(b), certifying the limited changes to the confirmed plan.

(g) Service of Chapter 12 Amended Plan After Confirmation by a CM/ECF Filer. An amended post confirmation plan and a passive notice containing the objection date must be provided to each creditor and party in interest, either by U.S. mail or electronically through the CM/ECF system. If an amended plan is filed that alters the treatment of the claims of a limited number of creditors, the debtor may be excused from serving the motion, notice, and amended plan on all creditors by filing L.B.F. 3015–2(c), certifying that service has been made on the affected creditors. Further, if an amended plan is filed to alter funding of the plan or to make technical amendments, but does not affect the payment of any creditor's claim, the debtor may be excused from serving the motion, notice, and amended plan on all creditors by filing L.B.F. 3015–2(d), certifying the limited changes to the confirmed plan.

(h) Filing and Service of Chapter 13 Amended Plan After Confirmation by Pro Se Debtor. A pro se debtor who wishes to amend a confirmed plan must file a motion to modify the confirmed plan with the clerk's office. The proposed modified plan and a proposed order must be attached to the motion to modify. The pro se debtor must, within five (5) days, mail a copy of the amended plan, the motion to modify, and a proposed order to each creditor and party in interest. The pro se debtor must also file a certificate of service, which complies with L.B.R. 9013–2. After the certificate of service is filed, the clerk will then issue and send to creditors and parties in interest a passive notice setting the objection date on the post confirmation amended plan.

(i) Filing and Service of Chapter 12 Amended Plan After Confirmation by Pro Se Debtor. A pro se debtor who wishes to amend a confirmed plan must file a motion to modify the confirmed plan with the clerk's office. The proposed modified plan and a proposed order must be attached to the motion to modify. The pro se debtor must, within five (5) days, mail a copy of the amended plan, the motion to modify, and a proposed order to each creditor and

party in interest. The pro se debtor must also file a certificate of service, which complies with L.B.R. 9013–2. After the certificate of service is filed, the clerk will then issue and send to creditors and parties in interest a passive notice setting the objection date on the post confirmation amended plan.

(j) Waiver of Objections to Chapter 12 or Chapter 13 Plans. The failure to file a timely objection, upon notice, is deemed a waiver of all objections to the amended plan and any prior plans, and the court may confirm the amended plan without further notice or hearing.

(k) Time for Filing Chapter 12 or Chapter 13 Amended Plans. Within thirty (30) days after an order is entered that determines whether a lien may be avoided, determines the priority or extent of a lien, or resolves an objection to a claim, the debtor must file an amended plan to provide for the allowed amount and priority of the claim, if the allowed amount or priority differs from the claim as stated in the plan.

[Effective January 1, 2005. Amended effective January 1, 2008; June 18, 2008; June 23, 2008; December 1, 2011; September 1, 2014.]

RULE 3015–3. CHAPTER 12 OR CHAPTER 13—CONFIRMATION HEARING

(a) Chapter 13 Pre–Confirmation Certifications. Debtor must file with the clerk a Pre–Confirmation Certification in conformity with L.B.F. 3015–3(a) and submit to the Chapter 13 Trustee a Certification Regarding Domestic Support Obligation(s) in conformity with L.B.F. 3015–3(b), if applicable, at least twenty-four (24) hours prior to the time of the hearing.

(b) Chapter 12 Pre–Confirmation Certification. Debtor must file with the clerk a Pre–Confirmation Certification in conformity with L.B.F. 3015–3(c) certifying compliance with 11 U.S.C. § 1225(a)(7) at least twenty-four (24) hours prior to the time of the hearing.

(c) Appearances at Hearing. Neither the debtor nor debtor's counsel need appear at the confirmation hearing if:

(1) No objections to the chapter 13 plan have been timely filed or any timely filed objections have been withdrawn; and

(2) The Pre–Confirmation Certifications have been filed in conformity with L.B.R. 3015–3(a).

If neither the debtor nor debtor's counsel appear at the hearing under this subsection and a party in interest appears and is permitted to lodge an untimely objection, the court will reschedule the hearing on confirmation. Otherwise, debtor and debtor's counsel must attend all scheduled confirmation hearings.

(d) Payment of Filing Fee. The entire case filing fee must be paid prior to the confirmation of any chapter 13 plan. Provided, the requirements of this subparagraph may be waived by the court, upon motion for cause.

[Former Rule 3015–4 effective January 1, 2008. Amended effective April 4, 2011. Redesignated as Rule 3015–3 effective December 1, 2011. Amended effective March 1, 2013; June 1, 2016.]

RULE 3015–4. CHAPTER 13—ADEQUATE PROTECTION PAYMENTS

For cases filed on or after October 17, 2005, the debtor must make pre-confirmation adequate protection payments as follows:

(a) Adequate Protection Payments to Lessors. Adequate protection payments to a lessor of personal property must be made by the debtor directly to the lessor if the debtor's plan so provides. If the debtor's plan provides for the lease payments to be made by the trustee, the debtor's plan payments must be made timely so that the trustee may begin prompt distribution.

(b) Adequate Protection Payments to Secured Creditors. Pre–confirmation adequate protection payments to a secured creditor must be made by the debtor directly to the secured creditor if the debtor's plan so provides. If the plan does not so provide, the adequate protection payments must be paid to the trustee and not directly to the secured creditor. The adequate protection payments must be made timely so that the trustee may begin prompt distribution.

(c) Creditor Identification. The debtor's plan must separately identify by creditor name, address, account number, and monthly payment amount each creditor entitled to receive adequate protection payments.

(d) Adequate Protection Payment Distribution. The trustee will distribute preconfirmation adequate protection payments to any creditor identified in the plan as receiving payments from trustee and for which a proof of claim has been filed, less the trustee's statutory compensation and expenses, as soon as practicable after receipt of said payment from the debtor.

[Former Rule 3015–5 effective January 1, 2008. Amended effective July 20, 2009; August 7, 2009; April 4, 2011. Redesignated as Rule 3015–4 effective December 1, 2011. Amended effective September 1, 2014.]

RULE 3015–5. ENTRY OF CHAPTER 13 DISCHARGE

A Chapter 13 discharge will not be entered unless the debtor has filed, after the completion of plan payments, the Chapter 13 Debtor's Certifications Regarding Domestic Support Obligations and Section 522(q) (Official Form 2830) and has completed an instructional course concerning personal financial management described in 11 U.S.C. §§ 111 and 1328(g)(1), and either the debtor or the course provider has filed a Certification About a Financial Management Course (Official Form 423).

[Former Rule 3015–6 effective April 4, 2011. Redesignated as Rule 3015–5 effective December 1, 2011. Amended effective September 1, 2014; June 1, 2016.]

COMMENTS:

L.B.R. 3015–5 was amended effective June 1, 2016, to provide for the use of Official Form 423—Certification About a Financial Management Court and to eliminate L.B.F. 3015–5.

RULE 3015–6. CHAPTER 12—INDIVIDUAL DEBTOR DISCHARGE

For all individual chapter 12 cases, a discharge will not be entered unless the debtor has filed, within seven (7) days after completion of plan payments, an Individual Chapter 12 Debtor's Certification Regarding Domestic Support Obligations (L.B.F. 3015–6), in conformity with the requirements of 11 U.S.C. § 1228(a) and (f).

[Effective March 1, 2013.]

RULE 3016–1. DISCLOSURE STATEMENT— GENERAL

(a) Contents. Unless the court orders otherwise, any disclosure statement or amended disclosure statement must include the following information in addition to all other information required by applicable law:

(1) an introductory narrative summarizing the plan, which must include:

(A) an identification of each class of claims or interests;

(B) the composition of each class as to number and type of creditor or interest;

(C) the amount of claims and interests (specifying any that are known to be disputed and how they will be treated under the plan);

(D) the amount (dollar and/or percentages) to be paid to each class and the timing of payments to be made under the plan; and

(E) all sources and amounts of funding in reasonable detail;

(2) a summary exhibit setting forth a liquidation analysis as if assets of the debtor were to be liquidated under chapter 7; and

(3) a narrative summarizing the scheduled assets and liabilities as of the date of the order for relief:

(A) reciting the disposition of assets during the chapter 11 case;

(B) describing the process for handling initial and subsequent disbursements under the plan; and

(C) identifying persons responsible for making disbursements under the plan.

(b) Disclosure Statement Accompanying Reorganization Plan. Unless a liquidating plan is proposed, each disclosure statement must also include a projected cash flow and budget, including plan payments over the shorter of the life of the plan or three fiscal years following confirmation, showing all anticipated income and expenses.

[Former Rule 3016–2 effective January 1, 2005. Renumbered as 3016–1 effective September 1, 2014.]

RULE 3017–1. DISCLOSURE STATEMENT—APPROVAL

(a) Notice and Hearing. Upon receipt of a disclosure statement, the court will issue an order and notice for hearing on the disclosure statement. The plan proponent filing the disclosure statement must mail the order and notice to all parties listed in F.R.B.P. 3017(a).

(b) Amended Disclosure Statements. With every amended disclosure statement, the plan proponent must file a certification in substantial compliance with L.B.F. 3017–1. The plan proponent must serve copies of the amended disclosure statement on parties in interest whose claims or interests may be affected by the changes and notify them of a new objection date as directed by the court.

(c) Transmission of Approved Disclosure Statement and Order. After entry of an order approving the disclosure statement, the plan proponent must mail the order, the plan or a court-approved summary of the plan, the disclosure statement, and a ballot for accepting or rejecting the plan conforming to Class [ ] Ballot for Accepting or Rejecting Plan of Reorganization (Official Form 314) to all creditors and interest holders. The ballot must state that ballots are to be returned to the plan proponent and not to the clerk.

[Effective January 1, 2005. Amended effective December 1, 2015.]

RULE 3018–1. BALLOTS— VOTING ON PLANS

(a) Service of Ballots and Report of Results of Balloting. Any ballot accepting or rejecting a plan must be served on the plan proponent as specified on the ballot. No less than seven (7) days before the confirmation hearing, the plan proponent must file a report of the balloting with the clerk and serve a copy on the debtor (unless the debtor is the plan proponent) and each committee. The proponent must retain the ballots.

(b) Form of Report of Balloting. The report of balloting must substantially conform to L.B.F. 3018–1.

[Effective January 1, 2005. Amended effective January 1, 2008; December 1, 2009; September 1, 2014.]

RULE 3019–1. CHAPTER 11—AMENDMENTS TO PLAN

With every plan that is amended or modified before confirmation, a plan proponent must file a certification in substantial compliance with L.B.F. 3019–1. The plan proponent must serve copies of the amended plan on parties in interest whose claims or interests may be affected by the changes and notify them of a new objection date as directed by the court.

[Effective January 1, 2005.]

RULE 3020–1. CHAPTER 11—INDIVIDUAL DEBTOR CONFIRMATION

For all individual chapter 11 cases, a confirmation order will not be entered unless the debtor has filed, at least seven (7) days before the confirmation hearing, an Individual Chapter 11 Debtor's Certification Regarding Domestic Support Obligations (L.B.F. 3020–1) in conformity with the requirements of 11 U.S.C. § 1129(a)(14).

[Effective March 1, 2013. Amended effective September 1, 2014.]

COMMENTS:

L.B.R. 3020–1 was amended effective September 1, 2014, to clarify that the requirement of the Individual Chapter 11 Debtor's Certification Regarding Domestic Support Obligations is a condition for confirmation, not discharge.

RULE 3022–1. FINAL REPORT/DECREE (CHAPTER 11)

(a) Motion. A motion for a final decree must certify that the estate is fully administered and list all pending adversary proceedings related to the case.

(b) Service of Motion. The motion must be served on all secured creditors and any committee appointed under 11 U.S.C. § 1102, or its authorized agent. If no committee of unsecured creditors has been appointed under § 1102, the motion must be served on the creditors included on the list filed under F.R.B.P. 1007(d).

[Effective January 1, 2005. Amended effective January 1, 2008.]

PART IV. THE DEBTOR: DUTIES AND BENEFITS

RULE 4001–1. AUTOMATIC STAY—RELIEF FROM

(a) **Filing a Motion for Relief from the Automatic Stay.** A motion for relief from the automatic stay must be filed using the self-scheduling procedures set forth in L.B.R. 9002–1. Unless service is made electronically through the ECF system, the movant must serve the motion and semi-passive notice upon the persons specified under F.R.B.P. 4001 and L.B.R. 4001–6.

(b) **Combination of Motions.** A motion for relief from the stay may not be combined with a request for any other relief.

(c) **Proposed Order.** Each motion for relief from the automatic stay must be accompanied by a proposed order granting the relief requested in the motion.

(d) **Contents of Motion.** The motion seeking relief must state the following:

(1) the location of the property;

(2) the priority of the movant's lien relative to any other liens against the property, if known without further inquiry;

(3) the contract amount of current monthly installments; and

(4) the stage to which debt enforcement or foreclosure actions had progressed when the order for relief was entered.

(e) **Debtor's Principal Residence.** If relief is sought for a post-petition default in a chapter 11 or 13 case with respect to property that is a debtor's principal residence, the movant must file L.B.F. 4001–1, signed by the movant, or an officer or employee of the movant, with the motion.

(f) **Concurrence in Motion.** The movant must seek the concurrence of the debtor and of the trustee, if one has been appointed in the case. The movant must file a certificate with the motion for relief stating whether concurrence was obtained. If a certificate of concurrence/nonconcurrence is not filed with the motion for relief, the court may deny the motion sua sponte.

[Effective January 1, 2005. Amended effective January 1, 2008; October 8, 2008; December 1, 2009; March 1, 2013; September 1, 2014.]

RULE 4001–2. CASH COLLATERAL

(a) **Filing a Motion to Authorize or Prohibit Use of Cash Collateral.** A motion seeking to authorize or prohibit the use of cash collateral must be filed using the self-scheduling procedures set forth in L.B.R. 9002–1. Unless service is made electronically through the ECF system, the movant must serve the motion and hearing required notice upon the persons specified under F.R.B.P. 4001 and L.B.R. 4001–6.

(b) **Required Disclosure of Certain Provisions of Financing Motion.** Each motion to use cash collateral must comply with L.B.R. 4001–3(c), (d), and (e), and interim and final relief must be granted, denied, or conditioned as provided under L.B.R. 4001–3(f) and (g).

[Effective January 1, 2005. Amended effective January 1, 2008; September 1, 2014.]

RULE 4001–3. OBTAINING CREDIT

(a) **Filing a Motion to Obtain Credit.** A motion seeking authority to obtain credit must be filed using the self-scheduling procedures set forth in L.B.R. 9002–1. Unless service is made electronically through the ECF system, the movant must serve the motion and semi-passive notice upon the persons specified under F.R.B.P. 4001 and L.B.R. 4001–6.

(b) **Credit Agreement.** Each motion for authority to obtain credit must be accompanied by the proposed credit agreement.

(c) **Required Disclosure of Certain Provisions of Financing Motion, Order, or Stipulation—Chapter 9 or Chapter 11 Cases.** All motions seeking authorization to use cash collateral and all motions for authority to obtain credit—collectively, the "Financing Motions"—must:

(1) recite whether the proposed form of order, underlying cash collateral stipulation, or loan agreement contains any provision of the type indicated below;

(2) identify the location of any such provision in the proposed form of order, cash collateral stipulation, or loan agreement; and

(3) state the justification for the inclusion of such provision:

(A) Provisions that grant cross-collateralization protection—other than replacement liens or other adequate protection—to the prepetition secured creditor (i.e., clauses that secure prepetition debt by postpetition assets in which the secured creditor would not otherwise have a security interest by virtue of its prepetition security agreement or applicable law).

(B) Provisions or findings of fact that bind the estate or parties in interest with respect to validity, perfection, priority, or amount of the secured creditor's prepetition lien or debt or the waiver of claims against the secured creditor without first giving parties in interest at least seventy-five (75) days from the entry of the order for relief and the creditors' committee, if formed, at least sixty (60) days from the date of its formation to investigate such matters.

(C) Provisions that seek to waive any rights the estate may have under 11 U.S.C. § 506(c).

(D) Provisions that grant to the prepetition secured creditor liens on the debtor's claims and causes of action arising under 11 U.S.C. §§ 544, 545, 547, 548, and 549.

(E) Provisions that deem prepetition secured debt to be postpetition debt or that use postpetition loans from a prepetition secured creditor to pay part or all of that secured creditor's prepetition debt, other than as provided under 11 U.S.C. § 552(b).

(F) Provisions that provide treatment for the professionals retained by a committee appointed by the United States trustee different from that provided for the professionals retained by the debtor with respect to a professional fee carveout, and provisions that limit the committee counsel's use of the carveout.

(G) Provisions that prime any secured lien without the consent of the lienholder.

(H) Provisions that release the secured creditor from lender liability.

(I) Provisions that grant the lender expedited relief from the automatic stay under 11 U.S.C. § 362 or relief from the automatic stay without further order of court.

(d) Summary of Essential Terms. Any Financing Motion must provide a summary of the essential terms of the proposed use of cash collateral or financing, including:

(1) the amount to be borrowed or advanced on both an interim and final basis;

(2) the terms of repayment;

(3) the interest rate;

(4) the description of any collateral;

(5) events of default; and

(6) limitations on the use of funds.

(e) Budget. Any Financing Motion must include a budget covering the time period during which the proposed financing will remain in effect. The budget must state in as much detail as is reasonably practical the amount of the projected receipts and disbursements during the period covered by the budget.

(f) Interim Relief. If a Financing Motion is filed with the court on or shortly after the date of the order for relief, the court may grant interim relief pending review by parties in interest of the proposed debtor in possession financing arrangements. Interim relief

will be granted only to avoid immediate and irreparable harm to the estate pending a final hearing. In the absence of extraordinary circumstances, the court will not approve interim financing orders that include any of the provisions previously identified under L.B.R. 4001–3(c)(3).

(g) Final Approval of Financing Motion. A final order may be entered only after notice and hearing under F.R.B.P. 4001. If formation of a creditors' committee is anticipated, a final hearing may not be held until at least fourteen (14) days following the organizational meeting of the creditors' committee contemplated by 11 U.S.C. § 1102 unless the court, upon motion, orders otherwise.

[Effective January 1, 2005. Amended effective January 1, 2008; December 1, 2009; September 1, 2014.]

RULE 4001–4. FILING A MOTION SEEKING TO PROHIBIT OR CONDITION THE USE, SALE, OR LEASE OF PROPERTY OTHER THAN CASH COLLATERAL

Unless service is made electronically through the ECF system, the movant must serve the motion seeking to prohibit or condition the use sale, or lease of property and semi-passive notice upon the persons specified under F.R.B.P. 4001 and L.B.R. 4001–6.

[Effective January 1, 2005. Amended effective January 1, 2008; September 1, 2014.]

RULE 4001–5. MOTIONS TO EXTEND THE AUTOMATIC STAY UNDER SECTION 362(c)(3) AND MOTIONS TO IMPOSE AUTOMATIC STAY UNDER SECTION 362(c)(4)

(a) Contents. If the stay is to be extended or imposed with regard to all creditors, then the motion must so indicate. If the motion seeks only to extend the stay or to impose the stay as to particular creditors, then the motion must identify those particular creditors. The motion also must state with particularity why the later filing has been made in good faith.

(b) Service. A motion that seeks to extend or impose the stay as to all creditors must be served upon all creditors. A motion that seeks to extend or impose the stay only as to particular creditors must be served upon those particular creditors.

(c) Affidavit. The movant may file a verified affidavit setting forth the substantial changes in the financial or personal affairs of the debtor since the dismissal of the next most previous bankruptcy case. In the absence of timely filed objections, the court may enter an order extending the automatic stay without a hearing where a sufficient affidavit has been filed.

[Former Rule 4001–5 effective January 1, 2008. Renumbered as Rule 4001–6 effective January 1. 2008. Amended effective December 1, 2009; September 1, 2014.]

RULE 4001–6. SERVICE OF MOTIONS UNDER F.R.B.P 4001

In addition to the parties identified in F.R.B.P. 4001, the following motions must also be served upon creditors listed on the schedules as holding claims secured by the asset(s) identified in the motion:

(a) A motion for relief from the stay;

(b) A motion seeking an order prohibiting or conditioning the use, sale, or lease of property;

(c) A motion to use cash collateral;

(d) A motion for authority to obtain credit;

(e) Any agreement regarding any of the preceding motions;

(f) A motion to extend, continue or impose the automatic stay; or

(g) A motion to confirm the termination or absence of the automatic stay.

[Effective January 1, 2005. Amended effective December 1, 2009.]

RULE 4003–1. EXEMPTIONS

(a) Notice of Response Date to Objection. When an objection is filed to a debtor's exemptions, the clerk will give twenty-one (21) days notice by mail of the time fixed for filing a response to the objection.

(b) Hearing Date for Objection to Exemptions. Except as provided in subdivision (c), the clerk will set a hearing date on the objection if a response is filed by the debtor.

(c) Request for Hearing Required. If the chapter 13 trustee files an objection to exemptions, the clerk

will not set a hearing date until requested by the debtor or the trustee.

[Effective January 1, 2005. Amended effective December 1, 2009.]

RULE 4004–1. MOTION TO DEFER ENTRY OF DISCHARGE ORDER

A motion to defer entry of the discharge order for the purposes of obtaining additional time to file the Certification About a Financial Management Course (Official Form 423) must indicate why debtor is unable to obtain and file the certification within the required time period.

[Effective January 1, 2008. Amended effective June 1, 2016.]

RULE 4006–1. CLOSING CHAPTER 7 OR CHAPTER 13 CASES WITHOUT DISCHARGE

If the Certification About a Financial Management Course (Official Form 423) is not filed in accordance with F.R.B.P. 1007(b)(7) and (c) and the time limits contained therein, the clerk may close the case without the issuance of an order of discharge and notify creditors thereof.

[Effective January 1, 2008. Amended effective December 1, 2009; September 1, 2014; June 1, 2016.]

RULE 4008–1. REAFFIRMATION

(a) General Procedure. A reaffirmation agreement must be substantially in compliance with L.B.F. 4008–1(a). A reaffirmation agreement must be accompanied by the Cover Sheet for Reaffirmation Agreement (Official Form 427). If the presumption arises that the reaffirmation agreement will impose an undue hardship on the debtor, and if the presumption is not rebutted to the satisfaction of the court by a statement on the reaffirmation agreement that identifies additional sources of funds to make the agreed payments, the court will set the matter for hearing.

(b) Hearings. Hearings will be held on all reaffirmation agreements filed by pro se debtors and debtors whose counsel has not signed the certification page of the agreement. Hearing will be held on any agreement which, in the judgment of the court, may impose an undue hardship on the debtor.

[Effective January 1, 2008. Amended effective December 1, 2009; June 1, 2016.]

COMMENTS:

L.B.R. 4008–1 was amended effective December 1, 2009, to provide for the filing of a reaffirmation cover sheet in accordance with F.R.B.P. 4008 and to delete the former requirement for submission of a proposed order complying with L.B.F. 4008–1(b), which form was eliminated as part of the amendments.

PART V. COURTS AND CLERKS

RULE 5001–1. CLERK'S OFFICE

Except as otherwise ordered by the court, or when closed by federal or official holiday, the clerk's offices in Wilkes–Barre and Harrisburg will be open to the public from 9:00 a.m. to 4:00 p.m., Monday through Friday.

[Effective January 1, 2005. Amended effective January 1, 2008; December 1, 2011; September 1, 2014.]

RULE 5004–1. DISQUALIFICATION

(a) **Motion.** A request for disqualification of a judge must be made by written motion. If a hearing is set, the clerk will provide to the movant an order setting the hearing date. The movant must serve the order upon:

(1) the debtor; and

(2) if disqualification from the entire case is not sought, all parties that are engaged in litigation before the court with regard to an adversary proceeding or contested matter from which the basis for disqualification arose unless service is made on such parties electronically through the ECF system.

(b) **Oral Motion.** The motion may be made orally in open court if grounds for disqualification are first presented during proceedings before the judge.

[Effective January 1, 2005. Amended effective January 1, 2008.]

RULE 5005–1. FILING PAPERS— REQUIREMENTS—PLACE OF FILING

Unless otherwise provided, a paper document that is permitted or required to be filed by the Local Bankruptcy Rules must be filed in the clerk's office. A paper document must not be filed with the judge or the judge's staff unless the bankruptcy clerk's office is closed. In the event a paper document is filed with the judge, the filing date must be noted thereon, and it must be transmitted to the clerk. A bankruptcy paper may be filed with the district court clerk's office only in an emergency.

[Effective January 1, 2005. Amended effective January 1, 2008; December 1, 2011.]

COMMENTS:

Subpart (b) of L.B.R. 5005–1 was reworded and renumbered as L.B.R. 9018–1 effective December 1, 2011.

RULE 5005–2. FILING PAPERS— NUMBER OF COPIES; TIME– STAMPED COPIES

(a) **Petition and Supporting Documents.** In all chapters, only the original petition and supporting documents must be filed.

(b) **No Copies of Electronic Filings Required.** Except when paper copies are required by a local rule or by court order, when a petition, pleading, or any other paper is filed electronically, no copies are required.

(c) **Stamped "Filed" Copies.** To receive a time-stamped copy of a document, the filing party must provide the clerk with a copy of the document and a self-addressed, stamped envelope.

[Effective January 1, 2005. Amended effective January 1, 2008.]

RULE 5005–3. ELECTRONIC FILING

(a) **Filing of Documents.** Pursuant to Miscellaneous Order 5:05–mp–50007, except as provided in paragraph (b) of this rule, documents must be filed, signed, and verified by electronic means in accordance with the Administrative Procedures available on the court's website (www.pamb.uscourts.gov). A document filed under this rule constitutes a written document for the purpose of these Local Bankruptcy Rules, the Federal Rules of Bankruptcy Procedure, and 11 U.S.C. § 107.

(b) **Filing of Proofs of Claim.** Notwithstanding the requirements of paragraph (a), pursuant to Miscellaneous Order 5:14–mp–00003,* claims may be filed, amended, or withdrawn through the court's Electronic Proof of Claim (ePOC) system without the need to register or login as a user in the court's ECF system (CM/ECF). Any claim filed, amended, or withdrawn electronically through the ePOC system will constitute the filer's approved signature and have the same force and effect as if the authorized individual signed a paper copy of the proof of claim form, amendment, or withdrawal.

(c) **Temporary Paper Filing.** An attorney who is not a registered CM/ECF filer may file initial papers in person, by facsimile, or by email after seeking permission from the court as set forth in Miscellaneous Order 5:05–mp–50007. Before any additional papers are filed, the attorney must apply for and obtain a CM/ECF login and password. Registration may be completed through the court's website: www.pamb.uscourts.gov using "Electronic Filing Registration" under the Court Info tab.

(d) **CM/ECF Filer Systems Failure.** A registered CM/ECF filer may file papers in person, by facsimile, or by email for up to seventy-two (72) hours when electronic filing is not possible due to a failure in the CM/ECF filer's systems, including, without limitation, hardware, software, or internet connection. Any filing made by means other than CM/ECF must be accompanied by an affidavit stating why the document was not filed electronically.

[Former Rule 5005–4 effective January 1, 2005. Amended effective January 1, 2008; December 1, 2011. Renumbered as Rule 5005–3 and amended effective September 1, 2014. Amended effective June 1, 2016.]

* [**Publisher's Note:** Miscellaneous Order 5–14–mp–00034 is reproduced herein under the heading "Electronic Case Filing", *post.*]

COMMENTS:

L.B.R. 5005–3 was amended effective June 1, 2016, to provide for temporary paper filings by an attorney who is not a registered CM/ECF filer and to provide for temporary paper filings for a registered CM/ECF filer who cannot file electronically due to a failure of his or her own systems.

RULE 5005–4. FILINGS DURING TECHNICAL FAILURES

In the event of a technical failure, as defined in L.B.R. 9001–1, an electronic filer may use any of the following filing methods:

(a) file the documents as a PDF attachment to an email sent to the following address: PAMB_ECF_Failure@pamb.uscourts.gov;

(b) file the documents in person by bringing the documents to the clerk's office in paper, accompanied by an electronic storage format (i.e., flash drive, CD–ROM) that contains the document in PDF format without any password requirement;

(c) file the documents via facsimile to: 570-829-0249 (Wilkes–Barre) or 717-901-2822 (Harrisburg); or

(d) seek appropriate relief from the court or proceed pursuant to any generally applicable order that may have been entered addressing the technical failure.

Electronic filers are cautioned that the court's ability to grant relief may be limited by F.R.B.P. 9006(b).

[Effective June 1, 2016.]

COMMENTS:

L.B.R. 5005–4 was adopted effective June 1, 2016, to provide for filing alternatives in the event of a technical failure as now defined in L.B.R. 9001–1.

RULE 5005–5. FILING PAPERS AFTER HOURS

(a) **After Hours Filings.** Except as otherwise authorized by the court, non–ECF filers may file petitions and other papers by facsimile only pursuant to the provisions of this rule.

(b) **Time and Manner of Filing.** Papers may be filed by facsimile to the Harrisburg or Wilkes–Barre facsimile numbers indicated on the court's website (www.pamb.uscourts.gov) when the clerk's office is not open. After 4:00 p.m. EST, and before Midnight (12:00 a.m.) EST, transmit by facsimile only the first page and the signature page of the document.

(c) **Filing of Original Document.** The entire original paper document, together with any required filing fee, must be filed in person and time-stamped by the clerk no later than 4:00 p.m. EST on the next business day after the facsimile filing when the clerk's office is open.

(d) **Clerk's Procedures Concerning Facsimile Documents.** If the original document is not timely filed after the facsimile transmittal, the clerk will note that fact and the facsimile will have no force or effect. The clerk's office will not acknowledge the filing of a document or assign a case number or adversary number to a document unless the original is timely filed pursuant to the provisions of this rule. Upon timely receipt of the original document and any required fee, the clerk will stamp the following notation on the document: "This document is deemed filed on _____(date) pursuant to L.B.R. 5005–5—Filing Papers After Hours." Documents filed in accordance with this rule will be deemed filed on the date and at the time printed on the document by the facsimile machine in the clerk's office which received the facsimile.

[Former Rule 5005–5 effective April 4, 2011. Amended effective December 1, 2011. Renumbered as Rule 5005–4 effective September 1, 2014. Renumbered as Rule 5005–5 and amended effective June 1, 2016.]

RULE 5010–1. REOPENING CASES

A motion to reopen a case, which may be granted summarily, must be accompanied by the appropriate filing fee unless waived by the court. The filing fee may be waived if the case is opened to correct an administrative error, to assert the protection of the discharge injunction, or for cause shown. The motion must be served on:

(a) the debtor; and

(b) any other party as directed by the court.

[Effective January 1, 2005. Amended effective January 1, 2008; April 4, 2011.]

RULE 5011–1. WITHDRAWAL OF REFERENCE

(a) **Filing of Motion.** The movant must file a motion, proposed order, and supporting brief with the clerk of the bankruptcy court. The clerk of the bankruptcy court will transmit the motion and supporting documents to the district court. All documents filed after the initial motion, proposed order, and supporting brief must be filed with the clerk of the district court.

(b) Motion Contents. The motion must address the following:

(1) whether the proceeding for which withdrawal is being sought is core under 28 U.S.C. § 157(b) or non-core under 28 U.S.C. § 157(c) and, if core, whether the bankruptcy court lacks the constitutional authority to enter a final order or judgment;

(2) whether withdrawal of the reference is permissive under 28 U.S.C. § 157(d);

(3) whether withdrawal of the reference is mandatory under 28 U.S.C. § 157(d).

(c) Notice of the Motion. The movant must provide notice to all creditors and parties in interest if the motion requests withdrawal of the entire bankruptcy case or provide notice to the parties in the adversary proceeding if the motion requests withdrawal of an adversary proceeding or counts within the proceeding.

(d) Objections to the Motion. Any party opposing the motion must file with the district court and serve on the movant and other interested parties an objection and brief within fourteen (14) days after service of the motion and a supporting brief.

(e) Bankruptcy Court Report and Recommendations. After the time for filing objections has expired, the bankruptcy judge assigned to the bankruptcy case will file with the district court, within fourteen (14) days, a report and recommendation on the motion to withdraw the reference. Once the report and recommendation is submitted by the bankruptcy judge, any party may object to the report and recommendations within fourteen (14) days after being served with a copy thereof. Thereafter, the motion will be ripe for disposition by the district court.

(f) Procedure After Grant of the Motion. If the district court grants the motion, all further proceedings will be governed by the Rules of Court for the Middle District of Pennsylvania.

[Effective June 1, 2016.]

COMMENTS:

L.B.R. 5011–1 was adopted effective June 1, 2016, to provide the procedure for filing a motion to withdraw the reference.

PART VI.   COLLECTION AND LIQUIDATION OF THE ESTATE

RULE 6002–1.   ACCOUNTING BY PRIOR CUSTODIAN OF PROPERTY OF THE ESTATE

A prior custodian must submit a report and accounting to the United States trustee that contains sufficient detail to inform the trustee or any other party in interest of the custodian's activities while in possession of what is now the property of the estate. No particular format is required under this rule.

[Effective January 1, 2005.]

RULE 6004–1.   USE, SALE, OR LEASE OF PROPERTY

(a) Sale on Notice. A sale of assets, other than in the ordinary course of business, under and subject to liens, may be conducted, on notice, pursuant to 11 U.S.C. § 363(b). The notice of sale is subject to the notice requirements of this rule.

(b) Sale Upon Motion. Any sale on motion is subject to the notice requirements of this rule. Any motion for a free and clear sale is subject to the notice requirements of this rule and to the additional requirements of L.B.R. 6004–5.

(c) Sale Notices. When the proposed use, sale, or lease of property is upon notice or motion (unless subject to the exceptions in F.R.B.P. 6004(d) or L.B.R. 9075–1), the required notice must include:

(1) the caption of the case;

(2) the name and address of the seller;

(3) a general description of the property to be sold;

(4) the place, date, and time the property may be examined prior to the sale or an explanation of how an interested party may be afforded an opportunity to examine the property prior to the sale;

(5) the terms and conditions of sale, including the terms of any pending offers, or minimum bid requirements, or breakup fee provisions;

(6) the date, time, and place of any public sale;

(7) whether the sale is subject to higher and better offers and how such offers must be submitted;

(8) in any private sale, the identity of the purchaser and any affiliation or relationship with the debtor or an insider of the debtor;

(9) the last date by which objections to the sale must be filed with the court—which must be not less than twenty-one (21) days after the notice is mailed, unless the court shortens the time under F.R.B.P. 9006 or directs another method of giving notice; and

(10) a statement that inquiries regarding the sale should be directed to the seller or their counsel or agent and not to the clerk.

(d) Service. Unless the court directs otherwise, and unless service is made electronically through the ECF system, the notice of sale must be served on the following:

(1) the debtor;

(2) the trustee, if any;

(3) indenture trustees, if any;

(4) all creditors;

(5) all committees appointed under the Bankruptcy Code, if any;

(6) the United States trustee;

(7) the United States as required by F.R.B.P. 2002(j); and

(8) all holders of liens or encumbrances against the property.

(e) Address for Service. Service of a notice of sale must be made at the address set forth in any request for notices filed under F.R.B.P. 2002(g)(1). If a request has not been filed, the notice must be served under F.R.B.P. 2002(g)(2) unless a different address is listed in a later-filed proof of claim. In the latter instance, the address stated in the proof of claim must be used.

[Effective January 1, 2005. Amended effective January 1, 2008; December 1, 2009; May 1, 2012; June 1, 2016.]

RULE 6004–2. OBJECTIONS TO SECTION 363(b) SALE

Any party who objects to a proposed sale must file an objection within the time period fixed by the notice of sale. The objecting party must serve a copy of the objection on the seller and the seller's counsel of record.

[Effective January 1, 2005.]

RULE 6004–3. PUBLIC SALE BIDDING PROCEDURES IN A CHAPTER 11 CASE

In the case of a public sale conducted in a chapter 11 case by other than a professional auctioneer, the seller must file a sale procedure motion which will detail the bidding procedures, including the following:

(1) any minimum bid requirements;

(2) any minimum bid increment requirements;

(3) whether any bidder who has a contractual right to a topping or breakup fee will receive a credit equal to the breakup or topping fee when bidding on the property; and

(4) a provision that all bidding must take place outside the presence of the court.

[Effective January 1, 2008; former Rule 6004–3 renumbered as Local Rule 6004–5. Amended effective May 1, 2012.]

RULE 6004–4. SPECIAL SALE PROVISIONS IN A CHAPTER 11 CASE

(a) Breakup/Topping Fees and Expense Reimbursement. When the seller in a chapter 11 case is seeking court approval of a breakup or topping fee or other bidding protections (such as the estate's proposed payment of out-of-pocket expenses incurred by a bidder or contract purchaser), the sale motion must include the following:

(1) the name of the party entitled to the breakup or topping fee;

(2) the dollar amount or the method to calculate the breakup or topping fee; and

(3) any relationship between the seller and the party eligible for the breakup or topping fee.

(b) Sale to Insider. If the seller seeks court approval of a sale to an insider of the debtor, the motion must include the following information:

(1) the name of the insider;

(2) the relationship of the insider to the debtor; and

(3) the measures that have and will be taken to ensure the fairness of the sale process.

(c) Agreements With Management. Any motion seeking approval of the private sale of an ongoing business must disclose the following:

(1) whether the proposed purchaser has entered into any agreements with management or key employees concerning compensation or future employment;

(2) the material terms of any agreements between the proposed purchaser and management or key employees; and

(3) what measures have or will be taken to ensure the fairness of the sale in light of such agreements with management or key employees.

(d) Tax Exemption. If the debtor is seeking to have a sale declared exempt from taxes under 11 U.S.C. § 1146(a), the sale motion must disclose the type of tax (i.e., recording tax, stamp tax, use tax, capital gains tax) for which the exemption is sought. The debtor must also identify the state or states in which the affected property is located. The sale motion must state whether or not the chapter 11 plan has been confirmed.

(e) Relief From F.R.B.P. 6004(h). If the seller seeks relief from the stay imposed by F.R.B.P.

6004(h), the sale motion must state the basis for the request.

[Effective January 1, 2008. Amended effective December 1, 2009; May 1, 2012.]

COMMENTS:

L.B.R. 6004–4(d) was amended effective December 1, 2009, to comply with the decision of Florida Dept. of Revenue v. Piccadilly Cafeterias, Inc., 128 S.Ct. 2326 (U.S. 2008).

RULE 6004–5. SALES OF PROPERTY FREE AND CLEAR OF LIENS— SECTION 363(f)

(a) **Notice.** All free and clear sales are subject to the applicable notice requirements of L.B.R. 6004–1(b), (c), and (d).

(b) **Motion.** A sale of property free and clear of liens must be commenced by motion, except as provided in subdivision (c) below. A motion for a free and clear sale must name as respondents all parties claiming an interest in the property.

(c) **Complaint.** A sale of property free and clear of liens must be brought as an adversary proceeding and commenced by a complaint under Part VII of the Federal Rules of Bankruptcy Procedure and Part VII of the Local Bankruptcy Rules when the seller also seeks:

(1) to determine the validity, priority, or extent of a lien or other interest in property, other than the avoidance of a lien or other transfer of property exempt under 11 U.S.C. § 522(f); or

(2) to obtain approval under 11 U.S.C. § 363(h) for the sale of both the interest of the estate and of a co-owner in the property unless the concurrence of the co-owner has been obtained.

(d) **Order.** When a motion is filed for a sale free and clear of liens, the clerk will issue an order fixing a response date and a hearing date. A hearing will be held only if a responsive pleading is timely filed, unless a hearing is requested by the moving party or is ordered by the court. Otherwise, an order granting the relief requested will be entered without a hearing.

(e) **Service of Motion.** The seller must serve a copy of the motion and the order referred to in subparagraph (d) upon all lienholders and other parties claiming an interest in the property and their counsel of record.

(f) **Service of Notice.** Unless the court directs otherwise, the seller must serve the notice on the respondent and any parties referenced in L.B.R.

6004–1(c), at least twenty-one (21) days before the hearing on the sale.

[Former Rule 6004–3 effective January 1, 2005; renumbered Rule 60045 and amended effective January 1, 2008. Amended effective December 1, 2009; May 1, 2012; September 1, 2014.]

RULE 6005–1. APPRAISERS, REAL ESTATE AGENTS, AND AUCTIONEERS

(a) **Form of Application.** All applications must conform to L.B.R. 2014–1.

(b) **Payment of Compensation.** An appraiser, real estate agent, or auctioneer may receive compensation and reimbursement of expenses from the proceeds of any sale approved by the court without filing a separate application for the approval of compensation and expenses under the following conditions:

(1) the terms for the payment of compensation and reimbursement of expenses were disclosed in the application for employment;

(2) the order approving retention of the appraiser, real estate agent, or auctioneer approved the compensation arrangement proposed in the application for employment; and

(3) the order approving the sale authorized the payment of compensation and expenses to the appraiser, real estate agent, or auctioneer.

[Effective January 1, 2005. Amended effective January 1, 2008.]

RULE 6006–1. EXECUTORY CONTRACTS

(a) **Motion.** A motion for the assumption, rejection, or assignment of an executory contract or unexpired lease must be filed in conformity with F.R.B.P. 6006.

(b) **Notice.** A notice for the assumption, rejection, or assignment of an executory contract or unexpired lease must contain the following:

(1) a date by which objections may be filed;

(2) a statement that in the event there are no objections filed an order may be entered approving the proposed assumption, rejection, or assignment without further notice; and

(3) the hearing date and time when any objection to the motion is to be heard.

(c) **Response.** No response is required to an objection.

[Effective January 1, 2005. Amended effective September 1, 2014.]

RULE 6007–1. ABANDONMENT OR DISPOSITION OF PROPERTY

(a) Proposed Abandonment A trustee or debtor in possession may abandon property by filing a notice of intent to abandon property with the clerk. The notice must contain sufficient information to allow parties in interest to make an informed decision regarding whether abandonment of a particular asset is in the best interest of the estate. The notice must provide that parties have fourteen (14) days from the mailing of the notice to file objections to the proposed abandonment. Unless service is made electronically through the ECF system, the trustee or debtor in possession must serve the passive notice upon the persons specified under F.R.B.P. 6007.

(b) Objection to Abandonment. An objection to a proposed abandonment of property of the estate must state specific grounds for the objection. No response is required to an objection.

(c) Filing of Motion to Compel Abandonment. Unless service is made electronically through the ECF system, the movant must serve the motion to compel abandonment and passive notice upon any party against whom relief is sought.

[Effective January 1, 2005. Amended effective January 1, 2008; December 1, 2009; September 1, 2014.]

PART VII. ADVERSARY PROCEEDINGS

RULE 7002–1. DISTRICT COURT RULES

Local Rules of the United States District Court for the Middle District of Pennsylvania LR 7.1 through 7.8 and 15.1 (www.pamd.uscourts.gov) apply in adversary proceedings unless modified by these rules.

[Effective January 1, 2005. Amended effective January 1, 2008; September 1, 2014.]

COMMENTS:

L.B.R. 7002–1 was amended effective September 1, 2014, to make District Court Rule 15.1, concerning amended pleadings, applicable to adversary proceedings.

RULE 7003–1. ADVERSARY PROCEEDING COVER SHEET

Any paper complaint filed under Part VII of the Federal Rules of Bankruptcy Procedure must be accompanied by an Adversary Proceeding Cover Sheet (Official Form 1040).

[Effective January 1, 2005. Amended effective January 1, 2008; September 1, 2014; June 1, 2016.]

RULE 7005–1. FILING OF DISCOVERY MATERIALS

(a) Discovery Motions. A party seeking a protective order, an order to compel discovery, or other relief under F.R.B.P. 7026 must attach to the motion only that portion of the deposition, interrogatory, request for document, or request for admissions that is the subject of the objection. An attachment to the motion must conform with the requirements of L.B.R. 5005–3 and any administrative order issued regarding electronic case filing.

(b) Documentation Not in Record. When discovery documentation not previously in the record is needed for appeal purposes, upon motion and order of the court, or by stipulation of counsel, the necessary discovery papers must be filed with the clerk. See Local Rule 5.4(d) of the Local Rules of the United States District Court for the Middle District of Pennsylvania (www.pamd.uscourts.gov).

(c) Original Response and Certificate of Service. A party who serves a discovery request must retain the original response as its custodian. Certificates of service of discovery materials must not be filed separately with the clerk. The original of any deposition upon oral examination must be retained by the party taking such deposition. See Local Rule 5.4(b) of the Local Rules of the United States District Court for the Middle District of Pennsylvania (www.pamd. uscourts.gov).

[Former Rule 7005–2 effective January 1, 2005. Amended effective January 1, 2008. Renumbered as Rule 7005–1 effective September 1, 2014.]

RULE 7007–1. MOTIONS IN ADVERSARY PROCEEDINGS

(a) Written Motion. A motion must be in writing unless made during a hearing or trial.

(b) Grounds and Relief to Be Stated. A motion filed in an adversary proceeding must contain a descriptive title of the motion in addition to the complete adversary caption. The caption must be substantially in compliance with the Caption for Use in Adversary Proceeding (Official Form 416D).

(c) Response. The response to any motion must be filed and served within fourteen (14) days after service of the motion. If no response is timely filed, the motion may be deemed uncontested, and the court may dispose of the motion.

(d) Continuances. A request for continuance of a trial date must be made in conformity with L.B.R. 9013–3.

(e) Hearing. Oral argument or hearing on a contested motion will be held only if requested by the court.

(f) Proposed Order. A proposed order of court as required under L.B.R. 9013–1(b) must be filed as an attachment to any motion and other pleading requesting relief in accordance with the procedures set forth in the Miscellaneous Order 5:05–mp–50007 and the Administrative Procedures available on the court's website (www.pamb.uscourts.gov).

[Effective January 1, 2005. Amended effective January 1, 2008; December 1, 2009; December 1, 2011; June 1, 2016.]

RULE 7008–1. STATEMENT OF CONSENT TO FINAL ORDERS OR JUDGMENT

In any adversary proceeding, each complaint, counterclaim, cross-claim, or third-party complaint must contain a statement that the pleader does or does not consent to the entry of final orders or judgment by the bankruptcy court.

[Effective June 1, 2016.]

RULE 7012–1. STATEMENT OF CONSENT TO FINAL ORDERS OR JUDGMENT IN RESPONSIVE PLEADINGS

In any adversary proceeding, each responsive pleading must contain a statement that the pleader does or does not consent to the entry of final orders or judgment by the bankruptcy court.

[Effective June 1, 2016.]

RULE 7016–1. PRE–TRIAL PROCEDURE

(a) Applicability of Fed. R. Civ. P. 16(b). Unless the court directs otherwise, an adversary proceeding is exempt from the provisions of Fed. R. Civ. P. 16(b), as incorporated in F.R.B.P. 7016.

(b) Scheduling Order. Notwithstanding subdivision (a), the court generally will issue a scheduling order.

(c) Pre–Trial Motions. The court may dispose of pre-trial motions in summary fashion at any time during their pendency.

[Effective January 1, 2005. Amended effective January 1, 2008.]

RULE 7021–1. MISJOINDER AND NON–JOINDER OF PARTIES

When an adversary is severed into two or more proceedings, a separate filing fee is payable to the clerk for each severed proceeding.

[Effective January 1, 2005.]

RULE 7041–1. NOTICE OF DISMISSAL OF ADVERSARY PROCEEDING

Before any adversary proceeding is involuntarily dismissed pursuant to F.R.B.P. 7041, a thirty (30) day notice will be given by the clerk to each party whose claim is to be dismissed and to the counsel of record for that party, if any.

[Effective January 1, 2005. Amended effective January 1, 2008.]

RULE 7055–1. DEFAULT—FAILURE TO PROSECUTE

Subject to L.B.R. 7041–1, an adversary complaint may be dismissed if neither a response nor a motion for default judgment has been filed within forty-five (45) days after the response date to the complaint. If a motion for default judgment is filed, the court may enter judgment by default against the defendant seven (7) days after the motion has been served on the defendant.

[Effective January 1, 2005. Amended effective December 1, 2009.]

RULE 7055–2. ORDER OF DEFAULT

The order of default may award damages for the amount to which the plaintiff is entitled if it is a sum certain or can be made certain by computation. If damages cannot be computed from the complaint, they must be assessed at a hearing at which the issues are limited to the amount of the damages.

[Effective January 1, 2005.]

RULE 7056–1. SUMMARY JUDGMENT— APPLICABILITY OF LOCAL RULE 56.1

Local Rule 56.1 for the United States District Court for the Middle District of Pennsylvania (www.pamd.uscourts.gov) applies in adversary proceedings.

[Effective January 1, 2005. Amended effective January 1, 2008.]

RULE 7067–1. REGISTRY FUNDS

(a) Deposit Funds into Court Registry Account. A party who wishes to deposit funds while litigation is pending may move the court to have such funds deposited into the court's registry account. The movant must attach a proposed order directing investment, which includes the following:

(1) the amount to be invested; and

(2) the mode of deposit (i.e., check, wire transfer).

(b) Investment of Registry Funds. Where, by order of the court, funds on deposit with the court are to be placed in some form of interest bearing account, the clerk is directed to use the Court Registry Investment System (CRIS), administered by the Administrative Office of the United States Courts. The Director of the United States Courts is designated as custodian for CRIS. The Director or the Director's designee will perform the duties of the custodian. CRIS will be the only investment mechanism authorized. Funds held in the CRIS remain subject to the control and jurisdiction of the court.

(c) Accounts in CRIS. An account for each case will be established in CRIS, titled in the name of the case giving rise to the deposit of funds. Money from each case deposited in CRIS will be "pooled" together with those on deposit with Treasury to the credit of other courts in CRIS and used to purchase Government Account Series securities through the Bureau of Public Debt, held at Treasury in an account in the name and credit of the Director of the Administrative Office of the United States Courts. Income generated from fund investments will be distributed to each case based on the ratio each account's principal and earnings has to the aggregate principal and income total in the fund. Income generated from fund investments will be distributed to each case. Reports showing the interest earned and the principal amounts contributed in each case will be made available to litigants and counsel.

(d) Motion to Withdraw Funds. In order to withdraw deposited funds, a motion for disbursement of invested registry funds and a proposed order must be filed with the court. The proposed order for disburse-

ment of invested registry funds must include the name and address of the payee in addition to the total amount of the principal and interest (if the interest is not known, the order may read "plus interest") that will be disbursed to each payee.

(e) Order for Payment. After entry of an order for disbursement, the parties to whom funds are to be disbursed must provide to the financial deputy their tax identification numbers or social security numbers and complete any forms required by the Internal Revenue Service for the reporting of earned interest. Disbursements may not be made until this information and the required Internal Revenue Service forms are submitted to the financial deputy.

(f) Deduction of Fees. The custodian is authorized and directed to deduct the investment services fee for the management of investments in CRIS and the registry fee for maintaining accounts deposited with the court. The investment services fee is assessed from interest earnings to the pool according to the Court's Miscellaneous Fee Schedule and is to be assessed before a pro rata distribution of earnings to court cases. The registry fee is assessed by the custodian from each case's pro rata distribution of the earnings and is to be determined on the basis of the rates published by the Director of the Administrative Office of the United States Courts as approved by the Judicial Conference of the United States.

[Effective January 1, 2005. Amended effective January 1, 2008; March 1, 2013; September 1, 2014.]

PART VIII.   APPEALS TO DISTRICT COURT OR BANKRUPTCY APPELLATE PANEL

RULE 8006–1.   DESIGNATION OF RECORD

Each designation of items to be included in the record of appeal must clearly indicate each document to be included in the record by listing its title, filing date, and document number, if any, as it appears on the case or adversary docket.

[Effective January 1, 2005.]

RULE 8007–1.   COMPLETION OF RECORD

The clerk is not responsible for the failure to transmit items not designated in accordance with L.B.R. 8006–1.

[Effective January 1, 2005.]

PART IX.   GENERAL PROVISIONS

RULE 9001–1.   DEFINITIONS

Unless inconsistent within the context of a particular rule, the following terms are defined for the purposes of the Local Bankruptcy Rules and Local Bankruptcy Forms as follows:

(a) *"Amended plan"* means a plan modified under the provisions of 11 U.S.C. §§ 942, 1127, 1223, 1229,

1323, and 1329. The terms "modified" and "amended" are used interchangeably.

(b) *"Chapter"* means one of the chapters of Title 11 of the Bankruptcy Code.

(c) *"Clerk"* means the office of the Clerk of the United States Bankruptcy Court for the Middle District of Pennsylvania.

(d) *"Contract amount"* means the amount of principal and interest payable each month under the terms of a note secured by a mortgage without the inclusion of late fees or other default fees or charges.

(e) *"Counsel of record"* means any attorney who has entered an appearance on the docket of a bankruptcy case or who has filed a paper on behalf of a party. An attorney remains counsel of record until an order authorizing withdrawal has been entered or another attorney has entered an appearance on behalf of the party.

(f) *"Electronic filer"* means a filing user registered with the clerk to file, serve, and receive documents through the electronic filing system established by the United States Bankruptcy Court for the Middle District of Pennsylvania.

(g) *"F.R.B.P."* means The Federal Rules of Bankruptcy Procedure.

(h) *"Hearing required notice"* is a notice that may provide an objection/response deadline and sets the matter for hearing. The hearing will take place at the date, time, and location indicated in the notice regardless of whether or not objections/responses are filed.

(i) *"Paper filer"* means an individual or entity that is not an electronic filer and files, serves, and receives paper documents in compliance with all rules and court orders.

(j) *"Party in interest"* means a person or entity who may be affected by a bankruptcy proceeding. In these rules, a party in interest also includes a creditor.

(k) *"Passive notice"* is a notice stating that if no response is filed, the court may enter the requested relief without further notice or hearing.

(l) *"Retainer agreement"* means an agreement between a client and an attorney in which the client deposits funds with the attorney for services to be performed whether entered before the filing of a bankruptcy petition or during the pendency of the case.

(m) *"Schedules and statements"* include all documents required to be filed by a debtor under 11 U.S.C. § 521.

(n) *"Semi passive notice"* is a notice setting an objection/response deadline and a proposed hearing date if objections/responses are filed. If no objections/responses are filed, the court may enter an order without conducting a hearing. If objections/responses are filed, the matter will proceed to hearing at the date, time, and location indicated in the notice. If a default order has not been signed and entered on the docket, the parties or their counsel are required to appear in court.

(o) *"Technical failure"* means any day on which the court's CM/ECF site is unable to accept filings contin-uously over a period of more than two (2) hours after 7:00 a.m.

[Effective January 1, 2005. Amended effective January 1, 2008; September 1, 2014; June 1, 2016.]

COMMENTS:

L.B.R. 9001–1 was amended effective September 1, 2014, to add definitions for the terms "Hearing required notice" and "semi passive notice".

RULE 9002–1. SELF–SCHEDULED MATTERS

(a) Filing a Self–Scheduled Matter. When a motion or other document is filed using self-scheduling, the electronic filer must use the Courtroom Hearing Scheduler ("CHS").

(b) Self–Scheduled Matters. A list of the matters that may be self-scheduled, as well as the filing procedures, are posted on the court's website under the Self–Scheduling Hearings button. (www.pamb. uscourts.gov).

(c) Matters Which Cannot Be Self–Scheduled. No matters other than those listed under the Self–Scheduling Hearings Button can be self-scheduled.

[Effective December 1, 2009. Amended effective October 15, 2010; September 1, 2014.]

COMMENTS:

L.B.R. 9002–1 was amended effective September 1, 2014, to refer electronic filers to the court's website to determine what matters can and cannot be self-scheduled.

RULE 9003–1. EX PARTE RELIEF

The following requests may be considered ex parte by the court:

(a) for conversion or dismissal under 11 U.S.C. §§ 1208(b) or 1307(b);

(b) for entry of a wage order under 11 U.S.C. §§ 1225(c) or 1325(c);

(c) for approval to pay filing fees in installments;

(d) for waiver of filing fees for documents including the bankruptcy petition;

(e) to limit notice;

(f) for admission pro hac vice;

(g) for emergency relief;

(h) for an extension of time to file documents required under 11 U.S.C. § 521;

(i) for protection from or application of disclosure of information under 11 U.S.C. § 107; and

(j) for relief after dismissal of an involuntary case.

[Effective January 1, 2005. Amended effective January 1, 2008; September 1, 2014.]

RULE 9004-1. CAPTION OF PLEADINGS

Unless additional information is required under 11 U.S.C. § 342(c), any pleading filed with the clerk in a contested matter must contain a caption substantially in compliance with L.B.F. 9004-1. Unless additional information is required under 11 U.S.C. § 342(c), any pleading filed with the clerk in an adversary proceeding must contain a caption substantially in compliance with the Caption for Use in Adversary Proceeding (Official Form 416D).

[Former Rule 9004-2 effective January 1, 2005. Amended effective January 1, 2008. Renumbered as Rule 9004-1 and amended effective September 1, 2014. Amended effective June 1, 2016.]

COMMENTS:

L.B.R. 9004-1 was amended effective June 1, 2016, to provide for the use of Official Form 416D—Caption for Use in Adversary Proceeding and to eliminate L.B.F. 9004-2.

RULE 9010-1. ATTORNEYS—NOTICE OF APPEARANCE

(a) General Appearance. An attorney who files with the clerk any application, motion, stipulation, or other document, other than as set forth in subdivision (b), is deemed to have entered an appearance for the party on whose behalf the document is filed.

(b) Limited Appearance. An attorney filing a proof of claim or interest is deemed to have entered an appearance only for the purpose of any objection that may be filed to that claim.

(c) Change of Address. When attorneys or parties representing themselves change their e-mail or physical addresses, they are required to provide notification as follows:

(1) Electronic filers must immediately update their addresses in the ECF system. If an address changes in a specific case, electronic filers must docket a Change of Address in each case in which the change should appear to enable the clerk to update the information.

(2) Paper filers must notify the clerk in writing of their new address so that the clerk may enter it in the ECF system. If an attorney has entered an appearance in more than one case, he also must file with the clerk a listing of all such cases so the new address may be entered by the clerk on the docket of each case.

(d) Withdrawal of Appearance. The debtor's attorney or an attorney in a pending adversary or contested matter may not withdraw his or her appearance except upon motion, after hearing and by order of the court, unless another attorney eligible to appear before the court enters his or her appearance simultaneously with the request for withdrawal of appearance. If an attorney leaves a law firm and the firm

remains counsel for certain cases, the law firm must submit a list of cases that the firm is retaining with its current address. If the firm has not entered an appearance in a case, it must enter an appearance in the cases it is retaining. An attorney may not submit a change of address as a substitute for filing a motion to withdraw.

(e) Notice to Parties. Unless service is made electronically through the ECF system, an attorney who files a request to note change of address must mail a copy of same to any attorney who has entered an appearance in an adversary proceeding or contested matter that is pending at the time the request is filed.

[Effective January 1, 2005. Amended effective January 1, 2008; October 8, 2008; December 1, 2009.]

RULE 9010-2. FACSIMILE AND E-MAIL ADDRESSES

In addition to the requirements of F.R.B.P. 9010(b), an attorney must provide the attorney's facsimile number and e-mail address, if any.

[Former Rule 9010-4 effective January 1, 2005. Renumbered as Rule 9010-2 and amended effective September 1, 2014.]

RULE 9011-1. ATTORNEYS' DUTIES

Subject to L.B.R. 9010-1(b), an attorney who files a petition in bankruptcy on behalf of a debtor, or who later enters an appearance on behalf of a debtor—other than as special counsel—is counsel of record in all matters arising during the administration of the case.

[Effective January 1, 2005. Amended effective December 1, 2009.]

RULE 9013-1. MOTION PRACTICE

(a) Title of Motion and Answer. The title of each motion must identify the party filing the motion and the nature of the relief sought. Any answer filed must identify the party filing the answer and the motion to which the party is responding. The answer must include in the caption the docket number reference of the document to which the party is responding.

(b) Orders to Accompany Motions. Each motion must be accompanied by a proposed form of order which, if entered by the court, would grant the relief sought by the motion in accordance with the procedures set forth in the Miscellaneous Order 5:05-mp-50007 and the Administrative Procedures available on the court's website (www.pamb.uscourts.gov).

(c) Service of Motion—Generally. Unless service is made electronically through the ECF system, the moving party must serve a copy of its motion and attachments on the following:

(1) the respondent;

(2) the debtor;

(3) any committee appointed pursuant to 11 U.S.C. § 1102; and

(4) such other entities as the court may direct.

(d) Service of Motion to Dismiss or Convert. Unless service is made electronically through the ECF system, the moving party must serve a copy of a motion to dismiss or convert a case to another chapter on the debtor and on debtor's counsel, in addition to those parties listed in paragraph (c).

(e) Service of Motion Against Counsel. Unless service is made electronically through the ECF system, the moving party must serve a copy of a motion seeking sanctions or other relief against a party's counsel on the party and on counsel.

[Effective January 1, 2005. Amended effective June 1, 2005; April 25, 2006; January 1, 2008. Amended effective December 1, 2011.]

RULE 9013–2.   CERTIFICATION OF SERVICE

In accordance with the procedures set forth in the Miscellaneous Order 5:05–mp–50007 and the Administrative Procedures available on the court's website (www.pamb.uscourts.gov), each document filed with the court must include a certificate of service containing the following information as to any paper filers on which service has been made:

(a) the title of the paper served;

(b) the names and addresses of all persons upon whom the paper has been served;

(c) the entities the persons served represent; and

(d) a description of when and how service was made.

[Former Rule 9013–3 effective January 1, 2005. Amended effective January 1, 2008; December 1, 2011. Renumbered as Rule 9013–2 effective September 1, 2014.]

RULE 9013–3.   CONTINUANCES

A request for a continuance must be made in writing and contain a certification that counsel making the request has sought the concurrence of all interested parties and that concurrence has been either granted or denied. A request may be denied if concurrence has not been obtained. If a request is the first request for a continuance of the matter, the request should be submitted using L.B.F. 9013–3. All further requests for a continuance must be made by motion. Requests received by the court within twenty-four (24) hours of the hearing will not be considered except in emergency situations, and the request will be granted only in the court's discretion. A party who obtains a continuance must immediately notify other parties of the continuance by email, telephone, facsimile transmission, or first class mail, whichever method is necessary to ensure that notice is received no later than twenty-four (24) hours prior to the time set for the hearing.

[Former Rule 5071–1 effective January 1, 2005; renumbered Rule 9013–4 and amended effective January 1, 2008. Amended effective December 1, 2009. Former Rule 9013–4 renumbered as Rule 9013–3 effective September 1, 2014.]

COMMENTS:

L.B.R. 9013–3 was amended effective December 1, 2009, to provide that a continuance request may be denied if concurrence has not been obtained from all interested parties.

RULE 9014–1.   DEFAULT AND SUMMARY JUDGMENT

F.R.B.P. 7055 and 7056 as well as L.B.R. 7055–1 and 7002–1 do not apply in contested matters except as otherwise provided in the Local Rules. If a response is required but none is filed, the court may, without hearing, grant the relief requested in the motion.

[Effective January 1, 2005.]

RULE 9015–1.   JURY TRIALS

The parties may consent to have a jury trial conducted by a bankruptcy judge under 28 U.S.C. § 157(e) by jointly or separately filing a statement of consent no later than thirty (30) days after time of demand or designation, whichever last occurs, if right to a jury trial applies; a timely demand has been filed under Fed. R. Civ. P. 38(b); and the bankruptcy judge has been specially designated to conduct the jury trial.

[Effective January 1, 2005. Amended effective January 1, 2008.]

RULE 9016–1.   SUBPOENA

A subpoena may be issued by an attorney as an officer of the court under Fed. R. Civ. P. 45(a)(3). The clerk must issue a subpoena signed, but otherwise blank, when requested by a pro se party.

[Effective January 1, 2005.]

RULE 9018–1.   DOCUMENTS UNDER SEAL

Any party who seeks to file documents under seal must file a motion to that effect. The documents proposed to be filed under seal must be placed in a prominently marked envelope with a cover sheet attached containing the case or adversary caption, related docket number of the motion to file under seal, title of the document to be filed under seal, and the legend "DOCUMENTS TO BE KEPT UNDER SEAL" in bold print. The envelope must be delivered directly to the respective Judge's chambers. The court will keep the documents segregated and under seal until the motion is decided. If the court grants the motion to file under seal, the clerk will electronically docket the cover sheet and will keep the documents segregated and under seal until the case or adversary proceeding is closed, at which time the sealed documents will be returned to the party that filed them. If the court denies the motion to file under seal, the clerk will return the segregated, proposed sealed documents to counsel for the moving party without any disclosure to third parties and such documents will not become part of the record in the case unless they are otherwise separately filed of record in accordance with the applicable rules.

[Effective December 1, 2011. Amended effective September 1, 2014.]

RULE 9019–1. SETTLEMENTS AND AGREED ORDERS

(a) Settlement of Adversary Matters and Contested Matters. In an adversary proceeding or contested matter, whenever the parties have reached a settlement, they must file a stipulation resolving the matter before the hearing date, submit a Request to Remove from the Hearing/Trial List (L.B.F. 9019–1), or announce the settlement at the hearing set on the matter. If a Request to Remove form is filed, within the time specified in the form, the moving party or plaintiff must file a stipulation or stipulated order and any requisite motion to compromise or settle. Failure to file a stipulation or stipulated order may result in the dismissal of the matter or proceeding. A motion to extend the time to comply with this rule or to re-list the matter for hearing may be filed within the period specified for filing a stipulation or stipulated order in the Request to Remove form, but the motion will be granted only upon cause shown.

(b) Hearing. When a matter has been settled and a stipulation has been filed or is expected to be filed within a period not to exceed sixty (60) days, the hearing before the court may be stricken by filing a Request to Remove form (L.B.F. 9019–1). A Request to Remove form must be filed with the court no later than twenty-four (24) hours before the hearing.

[Effective January 1, 2005. Amended effective January 1, 2008.]

RULE 9019–2. ALTERNATIVE DISPUTE RESOLUTION

(a) Setting Mediation. The court may set a case for mediation provided consideration is given to any reasons advanced by the parties as to why such mediation would not be in the best interest of justice. Once set for mediation, the matter can be removed from mediation by the court or on application by the mediator.

(b) Request for Mediation. The parties may request a case be assigned by the court to mediation by completing and filing L.B.F. 9019–2.

(c) Assigning Matters and Cases. The court may assign to mediation any adversary proceeding or contested matter or any issue within such adversary proceeding or contested matter.

(d) Certification of Mediators.

(1) The court may certify as many mediators as determined to be necessary under this rule.

(2) An individual may be certified to serve as a mediator if:

(A) he or she has been a member of the bar of the highest court of a state or the District of Columbia for a minimum of five (5) years;

(B) he or she is admitted to practice before this court;

(C) he or she has successfully completed a mediation training program established or recognized by the District Court or the Bankruptcy Court for the Middle District of Pennsylvania; and

(D) he or she has been determined by the appointing court to be competent to perform the duties of a mediator.

(3) The court will solicit qualified individuals to serve as mediators.

(4) Each individual certified as a mediator must take the oath or affirmation prescribed by 28 U.S.C. § 453 before serving as a mediator.

(5) The clerk must maintain a list of all persons certified as mediators.

(6) The appointing judge may remove anyone from the list of certified mediators for cause.

(7) Persons acting as mediators under this rule are assisting the court in performing its judicial function. They must be disqualified for bias or prejudice as provided by 28 U.S.C. § 144 and must disqualify themselves in any action in which they would be required under 28 U.S.C. § 455 to disqualify themselves if they were a justice or judge.

(e) Compensation and Expenses of Mediators. A mediator who accepts a case for mediation initially volunteers the time expended to prepare for and conduct a mediation conference or conferences lasting up to a total of four (4) hours. After completion of four (4) hours service, the mediator may either:

(1) continue to volunteer the mediator's time; or

(2) give the mediation parties the option to agree to pay the mediator his prevailing hourly rate for bank-

ruptcy services for the additional time spent on the mediation. The parties must each pay a pro rata share of the mediator's compensation, unless they agree among themselves to a different allocation. A motion to enforce a party's obligation to compensate a mediator is governed by F.R.B.P. 9014.

(f) Frequency of Service. An individual certified as a mediator will not be called upon more than twice in a twelve (12) month period to serve as a mediator without the prior approval of the mediator.

(g) Scheduling Mediation Conference.

(1) Upon referral of a case to mediation, the court will serve the order of referral to the mediator, all counsel, and any unrepresented party directing the mediator to establish the date, place, and time of the mediation session. The order will include the address, telephone number, email address, and facsimile number of the mediator, counsel, and unrepresented parties. The date of the mediation session must be a date within thirty (30) days from the date of the order of referral.

(2) The appointment is effective unless the designee rejects the appointment within seven (7) days.

(3) Upon docketing of the order of referral to mediation, the clerk must transmit to the mediator, either by email or regular mail, a copy of the docket sheet that reflects all filings to date. The mediator may identify to the clerk those filed documents which the mediator wishes to review for the mediation. Unless otherwise ordered by the court, the clerk will provide the mediator with electronic or paper copies of the requested documents free of charge.

(4) A mediator may change the date and time for the mediation session if the session takes place within forty-five (45) days of the date of the order of referral. Any continuance of the session beyond forty-five (45) days must be approved by the court.

(h) The Mediation Process.

(1) Not later than seven (7) days before the initial conference, each party must deliver or send a facsimile or email to the mediator a mediation conference memorandum no longer than two (2) pages, summarizing the nature of the case and the party's position on:

(A) the major factual and legal issues affecting liability and damages;

(B) the relief sought by each party; and

(C) the position of the parties relative to settlement.

(2) The memoranda required by this subdivision are solely for use in the mediation process and are not to be filed with the clerk.

(i) The Mediation Session.

(1) The mediation session must take place on the date and at the time set forth by the mediator. The mediation session must take place at a neutral setting as designated by the mediator that may include the mediator's office. A party must not contact or forward any document to the mediator unless the mediator requests the information or unless as otherwise provided under these rules.

(2) Counsel primarily responsible for the case and any unrepresented party must attend the mediation session. All parties or principals of parties with decision-making authority must attend the mediation session in person, unless attendance is excused by the mediator for good cause shown. Willful failure to attend the mediation conference must be reported to the court and may result in the imposition of sanctions. The participants must be prepared to discuss:

(A) all liability issues;

(B) all damage issues;

(C) all equitable and declaratory remedies if such are requested; and

(D) the position of the parties relative to settlement.

(3) Unless otherwise provided in this rule, and as may be necessary to the reporting of or the processing of complaints about unlawful or unethical conduct, nothing communicated during the mediation process—including any oral or written statement made by a party, attorney, or other participant, and any proposed settlement figure stated by the mediator or on behalf of any party—may be placed in evidence, made known to the trial court or jury, or construed for any purpose as an admission. No party may be bound by anything done or said during the mediation process except to enforce a settlement agreement or any other agreement achieved in that process.

(4) In the event the mediator determines that no settlement is likely to result from the mediation session, the mediator must terminate the session and promptly send a report to the court that there has been compliance with the requirements of these paragraphs, but that no resolution has been reached. In the event that a settlement is achieved at the mediation session, the mediator must send a written report to the judge to whom the case is assigned stating that a settlement has been achieved. The parties are responsible for the circulation of any required notice of settlement.

(5) Notwithstanding the above paragraph, the mediator must submit a written report to the court advising the court of the status of the mediation within sixty (60) days after the order of appointment of the mediator.

(6) No one may have a recording or transcript made of the mediation session, including the mediator, unless otherwise agreed to by the parties.

(7) The mediator cannot be called as a witness at trial.

(j) Neutral Evaluator. Anytime after an action or proceeding has been filed, the action may be referred to a neutral evaluator to be selected with the approval of the parties.

(k) Relationship to Other Procedures. Nothing in this rule modifies the provisions of Fed.R.Civ.P. 16 and 26, or L.B.R. 7016–1 or any order of court, nor does it preclude the use of any kind of mediation outside of the mediation process established by this rule or the use of any other means of alternative dispute resolution.

[Effective January 1, 2005. Amended effective January 1, 2008; December 1, 2009; October 15, 2010; March 1, 2013; September 1, 2014.]

RULE 9019–3. MORTGAGE MODIFI-CATION MEDIATION PROGRAM

(a) Program Description. The Mortgage Modification Mediation Program ("MMM Program") is available to any chapter 13 debtor seeking to modify a mortgage obligation with respect to his or her principal residence. In order to qualify for the MMM Program, debtor must meet the following criteria:

(1) Debtor has regular, verifiable income and is the owner/occupant of a residential property used as debtor's primary residence.

(2) Debtor has a mortgage balance of less than $729,750.00, and the mortgage payment is unaffordable due to financial hardship.

(3) Debtor will make monthly post-petition mortgage payments of seventy-five percent (75%) of debtor's current mortgage payment starting with the next monthly scheduled due date (plus any grace period, after the Motion to Participate is filed and granted). Debtor agrees that in the event debtor misses one of the modified mortgage payments, the lender and/or servicer for the mortgagee of record ("Mortgage Creditor") may file a motion for relief from the automatic stay and seek removal of debtor from the MMM Program.

(4) Debtor has filed complete bankruptcy schedules and must supply Mortgage Creditor with the last two (2) years' signed tax returns, last sixty (60) days' payment advices, and any other document Mortgage Creditor requests. Failure to supply the documents within thirty (30) days of admission to the MMM Program is grounds for dismissal from the MMM Program.

(5) If a mediator is used, debtor must pay a mediation fee of $125.00 to the mediator. Mortgage Creditor must also pay $125.00 to the mediator. Neither fee is refundable under any circumstances. Mediation is to be completed within sixty (60) days, unless otherwise extended consistent with the paragraphs contained herein.

(b) Application to the MMM Program.

(1) *Motion.* To seek admission to the MMM Program, debtor must file a Motion to Participate in the Mortgage Modification Mediation Program ("Motion to Participate"), together with the Notice of Filing of Motion to Participate in Mortgage Modification Mediation Program, L.B.F. 9019–3(a), and serve copies of same on Mortgage Creditor and any counsel of record. In the Motion to Participate, debtor must state whether he wishes to utilize the DMM Portal, or such other portal as may be designated by the court, (the "Portal") or to communicate directly with Mortgage Creditor and its counsel. Additional information related to the Portal is posted on the court's website at www.pamb.uscourts.gov and may be updated from time to time by the court.

(2) *Response.* Mortgage Creditor will have twenty-one (21) days to file a response to the Motion to Participate.

(A) Acceptance. If Mortgage Creditor agrees to participation, Mortgage Creditor will file a Consent to Participation in Mortgage Modification Mediation Program ("Creditor Consent Form"), L.B.F. 9019–3(b) and the court will enter an Order Granting Entry in MMM Program. Prior to filing the Creditor Consent Form, the parties will confer as to whether they wish to utilize the Portal or to communicate directly with one another outside the Portal for the modification process. The Creditor Consent Form will reflect the decision of the parties. Should the Creditor Consent Form not contain a designation as to whether or not the Portal will be used, the preference stated by debtor in the Motion to Participate will govern. Should both the Motion to Participate and the Creditor Consent Form fail to include a designation as to the Portal, the parties will be deemed to have opted not to use the Portal.

(B) Objection. If Mortgage Creditor objects to participation, a written response stating the basis for the objection must be filed with the court. Upon filed written objection, the Motion to Participate will be denied without prejudice to re-filing.

(C) Failure to Respond. If Mortgage Creditor fails to file either the Creditor Consent Form or an objection to participation within twenty-one (21) days, Mortgage Creditor will be deemed to have waived any objection and the court may enter an Order Granting Entry in MMM Program ("Participation Order") without further notice or hearing. The preference elected by debtor as to the Portal in the Motion to Participate will govern. Should the Motion to Participate fail to elect a preference, the parties will be deemed to have opted not to use the Portal.

(D) Re–filing the Motion to Participate. A Motion to Participate may be refiled after an objection by Mortgage Creditor, only with written concurrence of Mortgage Creditor unless the motion includes information demonstrating a material change in debtor's circumstances that either renders Mortgage Creditor's prior objection moot or otherwise rebuts the objection. If Mortgage Creditor files an objection to the refiled Motion to Participate, the court may set a hearing thereon or rule on the refiled Motion to Participate without a hearing.

(c) Proceeding in the MMM Program Using Portal.

(1) Within fourteen (14) days of entry of a Participation Order, unless not previously registered, Mortgage Creditor must, register with the Portal and post on the Portal the required loss mitigation application to be completed by debtor.

(2) Debtor must upload and submit a completed loss mitigation application on the Portal within thirty (30) days after Mortgage Creditor registers with the Portal. If Mortgage Creditor is registered with the Portal at the time the Participation Order is entered, debtor will be required to upload and submit a completed loss mitigation application on the Portal within thirty (30) days after such Participation Order is entered. Failure to do so may result in debtor being removed from the MMM Program upon written motion of Mortgage Creditor.

(3) Within fourteen (14) days after debtor's submission of the loss mitigation application, Mortgage Creditor must designate, via the Portal, a specific individual who is the single point of contact for the loss mitigation process. The designated representative will be responsible for all communications in the Portal with debtor. Mortgage Creditor must provide the designated representative's name, title, email address, and either a direct telephone number or direct extension. At the same time, Mortgage Creditor must acknowledge, via the Portal, receipt of debtor's loss mitigation application and advise debtor of any additional or missing information required for Mortgage Creditor to proceed with its review.

(4) Debtor must promptly submit any and all additional or missing information required for Mortgage Creditor to proceed with its review, but in no event may the documents be submitted more than twenty-one (21) days after the date they are requested by Mortgage Creditor. Mortgage Creditor must continue reviewing the loss mitigation application in good faith while awaiting submission of additional or missing information.

(5) Once the parties have opted to utilize the Portal, all material communications between debtor and Mortgage Creditor must be conducted exclusively through the Portal.

(6) In the event that the loan being reviewed under the MMM Program becomes subject to a transfer or the service rights are scheduled to be assigned to a new servicer, then no less than fourteen (14) days prior to the scheduled transfer/assignment, Mortgage Creditor must file a Proposed Order Substituting MMM Servicer, L.B.F. 9019–3(c), and update the Portal to identify the successor creditor ("Substituted Creditor"). In addition to updating the Portal, Mortgage Creditor must forthwith provide Substituted Creditor with all loss mitigation notes, applications, and correspondence related to the pending loss mitigation review. Substituted Creditor is responsible for ensuring all such documents are received from Mortgage Creditor and must continue the loss mitigation review without requiring a new Motion to Participate or initial application from debtor. Within thirty (30) days of the service transfer, Substituted Creditor must designate a representative who is the single point of contact for the loss mitigation process on behalf of Substituted Creditor. The designated representative is responsible for all communications in the Portal with debtor. Substituted Creditor must provide the designated representative's name, title, email address, and either a direct telephone number or direct extension. To the extent updated or additional documents are required by Substituted Creditor in order to complete the loss mitigation review, Substituted Creditor must request such information or documents contemporaneously with designating its single point of contact on the Portal.

(d) Proceeding in the MMM Program Outside the Portal.

(1) Upon entry of a Participation Order, Mortgage Creditor must provide debtor with the required loss mitigation package and document checklist within fourteen (14) days. Documents that may be requested include, but are not limited to, IRS Form 4506–T, utility bills, bank statements, payment advices, and federal tax returns.

(2) Within thirty (30) days of the entry of the Participation Order, debtor must provide the last two (2) years' signed tax returns, last sixty (60) days' payment advices, and any other document Mortgage Creditor requests. Failure to do so may result in debtor being removed from the MMM Program upon written motion of Mortgage Creditor.

(3) Within fourteen (14) days after debtor's submission of the loss mitigation application, Mortgage Creditor must designate, via written notice to debtor and debtor's counsel, a specific individual who is the single point of contact for the loss mitigation process. The designated representative is responsible for all communications with debtor with respect to the loss mitigation review. Mortgage Creditor must provide the designated representative's name, title, email address, and either a direct telephone number or direct exten-

sion. At the same time, Mortgage Creditor must acknowledge receipt of debtor's loss mitigation application and advise debtor of any additional or missing information required for Mortgage Creditor to proceed with its review.

(4) Debtor must promptly submit all additional or missing information required for Mortgage Creditor to proceed with its review, but in no event may the documents be submitted more than twenty-one (21) days after the date they are requested by Mortgage Creditor. Mortgage Creditor must continue reviewing the loss mitigation application in good faith while awaiting submission of additional or missing information.

(5) In the event that the loan being reviewed under the MMM Program becomes subject to a transfer or the service rights are scheduled to be assigned to a new servicer, then no less than fourteen (14) days prior to the scheduled transfer/assignment, Mortgage Creditor must file a Proposed Order Substituting MMM Servicer, L.B.F. 9019–3(c), identifying the successor creditor ("Substituted Creditor"). Mortgage Creditor must forthwith provide Substituted Creditor with all loss mitigation notes, applications, and correspondence related to the pending loss mitigation review. Substituted Creditor is responsible for ensuring all such documents are received from Mortgage Creditor and must continue the loss mitigation review without requiring a new Motion to Participate or initial application from debtor. Within thirty (30) days of the service transfer, Substituted Creditor must designate a representative who is the single point of contact for the loss mitigation process on behalf of Substituted Creditor and provide written notice thereof to debtor and debtor's counsel of record. The designated representative is responsible for all loss mitigation communications with debtor. Substituted Creditor must provide the designated representative's name, title, email address, and either a direct telephone number or direct extension. To the extent updated or additional documents are required by Substituted Creditor in order to complete the loss mitigation review, Substituted Creditor will request such information or documents contemporaneously with providing written notice of its single point of contact.

(e) Request for Status Conference and/or Appointment of Mediator.

(1) Upon the motion of either party, the court may schedule a status conference concerning the loss mitigation process. Such motion must include the grounds for requesting said conference along with a description of the efforts made to resolve any differences prior to requesting the status conference. The motion must be served upon the other party and his counsel. The court may, on its own initiative, schedule a status conference.

(2) At the time of the status conference, both parties must be prepared to provide the court with sufficient detail as to the status of the loss mitigation review so that the court can assess whether further two-party negotiations are likely to be productive and/or whether the appointment of a mediator may be beneficial to the parties.

(3) After the status conference, if the court determines that the appointment of a mediator may be beneficial, the court will issue an order of referral to the mediator, all counsel, and any unrepresented party, directing the mediator to establish the date, place, and time of the mediation session. The order will include the address, telephone number, email address, and facsimile number of the mediator, counsel, and unrepresented parties. The date of the mediation session will be a date within thirty (30) days from the date of the order of referral.

(4) The appointment is effective unless the mediator rejects the appointment within seven (7) days of the date of the order of referral.

(5) Upon docketing of the order of referral to mediation, the clerk must transmit to the mediator a copy of the docket sheet that reflects all filings to date. The mediator may specify those documents in the case that the mediator wishes to review for the mediation. Unless otherwise ordered by the court, the clerk will provide the mediator with electronic or paper copies of the requested documents.

(6) Mediation must be completed within thirty (30) days, but the mediator may extend the time to complete the mediation for a period up to forty-five (45) days from the date of the order of referral. Any continuance of the session beyond forty-five (45) days must be approved by the court.

(7) Debtor must pay a mediation fee of $125.00 to the appointed mediator. Mortgage Creditor (or, if applicable, Substituted Creditor) must also pay $125.00 to the appointed mediator. Neither fee is refundable under any circumstances.

(f) The Mediation Process.

(1) Not later than seven (7) days before the scheduled mediation session, debtor and Mortgage Creditor (or, if applicable, Substituted Creditor) must each deliver or send by facsimile or email to the mediator and the opposing party a mediation conference memorandum no longer than two (2) pages, summarizing the status of the loss mitigation process.

(2) The memoranda required by this subdivision are solely for use in the mediation process and are not to be filed with the clerk.

(g) The Mediation Session.

(1) The mediation session must take place on the date and at the time set by the mediator. The mediation session must take place at a neutral setting

as designated by the mediator that may include the mediator's office. A party must not contact or forward any document to the mediator unless the mediator requests the information or unless as otherwise provided under these rules. (2) Debtor must appear in person at the mediation session with counsel, unless unrepresented. Counsel for Mortgage Creditor (or, if applicable, Substituted Creditor) who is primarily responsible for the case must appear in person. A representative of Mortgage Creditor (or, if applicable, Substituted Creditor) must be available by phone for the mediation session. The participants must be prepared to discuss:

(A) the status of the loss mitigation process; and

(B) the position of the parties relative to settlement.

(2) Debtor must appear in person at the mediation session with counsel, unless unrepresented. Counsel for Mortgage Creditor (or, if applicable, Substituted Creditor) who is primarily responsible for the case must appear in person. A representative of Mortgage Creditor (or, if applicable, Substituted Creditor) must be available by phone for the mediation session. The participants must be prepared to discuss:

(3) Unless otherwise provided in this rule, and as may be necessary to the reporting or processing of complaints about unlawful or unethical conduct, nothing communicated during the mediation process—including any oral or written statement made by a party, attorney, or other participant, and any proposed settlement figure stated by the mediator or on behalf of any party—may be placed in evidence, made known to the trial court or jury, or construed for any purpose as an admission. No party may be bound by anything done or said during the mediation process except to enforce a settlement agreement or any other agreement achieved in that process.

(4) In the event the mediator determines that no settlement is likely to result from the mediation session, the mediator must terminate the session and promptly send a report to the court that there has been compliance with the requirements of L.B.R. 9019–3(g), but that no resolution has been reached. In the event that a settlement is achieved at the mediation session, the mediator must send a written report to the court stating that a settlement has been reached.

(5) Notwithstanding the above paragraph, the mediator must submit a written report to the court describing the status of the mediation no later than thirty (30) days after the completion of the mediation session.

(6) No one may have a recording or transcript made of the mediation session, including the mediator, unless otherwise agreed to by the parties.

(7) The mediator cannot be called as a witness at trial.

(h) Compensation and Expenses of Mediators. A mediator who accepts a case for mediation initially will receive a total of $250.00 from the parties for up three (3) hours' of actual mediation services for time expended to prepare and conduct a mediation conference or conferences. After completion of three (3) hours' service, the mediator may either

(1) continue to volunteer the mediator's time; or

(2) give the mediation parties the option to agree to pay the mediator his prevailing hourly rate for bankruptcy services for the additional time spent on the mediation. The parties must each pay a pro rata share of the mediator's compensation, unless they agree among themselves to a different allocation. A motion to enforce a party's obligation to compensate a mediator is governed by F.R.B.P. 9014.

(i) Frequency of Service. An individual certified as a mediator will not be called upon more than four (4) times in a twelve (12) month period to serve as a mediator under the MMM Program without the prior approval of the mediator.

(j) MMM Program Results.

(1) If the MMM Program is successful, Mortgage Creditor (or, if applicable, Substituted Creditor) will file a motion to approve final modification with a copy of the modification agreement.

(2) When debtor's primary residence remains property of the estate, notice of the filing of the motion to approve final modification must be provided to creditors and parties in interest. Such notice must be provided by Mortgage Creditor (or, if applicable, Substituted Creditor). A passive notice, pursuant to L.B.R. 2002–1(a), is required allowing a twenty-one (21) day objection period. A certificate of mailing evidencing compliance with this notice provision must be filed within seven (7) days following the date of the notice.

(3) If the MMM Program is unsuccessful and no loan modification is agreed to by the parties, debtor must file an amended/modified chapter 13 plan within twenty-one (21) days to address the pre-petition mortgage arrears and any post-petition arrears that may have accrued as a result of the reduced monthly payments. If an amended/modified chapter 13 plan is not timely filed, Mortgage Creditor (or, if applicable, Substituted Creditor) may file a motion for relief from the automatic stay.

(4) If within one hundred and twenty (120) days from the entry of the Participation Order, neither a motion to approve loan modification nor an amended/modified chapter 13 plan to address Mortgage Creditor's lien has been filed, debtor must file and serve a Loss Mitigation Status Report with an at-

tached printout of the current and complete account history from the Portal. If the parties opted not to use the Portal, the Loss Mitigation Status Report must include a history of the loss mitigation review process along with the outcome of same. Such Status Report is to be filed on the bankruptcy docket and, if applicable, in the Portal. The obligation to timely file a Loss Mitigation Status Report applies in all cases in the MMM Program unless the bankruptcy case has been dismissed or converted prior to the time for filing the Status Report, in which case no report is required. Upon the motion of any party, or on its own initiative, the court may set a hearing on the Status Report.

(k) Relationship to Other Procedures. Nothing in this rule modifies the provisions of F.R.C.P. 16 and 26, or L.B.R. 7016–1 or any order of court, nor does it preclude the use of any kind of mediation outside of the mediation process established by this rule or the use of any other means of alternative dispute resolution.

[Effective March 1, 2013. Amended effective September 1, 2014; June 1, 2016.]

COMMENTS:

L.B.R. 9019–3 was amended effective June 1, 2016, in part, to provide for optional use of a Portal to upload and exchange documents which will facilitate the mortgage modification process.

RULE 9023–1. MOTIONS FOR RECONSIDERATION

A motion for reconsideration must be filed within fourteen (14) days after the entry of the judgment, order, or decree concerned.

[Effective January 1, 2005. Amended effective December 1, 2009.]

RULE 9023–2. POST–TRIAL MOTIONS

(a) Post–Trial Motions to be Written. All motions after trial must be written and must contain a certification by counsel for the movant that he or she has sought concurrence in the motion from each party and that it has been either given or denied. In accordance with the procedures set forth in the Miscellaneous Order 5:05-mp-50007 and the Administrative Procedures available on the court's website (www. pamb.uscourts.gov), every motion must be accompanied by a proposed order. (See L.B.R. 9013–1(b)).

(b) Documents Supporting Post–Trial Motions. When allegations of fact not of record are relied upon in support of a motion, all pertinent affidavits, transcripts of depositions, and other documents must accompany the motion whenever practicable. In any event, such supporting documents must be filed within fourteen (14) days after the motion has been filed,

unless otherwise ordered by the court. Affidavits in support of a motion for new trial must be served with the motion as required by Fed. R. Civ. P. 59(c).

(c) Grounds. Post-trial motions must state with particularity any trial errors alleged as grounds for relief.

(d) Post–Trial Brief of Moving Party. The brief of the moving party must be filed within fourteen (14) days after the filing of the motion, unless, upon motion and for good cause shown, the court directs otherwise. If a supporting legal brief is not filed within the time provided, the motion may be deemed to be withdrawn.

(e) Post–Trial Brief of Respondent. The brief of the respondent must be filed within fourteen (14) days after service of the brief of the moving party, unless, upon motion and for good cause shown, the court directs otherwise. If a responsive legal brief is not filed within the time provided herein, the respondent may be deemed not to oppose such motion.

(f) After–Discovered Evidence. A motion for a new trial on the ground of after-discovered evidence must, in addition to all other requirements, be accompanied by the affidavits of the witnesses relied upon, stating the substance of their testimony and the reasons why it could not have been introduced at trial.

(g) Disposal of Post–Trial Motions. Notwithstanding the deadlines set forth in this rule, the court may summarily dispose of post-trial motions at any time during their pendency.

[Effective January 1, 2005. Amended effective January 1, 2008; December 1, 2009; December 1, 2011.]

RULE 9024–1. RELIEF FROM JUDGMENT OR ORDER

A motion filed under F.R.B.P. 9024 is governed by the provisions of L.B.R. 9023–1.

[Effective January 1, 2005.]

RULE 9029–1. ATTORNEY ADVISORY COMMITTEE

The court will appoint a committee of attorneys who regularly practice in the Bankruptcy Court for the Middle District of Pennsylvania to advise the court on issues identified by the court and by the members of the bar.

(a) Membership. The committee consists of the three (3) judges of the court, the Assistant United States trustee for the District, or his or her designee, the chapter 13 trustee, or his or her designee, the President of the Middle District Bankruptcy Bar Association, or his or her designee, the Chair of the Middle District Bankruptcy Bar Association Rules Committee, and eight (8) attorneys who are engaged in bankruptcy practice in the District and who represent the diverse interests of the District. The bankruptcy attorney members of the committee will be appointed by the Chief Judge after consultation with the other judges of the court and the President of the Middle District Bankruptcy Bar Association. The names of the committee members will be posted on the court's website (www.pamb.uscourts.gov). The clerk, or his or her designee, will serve as the secretary of the committee, and may invite staff to attend the meetings in order to facilitate the discussion of agenda items.

(b) Term of Office. Each bankruptcy attorney member of the committee will serve a three (3) year term, beginning January 1 of each year. In the event of a vacancy on the committee, the Chief Judge will select a bankruptcy attorney to fill the vacancy for the remainder of the term.

(c) Meetings. The committee will meet quarterly or as otherwise determined by the Chief Judge. All minutes of the committee meetings will be posted on the court's website (www.pamb.uscourts.gov).

(d) Duties. The committee will advise the court on matters of court administration and serve as a liaison between the bankruptcy bar and the court on administrative matters. The committee, or designated subcommittees thereof, will make any studies and render any reports and recommendations requested by the court. The committee, or designated subcommittees thereof, will recommend amendments to the Local Bankruptcy Rules and Forms.

[Effective April 4, 2011. Amended effective September 1, 2014; June 1, 2016.]

RULE 9037–1. REDACTION OF PERSONAL IDENTIFIERS IN FILINGS MADE WITH THE COURT

(a) Personal Identifiers. As used in this rule, the term "Personal Identifiers" includes:

(1) A social security number, taxpayer-identification number, or financial-account number showing more than the last four (4) digits;

(2) An individual's birth date showing more than the year; and

(3) The name of an individual, other than the debtor, known to be and identified as a minor.

(b) Redacted Documents. Any attorney, party, or other person filing documents with the court shall ensure that Personal Identifiers are redacted in accordance with F.R.B.P. 9037.

(c) Responsibility for Redaction. The clerk is not responsible for reviewing documents filed to ensure compliance with F.R.B.P. 9037. Unless the court orders otherwise, the clerk is not required to redact

any pleadings or documents filed in violation of F.R.B.P. 9037.

(d) Request to Redact. Any party in interest or person whose Personal Identifiers are contained in a document filed with the court may file a request to redact. A redaction request may be made using the court's Application Requesting Redaction of Personal Information form (L.B.F. 9037–1). The request must include the applicable redaction fee, unless the court has granted a waiver of the fee. A person making a redaction request must serve the request on the debtor, any individual whose Personal Identifiers have been exposed, the case trustee (if any), and the United States trustee. A certificate of service conforming to L.B.R. 9013–2 demonstrating service on the above-referenced parties must be filed within five (5) days of filing the request. If the request is approved, the clerk will promptly restrict the original documents from public view and make a notation on the docket that the original has been restricted from public view. Unless the court orders otherwise, the requesting party must then file the redacted document within fourteen (14) days of the court's approval.

[Effective September 14, 2015. Amended effective June 1, 2016.]

RULE 9070–1. EXHIBITS

(a) Paper Exhibits. Whenever the number of exhibits in any case to be presented at hearing or trial by either party exceeds fifteen (15), the party intending to offer such exhibits must tab, number, and index them in a binder. A complete copy of the exhibits must be provided to all parties at least seven (7) days prior to the trial or hearing, and to the court at the time of trial or hearing, unless otherwise ordered by the court. This requirement applies only to exhibits used in a party's case in chief and not to exhibits used for purposes of impeachment or rebuttal. Failure to timely exchange proposed exhibits in accordance with this rule may result in the court barring the admissions of any unexchanged exhibits.

(b) Electronic Exhibits. A party who wishes to electronically display exhibits must contact the assigned judge's courtroom deputy at least seven (7) days before the trial or hearing to coordinate with the court's automation department to allow for such electronic display. Any party using electronically displayed exhibits must, at the time of trial or hearing, provide the court with three (3) copies of the exhibits on digital storage devices, such as USB flash drives.

[Effective January 1, 2005. Amended effective January 1, 2008; December 1, 2009; June 1, 2016.]

RULE 9070–2. EXHIBITS AFTER FINAL JUDGMENT

Fourteen (14) days after entry of final, non-appealable judgment, each party is responsible for retrieving any exhibits, models, diagrams, or other physical evidence introduced at trial or hearing. If exhibits are not retrieved within the required time period, the clerk may dispose of the items without notice.

[Effective January 1, 2005. Amended effective January 1, 2008; December 1, 2009.]

RULE 9071–1. STIPULATIONS

Any proposed order requesting approval of a stipulation must be submitted as a separate document.

[Effective January 1, 2005.]

RULE 9073–1. HEARINGS

(a) **Testimony of Witnesses.** Unless otherwise directed, all hearings and trials are evidentiary in nature at which witnesses may testify.

(b) **Contested Matters—Procedure.**

(1) *Hearing.* Upon the filing of a motion, the clerk will set a date by which an answer or other responsive pleading must be filed. If a responsive pleading is not filed by the answer date, the court may grant the relief requested subject to the limitations of F.R.B.P. 9006(f). Except as otherwise provided in these rules, no hearing date on the motion will be set.

(2) *Motions.* Notwithstanding the language of paragraph (1), hearings are required and will be set on the following motions:

(a) for relief under 11 U.S.C. § 362(k);

(b) for sanctions under F.R.B.P. 9011;

(c) for contempt;

(d) to substantively consolidate under L.B.R. 1015–1(b);

(e) to dismiss the case with prejudice, including all motions filed pursuant to 11 U.S.C. § 109; and

(f) to disqualify counsel.

(3) *Approval of Sales of Property Free and Clear of Liens.* While not required in the absence of a responsive pleading, at the request of the movant, a hearing will be held regarding a motion for approval of sales of property free and clear of liens under L.B.R. 6004–5(c).

[Effective January 1, 2005. Amended effective January 1, 2008; October 8, 2008.]

RULE 9074–1. TELEPHONE OR VIDEO APPEARANCE

(a) **General Telephone Procedure.** An attorney or pro se party who wishes to participate in a matter telephonically must consult "Telephonic Court Appearance Information (CourtCall)" located on the court's website (www.pamb.uscourts.gov).

(b) **Request for Appearance by Video.** A request to appear by video must allege cause and be submitted in writing at least seven (7) days before the scheduled conference or hearing. Requests must include a certificate of concurrence or nonconcurrence from the other parties concerning the request. If the request is granted, the requestor must provide the court with the location and video conference numbers at the remote site. It is the responsibility of the requestor to arrange with the clerk's office for a test of the system prior to the date of the hearing or conference to ensure compatibility of the conferencing systems.

[Effective January 1, 2005. Amended effective January 1, 2008; March 12, 2009; December 1, 2009; October 15, 2010; December 1, 2011.]

RULE 9075–1. EMERGENCY ORDERS

(a) **General Procedure.** In any case where a party files a pleading that requires an immediate hearing date or is seeking emergency relief from the court (i.e., temporary restraining orders or preliminary injunctions), the proponent must proceed as follows:

(1) Any motion filed under this rule must state in the caption that it is an "Emergency Motion" or "Request for Expedited Consideration". Prior to filing the motion, movant must provide email notification of the intention to file the motion to the appropriate judge's chambers.

(2) All interested parties must be notified of the request by facsimile, email, or other electronic means prior to the filing of the request for expedited consideration.

(3) The emergency motion must specify the reasons why expedited consideration is necessary and attach a copy of the underlying pleading as an exhibit.

(4) A proposed order granting the motion for expedited relief and proposing a method of prompt service of the order and the underlying substantive motion must be filed with the emergency motion.

(b) **Emergency Sale.** A seller, without any notice or with such notice as the court directs, may conduct an emergency sale. Such sale may be conducted only upon leave of court obtained after filing a motion specifying the following:

(1) the property to be sold;

(2) the terms of the sale; and

(3) the reasons why the sale must be conducted without notice.

[Effective January 1, 2005. Amended effective January 1, 2008; December 1, 2009; September 1, 2014.]

COMMENTS:

L.B.R. 9075–1 was amended effective December 1, 2009, to modify the captioning requirements for requests for expedited relief or consideration and to delete provisions for facsimile transmission to the court.

L.B.R. 9075–1 was amended effective September 1, 2014, to provide for advanced notice of emergency filings by email to chambers.

APPENDIX

APPENDIX 2016–1. PROJECT CATEGORIES

ASSET ANALYSIS AND RECOVERY: Identification and review of potential assets including causes of action and non-litigation recoveries.

ASSET DISPOSITION: Sales, leases (§ 365 matters), abandonment, and related transaction work.

BUSINESS OPERATIONS: Issues related to debtor-in-possession operating in chapter 11 such as employee, vendor, tenant issues, and other similar problems.

CASE ADMINISTRATION: Coordination and compliance activities, including preparation of statement of financial affairs; schedules; list of contracts; United States trustee interim statements and operating reports; contacts with the United States trustee; general creditor inquiries.

CLAIMS ADMINISTRATION AND OBJECTIONS: Specific claim inquiries; bar date motions; analyses, objections, and allowances of claims.

EMPLOYEE BENEFITS/PENSIONS: Review issues such as severance, retention, 401K coverage and continuance of pension plan.

FEE/EMPLOYMENT APPLICATIONS: Preparations of employment and fee applications for self or others; motions to establish interim procedures.

FEE/EMPLOYMENT OBJECTIONS: Review of and objections to the employment and fee applications of others.

FINANCING: Matters under §§ 361, 363 and 364 including cash collateral and secured claims; loan document analysis.

LITIGATION: There should be a separate category established for each matter (e.g., XYZ Litigation).

MEETINGS OF CREDITORS: Preparing for and attending the conference of creditors, the § 341(a) meeting, and other creditors' committee meetings.

PLAN AND DISCLOSURE STATEMENT: Formulation, presentation, and confirmation; compliance with the plan confirmation order, related orders, and rules; disbursement and case closing activities, except those related to the allowance and objections to allowance of claims.

RELIEF FROM STAY PROCEEDINGS: Matters relating to termination or continuation of automatic stay under § 362.

The following categories are generally more applicable to accountants and financial advisors, but may be used by all professionals as appropriate.

ACCOUNTING/AUDITING: Activities related to maintaining and auditing books of account, preparation of financial statements, and account analysis.

BUSINESS ANALYSIS: Preparation and review of company business plan; development and review of strategies; preparation and review of cash flow forecasts and feasibility studies.

CORPORATE FINANCE: Review financial aspects of potential mergers, acquisitions, and disposition of company or subsidiaries.

DATA ANALYSIS: Management information systems review, installation and analysis, construction, maintenance, and reporting of significant case financial data, lease rejection, claims, etc.

LITIGATION CONSULTING: Providing consulting and expert witness services relating to various bankruptcy matters such as insolvency, feasibility, avoiding actions; forensic accounting, etc.

RECONSTRUCTION ACCOUNTING: Reconstructing books and records from past transactions and bringing accounting current.

TAX ISSUES: Analysis of tax issues and preparation of state and federal tax returns.

VALUATION: Appraise or review appraisals of assets.

[Effective October 18, 2000; redesignated effective January 1, 2005.]

LOCAL BANKRUPTCY FORMS

LOCAL BANKRUPTCY FORM 1007–1(c). CERTIFICATION
OF NO PAYMENT ADVICES

LOCAL BANKRUPTCY FORM 1007-1(c)

**IN THE UNITED STATES BANKRUPTCY COURT
FOR THE MIDDLE DISTRICT OF PENNSYLVANIA**

IN RE:

                   :   CHAPTER ____

                   :

                   :   CASE NO. __-___-bk-_____

                   :

                   :

Debtor(s)   :

CERTIFICATION OF NO PAYMENT ADVICES
pursuant to 11 U.S.C. § 521(a)(1)(B)(iv)

I, _____, hereby certify that within sixty (60) days before the date of filing the above-captioned bankruptcy petition, I did not receive payment advices (e.g. "pay stubs"), as contemplated by 11 U.S.C. § 521(a)(1)(B)(iv), from any source of employment. I further certify that I received no payment advices during that period because:

☐   I have been unable to work due to a disability throughout the sixty (60) days immediately preceding the date of the above-captioned petition.

☐   I have received no regular income other than Social Security payments throughout the sixty (60) days immediately preceding the date of the above-captioned petition.

☐   My sole source of regular employment income throughout the sixty (60) days immediately preceding the date of the above-captioned petition has been through self-employment from which I do not receive evidence of wages or a salary at fixed intervals.

☐   I have been unemployed throughout the sixty (60) days immediately preceding the date of the above-captioned petition.

☐   I did not receive payment advices due to factors other than those listed above. (Please explain) _____
_____
_____

I certify under penalty of perjury that the information provided in this certification is true and correct to the best of my knowledge and belief.

DATE: _____   _____
                                        Debtor

                                        _____

                                        Joint Debtor

[Effective December 1, 2009.]

LOCAL BANKRUPTCY FORM 2016–1. SUMMARY COVER SHEET FEES AND EXPENSES APPLICATION

LOCAL BANKRUPTCY FORM 2016-1

IN THE UNITED STATES BANKRUPTCY COURT
FOR THE MIDDLE DISTRICT OF PENNSYLVANIA

IN RE:

:	CHAPTER ____
:	
:	CASE NO. __-___-bk-_____
:	
:	
Debtor(s) :	

SUMMARY COVER SHEET
FEES AND EXPENSES APPLICATION

a.   Your applicant was appointed on _____, based on an application filed _____.

b.   Your applicant represents _____.

c.   This application is a _____ (state whether interim or final application).

d.   The total amount of compensation for which reimbursement is sought is _____ and is for the period from _____ to _____.

e.   The total amount of expenses for which reimbursement is sought is _____ and is for the period from _____ to _____.

f.   The dates and amounts of any retainer received are _____.

g.   The dates and amounts of withdrawals from the retainer by the Applicant are

_____.

h.   The dates and amounts of previous compensation allowed are:

_____

i.   The dates and amounts of previous compensation paid are:

_____

j.   There are/are no objections to prior fee applications of Applicant that have not been ruled upon by the Court in this bankruptcy case.

Applicant's Signature

_____

DATED: _____

[Effective October 18, 2000; redesignated and amended effective January 1, 2005.]

LOCAL BANKRUPTCY FORM 2016–2(a).   RIGHTS AND RESPONSIBILITIES AGREEMENT BETWEEN CHAPTER 13 DEBTORS AND THEIR ATTORNEYS

LOCAL BANKRUPTCY FORM 2016-2(a)

IN THE UNITED STATES BANKRUPTCY COURT
FOR THE MIDDLE DISTRICT OF PENNSYLVANIA

IN RE: *   CHAPTER 13
                                          *
        Debtor   *   CASE NO. __-___-bk-_____
                                          *

RIGHTS AND RESPONSIBILITIES AGREEMENT BETWEEN CHAPTER 13 DEBTORS AND THEIR ATTORNEYS

It is important for persons who file for bankruptcy under Chapter 13 to understand their rights and responsibilities. It is also important for them to know what their attorneys' responsibilities are and to appreciate the necessity of communicating openly with their attorneys to achieve successful results. These clients are entitled to expect certain services to be performed by their attorneys. The following Rights and Responsibilities Agreement has been adopted by the Bankruptcy Court for the Middle District of Pennsylvania. By signing this Rights and Responsibilities Agreement, attorneys and their clients accept the responsibilities outlined in this Agreement.

Under the rules of the Bankruptcy Court an attorney who files a bankruptcy case or who appears on behalf of a client filing for bankruptcy, other than as special counsel, is required to represent the client throughout the case, unless the client hires a new attorney or decides to represent himself or herself. However, an attorney may ask the Bankruptcy Court for permission to withdraw from a case. An attorney may request the Bankruptcy Court to approve additional fees, beyond those described in the Agreement, but only after the client has been given an opportunity to object and Court approval is obtained.

NOTICE TO ATTORNEYS: Attorneys have additional responsibilities which are imposed by the Bankruptcy Code and the Rules of Professional Conduct.

NOTICE TO CLIENTS: Your attorney may be unable to provide the services described in this Agreement if you do not provide accurate and complete information promptly and if you do not cooperate with your attorney during your case.

BEFORE THE CASE IS FILED:

You agree to:

1.   Provide your attorney with complete and accurate financial information, as promptly as possible, including any forms your attorney asks you to complete and copies of any documents that have been requested.

2.   Discuss your financial goals with your attorney.

3. Review all documents prepared by your attorney, advise your attorney about any necessary corrections or additions, and ask for explanations of any statements that you do not understand.

Your attorney agrees to:

1. Meet with you to review your debts, assets, liabilities, income, and expenses.

2. Discuss with you alternatives to bankruptcy, credit counseling, and the availability of relief under other chapters of the Bankruptcy Code.

3. Make all the disclosures required of your attorney as a debt relief agency.

4. Discuss the terms under which your attorney will represent you and prepare a written agreement describing the fee arrangement, including how your attorney will be paid.

5. Explain the expenses, in addition to attorneys fees, that will be incurred or may be incurred by you and how they must be paid.

6. Explain to you which payments must be made directly to creditors and which payments must be made to the Chapter 13 trustee.

7. Explain to you where to submit Chapter 13 plan payments, when to begin making payments, and the day of the month payments are due.

8. Explain to you the importance of insuring that your attorney is informed as to all changes in your contact information, including your phone number, mailing address, any email address, and place of employment.

9. Explain to you the consequences of failing to make direct payments to creditors, such as mortgage and auto payments, and failing to make payments to the Chapter 13 trustee.

10. Advise you concerning your obligation to attend the meeting of creditors.

11. Advise you of the necessity of maintaining appropriate insurance, such as homeowner's insurance and liability, collision, and comprehensive insurance on vehicles.

12. Timely prepare, file, and serve the bankruptcy petition, as well as statements, schedules, the plan, and other required documents and certificates, unless these documents are filed after the petition as permitted under the Bankruptcy Rules.

AFTER THE CASE IS FILED:

You agree to:

1. Begin making plan payments to the Chapter 13 trustee as instructed by your attorney.

2.   Attend the meeting of creditors and any other court proceeding for which you receive notice unless informed by your attorney that your presence is not necessary.

3.   Review and comply with notices you receive from the Court and respond to communications from your attorney.

4.   Keep your attorney and the Chapter 13 trustee informed of any changes to your contact information, including phone numbers and mailing addresses.

5.   Keep your attorney informed of any significant changes in your situation, including job loss or layoff, significant health problems requiring absence from work, and divorce or separation.

6.   Inform your attorney immediately if contacted by a creditor or if any action is taken against any of your assets or against you.

7.   Contact your attorney before buying, selling, or refinancing major assets such as a home or vehicle.

8.   Promptly provide copies of all documents requested by your attorney.

9.   Reimburse your attorney for all fees paid to third parties and charges advanced on your behalf (for example, credit counseling fees or credit report charges) unless your attorney agrees that these amounts will be paid through the plan.

The attorney agrees to provide all services necessary for representation and specifically to:

1.   Submit to the Chapter 13 trustee properly documented proof of all sources of income and most recently filed tax return for you.

2.   Appear at the meeting of creditors with you.

3.   Respond to objections to plan confirmation and, where necessary, prepare an amended plan.

4.   Prepare, file, and serve all statements, schedules, and the plan (if not filed with the petition) as well as any required amendments to any of these documents.

5.   Prepare, file, and serve motions to buy, sell, or refinance real estate or personal property.

6.   Review the file to ascertain if all required tax returns were filed and obtain and file the Pre-Confirmation Certification.

7.   Obtain the Domestic Support Obligation Certification, if necessary, and forward it to the Chapter 13 trustee.

8.   Attempt to obtain all secured Proofs of Claim, and/or prepare and file Proofs of Claim on behalf of creditors provided for in the plan, when appropriate.

9. Prepare, file, and serve objections to claims, if necessary.

10. Notify you of any pleading seeking relief against you and provide you with a deadline by which you must contact your attorney to discuss a response to the pleading, which also will explain possible consequences if you fail to respond.

11. Represent you at all hearings in which you have sought relief or have filed a response to a pleading seeking relief unless the matter has been settled. This does not include representation at adversary hearings.

12. Review any Transfer of Claims and any Notice of Mortgage Payment Change and advise of same, if necessary.

13. Prepare and serve any Motion to Suspend Trustee Payments.

14. Prepare and file any Motion for Wage Attachment for the Chapter 13 trustee or other secured creditor.

15. After your plan is confirmed, prepare and file any necessary motions to modify the confirmed plan and modified plans.

16. Explain to you what services will require the payment of additional legal fees and how those fees will be requested from the Court and that they may require the filing of an amended or modified plan. This explanation will include a discussion of what types of issues must be resolved through adversary proceedings.

17. Provide you with copies of all applications for the payment of fees for legal services, including time records, if required, before the applications are filed with the Bankruptcy Court.

18. Assist you in monitoring the status of your plan payments and in resolving any discrepancies between your records and those of the Chapter 13 trustee.

19. When appropriate, file motions to extend or impose the automatic stay.

20. If you qualify, assist you in attempting to obtain a mortgage modification. This only includes a modification which is necessary to obtain confirmation of the plan.

21. Respond promptly to your questions and communications throughout the term of the plan.

22. Advise you as to the requirement to complete an instructional course in personal financial management and the consequences of not doing so.

23. Advise you as to the requirements to complete the Debtors Certification Regarding Domestic Support Obligations and the consequences of not doing so.

24. Obtain a "No Position Letter" from the Chapter 13 trustee or file a Motion to Incur Debt and serve same.

25.   Timely notify you when a hearing has been rescheduled or when a hearing is no longer required.

26.   Review the Notice of Final Cure Payment and any response to the Notice of Final Cure Payment, and, if necessary, prepare and file a Motion for Determination of Final Cure and Payment of All Post-Petition Payments.

27.   Prepare a Motion for Early and/or Hardship Discharge if the facts and law support same.

SUMMARY OF AGREEMENT FOR PAYMENT OF ATTORNEY'S FEES

The Bankruptcy Court has adopted a "presumptively reasonable fee" of **$4000.00** for legal services provided through the confirmation of a Chapter 13 plan. If you operate a business and the Chapter 13 trustee requires you to provide a business examination report or if you hold the controlling interest in a corporation or LLC that is operating a business, the Court has determined that an additional **$1000.00** fee for legal services is also presumptively reasonable. In addition, if your plan provides for future mortgage payments to be made through the plan ("conduit plan") rather than directly to the mortgage company, an additional **$500.00** fee has been determined to be presumptively reasonable. Debtor(s') counsel will be allowed to charge an additional fee of $500.00 for amending the plan post-confirmation due to late Proofs of Claim being filed, adding post-petition payments to the plan, to resolve a Motion to Dismiss for material default, change in financial circumstances, or extending the plan term due to the Debtor(s) request. Counsel may elect either to accept an additional $500.00 fee for a post-confirmation plan amendment, or counsel may request compensation for same if the time and expense incurred exceeds $500.00. The cost of serving the modified plan will be your responsibility and must be reimbursed by you. Debtor(s') counsel will not be allowed to charge the additional legal fee of $500.00 for making minor changes, such as changing the name of a creditor. In addition, Debtor(s') counsel will be allowed to charge additional legal fees for preparing, filing, and serving a Motion to Sell Real or Personal Property. The fee will be disclosed in the Motion, Notice, and Order and served on all creditors. No fee application is required. The attorney fee will be paid at closing. In the event that the sale does not proceed to closing, Debtor(s') counsel will be allowed to file a Fee Application to collect said fees. Debtor(s') counsel will be allowed to collect the sale motion filing fee prior to filing the Motion to Sell, without Court approval.

These "presumptively reasonable fees" are neither minimum nor maximum fees for Chapter 13 cases. If an attorney agrees to perform the services set forth in this Rights and Responsibilities Agreement and to charge no more for these services than is described above, the attorney is not required to file a fee application detailing the work performed through the confirmation of a plan. If you and your attorney agree that you will pay for services provided based on an hourly rate, or through some other arrangement, the attorney must submit an application to the Court with time records to obtain approval of the fees. In addition, even if an attorney has agreed to accept a "presumptively reasonable fee" for services through the confirmation of a plan, the attorney must submit fee applications and obtain Court approval for any additional fees charged for services related to adversary proceedings or for services provided after a plan is confirmed.

In this case the parties agree that the legal fees for services to be provided through the confirmation of a plan, excluding adversary proceedings will be (complete one of the following boxes:)

☐ $_____ , the presumptively reasonable fee

☐ $_____ per hour, to be adjusted in accordance with the terms of the written fee agreement between you and your attorney (describe material terms of fee agreement or attach fee agreement) _____

_____

_____

Other than the initial retainer, your attorney may not receive fees directly from you after your bankruptcy case is filed. All other attorney's fees must be paid through the Chapter 13 Plan unless otherwise ordered by the Bankruptcy Court. These fees are separate from and in addition to any filing fees that you must pay when documents are filed by your attorney with the Bankruptcy Court.

If you dispute the legal services provided or the fees charged by your attorney, you may file an objection with the Bankruptcy Court. If your attorney believes that he or she cannot continue to represent you due to lack of cooperation or because of an ethical conflict, your attorney may request the Bankruptcy Court to permit him or her to withdraw from your case. You will receive notice of a request to withdraw and may contest the request at a hearing before the Court.

IN NO CASE SHALL YOUR ATTORNEY BE REQUIRED TO FILE A MOTION, PLAN, OBJECTION, OR ANSWER THAT IS NOT SUPPORTED BY CURRENT LAW.

Client: By signing this Rights and Responsibilities Agreement, I certify that have read the Agreement and understand and agree to carry out the terms to the best of my ability. I understand I am entitled to receive a signed copy of the Agreement.

Attorney: By signing this Agreement, your attorney certifies that he or she has reviewed this Agreement with you and answered your questions and that he or she agrees to perform the services described.

_____
Client   Date

_____
Client   Date

_____
Attorney   Date

Instructions: This Agreement is not to be filed with the Court. The original must be retained by the attorney and a copy provided to the client.

[Effective September 1, 2014.]

LOCAL BANKRUPTCY FORM 2016–2(b). APPLICATION OF ATTORNEY FOR CHAPTER 13 DEBTOR FOR COMPENSATION AND REIMBURSEMENT OF EXPENSES

LOCAL BANKRUPTCY FORM 2016-2(b)

IN THE UNITED STATES BANKRUPTCY COURT
FOR THE MIDDLE DISTRICT OF PENNSYLVANIA

IN RE: :   CHAPTER 13

                            :

                            :   CASE NO. __-____-bk-_____

                            :

                            :

       Debtor(s)   :

APPLICATION OF ATTORNEY FOR CHAPTER 13 DEBTOR
FOR COMPENSATION AND REIMBURSEMENT OF EXPENSES

(Name of applicant) _____ applies for approval of compensation as Chapter 13 Debtor(s)' counsel and for reimbursement of expenses pursuant to 11 U.S.C. § 330 as follows:

1.   Applicant is counsel for Debtor(s).

2.   Debtor(s) filed a petition for bankruptcy relief on _____ *(date)*.

3.   Applicant previously filed a Disclosure of Compensation of Attorney for Debtor(s) pursuant to Fed. R. Bankr. P. 2016(b), which is attached as Exhibit "A" to this Application.

4.   Debtor(s) and Applicant have executed a Rights and Responsibilities Agreement and a copy of the Agreement was provided to Debtor(s).

5.   This Application is _____ *(state whether an interim or a final application)*.

6.   *(Check all applicable items)*

        ( )   a.   Debtor(s)' Chapter 13 Plan was confirmed on _____ *(date)*.

        ( )   b.   The order approving the last post-confirmation modification of Debtor(s)' confirmed Chapter 13 plan was entered on _____ *(date)*.

        ( )   c.   Debtor(s) have not confirmed a Plan.

7.   The dates and amounts of previous compensation paid are:

      a.   as a retainer _____ *(list dates and amounts)*;

      b.   paid by the Chapter 13 Trustee through a confirmed Plan _____ _____ *(list dates and amounts)*;

    c.   other _____
               (*describe source, amount and date paid*).

8.   Compensation previously approved by the Court following the filing of an interim Application are: _____

      _____

      _____ (*dates and amounts*).

9.   If Applicant has not agreed with Debtor(s) to accept the Presumptively Reasonable Fee ("PRF"), or is filing a supplemental fee application after confirmation of the Plan in addition to the PRF, Applicant requests compensation in the amount of $_____ and reimbursement of expenses in the amount of $_____ for the period of _____ to _____. A chronological listing of services performed and itemization of expenses for which reimbursement is requested for this time is attached as Exhibit "B" to this Application.

10.   Legal services were provided by all professionals at the hourly rates set forth at the beginning of the chronological listing of services provided on Exhibit "B."

11.   (*Check one*)

    ( )   Debtor(s) have reviewed this Application prior to its filing and have approved the requested amounts.

    ( )   Debtor(s) have reviewed this Application prior to its filing and have not approved the request amounts.

    ( )   Debtor(s) have not reviewed this Application prior to its filing.

    ( )   Debtor(s) have not approved the requested amounts.

12.   Objections are pending to the following prior fee applications: (*list date application was filed and name of objector, if no objections pending state "none"*).

      _____

      _____

      _____

    WHEREFORE, your Applicant respectfully requests this Honorable Court to approve the requested compensation in the amount of $_____ and reimbursement of expenses in the amount of $_____ pursuant to 11 U.S.C. § 330, and if this is a Final Fee Application, to determine that all prior interim orders are final.

Dated: _____   _____

                                       Applicant's Signature

[Effective September 1, 2014.]

LOCAL BANKRUPTCY FORM 2016–2(c). REQUEST FOR PAYMENT OF CHAPTER 13 COMPENSATION AND EXPENSES

LOCAL BANKRUPTCY FORM 2016-2(c)

IN THE UNITED STATES BANKRUPTCY COURT
FOR THE MIDDLE DISTRICT OF PENNSYLVANIA

IN RE:	*	CHAPTER 13
	*	
Debtor	*	CASE NO. __-___-bk-_____
	*	

REQUEST FOR PAYMENT OF CHAPTER 13 COMPENSATION AND EXPENSES

Instructions: Complete **Part A** for payment of the presumptively reasonable fee, as described in L.B.R. 2016-2(c), being paid through a Chapter 13 plan and reimbursement of expenses. Complete **Part B** for payment of compensation and reimbursement of expenses awarded by separate Court order. Complete **Part C** for all requests for payment of compensation and reimbursement of expenses.

A. Presumptively reasonable fees under L.B.R. 2016-2(c)	
1. Amount agreed to by debtor	$
2. Less amount paid to attorney prior to filing petition	$
3. Balance of compensation to be paid through plan distributions	$
4. Expenses advanced to be paid through plan distributions: (describe expense and amount)	$

B. Compensation and reimbursement of expenses allowed upon application and order under LBR 2016-2(a)	
1. Retainer received	$
2. Compensation earned prepetition and paid to attorney prior to filing petition	$
3. Expenses reimbursed prepetition	$
4. Balance in retainer after deduction of prepetition compensation and expenses	$
5. Compensation and expenses to be approved by the Court and to be paid through plan distributions, less balance in client trust account	$

C. The undersigned hereby requests payment through the plan for compensation and reimbursement of expenses under 11 U.S.C. § 503(b)(2) in the following amount based on the information above:	$

Dated:_____   _____

                                 Attorney for Debtor

[Effective September 1, 2014. Amended effective June 1, 2016.]

LOCAL BANKRUPTCY FORM 3007-1. NOTICE OF OBJECTION TO CLAIM AND HEARING DATE

Effective 7/1/15

LOCAL BANKRUPTCY FORM 3007-1

IN THE UNITED STATES BANKRUPTCY COURT
FOR THE MIDDLE DISTRICT OF PENNSYLVANIA

IN RE:

                    :   CHAPTER ____

                    :

                    :

                    :   CASE NO. __-___-bk-_____

                    :

        Debtor(s)   :

                    :

                    :

                    :

        Objector   :

  v.   :

                    :

                    :

                    :

        Claimant   :

TO: _____ ("Claimant")

NOTICE OF OBJECTION TO CLAIM AND HEARING DATE

_____ has filed an objection to the proof of claim you filed in this bankruptcy case.

Your claim may be reduced, modified, or eliminated. You should read these papers carefully and discuss them with your attorney, if you have one.

If you do not want the court to eliminate or change your claim, you or your lawyer must attend the hearing on the objection, scheduled to be held:

United States Bankruptcy Court (Address of Court) (Address of Court) (Address of Court)	Date: _____ Time: _____

If you or your attorney do not attend the hearing on the objection, the court may decide that you do not oppose the objection to your claim.

                    _____
                    Attorney for Objector

                    _____
                    (Address)

                    _____

                    _____

                    _____
                    (Phone)

                    _____
                    (Facsimile)

                    _____
                    (Email)

                    _____
                    (Attorney ID No.)

Date of Notice: _____

[Effective October 18, 2000; redesignated and amended effective January 1, 2005; December 1, 2009; July 1, 2015.]

LOCAL BANKRUPTCY FORM 3015–1. CHAPTER 13 PLAN

LOCAL BANKRUPTCY FORM 3015-1

**IN THE UNITED STATES BANKRUPTCY COURT
FOR THE MIDDLE DISTRICT OF PENNSYLVANIA**

IN RE:

	: **CHAPTER 13**
	: **CASE NO. __-___-bk-_____**
	:
	: **CHAPTER 13 PLAN**
	:
Debtor(s)	: (Indicate if applicable)
	: ( ) # **MOTIONS TO AVOID LIENS**
	: ( ) # **MOTIONS TO VALUE COLLATERAL**
	:
	: ( ) **ORIGINAL PLAN**
	: ( ) **AMENDED PLAN**
	: (Indicate 1ST, 2ND, 3RD, etc.)

YOUR RIGHTS WILL BE AFFECTED

READ THIS PLAN CAREFULLY. If you oppose any provision of this plan you must file a timely written objection. This plan may be confirmed and become binding on you without further notice or hearing unless a written objection is filed before the deadline stated on the Notice issued in connection with the filing of the plan

---

PLAN PROVISIONS

DISCHARGE: (Check one)

(   )   The debtor will seek a discharge of debts pursuant to Section 1328(a).

(   )   The debtor is not eligible for a discharge of debts because the debtor has previously received a discharge described in Section 1328(f).

NOTICE OF SPECIAL PROVISIONS: (Check if applicable)

(   )   This plan contains special provisions that are not included in the standard plan as approved by the U.S. Bankruptcy Court for the Middle District of Pennsylvania. Those provisions are set out in Section 8 of this plan. Other than to insert text into the designated spaces or to expand the tables to include additional claims, the preprinted language of this form may not be altered. This does not mean that the Debtor is prohibited from proposing additional or different plan provisions in Section 8. The Debtor may propose additional or different plan provisions or specify that any of the provisions will not be applicable, provided however, that each such provision or deletion shall be set forth herein in Section 8.

1.   **PLAN FUNDING AND LENGTH OF PLAN**

    A.   Plan Payments

        1.   To date, the Debtor(s) has paid $_____ (enter $0 if no payments have been made to the Trustee to date). Debtor(s) shall pay to the Trustee for the remaining term of the plan the following payments. If applicable, in addition to monthly plan payments, Debtor(s) shall make conduit payments through the Trustee as set forth below. The total base plan is $_____, plus other payments and property stated in Section 1B below:

Start mm/yy	End mm/yy	Plan Payment	Estimated Conduit Payment	Total Payment

				Total Payments: $

        2.   If the plan provides for conduit mortgage payments, and the mortgagee notifies the Trustee that a different payment is due, the Trustee shall notify the Debtor and the attorney for the Debtor, in writing, to adjust the conduit payments and the plan funding accordingly. Debtor(s) is responsible for all post-petition mortgage payments due prior to the initiation of conduit mortgage payments.

        3.   Debtor(s) shall take appropriate action to ensure that all applicable wage attachments are adjusted to conform to the terms of the plan.

        4.   CHECK ONE:(   ) Debtor(s) is at or under median income

                (   ) Debtor(s) is over median income. Debtor(s) calculates that a minimum of $_____ must be paid to unsecured, non-priority creditors in order to comply with the Means Test.

    B.   Liquidation of Assets

        1.   In addition to the above specified plan payments, Debtor(s) shall dedicate to the plan proceeds in the estimated amount of $_____ from the sale of property known and designated as _____ _____. All sales shall be completed by

_____, 20_____. If the property does not sell by the date specified, then the disposition of the property shall be as follows:

_____

2.   Other payments from any source(s) (describe specifically) shall be paid to the Trustee as follows: _____

3.   The Debtor estimates that the liquidation value of this estate is $_____. (Liquidation value is calculated as the value of all non-exempt assets after the deduction of valid liens and encumbrances and before the deduction of Trustee fees and priority claims.)

2.   SECURED CLAIMS

A.   <u>Pre-Confirmation Distributions</u>. Adequate protection and conduit payments in the following amounts will be paid by the Debtor to the Trustee. The Trustee will disburse these payments for which a proof of claim has been filed as soon as practicable after receipt of said payments from the Debtor.

Name of Creditor	Address	Account #	Estimated Monthly Payment
			$
			$

The Trustee will not make a partial payment. If the Debtor makes a partial plan payment, or if it is not paid on time and the Trustee is unable to pay timely a payment due on a claim in this section, the Debtor's cure of this default must include any applicable late charges.

Upon receipt, Debtor shall mail to the Trustee all notices from mortgagees including statements, payment coupons, impound and escrow notices, and notices concerning changes of the interest rate on variable interest rate loans. If any such notice informs the Debtor that the amount of the payment has increased or decreased, the change in the plan payment to the Trustee will not require modification of this plan.

B.   <u>Mortgages and Other Direct Payments by Debtor</u>. Payments will be made outside the plan according to the original contract terms, with no modification of contract terms, unless otherwise agreed to by the contracting parties, and with liens retained. All mortgage and other lien claim balances survive the plan if not avoided or paid in full under the plan.

Name of Creditor	Description of Collateral	Contractual Monthly Payment	Principal Balance of Claim
		$	$
		$	$
		$	$
		$	$

C.   Arrears. The Trustee shall distribute the amount of pre-petition arrearages set forth in the allowed proof of claim to each secured creditor set forth below. If the Debtor or the Trustee objects to a proof of claim and the objection is sustained, or if the plan provides for payment of amounts greater than the allowed proof of claim, the creditor's claim will be paid in the amount allowed by the court.

Name of Creditor	Description of Collateral	Estimated Pre-petition Arrears to be Cured	Estimated Post-petition Arrears to be Cured	Estimated Total to be paid in plan
		$	$	$
		$	$	$
		$	$	$
		$	$	$

D.   Secured Claims Paid According to Modified Terms. These amounts will be paid in the plan according to modified terms, and liens retained until entry of discharge. The excess of the creditor's claim will be treated as an unsecured claim. Any claim listed as "NO VALUE" in the "Modified Principal Balance" column below will be treated as an unsecured claim. THE LIENS WILL BE AVOIDED OR LIMITED THROUGH THE PLAN OR DEBTOR(S) WILL FILE AN ADVERSARY ACTION TO DETERMINE THE EXTENT, VALIDITY, AND PRIORITY OF THE LIEN (Select method in last column):

Name of Creditor	Description of Collateral	Modified Principal Balance	Interest Rate	Total Payment	Plan* or Adversary Action
		$	% $		
		$	% $		
		$	% $		

* "PLAN" INDICATES THAT THE DEBTOR(S) PROPOSES TO AVOID OR LIMIT THE LIEN OF THE CREDITOR IN THIS PLAN. CONFIRMATION OF THE PLAN SHALL CONSTITUTE A FINDING OF VALUATION PURSUANT TO SECTION 506(a). NO ADVERSARY COMPLAINT OR MOTION WILL BE FILED AND THE LIEN WILL BE AVOIDED BY A CONFIRMATION ORDER UPON DISCHARGE. IF THE CREDITOR WISHES TO CONTEST THE AVOIDANCE OF THE LIEN, THE CREDITOR MUST FILE AN OBJECTION TO THIS PLAN. OTHERWISE CONFIRMATION OF THE PLAN WILL AVOID THE LIEN UPON DISCHARGE.

     E.   <u>Other Secured Claims</u>. (Including conduit payments)

Name of Creditor	Description of Collateral	Principal balance of Claim	Interest Rate	Total to be paid in plan
		$	% $	
		$	% $	
		$	% $	

     F.   <u>Surrender of Collateral</u>. Debtor(s) surrenders the following assets to secured creditors. Upon confirmation of the plan, bankruptcy stays are lifted as to the collateral to be surrendered. This provision does not prejudice a creditor's right to move to lift the stay prior to confirmation.

         Name of Creditor   **Description of Collateral to be Surrendered**

G.   Lien Avoidance. The Debtor moves to avoid the following judicial and/or nonpossessory, non-purchase money liens of the following creditors pursuant to Section 522(f) (this section should not be used for statutory or consensual liens such as mortgages):

Name of Creditor   **Description of Collateral**

THE DEBTOR(S) PROPOSES TO AVOID THE JUDICIAL LIEN OF THE CREDITOR(S) IN THIS PLAN. CONFIRMATION OF THE PLAN SHALL CONSTITUTE A FINDING OF VALUATION AND ALLOWANCE OF EXEMPTIONS PURSUANT TO § 522(f). NO ADVERSARY COMPLAINT OR MOTION WILL BE FILED AND THE JUDICIAL LIEN WILL BE AVOIDED BY A CONFIRMATION ORDER UPON DISCHARGE. IF THE CREDITOR(S) WISHES TO CONTEST THE AVOIDANCE OF THE LIEN, THE CREDITOR(S) MUST FILE A TIMELY OBJECTION TO THIS PLAN. OTHERWISE, CONFIRMATION OF THE PLAN WILL AVOID THE LIEN UPON DISCHARGE.

H.   Optional provisions regarding duties of certain mortgage holders and servicers. Property of the estate vests upon closing of the case, and Debtor elects to include the following provisions. (Check if applicable)

( )   Confirmation of the plan shall impose an affirmative duty on the holders and/or servicers of any claims secured by liens, mortgages and/or deeds of trust on the principal residence of the Debtor to do the following:

(1)   Apply the payments received from the Trustee on the pre-petition arrearage, if any, only to such arrearage. If the plan provides for an allowed payment of post-petition arrearages as set forth in Section 2C, apply those payments to only the post-petition arrearages.

(2)   Deem the pre-petition arrearage as contractually current upon confirmation of the plan for the sole purpose of precluding the imposition of late payment charges or other default-related fees and services based solely on the pre-petition default or defaults.

(3)   Apply the post-petition monthly mortgage payments made by the Debtor to the post-petition mortgage obligations as provided for by the terms of the underlying mortgage note. Late charges may be assessed on post-petition payments as provided by the terms of the mortgage and note.

3.   **PRIORITY CLAIMS**

A.   Allowed unsecured claims entitled to priority under section 1322(a) will be paid in full unless modified under Section 8:

Name of Creditor	Estimated Total Payment
	$
	$
	$

B.   <u>Administrative Claims</u>:

     (1)   Trustee fees.   Percentage fees payable to the Trustee will be paid at the rate fixed by the United States Trustee, not to exceed 10%.

     (2)   Attorney fees. Check only one box:

         ☐   In addition to the retainer of $_____ already paid by the Debtor, the amount of $_____ in the plan. This represents the unpaid balance of the presumptively reasonable fee specified in L.B.R. 2016-2(c); or

         ☐ $_____ per hour, to be adjusted in accordance with the terms of the written fee agreement between the Debtor and the attorney. Payment of such lodestar compensation shall require a separate fee application with the requested amount of compensation approved by the Court pursuant to L.B.R. 2016-2(b).

     (3)   Other administrative claims.

Name of Creditor	Estimated Total Payment
	$
	$
	$

4.   UNSECURED CLAIMS

A.   <u>Claims of Unsecured Nonpriority Creditors Specially Classified</u>. Includes unsecured claims, such as co-signed unsecured debts, that will be paid in full even though all other unsecured claims may not be paid in full.

Name of Creditor	Reason for Special Classification	Amount of Claim	Interest Rate	Total Payment
		$	%	$
		$	%	$

B.	All remaining allowed unsecured claims shall receive a pro-rata distribution of any funds remaining after payment of the other classes.

5.	**EXECUTORY CONTRACTS AND UNEXPIRED LEASES**. The following executory contracts and unexpired leases are assumed (and pre-petition arrears to be cured in the plan) or rejected (so indicate):

Name of Creditor	Description of Collateral	Monthly Payment	Interest Rate	Pre-petition Arrears	Total Payment	Assume/Reject
		$	%	$	$	
		$	%	$	$	

6.	**REVESTING OF PROPERTY: (Check One)**

( )	Property of the estate will vest in the Debtor upon confirmation. (Not to be used with Section 2H)

( )	Property of the estate will vest in the Debtor upon closing of the case.

7.	**STUDENT LOAN PROVISIONS**

A.	<u>Student loan provisions</u>. This plan does not seek to discharge student loan(s) except as follows:

(NOTE: If you are not seeking to discharge a student loan(s), do not complete this section.)

Name of Creditor	Monthly Payment	Interest Rate	Pre-petition Arrears	Total Payment
	$	%	$	$
	$	%	$	$

8.	**OTHER PLAN PROVISIONS**

A.	Include the additional provisions below or on an attachment. **(NOTE: The plan and any attachment must be filed as one document, not as a plan and exhibit.)**

9.   ORDER OF DISTRIBUTION:

Payments from the plan will be made by the Trustee in the following order:

Level 1: _____

Level 2: _____

Level 3: _____

Level 4: _____

Level 5: _____

Level 6: _____

Level 7: _____

Level 8: _____

If the above Levels are not filled-in, then the order of distribution of plan payments will be determined by the Trustee using the following as a guide:

Level 1:   Adequate protection payments.

Level 2:   Debtor's attorney's fees.

Level 3:   Domestic Support Obligations.

Level 4:   Priority claims, pro rata.

Level 5:   Secured claims, pro rata.

Level 6:   Specially classified unsecured claims.

Level 7:   General unsecured claims.

Level 8:   Untimely filed unsecured claims to which the Debtor has not objected.

GENERAL PRINCIPLES APPLICABLE TO ALL PLANS

All pre-petition arrears and cramdowns shall be paid to the Trustee and disbursed to creditors through the plan.

If a pre-petition creditor files a secured, priority or specially classified claim after the bar date, the Trustee will treat the claim as allowed, subject to objection by the Debtor. Claims filed after the bar date that are not properly served on the Trustee will not be paid. The Debtor is responsible for reviewing claims and filing objections, if appropriate.

Dated: _____   _____

                                                              Attorney for Debtor

                                                              _____

                                                              Debtor

                                                              _____

                                                              Joint Debtor

[Effective January 1, 2008. Amended effective March 12, 2009; October 15, 2010; April 4, 2011; March 1, 2013; September 1, 2014; June 1, 2016.]

LOCAL BANKRUPTCY FORM 3015–2(a). CERTIFICATION REGARDING SERVICE OF AMENDED CHAPTER 13 PLAN

LOCAL BANKRUPTCY FORM 3015-2(a)

**IN THE UNITED STATES BANKRUPTCY COURT
FOR THE MIDDLE DISTRICT OF PENNSYLVANIA**

IN RE:

:	**CHAPTER 13**
:	
:	**CASE NO. __-___-bk-_____**
:	
:	
Debtor(s) :	

CERTIFICATION REGARDING SERVICE OF AMENDED CHAPTER 13 PLAN
(Altering Treatment of Claims)

The undersigned, counsel for the above-captioned Debtor(s), hereby certifies that the

_____ Amended Chapter 13 Plan filed on _____ proposes to alter the treatment

of the claims of the following creditors included in the confirmed Chapter 13 Plan:

_____

I further certify that notice of the filing of the _____ Amended Chapter 13 Plan has

been served on the above listed creditors and the Chapter 13 trustee, as evidenced by the attached

certificate of service, and that no other party, other than the creditors listed above, will be

affected by the provisions of the _____ Amended Chapter 13 Plan.

_____
Counsel for Debtor(s)

Dated: _____

[Effective January 1, 2008. Amended effective June 23, 2008; March 1, 2013; September 1, 2014.]

LOCAL BANKRUPTCY FORM 3015–2(b).   CERTIFICATION REGARDING SERVICE OF AMENDED CHAPTER 13 PLAN

LOCAL BANKRUPTCY FORM 3015-2(b)

**IN THE UNITED STATES BANKRUPTCY COURT
FOR THE MIDDLE DISTRICT OF PENNSYLVANIA**

IN RE:

	:	**CHAPTER 13**
	:	
	:	
	:	**CASE NO. __-____-bk-_____**
	:	
Debtor(s)	:	

CERTIFICATION REGARDING SERVICE OF AMENDED CHAPTER 13 PLAN
(Altering Funding or Making Technical Amendments)

The undersigned, counsel for the above-captioned Debtor(s), hereby certifies that the

_____ Amended Chapter 13 Plan filed on _____ proposes to alter the funding

of, or to make technical amendments to, the Chapter 13 Plan confirmed on _____,

but does not affect the treatment of the claims of any creditors included in the confirmed Plan,

including the amounts to be paid, the timing of the payments or the treatment of collateral:

I further certify that the _____ Amended Chapter 13 Plan has been served on the

Chapter 13 trustee, and because none of the claims provided for in the plan will be affected by

the provisions of the _____ Amended Chapter 13 Plan, no further notice is required.

_____
Counsel for Debtor(s)

Dated:_____

[Effective January 1, 2008. Amended effective May 14, 2008; June 23, 2008; March 1, 2013.]

LOCAL BANKRUPTCY FORM 3015–2(c). CERTIFICATION REGARDING SERVICE OF AMENDED CHAPTER 12 PLAN (ALTERING TREATMENT OF CLAIMS)

LOCAL BANKRUPTCY FORM 3015-2(c)

IN THE UNITED STATES BANKRUPTCY COURT
FOR THE MIDDLE DISTRICT OF PENNSYLVANIA

IN RE: : **CHAPTER 12**
            :
            : **CASE NO. __-___-bk-_____**
            :
            :
Debtor(s)   :

CERTIFICATION REGARDING SERVICE OF AMENDED CHAPTER 12 PLAN
(Altering Treatment of Claims)

The undersigned, counsel for the above-captioned Debtor(s), hereby certifies that the

_____ Amended Chapter 12 Plan filed on _____ proposes to alter the treatment

of the claims of the following creditors included in the confirmed Chapter 12 Plan:

_____

I further certify that notice of the filing of the _____ Amended Chapter 12 Plan has

been served on the above listed creditors and the Chapter 12 trustee, as evidenced by the attached

certificate of service, and that no other party, other than the creditors listed above, will be

affected by the provisions of the _____ Amended Chapter 12 Plan.

         _____
         Counsel for Debtor(s)

Dated: _____

[Effective September 1, 2014.]

LOCAL BANKRUPTCY FORM 3015–2(d). CERTIFICATION REGARD-ING SERVICE OF AMENDED CHAPTER 12 PLAN (ALTERING FUNDING OR MAKING TECHNICAL AMENDMENTS)

LOCAL BANKRUPTCY FORM 3015-2(d)

**IN THE UNITED STATES BANKRUPTCY COURT
FOR THE MIDDLE DISTRICT OF PENNSYLVANIA**

IN RE: :   **CHAPTER 12**
                                                :
                                                :
                                                :   **CASE NO. __-___-bk-_____**
                                                :
                          Debtor(s)   :

CERTIFICATION REGARDING SERVICE OF AMENDED CHAPTER 12 PLAN
(Altering Funding or Making Technical Amendments)

The undersigned, counsel for the above-captioned Debtor(s), hereby certifies that the

_____ Amended Chapter 12 Plan filed on _____ proposes to alter the funding

of, or to make technical amendments to, the Chapter 12 Plan confirmed on _____,

but does not affect the treatment of the claims of any creditors included in the confirmed Plan,

including the amounts to be paid, the timing of the payments or the treatment of collateral:

I further certify that the _____ Amended Chapter 12 Plan has been served on the

Chapter 12 trustee, and because none of the claims provided for in the plan will be affected by the

provisions of the _____ Amended Chapter 12 Plan, no further notice is required.

_____
Counsel for Debtor(s)

Dated:_____

[Effective September 1, 2014.]

LOCAL BANKRUPTCY FORM 3015–3(a). CHAPTER 13 DEBTOR'S PRE–CONFIRMATION CERTIFICATION OF COMPLIANCE WITH POST PETITION DOMESTIC SUPPORT AND PREPETITION TAX RETURN FILING OBLIGATIONS

LOCAL BANKRUPTCY FORM 3015-3(a)

IN THE UNITED STATES BANKRUPTCY COURT
FOR THE MIDDLE DISTRICT OF PENNSYLVANIA

IN RE:

:	CHAPTER 13
:	
:	CASE NO. __-____-bk-_____
:	
:	
:	
Debtor(s) :	

CHAPTER 13 DEBTOR'S PRE-CONFIRMATION CERTIFICATION OF COMPLIANCE WITH POST PETITION DOMESTIC SUPPORT AND PREPETITION TAX RETURN FILING OBLIGATIONS

If a joint petition is filed, each spouse must complete and file a separate certification.

I, _____, upon oath or affirmation, hereby certify as follows:

1. That the below information is being supplied for compliance with the confirmation hearing date on _____.

2. That all post-petition amounts required to be paid under any and all Domestic Support Obligations have been paid as required by 11 U.S.C. § 1325(a)(8).

3. That all applicable Federal, State, and local tax returns, as required by 11 U.S.C. Section 1308 have been filed.

4. If this Certification is being signed by counsel for Debtor, that the Debtor was duly questioned about the statements in this Certification and supplied answers consistent with this Certification.

I hereby certify that the foregoing statements made by me are true. I am aware that if any of the foregoing statements made by me are willfully false, I am subject to punishment for perjury.

DATED:_____   BY: _____
                                              Counsel for Debtor

DATED:_____   BY: _____
                                              Debtor

[Effective January 1, 2008. Amended effective August 7, 2009; March 1, 2013.]

LOCAL BANKRUPTCY FORM 3015–3(b). CERTIFICATION REGARDING DOMESTIC SUPPORT OBLIGATION(S)

LOCAL BANKRUPTCY FORM 3015-3(b)

IN THE UNITED STATES BANKRUPTCY COURT
FOR THE MIDDLE DISTRICT OF PENNSYLVANIA

IN RE:

                      :   CHAPTER _____

                      :

                      :   CASE NO. __-___-bk-_____

                      :

                      :

Debtor(s)   :

CERTIFICATION REGARDING
DOMESTIC SUPPORT OBLIGATION(S)

       If there are domestic support obligation claims in a case, the Bankruptcy Abuse Prevention and Consumer Protection Act of 2005 requires the trustee to provide written notice to the holder of the claim and to the applicable state child support enforcement agency. In order for the trustee to comply with the Act, the Debtor/Obligor must complete the following information and verify the information is true and correct by signing at the bottom of this form.

1. Name of Person Entitled to Receive Domestic Support ("Recipient"):

Claim Holder _____
                   Last Name   First   Middle Initial

2. Address of Domestic Support Recipient:

Claim Holder _____
                Street   City

_____
                County   State   Zip

3. Telephone Number of Domestic Support Recipient:

Claim Holder _____
                (Area Code) Phone Number

4. If you are paying a Domestic Support Obligation pursuant to a Court Order, provide the following:

_____
Name of Court

_____
Address of Court

_____
Docket Number   PACSES Number

The undersigned hereby certifies that the foregoing statements are true and correct under penalty of perjury.

DATED: _____   BY: _____
                                          Debtor

[Effective January 1, 2008; December 19, 2008. Amended effective March 1, 2013; June 1, 2016.]

LOCAL BANKRUPTCY FORM 3015–3(c). CHAPTER 12 INDIVIDUAL DEBTOR'S PRE–CONFIRMATION CERTIFICATION OF COMPLI-ANCE WITH POST PETITION DOMESTIC SUPPORT OBLIGATIONS

LOCAL BANKRUPTCY FORM 3015-3(c)

IN THE UNITED STATES BANKRUPTCY COURT
FOR THE MIDDLE DISTRICT OF PENNSYLVANIA

IN RE:

                                 :   **CHAPTER 12**
                                 :
                                 :   **CASE NO. __-___-bk-_____**
                                 :
                                 :
                                 :
            Debtor(s)   :

CHAPTER 12 INDIVIDUAL DEBTOR'S PRE-CONFIRMATION CERTIFICATION OF COMPLIANCE WITH POST PETITION DOMESTIC SUPPORT OBLIGATIONS
If a joint petition is filed, each spouse must complete and file a separate certification.

I, _____, upon oath or affirmation, hereby certify as follows:

1.   That the below information is being supplied for compliance with the confirmation hearing date on _____.

2.   That all post-petition amounts required to be paid under any and all Domestic Support Obligations have been paid as required by 11 U.S.C. § 1225(a)(7).

3.   If this Certification is being signed by counsel for Debtor, that the Debtor was duly questioned about the statements in this Certification and supplied answers consistent with this Certification.

I hereby certify that the foregoing statements made by me are true. I am aware that if any of the foregoing statements made by me are willfully false, I am subject to punishment for perjury.

DATED:_____   BY: _____
                                               Counsel for Debtor

DATED:_____   BY: _____
                                               Debtor

[Effective March 1, 2013.]

LOCAL BANKRUPTCY FORM 3015–6. CHAPTER 12 INDIVIDUAL DEBTOR'S CERTIFICATIONS REGARDING DOMESTIC SUPPORT OBLIGATIONS AND 11 U.S.C. § 522(q)
LOCAL BANKRUPTCY FORM 3015-6

IN THE UNITED STATES BANKRUPTCY COURT
FOR THE MIDDLE DISTRICT OF PENNSYLVANIA

IN RE:

	:	**CHAPTER 12**
	:	
	:	**CASE NO. __-___-bk-_____**
	:	
	:	
Debtor(s)	:	

CHAPTER 12 INDIVIDUAL DEBTOR'S CERTIFICATIONS REGARDING DOMESTIC SUPPORT OBLIGATIONS AND 11 U.S.C. § 522(q)

If a joint petition is filed, each spouse must complete and file a separate certification.

Part I. Certification Regarding Domestic Support Obligations (check no more than one)

Pursuant to 11 U.S.C. § 1228, I certify that:

☐   I owed no domestic support obligation when I filed my bankruptcy petition, and I have not been required to pay any such obligation since then.

☐   I am or have been required to pay a domestic support obligation. I have paid all such amounts that my chapter 12 plan required me to pay. I have also paid all such amounts that became due between the filing of my bankruptcy petition and today.

Part II. If you checked the second box, you must provide the information below.

My current address is: _____

My current employer and my employer's
address: _____

Part III. Certification Regarding 11 U.S.C. § 522(q) (check no more than one)

Pursuant to 11 U.S.C. § 1228(f), I certify that:

☐   I have not claimed an exemption pursuant to 11 U.S.C. § 522(b)(3) and state or local law (1) in property that I or a dependent of mine uses as a residence, claims as a homestead, or acquired as a burial plot, as specified in 11 U.S.C. § 522(p)(1), and (2) that exceeds the aggregate value allowed in 11 U.S.C. § 522(q)(1), as amended.

☐   I have claimed an exemption in property pursuant to 11 U.S.C. § 522(b)(3) and state or local law (1) that I or a dependent of mine uses as a residence, claims as a homestead, or acquired as a burial plot, as specified in 11 U.S.C. § 522(p)(1), and (2) that exceeds the aggregate value allowed in 11 U.S.C. § 522(q)(1), as amended.

Part IV. Debtor's Signature

I certify under penalty of perjury that the information provided in these certifications is true and correct to the best of my knowledge and belief.

DATED: _____   BY: _____
                                                              Debtor

[Effective March 1, 2013.]

LOCAL BANKRUPTCY FORM 3017–1.　CERTIFICATION REGARDING AMENDED DISCLOSURE STATEMENT

IN THE UNITED STATES BANKRUPTCY
COURT FOR THE MIDDLE DISTRICT
OF PENNSYLVANIA

LOCAL BANKRUPTCY FORM 3017-1

**IN THE UNITED STATES BANKRUPTCY COURT
FOR THE MIDDLE DISTRICT OF PENNSYLVANIA**

IN RE:

:　　CHAPTER ____
:
:　　CASE NO. __-___-bk-_____
:
:
:
Debtor(s)　　　　:

**CERTIFICATION REGARDING
AMENDED DISCLOSURE STATEMENT**

The undersigned counsel for the plan proponent in the above-captioned case, hereby certifies that the Amended Disclosure Statement, filed _____, contains changes to the Disclosure Statement, filed _____, of such nature and degree that:

1. _____　notice must be circulated as if an original Disclosure Statement;

2. _____　notice need be sent only to the objectors to the last filed Disclosure Statement;

3. _____　no further notice is required and the Amended Disclosure Statement can be approved as submitted.

Dated: _____　　　　　_____
　　　　　　　　　　　　　　　　Counsel for Plan Proponent

[Effective October 18, 2000; redesignated and amended effective January 1, 2005.]

LOCAL BANKRUPTCY FORM 3018–1. SECTION 1126 BALLOT REPORT FORM

IN THE UNITED STATES BANKRUPTCY COURT
FOR THE MIDDLE DISTRICT OF PENNSYLVANIA

LOCAL BANKRUPTCY FORM 3018-1

IN THE UNITED STATES BANKRUPTCY COURT
FOR THE MIDDLE DISTRICT OF PENNSYLVANIA

IN RE:

                                :   CHAPTER _____

                                :

                                :   CASE NO. ___-___ -bk-_____

                                :

                                :

        Debtor(s)   :

SECTION 1126 BALLOT REPORT FORM

	# BALLOTS CAST	# ACCEPTING	# REJECTING	$ ACCEPTING	$ REJECTING	CLASS ACCEPTING	CLASS REJECTING
CLASS I							
CLASS II							
CLASS III							
CLASS IV							

The following classes are impaired: _____.

Copies of all ballots not accepted are attached. An explanation of why the ballots were rejected, if applicable, is attached.

PLAN ACCEPTED	YES	NO

The foregoing Report is accurate and complete.

Dated: _____   _____
                                        Counsel for Plan Proponent

[Effective January 1, 2005. Revised effective January 1, 2008.]

LOCAL BANKRUPTCY FORM 3019–1. CERTIFICATION REGARDING AMENDED PLAN OF REORGANIZATION

LOCAL BANKRUPTCY FORM 3019-1

IN THE UNITED STATES BANKRUPTCY COURT
FOR THE MIDDLE DISTRICT OF PENNSYLVANIA

IN RE:

              :   **CHAPTER 11**

              :

              :   **CASE NO. __-___-bk-_____**

              :

              :

     Debtor(s)   :

CERTIFICATION REGARDING
AMENDED PLAN OF REORGANIZATION

The undersigned counsel for the plan proponent in the above-captioned case, hereby certifies that

the Amended Plan of Reorganization, filed _____, contains changes to the Plan of

Reorganization, filed _____, of such nature and degree that:

1.   _____ notice must be circulated as if an original Plan of Reorganization;

2.   _____ notice need be sent only to the objectors to the last filed Plan of Reorganization;

3.   _____ no further notice is required and the Amended Plan of Reorganization can be confirmed as submitted. All pending objections to confirmation of the Plan of Reorganization have been resolved or settled by the modifications included in the Amended Plan of Reorganization, and the Amended Plan of Reorganization complies with the requirements of 11 U.S.C. § 1123 and § 1129.

Dated: _____   _____

                                           Counsel for Plan Proponent

[Effective January 1, 2005.]

LOCAL BANKRUPTCY FORM 3020–1. CHAPTER 11 INDIVIDUAL DEBTOR'S PRE–CONFIRMATION CERTIFICATION OF COMPLIANCE WITH POST PETITION DOMESTIC SUPPORT OBLIGATIONS

LOCAL BANKRUPTCY FORM 3020-1

**IN THE UNITED STATES BANKRUPTCY COURT
FOR THE MIDDLE DISTRICT OF PENNSYLVANIA**

IN RE:

            :   CHAPTER 11

            :   CASE NO. __-___-bk-_____

            :

            :

            :

     Debtor(s)   :

CHAPTER 11 INDIVIDUAL DEBTOR'S PRE-CONFIRMATION CERTIFICATION OF COMPLIANCE WITH POST PETITION DOMESTIC SUPPORT OBLIGATIONS
If a joint petition is filed, each spouse must complete and file a separate certification.

I, _____, upon oath or affirmation, hereby certify as follows:

1. That the below information is being supplied for compliance with the confirmation hearing date on _____.

2. That all post-petition amounts required to be paid under any and all Domestic Support Obligations have been paid as required by 11 U.S.C. § 1129(a)(14).

3. If this Certification is being signed by counsel for Debtor, that the Debtor was duly questioned about the statements in this Certification and supplied answers consistent with this Certification.

I hereby certify that the foregoing statements made by me are true. I am aware that if any of the foregoing statements made by me are willfully false, I am subject to punishment for perjury.

DATED:_____   BY: _____
                             Counsel for Debtor

DATED:_____   BY: _____
                             Debtor

[Amended effective September 1, 2014.]

LOCAL BANKRUPTCY FORM 4001–1. POST–PETITION PAYMENT HISTORY NOTE AND MORTGAGE

LOCAL BANKRUPTCY FORM 4001-1

IN THE UNITED STATES BANKRUPTCY COURT
FOR THE MIDDLE DISTRICT OF PENNSYLVANIA

IN RE:

                                    :   CHAPTER 13
                                    :
                                    :   CASE NO. __-___-bk-_____
                                    :
                                    :
        Debtor(s)   :

POST-PETITION PAYMENT HISTORY
NOTE AND MORTGAGE DATED _____

Recorded on _____, in _____ **County**, at _____.

Property Address:

_____

Mortgage Servicer:

_____

Post-petition mailing address for Debtor(s) to send payment:

_____

Mortgagor(s)/Debtor(s):

_____

Payments are contractually due:

Monthly____   Semi-monthly_____   Bi-weekly_____   Other _____

Each Monthly Payment is comprised of:
Principal and Interest......._____
R.E. Taxes..................... _____
Insurance..................... _____
Late Charge.................. _____
Other........................... _____ (Specify: _____)
TOTAL..................... _____

POST-PETITION PAYMENTS (Petition was filed on _____)

Payment amount due	Date payment was due	Date payment was received	Amount received	Check number	How payment was applied (mo./yr.)

[Continue on attached sheets if necessary]

TOTAL NUMBER OF POST-PETITION PAYMENTS PAST DUE: _____ as of _____.

TOTAL AMOUNT OF POST-PETITION ARREARS: _____ as of _____.

Dated: _____   _____
                                Mortgage Company

                                _____
                                (Print Name and Title)

(2)

[Effective January 1, 2005.   Amended effective April 4, 2011;   September 1, 2014.]

LOCAL BANKRUPTCY FORM 4008–1(a).
REAFFIRMATION AGREEMENT

B2400A/B ALT (Form 2400A/B ALT) (12/15)

> ☐ **Presumption of Undue Hardship**
>
> ☐ **No Presumption of Undue Hardship**
>
> (Check box as directed in Part D: Debtor's Statement in Support of Reaffirmation Agreement)

LOCAL BANKRUPTCY FORM 4008-1(a)

IN THE UNITED STATES BANKRUPTCY COURT
FOR THE MIDDLE DISTRICT OF PENNSYLVANIA

IN RE:

                :   CHAPTER ____

                :

                :   CASE NO. __-___-bk-_____

                :

                :

Debtor(s)   :

REAFFIRMATION AGREEMENT

[Indicate all documents included in this filing by checking each applicable box.]

☐ Part A; Disclosures, Instructions, and Notice to Debtor (pages 1–5)

☐ Part D: Debtor's Statement in Support of Reaffirmation Agreement

☐ Part B: Reaffirmation Agreement

☐ Part E: Motion for Court Approval

☐ Part C: Certification by Debtor's Attorney

*[Note: Complete Part E only if debtor was not represented by an attorney during the course of negotiating this agreement. **Note also:** If you complete Part E, you must prepare and file Form 2400C ALT - Order on Reaffirmation Agreement.]*

Name of Creditor: _____

☐ *[Check this box if]* Creditor is a Credit Union as defined in §19(b)(1)(a)(iv) of the Federal Reserve Act

PART A: DISCLOSURE STATEMENT, INSTRUCTIONS AND NOTICE TO DEBTOR

1.   **DISCLOSURE STATEMENT**

Before Agreeing to Reaffirm a Debt, Review These Important Disclosures:

SUMMARY OF REAFFIRMATION AGREEMENT
    This Summary is made pursuant to the requirements of the Bankruptcy Code.

AMOUNT REAFFIRMED

The amount of debt you have agreed to reaffirm $ _____

The amount of debt you have agreed to reaffirm includes all fees and costs (if any) that have accrued as of the date of this disclosure. Your credit agreement may obligate you to pay additional amounts which may come due after the date of this disclosure. Consult your credit agreement.

ANNUAL PERCENTAGE RATE

[The annual percentage rate can be disclosed in different ways, depending on the type of debt.]

a.   If the debt is an extension of "credit" under an "open end credit plan," as those terms are defined in § 103 of the Truth in Lending Act, such as a credit card, the creditor may disclose the annual percentage rate shown in (i) below or, to the extent this rate is not readily available or not applicable, the simple interest rate shown in (ii) below, or both.

(i)   The Annual Percentage Rate disclosed, or that would have been disclosed, to the debtor in the most recent periodic statement prior to entering into the reaffirmation agreement described in Part B below or, if no such periodic statement was given to the debtor during the prior six months, the annual percentage rate as it would have been so disclosed at the time of the disclosure statement: _____ %.

– And/Or –

(ii)   The simple interest rate applicable to the amount reaffirmed as of the date this disclosure statement is given to the debtor: _____ %. If different simple interest rates apply to different balances included in the amount reaffirmed, the amount of each balance and the rate applicable to it are:

$ _____ @ _____ %;
$ _____ @ _____ %;
$ _____ @ _____ %;

b.   If the debt is an extension of credit other than under an open end credit plan, the creditor may disclose the annual percentage rate shown in (i) below, or, to the extent this rate is not readily available or not applicable, the simple interest rate shown in (ii) below, or both.

(i)   The Annual Percentage Rate under §128(a)(4) of the Truth in Lending Act, as disclosed to the debtor in the most recent disclosure statement given to the debtor prior to entering into the reaffirmation agreement with respect to the debt or, if no such disclosure statement was given to the debtor, the annual percentage rate as it would have been so disclosed: _____ %.

– And/Or –

(ii)   The simple interest rate applicable to the amount reaffirmed as of the date this disclosure statement is given to the debtor: _____ %. If different simple interest rates apply to different balances included in the amount reaffirmed, the amount of each balance and the rate applicable to it are:

$ _____ @ _____ %;
$ _____ @ _____ %;
$ _____ @ _____ %;

c.   If the underlying debt transaction was disclosed as a variable rate transaction on the most recent disclosure given under the Truth in Lending Act:

The interest rate on your loan may be a variable interest rate which changes from time to time, so that the annual percentage rate disclosed here may be higher or lower.

d.   If the reaffirmed debt is secured by a security interest or lien, which has not been waived or determined to be void by a final order of the court, the following items or types of items on the debtor's goods or property remain subject to such security interest or lien in connection with the debt or debts being reaffirmed in the reaffirmation agreement described in Part B.

<u>Item or Type of Item</u>   <u>Original Purchase Price or Original Amount of Loan</u>

Optional — At the election of the creditor, a repayment schedule using one or a combination of the following may be provided:

Repayment Schedule:

Your first payment in the amount of $ _____ is due on _____ (date), but the future payment amount may be different. Consult your reaffirmation agreement or credit agreement, as applicable.

- - - Or - - -

Your payment schedule will be: _____ (number) payments in the amount of $_____ each, payable (monthly, annually, weekly, etc.) on the _____ (day) of each _____ (week, month, etc.), unless altered later by mutual agreement in writing.

- - - Or - - -

A reasonably specific description of the debtor's repayment obligations to the extent known by the creditor or creditor's representative.

2.   INSTRUCTIONS AND NOTICE TO DEBTOR

Reaffirming a debt is a serious financial decision. The law requires you to take certain steps to make sure the decision is in your best interest. If these steps are not completed, the reaffirmation agreement is not effective, even though you have signed it.

1.   Read the disclosures in this Part A carefully. Consider the decision to reaffirm carefully. Then, if you want to reaffirm, sign the reaffirmation agreement in Part B (or you may use a separate agreement you and your creditor agree on).

2.   Complete and sign Part D and be sure you can afford to make the payments you are agreeing to make and have received a copy of the disclosure statement and a completed and signed reaffirmation agreement.

3.   If you were represented by an attorney during the negotiation of your reaffirmation agreement, the attorney must have signed the certification in Part C.

4.   If you were not represented by an attorney during the negotiation of your reaffirmation agreement, you must have completed and signed Part E.

5.   The original of this disclosure must be filed with the court by you or your creditor. If a separate reaffirmation agreement (other than the one in Part B) has been signed, it must be attached.

6.   If the creditor is not a Credit Union and you were represented by an attorney during the negotiation of your reaffirmation agreement, your reaffirmation agreement becomes effective upon filing with the court unless the reaffirmation is presumed to be an undue hardship as explained in Part D. If the creditor is a Credit Union and you were represented by an attorney during the negotiation of your reaffirmation agreement, your reaffirmation agreement becomes effective upon filing with the court.

7.   If you were not represented by an attorney during the negotiation of your reaffirmation agreement, it will not be effective unless the court approves it. The court will notify you and the creditor of the hearing on your reaffirmation agreement. You must attend this hearing in bankruptcy court where the judge will review your reaffirmation agreement. The bankruptcy court must approve your reaffirmation agreement as consistent with your best interests, except that no court approval is required if your reaffirmation agreement is for a consumer debt secured by a mortgage, deed of trust, security deed, or other lien on your real property, like your home.

YOUR RIGHT TO RESCIND (CANCEL) YOUR REAFFIRMATION AGREEMENT

You may rescind (cancel) your reaffirmation agreement at any time before the bankruptcy court enters a discharge order, or before the expiration of the 60-day period that begins on the date your reaffirmation agreement is filed with the court, whichever occurs later. To rescind (cancel) your reaffirmation agreement, you must notify the creditor that your reaffirmation agreement is rescinded (canceled).

Frequently Asked Questions:

What are your obligations if you reaffirm the debt? A reaffirmed debt remains your personal legal obligation. It is not discharged in your bankruptcy case. That means if you default on your reaffirmed debt after your bankruptcy case is over, your creditor may be able to take your property or your wages. Otherwise, your obligations will be determined by the reaffirmation agreement which may have changed the terms of the original agreement. For example, if you are reaffirming an open end credit agreement, the creditor may be permitted by that agreement or applicable law to change the terms of that agreement in the future under certain conditions.

Are you required to enter into a reaffirmation agreement by any law? No, you are not required to reaffirm a debt by any law. Only agree to reaffirm a debt if it is in your best interest. Be sure you can afford the payments you agree to make.

What if your creditor has a security interest or lien? Your bankruptcy discharge does not eliminate any lien on your property. A "lien" is often referred to as a security interest, deed of trust, mortgage, or security deed. Even if you do not reaffirm and your personal liability on the debt is discharged, because of the lien your creditor may still have the right to take the property securing the lien if you do not pay the debt or default on it. If the lien is on an item of personal property that is exempt under your State's law or that the trustee has abandoned, you may be able to redeem the item rather than reaffirm the debt. To redeem, you must make a single payment to the creditor equal to the amount of the allowed secured claim, as agreed by the parties or determined by the court.

NOTE: When this disclosure refers to what a creditor "may" do, it does not use the word "may" to give the creditor specific permission. The word "may" is used to tell you what might occur if the law permits the creditor to take the action. If you have questions about reaffirming a debt or what the law requires, consult with the attorney who helped you negotiate this agreement reaffirming a debt. If you don't have an attorney helping you, the judge will explain the effect of reaffirming a debt when the hearing on the reaffirmation agreement is held.

PART B: REAFFIRMATION AGREEMENT

I (we) agree to reaffirm the debts arising under the credit agreement described below.

1.   Brief description of credit agreement.

2.   Description of any changes to the credit agreement made as part of this reaffirmation agreement:

SIGNATURE(S):

Borrower: Accepted by creditor:

_____   _____
(Print Name)   (Print Name of Creditor)

_____   _____
(Signature)   (Address of Creditor)

Date: _____   _____
                                             (Signature)

Co-borrower, if also reaffirming these debts: _____
                                             (Printed name and Title of Individual Signing for
Creditor)

_____   Date of creditor acceptance:
(Print Name)
                                             _____

_____
(Signature)

Date: _____

PART C: CERTIFICATION BY DEBTOR'S ATTORNEY (IF ANY).

[To be filed only if the attorney represented the debtor during the course of negotiating this agreement.]

    I hereby certify that (1) this agreement represents a fully informed and voluntary agreement by the debtor; (2) this agreement does not impose an undue hardship on the debtor or any dependent of the debtor; and (3) I have fully advised the debtor of the legal effect and consequences of this agreement and any default under this agreement.

    □ *[Check box, if applicable and the creditor is not a Credit Union.]* A presumption of undue hardship has been established with respect to this agreement. In my opinion, however, the debtor is able to make the required payment.

Printed Name of Debtor's Attorney: _____

Signature of Debtor's Attorney: _____

Date: _____

P.8

PART D: DEBTOR'S STATEMENT IN SUPPORT OF REAFFIRMATION AGREEMENT

*[Read and complete numbered paragraphs 1 and 2, OR, if the creditor is a Credit Union and the debtor is represented by an attorney, read section 3. Sign the appropriate signature line(s) and date your signature. If you complete sections 1 and 2 **and** your income less monthly expenses does not leave enough to make the payments under this reaffirmation agreement, check the box at the top of page 1 indicating "Presumption of Undue Hardship." Otherwise, check the box at the top of page 1 indicating "No Presumption of Undue Hardship."]*

1.   I believe this reaffirmation agreement will not impose an undue hardship on my dependents or me. I can afford to make the payments on the reaffirmed debt because my monthly income (take home pay plus any other income received) is $ _____, and my actual current monthly expenses including monthly payments on post-bankruptcy debt and other reaffirmation agreements total $ _____, leaving $ _____ to make the required payments on this reaffirmed debt.

I understand that if my income less my monthly expenses does not leave enough to make the payments, this reaffirmation agreement is presumed to be an undue hardship on me and must be reviewed by the court. However, this presumption may be overcome if I explain to the satisfaction of the court how I can afford to make the payments here:

_____

_____

(Use an additional page if needed for a full explanation.)

2.   I received a copy of the Reaffirmation Disclosure Statement in Part A and a completed and signed reaffirmation agreement.

Signed: _____
          (Debtor)

_____
          (Joint Debtor, if any)

Date: _____

— Or —

[If the creditor is a Credit Union and the debtor is represented by an attorney]

3.   I believe this reaffirmation agreement is in my financial interest. I can afford to make the payments on the reaffirmed debt. I received a copy of the Reaffirmation Disclosure Statement in Part A and a completed and signed reaffirmation agreement.

Signed: _____
          (Debtor)

_____   Date: _____
          (Joint Debtor, if any)

PART E: MOTION FOR COURT APPROVAL
[To be completed only if the debtor is not represented by an attorney during the course of negotiating this agreement.]

MOTION FOR COURT APPROVAL OF REAFFIRMATION AGREEMENT

I (we), the debtor(s), affirm the following to be true and correct:

I am not represented by an attorney in connection with this reaffirmation agreement.

I believe this reaffirmation agreement is in my best interest based on the income and expenses I have disclosed in my Statement in Support of this reaffirmation agreement, and because (provide any additional relevant reasons the court should consider):

Therefore, I ask the court for an order approving this reaffirmation agreement under the following provisions *(check all applicable boxes)*:

☐ 11 U.S.C. § 524(c)(6) (debtor is not represented by an attorney during the course of the negotiation of the reaffirmation agreement)

☐ 11 U.S.C. § 524(m) (presumption of undue hardship has arisen because monthly expenses exceed monthly income)

Signed: _____
     (Debtor)

_____
     (Joint Debtor, if any)

Date: _____

[Effective October 18, 2000. Revised effective January 1, 2005; November 21, 2005; January 1, 2008; December 1, 2009; October 15, 2010; December 1, 2011; June 1, 2016.]

LOCAL BANKRUPTCY FORM 9004–1.
CONTESTED MATTER CAPTION

LOCAL BANKRUPTCY FORM 9004-1
[Contested Matter Caption]

**IN THE UNITED STATES BANKRUPTCY COURT
FOR THE MIDDLE DISTRICT OF PENNSYLVANIA**

IN RE: :   CHAPTER ____

JOHN DOE   :
                                        :
                 Debtor(s)   :   CASE NO. __-____-bk-_____(judge's initials)
                                        :
XYZ MORTGAGE CO.   :
                 Movant   :
                                        :
      vs.   :
                                        :
JOHN DOE   :
                 Respondent   :

MOTION OF XYZ MORTGAGE CO. FOR RELIEF FROM THE STAY

[Former Local Bankruptcy Form 9004–2 effective January 1, 2005. Renumbered as Local Bankruptcy Form 9004–1 effective September 1, 2014.]

LOCAL BANKRUPTCY FORM 9013–3. REQUEST TO CONTINUE HEARING/TRIAL WITH CONCURRENCE

LOCAL BANKRUPTCY FORM 9013-3

IN THE UNITED STATES BANKRUPTCY COURT
FOR THE MIDDLE DISTRICT OF PENNSYLVANIA

IN RE:

     :   CHAPTER _____

     :

     :   CASE NO. __-___-bk-_____

     :

     :

Debtor(s)   :

     :   ADVERSARY NO. __-___-ap-_____

     :   (if applicable)

     :

     :

Plaintiff(s)/Movant(s)   :

vs.   :   Nature of Proceeding: _____

     :

     :   _____

     :

     :

Defendant(s)/Respondent(s)   :   Document #: _____

REQUEST TO CONTINUE HEARING/TRIAL WITH CONCURRENCE[1]

        This request must be filed at least twenty-four (24) hours prior to the hearing. All requests must be approved by the Court. Submitting a request is not an automatic continuance.

        The undersigned hereby requests a continuance with the concurrence of the opposing party (parties). This is a first request for a continuance.[2]

        Reason for the continuance.

_____

_____

_____

        Contemporaneous with the filing of this request, the undersigned has served a copy of this request upon all counsel participating in this proceeding.

Dated:_____   _____

                                    Attorney for_____

                                    Name: _____

_____   Phone Number: _____

[1] No alterations or interlineations of this document are permitted.

[2] If this is not a first request for a continuance, then a Motion to Continue must be filed.

[Effective January 1, 2008. Amended effective September 1, 2014.]

LOCAL BANKRUPTCY FORM 9019–1. REQUEST TO REMOVE FROM THE HEARING/TRIAL LIST

LOCAL BANKRUPTCY FORM 9019-1

**IN THE UNITED STATES BANKRUPTCY COURT
FOR THE MIDDLE DISTRICT OF PENNSYLVANIA**

IN RE:

                        :   CHAPTER _____

                        :   CASE NO. __-___-bk-_____

                        :

      Debtor(s)   :

                        :   ADVERSARY NO. __-___-ap-_____
                        :   (if applicable)

                        :

      Plaintiff(s)/Movant(s)   :
      vs.   :   Nature of Proceeding: _____

                        :   Pleading: _____

                        :

      Defendant(s)/Respondent(s)   :   Document #: _____

REQUEST TO REMOVE FROM THE HEARING/TRIAL LIST*

CHECK ONE:
☐   The undersigned hereby withdraws the above identified pleading with the consent of the opposition, if any.

☐   The undersigned counsel certifies as follows:

(1)   A settlement has been reached which will be reduced to writing, executed and filed within (please check only one).
     ☐   Thirty (30) days.
     ☐   Forty-five (45) days.
     ☐   Sixty (60) days.

(2)   If a stipulation is not filed or a hearing requested within the above-stated time frame, the Court may dismiss the matter without further notice.

(3)   Contemporaneous with the filing of this request, the undersigned has served a copy of this request upon all counsel participating in this proceeding.

Dated:_____   _____
                                   Attorney for_____

*No alterations or interlineations of this document are permitted. This request must be filed twenty-four (24) hours prior to the hearing.

[Effective October 18, 2000; redesignated and revised December 15, 2004. Revised effective January 31, 2006; January 1, 2008; March 1, 2013.]

LOCAL BANKRUPTCY FORM 9019–2.   REQUEST FOR MEDIATION

LOCAL BANKRUPTCY FORM 9019-2

IN THE UNITED STATES BANKRUPTCY COURT
FOR THE MIDDLE DISTRICT OF PENNSYLVANIA

IN RE:

	:	CHAPTER _____
	:	
	:	CASE NO. ___-___-bk-_____
	:	
Debtor(s)	:	
	:	ADVERSARY NO. ___-___-ap-_____
	:	(if applicable)
	:	
	:	
	:	
Plaintiff(s)/Movant(s)	:	
vs.	:	Nature of Proceeding: _____
	:	
	:	
	:	
Defendant(s)/Respondent(s)	:	

REQUEST FOR MEDIATION*

CHECK ONE:

☐   The undersigned requests this dispute be assigned to mediation.

☐   The undersigned certifies that the other party or parties to the dispute join in this request. (Check if applicable.)

     Contemporaneously with the filing of this request, the undersigned has served a copy of this request upon all the parties or their respective legal counsel.

Dated:_____   _____

                                            Attorney for_____

*No alterations or interlineations of this document are permitted.

[Effective March 1, 2013.]

LOCAL BANKRUPTCY FORM 9019–3(a). MOTION TO PARTICIPATE IN MORTGAGE MODIFICATION MEDIATION PROGRAM

LOCAL BANKRUPTCY FORM 9019-3(a)

IN THE UNITED STATES BANKRUPTCY COURT
FOR THE MIDDLE DISTRICT OF PENNSYLVANIA

IN RE:	:	CHAPTER 13
	:	
	:	
	:	CASE NO. ___-___-bk-_____
	:	
	:	
	:	
Debtor(s)	:	

MOTION TO PARTICIPATE IN
MORTGAGE MODIFICATION MEDIATION PROGRAM

The undersigned debtor [and joint debtor if applicable] (the "Debtor") moves as follows:

1. Debtor seeks to participate in the Mortgage Modification Mediation Program ("MMM Program") pursuant to L.B.R. 9019-3.

2. Debtor states the following preference for the MMM Program loss mitigation review process (check only ONE box):

    ☐ Debtor wishes to utilize the DMM Portal, or such other portal as may be designated by the Court, (the "Portal") for the modification process and hereby requests the concurrence of the Mortgage Creditor for use of the Portal.

    ☐ Debtor wishes to communicate directly with the Mortgage Creditor and its counsel during the modification process and will not utilize the Portal. Debtor hereby requests the concurrence of the Mortgage Creditor to opt out of the Portal.

3. By filing this Motion, Debtor certifies as follows:

    a. Debtor is the owner/occupant of a one- to four-unit residential property used as the Debtor's primary residence.

    b. Debtor has regular income.

    c. Debtor has an unpaid principal mortgage balance that is equal to or less than $729,750.00 (for a one-unit property).

    d. Debtor has a mortgage payment that is not affordable due to a financial hardship that can be documented.

4.   Debtor agrees to make post-petition mortgage payments to Mortgage Creditor of seventy-five percent (75%) of Debtor's current mortgage payment ("Modified Mortgage Payment").

5.   The first Modified Mortgage Payment will be due and must be received by Mortgage Creditor no later than the next monthly scheduled mortgage due date (plus any grace period) after the filing of this Motion. The only exception to this requirement is if Debtor does not know the identity of Mortgage Creditor at the time the payment is due; in that event Debtor will make the Modified Mortgage Payment to Debtor's attorney to be held in trust until Mortgage Creditor is identified.

6.   Debtor will continue to make the Modified Mortgage Payments to Mortgage Creditor each month until the MMM Program is concluded or a court order expressly states otherwise.

7.   Debtor has filed his or her Schedules and Statement of Financial Affairs which may be relied upon by Mortgage Creditor in evaluating Debtor's mortgage loan for modification.

8.   Debtor will submit a completed loss mitigation application to Mortgage Creditor as provided in L.B.R. 9019-3 within thirty (30) days of the entry of an order granting this Motion. Failure to timely submit a completed loss mitigation application may result in Debtor being removed from the MMM Program upon written motion of Mortgage Creditor.

9.   By filing this Motion, Debtor understands and consents to a modification of the automatic stay imposed by § 362(a) of the Bankruptcy Code as follows:

a.   The automatic stay is immediately modified to permit Mortgage Creditor to request information, evaluate and analyze Debtor's financial situation, and to fully participate in the mortgage modification process and negotiate loan modification terms.

b.   In the event Debtor misses a Modified Mortgage Payment, Mortgage Creditor may file a motion for relief from the automatic stay and seek removal of Debtor from the MMM Program.

c.   If a request for loan modification is denied, Debtor must file an amended/modified plan within twenty-one (21) days of receiving notice of the denial. The amended/modified plan must address the treatment of the pre-petition mortgage arrears and any post-petition arrears that may have accrued. If an amended/modified Chapter 13 Plan is not timely filed, Mortgage Creditor may file a motion for relief from the automatic stay. A rejection of an offered loan modification by Debtor shall be treated as a denial for the purposes of this paragraph.

10. If a loan modification is agreed upon, Debtor will cooperate in promptly formalizing any needed legal documents and seeking any necessary court approval for the mortgage modification.

11. If within one hundred and twenty (120) days from the entry of an order admitting Debtor into the MMM Program, no motion to approve loan modification has been filed and/or no amended/modified Chapter 13 plan has been filed, Debtor agrees to file a Loss Mitigation Status Report as required by L.B.R. 9019-3(j)(4).

WHEREFORE, Debtor requests that this Court enter an order authorizing Debtor and Mortgage Creditor to enter into the MMM Program.

Dated:_____   _____
                                    Attorney for Debtor(s)

Dated: _____   _____
                                    Debtor's Signature

Dated: _____   _____
                                    Joint Debtor's Signature

**IN THE UNITED STATES BANKRUPTCY COURT
FOR THE MIDDLE DISTRICT OF PENNSYLVANIA**

IN RE:

                                :   **CHAPTER 13**
                                :
                                :
                                :   **CASE NO. __-__-bk-_____**
                                :
                                :

      Debtor(s)   :

**NOTICE OF FILING OF MOTION TO PARTICIPATE
IN MORTGAGE MODIFICATION MEDIATION PROGRAM**

TO: _____, and its successors, assigns, and servicing agents ("Mortgage Creditor")

PLEASE TAKE NOTICE CONCERNING THE FOLLOWING:

On this date, Debtor filed a Motion to Participate in Mortgage Modification Mediation Program ("Motion to Participate")

Mortgage Creditor has twenty-one (21) days from the filing of the Motion to Participate to accept or object to Debtor's entry into the MMM Program.

If Mortgage Creditor agrees to participation, Mortgage Creditor will file a Consent to Participation in Mortgage Modification Mediation Program ("Creditor Consent Form"), L.B.F. 9019-3(b).

Prior to filing the Creditor Consent Form, the parties shall confer as to whether loss mitigation review will be done by DMM Portal, or such other portal as may be designated by the Court, (the "Portal") or between the parties outside of the Portal. The Creditor Consent Form shall reflect the decision of the parties.

If Mortgage Creditor objects to participation, a written objection must be filed with the Court. Upon written objection, the Motion to Participate will be denied without prejudice to re-filing.

If Mortgage Creditor fails to file the Creditor Consent Form or an objection to participation within twenty (21) days, the Motion to Participate may be granted without further notice or hearing and the preference elected by Debtor as to the Portal use will govern.

Should a mediator be appointed by the Court at any point during the loss mitigation process, Debtor and Mortgage Creditor will each pay $125.00 (the "Mediation Fee") to the mediator no later than fourteen (14) days after appointment of the mediator. Mediators do not accept personal checks for the Mediation Fee.

Should a mediator be appointed by the Court at any point during the loss mitigation process, Debtor agrees to appear and participate in good faith in the mediation session(s). The Mediation Fee is nonrefundable regardless of the outcome of the mediation session.

Dated: _____

                                                _____

                                                Attorney for Debtor(s)

                                                Address: _____

                                                _____

                                                Telephone: _____

                                                Facsimile: _____

                                                Email: _____

[Effective March 1, 2013. Amended effective June 1, 2016.]

LOCAL BANKRUPTCY FORM 9019–3(b). CONSENT TO PARTICIPATION IN MORTGAGE MODIFICATION MEDIATION PROGRAM

LOCAL BANKRUPTCY FORM 9019-3(b)

IN THE UNITED STATES BANKRUPTCY COURT
FOR THE MIDDLE DISTRICT OF PENNSYLVANIA

IN RE:

	:	**CHAPTER 13**
	:	
	:	
	:	**CASE NO. ___-___-bk-_____**
	:	
	:	
Debtor(s)	:	

CONSENT TO PARTICIPATION IN
MORTGAGE MODIFICATION MEDIATION PROGRAM

_____ ("Mortgage Creditor")
consents to Debtor's Motion to Participate in the Mortgage Modification Mediation Program
("MMM Program").

1.   The current monthly mortgage payment is _____, and seventy-five percent (75%) of
      same is _____.

2.   The parties have conferred and have chosen (check only ONE box):

      ☐   to use the DMM Portal, or such other portal as may be designated by the Court (the
            "Portal")

      ☐   not to use the Portal

3.   If the Portal is being used, Mortgage Creditor (to the extent not already registered), must
      register with the Portal and post the required loss mitigation application within fourteen (14)
      days after entry of the Order Granting Entry in MMM Program ("Participation Order"). If the
      parties are not using the Portal, Mortgage Creditor agrees to provide Debtor with the required
      loss mitigation package and document checklist advising Debtor of what information is
      needed to review for loss mitigation.

4.   Within fourteen (14) days of receiving Debtor's completed application, Mortgage Creditor
      will designate (via the Portal or in written correspondence, whichever is applicable) a specific
      individual who will be a single point of contact for all communication with Debtor during the
      loss mitigation review process.

5. If at any time during the loss mitigation review process the loan being reviewed becomes subject to a transfer to another creditor ("Substituted Creditor"), Mortgage Creditor agrees to file a Proposed Order Substituting MMM Servicer as required by L.B.R. 9019-3(c)(6) or 9019-3(d)(5), whichever is applicable. Mortgage Creditor further agrees to ensure that all loss mitigation notes, applications, and correspondence related to loss mitigation review are forwarded to Substituted Creditor.

6. If at any time during the loss mitigation review process the Court appoints a mediator as permitted under L.B.R. 9019-3(e), Mortgage Creditor agrees that a specialist from Mortgage Creditor's mortgage modification department or other representative with full authority to settle will participate in one or more mediation sessions with Debtor for the purpose of evaluating and considering Debtor's request for a permanent mortgage modification on Debtor's primary residence, and that attendance of a representative will be continuous throughout the mediation. The representative may participate by telephone or video conference.

7. If a mediator is appointed, Mortgage Creditor agrees to pay $125.00 to the mediator no later than fourteen (14) days after appointment of the mediator.

8. Mortgage Creditor agrees to engage in the loss mitigation review and mediation processes in good faith, and understands that failure to do so may result in the imposition of damages and sanctions. Mortgage Creditor understands that the goal of the MMM Program is to negotiate toward a permanent loan modification.

9. In the event a mortgage modification is agreed upon, Mortgage Creditor agrees to promptly file a motion to approve loan modification, attaching a copy of the modification agreement thereto, and to file any appropriate amendments or withdrawals of its proof of claim.

Dated:_____   _____
                                Attorneys for Mortgage Creditor

[Effective March 1, 2013. Amended effective June 1, 2016.]

LOCAL BANKRUPTCY FORM 9019–3(c). ORDER SUBSTITUTING MMM SERVICER

LOCAL BANKRUPTCY FORM 9019-3(c)

IN THE UNITED STATES BANKRUPTCY COURT
FOR THE MIDDLE DISTRICT OF PENNSYLVANIA

IN RE:

                   :   CHAPTER 13
                   :
                   :   CASE NO. __-____-bk-_____
                   :
                   :
    Debtor(s)   :

ORDER SUBSTITUTING MMM SERVICER

On _____ (Date of Motion to Participate) the above named Debtor(s) filed a

Motion to Participate in Mortgage Modification Mediation Program and Notice of Filing of Motion

to Participate in Mortgage Modification Mediation Program upon which the Court entered an Order

Granting Entry in MMM Program dated _____, (Date of Order) at Docket No. _____,

naming _____ (Full Name of Mortgage Creditor) ("Mortgage Creditor")

as the party responsible for representing Mortgage Creditor in the MMM Program and setting forth

certain deadlines for the then named Mortgage Creditor.

Subsequent to entry of the above-referenced Order, counsel for Mortgage Creditor was

notified that Mortgage Creditor is scheduled to change as of _____ (Date of Transfer)

(the "Transfer Date") and that as of the Transfer Date, the new servicer/lender will be _____

_____ (Full Name of Substituted Creditor) with an address of _____

_____ (Full Address of Substituted Creditor)

("Substituted Creditor"). On _____, (Date) Mortgage Creditor complied with all its

obligations to properly designate Substituted Creditor on the MMM Program Portal (if applicable)

and now it is incumbent on the Court to relieve Mortgage Creditor from any further responsibilities under the current Order Granting Entry in MMM Program and formally transfer those duties,

responsibilities, and obligations to Substituted Creditor.

After due consideration of the above, it is ORDERED that:

1. _____ (Mortgage Creditor) is relieved from any further

   responsibility pursuant to the Order Granting Entry in the MMM Program referred to

   above and that Order is VACATED as to it.

2. _____ (Substituted Creditor) is now designated as the current

   servicer responsible for completion of all MMM Program duties, responsibilities, and

   obligations previously imposed on Mortgage Creditor referred to in Paragraph 1,

   above. Substituted Creditor is now fully responsible for compliance with all MMM

   Program requirements as if originally designated in the Order Granting Entry in

   MMM Program in the first instance.

[Effective March 1, 2013.   Amended effective June 1, 2016.]

LOCAL BANKRUPTCY FORM 9037–1. APPLICATION REQUESTING REDACTION OF PERSONAL INFORMATION
LOCAL BANKRUPTCY FORM 9037-1

IN THE UNITED STATES BANKRUPTCY COURT
FOR THE MIDDLE DISTRICT OF PENNSYLVANIA

In re:

	CHAPTER:
* **Debtors**	**CASE NO.** __-___-bk-_____

APPLICATION REQUESTING REDACTION OF PERSONAL INFORMATION

_____ [insert name], hereby states that the following document(s) contain personally identifiable information as defined in Fed. R. Bankr. P. 9037 and requests that these document(s) be redacted pursuant to Local Rule 9037-1:

_____

_____

[specifically describe the document(s) you are seeking to redact, preferably indicating the docket number. For example, Docket. No. 32, Exhibit A to Certification in Support of Motion for Relief from the Automatic Stay].

I am [check appropriate box]:

    [ ] including the $25.00 redaction fee.

    [ ] requesting waiver of the redaction fee on the grounds that _____

_____

[Specify the reason(s) you believe you should not have to pay the redaction fee. For example, "I am the debtor and am seeking to redact personal identifiers from records that were filed by a creditor in the case."]

I understand that I must serve a copy of this application on the debtor, any individual whose personal identifiers have been exposed, the case trustee (if any), and the United States trustee. I must file proof of service of this application within five (5) days of filing it with the Court.

I declare under penalty of perjury that the foregoing is true and correct.

_____
Signature of Applicant

Date: _____, 20__

[Effective September 14, 2015.]

LOCAL BANKRUPTCY FORM 9074–1.   CERTIFICATION OF CONCURRENCE FOR TELEPHONIC TESTIMONY VIA COURTCALL

LOCAL BANKRUPTCY FORM 9074-1

IN THE UNITED STATES BANKRUPTCY COURT
FOR THE MIDDLE DISTRICT OF PENNSYLVANIA

IN RE:	:	CHAPTER _____
	:	
	:	CASE NO. __-___-bk-_____
	:	
	:	
Debtor(s)	:	
	:	ADVERSARY NO. __-___-ap-_____
	:	(if applicable)
	:	
	:	
Plaintiff(s)/Movant(s)	:	Nature of Proceeding: _____
vs.	:	
	:	
	:	Pleading: _____
	:	
	:	
Defendant(s)/Respondent(s)	:	Document #: _____

CERTIFICATION OF CONCURRENCE FOR TELEPHONIC TESTIMONY VIA COURTCALL

(Certification must be received at least 2 business days before the scheduled hearing. If a certification cannot be filed timely, leave to provide telephonic testimony must be obtained from the Court.)

1. HEARING INFORMATION

Hearing Type (e.g., Motion to Dismiss, Trial) _____

Hearing Date _____   Hearing Time _____

2. WITNESSES SCHEDULED TO PROVIDE TELEPHONIC TESTIMONY

3. I hereby certify that all parties participating in the above-described hearing have concurred in the telephonic appearance of the witness(es) set forth in paragraph 2 above.

_____   _____
Date   Signature of certifying attorney or pro se party

                                _____
                                Name of attorney or pro se party

[Effective April 4, 2011.]

ELECTRONIC CASE FILING
MISC. NO. 5–14–MP–00003.   IN RE ELECTRONIC
PROOF OF CLAIM SYSTEM (EPOC)

WHEREAS the Court is implementing an Electronic Proof of Claim (ePOC) system that permits the electronic filing of claims, amending a proof of claim, and withdrawing a proof of claim without requiring a login into the Court's Electronic Filing System (CM/ECF),

IT IS HEREBY ORDERED that notwithstanding the requirements of Local Rule 5005–4, Administrative Order Misc. Nos. 5–05–mp–50007, 5–04–mp–50007, 5–04–mp–50003, and/or 5–04–mp–50010, proofs of claim may be filed, amended and/or withdrawn through the ePOC system and without the need to register or login as a user in CM/ECF.

Any claims filed, amended and/or withdrawn electronically through the court's ePOC system shall constitute the filer's approved signature and have the same force and effects as if the individual signed a paper copy of the proof(s) of claim form, amendment or withdrawal.

With respect to all filings other than those stated herein, the provisions of the aforementioned Rules and Orders remain in full force and effect.

[Dated: April 4, 2014.]

ADMINISTRATIVE PROCEDURES FOR FILING, SIGNING AND VERIFYING PLEADINGS AND PAPERS BY ELECTRONIC MEANS
I.   REGISTRATION FOR THE ELECTRONIC FILING SYSTEM

A. Designation of Cases. Pursuant to Miscellaneous Order 5:05–mp–50007, all attorneys appearing in this Court must become "Filing Users" (i.e., hold a court-issued log-in to the Electronic Case Filing System and file documents only through the System as of April 1, 2006.) (Refer to notes at end of document marked "System"). Attorneys who are unable to file electronically may apply for an extension or waiver. Such requests shall be made by letter, addressed to the Clerk, showing good cause to file and serve pleadings in the traditional manner and setting forth why the attorney is unable to comply, what steps have been taken to comply and how long compliance will take. Requests will be determined by the Chief Judge or his designee. Counsel appearing pro hac vice shall, within ten (10) days of the order so admitting, register for electronic filing or comply with the waiver procedure described above, unless local counsel is a Filing User and will be responsible for filing all pleadings with the Court. Parties proceeding pro se shall not be required to file electronically. See Paragraph III.B.

B. Passwords. Each Filing User shall be entitled to one or more System passwords for each office from the Bankruptcy Court. The password permits the Filing User to participate in the electronic retrieval and filing of pleadings and other papers in accordance with the System. Registration for a password is governed by the following Paragraph (I.C.1.).

C. Registration.

1. Each user desiring to file pleadings or other papers electronically must complete and sign either an Application for an Attorney or an Application for Limited User (consisting of Creditor and/or Law Firm, Auditor, Transcription Company or Personal Financial Management Providers). Attorney users must either attend the necessary training required by the Court or complete the section on the top of the form "Attorney Access—Training Waived". The Registration

forms are available on the Court's website (www.pamb.uscourts.gov) under "Court Info, Case Management/Electronic Case Filing, Electronic Filing—Registration".

2. Each signed original registration form must be scanned in and attached as a PDF document when registering through the Court's website (www.pamb.uscourts. gov).

3. To ensure that the Clerk's Office has the correct Filing User's Internet e-mail address in the System, upon certification of requirements stated in Paragraph I.C.1., the Clerk's Office will send the Filing User a login and password via e-mail.

4. If any of the information on the Registration Form changes, e.g., mailing address, e-mail address, etc., the Filing User must update that information in the CM/ECF system. If an attorney is leaving his or her firm and some clients are remaining with the firm, the firm must file Substitutions of Counsel for those clients.

5. If an employee of the Filing User leaves his employment, the Filing User must change his password. All Filing Users must install and update Anti–Viral software at all locations from which CM/ECF is accessed. All disks must be checked for viruses and worms before being submitted for filing.

II. ELECTRONIC FILING AND SERVICE OF DOCUMENTS

A. Filing.

1. Filing Users shall file electronically all petitions, motions, pleadings, briefs, memoranda of law, proofs of claim, or other documents required to be filed with the Court in connection with a case. Pursuant to Miscellaneous Order 5:04–mp–50007, if a filing deadline for a pleading is fixed it must be completed before midnight local time in order to be considered filed that day.

2. The Clerk's Office shall not maintain a paper court file in any case assigned to the Electronic Filing System except as otherwise provided in Paragraph III.B. and as required by the National Archives and Records Administration regarding documents scanned by the Clerk's Office. The official court record shall be an electronic file maintained on the Court's server.

3. Requests for expedited consideration or hearing shall be by motion. For cases assigned to Judge France, the movant shall also contact the Courtroom Deputy by e-mail as soon as possible after filing the item needing expedited treatment. Requests to cancel hearings because of settlements or withdrawals shall be by e-mail to the Courtroom Deputy and by also filing a Request to Remove from the Hearing/Trial List. The e-mail address for cases assigned to Judge France is:

MDF_Calendar@pamb.uscourts.gov and for cases assigned to Judge Thomas is:

JJT_Calendar@pamb.uscourts.gov.

and for cases assigned to Judge Opel is:

RNO_Calendar@pamb.uscourts.gov

B. Service (See Local Rule 9013–2 and Miscellaneous Order 5:05–mp–50007).

1. Whenever a pleading or other paper is filed electronically in accordance with these procedures, the System shall generate a "Notice of Electronic Filing" to the Filing User and any other Filing User who has requested electronic notice in that case. (Refer to notes at end of document marked "Filing User.") If the recipient is a Filing User, the Clerk's Office e-mailing of the "Notice of Electronic Filing" shall be the equivalent of service of the pleading or other paper by first class mail, postage prepaid. Said Notice of Electronic Filing upon a Filing User shall constitute a Certificate of Service.

2. Except as otherwise provided in II.B.1. above, a certificate of service on all parties entitled to service or notice is still required notwithstanding the filing of a document electronically. The certificate must state the name and address of the

party served and the manner in which service was accomplished on each party so entitled. Sample language for a "Certificate of Service" can be found in the Local Recommended Forms or here as Form C.

3. A party who is not a Filing User is entitled to a paper copy of any electronically filed pleading or paper. The filing party must therefore provide the non-registered party with the pleading or paper according to the Federal Rules of Bankruptcy Procedure.

4. A Filing User may request the discontinuation of service by electronic notice in a particular bankruptcy case or adversary proceeding by making the appropriate docket entry. Upon the Court's receipt of said request, the Filing User will be administratively terminated in said case for the purpose of receiving notices. With regard to the specific case or adversary proceeding, the Filing User will no longer receive a "Notice of Electronic Filing" from the System nor will they receive notice by first class mail. Sample language for a "Request to Discontinue Service of Notices" can be found in the Local Recommended For or here as Form D.

C. Signatures.

1. Petitions, lists, schedules and statements, amendments, pleadings, affidavits, and other documents which must contain original signatures or which require verification under Federal Rule of Bankruptcy Procedure 1008 or an unsworn declaration as provided in 28 U.S.C. § 1746, shall be filed electronically. These shall indicate a signature of the party, e.g., "s/Jane Doe." (Refer to notes at end of document marked "Jane Doe.")

2. The attorney of record or the party originating the document shall maintain the original signed document for all bankruptcy cases pursuant to Miscellaneous Order 5:04–mp–50007. (Federal Rule of Bankruptcy Procedure 9011 applies.)

3. Pursuant to Miscellaneous Order 5:04–mp–50007, electronically filed documents must include a signature block for the Filing User and set forth the name, address, telephone number and the attorney's state bar registration number.

4. Miscellaneous Order 5:04–mp–50007 applies when a stipulation or other document requires two or more signatures.

D. Fees Payable to the Clerk's Office.

1. An Internet Credit Card payment system has been implemented effective November 1, 2004. Filing Users shall pay all filing fees due using this system. Payments should be made by the end of the day of filing. If payments are not timely made, the Filing user's password may be revoked and may not be reinstated until the payment is made.

2. If a case filing fee is to be paid in installments, the Filing User should electronically file an Application to pay in installments at the same time as filing the bankruptcy petition. Such cases must not be filed using the Case Upload feature of ECF as that feature requires full payment.

E. Orders Issued by the Court.

1. The Clerk's Office will electronically file all signed orders and all notices.

2. The Court may enter standard orders to grant or deny motions. Many orders will be in the form of a text-only docket entry "order," entered by court employees authorized to do so by the judge, which orders shall constitute the only Court order concerning the matter.

3. Any order filed electronically without the original signature of a judge, but with the judge's electronic signature, has the same force and effect as if the judge had affixed the judge's signature to a paper copy of the order.

4. Pursuant to Miscellaneous Order 5:04–mp–50007, upon entry of an order, the Clerk's Office will transmit a Notice of Electronic Filing to Filing Users which constitutes notice as required by F.R.B.P. 9022 and will give notice to non-Filing Users in paper format.

F. Proposed Orders/Notices Submitted to the Court.

Proposed orders shall be e-filed with the respective pleading in revisable pdf format.*

G. Title of Docket Entries. Filing Users shall be responsible for designating a docket entry title for the document by using one of the docket events prescribed by the Clerk's Office.

H. Correcting Documents Filed in Error.

1. A document incorrectly filed in a case may be the result of posting the wrong pdf file to a docket entry, or selecting the wrong document type from the menu, or entering the wrong case number and not catching the error before the transaction is completed.

2. As soon as possible after an error is discovered, the Filing User shall amend or withdraw the document filed in error. If not amended or withdrawn, the Filing User will be advised of the proper follow-up procedure by the Clerk's Office by a docket entry which will be e-mailed to the Filing User. The System will not permit Filing Users to make changes to the document(s) or docket entry filed in error once the transaction has been accepted.

I. Technical Failures.

1. The Court's CM/ECF site is deemed subject to a Technical Failure on a given day if the site is unable to accept filings continuously or intermittently over the course of any period of time greater than two hours after 7:00 a.m. In the event of a Technical Failure, a Filing User may do one of the following:

a) file the documents via electronic mail in a PDF attachment sent to the following e-mail address: PAMB_ECF_Failure@pamb.uscourts.gov;

b) file the documents in person by bringing the document to the Clerk's Office in paper format accompanied by an electronic pdf format (e.g. CD–ROM, USB);

c) file the documents via facsimile at one of the following numbers: 570–829–0249 (Wilkes–Barre) or 717–901–2822 (Harrisburg); or

d) seek appropriate relief from the Court. Filing User's are cautioned that the Court's ability to grant relief may be limited by Fed. R. Bankr. P. 9006(b).

2. Technical Problems on the Filing User's end, such as phone line problems, problems with the Filing User's Internet Service Provider (ISP), or hardware or software problems, will not constitute a Technical Failure under these procedures. A Filing User who cannot file a document electronically because of a technical problem on the Filing User's end may use one of the alternate methods specified above and must include an affidavit stating the reason for not filing the documents electronically.

J. Privacy. To address the privacy concerns created by Internet access to court documents, parties should modify or partially redact certain personal data identifiers appearing in pleadings or other filed papers (pursuant to F.R.B.P. 9037). This data and the suggested modifications are as follows:

1. Minors' names: Use the minors' initials;

2. Financial account numbers: Identify the name or type of account and the financial institution where maintained, but use only the last four numbers of the account number;

3. Social Security numbers: only the last four digits;

4. Dates of birth: Use only the year; and

5. Other data as directed by order of the Court.

III. MISCELLANEOUS FILING REQUIREMENTS

A. Exhibits to Pleadings. Pursuant to Miscellaneous Order 5:04–mp–50007, exhibits shall be excerpted and should be docketed as an attachment to the pleading.

B. Pro Se Filers. Except as otherwise advised by the Court, pro se debtors shall file fully signed paper originals of all documents.

C. Large Documents. Documents exceeding 60 pages or 3 MB will not be accepted by the system for filing. These documents must be subdivided, scanned/uploaded separately and filed as one pleading with attachments.

D. Concurrent Filings. If a motion, certificate of service, affidavit, exhibit and brief are filed on the same day, the Filing User must docket the brief separately. Regarding all other documents, the Filing User may either:

1) docket and upload the images of all documents in one docket entry or

2) docket and upload the images of all documents in separate docket entries.

E. Creditor Matrix. The creditor matrix is to be prepared with word processing software in single column format with a 1″ left margin (not centered). Creditors are to be single spaced with a double space separating one creditor from the next. The city, state and zip code are to be on the last line. The entire name and address must not exceed six lines. The word processing file is to be saved as a text (.txt) file and uploaded into the Electronic Case Filing System.

IV. LIMITED USE PASSWORD

A. Filing. Requests for notice under F.R.B.P. 2002, entries of appearance, claims, transfers/assignments/withdrawals of claims, reaffirmation agreements, withdrawals, changes of address, transcripts and auditor reports may be filed electronically by the person obtaining a limited use password from the Clerk's Office. Limited Users are not required to attend a training course, however, training is available for Limited Users. Each user desiring to file pleadings or other papers electronically must complete and sign an Application for Limited Use Password (consisting of Creditor and/or Law Firm, Auditor, Transcription Company or Personal Financial Management Providers). The Registration forms are available on the Court's website (www.pamb.uscourts.gov) under "Electronic Filing—Registration."

B. Transfer or Assignment of Claim. The Clerk's Office will comply with Federal Rule of Bankruptcy Procedure 3001(e)(2) if no "waiver of opportunity to object" is filed. If no timely objection is filed by alleged transferor, the transferee shall be substituted for the transferor without further notice or hearing.

V. PUBLIC ACCESS TO THE SYSTEM DOCKET

A. Public Access at the Court. Electronic access to the electronic docket and documents filed in the System is available for viewing to the public at no charge at the Clerk's Office during regular business hours. A fee for a paper copy of an electronic document is required in accordance with 28 U.S.C. § 1930.

B. Internet Access. Although any person can retrieve and view documents in the System and access information from it without charge at the Clerk's Office, electronic access to the System for viewing purposes is otherwise limited to subscribers to the Public Access to Court Electronic Records ("PACER") System. http://pacer.psc.uscourts.gov. The Judicial Conference of the United States has ruled that a user fee will be charged for remotely accessing certain detailed case information, such as reviewing filed documents and docket sheets, but excluding review of calendars and similar general information. (Refer to notes at end of document marked "Access Fee.")

C. Conventional Copies and Certified Copies. Conventional copies and certified copies of the electronically filed documents may be purchased at the Clerk's

Office. The fee for copying and certification will be in accordance with 28 U.S.C. § 1930.

NOTES:

Access Fee. According to a memorandum from the Administrative Office of the United States Courts dated April 30, 2001, non-judiciary CM/ECF users will be charged a fee beginning July 1, 2001, to access electronic data such as docket sheets and case documents obtained remotely through the PACER system.

The access fee does not apply to official recipients of electronic documents, i.e., parties legally required to receive service or to whom service is directed by the filer in the context of service under Federal Rules of Bankruptcy Procedure. Official recipients will receive the initial electronic copy of a document free to download as they see fit, but if they remotely access the document again, they will be charged the access fee.

Filing User. To determine whether another party or party's attorney is a Filing User the filer can select the System's "Utilities" category, and then click on "Mailings," then click on "Mailing Information for a Case." The Filing User then enters the case number and clicks on "Submit" and the System information will appear, stating whether or not the Filing User must mail a copy or if the System will electronically generate one.

System. "Electronic filing" means uploading a pleading or document directly from the registered user's computer, using the Court's Internet-based System, to file that pleading or document in the Court's case file. Sending a document or pleading to the Court via e-mail does not constitute "electronic filing" except in the instance of a Technical Failure as defined in these Procedures.

[Effective March 1, 2004. Amended effective November 22, 2004; May 10, 2005; July 28, 2006; June 28, 2007; January 4, 2010; May 16, 2012; November 12, 2014.]

* [**Publisher's note:** See also "Proposed Order Guidelines", *post*.]

PROPOSED ORDER GUIDELINES
DO'S AND DONT'S OF PROPOSED ORDERS

The Clerk's Office reviews Proposed Orders which are uploaded to the docket with the pleading for acceptable format prior to routing or approval.

Chambers has directed the Clerk's Office that Proposed Orders should be submitted following the below guidelines. If a proposed order received by the Clerk's Office cannot be quickly revised to comply with these guidelines using Adobe Acrobat or WordPerfect X3 the Clerk's Office has been directed to contact the submitting party for a new Proposed Order. This contact may be in the form of a phone call, email, or Notice to Filing Party.

NOTE: Throughout this document, graphic boxes are used to help with instruction. Any Proposed Order or Notice submitted to the court should **NEVER** include graphic boxes.

- DO NOT scan orders then submit them as Proposed Orders. Scanned documents are not revisable to the extent the court often needs.
- DO use a word processing program such as WordPerfect or Microsoft Word and publish, or save as a PDF which will create a revisable PDF document.
- DO refrain from using elaborate formatting such as (but not limited to) special characters (see Fonts below), borders, graphics, special date codes, data merging, special colors, hyperlinks, and column formats.
- MARGINS
  - DO try to use ½" margins (0.5") at the top and sides of the document. We understand some instances this will not be possible in order to create a nice

appearing document. However, as a general rule ½″ (0.5″) margins are acceptable.

- FONTS

  o DO try to use the same font style and point size throughout the document.

  o ONLY USE Fonts from the list below:
  Arial (Regular)
  Arial (Bold)
  Arial (Italic)
  Arial (Bold Italic)
  Courier (Regular)
  Courier (Bold)
  Courier (Oblique)
  Courier (Bold Oblique)
  Helvetica (Regular)
  Helvetica (Bold)
  Helvetica (Oblique)
  Helvetica (Bold Oblique)
  Times (Regular)
  Times (Bold)
  Times (Italic)
  Times (Bold Italic)
  Times New Roman (Bold)
  Times New Roman (Italic)
  Times New Roman (Bold Italic)
  Symbol
  ZapfDingbats

NOTE: If for some reason you absolutely cannot use one of the above-listed fonts, you will need to produce the PDF file with the **fonts embedded**. This can be done by changing a setting in your word processor or Adobe Acrobat program. Contact your software provider for assistance if needed.

Embedding fonts assures the PDF version of your document looks the same on all machines that may be viewing it. Embedding causes the document to carry its own copies of fonts you have used. If you don't embed your fonts, it is possible your document will look like gibberish or be missing essential information when viewed by other users.

- Acceptable PDF levels:

  o 1.2 Adobe Acrobat Version 3

  o 1.3 Adobe Acrobat Version 4

  o 1.4 Adobe Acrobat Version 5

  o 1.5 Adobe Acrobat Version 6

  o 1.6 Adobe Acrobat Version 7

  o 1.7 Adobe Acrobat Versions 8, 9 or 10

- COURT INFORMATION

  o DO start Orders with court information in CAPITAL LETTERS, centered at the ½″ top margin.

  o DO NOT include wording such as "Southern Division", or "Northern Tier", or "Harrisburg Office".

  o DO use the words "IN THE" and "FOR THE".

ACCEPTABLE:

IN THE UNITED STATES BANKRUPTCY COURT
FOR THE MIDDLE DISTRICT OF PENNSYLVANIA

- CAPTION—Always:
  - o Format using Party Names in ALL UPPERCASE LETTERS (i.e., JOHN DOE)
  - o Format Party Designation in mix of Upper and Lower case letters. (i.e., Debtor, Respondent, Movant)
  - o Include CHAPTER—Place above Case Number.
  - o Include CASE NUMBER—Place below Chapter.

  Correct Case Number formatting:
    - Office Number—"1" for Harrisburg or "5" for Wilkes–Barre
    - Year of filing (2 digits)
    - Designation of case matter—BK for bankruptcy, AP for adversary
    - Case number
    - Judge Initials
  - o Include the MATTER for which the order pertains. Place below the case number.
  - o When separating party information from Case/Chapter Number a SOLID LINE IS PREFERRED.

IN THE UNITED STATES BANKRUPTCY
FOR THE MIDDLE DISTRICT OF PENNSYLVANIA

DEBTOR NAME   CHAPTER 7
DEBTOR ALIAS(S)

                              CASE NUMBER: o-yy-bk-nnnnn-XXX

DEBTOR

                              MOTION FOR XXXXXXX

- o DEBTOR NAME(S)—Include names, alias(s) and Debtor designation.
  Place designation of Debtor on line below and to the right of the name.
- o PARTY NAME(S)—(if applicable) Include names, alias(s) and designation of Parties.
  Place below Debtor(s) name & designation.
- o DESIGNATION OF PARTY—Placed below, and to the right of their name.
- o MATTERS—"vs." should be used between the opposing party names.

Refer to LOCAL BANKRUPTCY FORMS 9004–2 and 9004–3 for proper formatting of Adversary and Contested Matters.

- BODY OF ORDER
  - o DO NOT use lines to separate the caption of the document from the body. Lines, due to the various methods in which they can be created, are frequently a problem to work with. They are frequently removed before orders are signed.
  Undesirable line separation example:

Plaintiff Full Name
Plaintiff Alias(s)

Plaintiff(s)   _____
                              ORDER OF COURT

---

o LINE SPACING—Avoid compressing text at the top of the page.

o DO adjust line spacing within the document so you utilize the page in creating a professional appearance. Generally, the caption area will be single spaced. The body of the order double spaced.

o UNACCEPTABLE STARTING LINES:

  ● And now, this ___ day of _____, 200x.
Due to the method the court uses for signing orders, and the statement included at the bottom of all orders by that process, the above date line is never needed.

  ● AND NOW, ...

  ● After notice and hearing ___ (If there was not a hearing in the matter, then do not state in the order that there was.)

o ACCEPTABLE STARTING LINES:

  ● Upon consideration of . . . . (This is the court's preferred language for Orders.)

  ● After notice and hearing . . . . (Acceptable IF there actually was a notice and/or hearing on the matter.)

  ● After notice and opportunity to be heard ___

o DO NOT use any kind of underscoring tool to create a blank within the body of the Order.
  (Example: A hearing will be held on _____, 2008 at _____ o'clock.)

o DO leave a blank space without any underscoring for hearing information. Extra points if you leave the exact number of spaces necessary to spell the month in which the order is being signed.

o SERVICE LIST

  ● DO NOT include a service list along with the order.

  ● DO NOT include within the order.

  ● DO NOT include as an additional page of the order.

● SIGNATURE AREA

o DO leave at least 3″ of space at the bottom of the page for the Judge's signature. If there is not 3″ of space left at the bottom of the page, DO NOT simply add another blank page. DO remove the last line from the preceding page onto the last page. The Judge will NOT sign a blank page.

o SIGNATURE LINES—DO NOT include Judge signature lines, titles, or name.
  The court's signature process includes all that is needed for signing. DO NOT put any text, underlines, title or Judge name where the Judge's signature should be placed.

o DO NOT include the text "By the Court," or "Dated:".
  The court's signature process automatically includes all this information for dating and signing.

● IF WE CANNOT WORK WITH WHAT IS SUBMITTED, you will receive notification requesting you submit the proposed document again until an acceptable document is received. This contact may be in the form of a phone call, email or a Notice to Filing Party.

[Effective May 16, 2012. Amended effective September 30, 2014.]

FORM A. ELECTRONIC CASE FILING SYSTEM ATTORNEY REGISTRATION FORM PLEASE TYPE

United States Bankruptcy Court
for the Middle District of Pennsylvania

This form shall be used to register for accounts on the Court's Case Management/Electronic Case Filing (CM/ECF) system. Registered attorneys will have privileges both to electronically submit documents and to view and retrieve electronic docket sheets and documents available for cases assigned to the CM/ECF system.

Full Participant—Training Required: If you are <u>not</u> electronically filing in another court, you must complete our in-person training prior to receiving a login an password.

Full Participant—Training Waived: If you are an electronic filer in another court's electronic filing system and do not wish to attend in-person training at the courthouse, please complete the following information: **I have filed cases electronically in another Bankruptcy or District Court in the District of _____ and therefore am requesting to waive the requirement to attend the CM/ECF training class to obtain my login/password. I understand that it is my responsibility to learn and use any and all updates to the electronic case filing procedures.**

The following information is required for registration:

First/Middle/Last Name: _____

Attorney Bar # and State: _____

Firm Name: _____

Firm Address: _____

_____

Voice Phone Number: _____ FAX Phone Number: _____

Internet E–Mail Address: _____

Additional E–Mail Address: _____

Does your E–Mail Software support HTML messages? Yes _____ No _____

By submitting this registration form, the undersigned agrees to abide by the following rules:

1. The CM/ECF system is for use only in cases designated by the U.S. Bankruptcy Court for the Middle District of Pennsylvania. The CM/ECF system may be used to file and view electronic documents, docket sheets, and notices.

2. <u>Each attorney desiring to file pleadings or other papers electronically must complete and sign an Attorney Registration Form.</u> An attorney's password issued by the Court combined with the user's identification (login), serves as and constitutes the attorney's signature. Therefore, an attorney must protect and secure the password issued by the Court. If there is any reason to suspect the password has been compromised in any way, such as resignation or reassignment of the person with authority to use the password, it is the duty and responsibility of the attorney to immediately notify the Court. The Court will immediately delete the password from the electronic filing system and issue a new password, if appropriate. If an attorney leaves his law firm, he should notify the Clerk's Office of his new addresses for mail and e-mail. If he does not and his firm returns e-mails from the Clerk's Office or notifies the Clerk's Office, his password will be changed, preventing access to the system until his addresses are formally updated.

3. Pursuant to Federal Rule of Civil Procedure 11 and Federal Rule of Bankruptcy Procedure 9011, every pleading, motion and other paper (except creditor lists,

schedules, statements or amendments thereto) shall be signed by at least one attorney of record or, if the party is not represented by an attorney, all papers shall be signed by the party. The electronic filing of a petition, pleading, motion or other paper by an attorney who is a registered participant in the electronic filing system shall constitute the signature of that attorney under Federal Rule of Civil Procedure 11 and Federal Rule of Bankruptcy Procedure 9011.

4. Registration as a Filing User constitutes: (1) consent to receive notice electronically and waiver of the right to receive notice by first class mail pursuant to Federal Rule of Civil Procedure 5(b)(2)(D) and Federal Rule of Bankruptcy Procedure 7005; (2) consent to electronic service and waiver of the right to service by personal service or first class mail pursuant to Federal Rule of Civil Procedure 5(b)(2)(D) and Federal Rule of Bankruptcy Procedure 7005, except with regard to service of a summons and complaint. Waiver of service and notice by first class mail applies to notice of the entry of an order or judgment. Notice by electronic means is complete as set forth in the general Order notwithstanding Federal Rule of Bankruptcy Procedure 9036.

5. A user accesses court information via the Court's Internet site or through the Public Access to Court Electronic Records ("PACER") Service Center. Although the Court manages the procedures for electronic filing, all electronic public access to case file documents occurs through PACER. A PACER login is required, in addition to, the password issued by the Court. To register for PACER, a user must complete the online form or submit a registration form, available on the PACER web site (http://pacer.psc.uscourts.gov).

6. By this registration, the undersigned agrees to abide by all of the rules and regulations in the most recent general Order, *Administrative Procedures for Filing, Signing and Verifying Pleadings and Papers by Electronic Means* currently in effect and any changes or additions that may be made to such Administrative Procedures in the future.

————————————————   ————————————————
Date   Attorney Signature

Your login and password will be sent to you by the Clerk's Office via e-mail to the addresses listed on this registration form.

If you are a Filing User in another federal electronic case filing system and wish to use that log-in for our Bankruptcy Court ECF system, please provide it **here**:
—————.

Revised: 11/13

[Effective March 1, 2004. Revised August 12, 2004; May 31, 2005; September 21, 2006; June 28, 2007; December 23, 2009; July 21, 2010; November 2013.]

FORM B. [RESERVED]

FORM C. CERTIFICATE OF SERVICE

**IN THE UNITED STATES BANKRUPTCY COURT
FOR THE MIDDLE DISTRICT OF PENNSYLVANIA**

IN THE MATTER OF:

>)
>) Chapter:
>)
>) Case Number:
>)
> DEBTOR(S)   )

CERTIFICATE OF SERVICE

I certify that I am more than 18 years of age and that on _____ (Date) _____ I served a copy of _____ on the following parties in this matter:

Name and Address	Mode of Service

I certify under penalty of perjury that the foregoing is true and correct.

Date: _____   Name: s/ _____
                                          Printed Name of Attorney
                               Address: _____

                               _____

[Effective March 1, 2004. Revised November 16, 2004; March 22, 2005.]

FORM D.   REQUEST TO DISCONTINUE SERVICE OF NOTICES

UNITED STATES BANKRUPTCY COURT
FOR THE MIDDLE DISTRICT OF PENNSYLVANIA

IN THE MATTER OF:

)	
)	Chapter:
)	
)	Case Number:
)	
DEBTOR(S))	

REQUEST TO DISCONTINUE SERVICE OF NOTICES

PLEASE TAKE NOTICE that the undersigned, appearing as counsel for _____
_____,
creditor and party-in-interest in the above-captioned matter, requests to be administratively terminated in this case for the purpose of receiving notices. The undersigned no longer wishes to receive notices from the Court, either by electronic form or first class mail.

Dated: _____   s/ _____
                                     _____
                                     _____
                                     _____

[Effective March 1, 2004. Revised November 12, 2004; March 3, 2005.]

FORM E.   APPLICATION FOR LIMITED USE PASSWORD
FOR ELECTRONIC CASE FILING SYSTEM

United States Bankruptcy Court
for the Middle District of Pennsylvania

APPLICATION FOR LIMITED USE PASSWORD
FOR ELECTRONIC CASE FILING SYSTEM

This form shall be used to apply for an account on the Court's Case Management/Electronic Case Filing (CM/ECF) system. The following information is required for registration:

This login provides filing users with limited access to the Case Management/Electronic Case Filing ("CM/ECF") system. **Limited User access is available for creditors and law firms, auditors, transcription companies and personal financial management providers.** A limited user has the ability to file selective entries.

Please check the appropriate limited use access you are registering for:

☐ **Creditor and/or Law Firm**
☐ **Transcription Company**
☐ **Auditor**
☐ **Personal Financial Management Provider**

If you are an Attorney and anticipate filing Motions, Answers,
etc., please complete the Attorney Registration Form

First/Middle/Last Name: _____

Attorney Bar # and State(if applicable): _____

Firm/Company Name: _____

Firm/Company Address: _____

_____

Voice Phone Number: _____ FAX Phone Number: _____

Internet E–Mail Address: _____

Additional E–Mail Address: _____

Does your E–Mail Software support HTML messages? Yes ☐ No ☐

By submitting this registration form, the undersigned agrees to abide by the following rules:

1. The CM/ECF system is for use only in cases designated by the U.S. Bankruptcy Court for the Middle District of Pennsylvania. The CM/ECF system may be used to file and view electronic documents, docket sheets, and notices.

2. This login provides filing users with limited access to the Case Management/Electronic Case Filing ("CM/ECF") system. Limited User access is available for creditors and law firms, auditors, transcription companies and personal financial management providers. A limited user has the ability to file selective entries. You must complete and sign an Application for Limited Use Password Form. A password issued by the Court combined with the user's identification (login), serves as and constitutes the user's signature. Therefore, users must protect and secure the password issued by the Court. If there is any reason to suspect the password has been compromised in any way, such as resignation or reassignment of the person with authority to use the password, it is the duty and responsibility of the user to immediately notify the Court. The Court will immediately delete the password from the electronic filing system and

issue a new password, if appropriate. If e-mails from the Clerk's Office are returned by the user, the password will be changed.

3. Pursuant to Federal Rule of Civil Procedure 11 and Federal Rule of Bankruptcy Procedure 9011, every pleading, motion and other paper (except creditor lists, schedules, statements or amendments thereto) shall be signed by at least one attorney of record or, if the party is not represented by an attorney, all papers shall be signed by the party. The electronic filing of a petition, pleading, motion or other paper by an attorney or unrepresented party who is a registered participant in the electronic filing system shall constitute the signature of that attorney or unrepresented party under Federal Rule of Civil Procedure 11 and Federal Rule of Bankruptcy Procedure 9011.

4. Registration as a Filing User constitutes: (1) consent to receive notice electronically and waiver of the right to receive notice by first class mail pursuant to Federal Rule of Civil Procedure 5(b)(2)(D) and Federal Rule of Bankruptcy Procedure 7005; (2) consent to electronic service and waiver of the right to service by personal service or first class mail pursuant to Federal Rule of Civil Procedure 5(b)(2)(D) and Federal Rule of Bankruptcy Procedure 7005, except with regard to service of a summons and complaint. Waiver of service and notice by first class mail applies to notice of the entry of an order or judgment. Notice by electronic means is complete as set forth in the general Order notwithstanding Federal Rule of Bankruptcy Procedure 9036.

5. A user accesses court information via the Court's Internet site or through the Public Access to Court Electronic Records ("PACER") Service Center. Although the Court manages the procedures for electronic filing, all electronic public access to case file documents occurs through PACER. A PACER login is required, in addition to, the password issued by the Court. To register for PACER, a user must complete the online form or submit a registration form, available on the PACER web site (http://pacer.psc.uscourts.gov).

6. I understand that, if I am a provider of a post-petition instructional course concerning personal financial management and I am filing a certificate of the debtor's completion of the course, the certificate must be timely filed in accordance with Fed.R.Bankr.P.1007(c). I understand that my limited filer privileges may be revoked if I do not file a certificate of a debtor's completion of the course in a timely manner, as failure to do so could result in the closing of the debtor's case with a discharge. I understand that, if my filing privileges are revoked by the court, the court will notify the Executive Office for U.S. Trustees of the revocation.

7. By this registration, the undersigned agrees to abide by all of the rules and regulations in the most recent general Order, *Administrative Procedures for Filing, Signing and Verifying Pleadings and Papers by Electronic Means* currently in effect and any changes or additions that may be made to such Administrative Procedures in the future.

8. I affirm that I am authorized to prepare and file the documents referenced in paragraph #2 above on behalf of _____.

_____   _____
Date   Signature

Your login and password will be sent to you by the Clerk's Office via e-mail to the addresses listed on this registration form.

If you are a Filing User in another federal electronic case filing system and wish to use that log-in for our

Bankruptcy Court ECF system, please provide it **here:** _____.

[Effective March 1, 2004. Revised August 12, 2004; June 13, 2005; September 21, 2006; June 28, 2007; December 23, 2009; July 2010; November 25, 2013.]

SELECTED ORDERS

MISC NO. 84–0203. IN RE: REFERRAL OF BANKRUPTCY MATTERS [DISTRICT COURT ORDER] [VACATED BY STANDING ORDER NO. 16–3, EFFECTIVE MARCH 11, 2016]

STANDING ORDER NO. 00–3. IN RE: STANDING ORDER OF REFERENCE IN BANKRUPTCY MATTERS [DISTRICT COURT ORDER] [VACATED BY STANDING ORDER NO. 16–3, EFFECTIVE MARCH 11, 2016]

MISC NO. 5–08–mp–50027. IN RE: AMENDED ORDER ADOPTING INTERIM FEDERAL BANKRUPTCY RULE 1007–I, AS AMENDED RETROACTIVELY EFFECTIVE DECEMBER 18, 2015

IT IS HEREBY ORDERED that Interim Bankruptcy Rule 1007–I (Lists, Schedules, Statements, and Other Documents; Time Limits; Expiration of Temporary Means Testing Exclusion), as amended, is adopted by this Court, retroactively effective December 18, 2015.

The amendment extends the temporary exclusion from the application of the means test for certain members of the National Guard and reserve components of the Armed Forces. A copy of revised Interim Rule 1007–I is posted at http://www.uscourts.gov/file/18071/download.

[Dated: January 5, 2016.]

Interim Rule 1007–I.[1] Lists, Schedules, Statements, and Other Documents; Time Limits; Expiration of Temporary Means Testing Exclusion

* * * * *

(b) Schedules, Statements, and Other Documents Required.

* * * * *

(4) Unless either: (A) § 707(b)(2)(D)(I) applies, or (B) § 707(b)(2)(D)(ii) applies and the exclusion from means testing granted therein extends beyond the period specified by Rule 1017(e), an individual debtor in a chapter 7 case shall file a statement of current monthly income prepared as prescribed by the appropriate Official Form, and, if the current monthly income exceeds the median family income for the applicable state and household size, the information, including calculations, required by § 707(b), prepared as prescribed by the appropriate Official Form.

* * * * *

(c) Time Limits. In a voluntary case, the schedules, statements, and other documents required by subdivision (b)(1), (4), (5), and (6) shall be filed with the petition or within 14 days thereafter, except as otherwise provided in subdivisions (d), (e), (f), (h), and (n) of this rule. In an involuntary case, the schedules, statements, and other documents required by subdivision (b)(1) shall be filed by the debtor within 14 days after the entry of the order for relief. In a voluntary case, the documents required by paragraphs (A), (C), and (D) of subdivision (b)(3) shall be filed with the petition. Unless the court orders otherwise, a debtor who has filed a statement under subdivision (b)(3)(B), shall file the documents required by subdivision (b)(3)(A) within 14 days of the order for relief. In a chapter 7 case, the debtor shall file the statement required by subdivision (b)(7) within 60 days after the first date set for the meeting of creditors under § 341 of the Code, and in a chapter 11 or 13 case no later than the date when the last payment was made by the debtor as required by the plan or the filing of a motion for a discharge under § 1141(d)(5)(B) or § 1328(b) of the Code. The court may, at any time and in its discretion, enlarge the time to file the statement required by subdivision (b)(7). The debtor shall file the statement required by subdivision (b)(8) no earlier than the date of the last payment made under the plan or the date of the filing of a motion for a discharge under §§ 1141(d)(5)(B), 1228(b), or 1328(b) of the Code. Lists, schedules, statements, and other documents filed prior to the conversion of a case to another chapter shall be deemed filed in the converted case unless the court directs otherwise. Except as provided in § 1116(3), any extension of time to file schedules, statements, and other documents required under this rule may be granted only on motion for cause shown and on notice to the United States trustee, any committee elected under § 705 or appointed under § 1102 of the Code, trustee, examiner, or other party as the court may direct. Notice of an extension shall be given to the United States trustee and to any committee, trustee, or other party as the court may direct.

* * * * *

(n) Time Limits for, and Notice to, Debtors Temporarily Excluded From Means Testing.

(1) An individual debtor who is temporarily excluded from means testing pursuant to § 707(b)(2)(D)(ii) of the Code shall file any statement and calculations required by subdivision (b)(4) no later than 14 days after the expiration of the temporary exclusion if the expiration occurs within the time specified by Rule 1017(e) for filing a motion pursuant to § 707(b)(2).

(2) If the temporary exclusion from means testing under § 707(b)(2)(D)(ii) terminates due to the circumstances specified in subdivision (n)(1), and if the debtor has not previously filed a statement and calculations required by subdivision (b)(4), the clerk shall promptly notify the debtor that the required statement and calculations must be filed within the time specified in subdivision (n)(1).

1 Interim Rule 1007–I has been adopted by the bankruptcy courts to implement the National Guard and Reservists Debt Relief Act of 2008, Public Law No. 110–438, as amended by Public Law No. 114–107. The amended Act, which provides a temporary exclusion from the application of the means test for certain members of the National Guard and reserve components of the Armed Forces, applies to bankruptcy cases commenced in the 11-year period beginning December 19, 2008.

STANDING ORDER NO. 16–3. AMENDED ORDER OF REFERENCE IN BANKRUPTCY MATTERS

WHEREAS, it having been determined that the Standing Order of Reference in Bankruptcy Matters entered on September 11, 2000 at No. 00–3 and the Order entered July 26, 1984 referring bankruptcy cases to the bankruptcy judges for the Middle District at Misc. No. 84–203 do not comport with the holding in *Stern v. Marshall* ___ U.S. ___, 131 S. Ct. 2594 (2011), **IT IS HEREBY ORDERED THAT** the Order entered re: Referral of Bankruptcy Matters at Misc. No, 84–203 and Standing Order of Reference No. 00–3 are **VACATED**.

IT IS FURTHER ORDERED THAT as provided in 28 U.S.C. § 157(a), any and all cases under title 11 and any and all proceedings arising under title 11 or arising in or related to a case under title 11 are referred to the bankruptcy judges for this district. If a bankruptcy judge or district judge determines that entry of a final order or judgment by a bankruptcy judge in a particular core proceeding as described in 28 U.S.C. § 157(b)(2) would not be consistent with Article III of the United States Constitution, the bankruptcy judge shall, unless the parties consent to the entry of a final order or judgment by the bankruptcy judge or the district court orders otherwise, hear the proceeding and submit proposed findings of fact and conclusions of law to the district court. The district court may treat any order of the bankruptcy court as proposed findings of fact and conclusions of law in the event the district court concludes that the bankruptcy judge could not have entered a final order or judgment consistent with Article III of the United States Constitution. In non-core cases that are otherwise related to a bankruptcy case, except as otherwise provided in 28 U.S.C. § 157, a bankruptcy judge may enter final orders and judgments if the parties consent. If the parties do not consent to a bankruptcy judge entering final orders or judgments, unless otherwise ordered by the district court, the bankruptcy judge shall hear the proceeding and submit proposed findings of fact and conclusions of law to the district court.

[Dated: March 11, 2016.]

UNITED STATES DISTRICT COURT FOR THE WESTERN DISTRICT OF PENNSYLVANIA

Including Amendments Received Through
June 1, 2016

LOCAL PATENT RULES

LOCAL CIVIL RULES OF COURT

LCvR 1.1   SCOPE OF RULES

A. Title and Citation. These rules shall be known as the Local Rules of the United States District Court for the Western District of Pennsylvania. They may be cited as "LCvR."

B. Scope of Rules. These rules shall apply in all proceedings in civil and criminal actions.

C. Relationship to Prior Rules; Actions Pending on Effective Date. These rules supersede all previous rules promulgated by this Court or any Judge of this Court. They shall govern all applicable proceedings brought in this Court after they take effect. They also shall apply to all proceedings pending at the time they take effect, except to the extent that in the opinion of the Court the application thereof would not be feasible or would work injustice, in which event the former rules shall govern.

D. Rule of Construction and Definitions. United States Code, Title 1, Sections 1 to 5, shall, as far as applicable, govern the construction of these rules. Unless the context indicates otherwise, the word "Judge" refers to both District Judges and Magistrate Judges.

[Effective September 1, 2009.]

LCvR 1.2   RULES AVAILABLE ON WEBSITE OR IN OFFICE OF CLERK OF COURT

Copies of these rules, as amended and with any appendices attached hereto, are available on the Court's website (www.pawd.uscourts.gov/) or in hard copy from the Clerk of Court's office for a reasonable charge to be determined by the Board of Judges. When amendments to these rules are made, notices of such amendments shall be provided on the Court's website, in the legal journals for each county and on the bulletin board in the Clerk of Court's office. When amendments to these rules are proposed, notice of such proposals and of the ability of the public to comment shall be provided on the Court's website, in the legal journals for each county and on the bulletin board in the Clerk of Court's office.

[Effective September 1, 2009.]

LCvR 3. ASSIGNMENT TO ERIE, JOHNSTOWN OR PITTSBURGH DOCKET

Where it appears from the complaint, petition or other pleading that the claim arose OR any plaintiff or defendant resides in: Crawford, Elk, Erie, Forest, McKean, Venango, or Warren County, the Clerk of Court shall give such complaint, petition or other pleading an Erie number and it shall be placed on the Erie docket. Should it appear from the complaint, petition or other pleading that the claim arose OR any plaintiff or defendant resides in: Bedford, Blair, Cambria, Clearfield or Somerset County, the Clerk of Court shall give such complaint, petition or other pleading a Johnstown number and it shall be placed on the Johnstown docket. All other cases or matters for litigation shall be docketed and processed at Pittsburgh. In the event of a conflict between the Erie and Johnstown dockets, the Clerk of Court shall place the action on the plaintiff's choice of those two dockets.

[Effective September 1, 2009. Amended effective February 1, 2013.]

LCvR 5.1 GENERAL FORMAT OF PAPERS PRESENTED FOR FILING

A. Filing and Paper Size. In order that the files in the Clerk of Court's office may be kept under the system commonly known as "flat filing," all papers presented to the Court or to the Clerk of Court for filing shall be flat and as thin as feasible. Further, all pleadings and other documents presented for filing to the Court or to the Clerk of Court shall be on 8½ by 11 inch size paper, white in color for scanning purposes and electronic case filing (ECF).

B. Lettering. The lettering or typeface shall be clearly legible and shall not be smaller than 12 point word processing font or, if typewritten, shall not be smaller than pica. The text must be double-spaced, but quotations more than two lines long may be indented and single-spaced. Headings and footnotes may be single-spaced. The font type and size used in footnotes shall be the same as that used in the body of the brief. Margins must be at least one inch on all four sides. Page numbers may be placed in the margins, but no text may appear there.

C. Printing on One Side. The lettering or typeface shall be on only one (1) side of a page.

D. Page Fasteners. All papers and other documents filed in this Court shall be securely fastened with a paper clip, binder clip or rubber band. The use of plastic strips, staples or other such fasteners is prohibited, with the exception that administrative and judicial records may be firmly bound.

E. Exhibits to Briefs. Exhibits to a brief or motion shall accompany the brief or motion, but shall not be attached to or bound with the brief or motion. Exhibits shall be secured separately, using either lettered or numbered separator pages to separate and identify each exhibit. Each exhibit also shall be identified by letter or number on the top right hand corner of the first page of the exhibit. Exhibits in support of a pleading or other paper shall accompany the pleading or other paper but shall not be physically bound thereto. In all instances where more than one exhibit is part of the same filing, there shall be a table of contents for the exhibits.

F. Separate Documents. Each motion and each brief shall be a separate document.

G. Exceptions on Motion. Exceptions to the provisions of this rule may be made only upon motion and for good cause or in the case of papers filed in litigation commenced in forma pauperis.

H. Withdrawal of Files. Records and papers on file in the office of the Clerk of Court may be produced pursuant to a subpoena from any federal or state Court, directing their production. Records and papers may be removed from the files only upon order of Court. Whenever records and papers are withdrawn, the person receiving them shall leave with the Clerk of Court a signed receipt describing the records or papers taken.

I. Exhibits. All exhibits received in evidence, or offered and rejected, upon the hearing of any cause or motion, shall be presented to the deputy clerk, who shall keep the same in custody, unless otherwise ordered by the Court, except that the clerk may without special order permit an official court reporter to withdraw exhibits, by means of a signed descriptive receipt, for the purpose of preparing the transcript.

J. Law Enforcement Evidence. In all cases where money, firearms, narcotics, controlled substances or any matter of contraband is introduced into evidence, such evidence shall be maintained for safekeeping by law enforcement during all times when court is not in session, and at the conclusion of the case. The law enforcement agent will be responsible for its custody if the evidence is required for any purpose thereafter. *See also* LCrR 23.

K. Exhibits Retained by Clerk. Trial exhibits shall be retained by the deputy clerk until it is determined whether an appeal has been taken from a final judgment. In the event of an appeal, exhibits shall be retained by the deputy clerk until disposition of the appeal. Otherwise, they may be reclaimed by counsel for a period of thirty (30) days after which the exhibits may be destroyed by the deputy clerk.

[Effective September 1, 2009.]

LCvR 5.2 DOCUMENTS TO BE FILED WITH THE CLERK OF COURT

A. Only Original to be Filed. As to any document required or permitted to be filed with the Court in paper form, only the original shall be filed with the Clerk of Court.

B. Attorney Identification. Any document signed by an attorney for filing shall contain under the signature line the name, address, telephone number, fax number, e-mail address (if applicable) and Pennsylvania or other state bar identification number. When listing the bar identification number, the state's postal abbreviation shall be used as a prefix (e.g., PA 12345, NY 246810).

C. No Faxed Documents. Documents shall not be faxed to a Judge without prior leave of Court. Documents shall not be faxed to the Clerk of Court's office, except in the event of a technical failure with the Court's Electronic Case Filing ("ECF") system. "Technical failure" is defined as a malfunction of Court owned/leased hardware, software, and/or telecommunications facility which results in the inability of a Filing User to submit a filing electronically. Technical failure does not include malfunctioning of a Filing User's equipment.

D. Redaction of Personal Identifiers. A filed document in a case (other than a social security case) shall not contain any of the personal data identifiers listed in this rule unless permitted by an order of the Court or unless redacted in conformity with this rule. The personal data identifiers covered by this rule and the required redactions are as follows:

1. *Social Security Numbers.* If an individual's Social Security Number must be included in a document, only the last four digits of that number shall be used;

2. *Names of Minor Children.* If the involvement of a minor child must be mentioned, only that child's initials shall be used;

3. *Dates of Birth.* If an individual's date of birth must be included, only the year shall be used;

4. *Financial Account Numbers.* If financial account numbers must be included, only the last four digits shall be used.

Additional personal data identifier in a criminal case document only:

5. *Home Addresses.* If a home address must be included, only the city and state shall be listed.

E. Personal Identifiers Under Seal. A party wishing to file a document containing the personal data identifiers listed above may file in addition to the required redacted document:

1. a sealed and otherwise identical document containing the unredacted personal data identifiers, or

2. a reference list under seal. The reference list shall contain the complete personal data identifier(s) and the redacted identifier(s) used in its(their) place in the filing. All references in the case to the redacted identifiers included in the reference list will be construed to refer to the corresponding complete personal data identifier. The reference list must be filed under seal, and may be amended as of right.

F. Unredacted Version Retained by Court. The sealed unredacted version of the document or the sealed reference list shall be retained by the Court as a part of the record.

G. Counsel and Parties Responsible. The responsibility for redacting these personal identifiers rests solely with counsel and the parties. The Clerk of Court will not review each document for compliance with this rule.

[Effective September 1, 2009.]

LCvR 5.3 PROOF OF SERVICE WHEN SERVICE IS REQUIRED BY FED. R. CIV. P. 5

Except as otherwise provided by these rules, the filing or submission to the Court by a party of any pleading or paper required to be served on the other parties pursuant to Fed. R. Civ. P. 5, shall constitute a representation that a copy thereof has been served upon each of the parties upon whom service is required. No further proof of service is required unless an adverse party raises a question of notice.

[Effective September 1, 2009.]

LCvR 5.4 FILING OF DISCOVERY MATERIALS

A. No Filing of Discovery Materials. Discovery requests and responses referenced in Fed. R. Civ. P. 5(d) shall not be filed with the office of the Clerk of Court except by order of Court.

B. Discovery Materials Necessary to Decide a Motion. A party making or responding to a motion or seeking relief under the Federal Rules of Civil Procedure shall file only that portion of discovery requests and responses as needed to decide the motion or determine whether relief should be granted.

C. Necessary Portions to Be Filed With Clerk of Court. When discovery requests and responses are needed for an appeal, upon an application and order of the Court, or by stipulation of counsel, the necessary portion of the discovery requests and responses shall be filed with the Clerk of Court.

D. Custodian of Discovery Materials. The party serving discovery requests or responses or taking depositions shall retain the original and be custodian of it.

[Effective September 1, 2009.]

LCvR 5.5   FILING OF DOCUMENTS BY ELECTRONIC MEANS

Except for documents filed by pro se litigants, or as otherwise ordered by the Court, documents must be filed, signed and verified by electronic means to the extent and in the manner authorized by the Court's Standing Order regarding Electronic Case Filing Policies and Procedures and the ECF User Manual. A document filed by electronic means in compliance with this Local Rule constitutes a written document for the purposes of applying these Local Rules, the Federal Rules of Civil Procedure and the Federal Rules of Criminal Procedure.

[Effective September 1, 2009.]

LCvR 5.6   SERVICE OF DOCUMENTS BY ELECTRONIC MEANS

Documents may be served through the Court's transmission facilities by electronic means to the extent and in the manner authorized by the Standing Order regarding Electronic Case Filing Policies and Procedures and the ECF User Manual. Transmission of the Notice of Electronic Filing constitutes service of the filed document upon each party in the case who is registered as a Filing User. Any other party or parties shall be served documents according to these Local Rules, the Federal Rules of Civil Procedure and the Federal Rules of Criminal Procedure.

[Effective September 1, 2009.]

LCvR 7.   MOTION PRACTICE AND STIPULATIONS

A. Motions Filed in Actions Pending in this Court. Motions in all civil actions pending in this Court shall comply with the applicable Federal Rules of Civil Procedure, the applicable Local Rules, the orders of the assigned Judge and the practices and procedures of the assigned Judge that are posted at the following internet link: http://www.pawd.uscourts.gov/pages/chamber.htm.

B. Motions Not Filed in Actions Pending in this Court. All motions of a civil nature that are not filed in a civil action pending in this Court shall comply with the applicable Federal Rules of Civil Procedure and the applicable Local Rules, shall be filed with the Clerk of Court upon payment of any appropriate filing fee, and shall be served on any interested parties. The Court's fee schedule is posted at the following internet link: http://www.pawd.uscourts.gov/pages/fee.htm.

C. Discovery Motions. In addition to the general requirements of this LCvR 7, any discovery motion filed pursuant to Fed. R. Civ. P. 26 through 37 shall comply with the requirements of LCvR 37.1 and 37.2, and any motion in limine shall comply with the requirements of LCvR 16.1.C.4.

D. Proposed Order of Court. All motions shall be accompanied by a proposed order of Court.

E. Stipulations. The parties, without Court approval, may file a stipulation one time which extends for a period not to exceed 45 days from the original due date the time for filing either an answer to a complaint or a motion pursuant to Fed. R. Civ. P. 12.

[Effective September 1, 2009. Amended effective February 1, 2013.]

LCvR 7.1   DISCLOSURE STATEMENT AND RICO CASE STATEMENT

A. Disclosure Statement.

1. *Disclosure Statement Required.* A corporation, association, joint venture, partnership, syndicate, or other similar entity appearing as a party or amicus in any proceeding shall file a Disclosure Statement, at the time of the filing of the initial pleading, or other Court paper on behalf of that party or as otherwise ordered by the Court, identifying all parent companies, subsidiaries, and affiliates that have issued shares or debt securities to the public. In emergency or any other situations where it is impossible or impracticable to file the Disclosure Statement with the initial pleading, or other Court paper, it shall be filed within seven days of the date of the original filing. For the purposes of this rule, "affiliate" shall be a person or entity that directly, or indirectly through one or more intermediaries, controls, is controlled by, or is under common control with, the specified entity; "parent" shall be an affiliate controlling such entity directly, or indirectly through intermediaries; and "subsidiary" shall be an affiliate controlled by such entity directly or indirectly through one or more intermediaries.

2. *Purpose of Disclosure Statement.* The purpose of this Disclosure Statement is to enable the Judges of this Court to determine the need for recusal pursuant to 28 U.S.C. § 455 or otherwise. Counsel shall have

the continuing obligation to amend the Disclosure Statement to reflect relevant changes.

3. *Disclosure Statement Contents.* The Disclosure Statement shall identify the represented entity's general nature and purpose and if the entity is unincorporated. The statement shall include the names of any members of the entity that have issued shares or debt securities to the public. No such listing need be made, however, of the names of members of a trade association or professional association. For purposes of this rule, a "trade association" is a continuing association of numerous organizations or individuals operated for the purpose of promoting the general commercial, professional, legislative, or other interests of the membership. The form of the Disclosure Statement is set forth in "Appendix LCvR 7.1A" to these Rules.

B. RICO Case Statement. Any party filing a civil action under 18 U.S.C. §§ 1961–1968 shall file with the complaint, or within fourteen (14) days thereafter, a RICO case statement in the form set forth at "Appendix LCvR 7. 1B" or in another form as directed by the Court.

[Effective September 1, 2009. Amended effective December 1, 2009.]

LCvR 8.   PLEADING UNLIQUIDATED DAMAGES

No party shall set forth in a pleading originally filed with this Court a specific dollar amount of unliquidated damages in a pleading except as may be necessary to invoke the diversity jurisdiction of the Court or to otherwise comply with any rule, statute or regulation which requires that a specific amount in controversy be pled in order to state a claim for relief or to invoke the jurisdiction of the Court.

[Effective September 1, 2009.]

LCvR 10.   PRO SE CIVIL RIGHTS ACTIONS BY INCARCERATED INDIVIDUALS

A. Approved Form Required. All pro se civil rights actions filed in this district by incarcerated individuals shall be submitted on the Court approved form supplied by the Clerk of Court. If the plaintiff does not use the Court approved form, the complaint must substantially follow the form. Any complaint that does not utilize or substantially follow the form, or does not comply with the requirements set forth herein, may be returned to the pro se petitioner with a copy of the court's standardized form, a statement of reasons for its return and a directive that the prisoner resubmit the claims outlined in the original filing in compliance with the Court's requirements.

A properly filed complaint must:

1. be submitted on the required form;

2. identify each defendant in the caption of the complaint; and

3. be signed by the plaintiff;

If additional pages are needed, they must be neatly written or typed, on one side only, of 8½ by 11 inch paper, white in color for scanning purposes and ECF.

B. Responsibilities; Service. All individuals filing pro se civil rights actions assume responsibilities inherent to litigation. Incarcerated individuals are not relieved of these responsibilities. One important obligation is the service of a properly filed complaint. Failure to comply with the requirements set forth herein may render the service of the complaint impossible and subject to dismissal for failure to prosecute.

To effectuate proper service, a plaintiff must provide:

1. an identical copy of the complaint for each named defendant. It is the plaintiff's responsibility, not that of the Clerk of Court or the Court, to submit these copies;

2. a completed United States Marshals 285 Form for each and every defendant named in the complaint. Additional copies of this form are available either through the United States Marshal's Office or the Clerk of Court;

3. a completed **Notice of Lawsuit and Waiver of Service of Summons** form for each and every defendant named in the complaint who **is not** an employee, or agency of, the federal government sued in his or her official capacity. Additional copies of this form are available through the Office of the Clerk of Court; and

4. a completed **Summons** form for each and every defendant that **is** an employee, or agency of, the federal government, as well as an identical copy of the complaint and a completed summons form for service on the Attorney General of the United States and the United States Attorney for the Western District of Pennsylvania.

C. Timing of Appointment of Counsel. Absent special circumstances, no motions for the appointment of counsel will be granted until after dispositive motions have been resolved.

D. Appeal. The pro se plaintiff shall have thirty (30) days to file an appeal with the Third Circuit Court of Appeals from a final decision of the District Court on a dispositive motion. Where it appears that the papers filed by a prisoner show that he had delivered his notice of appeal to the prison authorities within 30 days after the date of judgment from which the appeal is taken, the time for filing the formal notice of appeal shall be extended for a period not to exceed 30 days beyond the time required by Rule 4 of the Federal Rules of Appellate Procedure.

E. Powers of a Magistrate Judge. Within 21 days of commencement of a civil rights proceeding, the plaintiff shall execute and file a "CONSENT TO JURISDICTION BY UNITED STATES MAGISTRATE JUDGE" form, either consenting to the jurisdiction of the Magistrate Judge or electing to have the case randomly assigned to a District Judge. Respondent shall execute and file within 21 days of its appearance a form either consenting to the jurisdiction of the Magistrate Judge or electing to have the case randomly assigned to a District Judge. If all parties do not consent to Magistrate Judge jurisdiction, a District Judge shall be assigned and the Magistrate Judge shall continue to manage the case consistent with 28 U.S.C. § 636.

The "CONSENT TO JURISDICTION BY UNITED STATES MAGISTRATE JUDGE" form is available on this Court's website (www.pawd.uscourts.gov). If a party elects to have the case assigned to a District Judge, the Magistrate Judge shall continue to manage the case by deciding non-dispositive motions and submitting reports and recommendations on the petition and on dispositive motions, unless otherwise directed by the District Judge.

[Effective September 1, 2009. Amended effective December 1, 2009.]

Comment (June 2008)

With regard to LCvR 10.D, examples of final judgments are Court orders that: 1) grant a motion to dismiss, or a motion for judgment on the pleadings or a motion for summary judgment **AND** 2) end all claims against all defendants. If a Court order ends fewer than all claims against all defendants, it generally cannot be appealed to the Third Circuit Court of Appeals until there is a subsequent Court order that ends all of the remaining claims against all of the remaining defendants.

LCvR 16.1 PRETRIAL PROCEDURES

A. Scheduling and Pretrial Conferences—Generally.

1. There shall be two phases of pretrial scheduling as set forth in LCvR 16.1.B: (1) a discovery phase to be governed by an initial scheduling order; and (2) a post-discovery phase to be governed by a final scheduling order.

2. As soon as practicable but not later than thirty (30) days after the appearance of a defendant, the Court shall enter an order, which may be revised as set forth in LCvR 16.1.A.3 below, setting forth the date and time of an initial scheduling conference and the dates by which the parties shall confer and file the written report required by Fed. R. Civ. P. 26(f), which shall be in the form set forth at "Appendix LCvR 16.1A" to these Rules and shall be referred to as the Rule 26(f) Report. The Court may defer the initial scheduling conference if a motion that would dispose of all of the claims within the Court's original jurisdiction is pending.

3. The Court may conduct such further conferences as are consistent with the circumstances of the particular case and this Rule, and may revise any prior scheduling order for good cause.

4. Unrepresented parties are subject to the same obligations as those imposed upon attorneys representing a party. All counsel and unrepresented parties shall have sufficient knowledge of the claim asserted, defenses presented, relief sought, and legal issues fairly raised by the pleadings so as to allow for a meaningful discussion of all such matters at each conference.

5. Upon request or sua sponte, the Court may permit attendance by telephone of counsel or unrepresented parties at any conference.

6. Scheduling conferences shall not be conducted in any civil action involving Social Security claims, bankruptcy appeals, habeas corpus, government collection and prisoner civil rights, unless the Court to whom the case is assigned directs otherwise.

B. Scheduling Orders and Case Management.

1. *Initial Scheduling Order.* At the initial scheduling conference or as soon thereafter as practicable, the Court shall enter an initial scheduling order that sets forth dates for the following:

a. the topics identified in Fed. R. Civ. P. 16(b)(3)(A);

b. completion of fact discovery;

c. a post-discovery status conference to be held within thirty (30) days after the completion of fact discovery; and

d. designation, if appropriate, of the case for arbitration, mediation, early neutral evaluation, or appointment of a special master or other special procedure;

2. *Additional Topics.* The initial scheduling order may also address:

a. The topics identified in Fed. R. Civ. P. 16(b)(3)(B)(i)–(vi);

b. Dates for completion of expert discovery, including the dates for expert disclosures required by Fed. R. Civ. P. 26(a)(2) and the dates by which depositions of experts shall be completed;

c. Such limitations on the scope, method or order of discovery as may be warranted by the circumstances of the particular case to avoid duplication, harassment, delay or needless expenditure of costs; and

d. The date to file dispositive motions at an early stage of the proceedings (i.e., before completion of fact discovery or submission of experts' reports).

3. *Final Scheduling Order.* At the post-discovery status conference or as soon thereafter as practicable, the Court shall enter a final scheduling order that sets forth dates for the following:

a. Filing dispositive motions and responses thereto;

b. Filing motions in limine and motions to challenge the qualifications of any proposed expert witness and/or the substance of such expert's testimony;

c. Filing pretrial statements required by LCvR 16.1.C;

d. Further conferences before trial including the final pretrial conference.

4. *Additional Topics.* The final scheduling order may also include:

a. The presumptive trial date; and

b. Any other matters appropriate in the circumstances of the case.

5. *Requirement to Confer; Scheduling Motion Certificate.* Before filing a motion to modify any scheduling order, counsel or an unrepresented party shall confer with all other counsel and unrepresented parties in an effort to reach agreement on the proposed modification. Unless a motion to modify the scheduling order is filed jointly by all parties, any motion to modify shall be accompanied by a certificate of the movant denominated a Scheduling Motion Certificate stating that all parties have conferred with regard to the proposed modification and stating whether all parties consent thereto.

C. Pretrial Statements and Final Pretrial Conference.

1. By the date specified in the Court's scheduling order, which generally will be no sooner than 30 days after the close of discovery (including expert discovery), counsel for the plaintiff or an unrepresented plaintiff shall file and serve a pretrial statement. The pretrial statement shall include:

a. a brief narrative statement of the material facts that will be offered at trial;

b. a statement of all damages claimed, including the amount and the method of calculation of all economic damages;

c. the name, address and telephone number of each witness, separately identifying those whom the party expects to present and those whom the party may call if the need arises, and identifying each witness as a liability and/or damage witness;

d. the designation of those witnesses whose testimony is expected to be presented by means of a deposition and the designation of the portion of each deposition transcript (by page and line number) to be presented (and, if not taken stenographically, a transcript of the pertinent portions of the deposition testimony);

e. an appropriate identification of each document or other exhibit, including summaries of other evidence, separately identifying those that the party expects to offer and those that the party may offer if the need arises and assigning an exhibit number to those that the party expects to offer;

f. a list of legal issues that the party believes should be addressed at the final pretrial conference;

g. copies of all expert disclosures that the party made pursuant to Fed. R. Civ. P. 26(a)(2) with respect to expert witnesses identified in the pretrial statement pursuant to LCvR 16.1.C.1.c; and

h. copies of all reports containing findings or conclusions of any physician who has treated, examined, or has been consulted in connection with the injuries complained of, and whom a party expects to call as a witness at the trial of the case.

2. Within 30 days of filing of the plaintiff's pretrial statement, counsel for the defendant or an unrepresented defendant shall file a pretrial statement meeting the requirements set forth in LCvR 16.1.C.1, including defenses to the damages claims asserted against the defendant by any party and a statement of all damages claimed by the defendant in connection with a counterclaim, cross-claim or third party claim, including the amount and the method of calculation of all economic damages.

3. Within 30 days of the filing of the defendant's pretrial statement, counsel for any third-party defendant or an unrepresented third-party defendant shall file a pretrial statement meeting the requirements set forth above for plaintiffs and/or for defendants, as appropriate.

4. Before filing a motion in limine, counsel or an unrepresented party shall confer with all other counsel and unrepresented parties in an effort to reach agreement on the issue to be raised by the motion. In the event an agreement is not reached, the motion in limine shall be accompanied by a certificate of the movant denominated a Motion in Limine Certificate stating that all parties made a reasonable effort to reach agreement on the issue raised by the motion.

5. Following the filing of the pretrial statements, counsel and any unrepresented parties shall meet with the Court at a time fixed by the Court for a final pretrial conference. Prior to and in preparation for the conference, counsel and unrepresented parties shall:

a. make available for examination by opposing counsel or opposing unrepresented parties all exhibits identified in the pretrial statement and examine all exhibits made available by opposing counsel or opposing unrepresented parties;

b. confer and determine in a jury case whether counsel and any unrepresented parties can agree that the case shall be tried non-jury. If an agreement is reached, the parties shall report to the Court at the conference. If no agreement is reported, no inquiry shall be made by the Court and no disclosure shall be made by any counsel or unrepresented party identifying the counsel or party who failed to agree; and

c. unless previously filed or otherwise ordered, prepare a motion accompanied by or containing supporting legal authority for presentation at the final pretrial conference on any legal issues that have not been decided.

6. Unless otherwise ordered by the Court, the following shall be done at the final pretrial conference:

a. counsel and any unrepresented party shall indicate on the record whether the exhibits of any other party are agreed to or objected to, and the reason for any objection;

b. motions prepared pursuant to LCvR 16.1.C.5.c shall be presented, accompanied by or containing supporting legal authority;

c. counsel and any unrepresented party shall be prepared to disclose and discuss the evidence to be presented at trial, including (a) any anticipated use of trial technology in the presentation of evidence or in the opening statement or closing argument, and (b) any anticipated presentation of expert testimony and any challenges thereto;

d. counsel and any unrepresented parties shall advise the Court of any depositions that they anticipate will or may be taken after the final pretrial conference and the reason for the timing of the depositions. In the event that such deposition is for use at trial and the deposition will be taken other than by stenographic means, the party taking the deposition shall have the deposition transcribed and the transcript shall be made available for the Court to make rulings on any objections raised during the course of the deposition. Prior to use in the trial, the party offering the testimony shall edit any video recording to reflect the Court's ruling on objections;

e. counsel shall have inquired of their authority to settle and shall have their clients present or available by phone. The Court shall inquire whether counsel have discussed settlement;

f. counsel and any unrepresented party wishing to supplement his or her pretrial statement shall file and serve a motion to do so not less than seven (7) days before the final pretrial conference, which motion shall be granted in the absence of prejudice to another party;

g. if not previously done, the Court shall schedule the case for trial; and

h. such record shall be made of the conference as the Court orders or as any party may request.

7. Failure to fully disclose in the pretrial statements (or, as permitted by the Court, at or before the final pretrial conference) the substance of the evidence proposed to be offered at trial, may result in the exclusion of that evidence at trial, at a hearing or on a motion unless the parties otherwise agree or the Court orders otherwise. The only exception will be evidence used for impeachment purposes.

8. In the event that the civil action has not been tried within 12 months of the final pretrial conference, the Court upon request of any party shall schedule a status conference to discuss the possibility of settlement and establish a prompt trial date.

D. Procedures Following Inadvertent Disclosure. Unless a party requests otherwise, the following language will be included in the Scheduling Order to aid in the implementation of Fed. R. Evid. 502:

1. The producing party shall promptly notify all receiving parties of the inadvertent production of any privileged or trial preparation material. Any receiving party who has reasonable cause to believe that it has received privileged or trial preparation material shall promptly notify the producing party.

2. Upon receiving notice of inadvertent production, any receiving party shall immediately retrieve all copies of the inadvertently disclosed material and sequester such material pending a resolution of the producing party's claim either by the Court or by agreement of the parties.

3. If the parties cannot agree as to the claim of privilege, the producing party shall move the Court for a resolution within 30 days of the notice set forth in subparagraph (a). Nothing herein shall be construed to prevent a receiving party from moving the Court for a resolution, but such motion must be made within the 30–day period.

[Effective September 1, 2009. Amended effective December 1, 2009.]

LCvR 16.2 ALTERNATIVE DISPUTE RESOLUTION

A. Effective Date and Application. LCvR 16.2 shall govern all actions as the Board of Judges shall determine, from time to time, commenced on or after June 1, 2006, with the exception of Social Security cases and cases in which a prisoner is a party. Cases subject to LCvR 16.2 also remain subject to the other Local Rules of the Court.

B. Purpose. The Court recognizes that full, formal litigation of claims can impose large economic burdens on parties and can delay resolution of disputes for considerable periods. The Court also recognizes that an alternative dispute resolution ("ADR") procedure can improve the quality of justice by improving the parties' understanding of their case and their satisfaction with the process and the result. The Court adopts LCvR 16.2 to make available to litigants a broad range of Court-sponsored ADR processes to provide quicker, less expensive and potentially more satisfying alternatives to continuing litigation without impairing the quality of justice or the right to trial. The Court offers diverse ADR services to enable parties to pursue the ADR process that promises to deliver the greatest benefits to their particular case. In administering these Local ADR Rules and the ADR program, the Court will take appropriate steps to assure that no referral to ADR results in an unfair or unreasonable economic burden on any party.

C. ADR Options. The Court-sponsored ADR options for cases include:

1. Mediation

2. Early Neutral Evaluation

3. Arbitration

D. ADR Designation. At the Rule 26(f) "meet and confer" conference, the parties are required to discuss and, if possible, stipulate to an ADR process for that case. The Rule 26(f) written report shall (1) designate the specific ADR process that the parties have selected, (2) specify the time frame within which the ADR process will be completed, and (3) set forth any other information the parties would like the Court to know regarding their ADR designation. The parties shall use the form provided by the Court. When litigants have not stipulated to an ADR process before the Scheduling Conference contemplated by LCvR 16.1, the assigned Judge will discuss the ADR options with counsel and unrepresented parties at that conference. If the parties cannot agree on a process before the end of the Scheduling Conference, the Judge will make an appropriate determination and/or selection for the parties.

E. ADR Practices and Procedures. The ADR process is governed by the ADR Policies and Procedures, as adopted by the Board of Judges for the United States District Court for the Western District of Pennsylvania, which sets forth specific and more detailed information regarding the ADR process, and which can be accessed either on the Court's official website (www.pawd.uscourts.gov) or from the Clerk of Court.

[Effective September 1, 2009.]

LCvR 17.1 MINORS OR INCOMPETENT PERSONS—COMPROMISE SETTLEMENT, DISCONTINUANCE AND DISTRIBUTION

A. Court Approval Required. No action to which a minor is a party shall be compromised, settled, discontinued or dismissed except after approval by the Court pursuant to a petition presented by the guardian of the minor or the natural guardian of the minor, such as the circumstances might require.

B. Contents of Petition. In all such cases, the minor's attorney shall file with the Clerk of Court, as part of the record, a petition containing (1) a statement of the nature of the evidence relied on to show liability, (2) the elements of damage, (3) a statement of the services rendered by counsel, (4) the expenses incurred or to be incurred and (5) the amount of fees requested. The petition shall contain written statements of minor's attending physicians, setting forth the nature of the injuries and the extent of recovery. If required by the Judge, such statements of attending physicians shall be in affidavit form. The petition shall be verified by the affidavit of the minor's counsel. In claims for property damage, the extent of the damage shall be described and the statement shall be supported by the affidavit of the person who appraised the damage or made the repairs.

C. Contents of Court Order. When a compromise or settlement has been so approved by the Court, or when a judgment has been entered upon a verdict or by agreement, the Court, upon petition by the guardian or any party to the action, shall make an order approving or disapproving any agreement entered into by the guardian for the payment of counsel fees and other expenses out of the fund created by the compromise, settlement or judgment; or the Court may make such order as it deems proper fixing counsel fees and other proper expenses. The Court shall then order the balance of the fund to be paid to the guardian of the estate of the minor qualified to receive the fund except that if the amount payable to the minor does not exceed the sum of one hundred thousand dollars ($100,000.00), the Court may order the monies deposited in a federally insured bank or savings and loan in an account to be marked "not to be withdrawn until majority has been attained or further order of Court." If the amount of anticipated interest would cause the account to exceed $100,000.00, then the Court may order the deposit to be made in two or more savings institutions. If the minor has no guardian of his or her estate and the balance does not exceed ten thousand dollars ($10,000.00), the Court on its own motion or upon petition of any person entitled to apply for the appointment of a guardian for the minor may authorize the amount of the judgment to be paid to the guardian of the person, the natural guardian, the person by whom the minor is maintained, or the minor.

D. Payment of Funds. When a judgment has been entered in favor of a minor plaintiff and no petition has been filed under the provision of Subparagraph C of this rule, the amount of the judgment shall be paid only to a guardian of the estate of the minor qualified to receive the fund. If the minor has no such guardian and the judgment does not exceed ten thousand dollars ($10,000.00), the Court on its own motion or upon petition of any person entitled to apply for the appointment of a guardian for the minor may authorize the amount of the judgment to be paid to the guardian of the person, the natural guardian, the person by whom the minor is maintained, or the minor.

[Effective September 1, 2009.]

LCvR 17.2 SETTLEMENT PROCEDURE FOR SEAMAN SUITS

A. Court Approval Required. No suit in admiralty or civil action to which a seaman is a party shall be compromised, settled, discontinued or amicably or voluntarily dismissed except after approval by the Court pursuant to a petition presented by the seaman's attorney and upon payment to the Clerk of Court of the filing fee.

B. Contents of Petition. In all such cases, the seaman's attorney shall file with the Clerk of Court, as part of the record, a petition containing:

1. a statement of the essential facts relating to liability;

2. the elements of claimed damage, including a statement of amounts already paid to or on behalf of the seaman;

3. a statement of services rendered by counsel;

4. the expenses incurred or to be incurred by counsel; and

5. the amount of fees and expenses requested by counsel.

The petition shall also include copies of written statements of those physicians who have treated or examined the seaman setting forth the nature of the injuries and the extent of recovery and a copy of the release, if any, signed or to be signed by the seaman. The petition shall be verified by the seaman's attorney.

C. Seaman to Appear. No such compromise, settlement, discontinuance or dismissal shall be approved by the Court unless the seaman appears in open Court before the Judge to whom the petition is presented. At such time, the Court shall examine the seaman under oath in order to insure that the seaman's rights are fully protected and that he or she comprehends the nature of the action being taken by him or her and on his or her behalf before such petition and release shall be approved and order entered thereon.

D. Contents of Court Order. When a compromise or settlement has been so approved by the Court, or when a judgment has been entered on a verdict or by agreement, the Court, upon petition filed by the seaman's counsel, shall make an order approving or disapproving the agreement entered into by the attorney and the seaman for the payment of counsel fees and other expenses out of the fund created by the compromise, settlement or judgment; or the Court may make such order as it deems proper, fixing counsel fees and other proper expenses. The petition to be filed by counsel for the seaman in those instances where a judgment has been entered need only contain a statement of those matters referred to in LCvR 17.2.B.1–.5. The Court shall then order the balance of the fund to be paid to the seaman unless he or she be a minor or an incompetent, in which case the Court shall order the balance of the fund to be paid to a guardian of the estate of the seaman qualified to receive the fund.

[Effective September 1, 2009.]

LCvR 23. CLASS ACTIONS AND COLLECTIVE ACTIONS

The following procedures will govern class action and collective action proceedings in this district, except as otherwise provided in applicable federal statutes.

A. Class Action Information.

1. The caption of the complaint in any action sought to be maintained as a class action shall include in the legend "Complaint—Class Action."

2. If not included in the Complaint, a statement shall be filed with the Complaint under a separate heading styled "Class Action Statement," which shall contain the following information:

a. the proposed definition of the alleged class; and

b. information relating to the class action, including:

i. the size (or approximate size) of the alleged class;

ii. the alleged questions of law or fact claimed to be common to the class;

iii. the basis upon which the claims or defenses of the representative parties are typical of the claims or defenses of the class; and

iv. the basis upon which the representative parties will fairly and adequately protect the interests of the class.

B. Initial Disclosures. For any action sought to be maintained as a class action, the initial disclosures provided by all parties pursuant to Fed. R. Civ. P. 26(a)(1) shall include disclosures regarding the class certification allegations and any defenses thereto.

C. Matters to Be Addressed at Initial Scheduling Conference (hereafter "Pretrial Conference"). In addition to the requirements of Fed. R. Civ. P. 16, with respect to any case in which class claims are alleged, the parties should be prepared to address the following topics at the Pretrial Conference:

1. the timing of the filing of a motion for class certification;

2. the appointment of interim class counsel;

3. the scope of any discovery necessary for resolution of any class certification motion;

4. the briefing schedule; and

5. the timing of and plan for any methods for alternative dispute resolution to be utilized.

D. Time and Expense Records. Anyone seeking Court approval for payment for legal services rendered or costs advanced in a class action will maintain contemporaneous time and expense records. Upon request of Lead Class Counsel, time and expense records will be provided to that counsel or its designee on a periodic basis. The Court will inform counsel of any specific requirements that it has regarding record keeping at the Pretrial Conference.

E. Joint Report of the Parties. At least seven (7) days prior to the Pretrial Conference, the parties shall submit a "Joint Report of the Parties and Proposed Scheduling and Discovery Order—Class Action" setting forth their respective positions on the timing and scope of class certification discovery, the filing of a motion for class certification, and the appointment of class counsel. A form "Joint Report of the Parties and Proposed Scheduling and Discovery Order—Class Action" is available. *See* "Appendix LCvR 23.E." This is in lieu of the Fed. R. Civ. P. 26(f) Report. To the extent appropriate given the facts of the case, the parties are encouraged to stipulate to any facts regarding the approximate size and definition of the class, the qualifications of proposed class counsel, and any other matters relevant to the findings to be made by the Court under Fed. R. Civ. P. 23.

F. Order Following Pretrial Conference. After the Pretrial Conference, the Court will enter an order addressing the matters discussed at the Pretrial Conference. The Court may require the parties to draft a proposed order.

G. Conference Following Class Certification Decision. After resolution of the motion for class certification, the Court will schedule a conference to discuss how the case will proceed in light of the ruling on class certification. At this conference, the parties should be prepared to discuss the following topics:

1. if a party has sought appeal of the decision pursuant to Fed. R. Civ. P. 23(f), whether or not any party will seek a stay of proceedings before the District Court;

2. disclosures not otherwise provided in initial Fed. R. Civ. P. 26(a)(1) disclosure;

3. the completion of any remaining discovery; and

4. if applicable, a plan of notice.

H. Notice to the Class. If a class is certified and notice is required under either Fed. R. Civ. P. 23 or LCvR 100.2, or otherwise directed by the Court, prior to the conference following the class certification decision, the parties shall meet and make efforts to agree on the text of the proposed class notice, the manner of class notice, and the procedures to be used to identify the class. To the extent the parties cannot agree on these matters, they shall file jointly a proposed plan for class notice and the language on which they do agree. On the matters on which they disagree, the parties may provide briefs to supplement their position.

Once the Court approves a plan of class notice and a form of class notice, the Approved Class Notice shall be posted on the Court's website, in addition to any other notice procedures approved by the Court. Notice to be posted on the Court's website shall contain the following disclaimer:

CONTACT COUNSEL IDENTIFIED IN THIS NOTICE IF YOU HAVE ANY QUESTIONS. DO NOT CONTACT THE COURT.

I. Class Settlements. Parties seeking approval of any class settlement, voluntary dismissal, or compromise shall provide the Court with sufficient information for the Court to make findings with respect to the fairness and reasonableness of the settlement to the class.

J. Collective Actions. Civil actions containing Collective Action claims involving a group or groups of multiple plaintiffs who may elect to join or "opt into" the action as plaintiffs, *e.g.*, The Age Discrimination in Employment Act, 29 U.S.C. 621, *et seq.*, or the Fair Labor Standards Act, 29 U.S.C. 201, *et seq.*, shall be managed to the extent practicable in accordance with the provisions of LCvR 23, subject to the following:

1. The caption of a Complaint asserting a Collective Action claim shall include in the legend "Complaint—Collective Action." If not included in the Complaint, a statement shall be filed with the Complaint under a separate heading styled "Collective Action Statement," which shall contain the following:

a. the proposed definition of the alleged Collective Action;

b. the size (or approximate size) of the alleged Collective Action; and

c. the questions of law or fact claimed to be common to the Collective Action.

2. LCvR 23.H shall not apply to Collective Action claims.

3. If a Complaint seeking class certification of Class Action claims also asserts Collective Action

claims, the Class Action claims shall be governed by LCvR 23.

[Effective September 1, 2009.]

Comment (June 2008)

Counsel should acquaint themselves with the requirements of Fed. R. Civ. P. 23, the accompanying advisory committee notes, and the latest version of the Manual on Complex Litigation with respect to discovery and other practices in class actions.

LCvR 24. NOTICE OF CONSTITUTIONAL QUESTION

A. Notification to Court Required. In any action, suit, or proceeding in which the United States or any agency, officer, or employee thereof is not a party and in which the constitutionality of an Act of Congress affecting the public interest is drawn in question, or in any action, suit or proceeding in which a state or any agency, officer, or employee, thereof is not a party, and in which the constitutionality of any statute of that state affecting the public interest is drawn in question, the party raising the constitutional issue shall notify the Court of the existence of the question either by checking the appropriate box on the civil cover sheet or by stating on the pleading that alleges the unconstitutionality, immediately following the title of that pleading, "Claim of Unconstitutionality" or the equivalent.

B. Failure to Comply Not Waiver. Failure to comply with this rule will not be grounds for waiving the constitutional issue or for waiving any other rights the party may have. Any notice provided under this rule, or lack of notice, will not serve as a substitute for, or as a waiver of, any pleading requirement set forth in the federal rules or statutes.

[Effective September 1, 2009.]

LCvR 26.1 DISCOVERY MOTIONS

In addition to the general requirements of LCvR 7.1, any discovery motion filed pursuant to Fed. R. Civ. P. 26 through 37 shall comply with the requirements of LCvR 37.1 and 37.2.

[Effective September 1, 2009.]

LCvR 26.2 DISCOVERY OF ELECTRONICALLY STORED INFORMATION

A. Duty to Investigate. Prior to a Fed. R. Civ. P. 26(f) conference, counsel shall:

1. Investigate the client's Electronically Stored Information ("ESI"), such as email, electronic documents, and metadata, and including computer-based and other digital systems, in order to understand how such ESI is stored; how it has been or can be preserved, accessed, retrieved, and produced; and any other issues to be discussed at the Fed. R. Civ. P. 26(f) conference, including the issues in LCvR 26.2.C.

2. Identify a person or persons with knowledge about the client's ESI, with the ability to facilitate, through counsel, preservation and discovery of ESI.

B. Designation of Resource Person. In order to facilitate communication and cooperation between the parties and the Court, each party shall, if deemed necessary by agreement under LCvR 26.2.C.7 or by the Court, designate a single resource person through whom all issues relating to the preservation and production of ESI should be addressed.

C. Duty to Meet and Confer. At the Fed. R. Civ. P. 26(f) conference, and upon a later request for discovery of ESI, counsel shall meet and confer, and attempt to agree, on the discovery of ESI, including:

1. The steps the parties have taken to preserve ESI;

2. The scope of ESI discovery and an ESI search protocol, including methods to filter the data, such as application of search terms or date ranges;

3. Procedures to deal with inadvertent production of privileged information under LCvR 16.1.D;

4. Accessibility of ESI, including but not limited to the accessibility of back-up, deleted, archival, or historic legacy data;

5. The media, format and procedures for preserving and producing ESI, including the media, format, and procedures for the Fed. R. Civ. P. 26(a)(1) initial disclosures;

6. Allocation of costs of preservation, production, and restoration (if possible and/or necessary) of any ESI;

7. The need for a designated resource person, as discussed in Section B above; and

8. Any other issues related to ESI.

[Effective September 1, 2009.]

Comment (June 2008)

1. LCvR 26.2.A.1 imposes a duty for counsel to discuss ESI with their client. It does not, in any way, alter a party's and counsel's obligations under law to preserve evidence, including ESI, when litigation is reasonably anticipated. Nothing in this section precludes a party from moving the Court for an appropriate preservation order.

2. Regarding LCvR 26.2.A.2, the person may be an individual party, a party's employee, a third-party, or a party's attorney.

3. Regarding LCvR 26.2.B, the resource person must have sufficient familiarity with the party's ESI to meaningfully discuss technical issues and provide reliable information relative to the preservation and production of ESI. The resource person is permitted to, and, in fact, encouraged to, involve persons with technical expertise in these discussions, including the client, client's employee, or a third party. The

resource person may be an individual party, a party's employee, a third party, or a party's attorney, and may be the same person referenced in LCvR 26.2.A.2.

4. Regarding LCvR 26.2.C, the parties have an ongoing obligation to supplement their disclosures. *See* Fed. R. Civ. P. 26.

5. Regarding LCvR 26.2.C.1, it may be necessary to segregate ESI in order to properly preserve it.

6. Regarding LCvR 26.2.C.4, "accessibility" is used in the same manner as Fed. R. Civ. P. 26(b)(2)(B) ("A party need not provide discovery of [ESI] from sources that the party identifies as not reasonably accessible because of undue burden or cost.").

7. Regarding LCvR 26.2.C.5, the media, format, and procedures for preserving ESI may differ from the media, format, and procedures for producing ESI. For example, a party may preserve ESI in native format, and the parties may agree on production in a different format. *See* Fed. R. Civ. P. 34(b).

LCvR 26.3 CERTIFICATION BY SERVING OR FILING ELECTRONIC DOCUMENTS

Unless actual notice to the contrary is given in writing by the serving party, service under these Local Civil Rules of any electronic document containing an electronic representation of the original signature of any person shall constitute a certification by the server that as of the time of service he or she is in possession of the signer's actual original signature on a hard copy of the electronic document served. Service by a party or any counsel under LCvRs 33, 34 or 36 of responses to interrogatories, requests for production or requests for admission ("Written Discovery") shall constitute a certification by the server of such responses that no alteration has been made to the Written Discovery as originally served upon such party or counsel. The filing with the Court for any purpose by any party or counsel of Written Discovery or responses thereto served in electronic form pursuant to LCvRs 33, 34 and 36 shall constitute the certification by such party or counsel that the content of such electronic document so filed is the same as when it was served or received by the filing party.

[Effective September 1, 2009.]

LCvR 30. VIDEOTAPE DEPOSITIONS

A. Procedures.

1. Witnesses shall be placed under oath on the video-record.

2. Immediately upon the conclusion of the deposition, the operator shall label the recording by deponent's name, caption of the case, and case number.

B. Objections During Deposition.

1. Evidence objected to shall be taken subject to the objections. All objections shall be noted upon an

index listing pertinent videotape reel and videotape recorder counter numbered by the operator, which index shall be retained with the videotape recording.

[Effective September 1, 2009.]

LCvR 31. SERVING NOTICES AND WRITTEN QUESTIONS IN ELECTRONIC FORM

Any party serving any notice or written questions pursuant to the provisions of Rules 31(a)(3), 31(a)(5) or 31(b) of the Fed. R. Civ. P. may serve such notice or written questions in electronic form.

[Effective September 1, 2009.]

LCvR 33. SERVING AND RESPONDING TO INTERROGATORIES TO PARTIES IN ELECTRONIC FORM

A. Electronic Form. Any party may, pursuant to Rule 33 of the Fed. R. Civ. P., serve upon any other party interrogatories in Writable Electronic Form (as hereinafter defined) and require that written answers to such interrogatories also be provided in electronic form, except that a responding party shall retain the option to produce business records in the form and manner permitted pursuant to Fed. R. Civ. P. 33(d). Upon request by any party, interrogatories must be served upon that party in Writable Electronic Form. Unless the serving party specifically requests that the written answers be provided in hard-copy form, the responding party shall provide the written answers to such interrogatories in electronic form. Any party responding in electronic form to interrogatories may serve such response in a form that may not be altered.

B. Definition of Writable Electronic Form. "Writable Electronic Form" means a format that allows the recipient to copy or transfer the text of the document into the written answer or written response, or permits the written answer or written response to be typed directly into the document, and thus avoids the need to retype the text.

C. Hard Copy Form. In the event that the parties elect not to use the electronic form for interrogatories or written responses thereto, interrogatories shall be prepared in such a fashion that sufficient space for insertion of the written responses thereto is provided after each interrogatory or sub-section thereof. The original and two (2) copies shall be served upon the party to whom such interrogatories is directed. The responding party shall insert answers on the original interrogatories served upon him or her and shall retain the original and be the custodian of it. If there is not sufficient space on the original for insertion of written responses, the responding party may use and attach supplemental pages for the written responses. In lieu of the foregoing procedure, the responding party may retype each interrogatory with the response to such interrogatory appearing immediately thereafter.

[Effective September 1, 2009.]

LCvR 34. SERVING AND RESPONDING TO REQUESTS FOR PRODUCTION IN ELECTRONIC FORM

A. Electronic Form. Any party may, pursuant to Rule 34 of the Fed. R. Civ. P., serve upon any other party requests for production in Writable Electronic Form (as defined in LCvR 33.B) and require that written responses thereto also be provided in electronic form, except that a party producing documents or electronically stored information shall produce them in the manner and form as may be permitted or required pursuant to Fed. R. Civ. P. 34(b)(2)(E). Upon request by any party, requests for production must be served upon the requesting party in Writable Electronic Form. Unless the serving party specifically requests that the written responses be provided in hard-copy form, the responding party shall provide the written responses to such requests for production in electronic form. Any party responding in electronic form to requests for production may serve such written response in a form which may not be altered.

B. Hard Copy Form. In the event that the parties elect not to use the electronic form for requests for production or written responses thereto, requests for production shall be prepared in such a fashion that sufficient space for insertion of the written responses thereto is provided after each request or sub-section thereof. The original and two (2) copies shall be served upon the party to whom such request for production is directed. The responding party shall insert written responses on the original request for production served upon him or her and shall retain the original and be the custodian of it. If there is not sufficient space on the original for insertion of written responses, the responding party may use and attach supplemental pages for the written responses. In lieu of the foregoing procedure, the responding party may retype each request with the written response to each such request appearing immediately thereafter.

[Effective September 1, 2009.]

LCvR 36. SERVING AND RESPONDING TO REQUESTS FOR ADMISSION IN ELECTRONIC FORM

A. Electronic Form. Any party may, pursuant to Rule 36 of the Fed. R. Civ. P., serve upon any other party requests for admission in Writable Electronic Form (as defined in LCvR 33.B) and require that written answers thereto also be provided in electronic form. Upon request by any party, requests for admission must be served upon the requesting party in

Writable Electronic Form. Unless the serving party specifically requests that the written answers be provided in hard-copy form, the responding party shall provide the written answers to such requests for admission in electronic form. Any party responding in electronic form to requests for admission may serve such written response in a form which may not be altered.

B. Hard Copy Form. In the event that the parties elect not to use the electronic form for requests for admission or written responses thereto, requests for admission shall be prepared in such a fashion that sufficient space for insertion of the written responses thereto is provided after each request or sub-section thereof. The original and two (2) copies shall be served upon the party to whom such request for admission is directed. The responding party shall insert written answers on the original request for admission served upon him or her and shall retain the original and be the custodian of it. If there is not sufficient space on the original for insertion of written responses, the responding party may use and attach supplemental pages for the written responses. In lieu of the foregoing procedure, the responding party may retype each request with the written response to each such request appearing immediately thereafter.

[Effective September 1, 2009.]

LCvR 37.1 REFERRAL OF DISCOVERY MOTIONS BY CLERK OF COURT

All discovery motions shall be referred to the member of the Court to whom the case was assigned for disposition, except in cases where such matters may be required to be submitted to the emergency or miscellaneous judge, or the judge to whom matters may be temporarily referred by the judge to whom the case was assigned.

[Effective September 1, 2009.]

LCvR 37.2 FORM OF DISCOVERY MOTIONS

Any discovery motion filed pursuant to Fed. R. Civ. P. 26 through 37 shall include, in the motion itself or in an attached memorandum, a verbatim recitation of each interrogatory, request, answer, response, and objection which is the subject of the motion or a copy of the actual discovery document which is the subject of the motion.

[Effective September 1, 2009.]

LCvR 40. ASSIGNMENT OF ACTIONS

A. Civil Action Categories. All civil actions in the Court shall be divided into the following categories:

1. antitrust and securities cases;

2. labor-management relations;

3. habeas corpus;

4. civil rights;

5. patent, copyright, and trademark;

6. eminent domain;

7. all other federal question cases;

8. all personal and property damage tort cases, including maritime, F.E.L.A., Jones Act, motor vehicle, products liability, assault, defamation, malicious prosecution, and false arrest;

9. insurance, indemnity, contract, and other diversity cases; or

10. government collection cases (includes inter alia, Health & Human Services (formerly Health, Education and Welfare) student loans, Veterans Administration overpayment, Social Security overpayment, enlistment overpayment, Housing & Urban Development loans, General Accounting Office loans, mortgage foreclosures, Small Business Administration loans, civil and coal mine penalties, and reclamation fees).

B. Criminal Action Categories. All criminal cases in this jurisdiction shall be divided into the following categories:

1. narcotics and other controlled substances;

1a. narcotics and other controlled substances, 3 or more defendants;

2. fraud and property offenses;

2a. fraud and property offenses, 3 or more defendants;

3. crimes of violence;

4. sex offenses;

5. firearms and explosives;

6. immigration; or

7. all others.

C. Assignment of Civil Actions. Each civil action shall be assigned to a Judge who shall have charge of the case. The assignment shall be made by the Clerk of Court from a non-sequential list of all Judges arranged in each of the various categories. Sequences of Judges' names within each category shall be kept secret and no person shall directly or indirectly ascertain or divulge or attempt to ascertain or divulge the name of the Judge to whom any case may be assigned before the assignment is made by the Clerk of Court.

D. Related Actions. At the time of filing any civil or criminal action or entry of appearance or filing of the pleading or motion of any nature by defense counsel, as the case may be, counsel shall indicate on an appropriate form whether the action is related to any other pending or previously terminated actions in this Court. Relatedness shall be determined as follows:

1. all criminal actions arising out of the same criminal transaction or series of transactions are deemed related;

2. civil actions are deemed related when an action filed relates to property included in another action, or involves the same issue of fact, or it grows out of the same transaction as another action, or involves the validity or infringement of a patent involved in another action; and

3. all habeas corpus petitions filed by the same individual shall be deemed related. All pro se civil rights actions by the same individual shall be deemed related.

E. Assignment of Related Actions.

1. If the fact of relatedness is indicated on the appropriate form at time of filing, the Clerk of Court shall assign the case to the same Judge to whom the lower numbered related case is assigned.

2. If the fact of relatedness does not become known until after the case is assigned, the Judge receiving the later case may transfer the matter to the Judge to whom the earlier related case was assigned.

F. Erie or Johnstown Actions. All actions qualifying for the Erie or Johnstown calendars shall be assigned to Judges designated by the Court to hear such actions.

G. No Transfer of Actions. Except in the case of death, disability, recusal required or permitted by law or other exceptional circumstances approved by the Chief Judge, no civil action shall be transferred from one Judge to another where:

1. the action has already been transferred from one Judge to another;

2. the action has been pending for more than two years; or

3. there are dispositive motions pending.

[Effective September 1, 2009.]

LCvR 47.   VOIR DIRE OF JURORS

A. Examination of Jurors Before Trial. During the examination of jurors before trial, the Clerk of Court, or the representative of the Clerk of Court conducting such examination, shall state the following to the jurors collectively:

1. the name and county of residence of each of the parties;

2. the nature of the suit; and

3. the caption of the action.

B. Required Questions to Jurors Collectively. The following questions shall be posed to the jurors collectively:

1. Do you know any of the parties?

2. Do you know any of the attorneys in the case? Have they or their firms ever represented you or any members of your immediate family?

3. Do you know anything about this case?

4. Are you, or any member of your immediate family, employees, former employees, or stockholders in any of the corporate parties?

C. Required Questions to Each Juror. The following questions, where appropriate, shall, inter alia, be put to each juror individually:

1. How old are you?

2. Where do you live? How long have you lived there?

3. What is your educational background?

4. What is your present occupation? (If retired, what was your occupation?)

5. Who is your employer? (If retired, who was your employer?)

6. Are you married? If so, what is your spouse's occupation and who is your spouse's employer? (If your spouse is retired, what was his or her occupation and who was his or her employer?)

7. Do you have any children? If so, how old are they? For whom do they work, and what do they do?

8. Do you own your own home?

9. Do you drive a car?

10. Have you ever been a party to a lawsuit?

11. Any other question, which in the judgment of the trial Judge or the Judge in charge of miscellaneous matters after application being made, shall be deemed proper.

D. Jury List. Members of the bar of this Court shall be permitted to have a copy of each jury list on condition that a receipt be signed with the Clerk of Court at the date of delivery thereof which shall contain as the substance the following certification:

"I hereby certify that I and/or my firm or associates have litigation pending and in connection therewith, I will require a list of jurors. I further acknowledge to have received a copy of said list of jurors from the Clerk of Court and hereby agree that I will not, nor will I permit any person or agency, to call or contact any juror identified on said list at his or her home or any other place, nor will I call or contact any immediate member of said juror's family, which includes his or her spouse, children, mother, father, brother, or sister, in an effort to determine the background of

any member of said jury panel for acceptance or rejection of said juror.

                /s/_____

Date: _____"

[Effective September 1, 2009.]

LCvR 52. FINDINGS BY THE COURT

In all non-jury cases, civil or criminal, the Court may direct suggested findings of fact and conclusions of law to be filed, and require the parties and their counsel to set forth the pages of the record and the exhibit number with specific reference to that part of the exhibit or record which it is contended supports the findings or conclusions.

[Effective September 1, 2009.]

LCvR 54. COSTS

A. Jury Cost Assessment.

1. Whenever the Court finds, after 14 days notice and a reasonable opportunity to be heard, that any party or lawyer in any civil case before the Court has acted in bad faith, abused the judicial process, or has failed to exercise reasonable diligence in effecting the settlement of such case at the earliest practicable time, the Court may impose upon such party or lawyer the jury costs, including mileage and per diem, resulting therefrom.

2. The Court shall issue a rule to show cause and conduct a hearing of record to inquire into the facts prior to imposing any sanction.

B. Taxation of Costs.

1. Absent extenuating circumstances, the Clerk of Court will tax costs for a prevailing party only after the time for filing an appeal has expired. Generally, costs will not be taxed while an appeal is pending because of the possibility that the judgment may be reversed. However, if a party believes there is a reason why there should be an immediate taxation in a particular case, that party may make a written request for taxation prior to resolution of the appeal.

2. While there is no strict deadline for filing a bill of costs with the Court, a bill of costs must be filed within a reasonable period of time, which should be no later than 45 days after a final judgment is entered by the District Court.

3. Upon receipt of a bill of costs, the Clerk of Court will issue a schedule for objections and responses.

4. If after a bill of costs is filed the parties resolve the matter between themselves, the parties must im-

mediately notify the Clerk of Court in writing that the bill of costs is being withdrawn or has been resolved.

[Effective September 1, 2009. Amended effective December 1, 2009.]

LCvR 56.   MOTION FOR SUMMARY JUDGMENT

A.   Application. The procedures that follow shall govern all motions for summary judgment made in civil actions unless the Court, on its own motion, directs otherwise, based on the particular facts and circumstances of the individual action.

B.   Motion Requirements. The motion for summary judgment must set forth succinctly, but without argument, the specific grounds upon which the judgment is sought and must be accompanied by the following:

1. *A Concise Statement of Material Facts.* A separately filed concise statement setting forth the facts essential for the Court to decide the motion for summary judgment, which the moving party contends are **undisputed and material,** including any facts which for purposes of the summary judgment motion only are assumed to be true. The facts set forth in any party's Concise Statement shall be stated in separately numbered paragraphs. A party must cite to a particular pleading, deposition, answer to interrogatory, admission on file or other part of the record supporting the party's statement, acceptance, or denial of the material fact;

2. *Memorandum in Support.* The supporting memorandum must address applicable law and explain why there are no genuine issues of material fact to be tried and why the moving party is entitled to judgment as a matter of law; and

3. *Appendix.* Documents referenced in the Concise Statement shall be included in an appendix. Such documents need not be filed in their entirety. Instead, the filing party may extract and highlight the relevant portions of each referenced document. Photocopies of extracted pages, with appropriate identification and highlighting, will be adequate.

C.   Opposition Requirements. Within 30 days of service of the motion for summary judgment, the opposing party shall file:

1. *A Responsive Concise Statement.* A separately filed concise statement, which responds to each numbered paragraph in the moving party's Concise Statement of Material Facts by:

    a.   admitting or denying whether each fact contained in the moving party's Concise Statement of Material Facts is undisputed and/or material;

    b.   setting forth the basis for the denial if any fact contained in the moving party's Concise Statement of Material Facts is not admitted in its entire-

ty (as to whether it is undisputed or material), with appropriate reference to the record (See LCvR 56.B.1 for instructions regarding format and annotation); and

    c.   setting forth in separately numbered paragraphs any other material facts that are allegedly at issue, and/or that the opposing party asserts are necessary for the Court to determine the motion for summary judgment;

2. *Memorandum in Opposition.* The memorandum of law in opposition to the motion for summary judgment must address applicable law and explain why there are genuine issues of material fact to be tried and/or why the moving party is not entitled to judgment as a matter of law; and

3. *Appendix.* Documents referenced in the Responsive Concise Statement shall be included in an appendix. (See LCvR 56.B.3 for instructions regarding the appendix).

D.   Moving Party's Reply to Opposing Party's Submission. Within 14 days of service of the opposing party's submission in opposition to the motion for summary judgment, the moving party may reply to the opposing party's submission in the same manner as set forth in LCvR 56.C.

E.   Admission of Material Facts. Alleged material facts set forth in the moving party's Concise Statement of Material Facts or in the opposing party's Responsive Concise Statement, which are claimed to be undisputed, will for the purpose of deciding the motion for summary judgment be deemed admitted unless specifically denied or otherwise controverted by a separate concise statement of the opposing party.

[Effective September 1, 2009. Amended effective December 1, 2009.]

LCvR 66.   RECEIVERS

A.   Rule as Exercise of Vested Authority. In the exercise of the authority vested in the District Courts by Fed. R. Civ. P. 66, this rule is promulgated for the administration of estates by receivers, appointed by the Court, in civil actions.

B.   Inventories. Unless the Court otherwise orders, a receiver, as soon as practicable after his or her appointment and not later than thirty (30) days after he or she has taken possession of the estate, shall file an inventory of all the property and assets in his or her possession or in the possession of others who hold possession as his or her agent, and in a separate schedule an inventory of the property and assets of the estate not reduced to possession by him or her but claimed and held by others.

C.   Reports. Within three (3) months after the filing of the inventory, and at regular intervals of three (3) months thereafter until discharged, or at such other times as the Court may direct, the receiver shall file reports of his or her receipts and expenditures and of his or her acts and transactions in an official capacity.

D. Compensation of Receivers and Attorneys. No compensation for services of receivers and attorneys in connection with the administration of an estate shall be ascertained and awarded by the Court until after notice to such persons in interest as the Court may direct. The notice shall state the amount claimed by each applicant.

[Effective September 1, 2009.]

LCvR 67.1 BONDS AND OTHER SURETIES

A. By Non–Resident. In every action filed by a plaintiff who is not a resident of this district, the defendant, after answer to the complaint, may by petition and for good cause shown, have a rule upon the plaintiff to enter security for costs in such sum, in such manner and within such period of time as shall be determined by order of the Court upon hearing on the rule, all proceedings to stay meanwhile. If security for costs is not entered as ordered, the Court shall dismiss the action.

B. By Other Parties. The Court, on motion, may order any party to file an original bond for costs or additional costs in such an amount and so conditioned as the Court by its order may designate.

C. Qualifications of Surety. Every bond for costs under this rule must have as surety either (1) a cash deposit equal to the amount of the bond or (2) a corporation authorized to act as surety on official bond under 31 U.S.C. § 9304.

D. Persons Who May Not Be Sureties. No clerk, marshal, member of the bar, or other officer of this Court will be accepted as surety on any bond or undertaking in any action or proceeding in this Court.

[Effective September 1, 2009.]

LCvR 67.2 DEPOSIT IN COURT

A. Investment of Funds by Clerk of Court. The Clerk of Court will invest funds under Fed. R. Civ. P. 67 as soon as the business of his or her office allows.

B. Administrative Fee. All registry invested accounts are subject to an administrative handling fee at a rate established by the Judicial Conference of the United States. The fee will be assessed and funds will be withdrawn from each invested account in accordance with Judicial Conference directives and this may be accomplished by the authority herein and without further order of Court.

C. Motion Required for Deposit Into Interest Account. The posting party must move the Court to have registry funds deposited into an interest-bearing account, the Court Registry Investment System ("CRIS"), which is administered by the Administrative Office of the United States Courts under 28 U.S.C. § 2045, and shall be the only investment mechanism authorized. The proposed investment order should be reviewed by the Clerk of Court or his or her financial deputy to insure that all of the required investment information is included. It is the responsibility of the posting party to serve the Clerk of Court or his or her financial deputy with a copy of the signed investment order. In most instances, the office of the Clerk of Court can provide a standard investment order that would satisfy the requirements of the federal rules and these Local Rules.

D. Court Registry Investment System. CRIS is the designated depository for the Court. The Clerk of Court shall, upon an order from the Court, deposit funds subject to Fed. R. Civ. P. 67 into CRIS.

E. Petition Required for Investment. If the attorney for the party on whose behalf the deposit is made desires to invest funds in a manner other than at the designated depository of the Court, and if the investment is in accordance with the requirements of the federal rules, and specifically Fed. R. Civ. P. 67, a petition and proposed order may be presented for the Court's consideration.

F. IRS Regulations Applicable. Registry deposits involving designated or qualified settlement funds may be subject to IRS Regulations that require the appointment of an administrator outside of the Court to handle fiduciary and tax matters. A registry account may be a designated or qualified settlement fund if:

1. there has been a settlement agreement in the case;

2. the Court has entered an order establishing or approving a deposit into the registry as a settlement fund; and

3. the liability resolved by the settlement is of a kind described in 26 U.S.C. § 468B or 26 C.F.R. § 1.468B–1(c).

It is the responsibility of the depositing party to identify any registry deposit intended to be a designated or qualified settlement fund. Depositors should contact the office of the Clerk of Court prior to the deposit of settlement fund monies to insure that proper procedures are followed for the reporting of interest income and the payment of income tax on registry accounts.

[Effective September 1, 2009. Amended effective February 1, 2013.]

LCvR 67.3 WITHDRAWAL OF A DEPOSIT PURSUANT TO FED. R. CIV. P. 67

The Court's order for disbursement of invested registry funds must include the name and address of the payee(s) in addition to the total amount of the principal and interest (if the interest is not known, the order may read "plus interest") which will be disbursed to each payee. In order for the Clerk of Court to comply with the Internal Revenue Code and the rules thereunder, payees receiving earned interest must provide a W–9 Taxpayer Identification and Certification form to the office of the Clerk of Court prior to disbursement from the invested account. The disbursement order should be reviewed by the Clerk of Court or the financial deputy prior to being signed by the Judge in order to insure that the necessary information is provided.

[Effective September 1, 2009.]

LCvR 71A. CONDEMNATION OF PROPERTY

When the United States files separate land condemnation actions and concurrently files a single declaration of taking relating to those separate actions, the Clerk of Court is authorized to establish a master file so designated. If a master file is established, the declaration of taking shall be filed, and the filing of the declaration of taking therein shall constitute a filing of the same in each of the actions to which it relates when reference is made thereto in the separate actions.

[Effective September 1, 2009.]

LCvR 72. MAGISTRATE JUDGES

A. Duties Under 28 U.S.C. §§ 636(a)(1) and (2). Each Magistrate Judge appointed by this Court is authorized to perform the duties prescribed by 28 U.S.C. § 636(a)(1) and (2) and may:

1. exercise all the powers and duties conferred or imposed upon United States commissioners or Magistrate Judges by law or the Federal Rules of Criminal Procedure;

2. administer oaths and affirmations, impose conditions of release under 18 U.S.C. § 3142 and take acknowledgments, affidavits, and depositions;

3. conduct removal proceedings and issue warrants of removal in accordance with Fed. R. Crim. P. 40;

4. conduct extradition proceedings, in accordance with 18 U.S.C. § 3184; and

5. supervise proceedings conducted pursuant to letters rogatory, in accordance with 28 U.S.C. § 1782.

B. Disposition of Misdemeanor Cases—28 U.S.C. § 636(a)(3).

1. A Magistrate Judge may, upon the express consent of the defendant:

a. try persons accused of, and sentence persons convicted of, misdemeanors committed within this district in accordance with 18 U.S.C. § 3401; and

b. dismiss or quash a misdemeanor indictment or information, decide a motion to suppress evidence; and

c. direct the probation service of the Court to conduct a presentence investigation in any misdemeanor case.

2. A Magistrate Judge shall:

a. file the record of proceedings and all other official papers with the Clerk of Court within twenty-one (21) days after disposing of a misdemeanor or, in other cases, after completing his or her assigned duties;

b. transmit immediately to the Clerk of Court all fines collected or collateral forfeited.

3. An appeal from a judgment of a Magistrate Judge having been certified to the Court in accordance with the Rules of Procedure for Trials before Magistrate Judges (18 U.S.C. § 3402), the appellant shall, within fourteen (14) days, serve and submit a brief. The United States Attorney shall serve and submit a reply brief within fourteen (14) days after receipt of a copy of the appellant's brief;

4. In a case involving a petty offense as defined in 18 U.S.C. § 1(3), payment of a fixed sum may be accepted in lieu of appearance and as authorizing the termination of the proceeding;

5. There shall be maintained at the office of the Clerk of Court a list of those petty offenses for which collateral forfeiture may apply and the amounts of said collateral forfeiture. The list shall enumerate those offenses for which collateral forfeiture shall not apply and for which appearance shall be mandatory;

6. Nothing contained in this rule shall prohibit a law enforcement officer from arresting a person for the commission of any offense, including those for which collateral may be posted and forfeited, and requiring the person charged to appear before a Magistrate Judge or, upon arrest, taking him or her immediately before a Magistrate Judge;

C. Nondispositive Pretrial Matters.

1. In accordance with 28 U.S.C. § 636(b)(1)(A), a Magistrate Judge may hear and determine any pretrial motion or other pretrial matter, other than those motions specified in Rule 4 of the Rules Governing Section 2254 and Section 2255 Proceedings.

2. *Objections to Magistrate Judge's Determination.* Any party may object to a Magistrate Judge's

determination made under this rule within fourteen (14) days after the date of service of the Magistrate Judge's order, unless a different time is prescribed by the Magistrate Judge or District Judge. Such party shall file with the Clerk of Court, and serve on all parties, written objections which shall specifically designate the order or part thereof objected to and the basis for objection thereto. The opposing party shall be allowed fourteen (14) days after date of service to respond to the objections. The District Judge assigned to the case shall consider the objections and set aside any portion of the Magistrate Judge's order found to be clearly erroneous or contrary to law. The District Judge may also reconsider any matter sua sponte.

D. Dispositive Pretrial Motions and Prisoner Cases.

1. In accordance with 28 U.S.C. § 636(b)(1)(B) and (C), a Magistrate Judge may hear, conduct such evidentiary hearings as are necessary or appropriate, and submit to a District Judge proposed findings of fact and recommendations for the disposition of:

   a. applications for post-trial relief made by individuals convicted of criminal offenses;

   b. prisoner petitions challenging conditions of confinement; and

   c. motions for injunctive relief (including temporary restraining orders and preliminary injunctions), for judgment on the pleadings, for summary judgment, to dismiss or permit the maintenance of a class action, to dismiss for failure to state a claim upon which relief may be granted, to involuntarily dismiss an action, for judicial review of administrative determinations, and for review of default judgments.

2. *Objections to Magistrate Judge's Proposed Findings.* Any party may object to the Magistrate Judge's proposed findings, recommendations or report under this rule within fourteen (14) days after date of service. Such party shall file with the Clerk of Court, and serve on all parties, written objections which shall specifically identify the portions of the proposed, recommendations or report to which objection is made and the basis for such objections. Such party may be ordered to file with the Clerk of Court a transcript of the specific portions of any evidentiary proceedings to which objection is made. The opposing party shall be allowed fourteen (14) days after date of service to respond to the objections. A District Judge shall make a de novo determination of those portions to which objection is made and may accept, reject or modify in whole or in part, the findings and recommendations made by the Magistrate Judge. The District Judge, however, need not conduct a new hearing and may consider the record developed before the Magistrate Judge, making his or her own determina-

tion on the basis of that record, or recommit the matter to the Magistrate Judge with instructions.

E. Special Master References and Trials by Consent.

1. A Magistrate Judge may serve as a special master subject to the procedures and limitations of 28 U.S.C. § 636(b)(2) and Fed. R. Civ. P. 53.

2. Where the parties consent, a Magistrate Judge may serve as a special master in any civil case without regard to the provisions of Fed. R. Civ. P. 53(b).

3. The Magistrate Judges may, upon consent of the parties, conduct any and all proceedings in a jury or non-jury civil matter and order the entry of judgment in accordance with 28 U.S.C. § 636(c).

F. Other Duties. A Magistrate Judge is also authorized to:

1. exercise general supervision of the civil and criminal calendars of the Court, conduct calendar and status calls, and determine motions to expedite or postpone the trial of cases for the Judges;

2. conduct pretrial conferences, settlement conferences, omnibus hearings and related pretrial proceedings;

3. conduct arraignments in cases not triable by the Magistrate Judge to the extent of taking a not guilty plea or noting a defendant's intention to plead guilty or nolo contendere and ordering a presentence report in appropriate cases;

4. receive grand jury returns in accordance with Fed. R. Crim. P. 6(f), issue bench warrants and enter orders sealing the record in accordance with Fed. R. Crim. P. 6(e), 6(f) and 9(a);

5. conduct voir dire and select petit juries for the Court;

6. accept petit jury verdicts in civil cases in the absence of a District Judge;

7. conduct necessary proceedings leading to the potential revocation of probation;

8. issue subpoenas, writs of habeas corpus ad testificandum or habeas corpus ad prosequendum, or other orders necessary to obtain the presence of parties or witnesses or evidence needed for Court proceedings;

9. order the exoneration or forfeiture of bonds;

10. conduct proceedings for the collection of civil penalties of not more than $200 assessed under the Federal Boat Safety Act of 1971, in accordance with 46 U.S.C. § 484(d);

11. conduct examinations of judgment debtors in accordance with Fed. R.Civ. P. 69;

12. review petitions in civil commitment proceedings under Title III of the Narcotic Addict Rehabilitation Act;

13. approve deferred prosecution agreements in felony cases pending before the Magistrate Judge in which no indictment or information has been filed;

14. issue administrative inspection warrants and other compulsory process sought by administrative agencies of the United States; and

15. perform any additional duty as is not inconsistent with the Constitution and laws of the United States.

G. Assignment of Duties of Magistrate Judges. The Clerk of Court will assign each non-prisoner civil action to a District Judge or a Magistrate Judge by automated random selection such that a Magistrate Judge will be assigned a case, in the first instance, approximately one-third of the time. All prisoner civil cases and non-death penalty habeas cases will be assigned only to a Magistrate Judge.

In the event the action is assigned to a Magistrate Judge, each party shall execute and file within 21 days of its appearance a form, either consenting to the jurisdiction of the Magistrate Judge or electing to have the case randomly assigned to a District Judge. If a party elects to have the case assigned to a District Judge, the Magistrate Judge shall continue to manage the case by deciding non-dispositive motions and submitting reports and recommendations on dispositive motions, unless otherwise directed by the District Judge. If all parties do not consent to Magistrate Judge jurisdiction, a District Judge shall be assigned and the Magistrate Judge shall continue to manage the case consistent with 28 U.S.C. § 636.

H. Forfeiture of Collateral in Lieu of Appearance.

1. Pursuant to paragraph G(2) of the order of this Court of March 9, 1971, adopting rules for United States Magistrate Judges (LCvR 72.A), this list is established setting forth those petty offenses for which trial appearance shall be mandatory and the amounts of collateral forfeiture which may be acceptable in lieu of appearance.

2. Petty offenses for which trial appearance shall be mandatory:

   a. traffic offenses:

     i. indictable offenses;

     ii. offenses resulting in an accident where one of the following conditions are met:

     (a) two or more vehicles are involved;

     (b) personal injury has resulted; or

     (c) property damage in excess of $200 has resulted.

     iii. operation of a motor vehicle while under the influence of intoxicating liquor or a narcotic or habit producing drug, or permitting another person who is under the influence of intoxicating liquor or a narcotic or habit producing drug to operate a motor vehicle owned by the defendant or in his or her custody or control;

     iv. reckless driving;

     v. leaving the scene of an accident;

     vi. driving while under suspension or revocation of a driver's license;

     vii. driving without being licensed to drive;

     viii. exceeding the speed limit by more than 15 miles per hour; or

     ix. a second moving traffic offense within a 12–month period, as indicated by a notation on a driver's license.

   b. non-traffic offenses:

     i. drunkenness; or

     ii. disorderly conduct.

3. In all other petty offenses collateral forfeitures may be accepted by the duly authorized representative of the agency in an amount not greater than 25% of the maximum fine established by law for each offense, but in no event less than ten dollars ($10.00); provided, however, that the enforcing agencies shall file with the Clerk of Court a schedule of collateral forfeitures approved by the Chief Judge. However, in those petty offenses for which the maximum fine established by law is less than ten dollars ($10.00), collateral forfeitures may be accepted in an amount equal to the maximum fine.

[Effective September 1, 2009. Amended effective December 1, 2009.]

LCvR 77. SESSIONS OF COURT

Sessions of the Court shall be held at Pittsburgh, Erie and Johnstown at such times as may be required to expedite the business of the Court. The Clerk of Court shall post and make available to interested members of the bar, each Judge's tentative schedule of trials, both jury and non-jury, from time to time.

[Effective September 1, 2009.]

LCvR 83.1 FREE PRESS—FAIR TRIAL PROVISIONS

A. Release of Information in Civil Actions. A lawyer or law firm associated with a civil action shall not during its investigation or litigation make or participate in making an extrajudicial statement, other than a quotation from or reference to public records, that a reasonable person would expect to be disseminated by means of public communication if there is a substantial likelihood that such extrajudicial statement would materially prejudice such civil action and relates to:

1. evidence regarding the occurrence or transaction involved;

2. the character, credibility, or criminal record of a party, witness, or prospective witness;

3. the performance or results of any examinations or tests or the refusal or failure of a party to submit to such;

4. his or her opinion as to the merits of the claims or defenses of a party except as required by law or administrative rule; or

5. any other matter substantially likely to materially prejudice such civil action.

B. Matters on Which Extrajudicial Statements Are Not Precluded. Nothing in this rule is intended to preclude the issuance of extrajudicial statements made in connection with hearings or the lawful issuance of reports by legislative, administrative or investigative bodies, or to preclude any lawyer from replying to charges of misconduct that are publicly made against him or her.

C. Photography, Recording and Broadcasting.

1. Except as hereafter provided, all forms, means and manner of taking photographs, recording, broadcasting and televising are prohibited in any hearing room, corridor or stairway leading thereto, on any floor occupied entirely or in part by the United States District Court for the Western District of Pennsylvania, in any United States Courthouse or federal facility, or any other building designated by the United States District Court for the Western District of Pennsylvania as a place for holding Court or other judicial proceeding, whether or not Court is in session.

2. Exceptions:

a. Photographs may be taken and radio and television may be transmitted with the voluntary consent of the individual involved in and from the press rooms set aside for the use of members of the press and other communications media.

b. Subject to the approval of the presiding Judge, the broadcasting, televising, recording or photographing of investitive, ceremonial or naturalization proceedings in the Courtrooms of this district will be permitted under the following conditions:

i. available light is to be used;

ii. only one camera is to be used. The station owning that camera must make a tape available to all stations requesting one;

iii. the camera must remain in one position throughout. It must be in position before the opening of Court and remain there until the Court has recessed;

iv. microphones must be placed in fixed positions and remain there throughout; and

v. camera and microphone personnel shall not move about the Courtroom during the proceeding.

[Effective September 1, 2009.]

Comment (June 2008)

1. The amended Rule conforms to the standard set forth in *United States v. Wecht*, 484 F.3d 194, 205 (3d Cir. 2007) (exercising "supervisory authority to require that District Courts apply LCvR 83.1 to prohibit only speech that is substantially likely to materially prejudice ongoing criminal proceedings") and to the governing law of professional conduct. Former LCvR 83.1.A–E, governing free press and fair trial issues relating to criminal proceedings, has been moved to the Local Criminal Rules.

2. LCvR 83.1.C includes in the Local Rules the provisions of the standing order dated May 21, 1968.

LCvR 83.2 ADMISSION TO PRACTICE AND APPEARANCE OF ATTORNEYS AND STUDENTS

A. Admission to Practice—Generally.

1. *Roll of Attorneys.* The bar of this Court consists of those heretofore and those hereafter admitted to practice before this Court, who have taken the oath prescribed by the rules in force when they were admitted or prescribed by this rule.

2. *Eligibility; Member in Good Standing.* Any person who is eligible to become a member of the Bar of the Supreme Court of Pennsylvania or who is a member in good standing of the bar of the Supreme Court of Pennsylvania, or a member in good standing of the Supreme Court of the United States, or a member in good standing of any United States District Court, may be admitted to practice before the bar of this Court.

3. *Procedure For Admission.* No person shall be admitted to practice in this Court as an attorney, except on oral motion of a member of the bar of this Court. He or she shall, if required, offer satisfactory evidence of his or her moral and professional character and shall take the following oath or affirmation, to wit:

"I DO SOLEMNLY SWEAR (OR AFFIRM) THAT I WILL CONDUCT MYSELF AS AN ATTORNEY AND COUNSELOR OF THIS COURT, UPRIGHTLY AND ACCORDING TO LAW; AND THAT I WILL SUPPORT THE CONSTITUTION OF THE UNITED STATES. SO HELP ME GOD."

If admitted, the applicant shall, under the direction of the Clerk of Court, sign the roll of attorneys and pay such fee as shall have been prescribed by the Judicial Conference and by the Court.

5. *Agreements of Attorneys.* All agreements of attorneys relating to the business of the Court shall be in writing; otherwise, if disputed, they will be considered of no validity.

6. *Practice in Criminal Branch Prohibited.* No attorney shall be permitted to practice in the criminal branch of the federal law as counsel for any person accused of crime in the United States District Court for the Western District of Pennsylvania where said attorney is serving by appointment or election in any of the following categories in either the state of Pennsylvania or for the United States of America:

a. district attorney of any county in the Commonwealth of Pennsylvania;

b. assistant, deputy or special advisor of any district attorney of any county in the Commonwealth of Pennsylvania;

c. Attorney General of the Commonwealth of Pennsylvania;

d. assistant, deputy or special advisor of the Attorney General of the Commonwealth of Pennsylvania;

e. legal counsel for and any assistant or deputy of any agency of the United States government; or

f. magistrates or justices of the peace of any city, county or state.

B. *Pro Hac Vice Admissions.* All motions for admission pro hac vice must be accompanied by the filing fee. A motion for admission pro hac vice must be made by the attorney seeking to be admitted and must be accompanied by an affidavit from the attorney seeking to be admitted pro hac vice (hereinafter the "affiant"). The affidavit must include the affiant's name, law firm affiliation (if any), business address, and bar identification number. The affiant must attest in the affidavit that the affiant is a registered user of ECF in the United States District Court for the Western District of Pennsylvania, that the affiant has read, knows and understands the Local Rules of Court for the United States District Court for the Western District of Pennsylvania, and that the affiant is a member in good standing of the bar of any state or of any United States District Court. The affidavit must list the bars of any state or of any United States court of which the affiant is a member in good standing. The affiant must attach to the affidavit one current certificate of good standing from the bar or the court in which the affiant primarily practices. The affidavit also must list and explain any previous disciplinary proceedings concerning the affiant's practice of law that resulted in a non-confidential negative finding or sanction by the disciplinary authority of the bar of any state or any United States court. The Court will not rule on a motion for admission pro hac vice that does not include an affidavit containing the aforementioned information and attestations required by this rule.

The forms of the motion for admission pro hac vice and accompanying affidavit are set forth in "Appendix LCvR 83.2B–MOTION," and "Appendix LCvR 83.2B–AFFIDAVIT."

Comment (February 2013)

The Local Rules of Court for the United States District Court for the Western District of Pennsylvania and instructions for becoming a registered user of ECF in the United States District Court for the Western District of Pennsylvania are available on the Court's website. *"A Declaration pursuant to 28 U.S.C. § 1746 in lieu of an affidavit shall be sufficient to comply with the requirements of this Rule."*

C. Appearances and Withdrawals of Appearance.

1. *Appearance—How Entered.* In all criminal cases involving privately retained counsel, a notice of appearance of counsel shall be filed at or before the first appearance of counsel.

2. *Attorney Identification Number.* Any appearance by a Pennsylvania attorney shall contain a Pennsylvania attorney identification number.

3. *Separate Praecipe Unnecessary.* In a civil action, no separate praecipe for appearance need be filed by an attorney for an original party or for an intervenor. The endorsement of names of attorneys appearing on the first pleading or motion filed by a party shall constitute the entry of appearance of such attorneys. Appearance by other attorneys shall be by praecipe filed with the Clerk of Court.

4. *Withdrawal of Appearance.* In any civil proceeding, no attorney whose appearance has been entered shall withdraw his or her appearance except upon filing a written motion. The motion must specify the reasons requiring withdrawal and provide the name and address of the succeeding attorney. If the succeeding attorney is not known, the motion must set forth the name, address, and telephone number of the client and either bear the client's signature approving withdrawal or state specifically why, after due diligence, the attorney was unable to obtain the client's signature.

Comment (February 2013)

A motion for withdrawal of counsel's appearance that sets forth the basis for withdrawal should disclose that basis only in a manner consistent with the applicable provisions of the Pennsylvania Rules of Professional Conduct. See Pa. R. Prof. Conduct 1.16, comment 3.

D. Student Practice Rule.

1. *Purpose.* This rule is designed to provide law students with clinical instruction in federal litigation, and thereby enhance the competence of lawyers practicing before the United States District Courts.

2. *Student Requirements.* An eligible student must:

    a. be duly enrolled in a law school accredited by the American Bar Association:

    b. have completed a least three semesters of legal studies, or the equivalent;

    c. be enrolled for credit in a law school clinical program that has been approved by this Court;

    d. be certified by the Dean of the law school, or the Dean's designee, as being of good character, and having sufficient legal ability to fulfill the responsibilities of a legal intern to both the client and this Court;

    e. be certified by this Court to practice pursuant to this rule; and

    f. not accept personal compensation from a client or other source for legal services provided pursuant to this rule.

3. *Program Requirements.* A law school clinical practice program:

    a. must provide the student with academic and practice advocacy training, utilizing law school faculty or adjunct faculty, including federal government attorneys or private practitioners, for practice supervision;

    b. must grant the student academic credit for satisfactory participation therein;

    c. must be certified by this Court;

    d. must be conducted in such a manner as not to conflict with normal Court schedules;

    e. may accept compensation other than from a client; and

    f. must secure and maintain professional liability insurance for it activities.

4. *Supervisor Requirements.* A supervisor must:

    a. have faculty or adjunct faculty status at the law school offering the clinical practice program, and must be certified by the Dean of the law school as being of good character, and having sufficient legal ability and adequate training to fulfill the responsibilities of a supervisor;

    b. be admitted to practice before this Court;

    c. be present with the student at all times during Court appearance, and at all other proceedings, including depositions in which testimony is taken;

    d. co-sign all pleadings or other documents filed with this Court;

    e. assume full professional responsibility for the student's guidance in, and for the quality of, any work undertaken by the student pursuant to this rule;

    f. be available for consultation with represented clients;

    g. assist and counsel the student in all activities conducted pursuant to this rule, and review such activities with the student so as to assure the proper practical training of the student and the effective representation of the client; and

    h. be responsible for supplementing oral or written work of the student, where necessary, to ensure the effective representation of the client.

5. *Certification of Student, Program and Supervisor.*

    a. Students.

    (1) Certification by the law school Dean and approval by this Court shall be filed with the Clerk of Court, and unless it is sooner withdrawn, shall remain in effect until expiration of 18 months.

    (2) Certification to appear in a particular case may be withdrawn at any time, in the discretion of the Court, and without any showing of cause.

    b. Program.

    (1) Certification of a program by this Court shall be filed with the Clerk of Court and shall remain in effect indefinitely unless withdrawn by the Court.

    (2) Certification of a program may be withdrawn by this Court at any time.

    c. Supervisor.

    (1) Certification of a supervisor must be filed with the Clerk of Court, and shall remain in effect indefinitely unless withdrawn by this Court.

    (2) Certification of a supervisor may be withdrawn by the Court at any time.

    (3) Certification of a supervisor may be withdrawn by the Dean by mailing notice of such withdrawal to the Clerk of Court.

6. *Activities.* A certified student, under the personal supervision of the supervisor, as set forth in LCvR 83.2.C.4, may:

    a. represent any client including federal, state or local governmental bodies, in any civil or administrative matter, if the supervising lawyer and the client on whose behalf the student is appearing have consented in writing to that appearance; or

    b. engage in all activities on behalf of the clients that a licensed attorney may engage in.

7. *Limitation of Activities.* The Court retains the power to limit a student's participation in a particular case to such activities as the Court deems consistent with the appropriate administration of justice.

Comment (June 2008)

The amended Rule adds headings, modifies the numbering and clarifies and modernizes language in the Rule. More substantively, the amended Rule adds a section on pro hac vice admissions. In addition, it permits students to practice before the Court after completing three (as opposed to four) semesters of legal study.

[Effective September 1, 2009. Amended effective February 1, 2013.]

LCvR 83.3   RULES OF DISCIPLINARY ENFORCEMENT FOR ATTORNEYS

A. Introduction.

1. *Responsibility of Court.* The United States District Court for the Western District of Pennsylvania, in furtherance of its inherent power and responsibility to supervise the conduct of attorneys who are admitted to practice before it, or admitted for the purpose of a particular proceeding (pro hac vice), promulgates the following rules of Disciplinary Enforcement superseding all of its rules pertaining to disciplinary enforcement heretofore promulgated.

2. *Adoption of Rules of Professional Conduct.* Acts or omissions by an attorney admitted to practice before this Court, individually or in concert with others, that violate the rules of professional conduct adopted by this Court shall constitute misconduct and shall be grounds for discipline, whether or not the act or omission occurred in the course of an attorney-client relationship. The rules of professional conduct adopted by this Court are the rules of professional conduct adopted by the Supreme Court of Pennsylvania, as amended from time to time, except that Rule 3.10 has been specifically deleted as a rule of this Court, and as otherwise provided by specific order of this Court.

3. *Sanctions for Misconduct.* For misconduct defined in these rules, any attorney admitted to practice before this Court may be disbarred, suspended from practice before this Court, reprimanded or subjected to such other disciplinary action as the circumstances may warrant.

4. *Admission to Practice as Conferring Disciplinary Jurisdiction.* Whenever an attorney applies to be admitted or is admitted to this Court for purposes of a particular proceeding (pro hac vice), the attorney shall be deemed thereby to have conferred disciplinary jurisdiction upon this Court for any alleged misconduct of that attorney arising in the course of or in the preparation for such proceeding.

B. Disciplinary Proceeding.

1. *Reference to Counsel.* When misconduct or allegations of misconduct which, if substantiated, would warrant discipline on the part of an attorney admitted to practice before this Court shall come to the attention of a District Judge or Magistrate Judge of this Court, whether by complaint or otherwise, and the applicable procedure is not otherwise mandated by

these rules, or in the event a petition for reinstatement has been filed by a disciplined attorney, the Chief Judge shall in his or her discretion and with prior agreement of the Disciplinary Board of the Supreme Court of Pennsylvania appoint as counsel attorneys serving in the Office of Disciplinary Counsel of the Disciplinary Board or one or more members of the bar of this Court to investigate allegations of misconduct or to prosecute disciplinary proceedings under these rules or in conjunction with such a reinstatement petition, provided, however, that the respondent-attorney may move to disqualify an attorney so appointed who is or has been engaged as an adversary of the respondent-attorney in any matter. Counsel, once appointed, may not resign unless permission to do so is given by this Court.

2. *Recommendation of Counsel.* Should such counsel conclude after investigation and review that a formal disciplinary proceeding should not be initiated against the respondent-attorney because sufficient evidence is not present, or because there is pending another proceeding against the respondent-attorney, the disposition of which in the judgment of the counsel should be awaited before further action by this Court is considered or for any other valid reason, counsel shall file with this Court a recommendation for disposition of the matter, whether by dismissal, admonition, deferral, or otherwise setting forth the reasons therefor.

3. *Order to Show Cause.* Should such counsel conclude after investigation and review that a formal disciplinary proceeding should be initiated, counsel shall obtain an order of this Court upon a showing of probable cause requiring the respondent-attorney to show cause within thirty (30) days after service of that order upon that attorney, personally or by mail, why the attorney should not be disciplined.

4. *Hearings.* Upon the respondent-attorney's answer to the order to show cause, if any issue of fact is raised or the respondent-attorney wishes to be heard in mitigation, the Chief Judge shall set the matter for prompt hearing before one or more Judges of this Court, provided, however, that if the disciplinary proceeding is predicated upon the complaint of a Judge of this Court the hearing shall be conducted before a panel of three other Judges of this Court appointed by the Chief Judge, or if there are fewer than three Judges eligible to serve or the Chief Judge is the complainant, by the Chief Judge of the Court of Appeals. Where a Judge merely refers a matter and is not involved in the proceeding, he or she shall not be considered a complainant.

All such proceedings shall be conducted by counsel appointed pursuant to LCvR 83.3.B.1 or such other counsel as the Court may appoint for such purpose.

The Judge or Judges to whom a disciplinary proceeding is assigned by the Chief Judge may conduct a further hearing, and/or otherwise take additional testimony, or hear or receive oral or written argument, and shall make a recommendation based thereon to the Board of Judges. The Board, after consideration of the recommendation, shall enter such order as it shall determine by a majority vote of the active Judges in service at the next meeting of the board to be appropriate, including dismissal of the charges, reprimand, suspension for a period of time, disbarment, or such action as may be proper.

C. Attorneys Convicted of Crimes.

1. *Immediate Suspension.* Upon the filing with this Court of a certified copy of a judgment of conviction demonstrating that any attorney admitted to practice before this Court has been convicted in any Court of the United States, or the District of Columbia, or of any state, territory, commonwealth or possession of the United States, of a serious crime as hereinafter defined, the Chief Judge shall enter an order immediately suspending that attorney, whether the conviction resulted from a plea of guilty or nolo contendere or from a verdict after trial or otherwise, and regardless of the pendency of any appeal, until final disposition of a disciplinary proceeding to be commenced upon such conviction. A copy of such order shall immediately be served upon the attorney. Upon good cause shown, the Chief Judge may set aside such order when it appears in the interest of justice so to do upon concurrence of a majority of active Judges in service.

2. *Definition of Serious Crime.* The term "serious crime" shall include any felony and any lesser crime a necessary element of which, as determined by the statutory or common law definition of such crime in the jurisdiction where the judgment was entered, involves false swearing, misrepresentation, fraud, willful failure to file income tax returns, deceit, bribery, extortion, misappropriation, theft, or an attempt or a conspiracy or solicitation of another to commit a "serious crime."

3. *Certified Copy of Conviction as Evidence.* A certified copy of a judgment of conviction of an attorney for any crime shall be conclusive evidence of the commission of that crime in any disciplinary proceeding instituted against that attorney based upon the conviction.

4. *Mandatory Reference for Disciplinary Proceeding.* Upon the filing of a certified copy of a judgment of conviction of an attorney for a serious crime, the Court shall refer the matter for the institution of a disciplinary proceeding in which the sole issue to be determined shall be the extent of the final discipline to be imposed as a result of the conduct resulting in the conviction, provided that a disciplinary proceeding so instituted will not be brought to final hearing until all appeals from the conviction are concluded.

5. *Discretionary Reference for Disciplinary Proceedings.* Upon the filing of a certified copy of a judgment of conviction of an attorney for a crime not constituting a serious crime, the Court may refer the matter to counsel for whatever action counsel may deem warranted, including the institution of a disciplinary proceeding provided, however, that the Court may in its discretion make no reference with respect to convictions for minor offenses.

6. *Reinstatement Upon Reversal.* An attorney suspended under the provisions of this rule will be reinstated immediately upon the filing of a certificate demonstrating that the underlying conviction of a serious crime has been reversed but the reinstatement will not terminate any disciplinary proceeding then pending against the attorney, the disposition of which shall be determined by the Court on the basis of all available evidence pertaining to both guilt and the extent of discipline to be imposed.

D. Discipline Imposed by Other Courts.

1. *Notice by Attorney of Public Discipline.* Any attorney admitted to practice before this Court shall, upon being subjected to public discipline by any other Court of the United States or the District of Columbia, or by a Court of any state, territory, commonwealth or possession of the United States, promptly inform the Clerk of this Court of such action.

2. *Proceedings after Notice of Discipline.* Upon the filing of a certified or exemplified copy of a judgment or order demonstrating that an attorney admitted to practice before this Court has been disciplined by another Court, this Court shall forthwith issue a notice directed to the attorney containing:

a. A copy of the judgment or order from the other Court; and

b. An order to show cause directing that the attorney inform this Court within thirty (30) days after service of that order upon the attorney, personally or by mail, of any claim by the attorney predicated upon the grounds set forth in LCvR 83.3.D.4 that the imposition of the identical discipline by the Court would be unwarranted and the reasons therefor.

3. *Stay of Discipline in Other Jurisdiction.* In the event the discipline imposed in the other jurisdiction has been stayed there, any reciprocal discipline imposed in this Court shall be deferred until such stay expires.

4. *Reciprocal Discipline.* Upon the expiration of thirty (30) days from service of the notice issued pursuant to the provisions of LCvR 83.3.D.2, this Court shall impose the identical discipline unless the respondent-attorney demonstrates, or this Court finds, that upon the face of the record upon which the discipline in another jurisdiction is predicated it clearly appears that:

a. the procedure was so lacking in notice or opportunity to be heard as to constitute a deprivation of due process;

b. there was such an infirmity of proof establishing the misconduct as to give rise to the clear conviction that this Court could not, consistent with its duty, accept as final the conclusion on that subject;

c. the imposition of the same discipline by this Court would result in grave injustice; or

d. the misconduct established is deemed by this Court to warrant substantially different discipline.

In the event that an attorney files a timely answer alleging one or more of the elements set forth in LCvR 83.3.D.4, the Chief Judge shall set the matter for prompt hearing before one or more Judges of this Court who may order and conduct a further hearing, or take testimony or hear argument, and make a recommendation to the Board of Judges. The Board, after consideration of the recommendation, shall enter such order, as it shall determine by a majority vote of the active Judges in service at the next meeting of the Board, including dismissal of the charges, reprimand, suspension for a period of time, disbarment, or such action as may be proper.

5. *Conclusive Evidence of Final Adjudication.* In all other respects, a final adjudication in another Court that an attorney has been guilty of misconduct shall establish conclusively the misconduct for the purposes of a disciplinary proceeding in this Court.

6. *Appointment of Counsel.* This Court may at any stage appoint counsel to prosecute the disciplinary proceedings, pursuant to LCvR 83.3.B.I.

E. Disbarment on Consent or Resignation.

1. *Automatic Cessation of Right to Practice.* Any attorney admitted to practice before this Court who shall be disbarred on consent or resign from the bar of any other Court of the United States or the District of Columbia, or from the bar of any state, territory, commonwealth or possession of the United States, while an investigation into allegations of misconduct is pending, shall, upon the filing with this Court of a certified or exemplified copy of the judgment or order accepting such disbarment on consent or resignation, cease to be permitted to practice before this Court and be stricken from the roll of attorneys admitted to practice before this Court.

2. *Attorney to Notify Clerk of Disbarment.* Any attorney admitted to practice before this Court shall, upon being disbarred on consent or resigning from the bar of any other Court of the United States or the District of Columbia, or from the bar of any state, territory, commonwealth or possession of the United States, promptly inform the Clerk of this Court of such disbarment on consent or resignation.

F. Disbarment on Consent While Under Disciplinary Investigation or Prosecution.

1. *Consent to Disbarment.* Any attorney admitted to practice before this Court who is the subject of an investigation into, or a pending proceeding involving, allegations of misconduct may consent to disbarment, but only by delivering to this Court an affidavit stating that the attorney desires to consent to disbarment and that:

a. the attorney's consent is freely and voluntarily rendered; the attorney is not being subjected to coercion or duress; the attorney is fully aware of the implications of so consenting;

b. the attorney is aware that there is presently pending investigation or proceeding involving allegations that there exist grounds for the attorney's discipline, the nature of which the attorney shall specifically set forth;

c. the attorney acknowledges that the material facts so alleged are true; and

d. the attorney so consents because the attorney knows that if charges were predicated upon the matters under investigation, or if the proceeding were prosecuted, the attorney could not successfully defend himself or herself.

2. *Consent Order.* Upon receipt of the required affidavit, this Court shall enter an order disbarring the attorney.

3. *Public Record.* The Order disbarring the attorney on consent shall be a matter of public record. However, the affidavit required under the provisions of this rule shall not be publicly disclosed or made available for use in any other proceeding except upon order of this Court.

G. Reinstatement.

1. *After Disbarment or Suspension.* An attorney suspended for three (3) months or less shall be automatically reinstated at the end of the period of suspension upon the filing with the Court of an affidavit of compliance with the provisions of the order. An attorney suspended for more than three (3) months or disbarred may not resume practice until reinstated by order of this Court.

2. *Time of Application Following Disbarment.* A person who has been disbarred after hearing or by consent may not apply for reinstatement until the expiration of at least five (5) years from the effective date of this disbarment.

3. *Hearing on Application.* Petitions for reinstatement by a disbarred or suspended attorney under this rule shall be filed with the Chief Judge of this Court. Upon receipt of the petition, the Chief Judge shall refer the petition to counsel for investigation and recommendation, and shall assign the matter for a hearing, or other appropriate action, before one or

more Judges of this Court, provided, however, that if the disciplinary proceeding was predicated upon the complaint of a Judge of this Court, the hearing shall be conducted before a panel of three (3) other Judges of this Court appointed by the Chief Judge, or, if there are fewer than three (3) Judges eligible to serve or the Chief Judge was the complainant, by the Chief Judge of the Court of Appeals. The Judge or Judges assigned to the matter shall schedule a hearing, if necessary, at which the petitioner shall have the burden of demonstrating by clear and convincing evidence that he or she has the moral qualifications, competency and learning in the law required for admission to practice law before this Court and that his or her resumption of the practice of law will not be detrimental to the integrity and standing of the bar or to the administration of justice, or subversive of the public interest.

The Judge or Judges shall make a recommendation to the Board of Judges and the Board shall enter an appropriate order, as determined by a majority vote of the active Judges in service at the next meeting of the Board.

4. *Duty of Counsel.* In all proceedings upon a petition for reinstatement, cross-examination of the witnesses of the respondent-attorney and the submission of evidence, if any, in opposition to the petition shall be conducted by counsel.

5. *Deposit for Costs of Proceeding.* Petitions for reinstatement under this rule shall be accompanied by an advance cost deposit in an amount to be set from time to time by the Court to cover anticipated costs of the reinstatement proceeding.

6. *Conditions of Reinstatement.* If the petitioner is found unfit to resume the practice of law, the petition shall be dismissed. If the petitioner is found fit to resume the practice of law, the judgment shall reinstate him or her, provided that the judgment may make reinstatement conditional upon the payment of all or part of the costs of the proceedings, and upon the making of partial or complete restitution to parties harmed by the petitioner whose conduct led to the suspension or disbarment. Provided further, that if the petitioner has been suspended or disbarred for five (5) years or more, reinstatement may be conditioned, in the discretion of the Judge or Judges before whom the matter is heard, upon the furnishing of proof of competency and learning in the law, which proof may include certification by the bar examiners of a state or other jurisdiction of the attorney's successful completion of an examination for admission to practice subsequent to the date of suspension or disbarment.

7. *Successive Petitions.* No petition for reinstatement under this rule shall be filed within one (1) year following an adverse judgment upon a petition for reinstatement filed by or on behalf of the same person.

H. Service of Papers and Other Notices. Service of an order to show cause instituting a formal disciplinary proceeding or other papers or notices required by these rules shall be made by personal service or by registered or certified mail addressed to the respondent-attorney at the address most recently registered by him or her with the Clerk of Court. Service of any other papers or notices required by these rules shall be deemed to have been made if such paper or notice is addressed to the respondent-attorney at the address most recently registered with the Clerk of Court; or to counsel or respondent's attorney at the address indicated in the most recent pleading or other document filed by them in the course of any proceeding under these rules.

I. Duties of the Clerk of Court.

1. *Filing Certificate of Conviction.* Upon being informed that an attorney admitted to practice before this Court has been convicted of any crime, the Clerk of this Court shall determine whether the Clerk of the Court in which such conviction occurred has forwarded a certificate of such conviction to this Court. If a certificate has not been so forwarded, the Clerk of this Court shall promptly obtain a certificate and file it with this Court.

2. *Filing Disciplinary Judgment.* Upon being informed that an attorney admitted to practice before this Court has been subjected to discipline by another Court, the Clerk of this Court shall determine whether a certified or exemplified copy of the disciplinary judgment or order has been filed with this Court, and, if not, the Clerk of Court shall promptly obtain a certified or exemplified copy of the disciplinary judgment or order and file it with this Court.

3. *Filing Consent Order.* Upon being informed that an attorney admitted to practice before this Court has been disbarred on consent or resigned in another jurisdiction while an investigation into allegations of misconduct was pending, the Clerk of this Court shall determine whether a certified or exemplified copy of the disciplinary judgment or order striking the attorney's name from the rolls of those admitted to practice has been filed with the Court, and, if not, shall promptly obtain a certified or exemplified copy of such judgment or order and file it with the Court.

4. *Transmittal of Record to Other Courts.* Whenever it appears that any person convicted of any crime or disbarred or suspended or censured or disbarred on consent by this Court is admitted to practice law in any other jurisdiction or before any other court, the Clerk of this Court shall, within fourteen (14) days of that conviction, disbarment, suspension, censure, or disbarment on consent, transmit to the disciplinary authority in such other jurisdiction, or for such other

court, a certificate of the conviction or a certified or exemplified copy of the judgment or order of disbarment, suspension, censure, or disbarment on consent, as well as the last known office and residence addresses of the defendant or respondent.

5. *National Discipline Data Bank.* The Clerk of Court shall promptly notify the National Discipline Data Bank operated by the American Bar Association of any order imposing public discipline upon any attorney admitted to practice before this Court.

J. Retention of Control. Nothing contained in these rules shall be construed to deny to this Court such powers as are necessary for the Court to maintain control over proceedings conducted before it, such as proceedings for contempt under Title 18 of the United States Code or under Fed. R. Crim. P. 42.

K. Confidentiality. All investigations of allegations of misconduct, and disciplinary proceedings authorized by these rules shall be kept confidential until or unless:

1. the Judge or Judges to whom the matter is assigned determine otherwise;

2. the respondent-attorney requests in writing that the matter be public;

3. the investigation or proceeding is predicated on a conviction of the respondent-attorney for a crime; or

4. the Court determines that discipline is appropriate in accordance with LCvR 83.3.B.4.

This rule shall not prohibit counsel, appointed pursuant to LCvR 83.3.B.I or any member of this Court, from reporting to law enforcement authorities the suspected commission of any criminal offense.

[Effective August 1, 2001. Re-enacted January 11, 2003. Amended effective December 1, 2009.]

Comment (June 2008)

The amended Rule adds headings, modifies the numbering and clarifies and modernizes language in the Rule. The amendment reorganizes the Rule and clarifies the process whereby allegations of attorney misconduct are investigated and, if appropriate, prosecuted. The amended Rule clarifies that the word "Counsel" refers to a member of the bar of the Court appointed by the Chief Judge to perform the investigation and/or prosecution.

LCvR 100.1 TRANSFER OF MULTIDISTRICT LITIGATION

A. Composite Number Assigned. Whenever the Court consents to the transfer of a group of actions to this district in order to hold coordinated or consolidated pretrial proceedings as set forth in Title 28 U.S.C. § 1407, the group of actions shall be given the composite number previously assigned by the Judicial Panel on Multidistrict Litigation. Individual actions within the group shall be given specific civil action numbers.

B. Clerk of Court to Maintain Multidistrict Docket Sheet. The Clerk of Court shall maintain a multidistrict litigation docket sheet for the group of actions compositely numbered, as well as an individual docket sheet for each separate action. All pleadings, papers, depositions, interrogatories, and other documents or material, relating to two or more actions shall be entered only on the multidistrict litigation docket sheet. If such pleading or document relates to a single action only, it shall be entered on the individual action docket sheet.

C. No Separate Appearance Required. Counsel who entered an appearance in the transferor court prior to the transfer need not enter a separate appearance before this Court.

D. Notification of Representing Counsel. Upon receipt of an order of transfer, attorneys representing litigants in transferred cases shall notify the Clerk of this Court of the names, addresses and telephone numbers of attorneys of record. No litigant may list more than one attorney as its legal representative for the purpose of service.

E. Liaison Counsel to Be Designated. Prior to the first pretrial conference, counsel for plaintiffs and for defendants shall designate, subject to the approval of the Court, liaison counsel. Liaison counsel shall be authorized to receive notices on behalf of the parties by whom they have been designated. They shall be responsible for the preparation and transmittal of copies of such notices as they may receive as liaison counsel to each of the attorneys included on the list prepared in accordance with the preceding paragraph.

F. Only Original Documents to Be Filed. Unless the Judicial Panel on Multidistrict Litigation or this Court by order specifically otherwise directs for a specific case or group of cases, only the original of all documents shall be filed with the Clerk of this Court; provided, however, upon remand, it shall be the responsibility of the attorneys who filed a given document to furnish an adequate number of copies for transmittal to the transferor Court. The Clerk of Court shall notify counsel of the number of copies needed. The copies shall be furnished within thirty (30) days from the date of notification of remand. Upon receipt of an order of the Judicial Panel transferring or remanding cases, without further order of this Court, the Clerk of Court shall assemble the files, together with their documentation, and forward the files as directed by the Judicial Panel.

[Effective September 1, 2009.]

LCvR 100.2 PUBLICATION OF NOTICE OR ADVERTISEMENTS

Any notice or advertisement required by law or rule of Court to be published in any newspaper shall be a short analysis, setting forth the general purpose of such notice or advertisement, and shall also be published in the Pittsburgh Legal Journal, Erie County Law Journal, and/or Cambria County Legal Journal which are also designated as the official newspapers for this District or other publications ordered by the Court.

[Effective September 1, 2009.]

LCvR 2241. ACTIONS UNDER 28 U.S.C. § 2241

A. Scope. These rules shall apply in the United States District Court, Western District of Pennsylvania, in all proceedings initiated by federal prisoners under 28 U.S.C. § 2241. In filings submitted to this Court, these Local Rules shall be cited as "LCvR 2241. ___." In addition to these rules, all parties also should consult the applicable provisions of the federal habeas corpus statute at 28 U.S.C. §§ 2241–2266, as amended by the Antiterrorism and Effective Death Penalty Act of 1996 ("AEDPA"), P.L. 104–132, effective April 24, 1996.

B. The Petition.

1. *Naming the Respondent.* If the petitioner is currently serving a sentence imposed by a federal Court and he or she is challenging the execution of his or her sentence, petitioner must name as respondent the warden or custodian of the prison or correctional facility were petitioner is incarcerated.

2. *Form.*

a. Form of Petitions Required. A petitioner who files a petition seeking relief pursuant to 28 U.S.C. § 2241 may submit his or her petition on the standard form supplied by this Court. If the petitioner does not use the standard form, the petition must substantially follow the standard form supplied by this Court. Petitions that do not utilize the standard form shall contain all of the information required by the standard form. If the petitioner is represented by counsel, Electronic Case Filing (ECF) procedures apply.

b. Content. The petitioner is to state all grounds for relief, provide specific facts supporting each argument, and identify the relief requested. An accompanying memorandum of law is not required but will be accepted by the Clerk of Court at the time the petition is filed.

c. Where to Get the Standard Form. The standard form supplied by this Court for 28 U.S.C. § 2241 petitions can be obtained free of charge from the following sources: (i) this Court's website (www. pawd.uscourts.gov) (FORMS/MANUALS); (ii) this Court's Office of the Clerk of Court upon request; (iii) the Federal Public Defender's website (http://paw.fd.org); or (iv) the Federal Public Defender's Office upon request.

d. Requirements Concerning Filing Format. All filings in 28 U.S.C. § 2241 proceedings must by typed, word-processed or neatly written in ink. All filings must be submitted on paper sized 8½ by 11 inches. No writing or typing shall be made on the back of any filing.

e. Return of Petitions that Do Not Substantially Comply With Local Form Rules. If the form or other initial filing submitted by a pro se petitioner does not substantially comply with these Local Rules, the filing may be returned to the pro se petitioner with a copy of the Court's standard form, a statement of reasons for its return, and a directive that the petitioner resubmit the claims outlined in the original filing on the Court's form. A petitioner will be given 21 days or as directed by the Court to return his or her filing on the form supplied by this Court. A petitioner may seek leave of Court for an extension of time to return the form.

f. Certificate Required in Death Penalty Case. A petitioner challenging the execution of a sentence of death pursuant to a federal Court judgment shall file with the Clerk of Court a copy of the "Certificate of Death Penalty Case" required by the Third Circuit L.A.R. Misc. 111.2(a). The certificate will include the following information: names, addresses, and telephone numbers of parties and counsel; if set, the proposed date of execution of the sentence; and the emergency nature of the proceedings. Upon docketing, the Clerk of Court will transmit a copy of the certificate, together with a copy of the relevant documents, to the Clerk of the Court of Appeals as required by Third Circuit L.A.R. Misc. 111.2(a).

C. Filing the Petition. The original Section 2241 petition shall be filed with the Clerk of Court. Section 2241 petitions must be accompanied by the applicable filing fee or a motion requesting leave to proceed in forma pauperis.

D. The Answer and the Reply.

1. *The Answer.*

a. When Required. Upon undertaking preliminary review of the motion for relief under 28 U.S.C. § 2241, if the Court finds that there is no basis for dismissal, the Court must enter an order directing the respondent to file an Answer within the time frame permitted by the Court. The respondent is not required to file a Response to the petition unless a Judge so orders. An extension may be granted only for good cause shown.

b. Contents. The Response must address the allegations in the petition. All relevant documents should be attached to the Response as exhibits. In addition, the Response must state whether any claim in the petition is barred by a failure to exhaust administrative remedies, a procedural bar, or non-retroactivity.

2. *The Reply.* Although not required, the petitioner may file a Reply (also known as "a Traverse") within 30 days of the date the respondent files its Response. If the petitioner wishes to file a Reply after 30 days have passed, he or she must file a motion requesting to do so and an extension may be granted only for good cause shown.

E. Powers of a Magistrate Judge. Within 21 days of commencement of a Section 2241 proceeding in the Erie or Pittsburgh Divisions, the petitioner shall execute and file a "CONSENT TO JURISDICTION BY UNITED STATES MAGISTRATE JUDGE" form, either consenting to the jurisdiction of the Magistrate Judge or electing to have the case randomly assigned to a District Judge. Respondent shall execute and file within 21 days of its appearance a form either consenting to the jurisdiction of the Magistrate Judge or electing to have the case randomly assigned to a District Judge. If all parties do not consent to Magistrate Judge jurisdiction, a District Judge shall be assigned and the Magistrate Judge shall continue to manage the case consistent with 28 U.S.C. § 636.

The "CONSENT TO JURISDICTION BY UNITED STATES MAGISTRATE JUDGE" form is available on this Court's website (www.pawd.uscourts.gov) (CASE ASSIGNMENT SYSTEM). If a party elects to have the case assigned to a District Judge, the Magistrate Judge shall continue to manage the case by deciding non-dispositive motions and submitting reports and recommendations on the petition and on dispositive motions, unless otherwise directed by the District Judge.

F. Applicability of the Federal Rules of Civil Procedure. The Federal Rules of Civil Procedure may be applied to a proceeding under these rules.

G. Appeals.

1. Upon entry of a final decision decided pursuant to 28 U.S.C. § 2241, the Court shall set forth the judgment on a separate document and enter the judgment on the civil docket as required under Fed. R. Civ. P. 58(a)(1).

2. The time for filing a notice of appeal is governed by Fed. R. App. P. 4(a) and such time commences when the Court enters the judgment as described in said Rule.

H. The Appointment of Counsel. There is no constitutional right to counsel in proceedings brought pursuant to 28 U.S.C. § 2241. Financially eligible petitioners may, however, request that counsel be appointed at any time. *See* 18 U.S.C. § 3006A. The Court may appoint counsel for a petitioner who qualifies to have counsel appointed under 18 U.S.C. § 3006A. This Local Rule is not intended to alter or limit the appointment of counsel available pursuant to 18 U.S.C. § 3006A.

[Effective September 1, 2009. Amended effective December 1, 2009.]

Comment (June 2008)

All Section 2241 habeas cases in the Erie and Pittsburgh Divisions are assigned to a Magistrate Judge only.

LCvR 2254. ACTIONS UNDER 28 U.S.C. § 2254

A. Scope.

1. These rules shall apply in the United States District Court, Western District of Pennsylvania, in all proceedings initiated under 28 U.S.C. § 2254. In addition to these rules, all parties also should consult 28 U.S.C. § 2254 and the applicable provisions of the federal habeas corpus statute at 28 U.S.C. §§ 2241–2266, as amended by the Antiterrorism and Effective Death Penalty Act of 1996 ("AEDPA"), P.L. 104–132, effective April 24, 1996.

2. These Local Rules are intended to supplement, when necessary, the corresponding rules promulgated by the United States Supreme Court that are entitled "Rules Governing Section 2254 Proceedings for the United States District Courts." Those rules are cited herein as "the Federal 2254 Rules," and a specific Federal 2254 Rule is cited as "Federal 2254 Rule ___." All parties should consult the Federal 2254 Rules at the commencement of litigation to ensure compliance with the Federal 2254 Rules, as supplemented by these Local Rules. In filings submitted to this Court, these Local Rules shall be cited as "LCvR 2254. ___."

B. The Petition.

1. *Naming the Respondent.* If the petitioner is currently under a state Court judgment and he or she is challenging the state Court conviction/sentence, he or she must name as respondent the state officer who has custody (i.e., the warden or superintendent). The petitioner must also name as respondent the District Attorney of the county in which he or she was convicted and sentenced. If a petitioner is challenging parole proceedings, he or she must name as respondent the Pennsylvania Board of Probation and Parole.

2. *Form.*

a. Form of Petitions Required. A petitioner who files a petition seeking relief pursuant to 28 U.S.C. § 2254 may submit his or her petition on the standard form supplied by this Court. If the petitioner does not use the standard form, the petition must substantially follow the standard form supplied by this Court or the form attached to the Federal 2254 Rules. Petitions that do not utilize the standard forms shall contain all of the information required by the standard forms. If the petitioner is represented by counsel, the Electronic Case Filing (ECF) procedures apply.

b. Content. The petitioner is to state *all* grounds for relief, provide specific facts supporting each argument, and identify the relief requested. An accompanying memorandum of law is not required but will be accepted by the Clerk of Court at the time the petition is filed.

c. Where to Get the Standard Form. The standard form supplied by this Court for 28 U.S.C. § 2254 petitions can be obtained free of charge from the following sources: (i) this Court's website (www. pawd.uscourts.gov) (FORMS/MANUALS); (ii) this Court's Office of the Clerk of Court upon request; (iii) the Federal Public Defender's website (http:// paw.fd.org); or (iv) the Federal Public Defender's Office upon request.

d. Requirements Concerning Filing Format. All filings in 28 U.S.C. § 2254 proceedings must by typed, word-processed or neatly written in ink. All filings must be submitted on paper sized 8½ by 11 inches. No writing or typing shall be made on the back of any filing.

e. Return of Petitions that Do Not Substantially Comply With Local Form Rules. If the form or other initial filing submitted by a pro se petitioner does not substantially comply with Federal 2254 Rule 2, as supplemented by these Local Rules, the Clerk of Court will accept the petition and file it for the sole purpose of preserving the timeliness. If the Court so directs, the filing may be returned to a pro se petitioner with a copy of the Court's standard form, a statement of reasons for its return, and a directive that the petitioner resubmit the claims outlined in the original filing on the Court's form. A petitioner will be given 21 days to return his or her filing on the form supplied by this Court. A petitioner may seek leave of Court for an extension of time to return the form.

f. Certificate Required in Death Penalty Case. A petitioner challenging the imposition of a sentence of death pursuant to a state Court judgment shall file with the Clerk of Court a copy of the "Certificate of Death Penalty Case" required by the Third Circuit L.A.R. Misc. 111.2(a). The certificate will include the following information: names, addresses, and telephone numbers of parties and counsel; if set, the proposed date of execution of the sentence; and the emergency nature of the proceedings. Upon docketing, the Clerk of Court will transmit a copy of the certificate, together with a copy of the relevant documents, to the Clerk of the

Court of Appeals as required by Third Circuit L.A.R. Misc. 111.2(a).

C. Filing the Petition. The original Section 2254 petition shall be filed with the Clerk of Court. Section 2254 petitions must be accompanied by the applicable filing fee or for leave to proceed in forma pauperis.

D. Preliminary Review. These Local Rules provide no supplement to Federal 2254 Rule 4. Please consult that rule regarding preliminary review.

E. The Answer and the Reply.

1. *The Answer.*

a. When Required. Upon the directive of the Court, the respondent shall file an Answer to the petition in a form consistent with LCvR 2254.E.1.b–f.

The Respondent may, within the time frame permitted by the Court for the filing of the Answer, file a motion to dismiss if the respondent believes that there is a clear procedural bar to the action, such as the failure to exhaust, statute of limitations, abuse of the writ, and/or successive petitions. A motion to dismiss need not be in a form consistent with LCvR 2254.E.1.b–f. However, such a motion must be accompanied by a certified copy of all relevant state Court records.

b. Contents. The Answer is more than just a responsive pleading that simply admits or denies the allegations contained in the petition. In habeas petitions challenging a state conviction/sentence, the Answer shall contain a discussion of the relevant procedural and factual history of all state proceedings, including the state Court trial, direct appeal, and post-conviction proceedings. In habeas petitions challenging state parole proceedings, the Answer shall contain the relevant procedural and factual history of the parole proceedings and any state Court proceedings which related to the parole proceedings.

The Answer also shall address procedural issues, the merits of the petition, and shall contain accompanying legal argument and citation to appropriate authorities. All assertions of historical or procedural facts shall be accompanied by citations to the state Court record and shall appear in a style comporting with the designations employed in the index of materials prepared in accordance with LCvR 2254.E.1.d.

c. The respondent must also provide the Court with a certified copy of all relevant transcripts of the state trial and post-conviction proceedings; relevant documentary evidence admitted at those proceedings; briefs submitted by either party to any state Court relating to the matter; opinions and dispositive orders of the state Court or agency; other relevant state Court/agency records; and a certified copy of the docket sheets of all the state Courts/agencies involved. Care should be taken so that all items are photocopied accurately, legibly, and in full.

d. The respondent shall also submit an index of all material described in LCvR 2254.E.1.c. The pages of the records must be sequentially numbered so that citations to those records will identify the exact location where the information appears.

e. If any item identified in LCvR 2254.E.1.c is not available at the time the respondent submits an answer, the respondent shall notify the Court that the item is unavailable. Once the item becomes available, the respondent shall provide a supplemental lodging of the item and index within 21 days of its availability.

f. As set forth in this Court's "Electronic Case Filing Policies and Procedures," in addition to the items that must be filed electronically with the Answer, a respondent shall also submit the original state Court records, or a certified complete copy of those records. The records shall be submitted in the traditional manner on paper. The Clerk of Court shall note on the docket that the original state Court records have been received. State Court records are not part of this Court's permanent case file and will be returned to the appropriate state Court upon final disposition, including appeals.

2. *The Reply.* Although not required, the petitioner may file a Reply (also known as "a Traverse") within 30 days of the date the respondent files its Answer. If the petitioner wishes to file a Reply after 30 days have passed, he or she must file a motion requesting leave to do so. An extension may be granted only for good cause shown.

F. Discovery. These Local Rules provide no supplement to Federal 2254 Rule 6. Please consult that rule regarding discovery.

G. Expanding the Record. If either party intends to rely on any document(s) that are not a part of the state Court record, such party must include those documents in a separate appendix attached to the pleading by which those documents are being submitted. In addition, that party should address, in its documents filed with the Court, why reliance on those documents is proper under the federal habeas statute and Federal 2254 Rule 7.

H. Evidentiary Hearing. These Local Rules provide no supplement to Federal 2254 Rule 8. Please consult that rule regarding evidentiary hearings.

I. Second or Successive Petitions. These Local Rules provide no supplement to Federal 2254 Rule 9. Please consult that rule regarding second or successive petitions.

J. Powers of a Magistrate Judge. Within 21 days of commencement of a Section 2254 proceeding in the Erie or Pittsburgh Divisions, the petitioner shall execute and file a "CONSENT TO JURISDICTION BY UNITED STATES MAGISTRATE JUDGE" form, either consenting to the jurisdiction of the Magistrate Judge or electing to have the case randomly assigned to a District Judge. Respondent shall execute and file within 21 days of its appearance a form either consenting to the jurisdiction of the Magistrate Judge or electing to have the case randomly assigned to a District Judge. If all parties do not consent to Magistrate Judge jurisdiction, a District Judge shall be assigned and the Magistrate Judge shall continue to manage the case consistent with 28 U.S.C. § 636.

The "CONSENT TO JURISDICTION BY UNITED STATES MAGISTRATE JUDGE" form is available on this Court's website (www.pawd.uscourts.gov) (CASE ASSIGNMENT SYSTEM). If a party elects to have the case assigned to a District Judge, the Magistrate Judge shall continue to manage the case by deciding non-dispositive motions and submitting reports and recommendations on the petition and on dispositive motions, unless otherwise directed by the District Judge.

K. Applicability of the Federal Rules of Civil Procedure. These Local Rules provide no supplement to Federal 2254 Rule 11. Please consult that rule regarding applicability of the Federal Rules of Civil Procedure.

L. Appeals.

1. Upon entry of a final decision decided pursuant to 28 U.S.C. § 2254, the Court shall set forth the judgment on a separate document and enter the judgment on the civil docket as required under Fed. R. Civ. P. 58(a)(1).

2. The time for filing a notice of appeal is governed by Fed. R. App. P. 4(a) and such time commences when the Court enters the judgment as described above in said Rule.

M. The Appointment of Counsel. There is no constitutional right to counsel in proceedings brought pursuant to 28 U.S.C. § 2254. Financially eligible petitioners may, however, request that counsel be appointed at any time. *See* 18 U.S.C. § 3006A. Pursuant to Federal 2254 Rule 6(a), the Court may, if necessary for effective discovery, appoint counsel for a petitioner who qualifies to have counsel appointed under 18 U.S.C. § 3006A. Pursuant to Federal 2254 Rule 8(c), if an evidentiary hearing is warranted, the Court must appoint counsel to represent a moving party who qualifies to have counsel appointed under 18 U.S.C. § 3006A. This Local Rule is not intended to alter or limit the appointment of counsel available pursuant to Federal 2254 Rule 6(a), Federal 2254 Rule 8(c), or 18 U.S.C. § 3006A.

[Effective September 1, 2009. Amended effective December 1, 2009.]

Comment (June 2008)

All non-death penalty Section 2254 habeas cases in the Erie and Pittsburgh Divisions are assigned to a Magistrate Judge only. (Death penalty Section 2254 habeas cases continue to be assigned to District Judges only.)

LCvR 2255. ACTIONS UNDER 28 U.S.C. § 2255

A. Scope.

1. These rules shall apply in the United States District Court, Western District of Pennsylvania, in all proceedings initiated under 28 U.S.C. § 2255. In addition to these rules, all parties also should consult 28 U.S.C. § 2255 and the applicable provisions of the federal habeas corpus statute, 28 U.S.C. §§ 2241–2266, as amended by the Antiterrorism and Effective Death Penalty Act of 1996 ("AEDPA"), P.L. 104–132, effective April 24, 1996.

2. These Local Rules are intended to supplement, when necessary, the corresponding rules promulgated by the United States Supreme Court that are entitled "Rules Governing Section 2255 Proceedings for the United States District Courts." Those rules are cited herein as "the Federal 2255 Rules," and a specific Federal 2255 Rule is cited as "Federal 2255 Rule ___." All parties should consult the Federal 2255 Rules at the commencement of litigation to ensure compliance with the Federal 2255 Rules, as supplemented by these Local Rules. In filings submitted to this Court, these Local Rules shall be cited as "LCvR 2255. ___."

B. The Motion.

1. *Form.*

a. Form of Motions Required. Motions seeking relief under 28 U.S.C. § 2255 filed with this Court may be submitted on the standard form supplied by this Court. If the movant does not use the standard form, the motion must substantially follow the standard form supplied by this Court or the form attached to the Federal 2255 Rules. Motions that do not utilize the standard forms shall contain all of the information required by the standard forms.

b. Content. In the § 2255 motion, the movant is to state *all* grounds for relief, provide specific facts supporting each argument, and identify the relief requested. An accompanying memorandum of law is not required but will be accepted by the Clerk of Court at the time the motion is filed.

c. Where to Get the Standard Form. The standard form supplied by this Court for 28 U.S.C. § 2255 motions can be obtained free of charge from the following sources: (i) this Court's website (www.

pawd.uscourts.gov); (ii) this Court's Office of the Clerk of Court upon request; (iii) the Federal Public Defender's website (http://paw.fd.org); or (iv) the Federal Public Defender's Office upon request.

d. Requirements Concerning Filing Format. All filings in Section 2255 proceedings must by typed, word-processed or neatly written in ink. All filings must be submitted on paper sized 8½ by 11 inches. No writing or typing shall be made on the back of any filing.

e. Return of Motions that Do Not Substantially Comply With Local Form Rules. If the form or other initial filing submitted by a pro se movant does not substantially comply with Federal 2255 Rule 2, as supplemented by these Local Rules, the Clerk of Court will accept the motion and file it for the sole purpose of preserving the timeliness. If the Court so directs, the filing may be returned to a pro se movant with a copy of the Court's standard form, a statement of reasons for its return, and a directive that the movant resubmit the claims outlined in the original filing on the Court's form. A movant will be given 21 days to return his or her filing on the form supplied by this Court. A party may seek leave of Court for an extension of time to return the form.

f. Certificate Required in Death Penalty Case. A movant challenging the imposition of a sentence of death pursuant to a federal Court judgment shall file with the Clerk of Court a copy of the "Certificate of Death Penalty Case" required by the Third Circuit L.A.R. Misc. 111.2(a). The certificate will include the following information: names, addresses, and telephone numbers of parties and counsel; if set, the proposed date of execution of the sentence; and the emergency nature of the proceedings. Upon docketing, the Clerk of Court will transmit a copy of the certificate, together with a copy of the relevant documents, to the Clerk of the Court of Appeals as required by Third Circuit L.A.R. Misc. 111.2(a).

C. Filing and Serving the Motion.

1. The original Section 2255 motion shall be filed with the Office of the Clerk of Court.

2. Upon receiving the filing, the Clerk of Court will docket it at two places. The Clerk of Court will assign a civil case number for the motion, open that civil case, and enter the motion at that civil case number. At the same time, the Clerk of Court will file and docket the motion at the movant's related criminal case number. All filings related to the motion thereafter will be filed and docketed at the criminal case number only, with the exception of the final judgment order. The final judgment order will be filed and docketed at the civil case number only. If the movant is represented by counsel, Electronic Case Filing (ECF) procedures apply.

3. Following docketing of the filing, the Clerk of Court will deliver a copy of the filing to the United States Attorney by way of a Notice of Electronic Filing (NEF) or by hard copy. Although the United States Attorney has no obligation to do so, he or she may elect to respond to the motion prior to receipt of a District Court order directing that a response be filed.

D. Preliminary Review. These Local Rules provide no supplement to Federal 2255 Rule 4. Please consult that rule regarding preliminary review.

E. The Answer and the Reply.

1. *Order Directing Response.* Upon undertaking preliminary review of the motion for relief under 28 U.S.C. § 2255 (and the United States Attorney's initial response, if any), if the Court finds that there is no basis for dismissal, the Court must enter an order directing the United States Attorney to respond by way of an Answer, motion or other form of response within 45 days. An extension may be granted only for good cause shown.

2. *The Reply.* Although not required, the movant may file a Reply within 30 days of the date the United States Attorney files its Answer or other form of response. If the movant wishes to file a Reply after 30 days have passed, he or she must file a motion requesting leave to do so. An extension may be granted only for good cause shown.

F. Discovery. These Local Rules provide no supplement to Federal 2255 Rule 6. Please consult that rule regarding discovery.

G. Expanding the Record. These Local Rules provide no supplement to Federal 2255 Rule 7. Please consult that rule regarding expanding the record.

H. Evidentiary Hearing. Local Rules of Criminal Procedure [insert Local Rule here when that Rule is finalized] apply at a hearing under Federal 2255 Rule 8(d).

I. Second or Successive Motions. These Local Rules provide no supplement to Federal 2255 Rule 9. Please consult that rule regarding second or successive motions.

J. Powers of a Magistrate Judge. Motions filed under 28 U.S.C. § 2255 shall be assigned to District Judges only.

K. Appeals.

1. Upon entry of a final decision on a motion decided pursuant to 28 U.S.C. § 2255, the Court shall set forth the judgment on a separate document and enter the judgment on the civil docket as required under Fed. R. Civ. P. 58(a)(1).

2. The time for filing a notice of appeal is governed by Fed. R. App. P. 4(a) and such time commences when the Court enters the judgment as described above in subsection (a).

L. Applicability of the Federal Rules of Civil Procedure and the Federal Rules of Criminal Procedure. These Local Rules provide no supplement to Federal 2255 Rule 12. Please consult that rule regarding the applicability of the Federal Rules of Civil Procedure and the Federal Rules of Criminal Procedure.

M. The Appointment of Counsel. There is no constitutional right to counsel in proceedings brought under 28 U.S.C. § 2255. Financially eligible movants may, however, request that counsel be appointed at any time. *See* 18 U.S.C. § 3006A. Pursuant to Federal 2255 Rule 6(a), the Court may, if necessary for effective discovery, appoint counsel for a movant who qualifies to have counsel appointed under 18 U.S.C. § 3006A. Pursuant to Federal 2255 Rule 8(c), if an evidentiary hearing is warranted, the Court must appoint counsel to represent a moving party who qualifies to have counsel appointed under 18 U.S.C. § 3006A. This Local Rule is not intended to alter or limit the appointment of counsel available pursuant to Federal 2255 Rule 6(a), Federal 2255 Rule 8(c), or 18 U.S.C. § 3006A.

[Effective September 1, 2009. Amended effective December 1, 2009.]

LOCAL CRIMINAL RULES OF COURT

LCrR 1. CITATION AND APPLICABILITY TO PRO SE DEFENDANTS

These rules may be cited as "LCrR." Where the defendant is proceeding pro se, references in these rules to defense counsel shall be taken to include the pro se defendant.

[Effective September 1, 2009.]

LCrR 5. INITIAL APPEARANCE BEFORE MAGISTRATE JUDGE

A. Opportunity to Consult With Counsel. A defendant shall be given an opportunity to consult with counsel at his or her Initial Appearance and before an initial interview with Pretrial Service Officers. The Federal Public Defender, as directed by the Court, will provide advice of rights to defendants before their interview with Pretrial Services.

B. Notification of Counsel. It is the responsibility of the Magistrate Judge assigned to criminal duty to notify the Federal Public Defender, or the defendant's retained counsel if known, before the Initial Appearance.

C. Eligibility for Appointed Counsel. When a defendant requests appointment of counsel, and the Court determines that the defendant is eligible for appointed counsel, the Court will appoint counsel under the Criminal Justice Act at the time of the Initial Appearance.

D. Entry of Appearance. In all criminal cases involving privately retained counsel, a notice of appearance of counsel shall be filed at or before the first appearance of counsel. *See also* LCvR 83.2.C.1.

E. Withdrawal of Appearance. In any criminal proceeding, no attorney whose appearance has been entered shall withdraw his or her appearance except upon filing a written petition stating reasons for withdrawal, and only with leave of Court and upon reasonable notice to the client. *See also* LCvR 83.2.C.4.

[Effective September 1, 2009.]

LCrR 10. ARRAIGNMENTS

Arraignments may be conducted by the Magistrate Judge in cases triable by the Magistrate Judge and in other cases to the extent of taking a not guilty plea or noting a defendant's intention to plead guilty or nolo contendere and ordering a presentence report in appropriate cases. Upon the request of the defendant, the government shall provide available Fed. R. Crim. P. 16 material to the defendant at the time of the arraignment, and the Fed. R. Crim. P. 16 receipt shall be filed with the Court. Upon written request by the defendant, the Magistrate Judge may set a date for the filing of pretrial motions up to 45 days from the date of the arraignment, and order that the period of the extension shall be excluded from the time within which the trial of the case shall commence under the Speedy Trial Act, as necessary to provide the defendant with adequate time for investigation and preparation of motions. Any other motions for extension of time shall be filed with the District Judge.

[Effective September 1, 2009.]

Comment (February 2013)

Forms for Motions to Extend Time to File Pretrial Motions will be available to counsel at the time of the arraignment and may be approved by Order of the Magistrate Judge. The 45 day period will be excluded from the Speedy Trial Act 18 U.S.C. § 3161, et seq.

LCrR 12. PRETRIAL MOTIONS

A. Timing. Motions under Fed. R. Crim. P.12 and 41 shall be made within fourteen days after arraignment, unless the court extends the time at arraignment, or upon written application made within the said fourteen day period. The court, in its discretion, may, however, for good cause shown, permit a motion to be made and heard at a later date.

B. Requirements. All such motions shall contain a short and plain description of the requested relief and incorporate or be accompanied by a memorandum or brief setting forth the reasons and legal support for the granting of the requested relief.

C. Response. Any party opposing a motion may file and serve a response within fourteen days after service of the motion, unless the time period is otherwise extended by the Court. Every response shall incorporate or be accompanied by a memorandum or brief setting forth the reasons and legal support for the respondent's position.

D. Reply Memorandum. The movant may file and serve a reply memorandum within fourteen days after service of the response, unless the time period is otherwise extended by the Court.

E. Motion to Extend Time. Any motion to extend the time limits set forth above shall set forth the grounds upon which it is made and whether the continuance sought shall constitute, in whole or in part, excludable time as defined by 18 U.S.C. § 3161(h). Said motion to extend time shall be accompanied by a proposed form of Order that, if adopted, will state fully and with particularity the reasons for granting the motion as well as the proposed findings of the Court as to excludable time. Extensions of the time limits set forth above shall be excludable to the extent authorized by 18 U.S.C. § 3161(h). Extensions shall be granted by the Court where warranted by the ends of justice in accordance with the list of factors set forth in § 3161(h)(7)(B). The Court may consider good faith scheduling conflicts, additional time needed for reasonable preparation, the interests of the defendant and the government in maintaining continuity of counsel, and other unavoidable problems, such as emergencies and illness. This list is illustrative and not exclusive.

[Effective September 1, 2009. Amended effective December 1, 2009; February 1, 2013.]

LCrR 16. DISCOVERY AND INSPECTION

A. Compliance With Fed. R. Crim. P. 16. The parties shall comply with Fed. R. Crim. P. 16, including the reciprocal discovery provisions of Fed. R. Crim. P. 16(b).

B. Timing. Upon a defendant's request, the government shall make available the Rule 16 material at the time of the arraignment. If discovery is not requested by the defendant at the time of the arraignment, the government shall disclose such material within seven (7) days of a defendant's request. The government shall file a receipt with the Court which sets forth the general categories of information subject to disclosure under Rule 16, as well as any exculpatory evidence, and the items provided under each category.

C. Exculpatory Evidence. At the time of arraignment, and subject to a continuing duty of disclosure thereafter, the government shall notify the defendant of the existence of exculpatory evidence, and permit its inspection and copying by the defendant.

D. Voluntary Disclosure. Nothing in this rule shall be construed to prevent the government from voluntarily disclosing material to the defendant at an earlier time than that required by Fed. R. Crim. P. 16, Fed. R. Crim. P. 26.2 and 18 U.S.C. § 3500.

E. Obligation to Confer. Counsel shall confer and attempt to resolve issues regarding additional discovery before a motion to produce is filed with the Court.

F. Status Conference. The Court shall hold a status conference with counsel approximately 30 days after Arraignment, on a date certain to be set by the Court. Counsel must be prepared to discuss case scheduling matters, as well as the progress of discovery to date. The attendance of the defendant shall be at the discretion of the Court.

[Effective September 1, 2009. Amended effective December 1, 2009; February 1, 2013.]

LCrR 23. LAW ENFORCEMENT EVIDENCE

In all cases where money, firearms, narcotics, controlled substances or any matter of contraband is introduced into evidence, such evidence shall be maintained for safekeeping by law enforcement during all times when court is not in session, and at the conclusion of the case. The law enforcement agent will be responsible for its custody if the evidence is required for any purpose thereafter. *See also* LCvR 5.1.J.

[Effective September 1, 2009.]

LCrR 24.1   JURY LIST

Members of the bar of this court shall be permitted to have a copy of each jury list on condition that a receipt be signed with the Clerk of Court at the date of delivery thereof which shall contain as the substance the following certification:

> "I hereby certify that I and/or my firm or associates have litigation pending and in connection therewith, I will require a list of jurors. I further acknowledge to have received a copy of said list of jurors from the Clerk of Court and hereby agree that I will not, nor will I permit any person or agency, to call or contact any juror identified on said list at his or her home or any other place, nor will I call or contact any immediate member of said juror's family, which includes his or her spouse, children, mother, father, brother, or sister, in an effort to determine the background of any member of said jury panel for acceptance or rejection of said juror.
>
> /s/ _____
>
> Date: _____ "

[Effective September 1, 2009.]

LCrR 24.2   EXAMINATION OF JURORS BEFORE TRIAL

Jury selection in a criminal case shall be governed by Fed. R. Crim. P. 23 and 24 and by such procedures established by the trial judge. In its discretion, the Court may require potential jurors to complete a questionnaire before the formal voir dire process commences.

A. Examination of Jurors Before Trial. During the examination of jurors before trial, the Judge or a representative of the Clerk of Court conducting such examination, shall state the following to the jurors collectively:

1. The name of each of the defendants and the names of the attorneys for the parties; and

2. The nature of the case and the offenses charged.

B. Required Questions. The examination of jurors shall contain the following questions, or questions substantially similar thereto:

1. Do you know any of the defendants?

2. Do you know any of the attorneys in the case? Have they or their firms ever represented you or any members of your immediate family?

3. Do you know anything about this case?

4. (If appropriate) Are you or any member of your immediate family, employees, former employees or stockholders in any of the corporations or businesses involved in this case? The names of corporations and businesses involved in this case are:

5. Are you or any member of your immediate family employed by the federal government (with the exception of military service)? What do they do?

6. Are you or any member of your immediate family employed by any law enforcement agency?

C. **Questions to Individual Jurors.** The following questions, where appropriate, shall, inter alia, be put to each juror individually:

1. What is your present occupation?

2. Who is your employer?

3. If you are retired, who was your last employer and what was your occupation?

4. Are you married? If so, what is your spouse's occupation and who is your spouse's employer?

5. Do you have any children? Do any of them work in the Western District of Pennsylvania? For whom do they work and what do they do?

6. Have you ever been a witness or defendant in a criminal case?

7. Have you ever been the victim of a crime?

8. Any other question which in the judgment of the Court shall be deemed proper.

[Effective September 1, 2009.]

LCrR 24.3 COMMUNICATION WITH A TRIAL JUROR

A. **During Trial.** During the trial, no party, attorney for a party, or person acting on behalf of a party or attorney, shall communicate directly or indirectly with any of the following: (1) a juror, (2) an excused juror, (3) an alternate juror or (4) a family member or person living within the same household as a juror, excused juror or alternate juror.

B. **After Trial.** After a verdict is rendered or a mistrial is declared, the Court shall inform the jury that no juror is required to speak to anyone, but that a juror may do so if the juror wishes.

[Effective September 1, 2009.]

LCrR 24.4 JUROR NOTE TAKING

Jurors may be permitted to take notes in the discretion of the Court. If jurors are permitted to take notes, the Court will provide jurors with the necessary materials, and shall retain custody of the notes when Court is not in session or the jury is not deliberating. After the jury is discharged by the Court, the notes shall be destroyed.

[Effective September 1, 2009.]

LCrR 28. INTERPRETERS

A court certified interpreter will be provided by the Court and present for all proceedings involving defendants who are not proficient in English.

[Effective September 1, 2009.]

LCrR 32. PROCEDURE FOR GUIDELINE SENTENCING

The following procedures hereby are established to govern sentencing proceedings in this Court, in addition to the requirements of Fed. R. Crim. P. 32; the Sentencing Reform Act of 1984, 18 U.S.C. § 3551 *et seq.*; and the advisory United States Sentencing Guidelines ("U.S.S.G."), as promulgated under that Act and by the Sentencing Commission Act, 28 U.S.C. § 991 *et seq.*

A. **Timing of Sentencing.** Unless the Court orders otherwise, sentencing proceedings shall be scheduled no earlier than 14 weeks following the entry of a plea of guilty or nolo contendere, or the entry of a verdict of guilty.

B. **Presentence Investigation and Report.** Counsel is directed to the requirements of Fed. R. Crim. P. 32(c) and Fed. R. Crim. P. 32(d) regarding Presentence Investigations and Reports.

C. **Presentence Procedures.** No later than 7 weeks prior to the date set for sentencing, the United States Probation Office ("USPO") shall disclose the tentative Presentence Investigation Report ("PSR") to only the defendant, the defendant's attorney, and the attorney for the government. *See* Fed. R. Crim. P. 32(e)(2) and § 6A1.2(a) of the U.S.S.G.

1. *Confidentiality.* The PSR is a confidential court document. No copies or dissemination of the PSR shall be made without the express permission or Order of this Court, except that, pursuant to Third Circuit Local Appellate Rule 30.3(c), copies may be made for the United States Court of Appeals in any appeal from the sentence. The unauthorized copying

or disclosure of the PSR may be treated as a contempt of court and be punished accordingly.

2. *Administrative Resolution.* If a party disputes facts or factors material to sentencing contained in the PSR, or seeks the inclusion of additional facts or factors material to sentencing, that party shall have the obligation to pursue the administrative resolution of that matter through informal presentence conferences with opposing counsel and the USPO.

    a. The party seeking administrative resolution of such facts and factors shall do so within 2 weeks from the disclosure of the tentative PSR.

    b. No later than 2 weeks after the disclosure of the tentative PSR, following any good faith efforts to resolve disputed, or include additional, material facts or factors described above, the USPO shall notify the attorneys for the government and the defendant of those matters that have, or have not, been administratively resolved.

3. *Disclosure of PSR to Court.* Following the 2 week time period for administrative resolution, and no later than 5 weeks before sentencing, pursuant to Fed. R. Crim. P. 32(g), the USPO shall disclose the PSR, as may be amended, to the Court, the defendant, the attorney for the defendant, and the attorney for the government.

4. *Objections; Positions of the Parties.* No later than 4 weeks before sentencing, the parties each shall file with the court a pleading entitled "Position of [Defendant or Government, as appropriate] With Respect to Sentencing Factors," pursuant to Fed. R. Crim. P. 32(f) and § 6A1.2(b) of the U.S.S.G. This pleading shall set forth any objections to the PSR and any anticipated grounds for: (a) departure from the advisory guideline sentencing range; or, (b) a sentence outside of the advisory guideline sentencing range, pursuant to the provisions of 18 U.S.C. § 3553(a). The party's Position With Respect to Sentencing shall be accompanied by a written statement certifying that filing counsel has conferred with opposing counsel and with the USPO in a good faith effort to resolve any disputed matters.

5. *Responses to Objections and Positions.* A party may file a response to the opposing party's Position With Respect to Sentencing Factors no later than 3 weeks prior to the sentencing.

6. *Action on Objections; Addendum.* After receiving counsel's objections and any responses thereto, the USPO shall conduct such further investigation as appropriate. The USPO may meet or otherwise confer with counsel to discuss unresolved factual or legal issues.

    a. No later than 2 weeks before sentencing, the USPO shall serve an addendum which shall set forth any unresolved objections to the PSR, the grounds for those objections, the responses thereto, and the USPO's comments thereon.

    b. The USPO shall certify that the PSR, together with any revision thereof and any addendum thereto, have been disclosed to the defendant and all counsel of record, and that the addendum fairly sets forth any remaining objections and responses.

7. *Court's Tentative Findings and Rulings.* Prior to the sentencing hearing, the Court shall notify the parties and the USPO of the Court's tentative findings and rulings, to the extent practicable, concerning disputed facts or factors. Reasonable opportunity shall be provided to the parties, prior to the imposition of sentence, for the submission of oral or written objections to the Court's tentative findings and rulings.

8. *Supplemental Information and Memoranda.* No later than 1 week before sentencing, a party may file supplemental information or a memorandum with respect to sentencing of the defendant, and shall serve the same upon the USPO. If counsel for the defendant intends to submit letters to the Court for consideration at sentencing, said letters should be electronically filed at least seven calendar days before sentencing. Opposing counsel may file a response to any supplemental information or memorandum no later than three days before sentencing.

9. *Additional Information and Memoranda.* For good cause shown, the Court may allow additional information and memoranda, and the responses thereto, to be raised at any time prior to the imposition of sentence.

10. *Introducing Evidence.* When any fact or factor material to the sentencing determination is reasonably in dispute, the parties shall be given an adequate opportunity to introduce evidence and to present information to the Court regarding that fact or factor, in accordance with § 6A1.3(a) of the U.S.S.G.

11. *Court Determinations.* Except with respect to any objection made pursuant to Fed. R. Crim. P. 32(f) and LCrR 32.C.5, above, the Court may accept as accurate any undisputed portion of the PSR as a finding of fact. However, with respect to disputed portions of the PSR, the Court shall make determinations pursuant to Fed. R. Crim. P. 32(i)(3) and § 6A1.3 of the U.S.S.G.

D. Judicial Modifications. For good cause shown, the time limits set forth in LCrR 32 may be modified by the Court.

E. Pre–Plea Presentence Investigations and Reports. Under appropriate circumstances, and with the written consent of the defendant pursuant to Fed. R. Crim. P. 32(e)(1), the Court may order the USPO to conduct a Presentence Investigation and prepare a PSR for a defendant prior to the entry of a plea of guilty or nolo contendere. The scope of any pre-plea PSR shall be determined by the Court.

[Effective September 1, 2009. Amended effective February 1, 2013.]

LCrR 41. INSPECTION AND COPYING OF SEIZED PROPERTY

Under appropriate circumstances, upon the filing of a motion and a showing of good cause by the party seeking relief, the Court may enter an order which permits such party (1) to have reasonable access to seized property, including documents, for inspection; or (2) to obtain copies of seized documents or property other than contraband. The moving party shall bear the cost of copying, unless otherwise ordered by the Court for good cause shown. In fashioning an order for relief under this Rule, the Court shall consider, among other things, the burden of compliance with the order upon the government, as well as the needs of the party seeking relief. Nothing herein is intended to limit any remedies which may be available under Fed. R. Crim. P. 41(g).

[Effective September 1, 2009.]

LCrR 46. TYPES OF BAIL IN CRIMINAL CASES

Provided that a bond in the form available at the office of the Clerk of Court is executed, any of the following may be accepted as security:

A. United States currency, or a certificate of deposit of a federally insured bank or savings and loan association, or federal, state or local government securities or bonds, or corporate securities or bonds of companies listed on the New York Stock Exchange, or a combination thereof, in the face amount of the bail, provided that the instruments are payable on demand, and provided further that, if the instruments are payable to one or more persons, the Clerk of Court or the appropriate judicial officer is satisfied that the endorsements of all owners have been secured as obligers.

B. Real property in the Commonwealth of Pennsylvania, including realty in which the defendant has an interest, in which the market value of the property after subtracting the current value of all mortgages, liens and judgments, equals the amount of the bond. *See also* Fed. R. Crim. P. 46(e).

The Clerk of Court shall maintain in its office and on its official website the procedures and requirements for posting of property bonds.

C. A surety company or corporation authorized by the Secretary of Treasury of the United States to act as surety on official bonds under the Act of August 13, 1894 (28 Stat. 279, as amended, U.S.C. Title 6, 1–13).

D. Such other property as the court deems sufficient pursuant to the Bail Reform Act of 1984, 18 U.S.C. § 3142(c)(2)(K).

[Effective September 1, 2009.]

LCrR 49. ELECTRONIC CASE FILING; SEALING OF DOCUMENTS

A. Electronic Case Filing Policies and Procedures. Counsel must comply with the Electronic Case Filing Policies and Procedures promulgated by the Court which govern all criminal cases and matters. All documents must comply with the privacy protection provisions set forth in Fed. R. Crim. P. 49.1 and LCvR 5.2.D.

B. Filing by Electronic Means. Documents may be filed, signed and verified by electronic means to the extent and in the manner authorized by the Court's Standing Order regarding Electronic Case Filing Policies and Procedures and the ECF User Manual. A document filed by electronic means in compliance with this Local Rule constitutes a written document for the purposes of applying these Local Rules, the Federal Rules of Civil Procedure and the Federal Rules of Criminal Procedure. *See also* LCvR 5.5.

C. Service by Electronic Means. Documents may be served through the Court's transmission facilities by electronic means to the extent and in the manner authorized by the Standing Order regarding Electronic Case Filing Policies and Procedures and the ECF User Manual. Transmission of the Notice of Electronic Filing constitutes service of the filed document upon each party in the case who is registered as a Filing User. Any other party or parties shall be served documents according to these Local Rules, the Federal Rules of Civil Procedure and the Federal Rules of Criminal Procedure. *See also* LCvR 5.6.

D. Filing Under Seal. The following documents shall be accepted by the Clerk for filing under seal without the necessity of a separate sealing order: (1) Motions setting forth the substantial assistance of a defendant in the investigation or prosecution of another person pursuant to U.S.S.G. § 5K1.1 or Fed. R. Crim. P. 35; (2) Motions for writs to produce incarcerated witnesses for testimony; (3) Motions for subpoenas for witnesses; (4) Motions by counsel seeking authorization for the expenditure of funds under the Criminal Justice Act, or seeking reimbursement for expenses incurred or attorney's fees. Such documents should be presented to the Clerk in hard copy for scanning and docketing under seal.

E. Provision of Sealed Documents to Opposing Party. Counsel of record may exchange copies of sealed documents, without obtaining leave of court, if the document is provided in an ongoing criminal case.

[Effective September 1, 2009.]

LCrR 57. ASSIGNMENT OF CASES

A. Criminal Action Categories. All criminal cases in this district shall be divided into the following categories:

1. Narcotics and Other Controlled Substances.

1a. Narcotics and Other Controlled Substances, 3 or more Defendants.

2. Fraud and Property Offenses.

2a. Fraud and Property Offenses, 3 or more Defendants.

3. Crimes of Violence.

4. Sex Offenses.

5. Firearms and Explosives.

6. Immigration.

7. All Others.

See also LCvR 40.B.

B. Assignment of Criminal Cases to District Judges. All criminal cases shall be assigned by the Clerk of Court at the earlier of (1) the time of filing of the indictment or information; (2) when any appeal is taken from a Magistrate Judge's decision on bail; (3) upon the filing of a motion for return of seized property; (4) upon the filing of a motion to quash a subpoena; (5) upon the filing of a motion to dismiss the complaint; (6) upon the filing of any motions of a similar nature that a Magistrate Judge concludes must be handled by a District Judge; or, (7) at the time of filing any motion in a case at the magisterial stage for a competency determination.

C. Related Actions. At the time of filing any criminal action or entry of appearance or any initial pleading or motion by defense counsel, as the case may be, counsel shall indicate on an appropriate form whether the action is related to any other pending or previously terminated actions in this Court. For the purpose of completing the form, all criminal actions arising out of the same criminal transaction or series of transactions are deemed related.

[Effective September 1, 2009.]

LCrR 58. PROCEDURES FOR MISDEMEANORS AND OTHER PETTY OFFENSES

See LCvR 72.

[Effective September 1, 2009.]

LCrR 83. FREE PRESS—FAIR TRIAL PROVISIONS

A. Release of Information in Criminal Litigation. A lawyer or law firm shall not release or authorize the release of information or opinion that a reasonable person would expect to be disseminated by means of public communication, in connection with pending or imminent criminal litigation with which he or she or the firm is associated, if there is a substantial likelihood that such release would materially prejudice ongoing criminal proceedings.

B. Release Beyond Public Record. With respect to a pending investigation of any criminal matter, a lawyer participating in or associated with the investigation shall refrain from making any extrajudicial statement that a reasonable person would expect to be disseminated by means of public communication, that goes beyond the public record, if there is a substantial likelihood that such statement would materially prejudice such pending investigation.

C. Subjects Likely to Be Materially Prejudicial. From the time of arrest, issuance of an arrest warrant, or the filing of a complaint, information, or indictment in any criminal matter until the commencement of trial or disposition without trial, extrajudicial statements by a lawyer or law firm associated with the prosecution or defense that a reasonable person would expect to be disseminated by means of public communication relating to the following subjects are substantially likely to be considered materially prejudicial to ongoing criminal proceedings:

1. the prior criminal record (including arrests, indictments, or other charges of crime), or the character or reputation of the accused, except that the lawyer or law firm may make a factual statement of the accused's name, age, residence, occupation, and family status, and if the accused has not been apprehended, a lawyer associated with the prosecution may release any information necessary to aid in his or her apprehension or to warn the public of any dangers he or she may present;

2. the existence or contents of any confession, admission, or statement given by the accused, or the refusal or failure of the accused to make any statement;

3. the performance of any examinations or tests or the accused's refusal or failure to submit to an examination or test;

4. the identity, testimony or credibility of prospective witnesses, except that the lawyer or law firm may announce the identity of the victim if the announcement is not otherwise prohibited by law;

5. the possibility of a plea of guilty to the offense charged or a lesser offense; or

6. any opinion as to the accused's guilt or innocence or as to the merits of the case or the evidence in the case, except that counsel may announce without further comment that the accused asserts innocence or denies the charges made against him or her.

Unless otherwise prohibited by law, the foregoing shall not be construed to preclude the lawyer or law firm during this period, in the proper discharge of his or her or its official or professional obligations, from announcing the fact, time and place of arrest, the identity of the investigating and arresting officer or agency, and the length of the investigation; from disclosing the nature, substance, or text of the charge, including a brief description of the offense charged; from quoting or referring without comment to public records of the Court in the case; from announcing the scheduling or result of any stage in the judicial process; from requesting assistance in obtaining evidence; or from announcing without further comment that the accused asserts innocence or denies the charges made against him or her.

[Effective September 1, 2009.]

LOCAL BANKRUPTCY APPELLATE RULES OF COURT

LBR 8007–2. APPEAL TO THE DISTRICT COURT FROM THE BANKRUPTCY COURT

A. Appeals to the United States District Court from the United States Bankruptcy Court for the Western District of Pennsylvania pursuant to 28 U.S.C. § 158, shall be taken in the manner prescribed in Part VIII of the Federal Rules of Bankruptcy Procedure (hereinafter FRBP), Rule 8001, *et seq.*

B. Where, after a notice of appeal to the United States District Court has been filed in the Bankruptcy Court, the appellant fails to designate the contents of the record on appeal or fails to file a statement of issues on appeal within the time required by FRBP 8006, or fails to provide, when appropriate, evidence that a transcript has been ordered and that payment therefor has been arranged, or fails to take any other action to enable the bankruptcy clerk to assemble and transmit the record:

1. the bankruptcy clerk shall provide fourteen (14) days notice to the appellant and appellee of an intention to transmit a partial record consistent with Subsection B.2. of this rule;

2. after the 14 day notice period required by subsection B.1. of this rule has expired, the clerk of the bankruptcy court shall thereafter promptly forward to the clerk of the United States District Court a partial record consisting of a copy of the order or judgment appealed from, any opinion, findings of fact, and conclusions of law by the court, the notice of appeal, a copy of the docket entries, any documents filed as part of the appeal, and any copies of the record which have been designated by the parties pursuant to FRBP 8006; the record as transmitted shall be deemed to be the complete record for purposes of the appeal; and

3. the district court may dismiss said appeal for failure to comply with FRBP 8006 upon its own motion, or upon motion filed in the district court by any party in interest or the United States trustee.

C. Notwithstanding any counter designation of the record or statement of issues filed by the appellee, if the appellee fails to provide, where appropriate, evidence that a transcript has been ordered and that payment therefore has been arranged, or the appellee fails to take any other action to enable the bankruptcy clerk to assemble and transmit the record pursuant to FRBP 8006, the bankruptcy clerk shall transmit the copies of the record designated by the parties and this shall be deemed to be the complete record on appeal.

[Effective September 1, 2009. Amended effective December 1, 2009.]

LBR 9015–1. JURY TRIAL IN BANKRUPTCY COURT

A. In accordance with 28 U.S.C. § 157(e), the bankruptcy judges of this Court are specially designated to conduct jury trials where the right to a jury applies. This jurisdiction is subject to the express consent of all parties.

B. The jurors will be drawn from the same qualified jury wheels, consisting of the same counties, that are used in this Court.

[Effective September 1, 2009.]

LOCAL ADMIRALTY RULES

RULE (a). AUTHORITY AND SCOPE

LAR(a)(1) Authority. The local admiralty rules for the United States District Court for the Western District of Pennsylvania are promulgated as authorized by and subject to the limitations of Federal Rule of Civil Procedure 83.

LAR(a)(2) Scope.

A. General. These local admiralty rules apply only to civil actions that are governed by the Supplemental Rules for Certain Admiralty or Maritime Claims and Asset Forfeiture Actions (Supplemental Rule or Rules). All other local civil rules are applicable in these cases; except as may otherwise be provided herein and further, to the extent that another local civil rule is inconsistent with the applicable local admiralty rules, the local admiralty rules shall govern.

B. Settlement Procedure for Seaman Suits. The procedure for the compromise, settlement, discontinuance or dismissal of seaman suits shall be as set forth in LCvR 17.2.

LAR(a)(3) Citation. The local admiralty rules may be cited by the letters "LAR" and the lower case letters and numbers in parentheses that appear at the beginning of each section. The lower case letter is intended to associate the local admiralty rule with the Supplemental Rule that bears the same capital letter.

LAR(a)(4) Officers of Court. As used in the local admiralty rules, "judicial officer" means a United States district judge or a United States magistrate judge; "clerk of court" means the clerk of the district court and includes deputy clerks of court; and "marshal" means the United States marshal and includes deputy marshals.

[Effective September 1, 2009.]

RULE (b). MARITIME ATTACHMENT AND GARNISHMENT

LAR(b)(1) Affidavit that Defendant Is Not Found Within the District. The affidavit required by Supplemental Rule B(1)(b) to accompany the complaint shall list the efforts made by and on behalf of plaintiff to find and serve the defendant within the district.

[Effective September 1, 2009.]

RULE (c). ACTIONS IN REM: SPECIAL PROVISIONS

LAR(c)(1) Intangible Property. The summons issued pursuant to Supplemental Rule C(3) shall direct the person having control of intangible property to show cause no later than 14 days after service why the intangible property should not be delivered to the court to abide the judgment. A judicial officer for good cause shown may lengthen or shorten the time. Service of the summons has the effect of an arrest of the intangible property and brings it within the control of the court. The person who is served may deliver or pay over to the marshal the intangible property proceeded against to the extent sufficient to satisfy the plaintiff's claim. If such delivery or payment is made, the person served is excused from the duty to show cause. The claimant of the property may show cause as provided in Supplemental rule C(6) why the property should not be delivered to the court.

LAR(c)(2) Publication of Notice of Action and Arrest. The notice required by Supplemental Rule C(4) shall be published once in a newspaper named in LAR(g)(3), and plaintiff's attorney shall file a copy of the notice as it was published with the clerk. The notice shall contain:

A. The court, title, and number of the action;

B. The date of the arrest;

C. An identification of the property arrested;

D. The name, address, and telephone number of the attorney for plaintiff;

E. A statement that the claim of the person who is entitled to possession or who claims an interest pursuant to Supplemental Rule C(6) must be filed with the clerk and served on the attorney for plaintiff within 14 days after publication;

F. A statement that an answer to the complaint must be filed and served within 30 days after publication, and that otherwise, default may be entered and condemnation ordered;

G. A statement that applications for intervention under Federal Rule 24 by person claiming maritime liens or other interests shall be filed within the time fixed by the court; and

H. The name, address, and telephone number of the marshal.

LAR(c)(3) Default in Action In Rem.

A. *Notice Required.* A party seeking a default judgment in an action in rem must satisfy the judge that due notice of the action and arrest of the property has been given (1) by publication as required by LAR (c)(2), (2) by service upon the master or other person having custody of the property, and (3) by service under Federal Rule 5(b) upon every other person who has not appeared in the action and is known to have an interest in the property.

B. *Persons with Recorded Interests.*

1. If the defendant property is a vessel documented under the laws of the United States, the party seeking the default must attempt to notify all persons named in the United States Coast Guard certificate of ownership.

2. If the defendant property is a vessel numbered as provided in the Federal Boat Safety Act, plaintiff must attempt to notify the persons named in the records of the issuing authority.

3. If the defendant property is of such character that there exists a governmental registry of recorded property interests and/or security interests in the property, the plaintiff must attempt to notify all persons named in the records of each such registry.

LAR(c)(4) Entry of Default and Default Judgment. After the time for filing an answer has expired, the plaintiff may move for entry of default under Federal Rule 55(a). Default will be entered upon showing that:

A. Notice has been given as required by LAR(c)(3)(a) and,

B. Notice has been attempted as required by LAR(c)(3)(b), where appropriate, and

C. The time for answer has expired, and

D. No one has appeared to claim the property.

The plaintiff may move for judgment under Federal Rule 55(b) at any time after default has been entered.

LAR(c)(5) Undertakings in Lieu of Arrest. If, before or after commencement of suit, plaintiff accepts any written undertaking to respond on behalf of the vessel or other property sued in return for his/her forgoing the arrest or stipulating to the release of such vessel or other property, the undertaking shall become a defendant in place of the vessel or other property sued and be deemed referred to under the name of the vessel or other property in any pleading, order or judgment in any action referred to in the undertaking.

[Effective September 1, 2009; amended effective December 1, 2009.]

RULE (d). POSSESSORY, PETITORY AND PARTITION ACTIONS

LAR(d)(1) Return Date. In a possessory action under Supplemental Rule D, a judicial officer may order that the claim and answer be filed on a date earlier than 21 days after arrest. The order may also set a date for expedited hearing of the action.

[Effective September 1, 2009; amended effective December 1, 2009.]

RULE (e). ACTIONS IN REM AND QUASI IN REM: GENERAL PROVISIONS

LAR(e)(1) Itemized Demand for Judgment. The demand for judgment in every complaint filed under Supplemental Rule B or C shall allege the dollar amount of the debt or damages for which the action was commenced. The demand for judgment shall also allege the nature of other items of damage. The amount of the special bond posted under Supplemental Rule E(5)(a) may be based upon these allegations.

LAR(e)(2) Verification of Pleadings. Every complaint filed in Supplemental Rule B, C, and D actions shall be verified upon oath or solemn affirmation, or in the form provided by 28 U.S.C. § 1746, by a party or by an authorized officer of a corporate party. If no party or authorized corporate officer is present within the district, verification of a complaint may be made by an agent, attorney in fact, or attorney of record, who shall state the sources of the knowledge, information and belief contained in the complaint; declare that the document verified is true to the best of that knowledge, information, and belief; state why verification is not made by the party or an authorized corporate officer; and state that the affiant is authorized so to verify. A verification not made by a party or authorized corporate officer will be deemed to have been made by the party as if verified personally. If the verification was not made by a party or authorized corporate officer, any interested party may move, with or without requesting a stay, for the personal oath of a party or an authorized corporate officer, which shall be procured by commission or as otherwise ordered.

LAR(e)(3) Review by Judicial Officer. Unless otherwise required by the judicial officer, the review of complaints and papers called for by Supplemental Rules B(1) and C(3) does not require the affiant party or attorney to be present. The applicant for review shall include a form of order to the clerk which, upon signature by the judicial officer, will direct the arrest, attachment or garnishment sought by the applicant. In exigent circumstances, the certification of the plaintiff or his/her attorney under Supplemental Rules B and C shall consist of an affidavit.

LAR(e)(4) Instructions to the Marshal. The party who requests a warrant of arrest or process of attachment or garnishment shall provide instructions to the marshal.

LAR(e)(5) Property in Possession of United States Officer. When the property to be attached or arrested is in the custody of an employee or officer of the United States, the marshal will deliver a copy of the complaint and warrant of arrest or summons and process of attachment or garnishment to that officer or employee if present, and otherwise to the custodian of the property. The marshal will instruct the officer or employee or custodian to retain custody of the property until ordered to do otherwise by a judicial officer.

LAR(e)(6) Security for Costs. In an action under the Supplemental Rules, a party may move upon notice to all parties for an order to compel an adverse party to post security for costs with the clerk pursuant to Supplemental Rule E(2)(b). Unless otherwise ordered, the amount of security shall be $250. The party so ordered shall post the security within seven days after the order is entered. A party who fails to post security when due may not participate further in the proceedings. A party may move for an order increasing the amount of security for costs.

LAR(e)(7) Adversary Hearing. The adversary hearing following arrest or attachment or garnishment that is called for in Supplemental Rule E(4)(f) shall be conducted by a judicial officer within three court days, unless otherwise ordered.

LAR(e)(8) Appraisal. An order for appraisal of property so that security may be given or altered will be entered by the clerk at the request of any interested party. If the parties do not agree in writing upon an appraiser, a judicial officer will appoint the appraiser. The appraiser shall be sworn to the faithful and impartial discharge of the appraiser's duties before any federal or state officer authorized by law to administer oaths. The appraiser shall give one day's notice of the time and place of making the appraisal to counsel of record. The appraiser shall promptly file the appraisal with the clerk and serve it upon counsel of record. The appraiser's fee normally will be paid by the moving party, but it is a taxable cost of the action.

LAR(e)(9) Security Deposit for Seizure of Vessels. The first party who seeks arrest or attachment of a vessel or property aboard a vessel shall deposit with the marshal the sum estimated by the marshal to be sufficient to cover the expenses of the marshal including, but not limited to, dockage, keepers, maintenance and insurance for at least 30 days. The marshal is not required to execute process until the deposit is made. That party shall advance additional sums from time to time as requested to cover the marshal's estimated expenses until the property is released or disposed of as provided in Supplemental Rule E. If the first party fails to deposit requested funds, the marshal may seek relief from the district court including, but not limited to, the right to request the release of the property from arrest or attachment with a reservation of the right to proceed against the first party for any balance due.

LAR(e)(10) Intervenors' Claims.

A. *Presentation of Claim.* When a vessel or other property has been arrested, attached, or garnished, and is in the hands of the marshal or custodian substituted therefor, anyone having a claim against the vessel or property is required to present the claim by filing an intervening complaint, and not by filing an original complaint, unless otherwise ordered by a judicial officer. Upon the satisfaction of the requirements of Federal Rule 24, the clerk shall forthwith deliver a conformed copy of the complaint to the marshal, who shall deliver the copy to the vessel or custodian of the property. Intervenors shall thereafter be subject to the rights and obligations of parties, and the vessel or property shall stand arrested, attached, or garnished by the intervenor. An intervenor shall not be required to advance a security deposit to the marshal for seizure of a vessel as required by LAR(e)(9).

B. *Sharing Marshal's Fees and Expenses.* In the absence of an order to the contrary after hearing, no intervenor shall be required to make contribution to the plaintiff for any of the costs enumerated in LAR (e)(9).

LAR(e)(11) Custody of Property.

A. *Safekeeping of Property.* When a vessel or other property is brought into the marshal's custody by arrest or attachment, the marshal shall arrange for adequate safekeeping, which may include the placing of keepers on or near the vessel. A substitute custodian in place of the marshal may be appointed by order of the court.

B. *Insurance.* The marshal may order insurance to protect the marshal, his/her deputies, keepers, and substitute custodians, from liabilities assumed in arresting and holding the vessel, cargo, or other property, and in performing whatever services may be undertaken to protect the vessel, cargo, or other property, and to maintain the court's custody. The party who applies for arrest or attachment of the vessel, cargo, or other property shall reimburse the marshal for premiums paid for the insurance and shall be an added insured on the policy. The party who applies for removal of the vessel, cargo, or other property to another location, for designation of a substitute custodian, or for other relief that will require an additional premium, shall reimburse the marshal therefor. The premiums charged for the liability insurance are taxable as administrative costs while the vessel, cargo, or other property is in custody of the court.

C. *Cargo Handling, Repairs, and Movement of the Vessel.* Following arrest or attachment of a vessel, no cargo handling, repairs, or movement may be made without an order of court. The applicant for such an order shall give notice to the marshal and to all parties of record unless the applicant avers that exigent circumstances exist. Upon proof of adequate insurance coverage of the applicant to indemnify the marshal for his/her liability, the court may direct the marshal to permit cargo handling, repairs, movement of the vessel, or other operations. Before or after the marshal has taken custody of a vessel, cargo, or other property, any party of record may move for an order to dispense with keepers or to remove or place the vessel, cargo, or other property at a specified facility, to designate a substitute custodian, or for similar relief. Notice of the motion shall be given to the marshal and to all parties of record. The judicial officer will require that adequate insurance on the property will be maintained by the successor to the marshal, before issuing the order to change arrangements.

D. *Claims by Suppliers for Payment of Charges.* A person who furnishes supplies or services to a vessel, cargo, or other property in custody of the court who has not been paid and claims the right to payment as an expense of administration shall submit an invoice to the clerk in the form of a verified claim at any time before the vessel, cargo, or other property is released or sold. The supplier must serve copies of the claim on the marshal, substitute custodian if one has been appointed, and all parties of record. The court may consider the claims individually or schedule a single hearing for all claims.

LAR(e)(12) Sale of Property.

A. *Notice.* Notice of sale of arrested or attached property shall be published in one or more newspapers to be specified in the order of sale. Unless otherwise ordered by a Judge upon a showing of urgency or impracticality or unless otherwise provided by law, such notice shall be published for at least six days before the date of sale.

B. *Payment of Bid.* These provisions apply unless otherwise ordered in the order of sale: The person whose bid is accepted shall immediately pay the marshal the full purchase price if the bid is $1,000 or less. If the bid exceeds $1,000, the bidder shall immediately pay a deposit of at least $1,000 or 10% of the bid, whichever is greater, and shall pay the balance within three court days after the day on which the bid was accepted. If an objection to the sale is filed within that three-day period, the bidder is excused from paying the balance of the purchase price until three court days after the sale is confirmed. Payment shall be made in cash, by certified check, or by cashier's check.

C. *Late Payment.* If the successful bidder does not pay the balance of the purchase price when it falls due, the bidder shall pay the marshal the cost of keeping the property from the due date until the balance is paid, and the marshal may refuse to release the property until this charge is paid.

D. *Default.* If the successful bidder does not pay the balance of the purchase price within the time allowed, the bidder is deemed to be in default. In such a case, the judicial officer may accept the second highest bid or arrange a new sale. The defaulting bidder's deposit shall be forfeited and applied to any additional costs incurred by the marshal because of the default, the balance being retained in the registry of the court awaiting its order.

E. *Report of Sale by Marshal.* At the conclusion of the sale, the marshal shall forthwith file a written report with the court of the fact of sale, the date, the price obtained, the name and address of the successful bidder, and any other pertinent information.

F. *Time and Procedure for Objection to Sale.* An interested person may object to the sale by filing a written objection with the clerk within three court days following the sale, serving the objection on all parties of record, the successful bidder, and the marshal, and depositing a sum with the marshal that is sufficient to pay the expense of keeping the property for at least seven days. Payment to the marshal shall be in cash, certified check, or cashier's check.

G. *Confirmation of Sale.* A sale shall be confirmed by order of the court within five court days but no sooner than three court days after the sale unless an objection to the sale has been filed, in which case the court shall hold a hearing on the confirmation of the sale. The marshal shall transfer title to the purchaser upon the order of the court.

H. *Disposition of Deposits.*

1. Objection Sustained. If an objection is sustained, sums deposited by the successful bidder will be returned to the bidder forthwith. The sum deposited by the objector will be applied to pay the fees and expenses incurred by the marshal in keeping the property until it is resold, and any balance remaining shall be returned to the objector. The objector will be reimbursed for the expense of keeping the property from the proceeds of a subsequent sale.

2. Objection Overruled. If the objection is overruled, the sum deposited by the objector will be applied to pay the expense of keeping the property from the day the objection was filed until the day the sale is confirmed, and any balance remaining will be returned to the objector forthwith.

I. *Title to Property.* Failure of a party to give the required notice of the action and arrest of the vessel, cargo, or other property, or required notice of the sale, may afford ground for objecting to the sale but does not affect the title of a bona fide purchase of the property without notice of the failure.

[Effective September 1, 2009. Amended effective December 1, 2009.]

RULE (f). LIMITATION OF LIABILITY

LAR(f)(1) Security for Costs. The amount of security for costs under Supplemental Rule F(1) shall be $250, and it may be combined with the security for value and interest, unless otherwise ordered.

LAR(f)(2) Order of Proof at Trial. Where the vessel interests seeking statutory limitation of liability have raised the statutory defense by way of answer or complaint, the plaintiff in the former or the damage claimant in the latter shall proceed with its proof first, as is normal at civil trials.

[Effective September 1, 2009.]

RULE (g). SPECIAL RULES

LAR(g)(1) Suits Under 28 U.S.C. §§ 1915 and 1916. In any case where a plaintiff is permitted to institute his/her action in rem or quasi in rem by the attachment of tangible property without the prepayment of the security required in LAR(e), no such process for attachment shall issue except upon proof of twenty-four (24) hours written notice to the owner of the res or his/her agent of the filing of the complaint unless such notice requirement is waived by a judicial officer.

LAR(g)(2) Use of State Procedures. When the plaintiff invokes a state procedure in order to attach or garnish under Federal Rule 4(e), the process of attachment or garnishment shall so state.

LAR(g)(3) Newspapers for Publishing Notices. Every notice required to be published under the Local Admiralty Rules or any rules or statutes applying to admiralty and maritime proceedings except LAR(e)(12) shall be published in at least one of the following newspapers of general circulation in the district: The Pittsburgh Post–Gazette or The Pittsburgh Tribune Review for all proceedings in Pittsburgh; (the Erie Times or Morning News for all proceedings in Erie, and in the Johnstown Tribune Democrat for all proceedings in Johnstown.) LR 100.2 shall not apply to notices published pursuant to this LAR(g)(3) or under LAR(e)(12)(A).

[Effective September 1, 2009.]

LOCAL PATENT RULES

1. SCOPE OF RULES

LPR 1.1   AUTHORITY

The Local Patent Rules for the United States District Court for the Western District of Pennsylvania are promulgated as authorized by and subject to the limitations of Federal Rule of Civil Procedure 83.

[Effective September 1, 2009.]

LPR 1.2   CITATION

These are the Local Rules of Practice for Patent Cases before the United States District Court for the Western District of Pennsylvania. They should be cited as "LPR," followed by the applicable rule number and subsection.

[Effective September 1, 2009.]

LPR 1.3   APPLICATION AND CONSTRUCTION

These rules apply to all civil actions filed in or transferred to this Court that allege infringement of a utility patent in a complaint, counterclaim, cross-claim or third party claim, or that seek a declaratory judgment that a utility patent is not infringed, is invalid or is unenforceable. The Court may accelerate, extend, eliminate, or modify the obligations or deadlines set forth in these Local Patent Rules based on the circumstances of any particular case, including, without limitation, the complexity of the case or the number of patents, claims, products, or parties involved. If any motion filed prior to the Claim Construction Hearing provided for in LPR 4.4 raises claim construction issues, the Court may, for good cause shown, defer the motion until after completion of the disclosures, filings, or ruling following the Claim Construction Hearing. The Local Civil Rules of this Court shall also apply to these actions, except to the extent that they are inconsistent with these Local Patent Rules.

[Effective September 1, 2009. Amended effective August 1, 2015.]

LPR 1.4   EFFECTIVE DATE

These Local Patent Rules shall take effect on December 5, 2015 and shall apply to any case filed thereafter. The parties to any other pending civil action in which the infringement, validity, or enforceability of a utility patent is an issue shall meet and confer promptly after December 5, 2015, for the purpose of determining whether any provisions in these Local Patent Rules should be made applicable to that case. No later than seven (7) calendar days after the parties meet and confer, the parties shall file a stipulation setting forth a proposed order that relates to the application of these Local Patent Rules. Unless and until an order is entered applying these Local Patent Rules to any pending case, the Local Civil Rules and Local Patent Rules previously applicable to pending patent cases shall govern.

[Effective September 1, 2009. Amended effective August 1, 2015; December 5, 2015.]

LPR 1.5   ALTERNATIVE DISPUTE RESOLUTION

Unless the Court orders otherwise, the default form of alternative dispute resolution in any case governed by these Local Patent Rules shall be Early Neutral Evaluation, which shall occur in accordance with the timing and procedures stated in the ADR Policies and Procedures, as adopted by the Board of Judges for the United States District Court for the Western District of Pennsylvania. See, e.g., ¶ 4.4.B ADR Policies & Procedures (W.D. Pa.) (found at http://www.pawd.uscourts.gov/Applications/pawd_adr/Documents/ADRPolicies.pdf) However, if all parties (1) mutually agree to employ some other form of alternative dispute resolution, such as Mediation or Arbitration, and (2) mutually agree to the timing therefor, then, unless the Court orders otherwise, the deadline for completing such Mediation or Arbitration shall be 60 calendar days after the Court's decision on claim construction.

[Effective September 1, 2009. Amended effective August 1, 2015.]

2. GENERAL PROVISIONS

LPR 2.1   GOVERNING PROCEDURE

(a) **Planning Meeting and Report.** When the parties confer with each other pursuant to Federal Rule of Civil Procedure 26(f), in addition to the matters covered by Federal Rule of Civil Procedure 26, the parties must discuss and address in the statement filed pursuant to Federal Rule of Civil Procedure 26(f), the following topics:

(1) Proposed modification of the deadlines provided for in these Local Patent Rules and/or set forth in the Court's Scheduling Order (see Model Scheduling Order at "Appendix LPR 2.1" for types of deadlines that

might be included) and the effect of any such modification on the date and time of the Claim Construction Hearing, if any;

(2) Whether the parties believe that appointment of a special master may be helpful to the parties and the Court and if so, the joint nomination of a special master to be appointed in the case for purposes of claim construction, based upon mutual agreement of the parties;

(3) Any anticipated motions or proceedings that might affect the deadlines set by these Local Patent Rules, including motions for preliminary injunction; to add or substitute parties; to consolidate; or to stay due to any currently known related, concurrent, or intended patent office proceedings, ITC proceedings, or court cases;

(4) Any issues that might be the proper subject of an early motion for summary judgment or partial summary judgment;

(5) The format of the Claim Construction Hearing, including whether the Court will hear live testimony at the Claim Construction Hearing, the order of presentation, and the estimated length of the hearing;

(6) Whether the parties should provide a tutorial to the Court concerning the technology at issue, including the format and timing of such tutorial;

(7) The need for and any specific procedures or limits on discovery relating to claim construction, including depositions of witnesses, including expert witnesses;

(8) Whether parties are willing to go to trial in front of a Magistrate Judge;

(9) Whether the parties request a claim construction status conference to be held after the Joint Disputed Claim Terms Chart and Prehearing Statement provided for in LPR 4.2 has been filed, and

(10) The form(s) of alternative dispute resolution (Early Neutral Evaluation, Arbitration, or Mediation) that will be utilized in the case, along with the following information:

- the joint nomination of the neutral(s) to be appointed by the Court for purposes of alternative dispute resolution, based upon mutual agreement of the parties;
- percentage of payment responsibility by each party for any fees and expenses associated with the neutral(s);
- the date(s) on which the selected form of alternative dispute resolution will occur; and
- identification of each party representative(s) who will attend the selected alternative dispute resolution session(s).

(b) Initial Scheduling Conference. In addition to the items in section (a) above, each party should be prepared to discuss the technology at issue during the initial scheduling conference. This includes the general technology at issue, the patent(s) in suit, and each accused apparatus, product, device, process, method, act or other instrumentality of each opposing party that is accused of infringing ("Accused Instrumentality"). In addition to the foregoing, each party is expected to bring a sample or representation (e.g., photographs, video, specification, etc.) of each Accused Instrumentality, if possible. Finally, each party should be prepared for a preliminary discussion on damages.

(c) Further Scheduling Conferences. To the extent that some or all of the matters provided for in LPR 2.1 are not resolved or decided at the Initial Scheduling Conference, the parties shall propose dates for further Scheduling Conferences at which such matters shall be addressed.

[Effective September 1, 2009. Amended effective August 1, 2015.]

LPR 2.2   CONFIDENTIALITY

(a) Automatic Protective Order. All documents or information produced under these Local Patent Rules shall be governed by the terms and conditions of the Protective Order in "Appendix LPR 2.2." Such Protective Order shall be deemed automatically entered upon the filing or transfer of any civil action to which these Local Patent Rules apply pursuant to LPR 1.3, unless otherwise modified by agreement of the parties or Order of Court.

(b) Additional Model Language. Appendix LPR 2.2a contains model language for additional provisions for the Protective Order. This language is provided for consideration by the Court and the parties should the circumstances warrant inclusion of such additional provisions in the Protective Order.

[Effective September 1, 2009. Amended effective August 1, 2015.]

LPR 2.3   CERTIFICATION OF INITIAL DISCLOSURES

All statements, disclosures, or charts filed or served in accordance with these Local Patent Rules must be dated and signed by counsel of record (or by the party if unrepresented by counsel). Pursuant to Rules 11 and 26(g) of the Federal Rules of Civil Procedure, counsel's signature (or the signature of the unrepresented party) shall constitute a certification that to the best of his or her knowledge, information, and belief, formed after an inquiry that is reasonable under the circumstances, the information contained in the statement, disclosure, or chart is complete and correct at the time it is made.

[Effective September 1, 2009.]

LPR 2.4   ADMISSIBILITY OF DISCLOSURES

Except as hereinafter provided, statements, disclosures, or charts governed by these Local Patent Rules are admissible to the extent permitted by the Federal Rules of Evidence or Civil Procedure. However, the statements or disclosures provided for in LPR 4.1 and 4.2 are not admissible for any purpose other than in connection with motions seeking an extension or modification of the time periods within which actions contemplated by these Local Patent Rules must be taken, or concerning the scope, length, or substance of the Claim Construction proceedings set forth in LPR 4.3 and 4.4.

[Effective September 1, 2009. Amended effective August 1, 2015.]

LPR 2.5   RELATIONSHIP TO FEDERAL RULES OF CIVIL PROCEDURE

(a) Objections on Grounds of Prematurity. Except as provided in this paragraph or as otherwise ordered, it shall not be a legitimate ground for objecting to an opposing party's discovery request (e.g., interrogatory, document request, request for admission, deposition question) or declining to provide information otherwise required to be disclosed pursuant to Federal Rule of Civil Procedure 26(a)(1) that the discovery request or disclosure requirement is premature in light of or otherwise conflicts with, these Local Patent Rules. A party may object, however, to the following categories of discovery requests (or decline to provide information in its initial disclosures under Federal Rule of Civil Procedure 26(a)(1)) on the ground that they are premature in light of the timetable provided in the Local Patent Rules:

(1) Requests seeking to elicit a party's claim construction position. **See LPR 4.1–4.3;**

(2) Requests seeking to elicit from the patent claimant a comparison of the asserted claims and the accused apparatus, device, process, method, act, or other instrumentality. **See LPR 3.2–3.3;**

(3) Requests seeking to elicit from an accused infringer a comparison of the asserted claims and the prior art. **See LPR 3.4–3.5; and**

(4) Requests seeking to elicit the identification of any advice of counsel, and related documents. **See LPR 3.9.**

Where a party properly objects to a discovery request (or declines to provide information in its initial disclosures under Federal Rule of Civil Procedure 26(a)(1)) as set forth above, that party shall provide the requested information on the date on which it is required to provide the requested information to an opposing party under these Local Patent Rules, unless there exists another legitimate ground for objection.

The parties are reminded that the obligations under Federal Rule of Civil Procedure 26(e) to supplement disclosure and discovery responses shall apply to all Patent Initial Disclosures and all other discovery responses associated with these Local Patent Rules.

[Effective September 1, 2009. Amended effective August 1, 2015.]

3.   PATENT INITIAL DISCLOSURES

LPR 3.1   INITIAL DISCLOSURES

Not later than fourteen (14) days after the Initial Scheduling Conference, the parties shall exchange the initial disclosures required by Federal Rule of Civil Procedure 26(a)(1) ("Initial Disclosures") and shall exchange the documents specified below, subject to the terms of the Protective Order as set forth in LPR 2.2.

With the Initial Disclosures of the party asserting a claim of patent infringement, such party shall produce or make available for inspection and copying, among other items:

All Documents (e.g., contracts, purchase orders, invoices, advertisements, marketing materials, offer letters, beta site testing agreement, and third party or joint development agreements) sufficient to evidence each discussion with, disclosure to, or other manner of providing to a third party, or sale of or offer to sell or other manner of transfer, the claimed invention prior to the date of application for the patent in suit. A party's production of a document as required herein shall not constitute an admission that such document evidences or is prior art under 35 U.S.C. § 102;

All documents evidencing the conception, reduction to practice, design, and development of each claimed invention, which were created on or before the date of application for the patent in suit or a priority date otherwise identified for the patent in suit, whichever is earlier;

All documents evidencing communications to and from the U.S. Patent Office for each patent in suit and for each patent on which a claim for priority is based; and

All documents evidencing ownership of the patent rights by the party asserting patent infringement.

The producing party shall separately identify by production number which documents correspond to each category.

With the Initial Disclosures of the party opposing a claim of patent infringement, such party shall produce or make available for inspection and copying, among other items:

Source code, specifications, schematics, flow charts, artwork, formulas, drawings and/or other documentation, including sales literature, sufficient to show the operation of any aspects or elements of each accused apparatus, product, device, process, method or other accused instrumentality identified with specificity in the pleading of the party asserting patent infringement; and

A copy of each item of prior art, of which the opposing party is aware, that allegedly anticipates each asserted patent and its related claims or renders them obvious.

[Effective September 1, 2009. Amended effective December 1, 2009; August 1, 2015.]

LPR 3.2 DISCLOSURE OF ASSERTED CLAIMS AND INFRINGEMENT CONTENTIONS

(a) Timing. Not later than thirty (30) calendar days after the Initial Scheduling Conference, a party claiming patent infringement must serve on all parties a "Disclosure of Asserted Claims and Infringement Contentions."

(b) Asserted Claims and Infringement Contentions. Separately for each opposing party, the "Disclosure of Asserted Claims and Infringement Contentions" shall contain the following information:

(1) Each claim of each patent in suit that is allegedly infringed by each opposing party, including for each claim the applicable statutory subsection of 35 U.S.C. § 271;

(2) Separately for each asserted claim, each accused apparatus, product, device, process, method, act, or other instrumentality ("Accused Instrumentality") of each opposing party of which the party claiming infringement is aware. This identification shall be as specific as possible. Each product, device, and apparatus must be identified by name, if known, or by any product, device, or apparatus which, when used, allegedly results in the practice of the claimed method or process;

(3) A chart identifying specifically where each element of each asserted claim is found within each Accused Instrumentality, including for each element that such party contends is governed by 35 U.S.C. § 112(6) [or 35 U.S.C. § 112(f) for patents having an effective date after March 16, 2013], a description of the claimed function of that element and the identity of the structure(s), act(s), or material(s) in the Accused Instrumentality that performs the claimed function;

(4) Whether each element of each asserted claim is claimed to be literally present or present under the doctrine of equivalents in the Accused Instrumentality, and if present under the doctrine of equivalents, the asserting party shall also explain each function, way, and result that it contends are equivalent, and why it contends that any differences are not substantial;

(5) For each claim which is alleged to have been indirectly infringed, an identification of any direct infringement and a description of the acts of the alleged indirect infringer(s) that contribute to or that are inducing direct infringement;

(6) To the extent any alleged direct infringement is based on the joint acts of multiple parties, an identification of each such party and a description of the relevant role of each such party;

(7) For any patent that claims priority to an earlier application, the priority date to which each asserted claim allegedly is entitled;

(8) If a party claiming patent infringement wishes to preserve the right to rely, for any purpose, on the assertion that its own apparatus, product, device, process, method, act, or other instrumentality practices the claimed invention, the party must identify, separately for each asserted claim, each such apparatus, product, device, process, method, act, or other instrumentality that incorporates or reflects that particular claim and;

(9) If a party claiming patent infringement alleges willful infringement, the bases for such allegation.

(10) Nothing in this provision shall be construed to modify any party's pleading obligations under the Federal Rules of Civil Procedure.

[Effective September 1, 2009. Amended effective August 1, 2015.]

LPR 3.3 DOCUMENT PRODUCTION ACCOMPANYING DISCLOSURE

With the "Disclosure of Asserted Claims and Infringement Contentions," the party claiming patent infringement shall supplement its Initial Disclosures, if applicable, based upon the Initial Disclosures of the opposing party.

[Effective September 1, 2009.]

LPR 3.4 NON–INFRINGEMENT AND/OR INVALIDITY CONTENTIONS

(a) Timing. Not later than fourteen (14) calendar days after service upon it of the "Disclosure of Asserted Claims and Infringement Contentions," each party asserting non-infringement and/or invalidity of a patent, shall serve upon all parties its "Non–Infringement and/or Invalidity Contentions."

(b) Non–Infringement Contentions. Non–Infringement Contentions shall contain a chart, responsive to the chart required by LPR 3.2, that states as to each identified element in each asserted claim, whether such element is present literally or under the doctrine of equivalents in each Accused Instrumentality, and, if denied, the specific reasons for such denial.

(c) Invalidity Contentions. Invalidity Contentions must contain the following information:

(1) The identity of each item of prior art that allegedly anticipates each asserted claim or renders it obvious. Each prior art patent shall be identified by its number, country of origin, and date of issue. Each prior art publication must be identified by its title, date of publication, and where feasible, author and publisher.

(2) With respect to prior art that anticipates any asserted claim, the facts, documents, witnesses, entities and times that establish that an asserted claim was, before the applicable priority date, patented, described in a printed publication, known, on sale, in public use, otherwise available to the public, derived from another, or is otherwise invalid according to the applicable provisions of § 102.

(3) With respect to a combination of items of prior art that allegedly make a claim obvious, each such combination, and the reasons a person of ordinary skill in the art would combine such items.

(4) A chart identifying where specifically in each alleged item of prior art each element of each challenged claim is found, including for each element that such party contends is governed by 35 U.S.C. § 112(6) [or 35 U.S.C. § 112(f) for patents having an effective date after March 16, 2013], a description of the claimed function of that element and the identity of the structure(s), act(s), or material(s) in each item of prior art that performs the claimed function.

(5) A detailed explanation of any grounds of invalidity of any of the asserted claims based on ineligible subject matter under 35 U.S.C. § 101, indefiniteness under 35 U.S.C. § 112, or enablement or written description under 35 U.S.C. § 112.

[Effective September 1, 2009. Amended effective December 1, 2009; August 1, 2015.]

LPR 3.5   DOCUMENT PRODUCTION ACCOMPANYING INVALIDITY CONTENTIONS

With the "Non-infringement and/or Invalidity Contentions," the party asserting non-infringement and/or invalidity of a patent shall supplement its Initial Disclosures and, in particular, must produce or make available for inspection and copying:

Any additional documentation showing the operation of any aspects or elements of an Accused Instru-

mentality identified by the patent claimant in its LPR 3.2 chart; and

A copy of any additional items of prior art identified pursuant to LPR 3.4 that does not appear in the file history of the patent(s) at issue.

The party asserting non-infringement and/or invalidity of a patent shall also produce summary sales and/or use information reflecting the quantity of the Accused Instrumentality sold and/or used in the United States and the revenues from those sales and/or uses, to the extent known.

[Effective September 1, 2009. Amended effective August 1, 2015.]

LPR 3.6   GOOD FAITH DAMAGES ESTIMATE

Not later than fourteen (14) calendar days after production of the summary sales and use information set forth in LPR 3.5, the party asserting patent infringement shall serve upon the party asserting non-infringement a good faith estimate of its expected damages, including a summary description of the method used to arrive at that estimate. If such damages estimate is based upon a reasonable royalty, the party asserting patent infringement shall also produce any and all license agreements concerning each patent in suit and any related patent.

[Effective August 1, 2015.]

LPR 3.7   DISCLOSURE REQUIREMENT IN PATENT CASES INITIATED BY DECLARATORY JUDGMENT

(a) Non–Infringement and/or Invalidity Contentions If No Claim of Infringement. In all cases in which a party files a complaint or other pleading seeking a declaratory judgment that a patent is not infringed, is invalid, or is unenforceable, LPR 3.2 and 3.3 shall not apply unless and until a claim for patent infringement is made by a party. If the defendant does not assert a claim for patent infringement in its answer to the complaint, no later than thirty (30) calendar days after the Initial Scheduling Conference, the party seeking a declaratory judgment must serve upon each opposing party its Non-infringement and/or Invalidity Contentions that conform to LPR 3.4 and produce or make available for inspection and copying the documentation described in LPR 3.5.

(b) Application of Rules When No Specified Triggering Event. If the filings or actions in a case do not trigger the application of these Local Patent Rules under the terms set forth herein, the parties shall, as soon as such circumstances become known, meet and confer for the purpose of agreeing on the application of these Local Patent Rules to the case.

(c) Inapplicability of Rule. This LPR 3.7 shall not apply to cases in which a request for a declaratory judgment that a patent is not infringed, is invalid, or is unenforceable is filed in response to a complaint for infringement of the same patent.

[Former LPR 3.6 adopted effective September 1, 2009. Renumbered and amended effective August 1, 2015.]

LPR 3.8 AMENDMENT TO CONTENTIONS

(a) Leave Not Required. Not later than twenty-one (21) days after entry of a Claim Construction Order, a party claiming patent infringement may amend, modify or supplement its Infringement Contentions without leave of Court if the Court adopts a claim construction different from that proposed by the party claiming patent infringement and that party believes, in good faith, that the claim construction necessitates the proposed amendment, modification or supplement. Not later than thirty-five (35) days after entry of a Claim Construction Order, a party opposing a claim of patent infringement may amend, modify or supplement its Invalidity and/or Non–Infringement Contentions without leave of Court if (1) a party claiming patent infringement amends, modifies or supplements its Infringement Contentions pursuant to this Rule or (2) the Court adopts a claim construction different from that proposed by the party opposing patent infringement and that party believes, in good faith, that the claim construction necessitates the proposed amendment, modification, or supplement.

(b) Leave Required. Except otherwise provided in LPR 3.8(a), any amendment, modification, or supplement of any Infringement or Non–Infringement and/or Invalidity Contentions may be made only by order of the Court or Court-approved stipulation of the parties. Leave may be granted if the motion is made in a timely fashion, for good cause, and without purpose of delay or undue prejudice to the non-moving party. Non-exhaustive examples of circumstances that may support a finding of good cause can include: information newly discovered, through due diligence, regarding an accused product or prior art; information discovered or provided by a party's consultant or expert after a party's contentions have been served; a new product launches; amendments to the complaint or counterclaim adding or removing one or

more asserted patents; and information learned from or positions taken in the claim construction proceedings or in the exchange of contentions pursuant to LPR 3.2–3.7.

[Former LPR 3.7 adopted effective September 1, 2009. Renumbered and amended effective August 1, 2015.]

LPR 3.9 ADVICE OF COUNSEL

(a) Timing. Not later than 60 days prior to the close of fact discovery, as set forth in the Court's Scheduling Order, any party relying upon advice of counsel as part of a patent-related claim or defense for any reason shall:

(1) Produce or make available for inspection and copying any written advice and documents related thereto for which the attorney-client and work product protection have been waived;

(2) Provide a written summary of any oral advice and produce or make available for inspection and copying that summary and documents related thereto for which the attorney-client and work product protection have been waived; and

(3) Serve a privilege log identifying any other documents, except those authored by counsel acting solely as trial counsel, relating to the subject matter of the advice which the party is withholding on the grounds of attorney-client privilege or work product protection.

(b) Depositions. After such information becomes discoverable, an opposing party shall be entitled to take the deposition of any attorneys rendering the advice relied upon and any persons who received such advice, including but not limited to any person who claims to have relied upon such advice, subject to any limitations otherwise imposed by these Rules, the Federal Rules of Civil Procedure, or the Court's Scheduling Order, and prior to the close of fact discovery, unless otherwise ordered by the Court.

(c) Failure to Comply. A party who does not comply with the requirements of this Rule shall not be permitted to rely upon advice of counsel for any purpose absent a stipulation of all parties, with approval by the Court, or otherwise by order of the Court.

[Effective August 1, 2015.]

4. CLAIM CONSTRUCTION PROCEEDINGS

LPR 4.1 EXCHANGE OF PROPOSED CLAIM TERMS AND PHRASES FOR CONSTRUCTION

(a) Exchange of Proposed Claim Terms and Phrases. Not later than fourteen (14) days after: (i)

service of the Non-infringement and/or Invalidity Contentions pursuant to LPR 3.4; or (ii) an agreement of the parties to expedite claim construction following the Initial Scheduling Conference pursuant to LPR 2.1, each party shall simultaneously exchange a list of claim terms and phrases which that party contends should be construed by the Court, and identify any claim element which that party contends should be governed by 35 U.S.C. § 112(6) (pre–AIA) or 35 U.S.C. § 112(f) (AIA).

(b) Exchange of Proposed Constructions. Not later than fourteen (14) days after the exchange of the "Proposed Claim Terms and Phrases for Construction" pursuant to LPR 4.1(a), the parties shall simultaneously exchange a preliminary proposed construction of each claim term or phrase which the parties collectively have identified for claim construction purposes. Each such preliminary claim construction shall also, for each element which any party contends is governed by 35 U.S.C. § 112(6) (pre–AIA) or 35 U.S.C. § 112(f) (AIA), identify the structure(s), act(s), or material(s) corresponding to that element.

[Effective September 1, 2009. Amended effective December 1, 2009; August 1, 2015.]

LPR 4.2   PREPARATION AND FILING OF JOINT DISPUTED CLAIM TERMS CHART AND PREHEARING STATEMENT

(a) Meet and Confer. Not later than seven (7) days after the exchange set forth in LPR 4.1(b), the parties shall meet and confer to identify claim terms and phrases that are in dispute, and claim terms and phrases that are not in dispute, and shall prepare and file a Joint Disputed Claim Terms Chart listing claim terms and phrases and corresponding intrinsic evidence for each disputed claim term and phrase, asserted by each party. Reasonable efforts shall be made by the parties to limit the terms in dispute by narrowing or resolving any differences between the respective constructions. The Joint Disputed Claim Terms Chart shall be in the format shown in "Appendix LPR 4.2." Each party shall also file with the Joint Disputed Claim Terms Chart an appendix containing a copy of each exhibit of intrinsic evidence cited by the party in the Joint Disputed Claim Terms Chart.

(b) Prehearing Statement. At the same time, the parties shall jointly file a Prehearing Statement that contains the following information:

(1) The construction of those claim terms and phrases on which the parties agree;

(2) The anticipated length of time necessary for the Claim Construction Hearing; and

(3) Whether any party proposes to call one or more witnesses at the Claim Construction Hearing, the identity of each such witness, and for each such witness, a copy of his or her CV (if available) and a brief summary of his or her anticipated testimony.

[Effective September 1, 2009. Amended effective December 1, 2009; August 1, 2015.]

LPR 4.3   CLAIM CONSTRUCTION BRIEFING AND EXTRINSIC EVIDENCE

(a) Opening Submission. Not later than thirty (30) calendar days after filing of the Joint Disputed Claim Terms Chart pursuant to LPR 4.2, the Plaintiff (including the Plaintiff alleging non-infringement in a declaratory judgment action), shall serve and file an Opening Claim Construction Brief including a proposed construction of each claim term and phrase which the parties collectively have identified as being in dispute. Notwithstanding the above, the parties may stipulate that the Defendant (including the Defendant alleging infringement in a declaratory judgment action) will serve and file the Opening Claim Construction Brief. Such Opening Claim Construction Brief shall also, for each element which the party contends is governed by 35 U.S.C. § 112(6) (pre–AIA) or 35 U.S.C. § 112(f) (AIA), describe the claimed function of that element and identify the structure(s), act(s), or material(s) corresponding to that element. For purposes of this rule, if there is no claim of patent infringement present in the complaint as originally filed, then the party first alleging infringement or non-infringement of the subject patent shall serve and file the Opening Claim Construction Brief.

At the same time the party serves its Opening Claim Construction Brief, that party shall serve and file an identification of extrinsic evidence, including testimony of lay and expert witnesses the party contends supports its claim construction. The party shall identify each such item of extrinsic evidence by production number or produce a copy of any such item not previously produced. With respect to any such witness, lay or expert, the party shall also serve and file an affidavit signed by the witness that sets forth the substance of that witness' proposed testimony sufficient for the opposing party to conduct meaningful examination of the witness(es) and promptly make the witness available for deposition concerning the proposed testimony.

(b) Responsive Submission. Not later than twenty-one (21) days after service of the Opening Claim Construction Brief, the opposing party shall serve and file a Response to Opening Claim Construction Brief including the party's proposed construction of each claim term and phrase which the parties collectively have identified as being in dispute. Such Response shall also, for each element which the opposing party contends is governed by 35 U.S.C. § 112(6) (pre–AIA) or 35 U.S.C. § 112(f) (AIA), describe the claimed function of that element and identify the structure(s), act(s), or material(s) corresponding to that element. Such Response shall further include a concise statement not to exceed five (5) pages as to whether the party objects to the opening party's offer of extrinsic evidence.

At the same time the opposing party serves its Response, that party shall serve and file an identification of extrinsic evidence, including testimony of lay and expert witnesses the party contends supports its claim construction. The party shall identify each such item of extrinsic evidence by production number or produce a copy of any such item not previously produced. With respect to any such witness, lay or expert, the party shall also serve and file an affidavit signed by the witness that sets forth the substance of that witness' proposed testimony sufficient for the opposing party to conduct meaningful examination of the witness(es) and promptly make the witness available for deposition concerning the proposed testimony.

(c) Reply Submission. Not later than fourteen (14) days after service of the Response, the opening party may serve and file a Reply directly rebutting the opposing party's Response. Such Reply shall further include a concise statement not to exceed five (5) pages as to whether the party objects to the opposing party's offer of extrinsic evidence. In the event the opposing party identifies a lay or expert witness whose testimony will support its claim construction, the date for the filing of a Reply Claim Construction Brief shall be extended by seven (7) calendar days.

(d) Surreply Submission. In the event that the party bearing the burden of proof on the issue of infringement is the party filing the Response, that party may file a Surreply directly rebutting the opposing party's Reply without leave of Court. Such Surreply shall be filed no later than fourteen (14) days after the service of the Reply and shall not exceed five (5) pages.

(e) Status Conference. Prior to the Claim Construction Hearing, the Court may schedule a status conference or issue an order stating whether it will receive extrinsic evidence and, if so, the particular evidence that it will exclude and that it will receive, and any other matter the Court deems appropriate concerning the conduct of the hearing. Should the Court not conduct a conference or issue an order in advance of the Claim Construction Hearing, such matters will be addressed, as necessary, at the Hearing.
[Effective September 1, 2009. Amended effective December 1, 2009; August 1, 2015.]

LPR 4.4 CLAIM CONSTRUCTION HEARING

Subject to the convenience of the Court's calendar, promptly following submission of the Reply specified in LPR 4.3(c) [or the Surreply specified in LPR 4.3(d) if applicable], the Court shall conduct a Claim Construction Hearing.
[Effective September 1, 2009. Amended effective December 1, 2009; August 1, 2015.]

LPR 4.5 SPECIAL MASTER REPORT AND RECOMMENDATION ON CLAIM CONSTRUCTION

If a Special Master for the purpose of claim construction is appointed, the Special Master shall be empowered to hold hearings and receive and report evidence on the issue of claim construction.

Unless otherwise ordered by the Court, within thirty (30) calendar days following the hearing on the issue of claim construction, the Special Master shall submit to the Court a report and recommendation on the issue of claim construction. Either party may file objections to — or a motion to adopt or modify — the Special Master's report and recommendation, no later than fourteen (14) days from the time the Special Master's report and recommendations are submitted. A party may file a response to such objection or motion within fourteen (14) days of the initial filing of such objection or motion.

The compensation to be paid to the Special Master shall be fixed and determined by the Court pursuant to Federal Rule of Civil Procedure 53(a). Unless otherwise ordered by the Court, the parties shall equally split the costs and fees for services rendered by the Special Master.
[Effective September 1, 2009. Amended effective December 1, 2009; August 1, 2015.]

5. EXPERT WITNESSES

LPR 5.1 DISCLOSURE OF EXPERTS AND EXPERT REPORTS

For issues other than claim construction to which expert testimony shall be directed, expert witness disclosures and depositions shall be governed by this Rule.

No later than thirty (30) calendar days after (1) the normal close of discovery pursuant to the Court's case management order, or (2) the Court's ruling on claim construction, whichever is later, each party shall make its initial expert witness disclosures required by Rule 26 on the issues on which each bears the burden of proof.

No later than thirty (30) calendar days after the first round of disclosures, each party shall make its initial expert witness disclosures required by Rule 26 on the issues on which the opposing party bears the burden of proof.

Unless otherwise ordered by the Court, no later than fourteen (14) days after the second round of disclosures, each party shall make any rebuttal expert witness disclosures permitted by Rule 26.

[Effective September 1, 2009. Amended effective December 1, 2009; August 1, 2015.]

LPR 5.2 DEPOSITIONS OF EXPERTS

Depositions of expert witnesses disclosed under this Rule, if any, shall commence within seven (7) calendar days after rebuttal reports are served and shall be completed within thirty (30) calendar days after commencement of the deposition period.

[Effective September 1, 2009.]

APPENDICES TO RULES
APPENDIX LCvR 7.1A   DISCLOSURE STATEMENT
IN THE UNITED STATES DISTRICT COURT
FOR THE WESTERN DISTRICT OF PENNSYLVANIA

```
_____      )
                              )   Civil Action No. _____
                              )
              vs.             )        or
                              )
                              )   Criminal Action No. _____
_____      )
```

DISCLOSURE STATEMENT

Pursuant to LCvR 7.1 of the Western District of Pennsylvania and to enable Judges and Magistrate Judges to evaluate possible disqualification or recusal, the undersigned counsel for _____, in the above captioned action, certifies that the following are parents, subsidiaries and/or affiliates of said party that have issued shares or debt securities to the public:

or

Pursuant to LCvR 7.1 of the Western District of Pennsylvania and to enable Judges and Magistrate Judges to evaluate possible disqualification or recusal, the undersigned counsel for _____, in the above captioned action, certifies that there are no parents, subsidiaries and/or affiliates of said party that have issued shares or debt securities to the public.

```
_____        _____
Date                          Signature of Attorney or Litigant
```

[Effective September 1, 2009.]

APPENDIX LCvR 7.1B   RICO CASE STATEMENT
IN THE UNITED STATES DISTRICT COURT
FOR THE WESTERN DISTRICT OF PENNSYLVANIA

```
_____      )
                              )
                              )
              vs.             )   Civil Action No. _____
                              )
                              )
_____      )
```

RICO CASE STATEMENT

Pursuant to LCvR 7.1B, any party filing a civil action under 18 U.S.C. §§ 1961–1968 shall set forth those facts upon which such party relied to initiate the RICO claim as a result of the "reasonable inquiry" required by Fed. R. Civ. P. 11. The statement shall be in paragraph form corresponding by number and letter to the paragraphs and subparagraphs appearing below and shall provide in detail and with specificity the information required herein.

1.   State whether the alleged unlawful conduct is in violation of any or all of the provisions of 18 U.S.C. §§ 1962(a), (b), (c) or (d).

2.   List each defendant and state the alleged misconduct and basis of liability of each defendant.

3.   List alleged wrongdoers, other than the defendants listed above, and state the alleged misconduct of each.

4.   List the alleged victims and state how each victim has been allegedly injured.

5.   Describe in detail the pattern of racketeering activity or collection of unlawful debts alleged for each RICO claim. The description of the pattern of racketeering shall include the following information:

   a.   A list of the alleged predicate acts and the specific statutes which were allegedly violated;

   b.   The date of each predicate act, the participants in each such predicate act and the relevant facts surrounding each such predicate act;

   c.   The time, place and contents of each alleged misrepresentation, the identity of persons by whom and to whom such alleged misrepresentation was made and if the predicate act was an offense of wire fraud, mail fraud or fraud in the sale of securities. The "circumstances constituting fraud or mistake" shall be stated with particularity as provided by Fed. R. Civ. P. 9(b);

   d.   Whether there has been a criminal conviction for violation of any predicate act and, if so, a description of each such act;

   e.   Whether civil litigation has resulted in a judgment in regard to any predicate act and, if so, a description of each such act;

   f.   A description of how the predicate acts form a "pattern of racketeering activity."

6.   State whether the alleged predicate acts referred to above relate to each other as part of a common plan, and, if so, describe in detail the alleged enterprise for each RICO claim. A description of the enterprise shall include the following information:

   a.   The names of each individual partnership, corporation, association or other legal entity which allegedly constitute the enterprise;

   b.   A description of the structure, purpose, function and course of conduct of the enterprise;

   c.   Whether each defendant is an employee, officer or director of the alleged enterprise;

   d.   Whether each defendant is associated with the alleged enterprise;

   e.   Whether it is alleged that each defendant is an individual or entity separate from the alleged enterprise, or that such defendant is the enterprise itself, or a member of the enterprise; and

   f.   If any defendant is alleged to be the enterprise itself, or a member of the enterprise, an explanation whether each such defendant is a perpetrator, passive instrument or victim of the alleged racketeering activity.

7.   State and describe in detail whether it is alleged that the pattern of racketeering activity and the enterprise are separate or have merged into one entity.

8.   Describe the alleged relationship between the activities of the enterprise and the pattern of racketeering activity. Discuss how the racketeering activity differs from the usual and daily activities of the enterprise, if at all.

9.   Describe what benefits, if any, the alleged enterprise receives from the alleged pattern of racketeering.

10. Describe the effect of the activities of the enterprise on interstate or foreign commerce.

11. If the complaint alleges a violation of 18 U.S.C. § 1962(a), provide the following information:

    a. The recipient of the income derived from the pattern of racketeering activity or through the collection of an unlawful debt; and

    b. A description of the use or investment of such income.

12. If the complaint alleges a violation of 18 U.S.C. § 1962(b), describe in detail the acquisition or maintenance of any interest in or control of the alleged enterprise.

13. If the complaint alleges a violation of 18 U.S.C. § 1962(c), provide the following information:

    a. The identity of each person or entity employed by, or associated with, the enterprise and

    b. Whether the same entity is both the liable "person" and the "enterprise" under § 1962(c).

14. If the complaint alleges a violation of 18 U.S.C. § 1962(d), describe in detail the alleged conspiracy.

15. Describe the alleged injury to business or property.

16. Describe the direct causal relationship between the alleged injury and the violation of the RICO statute.

17. List the damages sustained by each plaintiff for which each defendant is allegedly liable.

18. List all other federal causes of action, if any, and provide the relevant statute numbers.

19. List all pendent state claims, if any.

20. Provide any additional relevant information that would be helpful to the court in processing the RICO claim.

[Effective September 1, 2009.]

APPENDIX LCvR 16.1A FED R. CIV. P.
26(F) REPORT OF THE PARTIES
IN THE UNITED STATES DISTRICT COURT FOR THE
WESTERN DISTRICT OF PENNSYLVANIA

[CAPTION]
[JUDICIAL OFFICER(S)]

FED. R. CIV. P. 26(f) REPORT OF THE PARTIES

Counsel for the parties and unrepresented parties shall confer regarding the matters identified herein and prepare a signed report in the following form to be filed at least 21 days before the Initial LCvR 16.1 Scheduling Conference or at such other time as ordered by the court. This report form may be downloaded from the Court's website as a word-processing document and the information filled in as requested on the downloaded form. The dates to be provided in the report are suggested dates and may be accepted or modified by the Court.

1. Identification of counsel and unrepresented parties. Set forth the names, addresses, telephone and fax numbers and e-mail addresses of each unrepresented party and of each counsel and identify the parties whom such counsel represent:

2. Set forth the general nature of the case (patent, civil rights, anti-trust, class action, etc.):

3. Date Rule 26(f) Conference was held, the identification of those participating therein and the identification of any party who may not yet have been served or entered an appearance as of the date of said Conference:

4. Date of Rule 16 Initial Scheduling Conference as scheduled by the Court: (Lead Trial Counsel and unrepresented parties shall attend the Rule 16 Initial Scheduling Conference with their calendars in hand for the purpose of scheduling other pre-trial events and procedures, including a Post–Discovery Status Conference; Counsel and unrepresented parties shall attend the Rule 16 Initial Scheduling Conference prepared to discuss the anticipated number of depositions and identities of potential deponents and the anticipated dates by which interrogatories, requests for production of documents and requests for admissions will be served):

5. Identify any party who has filed or anticipates filing a dispositive motion pursuant to Fed. R. Civ. P. 12 and the date(s) by which any such anticipated motion may be filed:

6. Designate the specific Alternative Dispute Resolution (ADR) process the parties have discussed and selected, if any, and specify the anticipated time frame for completion of the ADR process. Set forth any other information the parties wish to communicate to the court regarding the ADR designation:

7. Set forth any change that any party proposes to be made in the timing, form or requirements of Fed. R. Civ. P. Rule 26(a) disclosures, whether such change is opposed by any other party, whether any party has filed a motion seeking such change and whether any such motion has been ruled on by the Court:

8. Subjects on which fact discovery may be needed. (By executing this report, no party shall be deemed to (1) have waived the right to conduct discovery on subjects not listed herein or (2) be required to first seek the permission of the Court to conduct discovery with regard to subjects not listed herein):

9. Set forth suggested dates for the following (The parties may elect by agreement to schedule a Post–Discovery Status Conference, as identified in Paragraph 12, below, at the conclusion of Fact–Discovery rather than at the conclusion of Expert Discovery. In that event, the parties should provide suggested dates only for the events identified in sub-paragraphs 9.a through 9.e, below. The parties shall provide such information even if dispositive motions pursuant to Fed. R. Civ. P. 12 have been or are anticipated to be filed. If there are dates on which the parties have been unable to agree, set forth the date each party proposes and a brief statement in support of each such party's proposed date. Attach to this report form a proposed Court Order setting forth all dates agreed to below and leaving a blank for the insertion of a date by the Court for any date not agreed to):

a. Date(s) on which disclosures required by Fed. R. Civ. P. 26(a) have been or will be made:

b. Date by which any additional parties shall be joined:

c. Date by which the pleadings shall be amended:

d. Date by which fact discovery should be completed:

e. If the parties agree that discovery should be conducted in phases or limited to or focused on particular issues, identify the proposed phases or issues and the dates by which discovery as to each phase or issue should be completed:

f. Date by which plaintiff's expert reports should be filed:

g. Date by which depositions of plaintiff's expert(s) should be completed:

h. Date by which defendant's expert reports should be filed:

i. Date by which depositions of defendant's expert(s) should be completed:

j. Date by which third party expert's reports should be filed:

k. Date by which depositions of third party's expert(s) should be completed:

10. If the parties agree that changes should be made to the limitations on discovery imposed by the Federal Rules of Civil Procedure or Local Rule or that any other limitations should be imposed on discovery, set forth such changes or limitations:

11. Set forth whether the parties have considered the need for special deadlines, procedures or orders of court dealing with discovery of electronically-stored information (electronic discovery), including the need for the preservation of discoverable information and the protection of the right to assert privilege(s) after the production of privileged information and if so, set forth the results of such consideration. In particular, answer the following questions:

a. ESI. Is either party seeking the discovery of ESI in this case? ☐ Yes ☐ No

If disputed, identify the nature of the dispute _____

b. Metadata: Will any metadata be relevant in this case? ☐ Yes ☐ No

If yes, with respect to what ESI _____

If disputed, identify the nature of the dispute _____

c. Format. Have the parties agreed on the format(s) for production of ESI? ☐ Yes ☐ No

If no, what disputes remain outstanding _____

d. Clawback Agreement. Will the parties be using the Form Inadvertent Production Provision of LCvR 16.1.D? ☐ Yes ☐ No

If no, will an alternative provision be proposed? ☐ Yes (Please attach) ☐ No

e. Search terms. Have the parties agreed on any protocol for review of electronic data? ☐ Yes ☐ No

If yes, please describe _____

If no, please identify what issues remain outstanding _____

f. Accessibility. Have the parties agreed on what ESI is "reasonably accessible" as defined in R. 26(b)(2)(B)? ☐ Yes ☐ No

If no, please identify the nature of the dispute _____

g. Preservation. Are there any unresolved issues pertaining to the preservation of ESI? If so, please describe _____

h. Other. Identify all outstanding issues or disputes concerning ESI _____

12. Set forth whether the parties have elected to schedule the Post–Discovery Status Conference following the completion of Fact Discovery or Expert Discovery; in either event the parties shall be prepared at the Post–Discovery Status Conference to discuss and/or schedule the following: (The parties are *not* required during their Rule 26(f) Conference to consider or propose dates for the items identified below. Those dates will be determined, if necessary, at the Post–Discovery Status Conference. Lead trial counsel for each party and each unrepresented party are required to attend the Post–Discovery Status Conference with their calendars in hand to discuss those items listed below that require scheduling. In addition, a representative with settlement authority of each party shall be required to attend; representatives with settlement authority of any insurance company providing any coverage shall be available throughout the Conference by telephone):

a. Settlement and/or transfer to an ADR procedure;

b. Dates for the filing of expert reports and the completion of expert discovery as itemized in sub-paragraphs 9.f. through 9.k., above, if the parties elected to defer such discovery until after the Post–Discovery Status Conference;

c. Dates by which dispositive motions pursuant to Fed. R. Civ. P. 56, replies thereto and responses to replies should be filed;

d. Dates by which parties' pre-trial statements should be filed;

e. Dates by which in limine and *Daubert* motions and responses thereto should be filed;

f. Dates on which motions in limine and *Daubert* motions shall be heard;

g. Dates proposed for final pre-trial conference;

h. Presumptive and final trial dates.

13. Set forth any other order(s) that the parties agree should be entered by the court pursuant to Fed. R. Civ. P. 16(b) or 26(c):

14. Set forth whether the parties anticipate that the court may have to appoint a special master to deal with any matter and if so, specify the proposed role of any such master and any special qualifications that such master may require to perform such role:

15. If the parties have failed to agree with regard to any subject for which a report is required as set forth above, except for proposed dates required in paragraph 9, above, briefly set forth the position of each party with regard to each matter on which agreement has not been reached:

16. Set forth whether the parties have considered the possibility of settlement of the action and describe briefly the nature of that consideration:

Respectfully submitted,

_____

_____

_____

_____

_____

_____

———————————————————

———————————————————

(Signatures of counsel and unrepresented parties)

[Effective September 1, 2009.]

APPENDIX LCvR 23.E   FED. R. CIV. P. 26(f) JOINT
REPORT OF THE PARTIES (CLASS ACTION)

FED. R. CIV. P. 26(f) JOINT REPORT OF THE PARTIES (CLASS ACTION)

1. **Identification of counsel and unrepresented parties.**

2. **Set forth the general nature of the case** (anti-trust, consumer finance, securities, employment, etc.):

3. **Date Rule 26(f) Conference was held, the identification of those partici-pating therein and the identification of any party who may not yet have been served or entered an appearance as of the date of said Conference:**

4. **Date of Rule 16 Initial Scheduling Conference as scheduled by the Court:** *(Lead Trial Counsel and unrepresented parties shall attend the Rule 16 Initial Scheduling Conference with their calendars in hand for the purpose of scheduling other pre-trial events and procedures, including a Post–Discovery Status Confer-ence; Counsel and unrepresented parties shall attend the Rule 16 Initial Schedul-ing Conference prepared to discuss the anticipated number of depositions and identities of potential deponents and the anticipated dates by which interrogatories, requests for production of documents and requests for admissions will be served):*

5. **Identify any party who has filed or anticipates filing a dispositive motion pursuant to Fed. R. Civ. P. 12 and the date(s) by which any such anticipated motion may be filed:**

6. **Designate the specific Alternative Dispute Resolution (ADR) process the parties have discussed and selected, if any, and specify the anticipated time frame for completion of the ADR process. Set forth any other information the parties wish to communicate to the court regarding the ADR designation:**

7. **Set forth any change that any party proposes to be made in the timing, form or requirements of Fed. R. Civ. P. Rule 26(a) disclosures, whether such change is opposed by any other party, whether any party has filed a motion seeking such change and whether any such motion has been ruled on by the Court:**

8. **Discovery prior to Class Certification must be sufficient to permit the Court to determine whether the requirements of Fed. R. Civ. P. Rule 23 are satisfied, including a preliminary inquiry into the merits of the case to ensure appropriate management of the case as a Class Action. However, in order to ensure that a class certification decision be issued at an early practicable time, priority shall be given to discovery on class issues. Once Class Certification is decided, the Court may, upon motion of a party, enter a second scheduling and discovery order, if necessary.**

9. **Subjects on which class certification discovery may be needed.** (By executing this report, no party shall be deemed to (1) have waived the right to conduct discovery on subjects not listed herein or (2) be required to first seek the permission of the Court to conduct discovery with regard to subjects not listed herein):

10. **Set forth suggested dates for the following** *(The parties shall provide such information even if dispositive motions pursuant to Fed. R. Civ. P. 12 have been or are anticipated to be filed, except to the extent discovery and other proceedings have been or will be stayed under the Private Securities Litigation Reform Act or otherwise. If there are dates on which the parties have been unable to agree, set forth the date each party proposes and a brief statement in support of each such party's proposed date. Attach to this report form a proposed Court Order setting forth all dates agreed to below and leaving a blank for the insertion of a date by the Court for any date not agreed to):*

a.   Date(s) on which disclosures required by Fed. R. Civ. P. 26(a) have been or will be made:

b.   Date by which any additional parties shall be joined:

c.   Date by which the pleadings shall be amended:

d.   Date by which class certification discovery shall be completed:

e.   Date by which plaintiffs' expert reports as to class certification shall be filed:

f.   Date by which defendants' expert reports as to class certification shall be filed:

g.   Date by which depositions of class certification experts must be completed:

h.   Plaintiffs' Motion for Class Certification, Memorandum in Support, and all supporting evidence shall be filed by _____:

i.   Defendants' Memorandum in Opposition to Class Certification and all supporting evidence shall be filed by _____:

j.   Plaintiffs' Reply Memorandum in support of class certification, if any, shall be filed by _____:

k.   The Class Certification hearing shall be as scheduled by the Court.

11.   After the resolution of the motion for class certification, the Court shall hold a Post–Certification Determination Conference to discuss how the case shall proceed in light of the disposition of the Class motion. If the parties wish to establish a schedule for post-Class Certification pretrial matters at this time, set forth suggested dates for the following:

a.   Date by which fact discovery should be completed:

b.   Date by which plaintiff's expert reports should be filed:

c.   Date by which depositions of plaintiff's expert(s) should be completed:

d.   Date by which defendant's expert reports should be filed:

e.   Date by which depositions of defendant's expert(s) should be completed:

g.   Date by which third party expert's reports should be filed:

h.   Date by which depositions of third party's experts should be completed.

12.   If the parties agree that changes should be made to the limitations on discovery imposed by the Federal Rules of Civil Procedure or Local Rule or that any other limitations should be imposed on discovery, set forth such changes or limitations:

13.   Set forth whether the parties have considered the need for special deadlines, procedures or orders of court dealing with discovery of electronically-stored information (electronic discovery), including the need for the preservation of discoverable information and the protection of the right to assert privilege(s) after the production of privileged information and if so, set forth the results of such consideration:

14.   Set forth whether the parties have elected to schedule the Post–Discovery Status Conference following the completion of Fact Discovery or Expert Discovery; in either event the parties shall be prepared at the Post–Discovery Status Conference to discuss and/or schedule the following: *(The parties are not required during their Rule 26(f) Conference to consider or propose dates for the items identified below. Those dates will be determined, if necessary, at the Post–Discovery Status Conference. Lead trial counsel for each party and each unrepresented party are required to attend the Post–Discovery Status Conference with their calendars in hand to discuss those items listed below that require scheduling. In addition, a representative with settlement authority of each party shall be required*

to attend; representatives with settlement authority of any insurance company providing any coverage shall be available throughout the Conference by telephone):

a. Settlement and/or transfer to an ADR procedure;

b. Dates for the filing of expert reports and the completion of expert discovery as itemized in sub-paragraphs 11.b. through 11.h., above, if the parties elected to defer such discovery until after the Post–Discovery Status Conference;

c. Dates by which dispositive motions pursuant to Fed. R. Civ. P. 56, replies thereto and responses to replies should be filed;

d. Dates by which parties' pre-trial statements should be filed;

e. Dates by which *in limine* and *Daubert* motions and responses thereto should be filed;

f. Dates on which motions *in limine* and *Daubert* motions shall be heard;

g. Dates proposed for final pre-trial conference;

h. Presumptive and final trial dates.

15. Set forth any other order(s) that the parties agree should be entered by the court pursuant to Fed. R. Civ. P. 16(b) or 26(c):

16. Set forth whether the parties anticipate that the court may have to appoint a special master to deal with any matter and if so, specify the proposed role of any such master and any special qualifications that such master may require to perform such role:

17. If the parties have failed to agree with regard to any subject for which a report is required as set forth above, except for proposed dates required in paragraph 10 and/or 11, above, briefly set forth the position of each party with regard to each matter on which agreement has not been reached:

18. Set forth whether the parties have considered the possibility of settlement of the action and describe briefly the nature of that consideration:

Respectfully submitted,

[Effective September 1, 2009.]

APPENDIX LCvR 83.2B   MOTION AND AFFIDAVIT

APPENDIX LCvR 83.2B–MOTION
IN THE UNITED STATES DISTRICT COURT
FOR THE WESTERN DISTRICT OF PENNSYLVANIA

_____   )

)

          vs.   ) Civil Action No. _____

)

_____   )

)

MOTION FOR ADMISSION PRO HAC VICE OF _____

[Affiant], undersigned counsel for [Plaintiff/Defendant] _____, hereby moves that [Affiant] be admitted to appear and practice in this Court in the above-captioned matter as counsel pro hac vice for [Plaintiff/Defendant] _____ in the above-captioned matter pursuant to LCvR 83.2 and LCvR 83.3 and this Court's Standing Order Regarding Pro Hac Vice Admissions dated May 31, 2006 (Misc. No. 06–151).

In support of this motion, undersigned counsel attaches the Affidavit for Admission Pro Hac Vice of [Affiant] filed herewith, which, it is averred, satisfies the requirements of the foregoing Local Rules and Standing Order.

Respectfully submitted,

Dated: _____   _____
                                 [Affiant's name] (Bar. ID NO. _____)
                                 [Affiant's Address/Contact Details]

                                 Counsel for [Plaintiff/Defendant]
                                 _____

APPENDIX LCvR 83.2B–AFFIDAVIT
IN THE UNITED STATES DISTRICT COURT
FOR THE WESTERN DISTRICT OF PENNSYLVANIA

_____   )
)
          vs.   ) Civil Action No. _____
)
_____   )
)

AFFIDAVIT OF _____ IN SUPPORT OF MOTION FOR ADMISSION PRO HAC VICE

[I, _____, make this affidavit in support of the motion for my admission to appear and practice in this Court in the above-captioned matter as counsel pro hac vice for [Plaintiff/Defendant] _____ in the above-captioned matter pursuant to LCvR 83.2 and LCvR 83.3 and this Court's Standing Order Regarding Pro Hac Vice Admissions dated May 31, 2006 (Misc. No. 06–151).

I, _____, being duly sworn, do hereby depose and say as follows:

1. I am a [Lawyer/Partner/Associate] of the law firm [_____].
2. My business address is _____.
3. I am a member in good standing of the bar[s] of _____.
4. My bar identification number(s) [is/are] _____.

5. A current certificate of good standing from _____ is attached to this Affidavit as Exhibit ___.

6. [if applicable] The following are a complete list of any previous disciplinary proceedings concerning my practice of law that resulted in a non-confidential negative finding or sanction by the disciplinary authority of the bar of any state or any United States court: _____: [Insert additional explanation as appropriate.]

7. I attest that I am a registered user of ECF in the United States District Court for the Western District of Pennsylvania.

8. I attest that I have read, know and understand the Local Rules of Court for the United States District Court for the Western District of Pennsylvania

9. Based upon the foregoing, I respectfully request that I be granted pro hac vice admission in this matter.

I certify and attest that the foregoing statements made by me are true. I am aware that if any of the foregoing statements made by me are false, I am subject to punishment.

Dated: _____   _____
                                            [Affiant]

[Effective February 1, 2013.]

APPENDIX LPR 2.1   MODEL SCHEDULING ORDER FOR USE IN PATENT CASES

IN THE UNITED STATES DISTRICT COURT
FOR THE WESTERN DISTRICT OF PENNSYLVANIA

Plaintiff v. Defendant.   )   Civil Action No.

MODEL SCHEDULING ORDER FOR USE IN PATENT CASES

AND NOW, this ___ day of _____, 20 ___,

IT IS ORDERED that this action is placed under the Local Patent Rules of this Court for pretrial proceedings and all provisions of these Rules will be strictly enforced.

IT IS FURTHER ORDERED that counsel shall confer with their clients prior to all scheduling, status, or pretrial conferences to obtain authority to participate in settlement negotiations which may be conducted or ordered by the Court.

IT IS FURTHER ORDERED that compliance with provisions of Local Rule 16 and the Local Patent Rules shall be completed as follows:

(1) The parties shall move to amend the pleadings or add new parties by _____;

(2) The party claiming patent infringement must serve on all parties a Disclosure of Asserted Claims and Infringement Contentions by _____; *[30 calendar days after the Initial Scheduling Conference; LPR 3.2]*

(3) The party claiming non-infringement and/or invalidity must serve on all parties a Disclosure of Non-infringement and/or Invalidity Contentions by _____; *[14 days after service of Disclosure of Asserted Claims and Infringement Contentions; LPR 3.4]*

(4) Each party will simultaneously exchange Proposed Claim Terms and Phrases for Construction by _____; *[14 days after service of the Non-infringement and/or Invalidity Contention; LPR 4.1(a)]*

(4a) Each party will simultaneously exchange a preliminary proposed construction of each term or phrase by _____; *[not later than 14 days after the exchange of proposed claim terms and phrases; LPR 4.1(b)]*

(5) The parties shall meet and confer by _____ to identify claim terms and phrases that are in dispute, and claim terms and phrases that are not in dispute and prepare and file a Joint Disputed Claim Terms Chart and Prehearing Statement. Each party shall also file with the Joint Disputed Claim Terms Chart and Prehearing Statement an appendix containing a copy of each item of intrinsic evidence cited by the party in the Joint Disputed Claim Terms Chart; *[Not later than 7 days after the exchange of preliminary constructions; LPR 4.2]*

(6) It is hereby Ordered that _____ is appointed Special Master pursuant to Federal Rule of Civil Procedure 53 to serve in accordance with the LPRs in this action;

(7) The parties have agreed to submit this case to _____ *[Early Neutral Evaluation, Mediation, or Arbitration]*. As such, it is hereby Ordered that _____ is/are appointed as the *[Early Neutral Evaluator, Mediator, or Arbitrator]* to serve in accordance with the ADR Policies and Procedures in this action;

(8) The above-mentioned alternative dispute resolution shall take place on _____ and on such other dates as the parties may agree; *[if Mediation is selected, then the deadline shall be 60 calendar days after the Court's decision on claim construction, unless the Court rules otherwise; LPR 2.1]*

(9) Plaintiff shall file and serve an Opening Claim Construction Brief and an identification of extrinsic evidence by _____; *[30 calendar days after filing of the joint disputed claim terms chart; LPR 4.3]*

(10) The Opposing Party shall file and serve a response to the Opening Claims Construction Brief, an identification of extrinsic evidence and any objections to extrinsic evidence by _____; *[21 days after service of the opening claim construction brief; LPR 4.3]*

(11) The opening party may serve and file a Reply directly rebutting the opposing party's Response, and any objections to extrinsic evidence by _____; *[14 days after opposing party's response is served (or 21 days if the opposing party's response includes testimony from a lay or expert witness); LPR 4.3]*

(12) If the Opposing Party bears the burden of proof on infringement, it may file a Surreply directly rebutting the opening party's Reply by _____; *[14 days after opening party's Reply is served; LPR 4.3]*

(13) The Court will conduct a hearing on the issue of Claim Construction on _____;

(14) The Report and Recommendation of the Special Master on the issue of claim construction shall be due on _____; *[Unless otherwise ordered by the Court, 30 calendar days after the hearing on claim construction; LPR 4.5]*

(15) The parties shall complete fact discovery by 60 days after the Court issues a ruling on claim construction, and all interrogatories, depositions, requests for admissions, and requests for production shall be served within sufficient time to allow responses to be completed prior to the close of discovery;

(16) Each party shall make its initial expert witness disclosures, as required under Rule 26, on the issues on which each bears the burden of proof by _____, *[30 calendar days after the normal close of discovery pursuant to the Court's case management order, or the court's ruling on claim construction, whichever is later; LPR 5.1]*

(17) Each party shall make its initial expert witness disclosures, as required under Rule 26, on the issues on which the opposing party bears the burden of proof by _____; *[30 calendar days after the first round of expert disclosures; LPR 5.1]*

(18) Rebuttal expert witness disclosures are to be made by _____; *[14 days after second round of expert disclosures; LPR 5.1]*

(19) Expert Depositions, if any, shall begin by _____; *[within 7 calendar days after service of the rebuttal expert reports]* and be completed by _____; *[30 calendar days after commencement of deposition period; LPR 5.2]*

(20) Motions for summary judgment with evidentiary material and accompanying brief, if appropriate, shall be filed by _____, and responses to such motions shall be filed within _____ *calendar* days thereafter. Reply and surreply briefs shall not be filed unless approved/requested by the Court;

(21) Plaintiff's pretrial narrative statement shall comply with Rule 16.1.C.1, and be filed by _____;

(22) Defendant's pretrial narrative statement shall comply with Rule 16.1.C.2, and be filed by _____;

(23) The parties shall not amend or supplement their pretrial narrative statements without leave of Court;

(24) All parties shall file an indication whether or not they are willing to proceed to trial in front of a Magistrate Judge by _____;

(25) The Court shall conduct a pretrial conference on _____ 20 _____, at _____ (time) Room _____ U.S. Post Office & Courthouse, Seventh Avenue and Grant Street, Pittsburgh, Pennsylvania, and all trial counsel must attend; and

(26) The trial shall commence on _____, 20 _____, at _____ (time), Courtroom No. _____.

_____
United States District Judge

cc: All Counsel of Record

[Effective September 1, 2009. Amended effective December 1, 2009; February 1, 2013; August 1, 2015.]

APPENDIX LPR 2.2   PROTECTIVE ORDER
IN THE UNITED STATES DISTRICT COURT
FOR THE WESTERN DISTRICT OF PENNSYLVANIA

Plaintiff v. Defendant.   )   Civil Action No.

PROTECTIVE ORDER

Pursuant to Rule 26(c) of the Federal Rules of Civil Procedure, the following Protective Order has been entered by Court.

Proceedings and Information Governed.

1.   This Order and any amendments or modifications hereto ("Protective Order") shall govern any document, information, or other thing furnished by any party, to any other party, and includes non-parties who receive a subpoena in connection with this action.   The information protected includes, but is not limited to, answers to interrogatories, answers to requests for admission, responses to requests for production of documents, deposition transcripts and videotapes, deposition exhibits, and other writings or things produced, given, or filed in this action that are designated by a party as "Confidential Information," "Confidential Attorney Eyes Only Information," or "Highly Confidential—Source Code Information" (collectively, "Protected Information") in accordance with the terms of this Order, as well as to any copies, excerpts, abstracts, analyses, summaries, descriptions, or other forms of recorded information containing, reflecting, or disclosing such information.

Designation and Maintenance of Information.

2.   For purposes of this Protective Order:

(a) The "Confidential Information" designation shall mean that the document is comprised of trade secrets or commercial information which is not publicly known and is of technical or commercial advantage to its possessor, in accordance with Federal Rule of Civil Procedure 26(c)(7), or other information required by law or agreement to be kept confidential.

(b) The "Confidential Attorney Eyes Only Information" designation shall mean that the document is comprised of Confidential Information that the producing party deems especially sensitive, which may include, but is not limited to, confidential research and development, financial, technical, marketing, any other sensitive trade secret information, or information capable of being utilized for the preparation or prosecution of a patent application dealing with such subject matter.

(c) The "Highly Confidential—Source Code Information" designation shall mean extremely sensitive "Confidential Information" representing computer code and associated comments and revision histories, formulas, engineering specifications, or schematics that define or otherwise describe in detail the algorithms or structure of software or hardware designs, disclosure of which to another party or non-party would create a substantial risk of serious harm that could not be avoided by less restrictive means.

(d) Protected Information does not include, and this Protective Order shall not apply to, information that is already in the knowledge or possession of the party to whom disclosure is made unless that party is already bound by agreement not to disclose such information, or information that has been disclosed to the public or third persons in a manner making such information no longer confidential.

3.   Protected Information may be designated in the following manner.

(a) Documents and things produced during the course of this litigation within the scope of paragraph 2(a) above, may be designated by the producing party as containing Confidential Information by placing on each page and each thing a legend substantially as follows:

CONFIDENTIAL INFORMATION
SUBJECT TO PROTECTIVE ORDER

(b) Documents and things produced during the course of this litigation within the scope of paragraph 2(b) above may be designated by the producing party as containing Confidential Attorney Eyes Only Information by placing on each page and each thing a legend substantially as follows:

CONFIDENTIAL ATTORNEY EYES ONLY INFORMATION
SUBJECT TO PROTECTIVE ORDER

(c) Documents and things produced during the course of this litigation within the scope of paragraph 2(c) above may be designated by the producing party as containing Highly Confidential—Source Code Information by placing on each page and each thing a legend substantially as follows:

HIGHLY CONFIDENTIAL—SOURCE CODE INFORMATION
SUBJECT TO PROTECTIVE ORDER

(d) A party may designate information disclosed at a deposition as Protected Information by requesting the reporter to so designate the transcript or any portion thereof at the time of the deposition. If no such designation is made at the time of the deposition, any party shall have fourteen (14) calendar days after the date of the deposition to designate, in writing to the other parties and to the court reporter, whether the transcript is to be designated as Protected Information. If no such designation is made at the deposition or within such fourteen (14) calendar day period (during which period, the transcript shall be treated as Confidential Attorneys Eyes Only Information, unless the disclosing party consents to less confidential treatment of the information), the entire deposition will be considered devoid of Protected Information. Each party and the court reporter shall attach a copy of any final and timely written designation notice to the transcript and each copy thereof in its possession, custody or control, and the portions designated in such notice shall thereafter be treated in accordance with this Protective Order.

(e) It is the responsibility of counsel for each party to maintain materials containing Protected Information in a secure manner and appropriately identified so as to allow access to such information only to such persons and under such terms as is permitted under this Protective Order.

Inadvertent Failure to Designate.

4. The inadvertent failure to designate or withhold any information as confidential or privileged will not be deemed to waive a later claim as to its confidential or privileged nature, or to stop the producing party from designating such information as confidential at a later date in writing and with particularity. The information shall be treated by the receiving party as confidential from the time the receiving party is notified in writing of the change in the designation.

Challenge to Designations.

5. A receiving party may challenge a producing party's designation at any time. Any receiving party disagreeing with a designation may request in writing that the producing party change the designation. The producing party shall then have

fourteen (14) days after receipt of a challenge notice to advise the receiving party whether or not it will change the designation. If the parties are unable to reach agreement after the expiration of this fourteen (14) day time frame, and after the conference required under Local Rule 37.1, the receiving party may at any time thereafter seek a Court Order to alter the confidential status of the designated information. Until any dispute under this paragraph is ruled upon by the Court, the designation shall remain in full force and effect and the information shall continue to be accorded the confidential treatment required by this Protective Order.

Disclosure and Use of Confidential Information.

6. Information designated as Confidential Information or Protected Information may only be used for purposes of preparation, trial and appeal of this action. Protected Information may not be used under any circumstances for prosecuting any patent application, for patent licensing or for any other purpose. The provisions of LCvR 16.1.D, relating to the inadvertent disclosure of privileged information, shall apply in all cases governed by this Protective Order.

7. Subject to paragraph 9 below, Confidential Information may be disclosed by the receiving party only to the following individuals provided that such individuals are informed of the terms of this Protective Order: (a) two (2) employees of the receiving party who are required in good faith to provide assistance in the conduct of this litigation, including any settlement discussions, and who are identified as such in writing to counsel for the designating party in advance of the disclosure; (b) two (2) in-house counsel who are identified by the receiving party; (c) outside counsel for the receiving party; (d) supporting personnel employed by (b) and (c), such as paralegals, legal secretaries, data entry clerks and legal clerks; (e) experts or consultants; (f) any persons requested by counsel to furnish services such as photocopying, document coding, image scanning, mock trial, jury profiling, translation services, court reporting services, demonstrative exhibit preparation, or the creation of any computer database from documents; and (g) the Court and its personnel.

8. Subject to paragraph 9 below, Confidential Attorney Eyes Only Information may be disclosed by the receiving party only to the following individuals provided that such individuals are informed of the terms of this Protective Order: (a) two (2) in-house counsel who are identified by the receiving party; (b) outside counsel for the receiving party; (c) supporting personnel employed by (a) and (b), such as paralegals, legal secretaries, data entry clerks and legal clerks; (d) experts or consultants; (e) any persons requested by counsel to furnish services such as photocopying, document coding, image scanning, mock trial, jury profiling, translation services, court reporting services, demonstrative exhibit preparation, or the creation of any computer database from documents; and (f) the Court and its personnel.

9. Further, prior to disclosing Confidential Information or Confidential Attorney Eyes Only Information to a receiving party's proposed expert, consultant or employees, the receiving party shall provide to the producing party a signed Confidentiality Agreement in the form attached as Exhibit A, the resume or curriculum vitae of the proposed expert or consultant, the expert or consultant's business affiliation, and any current and past consulting relationships in the industry. The producing party shall thereafter have fourteen (14) days from receipt of the Confidentiality Agreement to object to any proposed individual. Such objection must be made for good cause and in writing, stating with particularity the reasons for objection. Failure to object within fourteen (14) days shall constitute approval. If the parties are unable to resolve any objection, the receiving party may apply to the Court to resolve the matter. There shall be no disclosure to any proposed individual during the fourteen (14) day objection period, unless that period is waived by the producing party, or if any objection is made, until the parties have resolved the objection or the Court has ruled upon any resultant motion.

10. Counsel shall be responsible for the adherence by third-party vendors to the terms and conditions of this Protective Order. Counsel may fulfill this obligation by obtaining a signed Confidentiality Agreement in the form attached as Exhibit B.

11. Confidential Information or Confidential Attorney Eyes Only Information may be disclosed to a person, not already allowed access to such information under this Protective Order, if:

(a) the information was previously received or authored by the person or was authored or received by a director, officer, employee, or agent of the company for which the person is testifying as a Rule 30(b)(6) designee;

(b) the designating party is the person or is a party for whom the person is a director, officer, employee, consultant or agent; or

(c) counsel for the party designating the material agrees that the material may be disclosed to the person.

In the event of disclosure under this paragraph, only the reporter, the person, his or her counsel, the Court and its personnel, and persons to whom disclosure may be made, and who are bound by the Protective Order, may be present during the disclosure or discussion of the Protected Information. Disclosure of material pursuant to this paragraph shall not constitute a waiver of the confidential status of the material so disclosed.

Disclosure and Use of Highly Confidential—Source Code Information.

12. To the extent production of source code becomes necessary in this case, a producing party may designate source code as Highly Confidential—Source Code Information if it comprises or includes confidential, proprietary, or trade secret source code.

13. The parties agreed to cooperate in good faith so as to protect the producing party's source code while not unreasonably hindering the receiving party's ability to efficiently and effectively conduct the prosecution or defense of this action.

14. Protected Information designated as Highly Confidential—Source Code shall be subject to all of the protections afforded to Confidential Attorney Eyes Only Information and may be disclosed only to the authorized individuals to whom Confidential Attorney Eyes Only Information may be disclosed, as set forth in paragraph 8, with the exception of the two in-house counsel specified in paragraph 8(a). Disclosure of this information to the individuals identified in paragraph 8(e) may only be made if the disclosure is reasonably necessary for this litigation and the individuals have signed the Confidentiality Agreement in the form attached as Exhibit B.

15. Any source code produced in discovery shall be made available for inspection, in a format allowing it to be reasonably reviewed and searched, during normal business hours (8:00 a.m. to 6:00 p.m. on open business days) or at other mutually agreeable times, at an office of the producing party's counsel or another mutually agreed upon location. The source code shall be made available for inspection on a secured computer in a secured room without internet access or network access to other computers, and the receiving party shall not copy, remove, or otherwise transfer any portion of the source code onto any recordable media or recordable device. The producing party shall provide the receiving party with information explaining how to start, log on to, and operate the computer(s) in order to access the source code. The producing party may visually monitor the activities of the receiving party's representatives during any source code review, but only to ensure that there is no unauthorized recording, copying, or transmission of the source code.

16. The receiving party may request paper copies of limited portions of source code that are reasonably necessary for the preparation of court filings, pleadings, expert reports, or other papers, or for deposition or trial, but shall not request paper copies for the purposes of reviewing the source code other than electronically as set forth in paragraph 15 in the first instance. The producing party shall provide all such source code in paper form including bates numbers and the label specified in

paragraph 3(c). The producing party may challenge the amount of source code requested in hard copy form pursuant to the dispute resolution procedure and timeframes set forth in paragraph 5 whereby the producing party is the "receiving party" and the receiving party is the "producing party" for purposes of the dispute resolution provisions of that paragraph.

17. The receiving party shall maintain a record of any individual who has inspected any portion of the source code in electronic or paper form. The receiving party shall maintain all paper copies of any printed portions of the source code in a secured, locked area under the supervision and control of an individual authorized to be in possession of the information. The receiving party may also temporarily keep paper copies of any printed portions of the source code at (a) the Court for any proceedings where the use of the source code may be relevant; (b) the site of any depositions where the use of the source code may be relevant; and (c) any intermediate location reasonably necessary to transport the copies (e.g., at a hotel prior to a Court proceeding or deposition) as long as the receiving party takes reasonable steps to secure the copies.

18. Highly Confidential—Source Code Information may only be transported by the receiving party at the direction of a person authorized to be in possession of the information by hand carry, Federal Express, or other similar reliable courier. Highly Confidential—Source Code Information may not be transported or transmitted electronically over a network of any kind, including a LAN, intranet, or the internet, except as required by the Court pursuant to paragraph 19 below.

19. The receiving party shall not create any electronic or other images of the paper copies and shall not convert any of the information contained in the paper copies into any electronic format without the producing party's permission, except as is necessary to create documents that, pursuant to the Court's rules, procedures, or orders, must be filed or served electronically. The receiving party shall only make additional paper copies if such additional copies are (1) necessary to prepare court filings, pleadings, or other papers (including a testifying expert's expert report), (2) necessary for deposition, or (3) otherwise necessary for the preparation of its case. Any paper copies used during a deposition shall be retrieved by the producing party at the end of each day and must not be given to or left with a court reporter or any other unauthorized individual.

Non–Party Information.

20. The existence of this Protective Order shall be disclosed to any person producing documents, tangible things or testimony in this action who may reasonably be expected to desire confidential treatment for such documents, tangible things or testimony. Any such person may designate documents, tangible things, or testimony confidential pursuant to this Protective Order.

Filing Documents With the Court.

21. In the event that any party wishes to submit Protected Information to the Court, such party shall follow the procedures prescribed by the Court, including obtaining leave of Court prior to filing any documents under seal.

No Prejudice.

22. Producing or receiving confidential information, or otherwise complying with the terms of this Protective Order, shall not (a) operate as an admission by any party that any particular Protected Information contains or reflects trade secrets or any other type of confidential or proprietary information; (b) prejudice the rights of a party to object to the production of information or material that the party does not consider to be within the scope of discovery; (c) prejudice the rights of a party to seek a determination by the Court that particular materials be produced; (d) prejudice the rights of a party to apply to the Court for further protective orders; or (e) prevent the parties from agreeing in writing to alter or waive the provisions or protections provided for herein with respect to any particular information or material.

Conclusion of Litigation.

23. Within sixty (60) calendar days after final judgment in this action, including the exhaustion of all appeals, or within sixty (60) calendar days after dismissal pursuant to a settlement agreement, each party or other person subject to the terms of this Protective Order shall be under an obligation to destroy or return to the producing party all materials and documents containing Protected Information, and to certify to the producing party such destruction or return. However, outside counsel for any party shall be entitled to retain all court papers, trial transcripts, exhibits, and attorney work provided that any such materials are maintained and protected in accordance with the terms of this Protective Order.

Other Proceedings.

24. By entering this Order and limiting the disclosure of information in this case, the Court does not intend to preclude another court from finding that information may be relevant and subject to disclosure in another case. Any person or parties subject to this Protective Order that may be subject to a motion to disclose another party's information designated as Protected Information pursuant to this Protective Order, shall promptly notify that party of the motion so that it may have an opportunity to appear and be heard on whether that information should be disclosed.

Remedies.

25. It is Ordered by the Court that this Protective Order will be enforced by the sanctions set forth in Rule 37(b) of the Federal Rules of Civil Procedure and such other sanctions as may be available to the Court, including the power to hold parties or other violators of this Protective Order in contempt. All other remedies available to any person(s) injured by a violation of this Protective Order are fully reserved.

26. Any party may petition the Court for good cause shown, in the event such party desires relief from a term or condition of this Order.

Exhibit A

IN THE UNITED STATES DISTRICT COURT
FOR THE WESTERN DISTRICT OF PENNSYLVANIA

Plaintiff v. Defendant.   )   Civil Action No.

**CONFIDENTIALITY AGREEMENT FOR EXPERT,
CONSULTANT OR EMPLOYEES OF ANY PARTY**

I hereby affirm that:

Information, including documents and things, designated as "Protected Information," as defined in the Protective Order entered in the above-captioned action (hereinafter "Protective Order"), is being provided to me pursuant to the terms and restrictions of the Protective Order.

I have been given a copy of and have read the Protective Order.

I am familiar with the terms of the Protective Order and I agree to comply with and to be bound by such terms.

I submit to the jurisdiction of this Court for enforcement of the Protective Order.

I agree not to use any Protected Information disclosed to me pursuant to the Protective Order except for purposes of the above-captioned litigation and not to disclose any such information to persons other than those specifically authorized by said Protective Order, without the express written consent of the party who designated such information as confidential or by order of this Court. I also agree to notify any stenographic, clerical, or technical personnel who are required to assist me of the terms of this Protective Order and of its binding effect on them and me.

I understand that I am to retain all documents or materials designated as or containing Protected Information in a secure manner, and that all such documents and materials are to remain in my personal custody until the completion of my assigned duties in this matter, whereupon all such documents and materials, including all copies thereof, and any writings prepared by me containing any Protected Information are to be returned to counsel who provided me with such documents and materials.

Exhibit B

IN THE UNITED STATES DISTRICT COURT
FOR THE WESTERN DISTRICT OF PENNSYLVANIA

Plaintiff v. Defendant.   )   Civil Action No.

CONFIDENTIALITY AGREEMENT FOR THIRD—PARTY VENDORS

I hereby affirm that:

Information, including documents and things, designated as "Protected Information," as defined in the Protective Order entered in the above-captioned action (hereinafter "Protective Order"), is being provided to me pursuant to the terms and restrictions of the Protective Order.

I have been given a copy of and have read the Protective Order.

I am familiar with the terms of the Protective Order and I agree to comply with and to be bound by such terms.

I submit to the jurisdiction of this Court for enforcement of the Protective Order.

I agree not to use any Protected Information disclosed to me pursuant to the Protective Order except for purposes of the above-captioned litigation and not to disclose any such information to persons other than those specifically authorized by said Protective Order, without the express written consent of the party who designated such information as confidential or by order of this Court.

[Effective September 1, 2009. Amended effective December 1, 2009; August 1, 2015.]

APPENDIX LPR 2.2a   PROSECUTION BAR

Prosecution Bar

Absent written consent from the producing party, any individual (including in-house counsel and outside counsel) who reviews Confidential Attorney Eyes Only Information relating to the producing party's technical or scientific information (as opposed to financial, marketing, or other types of information not related to the technical subject matter of the patents in suit) ("Technical Confidential Attorney Eyes Only Information") or Highly Confidential—Source Code Information shall not be involved in the prosecution of patents or patent applications relating to [(insert subject matter)], including without limitation the patents asserted in this action and any patent or application claiming priority to or otherwise related to the patents asserted in this action, before any foreign or domestic agency, including the United States Patent and Trademark Office. For purposes of this paragraph, "prosecution" includes directly or indirectly drafting, amending, advising, or otherwise affecting the scope or maintenance of patent claims. To avoid any doubt, "prosecution" as used in this paragraph does not include representing a party challenging a patent before a domestic or foreign agency (including, but not limited to, a reissue protest, ex parte reexamination, inter partes reexamination, or other similar proceeding). This Prosecution Bar shall begin when the Technical Confidential Attorney Eyes Only Information or Highly Confidential—Source Code Information is first reviewed by the affected individual and shall end [___ months/years] after final termination of this action, including appeals.

Documents and things produced during the course of this litigation that contain Technical Confidential Attorneys Eyes Only Information should be designated by the producing party as containing Technical Confidential Attorneys Eyes Only Information by placing on each page and each thing a legend substantially as follows:

TECHNICAL CONFIDENTIAL ATTORNEYS EYES ONLY INFORMATION SUBJECT TO PROTECTIVE ORDER AND PROSECUTION BAR

[Effective August 1, 2015.]

APPENDIX LPR 4.2   JOINT DISPUTED CLAIM TERMS CHART

JOINT DISPUTED CLAIM TERMS CHART** Plaintiff
v. Defendant, Civ. Action No. 00–000–XXX

Disputed Claim Term	Plaintiff Proposed Construction	Plaintiff Citation To Intrinsic Evidence	Defendant Proposed Construction	Defendant Citation To Intrinsic Evidence
1. "Term 1"				
2. "Term 2"				
3. "Term 3"				
4. "Term 4"				

[Effective September 1, 2009.]

** This chart shall not contain legal argument.

ELECTRONIC CASE FILING

MISC. 05–186.   IN RE: ELECTRONIC CASE FILING POLICIES AND PROCEDURES

ORDER

Effective July 1, 2005, the court will establish an Electronic Case Filing system, referred to in this Order as "ECF." ECF is designed to capitalize on the use of automated technology in the administration of justice by promoting cost savings, more efficient maintenance of court records, and improved public access to case file information. As delineated in Local Rules 5.4 and 5.5, ECF permits electronic filing, signing and verification of pleadings and other papers with the clerk of court through the court's public web site, allows parties to use the court's transmission facilities to make service when appropriate, and authorizes the clerk of court to serve notice of orders and judgments when appropriate, and

This Order details the policies and procedures to be followed by parties participating in ECF, and is intended to be applied and interpreted in connection with the court's ECF User Manual. The court is satisfied that these procedures, read in conjunction with the Electronic Filing User Manual, are consistent with the policies of the Judicial Conference of the United States and all applicable Federal Rules of Civil and Criminal Procedure.

IT IS HEREBY ORDERED THAT:

1.   The court adopts the attached Electronic Case Filing Policies and Procedures and directs that they be applied and interpreted in connection with the court's ECF User Manual.

2.   The clerk of court may amend the ECF User Manual from time to time as appropriate, and shall make copies of this Order and the User Manual available to the bar and public at the clerk's office and on the court's public web site at www. pawd.uscourts.gov.

[Dated: April 20, 2005.]

ELECTRONIC CASE FILING POLICIES AND PROCEDURES

1. Definitions.

1.1 "Electronic Filing System" refers to the court's automated system that receives and stores documents filed in electronic form. The program is part of the CM/ECF (Case Management/Electronic Case Files) software which was developed for the Federal Judiciary by the Administrative Office of the United States Courts.

1.2 "Filing User" is an individual who has a court-issued login and password to file documents electronically.

1.3 "Notice of Electronic Filing" is a notice automatically generated by the Electronic Filing System at the time a document is filed with the system, setting forth the time of filing, the name of the party and attorney filing the document, the type of document, the text of the docket entry, the name of the party and/or attorney receiving the notice, and an electronic link (hyperlink) to the filed document, which allows recipients to retrieve the document automatically.

1.4 "PACER" (Public Access to Court Electronic Records) is an automated system that allows an individual to view, print and download court docket information over the internet.

1.5 "PDF/A" refers to Portable Document Format. A document file created with a word processor, or a paper document which has been scanned, must be converted to portable document format to be filed electronically with the court. Converted files contain the extension ".pdf".

1.6 "Proposed Order" is a draft document submitted by an attorney for a judge's signature. A proposed order shall accompany a motion or other request for relief as an electronic attachment to the document.

1.7 "Technical Failure" is defined as a malfunction of court owned/leased hardware, software, and/or telecommunications facility which results in the inability of a Filing User to submit a filing electronically. Technical failure does not include malfunctioning of a Filing User's equipment.

2. Scope of Electronic Filing. All civil, criminal and miscellaneous cases shall be assigned to the Electronic Filing System. Except as expressly provided herein or by order of court, or in exceptional circumstances including technical failures, a Filing User shall electronically file all documents required to be filed with the court.

The filing of initial papers may be accomplished electronically under procedures outlined in the court's ECF User Manual. In a case removed to the federal court, parties are required to electronically file all documents previously filed in the state court. Service of the summons and complaint must be made under Federal Rule of Civil Procedure 4.

This Court is a mandatory ECF court. All attorneys must be a registered Filing User. Pro Hac Vice movants/admittees must comply with Local Civil Rule 83.2(B).

A party who is not represented by counsel may file papers with the clerk in the traditional manner, but is not precluded from filing electronically.

Effective June 12, 2006, a processing fee and sanctions of $150.00 per document will be imposed each time an attorney files a document by means other than the Court's CM/ECF system, unless leave of Court has been granted to file the document under seal. Attorneys shall pay a processing fee and sanctions of $150.00 per document for failure to file a document with this Court electronically by use of the CM/ECF system. This fee must be paid from the funds of the attorney or his/her law firm. Counsel shall not charge to or collect the $150.00 from the client as a fee, cost, expense, or other charge in this case. (See Standing Order at Misc 06–34—In Re: Compliance With Electronic Case Filing Registration Requirements)

3. Eligibility, Registration, Passwords. An attorney admitted to the Bar of this court, including an attorney admitted pro hac vice, may register as a Filing User by completing and submitting the prescribed registration form electronically under the Court's CM/ECF Electronic Filing link "Request CM/ECF User Account" at http://www.pawd.uscourts.gov. Registration as a Filing User constitutes consent to electronic service of all documents as provided in this Court's Electronic Case Filing Policies and Procedures in accordance with the Federal Rules of Civil Procedure and the Federal Rules of Criminal Procedure.

A person who is a party to an action who is not represented by an attorney may register as a Filing User in the Electronic Filing System solely for purposes of the action. If during the course of the action the person retains an attorney who appears on the person's behalf, the attorney must advise the clerk to terminate the person's registration as a Filing User upon the attorney's appearance.

When registering, an individual must have an established PACER account and certify that ECF training has been completed. An individual may register more than one Internet e-mail address. Once the registration is processed by the clerk, the Filing User will receive notification of the user login and password. A Filing User shall protect the security of the User's password and immediately notify the clerk if the Filing User learns that the password has been compromised.

Once registration is complete, a Filing User may not withdraw from participation in the Electronic Filing System except by leave of court.

Once registered, a Filing User shall be responsible for maintaining his/her account, including, but not limited to change of address, firm, phone number, e-mail notification address, etc.

4. **Consequences of Electronic Filing.** Electronic transmission of a document to the Electronic Filing System in accordance with this Court's Electronic Case Filing Policies and Procedures, together with the transmission of a Notice of Electronic Filing from the court, constitutes filing of the document for all purposes of the Federal Rules of Civil Procedure, the Federal Rules of Criminal Procedure and the Local Rules of this court, and constitutes entry of the document on the docket kept by the clerk under Fed.R.Civ.P. 58 and 79, and Fed.R.Crim.P. 49 and 55.

When a document has been filed electronically, the official record of that document is the electronic recording as stored by the court, and the filing party is bound by the document as filed. A document filed electronically is deemed filed on the "**filed on**" date on the Notice of Electronic Filing from the court.

The fact that a party files a document electronically does not alter the filing deadline for that document. Electronic filing must be completed before midnight Eastern time in order to be considered timely filed that day. In accordance with Rule 6(d) of the Federal Rules of Civil Procedure and Rule 45(c) of the Federal Rules of Criminal Procedure, service by electronic means is treated the same as service by mail for the purposes of adding three (3) days to the prescribed period to respond.

5. **Entry of Court Orders and Related Papers.** A document entered or issued by the court will be filed in accordance with this Court's Electronic Case Filing Policies and Procedures and such filing shall constitute entry on the docket kept by the clerk under Fed.R.Civ.P. 58 and 79 and Fed.R.Crim.P. 55.

All signed orders will be filed electronically by the court or court personnel. An order filed electronically without the original signature of a judge shall have the same force and effect as if the judge had affixed a signature to a paper copy of the order and the order had been entered on the docket in a conventional manner.

A Filing User submitting a document that requires a judge's signature shall submit the document as an electronic attachment to a motion or other request for relief in accordance with the procedure for a "Proposed Order" as outlined in the court's ECF User Manual.

6. **Notice of Court Orders and Judgments.** Immediately upon the entry of an order or judgment in an action, the clerk will transmit to Filing Users in the case, in electronic form, a Notice of Electronic Filing. Electronic transmission of the Notice of Electronic Filing constitutes the notice required by Fed.R.Civ.P. 77(d) and Fed.R.Crim.P.49(c). The clerk must give notice in paper form to a person who is not a registered filing user.

7. **Attachments and Exhibits.** A Filing User must submit in electronic form all documents referenced as exhibits or attachments in accordance with the court's ECF User Manual, unless otherwise ordered by the court. A Filing User shall submit as exhibits or attachments only those excerpts of the referenced documents that are directly germane to the matter under consideration by the court. Excerpted material must be clearly and prominently identified as such. Filing Users who file excerpts of documents as exhibits or attachments under this rule do so without prejudice to their right to timely file additional excerpts or the complete document. Responding parties may timely file additional excerpts or the complete document that they believe are/is directly germane.

8. **Sealed Documents.** A document subject to a sealing order must be filed in the traditional manner on one-sided paper in a sealed envelope marked "sealed" accompanied by a disk or CD–ROM containing the document in PDF/A format. Each pdf must be no larger than 2.5MB. Only the motion to file a document under seal may be filed electronically, unless prohibited by law. When filing a motion for leave to file a document under seal, the filer must state in the motion why a means other than sealing is not available or unsatisfactory to support the necessity of the seal.

When leave has been granted to file a document under seal, the filing party must first electronically file a redacted public version of the document, unless otherwise ordered by the Court. It is the filer's responsibility to present the sealed version of the document to the clerk's office for filing in the traditional manner on paper in a sealed envelope marked "sealed" and with appropriate court and case identifying information, accompanied by a disk or CD–ROM containing the document in PDF/A format. The Clerk of Court will not docket the sealed version of the document until the party electronically files the redacted public document.

The Court may establish a practice, when sealing documents, to specify a date by which the seal will be vacated or state that the document will be sealed permanently. If no specific date is provided to vacate the seal or the record is not designated as being permanently sealed, the Judge who chairs the Joint IT Committee and the Chief Deputy of the Clerk's Office will implement a policy to unseal documents, only upon written notice to the litigants prior to unsealing.

The order of the court authorizing the filing of document(s) under seal may be filed electronically, unless prohibited by law.

Refer to this Court's policy governing all sealed matters–Misc No. 05–45 (See Exhibit A)

9. Special Filing Requirements and Exceptions.

9.1 *Special Filing Requirements.* The documents listed below shall be presented for filing in the traditional manner on paper and accompanied by a disk or CD–ROM containing the document in PDF/A format:

Sealed (subject to policy on sealed matters—Misc No. 05–45—Exhibit A)

Cases filed sealed by STATUTE (such as, Qui Tam Cases).

9.2 *Mandatory Exceptions.* In addition to the provision in LCrR49D, the following are excluded from the Electronic Filing System and shall be filed solely on paper:

ALL GRAND JURY MATTERS:

The following documents are examples of grand jury matters:

  1) Motion to Empanel Grand Jury and orders ruling on them;

  2) Motions to Quash Grand Jury subpoenas and orders ruling on them;

  3) Motions to Enforce Grand Jury subpoenas and orders ruling on them;

  4) Motions for immunity and orders ruling on them;

  5) Motions for appointment of counsel before a Grand Jury and orders ruling on them.

9.3 Social Security Administrative Transcripts shall be filed electronically by the U.S. Attorney's Office.

9.4 Original State Court Records presented in 28 U.S.C. Section 2254 cases shall be filed in the traditional manner on paper. Records received will be noted on the docket, however, will not be available for view electronically. State Court records are NOT part of this court's permanent case file and are returned to the appropriate State Court upon final disposition.

9.5 Transcripts of this Court (both civil and criminal) shall be filed electronically in PDF/A Format. The Judicial Conference has established a policy regarding the electronic availability of transcripts of court proceedings. The policy establishes a procedure whereby counsel can request the redaction from the transcript of specific personal data identifiers before the transcript is remotely electronically available to the public and also recognizes the court reporters' statutory authority to sell copies of the transcript.

  9.5.1 A transcript filed by a court reporter or transcriber will be available at the office of the clerk for inspection only for a period of 90 days after it has been filed. A party must file a Notice of Intent to Request Redaction of Specific Personal Data Identifiers within seven days of the filing of the official transcript by the court reporter. Neither the court nor court reporters will review the original transcript for specific personal data identifiers. A Notice of Intent to Request Redaction of Specific Personal Data Identifiers form is available under the Forms section on the court's website at http://www.pawd.uscourts.gov/ (See Exhibit B)

During the 90 day restriction period, a copy of the officially transcribed transcript may be purchased from the court reporter/transcriber at the rate established by the Judicial Conference and will be available for inspection only on the public terminal in the clerk's office. After the 90 day period has ended, the filed transcript will be available for inspection and copying in the clerk's office and for download from the court's CM/ECF system through the PACER system.

Following the filing of a notice of Intent to Request Redaction of Specific Personal Identifiers, the parties have 21 days from the date the transcript is filed with the clerk, or longer IF ordered by the court, to submit a statement to the court reporter/transcriber indicating where the specific personal data identifiers appear in the transcript by page and line and how they are to be redacted. See 14.1 of these Procedures for Redacted Identifiers. The court reporter/transcriber shall have 31 days from the date of the filing of the official transcript with the clerk of court to electronically file the redacted transcript. The redacted transcript filed with the clerk will be made available to the general public and remotely electronically available once the initial 90 day restriction period of the original transcript is lifted. The original or unredacted transcript will remain restricted. **Note:** If a party fails to submit the statement within this time frame, the transcript will be made remotely electronically available without redaction of specific personal data identifiers 90 days after the initial filing of the transcript with the clerk.

Note: The 90 day restriction time calculation begins with the electronic filing of the initial official transcript by the court reporter or transcriber and does not begin again should a redacted transcript be subsequently filed. The initial calculated release date of the 90 day restriction applies to the redacted transcript.

10. Retention Requirements. A document that is electronically filed and requires an original signature other than that of the Filing User must be maintained in paper form by counsel and/or the firm representing the party on whose behalf the document was filed until one year after all periods for appeals expire. Such papers in criminal cases shall be retained by the United States Attorney. On request of the court, said counsel must provide the original document for review.

11. Signatures. The user login and password required to submit documents to the Electronic Filing System serve as the Filing User's signature on all electronic documents filed with the court. They serve as a signature for purposes of Fed.R.Civ.P.11, all other Federal Rules of Civil Procedure, the Federal Rules of Criminal Procedure, the Local Rules of this court, and any other purpose for which a signature is required in connection with proceedings before the court.

Each document filed electronically must indicate in the caption that it has been electronically filed. An electronically filed document must include a signature block in compliance with Local Rule 5.2(B), and must set forth the name, address, telephone number, fax number, e-mail address, and the attorney's Pennsylvania or other state bar identification number, if applicable. When listing the attorney identification number, the state's postal abbreviation shall be used as a prefix (e.g., PA12345, NY2243316). In addition, the name of the Filing User under whose login and password the document is submitted must be preceded by an "s/" and typed in the space where the signature would otherwise appear. No Filing User or other person may knowingly permit or cause to permit a Filing User's password to be used by anyone other than an authorized agent of the Filing User. A document containing the signature of a defendant in a criminal case shall be electronically filed as a scanned document in PDF format that contains an image of the defendant's original signature. The Filing User is required to verify the readability of the scanned document before filing it electronically with the court.

A document requiring signatures of more than one party must be filed electronically either by: (1) submitting a scanned document containing all necessary signatures; (2) representing the consent of the other parties on the document; or (3) in any other manner approved by the court.

12. Service of Documents by Electronic Means.

12.1 *Service of Process.* Fed.R.Civ.P. 5(b) and Fed.R.Crim.P. 49(b) do **not** permit electronic service of process for purposes of obtaining personal jurisdiction, i.e., Rule 4 service. Therefore, service of process must be effected in the traditional manner.

12.2 *Other Types of Service*:

12.2.1 Filing User. Upon the electronic filing of a pleading or other document, the court's ECF System will automatically generate and send a Notice of Electronic Filing to all Filing Users associated with that case. Transmission of the Notice of Electronic Filing constitutes service of the filed document.

The Notice of Electronic Filing includes the time of filing, the name of the party and attorney filing the document, the type of document, the text of the docket entry, and an electronic link (hyperlink) to the filed document, allowing anyone receiving the notice by e-mail to retrieve the document automatically. If the Filing User becomes aware that the Notice of Electronic Filing was not transmitted successfully to a party, or that the notice is deficient, i.e. the electronic link to the document is defective, the filer shall serve the electronically filed document by e-mail, hand delivery, facsimile, or by first-class mail postage prepaid immediately upon notification of the deficiency of the Notice of Electronic Filing.

12.2.2 Individual who is not a Filing User. A Non–Filing User is entitled to receive a paper copy of any electronically filed document from the party making such filing. Service of such paper copy must be made according to the Federal Rules of Civil Procedure, the Federal Rules of Criminal Procedure and the Local Rules of Court.

13. Technical Failures.
The clerk shall deem the court's Electronic Case Filing Web Site to be subject to a technical failure if the site is unable to accept filings continuously or intermittently for **more** than one hour occurring after 12:00 noon (Eastern Time) that day. If a Filing User experiences technical failure, the document may be submitted to the court that day in an alternative manner, provided that it is accompanied by an affidavit of the Filing User's failed attempts to file electronically at least two times in one hour increments after 12:00 noon. The following methods of filing are acceptable as a result of a technical failure:

13.1 via electronic mail in a PDF/A attachment, sent to the e-mail address for technical failures listed in the ECF User Manual;

13.2 in person, by bringing the document to the clerk's office on paper accompanied by a disk or CD–ROM which contains the document in PDF/A format;

13.3 Problems on the filer's end, such as phone line problems, problems with the filer's Internet Service Provider (ISP), or hardware or software issues, do not constitute a technical failure under these procedures nor excuse an untimely filing.

Should, however, a technical failure of the filer's equipment cause the filing party to miss a filing deadline, the filer shall electronically file, within 24 hours of failure, a motion for leave to file said document(s) out of time along with a completed "Verification of Technical Failure–Filer's equipment" (Exhibit C).

If filing said motion for leave electronically within 24 hours is impossible, the filing party must hand deliver the motion and verification to the Clerk's Office on paper accompanied by a disk or CD–ROM which contains the document(s) in PDF/A format OR by mailing same to the Clerk's Office and postmarked accordingly, for filing. If leave is granted, the filer shall electronically file said document(s) forthwith.   Service of motion and verification shall be made on all parties of record by filing party.

Counsel should be aware that the Court will be monitoring filers for abuse of this procedure.

The initial point of contact for a Filing User experiencing technical difficulty filing a document electronically shall be the case assigned docket clerk whose phone number can be found on the Court's website at www.pawd.uscourts.gov under the CM/ECF link for help.

A Filing User who suffers prejudice as a result of a technical failure may seek appropriate relief from the court.

14. Public Access.   A person may retrieve information from the Electronic Filing System at the court's Internet site by obtaining a PACER login and password.   A person who has PACER access may retrieve docket sheets and documents in all cases, except for social security cases, in which only participants in the case may retrieve certain documents.   Any case or document under seal shall not be available to the public through electronic or any other means.

14.1 *Sensitive Information.*   As the public may access certain case information over the Internet through the court's Electronic Filing System, sensitive information should not be included in any document filed with the court unless such inclusion is necessary and relevant to the case.   In accordance with Local Rule 5.2(D), if sensitive information must be included, the following specific personal data identifiers must be partially redacted from the document, whether it is filed traditionally or electronically: Social Security numbers to the last four digits, financial account numbers to the last four digits, dates of birth to the year and the names of minor children to the initials.[1]

Note: In criminal case documents only, home addresses also must be redacted to the city and state.

In compliance with the E–Government Act of 2002, a party wishing to file a document containing the specific personal data identifiers specified above must file a motion for leave to file the unredacted document or reference list under seal.   If the motion to seal is granted, the party may file: 1) a sealed and otherwise identical document containing the unredacted personal identifiers; or 2) a reference list under seal.   The reference list shall contain the complete personal data identifier(s) and the redacted identifier(s) used in its (their) place in the filing.   All references in the case to the redacted identifiers included in the reference list will be construed to refer to the corresponding complete personal data identifier.

In addition, caution must be exercised when filing documents that contain the following:

1) Personal identifying number, such as a driver's license number;

2) medical records, treatments and diagnosis;

3) employment history;

4) individual financial information; and

5) proprietary or trade secret information

Additional items for criminal cases only:

6) information regarding an individual's cooperation with the government;

7) information regarding the victim of any criminal activity;

8) national security information; and

9) sensitive security information as described in 49 U.S.C. Section 114(s).

14.2   Documents for which public access will not be provided in criminal cases.

The following documents shall not be included in the public criminal case file and will not be made available to the public at the courthouse or via remote electronic access:

1) Un-executed summonses or warrants of any kind (e.g., search warrants, arrest warrants);

2) Pretrial bail or pre-sentence investigation reports;

3) Statements of Reasons in the judgment of conviction;

4) Juvenile records;

5) Financial Affidavits filed in seeking representation pursuant to the Criminal Justice Act;

6) Ex Parte requests for authorization of investigative, expert or other services pursuant to the Criminal Justice Act; and

7) Sealed documents

Counsel is strongly urged to share this information with all clients so that an informed decision about the inclusion of certain materials may be made. If a redacted document is filed, it is the sole responsibility of counsel and the parties to be sure that pleadings and other papers comply with the rules and orders of this court requiring redaction of personal identifiers. The clerk will not review each filing for redaction.

15. Hyperlinks. In order to preserve the integrity of the court record, attorneys wishing to insert hyperlinks in court filings shall continue to use the traditional citation method for the cited authority, in addition to the hyperlink. The Judiciary's policy on hyperlinks is that a hyperlink contained in a filing is no more than a convenient mechanism for accessing material cited in the document. A hyperlink reference is extraneous to any filed document and is not part of the court's record.

EXHIBIT A

IN THE UNITED STATES DISTRICT COURT
FOR THE WESTERN DISTRICT OF PENNSYLVANIA

IN RE: CONFIDENTIALITY AND PROTECTIVE ORDERS IN CIVIL MATTERS

ORDER

AND NOW, this 27TH day of January 2005, as APPROVED by the Board of Judges on January 26, 2005,

It is hereby ORDERED that effective July l, 2005, any provision in a Confidentiality or Protective Order filed prior to June 30, 2005 that permits the parties to designate documents as confidential and file said documents with the Court under seal is NULL and VOID.

IT IS FURTHER ORDERED, that for Confidentiality or Protective Orders filed on or after July 1, 2005, the Court will not recognize any provision of said orders which allow for the automatic sealing of documents that are filed with the Court.

On or after July 1, 2005, parties wishing to file documents under seal must obtain prior leave of Court for each document that is requested to be filed under seal.

Donetta W. Ambrose
Chief U.S. District Judge

Revised 3/08

EXHIBIT B

IN THE UNITED STATES DISTRICT COURT
FOR THE WESTERN DISTRICT OF PENNSYLVANIA

_____   Case No. _____

Plaintiff(s)

vs

_____

Defendant(s)

NOTICE OF INTENT TO REQUEST REDACTION OF
SPECIFIC PERSONAL DATA IDENTIFIERS

Notice is hereby given that a statement of redaction of specific personal data identifiers will be submitted to the court reporter/transcriber within 21 days from the filing of the transcript with the clerk.

s/ _____

ID Bar Number
Attorney for (Plaintiff/Defendant)

Address

City/State/Zip

Phone: (xxx) xxx-xxxx

E-mail: xxx@xxxx.xxx

Date: _____

CERTIFICATE OF SERVICE

I hereby certify that on _____, I electronically filed the foregoing with the Clerk of Court using the CM/ECF system which will send notification of such filing to the following: _____. I hereby certify that I have personally served _____, court reporter/transcriber and that I have mailed by U.S. Postal Service, the document to the following non–CM/ECF participant(s) _____.

s/ _____

EXHIBIT C

IN THE UNITED STATES DISTRICT COURT
FOR THE WESTERN DISTRICT OF PENNSYLVANIA

Plaintiff   Case No.
   vs.
Defendant

Verification of Technical Failure Filer's Equipment

Please take notice that [Plaintiff/Defendant, Name of Party] was unable to file [Title of Document] in timely manner because of technical difficulties. The deadline for filing the [Title of Document] was [Filing Deadline Date]. The reason(s) that I was unable to file the [Title of Document] in a timely manner and the good faith efforts I made prior to the filing deadline to both file in a timely manner and to inform the Court and the other parties that I could not do so are set forth below.

[Statement of reasons and good faith efforts to file and to inform (including dates and times)]

I declare under penalty of perjury that the foregoing is true and correct.

Respectfully submitted,

s/[Name of Registrant]

ID Bar Number
Attorney for (Plaintiff/Defendant)

Address

City, State, Zip Code

Phone: (xxx) xxx-xxxx

E-mail: xxx@xxxx.xxx

[Amended effective January 1, 2011; January 1, 2012; March 1, 2013; June 1, 2013.]

1Documents in social security cases are excluded from the redaction requirement as they are not electronically available to the public over the Internet, pursuant to the privacy policy of the Judicial Conference of the United States

ALTERNATIVE DISPUTE RESOLUTION
POLICIES AND PROCEDURES

1. Definitions.

1.1 **"Mediation"** refers to a nonadjudicative, third-party intervention wherein an impartial neutral, selected by the parties, facilitates negotiations between the parties to help them reach a mutually acceptable agreement. The parties are responsible for negotiating a settlement. The neutral's role is to assist the process in ways acceptable to the disputants.

1.2 **"Early Neutral Evaluation"** refers to a nonadjudicative, third-party intervention by an impartial experienced attorney, selected by the parties, with subject matter expertise. After reviewing concise presentations of the parties' claims, the neutral provides a non-binding evaluation of the case and thereafter is available to assist the parties in reaching an agreement.

1.3 **"Arbitration"** involves the referral of a dispute to an impartial third party (or a panel of three), selected by the parties, who, after giving the parties an opportunity to present evidence and arguments, renders a non-binding determination in settlement of the claim(s). Arbitration in the federal district court is further defined in 28 U.S.C. § 654. Parties may agree to be bound by the arbitrator's decision which is non appealable.

1.4 Other ADR Processes. See Section 7.

2. General Provisions.

2.1 *Staff and Responsibilities.* An ADR Coordinator will oversee the Court's ADR programs and must have expertise in ADR procedures. The ADR Coordinator is responsible for designing, implementing, administering and evaluating the Court's ADR programs. These responsibilities include educating litigants, lawyers, Judges, and Court staff about the ADR program and rules. In addition, the ADR Coordinator must be responsible for overseeing, screening and orienting neutral arbitrators, mediators and evaluators (hereinafter "neutrals") to serve in the Court's ADR programs.

2.2 *ADR Internet Site.* www.pawd.uscourts.gov, contains information about the Court's ADR processes, information about neutrals and their fees, answers to frequently asked questions, various forms approved by the Court, and information about becoming a neutral in the Court's programs.

2.3 *Contacting the ADR Coordinator.* The ADR Coordinator's contact information is:

ADR Coordinator

United States District Court

For the Western District of PA

700 Grant Street

Pittsburgh, PA 15219

Telephone: (412) 208–7458

Fax: (412) 208–7517

E–Mail: ADRCoordinator@pawd.uscourts.gov

The Court encourages litigants and counsel to consult the ADR Internet site (www.pawd.uscourts.gov) and to contact the ADR Coordinator to discuss the suitability of ADR options for their cases or for assistance in tailoring an ADR process to a specific case.

2.4 *ADR Judge.* The Court has appointed a United States District Judge (who serves as the Chair of the Court's Standing Committee on Case Management and

ADR) to serve as the ADR Judge. The ADR Judge is responsible for overseeing the ADR program, consulting with the ADR Coordinator on matters of policy, program design and evaluation, education, training and administration. When necessary, the Chief District Judge may appoint another Judicial Officer of this Court to perform, temporarily, the duties of the ADR Judge.

If a party files a motion with the court alleging matters such as bad faith or requesting enforcement of a settlement reached as a result of the ADR process, the assigned judicial officer may adjudicate the motion or may elect to request another judge to do so. Should the latter occur, the matter will be referred internally to another judge who is a member of the Case Management and ADR Committee, to decide the motion.

2.5 *Neutrals.*

A. Panel. The ADR Coordinator must maintain a panel of neutrals serving in the Court's ADR programs. Neutrals will be selected from time to time by the Court from applications submitted by lawyers willing to serve or by other persons as set forth in section B(1)(b) below.

B. Qualifications and Training. Each person serving as a neutral in a Court ADR program must be a member of the bar of this Court, a member of the faculty of an accredited law school, or be approved by this Court to serve as a neutral and be determined by the ADR Judge to be competent to perform the applicable duties, and must successfully complete initial and periodic training sessions as required by the Court and be a registered user of the Electronic Case Filing (ECF) system for the United States District Court, Western District of Pennsylvania. (**All neutrals, including those who are retained privately, are required to be registered users of the Court's ECF system.**) Additional minimum requirements for serving on the Court's panel of neutrals, which the Court may modify in individual circumstances for good cause, are as follows:

1. Mediators.

a. Attorney Mediators. Mediators who are attorneys must have been admitted to the practice of law for at least seven years and must have:

i. substantial experience with civil litigation in federal court;

ii. completed 40 hours of mediation training, including training in the facilitative method of mediation. At least 16 hours of mediation training must be participating in simulated facilitative mediations;

iii. strong mediation process skills and the temperament and training to listen well, facilitate communication across party lines and assist the parties with settlement negotiations.

b. Non–Attorney Mediators. Non-attorney mediators may be appointed to a case only with the consent of the parties. Mediators who are not attorneys may be selected to serve on the Court's panel of mediators if they are knowledgeable about civil litigation in federal courts and have:

i. appropriate professional credentials in another discipline;

ii. 40 hours of mediation training, including training in the facilitative method of mediation;

iii. experience mediating at least five cases; and

iv. strong mediation process skills and the temperament and training to listen well, facilitate communication across party lines and assist the parties with settlement negotiations.

c. All Mediators. All mediators must adhere to the Model Standards of Conduct for Mediators as last adopted or amended by the American Arbitration Association, American Bar Association and Association for Conflict Resolution, as well as any other applicable standards of professional conduct which may be required by the Court. (Available at http://www.abanet. org/dispute/docu-ments/model_standards_conduct_april2007.pdf.)

2. Early Neutral Evaluators. Evaluators must have been admitted to the practice of law for at least 15 years and must have:

a. substantial experience with civil litigation in federal court;

b. substantial expertise in the subject matter of the cases assigned to them; and

c. the temperament and training to listen well, facilitate communication across party lines and, if called upon, assist the parties with settlement negotiations.

d. agreed to adhere to the Model Standards of Conduct for Mediators as last adopted or amended by the American Arbitration Association, American Bar Association and Association for Conflict Resolution, as well as any other applicable standards of professional conduct which may be required by the Court. (Available at http://www.abanet.org/dispute/documents/model_standards_conduct_april2007.pdf.)

3. Arbitrators. Arbitrators must have been admitted to the practice of law for at least 10 years and must have:

a. For not less than five years, committed 50% or more of their professional time to matters involving litigation; or

b. Substantial experience serving as a neutral in dispute resolution proceed-ings; and

c. agree to adhere to the Model Standards of Conduct for Arbitrators. (Available at http://www.abanet.org/dispute/commercial_disputes.pdf.)

C. Immunities. All persons serving as neutrals in any of the Court's ADR programs are performing quasi-judicial functions and are entitled to the immuni-ties and protections that the law accords to persons serving in such capacity.

2.6 *Evaluation of ADR Programs.* Congress has mandated that the Court's ADR programs be evaluated. Neutrals, counsel and parties must promptly respond to any inquiries or questionnaires from persons authorized by the Court to evaluate the programs. Responses to such inquiries will be used for research and monitoring purposes only and the sources of specific information will not be disclosed to the assigned Judicial Officer in any report.

2.7 *Attendance at Session.*

A. Parties. Each party must attend the selected ADR process session unless excused under paragraph D below. This requirement reflects the Court's view that the principal values of Alternate Dispute Resolution include affording liti-gants an opportunity to articulate their positions and to hear, first hand, both their opponent's version of the matters in dispute and a neutral assessment of the merits of the case.

1. Corporation or Other Entity. A party other than a natural person (e.g., a corporation or an association) satisfies this attendance requirement if represent-ed by a decision maker(s) (other than outside counsel) who has full settlement authority and who is knowledgeable about the facts of the case.

2. Government Entity. A unit or agency of government satisfies this attendance requirement if represented by a person who has, to the greatest extend feasible, full settlement authority, and who is knowledgeable about the facts of the case, the governmental unit's position, and the procedures and policies under which the governmental unit decides whether to accept proposed settlements. If the action is brought by the government on behalf of one or more individuals, at least one such individual also must attend.

3. Any party who fails to have physically in attendance the necessary decision maker(s) will be subject to sanctions.

B. Counsel. Each represented party must be accompanied at the selected ADR process session by the lawyer who will be primarily responsible for handling the trial of the matter. If a party is proceeding pro se, a request may be made to the Court to name a pro bono attorney to represent the pro se litigant at the selected ADR process session.

C. Insurers. Insurer representatives, including, if applicable, risk pool representatives, are required to attend in person unless excused under paragraph D below, if their agreement would be necessary to achieve a settlement.

D. Request to be Excused. A person who is required to attend the selected ADR process session may be excused from attending in person only after a showing that personal attendance would impose an extraordinary or otherwise unjustifiable hardship. A person seeking to be excused must file a motion with the assigned Judicial Officer, no fewer than 15 days before the date set for the session, simultaneously copying the Arbitration Clerk (if applicable), all other counsel and unrepresented parties and the neutral(s). The motion seeking excuse from the selected ADR process session must:

1. Set forth with specificity all considerations that support the request;

2. State realistically the amount in controversy in the case;

3. Indicate whether the other party or parties join in or object to the request; and

4. Be accompanied by a proposed order.

E. Participation by Telephone. A person excused from attending the selected ADR process session in person must be available to participate by telephone.

3. Mediation.

3.1 *Description.* Mediation is a flexible, non-binding, confidential process in which a neutral person (the mediator), selected by the parties, facilitates settlement negotiations. The mediator improves communication across party lines, helps parties articulate their interests and understand those of their opponent, probes the strengths and weaknesses of each party's legal positions, identifies areas of agreement and helps generate options for a mutually agreeable resolution to the dispute. The mediator generally does not give an overall evaluation of the case. A hallmark of mediation is its capacity to expand traditional settlement discussion and broaden resolution options, often by exploring litigant needs and interests that may be formally independent of the legal issues in controversy.

3.2 *Eligible Cases.* Appropriate civil cases may be referred to mediation by order of the assigned Judicial Officer.

3.3 *Mediators.*

A. Referral. No later than the Initial Case Management Conference (Rule 16) the parties are to choose a mediator who is available during the appropriate period and has no apparent conflict of interest.

B. Compensation. Unless otherwise agreed by all parties or ordered by the Court, one-half the cost of the mediator's services must be borne by the plaintiff(s) and one-half by the defendant(s) at the rate contained in the neutral's fee schedule filed with the Court. In a case with third-party defendants, the cost must be divided into three equal shares. A neutral must not charge or accept in connection with a particular case a fee or thing of value from any source other than the parties. The Court may review the reasonableness of the fee and, if necessary, enter an Order modifying the fee. Compensation must be paid directly to the neutral upon the conclusion of the ADR process, or as otherwise agreed to by the parties and the mediator. Failure to pay the mediator must be brought to the Court's attention.

C. Fee Waiver. A party who demonstrates a financial inability to pay all or part of that party's pro rata share of the neutral's fee may request the Court to appoint a mediator who has agreed to serve pro bono. The Court may waive all or part of that party's share of the fee. Other parties to the case who are able to pay the fee must bear their pro rata portions of the fee.

3.4   *Timing and Scheduling the Mediation.*

A.   Scheduling by Mediator.   Promptly after being chosen to mediate a case, the mediator shall, after consulting with all parties, fix the date and place of the mediation within the deadlines set by paragraph B below, or the order referring the case to mediation.

B.   Deadline for Conducting Mediation.   Unless otherwise ordered, the mediation shall be held within 60 days after the Initial Case Management Conference (Rule 16) or issuance of the Initial Case Management Order, whichever occurs first.

3.5   *Request to Extend the Deadline.*

A.   Motion Required.   Requests for extension of the deadline for conducting a mediation must be made no later than 15 days before the session is to be held and must be directed to the assigned Judicial Officer, in a motion under LR 7.1, with a copy to the other parties and the mediator.

B.   Content of Motion.   Such motion must:

1.   Detail the considerations that support the request;

2.   Indicate whether the other parties concur in or object to the request; and

3.   Be accompanied by a proposed order setting forth a new deadline by which the mediation must be held.

3.6   *Telephone Conference Before Mediation.*   The mediator must schedule a brief joint telephone conference with counsel and any unrepresented parties before the mediation session to discuss matters such as the scheduling of the mediation, the procedures to be followed, the nature of the case, and which client representatives will attend.

3.7   *No Written Mediation Statements Required.*   Written mediation statements are not required for mediations.

3.8   *Procedure at Mediation.*

A.   Procedure.   The mediation must be informal and must employ a facilitative method.   Mediators have discretion to structure the mediation so as to maximize the benefits of the process.

B.   Separate Caucuses.   The mediator may hold separate, private caucuses with each side or each lawyer or, if the parties agree, with the parties only.   The mediator may not disclose communications made during such a caucus to another party or counsel without the consent of the party who made the communication.

3.9.   *Follow Up.*   At the close of the mediation session, the mediator and parties shall jointly determine whether it would be appropriate to schedule any additional ADR activity.   Additional ADR activities to which the parties may agree include, but need not be limited to: written or telephonic reports by the parties to one another or to the mediator; exchange of specified information; another mediation session; or asking the Court for a settlement conference.

3.10   *Report of the Neutral.*   Within five (5) days of the conclusion of the mediation, the mediator must electronically file the "Report of Neutral" which includes the caption and case number, the date of the mediation, whether any follow up is scheduled, whether the case resolved in whole or in part, and any stipulations the parties agree may be disclosed.

4.   Early Neutral Evaluation.

4.1   *Description.*   In Early Neutral Evaluation (ENE) the parties and their counsel, in a confidential session, make compact presentations of their claims and defenses, including key evidence as developed at that juncture, and receive a non-binding evaluation by an experienced neutral lawyer, selected by the parties, with subject matter expertise. The evaluator also helps identify areas of agreement, offers case-planning suggestions and, if requested by the parties, settlement assistance.

4.2 *Eligible Cases.* Subject to the availability of an evaluator with subject matter expertise, appropriate civil cases may be referred to ENE by order of the assigned Judicial Officer.

4.3 *Evaluators.*

A. Referral. No later than the Initial Case Management Conference (Rule 16) the parties are to choose an evaluator who has expertise in the subject matter of the lawsuit, is available during the appropriate period and has no apparent conflict of interest.

B. Compensation. Unless otherwise agreed by all parties or ordered by the Court, one-half the cost of the evaluator's services must be borne by the plaintiff(s) and one-half by the defendant(s) at the rate contained in the evaluator's fee schedule filed with the Court. In a case with third-party defendants, the cost must be divided into three equal shares. An evaluator must not charge or accept in connection with a particular case a fee or thing of value from any source other than the parties. The Court may review the reasonableness of the fee and, if necessary, enter an Order modifying the fee.

Compensation must be paid directly to the evaluator upon the conclusion of the ADR process, or as otherwise agreed to by the parties and the evaluator. Failure to pay the evaluator must be brought to the Court's attention.

C. Fee Waiver. A party who demonstrates a financial inability to pay all or part of that party's pro rata share of the neutral's fee may request the Court to appoint an evaluator who has agreed to serve pro bono. The Court may waive all or part of that party's share of the fee. Other parties to the case who are able to pay the fee must bear their pro rata portions of the fee.

4.4 *Timing and Scheduling the Early Neutral Evaluation.*

A. Scheduling by Evaluator. Promptly after being appointed to a case, the evaluator must, after consulting with all parties, fix the date and place of the ENE within the deadlines set by paragraph B below, or the order referring the case.

B. Deadline for Conducting Session. Unless otherwise ordered, the ENE must be held within 60 days after the Initial Case Management Conference (Rule 16) or the issuance of the Initial Case Management Order (Rule 16), whichever occurs first.

4.5 *Requests to Extend Deadline.*

A. Motion Required. Requests for extension of the deadline for conducting an ENE must be made no later than 15 days before the ENE is to be held and must be directed to the assigned Judicial Officer, in a motion under Civil LR 7.1, with a copy to the other parties and the evaluator.

B. Content of Motion. Such motion must:

1. Detail the considerations that support the request;

2. Indicate whether the other parties concur in or object to the request; and

3. Be accompanied by a proposed order setting forth a new deadline by which the ENE must be held.

4.6 *Ex Parte Contact Prohibited.* Except with respect to scheduling matters, there must be no ex parte communications between parties or counsel and the evaluator, including private caucuses to discuss settlement, until after the evaluator has either delivered orally his or her evaluation or, if so requested by the parties, has committed his or her evaluation to writing, or all parties have agreed that ex parte communications with the evaluator may occur.

4.7 *Telephone Conference Before Early Neutral Evaluation.* The evaluator must schedule a brief joint telephone conference with counsel before the ENE to discuss matters such as the scheduling, the procedures to be followed, the nature of the case, and which client representatives will attend.

4.8 *Written Statements.*

A. Time for Submission. No later than 10 calendar days before the ENE, each party must submit directly to the evaluator, and must serve on all other parties, a written Statement.

B. Prohibition Against Filing. The Statements constitute confidential information, must not be filed and the assigned Judicial Officer must not have access to them.

C. Content of Statement. The Statements must be concise and should include any information that may be useful to the evaluator, for example:

1. Identify, by name and title or status:

a. The person(s) with decision-making authority, who, in addition to counsel, will attend the ENE as representative(s) of the party, and

b. Persons connected with a party opponent (including an insurer representative) whose presence might substantially improve the utility of the ENE or the prospects for settlement;

2. Describe briefly the substance of the suit, addressing the party's views of the key liability issues and damages and discussing the key evidence;

3. Address whether there are legal or factual issues whose early resolution would reduce significantly the scope of the dispute or contribute to settlement negotiations;

4. Identify the discovery that is necessary to equip the parties for meaningful settlement negotiations;

5. Describe the history and status of any settlement negotiations; and

6. Include copies of documents out of which the suit arose (*e.g.,* contracts), or whose availability would materially advance the purposes of the evaluation session, (*e.g.,* medical reports or documents by which special damages might be determined).

4.9 *Procedure at an Early Neutral Evaluation.*

A. Components of Early Neutral Evaluation. Unless otherwise agreed to by the parties and evaluator, the evaluator must:

1. Permit each party (through counsel or otherwise), orally and through documents or other media, to present its claims or defenses and to describe the principal evidence on which they are based;

2. Help the parties identify areas of agreement and, where feasible, enter stipulations;

3. Assess the relative strengths and weaknesses of the parties' contentions and evidence, and explain the reasoning that supports these assessments;

4. Estimate, where feasible, the likelihood of liability and the dollar range of damages;

5. Help the parties devise a plan for sharing the important information and/or conducting the key discovery that will equip them as expeditiously as possible to enter meaningful settlement discussions or to position the case for disposition by other means;

6. Help the parties assess litigation costs realistically; and

7. If the parties are interested, help them, through private caucusing or otherwise, explore the possibility of settling the case; and

8. Determine whether some form of follow up to the session would contribute to the case development process or to settlement.

B. Process Rules. The session must be informal. Rules of evidence must not apply. There must be no formal examination or cross-examination of witnesses and no recording of the presentations or discussion must be made.

C. Evaluation. The evaluation must be presented orally to all parties (including, as applicable, party representatives, insurers and risk pool representatives), and may be supplemented by a written evaluation within ten days of the ENE if so requested by the parties. The evaluation constitutes confidential information which shall not be disclosed to the assigned Judicial Officer or anyone else except as provided in Section 6.D.

Comment: See Prohibition Against Disclosing ENE Communications to Settlement Judges, 494 F. Supp. 2d 1097 (N.D. CA. 2007).

D. Settlement Discussions. At any point during the ENE, if all parties agree, they may proceed to mediation and/or discuss settlement.

4.10 *Follow Up.* At the close of the ENE session, the neutral evaluator and parties shall jointly determine whether it would be appropriate to schedule any additional ADR activity. Additional ADR activities to which the parties may agree include, but need not be limited to: written or telephonic reports by the parties to one another or to the neutral evaluator; exchange of specified information; a mediation session; or asking the court for a settlement conference

4.11 *Limitation on Authority of Evaluator.* Evaluators have no authority to compel parties to conduct or respond to discovery or to file motions. Nor do evaluators have authority to determine what the issues in any case are, to impose limits on parties' pretrial activities, or to impose sanctions.

4.12 *Report of the Neutral.* Within five (5) days of the conclusion of the ENE, the evaluator must electronically file "Report of Neutral" which includes the caption and case number, the date of the session, whether any follow up is scheduled, whether the case resolved in whole or in part, and any stipulations the parties agree may be disclosed.

5. Court Sponsored Arbitration (in accordance with 28 U.S.C. § 651.)

(For private arbitration, see Section 7.)

5.1 *Description.* Arbitration is an adjudicative process in which an arbitrator or a panel of three arbitrators, selected by the parties, issues a non-binding judgment ("award") on the merits after an expedited, adversarial hearing. Either party may reject the non-binding award and request a trial de novo. An arbitration occurs earlier in the life of a case than a trial and is less formal and less expensive. Because testimony is taken under oath and is subject to cross-examination, arbitration can be especially useful in cases that turn on credibility of witnesses. Arbitrators do not facilitate settlement discussions.

5.2 *Eligible Cases.* A case may be referred to arbitration by order of the assigned Judicial Officer.

5.3 *Arbitrators.*

A. Selection. After entry of an order referring the case to arbitration, the parties must choose an arbitrator from the Court's panel or, if the parties cannot decide, an arbitrator must be randomly selected by the Arbitration Clerk. The parties have the option of choosing a panel of three arbitrators. If the parties cannot agree upon the panel of three, one or more arbitrators may be selected by the Arbitration Clerk.

B. Notification by Clerk. The Arbitration Clerk must promptly notify the person or persons who is selected to serve. If any person so selected is unable or unwilling to serve, the Arbitration Clerk will secure another arbitrator after conferring with the parties. When the requisite number of arbitrators has agreed to serve, the Arbitration Clerk must promptly send written notice of the selections to the arbitrator(s) and to the parties. When a panel of three arbitrators is selected, the Arbitration Clerk must designate the person to serve as the panel's presiding arbitrator.

C. Compensation. Arbitrators are paid by the Court $250, per Judicial Conference Policy, per day or portion of each day of hearing in which they serve as a single arbitrator or $100 for each day or portion of each day in which they serve as a member of a panel of three. No party may offer or give the arbitrator(s) any gift. No compensation is permitted for preparation time on the case.

D. Payment and Reimbursement. When filing an award, arbitrators must submit a voucher on the form prescribed by the Arbitration Clerk for payment of compensation and for reimbursement of any reasonable transportation expenses necessarily incurred in the performance of duties. No reimbursement will be made for any other expenses.

5.4 *Timing and Scheduling the Hearing.*

A. Scheduling by Arbitrator. Promptly after being appointed to a case, the arbitrator(s) must arrange for the pre-session phone conference and, after consulting with all parties, must fix the date and place for the arbitration within the deadline fixed by the assigned Judicial Officer, or if no such deadline is fixed, within 90 days after the notice of appointment. Counsel and unrepresented parties must respond promptly to and cooperate fully with the arbitrator(s) with respect to scheduling the pre-session phone conference and the arbitration hearing. The hearing date must not be continued or vacated except for emergencies as established in writing and approved by the assigned Judicial Officer. If the case is resolved before the hearing date, or if due to an emergency a participant cannot attend the arbitration, counsel or an unrepresented party must notify the arbitrator(s) immediately upon learning of such settlement or emergency.

B. Place and Time. The hearing may be held at any location within the Western District of Pennsylvania selected by the arbitrator(s), including a room at a federal courthouse, if available. In selecting the location, the arbitrator(s) must consider the convenience of the parties and witnesses. Unless the parties agree otherwise, the hearing must be held during normal business hours.

5.5 *Ex Parte Contact Prohibited.* Except with respect to scheduling matters, there must be no ex parte communications between parties or counsel and an arbitrator.

5.6 *Written Arbitration Statements.*

A. Time for Submission. No later than 10 calendar days before the arbitration session, each party must submit directly to the arbitrator(s), and must serve on all other parties, a written Arbitration Statement.

B. Prohibition against Filing. The statements must not be filed and the assigned Judicial Officer must not have access to them.

C. Content of Statement. The statements must be concise and must:

1. Summarize the claims and defenses;

2. Identify the significant contested factual and legal issues, citing authority on the questions of law;

3. Identify proposed witnesses; and

4. Identify, by name and title or status, the person(s) with decision-making authority, who, in addition to counsel, will attend the arbitration as representative(s) of the party.

D. Modification of Requirement by Arbitrator(s). After jointly consulting counsel for all parties and any unrepresented parties, the arbitrator(s) may modify or dispense with the requirements for the written Arbitration Statements.

5.7 *Telephone Conference Before Arbitration.* The arbitrator(s) must schedule a brief joint telephone conference with counsel and any unrepresented parties before the arbitration to discuss matters such as the scheduling of the arbitration, the procedures to be followed, whether supplemental written material should be submitted, which witnesses will attend, how testimony will be presented, including expert testimony, and whether and how the arbitration will be recorded.

5.8 *Authority of Arbitrators and Procedures at Arbitration.*

A. Authority of Arbitrators. Arbitrators must be authorized to:

1. Administer oaths and affirmations;

2. Make reasonable rulings as are necessary for the fair and efficient conduct of the hearing; and

3. Make awards.

B. Prohibition on Facilitating Settlement Discussions. Arbitrators are not authorized to facilitate settlement discussions. If the parties desire assistance with settlement, the parties or arbitrator(s) may request that the case be referred to mediation (see Section 3 above), or a settlement conference before the Court.

C. Presumption against Bifurcation. Except in extraordinary circumstances, the arbitrator(s) must not bifurcate the arbitration.

D. Quorum. Where a panel of three arbitrators has been named, any two members of a panel must constitute a quorum, but the concurrence of a majority of the entire panel must be required for any action or decision by the panel, unless the parties stipulate otherwise.

E. Testimony.

1. Subpoenas. Attendance of witnesses and production of documents may be compelled in accordance with F.R.Civ.P. 45.

2. Oath and Cross-examination. All testimony must be taken under oath or affirmation and must be subject to such reasonable cross-examination as the circumstances warrant.

3. Evidence. In receiving evidence, the arbitrator(s) must be guided by the Federal Rules of Evidence, but must not thereby be precluded from receiving evidence which the arbitrator(s) consider(s) relevant and trustworthy and which is not privileged.

F. Transcript or Recording. A party may cause a transcript or recording of the proceedings to be made but must provide a copy to any other party who requests it and who agrees to pay the reasonable costs of having a copy made.

G. Default of Party. The unexcused absence of a party must not be a ground for continuance, but damages must be awarded against an absent party only upon presentation of proof thereof satisfactory to the arbitrator(s).

5.9 *Award and Judgment.*

A. Form of Award. An award must be made after an arbitration under this Rule. Such an award must state clearly and concisely the name or names of the prevailing party or parties and the party or parties against which it is rendered, and the precise amount of money, if any, awarded. It must be in writing and (unless the parties stipulate otherwise) be signed by the arbitrator or by at least two members of a panel. No arbitrator must participate in the award without having attended the hearing. Costs within the meaning of F.R.Civ.P. 54 and Civil LR 54.1 may be assessed by the arbitrator(s) as part of an arbitration award.

B. Filing and Serving the Award. Within 10 days after the arbitration hearing is concluded, the arbitrator(s) must deliver the award to the Arbitration Clerk in an unsealed envelope with a cover sheet stating: "Arbitration Award." The cover sheet also must list the case caption, case number and name(s) of the arbitrator, but must not specify the content of the award. The Clerk must note the entry of the arbitration award on the docket and promptly serve copies of the arbitration award on the parties.

C. Sealing of Award. Each filed arbitration award must promptly be sealed by the Clerk. The award must not be disclosed to any Judicial Officer who might be assigned to the case until the Court has entered final judgment in the action or the action has been otherwise terminated, except as necessary to assess costs or prepare the report required by Section 903(b) of the Judicial Improvements and Access to Justice Act.

D. Entry of Judgment on Award. If no party has filed a demand for trial de novo (or a notice of appeal, which must be treated as a demand for trial de novo) the Clerk must enter judgment on the arbitration award in accordance with F.R.Civ.P. 58. A judgment so entered must be subject to the same provisions of law and must have the same force and effect as a judgment of the Court in a civil action, except that the judgment must not be subject to review in any other court by appeal or otherwise.

5.10 *Trial de Novo.*

A. Time for Demand. If any party files and serves a demand for trial de novo within 14 days of entry of the filing of the arbitration award, no judgment thereon must be entered by the Clerk and the action must proceed in the normal manner before the assigned Judicial Officer. Failure to file and serve a demand for trial de novo within this 14-day period waives the right to trial de novo.

B. Limitation on Admission of Evidence. At the trial de novo the Court must not admit any evidence indicating that there has been an arbitration proceeding, the nature or amount of any award, or any other matter concerning the conduct of the arbitration proceeding, unless:

    1. The evidence would otherwise be admissible in the trial under the Federal Rules of Evidence, or

    2. The parties have otherwise stipulated.

C. Award Not to be Attached. A party filing a demand for a trial de novo must not attach the arbitration award.

5.11 *Stipulation to Binding Arbitration.* At any time before the arbitration hearing, the parties may stipulate in writing to waive their rights to request a trial de novo. Such stipulation must be submitted to the assigned Judicial Officer for approval and must be filed. In the event of such stipulation, judgment must be entered on the arbitration award after the award is received by the Arbitration Clerk.

5.12 *Federal Arbitration Act.* Nothing in these ADR Policies and Procedures Rules limits any party's right to agree to arbitrate any dispute, regardless of the amount, pursuant to Title 9, United States Code, or any other provision of law.

6. Confidentiality.

A. General Rule. Except as provided in subsection D of this Section 6, this Court, the ADR Coordinator, all neutrals, all counsel, all parties and any other person who participates (in person or by telephone) in (i) any ADR process described in Sections 1 through 5 of these Policies and Procedures, or (ii) any private ADR process pursuant to Court order, shall treat as "confidential information" (i) the contents of all documents created for or by the neutral, (ii) all communications and conduct during the ADR process, and (iii) all "communications in connection with" the ADR process.

B. "Communications in connection with" any ADR process include nonverbal, oral and written communications made by, between, or among (i) a party, (ii) counsel for a party, (iii) a neutral, (iv) a member of the neutral's staff, (v) the ADR Coordinator, or (vi) any other person present to further the ADR process, when the communication occurs (x) during any ADR process, or (y) before or after any

ADR process and is made by or to the neutral, a member of the neutral's staff, or the ADR Coordinator.

C. "Confidential Information":

1. shall only be disclosed to those involved in the ADR process, and shall not be disclosed to any other person, specifically including the assigned Judicial Officer or his or her staff;

2. shall not be used for any purpose, including impeachment, in any pending or future proceeding.

D. Limited Exceptions to Confidentiality. This Section 6 does not prohibit:

1. Disclosure of any confidential information the neutral is required to report to the Court pursuant to (a) Sections 3.3B or 4.3B hereof, both of which provide that a failure to pay the neutral must be brought to the Court's attention, or (b) Sections 3.10 or 4.12 hereof, both of which address the mandatory report of the neutral.

2. Disclosure to the Court in writing of the failure of any party, party representative, insurer or risk pool representative to appear as required pursuant to Sections 3.8, 4.9 or 5.8 of these Policies and Procedures and as designated in a Court Order. The disclosure permitted by this exception is only that the party, party representative, or insurer or risk pool representative failed to appear and does not include any portion of any communication in connection with the ADR process relating to the failure to appear.

3. Disclosure of specifically identified confidential information when all parties agree in writing that such specifically identified information may be disclosed.

4. Disclosure of confidential information by the neutral to the extent that such disclosure is necessary for the neutral to respond to, or defend against, a claim or allegation of professional misconduct or malfeasance.

5. Disclosure of a written settlement document signed by the parties in an action or proceeding to enforce the settlement agreement expressed in the document, unless the settlement document by its terms states that it is unenforceable or not intended to be legally binding.

6. To the extent that the communication or conduct is relevant and admissible evidence in a pending criminal proceeding, as determined by a court, disclosure of:

a. a threat of bodily injury;

b. a threat to damage real or personal property under circumstances constituting a felony; or

c. conduct causing direct bodily injury.

7. Disclosure of a fraudulent communication made during a mediation or ENE process to the extent that such communication is relevant and admissible evidence in a pending action to enforce or set aside an agreement reached in the mediation or ENE process as a result of that fraudulent communication.

8. Disclosure of any document which, although referenced or used in an ADR process, exists independently of the ADR process.

9. Disclosure of an arbitration award if no party timely files a demand for trial de novo (or a Notice of Appeal) as provided in Section 5.11.A of these Policies and Procedures.

E. Miscellaneous

1. The neutral shall not be called to testify as to what transpired in an ADR process.

2. No one shall make any recording or transcript of any ADR session or proceeding without the prior written consent of all parties and other person participating in the ADR session.

3. A mediator or neutral evaluator shall: (a) ask the parties to sign an agreement to mediate or to engage in ENE; (b) ask all persons participating in a mediation or ENE to sign a confidentiality agreement, as part of the mediation or ENE agreement or as a separate document; and (c) clarify by agreement or engagement letter (i) that he or she serves only as a neutral and not as legal counsel for any participant and (ii) all fees and expenses that will be charged and payment terms.

7. Other ADR Processes.

7.1 *Private ADR.* There are numerous private sector providers of ADR services including arbitration, mediation, fact-finding, neutral evaluation and private judging. Private providers may be lawyers, law professors, retired judges or other professionals with expertise in dispute resolution techniques. Virtually all private sector providers charge fees for their services. The Court is willing to refer cases to private providers with the stipulation of the parties. The assigned Judicial Officer will take appropriate steps to assure that a referral to private ADR does not result in an imposition on any party of an unfair or unreasonable economic burden. At the conclusion of the private ADR session, with the exception of private arbitration, the neutral is to complete and file the Report of the Neutral, indicating that the session was held and if the session resulted in a settlement.

At the conclusion of the private arbitration, the arbitrator is to file a report only indicating the date that the arbitration was held.

7.2 *Special Masters.* The Court may appoint special masters to serve a wide variety of functions, including, but not limited to: discovery manager, fact finder or host of settlement negotiations. Generally the parties pay the master's fees.

7.3 *Non–Binding Summary Bench or Jury Trial.* A summary bench or jury trial is a flexible, non-binding process designed to promote settlement in complex, trial-ready cases headed for protracted trials. The process provides litigants and their counsel with an advisory verdict after a short hearing in which the evidence may be presented in condensed form, usually by counsel and sometimes through witnesses. This procedure, as ordinarily structured, provides the litigants an opportunity to ask questions and hear the reactions of the Judicial Officer or jury. The Judicial Officer's or jury's non-binding verdict and reactions to the legal and factual arguments are used as bases for subsequent settlement negotiations.

[Effective March 26, 2008. Revised effective February 1, 2012.]

JURY PLAN

PLAN OF THE UNITED STATES DISTRICT COURT FOR THE WESTERN DISTRICT OF PENNSYLVANIA FOR THE RANDOM SELECTION OF GRAND AND PETIT JURORS

Pursuant to 28 U.S.C. § 1863, the following Plan[1] is hereby adopted by this Court, subject to approval by a reviewing panel for the Third Circuit Judicial Council and to such rules and regulations as may be adopted from time to time by the Judicial Conference of the United States. In case of any conflict between this Plan and any statute, the statutory provisions shall govern.

Section 1. Declaration of Policy. All citizens shall have the opportunity to be considered for service on grand and petit juries in this Court and shall have an obligation to serve when summoned for this purpose.

Section 2. Discrimination Prohibited. No citizen shall be excluded from service as a grand or petit juror on account of race, color, religion, sex, national origin or economic status.

Section 3. Applicability of Plan. The Western District of Pennsylvania is divided into three divisions for jury selection purposes as follows:

The Pittsburgh Division consists of the counties of Allegheny, Armstrong, Beaver, Butler, Clarion, Fayette, Greene, Indiana, Jefferson, Lawrence, Mercer, Washington, and Westmoreland.

The Erie Division consists of the counties of Crawford, Elk, Erie, Forest, McKean, Venango, and Warren.

The Johnstown Division consists of the counties of Bedford, Blair, Cambria, Clearfield and Somerset.

The Provisions of this Plan shall apply to each division in the district, unless specifically indicated otherwise.

Section 4. Management and Supervision of Jury Selection Process. The Clerk of the Court shall manage the jury selection process under the supervision and control of the Chief Judge or such other district judge as the Chief Judge may designate.

For purposes of definition when used in this Plan, "Clerk" and "Clerk of Court" shall mean the Clerk of the district court, any authorized deputy clerk, and any other person authorized by the Court to assist the Clerk in the performance of the selection procedures authorized by the Plan.

Section 5. Plan for Random Jury Selection. Voter registration lists represent a fair cross section of the community in each division of the Western District of Pennsylvania. Accordingly, names of grand and petit jurors selected to serve on or after the effective date of this Plan shall be selected at random from the voter registration lists of all the counties within the relevant divisions.

"Voter registration lists" or "voters lists" referred to throughout this Plan shall mean the voter registration lists for a statewide primary or general election as maintained by the counties. Voter registration lists are exclusively obtained electronically from the Statewide Uniform Registry of Electors ("SURE") through the Department of State for all the appropriate jurisdictional counties.

This Plan's reference to random selection shall mean a purely random selection of all names, or a selection where only the first selected name shall be chosen by a purely random method, with each subsequent name for that drawing chosen systematically at regular intervals through the remainder of the source list. Either selection process used must insure: a) that names chosen will represent all segments of the source file from which drawn, b) that the mathematical odds of any single name being picked are substantially equalized, and c) that the possibility of human discretion or choice affecting the selection of any individual's name is eliminated.

The Judges of the Court have determined that the initial selection of persons to be considered for service as grand and petit jurors from the lists of the voters and placed in the master wheel shall be made at random in such a total number as may be deemed sufficient for a two-year period.

The number of names drawn from each county shall be substantially in the same proportion to the total number drawn from all counties within the division as the number of names on that county's list of voters bears to the total number of names on the lists of voters for all counties within the division. For example, if there are exactly 240,000 names on the list of voters of all counties within the division, and there are 48,000 names on County "A's" list (twenty percent of the total), then the number of County "A's" names initially selected should be substantially twenty percent of the total number selected from all counties within the division.

For the purpose of calculating from the lists of voters the total number of voters in the respective divisions within the district, the Clerk will add together the totals obtained for each county. The number taken as the total for each county may be based, at the Clerk's option, upon such total number as is published by the State Bureau of Elections or furnished by the Boards of Elections for the respective counties.

After determining the total number of names needed for the master jury wheel, the Clerk shall proceed through the use of a properly programmed data computer or through a combination of manual, computer or electronic methods to make the initial selection of names from the list of voters of each county.

a) *Determining a Quotient.* The Clerk shall maintain separate master jury wheels for each of the divisions within the District, and shall place in each master jury wheel the names of all persons randomly selected from the voter registration lists for that division. The number of names to be placed initially in each master jury wheel shall be at least one-half of one percent of the total number of voters registered in each division, and each master jury plan shall contain no less than 1,000 names.

For each division, the Clerk shall make the randomized selection by taking the total number of registered voters of the counties in that division of the court and dividing that number by the minimum number of names to be placed in the master jury wheel, and the number obtained will be the "quotient." The quotient is the ratio of selected to unselected names. For example, if the Clerk should determine that to supply court jury requirements for two years he or she will need 10,000 names in the master wheel, and if there are a total of 1,000,000 names on all county voter lists, the "quotient" to be used would be 1,000,000 divided by 10,000 or 100. The clerk would therefore take every "100th" name from the lists of voters for the master wheel.

b) *Determining a Starting Number.* After determining the "quotient," the Clerk shall establish a starting number.

This number will locate on the voter list, whether it is on paper, a computer tape or disk, or some other electronic media record, the first name to be selected. The Clerk will draw a starting number manually by lot from numbered cards in a drum or box. Numbers used for this drawing should begin with number one and end with the same number as the "quotient." In other words, the range of numbers from which a starting number is drawn is exactly the same range between number one and whatever the "quotient" number happens to be. As an example of how both the starting number and quotient are used, if we suppose the quotient to be 100 and the starting number drawn is 12, the first name chosen for each county would be the 12th name on its list of voters, the second name would be the 112th, the third the 212th, and continue in the same sequence to the end of the list.

Section 6. Selecting the Names by Manual Methods. In the event that circumstances prevent or render impossible the foregoing method of random selection from being followed, the Court may utilize an alternate manual method of random selection on a temporary basis.

When selection from any county's list of voters is made manually, names will be chosen by counting names down the list, either in a numerical sequence if the names are numbered, or if they are not numbered, in any other logical consistent sequence. Utilizing this process, the entire list must be covered and the specific names selected will be according to the established "quotient" and "starting number" formula described above.

Section 7. Selecting the Names by Machine Method. As noted in Section 5, all voter registration lists are exclusively obtained in electronic media format from the Statewide Uniform Registry of Electors ("SURE").

Consequently, a properly programmed electronic data processing system, or a combination system employing both manual and electronic methods may, at the Clerk's option and after consultation with the Chief Judge, be used to select master wheel names from voter lists of any or all counties in the District, provided that the required proportions of names for each county are maintained.

Similarly, the Judges of the Court have determined that an electronic data processing system or a combination electronic and manual system may, at the option of the Clerk and the Chief Judge, be used to select names from the master wheel for the purpose of determining qualification of jury service and from the qualified wheel for summoning persons to serve summoned to serve as grand or petit jurors, and the recording of names of prospective jurors on any papers and records needed by the court to administer the selection and payment of jurors.

The Clerk shall post a general notice for public review in the Clerk's office and on the Court's internet website explaining the process by which names are periodically and randomly drawn.

Section 8. Master Jury Wheels For Each Division. The physical form of record on which names for the master wheel is kept may include paper lists, data processing files, computer tapes, computer disks, or some other electronic format. Pursuant to 28 U.S.C. § 1863(b)(4), the minimum number of names to be placed in the master jury wheel shall be at least ½ of 1% of the total number of names on all county voter lists of the Pittsburgh, Johnstown and Erie divisions, respectively.

The Chief Judge, or such other district judge as the Chief Judge may designate, may order additional names to be placed in the master wheel from time to time, as necessary. The master jury wheel shall be emptied and refilled every two years and refilled within four months after a November general election.

Section 9. Drawing of Names from the Master Jury Wheels: Completion of Juror Qualification Forms. The Clerk or a designated deputy clerk in each of the Court's divisions shall, at periodic intervals, draw at random from the master jury wheel the names of as many persons as may be required to maintain an adequate number of names in the qualified wheel.

The Clerk may have prepared, by manual, computer, or electronic means, alphabetized lists of the names drawn. These lists shall not be exhibited to any person except as provided herein and in accordance with 28 U.S.C. §§ 1867(f), 1868. The Clerk shall, by manual, computer, or electronic means, prepare and have mailed to every person whose name is so drawn, a juror qualification questionnaire form, accompanied by instructions to execute and return the questionnaire duly signed and sworn, to the Clerk by mail or through the Court's internet website within ten days, in accordance with 28 U.S.C. § 1864(a).

A second juror qualification questionnaire form will be mailed to any person who fails to complete and return the initial juror qualification questionnaire as instructed. If the person fails to complete and return the second juror qualification questionnaire, such person may be summoned by the Clerk to appear and fill out such form.

Any such person who fails to appear as directed, or who appears to have willfully misrepresented a material fact on any such form for the purpose of securing or avoiding service as a juror, may be ordered by the Court to appear and explain his/her failure to appear or his/her alleged misrepresentation(s).

Section 10. Qualifications for Jury Service.

(a) Upon recommendation of the Clerk, the Chief Judge or such other district judge as the Chief Judge may designate, or the Clerk under supervision of the Court, shall determine solely on the basis of information provided on the jury qualification form and other competent evidence whether a person is qualified, unqualified, exempt, or to be excused from jury service. The Clerk shall enter such determination on the juror qualification form or in the juror record in the database of a computer program or on such other qualifying reports that contain the list of names drawn from the master wheel.

(b) In making such determination, the Court shall deem any person qualified to serve on grand and petit juries in the district unless he or she:

(1) is not a citizen of the United States, is less than eighteen years old, or has not resided for a period of one year within the judicial district;

(2) is unable to speak the English Language or is unable to read, write, and understand the English Language with a degree of proficiency sufficient to fill out satisfactorily the juror qualification questionnaire form;

(3) is incapable, by reason of mental or physical infirmity, to render satisfactory jury service;

(4) has a charge pending against him or her for the commission of a crime, or has been convicted in a State or Federal Court of record, of a crime punishable by imprisonment for more than one year and his or her civil rights have not been restored.

Section 11. Excuses on Individual Request.
The district court hereby finds that jury service by members of the following occupation classes or groups of persons may entail undue hardship or extreme inconvenience to the members thereof, and the excuse of such members for the life of the unexpired master wheel will not be inconsistent with 28 U.S.C. §§ 1861, 1862 and shall be granted individually upon written request:

(1) Any person 70 years of age and over;

(2) Any person who has served on a federal grand or petit jury panel within the past 2 years;

(3) Any person not gainfully employed full-time outside the home and having sole, full-time active custody of a child or children under 8 years of age, and the health and/or safety of such child or children would be jeopardized by that person's absence for jury; or any person not gainfully employed full-time outside the home who is likewise essential to the care of aged or infirm persons and who reside full time in the same household. This category does not apply to health care workers and/or those employed as caregivers;

(4) Any person whose presence is so essential to the operation of a business, that such business must close or cease to function during that person's their absence for jury duty;

(5) Any volunteer safety personnel who serve in an official capacity without compensation as firefighters, members of rescue squads or ambulance crews of a public agency of the United States, or any state, district, territory or possession of the United States, or any unit of local government, department or instrumentality of any of the foregoing. "Public Agency" for this purpose means the United States, any state of the United States, the District of Columbia, or any unit of local government, department, or instrumentality of the foregoing.

(6) In addition to the foregoing categories of persons, upon appearing for jury service, a Judge may determine that a prospective juror shall be excused from jury service, upon a request and showing that jury service would entail undue hardship or extreme inconvenience to the juror and that the excuse will not be inconsistent with the Act.

Section 12. Exemptions from Jury Service. Only the following persons who are barred from jury service under the provisions of 28 U.S.C. § 1863(b)(6) shall be exempt from jury service under this Plan:

(1) Members in active service in the Armed Forces of the United States.

(2) Members of the regular fire or police departments of any state, district, territory, possession or subdivision thereof;

(3) Full-time public officers in the executive, legislative, or judicial branches of the Government of the United States, or of any State, the District of Columbia, any territory or possession of the United States, or any subdivision of a State, the District of Columbia, or such territory or possession, who are actively engaged in the performance of official duties. "Public officer" shall mean a person who is either elected to public office or who is directly appointed by a person elected to public office.

Section 13. Qualified Jury Wheel for Each Division. The Clerk, designated deputy clerk, or another person authorized by the court to assist the Clerk in the performance of jury functions for the Pittsburgh, Johnstown and Erie divisions, shall maintain separate qualified jury wheels for each division and shall place in such wheels the names of all persons drawn from the master jury list in each division, who are not disqualified, exempt or excused pursuant to this Plan.

The qualified wheel for each division shall be emptied and refilled every two (2) years and within seven (7) months after a November general election in order that names shall be drawn no sooner than June 1st, unless otherwise ordered by the Court.

From time to time the Court may direct the Clerk to draw from the qualified wheel, via random manual or electronic selection, such number of persons as may be required for grand and petit jury arrays and supplemental arrays and to print their names and addresses on summons forms.

A supplemental array is a small list of prospective jurors which may be added to a regular array as necessary, when a regular array needs to be supplemented because of the number of jurors excused or because of increased jury requirements. Such supplemental array will become a part of the regular array until that array is terminated.

Lists of those juror names drawn from the qualified jury wheel and summoned for a term of court shall be made available to members of the bar who have cases pending on the current trial list and in accordance with Local Rules and the administrative practices of this Court.

From time to time, as grand juries are required in each court division, the Clerk shall order a random drawing from the qualified wheel of a sufficient number of names to realize, after excuses, a grand jury panel.

When the court orders a grand or petit jury to be drawn, the Clerk shall issue summonses for the required number of jurors. Each person drawn for jury service may be served in the manner prescribed in 28 U.S.C. § 1866(b). An alphabetical list may be prepared by the Clerk of persons assigned to each grand or petit jury.

Requests by summoned jurors to be excused from jury service shall be in writing, and received by the Clerk prior to the date summoned, except in emergency situations. Excuses from jury service will be by Order of the Court or by the Clerk, under the supervision of the Court. The clerk is specifically authorized to grant temporary excuses, under the supervision of the Court, upon a showing of undue hardship or extreme inconvenience and for such period of time as the clerk deems necessary. Permanent exclusions and excuses will be by Order of the Court or by the Clerk, under the supervision of the Court.

Except as provided elsewhere in this Plan, no person or class of persons shall be disqualified, excluded, excused or exempted from service as jurors; provided, however, that any person summoned for jury service may be:

1. Excused for a temporary period by the Court, or by the Clerk under the supervision of the Court, upon a showing of undue hardship or extreme inconvenience, for such period as is deemed necessary. At the conclusion of such temporary excuse period, the name of such person shall be reinserted into the qualified jury wheel for selection pursuant to 28 U.S.C. § 1886(a).

2. Excluded by the Court on the ground that such person may be unable to render impartial jury service, or that his or her service as a juror would be likely to disrupt the proceedings.

3. Excluded upon peremptory challenge as provided by law.

4. Excluded pursuant to the procedure specified by law upon a challenge by any party for good cause shown.

5. Excluded upon determination of the Court, after hearing in open court, that his or her service as a juror would be likely to threaten the secrecy of the proceedings, or otherwise adversely affect the integrity of jury deliberations, and that exclusion of such person will not be inconsistent with the policy stated in 28 U.S.C. §§ 1861, 1862.

Jurors who do not make a request in advance to be excused, and who report for jury service and request immediate release will not be paid by the Court for their service unless they can prove circumstances that warranted their travel to the courthouse.

Whenever a person is disqualified, excused, exempt or excluded from jury service, the Clerk shall note the same on the manual record or electronic tracking program being used at the time.

In any two-year, period, no person shall be required to (1) serve as a petit juror for more than 30 days, except when necessary to complete service in a particular case, or (2) serve on more than one grand jury, or (3) serve as both a grand and a petit juror.

Any person summoned for jury service who failed to appear as directed may be ordered by the district court to appear forthwith and show cause for his or her failure to comply with the summons. Any person who fails to show good cause for noncompliance to a summons may be fined not more than $1000, imprisoned not more than three days, or ordered to perform community service, or any combination thereof.

Section 14. Assignment to Panels. The names of all jurors reporting for petit jury service shall be placed in the jury wheel in the jury rooms in Pittsburgh, Johnstown or Erie, or will be available in the database of a computer program available to the court divisions. Names shall be drawn at random from the wheel or computer program and assigned to cases. After challenges are made during jury selection, the names remaining shall be placed immediately in the wheel or computer program for service on other cases. The system shall be employed to optimize the use of summoned jurors.

If a juror who has been selected for a case and who has given appropriate oath or affirmation, thereafter fails to appear at any session of court at the time and place fixed by the Court, he or she shall be adjudged in contempt of Court. Notwithstanding any sentence imposed by the Court, that juror shall not be paid juror's fees for any days served on the case for which that juror had been selected unless good cause is shown for failure to appear.

Section 15. Disclosure of Records.

(a) Names drawn from the qualified jury wheel to serve as petit jurors shall not be disclosed to the public or media until the jurors have been summoned and have appeared at the courthouse. The Court in any case may order that the names be kept confidential when the interests of justice so require, and may otherwise restrict the disclosure of juror information in accordance with local rules of court. Any request for disclosure shall be made to the Court by written motion.

(b) The contents of records or papers used by the Clerk in connection with the jury selection process shall not be disclosed except pursuant to this Plan or as may be necessary in the preparation or presentation of a motion challenging compliance with the selection procedures of the district court Plan. The parties in a case shall be allowed to inspect, reproduce, and copy such records or papers at all reasonable times during the pendency of such motion. Any person who discloses the contents of any record or paper shall be subject to penalty as provided in the Jury Selection and Service Act of 1968 as amended.

(c) Names of grand jurors shall not be disclosed except upon special order of the Court.

Section 16. Non–Citizens Report. The Chief Judge or the Clerk may, upon being advised that any potential juror identified him/herself, or has been determined to be, a non-citizen of the United States, notify the Department of State, Bureau of Elections. Any individual claiming to be a non-citizen shall provide proof of his/her non-citizen status in writing upon request by the Clerk.

Section 17. Authorization to Use a Contractor. The Court authorizes the Clerk to designate and contract for a competent electronic data processing service to perform any of the automated methods, tasks and procedures required by this plan, including but not limited to the creation of master wheels, the selection of prospective juror names, and the mailing of juror qualification forms. The selection of prospective juror names will be conducted pursuant to instructions by the Clerk and the contractor will certify that the work has been completed pursuant to those instructions.

Section 18. Protection of Jurors Employment.

(a) No employer shall discharge, threaten to discharge, intimidate, or coerce any permanent employee by reason of such employee's jury service, or the attendance or scheduled attendance in connection with such service, in any court of the United States.

(b) Any employer who violates the provisions of this section—

(1) shall be liable for damages for any loss of wages or other benefits suffered by an employee by reason of such violation;

(2) may be enjoined from further violations of this section and ordered to provide other appropriate relief, including but not limited to the reinstatement of any employee discharged by reason of his jury service; and

(3) shall be subject to a civil penalty of not more than $5000 for each violation as to each employee and may be ordered to perform community service.

[Entered January 29, 2009, as approved by the Judicial Council for the Third Circuit effective April 1, 2009.]

1 Approved by the Judicial Council on September 23, 1968, effective December 22, 1968; as modified and approved by the Judicial Council on February 27, 1969, September 3, 1969, March 31, 1971, December 8, 1971, July 7, 1972, May 14, 1973, November 18, 1977, March 19, 1979, March 13, 1980, October 14, 1983, October 24, 1984, June 3, 1988, March 17, 1989, January 2, 1990, March 29, 2001, and March 20, 2009, effective April 1, 2009.

SELECTED ORDERS

GENERAL ORDER 13–MC–44.   ORDER REGARDING DEPOSIT AND INVESTMENT OF REGISTRY FUNDS

The Court, having determined that it is necessary to adopt local procedures to ensure uniformity in the deposit and investment of funds in the Court's Registry,

IT IS ORDERED that the following shall govern the receipt, deposit and investment of registry funds:

I.   Receipt of Funds

A.   No money shall be sent to the Court or its officers for deposit in the Court's registry without a court order signed by the presiding judge in the case or proceeding.

B.   The party making the deposit or transferring funds to the Court's registry shall serve the order permitting the deposit or transfer on the Clerk of Court.

C.   Unless provided for elsewhere in this Order, all monies ordered to be paid to the Court or received by its officers in any case pending or adjudicated shall be deposited with the Treasurer of the United States in the name and to the credit of this Court pursuant to 28 U.S.C. § 2041 through depositories designated by the Treasury to accept such deposit on its behalf.

II.   Investment of Registry Funds

A.   Where, by order of the Court, funds on deposit with the Court are to be placed in some form of interest-bearing account, the Court Registry Investment System ("CRIS"), administered by the Administrative Office of the United States Courts under 28 U.S.C. § 2045, shall be the only investment mechanism authorized.

B.   The Director of Administrative Office of the United States Courts is designated as custodian for CRIS.   The Director or the Director's designee shall perform the duties of custodian.   Funds held in the CRIS remain subject to the control and jurisdiction of the Court.

C.   Money from each case deposited in the CRIS shall be "pooled" together with those on deposit with Treasury to the credit of other courts in the CRIS and used to purchase Government Account Series securities through the Bureau of Public Debt, which will be held at Treasury, in an account in the name and to the credit of the Director of Administrative Office of the United States Courts.   The pooled funds will be invested in accordance with the principals of the CRIS Investment Policy as approved by the Registry Monitoring Group.

D.   An account for each case will be established in the CRIS titled in the name of the case giving rise to the investment in the fund.   Income generated from fund investments will be distributed to each case based on the ratio each account's principal and earnings has to the aggregate principal and income total in the fund. Reports showing the interest earned and the principal amounts contributed in each case will be prepared and distributed to each court participating in the CRIS and made available to litigants and/or their counsel.

III.   Deductions of Fees

A.   The custodian is authorized and directed by this Order to deduct the investment services fee for the management of investments in the CRIS and the registry fee for maintaining accounts deposited with the Court.

B. The investment services fee is assessed from interest earnings to the pool according to the Court's Miscellaneous Fee Schedule and is to be assessed before a pro rata distribution of earnings to court cases.

C. The registry fee is assessed by the custodian from each case's pro rata distribution of the earnings and is to be determined on the basis of the rates published by the Director of the Administrative Office of the United States Courts as approved by the Judicial Conference of the United States.

IV. Transition From Former Investment Procedure

A. The Clerk of Court is further directed to develop a systematic method of redemption of all existing investments and their transfer to the CRIS.

B. Parties not wishing to transfer certain existing registry deposits into the CRIS may seek leave to transfer them to the litigants or their designees on proper motion and approval of the judge assigned to the specific case.

C. This Order supersedes and abrogates all prior orders of this Court regarding the deposit and investment of registry funds.

[Dated: February 1, 2013.]

MISC. NO. 03–451. IN RE: THE USE AND POSSESSION OF ELECTRONIC DEVICES IN THE COURTHOUSE

1. This Order, effective February 14, 2013, applies to the United States courthouses in Pittsburgh, Erie and Johnstown, and, with the exception of Local Rule 83.1, supersedes any prior orders or policies of this Court governing electronic devices in the courthouse.

2. This Court's policy set forth in L.R. 83.1.C. prohibiting "taking of photographs, recording, broadcasting and televising" in any "hearing room, corridor or stairway leading thereto, on any floor occupied entirely or in part by the United States District Court for the Western District of Pennsylvania," except as provided therein, is acknowledged and reaffirmed.

3. Except as otherwise ordered by the presiding judicial officer in a particular case, any attorney with business in this Court may possess in a courthouse cell phones, mobile devices, notebooks, laptops or other similar devices (hereinafter, "electronic devices"), for purposes not prohibited by L.R. 83.1. Except as otherwise ordered by the presiding judicial officer in a particular case, electronic devices may be used to send or receive messages from outside courtrooms only.

4. Jurors reporting for jury duty may possess electronic devices in a courthouse for purposes not prohibited by L.R. 83.1. Unless otherwise ordered by the presiding judicial officer, jurors' electronic devices may only be used in the jury room and may not be brought into a courtroom. Jurors shall deposit all electronic devices in receptacles provided for that purpose prior to entering the jury room to commence deliberations.

5. For the purposes of this Order, "members of the news media" shall consist of representatives of a person or entity that regularly and customarily is engaged in the business of gathering, marketing and disseminating the news.

6. Except as otherwise ordered by the presiding judicial officer in a particular case, members of the news media may possess electronic devices in a courthouse for purposes not prohibited by L.R. 83.1. Unless otherwise ordered by the presiding judicial officer in a particular case, electronic devices may not be used in a courtroom. In order to prevent a breach of security occasioned by the presentation of false media credentials to court security officers, except as otherwise ordered,

members of the news media must produce employer-issued photo identification upon seeking entry to a courthouse with electronic devices.

7. Except as otherwise authorized (which may include authorization by a presiding judicial officer for naturalizations, investitures, ceremonial occasions and other events) members of the public (other than attorneys, jurors and news media) may not possess electronic devices in a courthouse. All electronic devices possessed by members of the public seeking entry to a courthouse must be surrendered to the Court Security Officers at the entrance to the courthouse, and will be returned upon exiting the courthouse.

8. Except as otherwise ordered by the presiding judicial officer, all electronic devices must be turned off prior to entering courtrooms and judicial chambers.

9. A judicial officer may prohibit electronic devices in that judicial officer's courtroom and chambers and may direct screening procedures to be conducted by the United States Marshal Service.

10. Court staff, court security officers and deputy marshals may confiscate electronic devices being used in violation of these rules.

11. Nothing in this Order is intended to prevent courthouse employees from using and possessing electronic devices in the courthouse.

12. Any disputes regarding the possession or use of electronic devices hereunder may be referred to the Chief Judge for resolution.

13. The United States Marshal shall post copies of this Order at all entrances to the federal courthouses in the Western District of Pennsylvania and violators of this Order will be subject to sanction for contempt of court.

IT IS SO ORDERED.

[Dated: February 14, 2013.]

INDEX TO UNITED STATES DISTRICT COURT
FOR THE WESTERN DISTRICT OF PENNSYLVANIA

FORMS—Cont'd

Admiralty—Cont'd

Petitions, disposition of actions, **LCvR 17.2**

Attorneys, this index

Children and minors, petitions, actions and proceedings, disposition, **LCvR 17.1**

Class actions, **LCvR 23; APPENDIX LCvR 23.E**

Collective actions, **LCvR 23**

Constitutional questions, notice, **LCvR 24**

Court sponsored arbitration,

Judgments and decrees, **ADRPP 5.9**

Statements, **ADRPP 5.6**

Crimes and offenses,

Pretrial motions, **LCrR 12**

Related actions, notice, **LCrR 57**

Deposits, courts, investments, withdrawals, orders, **LCvR 67.3**

Discovery, motions, **LCvR 37.2**

Early neutral evaluation, statements, **ADRPP 4.8**

Habeas corpus, **LCvR 2241, 2254**

Interrogatories, **LCvR 33**

Jury, this index

Parties, this index

Patents, this index

Pretrial statements, **LCvR 16.1**

Related actions, assignments, cases, **LCvR 40**

Sentence and punishment,

Guidelines, procedures, pleadings, **LCrR 32**

Motions, **LCvR 2255**

Summary judgment, motions, **LCvR 56**

FREE PRESS

Generally, **LCvR 83.1**

Crimes and offenses, **LCrR 83**

GARNISHMENT

Admiralty,

Affidavits, **LAR (b)**

State law procedure, notice, **LAR (g)**

GOOD FAITH

Patents,

Contentions, amendments, **LPR 3.8**

Damages, estimates, **LPR 3.6**

GRAND JURY

Jury selection plan, **JSP § 1 et seq.**

GUIDELINES

Sentence and punishment, procedures, **LCrR 32**

GUILTY PLEAS

Sentence and punishment, guidelines, procedures, investigations and investigators, reports, time, **LCrR 32**

HABEAS CORPUS

Generally, **LCvR 2241, 2254, 2255**

HEARINGS

Alternative dispute resolution, attendance, **ADRPP 2.6**

Attorneys, disciplinary proceedings, **LCvR 83.3**

HEARINGS—Cont'd

Court sponsored arbitration,

Procedure, **ADRPP 5.8**

Time, **ADRPP 5.4**

Early neutral evaluation, procedure, **ADRPP 4.9**

Magistrate judges, **LCvR 72**

Mediation, procedure, **ADRPP 3.8, 3.9**

Sanctions, compromise and settlement, jury, costs, **LCvR 54**

Sentence and punishment, motions, application of rules, **LCvR 2255**

HYPERLINKS

Electronic case filing, **ECFPP 15**

IDENTITY AND IDENTIFICATION

Attorneys, filing, **LCvR 5.2, 83.2**

Patents, claim construction proceedings, evidence, **LPR 4.3**

IN REM PROCEEDINGS

Admiralty, **LAR (c), (e)**

INCOME TAX—FEDERAL

Deposits, courts,

Designated or qualified settlement funds, application of law, **LCvR 67.2**

Withdrawals, **LCvR 67.3**

INFORMATION

Attorneys, extrajudicial statements, limitations, **LCvR 83.1; LCrR 83**

Class actions, **LCvR 23**

INITIAL DISCLOSURE

Patents, **LPR 3.1 et seq.**

INJUNCTIONS

Jury, labor and employment, retaliation, **JSP § 18**

INSPECTION AND INSPECTORS

Crimes and offenses, **LCrR 10, 16**

Searches and seizures, motions, **LCrR 41**

INTERNET

Alternative dispute resolution, information, **ADRPP 2.2, 2.3**

Civil rules, copies, **LCvR 1.2**

INTERPRETERS AND TRANSLATORS

Crimes and offenses, **LCrR 28**

INTERROGATORIES

Generally, **LCvR 33**

Service of process, electronic transactions, certificates and certification, **LCvR 26.3**

INTERVENTION

Admiralty, claims, in rem and quasi in rem actions, **LAR (e)**

INVENTORIES

Receivers and receivership, **LCvR 66**

INVESTIGATIONS AND INVESTIGATORS

Attorneys, disciplinary proceedings, **LCvR 83.3**

UNITED STATES BANKRUPTCY COURT FOR THE WESTERN DISTRICT OF PENNSYLVANIA

Including Amendments Received Through
June 1, 2016

PART I. COMMENCEMENT OF CASE: PROCEEDINGS RELATING TO PETITION AND ORDER FOR RELIEF

RULE 1001–1. CITATION OF LOCAL BANKRUPTCY RULES (W.PA.LBR)

The Local Bankruptcy Rules of the United States Bankruptcy Court for the Western District of Pennsylvania (hereinafter "the Court") shall be cited as W.PA.LBR ——— [Local Bankruptcy Rule number]. The citations in the Local Bankruptcy Rules may be modified to correspond to changes in the Bankruptcy Code, Official Forms, and Federal Rules of Bankruptcy Procedure.

[Effective July 1, 2004. Amended effective March 1, 2012.]

RULE 1001–2. APPLICABILITY OF LOCAL BANKRUPTCY RULES AND RULES OF CONSTRUCTION

(a) These Rules supersede all previous local bankruptcy rules promulgated by this Court. They shall govern all applicable cases and proceedings brought in this Court after they take effect. They also shall apply to all proceedings pending at the time they take effect, in so far as just and practical.

(b) Local Bankruptcy Rules of general applicability also apply when there are specific rules governing a particular matter unless expressly stated otherwise in these Local Bankruptcy Rules or an order of Court.

(c) Where appropriate in order to correct errors, adjust scheduling, or to accomplish substantial justice, a Presiding Judge may modify the applicability of any Local Bankruptcy Rule in a particular case or matter.

(d) The provisions of the Local Bankruptcy Rules are severable, and if any Local Bankruptcy Rule or provision thereof shall be held to be unenforceable, other Local Bankruptcy Rules and provisions will not be affected.

[Effective July 1, 2004. Amended effective December 1, 2009; March 1, 2012.]

RULE 1001–3. EFFECTIVE DATE OF RULES

These Rules shall take effect on April 1, 2016.

[Effective July 1, 2004. Amended effective March 1, 2012; July 1, 2013; April 1, 2016.]

RULE 1001–4. STANDING ORDERS

(a) The Court may issue Standing Orders that supplement and/or amend these Rules.

(b) Standing Orders shall be filed on the Miscellaneous Docket and posted on the Court's website, addressing but not limited to the following:

(1) temporary measures inappropriate for inclusion in these Rules (*e.g.*, the closure of the Court during a holiday, inclement weather or emergency);

(2) matters requiring prompt action (*e.g.*, accommodating changes to the Bankruptcy Code or federal rules), and/or addressing matters where the Court determines that there is an immediate need to revise or enact a rule;

(3) the assignment or reassignment of cases, or

(4) the adoption and implementation of the latest version of these Local Rules and corresponding Local Forms.

(c) Standing Orders issued under subpart (b)(2) of this Rule shall be incorporated into and superseded by these Rules during the ensuing, annual, formal revision process, including review and comment by the Standing Local Rules Committee, a public comment period and approval by both the District Court for the Western District of Pennsylvania and the Judicial Council for the Third Circuit Court of Appeals.

[Effective April 1, 2016.]

RULE 1002–1. DIVISION OF BUSINESS & CLERK'S OFFICE HOURS

(a) The Court operates in Divisions: the Pittsburgh Division and the Erie Division.

(1) The Pittsburgh Division of the Court is comprised of the Pittsburgh Counties and the Johnstown Counties. The counties of Allegheny, Armstrong, Beaver, Butler, Fayette, Greene, Lawrence, Washington, and Westmoreland constitute the Pittsburgh Counties. The counties of Bedford, Blair, Cambria, Indiana, Somerset, and Clearfield constitute the Johnstown Counties.

(2) The Erie Division is comprised of the counties of Erie, Clarion, Elk, Jefferson, McKean, Warren, Crawford, Forest, Mercer, and Venango.

(3) The bankruptcy petition shall indicate the county of the debtor's residence, or principal place of business, as the case may be.

(b) The Clerk's Office shall maintain public office hours from 9:00 a.m. until 4:30 p.m. on weekdays, except for legal holidays or as otherwise ordered by the Chief Bankruptcy Judge.

[Effective July 1, 2004. Amended effective March 1, 2012; April 1, 2016.]

RULE 1002–2. COMPLEX CHAPTER 11 CASES

(a) A "Complex Chapter 11 Case" is defined as a case filed in the Western District of Pennsylvania under chapter 11 of the Bankruptcy Code that requires special scheduling and other procedures because of a combination of factors, including, but not limited to, one (1) or more of the following factors:

(1) the need for expedited hearings for consideration of case management and administrative orders, the use of cash collateral, debtor in possession financing, retaining professionals on an interim basis, maintaining existing bookkeeping systems, paying employees wages and benefits, utility deposit orders for a limited period, and other matters vital to the survival of the business;

(2) the size of the case;

(3) the large number of parties in interest in the case;

(4) the fact that claims against the debtor and/or equity interests in the debtor are publicly traded;

(5) the need for special noticing and hearing procedures.

(b) To secure designation as a Complex Chapter 11 Case, the party shall file a motion. The motion shall substantially conform to Local Bankruptcy Form 2 (Ex Parte Motion for Designation as Complex Chapter 11 Bankruptcy Case).

(c) Generally, requests for relief will be heard on at least forty-eight (48) hours' notice to the parties specified in W.PA.LBR 1002–2(d). If immediate relief is requested, the Court, in its sole discretion, may preliminarily grant the relief requested without notice and hearing, provided, however, that the Court shall direct that any such order entered be served, together with a notice of objection and hearing dates, prior to entry of a final order. Upon the request of a party in interest, the Court may issue an order substantially in the form of Local Bankruptcy Form 3 (Initial Order for Complex Chapter 11 Bankruptcy Case).

(d) Any motion filed under this Local Bankruptcy Rule, together with notice providing the time by which any objection shall be filed and the date, time, and place of hearing, shall be served on:

(1) the three (3) largest secured creditors;

(2) any committee appointed under the Bankruptcy Code or its authorized agent or, if no committee has been appointed, on the twenty (20) largest unsecured creditors;

(3) the Office of the United States Trustee, and

(4) any other entity that the Court may direct.

(e) The Court may require agenda letters and paper copies of documents in complex cases.

[Effective July 1, 2004. Amended effective May 3, 2005; December 1, 2009; March 1, 2012.]

RULE 1003–1. DESIGNATION OF PRINCIPAL IN INVOLUNTARY CASES

All involuntary petitions relating to corporate and partnership debtors shall include a designation of the individual who is the principal operating officer or managing general partner, as the case may be, of the alleged debtor together with the address and phone number of the person so designated. If the identity or location of the principal operating officer or managing general partner is not known, a declaration shall be filed to that effect.

[Effective July 1, 2004. Amended effective March 1, 2012.]

RULE 1006–1. FILING FEES, INSTALLMENT PAYMENTS

(a) In accordance with W.PA.LBR 1017–2, the Court shall immediately issue an order of dismissal in any case where an installment payment has not been received by the due date unless, prior to the entry of any such order of dismissal, the debtor files an application to extend the installment payment schedule or requests in writing a hearing to show cause why the case should not be dismissed. The individual debtor and the attorney for the debtor are responsible for knowing the due dates of installment payments. The Clerk will not send reminders or notices that installment payments are due.

(b) Whenever a case is dismissed prior to the filing fees being paid in full, the debtor shall remit the balance of the fees to the Clerk within fourteen (14) days after the entry of the order of dismissal.

(c) A motion to reopen a case or to vacate an order of dismissal shall be accompanied by the filing fee for a motion to reopen a case and any balance due on the original filing fee for the bankruptcy petition.

[Effective July 1, 2004. Amended effective December 1, 2009; March 1, 2012.]

RULE 1007-1. MAILING MATRICES

(a) For purposes of this Local Bankruptcy Rule, the term "Mailing Matrix" is an alphabetical listing by name and address, including ZIP Code, of counsel of record for the debtor, each scheduled creditor and equity security holder of the debtor, and nondebtor parties to executory contracts or unexpired leases in which a debtor is a party.

(1) If the debtor is a corporation, the Mailing Matrix shall include the names and addresses, including ZIP Codes, of all current officers and directors.

(2) If a debtor is a partnership, the Mailing Matrix shall include the names and addresses, including ZIP Codes, of all general and limited partners.

(3) If a debtor is a limited liability company, the Mailing Matrix shall include the names and addresses, including ZIP Codes, of all members and managers.

(b) When the debtor lists any federal agency, other than the Office of the United States Trustee, on a Mailing Matrix, the debtor shall also list the name of the agency, c/o The United States Attorney's Office for the Western District of Pennsylvania, at the address listed in the Address Appendix located in the Local Bankruptcy Rules section of the Court's website. When the Internal Revenue Service is a party, the debtor shall include the name and address of the IRS Insolvency Unit at the address listed in the Address Appendix located in the Local Bankruptcy Rules section of the Court's website.

(c) Mailing Matrices shall be filed electronically, unless a party is not represented by an attorney (pro se) or has been granted by order of Court permission to file the Mailing Matrix on paper.

(d) In all voluntary cases, the Mailing Matrix is due when the petition is filed. If the Mailing Matrix is not timely filed, the case will be dismissed automatically by the Court. An order extending the time to file the bankruptcy schedules or other documents needed to complete the bankruptcy petition shall not constitute an extension of time to file the Mailing Matrix unless so stated in the order.

(e) At the time of filing the petition, the debtor shall file on the Case Management/Electronic Case Files System ("CM/ECF System") Local Bankruptcy Form 29 (Notice Regarding Filing of Mailing Matrix) with the Mailing Matrix as an attachment. After docketing Local Bankruptcy Form 29, the debtor immediately shall upload the Mailing Matrix into the CM/ECF System as a text file (with a .txt extension). Mailing Matrices shall be stricken if not filed in a text (.txt) format.

(f) If one (1) or more creditors is added to the creditor maintenance system in CM/ECF, the debtor shall file Local Bankruptcy Form 30 (Notice Regarding Modification to Mailing Matrix) on the CM/ECF System. After docketing Local Bankruptcy Form 30, the debtor shall upload into the CM/ECF System a supplemental Mailing Matrix as a text file containing only the names and addresses of the added creditors.

(g) The debtor is to assure that the Mailing Matrix is kept current and accurate at all times.

[Effective July 1, 2004. Amended effective March 1, 2012; July 1, 2013; April 1, 2016.]

RULE 1007-3. DISCLOSURE OF RELATED CASES AND PROCEEDINGS

(a) At the time a petition is filed commencing a case under the Bankruptcy Code, or at any time during which a case is pending and such information becomes known, the debtor or counsel for the debtor shall file with the Court a statement disclosing the name, case number, location of the Bankruptcy Court having jurisdiction, and the name of the Bankruptcy Judge to whom the case is assigned for each related case that has been previously filed or that is then pending.

(b) As used in this Local Bankruptcy Rule, the term "Related Case" includes, but is not limited to, bankruptcy cases, ancillary or miscellaneous proceedings, and adversary proceedings, whether or not presently pending, involving:

(1) a spouse or former spouse of the debtor;

(2) an affiliate (as defined by 11 U.S.C. § 101);

(3) an insider (as defined by 11 U.S.C. § 101); or

(4) the same debtor, entity, or person, including aliases or fictitious names used by that debtor, entity, or person, having previously filed a case or proceeding whether in this or any other district.

[Effective July 1, 2004. Amended effective March 1, 2012.]

RULE 1007-4. PROOF OF INCOME

(a) The debtor shall file with the Clerk copies of the payment advices described in 11 U.S.C. § 521(a)(1)(B)(iv). Debtors shall file payment advices in accordance with Fed. R. Bankr. P. 9037, Privacy Protection for Filings Made with the Court, which instructs parties to redact personal information such as the first five (5) numbers of a debtor's Social Security number and personal identifying numbers such as employee identification numbers. If the debtor does not have the required payment advices, then the debtor shall file a certification with the Clerk explaining the reason payment advices are not available.

(b) Each individual debtor shall also report to the trustee not later than fourteen (14) days before the date first set for the first meeting of creditors any other source of income not listed on debtor's payment advices.

(c) Chapter 13 debtors that are self-employed (including debtors acting as landlords) shall submit a completed Local Bankruptcy Form 5 (Chapter 13 Business Case Questionnaire) to the trustee at least fourteen (14) days prior to the first scheduled meeting of creditors.

[Effective July 1, 2004. Amended effective October 17, 2005; December 1, 2009; March 1, 2012.]

RULE 1007–5. DOMESTIC SUPPORT CERTIFICATION

(a) Debtors in chapter 12 or chapter 13 cases who are subject to a domestic support obligation, whether the obligation arose before or after the commencement of the case, shall at the time of making the last payment called for under the plan:

(1) certify to the chapter 12 or chapter 13 trustee that all prefiling and postfiling payments have been made on domestic support obligations substantially conforming to Local Bankruptcy Form 21 (Domestic Support Obligation Certification); and

(2) provide the chapter 12 or chapter 13 trustee with the name and address of any holders of a domestic support obligation, the name and address of the debtor responsible for the obligation, and the name and address of the most recent employer of the debtor responsible for the obligation substantially conforming to Local Bankruptcy Form 22 (Domestic Support Obligation Claim Holder Report).

[Effective March 1, 2012.]

RULE 1007–6. LIST OF 20 LARGEST UNSECURED CREDITORS

The List of 20 Largest Unsecured Creditors shall be filed with every voluntary chapter 11 petition. The bankruptcy case shall be dismissed if the List of 20 Largest Unsecured Creditors is not filed with the petition. In the event that there are fewer than twenty (20) creditors, the list shall so state.

[Effective March 1, 2012.]

RULE 1009–1. AMENDMENTS BY DEBTOR

(a) No petition may be amended to add an additional debtor after the order for relief has been entered.

(b) The trustee or any creditor may file objections to an amendment by the debtor of the schedules or statement of financial affairs within thirty (30) days after the conclusion of the meeting of creditors or the filing of that amendment, whichever is later, unless further time is granted by the Court.

(c) Each debt newly listed by an amendment to the schedules of liabilities shall also state when such debt was incurred and the amount and nature of such debt.

(d) All amendments shall include:

(1) a caption indicating that the document is an "Amendment to [Note: Filer to specify.]";

(2) a clear description of the material added or deleted;

(3) a certificate of service by the debtor or debtor's attorney that notice has been given as required by the Federal Rules of Bankruptcy Procedure and these Local Bankruptcy Rules;

(4) a supplemental Mailing Matrix and Local Bankruptcy Form 30 (Notice Regarding Modification to Mailing Matrix) shall be filed pursuant to W.PA.LBR 1007–1(f);

(5) the payment of any fees required by 28 U.S.C. § 1930; and

(6) a completed amendment cover sheet substantially conforming to Local Bankruptcy Form 6 (Amendment Cover Sheet).

(e) The debtor shall immediately give notice to each creditor added by an amendment to the schedules and file a certificate of service. The notice shall include a copy of the amendment filed with the Court and a copy of the original § 341 Meeting Notice that lists the full Social Security number of debtor.

(f) When the debtor files an amendment modifying the Social Security number, the amendment including the full Social Security number shall be served on creditors and all parties in interest. The amendment filed with the Court shall have the first five (5) numbers of the Social Security number redacted. The certificate of service filed with the amendment shall list the parties served and aver that the recipients received a copy of the amendment that included the full Social Security number. The caption of Official Form 21 (Statement of Social Security Number) shall be modified to include the word "amendment" at the end of the caption, and the completed form shall be submitted on paper, not filed, with the Clerk.

[Effective July 1, 2004. Amended effective May 3, 2005; March 1, 2012.]

RULE 1017–1. DISMISSAL OR CONVERSION OF BANKRUPTCY CASE

(a) A motion to dismiss a voluntary or involuntary bankruptcy petition shall set forth the reasons for the dismissal. The motion shall also set forth whether any arrangement or agreement has been made with any creditor or other person in connection with such application for dismissal and the terms thereof. In addition, any payment or consideration received or anticipated, lump sum or otherwise, shall be identified.

(b) A motion filed by a party other than the debtor to convert a chapter 11 case to a chapter 7 or to dismiss the case shall be scheduled initially for a hearing at a motion Court time on notice by the movant upon all creditors or, at the option of the moving party, only upon:

(1) counsel for debtor;

(2) United States trustee;

(3) any person who has filed a request for notices in the case;

(4) the IRS Office of the District Counsel in Pittsburgh at the address listed in the Address Appendix located in the Local Bankruptcy Rules section of the Court's website;

(5) the Commonwealth of Pennsylvania Department of Revenue at the address listed in the Address Appendix located in the Local Bankruptcy Rules section of the Court's website;

(6) the Commonwealth of Pennsylvania Department of Labor and Industry, at the address listed in the Address Appendix located in the Local Bankruptcy Rules section of the Court's website;

(7) other taxing body creditors;

(8) all secured creditors;

(9) the attorney for the creditors' and other committees or, if none, then on the seven (7) largest unsecured creditors; and

(10) creditors claiming they are owed domestic support obligation.

(c) A motion filed by a party other than the debtor to convert or dismiss a chapter 13 case shall be scheduled initially for a hearing before the Presiding Judge on a chapter 13 motions day.

(d) Upon the filing by the chapter 13 trustee of a Certificate of Default Recommending Dismissal of Case based upon plan payment defaults, the debtor shall file and serve a written response accompanied by documentation that at least one (1) full plan payment was sent to the chapter 13 trustee's lock box after the date of the Certificate of Default.

(1) The debtor's failure to respond in accordance with the requirement of the order will result in the dismissal of the case without a hearing.

(2) The response shall set forth in detail the basis for denial of the chapter 13 trustee's request for dismissal and any prospective plan changes designed to cure the existing default. Proof of one (1) full plan payment shall be attached to any response, including an amended plan.

(3) If the response proposes that additional payments will be made prior to the hearing scheduled on the motion, verification of such payments shall be made to the Court contemporaneously with delivery of payment to the chapter 13 trustee.

(4) If the response indicates that the plan payment is to be increased in order to cure the existing default, the new payment shall be identified in the response, and the plan shall be deemed amended as of the date of the response to include the adjusted payment.

(5) If the response expresses the debtor's intent to amend the plan other than by a payment increase, the amended plan is to be filed along with the response and served on all parties in interest. Upon the filing of the amended plan, the Court shall cancel the hearing previously set for consideration of the chapter 13 trustee's request for dismissal, and a conciliation conference and plan confirmation hearing will be scheduled. If the debtor fails to make any plan payment prior to the conciliation conference and plan confirmation hearing, on Supplemental Certificate of Default filed and served by the chapter 13 trustee, the case will be dismissed and the hearing canceled.

[Effective July 1, 2004. Amended effective March 1, 2012.]

RULE 1017–2. DISMISSAL OF BANKRUPTCY CASE FOR DEFICIENT FILING

(a) The Clerk shall serve electronically upon debtor's counsel, or by postal mail if the debtor is not represented by counsel, a Notice of Deficient Filing if the debtor fails to timely file all of the documents necessary to initiate the case as required by the Bankruptcy Code, the Federal Rules of Bankruptcy Procedure, these Local Bankruptcy Rules, and/or any order of this Court.

(b) Pursuant to the United States trustee's motion to dismiss, as authorized by General Order #91–1, the Notice of Deficient Filing will identify the filing deficiencies and set forth a date for dismissal of the case.

(c) At any time before the date set for entry of an order of dismissal, the debtor:

(1) may file a motion requesting a hearing at which debtor shall show cause why the case should not be dismissed for deficiencies; or

(2) may file a motion and proposed order seeking an extension of time to comply with the Notice of Deficient Filing.

[Effective July 1, 2004. Amended effective March 1, 2012.]

RULE 1019–1. MAILING MATRIX IN CONVERTED CASES

Local Bankruptcy Form 30 (Notice Regarding Modification to Mailing Matrix) and a supplemental Mailing Matrix, which meets the requirements of W. PA. LBR 1007–1 and lists the names and addresses of nonscheduled prepetition and postpetition creditors and executory contract holders, shall be filed by the debtor. If the debtor is the filing party, then all postpetition creditors shall be served with a copy of the motion.

[Effective March 1, 2012.]

PART II. OFFICERS AND ADMINISTRATION; NOTICES; MEETINGS; EXAMINATIONS; ELECTIONS; ATTORNEYS AND ACCOUNTANTS

RULE 2002–1. CERTIFICATES OF SERVICE

(a) Any entity who serves a document in satisfaction of a notice requirement shall file a certificate of service with the Clerk within seven (7) calendar days after the date of service. A certificate of service of any document in an expedited matter shall be filed immediately after service is made.

(b) Service in paper copy format shall be made on each party in interest who is not a Notice of Electronic Filing (NEF) recipient.

(c) The certificate of service shall conform substantially to Local Bankruptcy Form 7 (Certificate of Service).

(d) It is the responsibility of the filer to compare the actual NEF generated by CM/ECF upon filing the document with the list of NEF recipients identified in the certificate of service. The filer shall file an amended certificate of service where there is a discrepancy between the original certificate of service and the actual NEF.

[Effective July 1, 2004. Amended effective December 1, 2009; March 1, 2012; July 1, 2013.]

RULE 2002–2. DUTY TO MAINTAIN CURRENT ADDRESS

It is the responsibility of parties in interest and counsel to assure that their postal and e-mail addresses are kept current in each case pending entry of a final decree.

[Effective July 1, 2004. Amended effective March 1, 2012.]

RULE 2004–1. EXAMINATION

(a) The purpose of this Rule is to avoid a motion and Court order for a 2004 examination unless an objection is filed.

(b) Before giving notice of a proposed examination, the movant shall confer with the proposed examinee (through counsel, if represented) to arrange for an agreeable date, place, and time for the examination. Failure by the movant to attempt to confer shall be grounds to quash under W.PA.LBR 2004–1(e).

(c) Not less than twenty-eight (28) days' written notice of a proposed examination shall be given to the entity to be examined, its counsel, and to other affected parties. The entity to be examined and other affected parties shall have fourteen (14) days after service to respond or object to the proposed examination. The notice shall apprise the party of the scope of the examination and categories of documents to be produced.

(d) If no response or objection is served, the notice to conduct an examination need not be filed, and the examination may occur as the parties agree.

(e) When an examinee or party in interest objects to the examination, the burden is on the party seeking the examination to file a motion to compel the examination, in accord with Fed. R. Bankr. P. 2004(a). A certificate shall be attached to any motion to compel explaining the efforts made to meet and confer and certifying that such efforts were unsuccessful. All parties in interest, including the examinee and its counsel, shall be served with the motion.

(f) If anyone has been unreasonable in seeking or resisting discovery pursuant to Fed. R. Bankr. P. 2004, the Court may impose sanctions. The Court may condition the taking of an examination on terms that are just and promote efficient administration.

(g) This Rule does not apply to adversary proceedings and to contested matters.

(1) The discovery provisions of Part VII of the Local Bankruptcy Rules apply in adversary proceedings.

(2) Fed. R. Bankr. P. 9014 applies to discovery in contested matters.

[Effective July 1, 2004. Amended effective November 22, 2004; December 1, 2009; March 1, 2012.]

RULE 2015–1. DUTY TO KEEP RECORDS, FILE REPORTS, AND MAKE PAYMENTS, INCLUDING TAXES

(a) Within sixty (60) days of the date of the initial filing of a bankruptcy petition, each debtor or debtor in possession shall file any and all federal, state, and local tax returns which are due but unfiled as of the date of the filing of the bankruptcy petition. The returns shall include all income, estate, gift, sales, excise, employment, real estate, school district, and other tax returns.

(b) For purposes of proper service, the party shall use the current address, if listed, in the Address Appendix located in the Local Bankruptcy Rules section of the Court's website.

(c) Any entity whose address is listed in the Address Appendix located in the Local Bankruptcy Rules section of the Court's website shall file a notice with the Clerk of any change of address necessary for the parties to comply with these Rules on or before the effective date of the change.

(d) Payments to the chapter 13 trustee shall be made in accordance with instructions provided by the chapter 13 trustee.

(e) Where applicable, a debtor in possession or a trustee in a chapter 11, a chapter 12 debtor, or a chapter 13 debtor case shall comply with the following:

(1) All checks issued by a debtor in possession under chapter 11 shall bear the legend: "Debtor in Possession Account, Bankruptcy Case No. xx-xxxxx."

(2) Any instrument used to make a chapter 12 or chapter 13 plan payment shall include the debtor's name and case number.

(3) Keep current, and pay when due, all debts arising after the entry of the order for relief, including any debt arising from rentals or other money due on account of real estate leases and utility services, as well as any federal, state, and local employment, income, or other tax, as required by law.

(4) Submit to the Pennsylvania Department of Revenue Bankruptcy Division, at the address listed on the Address Appendix, a certified or cashier's check in full payment of the following taxes in the manner hereafter set forth:

(A) all Pennsylvania sales tax collected pursuant to 72 P.S. § 7202, *et seq.* shall be remitted together with the proper tax returns, no later than the end of the seventh day following the last day of each month in which such sales taxes were required to be collected; and

(B) all employer withholding tax (personal income tax) withheld pursuant to 72 P.S. § 7316, *et seq.* shall be remitted together with the proper tax returns, no later than the end of the second business day after the payment of wages to employees.

(5) Submit, no later than the last day of the month following the end of the contributions withheld, pursuant to 43 P.S. § 785 and § 781.4, to the Local Office of the Field Accounting Service of the Pennsylvania Department of Labor and Industry, Office of Unemployment Compensation Tax Services.

(6) In the case of self-employed debtors, submit estimated income tax payments by April 15, June 15, September 15, and January 15 to the IRS and Pennsylvania Department of Revenue Bankruptcy Division, respectively.

(7) Timely file all federal, state, and local tax returns with the applicable taxing bodies during the pendency of the bankruptcy case.

(f) The debtor in possession or trustee in a chapter 11 case shall:

(1) timely file all federal, state, and local tax returns with the applicable taxing bodies during the pendency of the bankruptcy case;

(2) file with the Clerk monthly statements of operations for the preceding month ("Monthly Operating Report") no later than the twentieth day of the next month. The initial Monthly Operating Report shall include:

(A) the name and location of each depository or place of investment holding funds of the estate;

(B) the applicable account number or numbers; and

(C) whether the debtor is operating on a "cash" or "accrual" basis.

(g) After a confirmation order is entered, the reorganized debtor shall file quarterly reports until the case is closed.

(h) A chapter 13 debtor engaged in business shall:

(1) timely file all federal, state, and local tax returns with the applicable taxing bodies during the pendency of the bankruptcy case;

(2) serve the chapter 13 trustee with an initial chapter 13 "Business Case Questionnaire" on a form substantially in compliance with Local Bankruptcy Form 5 (Chapter 13 Business Case Questionnaire) at least fourteen (14) days prior to the first date set for the meeting of creditors. The initial questionnaire shall include:

(A) the name and location of each depository or place of investment holding funds of the estate;

(B) the applicable account number or numbers; and

(C) whether the debtor is operating on a "cash" or "accrual" basis; and

(3) beginning with the first full month following the petition filing and continuing monthly thereafter, serve the chapter 13 trustee with a "Report of Operations" no later than the twentieth day of the month covering each preceding month. The Reports of Operations shall not be filed with the Court.

[Effective July 1, 2004. Amended effective March 1, 2012; April 1, 2016.]

RULE 2016–1. PROFESSIONAL FEES AND EXPENSES

(a) Fee applications are required in all cases, except those originally filed Chapter 7 cases where counsel for the debtor is compensated via a lump sum payment prior to filing, and in those Chapter 13 cases when counsel opts for compensation pursuant to the "no-look fee" provisions of this Local Bankruptcy Rule.

(b) No compensation or expenses will be allowed, or paid by the estate or any third-party source, to any professional for services rendered in any case unless:

(1) a motion to approve employment has been filed; and

(2) an order granting the motion has been entered, except that counsel for debtors in Chapter 13 cases are not required to file such a motion or obtain such an order.

(c) An application for fees and expenses filed pursuant to W.PA.LBR 2016–1(b) shall include the following:

(1) the date of the order appointing the professional, with a copy thereof attached as an exhibit;

(2) a statement indicating whether the application is for final or interim compensation and expenses, the total amounts thereof, and the period covered by the application;

(3) the dates and amounts of previous compensation requested and the amounts approved, if any, including any retainers paid, with copies of the orders approving the prior payments, the retention agreement, an itemization of fees and expenses paid from any source other than the debtor's estate, a copy of the attorney disclosure statement previously filed pursuant to Fed. R. Bankr. P. 2016, attached as exhibits;

(4) a list of all timekeepers included in the application, including, but not limited to: the attorneys, paraprofessionals, or other professionals contributing services, number of years in practice, their billing rates, total hours, total dollars, and the blended hourly rate;

(5) a chronological listing of time and services performed ("Chronological Listing") or a listing of time and services by category of service arranged chronologically ("Category Listing"), attached to the Applica-

tion. Regardless of the approach utilized, both a Chronological Listing and a Category Listing shall include the date, the professional or other timekeeper, a description of the service, and the time involved;

(A) If a Category Listing is provided, each category shall be preceded by a heading generally describing the services within that category and a brief statement detailing the result to the estate. A separate category shall be included for preparation of the fee application and another for all administrative services such as file maintenance, docket review, typing, filing and service of documents, etc.

(B) If a Chronological Listing is provided, a separate summary of time and service by category shall be attached, and each category shall be given an identifying number. This identifying number shall be placed beside each chronological entry to identify the category number into which it falls. A separate category shall be included in the summary for preparation of the fee application and another for all administrative services such as file maintenance, docket review, typing, filing and service of documents, etc.

(C) In Chapter 13 cases, if the professional or other timekeeper has performed services in connection with the debtor's participation in the Loss Mitigation Program, described in W.PA.LBR 9020–1, the application for fees and expenses shall:

(i) separately itemize any fees for services rendered and expenses incurred in connection with the debtor's participation in the Loss Mitigation Program; and,

(ii) otherwise comply with the requirements of W.PA.LBR 9020–7(c).

(6) an itemization of the expenses for which reimbursement is requested:

(A) Expenses shall be billed and allowed only at actual cost without overhead or add-ons; and

(B) If compensation for travel time is requested, unless appropriate, special circumstances are set forth, typically only fifty percent (50%) of the applicable hourly rate of the professional will be allowed for travel;

(7) a statement that the professional or other timekeeper is a disinterested person and does not represent or hold an interest adverse to the interest of the estate on the matter on which he was employed;

(8) a history of the case in narrative form;

(9) a summary cover sheet substantially conforming to Local Bankruptcy Form 9 (Summary Cover Sheet). A fee application filed without a completed cover sheet shall be dismissed without prejudice to refiling;

(10) a proposed order of Court;

(11) in complex Chapter 11 cases, a spreadsheet which reflects all fees that are requested pursuant to the application and a cumulative total for professional by category; and

(12) if the Court enters an administrative fee order in a particular case, the terms of the order shall govern;

(d) All entries in a fee application shall:

(1) list each service or task separately and state in increments not exceeding one-tenth (⅒) of an hour the amount of time expended in its performance;

(2) identify the subject matter of any correspondence or phone call and the party with whom the professional or other timekeeper has communicated if the service involves telephone and/or written correspondence;

(3) identify where appropriate, and in the interest of clarity, the subject matter of any hearing or trial with specificity, including the case or adversary number, if the service involved attendance at a hearing or trial;

(4) identify any document with specificity if the service involves preparation of that document; and

(5) include all other information necessary to a full understanding of the services performed and the person and time involved.

(e) Unless leave to seek interim compensation has been allowed by order of the Court, all fee applications filed in Chapter 7 cases will be considered only after:

(1) the trustee in the case has filed a final account;

(2) there has been a proposed order of final distribution submitted for the Court's consideration in which the allowed fees are included; and

(3) notice has been given to all parties in interest of:

(A) the last date to file objections thereto; and

(B) the hearing date and time, if any.

(f) The Chapter 13 "no look attorney fee" shall be limited to a maximum of $4,000.00 and the Chapter 13 "no-look expense charge" shall be limited to a maximum in the amount of $500 (allowable expenses charged include the petition filing fee, postage, copying, certifications and other costs incurred in the administration of the case.) When the fee and expenses charged by counsel is less than or equal to either or both of the no-look fee and expense charge, no fee application is required. The no-look attorney fee and expense charge:

(1) shall include any retainer received;

(2) shall be reduced on a dollar-for-dollar basis for anything paid directly by the client, for instance if the client pays the petition filing fee directly, the no-look

expense charge shall be equal to $500 less the filing fee; and,

(3) does not preclude the award of additional fees and/or expenses by the Court upon the filing of a fee application consistent with these Local Bankruptcy Rules requiring in such case a detailed statement and accounting of fees and expenses charged; *provided however*, in order to "opt out" of the no-look fee provisions of this Local Bankruptcy Rule:

(A) counsel shall have entered into a written fee agreement at the commencement of the representation providing the alternative of opting out of the no-look fee compensation option and for payment of additional fees in the event of unforeseen, future case complications; and

(B) to the extent counsel seeks such additional compensation, counsel is required to file a cumulative fee application subject to the other provisions of this Local Bankruptcy Rule.

(g) If counsel opts to be paid via the no-look fee, counsel shall nevertheless advise and represent the debtor(s) in a manner consistent with applicable professional standards and be required to perform all matters necessary to properly and timely complete the bankruptcy case, including the following services:

(1) the debtor(s) will be interviewed by counsel and appropriately briefed on the Chapter 13 process;

(2) accurate and complete schedules, statements of financial affairs, and related documents will be prepared by counsel;

(3) all documents will be explained;

(4) counsel will file a Chapter 13 plan that meets with the requirements of Local Bankruptcy Form 10 (Chapter 13 Plan) and is capable of confirmation;

(5) in addition to the first meeting of creditors, counsel will attend all hearings and will remain counsel of record until the case is either completed or dismissed, unless the Court has issued an order discharging the attorney as counsel of record;

(6) counsel will file all motions and objections contemplated in the confirmed plan in a timely fashion; and

(7) counsel will complete representation without additional charge to the debtor(s) for the duration of the Chapter 13 case.

(h) Counsel fees paid through the Chapter 13 plan shall be at the monthly rate and level set forth in the plan.

(i) Additional fees may be paid through the Chapter 13 plan if either:

(1) the confirmed Chapter 13 plan contemplated such fees without decreasing the percentage or amount originally to be paid to other creditors

through the plan, and proper application for allowance and payment is filed and approved; or

(2) in instances where the additional fees are not contemplated in the plan, assuming the plan is amended within fourteen (14) days after the application for fees is allowed and such fees are paid from plan resources without decreasing the percentage or amount to be paid to other creditors through the plan.

(j) Notwithstanding W.PA.LBR 2016–1(i), the Court recognizes that additional services provided by debtor's counsel may provide a benefit to the estate. Upon counsel's request, the Court may determine that the benefit to the estate warrants a diminution in the dividend paid to unsecured creditors and an amendment to the plan is not necessary. In such cases, any fee application filed shall specify:

(1) in detail, the benefit received by the estate; and

(2) whether and to what extent the unsecured creditors would receive a lower dividend under the existing plan if the fee application were granted and the fees were paid by the trustee from debtor's plan payments.

[Effective July 1, 2004. Amended effective March 1, 2012; July 1, 2013; August 1, 2015; April 1, 2016.]

RULE 2016–2. BANK SERVICE FEES ON CHAPTER 7 ESTATE ACCOUNTS

(a) Chapter 7 trustees are authorized to incur and pay any actual, necessary expense as contemplated by 11 U.S.C. § 330, for bank fees and charges directly related to the administration of estate accounts.

(b) The Court retains authority to review and approve such expenses during the administration of the case.

[Effective April 1, 2016.]

PART III. CLAIMS AND DISTRIBUTION TO CREDITORS AND EQUITY INTEREST HOLDERS; PLANS

RULE 3002–1. FILING CLAIMS

(a) If the amendment adding creditor(s) to schedules is filed after the claims bar date has expired or will expire within thirty (30) days of the amendment, the affected creditor(s) shall file a proof of claim within thirty (30) days of the date notice of the amendment is sent.

(b) A wage claimant who files a proof of claim listing the redacted Social Security number shall provide the full Social Security number to the trustee upon the trustee's written request. The trustee shall inform the wage claimant that the full Social Security number shall not be filed with the Court.

(c) The Clerk shall notify parties in interest of the bar date when proofs of claims are required to be filed in the case.

(d) The Clerk shall set a bar date for governmental entities to file proofs of claim in each bankruptcy case filed in the Western District of Pennsylvania. The bar date shall be included on the docket of the case. The bar date for governmental entities shall not be modified when a case is converted to a different chapter of the Bankruptcy Code. Governmental entities shall file proofs of claim within the greater of one hundred eighty (180) days from the date the order for relief was first entered in the case or the bar date set for other creditors after conversion.

(e) The bar date for governmental entities shall not be modified when the chapter 7 trustee files a Notice of Assets and the Clerk notifies parties to file claims. Governmental entities shall file proofs of claim within the greater of one hundred eighty (180) days from the date the order for relief was first entered in the case or the proof of claim deadline date set for other creditors by the Clerk.

(f) Any entity filing more than ten (10) claims in a calendar year shall file claims electronically in the CM/ECF System.

[Effective July 1, 2004. Amended effective March 1, 2012.]

RULE 3002–2. AMENDING CLAIMS

(a) All amended claims shall include:

(1) a caption indicating that the document is an amendment to a prior claim, i.e., "Amendment to Claim No. _____, Filed by _____"; and

(2) a clear description of the material added or deleted; and

(3) a certificate of service by the creditor that notice has been served on the debtor, trustee, and any creditor and attorney for the creditor originally on the claim.

(b) Amendments made for the sole purpose of redacting personal identifiers pursuant to Fed. R. Bankr. P. 9037 shall comply with the requirements of W.PA.LBR 9037–1, and shall not be combined with any other amendment of the claim.

[Effective July 1, 2004. Amended effective March 1, 2012. Amended on an interim basis effective November 1, 2012, permanently effective July 1, 2013.]

RULE 3002–3. ADDITIONAL REQUIREMENTS FOR CLAIMS IN CHAPTER 12 AND 13 CASES

(a) Subject to the requirements of Fed. R. Bankr. P. 9037, the following shall be included in the claim form:

(1) Creditor's account number conspicuously stated.

(2) Sufficient identification of collateral.

(3) A holder of a claim secured by real property shall separately state the following:

(A) arrearage, late fees, attorney's fees and fore-closure costs incurred through the date of filing of the debtor's bankruptcy petition, principal balance, applicable interest rate and amount of the regular monthly payment.

(B) if regular payment includes an escrow component, it shall be clearly identified and the amount stated.

(C) the Mortgage and Note and any Assignments of Claim shall be attached to the claim.

(D) any postpetition arrearage shall be separately stated and itemized.

(b) Claims resulting from the rejection of an executory contract shall be filed and served on the chapter 13 trustee, the debtor, and debtor's attorney, if represented, by the later of the claims bar date or thirty (30) days after the date of rejection. Executory contracts may be rejected in the confirmed plan.

(c) Any creditor who asserts a deficiency shall file a proof of claim or amend a filed proof of claim to assert the deficiency.

(d) If an amended proof of claim is filed after the deadline for filing claims, such claim shall be served by the creditor on the chapter 13 trustee, the debtor, and debtor's attorney, if represented.

(e) All objections to the amended proof of claim shall be filed and served within ninety (90) days after the amended proof of claim is filed and served.

(f) The chapter 13 trustee will promptly place all funds intended for a specific creditor on reserve:

(1) upon notice from an assignor or transferee that a claim has been transferred;

(2) whenever the trustee receives:

(A) a returned check;

(B) a statement from a creditor indicating that the account has been assigned;

(C) a statement from a creditor indicating that the account has been paid in full; or

(D) any other statement from a creditor indicating that the creditor is not owed anything on a claim; or

(3) in any circumstance where a creditor seeks to change the payee name for a claim.

(g) Within twenty-one (21) days of placing funds on reserve, the chapter 13 trustee shall file a "Notice of Funds on Reserve" with the Court which certifies that the debtor(s), the original creditor, the putative creditor, and if known, counsel for the debtor(s), original creditor and putative creditor were served with the Notice and the date of such service.

(h) No funds will be distributed by the chapter 13 trustee to any purported assignee or transferee without a "transferred proof of claim" filed in accordance with Fed. R. Bankr. P. 3001(e) and notice issued in accordance therewith by the Clerk with an opportunity to object.

(i) Transferred or assigned proofs of claim shall include the following:

(1) the case number;

(2) the claim to be paid;

(3) the nature of the collateral supporting the claim;

(4) the appropriate address for payment; and

(5) copies of all assignments and authorizations for loan service applicable to the transfer and in support of the claim.

(j) Copies of each proof of claim and each amended, assigned, and/or transferred proof of claim, including all attachments, shall be served on the chapter 13 trustee, the debtor, and the debtor's counsel, if represented.

[Effective March 1, 2012. Amended effective July 1, 2013.]

RULE 3002–4. NOTICE OF MORTGAGE PAYMENT CHANGE

A narrative summary of the chain of title, copies of all applicable lien assignments(s) and other appropriate evidence of the Creditor's authority to act and be paid, shall be filed as attachments to the Notice of Mortgage Payment Change if filed by a Creditor who, at the time of filing, is not a Creditor of record.

[Effective April 1, 2016.]

RULE 3002–5. NOTICE OF POSTPETITION FEES, EXPENSES, AND CHARGES

(a) A holder of a claim: (i) for rent for debtor's residence or (ii) secured by a security interest in the debtor's assets asserting recovery against the debtor and/or against the debtor's assets for fees, expenses, or charges, incurred in connection with the claim after the bankruptcy case was filed, shall file a separate "Notice of Postpetition Fees, Expenses, and Charges," which:

(1) shall be filed as a supplement to the holder's proof of claim;

(2) shall be served no later than one hundred eighty (180) days after the date when the fees, expenses, or charges are incurred;

(3) shall not be subject to Fed. R. Bank. P. 3001(f);

(4) shall be served on the debtor(s), counsel to the debtor(s), and the Chapter 13 trustee;

(5) need not be filed if fees, expenses, and charges were included in a previously filed "Notice of Mortgage Payment Change"; and

(6) if not timely filed, shall result in the disallowance of any additional sums claimed by the creditor for the period in question.

(b) After a Notice of Postpetition Fees, Expenses, and Charges is docketed, the Court will issue an order requiring the debtor(s) within twenty-one (21) days to file:

(1) an amended Chapter 13 plan;

(2) a declaration certifying that the existing Chapter 13 plan is sufficient to pay the modified debt; or

(3) an objection to the Notice of Postpetition Fees, Expenses, and Charges.

(c) If a Notice of Postpetition Fees, Expenses, and Charges is timely filed in the proper form and the debtor fails to timely file an objection, the postpetition fees, expenses, and/or charges shall be allowed without further order, notice, or hearing. However, no such postpetition fees, expenses, and/or charges shall be paid by the chapter 13 trustee until such time as the debtor or debtor's counsel files an amended chap-

ter 13 plan or a declaration certifying that the existing chapter 13 plan is sufficient to pay the modified debt.

[Effective March 1, 2012. Amended effective July 1, 2013; April 1, 2016.]

RULE 3003–1. PROOFS OF CLAIM BAR DATE IN CHAPTER 11 CASES

The deadline for creditors other than governmental units to file proofs of claim in chapter 11 cases is ninety (90) days after the first date set for the meeting of creditors.

[Effective March 1, 2012.]

RULE 3011–1. UNCLAIMED FUNDS

Requests for disbursement of unclaimed funds shall be made pursuant to 28 U.S.C. § 2042 by filing a motion and serving a copy of the motion on all interested parties, including the debtor, United States attorney, United States trustee, and former and/or current case trustee(s).

[Effective July 1, 2004. Amended effective March 1, 2012.]

RULE 3015–1. USE OF PLAN FORM IN CHAPTER 13 CASES

In chapter 13 cases, the plan shall be filed in substantial conformity to Local Bankruptcy Form 10 (Chapter 13 Plan).

[Effective July 1, 2004. Amended effective March 1, 2012.]

RULE 3015–2. WAGE ORDERS IN CHAPTER 13 CASES

(a) The plan filed by a chapter 13 debtor with attachable income shall be accompanied by a motion for a wage attachment(s) and order(s) in an amount(s) sufficient to cover plan payments. The motion and order shall substantially comply with Local Bankruptcy Form 11 (Ex Parte Motion for Order to Pay Trustee Pursuant to Wage Attachment and Order to Pay Trustee Pursuant to Wage Attachment).

(b) When a bankruptcy case is filed by one (1) debtor, "Doc. No. WO–1" shall be included in the caption of the motion for wage attachment and the proposed order. Any motion to amend shall include "Doc. No. WO–1" in the caption.

(c) When a joint case is filed, the name of the debtor whose wages are to be attached shall be stated in the caption of the motion and in the proposed order. "Doc. No. WO–1" shall be included in the caption of the first joint debtor requesting a wage attachment. "Doc. No. WO–2" shall be included in the caption of a subsequent motion requesting a wage attachment filed by the other joint debtor.

(d) Any motion to amend a wage attachment shall be filed at the original motion number for the first or second joint debtor (WO–1 or WO–2) and shall be marked "Amended Motion for Wage Attachment" in the caption.

(e) Any motion to amend the amount of the wage deduction shall request only the exact amount to be attached.

(f) If a debtor has more than one (1) employer, separate wage attachment motions and proposed orders granting the requested relief shall be filed for each employer from whom wages are to be attached. A motion naming more than one (1) employer as a respondent will be dismissed without prejudice for failure to comply with this Local Bankruptcy Rule.

(g) The debtor shall state the pay frequency when providing the statement of the payment amount, e.g., $535.00 biweekly, or $267.50 weekly, in addition to providing the calculation of the monthly amount. If the payroll period is unknown, a monthly basis shall be used. If the payroll period is known, the payment amount shall be calculated as follows:

Payment Frequency	Calculation of Monthly Amount
Weekly (52 pays/year)	amount to be attached multiplied by 12; then divided by 52 and rounded upwards
Biweekly (every 2 weeks = 26 pays/year)	amount to be attached multiplied by 12; then divided by 26 and rounded upwards
Semimonthly (twice each month = 24 pays/year)	amount to be attached divided by 2; then rounded upwards

(h) Automated Clearing House (ACH) payments are made by entering into a contract with the chapter 13 trustee and not by motion and order. Therefore, no motion shall be filed to commence or terminate ACH payments.

(i) The debtor shall serve a copy of the signed order granting the wage attachment on the entity or entities required to remit payment to the trustee. The order shall be accompanied by a notification of debtor's complete, nine-digit Social Security number substantially conforming to Local Bankruptcy Form 12 (Notification of Debtor's Social Security Number). Debtor shall file a certificate of service regarding service of the order and notification, but the Social Security number shall not be included on the certificate.

[Effective July 1, 2004. Amended effective March 1, 2012.]

RULE 3015–3. PLAN CONFIRMATION HEARINGS & CONCILIATION

(a) Objections to the debtor(s)' Chapter 13 plan shall be filed at least 7 days prior to the first date set for the meeting of creditors as scheduled by the Notice of Chapter 13 Bankruptcy Case, Meeting of Creditors & Deadlines (the "341 Notice").

(b) The 341 Notice shall schedule a plan confirmation hearing (the "Initial Confirmation Hearing") to be held immediately following the meeting of creditors, as authorized by 11 U.S.C. § 1324(b). Initial Confirmation Hearings shall be conciliated by the Chapter 13 Trustee or her designee.

(c) Objections to holding the Initial Confirmation Hearing immediately following the meeting of creditors ("Hearing Objections") shall be filed at least 14 days prior to the first date set for the meeting of creditors as scheduled by the 341 Notice. A party filing a Hearing Objection that is not withdrawn prior to the first date set for the meeting of creditors shall attend the Initial Confirmation Hearing.

(d) In the absence of a pending Hearing Objection, the Court shall deem the Initial Confirmation Hearing as a Final Confirmation Hearing. If there is a timely filed Hearing Objection as of the date of the first meeting of creditors, then the Court shall deem the Initial Confirmation Hearing as an "Interim Confirmation Hearing" and schedule a Final Confirmation Hearing not earlier than 20 days, and not later than 45 days, after the date of the first meeting of creditors.

(e) Promptly after the conclusion of each conciliated confirmation hearing, the Chapter 13 Trustee shall submit to the Court a recommendation that the Chapter 13 Trustee deems appropriate under the circumstances, including but not limited to: continuation of the conciliation, confirmation of the plan and/or dismissal or conversion of the case.

[Effective March 1, 2012. Amended effective April 1, 2016.]

RULE 3015–4. CONTINUED CHAPTER 13 CONCILIATION CONFERENCES

(a) If the chapter 13 trustee determines during the initial conciliation conference that a continuance is necessary, the trustee shall announce to the parties in attendance the time, date, and location of the rescheduled chapter 13 conciliation conference.

(b) The case docket shall reflect the time, date, and location of any rescheduled chapter 13 conciliation conference that is continued by the chapter 13 trustee during the conference. Generally, parties shall review the case docket to determine if an entry has been made rescheduling the conciliation conference. Attorneys filing electronically in a case shall receive in electronic form a Notice of Electronic Filing (NEF) from the Clerk that includes the docket entry reflecting the continued time, date, and location of the conciliation conference.

[Effective March 1, 2012.]

RULE 3016–1. USE OF DISCLOSURE STATEMENT FORM IN CHAPTER 11 CASES

The disclosure statement filed in chapter 11 cases shall substantially conform to Local Bankruptcy Form 13 (Disclosure Statement To Accompany Plan), except in a case designated as a complex chapter 11.

[Effective July 1, 2004. Amended effective March 1, 2012.]

RULE 3016–2. PLAN SUMMARY IN CHAPTER 11 CASES

(a) A summary shall be filed with the plan and contain a concise description of the provisions of the plan. The plan summary shall provide an explanation of the plan in narrative form and shall be no more than two (2) pages.

(b) A description of any releases provided by the plan and the consideration given by the party to be released shall be set forth clearly as a separately labeled paragraph.

(c) A description of any liens which are to be avoided according to the plan shall be set forth as a separately labeled paragraph.

[Effective July 1, 2004. Amended effective March 1, 2012.]

RULE 3017–1. HEARING ON DISCLOSURE STATEMENT

(a) The responsibility for service shall be upon the proponent of the disclosure statement.

(b) All objections to the disclosure statement shall be filed with the Clerk. In addition to any entities listed in Fed. R. Bankr. P. 3017, any objections to the disclosure statement shall be served upon the plan proponent and proponent's counsel.

[Effective July 1, 2004. Amended effective March 1, 2012.]

RULE 3018–1. BALLOTING

(a) All ballots submitted in connection with a plan shall identify the proponent of the plan and the date of the plan for which the ballot is to be cast.

(b) All ballots shall be returned to counsel for the proponent of the plan or his designated agent. The address for return of the ballot shall be noted on the ballot.

(c) Counsel for the proponent of the plan shall electronically file the ballots at least two (2) business days prior to the confirmation hearing and bring the original ballots to the hearing.

(d) At least two (2) business days prior to the plan confirmation hearing, counsel for the proponent of the plan shall file a summary of the ballots including certification that all ballots received have been accounted for and tabulated and that the summary is an accurate representation of the ballots received.

(e) An amended summary of ballots shall be filed within two (2) days after the plan hearing to account for any ballots cast with the approval of the Court after the time fixed for voting on the plan.

(f) In cases where the plan includes nondebtor releases, permanent injunctions, and/or exculpations, the ballot shall include a separate section for the voting creditor to choose whether to accept or reject those provisions.

[Effective July 1, 2004. Amended effective March 1, 2012.]

RULE 3021–1. DISTRIBUTION UNDER CHAPTER 9, 11, AND 13 PLANS

(a) Each creditor shall assure that its current address is on file with the Clerk. Distribution by the disbursing agent shall be to the most recent address on file with the Clerk. The distribution of any proceeds pursuant to a confirmed plan shall be mailed to the address of the creditor as designated pursuant to Fed. R. Bankr. P. 2002(g), if one has been filed.

(b) Within ninety (90) days of confirmation of a Chapter 9 or Chapter 11 plan and each ninety (90) days thereafter until the case is closed, the disbursing agent shall file with the Clerk a brief and accurate accounting of all sums received, all sums disbursed to date, the sums remaining with the disbursing agent, and the proposed disposition thereof.

(c) Following confirmation of a plan, the Chapter 13 trustee shall make distribution to secured and priority creditors in accordance with the terms of the plan. Claims identified in the plan or proofs of claim filed shall be treated for distribution purposes as follows:

(1) after the filing of a plan and prior to confirmation of such plan, the Chapter 13 trustee is authorized to make distribution of the designated monthly payments as provided in the plan on secured nontax claims, attorney's fees, and utility accounts;

(2) the debtor or debtor's attorney, if represented, shall review the proofs of claim filed and shall file

objections to any disputed claims within ninety (90) days after the claims bar date or, for late filed or amended claims, within ninety (90) days after they are filed and served. Absent an objection, the proof of claim will govern as to the classification and amount of the claim. Objections filed after the ninety (90) days specified herein shall be deemed untimely.

(d) In Chapter 13 cases, failure of an unsecured creditor to file a claim shall inure to the benefit of the other unsecured creditors in the same class. The Chapter 13 trustee shall increase the percentage to be paid accordingly, provided that payments shall not exceed one hundred percent (100%) of the total amount of the allowed unsecured claims (including interest if provided in the plan for such claims). Distributions to unsecured creditors shall be made on a pro rata basis as calculated by the Chapter 13 trustee and not on a per capita basis.

(e) If a secured creditor obtains relief from the automatic stay, the Chapter 13 trustee shall suspend distributions to all creditors with claims secured by the collateral released from the automatic stay, following the Chapter 13 trustee's receipt of notice of the grant of relief. However, the Chapter 13 trustee shall continue to make distribution to other creditors in accordance with the terms of the plan.

(f) In the event that a Chapter 13 plan is not confirmed, then the trustee shall refund all payments to the debtor if the case is dismissed, or to the Chapter 7 trustee if the case is converted.
[Effective July 1, 2004. Amended effective March 1, 2012; August 1, 2015; April 1, 2016.]

RULE 3022–1. MOTION FOR FINAL DECREE IN CHAPTER 11 CASES

(a) The agent designated to administer the plan, or if none then the plan proponent, shall file and serve on all parties in interest a motion for final decree within the time period set forth in the confirmation order. If no confirmation order is issued, a motion for final decree shall be served within ninety (90) days after confirmation.

(b) Every motion for final decree shall have a completed Local Bankruptcy Form 14 (Report for Bankruptcy Judges in Cases To Be Closed—Chapter 11 Cases) attached.
[Effective July 1, 2004. Amended effective March 1, 2012.]

PART IV. THE DEBTOR: DUTIES AND BENEFITS

RULE 4001–1. MOTIONS FOR RELIEF FROM STAY COMBINED WITH OTHER REQUESTS FOR RELIEF

(a) Motions for relief from stay shall not be combined with requests for any type of relief other than for adequate protection.

(b) If a motion combining relief from stay with a request for any type of relief other than for adequate protection is not dismissed, the movant is deemed to have waived the time periods set forth in 11 U.S.C. § 362(e).

[Effective July 1, 2004. Amended effective March 1, 2012.]

RULE 4001–2. USE OF CASH COLLATERAL AND OBTAINING FINANCING

(a) A preliminary hearing may commence no earlier than forty-eight (48) hours after service of the motion and notice of the hearing. In addition to the CM/ECF System, the movant may use any means reasonably calculated to accomplish expedited notice and service (e.g., hand delivery, facsimile, direct e-mail, or next-day delivery) upon an authorized representative of a party adversely affected by the relief requested, and shall note on the certificate of service the manner in which service was effected.

(b) Except as provided herein and elsewhere in these Local Bankruptcy Rules, all cash collateral and financing requests under 11 U.S.C. §§ 363 and 364 shall be heard by motion filed pursuant to Fed. R. Bankr. P. 2002, 4001, and 9014 ("financing motions").

(1) All financing motions shall (a) recite whether the proposed form of order and/or underlying cash collateral stipulation or loan agreement contains any provision of the type indicated below; (b) identify the location of any such provision in the proposed form of order, cash collateral stipulation and/or loan agreement; and (c) justify the inclusion of such provision:

(A) Provisions that grant cross-collateralization protection (other than replacement liens or other adequate protection) to the prepetition secured creditors (i.e., clauses that secure prepetition debt by postpetition assets in which the secured creditor would not otherwise have a security interest by virtue of its prepetition security agreement or applicable law);

(B) Provisions or findings of fact that bind the estate or other parties in interest with respect to the validity, perfection, or amount of the secured creditor's prepetition lien or the waiver of claims against the secured creditor without first giving parties in interest at least (a) one hundred twenty (120) days from the date of the order, or (b) ninety

(90) days from the date a committee is formed and retains counsel, to investigate such matters;

(C) Provisions that seek to waive or release, without notice and/or hearing, whatever rights the estate may have under applicable law, including without limitation, chapter 5 of the United States Bankruptcy Code;

(D) Provisions that immediately grant to the prepetition secured creditor liens on the debtor's claims and causes of action arising under 11 U.S.C. §§ 544, 545, 547, 548, and 549;

(E) Provisions that deem prepetition secured debt to be postpetition debt or that use postpetition loans from a prepetition secured creditor to pay part or all of that secured creditor's prepetition debt, other than as provided in U.S.C. § 552(b);

(F) Provisions that provide disparate treatment for the professionals retained by a creditors' committee from those professionals retained by the debtor with respect to a professional fee carve-out; and

(G) Provisions that prime any secured lien without the consent of that lienor.

(2) All financing motions shall also provide a summary of the essential terms of the proposed use of cash collateral and/or financing (e.g., the maximum borrowing available on a final basis, the interim borrowing limit, borrowing conditions, interest rate, maturity, events of default, use of funds limitations, and protections afforded under 11 U.S.C. §§ 363 and 364).

(c) The Court may grant interim relief pending review by interested parties of the proposed debtor in possession financing arrangements. Such interim relief shall include only what is necessary to avoid immediate and irreparable harm to the estate pending a final hearing. In the absence of extraordinary circumstances, the Court shall not approve interim financing orders that include any of the provisions previously identified in W.PA.LBR 4001–2(B)(i)(A)–(G).

(d) A final order shall be entered only after notice and a hearing pursuant to Fed. R. Bankr. P. 4001.

[Effective July 1, 2004. Amended effective March 1, 2012.]

RULE 4001–3. RENT DEPOSITS

(a) A rent deposit submitted under 11 U.S.C. § 362(l)(1)(B) by a debtor filing a bankruptcy petition in the Court's electronic filing system shall be delivered to the Clerk within three (3) days of the filing date of the petition and shall be in the form of a cashier's check, certified check, attorney's client account check, or money order payable to the lessor.

(b) A rent deposit submitted under 11 U.S.C. § 362(l)(1)(B) by a debtor filing a bankruptcy petition conventionally on paper shall be filed at the same time as the petition. The deposit shall be in the form of a cashier's check, certified check, attorney's client account check, or money order payable to the lessor.

[Effective July 1, 2004. Amended effective March 1, 2012; July 1, 2013.]

RULE 4001–4. POSTCONFIRMATION MATTERS IN CHAPTER 13 CASES

(a) Notwithstanding any provision in a chapter 13 plan revesting property of the estate in the debtor, all sales of real and personal property shall be conducted in accordance with the Federal Rules of Bankruptcy Procedure and Local Bankruptcy Rules. The Notice of Sale shall state the proposed disposition of sale proceeds.

(b) Any postpetition extensions of credit sought by the debtor shall be in the form of a motion subject to the Federal Rules of Bankruptcy Procedure and Local Bankruptcy Rules. Such motion shall be served on the Chapter 13 trustee and all parties in interest.

(c) A motion seeking real estate/mortgage financing shall include the following information:

(1) the identity of the property that is subject to the financing;

(2) the identity of the source of funds;

(3) a description of the terms of the financing, including:

(A) whether it will be the first mortgage on the subject property;

(B) the amount of principal borrowed;

(C) the interest rate;

(D) the term of the loan and its amortization schedule;

(E) the amount of the monthly payment; and

(F) all other material terms of the financing agreement;

(4) whether the new mortgage financing is to be incorporated into the existing plan or is designed to complete payments under the plan;

(5) the status of plan payments at the time that the motion is filed;

(6) if a discharge is sought through the financing, whether the provisions of 11 U.S.C. § 1328 are met; and

(7) the date the loan is expected to close.

(d) A motion seeking approval of motor vehicle financing shall include the following:

(1) the type and cost of vehicle being purchased;

(2) the source of funds;

(3) the terms of financing, including:

(A) the principal borrowed;

(B) the interest rate;

(C) the term of the loan and its amortization schedule;

(D) the amount of the monthly payment; and

(E) all other material terms of the financing agreement;

(4) how the new payment will be incorporated into the chapter 13 plan;

(5) the status of plan payments at the time the motion is filed;

(6) whether any further plan modification is necessary;

(7) the date the loan is expected to close;

(8) if the treatment of other creditors will be changed as a result of this financing, a statement of the rationale and underlying facts in support of that change;

(9) if the plan payment is to be changed as a result of the financing, sufficient facts to demonstrate the feasibility of the plan amendment;

(10) whether the standards of 11 U.S.C. § 1325(b) are met; and

(11) whether and when an amended plan will be filed.

[Effective July 1, 2004. Amended effective March 1, 2012.]

RULE 4002–1. PROOF OF FEDERAL INCOME TAX RETURNS

If debtor did not file the federal income tax return required under applicable law for the most recent tax year ending immediately before the commencement of the case not later than seven (7) days before the date first set for the first meeting of creditors, then debtor shall submit to the trustee documentary proof of income from any source whatsoever, including, but not limited to, wages, salaries, commission, workmen's compensation, public assistance, aid to families with dependent children, alimony, support, gambling or lottery winnings, pensions, distributions from trust funds, interest, dividends, etc., not later than seven (7) days before the date first set for the first meeting of creditors. Any debtor who does not have documentary proof of income required by this Rule, or who had no income during the period, shall file a verified statement to that effect and serve a copy on the trustee.

[Effective March 1, 2012.]

RULE 4002–2. PROOF OF INSURANCE

All Chapter 13 debtors shall submit to the Chapter 13 Trustee proof of insurance for all of the debtors' motor vehicles, motor homes, and improved real estate, within 14 days after their initial Chapter 13 Plan is filed.

[Effective April 1, 2016.]

RULE 4004–4. MOTIONS FOR DISCHARGE IN CHAPTER 11 CASES BROUGHT BY INDIVIDUALS

Within ninety (90) days after final distribution of all plan payments, the debtor shall:

(a) file a combined motion to reopen the case and to waive the filing fee; and

(b) file a motion seeking discharge with a final report and account certifying that all plan payments have been made, that debtor has completed the financial management course, and that all domestic support obligations (if any) are current. The report shall include a list of all creditors, the amount of each creditor's claim, and the principal and interest paid to each creditor.

[Effective March 1, 2012.]

PART V.   BANKRUPTCY COURTS AND CLERKS

RULE 5001–1.   SEAL OF THE COURT

The official seal of the Court shall bear the inscription "UNITED STATES BANKRUPTCY COURT" and shall be used by the Clerk for all documents required to be under seal of the Court. In lieu of an original seal, the Clerk or his deputy may place the official graphic of the seal on electronic documents issued by the Court.

[Effective July 1, 2004. Amended effective March 1, 2012.]

RULE 5005–1.   MANDATORY ELECTRONIC FILING

(a) Electronic filing through the Court's Case Management/Electronic Case Files System (the "CM/ECF System") is mandatory in this District for attorneys. Filers not represented by an attorney (pro se) may file paper documents with the Clerk, who shall promptly file such documents using the CM/ECF System.

(b) The Court shall sanction violators of this Local Bankruptcy Rule in the amount of $150.00 per paper filing. Counsel shall not charge to or collect the

$150.00 from the client as a fee, cost, expense, or other charge in the case.

[Effective July 1, 2004. Amended effective March 1, 2012.]

RULE 5005–2. REGISTRATION AS A FILING USER

(a) A "Filing User" is anyone having a Court-issued CM/ECF System log-in and password. Any attorney appearing before the Court shall be registered as a Filing User. Pursuant to W.PA.LBR 9010–1 and Local Bankruptcy Form 18 (Motion for *Pro Hac Vice* Admission), *pro hac vice* admission requires association with a local registered Filing User.

(b) Any attorney admitted to the Bar of the Western District of Pennsylvania (including those admitted *pro hac vice*), United States trustees and their assistants, private trustees, and others as the Court deems appropriate may apply for registration as a Filing User after attending CM/ECF System training provided by the Clerk.

(c) The Court may grant a *pro se* party to a pending action permission to apply for registration as a Filing User, subject to attending CM/ECF System training provided by the Clerk. If granted, the *pro se* party's Filing User status is limited solely to the specific pending action. If, during the course of the action, an attorney appears on the party's behalf, that attorney shall immediately advise the Clerk to terminate the *pro se* party's registration as a Filing User.

(d) Applications for registration as a Filing User shall be submitted through the Court's website.

[Effective July 1, 2004. Amended effective November 22, 2004; March 1, 2012; August 1, 2015; April 1, 2016.]

RULE 5005–3. REGISTRATION AS A LIMITED FILING USER

(a) An individual who is registered as a CM/ECF System participant in another district and/or who has attended CM/ECF System training provided by the Clerk may apply for registration as a Limited Filing User. A Limited Filing User's CM/ECF System account is limited to filing proofs of claim, notice requests, withdrawals of claims, transfers of claims, objections to transfer of claim, reaffirmation agreements, notices of mortgage payment change, and notices of postpetition fees, expenses, and charges.

(b) A Limited Filing User will not receive electronic notification of documents or docket activity.

(c) Applications for registration as a Limited Filing User shall be submitted through the Court's website.

[Effective July 1, 2004. Amended effective May 3, 2005; March 1, 2012; August 1, 2015; April 1, 2016.]

RULE 5005–4. TERMINATION OF REGISTERED FILING USER STATUS

(a) An attorney may terminate his or her status as a registered Filing User in a specific case only upon the granting of a motion for withdrawal of appearance in that case pursuant to W.PA.LBR 9010–2(b).

(b) An attorney may terminate his or her status as a registered Filing User in the entire CM/ECF System only by using Local Bankruptcy Form 4C (Notice of Termination of CM/ECF Privileges), which shall be delivered to the Clerk by certified mail.

(c) Termination of registered Filing User status due to special circumstances (for example, death or mental incapacity) may be made by motion to the Court by an appropriate representative.

(d) At its discretion, the Court may terminate an individual's status as a registered Filing User for reasons that include, but are not limited to, an egregious or recurring violation of these Local Bankruptcy Rules and/or Federal Rules of Bankruptcy Procedure and/or in response to a finding of misconduct by any duly empowered tribunal.

[Effective March 1, 2012.]

RULE 5005–5. CM/ECF SYSTEM PASSWORDS

(a) Each Filing User shall maintain control and security over his or her CM/ECF System log-in and password. A Filing User shall not voluntarily share, transfer or assign the use of his or her CM/ECF System log-in and/or password. A Filing User who suspects that his or her password has been compromised shall immediately notify the Clerk.

(b) Violation of this Local Bankruptcy Rule may result in the termination of the Filing User's CM/ECF System account, sanctions and/or other disciplinary action at the discretion of the Court.

[Effective March 1, 2012. Amended effective July 1, 2013.]

RULE 5005–6. SIGNATURES

(a) A Filing User's CM/ECF System log-in and password serve as the Filing User's signature on all electronic documents filed with the Court for purposes of the Federal Rules of Bankruptcy Procedure, the Local Bankruptcy Rules of this Court, and any other purpose for which a signature is required in connection with proceedings before the Court.

(b) Electronically filed documents shall comply with Fed. R. Bankr. P. 9011 and set forth the Filing User's name, address, telephone number, e-mail address, and state Bar registration number, if applicable. In addition, the name of the Filing User under whose log-in and password the document is submitted shall be preceded by an "/s/" and typed in the space where the signature would otherwise appear.

(c) When a settlement agreement or similar document requiring multiple signatures is filed electronically, the filing party shall comply with instructions set forth by the Judge assigned to the case on the Court's website. If the Judge does not have specific instructions, then the document bearing all the necessary signatures shall be electronically filed either by:

(1) submitting a scanned document containing all necessary signatures, with Local Bankruptcy Form 26 (Settlement and Certification of Counsel) attached;

(2) representing the consent of the parties on the document; or

(3) in any other manner approved by the Court.

[Effective March 1, 2012.]

RULE 5005–7. DECLARATION OF ELECTRONIC FILING

(a) The signature of the debtor(s) authorizing the electronic filing of the bankruptcy case shall be accomplished by filing an original executed paper version of Local Bankruptcy Form 1A (Declaration Re: Electronic Filing), or Local Bankruptcy Form 1B if the debtor is not represented by counsel, within fourteen (14) days of the electronic filing of the petition. Both debtors shall sign the authorization when a joint petition is filed.

(b) The attorney representing the debtor shall notify the Court forthwith if the debtor(s) fails to sign the declaration.

(c) The case shall be dismissed without prejudice when the Court is notified that the debtor has failed to sign the declaration or if the declaration is not filed within fourteen (14) days of the date the petition is filed.

[Effective March 1, 2012.]

RULE 5005–8. NOTICE AND SERVICE

(a) The CM/ECF System automatically generates a Notice of Electronic Filing ("NEF") when a document is filed. The NEF contains a hyperlink to the document filed and identifies by e-mail address each Filing User to whom the CM/ECF System automatically transmits the NEF. The generation of an NEF by the CM/ECF System creates a presumption of effective notice and service as to each Filing User identified in the NEF.

(b) By registering as a Filing User with the Court, a Filing User consents to electronic notice in the form of a CM/ECF System-generated NEF, and waives his or her right to receive notice by first-class mail, including, but not limited to, the entry of an order or judgment pursuant to Fed. R. Bankr. P. 9022.

(c) By registering as a Filing User with the Court, a Filing User consents to electronic service in the form of a CM/ECF System-generated NEF which contains a hyperlink to a PDF of the document(s) being served, and waives his or her right to service by personal service or first-class mail, except with regard to service of a summons and complaint pursuant to Fed. R. Bankr. P. 7004, a motion initiating a contested matter under Fed. R. Bankr. P. 9014, and/or a subpoena under Fed. R. Bankr. P. 9016.

(d) As to persons who are not Filing Users, notice and service shall be effectuated by nonelectronic means in accordance with all applicable Local Bankruptcy Rules and Federal Rules of Bankruptcy Procedure.

(e) A certificate of service shall identify the specific method of service upon each person served.

[Effective March 1, 2012. Amended effective July 1, 2013.]

RULE 5005–9. E–MAIL ACCOUNTS

(a) A Filing User shall maintain a current primary e-mail address in the CM/ECF System. Filing Users may also register a secondary e-mail address. It is the Filing User's responsibility to ensure that the primary and secondary e-mail accounts are active and fully functional.

(b) The CM/ECF System will automatically send Notices of Electronic Filing (NEFs) to the registered primary and secondary e-mail addresses of all Filing Users in a case. Filing Users are responsible for monitoring the docket activity in each of his or her cases, independently of the NEFs sent to the Filing User's registered e-mail accounts. Problems with a Filing User's e-mail account will not defeat the presumption of effective notice and service pursuant to W.PA.LBR 5005–8(a).

(c) If the CM/ECF System reports repeated e-mail delivery errors to a Filing User's primary or secondary e-mail addresses, the Chief Judge shall issue a Rule to Show Cause to the Filing User.

[Effective March 1, 2012.]

RULE 5005–10. PAYMENT OF COURT FEES

(a) Unless another form of payment is required by the Court, filers shall pay by credit card, through the CM/ECF System, all applicable filing fees at the time of filing or by the end of the day.

(b) If fees are not paid within four (4) days of the date incurred, the Filing User shall be locked out of the CM/ECF System until full payment is made.

[Effective March 1, 2012.]

RULE 5005–11. COURT–ISSUED DOCUMENTS

(a) All orders, decrees, judgments, and proceedings of the Court shall be filed through the CM/ECF System, constituting entry on the docket pursuant to Fed. R. Bankr. P. 5003 and 9021.

(b) Any order or other Court-issued document filed electronically without the original signature of a Judge or the Clerk has the same force and effect as if the Judge or Clerk had physically signed the document.

(c) Except as may be otherwise provided in the Federal Rules of Bankruptcy Procedure, orders may be issued as "text-only" entries on the docket, without an attached document. Such orders are official and binding.

[Effective March 1, 2012.]

RULE 5005–12. ATTACHMENTS AND EXHIBITS

(a) Each abstract, exhibit, and excerpt shall be electronically filed as a separate Portable Document Format ("PDF") file attached to the docket entry to which it refers.

(b) Filing Users shall provide a description of each attachment or exhibit at the time of filing, using the description input field provided by the CM/ECF System. Descriptions shall clearly and concisely identify the content and/or type of document being attached.

(c) Filing Users shall submit as exhibits or attachments only those excerpts of the referenced documents that are directly germane to the matter under consideration by the Court. All excerpted material shall be clearly and prominently identified as such. Filing an excerpt as an attachment or exhibit does not prejudice the filing of additional excerpts or the complete document. Responding parties may timely file additional excerpts or the complete document that they believe are directly germane. The Court may require parties to file additional excerpts or the complete document.

(d) With respect to loan documentation, in lieu of the entire document, a one-page Local Bankruptcy Form 28 (Document and Loan History Abstract) may be filed.

(e) A party filing a pleading containing a Document and Loan History Abstract, or an excerpted exhibit, shall have a paper copy of the entire document at any hearing pertaining to the pleading.

(f) A party filing a pleading containing an excerpt or abstract shall, upon request of any party in interest, provide a copy of the entire exhibit. Unless otherwise directed by the Court, the copy may be provided in electronic format.

[Effective March 1, 2012.]

RULE 5005–13. DOCUMENT FORMAT AND QUALITY

(a) All documents filed through the CM/ECF System shall be in a Portable Document Format ("PDF").

(b) All documents created by the Filing User shall be:

(1) on 8.5″ by 11″ paper;

(2) sequentially page numbered;

(3) sequentially paragraph numbered except as to briefs;

(4) created in a font size no smaller than 12 Courier or an equivalent font size, including footnotes; and

(5) converted directly to PDF format using the word processing software (i.e., shall not be scanned into PDF format).

(c) Only documents not created by the filing party (e.g., lease agreements, mortgages, etc.) may be scanned into PDF format. Scanned documents shall be legible, properly aligned, and free of water marks or other marks caused by poorly maintained scanning equipment or text from other pages bleeding through the page.

(d) All PDF documents filed through the CM/ECF System shall be flattened and fully text-searchable.

[Effective March 1, 2012.]

RULE 5005–14. HYPERLINKS

(a) Electronically filed documents may contain hyperlinks to other portions of the same document and/or hyperlinks to a location on the Internet that contains a source document for a citation.

(b) Hyperlinks to cited authority shall not replace standard citation format. Complete citations shall be included in the text of the filed document.

(c) Neither a hyperlink, nor any site to which it refers, shall be considered part of the record. Hyperlinks are simply convenient mechanisms for accessing material cited in a filed document.

(d) The Court accepts no responsibility for, and does not endorse, any product, organization, or content at any hyperlinked site, or at any site to which that site may be linked. The Court accepts no responsibility for the availability or functionality of any hyperlink.

[Effective March 1, 2012.]

RULE 5005–15. PAPER RETENTION REQUIREMENTS

(a) Documents that are electronically filed and require original signatures other than that of the Filing User, such as the debtor, corporate officers, etc., shall be maintained in paper form by the Filing User for six (6) years from the date of case closing.

(b) On request of the Court, the Filing User shall provide original documents for review.

(c) Failure to maintain documents for the specified period shall subject the Filing User to sanctions, including, without limitation, disgorgement of fees.

[Effective March 1, 2012.]

RULE 5005–16. WITHDRAWAL OF FILES FROM THE CLERK'S OFFICE

(a) Records and papers on file in the Clerk's Office may be produced pursuant to subpoena from any federal or state court directing their production.

(b) At the Clerk's discretion, records or papers in the files of the Court may be temporarily removed by United States District Court Judges, United States Magistrate Judges, the United States attorney, the United States trustee, the standing chapter 13 trustee, and panel member trustees of this District upon receipt of a signed requisition. Otherwise, records and papers may be removed from the files only upon order of the Court.

(c) Whenever records or papers are withdrawn, the person receiving them shall leave with the Clerk a signed receipt describing the records or papers taken, and shall return them within the time specified by the Clerk.

[Effective March 1, 2012.]

RULE 5005–20. DOCUMENTS FILED UNDER SEAL

(a) Filing Users shall electronically file a motion to file documents under seal. Documents that contain confidential, scandalous, or defamatory matter shall be filed using docket events specified by the Clerk, and access to the documents shall be limited to parties authorized by the Judge. In the event the motion to file documents under seal is denied, the motion to seal documents and attachments, as well as any associated documents electronically filed by the movant, shall be made publicly accessible on the docket.

(b) A party who is not a Filing User shall file on paper a motion to file documents under seal and related documents containing confidential, scandalous, or defamatory matter. The document to be sealed shall be in a secured envelope. Affixed to the outside of the envelope shall be a statement containing a case caption, a case number, the nature of the document, and a notation that the document is being filed under seal.

(c) The motion to file documents under seal shall include a proposed order which grants the relief requested and further states: "The docket entry for the document(s) filed under seal shall describe the document(s) as follows: [Note: Filer to include a docket description for the sealed document.]" The docket entry for a sealed document shall describe the nature of the document filed without divulging confidential, scandalous, or defamatory information.

(d) A motion to file documents under seal shall be available for public review on the docket unless it contains confidential, scandalous, or defamatory matter, in which case the motion itself shall be filed under seal.

(e) The docket entry for a sealed document shall describe the nature of the document filed without divulging confidential, scandalous, or defamatory information.

(f) The Judge shall determine who shall scan the document and enter it into the electronic filing system as well as the parties that can view it. The document shall be destroyed after it is entered into the electronic filing system.

(g) The filing party shall keep the original documents for a period of six (6) years from the date of submission.

[Effective March 1, 2012.]

RULE 5005–21. TECHNICAL FAILURES OF THE CM/ECF SYSTEM

A Filing User whose filing is made untimely as a result of a technical failure of the CM/ECF System may seek appropriate relief from the Court.

[Effective March 1, 2012.]

RULE 5005–22. FACSIMILE DOCUMENTS AND E–MAILED DOCUMENTS

Documents may not be transmitted to the Clerk's Office for filing by facsimile, e-mail, text message, or any other electronic means other than CM/ECF, except as authorized by the Court. Any documents transmitted by facsimile or e-mail to the Clerk's Office without prior Court authorization shall be discarded without review.

[Effective April 1, 2016.]

RULE 5007–1. REQUESTS FOR TRANSCRIPTS

(a) Parties may request transcripts or an audio recording on cassette or compact disk by either filing a transcript request with the Clerk on a form available from the Clerk and the Court's website or by verbal request made to an Electronic Court Reporter Operator ("ECRO"). If a verbal request is made, the party requesting the transcript shall provide the ECRO with a written request containing the details of the request and payment as described below before the request will be processed.

(b) W.PA.LBR 8006–1 shall apply to a request in connection with an appeal.

(c) The requesting party shall provide the ECRO with:

(1) the name of the case;

(2) the bankruptcy and motion or adversary numbers;

(3) the date of the hearing;

(4) the name of the Judge who heard the matter; and

(5) the requesting party's name, telephone number, and mailing address and/or e-mail address and/or fax number.

(d) The ECRO shall estimate the cost of the transcript and the party requesting the transcript shall provide appropriate payment before the transcript request is processed. Checks written on a firm's business account will be accepted. Pro se litigants shall submit payment by money order, certified check, or cashier's check.

(e) When the completed transcript is received by the ECRO, the ECRO shall notify the requesting party that the transcript is available and shall notify the requesting party whether the actual cost of the transcript exceeded the estimate. If the actual cost of the transcript exceeded the estimate, the transcript will not be released until the additional payment is made. If the actual cost is less than the amount paid, the excess amount will be refunded.

(f) If the requesting party wants an expedited transcript, the requesting party shall notify the ECRO at the time the transcript is ordered. There is extra cost associated with expedited transcripts.

(g) Requests to redact personal identifiers from transcripts shall comply with W.PA.LBR 9037–1.

[Effective July 1, 2004. Amended effective March 1, 2012. Amended on an interim basis effective November 1, 2012, permanently effective July 1, 2013.]

RULE 5095–1. DEPOSITS (OTHER THAN UNCLAIMED FUNDS) INTO A REGISTRY FUND

(a) A motion seeking Court approval of deposits into a registry fund shall be filed with the Court. The Clerk will not accept funds for a registry account without an order of Court.

(b) Upon entry of an order allowing the deposit of funds, the Clerk shall place the funds in a depository that will provide collateral for the full amount of the deposit. The Clerk shall not accept the funds until adequate collateral is pledged by the depository.

(c) An administrative handling fee will be assessed and funds will be withdrawn from each invested account at a rate established by the Judicial Conference of the United States.

[Effective July 1, 2004. Amended effective March 1, 2012.]

RULE 5095–2. WITHDRAWALS (OTHER THAN UNCLAIMED FUNDS) FROM A REGISTRY FUND

(a) In order to withdraw deposited funds, a motion for disbursement of invested registry funds and a proposed order shall be filed. The proposed order for disbursement of invested registry funds shall include the name and address of the payee(s) and the total amount of the principal and interest (if the interest is not known, the order may read "plus interest") which will be disbursed to each payee. Interest will be distributed pro rata among the payees unless the motion requests and the order signed by the Court provides otherwise. The proposed order shall specify whether the payment is to be delivered to the payee or to counsel.

(b) The tax identification number or Social Security number of each payee receiving earned interest shall be provided to the Clerk in compliance with the Clerk's instructions. No disbursement shall be made until the Clerk receives this information and any other information concerning payment required by the Internal Revenue Service.

[Effective March 1, 2012.]

PART VI. COLLECTION AND LIQUIDATION OF THE ESTATE

RULE 6002–1. DEADLINE FOR ACCOUNT OF PRIOR CUSTODIAN

The custodian shall file and serve on the United States trustee the required report and account within thirty (30) days from the date the custodian acquires knowledge of the commencement of the case.

[Effective July 1, 2004. Amended effective March 1, 2012.]

RULE 6004–1. SALE OF ESTATE PROPERTY OUTSIDE THE ORDINARY COURSE OF BUSINESS

(a) All sales of property not in the ordinary course of debtor's business shall be by motion, except where Fed. R. Bankr. P. 7001(2) or (3) is applicable.

(b) Unless a specific Judge employs the self-scheduling procedure, the Court will schedule any requested sale by separate order. If the seller anticipates that the sale hearing will take more than a limited time, the seller shall so notify the appropriate Court personnel.

(c) In the event of a sale not in the ordinary course of business, pursuant to Fed R. Bankr. P. 6004(f), the following shall apply:

(1) The Notice of Sale shall contain the following information and shall be uploaded to the Electronic Access to Sales Information (EASI) system on the Court's website under "Notice of Sale":

(A) the case name and number and the adversary name and number or document number of the motion;

(B) a brief description of the property to be sold, such as "1988 Dodge Truck" for personalty, or in the case of realty, the complete street address, deed book volume, and page number;

(C) the date, time, and place of sale hearing;

(D) the date by which objections to the sale shall be filed and served;

(E) a statement of the amount of the initial offer and that higher or better offers will be considered at the hearing;

(F) the name, address, and telephone number of the person to contact for terms and conditions of sale or to examine the property; and

(G) hand money requirements at the time of the hearing.

(2) Notice of any proposed sale shall be advertised by the seller by publication in a newspaper of general circulation in the county in which the property is located and in the Legal Journal of such county if one exists and shall contain the case name and number, a brief description of the property to be sold, the date of the sale hearing, and a reference to the Court's EASI website where additional information regarding the sale shall be uploaded pursuant to subsection (c)(1). The publication shall be made no more than thirty (30) nor less than fourteen (14) calendar days before the scheduled date of sale.

(3) Proofs of publication of the advertising shall be filed when received by movant. If a representation is made to the Court at the time of the sale hearing that publication was made but the proofs of publication are not yet received, the proofs of publication shall be filed upon receipt by the movant.

(4) An itemized Report of Sale shall be filed with the Court within seven (7) calendar days of the date of consummation of the sale.

(d) Notices shall meet the following requirements:

(1) Other than to parties receiving notice via the CM/ECF System, the seller shall send the Notice of Sale by first-class mail to:

(A) the debtor and debtor's counsel;

(B) the trustee and trustee's counsel, if any;

(C) all indenture trustees and their counsel, if any;

(D) lien holders;

(E) all creditors;

(F) all committees appointed pursuant to the Bankruptcy Code or to their authorized agents and their counsel, if any;

(G) the United States as required by Fed. R. Bankr. P. 2002(j); and

(H) the United States trustee.

(2) The seller may file a motion, served on all creditors and parties in interest, to establish a procedure for selling less than substantially all the assets of the estate or those assets of less than substantial value. The motion to establish sale procedure may provide that the Notice of Sale be served on a limited list of creditors and parties in interest. Each such list shall be set forth with particularity in the motion to establish the sale procedure.

(3) Any notice required to be served under these procedures shall be addressed as directed in a request for notices filed with the Clerk, but if a different address is stated in a proof of claim duly filed, that address shall be used; otherwise, the address shown in the list of creditors in the schedules shall be used.

[Effective July 1, 2004. Amended effective March 1, 2012; July 1, 2013.]

RULE 6004–2. SALE OF PROPERTY WITHOUT PUBLICATION IN CHAPTER 13 CASES

(a) The debtor in a chapter 13 case may conduct a private sale without meeting the requirements for publication in W.PA.LBR 6004–1 when all or a portion of the funds received by the debtor for the sale or refinancing of real property is designated to pay one hundred percent (100%) of the amount owed to creditors with allowed claims.

(b) A stipulation signed by debtor's counsel and the chapter 13 trustee to sell property without publication shall be served on all parties in interest, including the creditors and lien holders.

[Effective March 1, 2012.]

RULE 6006–1. NOTICE OF ASSUMPTION OR REJECTION OF EXECUTORY CONTRACTS

In proceedings proposing assumption or rejection of executory contracts or unexpired leases, notice of such proceedings shall be served upon the trustee, if any, all parties to such contracts or leases, and to counsel for any committee of creditors or equity security holders appointed or elected under the Bankruptcy Code. If there is no such counsel, then service shall be made upon each of the committee members and, if no committee has been appointed, upon the seven (7) largest unsecured creditors.

[Effective July 1, 2004. Amended effective March 1, 2012.]

PART VII. ADVERSARY PROCEEDINGS

RULE 7004–1. NOTICE OF CONSTITUTIONAL QUESTION

(a) Any party who draws in question the constitutionality of an act of Congress affecting the public interest in any action to which the United States or an officer, agency, or employee thereof is not a party, shall include in the caption under the case number in bold-face type and all capital letters the words **CONSTITUTIONAL QUESTION RAISED,** shall serve a copy on the Attorney General of the United States, shall file a certificate of service simultaneously, and shall otherwise comply with the service requirements of Fed. R. Bankr. P. 7004.

(b) Any party who draws in question the constitutionality of a state law affecting the public interest, in any action to which the state or an officer, agency, or employee thereof is not a party, shall include in the caption under the case number in bold-face type and all capital letters the words **CONSTITUTIONAL QUESTION RAISED,** shall serve a copy on the Attorney General of the state, shall file a certificate of service simultaneously, and shall otherwise comply with the service requirements of Fed. R. Bankr. P. 7004.

[Effective July 1, 2004. Amended effective March 1, 2012.]

RULE 7005–1. FILING OF DISCOVERY MATERIALS

(a) Depositions, interrogatories, requests for documents, requests for admissions, and responses thereto shall not be filed with the Clerk.

(b) A party seeking a protective order, to compel discovery, or other relief pursuant to Fed. R. Bankr. P. 7026 shall file as an attachment to the motion only that portion of the deposition, interrogatory, request for document, or request for admissions that is the subject of an objection.

(c) When discovery material is essential to an appeal, upon application by a party in interest and order of Court, the necessary portion of the discovery material shall be filed with the Clerk.

(d) The party serving discovery or taking depositions shall retain the original as the custodian thereof.

[Effective July 1, 2004. Amended effective March 1, 2012.]

RULE 7008–1. MOTIONS IN ADVERSARY PROCEEDINGS

(a) All motions shall be in writing unless made during a hearing or trial.

(b) Motions filed within adversary proceedings shall contain a descriptive title of the motion in addition to the complete adversary caption. The caption shall conform to Official Form 16D (Caption for Use in Adversary Proceeding).

(c) The response to any motion shall be filed and served within fourteen (14) days after service of the motion plus an additional three (3) days as provided by Fed. R. Bankr. P. 9006(f) when service is by mail. If no response is timely filed, the motion shall be deemed uncontested, and the Court shall dispose of the motion. Replies and surreplies are not permitted unless ordered by the Court. If permitted, replies and surreplies shall be filed and served within seven (7) days, plus an additional three (3) days as provided by Fed. R. Bankr. P. 9006(f) when service is by mail, after service of the response or reply, as applicable.

(d) The movant shall file a brief, if any, and any supporting affidavits as an attachment to the motion, and the respondent shall file a brief, if any, and any supporting affidavits as attachments to the response. Briefs shall be limited to twenty (20) pages.

(e) If authorized, reply and surreply briefs shall be limited to five (5) pages, and shall address only matters not addressed in the initial brief. The deadlines for such briefs shall be set forth in the order granting their authorization.

(f) Motions for continuance of a trial date shall be considered by the Court only upon motion filed and served at least seven (7) calendar days before the scheduled trial.

(g) Any request for oral argument or hearing on a contested motion within an adversary proceeding shall be in writing and referenced in the caption.

(h) A proposed order of Court shall be filed as an attachment to all motions and all other requests for relief.

(i) When briefing is complete, the moving party shall file a certification that briefing is completed substantially in compliance with Local Bankruptcy Form 16 (Certification That Briefing Completed). The Court may not act until the certificate is filed with the Clerk. In addition, when briefing is complete, a tabbed binder with all related pleadings, documents, exhibits, and an index shall be delivered to the Judge's Chambers.

[Effective July 1, 2004. Amended effective November 22, 2004; December 1, 2009; March 1, 2012.]

RULE 7008–2. REVIEW OF PROPOSED FINDINGS OF FACT AND CONCLUSIONS OF LAW

(a) This Local Rule applies to non-core proceedings and any core proceeding in which a final order or judgment must be entered by a United States District Judge.

(b) A party objecting to the Bankruptcy Judge's proposed findings of fact and conclusions of law shall arrange for the transcription of the record or such portions of it as all parties may agree upon and file a Notice of Transcript Order within fourteen (14) days of the date the objection is filed.

(c) A party objecting to the Bankruptcy Judge's proposed findings or conclusions must file a motion to determine the portion of the record to be transcribed within fourteen (14) days of the date the objection is filed when the parties cannot agree. The objecting party shall arrange for the transcription of the record as determined by the Court and file a Notice of Transcript Order within seven (7) days of the date an order is entered on the motion.

(d) The Notice of Transcript Order shall comply with the caption requirements of W.PA.LBR. 9004–1, reference the date that the proposed findings of fact and conclusions of law were issued, provide the date and time of the hearing that will be transcribed, and provide the date that the transcript was ordered.

(e) A party objecting to the Bankruptcy Judge's proposed findings and conclusions of law shall file all of the exhibits admitted into evidence as a single document prior to filing the objection. The objection shall identify all of the exhibits and the docket number at which the exhibits were filed.

(f) The Clerk shall transmit the proposed findings of fact and conclusions of law, the Clerk's notice to the parties, objections, and responses to the District Court without a transcript when the Notice of Transcript Order is not timely filed.

[Effective July 1, 2013. Amended effective August 1, 2015; April 1, 2016.]

RULE 7010–1. CAPTIONS OF ADVERSARY PROCEEDINGS AND OF MOTIONS FILED WITHIN ADVERSARIES

(a) The caption of an adversary proceeding shall conform to Official Form 16D (Caption for Use in Adversary Proceeding). Additionally, the initials of the Presiding Judge shall be appended to the bankruptcy case number.

(b) Motions filed within adversary proceedings shall contain a descriptive title of the motion in addition to the complete adversary caption and adversary proceeding number.

(c) Responses or replies to motions filed within adversary proceedings shall contain the adversary caption and number and the same caption as the motion, but the description shall indicate that it is a response or reply.

[Effective July 1, 2004. Amended effective March 1, 2012.]

RULE 7014–1. SERVICE OF DOCUMENTS ON THIRD–PARTY DEFENDANTS

In every action in which there is a joinder of a third-party defendant, the third-party plaintiff shall deliver to the newly joined third-party defendant, within fourteen (14) days after the filing of an appearance or a responsive pleading by the joined third-party defendant, copies of all docket sheets, documents of record, and docketed items in the case.

[Effective July 1, 2004. Amended effective December 1, 2009; March 1, 2012.]

RULE 7016–1. PRETRIAL PROCEDURE

Pretrial procedures are governed by pretrial orders entered in each case and any additional requirements set forth by the Presiding Judge.

[Effective July 1, 2004. Amended effective March 1, 2012.]

RULE 7026–1. DISCOVERY OF ELECTRONIC DOCUMENTS ("E–DISCOVERY")

(a) If the parties cannot agree on how to conduct e-discovery before the first pretrial conference, the following default standards shall apply.

(b) Each party shall designate an "e-discovery liaison," through whom all e-discovery requests and responses are made.

(1) The e-discovery liaison shall be:

(A) familiar with and able to explain the party's electronic systems;

(B) knowledgeable about the technical aspects of e-discovery, including electronic document storage, organization, and format issues; and

(C) prepared to participate in e-discovery dispute resolutions.

(2) At all times, counsel of record shall be responsible for compliance with e-discovery requests. However, the e-discovery liaisons shall be responsible for organizing each party's e-discovery efforts to insure consistency and thoroughness.

(c) At least seven (7) days prior to the first pretrial conference, the parties shall exchange the following:

(1) A list of the most likely custodians of relevant electronic materials, including a brief description of each person's title and responsibilities;

(2) The name of the individual responsible for that party's electronic document retention policies ("the retention coordinator");

(3) The name of the party's e-discovery liaison;

(4) A list of each relevant electronic system that has been in place at all relevant times and a general description of each system, including: (a) the nature, (b) scope, (c) character, (d) organization, (e) formats employed in each system, and (f) whether the electronic documents are of limited accessibility (for example, documents created or used by electronic media no longer in use, maintained in redundant electronic storage media, or for which retrieval involves substantial cost);

(5) A general description of the party's electronic document retention policies for the systems identified above; and

(6) Any problems reasonably anticipated to arise with e-discovery.

(d) Discovery shall proceed in a sequenced fashion.

(1) After receiving requests for document production, a party shall search its documents, other than those identified as limited accessibility electronic documents, and produce responsive electronic documents in accordance with Fed. R. Civ. P. 26(b)(2).

(2) Electronic searches of documents identified as of limited accessibility shall not be conducted until the initial electronic document search has been completed. Requests for information expected to be found in limited accessibility documents shall be narrowly focused with some basis in fact supporting the request.

(3) On-site inspections of electronic media pursuant to Fed. R. Civ. P. 34(b) shall not be permitted absent exceptional circumstances, where good cause and specific need have been demonstrated.

(e) If a party intends to employ an electronic search, the party shall disclose any restrictions as to scope and method which might affect its ability to conduct a complete search. The parties shall reach an agreement as to the method of searching, and the words, terms, and phrases to be searched with the assistance of the respective e-discovery liaisons. The parties also shall reach an agreement as to the timing and conditions of any additional searches which may become necessary in the normal course of discovery. To minimize the expense, the parties may consider limiting the scope of the electronic search (e.g., time frames, fields, document types).

(f) Unless the parties otherwise agree, electronic documents shall be produced as image files, such as Portable Document Format (PDF) or Tagged Image File Format (TIFF). The producing party shall preserve the integrity of the electronic document's contents, i.e., the original formatting, its metadata and, where applicable, its revision history. For production of electronic documents in their native format, particularized need shall be shown.

(g) Within the first thirty (30) days of discovery, each party shall outline the steps each shall take to segregate and preserve the integrity of all relevant electronic documents (akin to the standard protective order). If spoliation is at issue, a Fed. R. Civ. P. 30(b)(6) deposition of the retention coordinator shall be scheduled at a mutually convenient time. The retention coordinators shall:

(1) take steps to ensure that e-mail of identified custodians is retained and not permanently deleted in the ordinary course of business and that electronic documents maintained by the individual custodians are not altered; and

(2) provide notice as to the criteria used for spam and/or virus filtering of e-mail and attachments; e-mails and attachments filtered out by such systems need not be produced provided that the criteria underlying the filtering are reasonable.

(h) Within seven (7) days of identifying the relevant document custodians, the retention coordinators shall implement the above procedures, and each party's counsel shall file a statement of compliance as such with the Court.

(i) Electronic documents that contain privileged information or attorney work product shall be immediately returned if the documents appear on their face to have been inadvertently produced or upon written notice of the inadvertent production.

(j) The costs of discovery will be borne in accordance with the applicable rules. However, the Court will apportion the costs of electronic discovery upon a showing of good cause.

[Effective March 1, 2012.]

RULE 7026–2. ELECTRONIC DISCOVERY SPECIAL MASTER

Any party may request, and the Court may order, sua sponte, that any dispute concerning electronic discovery be referred to an Electronic Discovery Special Master, pursuant to United States District Court for the Western District of Pennsylvania, General Order No. 2:11–mc–94 (In Re: Use of Special Masters for Electronic Discovery by United States Bankruptcy Judges).

[Effective March 1, 2012.]

RULE 7037–1. DISCOVERY DISPUTES

(a) An objection to interrogatories, depositions, requests, or applications pursuant to Fed. R. Bankr. P. 7026 through 7037, as well as all motions and responses concerning discovery matters, shall be filed and have attached as an exhibit only the specific portion that is the subject of the objection.

(b) An objection to discovery matters shall not extend the time to answer or respond to portions to which no objection was made.

(c) Any party opposing the requested relief shall file only those additional portions of the interrogatories, requests for documents, or requests for admission, and the responses to same that are necessary for the Court's consideration of the matter.

(d) If a discovery dispute is not resolved, the party initiating discovery shall file and serve a motion to compel. Only those portions of the interrogatories, depositions, requests for documents, or request applications that are germane to the motion shall be filed. Any party opposing the requested relief shall file only those additional portions of the interrogatories, depositions, requests, or applications, and the responses to same that are necessary for the Court's consideration of the matter.

(e) Compliance with discovery orders shall be effected within fourteen (14) days of the entry of the order.

(f) Should a party fail to comply with an order of Court concerning discovery motions, the party objecting to such failure to comply shall place the matter before the Court by filing and serving a motion for supplementary relief.

(g) Counsel are required to participate in pretrial discovery conferences in order to decrease, in every way possible, the filing of unnecessary discovery motions. No motion concerning discovery matters may be filed until counsel makes a good-faith effort with opposing counsel to resolve the discovery matters in dispute. The Court shall dismiss any motion concerning discovery matters not accompanied by a certificate of counsel that a good-faith effort has been made to resolve the discovery matters at issue. The certification shall be filed as an attachment to the motion.

[Effective July 1, 2004. Amended effective December 1, 2009; March 1, 2012.]

RULE 7065–1. TEMPORARY RESTRAINING ORDERS

(a) A party shall file an adversary complaint and a motion for preliminary injunction along with an application for a temporary restraining order.

(b) A party filing an application for a temporary restraining order with an attached proposed order and any party filing a response shall deliver a paper copy to the Presiding Judge's Chambers to notify the Court that the application or response has been filed.

[Effective July 1, 2004. Amended effective March 1, 2012.]

PART VIII. APPEALS TO DISTRICT COURT OR BANKRUPTCY APPELLATE PANEL

RULE 8006–1. REQUESTS FOR COMPLETE OR PARTIAL TRANSCRIPTS ON APPEAL

(a) The requirements for ordering transcripts are set forth in W.PA.LBR 5007–1. In addition to designating a transcript as part of the record on appeal, the requesting party shall file and serve notice that a transcript has been requested.

(b) The request for a transcript by an appellant, shall be filed not later than two (2) days after filing the designation of the record and statement of issues to be presented.

(c) Not later than two (2) days after the filing by appellee of a designation of any additional items to be included in the record, an appellee shall file any request for a transcript.

(d) If an appellee has filed a cross-appeal, the appellee as cross-appellant, shall file any request for a transcript not later than two (2) days after the filing by such party of a statement of the issues to be presented on the cross-appeal and any designation of additional items to be included in the record.

(e) A cross-appellee shall file any request for a transcript no later than two (2) days after the filing by such party of a designation of any additional items to be included in the record on the cross-appeal.

(f) Parties shall comply with W.PA.LBR 9037–1 when requesting redaction of personal identifiers from transcripts.

[Effective July 1, 2004. Amended effective March 1, 2012.]

RULE 8007–1. APPEAL TO THE DISTRICT COURT FROM THE BANKRUPTCY COURT

(a) When, after a Notice of Appeal to the United States District Court has been filed in the Bankruptcy Court, the appellant fails to designate the contents of the record on appeal or fails to file a statement of issues on appeal within the time required by the Federal Rules of Bankruptcy Procedure, or fails to provide, when appropriate, evidence that a transcript has been ordered and that payment therefor has been arranged, or fails to take any other action to enable the Bankruptcy Clerk to assemble and transmit the record:

(1) The Clerk of the Bankruptcy Court shall provide fourteen (14) days' notice to the appellant and appellee of an intention to transmit a partial record consistent with W.PA.LBR 8007–1(b); and

(2) After the 14–day notice period has expired, the Clerk of the Bankruptcy Court shall thereafter promptly forward to the Clerk of the United States District Court a partial record consisting of a copy of the order or judgment appealed from, any opinion, findings of fact, and conclusions of law by the Court, the Notice of Appeal, a copy of the docket entries, any documents filed as part of the appeal, and any copies of the record which have been designated by the parties pursuant to Fed. R. Bankr. P. 8006. The record as transmitted shall be deemed to be the complete record for purposes of the appeal; and

(b) Notwithstanding any counter designation of the record or statement of issues filed by the appellee, if the appellee fails to provide, where appropriate, evidence that a transcript has been ordered and that payment therefor has been arranged, or the appellee fails to take any other action to enable the Bankruptcy Clerk to assemble and transmit the record pursuant to Fed. R. Bankr. P. 8006, the Clerk of the Bankruptcy Court shall transmit the copies of the record designated by the parties, and this shall be deemed to be the complete record on appeal.

[Effective July 1, 2004. Amended effective December 1, 2009; March 1, 2012.]

RULE 8007–2. TRANSMISSION OF THE RECORD ON APPEAL

In accordance with Miscellaneous Order # 12–284 of the District Court, the Clerk shall not transmit to the District Court paper copies of documents listed on designations of record on appeal. The Bankruptcy Court Clerk shall transmit the record on appeal by way of an e-mail to the District Court Clerk, identifying the corresponding Bankruptcy Court docket entry number of each document designated by the parties to the appeal and attaching electronic copies of the respective designations of the record. The District Court shall access the designated documents by way of the ECF and PACER systems.

[Effective July 1, 2013.]

PART IX. GENERAL PROVISIONS

RULE 9004–1. CAPTIONS OF PLEADINGS AND ORDERS

Except as specified herein, any document filed in the general case or miscellaneous docket of a bankruptcy proceeding, including, but not limited to, any proposed order, pleading, notice, declaration, motion, application, response, or reply, shall contain a caption substantially conforming to Official Form 16D (Caption for Use in Adversary Proceeding), governing adversary captions except that the party seeking relief shall be designated as "Movant," and the party against whom relief is sought shall be designated as "Respondent." When there is no entity to be named as a respondent, the words "No Respondent(s)" shall be stated. In the caption of each motion and any response thereto, the case number shall be entered as well as the chapter number. "Document No." shall be stated instead of "Adversary Proceeding No." A certificate of service, proposed order, or any subsequent pleading to a motion, objection, or other request for relief shall include in the caption the hearing date and time, the objection date, and the document number of the document to which it pertains. The foregoing requirement as to captions shall not apply as to a bankruptcy petition and other related preliminary filings in a bankruptcy case (Official Forms 1 through 15, 18, 19, 21, 22, 23, 25, and 26, or any Supplement or Attachment thereto); Directors Procedural Forms 13S through 231A–B, 253; Local Bankruptcy Forms 1A–1B, 10, and 13; a chapter 11 plan of reorganization; a plan of reorganization in a small business case; a chapter 12 plan; and a chapter 13 plan and related disclosure statements.

[Effective July 1, 2004. Amended effective March 1, 2012; July 1, 2013.]

RULE 9006–1. TIME

(a) To the extent a matter is self-scheduled pursuant to the scheduling practices of a particular judge, every request for relief, however made, shall be served on the same day that it is filed. Otherwise, the matter shall be served in the manner required by the directive of the Court.

(b) Every responsive pleading shall be filed and served within fourteen (14) days from the date the motion is filed and served.

(c) All references to days mean calendar days unless otherwise noted.

[Effective July 1, 2004. Amended effective November 22, 2004; December 1, 2009; March 1, 2012.]

RULE 9010–1. ADMISSION TO PRACTICE

(a) Attorneys who are admitted to the Bar of the United States District Court for the Western District of Pennsylvania are admitted to the Bar of this Court.

(b) No one, other than an attorney regularly admitted to practice in this Court, shall appear in any proceeding except upon motion filed with the Clerk and order entered by the Court. Every motion to be admitted pro hac vice shall be signed and filed by an attorney admitted to practice in this District. The motion shall substantially conform to Local Bankruptcy Form 18 (Motion for Pro Hac Vice Admission). The party seeking pro hac vice admission shall pay the required fees of $40.00 contemporaneously with filing the motion. If a motion for pro hac vice is made orally in open Court, it shall be followed promptly by the filing of a written motion signed by local counsel and the applicant. The Court may require counsel to provide evidence of admission in another district. An attorney admitted pro hac vice and local counsel shall appear at Court hearings and be prepared to address all issues set for argument.

(c) An attorney not admitted to practice by the United States District Court for the Western District of Pennsylvania may not be admitted pro hac vice in this Court unless associated with an attorney, as local counsel, who is a member of the Bar of this Court and who shall act as local counsel during the term of applicant's admission and who maintains an office in this District for the regular transaction of business, upon whom all documents, pleadings, and notices shall be served and who shall be required to sign all papers filed with the Clerk. Local counsel is not necessary for:

(1) the filing or prosecution of a proof of claim or response to an objection to a proof of claim. The Court may, however, direct counsel to claimant to associate with local counsel if the claim litigation will involve extensive discovery or trial time.

(2) an attorney not admitted in the United States District Court for the Western District of Pennsylvania but admitted in another United States District Court representing the United States of America (or any officer or agency thereof) or any State (or officer or agency thereof) provided that a certification is filed, signed by that attorney, stating (a) the courts in which the attorney is admitted, (b) that the attorney is in good standing in all jurisdictions in which the attorney has been admitted, and (c) that the attorney will be bound by the Local Bankruptcy Rules of this Court and submits to the jurisdiction of this Court for disciplinary purposes in connection with the matter in which the attorney is appearing.

(d) No attorney shall be given pro hac vice status on more than 3 occasions. At that point, general admission before the United States District Court for the Western District of Pennsylvania is required.

(e) The Local Rules of the United States District Court for the Western District of Pennsylvania as amended from time to time shall apply as to discipline of attorneys.

[Effective July 1, 2004. Amended effective March 1, 2012.]

RULE 9010–2. ENTRY, WITHDRAWAL AND/OR SUBSTITUTION OF APPEARANCE

(a) A separate Notice of Appearance need not be filed by an attorney for an original party to an action or for an intervenor. The endorsement of names of attorneys appearing on the first pleading or motion filed by a party shall constitute the entry of appearance for such attorneys and their law firms. Thereafter, pursuant to W.PA.LBR 5005–8, service and notice to the attorney(s) appearing on the first pleading or motion will be provided by way of electronic Notice of Electronic Filing ("NEF") only to the Filing User unless an attorney enters a separate Notice of Appearance.

(b) All parties filing any document, including pleadings, shall appear in person or through counsel for the scheduled hearing on that matter unless such appearance has been excused by the Court.

(c) Only natural persons may appear in Court without counsel.

(d) Child support creditors need not appear by counsel; provided, however, that they shall first complete and file Local Bankruptcy Form 19 (Appearance of Child Support Creditor or Representative).

(e) An attorney may withdraw an entry of appearance and/or substitute appearance only with leave of Court, upon filing a written motion stating the reasons for withdrawal and/or substitution and certifying that each affected client has expressly consented to the withdrawal and/or substitution.

(f) In the event that the consent of an affected client cannot be obtained, movant shall file a motion pursuant to subpart (e), above, which shall include "IN THE ABSENCE OF CLIENT CONSENT" in the title of the motion, and the Court shall schedule a hearing on the motion.

(g) An attorney intending to file a motion pursuant to subpart (e) or (f), above, in more than twenty (20) cases may contact the Clerk of Court to request the opening of a Miscellaneous Proceeding for the filing of an omnibus motion for the withdrawal and/or substitution of appearance in all cases. If the Chief Bankruptcy Judge determines that omnibus relief is appropriate, the Clerk shall open a Miscellaneous Proceeding and the movant shall file an omnibus motion for withdrawal and/or substitution of appearance with a list of all affected cases attached as an exhibit to the motion. For each case listed in the exhibit, the movant shall provide the case number, Presiding Judge, debtor(s)' full name(s), and the full name of the movant's client. The movant is responsible for the preparation and accuracy of the information set forth in the exhibit. The movant shall file a certificate of service demonstrating that the omnibus motion was timely served on each of the movant's clients identified in the exhibit. The movant shall pay any applicable fee as set forth in the Fee Schedule available on the Court's website.

[Effective July 1, 2004. Amended effective March 1, 2012; April 1, 2016.]

RULE 9010–3. AGREEMENTS OF ATTORNEYS

(a) All agreements of attorneys shall be filed with the Court for approval; otherwise, they will be considered of no validity.

(b) No agreement contrary to the Federal Rules of Bankruptcy Procedure, these Local Bankruptcy Rules, or a separate order of Court will be considered valid including, without limitation, agreements to extend time.

[Effective July 1, 2004. Amended effective March 1, 2012.]

RULE 9013–1. MOTIONS AND CONTESTED MATTERS

(a) All written motions, applications, objections or other requests for relief shall be accompanied by a proposed order filed as an attachment to the motion.

(b) Periodic motions days may be established by each Judge. No witnesses shall be heard on motions days.

(c) Any affirmative request for relief shall be brought by motion and may not be included in any response to a motion.

[Effective July 1, 2004. Amended effective November 22, 2004; December 1, 2009; March 1, 2012.]

RULE 9013–2. PROCEDURE FOR EXPEDITED HEARINGS

(a) A motion including a request for expedited hearing shall specify:

(1) the substantive relief sought;

(2) just cause to request consideration of the underlying matter on an expedited basis;

(3) the specific harm the movant shall incur if a hearing is not granted on an expedited basis; and

(4) the need for an expedited hearing has not been caused by any lack of due diligence on the part of the attorney or the attorney's client but has been brought about solely by circumstances beyond their control.

(b) The request for expedited hearing shall be set forth in the title to the motion.

(c) A proposed order granting the relief requested shall be filed as an attachment to the motion. A second proposed order substantially conforming to Local Bankruptcy Form 20 (Notice and Order Setting Hearing on an Expedited Basis) shall be filed as an attachment to the motion and shall provide that the request for expedited hearing is granted and shall contain blank spaces for the Court to enter the date, time, place of hearing, and the date by which responses shall be filed and served.

(d) Once the hearing is scheduled, movant shall serve on the respondent and all other applicable parties of interest a copy of the completed order scheduling the hearing and the accompanying motion, by hand delivery, and where addresses and numbers are known or readily ascertainable, alternate service by facsimile, electronic transmission, and any other method of service approved by the Court.

(e) Parties filing a motion for expedited hearing shall immediately notify Chambers of the Judge assigned the case that the motion has been entered on the docket.

[Effective July 1, 2004. Amended effective March 1, 2012.]

RULE 9013–3. MOTIONS SEEKING: (1) RELIEF FROM THE AUTOMATIC STAY; (2) LIEN AVOIDANCE; (3) ABANDONMENT; (4) SALE APPROVAL; AND/OR (5) TO EXTEND/IMPOSE THE AUTOMATIC STAY

(a) All motions seeking relief from the automatic stay shall plead the following with particularity:

(1) the movant's name and proof of claim number, if any;

(2) a description of any affected property and whether it appears in the schedules;

(3) the value of any affected property and the source of the valuation;

(4) the amount and date of the loan at origination;

(5) the date and type of perfection (e.g., date of lien on title, date and location of UCC filing, date and mortgage book volume and page number, etc.);

(6) the current balance (principal, interest, interest rate, charges, costs, fees, and accruing daily interest);

(7) the balance owed as of the date of the motion;

(8) an itemized statement of the default and the amount necessary to cure as of the filing date of the motion;

(9) the amount of any plan payment arrearages;

(10) a separate itemized statement of the postpetition default;

(11) the value of any claimed exemption in the affected property;

(12) the amount of any equity in the affected property; and

(13) all known liens against any affected property, including:

(A) the name and address of the holder;

(B) the date incurred;

(C) the current balance owed; and

(D) the type of lien (e.g., mortgage, judgment, etc.).

(b) All motions seeking lien avoidance shall plead the following with particularity:

(1) a description of the affected property and whether it appears in the schedules;

(2) the name of each person or entity having an ownership interest in the affected property;

(3) the value of the affected property and the source of the valuation;

(4) the value of any claimed exemption in the affected property; and

(5) all known liens against the affected property, including:

(A) the name and address of the holder, and in the case of a judgment lien, counsel for the holder in the underlying lawsuit;

(B) the current balance owed;

(C) the date incurred;

(D) the type of lien (e.g., mortgage, judgment, etc.); and

(E) the identification of record location of each lien on the property subject to the action (i.e., in the case of a mortgage lien, the mortgage book volume and page number, and in the case of a judgment lien, the name of the court, identification of the case number, and date when the judgment was entered).

(c) All sale motions shall plead the following with particularity:

(1) the full name, address, and account number, if available, of all respondents, with only entities holding a lien, claim, or encumbrance against the affected property named as respondents;

(2) the value of the affected property and the source of the valuation, e.g., appraisal, book value, personal opinion, recent comparable sales;

(3) an appropriate description of the affected property and where it appears in the schedules:

(A) For sale of real estate, the formal deed description is not necessary. The current deed book and page number (or other recording information if deed book and page number are not available), street address, tax identification number, and basic description of the real estate use (e.g., commercial building, single-family residence) as well as a brief description of any other relevant appurtenances, shall be included; and

(B) For sale of personalty, an itemized list of the specific property subject to sale, individually identified without an "in bulk" reference (unless it would be impractical to do otherwise), shall be included;

(4) the name and address of each person or other entity having an ownership interest in the affected property;

(5) the value of any claimed exemption in the affected property;

(6) identification of the specific disbursements, costs, and expenses of sale to be made at the time of closing:

(A) Unless an exact payoff amount for the specific lien, claim, and/or encumbrances is capable of being set forth in a finite amount, the per diem and other charges or assessments to be made at closing shall be identified in the respective payoffs listed; and

(B) In the event a request for payment of attorney fees and expenses in excess of $750.00 is requested to be paid at closing, an itemization of attorney time and billing in support of the request shall be appended to the motion as a separate exhibit, in a form consistent with the requirements of these Local Bankruptcy Rules;

(7) all liens, claims, and encumbrances against the affected property, including:

(A) the name and address of the holder, and in the case of a judgment lien, counsel for the holder in the underlying lawsuit;

(B) the current balance owed;

(C) the date incurred;

(D) the type of lien (e.g., mortgage, judgment, etc.); and

(E) the identification of record location of each lien on the property subject to the action (i.e., in the case of a mortgage lien, the mortgage book volume and page number, and in the case of a judgment lien, the name of the court, identification of the case number, and date when the judgment was entered);

(8) the name and address of the purchaser(s), including:

(A) the relationship, if any, of the purchaser to the debtor;

(B) the purchase price;

(C) all conditions of sale; and

(D) a copy of any agreement of sale to be approved by the Court as a separate attachment; and

(9) a proposed order in the form required by the assigned Judge.

(A) The order shall include the identity of every respondent and identity of the respective liens, claims, and encumbrances to be transferred to proceeds of sale, in the same manner as required by W.PA.LBR 9013–3(c)(1); and

(B) Identity of the specific disbursements, costs, and expenses of sale to be paid at closing, in the same manner required by W.PA.LBR 9013–3(c)(6).

(10) as to the procedural requirements for sale of estate property outside the ordinary course of business, see W.PA.LBR 6004–1.

(d) All motions seeking abandonment of property shall plead the following with particularity:

(1) a description of the affected property and whether it appears in the schedules;

(2) the value of the affected property and the source of the valuation;

(3) the value of any claimed exemption in the affected property;

(4) the basis for any assertion that the affected property is either burdensome to the estate or is of inconsequential value and benefit thereto; and

(5) all known liens against the affected property, including:

(A) the name and address of the holder, and in the case of a judgment lien, counsel for the holder in the underlying lawsuit;

(B) the current balance owed;

(C) the date incurred;

(D) the type of lien (i.e., mortgage, judgment, etc.); and

(E) the identification of record location of each lien on the property subject to the action (i.e., in the case of a mortgage lien, the mortgage book volume and page number, and in the case of a judgment lien, the name of the court, identification of the case number, and date when the judgment was entered).

(e) All motions seeking to extend or re-impose the automatic stay shall plead the following with particularity:

(1) all creditors against whom the relief is sought shall be listed in the caption, notice, and motion;

(2) whether the automatic stay was in effect upon commencement of the case, and if so, the date on which the automatic stay expires;

(3) each bankruptcy case number for all bankruptcy cases in which the debtor was a debtor within the one-year period prior to the date when the current case was filed;

(4) the reasons that each of the debtor's previous bankruptcy cases was dismissed;

(5) whether presumption is in effect that the debtor did not file the case at issue in good faith and the reason for the presumption;

(6) with particularity the substantial change in circumstances that occurred since the dismissal of the previous case; and

(7) a verification executed by the debtor attached to the motion.

[Effective July 1, 2004. Amended effective November 22, 2004; March 1, 2012.]

RULE 9013–4. FILING OF PROPOSED ORDERS

(a) All documents requesting relief shall have an appropriate proposed order of Court, that is, one that specifies the relief sought and not merely incorporating by reference the content of the foregoing document, filed as a separate attachment. If a proposed order is not attached, the Court shall dismiss the matter without scheduling a hearing thereon and without prejudice to its being refiled in compliance with these Local Bankruptcy Rules, Federal Rules of Bankruptcy Procedure, and Court orders or procedures.

(b) Proposed orders electronically filed with motions, petitions applications, objections, or other requests for relief shall be filed with the motion as a separate attachment.

[Effective July 1, 2004. Amended effective March 1, 2012.]

RULE 9013–5. SCHEDULING HEARINGS

(a) Parties are directed to ascertain, and shall comply with, procedures stated on the Court's website for the scheduling practices of each Judge.

(b) The moving party shall serve all parties in interest with the motion, proposed order, and notice of hearing. For chapter 7 final accounts and proposed distributions, use the form prescribed by the United States Trustee. For fee applications in chapter 7 and

13 cases, use Local Bankruptcy Form 8 (Summary Cover Sheet and Notice of Hearing on Professional Fees in Chapters 7, 12 and 13). For fee applications in chapter 11 and 15 cases, use Local Bankruptcy Form 9 (Summary Cover Sheet for Fee Applications in Chapter 11 and Chapter 15).

(c) If nothing is filed on the docket in response to a motion, then the moving party, assuming no agreement with the opposing party/counsel to the contrary, shall file with the Clerk a Certification of No Objection substantially in compliance with Local Bankruptcy Form 25 (Certification of No Objection). The Certification shall be filed no later than two (2) days after the objection deadline has expired. If the Court grants the relief by default, the hearing is canceled.

(d) If a disputed matter has been settled prior to the hearing, counsel for movant shall file a Settlement and Certification of Counsel substantially in compliance with Local Bankruptcy Form 26 (Settlement and Certification of Counsel). A proposed consent order shall be filed as an attachment to the Settlement and Certification of Counsel.

(e) Initial hearings on motions shall be brief, not more than ten (10) minutes in any case. No testimony will be heard. If there is an issue of fact, a discovery schedule, if appropriate, and an evidentiary hearing will be fixed by the Court at the initial hearing. If there is no issue of fact, the Court may dispose of the matter at such hearing, or on briefs, or as the Court may determine. Matters which are settled after responses are filed shall be heard prior to other matters scheduled for the same time upon request of the parties at the hearing.

(f) If a filing is not in substantial compliance with these Local Bankruptcy Rules or procedures, an order may be entered dismissing the motion without prejudice, and movant shall promptly notify respondent thereof.

(g) A motion for relief from default orders is governed by Fed. R. Bankr. P. 9023 or 9024 as applicable.

(h) A movant who files a motion for relief from stay and selects a hearing date in accordance with a Judge's scheduling practice shall be deemed to have waived the 30–day period specified in 11 U.S.C. § 362(e) when the hearing is scheduled for a date more than thirty (30) days after the date the motion is filed. If a hearing date is not available within the 30–day period, a movant who would be harmed by a delay of the hearing beyond the 30–day period specified in 11 U.S.C. § 362(e) shall file a motion for expedited hearing.

[Effective July 1, 2004. Amended effective May 3, 2005; March 1, 2012.]

RULE 9013–6. EXTENSION OF TIME TO ASSUME CONTRACT OR LEASE OR TO FILE A PLAN

If the time has not expired within which an executory contract or an unexpired lease may be assumed or rejected or within which the debtor retains the exclusive right to file a plan of reorganization, in only such instances, when a motion to extend time is filed, then the time shall be extended until the disposition of the motion.

[Effective July 1, 2004. Amended effective March 1, 2012.]

RULE 9014–1. FILING AND SERVICE OF RESPONSIVE PLEADINGS IN CONTESTED MATTERS

Every responsive pleading shall be filed and served within fourteen (14) days from the date the motion is filed. Respondent shall have an additional three (3) days to file a response to any motion served by mail. A written response is required for every written request for relief. Failure to timely file a response may result in the Court granting the relief by default.

[Effective July 1, 2004. Amended effective November 22, 2004; March 1, 2012.]

RULE 9015–1. JURY DEMAND

(a) The party making a jury trial demand shall file the demand with the Clerk of the Bankruptcy Court and serve all parties in interest. If the demand is made by the moving party, it shall be endorsed on the front of the initial motion or pleading. The last date on which a demand for jury trial may be made by any party is fourteen (14) days after:

(1) an answer is filed and served to a complaint, cross-claim, or counterclaim; or

(2) a response to a motion or objection is filed and served.

(b) With respect to removed actions, Fed. R. Civ. P. 81(c) applies. In such cases, demand for jury trial shall be made within thirty (30) days after filing the Notice of Removal.

(c) Within thirty (30) days of filing the demand, the party making the demand shall file with the Clerk and serve on all parties in interest:

(1) the consent of all parties to trial by jury in the Bankruptcy Court and the Bankruptcy Court's entry of final orders or judgments with respect to the same; or

(2) a motion to withdraw the reference to the District Court. All proceedings shall continue in the Bankruptcy Court unless and until an Order is issued by the District Court withdrawing the reference.

(d) The failure to comply with this Local Bankruptcy Rule shall be deemed to be a waiver of trial by jury in the Bankruptcy Court.

[Effective July 1, 2004. Amended effective December 1, 2009; March 1, 2012.]

RULE 9015–2. JURY SELECTION SYSTEM

(a) The plan for random selection of jurors adopted by the United States District Court for the Western District of Pennsylvania with the approval of its reviewing panel under 28 U.S.C. § 1863 governs jury selection by the United States Bankruptcy Court for the Western District of Pennsylvania.

(b) The Clerk of the Bankruptcy Court shall request that the Clerk of the District Court furnish a sufficient number of jurors for use in scheduled jury trials. If not selected or serving in the Bankruptcy Court, such jurors shall be released to the District Court.

(c) The Clerk of the Bankruptcy Court shall cooperate with the Clerk of the District Court in the implementation of those jury utilization techniques which are employed by the District Court in the interest of efficient and economical use of jurors.

[Effective July 1, 2004. Amended effective March 1, 2012.]

RULE 9019–1. SETTLEMENTS

A motion requesting Court approval of a settlement shall delineate the reasons for settling the matter and shall attach a copy of the proposed settlement agreement.

[Effective July 1, 2004; Amended effective November 22, 2004; March 1, 2012.]

RULE 9019–2. SCOPE AND EFFECT OF MEDIATION

(a) The Court may assign any matter to the Mediation Program for the Western District of Pennsylvania (the "Mediation Program") sua sponte, upon motion or stipulation of the parties to the matter or the United States trustee. The Court may order additional parties to participate in the mediation as necessary.

(b) The Court may assign to mediation any dispute arising in the bankruptcy case or in any adversary proceeding, contested matter, or otherwise. Fed. R. Bankr. P. 7016 is hereby made applicable to all matters in which mediation is requested in accordance with the Mediation Program.

(c) The assignment of a matter to mediation does not relieve the parties to that matter from complying with any other Court orders or applicable provisions of the Bankruptcy Code, the Federal Rules of Bankruptcy Procedure, or the Local Bankruptcy Rules of this Court. The assignment to mediation stays all discovery, pretrial, hearing dates, and trial schedules. The Court will issue a scheduling order and set deadlines for the mediation to conclude and for the discovery, pretrial, and trial to resume.

[Effective July 1, 2004. Amended effective March 1, 2012.]

RULE 9019–3. MEDIATORS

(a) The Clerk shall establish and maintain a register of persons (the "Register") qualified and designated by the Court to serve as mediators in the Mediation Program. The Chief Bankruptcy Judge shall appoint a Judge of this Court to serve as the "Mediation Program Administrator." The Mediation Program Administrator or designee shall receive applications for designation to the Register, maintain the Register, track and compile reports on the Mediation Program, and otherwise administer the program.

(b) Each applicant shall submit to the Mediation Program Administrator a statement of professional qualifications, experience, training, and other information relevant to designation to the Register, using Local Bankruptcy Form 31 (Application for Admission to Bankruptcy Mediation Program Register).

(c) Each applicant shall agree to serve in a pro bono capacity for his or her initial mediation appointment. Thereafter, the applicant shall serve in a pro bono capacity for one (1) out of every five (5) subsequent appointments as a mediator.

(d) Not later than March 1 of every year using Local Bankruptcy Form 31 (Application for Admission to Bankruptcy Mediation Program Register), each applicant accepted for designation to the Register shall reaffirm the continued existence and accuracy of the qualifications, statements, and representations made in the application, and file amendments as needed.

(e) The Court in its sole and absolute determination on any basis shall grant or deny an application. If the Court grants the application, the applicant's name shall be added to the Register.

(f) A person shall be removed from the Register either at the person's request or by Court order entered on the sole and absolute determination of the Court. If removed by Court order, the person shall be eligible to file an application for reinstatement after one (1) year.

(g) Before serving as a mediator, each person designated as a mediator shall take the following oath or affirmation:

"I, _____, do solemnly swear [or affirm] that I will faithfully and impartially discharge and perform all the duties incumbent upon me as a mediator in the Mediation Program of the United States Bankruptcy Court for the Western District of Pennsylvania without respect to persons and will do so equally with respect to the poor and to the rich."

(h) Upon assignment of a matter to mediation and unless special circumstances exist as determined by the Court, the parties shall select a mediator and may choose an alternate mediator from the Register whose appointment shall be authorized by the Court. If the parties fail to make such selection within the time frame as set by the Court, then the Court shall appoint a mediator and may appoint an alternate mediator.

(i) If the mediator is unable or elects not to serve, the mediator shall file and serve on all parties to the mediation and on the alternate mediator, within seven (7) calendar days after receipt of a Notice of Appointment, a Notice of Inability or Election Not to Accept the Appointment. The alternate mediator then shall become the mediator, if the alternate does not file and serve on all parties to the mediation a Notice of Inability or Election Not to Accept the Appointment within seven (7) calendar days after receipt of the original mediator's Notice of Inability or Election Not to Accept the Appointment. If neither the mediator nor the alternate mediator can serve, the Court shall appoint another mediator and alternate mediator.

(j) Any person selected as a mediator may be disqualified for bias or prejudice in the same manner that a Judge may be disqualified under 28 U.S.C. § 144. Any person selected as a mediator shall be disqualified in any matter where 28 U.S.C. § 455 would require disqualification if that person were a Judge.

(k) Promptly after receiving Notice of Appointment, the mediator shall make inquiry sufficient to determine whether there is a basis for disqualification under W.PA.LBR 9019–3(j). The inquiry shall include, but shall not be limited to, a search for conflicts of interests in the manner prescribed by the applicable rules of professional conduct for attorney mediators, and by the applicable rules pertaining to the mediator's profession for nonattorney mediators. Within seven (7) calendar days after receiving Notice of Appointment, the mediator shall file with the Court and serve on the parties to the mediation either (1) a statement that there is no basis for disqualification under W.PA.LBR 9019–3(j), and that the mediator has no actual potential conflict of interest, or (2) a Notice of Withdrawal.

(l) A party to the mediation who believes that the assigned mediator and/or the alternate mediator has a conflict of interest shall promptly bring the issue to the attention of the mediator and/or the alternate mediator, as applicable, and to the other parties to the mediation. If the mediator does not withdraw, and the movant is dissatisfied with this decision, the issue shall be brought to the Court's attention by the mediator or any of the parties to the mediation. The Court shall take such action as the Court deems necessary or appropriate to resolve the alleged conflict of interest.

(m) Aside from proof of actual fraud or unethical conduct, there shall be no liability on the part of, and no cause of action shall arise against, any person who is appointed as a mediator pursuant to this Local Bankruptcy Rule on account of any act or omission in the course and scope of such person's duties as a mediator.

(n) Once eligible to serve as a mediator for compensation, which shall be at reasonable rates and subject to judicial review, the mediator may require compensation or reimbursement of expenses as agreed by the parties to the mediation. Prior Court approval shall also be required if the estate is to be charged. If the mediator consents to serve without compensation, and at the conclusion of the first full day of the mediation conference, it is determined by the mediator and the parties to the mediation that additional time will be both necessary and productive in order to complete the mediation, then:

(1) if the mediator consents to continue to serve without compensation, the parties to the mediation may agree to continue the mediation conference; and

(2) if the mediator does not consent to continue to serve without compensation, the mediator's fees and expenses shall be on such terms as are satisfactory to the mediator and the parties to the mediation, subject to Court approval.

(o) Where the parties have agreed to pay mediation fees and expenses, they shall share equally all such fees and expenses unless the parties to the mediation agree to some other allocation. The Court may, in the interest of justice, determine a different allocation.

(p) If the Court determines that a party to a matter assigned to mediation cannot afford to pay the fees and costs of the mediator, the Court may appoint a mediator to serve pro bono as to that party.

[Effective March 1, 2012. Amended effective July 1, 2013.]

RULE 9019–4. THE MEDIATION PROCESS

(a) After consulting with all counsel and pro se parties, the mediator shall schedule a convenient time and place for the mediation conference, and promptly give all counsel and pro se parties written notice of the time and place of the mediation conference. The mediator shall schedule the mediation to begin as soon as practicable.

(b) Unless the mediator directs otherwise, not less than seven (7) calendar days before the mediation conference, each party shall submit directly to the mediator any materials the mediator directs to be prepared or assembled. The mediator shall so direct not less than fourteen (14) calendar days before the mediation conference. Prior to the mediation conference, the mediator may confer with the participants to determine what materials would be helpful. The submissions shall not be filed with the Court, and the Court shall not have access to them. The mediator will not share one party's materials with another party unless expressly authorized to do so by the party providing the materials to the mediator.

(c) The following persons personally shall attend the mediation conference:

(1) each party that is a natural person;

(2) if the party is not a natural person, including a governmental entity, a representative who is not the party's attorney of record and who has full authority to negotiate and settle the matter on behalf of the party;

(3) if the party is a governmental entity that requires settlement approval by an elected official or legislative body, a representative who has authority to recommend a settlement to the elected official or legislative body;

(4) the attorney who has primary responsibility for each party's case; and

(5) other interested parties such as insurers or indemnitors or one (1) or more of their representatives, whose presence is necessary for a full resolution of the matter assigned to mediation.

(d) A person required to attend the mediation is excused from personal appearance if all parties and the mediator agree that the person need not attend. The Court for cause may excuse a person's attendance. The mediator may require telephonic attendance in lieu of personal appearance.

(e) Willful failure to attend any mediation conference, and any other material violation of this Local Bankruptcy Rule, shall be reported to the Court by the mediator and may result in the imposition of sanctions by the Court. Any such report of the mediator shall comply with the confidentiality requirement of W.PA.LBR 9019–5.

(f) The mediator may establish procedures for the mediation conference.

[Effective March 1, 2012.]

RULE 9019–5. CONFIDENTIALITY OF MEDIATION PROCEEDINGS

(a) The mediator and the participants in mediation are prohibited from divulging, outside of the mediation, any oral or written information disclosed by the parties or by witnesses in the course of the mediation. No person may rely on or introduce, as evidence in any arbitral, judicial, or other proceedings, evidence pertaining to any aspect of the mediation effort, including, but not limited to:

(1) views expressed or suggestions made by a party with respect to a possible settlement of the dispute;

(2) the fact that another party had or had not indicated willingness to accept a proposal for settlement made by the mediator;

(3) proposals made or views expressed by the mediator;

(4) statements or admissions made by a party in the course of the mediation; and

(5) documents prepared for the purpose of, in the course of, or pursuant to the mediation.

(b) Without limiting the foregoing, Rule 408 of the Federal Rules of Evidence and any applicable federal or state statute, rule, common law, or judicial precedent relating to the privileged nature of settlement discussions, mediation, or other alternative dispute resolution procedure shall apply.

(c) Information otherwise discoverable or admissible in evidence, however, does not become exempt from discovery, or inadmissible in evidence, merely by being used by a party in a mediation.

(d) The mediator shall not be compelled to disclose to the Court or to any person outside the mediation conference any of the records, reports, summaries, notes, communications, or other documents received or made by a mediator while serving in such capacity. The mediator shall not testify or be compelled to testify in regard to the mediation in connection with any arbitral, judicial, or other proceeding. The mediator shall not be a necessary party in any proceedings relating to the mediation.

(e) The parties, the mediator, and all mediation participants shall protect proprietary information and in-camera submissions. All such materials shall be kept confidential and shall not be used outside the mediation by any adverse party.

(f) The disclosure by a party of privileged information to the mediator does not waive or otherwise adversely affect the privileged nature of the information.

[Effective March 1, 2012.]

RULE 9019–6. POSTMEDIATION PROCEDURES

(a) The mediator is not required to prepare written comments or recommendations to the parties. Mediators may present a written settlement recommendation memorandum to attorneys or *pro se* litigants, but not to the Court.

(b) If a settlement is reached at a mediation, a party designated by the mediator shall submit a fully executed stipulation and proposed order to the Court within twenty-one (21) calendar days after the end of the mediation. If the party fails to prepare the stipulation and order, the Court may impose appropriate sanctions.

(c) Promptly after the mediation conference, the mediator shall file with the Court, and serve on the parties and the Mediation Program Administrator, Local Bankruptcy Form 32 (Mediator's Certificate of Completion of Mediation Conference) showing compliance or noncompliance with the mediation conference requirements of this Local Bankruptcy Rule and whether or not a settlement has been reached. Regardless of the outcome of the mediation conference, the mediator shall not provide the Court with any details of the substance of the conference.

(d) Whether or not the mediation conference results in a settlement, within seven (7) days of the conclusion of the mediation the mediator shall file on the docket of the case the Mediator's Certificate of Completion of Mediation Conference (Local Bankruptcy Form 32) and submit to the Mediation Administrator the Report of Mediation Conference & Mediator Survey through the Court's website at: http://www.pawb.uscourts.gov/bankruptcy–mediators–upload.

[Effective March 1, 2012. Amended effective October 1, 2013; August 1, 2015; April 1, 2016.]

RULE 9019–7. TERMINATION OF MEDIATION

(a) Any matter assigned to mediation may be withdrawn from mediation by the Court at any time.

(b) Upon the filing of Local Bankruptcy Form 32 (Mediator's Certificate of Completion of Mediation Conference) or the entry of an order withdrawing a matter from mediation pursuant to W.PA.LBR 9019–7(a), the mediation will be deemed terminated, and the mediator excused and relieved from further responsibilities in the matter without further Court order.

(c) If the mediation conference does not result in a resolution of all of the disputes in the assigned matter, the matter shall proceed to trial or hearing pursuant to the Court's scheduling orders.

[Effective March 1, 2012.]

RULE 9020–1. LOSS MITIGATION PROGRAM

(a) The Loss Mitigation Program ("LMP") is a structured process to facilitate consensual resolutions when residential property is at risk of foreclosure.

(b) For purposes of the LMP, the following definitions apply in W.PA.LBR 9020–1 through 9020–7:

(1) "Core LMP Package" refers collectively to all of the forms and supporting documentation that the Creditor requires to initiate the assessment of loss mitigation options.

(2) "Creditor" refers to any mortgage holder, servicer or trustee of an Eligible Loan.

(3) "Debtor" means any individual debtor in a case filed under Chapter 7, 11, 12 or 13 of the Bankruptcy Code, including joint debtors.

(4) "Document Preparation Software" refers to a secure online program that facilitates the preparation of the Core LMP Package by populating the Primary LMP Documents and generating a customized checklist. A list of approved Document Preparation Software providers and related information shall be posted on the Court's website.

(5) "Eligible Loan" means any mortgage, lien or extension of money or credit secured by Eligible Property, regardless of whether the loan is considered to be subprime or non-traditional, was in foreclosure prior to the bankruptcy filing, is the first or junior mortgage or lien on the Eligible Property, and/or has been pooled, securitized or assigned to a creditor or trustee.

(6) "Eligible Property" means any real property used as the debtor's principal residence in which the debtor holds an interest.

(7) "LMP Period" is the time during which the LMP is in effect prior to its expiration or termination by Court order.

(8) "Loss Mitigation" includes the full range of solutions that may prevent either the loss of a debtor's Eligible Property to foreclosure, increased costs to the lender, or both, including but not limited to, loan modification, loan refinance, forbearance, short sale, or surrender of the Eligible Property in full satisfaction of obligations arising under an Eligible Loan.

(9) "Portal" refers to a secure online service that allows LMP documents to be submitted, retrieved and tracked. A list of approved Portals and related information shall be posted on the Court's website.

(10) "Primary LMP Documents" refers collectively to the documentation that is generated by the Document Preparation Software.

(c) Unless otherwise ordered by the Court, the Local Bankruptcy Rules apply to the LMP, including but not limited to the caption requirements set forth in W.PA.LBR 9004–1, the certificate of service requirements set forth in W.PA.LBR 2002–1 and the notice requirements set forth in W.PA.LBR 5005–8.

[Effective July 1, 2013. Amended effective April 1, 2014; April 1, 2016.]

RULE 9020–2. LOSS MITIGATION PROGRAM COMMENCEMENT

(a) At any time after the commencement of the case until three (3) days before the first date scheduled for the First Meeting of Creditors, a debtor with Eligible Property secured by an Eligible Loan may request the commencement of the LMP by filing a Motion for Loss Mitigation (substantially in the form of Local Bankruptcy Form 39). The Motion for Loss Mitigation shall be served on the Creditor and all other creditors whose claims are secured by liens against the Eligible Property.

(b) Prior to filing a Motion for Loss Mitigation, the debtor's counsel (or the debtor if not represented by counsel) shall:

(1) perform adequate due diligence concerning the debtor's eligibility for loss mitigation by reviewing all of the loan documentation in the debtor's possession and confirming all information necessary to make the certifications required on the Certification of LMP Eligibility and Readiness (Local Bankruptcy Form 40);

(2) fully and completely prepare the Primary LMP Documents using Court-approved Document Preparation Software; and

(3) if the Creditor is registered on the Portal, download the Core LMP Package from the Portal and fully prepare all documentation that may be required and posted by the Creditor in addition to the Primary LMP Documents.

(c) A Certification of LMP Eligibility and Readiness (substantially in the form of Local Bankruptcy Form 40) and a proposed Loss Mitigation Order (substantially in the form of Local Bankruptcy Form 41) shall be attached to any Motion for Loss Mitigation.

(d) The deadline for filing an objection to a Motion for Loss Mitigation is fourteen (14) days from the service of the motion. Objections shall identify with specificity the grounds for the objection. If no objection is filed, the Court may enter a Loss Mitigation Order without further notice or hearing.

[Effective July 1, 2013. Amended effective April 1, 2014; April 1, 2016.]

RULE 9020–3. LOSS MITIGATION PROGRAM PARTICIPATION & DUTIES

(a) The debtor and Creditor are the primary LMP participants. Any interested party may request by motion, or the Court may on its own direct, that a co-obligor, additional creditors or other third parties articipate in the LMP in furtherance of pursuing a bal resolution.

(b) The Chapter 13 Trustee may participate in the LMP to the extent that such participation would be consistent with the Chapter 13 Trustee's duties under the Bankruptcy Code.

(c) LMP participants shall act in good faith. A party failing to participate in good faith may be subject to sanctions after notice and a hearing.

(d) During the LMP all material communications between the debtor and Creditor shall be conducted exclusively through the Portal.

(e) On behalf of each participating party, a person with complete knowledge of the file so as to be reasonably capable of answering questions posed by the Court related to the LMP shall attend all LMP-related hearings and conferences before the Court. Attendance at all hearings and conferences related to the LMP shall be in person unless participation by telephone or videoconference is expressly authorized by the Court.

(f) A debtor who files a Motion for Loss Mitigation immediately shall make (or cause to be made) adequate protection payments to the Creditor in an amount that is at least sixty percent (60%) of the monthly principal and interest payment that is contractually due, plus one hundred percent (100%) of any required monthly escrow payment. If the Creditor objects to the amount of the adequate protection payment, then after adequate notice, the Court shall hold a hearing to consider the objection.

(g) If the debtor is required to direct adequate protection payments to a different address than the debtor utilized prior to the filing of the bankruptcy case, the Creditor shall promptly advise the debtor of the correct address and any other requirements to ensure the proper posting and processing of the payments. In Chapter 13 cases, the debtor immediately shall file a motion and proposed order requesting the Court to authorize the Chapter 13 Trustee to make payments to the specified payee at the specified address.

(h) In the event that the Eligible Loan is transferred or the service rights are assigned to a new servicer, then immediately on notice of the same the debtor shall file a proposed Order Substituting LMP Servicer (substantially in the form of Local Bankruptcy Form 46) and initiate the change of Creditor in the Portal.

(i) If a relief from stay motion pursuant to section 362(d) is pending when a Loss Mitigation Order is entered or if such a motion is filed during the LMP period, the Court may condition the stay upon fulfillment of the debtor's obligations under the Loss Mitigation Order. If the debtor fails to comply with the debtor's LMP duties or the Loss Mitigation Order, the Creditor may apply to terminate the LMP pursuant to W.PA.LBR 9020–5. Additionally, unless the

Creditor specifically objects in writing, it is deemed to consent to a waiver of the deadlines set forth in section 362(e) of the Bankruptcy Code until thirty (30) days after the conclusion of the LMP.

[Effective July 1, 2013. Amended effective April 1, 2014; April 1, 2016.]

RULE 9020–4. LOSS MITIGATION PROGRAM DEADLINES

(a) The LMP commences upon the entry of a Loss Mitigation Order. The Court, at its discretion, may alter any of the deadlines set forth in these Local Rules. Where there is a conflict between the Loss Mitigation Order and these Local Rules, the Order governs.

(b) If not previously registered, within fourteen (14) days after the entry of the Loss Mitigation Order, the Creditor shall register and post its entire Core LMP Package on the Portal.

(c) Within seven (7) days after entry of the Loss Mitigation Order or the Creditor's registration on the Portal, whichever occurs later, the debtor shall upload and submit a through the Portal debtor's completed Core LMP Package.

(d) Within fourteen (14) days after the debtor's submission of the Core LMP Package, the Creditor shall designate, via the Portal, a specific individual who, on behalf of the Creditor, is the single point of contact for the LMP and is responsible for communicating with the debtor. The Creditor shall provide the designee's name, title, email address and either a direct telephone number or direct extension. At the same time, Creditor shall acknowledge, via the Portal, receipt of debtor's Core LMP Package and advise debtor of any additional or missing information required for Creditor to proceed with its review. The Creditor shall immediately notify the debtor if there is a substituted designee and/or any change in the designee's contact information.

(e) Within sixty (60) days after the entry of the Loss Mitigation Order, the debtor, on notice to the Creditor, shall file and serve an LMP Status Report with an attached printout of the current and complete account history from the Portal. The LMP Status Report shall be completed in accordance with the instructions provided in the Portal.

(f) Within seven (7) days after the conclusion of the LMP Period, the debtor, on notice to the Creditor, shall file and serve an LMP Final Report with an attached printout of the current and complete account history from the Portal. The LMP Final Report shall be completed in accordance with the instructions provided in the Portal. The obligation to timely file an LMP Final Report applies in all cases where a Loss Mitigation Order was issued, regardless of whether the case was subsequently dismissed or converted.

(g) If the LMP participants agree to the terms of a loan modification on a trial/interim basis, the debtor shall file a proposed order to approve the interim trial loan modification (substantially in the form of Local Bankruptcy Form 47) not less than fourteen (14) days before the first modification payment is due. In Chapter 13 cases, when trial payments are included as part of the trial loan modification, the proposed order must be filed not less than fourteen (14) days prior to the Chapter 13 Trustee's distribution date preceding the month in which the first trial payment is to begin.

[Effective July 1, 2013. Amended effective October 1, 2013; April 1, 2014; April 1, 2016.]

RULE 9020–5. LOSS MITIGATION PROGRAM DURATION

(a) The LMP Period shall be ninety (90) days unless otherwise specified in the Loss Mitigation Order.

(b) A request to extend the LMP Period shall be made by way of a Motion to Extend the Loss Mitigation Period (substantially in the form of Local Bankruptcy Form 42). A proposed order (substantially in the form of Local Bankruptcy Form 43) and a complete and current printout of the account history from the Portal shall be attached to the Motion.

(c) A request to terminate the LMP process shall be made by way of Motion to Terminate the Loss Mitigation Program (substantially in the form of Local Bankruptcy Form 44). A proposed order (substantially in the form of Local Bankruptcy Form 45) and a complete and current printout of the account history from the Portal shall be attached to the Motion.

(d) Requests to extend or terminate the LMP process shall be served on all parties in interest, including, where applicable, the trustee or Chapter 13 Trustee.

(e) The deadline for objecting to a request to extend or terminate the LMP process is seven (7) business days from the service of the motion.

(f) Where a timely objection is filed, the Court may schedule a hearing to determine whether granting the relief requested is appropriate under the circumstances.

[Effective July 1, 2013. Amended effective April 1, 2014; April 1, 2016.]

RULE 9020–6. LOSS MITIGATION PROGRAM RESOLUTION

(a) LMP participants shall seek the Court's authorization to enter into any agreement reached during the LMP process, including, but not limited to, a stipulation, sale, plan of reorganization, amended plan of reorganization, or loan modification, by way of a motion that complies with W.PA.LBR 9010–3 and W.PA.LBR 9019–1.

(b) Dismissal of the bankruptcy case shall not be made a requirement of an agreement reached through the LMP.

(c) Consent to the resolution shall be acknowledged in writing by an authorized representative of the Creditor, the debtor, and the debtor's attorney, if applicable.

(d) If parties agree to a final or long-term loan modification, the debtor shall file a Motion to Authorize the Loan Modification, which shall be served immediately on any applicable trustee and all creditors whose claims are secured by liens against the Eligible Property. The motion shall contain a detailed analysis of the proposed loan modification, and shall include a Loan Modification Summary (substantially in the form of Local Bankruptcy Form 48). A copy of the loan modification agreement shall accompany the motion. In a Chapter 13 case, the proposed order shall include the following provisions, where applicable:

(1) If the loan modification approved by the Court impacts on the provisions of the debtor's Chapter 13 plan, a modified plan shall be filed within fourteen (14) days of the entry of the order approving the loan modification.

(2) If the loan modification approved by the Court results in a material change in the debtor's expenses, the debtor shall file an amendment to the impacted schedules reflecting income and expenses (Schedules I and J) within fourteen (14) days of the entry of the order approving the loan modification.

(e) Where a debtor is represented by counsel, a resolution may be authorized by the Court without further notice, or upon such notice as the Court directs. Where a debtor is not represented by counsel, prior to authorizing a resolution the Court may conduct a hearing at which the debtor shall appear in person. To be authorized by the Court, a proposed resolution must be in the best interests of the debtor and the bankruptcy estate.

(f) In the event a debtor satisfies all payment obligations under a trial/interim loan modification order, the Creditor shall extend an offer to enter into a final loan modification agreement within fourteen (14) days of receipt of the last interim payment. If the debtor accepts the offer, then the debtor immediately shall file and serve a Motion to Authorize the Loan Modification pursuant to W.PA.LBR 9020–6(d). If the debtor rejects the offer, then the debtor immediately shall file and serve either a Motion to Extend the Loss Modification Period (pursuant to W.PA.LBR 20–5(b)) or a Motion to Terminate the Loss Modification Program (pursuant to W.PA.LBR 9020–5(c))

that sets forth the specific reasons for rejecting the offer.

[Effective July 1, 2013. Amended effective April 1, 2014; April 1, 2016.]

RULE 9020–7. LOSS MITIGATION PROGRAM FEES, COSTS & CHARGES

(a) Use of the Document Preparation Software requires the debtor to pay a fee of up to $40.00 to the provider of the Document Preparation Software. Use of the Portal requires the debtor to pay a fee of up to $40 to the administrator of the Portal. If use of the Document Preparation Software and/or the Portal creates an undue hardship, the debtor may file a motion specifying why the use of the Document Preparation Software and/or the Portal creates an undue hardship and requesting permission to prepare and exchange documents and communications with the Creditor in another manner.

(b) If a proposed LMP resolution provides for a Creditor to receive payment or reimbursement of any fee, cost or charge that arose from the LMP process, all such fees, costs and charges shall be disclosed to the debtor, the trustee, the U.S. Trustee, and to the Court prior to approval of the resolution. Counsel for the Creditor may be entitled to receive a reasonable fee for all work involved with the LMP and shall clearly delineate such fee in the LMP resolution or by amended proof of claim.

(c) Counsel for the debtor is entitled to receive reasonable compensation for all work involved in connection with the LMP process and shall file an application for allowance of attorney fees and costs with the Court, or alternatively accept a "no look" fee in a reasonable amount not to exceed $1,000 to be paid as an administrative expense. Debtor's counsel may also treat the Document Preparation Software fee of up to $40 and the Portal fee of up to $40 as administrative expenses. Counsel for the debtor shall request compensation for LMP work in excess of the no look fee by way of a fee application substantially conforming to W.PA.LBR 2016–1 which shall separately itemize and designate fees and expenses arising from LMP–related services. No fees or expenses arising from LMP–related services may be paid until an LMP Final Report is filed pursuant to W.PA.LBR 9020–4(f).

[Effective July 1, 2013. Amended effective April 1, 2014; February 15, 2015; August 1, 2015; April 1, 2016.]

RULE 9037–1. REDACTION OF PERSONAL IDENTIFIERS

(a) Parties to transcripts and filers of any documents on the docket or claims register are responsible for reviewing each document in advance for personal identifiers and redacting information as required by Fed. R. Bankr. P. 9037.

(b) If, despite subsection (a), personal identifiers are disclosed in a filed document, the applicable corrective steps shall be taken, including:

(1) If the document is a transcript:

(A) Within seven (7) days of the filing of the transcript, any party intending to redact any portion of the transcript shall file Local Bankruptcy Form 35 (Notice of Intent to Request Redaction of Transcript), with an attached certificate of service demonstrating that Form 35 was served upon the transcriber, all persons whose testimony was transcribed, the debtor and all persons whose personal identifiers are to be redacted.

(B) The party requesting redaction shall serve upon the transcriber, all persons whose testimony was transcribed, the debtor and all persons whose personal identifiers were redacted, Local Bankruptcy Form 36 (Transcript Redaction Request) within twenty-one (21) days after the original transcript was filed. Local Bankruptcy Form 36 shall not be filed on the docket.

(C) Upon the transcriber's receipt of Local Bankruptcy Form 36 (Transcript Redaction Request), no unredacted copies of the transcript shall be sold or otherwise made available.

(D) Transcribers shall file a redacted version of the transcript within thirty-one (31) days after the original transcript was filed.

(2) If the document is a proof of claim:

(A) Regardless of whether the case is open or closed, the creditor shall immediately file a redacted claim on the claims register as an amended claim in compliance with the requirements of W.PA.LBR 3002–2(a).

(B) If the case is open at the time of the amendment, the creditor shall file Local Bankruptcy Form 37 ("Request to Restrict Public Access to Claim").

(C) If the case is closed at the time of the amendment, the creditor shall file a motion to reopen. The creditor shall attach Local Bankruptcy Form 37 to the motion to reopen.

(D) The creditor shall attach to Local Bankruptcy Form 37 a certificate of service demonstrating that Form 37 was served upon the debtor and all persons whose personal identifiers were redacted.

(3) Any other document filed on the docket:

(A) If the case is open at the time of the request, the filer of the original document shall file Local Bankruptcy Form 38 ("Request to Restrict Public Access to [specify document]").

(B) If the case is closed at the time of the amendment, the filer of the original document shall file a motion to reopen. The movant shall attach Local Bankruptcy Form 38 to the motion to reopen.

(C) The movant shall attach to Local Bankruptcy Form 38 a certificate of service demonstrating that Form 38 was served upon the debtor and all persons whose personal identifiers were redacted.

(c) Amendments to any filed documents made to redact personal identifiers pursuant to Fed. R. Bankr. P. 9037 shall not be combined with any other amendment to the original document.

(d) Motions requesting the Court to restrict public access to a document shall not be combined with any other motion, except for a motion to reopen pursuant to subsections (b)(2)(C) or (b)(3)(B).

[Adopted on an interim basis effective November 1, 2012, permanently effective July 1, 2013. Amended effective August 1, 2015; April 1, 2016.]

RULE 9070–1. EXHIBITS

All exhibits, models, or diagrams, documentary or physical, introduced at a trial or hearing shall be removed by the parties to the litigation or their counsel within fourteen (14) calendar days after final judgment, order, or other final disposition of the trial or hearing, whichever is later. If the exhibits, models, or diagrams are not removed within the 14–day period, the Clerk shall destroy them or make such other disposition of them as the Clerk may deem appropriate. It shall be the responsibility of counsel to produce any and all exhibits as designated on appeal.

[Effective July 1, 2004. Amended effective December 1, 2009; March 1, 2012; July 1, 2013.]

SELECTED LOCAL FORMS
LOCAL BANKRUPTCY FORM NO. 1A. DECLARATION RE: ELECTRONIC FILING OF PETITION, SCHEDULES & STATEMENTS

IN THE UNITED STATES BANKRUPTCY COURT
FOR THE WESTERN DISTRICT OF PENNSYLVANIA

In Re: Bankruptcy No.

         Debtor

DECLARATION RE: ELECTRONIC FILING OF PETITION, SCHEDULES & STATEMENTS

PART I – DECLARATION OF PETITIONER

I, _____, and I, _____, the undersigned debtor, certify that the information I give to my attorney for the preparation of the petition, statements, schedules and mailing matrix is true and correct. I consent to my attorney sending my petition, this declaration, statements and schedules to the United States Bankruptcy Court. I understand that this DECLARATION RE: ELECTRONIC FILING is to be submitted to the Clerk once all schedules have been electronically docketed but, in any event, no later than fourteen (14) days following the date the petition was electronically filed unless the time is extended by order of court. I understand that failure to timely submit the signed original of this DECLARATION will result in dismissal of my case pursuant to 11 U.S.C. § 707(a)(3) without further notice.

☐ [If petitioner is an individual] I declare under penalty of perjury that the information provided in this petition and the Social Security number(s) listed below are true and correct:

_____   Debtor has a Social Security number and it is: _____
Name of Debtor   Check here if Debtor does not have a Social Security number: _____

_____   Joint Debtor has a Social Security number and it is: _____
Name of Joint Debtor   Check here if Joint Debtor does not have a Social Security number: _____

☐ [If petitioner is a corporation or partnership] I declare under penalty of perjury that the information provided in this petition is true and correct, and that I have been authorized to file this petition on behalf of the debtor. The debtor requests relief in accordance with the chapter specified in this petition.

Dated: _____   Signed: _____   _____
                           (Type Debtor name here)   (Joint Debtor, if applicable, type name)

                 Title: _____   EIN: _____
                           (Corporate or Partnership Filing)

                          Phone Number of Signer   Address of Signer

PART II – DECLARATION OF ATTORNEY

I further declare that before filing any document I will have examined the debtor's petition and that the information is complete and correct to the best of my knowledge, information and belief. The debtor will have signed this form before I submit the petition, schedules, statements and mailing matrix. I will give the debtor a copy of all forms and information to be filed with the United States Bankruptcy Court, and have followed all other requirements for electronic case filing. I further declare that I have examined the above debtor's petition, schedules, and statements and, to the best of my knowledge, information and belief, they are true, correct, and complete. If debtor is an individual, I further declare that I have informed the petitioner that [he or she] may proceed under chapter 7, 11, 12 or 13 of Title 11, United States Code, and have explained the relief available under each such chapter. This declaration is based on all information of which I have knowledge.

☐ Check box if debtor is a servicemember as defined by the Servicemembers Civil Relief Act of 2003. If debtor becomes entitled to protections of the Act during the bankruptcy case, he shall file an affidavit advising the Court within fourteen (14) days of the date of his change in status.

Dated: _____

                        _____
                        Attorney for Debtor (Signature)

                        _____
                        Typed Name

                        _____
                        Address

                        _____
                        Phone No.

                        _____
                        List Bar I.D. and State of Admission

PAWB Local Form 1A (07/13)

[Effective March 1, 2012. Amended effective July 1, 2013.]

LOCAL BANKRUPTCY FORM NO. 1B. DECLARATION RE: ELECTRONIC FILING OF PETITION, SCHEDULES & STATEMENTS FOR INDIVIDUAL DEBTOR NOT REPRESENTED BY COUNSEL

IN THE UNITED STATES BANKRUPTCY COURT
FOR THE WESTERN DISTRICT OF PENNSYLVANIA

In Re: :   Bankruptcy No.
                                          :
                                          :
         Debtor   :

DECLARATION RE: ELECTRONIC FILING OF PETITION, SCHEDULES & STATEMENTS FOR INDIVIDUAL DEBTOR NOT REPRESENTED BY COUNSEL

I, _____, and I, _____, the undersigned debtor, certify that the Bankruptcy petition, statements, schedules and mailing matrix presented to the Clerk for filing is true and correct. I understand that this DECLARATION RE: ELECTRONIC FILING is to be submitted to the Clerk once all schedules have been filed but, in any event, no later than fourteen (14) days following the date the petition was filed unless the time is extended by order of court. I understand that failure to timely submit the signed original of this DECLARATION will result in dismissal of my case pursuant to 11 U.S.C. § 707(a)(3) without further notice.

☐ Check box if debtor is a servicemember as defined by the Servicemembers Civil Relief Act of 2003. If debtor becomes entitled to protections of the Act during the bankruptcy case, he shall file an affidavit advising the Court within fourteen (14) days of the date of his change in status.

I declare under penalty of perjury that the information provided in this petition and the Social Security number(s) listed below are true and correct:

_____
Signature of Debtor

Debtor has a Social Security number and it is: _____
Check here if Debtor does not have a Social Security number: _____

_____
Signature of Joint Debtor

Joint Debtor has a Social Security number and it is: _____
Check here if Joint Debtor does not have a Social Security number: _____

Dated: _____

_____
Address

_____

_____
Phone No.

PAWB Local Form 1B (07/13)

[Effective March 1, 2012. Amended effective July 1, 2013.]

LOCAL BANKRUPTCY FORM NO. 2.   EX PARTE MOTION FOR DESIGNATION AS COMPLEX CHAPTER 11 BANKRUPTCY CASE

IN THE UNITED STATES BANKRUPTCY COURT
FOR THE WESTERN DISTRICT OF PENNSYLVANIA

In Re:	:	Bankruptcy No.
Debtor	:	
	:	Chapter 11
Movant	:	
	:	Related to Document No.
v.	:	
	:	
Respondent (if none, then "No Respondent")	:	Hearing Date and Time:

EX PARTE MOTION FOR DESIGNATION AS COMPLEX CHAPTER 11 BANKRUPTCY CASE

This bankruptcy case was filed on _____. The undersigned party in interest believes that this case qualifies as a Complex Chapter 11 Bankruptcy Case pursuant to Local Bankruptcy Rules because:

_____ There is a need for expedited consideration of the following "First Day" motions.

_____ The debtor has total debt of more than $_____ million and unsecured non-priority debt of more than $_____ million.

_____ There are more than _____ parties in interest in this case.

_____ Claims against the debtor are publicly traded.

_____ Equity interests in the debtor are publicly traded.

_____ Other: (Substantial explanation is required. Attach additional sheets if necessary.)

DATE: _____   By: _____
                                          Signature

                                          _____
                                          Typed Name

                                          _____
                                          Address

                                          _____
                                          Phone No.

                                          _____
                                          List Bar I.D. and State of Admission

PAWB Local Form 2 (07/13)

[Effective March 1, 2012.   Amended effective July 1, 2013.]

LOCAL BANKRUPTCY FORM NO. 3. INITIAL ORDER FOR COMPLEX CHAPTER 11 BANKRUPTCY CASE

IN THE UNITED STATES BANKRUPTCY COURT
FOR THE WESTERN DISTRICT OF PENNSYLVANIA

In Re: :   Bankruptcy No.
                                                              :
            Debtor(s)   :
                                                              :   Chapter 11

INITIAL ORDER FOR COMPLEX CHAPTER 11 BANKRUPTCY CASE

This bankruptcy case was filed on _____. An Ex Parte Motion for Designation as a Complex Chapter 11 Case was filed. After review of the initial pleadings filed in this case, the Court concludes that this is a Complex Chapter 11 Case and issues this scheduling order.

1.   The Debtor shall maintain a Service List identifying the parties that must be served whenever a motion or other pleading requires notice. Upon establishment of such a list, notices of motions and other matters will be limited to the parties on the Service List.

        a.   The Service List shall initially include the Debtor, Debtor's counsel, counsel for the unsecured creditors' committee, U.S. Trustee, all secured creditors, the twenty (20) largest unsecured creditors, any indenture trustee, and any party that files a request for notice.

        b.   Any party in interest that wishes to receive notice, other than as listed on the Service List, shall be added to the Service List merely by request filed of record with the Clerk and served on the Debtor and Debtor's counsel.

        c.   Parties on the Service List are encouraged to give a fax number or e-mail address for service of process, and parties are encouraged to authorize service by fax or e-mail. Consent to fax or e-mail service may be included in the party's notice of appearance and request for service.

        d.   The Service List shall be filed within three (3) calendar days after entry of this Order. Debtors shall update the Service List and file with the Clerk a copy of the updated Service List upon request of a party to be added.

2.   The Court hereby establishes the following dates and times for hearing all motions and other matters in this case in Courtroom _____ at _____.

3.   If a matter is properly noticed for hearing and the parties reach agreement on a settlement of the dispute prior to the hearing, the parties may announce the settlement at the scheduled hearing. If the Court determines that the notice of the dispute and the hearing is adequate notice of the effects of the settlement, the Court may approve the settlement at the hearing without further notice of the terms of the settlement.

4.   The debtor shall give notice of this Order to all parties in interest within seven (7) calendar days. If any party in interest objects to the provisions of this Order, that party shall file and serve a motion for reconsideration and proposed order within fourteen (14) days of the date of this Order articulating the objection and the relief requested.

Date: _____   _____
                                                United States Bankruptcy Judge

PAWB Local Form 3 (07/13)

[Effective March 1, 2012. Amended effective July 1, 2013.]

LOCAL BANKRUPTCY FORM NO. 4A. REGISTRATION FORM TO FILE ELECTRONICALLY [RESERVED EFFECTIVE AUGUST 1, 2015.]

LOCAL BANKRUPTCY FORM NO. 4B. LIMITED FILING USER REGISTRATION FORM AND AGREEMENT [RESERVED EFFECTIVE AUGUST 1, 2015.]

LOCAL BANKRUPTCY FORM NO. 4C.   NOTICE OF TERMINATION OF CM/ECF PRIVILEGES

IN THE UNITED STATES BANKRUPTCY COURT
WESTERN DISTRICT OF PENNSYLVANIA

NOTICE OF TERMINATION OF CM/ECF PRIVILEGES

I, _____, the undersigned, hereby certify that I am not an attorney of record on any pending case before the Bankruptcy Court for the Western District of Pennsylvania (the "Court").

I am instructing the Clerk of Court to terminate my status as a registered Filing User in the Court's CM/ECF System, pursuant to W.PA.LBR 5005-4.

I understand that I will no longer be able to file documents electronically or receive Notices of Electronic Filing when entries are made on cases.

I shall mail this signed **Notice of Termination of CM/ECF Privileges** to the Clerk of Court by certified U.S. mail.

EXECUTED ON [date]:

By: _____
Signature

_____
Typed Name

_____
Address

_____
Phone No.

_____
Bar I.D. and State of Admission

PAWB Local Form 4C (07/13)

[Effective March 1, 2012. Amended effective July 1, 2013.]

LOCAL BANKRUPTCY FORM NO. 5. CHAPTER 13 BUSINESS CASE QUESTIONNAIRE

IN THE UNITED STATES BANKRUPTCY COURT
FOR THE WESTERN DISTRICT OF PENNSYLVANIA

In Re: :   Bankruptcy No.

                          Debtor   :

                                                   :   Chapter 11

Movant   :

          v.   :   Related to Document No.

                                                   :

                                                   :

Respondent (if none, then "No Respondent")   :

CHAPTER 13 BUSINESS CASE QUESTIONNAIRE

Local Bankruptcy Rule 1007-4 requires chapter 13 debtors that are self-employed (including debtors acting as landlords), to complete and submit this Questionnaire to the Trustee along with all documents set forth in the Checklist which follows the signature page of the Questionnaire. You must answer all items in the Questionnaire. Use a separate page if additional room is needed, but be sure to reference the additional page next to the item you are answering. All information must be complete and organized. Failure to provide detailed and accurate information may result in the Trustee filing a motion to dismiss your case.

- You must send this completed Questionnaire along with all required attachments to Ronda J. Winnecour, Trustee, U.S. Steel Tower, Suite 3250, 600 Grant Street, Pittsburgh, PA 15219 so that it reaches the Trustee at least fourteen (14) days prior to your first scheduled meeting of creditors. If you fail to do so, the Trustee may require your appearance at an additional meeting or file a motion to dismiss your case.
- Do not file this Questionnaire with the Clerk of the Bankruptcy Court.
- The Questionnaire must be dated.
- The Questionnaire must contain the original signature of all debtors in the case.
- A copy of the Questionnaire should be kept by the debtor for future reference.
- If you have questions concerning this Questionnaire, please contact your attorney.

Debtor (s)' Name(s) _____

Chapter 13 Case No. _____

Name of Business _____

List all past names used by Business _____

_____

Location where business is operated _____

_____

Description of Business Activities/Type of Business _____

_____

What circumstances led you to file this bankruptcy? _____

_____

_____

PAWB Local Form 5 (07/13)

How do you expect these circumstances to change so that you will be able to fund a Chapter 13 Plan? _____

_____

_____

_____

1.   Type of Business Organization, circle one:

      Corporation   Sole Proprietorship   Partnership   Other

      Has business ever been incorporated? _____ Yes _____ No

      Date business began _____

      Federal ID number (if applicable) _____   State ID number _____

2.   If your business is a Partnership, please answer (a) to (c) below:

      (a) Names of Partners _____

      _____

      (b) Percentage of your ownership: Debtor _____ %   Joint Debtor _____ %

      (c) Is there a written partnership agreement? _____ Yes _____ No

      If yes, please include a copy of the agreement with this Questionnaire when you return it to the Trustee.

3.   If your business is a Corporation, please answer (a) to (g) below:

      (a) Who are the shareholders? _____

      _____

      (b) How many shares have been issued and are outstanding? _____

      (c) What is your percentage ownership?   Debtor _____ %   Joint Debtor _____ %

      (d) State of incorporation _____

      (e) Is the corporation in good standing with the Secretary of State? _____ Yes _____ No

      If no, why not? _____

      _____

      _____

      (f) Fair Market Value of Corporate Assets, including going concern value $_____

      Basis of value _____

      (g) Amount of Corporate Debts $_____

4.   Is the business cyclical? _____ Yes _____ No

      If yes, when is the busy season? _____

      If yes, when is the slow season? _____

5.   Do you have an accountant or bookkeeper? _____ Yes _____ No

If yes, please provide the name, address and phone number of this individual _____

_____

Do you understand that you are required to file monthly operating reports with the Court and serve the Trustee with a copy by the 15th of each month that you are in bankruptcy? _____ Yes _____ No

6.   Are all tax returns which should have been filed to this point in time filed? _____ Yes _____ No

If no, list years that are delinquent, type of return owed, and entity to which return is owed:

Year   Entity(s) and Type of Return Due

_____   _____

_____   _____

_____   _____

_____   _____

_____   _____

Do you understand that while you are in Chapter 13, you are individually responsible for keeping current with all of your post-petition business as well as personal tax obligations? _____ Yes _____ No

Do you understand that the Court in this District has entered a General Order which requires all delinquent tax returns to be filed within sixty (60) days from the date that you filed your bankruptcy case?

_____ Yes _____ No

7.   Have you filed estimated quarterly income tax returns with the IRS? _____ Yes _____ No

If yes, please provide copies of the last three (3) estimated returns filed, with proof of payment.

If no, explain why not _____

_____

8.   Does the business have employees? _____ Yes _____ No

If yes, how many? _____ Are any of these persons related to you? _____ Yes _____ No

Does the business withhold from their wages? _____ Yes _____ No

If yes, where do you deposit the withholdings and how often?

          i. _____

          ii. _____

Please provide copies of proof of payment of employee withholding taxes for the three (3) months prior to the month that your case was filed.

Do you understand that you must keep the withholding funds separate from your general operating funds?
_____Yes _____No

If you do not withhold, how are the employees compensated? _____

_____

Do you have subcontractors? _____ Yes _____ No

Are 1099s issued? _____ Yes _____ No

9.   Is your business required to collect sales tax? _____ Yes _____ No

If yes, has your business collected and remitted sales taxes on a regular basis? _____ Yes _____ No

If no, explain why _____

_____

Do you understand that you must keep the sales tax funds separate from your general operating funds?

_____ Yes _____ No

Please provide copies of proof of payment of sales taxes for three (3) months prior to the month your case was filed.

10.   Are you leasing office space? _____ Yes _____ No

If yes, answer (a) to (e) below:

(a) Address of Property _____

_____

(b) Landlord's Name and Address

_____

_____

(c) Monthly Rental Payment $_____

(d) Term of lease _____

(e) Do you wish to continue the lease? _____ Yes _____ No

11.   Does the business lease business equipment or autos? _____ Yes _____ No

If yes, answer (a) to (e) below:

(a) Description of leased/rented items? _____

_____

(b) Person or entity's name and address from which items are rented or leased _____

_____

_____

    (c) Payment terms _____

    (d) Term of lease _____

    (e) Do you wish to continue the lease? _____ Yes _____ No

12.   Does the business have any outstanding contracts? _____ Yes _____ No

    If yes, please describe _____

    _____

13.   If you rent real property owned by you to others, please complete the following:

Address of Tenant	Date Lease Began	Date Lease Ends	Amount of Monthly Rent

14.   Is the business required to have any business licenses or permits? _____ Yes _____ No

    If yes, please list:_____

    _____

    If yes, are licenses/permits current? _____ Yes _____ No

15.   Does the business carry the following insurance policies?

    Commercial Liability? _____ Yes _____ No   Policy No. _____   Exp. Date _____

    Workmans Compensation? _____ Yes _____ No   Policy No. _____   Exp. Date _____

    Fire Building? _____ Yes _____ No   Policy No. _____   Exp. Date _____

    Fire Contents? _____ Yes _____ No   Policy No. _____   Exp. Date _____

    Automobile Coverage? _____ Yes _____ No   Policy No. _____   Exp. Date _____

    Liquor liability? _____ Yes _____ No   Policy No. _____   Exp. Date _____

    List Others _____

    Are all policies current? _____ Yes _____ No

    List insurance agency(s) _____

    _____

Do you know that in order to continue the operation of your business, it is your responsibility to obtain and maintain comprehensive liability insurance for the operation for your business?

_____ Yes   _____ No

16.   Does the business keep inventory on hand? _____ Yes _____ No

If yes, what would you estimate the market value of your inventory to be? $_____

When was the last physical count of your inventory? _____

What was the value of the inventory at that time? $_____

            Please provide a list of your inventory.

17.   What is the balance of the business accounts receivable? $_____

What amount of the receivables is reasonably collectible? $_____

Please provide a copy of your accounts receivable ledger.

Have you pledged your receivables, rents, profits, or other cash as collateral for any loans?

_____ Yes   _____ No

If yes, please identify _____

Do you understand that if you have borrowed money from any creditor and as security or collateral for the loan you have pledged accounts receivables, rents, or other cash, you may not use the accounts receivables, rents or cash without express written consent from the Creditor, or an order from the Bankruptcy Court allowing the use? _____ Yes _____ No

18.   If you were to buy your business today, how much would you pay for it? $_____

            I/We declare under penalty of perjury that the foregoing statement of information is true and correct to the best of my/our knowledge, information, and belief.

Dated:_____   _____

                                        Debtor's signature

                                        _____

                                        Joint Debtor's signature

CHECKLIST OF DOCUMENTS
THAT MUST BE RETURNED WITH YOUR QUESTIONNAIRE

You must send <u>copies</u> of the following documents to Ronda J. Winnecour, the Trustee, along with your completed Questionnaire within fifteen (15) days before the first scheduled § 341 meeting date. Failure to do so may cause the Trustee to require your attendance at an additional meeting or file a motion to dismiss your case.

_____ Operating statements showing income and expenses for the business for the twelve (12) months prior to the time of filing your bankruptcy case.

_____ Bank statements for all accounts for the twelve (12) months prior to the time of filing your bankruptcy case.

_____ Federal income tax returns with all accompanying schedules for the two (2) years prior to filing your bankruptcy case.

_____ State income tax returns with all accompanying schedules for the two (2) years prior to filing your bankruptcy case.

_____ Appraisals or other third party valuations of real estate, equipment, inventories and other business property listed in your bankruptcy schedules.

_____ Financial statements furnished to third parties such as banks and trade creditors within the two (2) years prior to filing your bankruptcy case, including but not limited to the balance sheet, income statement and cash flow statement.

_____ Current schedule of accounts receivable and accounts payable.

_____ Current insurance policies that cover the assets listed in your bankruptcy schedules.

_____ The business's check register for the three (3) months prior to filing your bankruptcy case.

_____ If your business has employees, proof of payment of employee withholding taxes for the three (3) months prior to the month your case was filed.

_____ If your business is required to collect and remit sales taxes, proof of payment of sales taxes for the three (3) months prior to the month your case was filed.

_____ The last three (3) federal quarterly income tax returns with proof of payment.

_____ Any partnership agreement that exists.

_____ List of your inventory and equipment.

MONTHLY OPERATING REPORT FOR CHAPTER 13 CASES

Debtor's name _____

Case No. _____

Month _____   Year _____

Gross receipts for month: _____

(If more than one source, list each)   _____

                                        _____

         TOTAL GROSS RECEIPTS: $_____

Business expenses paid:

Description   Amount

_____   _____

_____   _____

_____   _____

_____   _____

_____   _____

_____   _____

_____   _____

_____   _____

_____   _____

_____   _____

_____   _____

                      TOTAL EXPENSES: $_____

       NET PROFIT OR (LOSS) FOR MONTH: $_____

Reports for each month are due by the 15th day of the following month and should be mailed to:

Chapter 13 Trustee, U.S. Steel Tower, Suite 3250, 600 Grant Street, Pittsburgh, PA 15219

USE ADDITIONAL SHEETS IF NEEDED

BANKRUPTCY RULE 2015 AND SECTION 1304(c)
DUTY OF CHAPTER 13 DEBTORS ENGAGED IN A BUSINESS
TO KEEP RECORDS, MAKE REPORTS AND GIVE NOTICE OF CASE

Bankruptcy Rule 2015 and Section 1304(c) of the Bankruptcy Code requires debtors engaged in business that file a Chapter 13 bankruptcy petition to:

- Keep a record of receipts and the disposition of money and property received.

- File with the Court, the Trustee, and with any governmental unit charged with responsibility for collection or determination of any tax arising out of such operation, periodic reports and summaries of the operation of the business, including a statement of receipts and disbursements, which shall include a statement, if payments are made to employees, or the amounts of deductions for all taxes required to be withheld or paid for on behalf of employees and the place where these amounts are deposited.

- As soon as possible after the commencement of the case, give notice of the case to every entity known to be holding money or property subject to withdrawal, including every bank, savings or buildings and loan association, public utility company, and the landlord with whom the debtor has a deposit, and to every insurance company which has issued a policy having a cash surrender value payable to the debtor, except that notice need not be given to any entity who has knowledge or has previously been notified of the case.

[Effective March 1, 2012. Amended effective July 1, 2013.]

LOCAL BANKRUPTCY FORM NO. 6.   AMENDMENT COVER SHEET

IN THE UNITED STATES BANKRUPTCY COURT
FOR THE WESTERN DISTRICT OF PENNSYLVANIA

In Re: :   Bankruptcy No.
                                                 :
                          Debtor   :
                                                 :   Chapter
                                                 :
Movant   :
                                                 :   Related to Document No.
             v.   :
                                                 :
                                                 :
                                                 :
Respondent (if none, then "No Respondent")   :

AMENDMENT COVER SHEET

Amendment(s) to the following petition, list(s), schedule(s), or statement(s) are transmitted herewith:

_____   Voluntary Petition - *Specify reason for amendment*:

        Official Form 6 Schedules (Itemization of Changes Must Be Specified)
_____   Summary of Schedules
_____   Schedule A - Real Property
_____   Schedule B - Personal Property
_____   Schedule C - Property Claimed as Exempt
_____   Schedule D - Creditors holding Secured Claims
            Check one:
            _____   Creditor(s) added
            _____   NO creditor(s) added
            _____   Creditor(s) deleted
_____   Schedule E - Creditors Holding Unsecured Priority Claims
            Check one:
            _____   Creditor(s) added
            _____   NO creditor(s) added
            _____   Creditor(s) deleted
_____   Schedule F - Creditors Holding Unsecured Nonpriority Claims
            Check one:
            _____   Creditor(s) added
            _____   NO creditor(s) added
            _____   Creditor(s) deleted
_____   Schedule G - Executory Contracts and Unexpired Leases
            Check one:
            _____   Creditor(s) added
            _____   NO creditor(s) added
            _____   Creditor(s) deleted
_____   Schedule H - Codebtors
_____   Schedule I - Current Income of Individual Debtor(s)
_____   Schedule J - Current Expenditures of Individual Debtor(s)
_____   Statement of Financial Affairs
_____   Chapter 7 Individual Debtor's Statement of Intention
_____   Chapter 11 List of Equity Security Holders
_____   Chapter 11 List of Creditors Holding 20 Largest Unsecured Claims
_____   Disclosure of Compensation of Attorney for Debtor
_____   Other: _____

PAWB Local Form 6 (07/13)   Page 1 of 2

NOTICE OF AMENDMENT(S) TO AFFECTED PARTIES

Pursuant to Fed.R.Bankr.P. 1009(a) and Local Bankruptcy Rule 1009-1, I certify that notice of the filing of the amendment(s) checked above has been given this date to the U.S. Trustee, the trustee in this case, and to entities affected by the amendment as follows:

Date: _____   _____
                                 Attorney for Debtor(s) [or *pro se* Debtor(s)]

                                 _____
                                 (Typed Name)

                                 _____
                                 (Address)

                                 _____
                                 (Phone No.)

                                 _____
                                 List Bar I.D. and State of Admission

Note: An amended matrix of creditors added by the amendment must be submitted on disk with the amendment. Attorneys filing electronically on the Case Management/Electronic Case Filing System may add creditors to the case electronically.

[Effective March 1, 2012. Amended effective July 1, 2013.]

LOCAL BANKRUPTCY FORM NO. 7. CERTIFICATE OF SERVICE OF (SPECIFY DOCUMENT SERVED)

IN THE UNITED STATES BANKRUPTCY COURT
FOR THE WESTERN DISTRICT OF PENNSYLVANIA

In Re:	:	Bankruptcy No.
	:	Chapter
Debtor	:	
	:	
	:	Related to Document No.
Movant	:	
	:	
v.	:	Hearing Date and Time:
	:	
	:	
Respondent (if none, then "No Respondent")	:	

CERTIFICATE OF SERVICE OF (Specify Document Served)

       I certify under penalty of perjury that I served the above captioned pleading on the parties at the addresses specified below or on the attached list on (date) _____.

       The type(s) of service made on the parties (first-class mail, electronic notification, hand delivery, or another type of service) was: _____.

       If more than one method of service was employed, this certificate of service groups the parties by the type of service. For example, the full name, email address, and where applicable the full name of the person or entity represented, for each party served by electronic transmission is listed under the heading "Service by NEF," and the full name and complete postal address for each party served by mail, is listed under the heading "Service by First-Class Mail."

EXECUTED ON: _____

          By: _____

                  Signature

                  _____

                  Typed Name

                  _____

                  Address

                  _____

                  Phone No.

                  _____

                  List Bar I.D. and State of Admission

PAWB Local Form 7 (07/13)

[Effective March 1, 2012. Amended effective July 1, 2013.]

LOCAL BANKRUPTCY FORM NO. 8. SUMMARY COVER SHEET AND NOTICE OF HEARING ON PROFESSIONAL FEES IN CHAPTERS 7, 12 AND 13

IN THE UNITED STATES BANKRUPTCY COURT
WESTERN DISTRICT OF PENNSYLVANIA

In Re: :   Bankruptcy No.
                                                :
                          Debtor   :
                                                :   Chapter
                                                :
Movant   :
                                                :   Related to Document No.
            v.   :
                                                :
                                                :   Hearing Date and Time
Respondent (if none, then "No Respondent")   :

SUMMARY COVER SHEET AND NOTICE OF HEARING ON PROFESSIONAL FEES IN CHAPTERS 7, 12 AND 13 ON BEHALF OF
_____

To All Creditors and Parties in Interest:

1. Applicant represents _____
2. This is (check one)
    _____ a final application
    _____ an interim application
    for the period _____ to _____
3. Previous retainer paid to Applicant: $_____
4. Previous interim compensation allowed to Applicant: $_____
5. Applicant requests additional:
    Compensation of $_____
    Reimbursement of Expenses of $_____
6. A hearing on the Application will be held in Courtroom _____, _____, at _____.m., on _____, _____.
7. Any written objections must be filed with the court and served on the Applicant on or before _____, _____, (fourteen (14) days from the date of this notice plus an additional three (3) days if served by mail). Copies of the application are available from the applicant.

Date of service:

_____
Signature of Applicant or Attorney for Applicant

_____
Typed Name

_____
Address

_____
Phone No.

_____
List Bar I.D. and State of Admission

(Note: 1. Scheduling dates in this Notice shall comply with Local Rules. 2. The full application need be served only upon Debtor, counsel for Debtor, the U.S. Trustee, and the trustee and counsel for the trustee. 3. Applicant shall serve this Notice on all creditors and parties in interest including any person who has filed a request for notices. 4. A certificate of service shall be filed with this Notice and the application.)
PAWB Local Form 8 (07/13)

[Effective March 1, 2012. Amended effective July 1, 2013.]

LOCAL BANKRUPTCY FORM NO. 9.   SUMMARY COVER SHEET FOR FEE APPLICATIONS IN CHAPTER 11 AND CHAPTER 15

IN THE UNITED STATES BANKRUPTCY COURT
FOR THE WESTERN DISTRICT OF PENNSYLVANIA

In Re: :   Bankruptcy No.
                                                :
                        Debtor   :
                                                :   Chapter
                                                :
Movant   :
                                                :   Related to Document No.
            v.   :
                                                :
                                                :   Hearing Date and Time:
Respondent (if none, then "No Respondent")   :

SUMMARY COVER SHEET
FOR FEE APPLICATIONS IN CHAPTER 11 AND CHAPTER 15

1.   Your applicant was appointed on _____.
     (Attach a copy of the order approving appointment.)

2.   Your applicant represents _____.

3.   The total amount of the compensation requested is $_____ for the period from
     _____ to _____.

4.   The compensation is _____.
     (State whether interim or final compensation.)

5.   A retainer of $_____ was paid on _____.

6.   The amount of compensation previously requested is $_____.

7.   The amount of compensation previously approved is $_____.

8.   The amount of compensation previously paid is $_____.

9.   The total amount of expenses for which reimbursement is sought is $_____ and is
     for the period from _____ to _____.

10. The amount of expenses previously requested is $_____.

11. The amount of expenses previously approved is $_____.

12. The amount of expenses previously paid is $_____.

13. The blended hourly rate for this application is $_____.

14.   Other factors bearing on fee application:

_____

_____

_____

DATE: _____   By: _____
                                   Signature

                                   _____
                                   Typed Name

                                   _____
                                   Address

                                   _____
                                   Phone No.

                                   _____
                                   List Bar I.D. and State of Admission

APPENDIX
EXAMPLE OF CATEGORY LISTING OF TIME AND SERVICES
PURSUANT TO W.PA.LBR 2016-1(c)(5)(A)

IN THE UNITED STATES BANKRUPTCY COURT
WESTERN DISTRICT OF PENNSYLVANIA

In Re:	:	Bankruptcy No.
	:	
Debtor	:	
	:	Chapter
	:	
Movant	:	
	:	Related to Document No.
v.	:	
	:	
	:	Hearing Date and Time:
Respondent (if none, then "No Respondent")	:	

PART "A"

Category Listing of time and services or tasks by category on behalf of Acme Shoe Company, Debtor, during the period from May 1, 1985 to the closing of the case.

CATEGORY 1. - Sale of real estate at 320 Grant Avenue, Pittsburgh, PA to Jones Company for $_____ including negotiations with purchaser, drafting Agreement of Sale, lien search, preparation and filing of Motion and Order for sale, hearing on sale and closing on sale and preparation and filing of report of sale. After payment of all liens and expenses of sale the estate netted $_____ .

DATE	ATTY	DESCRIPTION OF SERVICE	HOURS
5/1/85	RB	Conference with Jones Company representatives re: potential purchase of 320 Grant Avenue	
5/3/85	RB	Preparation of Agreement of Sale for 320 Grant Avenue	

TOTAL IN CATEGORY 1:

CATEGORY 2. - Distribution to Creditors per Order of August 14, 2002, including preparation and filing of Motion, obtaining Order of Court and making the distribution of $_____ to priority creditors and $_____ as a _____ % distribution to Class 4 general creditors.

DATE	ATTY	DESCRIPTION OF SERVICE	HOURS
9/17/85	JS	Review & Sign Distribution Checks	
9/18/85	JS	Covering letters to all creditors, Anderson, Wagner, Bernstein & Debtor re the distribution	

TOTAL IN CATEGORY 2:

CATEGORY 3. - Tax returns and tax refund including arranging for filing of final returns, numerous calls and letters to Pennsylvania Department of Revenue resulting in tax refund of $12,435.04.

5/02/85	JS	Telephone Call: Virginia Vatz of Pa. Dept. of Revenue re tax refund
5/04/85	JS	Letter: PA Dept. of Revenue re status of tax returns

TOTAL IN CATEGORY 3:

TOTAL TIME IN ALL CATEGORIES:

DISBURSEMENTS

6/24/85	JS	Copy Expense
8/23/85	JS	Copy Expense and postage on distribution

TOTAL DISBURSEMENTS:

BILLING SUMMARY

JS	Hrs.	Min.	$135.00	$
RB	Hrs.	Min.	$125.00	-
CLIENT TOTAL	-			$
CURRENT BILLING:				$
CURRENT EXPENSES:				
TOTAL AMOUNT DUE:				$

EXAMPLE OF CHRONOLOGICAL SUMMARY OF TIME AND SERVICES
PURSUANT TO W.PA.LBR 2016-1(c)(5)(B)

IN THE UNITED STATES BANKRUPTCY COURT
WESTERN DISTRICT OF PENNSYLVANIA

In Re:		:	Bankruptcy No.
	Debtor	:	
		:	Chapter
		:	
Movant		:	
		:	Related to Document No.
	v.	:	
		:	
		:	
Respondent (if none, then "No Respondent")		:	

PART A

CHRONOLOGICAL SUMMARY OF TIME AND SERVICES
RENDERED ON BEHALF OF DEBTOR DURING PERIOD
FROM MAY 1, 1985 TO CONCLUSION OF CASE

DATE	ATTY	DESCRIPTION OF SERVICE	HOURS
5/1/85	RB	Conference with Jones Co. representative re: potential purchase of 320 Grant Avenue	
5/2/85	JS	Telephone call: Virginia Vatz and Pa. Dept. of Revenue Re: tax refund	
5/3/85	RB	Preparation of Agreement of Sale for 320 Grant Avenue	
5/4/85	JS	Letter: Pa. Dept. of Revenue re: status of tax claim	
9/17/85	JS	Review & Sign: Distribution checks	
9/18/85	JS	Covering letters to all creditors, Anderson, Wagner, Bernstein & Debtor re: the distributions	

TOTAL HOURS

			DISBURSEMENTS
6/24/85	JS	Copy Expense	$
8/23/85	JS	Copy Expense and postage on distribution	$
		TOTAL DISBURSEMENTS	$

BILLING SUMMARY

JS	2 Hrs. 0 Min.	$135.00		$
RB	2 Hrs. 0 Min.	$125.00		$
	CLIENT TOTAL:			$
	CURRENT BILLING:			$
	CURRENT EXPENSES:			$
	TOTAL AMOUNT DUE:			$

IN THE UNITED STATES BANKRUPTCY COURT
WESTERN DISTRICT OF PENNSYLVANIA

In Re: :   Bankruptcy No.
                                                :
                          Debtor   :
                                                :   Chapter
                                                :
Movant   :
                                                :   Related to Document No.
            v.   :
                                                :
                                                :   Hearing Date and Time:
Respondent (if none, then "No Respondent")   :

PART "B"

CATEGORY LISTING OF TIME AND SERVICES
ON BEHALF OF ACME SHOE COMPANY, DEBTOR, DURING THE PERIOD
FROM MAY 1, 1985 TO THE CLOSING OF THE CASE.

I.   Category 1. - Sale of real estate at
      320 Grant Avenue, Pittsburgh, PA to
      Jones Company for $30,000.00 including
      negotiations with purchaser, drafting Agreement
      of Sale, lien search, preparation and filing
      of Motion and Order for sale, hearing on
      sale and closing on sale and preparation and
      filing of report of sale. After payment of
      all liens and expenses of sale the estate
      netted $24,500.00   hrs.   min.

II.   Category 2. - Distribution to Creditors
      per Order of August 14, 1985, including
      preparation and filing of Motion, obtaining
      Order of Court and making the distribution
      of $36,533.61 to priority creditors and
      $21,794.45 as a 4% distribution to Class 4
      general creditors   hrs.   min.

III. Category 3. - Tax returns and tax refund
      including arranging for filing of final
      returns, numerous calls and letters to
      Pennsylvania Department of Revenue
      resulting in tax refund of $12,435.04   hrs.   min.

                                          TOTAL   hrs.

PAWB Local Form 9 (07/13)

[Effective March 1, 2012. Amended effective July 1, 2013.]

LOCAL BANKRUPTCY FORM NO. 10. CHAPTER 13 PLAN

IN THE UNITED STATES BANKRUPTCY COURT
WESTERN DISTRICT OF PENNSYLVANIA

Bankruptcy Case Number_____

Debtor#1: _____ Last Four (4) Digits of SSN: _____

Debtor#2: _____ Last Four (4) Digits of SSN: _____
Check if applicable   □ **Amended Plan**   □ **Plan expected to be completed within the next 12 months**

CHAPTER 13 PLAN DATED _____
COMBINED WITH CLAIMS BY DEBTOR PURSUANT TO RULE 3004

UNLESS PROVIDED BY PRIOR COURT ORDER THE OFFICIAL PLAN FORM MAY NOT BE MODIFIED

PLAN FUNDING
Total amount of $_____ per month for a plan term of _____ months shall be paid to the Trustee from future earnings as follows:

Payments:	By Income Attachment	Directly by Debtor	By Automated Bank Transfer
D#1	$_____	$_____	$_____
D#2	$_____	$_____	$_____

(Income attachments must be used by Debtors having attachable income)   (SSA direct deposit recipients only)

Estimated amount of additional plan funds from sale proceeds, etc.: $_____
The Trustee shall calculate the actual total payments estimated throughout the plan.
The responsibility for ensuring that there are sufficient funds to effectuate the goals of the Chapter 13 plan rests with the Debtor.

PLAN PAYMENTS TO BEGIN: no later than one month following the filing of the bankruptcy petition.

FOR AMENDED PLANS:
     i.   The total plan payments shall consist of all amounts previously paid together with the new monthly payment for the remainder of the plan's duration.
     ii.   The original plan term has been extended by _____ months for a total of _____ months from the original plan filing date;
     iii.   The payment shall be changed effective_____
     iv.   The Debtor (s) have filed a motion requesting that the court appropriately change the amount of all wage orders.

The Debtor agrees to dedicate to the plan the estimated amount of sale proceeds: $_____ from the sale of this property (describe) _____. All sales shall be completed by_____. Lump sum payments shall be received by the Trustee as follows: _____.
Other payments from any source (describe specifically) _____ shall be received by the Trustee as follows: _____.

The sequence of plan payments shall be determined by the Trustee, using the following as a general guide:

     Level One: Unpaid filing fees.
     Level Two: Secured claims and lease payments entitled to Section 1326 (a)(1)(C) pre-confirmation adequate protection payments.
     Level Three: Monthly ongoing mortgage payments, ongoing vehicle and lease payments, installments on professional fees, and post-petition utility claims.
     Level Four: Priority Domestic Support Obligations.
     Level Five: Mortgage arrears, secured taxes, rental arrears, vehicle payment arrears.
     Level Six: All remaining secured, priority and specially classified claims, miscellaneous secured arrears.
     Level Seven Allowed general unsecured claims.
     Level Eight: Untimely filed unsecured claims for which the Debtor has not lodged an objection.

1.   UNPAID FILING FEES _____

Filing fees: the balance of $_____ shall be fully paid by the Trustee to the Clerk of Bankruptcy Court from the first available funds.

2. PERSONAL PROPERTY SECURED CLAIMS AND LEASE PAYMENTS ENTITLED TO PRECONFIRMATION ADEQUATE PROTECTION PAYMENTS UNDER SECTION 1326 (a)(1)(C)

Creditors subject to these terms are identified below within parts 3b, 4b, 5b or 8b. Timely plan payments to the Trustee by the Debtor(s) shall constitute compliance with the adequate protection requirements of Section 1326 (a)(1)(C). Distributions prior to final plan confirmation shall be made at Level 2. Upon final plan confirmation, these distributions shall change to level 3. Leases provided for in this section are assumed by the Debtor(s).

3(a). LONG TERM CONTINUING DEBTS CURED AND REINSTATED, AND LIEN (if any) RETAINED

Name of Creditor (include account #)	Description of Collateral (Address or parcel ID of real estate, etc.)	Monthly Payment (If changed, state effective date)	Pre-petition arrears to be cured (w/o interest, unless expressly stated)

3(b). *Long term debt claims secured by PERSONAL property entitled to §1326 (a)(1)(C) preconfirmation adequate protection payments:*

4. SECURED CLAIMS TO BE PAID IN FULL DURING TERM OF PLAN, ACCORDING TO ORIGINAL CONTRACT TERMS, WITH NO MODIFICATION OF CONTRACTUAL TERMS AND LIENS RETAINED UNTIL PAID

4(a). *Claims to be paid at plan level three (for vehicle payments, do not use "pro rata" but instead, state the monthly payment to be applied to the claim):*

Name of Creditor	Description of Collateral	Contractual Monthly Payment (Level 3)	Principal Balance Of Claim	Contract Rate of Interest

4(b). *Claims entitled to preconfirmation adequate protection payments pursuant to Section 1326 (a)(1)(C) (Use only if claim qualifies for this treatment under the statute, and if claims are to be paid at level two prior to confirmation, and moved to level three after confirmation):*

Name of Creditor	Description of Collateral	Contractual Monthly Payment (Level 3)	Principal Balance Of Claim	Contract Rate of Interest

5. SECURED CLAIMS TO BE FULLY PAID ACCORDING TO MODIFIED TERMS AND LIENS RETAINED

5(a). *Claims to be paid at plan level three (for vehicle payments, do not use "pro rata"; instead, state the monthly payment to be applied to the claim)*

Name of Creditor	Description of Collateral	Modified Principal Balance	Interest Rate	Monthly Payment at Level 3 or Pro Rata

PAWB Local Form 10 (07/13)   Page 2 of 6

5(b). *Claims entitled to preconfirmation adequate protection payments pursuant to Section 1326 (a)(1)(C) (Use only if claim qualifies for this treatment under the statute, and if claims are to be paid at level two prior to confirmation, and moved to level three after confirmation):*

Name of Creditor	Description of Collateral	Modified Principal Balance	Interest Rate	Monthly Payment at Level 3 or Pro Rata

6. SECURED CLAIMS NOT PAID DUE TO SURRENDER OF COLLATERAL; SPECIFY DATE OF SURRENDER

7. THE DEBTOR PROPOSES TO AVOID OR LIMIT THE LIENS OF THE FOLLOWING CREDITORS:

Name the Creditor and identify the collateral with specificity.	Name the Creditor and identify the collateral with specificity.

8. LEASES. Leases provided for in this section are assumed by the debtor(s). Provide the number of lease payments to be made by the Trustee.

8(a). *Claims to be paid at plan level three (for vehicle payments, do not use "pro rata"; instead, state the monthly payment to be applied to the claim):*

Name of Creditor (include account#)	Description of leased asset	Monthly payment amount and number of payments	Pre-petition arrears to be cured (Without interest, unless expressly stated otherwise)

8(b). *Claims entitled to preconfirmation adequate protection payments pursuant to Section 1326 (a)(1)(C) (Use only if claim qualifies for this treatment under the statute, and if claims are to be paid at level two prior to confirmation, and moved to level three after confirmation):*

Name of Creditor (include account#)	Description of leased asset	Monthly payment amount and number of payments	Pre-petition arrears to be cured (Without interest, unless expressly stated otherwise)

9. SECURED TAX CLAIMS FULLY PAID AND LIENS RETAINED

Name of Taxing Authority	Total Amount of Claim	Type of Tax	Rate of Interest *	Identifying Number(s) if Collateral is Real Estate	Tax Periods

* *The secured tax claims of the Internal Revenue Service, Commonwealth of Pennsylvania and County of Allegheny shall bear interest at the statutory rate in effect as of the date of confirmation of the first plan providing for payment of such claims.*

10. PRIORITY DOMESTIC SUPPORT OBLIGATIONS:

If the Debtor (s) is currently paying Domestic Support Obligations through existing state court order(s) and leaves this section blank, the Debtor (s) expressly agrees to continue paying and remain current on all Domestic Support Obligations through existing state court orders. If this payment is for prepetition arrearages only, check here: ☐ As to "Name of Creditor," specify the actual payee, e.g. PA SCDU, etc.

Name of Creditor	Description	Total Amount of Claim	Monthly Payment or Prorata

11. PRIORITY UNSECURED TAX CLAIMS PAID IN FULL

Name of Taxing Authority	Total Amount of Claim	Type of Tax	Rate of Interest (0% if blank)	Tax Periods

12. ADMINISTRATIVE PRIORITY CLAIMS TO BE FULLY PAID

    a. Percentage fees payable to the Chapter 13 Fee and Expense Fund shall be paid at the rate fixed by the United States Trustee.

    b. Attorney fees are payable to _____. In addition to a retainer of $_____ already paid by or on behalf of the Debtor, the amount of $_____ is to be paid at the rate of $_____ per month. Including any retainer paid, a total of $_____ has been approved pursuant to a fee application. An additional $_____ will be sought through a fee application to be filed and approved before any additional amount will be paid thru the Plan.

13. OTHER PRIORITY CLAIMS TO BE PAID IN FULL

Name of Creditor	Total Amount of Claim	Interest Rate (0% if blank)	Statute Providing Priority Status

14. POST-PETITION UTILITY MONTHLY PAYMENTS. This provision completed only if utility provider has agreed to this treatment.

These payments comprise a single monthly combined payment for post-petition utility services, any post-petition delinquencies and unpaid security deposits. The claim payment will not change for the life of the plan. Should the utility file a motion requesting a payment change, the Debtor will be required to file an amended plan. These payments may not resolve all of the post-petition claims of the utility. The utility may require additional funds from the Debtor (s) after discharge.

PAWB Local Form 10 (07/13)   **Page 4 of 6**

Name of Creditor	Monthly Payment	Post-petition Account Number

15. CLAIMS OF UNSECURED NONPRIORITY CREDITORS TO BE SPECIALLY CLASSIFIED. If the following is intended to be treated as long term continuing debt treatment pursuant to Section 1322(b)(5) of the Bankruptcy Code, check here: ☐

Name of Creditor	Principal Balance or Long Term Debt	Rate of Interest (0% if blank)	Monthly Payments	Arrears to be Cured	Interest Rate on Arrears

16. CLAIMS OF GENERAL, NONPRIORITY UNSECURED CREDITORS

Debtor(s) ESTIMATE that a total of $_____ will be available for distribution to unsecured, non-priority creditors. Debtor(s) UNDERSTAND that a MINIMUM of $_____ shall be paid to unsecured, non-priority creditors in order to comply with the liquidation alternative test for confirmation. The total pool of funds estimated above is NOT the MAXIMUM amount payable to this class of creditors. Instead, the actual pool of funds available for payment to these creditors under the plan base will be determined only after audit of the plan at time of completion. The estimated percentage of payment to general unsecured creditors is _____ %. The percentage of payment may change, based upon the total amount of allowed claims. Late-filed claims will not be paid unless all timely filed claims have been paid in full. Thereafter, all late-filed claims will be paid pro-rata unless an objection has been filed within thirty (30) days of filing the claim. Creditors not specifically identified in Parts 1 - 15, above, are included in this class.

GENERAL PRINCIPLES APPLICABLE TO ALL CHAPTER 13 PLANS

This is the voluntary Chapter 13 reorganization plan of the Debtor (s). The Debtor (s) understand and agree that the Chapter 13 plan may be extended as necessary by the Trustee, to not more than sixty (60) months, in order to insure that the goals of the plan have been achieved. Property of the estate shall not re-vest in the Debtor (s) until the bankruptcy case is closed.

The Debtor (s) shall comply with the tax return filing requirements of Section 1308, prior to the Section 341 Meeting of Creditors, and shall provide the Trustee with documentation of such compliance at or before the time of the Section 341 Meeting of Creditors. Counsel for the Debtor(s), or Debtor (if not represented by counsel), shall provide the Trustee with the information needed for the Trustee to comply with the requirements of Section 1302 as to notification to be given to Domestic Support Obligation creditors, and Counsel for the Debtor(s), or Debtor (if pro se) shall provide the Trustee with the calculations relied upon by Counsel to determine the Debtor (s)' current monthly income and disposable income.

As a condition to eligibility of the Debtor(s) to receive a discharge upon successful completion of the plan, Counsel for the debtor(s), or the debtor(s) if not represented by counsel, shall file with the Court Local Bankruptcy Form 24 (Debtor's Certification of Discharge Eligibility) within forty-five (45) days after making the final plan payment.

All pre-petition debts are paid through the Trustee. Additionally, ongoing payments for vehicles, mortgages and assumed leases are also paid through the Trustee, unless the Court orders otherwise.

Percentage fees to the Trustee are paid on all distributions at the rate fixed by the United States Trustee. The Trustee has the discretion to adjust, interpret and implement the distribution schedule to carry out the plan. The Trustee shall follow this standard plan form sequence unless otherwise ordered by the Court.

The provisions for payment to secured, priority and specially classified creditors in this plan shall constitute claims in accordance with Bankruptcy Rule 3004. Proofs of claim by the Trustee will not be required. The Clerk shall be entitled to rely on the accuracy of the information contained in this plan with regard to each claim. If the secured, priority or specially classified creditor files its own claim, then the creditor's claim shall govern, provided the Debtor (s) and Debtor (s)' counsel have been given notice and an opportunity to object. The Trustee is authorized, without prior notice, to pay claims exceeding the amount provided in the plan by not more than $250.

Any Creditor whose secured claim is modified by the plan, or reduced by separate lien avoidance actions, shall retain its lien until the plan has been fully completed, or until it has been paid the full amount to which it is entitled under applicable non-bankruptcy law, whichever occurs earlier. Upon payment in accordance with these terms and successful completion of the plan by the Debtor (s), the creditor shall promptly cause all mortgages and liens encumbering the collateral to be satisfied, discharged and released

Should a pre-petition Creditor file a claim asserting secured or priority status that is not provided for in the plan, then after notice to the Trustee, counsel of record, (or the Debtor (s) in the event that they are not represented by counsel), the Trustee shall treat the claim as allowed unless the Debtor(s) successfully objects.

Both of the preceding provisions will also apply to allowed secured, priority and specially classified claims filed after the bar date. LATE-FILED CLAIMS NOT PROPERLY SERVED ON THE TRUSTEE AND THE DEBTOR(S)' COUNSEL OF RECORD (OR DEBTOR, IF PRO SE) WILL NOT BE PAID. The responsibility for reviewing the claims and objecting where appropriate is placed on the Debtor.

BY SIGNING THIS PLAN THE UNDERSIGNED, AS COUNSEL FOR THE DEBTOR(S), OR THE DEBTOR(S) IF NOT REPRESENTED BY COUNSEL, CERTIFY THAT I/WE HAVE REVIEWED ANY PRIOR CONFIRMED PLAN(S), ORDER(S) CONFIRMING PRIOR PLAN(S), PROOFS OF CLAIM FILED WITH THE COURT BY CREDITORS, AND ANY ORDERS OF COURT AFFECTING THE AMOUNT(S) OR TREATMENT OF ANY CREDITOR CLAIMS, AND EXCEPT AS MODIFIED HEREIN, THAT THIS PROPOSED PLAN CONFORMS TO AND IS CONSISTENT WITH ALL SUCH PRIOR PLANS, ORDERS AND CLAIMS. FALSE CERTIFICATIONS SHALL SUBJECT THE SIGNATORIES TO SANCTIONS UNDER FED.R.BANK.P. 9011.

Attorney Signature_____

Attorney Name and Pa. ID #_____

Attorney Address and Phone _____

Debtor Signature_____

Debtor Signature_____

[Effective March 1, 2012. Amended effective July 1, 2013.]

LOCAL BANKRUPTCY FORM NO. 11. EX PARTE MOTION FOR ORDER TO PAY TRUSTEE PURSUANT TO WAGE ATTACHMENT

IN THE UNITED STATES BANKRUPTCY COURT
FOR THE WESTERN DISTRICT OF PENNSYLVANIA

In Re: :   Bankruptcy No.
                                                :
                          Debtor(s)   :
                                                :   Chapter 13
Trustee, or Debtors(s), Movant   :
                                                :   Motion No. ⌐ WO-1
                          v.   :   Motion No. ☐ WO-2
                                                :
Respondents   :

EX PARTE MOTION FOR ORDER TO PAY TRUSTEE PURSUANT TO WAGE ATTACHMENT

The undersigned respectfully represents as follows:

1.   A Chapter 13 case was filed.

2.   It appears that the Debtor receives regular income which may be attached under 11 U.S.C. §1326 to fund the Chapter 13 Plan.

3.   The likelihood of success in the case will be much greater if the Debtor's income is attached to fund the plan.

WHEREFORE, the Chapter 13 Trustee and/or the Debtor respectfully request that this Court enter an Order to Pay Trustee in the form attached.

_____
Signature of Chapter 13 Trustee or Attorney for Debtor(s)

_____
Typed Name of Chapter 13 Trustee or Attorney for Debtor(s)

_____
Address of Chapter 13 Trustee or Attorney for Debtor(s)

_____
Phone No. and Pa. I.D. No. of Chapter 13 Trustee or Attorney for Debtor(s)

IN THE UNITED STATES BANKRUPTCY COURT
FOR THE WESTERN DISTRICT OF PENNSYLVANIA

In Re: :   Bankruptcy No.
                                                    :
                    Debtor   :
                                                    :   Chapter 13
                                                    :
Standing Chapter 13 Trustee or Debtor(s)   :
Movant   :
                                                    :   Related to Document No.
                v.   :
                                                    :
                                                    :
Respondent(s)   :

ORDER TO PAY TRUSTEE PURSUANT TO WAGE ATTACHMENT

The above-named Debtor(s) having filed a Chapter 13 petition and Debtor(s) or Trustee having moved to attach wages to fund the Chapter 13 Plan:

IT IS, THEREFORE, ORDERED that until further order of this Court, the entity from which the Debtor receives income:

shall deduct from that income the sum of $_____, beginning on the next pay day following receipt of this order and shall deduct a similar amount each pay period thereafter, including any period for which the Debtor receives a periodic or lump sum payment as a result of vacation, termination, or other benefit arising out of present or past employment, or from any other benefits payable to the Debtor, and shall remit the deducted sums ON AT LEAST A MONTHLY BASIS to:

> RONDA J. WINNECOUR
> CHAPTER 13 TRUSTEE, W.D.PA.
> P.O. BOX 84051
> CHICAGO, IL 60689-4002

IT IS FURTHER ORDERED that the above-named entity shall notify the Chapter 13 Trustee if the Debtor's income is terminated and the reason therefor.

IT IS FURTHER ORDERED that the Debtors shall serve this order and a copy of the Notification of Debtor's Social Security Number, Local Bankruptcy Form 12, that includes the debtor's full Social Security number on the above-named entity. Debtor shall file a certificate of service regarding service of the order and local form, but the Social Security number shall not be included on the certificate.

IT IS FURTHER ORDERED that all remaining income of the Debtor, except the amounts required to be withheld for taxes, Social Security, insurance, pension, or union dues shall be paid to the Debtor in accordance with usual payment procedures.

IT IS FURTHER ORDERED THAT NO OTHER DEDUCTIONS FOR GARNISHMENT, WAGE ASSIGNMENT, CREDIT UNION, OR OTHER PURPOSE SHALL BE MADE FROM THE INCOME OF DEBTOR WITH THE SOLE EXCEPTION OF ANY SUPPORT PAYMENTS.

IT IS FURTHER ORDERED that this order supersedes previous orders made to the above-named entity in this case.

IT IS FURTHER ORDERED that the above-named entity shall not charge any fee to the Debtor for the administration of this attachment order, except as may be allowed upon application to and order of this Court.

DATED this _____ day of _____, _____.

                                        _____
                                        United States Bankruptcy Judge

PAWB Local Form 11 (05/16)   Page 2 of 2

[Effective March 1, 2012. Amended effective July 1, 2013; May 1, 2016.]

LOCAL BANKRUPTCY FORM NO. 12. NOTIFICATION
OF DEBTOR'S SOCIAL SECURITY NUMBER

IN THE UNITED STATES BANKRUPTCY COURT
FOR THE WESTERN DISTRICT OF PENNSYLVANIA

In Re: :   Bankruptcy No.
                                                :
              Debtor(s)   :
                                                :   Chapter
                                                :
Movant(s)   :
                                                :   Related to Document No.
          v.   :
                                                :
                                                :
Respondent(s)   :

NOTIFICATION OF DEBTOR'S SOCIAL SECURITY NUMBER

Name of employer or other party subject to wage attachment:

Debtor's name:

Debtor's nine-digit Social Security number: __ __ __ - __ __ - __ __ __ __

Debtor's address:

Debtor's phone number:

This notification is accompanied by a Wage Attachment Order issued by a United States Bankruptcy Judge regarding attachment of the debtor's wages. The debtor's Social Security number is being provided to assist in complying with the court order.

NOTE: BECAUSE THIS NOTICE DISCLOSES THE DEBTOR'S FULL SOCIAL SECURITY NUMBER, IT IS TO BE MAILED TO THE EMPLOYER BUT SHALL NOT BE FILED WITH THE BANKRUPTCY COURT.

DATE: _____

                          Signature: Attorney for Debtor(s) [or pro se Debtor(s)]

                          _____
                          (Typed Name)

                          _____
                          (Address)

                          _____
                          (Phone No.)

                          _____
                          List Bar I.D. and State of Admission

PAWB Local Form 12 (07/13)

[Effective March 1, 2012. Amended effective July 1, 2013.]

LOCAL BANKRUPTCY FORM NO. 13. DISCLOSURE STATEMENT TO ACCOMPANY PLAN

IN THE UNITED STATES BANKRUPTCY COURT
FOR THE WESTERN DISTRICT OF PENNSYLVANIA

In Re: Bankruptcy No.

DISCLOSURE STATEMENT
TO ACCOMPANY PLAN DATED _____

☐ Chapter 11 Small Business (Check box only if debtor has elected to be considered a small business under 11 U.S.C. §1121(e))

Debtor furnishes this disclosure statement to creditors in the above-captioned matter pursuant to Bankruptcy Code §1125 to assist them in evaluating debtor's proposed Chapter 11 plan, a copy of which is attached hereto. Creditors may vote for or against the plan of reorganization. Creditors who wish to vote must complete their ballots and return them to the following address before the deadline noted in the order approving the disclosure statement and fixing time. The Court will schedule a hearing on the plan pursuant to 11 U.S.C. §1129.

Address for return of ballots:

I.   Background

   1.   Name of Debtor

   2.   Type of Debtor (individual, partnership, corporation)

   3.   Debtor's Business or Employment

   4.   Date of Chapter 11 Petition

5.   Events that Caused the Filing:

6.   Anticipated Future of the Company & Source of this Information and Opinion

7.   Summarize all Significant Features of the Plan Including When and How Each Class of
      Creditor Will Be Paid and What, If Any, Liens Will Be Retained By Secured Creditors or
      Granted to Any Creditor Under the Plan

8.   Are All Monthly Operating Statements Current and on File With The Clerk of Court?
                    Yes _____   No _____

      If Not, Explain:

9.   Does the plan provided for releases of nondebtor parties? Specify which parties and
      terms of release.

10.   Identify all executory contracts that are to be assumed or assumed and assigned.

11.   Has a bar date been set?   Yes _____   No _____
      (If not, a motion to set the bar date has been filed simultaneously with the filing of this
      disclosure statement.)

12.   Has an election under 11 U.S.C. §1121(e) been filed with the Court to be treated as a
      small business?
                    Yes _____   No _____

13.   Specify property that will be transferred subject to 11 U.S.C. §1146(c).

II. Creditors

A. Secured Claims

SECURED CLAIMS

Creditor	Total Amount Owed	Arrearages	Type of Collateral Priority of Lien (1, 2, 3)	Disputed (D) Liquidated (L) Unliquidated (U)	Will Liens Be Retained Under the Plan? (Y) or (N)
TOTAL	$	$			

B.   Priority Claims

PRIORITY CLAIMS

Creditor	Total Amount Owed	Type of Collateral	(D) (L) (U) *
TOTAL	$		

* Disputed (D), Liquidated (L), or Unliquidated (U)

C.   Unsecured Claims

       1.   Amount Debtor Scheduled (Disputed and Undisputed) $
       2.   Amount of Unscheduled Unsecured Claims[1] $
       3.   Total Claims Scheduled or Filed $
       4.   Amount Debtor Disputes $
       5.   Estimated Allowable Unsecured Claims $

D.   Other Classes of Creditors

       1.   Amount Debtor Scheduled (Disputed and Undisputed) $
       2.   Amount of Unscheduled Claims[1] $
       3.   Total Claims Scheduled or Filed $
       4.   Amount Debtor Disputes $
       5.   Estimated Allowable Claims $

E.   Other Classes of Interest Holders

       1.   Amount Debtor Scheduled (Disputed and Undisputed) $
       2.   Amount of Unscheduled Claims[1] $
       3.   Total Claims Scheduled or Filed $
       4.   Amount Debtor Disputes $
       5.   Estimated Allowable Claims $

---

[1] Includes (a.) unsecured claims filed by unscheduled creditors; (b.) that portion of any unsecured claim filed by a scheduled creditor that exceeds the amount debtor scheduled; and (c.) any unsecured portion of any secured debt not previously scheduled.

PAWB Local Form 13 (07/13)

III.   <u>Assets</u>

ASSETS

Assets	Value	Basis for Value Priority of Lien	Name of Lien Holder (if any) (Fair Market Value/ Book Value)	Amount of Debtor's Equity (Value Minus Liens)
	$ TOTAL			$ TOTAL

1.   Are any assets which appear on Schedule A or B of the bankruptcy petition not listed above?

     If so, identify asset and explain why asset is not in estate:

2.   Are any assets listed above claimed as exempt? If so attach a copy of Schedule C and any amendments.

PAWB Local Form 13 (07/13)   Page 6 of 21

IV.   SUMMARY OF PLAN

1.   Effective Date of Plan:

2.   Will cramdown be sought? ___ Yes ___ No
If Yes, state bar date: _____

3.   Treatment of Secured **Non-Tax** Claims

SECURED NON-TAX CLAIMS

Name of Creditor	Class	Amount Owed	Summary of Proposed Treatment
TOTAL		$	

4.   Treatment of Secured Tax Claims

SECURED TAX CLAIMS

Name of Creditor	Class	Amount Owed	Summary of Proposed Treatment
TOTAL		$	

5.   Treatment of Administrative Non-Tax Claims[2]

ADMINISTRATIVE NON-TAX CLAIMS

Name of Creditor*	Amount Owed	Type of Debt**	Summary of Proposed Treatment and Date of First Payment

6.   Treatment of Administrative Tax Claims

ADMINISTRATIVE TAX CLAIMS

Name of Creditor*	Amount Owed	Type of Debt**	Summary of Proposed Treatment and Date of First Payment

* Identify and Use Separate Line for Each Professional and Estimated Amount of Payment
** Type of Debt (P=Professional, TD=Trade, TX=Taxes)

PAWB Local Form 13 (07/13)

[2] Include all §503(b) administrative claims.

7.   Treatment of Priority Non-Tax Claims

PRIORITY NON-TAX CLAIMS

Name of Creditor	Class	Amount Owed	Date of Assessment	Summary of Proposed Treatment

8.   Treatment of Priority Tax Claims[3]

PRIORITY TAX CLAIMS

Name of Creditor	Class	Amount Owed	Date of Assessment	Summary of Proposed Treatment

[3] Include dates when any §507(a)(7) taxes were assessed.

PAWB Local Form 13 (07/13)

9.   Treatment of General Unsecured Non-Tax Claims

GENERAL UNSECURED NON-TAX CLAIMS

Creditor	Class	Total Amount Owed	Percent of Dividend
TOTAL		$	

10. Treatment of General Unsecured Tax Claims

GENERAL UNSECURED TAX CLAIMS

Creditor	Class	Total Amount Owed	Percent of Dividend
TOTAL		$	

11.   Will periodic payments be made to unsecured creditors?

Yes _____   No _____   First payment to begin _____

If so:

Amount of each payment (aggregate to all unsecured claimants)
Estimated date of first payment:
Time period between payments:
Estimated date of last payment:
Contingencies, if any:

State source of funds for planned payments, including funds necessary for capital replacement, repairs, or improvements:

Other significant features of the plan:

Include any other information necessary to explain this plan:

V.   Comparison of Plan with Chapter 7 Liquidation

If debtor's proposed plan is not confirmed, the potential alternatives would include proposal of a different plan, dismissal of the case or conversion of the case to Chapter 7. If this case is converted to Chapter 7, a trustee will be appointed to liquidate the debtor's non-exempt assets. In this event, all secured claims and priority claims, including all expenses of administration, must be paid in full before any distribution is made to unsecured claimants.

Total value of Chapter 7 estate (See Section III)	$
1. Less secured claims (See Section II A)	$
2. Less administrative claims (See Section IV-5-6	
and include approximate Chapter 7 expenses)	$
3. Less other priority claims (See Section II B)	$
Total Amount Available for Distribution to Unsecured Creditors	$
Divided by total allowable unsecured claims of (See Section II C)	$
Percentage of Dividend to Unsecured Creditors:	%

Will the creditors fare better under the plan than they would in a Chapter 7 liquidation?

Yes _____   No _____

Explain:

VI.   Feasibility

A.   Attach Income Statement for Prior 12 Months.

B.   Attach Cash Flow Statement for Prior 12 Months.

C.   Attach Cash Flow Projections for Next 12 Months.

Estimated amount to be paid on effective date of plan, including administrative expenses.

$ _____

Show how this amount was calculated.

$ _____   Administrative Class
  $ _____   Taxes
  $ _____   Unsecured Creditors
  $ _____   UST Fees

  $ _____   TOTAL

What assumptions are made to justify the increase in cash available for the funding of the plan?

Will funds be available in the full amount for administrative expenses on the effective date of the plan? From what source? If not available, why not and when will payments be made?

Cash on hand $\underline{\hspace{2cm}}$ (Current). Attach current bank statement.

Cash on hand $\underline{\hspace{2cm}}$ (Estimated amount available on date of confirmation)

If this amount is less than the amount necessary at confirmation, how will debtor make up the shortfall?

VII.   Management Salaries

MANAGEMENT SALARIES

Position/Name of Person Holding Position	Salary at Time of Filing	Proposed Salary (Post-Confirmation)

VIII.   Identify the Effect on Plan Payments and Specify Each of the Following:

1.   What, if any, litigation is pending?

2.   What, if any, litigation is proposed or contemplated?

IX.   Additional Information and Comments

X.   Certification

The undersigned hereby certifies that the information herein is true and correct to the best of my knowledge and belief formed after reasonable inquiry.

If Debtor is a corporation, attach a copy of corporate resolution authorizing the filing of this Disclosure Statement and Plan.

If Debtor is a general partnership, attach a copy of the consent agreement of all general partners to the filing of the bankruptcy.

_____   _____
Signature of Debtor   Date
or Authorized Representative

_____   _____
Signature of Debtor   Date
or Authorized Representative

_____   _____
Debtor's Counsel   Date

OPTIONAL TABLE

6. Treatment of Other Claims

  N/A

OTHER CLASSES OF CREDITORS

Creditor	Class	Total Amount Owed	Percent of Dividend

A. Will periodic payments be made?

  Yes ___ No ___
  If so:

  Amount of each payment (aggregate to all claimants) $ _____
  Estimated date of first payment _____
  Time period between payments _____
  Estimated date of last payment _____
  Contingencies, if any:

PAWB Local Form 13 (07/13)   Page 17 of 21

OPTIONAL TABLE

7.   Treatment of Interest Holders (Other Than Equity Holders)

OTHER CLASSES OF INTEREST HOLDERS

Creditor	Class	Total Amount Owed	Percent of Dividend

8.   Treatment of Equity Holders (Specify how the market test of *Bank of America National Trust and Savings Association v. 203 North LaSalle Street Partnership*, 526 U.S. 434, 110 S.Ct. 141 (1999), is met)

EQUITY HOLDERS

Creditor	Class	Total Amount Owed	Percent of Dividend

A.   Will periodic payments be made?

     Yes _____   No _____

If so:

     Amount of each payment (aggregate to all claimants) $ _____

     Estimated date of first payment   _____

     Time period between payments   _____

     Estimated date of last payment   _____

     Contingencies, if any:

PAWB Local Form 13 (07/13)

HISTORIC SUMMARY

1994

POST PETITION PERIODS	MONTH ONE	MONTH TWO	MONTH THREE	MONTH FOUR	MONTH FIVE	MONTH SIX	MONTH SEVEN	MONTH EIGHT	MONTH NINE	MONTH TEN	MONTH ELEVEN	MONTH TWELVE
1. TOTAL CASH FLOW FROM OPERATIONS:	$10,000	$12,000	$14,000	$9,000	$15,000	$18,000	$14,000	$22,000	$35,000	$30,000	$38,000	$36,000
2. LESS TOTAL DISBURSEMENTS EXCLUDING PAYMENTS TO CREDITORS IN A PLAN:	$10,000	$14,000	$12,000	$10,000	$12,000	$15,000	$12,500	$16,000	$30,000	$23,000	$30,000	$30,000
3. TOTAL NET CASH FLOW:-	0	(2,000)	2,000	(1,000)	3,000	3,000	1,500	6,000	5,000	7,000	8,000	6,000

DEFINITIONS

TOTAL CASH FLOW FROM OPERATIONS:

THE TOTAL AMOUNT OF FUNDS COLLECTED IN A SPECIFIC PERIOD FROM CASH SALES, COLLECTION OF ACCOUNTS RECEIVABLE, AND OTHER INCOME, EXCLUDING LOANS PROCEEDS, CASH CONTRIBUTIONS FROM INSIDERS, AND SALES TAXES COLLECTED.

TOTAL DISBURSEMENTS EXCLUDING PAYMENTS TO CREDITORS IN A PLAN:

THE TOTAL DISBURSEMENTS IN A SPECIFIC PERIOD FOR PRODUCTION COSTS, GENERAL AND ADMINISTRATIVE COSTS, EXCLUDING PAYMENTS TO CREDITORS TO BE PAID UNDER THE TERMS OF THE PLAN.

PROJECTED SUMMARY

POST PETITION PERIODS	MONTH ONE	MONTH TWO	MONTH THREE	MONTH FOUR	MONTH FIVE	MONTH SIX	MONTH SEVEN	MONTH EIGHT	MONTH NINE	MONTH TEN	MONTH ELEVEN	MONTH TWELVE
4. TOTAL PROJECTED CASH FLOW FROM OPERATIONS:	$38,000	$40,000	$41,000	$43,000	$45,000	$45,000	$46,000	$47,000	$48,000	$48,000	$48,000	$50,000
5. LESS TOTAL PROJECTED DISBURSEMENTS EXCLUDING PMTS TO CREDITORS IN A PLAN:	$30,000	$32,000	$32,000	$32,000	$33,000	$33,000	$35,000	$35,000	$38,000	$38,000	$38,000	$39,000
6. ANTICIPATED CASH FLOW AVAILABLE FOR PLAN:	8,000	8,000	9,000	11,000	12,000	12,000	11,000	12,000	10,000	10,000	10,000	11,000

DEFINITIONS

TOTAL PROJECTED CASH FLOW FROM OPERATIONS:
TOTAL AMOUNT OF PROJECTED FUNDS COLLECTED IN A SPECIFIC PERIOD FROM CASH SALES, COLLECTION OF ACCOUNTS RECEIVABLE, AND OTHER INCOME, EXCLUDING LOANS PROCEEDS, CASH CONTRIBUTIONS FROM INSIDERS, AND SALES TAXES COLLECTED.

TOTAL DISBURSEMENTS EXCLUDING PAYMENTS TO CREDITORS IN A PLAN:
TOTAL PROJECTED DISBURSEMENTS IN A SPECIFIC PERIOD FOR PRODUCTION COSTS, GENERAL AND ADMINISTRATIVE COSTS, EXCLUDING PAYMENTS TO CREDITORS TO BE PAID UNDER THE TERMS OF THE PROPOSED PLAN.

PLAN FEASIBILITY

POST PETITION PERIODS	MONTH ONE	MONTH TWO	MONTH THREE	MONTH FOUR	MONTH FIVE	MONTH SIX	MONTH SEVEN	MONTH EIGHT	MONTH NINE	MONTH TEN	MONTH ELEVEN	MONTH TWELVE
ANTICIPATED RECEIPTS AVAILABLE FOR PLAN (SEE LINE 6, ABOVE):	$8,000	$8,000	$9,000	$11,000	$12,000	$12,000	$11,000	$12,000	$10,000	$10,000	$10,000	$11,000
LESS PROPOSED PLAN PAYMENTS (SEE SECTION IV):	$5,000	$5,000	$5,000	$5,000	$5,000	$5,000	$5,500	$5,000	$5,000	$5,000	$5,000	$5,000
OVERAGE/(SHORTAGE) OF CASH FLOW AVAILABLE TO FUND PLAN:	3,000	3,000	4,000	6,000	7,000	7,000	5,500	7,000	5,000	5,000	5,000	6,000

PAWB Local Form 13 (07/13)

Page 21 of 21

[Effective March 1, 2012. Amended effective July 1, 2013.]

1025

LOCAL BANKRUPTCY FORM NO. 14.   REPORT FOR BANKRUPTCY JUDGES IN CASES TO BE CLOSED—CHAPTER 11 CASES

IN THE UNITED STATES BANKRUPTCY COURT
FOR THE WESTERN DISTRICT OF PENNSYLVANIA

In Re: :   Bankruptcy No.
                                  :
             Debtor(s)   :
                                  :   Chapter 11
                                  :
Movant(s)   :   Related to Document No.
            v.   :
                                  :
Respondent(s)   :

REPORT FOR BANKRUPTCY JUDGES IN CASES TO BE CLOSED

CHAPTER 11 CASES

_____Plan Confirmed   _____Plan Not Confirmed

If plan was confirmed and the case is still in Chapter 11, what percentage dividend was (or is) to be paid under the plan to the general unsecured class of creditors? _____%

I certify under penalty of perjury that the information provided on this form is true and correct to the best of my knowledge, information, and belief and that all estimated payments have been designated appropriately as such.

DATE _____   PREPARER _____   SIGNATURE _____

PAWB Local Form 14 (07/13)

[Effective March 1, 2012.   Amended effective July 1, 2013.]

LOCAL BANKRUPTCY FORM NO. 15.   [RESERVED]

LOCAL BANKRUPTCY FORM NO. 16.   CERTIFICATION
THAT BRIEFING COMPLETED

IN THE UNITED STATES BANKRUPTCY COURT
FOR THE WESTERN DISTRICT OF PENNSYLVANIA

In Re: :   Bankruptcy No.
                                                    :
                    Debtor(s)   :   Adversary No.
                                                    :
                                                    :
Plaintiff/Movant   :
                                                    :
            v.   :
                                                    :
                                                    :
Defendant/Respondent   :

CERTIFICATION THAT BRIEFING COMPLETED

I hereby certify that briefs in the above-captioned matter have been filed by the parties or that the deadline for filing all briefs has expired and the matter is ready for trial or other disposition by the Court.

DATE: _____   By: _____
                                            Signature

                                            _____
                                            Typed Name

                                            _____
                                            Address

                                            _____
                                            Phone No.

                                            _____
                                            List Bar I.D. and State of Admission

PAWB Local Form 16 (07/13)

[Effective March 1, 2012.   Amended effective July 1, 2013.]

LOCAL BANKRUPTCY FORM NO. 17. MOTION FOR WITHDRAWAL OF APPEARANCE AND TERMINATION OF CM/ECF RECORD

IN THE UNITED STATES BANKRUPTCY COURT
FOR THE WESTERN DISTRICT OF PENNSYLVANIA

In Re:	:	Bankruptcy No.
Debtor(s)	:	
	:	Chapter
	:	
Movant(s)	:	
v.	:	Related to Document No.
	:	
	:	
Respondent(s)	:	

MOTION FOR WITHDRAWAL OF APPEARANCE AND TERMINATION OF CM/ECF RECORD

AND NOW comes [attorney's name], counsel to [client's name] in the above-captioned case, and certifies to this Honorable Court that [he/she] (a) has satisfied the interest of [his/her] client [client's name] in the above-captioned case, and (b) has informed and received the consent of [client's name] to withdraw [his/her] appearance in the above-captioned case. Having so certified, and pursuant to W.PA.LBR 9010-2(b), [attorney's name] requests that this Honorable Court grant [his/her] request for leave for withdrawal of [his/her] appearance and termination of [his/her] CM/ECF record in this case.

Date: [date]   Movant/Attorney: _____

[attorney's address]
[attorney's telephone number]
[attorney's Bar ID No.]

ORDER

Based on the foregoing Motion for Withdrawal of Appearance, and pursuant to W.PA.LBR 9010-2(b), it is hereby ORDERED that [attorney's name] is GRANTED leave to withdraw from the above-captioned case, and the Clerk shall terminate the corresponding CM/ECF attorney record in this case.

Date: [date]   _____
                      United States Bankruptcy Judge

PAWB Local Form 17 (07/13)

[Effective March 1, 2012. Amended effective July 1, 2013.]

LOCAL BANKRUPTCY FORM NO. 18. MOTION
FOR PRO HAC VICE ADMISSION

IN THE UNITED STATES BANKRUPTCY COURT
FOR THE WESTERN DISTRICT OF PENNSYLVANIA

In Re: :   Bankruptcy No.
                                                    :   Chapter
                        Debtor   :
           Movant   :
                                                    :   Related to Document No.
                 v.   :
                                                    :
           Respondent (if applicable)   :   Hearing Date and Time:

MOTION FOR *PRO HAC VICE* ADMISSION

1.   This motion for admission *pro hac vice* is being filed on behalf of: (*Applicant's name, firm name, address, phone number, email address, Bar I.D. Number and State of Admission*) by (*Movant's name as identified in Paragraph 4 below*).

2.   Applicant represents _____ *(Name and address of client)* _____. Accompanying this Motion is the required $40 filing fee paid using the Movant's CM/ECF account at the time of filing.

3.   Applicant is a member in good standing of the Bar of_____, is not the subject of any pending disciplinary matters, is personally familiar with the *Local Bankruptcy Rules* of the United States Bankruptcy Court for the Western District of Pennsylvania and shall abide by those *Local Bankruptcy Rules*.

4.   Applicant will be associated with the following attorney acting in this matter as local counsel, who is a member of the Bar of the Bankruptcy Court for the Western District of Pennsylvania: (*Movant's name, firm name, address, phone number, email address, Bar I.D. Number and State of Admission*).

5.   Applicant and Movant have read and shall comply with Local Bankruptcy Rules 9010-1(b), 9010-1(c) and 9010-1(d).

6.   Applicant has previously received *Pro Hac Vice* admission to this Court by Orders dated _____ in the following matters: (*Applicant must identify each prior admission*).

_____   By: _____
Date   Signature of Movant

                               _____
                               Typed Name

                               _____
                               Address

                               _____
                               Phone No.

                               _____
                               List Bar I.D. and State of Admission

PAWB Local Form 18 (07/13)

[Effective March 1, 2012. Amended effective July 1, 2013.]

LOCAL BANKRUPTCY FORM NO. 19.   APPEARANCE OF CHILD SUPPORT CREDITOR OR REPRESENTATIVE

IN THE UNITED STATES BANKRUPTCY COURT
WESTERN DISTRICT OF PENNSYLVANIA

In Re: :   Bankruptcy No.
                                                :
                   Debtor   :
                                                :   Chapter
                                                :
Movant   :
                                                :   Related to Document No.
                   v.   :
                                                :
                                                :   Hearing Date and Time:
                                                :
Respondent(s)   :

APPEARANCE OF CHILD SUPPORT CREDITOR*
OR REPRESENTATIVE

I certify under penalty of perjury that I am a child support creditor* of the above-named debtor, or the authorized representative of such child support creditor, with respect to the child support obligations which is set out below.

Name:
Organization:
Address:

Telephone Number:

_____   X_____
Date   Child Support Creditor* or Authorized Representative

Summary of Child Support Obligation

Amount of arrears: If Child Support has been assigned:

$_____   Amount of Support which is owed under
                                                assignments:

Amount currently due per week or per month: $_____
on a continuing basis:

                                                Amount owed primary child support
                                                Creditor (balance not assigned):

$_____ $_____
  (per week)   (per month)

Attach an itemized statement of account

---

* Child support creditor includes both creditor to whom the debtor has a primary obligation to pay child support as well as any entity to whom such support has been assigned to the Federal Government or to any State or political subdivision of a State.
PAWB Local Form 19 (07/13)

[Effective March 1, 2012. Amended effective July 1, 2013.]

LOCAL BANKRUPTCY FORM NO. 20. NOTICE AND ORDER SETTING HEARING ON AN EXPEDITED BASIS

IN THE UNITED STATES BANKRUPTCY COURT
FOR THE WESTERN DISTRICT OF PENNSYLVANIA

In Re:	)	
	)	Bankruptcy No.
Debtor	)	Adversary No.
	)	Document No.
Plaintiff/Movant	)	Chapter
	)	Hearing Date & Time:
v.	)	_____
	)	
Defendant/Respondent	)	

NOTICE AND ORDER SETTING HEARING ON AN EXPEDITED BASIS

NOTICE IS HEREBY GIVEN THAT an Expedited Motion for _____ has been filed in the above-referenced case by _____.

A hearing has been scheduled for _____ at _____ in _____.

Responses to the motion shall be filed with the Clerk of the Bankruptcy Court and served on parties in interest on or before _____.

A courtesy copy of all responses shall be delivered to chambers with the filing.

Service shall be made as directed below. A certificate of service shall be filed with the Clerk immediately.

_____   _____
Date   United States Bankruptcy Judge

Movant is to complete this notice and file it with the motion for expedited hearing and proposed order granting the substantive relief requested, leaving blank the hearing and response dates. If the Court determines that a hearing is necessary, response and hearing dates will be provided to movant. Movant shall serve a copy of this completed scheduling order and the motion by hand delivery or facsimile on the respondent, trustee, debtor, debtor's attorney, all secured creditors whose interests may be affected by the relief requested, U.S. Trustee and the attorney for any committee. If there is no committee counsel, serve all members of each committee. Movant shall deliver a paper copy of the motion and this notice of hearing to chambers.

PAWB Local Form 20 (07/13)

[Effective March 1, 2012. Amended effective July 1, 2013.]

LOCAL BANKRUPTCY FORM NO. 21. DOMESTIC SUPPORT OBLIGATION CERTIFICATION

IN THE UNITED STATES BANKRUPTCY COURT
FOR THE WESTERN DISTRICT OF PENNSYLVANIA

In Re: :   Bankruptcy No.
                                                :
                        Debtor   :
                                                :   Chapter 13
                                                :
Movant   :
                                                :   Related to Document No.
            v.   :
                                                :
                                                :
                                                :
Respondent(s)   :

DOMESTIC SUPPORT OBLIGATION CERTIFICATION

I, the debtor named below, state as follows:

☐   I do not have any obligation to pay alimony, maintenance, or support to a spouse, former
       spouse, child, child's parent, legal guardian, or responsible relative.
OR
☐   I owe the following obligation(s) for alimony, maintenance, or support:
       ☐ alimony   ☐ child support   ☐ other   owed to:

       Name: _____

       Address: _____

       Phone: _____

       I am ☐ current   OR ☐ in arrears on this obligation.

I HEREBY CERTIFY under penalties of perjury that the information in this certificate, including any
additional sheets provided, is true, correct, and complete as of the date provided below.

       Signature of Debtor: _____

       Type or Print Name of Debtor: _____

       Date Certificate is Signed: _____

       Chapter 13 Case Number: _____

PAWB Local Form 21 (07/13)

[Effective March 1, 2012. Amended effective July 1, 2013.]

LOCAL BANKRUPTCY FORM NO. 22. DOMESTIC SUPPORT OBLIGATION CLAIM HOLDER REPORT

IN THE UNITED STATES BANKRUPTCY COURT
FOR THE WESTERN DISTRICT OF PENNSYLVANIA

In Re: :   Bankruptcy No.
                              Debtor   :
                                                :   Chapter 13
                                                :
Movant   :
                                                :   Related to Document No.
          v.   :
                                                :
                                                :
Respondent(s)   :

**DOMESTIC SUPPORT OBLIGATION
CLAIM HOLDER REPORT**

Debtor Daytime Phone:_____ Evening: _____

Attorney Name:_____

Name of Claim Holder:_____

Address of Claim Holder:_____

_____
Mailing Address   City/State   ZIP Code

Support Type:
   Spousal Support _____ Child Support _____
   Both _____

The following information must be completed for each support obligation:

   Name of Applicable State Agency Where Claim Holder Resides:
   _____

   Payment Address:
   _____
   _____

   _____
   Mailing Address   City/State   ZIP Code

   Account #: _____   Agency Phone #: _____
   Monthly Payment Amount: $_____ Monthly Due Date: _____
   Date Payment Late: _____ Years Remaining: _____

   Are ongoing payments being made to the claim holder by Wage Orders? Yes_____ No_____

Is the Debtor currently employed? Yes_____ No_____

   If yes, Employer Information:

   _____
   Mailing Address   City/State   ZIP Code
PAWB Local Form 22 (07/13)

[Effective March 1, 2012. Amended effective July 1, 2013.]

LOCAL BANKRUPTCY FORM NO. 23.   [RESERVED]

LOCAL BANKRUPTCY FORM NO. 24.   DEBTOR'S CERTIFICATION OF DISCHARGE ELIGIBILITY

IN THE UNITED STATES BANKRUPTCY COURT
FOR THE WESTERN DISTRICT OF PENNSYLVANIA

In Re: :   Bankruptcy No.
                                              :
                          Debtor(s)   :
                                              :   Chapter 13
Trustee, or Debtors(s), Movant   :
                                              :
              v.   :
                                              :
Respondents   :

DEBTOR'S CERTIFICATION OF DISCHARGE ELIGIBILITY

1.   The Debtor has made all payments required by the Chapter 13 Plan.

2.   Include whichever one of the two following statements applies:
[The Debtor is not required to pay any Domestic Support Obligations] OR [The Debtor is required to pay Domestic Support Obligations and the Debtor has paid any amounts payable under a Court Order or Statute that were due on or before the date of this Certification (including amounts due before the petition was filed, but only to the extent provided for in the Plan).]

3.   The Debtor is entitled to a discharge under the terms of Section 1328 of the Bankruptcy Code. The Debtor has not received a prior discharge in a bankruptcy case within the time frames specified in Section 1328(f)(1) of the Bankruptcy Code. Section 1328(h) of the Bankruptcy Code does not render the Debtor ineligible for a discharge.

4.   On [date], at docket number [number], Debtor complied with Federal Rule of Bankruptcy Procedure 1007(c) by filing a *Certification of Completion of Postpetition Instructional Course in Personal Financial Management*, with the *Certificate of Completion* attached to the form.

This Certification is being signed under penalty of perjury by (*include whichever one of the two following statements applies):*[Debtor(s) carefully examined and understand each of the Bankruptcy Code sections referenced in this Certification.] *OR* [Undersigned Counsel duly questioned Debtor(s) about the statements in this Certification and verified the answers in support of this Certification.]

Dated: _____   By: _____
                                 Signature

                                 _____
                                 Name of Filer - Typed

                                 _____
                                 Address of Filer

                                 _____
                                 Email Address of Filer

                                 _____
                                 Phone Number of Filer

                                 _____
                                 Bar I.D. and State of Admission

PAWB Local Form 24 (07/13)

[Effective March 1, 2012. Amended effective July 1, 2013.]

LOCAL BANKRUPTCY FORM NO. 25.   CERTIFICATION OF NO OBJECTION

IN THE UNITED STATES BANKRUPTCY COURT
WESTERN DISTRICT OF PENNSYLVANIA

In Re:	:	
	:	Bankruptcy No.
Debtor	:	Chapter
	:	Document No.
Movant	:	Hearing Date & Time:
	:	
v.	:	
	:	
Respondent(s)	:	

CERTIFICATION OF NO OBJECTION REGARDING
(Insert Pleading Title and Document Number)

The undersigned hereby certifies that, as of the date hereof, no answer, objection or other responsive pleading to the [Application/Motion] filed on _____ has been received. The undersigned further certifies that the Court's docket in this case has been reviewed and no answer, objection or other responsive pleading to the [Application/Motion] appears thereon. Pursuant to the Notice of Hearing, objections to the [Application/Motion] were to be filed and served no later than _____.

It is hereby respectfully requested that the Order attached to the [Application/Motion] be entered by the Court.

Dated: _____   By: _____
                                           Signature

                                           _____
                                           Typed Name

                                           _____
                                           Address

                                           _____
                                           Phone No.

                                           _____
                                           List Bar I.D. and State of Admission

PAWB Local Form 25 (07/13)

[Effective March 1, 2012.   Amended effective July 1, 2013.]

LOCAL BANKRUPTCY FORM NO. 26.   SETTLEMENT AND CERTIFICATION OF COUNSEL

IN THE UNITED STATES BANKRUPTCY COURT
WESTERN DISTRICT OF PENNSYLVANIA

In Re: :
                                                :   Bankruptcy No.
        Debtor   :   Chapter
                                                :   Document No.
        Movant   :   Hearing Date & Time:
                                                :
        v.   :
                                                :
Respondent(s)   :

SETTLEMENT AND CERTIFICATION OF COUNSEL REGARDING
(Insert Pleading Title)

The undersigned hereby certifies that agreement has been reached with the respondent(s) regarding the [Application/Motion] filed on _____ . (State "None" if no prior Motion or Application.)

The signature requirements of W.PA.LBR 5005-6 have been followed in obtaining the agreement of all parties and is reflected in the attached document.

The undersigned further certifies that:

☐   An agreed order and a black-lined version showing the changes made to the order originally filed with the court as an attachment to the motion is attached to this Certificate of Counsel. Deletions are signified by a line in the middle of the original text (strikeout) and additions are signified by text in italics. It is respectfully requested that the attached order be entered by the Court.

☐   No other order has been filed pertaining to the subject matter of this agreement.

☐   The attached document does not require a proposed order.

Dated: _____   By: _____
                                         Signature

                                        _____
                                         Typed Name

                                        _____
                                         Address

                                        _____
                                         Phone No.

                                        _____
                                         List Bar I.D. and State of Admission

PAWB Local Form 26 (07/13)

[Effective March 1, 2012. Amended effective July 1, 2013.]

LOCAL BANKRUPTCY FORM NO. 27.   [RESERVED]

LOCAL BANKRUPTCY FORM NO. 28. DOCUMENT AND LOAN HISTORY ABSTRACT

IN THE UNITED STATES BANKRUPTCY COURT
FOR THE WESTERN DISTRICT OF PENNSYLVANIA

In Re: :
                                   :   Bankruptcy No.

       Debtor   :   Chapter
                                     :   Document No.

       Movant   :   Hearing Date & Time:
                                     :

          v.   :
                                     :

       Respondent(s)   :

DOCUMENT AND LOAN HISTORY ABSTRACT
(COMPLETE A SEPARATE ABSTRACT FOR
THE ORIGINAL TRANSACTION AND EACH ASSIGNMENT)

TYPE OF
INSTRUMENT

___ Mortgage   ___ Retail Installment Contract
___ Assignment   ___ UCC Financing Statement
___ Lease   ___ Promissory Note / Security Agreement
___ Other (describe) _____

PARTIES   _____ Borrower/Lessee
                     _____ Lender/Lessor

DATE OF INSTRUMENT _____ # OF PAGES _____

ESSENTIAL
TERMS

_____ Original Principal Balance
_____ Term
_____ Interest Rate
_____ First Payment Due
_____ Payment Amount
_____ Frequency of Payments (weekly, monthly, yearly, etc.)
_____ First Payment Due Date
Last Payment Applied to Installment due on _____
_____ Amount in Arrears
_____ Total Amount of Claim on Date of Filing of Petition
_____ Total Amount of Claim on Date of Filing of Motion

SECURED (LEASED) PROPERTY DESCRIPTION

___ Real Property   ___ Motor Vehicle   ___ Other
_____ Address/Description

Lien Recording

_____ Recorder of Deeds
_____ County/Commonwealth/State
_____ Secretary of State/Commonwealth/State
_____ Bureau of Motor Vehicles (Commonwealth/State _____)
_____ Other (Describe) _____
_____ Recording Date
_____ Book & Page/Instrument Number

OTHER ESSENTIAL INFORMATION:
PROOF OF CLAIM FILED WITH CLERK, U.S. BANKRUPTCY COURT _____ (Yes/No)

PAWB Local Form 28 (07/13)

[Effective March 1, 2012. Amended effective July 1, 2013.]

LOCAL BANKRUPTCY FORM NO. 29.   NOTICE REGARDING FILING OF MAILING MATRIX

IN THE UNITED STATES BANKRUPTCY COURT
FOR THE WESTERN DISTRICT OF PENNSYLVANIA

In Re: :   Bankruptcy No.
                                             :
                        Debtor   :
                                             :   Chapter
                                             :
Movant   :
                                             :   Related to Document No.
            v.   :
                                             :
                                             :
Respondent (if none, then "No Respondent")   :

NOTICE REGARDING FILING OF MAILING MATRIX

In accordance with Local Bankruptcy Rule 1007-1(e) I, _____,
counsel for the debtor(s) in the above-captioned case, hereby certify that the following list of creditors'
names and addresses was uploaded through the creditor maintenance option in CM/ECF to the above-
captioned case.

                              By: _____
                                     Signature

                                     _____
                                     Typed Name

                                     _____
                                     Address

                                     _____
                                     Phone No.

                                     _____
                                     List Bar I.D. and State of Admission

PAWB Local Form 29 (07/13)

[Effective March 1, 2012.   Amended effective July 1, 2013.]

LOCAL BANKRUPTCY FORM NO. 30. NOTICE REGARDING MODIFICATION TO MAILING MATRIX

IN THE UNITED STATES BANKRUPTCY COURT
FOR THE WESTERN DISTRICT OF PENNSYLVANIA

In Re: :   Bankruptcy No.
                                                  :
                      Debtor   :
                                                  :   Chapter
                                                  :
Movant   :
                                                  :   Related to Document No.
            v.   :
                                                  :
                                                  :
                                                  :
Respondent (if none, then "No Respondent")   :

NOTICE REGARDING MODIFICATION TO MAILING MATRIX

In accordance with Local Bankruptcy Rule 1007-1(f) I, _____,

counsel for the debtor(s) in the above-captioned case, hereby certify that the following list of creditors'

names and addresses was uploaded through the creditor maintenance option in CM/ECF to the above-

captioned case regarding the filing of an amendment to the schedules.

                    By: _____
                             Signature

                             _____
                             Typed Name

                             _____
                             Address

                             _____
                             Phone No.

                             _____
                             List Bar I.D. and State of Admission

PAWB Local Form 30 (07/13)

[Effective March 1, 2012. Amended effective July 1, 2013.]

LOCAL BANKRUPTCY FORM NO. 31. APPLICATION FOR ADMISSION TO BANKRUPTCY MEDIATION PROGRAM REGISTER

IN THE UNITED STATES BANKRUPTCY COURT
FOR THE WESTERN DISTRICT OF PENNSYLVANIA

APPLICATION FOR ADMISSION TO
BANKRUPTCY MEDIATION PROGRAM REGISTER

General Instructions

(1)   Each applicant shall read Local Bankruptcy Rules 9019-2 through 9019-7.

(2)   If additional space is needed to respond fully to any item on this application, the response(s) shall be set forth in an attached, signed separate page with an identification of the question number to which it responds.

(3)   Attorney applicants shall complete Parts I, II and IV of this Application.

(4)   Non-attorney applicants shall complete Parts I, III and IV of this Application.

Part I. ALL APPLICANTS.

Name: _____

Firm: _____

Office Address: _____
                                        Street

_____
     City   State   Zip Code

Office Phone: _____

Office Fax: _____

E-Mail: _____

Pa. I.D. or other Professional Association I.D. _____

Part II. ATTORNEY APPLICANTS

1.   List each state and federal court in which you currently are licensed to practice law:

Court   Date of Admission

_____
_____
_____
_____
_____
_____

2.   If you have bankruptcy experience, list the three most recent adversary proceedings or contested matters in which you have served as attorney of record for a party-in-interest from commencement through conclusion (i.e., judgment, order, or stipulation).

Case Title   Case Number   Dates   Representation

a. _____
_____

b. _____
_____

c. _____
_____

3.   If you have bankruptcy experience, list the most recent three bankruptcy cases in which you have served as the principal attorney of record (without regard to the party represented) from commencement to conclusion.

Case Title   Case Number   Dates   Representation

a. _____
_____
_____

b. _____
_____
_____

c. _____
_____
_____

4.   If you have participated in mediation or other ADR processes (either as a neutral or in another role), list the three most recent of those matters below.

Case Title	Case Number	Dates	Representation

a. _____

b. _____

c. _____

Part III. NON-ATTORNEY APPLICANTS

1.   If you have participated in mediation or other ADR processes (either as a neutral or in another role), list no more than three of those matters below.

Case Title	Case Number	Dates	Representation

a. _____

b. _____

c. _____

Part IV. ALL APPLICANTS

1.   List any professional licenses you hold (other than bar admission) and include the number of years you have practiced in each profession listed (e.g., accountant, real estate broker, appraiser, engineer).

Profession	Accrediting Organization	Years of Practice

_____

_____

_____

_____

2.   List any professional organizations of which you are or were an active member, the length of your membership, and any positions held and/or projects completed.

Organization   No. of Years   Active/Retired   Positions/Projects

_____
_____
_____
_____

3.   List any relevant bankruptcy or mediation experience not included in any response above.

_____
_____
_____
_____
_____

4.   List any mediation or other alternative dispute resolution training that you have completed and that has qualified for continuing professional education credit or has been approved by a court of competent jurisdiction within the past three years.

Course Title   Trainer/School   Court/Sponsor   CLE Credit Hours   Dates

_____
_____
_____
_____

5.   List speaking engagements, panel/seminar participation teaching experience, etc., within the past three years.

_____
_____
_____
_____

6.   List any other relevant experience, training, skills, honors, publications, or other information which you would like considered in connection with this application.

_____
_____
_____
_____
_____

7.   Have you been removed from any professional organization, or have you resigned from any professional organization while an investigation into allegations of professional misconduct was pending?

Yes _____   No _____

If so, please explain the circumstances of such removal or resignation.

_____

_____

_____

8.   Check the city(ies) in which you are willing to conduct mediation conferences:

_____ Pittsburgh   _____ Johnstown

_____ Erie   _____ Other (specify): _____

I hereby certify that I have read Local Bankruptcy Rules 9019-2 through 9019-7, that I meet the qualifications set forth therein for admission to this Court's Register of mediators, and that I will fully comply with the relevant provisions of this Court's General Orders, Local Rules, Local Forms, and any modifications thereto relating to mediation. I will immediately contact the Mediation Program Administrator, and any parties for whom I have accepted appointment as a mediator, upon learning I am no longer qualified to serve pursuant to the provisions of Local Bankruptcy Rule 9019-3.

If I am applying for appointment as an attorney mediator, I certify that I am a member in good standing of the state and federal bar(s) listed above. If I am applying for appointment as a non-attorney mediator, I certify that I am a member in good standing of my profession.

I consent to disclosure of the information contained in this Application to Court personnel and to the parties and their representatives whose matters have been referred to the Bankruptcy Mediation Program of this Court.

I declare under penalty of perjury that the information contained in this Application is true and correct.

Executed on _____, _____ at _____, _____.
                      (date)   (year)   (city)   (state)

By typing my name in the box below, it is my intent to affix my signature to this application as though it were my handwritten signature. I understand and accept that this digital signature shall have the full force and effect of a handwritten signature.

_____

[Effective March 1, 2012. Amended effective July 1, 2013.]

LOCAL BANKRUPTCY FORM NO. 32. MEDIATOR'S CERTIFICATE OF COMPLETION OF MEDIATION CONFERENCE

IN THE UNITED STATES BANKRUPTCY COURT
FOR THE WESTERN DISTRICT OF PENNSYLVANIA

In re:)   Bankruptcy No. _____
_____ ,   )
                Debtor   )
_____   )
)   Motion No. _____
_____ ,   )
         Plaintiff/Movant   )   Adversary No. _____
)
             vs.   )
)
_____   )
     Defendant/Respondent   )
_____   )

MEDIATOR'S CERTIFICATE OF COMPLETION OF MEDIATION CONFERENCE

      1.   I hereby certify that pursuant to an order of assignment of this Court to the Bankruptcy Mediation Program dated _____, a Mediation Program Conference was held on _____ /was not held.
(list all date(s) on which conference was held)

      2.   A settlement/resolution of this matter was _____/was not_____ reached.

Dated: _____   Mediator: _____
                                            Signature

                              Type or print:

                              Name:_____

                              Address:_____

                                          _____

                              Telephone:_____

PAWB Local Form 32 (07/13)

[Effective March 1, 2012. Amended effective July 1, 2013.]

LOCAL BANKRUPTCY FORM NO. 33.   [RESERVED EFFECTIVE JUNE 15, 2016]

LOCAL BANKRUPTCY FORM NO. 34. [RESERVED EFFECTIVE JUNE 15, 2016]

U.S. BANKRUPTCY COURT

LOCAL BANKRUPTCY FORM NO. 35. NOTICE
OF INTENT TO REQUEST REDACTION

IN THE UNITED STATES BANKRUPTCY COURT
FOR THE WESTERN DISTRICT OF PENNSYLVANIA

In Re:	:	Bankruptcy No.
	:	Adversary Proceeding No.
Debtor	:	
	:	Chapter
	:	
Movant	:	
	:	Related to Document No.
v.	:	
	:	
	:	
Respondent (if none, then "No Respondent")	:	

NOTICE OF INTENT TO REQUEST REDACTION

WHEREAS, on [INSERT DATE] a transcript was filed in the above-captioned case at Document No. [INSERT DOCUMENT NUMBER],

NOTICE IS HEREBY GIVEN THAT:

Pursuant to W.PA.LBR 5007-1 and Rule 9037 of the *Federal Rules of Bankruptcy Procedure,* I have reviewed the above-referenced transcript and intend to serve upon the transcriber, [INSERT NAME OF TRANSCRIBER], and all parties in interest, within twenty-one (21) days after [INSERT THE ABOVE-REFERENCED DATE OF FILING], a detailed request to redact information from that transcript.

I understand that the above-referenced transcriber has until thirty-one (31) days after [INSERT THE ABOVE-REFERENCED DATE OF FILING] to deliver a redacted version of the transcript to the Court.

I HEREBY CERTIFY THAT:

On [INSERT DATE] I filed a copy of this *Notice* with the Court and served a copy on: [INSERT RECIPIENTS OF ELECTRONIC SERVICE] electronically using the CM/ECF system and [INSERT RECIPIENTS (INCLUDING TRANSCRIBER) OF REGULAR MAIL SERVICE] using the United States Postal Service.

Date: _____   Signed: _____

_____
Name of Filer - Typed

_____
Address

_____
Phone No.

_____
Bar I.D. and State of Admission

_____
Name of Party Represented

PAWB Local Form 35 (07/13)

[Effective March 1, 2012. Amended effective July 1, 2013.]

LOCAL BANKRUPTCY FORM NO. 36.   REDACTION REQUEST

IN THE UNITED STATES BANKRUPTCY COURT
FOR THE WESTERN DISTRICT OF PENNSYLVANIA

In Re:	:	Bankruptcy No.
	:	Adversary Proceeding No.
Debtor	:	
	:	Chapter
	:	
Movant	:	
	:	Related to Document No.
v.	:	
	:	
	:	
Respondent (if none, then "No Respondent")	:	

REDACTION REQUEST

To: [INSERT COURT REPORTER/TRANSCRIBER]

From: [INSERT NAME OF PERSON MAKING THE REQUEST]
Address:

Telephone:

On behalf of: [INSERT NAME OF PARTY REPRESENTED or "SELF"]

RE: Western District of Pennsylvania Bankruptcy Case Number _____
Document Number _____
Hearing Dated _____

Request Date: _____

Pursuant to W.PA.LBR 5007-1 and understanding that the redaction of any information other than the identifiers specifically enumerated in Rule 9037 of the *Federal Rules of Bankruptcy Procedure* requires a separate motion and Court approval, the undersigned hereby requests the following redaction of personal identifiers in the above-referenced transcript.

Page(s)	Line(s)	Identifier as is	Identifier as redacted

Page(s)	Line(s)	Identifier as is	Identifier as redacted

Date: _____

Signed: _____

_____
Name of Filer - Typed

_____
Address

_____
Phone No.

_____
Bar I.D. and State of Admission

_____
Name of Party Represented

This form must be served on the transcriber identified above and all parties in interest; it should not be filed with the Court.

PAWB Local Form 36 (07/13)   Page 2 of 2

[Effective March 1, 2012. Amended effective July 1, 2013.]

LOCAL BANKRUPTCY FORM NO. 37. REQUEST TO RESTRICT PUBLIC ACCESS TO CLAIM

IN THE UNITED STATES BANKRUPTCY COURT
FOR THE WESTERN DISTRICT OF PENNSYLVANIA

In Re:	:	Bankruptcy No.
	:	Adversary Proceeding No.
Debtor	:	
	:	Chapter
	:	
Movant	:	
	:	Related to Claim No.
v.	:	
	:	
	:	
Respondent (if none, then "No Respondent")	:	

REQUEST TO RESTRICT PUBLIC ACCESS TO CLAIM

Pursuant to W.PA.LBR 9037-1 and understanding that the redaction of any information other than the identifiers specifically enumerated in Fed. R. Bankr. P. 9037 requires a separate motion and Court approval, under penalty of perjury, the UNDERSIGNED HEREBY CERTIFIES that:

1.   [creditor's name] filed a proof of claim, Claim No. [specify the number of the unredacted claim] in the above-captioned case on [date of filing original claim] which contains one or more of the identifiers enumerated in Fed. R. Bankr. P. 9037.

2.   On [date of filing the redacted claim], [creditor's name] filed an amended claim on the claims register in compliance with W.PA.LBR 3002-2(a), a copy of which is attached hereto, and the only change made to the original claim is the redaction of personal identifiers.

3.   I am requesting that the Court take whatever steps are necessary to restrict public access to the unredacted claim.

Date: _____   Signed: _____

                                         On behalf of: _____
                                                       Name of Creditor

                                         _____
                                         Name of Filer - Typed

                                         _____
                                         Address of Filer

                                         _____
                                         Email Address of Filer

                                         _____
                                         Phone Number of Filer

                                         _____
                                         Bar I.D. and State of Admission

PAWB Local Form 37 (07/13)

[Effective March 1, 2012. Amended effective July 1, 2013.]

U.S. BANKRUPTCY COURT

LOCAL BANKRUPTCY FORM NO. 38. REQUEST TO RESTRICT PUBLIC ACCESS TO [SPECIFY DOCUMENT]

IN THE UNITED STATES BANKRUPTCY COURT
FOR THE WESTERN DISTRICT OF PENNSYLVANIA

In Re: :   Bankruptcy No.
                               :   Adversary Proceeding No.
              Debtor   :
                               :   Chapter
                               :
Movant   :
                               :   Related to Document No.
        v.   :
                               :
                               :
Respondent (if none, then "No Respondent")   :

REQUEST TO RESTRICT PUBLIC ACCESS TO [specify document]

Pursuant to W.PA.LBR 9037-1 and understanding that the redaction of any information other than the identifiers specifically enumerated in Fed. R. Bankr. P. 9037 requires a separate motion and Court approval, under penalty of perjury, the **UNDERSIGNED HEREBY CERTIFIES** that:

        1.   A [specify the document to be redacted] was filed in the above-captioned case on [date of filing original document] at document # [state the docket entry number] which contains one or more of the identifiers enumerated in Fed. R. Bankr. P. 9037.

        2.   Attached hereto is an amended version of the [specify the document], and the only change made to the original document is the redaction of personal identifiers.

        3.   I am requesting that the Court accept the attached [specify the document] in substitution for the unredacted version, and to take whatever steps are necessary to restrict public access to the unredacted version.

Date: _____   Signed: _____

                                                 _____
                                                 Name of Filer - Typed

                                                 _____
                                                 Address

                                                 _____
                                                 Email Address

                                                 _____
                                                 Phone No.

                                                 _____
                                                 Bar I.D. and State of Admission

PAWB Local Form 38 (07/13)

[Effective March 1, 2012. Amended effective July 1, 2013.]

LOCAL BANKRUPTCY FORM NO. 39.   MOTION
FOR LOSS MITIGATION

IN THE UNITED STATES BANKRUPTCY COURT
FOR THE WESTERN DISTRICT OF PENNSYLVANIA

In Re: :   Bankruptcy No.
                                                :   Chapter
                        Debtor   :
                                                :
                                                :
Movant   :
                                                :
            v.   :
                                                :
                                                :
Respondent (if none, then "No Respondent")   :

MOTION FOR LOSS MITIGATION

1.   The Debtor(s) in this case hereby request the commencement of the Court's *Loss Mitigation Program* (LMP) as set forth in *W.PA.LBR 9020-1 through 9020-7* with respect to property located at: [FULL ADDRESS OF THE ELIGIBLE PROPERTY].

2.   The Creditor is [FULL NAME OF CREDITOR] and [is / is not] registered on the Portal.

3.   The Creditor is the holder of a [first / second / third] mortgage.

4.   A *Certification of LMP Eligibility and Readiness* (Local Bankruptcy Form 40) and a *Proposed Loss Mitigation Order* (Local Bankruptcy Form 41) are attached to this Motion pursuant to *W.PA.LBR 9020-2(c)*.

5.   Pursuant to *W.PA.LBR 9020-2(d)*, any objection to the relief requested herein must be filed within fourteen (14) days of service of the Motion.

Date: _____   Signed: _____

                                        On behalf of: _____
                                                        Name of Debtor(s)

                                        _____
                                        Name of Attorney - Typed

                                        _____
                                        Postal Address of Attorney

                                        _____
                                        Email Address of Attorney

                                        _____
                                        Phone Number of Attorney

                                        _____
                                        Attorney's Bar I.D. and State of Admission

[Amended effective April 1, 2014.]

LOCAL BANKRUPTCY FORM NO. 40.   CERTIFICATION OF LMP ELIGIBILITY AND READINESS

IN THE UNITED STATES BANKRUPTCY COURT
FOR THE WESTERN DISTRICT OF PENNSYLVANIA

In Re: :   Bankruptcy No.
                                                :   Chapter
                     Debtor   :
                                                :
                                                :
Movant   :
                                                :
         v.   :
                                                :
                                                :
Respondent (if none, then "No Respondent")   :

CERTIFICATION OF LMP ELIGIBILITY AND READINESS

I.   CERTIFICATION OF THE DEBTOR(S)

[I _____ am / We _____ and _____ are] the [debtor / debtors] in this case and hereby certify that:

1.   [I / We] will participate in the Court's *Loss Mitigation Program* (LMP) as set forth in *W.PA.LBR 9020-1 through 9020-7* [in full cooperation with my / our undersigned counsel (if represented by an attorney)] in good faith.

2.   [I / We] understand and agree to the ongoing obligation to promptly provide information and documentation that may be reasonably requested by the Creditor during the LMP process.

3.   [I / We] will make (or cause to be made) adequate protection payments to [FULL NAME OF CREDITOR] in the amount of $ _____ each month during the LMP period, pursuant to *W.PA.LBR 9020-3(f)*, unless and until otherwise ordered by the Court.

4.   [I / We] understand that commencing the LMP is voluntary, and that [I am / we are] not required to enter into any agreement or settlement with any other party, and no other party is required to enter into any agreement or settlement with [me / us] as part of the LMP.

5.   [I / We] understand that [I am / we are] not required to request dismissal of this case as part of any resolution or settlement that is offered or agreed to during the LMP.

6.   [I / We] understand that if [I / we] do not fully comply with the requirements of the LMP, our participation in the LMP may be terminated.

Date: _____   _____
                                     Debtor

Date: _____   _____
                                     Joint Debtor (if any)

II. CERTIFICATION OF COUNSEL TO DEBTOR(S)

I, [ATTORNEY NAME] represent [NAME(S) OF DEBTOR(S)] (my "Client(s)") in this case and hereby certify that:

1.   I have discussed the details of the Court's *Loss Mitigation Program* (LMP) set forth in *W.PA.LBR 9020-1 through 9020-7* with my Client(s).

2.   I performed adequate due diligence to determine my Client's eligibility for the LMP. As part of this process, I obtained and reviewed all loan documentation from my Client and confirmed all pertinent details of the Eligible Loan, including but not limited to, the following: (i) the complete loan number; (ii) the original loan amount, origination date and maturity date; (iii) the principal balance and interest rate; (iv) monthly principal, interest and escrow payments; (v) the specific amount of any arrears; (vi) any applicable balloon payments or other conditions of repayment; and (vii) the details of any previous activities related to modification of the loan. I also confirmed that the debtor is named on the applicable loan documentation and I identified the complete name of the Creditor as registered on the Portal (to the extent the Creditor is registered on the Portal).

3.   In light of my due diligence, I [am aware of no reasons why the commencement of the LMP in this case would be futile or otherwise contrary to reasonable expectations of a successful outcome.] OR [I have a colorable argument for LMP notwithstanding the following fact(s) which might hinder the pursuit of a successful outcome: [IF KNOWN, COUNSEL MUST SPECIFY THESE FACT(S), for example, the debt-to-income ratio is outside of the standard range for loan modification, the loan was recently denied for modification, the loan is currently under a modification, and any similarly problematic facts]. I am moving for the commencement of the LMP because [FOR EACH OF THE AFOREMENTIONED FACTS, PROVIDE SPECIFIC REASONS WHY LMP IS SOUGHT IN GOOD FAITH].

4.   I have fully complied with the requirements set forth in *W.PA.LBR 9020-2(b)(1), (2), and (3)* and I am prepared to upload the required documents to the Portal upon entry of the Loss Mitigation Order.

Date: _____   Signed: _____

                                           Name of Attorney - Typed

                                           Postal Address of Attorney

                                           Email Address of Attorney

                                           Phone Number of Attorney

                                           Attorney's Bar I.D. and State of Admission

PAWB Local Form 40 (04/14)   Page 2 of 2

[Amended effective April 1, 2014.]

LOCAL BANKRUPTCY FORM NO. 41. LOSS MITIGATION ORDER

IN THE UNITED STATES BANKRUPTCY COURT
FOR THE WESTERN DISTRICT OF PENNSYLVANIA

In Re:	:	Bankruptcy No.
	:	Chapter
Debtor	:	
	:	
	:	Related to Document No.
Movant	:	
	:	
v.	:	Hearing Date and Time:
	:	
	:	

Respondent (if none, then "No Respondent"):

LOSS MITIGATION ORDER

A **Motion for Loss Mitigation** was filed by _____ on _____. The Parties have had notice and an opportunity to object and the Court has reviewed any objections filed thereto.

AND NOW, this _____ day of _____, 20_____, it is hereby *ORDERED* that:

(1)   The following parties are directed to participate in the Court's **Loss Mitigation Program (LMP)** as set forth in *W.PA.LBR 9020-1* through *9020-7*.

Debtor: _____

Creditor: _____

(2)   **During the Loss Mitigation Period**, the Debtor shall make (or cause to be made) adequate protection payments in the amount of $ _____ per month to the Creditor or the Creditor's designee pursuant to *W.PA.LBR 9020-3(g)*.

(3)   **Within fourteen (14) days from the entry of this Order**, the Creditor shall register and post its entire Core LMP Package on the Portal (if not previously registered) pursuant to *W.PA.LBR 9020-4(b)*.

(4)   **Within seven (7) days from the entry of this Order** or Creditor's registration on the Portal, whichever is later, the Debtor shall upload a completed Core LMP Package through the Portal pursuant to *W.PA.LBR 9020-4(c)*.

(5)   **Within fourteen (14) days of the debtor's submission of the Core LMP Package**, the Creditor shall acknowledge receipt and designate a single point of contact for Debtor's review, pursuant to *W.PA.LBR 9020-4(d)*.

(6)   **Within sixty (60) days from the entry of this Order**, the Debtor shall file and serve upon all interested parties an LMP Status Report, pursuant to *W.PA.LBR 9020-4(e)*.

PAWB Local Form 41 (04/14)   Page1 of 2

(7)   *Ninety (90) days from the entry of this Order,* the LMP Period shall terminate unless extended pursuant to *W.PA.LBR 9020-5(b).*

(8)   *Within seven (7) days of the termination of the Loss Mitigation Period,* the Debtor shall submit an LMP Final Report pursuant to *W.PA.LBR 9020-4(f).*

(9)   Debtor shall *immediately* serve a copy of this Order on Creditor and file a certificate of service evidencing same.

_____
United States Bankruptcy Judge

[Amended effective April 1, 2014.]

LOCAL BANKRUPTCY FORM NO. 42. MOTION TO EXTEND THE LOSS MITIGATION PERIOD

IN THE UNITED STATES BANKRUPTCY COURT
FOR THE WESTERN DISTRICT OF PENNSYLVANIA

In Re:	:	Bankruptcy No.
	:	Chapter
Debtor	:	
	:	
	:	[Related to Document No.]
Movant	:	
	:	
v.	:	[Hearing Date and Time:]
	:	
	:	
Respondent (if none, then "No Respondent")	:	

MOTION TO EXTEND THE LOSS MITIGATION PERIOD

[FULL NAME OF MOVANT] hereby requests an extension of the Loss Mitigation Period in this case, pursuant to *W.PA.LBR 9020-5(b)*, and in support for said request attests as follows:

Part 1: LMP Background

[In separately numbered paragraphs, and in chronological order, identify each docket event related to the LMP in this case; for example "1.   On October 11, 2013, Debtor filed a *Motion For Loss Mitigation* at Docket N0. 23." Include in the chronology an account of each hearing and conference related to the LMP in this case; for example "13. On December 15, 2013 a status conference was held before the Honorable Thomas P. Agresti, resulting in the entry of an Order on December 16, 2013 at Docket No. 25. Said Order required Debtor to submit IRS Form 4506T to the creditor via the Portal on or before January 3, 2014."]

Part 2: LMP Progress

[In separately numbered paragraphs, and in chronological order, identify each of the specific steps taken by the debtor and creditor towards arriving at a consensual resolution as of the date of this Motion]

Part 3: Reasons Supporting an Extension of the LMP Period

[In separately numbered paragraphs, set forth the specific reasons why the creditor and debtor are unable to reach a consensual resolution on or before the present LMP termination date as ordered by the Court, and set forth the specific reasons why an extension of the LMP Period should be granted by the Court.]

A proposed order (substantially in the form of Local Bankruptcy Form 43) and a complete and current printout of the entire account history from the Portal are attached hereto pursuant to *W.PA.LBR 9020-5(b)*.

Date: _____   Signed: _____

                                  On behalf of: _____
                                                    Name of Debtor(s)

                                  _____
                                  Name of Attorney - Typed

                                  _____
                                  Postal Address of Attorney

                                  _____
                                  Email Address of Attorney

                                  _____
                                  Phone Number of Attorney

                                  _____
                                  Attorney's Bar I.D. and State of Admission

[Amended effective April 1, 2014.]

LOCAL BANKRUPTCY FORM NO. 43. PROPOSED ORDER EXTENDING THE LOSS MITIGATION PERIOD

IN THE UNITED STATES BANKRUPTCY COURT
FOR THE WESTERN DISTRICT OF PENNSYLVANIA

In Re: :   Bankruptcy No.
                                              :   Chapter
                    Debtor   :
                                              :
                                              :   Related to Document No.
Movant   :
                                              :
        v.   :   Hearing Date and Time:
                                              :
                                              :
Respondent   :
        (if none, then "No Respondent"):

ORDER

A *Loss Mitigation Order* dated_____ , was entered in the above matter at Document

No. _____. On_____[date]_____, a *Motion to Extend the Loss Mitigation Period* was filed

by__[movant]_____ at Document No._____.

AND NOW, this_____day of_____, 20____, it is hereby *ORDERED,*
ADJUDGED AND DECREED that the loss mitigation period is *extended up to and including*
_____, 20 ____.

                                              _____
                                              United States Bankruptcy Judge

PAWB Local Form 43 (04/14)   Page 1 of 1

[Amended effective April 1, 2014.]

LOCAL BANKRUPTCY FORM NO. 44.   MOTION TO TERMINATE THE LOSS MITIGATION PROGRAM

IN THE UNITED STATES BANKRUPTCY COURT
FOR THE WESTERN DISTRICT OF PENNSYLVANIA

In Re: :   Bankruptcy No.
                                                :   Chapter
                        Debtor   :
                                                :
                                                :   [Related to Document No.]
Movant   :
                                                :
          v.   :   [Hearing Date and Time:]
                                                :
                                                :
Respondent (if none, then "No Respondent")   :

MOTION TO TERMINATE THE LOSS MITIGATION PROGRAM

[FULL NAME OF MOVANT] hereby requests the termination of the Loss Mitigation Program in this case, pursuant to *W.PA.LBR 9020-5(c)*, and in support for said request attests as follows:

Part 1: LMP Background

[In separately numbered paragraphs, and in chronological order, identify each docket event related to the LMP in this case; for example "1.   On October 11, 2013, Debtor filed a *Motion For Loss Mitigation* at Docket N0. 23." Include in the chronology an account of each hearing and conference related to the LMP in this case; for example "13.   On December 15, 2013 a status conference was held before the Honorable Thomas P. Agresti, resulting in the entry of an Order on December 16, 2013 at Docket No. 25. Said Order required Debtor to submit IRS Form 4506T to the creditor via the Portal on or before January 3, 2014."]

Part 2: LMP Progress

[In separately numbered paragraphs, and in chronological order, identify each of the specific steps taken by the debtor and creditor towards arriving at a consensual resolution as of the date of this Motion]

Part 3: Reasons Supporting a Termination of the LMP Period

[In separately numbered paragraphs, set forth the specific reasons why the creditor and debtor are unable to reach a consensual resolution, and/or set forth the specific reasons why the Court should terminate the Loss Mitigation Program in this case.]

A proposed order substantially in the form of Local Bankruptcy Form 45, and a complete and current printout of the entire account history from the Portal, are attached hereto pursuant to *W.PA.LBR 9020-5(c)*

Date: _____

Signed: _____

On behalf of: _____
                        Name of Debtor(s)

_____
Name of Attorney - Typed

_____
Postal Address of Attorney

_____
Email Address of Attorney

_____
Phone Number of Attorney

_____
Attorney's Bar I.D. and State of Admission

[Amended effective April 1, 2014.]

LOCAL BANKRUPTCY FORM NO. 45.   PROPOSED ORDER
TERMINATING THE LOSS MITIGATION PROGRAM

IN THE UNITED STATES BANKRUPTCY COURT
FOR THE WESTERN DISTRICT OF PENNSYLVANIA

In Re: :   Bankruptcy No.
                                          :   Chapter
                         Debtor   :
                                          :
                                          :   Related to Document No.
Movant   :
                                          :
         v.   :   Hearing Date and Time:
                                          :
                                          :
                                          :
Respondent   :
         (if none, then "No Respondent") :

ORDER

        A *Loss Mitigation Order* dated _____, was entered in the above matter at Document

No. _____. On ____[date]_____, a *Motion to Terminate the Loss Mitigation Program* was

filed by___[movant]_____ at Document No. ____.

        AND NOW, this _____ day of _____, 20___, it is hereby *ORDERED,*

ADJUDGED AND DECREED that the loss mitigation program in this case is *terminated, effective*

_____, *20* _____, and the Final Report is due seven (7) days thereafter pursuant to W.PA.LBR

9020-4(f).

                                                  _____
                                                  United States Bankruptcy Judge

[Amended effective April 1, 2014.]

LOCAL BANKRUPTCY FORM NO. 46.   ORDER
SUBSTITUTING LMP SERVICER
IN THE UNITED STATES BANKRUPTCY COURT
FOR THE WESTERN DISTRICT OF PENNSYLVANIA

In Re: :   Bankruptcy No.
                                          :   Chapter
                     Debtor   :
                                          :
                                          :   Related to Document No.
Movant   :
                                          :
         v.   :   Hearing Date and Time:
                                          :
                                          :
Respondent   :
    (if none, then "No Respondent")   :

ORDER SUBSTITUTING LMP SERVICER

On [DATE OF NOTICE OF REQUEST FOR LMP] the above named Debtor(s) filed a
Motion for Loss Mitigation upon which the Court entered a *Loss Mitigation Order* dated [DATE OF
DOCKETING], at Document No. __, naming [FORMER SERVICER] ("Former Servicer") as the Party
responsible for representing the creditor in the LMP and setting forth certain deadlines for the then
named Respondent.

Subsequent to entry of the above-referenced Order, the Debtor(s) was notified that the
Former Servicer changed and that the current Servicer/Lender is _____ [FULL AND
COMPLETE NAME OF CURRENT SERVICER] with an address of [FULL AND COMPLETE
ADDRESS OF CURRENT SERVICER] ("Current Servicer"). On ___[DATE], the Debtor complied
with all its obligations to properly designate the Current Servicer on the LMP Portal and now it is
incumbent on the Court to relieve the Former Servicer from any further responsibilities under the current
Loss Mitigation Order and formally transfer those duties, responsibilities and obligations to the Current
Servicer.

AND NOW, this *[DAY]* of *[MONTH, 20__]*, for the foregoing reasons it is hereby *ORDERED, ADJUDGED and DECREED* that:

(1)   [FORMER SERVICER] is relieved from any further responsibility pursuant to the *Loss Mitigation Order* referred to above and that *Order* is *VACATED* as to it.

(2)   [CURRENT SERVICER] is now designated as the Current Servicer responsible for completion of all LMP duties, responsibilities and obligations previously imposed on the Former Servicer referred to in Paragraph 1, above. The Current Servicer is now fully responsible for compliance with all LMP requirements as if originally designated in the *Loss Mitigation Order* in the first instance.

(3)   Within three (3) days of entry of this *Order*, the party filing this proposed order shall upload this signed *Order* on the LMP Portal and serve this *Order* electronically on the Chapter 13 Trustee at the following email address: **LMP@chapter13trusteewdpa.com.** The Debtor shall not be entitled to rely on CM/ECF or United States Mail for service of this *Order* on the Chapter 13 Trustee. The Debtor(s) Certificate of Service shall reflect service upon the above identified email address.

(4)   The Chapter 13 Trustee is authorized and directed to make payments to the [CURRENT SERVICER], beginning with the next distribution date that is not less than ten (10) days from service of this *Order* upon the Chapter 13 Trustee.

_____
UNITED STATES BANKRUPTCY JUDGE

Case administrator to serve:
     Debtor(s)
     Counsel for Debtor(s)
     Ronda J. Winnecour, Esq. Ch 13 Trustee
     |Counsel for Creditor|

[Amended effective April 1, 2014.]

LOCAL BANKRUPTCY FORM NO. 47. INTERIM MORTGAGE MODIFICATION ORDER

IN THE UNITED STATES BANKRUPTCY COURT
FOR THE WESTERN DISTRICT OF PENNSYLVANIA

In Re: :   Bankruptcy No.
                                          :   Chapter
                 Debtor   :
                                          :
                                          :   Related to Document No.
Movant   :
                                          :
          v.   :   Hearing Date and Time:
                                          :
                                          :
Respondent   :
   (if none, then "No Respondent")   :

INTERIM MORTGAGE MODIFICATION ORDER

On [DATE OF TRIAL MODIFICATION AGREEMENT] the above named Debtor(s) and Respondent [NAME OF LENDER/SERVICER] ("Creditor") entered into a trial modification (the "Trial Modification"), through the Court's *Loss Mitigation Program* (LMP), with respect to the [FIRST/SECOND/THIRD] mortgage on the Debtor's residence. The terms of the Trial Modification require monthly payments in the amount of [$ AMOUNT] ("Trial Payments") to begin on **[DUE DATE OF FIRST TRIAL PAYMENT]** and to continue in that amount until **[DUE DATE OF LAST TRIAL PAYMENT]** (the "Trial Modification Period"). In light of the need for an immediate change in the distribution to the Creditor, the Debtor(s) request the Court to enter this *Interim Mortgage Modification Order* until a final, permanent modification can be presented to the Court for approval.

AND NOW, this _____ day of _____, 20__, for the foregoing reasons it is hereby *ORDERED, ADJUDGED and DECREED* that:

(1)   The Chapter 13 Trustee is authorized and directed to modify the distributions to the above-named Creditor for the Trial Modification Period. Each Trial Payment shall be made in the

Amount of [$AMOUNT] for the following months: [Month 1], [Month 2], [Month 3]. Following the Trial Modification Period, the Chapter 13 Trustee shall continue to make distributions in the same amount as the Trial Payments until further Order of Court.

(2)   In the event that a Permanent Modification is reached between the Parties, the Debtor *immediately* shall file a *Motion to Authorize the Loan Modification* in compliance with *W.PA.LBR 9020-6(d)*.

(3)   The LMP Period is extended until fourteen (14) days after the expiration of the Trial Modification Period. If the Debtor has not filed a *Motion to Authorize the Loan Modification* within fourteen (14) days after the expiration of the Trial Modification Period, then the Debtor shall *immediately* file and serve either a *Motion to Extend the Loss Modification Period* pursuant to *W.PA.LBR 9020-5(b)* or a *Motion to Terminate the Loss Modification Program* pursuant to *W.PA.LBR 9020-5(c)* that sets forth the specific reasons why an agreement was not reached.

(4)   Any Party may seek a further hearing regarding the amendment or termination of this *Order* at any time during the Trial Modification Period by filing an appropriate Motion.

(5)   Within three (3) days of entry of this *Order*, Debtor shall serve this *Order* electronically on the Chapter 13 Trustee at the following email address: **LMP@chapter13trusteewdpa.com** and Debtor shall not be entitled to rely on CM/ECF or United States Mail for service of this *Order* on the Chapter 13 Trustee. The Debtor(s) Certificate of Service shall reflect service upon the above identified email address.

_____
UNITED STATES BANKRUPTCY JUDGE

Case administrator to serve:
    Debtor(s)
    Counsel for Debtor(s)
    |Counsel for Creditor|
    Ronda J. Winnecour, Esq. Ch 13 Trustee

PAWB Local Form 47 (04/14)

[Amended effective April 1, 2014.]

U.S. BANKRUPTCY COURT

LOCAL BANKRUPTCY FORM NO. 48. LOAN MODIFICATION SUMMARY

IN THE UNITED STATES BANKRUPTCY COURT
FOR THE WESTERN DISTRICT OF PENNSYLVANIA

In Re: :   Bankruptcy No.
                          :   Chapter
         Debtor   :
                          :
                          :   Related to Document No.
Movant   :
                          :
       v.   :   Hearing Date and Time:
                          :
                          :
Respondent (if none, then "No Respondent") :

LOAN MODIFICATION SUMMARY

Property Valuation: $ _____   Source: _____

Original Loan Amount: $ _____   Origination Date: _____

Prepetition Arrears: $ _____

As of Petition Date		Under Proposed Modification
	Principal Balance	
	Interest Rate	
	Maturity Date	
	P&I Payment	
	Escrow Payment	
	Total Payment	
	Balloon Payment	
	Cumulative Interest	
	LTV	
	Ch. 13 Payment	
	Ch. 13 Pmt. (Arrears)	

Any other term(s) in which there is a substantive difference between the original loan and the proposed modified loan:

PAWB Local Form 48 (04/14)   Page 1 of 1

[Amended effective April 1, 2014.]

ECF PROCEDURES

[**Publisher's Note:** For Electronic Filing Rules,
please refer to Rules 5005–1 through 5005–21, *ante.*]

SELECTED GENERAL ORDERS
GENERAL ORDER 91–1.   GOVERNING DISMISSAL OF CASES AND IMPOSITION OF SANCTIONS FOR INCOMPLETE FILINGS

WHEREAS pertinent sections of the Bankruptcy Code including 11 U.S.C. Sections 707(a)(3), 1112(e), and 1307(c)(9) require that a case not be dismissed for failure to prosecute unless a motion therefor is filed by the Unites States Trustee, and

WHEREAS, given the level of filings in this District, it is impractical and infeasible to file a separate motion for each case wherein a debtor has failed to prosecute a case by not timely filing all documents required by the Bankruptcy Code, Bankruptcy Rules, and the local rules, and

WHEREAS, given the level of filings in this District, it is impractical and infeasible to file a separate motion for each case wherein a debtor has failed to prosecute a case by failing to respond or to file full and complete answers to all questions contained in the documents required by the Bankruptcy Code, Bankruptcy Rules, and the Local rules, and

WHEREAS, an efficient system exists in the Clerk's Office to provide notice of deficient filings to all debtors, and

WHEREAS, an efficient system exists via the panel trustees, the standing Chapter 13 trustee, and the Bankruptcy Analysts of the United States Trustee's Office for the Western District of Pennsylvania to provide notice to all debtors of incomplete answers to questions contained in the various documents required to be filed.

NOW, THEREFORE, this 2nd day of August, 1991, IT IS HEREBY ORDERED that in any voluntarily filed cases there shall be deemed filed a Motion To Dismiss, or in the alternative, a Motion for the Imposition of Sanctions, for failure to prosecute the case, where the debtor has failed to file any documents required by the bankruptcy Code, Bankruptcy Rules, or local rules or has failed to answer or respond fully to all questions in said documents, and

IT IS FURTHER ORDERED that the Clerk, the U.S. Trustee, or the trustee shall provide, when applicable, to the debtor or debtor's attorney, a notice,

(1) That the U.S. Trustee is deemed to have filed a Motion To Dismiss the bankruptcy case, or in the alternative, a Motion for Imposition of Sanctions, based upon deficiencies in the documents required to be filed by the debtor pursuant to the Bankruptcy Code, Bankruptcy Rules or Local Bankruptcy Rules;

(2) Indicating the nature of the case as being asset or no-asset, voluntary or involuntary; recommending either the dismissal of the case or the imposition of sanctions and specifying such deficiencies;

(3) That the debtor shall provide a verification that all property of and all claims against debtor, whether or not debtor is continuing to pay them or considers them nondischargeable debts, have been listed in the schedules;

(4) That the Motion will be granted and the case dismissed, or in the alternative, sanctions imposed, including but not limited to, denial of the debtor's discharge after distribution of any estate assets if the specified documentary deficiencies are not corrected within fourteen (14) days, or within such further time as the court may allow by order;

(5) That the debtor may request a hearing on the deemed filed motion to dismiss or motion to impose sanctions; however, a request for a hearing does not stay the due date for correcting any deficiencies; and

In the event that the trustee recommends imposition of sanctions, the court shall set a hearing to determine what, if any, sanctions shall be imposed.

IT IS FURTHER ORDERED that the Clerk shall publish the entry of this Amended General Order in the Pittsburgh Legal Journal, the Erie County Legal Journal and the Cambria County Legal Journal.

This Amended General Order shall become effective on the 3rd day of September, 1991.

[Dated: August 2, 1991. Amended effective December 1, 2009.]

GENERAL ORDER 92–2.   ADMINISTRATION OF CHAPTER 13 CASES

AND NOW, this 24th day of February, 1992, it appearing to the Court that the use of consumer credit reports will enhance the Trustee's ability to perform his duty to investigate the financial affairs of debtors in Chapter 13 cases, it is hereby Ordered and Decreed as follows:

1.   The Chapter 13 Trustee is authorized to obtain consumer credit reports from any and all consumer reporting agencies which the Trustee may select for such purpose, in any and all Chapter 13 cases selected by the Chapter 13 Trustee for further investigation.

2.   The Trustee is authorized to utilize the information contained in such consumer credit reports for comparison with the disclosures in the bankruptcy schedules, as a source of questions during meetings of creditors, and for all other proper purposes during hearings in bankruptcy proceedings, subject to the customary proscriptions of the Federal Rules of Evidence.

3.   This Order shall constitute authorization to consumer credit reporting agencies pursuant to 15 U.S.C. Section 1681(b)(1) to issue such consumer credit reports in all Chapter 13 cases selected in his discretion by the Chapter 13 Trustee.

4.   Nothing herein shall transform the Office of the Chapter 13 Trustee into a consumer credit reporting agency. All rights of debtors to obtain in consumer reports directly from reporting agencies are preserved. Comments and corrections, if any, are to be made directly by debtors to those credit reporting agencies from which the Trustee obtains the reports.

5.   This order extends indefinitely the prior Order dated September 27, 1991 and applies to all Chapter 13 cases filed in this District.

[Dated: February 24, 1992.]

GENERAL ORDER 2013–4.   IN RE: COURT SECURITY AND ELECTRONIC DEVICES IN THE COURTHOUSE
ORDER

The within *Order* applies to the United States Bankruptcy Courthouses in Pittsburgh, Erie and Johnstown and supersedes any prior orders or policies of this Court governing Court security or electronic devices in the Bankruptcy Courthouses.

AND NOW, this **30th** day of **May**, **2013**, it is hereby **ORDERED** as follows:

(1) Any person entering the United States Bankruptcy Court is prohibited from doing so with a weapon, i.e., a firearm, mace, knife, stun gun, or any other instrument considered as a weapon, concealed or otherwise, unless authorized to do so by the Court.

(2) Any person seeking entry to the United States Bankruptcy Court shall enter through the security equipment installed therein. Should the equipment be activated by the sounding of an alarm or meter reading, that person shall be denied entry to the United States Bankruptcy Court until the person clears the security equipment and other security measures in place to the satisfaction of the Court security personnel.

(3) The United States Marshal for the Western District of Pennsylvania shall provide for the inspection and, if necessary, temporary storage of packages, cellular telephones, pagers, computers and other electronic devices in the custody of any person entering or leaving the United States Bankruptcy Court.

(4) Any confiscated weapon or other property left unclaimed with the Court security personnel after thirty (30) days will be destroyed by the United States Marshals Service.

(5) Except as otherwise ordered by the presiding judicial officer in any particular case:

(A) All forms, means and manner of taking photographs, recording, broadcasting and televising are prohibited in any room, corridor or stairway leading thereto, on any floor occupied entirely or in part by the United States Bankruptcy Court for the Western District of Pennsylvania, or any other building designated as a place for holding judicial proceedings whether or not Court is in session.

(B) Any Attorney with business in this Court may possess in the Bankruptcy Courthouse cell phones, mobile devices, laptops or other similar devices (hereinafter, "electronic devices"). Electronic devices may be used to send or receive messages only from outside the courtrooms.

(C) For purposes of this Order, "members of the news media" shall consist of representatives of the person or entity that regularly and customarily is engaged in the business of gathering, marketing and/or disseminating the news. Members of the news media may possess electronic devices in the Bankruptcy Courthouse for purposes not prohibited by this rule. Electronic devices may not be used in a courtroom by the media. In order to prevent a breach of security occasioned by the presentation of false media credentials to court security officers, except as otherwise ordered, members of the news media must produce employer-issued photo identification upon seeking entrance into the Bankruptcy Courthouse with electronic devices.

(D) All electronic devices shall be turned off prior to entering courtrooms and judicial chambers.

(E) In those rare instances in which jurors report for duty, those persons may possess electronic devices in the Bankruptcy Courthouse for purposes not prohibited by this rule. Electronic devices may only be used in the jury room and may not be brought into a courtroom. Jurors shall deposit all electronic devices in the receptacles provided for that purpose prior to entering into the jury room to commence deliberations.

(F) Unless exempted above, except for purposes of investitures, ceremonial occasions and other similar events, members of the public may not possess electronic devices in the Bankruptcy Courthouse. All electronic devices possessed by members of the public seeking entry into the Bankruptcy Courthouse must be surrendered to the Court Security Officers at the entrance to the Bankruptcy Courthouse, and will be returned upon exiting the Bankruptcy Courthouse.

(6) In addition to any of the foregoing, a judicial officer may, in the judicial officer's discretion, prohibit electronic devices in that judicial officer's courtroom and chambers and may direct screening procedures to be conducted by the Court Security Officers/United States Marshal Service.

(7) Court staff, court security officers and deputy marshals may confiscate electronic devices being used in violation of these rules.

(8) Nothing in this *Order* is intended to prevent Bankruptcy Courthouse employees from using and possessing electronic devices in the Bankruptcy Courthouse.

(9) Except as to the decisions made by a specific judicial officer in regard to his or her chambers and courtroom, any disputes regarding the possession or use of electronic devices hereunder may be referred to the Chief Judge for resolution.

(10) The Court Security Officers/United States Marshal shall post copies of this Order at all entrances to the Bankruptcy Courthouse. Violators of this *Order* will be subject to sanction for contempt of court.

(11) The within *Order* is **IMMEDIATELY** effective.

[Dated: May 30, 2013.]

GENERAL ORDER 2013–16. IN RE: DEPOSIT AND INVESTMENT OF REGISTRY FUNDS
ORDER

The Court, having determined that it is necessary to adopt local procedures to ensure uniformity in the deposit and investment of funds in the Court's Registry,

AND NOW, this **11th** day of **December, 2013,** it is hereby **ORDERED** that the following shall govern the receipt, deposit and investment of registry funds:

I. Receipt of Funds

(A) No money shall be sent to the Court or its officers for deposit in the Court's registry without a court order signed by the presiding judge in the case or proceeding.

(B) The party making the deposit or transferring funds to the Court's registry shall serve the order permitting the deposit or transfer on the Clerk of Court.

(C) Unless provided for elsewhere in this Order, all monies ordered to be paid to the Court or received by its officers in any case pending or adjudicated shall be deposited with the Treasurer of the United States in the name and to the credit of this Court pursuant to 28 U.S.C. § 2041 through depositories designated by the Treasury to accept such deposit on its behalf.

II. Investment of Registry Funds

(A) Where, by order of the Court, funds on deposit with the Court are to be placed in some form of interest-bearing account, or invested in a court-approved, interest-bearing instrument in accordance with Rule 67 of the Federal Rules of Civil Procedure, the Court Registry Investment System ("CRIS"), administered by the Administrative Office of the United States Courts under 28 U.S.C. § 2045, shall be the only investment mechanism authorized.

(B) The Director of Administrative Office of the United States Courts is designated as custodian for CRIS. The Director or the Director's designee shall perform the duties of custodian. Funds held in the CRIS remain subject to the control and jurisdiction of the Court.

(C) Money from each case deposited in the CRIS shall be "pooled" together with those on deposit with Treasury to the credit of other courts in the CRIS and used to purchase Government Account Series securities through the Bureau of Public Debt, which will be held at Treasury, in an account in the name and to the credit of the Director of Administrative Office of the United States Courts. The pooled funds will be invested in accordance with the principals of the CRIS Investment Policy as approved by the Registry Monitoring Group.

(D) An account for each case will be established in the CRIS titled in the name of the case giving rise to the investment in the fund. Income generated from fund investments will be distributed to each case based on the ratio each account's principal and earnings has to the aggregate principal and income total in the fund. Reports showing the interest earned and the principal amounts contributed in each case will be prepared and distributed to each court participating in the CRIS and made available to litigants and/or their counsel.

III.   Deductions of Fees

(A) The custodian is authorized and directed by this Order to deduct the investment services fee for the management of investments in the CRIS and the registry fee for maintaining accounts deposited with the Court.

(B) The investment services fee is assessed from interest earnings to the pool according to the Court's Miscellaneous Fee Schedule and is to be assessed before a pro rata distribution of earnings to court cases.

(C) The registry fee is assessed by the custodian from each case's pro rata distribution of the earnings and is to be determined on the basis of the rates published by the Director of the Administrative Office of the United States Courts as approved by the Judicial Conference of the United States.

IV.   Transition From Former Investment Procedure

(A) The Clerk of Court is further directed to develop a systematic method of redemption of all existing investments and their transfer to the CRIS.

(B) Parties not wishing to transfer certain existing registry deposits into the CRIS may seek leave to transfer them to the litigants or their designees on proper motion and approval of the judge assigned to the specific case.

(C) This Order supersedes and abrogates all prior orders and local rules of this Court regarding the deposit and investment of registry funds.

[Dated: December 11, 2013.]

RULES OF PROCEDURE OF THE JUDICIAL PANEL ON MULTIDISTRICT LITIGATION

Renumbered and Amended Effective November 2, 1998

Including Amendments Effective
July 6, 2011

I. RULES FOR MULTIDISTRICT LITIGATION UNDER 28 U.S.C. § 1407

RULE 1.1 DEFINITIONS

(a) "Panel" means the members of the United States Judicial Panel on Multidistrict Litigation appointed by the Chief Justice of the United States pursuant to 28 U.S.C. § 1407.

(b) "Chair" means the Chair of the Panel appointed by the Chief Justice of the United States pursuant to Section 1407, or the member of the Panel properly designated to act as Chair.

(c) "Clerk of the Panel" means the official that the Panel appoints to that position. The Clerk of the Panel shall perform such duties that the Panel or the Panel Executive delegates.

(d) "Electronic Case Filing (ECF)" refers to the Panel's automated system that receives and stores documents filed in electronic form. All attorneys filing pleadings with the Panel must do so using ECF. All pro se individuals are non-ECF users, unless the Panel orders otherwise.

(e) "MDL" means a multidistrict litigation docket which the Panel is either considering or has created by transferring cases to a transferee district for coordinated or consolidated pretrial proceedings pursuant to Section 1407.

(f) "Panel Executive" means the official appointed to act as the Panel's Chief Executive and Legal Officer. The Panel Executive may appoint, with the approval of the Panel, necessary deputies, clerical assistants and other employees to perform or assist in the performance of the duties of the Panel Executive. The Panel Executive, with the approval of the Panel, may make such delegations of authority as are necessary for the Panel's efficient operation.

(g) "Pleadings" means all papers, motions, responses, or replies of any kind filed with the Panel, including exhibits attached thereto, as well as all orders and notices that the Panel issues.

(h) "Tag-along action" refers to a civil action pending in a district court which involves common questions of fact with either (1) actions on a pending motion to transfer to create an MDL or (2) actions previously transferred to an existing MDL, and which the Panel would consider transferring under Section 1407.

(i) "Transferee district" is the federal district court to which the Panel transfers an action pursuant to Section 1407, for inclusion in an MDL.

(j) "Transferor district" is the federal district court where an action was pending prior to its transfer pursuant to Section 1407, for inclusion in an MDL, and where the Panel may remand that action at or before the conclusion of pretrial proceedings.

[Former Rule 1 adopted May 3, 1993, effective July 1, 1993. Renumbered Rule 1.1 September 1, 1998, effective November 2, 1998. Amended September 8, 2010, effective October 4, 2010.]

RULE 2.1   RULES AND PRACTICE

(a) Customary Practice. The Panel's customary practice shall govern, unless otherwise fixed by statute or these Rules.

(b) Failure to Comply With Rules. When a pleading does not comply with these Rules, the Clerk of the Panel may advise counsel of the deficiencies and set a date for full compliance. If counsel does not fully comply within the established time, the Clerk of the Panel shall file the non-complying pleading, but the Chair may thereafter order it stricken.

(c) Admission to Practice Before the Panel. Every member in good standing of the Bar of any district court of the United States is entitled to practice before the Panel, provided, however, that he or she has established and maintains a CM/ECF account with any United States federal court. Any attorney of record in any action transferred under Section 1407 may continue to represent his or her client in any district court of the United States to which such action is transferred. Parties are not required to obtain local counsel.

(d) Pendency of Motion or Conditional Order. The pendency of a motion, order to show cause, conditional transfer order or conditional remand order before the Panel pursuant to 28 U.S.C. § 1407 does not affect or suspend orders and pretrial proceedings in any pending federal district court action and does not limit the pretrial jurisdiction of that court. An order to transfer or remand pursuant to 28 U.S.C. § 1407 shall be effective only upon its filing with the clerk of the transferee district court.

(e) Reassignment. If for any reason the transferee judge is unable to continue those responsibilities, the Panel shall make the reassignment of a new transferee judge.

[Former Rule 5 adopted May 3, 1993, effective July 1, 1993. Renumbered Rule 1.2 September 1, 1998, effective November 2, 1998. Former Rule 4 adopted May 3, 1993, effective July 1, 1993. Renumbered Rule 1.3 and amended September 1, 1998, effective November 2, 1998. Former Rule 6 adopted May 3, 1993, effective July 1, 1993. Renumbered Rule 1.4 September 1, 1998, effective November 2, 1998. Former Rule 18 adopted May 3, 1993, effective July 1, 1993. Renumbered Rule 1.5 September 1, 1998, effective November 2, 1998. Former Rules 1.2, 1.3, 1.4, and 1.5 redesignated and amended September 8, 2010, effective October 4, 2010.]

RULE 3.1   ELECTRONIC RECORDS AND FILES; COPY FEES

(a) Electronic Record. Effective October 4, 2010, the official Panel record shall be the electronic file maintained on the Panel's servers. This record includes, but is not limited to, Panel pleadings, documents filed in paper and then scanned and made part of the electronic record, and Panel orders and notices filed. The official record also includes any documents or exhibits that may be impractical to scan. These documents and exhibits shall be kept in the Panel offices.

(b) Maintaining Records. Records and files generated prior to October 4, 2010, may be (i) maintained at the Panel offices, (ii) temporarily or permanently removed to such places at such times as the Clerk of the Panel or the Chair shall direct, or (iii) transferred whenever appropriate to the Federal Records Center.

(c) Fees. The Clerk of the Panel may charge fees for duplicating records and files, as prescribed by the Judicial Conference of the United States.

[Former Rule 2 adopted May 3, 1993, effective July 1, 1993. Renumbered Rule 5.1 and amended September 1, 1998, effective November 2, 1998. Former Rule 5.1 redesignated and amended September 8, 2010, effective October 4, 2010.]

RULE 3.2   ECF USERS: FILING REQUIREMENTS

(a) Form of Pleadings. This Rule applies to pleadings that ECF users file with the Panel.

(i) Each pleading shall bear the heading "Before the United States Judicial Panel on Multidistrict Litigation," the identification "MDL No. ___" and the descriptive title designated by the Panel. If the Panel has not yet designated a title, counsel shall use an appropriate description.

(ii) The final page of each pleading shall contain the name, address, telephone number, fax number and email address of the attorney or party designated to receive service of pleadings in the case, and the name of each party represented.

(iii) Each brief submitted with a motion and any response to it shall not exceed 20 pages, exclusive of exhibits. Each reply shall not exceed 10 pages and shall address arguments raised in the response(s). Absent exceptional circumstances and those set forth in Rule 6.1(d), the Panel will not grant motions to exceed page limits.

(iv) Each pleading shall be typed in size 12 point font (for both text and footnotes), double spaced (text only), in a letter size document (8 ½ × 11 inch) with sequentially numbered pages.

(v) Each exhibit shall be separately numbered and clearly identified.

(vi) Proposed Panel orders shall not be submitted.

(b) Place of Filing. Counsel shall sign and verify all pleadings electronically in accordance with these Rules and the Panel's Administrative Policies and Procedures for Electronic Case Filing found at www.jpml.uscourts.gov. A pleading filed electronically constitutes a written document for the purpose of these Rules and the Federal Rules of Civil Procedure and is deemed the electronically signed original thereof. All pleadings, except by pro se litigants, shall conform with this Rule beginning on October 4, 2010.

(i)* Pleadings shall not be transmitted directly to any Panel member.

(c) Attorney Registration. Only attorneys identified, or to be identified, pursuant to Rule 4.1, shall file pleadings. Each of these attorneys must register as a Panel CM/ECF user through www.jpml.uscourts.gov. Registration/possession of a CM/ECF account with any United States federal court shall be deemed consent to receive electronic service of all Panel orders and notices as well as electronic service of pleadings from other parties before the Panel.

(d) Courtesy Copy of Specified Pleadings. Counsel shall serve the Clerk of the Panel, for delivery within 1 business day of filing, with a courtesy paper copy of any of the following pleadings: (i) a motion to transfer and its supporting brief; (ii) a response to a show cause order; (iii) a motion to vacate a conditional transfer order or a conditional remand order; (iv) any response, reply, supplemental information or interested party response related to the pleadings listed in (i), (ii) and (iii); and (v) a corporate disclosure statement. No courtesy copies of any other pleadings are required. Courtesy copies of pleadings totaling 10

pages or less (including any attachments) may be faxed to the Panel. The courtesy copy shall include all exhibits, shall be clearly marked "Courtesy Copy—Do Not File," shall contain the CM/ECF pleading number (if known), and shall be mailed or delivered to:

Clerk of the Panel
United States Judicial Panel on Multidistrict
  Litigation
Thurgood Marshall Federal Judiciary Building
One Columbus Circle, NE,
Room G–255, North Lobby
Washington, DC 20002–8041

(e) Privacy Protections. The privacy protections contained in Rule 5.2 of the Federal Rules of Civil Procedure shall apply to all Panel filings.

[Former Rule 3 adopted May 3, 1993, effective July 1, 1993. Renumbered Rule 5.11 and amended September 1, 1998, effective November 2, 1998; renumbered Rule 5.1.1 and amended March 25, 2010, effective April 1, 2010. Former Rule 7 adopted May 3, 1993, effective July 1, 1993. Renumbered Rule 5.12 and amended September 1, 1998, effective November 2, 1998. Amended April 2, 2001, effective April 2, 2001; paragraph (a) suspended in part by Order filed April 19, 2005; renumbered Rule 5.1.2 and amended March 25, 2010, effective April 1, 2010. Former Rule 9 adopted May 3, 1993, effective July 1, 1993. Renumbered Rule 7.1 and amended September 1, 1998, effective November 2, 1998. Amended April 2, 2001, effective April 2, 2001. Former Rules 5.1.1, 5.1.2, and 7.1 redesignated in part and amended September 8, 2010, effective October 4, 2010. Amended effective July 6, 2011.]

* So in original. No subdivision (ii) promulgated.

RULE 3.3 NON–ECF USERS: FILING REQUIREMENTS

(a) Definition of Non–ECF Users. Non–ECF users are all pro se individuals, unless the Panel orders otherwise. This Rule shall apply to all motions, responses and replies that non-ECF users file with the Panel.

(b) Form of Pleadings. Unless otherwise set forth in this Rule, the provisions of Rule 3.2 shall apply to non-ECF users.

(i) Each pleading shall be flat and unfolded; plainly written or typed in size 12 point font (for both text and footnotes), double spaced (text only), and printed single-sided on letter size (8 ½ × 11 inch) white paper with sequentially numbered pages; and fastened at the top-left corner without side binding or front or back covers.

(ii) Each exhibit shall be separately numbered and clearly identified. Any exhibits exceeding a cumulative total of 50 pages shall be bound separately.

(c) Place of Filing. File an original and one copy of all pleadings with the Clerk of the Panel by mailing or delivering to:

Clerk of the Panel
United States Judicial Panel on Multidistrict
  Litigation
Thurgood Marshall Federal Judiciary Building
One Columbus Circle, NE,
Room G–255, North Lobby
Washington, DC 20002–8041

(i) Pleadings not exceeding a total of 10 pages, including exhibits, may be faxed to the Panel office.

(ii) The Clerk of the Panel shall endorse the date for filing on all pleadings submitted for filing.

[Former Rule 3 adopted May 3, 1993, effective July 1, 1993. Renumbered Rule 5.11 and amended September 1, 1998, effective November 2, 1998; renumbered Rule 5.1.1 and amended March 25, 2010, effective April 1, 2010. Former Rule 7 adopted May 3, 1993, effective July 1, 1993. Renumbered Rule 5.12 and amended September 1, 1998, effective November 2, 1998. Amended April 2, 2001, effective April 2, 2001; paragraph (a) suspended in part by Order filed April 19, 2005; renumbered Rule 5.1.2 and amended March 25, 2010, effective April 1, 2010. Former Rule 9 adopted May 3, 1993, effective July 1, 1993. Renumbered Rule 7.1 and amended September 1, 1998, effective November 2, 1998. Amended April 2, 2001, effective April 2, 2001. Former Rules 5.1.1, 5.1.2, and 7.1 redesignated in part and amended September 8, 2010, effective October 4, 2010.]

RULE 4.1   SERVICE OF PLEADINGS

(a) **Proof of Service.** The Panel's notice of electronic filing shall constitute service of pleadings. Registration/possession by counsel of a CM/ECF account with any United States federal court shall be deemed consent to receive electronic service of all pleadings. All pleadings shall contain a proof of service on all other parties in all involved actions. The proof of service shall indicate the name and manner of service. If a party is not represented by counsel, the proof of service shall indicate the name of the party and the party's last known address. The proof of service shall indicate why any person named as a party in a constituent complaint was not served with the Section 1407 pleading.

(b) **Service Upon Transferor Court.** The proof of service pertaining to motions for a transfer or remand pursuant to 28 U.S.C. § 1407 shall certify that counsel has transmitted a copy of the motion for filing to the clerk of each district court where an affected action is pending.

(c) **Notice of Appearance.** Within 14 days after the issuance of a (i) notice of filing of a motion to initiate transfer under Rule 6.2, (ii) notice of filed opposition to a CTO under Rule 7.1, (iii) a show cause order under Rules* 8.1, (iv) notice of filed opposition to a CRO under Rule 10.2, or (v) notice of filing of a motion to remand under Rule 10.3, each party or designated attorney as required hereinafter shall file a Notice of Appearance notifying the Clerk of the Panel of the name, address and email address of the attorney designated to file and receive service of all pleadings. Each party shall designate only one attorney. Any party not represented by counsel shall be served by mailing such pleadings to the party's last known address. Except in extraordinary circumstances, the Panel will not grant requests for an extension of time to file the Notice of Appearance.

(d) **Liaison Counsel.** If the transferee district court appoints liaison counsel, this Rule shall be satisfied by serving each party in each affected action and all liaison counsel. Liaison counsel shall receive copies of all Panel orders concerning their particular litigation and shall be responsible for distribution to the parties for whom he or she serves as liaison counsel.

[Former Rule 8 adopted May 3, 1993, effective July 1, 1993. Renumbered Rule 5.2 and amended September 1, 1998, effective November 2, 1998; March 26, 2009, effective December 1, 2009. Former Rule 5.2 redesignated and amended September 8, 2010, effective October 4, 2010. Technical revisions effective July 6, 2011.]

* So in original.

RULE 5.1   CORPORATE DISCLOSURE STATEMENT

(a) **Requirements.** A nongovernmental corporate party must file a disclosure statement that: (1) identifies any parent corporation and any publicly held corporation owning 10% or more of its stock; or (2) states that there is no such corporation.

(b) **Deadline.** A party shall file the corporate disclosure statement within 14 days after issuance of a notice of the filing of a motion to transfer or remand, an order to show cause, or a motion to vacate a conditional transfer order or a conditional remand order.

(c) **Updating.** Each party must update its corporate disclosure statement to reflect any change in the information therein (i) until the matter before the Panel is decided, and (ii) within 14 days after issuance of a notice of the filing of any subsequent motion to transfer or remand, order to show cause, or motion to vacate a conditional transfer order or a conditional remand order in that docket.

[Former Rule 2 adopted May 3, 1993, effective July 1, 1993. Renumbered Rule 5.1 and amended September 1, 1998, effective November 2, 1998. Former Rule 5.3 redesignated and amended September 8, 2010, effective October 4, 2010. Amended effective July 6, 2011.]

RULE 5.1.3   FILING OF PAPERS: COMPUTER GENERATED DISK REQUIRED [DELETED SEPT. 8, 2010, EFF. OCT. 4, 2010]

[Added May 22, 2000, effective June 1, 2000. And amended July 30, 2007, effective July 30, 2007; renumbered Rule 5.1.3 and amended March 25, 2010, effective April 1, 2010. Deleted September 8, 2010, effective October 4, 2010.]

RULE 6.1   MOTION PRACTICE

(a) Application. This Rule governs all motions requesting Panel action generally. More specific provisions may apply to motions to transfer (Rule 6.2), miscellaneous motions (Rule 6.3), conditional transfer orders (Rule 7.1), show cause orders (Rule 8.1), conditional remand orders (Rule 10.2) and motions to remand (Rule 10.3).

(b) Form of Motions. All motions shall briefly describe the action or relief sought and shall include:

(i) a brief which concisely states the background of the litigation and movant's factual and legal contentions;

(ii) a numbered schedule providing

(A) the complete name of each action involved, listing the full name of each party included as such on the district court's docket sheet, not shortened by the use of references such as "et al." or "etc.";

(B) the district court and division where each action is pending;

(C) the civil action number of each action; and

(D) the name of the judge assigned each action, if known;

(iii) a proof of service providing

(A) a service list listing the full name of each party included on the district court's docket sheet and the complaint, including opt-in plaintiffs not listed on the docket sheet; and

(B) in actions where there are 25 or more plaintiffs listed on the docket sheet, list the first named plaintiff with the reference "et al." if all the plaintiffs are represented by the same attorney(s);

(iv) a copy of all complaints and docket sheets for all actions listed on the Schedule; and

(v) exhibits, if any, identified by number or letter and a descriptive title.

(c) Responses and Joinders. Any other party may file a response within 21 days after filing of a motion. Failure to respond to a motion shall be treated as that party's acquiescence to it. A joinder in a motion shall not add any action to that motion.

(d) Replies. The movant may file a reply within 7 days after the lapse of the time period for filing a response. Where a movant is replying to more than one response in opposition, the movant may file a consolidated reply with a limit of 20 pages.

(e) Alteration of Time Periods. The Clerk of the Panel has the discretion to shorten or enlarge the time periods set forth in this Rule as necessary.

(f) Notification of Developments. Counsel shall promptly notify the Clerk of the Panel of any development that would partially or completely moot any Panel matter.

[Former Rule 10 adopted May 3, 1993, effective July 1, 1993. Renumbered Rule 7.2 and amended September 1, 1998, effective November 2, 1998. Amended April 2, 2001, effective April 2, 2001; March 26, 2009, December 1, 2009. Former Rule 7.2 redesignated in part and amended September 8, 2010, effective October 4, 2010.]

RULE 6.2   MOTIONS TO TRANSFER FOR COORDINATED OR CONSOLIDATED PRETRIAL PROCEEDINGS

(a) Initiation of Transfer. A party to an action may initiate proceedings to transfer under Section 1407 by filing a motion in accordance with these Rules. A copy of the motion shall be filed in each district court where the motion affects a pending action.

(b) Notice of Filing of Motion to Transfer. Upon receipt of a motion, the Clerk of the Panel shall issue a "Notice of Filing of Motion to Transfer" to the service list recipients. The Notice shall contain the following: the filing date of the motion, caption, MDL docket number, briefing schedule and pertinent Panel policies. After a motion is filed, the Clerk of the Panel shall consider any other pleading to be a response unless the pleading adds an action. The Clerk of the Panel may designate such a pleading as a motion, and distribute a briefing schedule applicable to all or some of the parties, as appropriate.

(c) Notice of Appearance. Within 14 days of issuance of a "Notice of the Filing of a Motion to Transfer," each party or designated attorney shall file a Notice of Appearance in accordance with Rule 4.1(c).

(d) Notice of Potential Tag-along Actions. Any party or counsel in a new group of actions under consideration for transfer under Section 1407 shall promptly notify the Clerk of the Panel of any potential tag-along actions in which that party is also named or in which that counsel appears.

(e) Interested Party Responses. Any party or counsel in one or more potential tag-along actions as well as amicus curiae may file a response to a pending motion to transfer. Such a pleading shall be deemed an Interested Party Response.

(f) Amendment to a Motion. Before amending a motion to transfer, a party shall first contact the Clerk of the Panel to ascertain whether such amendment is feasible and permissible considering the Panel's hearing schedule. Any such amendment shall be entitled "Amendment to Motion for Transfer," and shall clearly and specifically identify and describe the nature of the amendment.

(i) Where the amended motion includes new civil actions, the amending party shall file a "Schedule of Additional Actions" and a revised Proof of Service.

(ii) The Proof of Service shall state (A) that all new counsel have been served with a copy of the amendment and all previously-filed motion papers, and (B) that all counsel previously served with the original motion have been served with a copy of the amendment.

(iii) The Clerk of the Panel may designate the amendment with a different denomination (*e.g.*, a notice of potential tag-along action(s)) and treatment.

(h) Oral Argument*. The Panel shall schedule oral arguments as needed and as set forth in Rule 11.1.

[Former Rule 10 adopted May 3, 1993, effective July 1, 1993. Renumbered Rule 7.2 and amended September 1, 1998, effective November 2, 1998. Amended April 2, 2001, effective April 2, 2001; March 26, 2009, December 1, 2009. Former Rule 15 adopted May 3, 1993, effective July 1, 1993. Renumbered Rule 6.2 and amended September 1, 1998, effective November 2, 1998. Former Rule 7.2 redesignated in part and amended September 8, 2010, effective October 4, 2010. Technical revisions effective July 6, 2011.]

* So in original.

RULE 6.3 MOTIONS FOR MISCELLANEOUS RELIEF

(a) Definition. Motions for miscellaneous relief include, but are not limited to, requests for extensions of time, exemption from ECF requirements, page limit extensions, or expedited consideration of any motion.

(b) Panel Action. The Panel, through the Clerk, may act upon any motion for miscellaneous relief, at any time, without waiting for a response. A motion for extension of time to file a pleading or perform an act under these Rules must state specifically the revised date sought and must be filed before the deadline for filing the pleading or performing the act. Any party aggrieved by the Clerk of the Panel's action may file objections for consideration. Absent exceptional circumstances, the Panel will not grant any extensions of time to file a notice of opposition to either a conditional transfer order or a conditional remand order.

[Former Rule 15 adopted May 3, 1993, effective July 1, 1993. Renumbered Rule 6.2 and amended September 1, 1998, effective November 2, 1998. Former Rule 6.2 redesignated and amended September 8, 2010, effective October 4, 2010.]

RULE 7.1 CONDITIONAL TRANSFER ORDERS (CTO) FOR TAG–ALONG ACTIONS

(a) Notice of Potential Tag-along Actions. Any party or counsel in actions previously transferred under Section 1407 shall promptly notify the Clerk of the Panel of any potential tag-along actions in which that party is also named or in which that counsel appears. The Panel has several options: (i) filing a CTO under Rule 7.1, (ii) filing a show cause order under Rule 8.1, or (iii) declining to act (Rule 7.1(b)(i)).

(b) Initiation of CTO. Upon learning of the pendency of a potential tag-along action, the Clerk of the Panel may enter a conditional order transferring that action to the previously designated transferee district court for the reasons expressed in the Panel's previous opinions and orders. The Clerk of the Panel shall serve this order on each party to the litigation but shall not send the order to the clerk of the transferee district court until 7 days after its entry.

(i)* If the Clerk of the Panel determines that a potential tag-along action is not appropriate for inclusion in an MDL proceeding and does not enter a CTO, an involved party may move for its transfer pursuant to Rule 6.1.

(c) Notice of Opposition to CTO. Any party opposing the transfer shall file a notice of opposition with the Clerk of the Panel within the 7–day period. In such event, the Clerk of the Panel shall not transmit the transfer order to the clerk of the transferee district court, but shall notify the parties of the briefing schedule.

(d) Failure to Respond. Failure to respond to a CTO shall be treated as that party's acquiescence to it.

(e) Notice of Appearance. Within 14 days after the issuance of a "Notice of Filed Opposition" to a CTO, each opposing party or designated attorney shall file a Notice of Appearance in accordance with Rule 4.1(c).

(f) Motion to Vacate CTO. Within 14 days of the filing of its notice of opposition, the party opposing transfer shall file a motion to vacate the CTO and brief in support thereof. The Clerk of the Panel shall set the motion for the next appropriate hearing session. Failure to file and serve a motion and brief shall be treated as withdrawal of the opposition and the Clerk of the Panel shall forthwith transmit the order to the clerk of the transferee district court.

(g) Notification of Developments. Parties to an action subject to a CTO shall notify the Clerk of the Panel if that action is no longer pending in its transferor district court.

(h) Effective Date of CTO. CTOs are effective when filed with the clerk of the transferee district court.

[Former Rule 12 adopted May 3, 1993, effective July 1, 1993. Renumbered Rule 7.4 and amended September 1, 1998, effective November 2, 1998. Amended April 2, 2001, effective April 2, 2001; March 26, 2009, December 1, 2009. Former Rule 7.4 redesignated and amended September 8, 2010, effective October 4, 2010. Technical revisions effective July 6, 2011.]

* So in original. No subdivision (ii) promulgated.

RULE 7.2 MISCELLANEOUS PROVISIONS CONCERNING TAG–ALONG ACTIONS

(a) **Potential Tag-alongs in Transferee Court.** Potential tag-along actions filed in the transferee district do not require Panel action. A party should request assignment of such actions to the Section 1407 transferee judge in accordance with applicable local rules.

(b) **Failure to Serve.** Failure to serve one or more of the defendants in a potential tag-along action with the complaint and summons as required by Rule 4 of the Federal Rules of Civil Procedure does not preclude transfer of such action under Section 1407. Such failure, however, may constitute grounds for denying the proposed transfer where prejudice can be shown. The failure of the Clerk of the Panel to serve a CTO on all plaintiffs or defendants or their counsel may constitute grounds for the Clerk to reinstate the CTO or for the aggrieved party to seek § 1407(c) remand.

[Former Rule 13 adopted May 3, 1993, effective July 1, 1993. Renumbered Rule 7.5 and amended September 1, 1998, effective November 2, 1998. Amended April 2, 2001, effective April 2, 2001. Former Rule 7.5 redesignated and amended September 8, 2010, effective October 4, 2010. Amended effective July 6, 2011.]

RULE 8.1 SHOW CAUSE ORDERS

(a) **Entry of Show Cause Order.** When transfer of multidistrict litigation is being considered on the initiative of the Panel pursuant to 28 U.S.C. § 1407(c)(i), the Clerk of the Panel may enter an order directing the parties to show cause why a certain civil action or actions should not be transferred for coordinated or consolidated pretrial proceedings. Any party shall also promptly notify the Clerk of the Panel whenever they learn of any other federal district court actions which are similar to those which the show cause order encompasses.

(b) **Notice of Appearance.** Within 14 days of the issuance of an order to show cause, each party or designated attorney shall file a Notice of Appearance in accordance with Rule 4.1(c).

(c) **Responses.** Unless otherwise provided by order, any party may file a response within 21 days of the filing of the show cause order. Failure to respond to a show cause order shall be treated as that party's acquiescence to the Panel action.

(d) **Replies.** Within 7 days after the lapse of the time period for filing a response, any party may file a reply.

(e) **Notification of Developments.** Counsel shall promptly notify the Clerk of the Panel of any develop-ment that would partially or completely moot any matter subject to a show cause order.

[Former Rule 7.3 adopted May 3, 1993, effective July 1, 1993. Renumbered Rule 7.3 and amended September 1, 1998, effective November 2, 1998; March 26, 2009, effective December 1, 2009. Former Rule 7.3 redesignated and amended September 8, 2010, effective October 4, 2010.]

RULE 9.1 TRANSFER OF FILES; NOTIFICATION REQUIREMENTS

(a) **Notice to Transferee Court Clerk.** The Clerk of the Panel, via a notice of electronic filing, will notify the clerk of the transferee district whenever a Panel transfer order should be filed in the transferee district court. Upon receipt of an electronically certified copy of a Panel transfer order from the clerk of the transferee district, the clerk of the transferor district shall transmit the record of each transferred action to the transferee district and then, unless Rule 9.1(b) applies, close the transferred action in the transferor district.

(b) **Retention of Claims.** If the transfer order provides for the separation and simultaneous remand of any claim, cross-claim, counterclaim, or third-party claim, the clerk of the transferor district shall retain jurisdiction over any such claim and shall not close the action.

(c) **Notice to Clerk of Panel.** The clerk of the transferee district shall promptly provide the Clerk of the Panel with the civil action numbers assigned to all transferred actions and the identity of liaison counsel, if or when designated. The clerk of the transferee district shall also promptly notify the Clerk of the Panel of any dispositive ruling that terminates a transferred action.

[Former Rule 19 adopted May 3, 1993, effective July 1, 1993. Renumbered Rule 1.6 and amended September 1, 1998, effective November 2, 1998. Former Rule 1.6 redesignated in part and amended September 8, 2010, effective October 4, 2010.]

RULE 10.1 TERMINATION AND REMAND

(a) **Termination.** Where the transferee district court terminates an action by valid order, including but not limited to summary judgment, judgment of dismissal and judgment upon stipulation, the transferee district court clerk shall transmit a copy of that order to the Clerk of the Panel. The terminated action shall not be remanded to the transferor court and the transferee court shall retain the original files and records unless the transferee judge or the Panel directs otherwise.

(b) **Initiation of Remand.** Typically, the transferee judge recommends remand of an action, or a part of it, to the transferor court at any time by filing a suggestion of remand with the Panel. However, the Panel may remand an action or any separable claim, cross-claim, counterclaim or third-party claim within it, upon

(i) the transferee court's suggestion of remand,

(ii) the Panel's own initiative by entry of an order to show cause, a conditional remand order or other appropriate order, or

(iii) motion of any party.

[Former Rule 14 adopted May 3, 1993, effective July 1, 1993. Renumbered Rule 7.6 and amended September 1, 1998, effective November 2, 1998. Amended April 2, 2001, effective April 2, 2001; March 26, 2009, effective December 1, 2009. Former Rule 7.6 redesignated in part and amended September 8, 2010, effective October 4, 2010.]

RULE 10.2   CONDITIONAL REMAND ORDERS (CRO)

(a) Entering a CRO. Upon the suggestion of the transferee judge or the Panel's own initiative, the Clerk of the Panel shall enter a conditional order remanding the action or actions to the transferor district court. The Clerk of the Panel shall serve this order on each party to the litigation but shall not send the order to the clerk of the transferee district court for 7 days from the entry thereof.

(i)* The Panel may, on its own initiative, also enter an order that the parties show cause why a matter should not be remanded. Rule 8.1 applies to responses and replies with respect to such a show cause order.

(b) Notice of Opposition. Any party opposing the CRO shall file a notice of opposition with the Clerk of the Panel within the 7–day period. In such event, the Clerk of the Panel shall not transmit the remand order to the clerk of the transferee district court and shall notify the parties of the briefing schedule.

(c) Failure to Respond. Failure to respond to a CRO shall be treated as that party's acquiescence to it.

(d) Notice of Appearance. Within 14 days after the issuance of a "Notice of Filed Opposition" to a CRO, each opposing party or designated attorney shall file a Notice of Appearance in accordance with Rule 4.1(c).

(e) Motion to Vacate CRO. Within 14 days of the filing of its notice of opposition, the party opposing remand shall file a motion to vacate the CRO and brief in support thereof. The Clerk of the Panel shall set the motion for the next appropriate Panel hearing session. Failure to file and serve a motion and brief shall be treated as a withdrawal of the opposition and the Clerk of the Panel shall forthwith transmit the order to the clerk of the transferee district court.

(f) Effective Date of CRO. CROs are not effective until filed with the clerk of the transferee district court.

[Former Rule 14 adopted May 3, 1993, effective July 1, 1993. Renumbered Rule 7.6 and amended September 1, 1998, effective November 2, 1998. Amended April 2, 2001, effective April 2, 2001; March 26, 2009, effective December 1, 2009. Former Rule 7.6 redesignated in part and amended September 8, 2010, effective October 4, 2010. Technical revisions effective July 6, 2011.]

* So in original. No subdivision (ii) promulgated.

RULE 10.3   MOTION TO REMAND

(a) Requirements of the Motion. If the Clerk of the Panel does not enter a CRO, a party may file a motion to remand to the transferor court pursuant to these Rules. Because the Panel is reluctant to order a remand absent the suggestion of the transferee judge, the motion must include:

(i) An affidavit reciting whether the movant has requested a suggestion of remand and the judge's response, whether the parties have completed common discovery and other pretrial proceedings, and whether the parties have complied with all transferee court orders.

(ii) A copy of the transferee district court's final pretrial order, if entered.

(b) Filing Copy of Motion. Counsel shall file a copy of the motion to remand in the affected transferee district court.

(c) Notice of Appearance. Within 14 days of the issuance of a "Notice of Filing" of a motion to remand, each party or designated attorney shall file a Notice of Appearance in accordance with Rule 4.1(c).

[Former Rule 14 adopted May 3, 1993, effective July 1, 1993. Renumbered Rule 7.6 and amended September 1, 1998, effective November 2, 1998. Amended April 2, 2001, effective April 2, 2001; March 26, 2009, effective December 1, 2009. Former Rule 7.6 redesignated in part and amended September 8, 2010, effective October 4, 2010. Technical revisions effective July 6, 2011.]

RULE 10.4   TRANSFER OF FILES ON REMAND

(a) Designating the Record. Upon receipt of an order to remand from the Clerk of the Panel, the parties shall furnish forthwith to the transferee district clerk a stipulation or designation of the contents of the record or part thereof to be remanded.

(b) Transfer of Files. Upon receipt of an order to remand from the Clerk of the Panel, the transferee district shall transmit to the clerk of the transferor district the following concerning each remanded action:

(i) a copy of the individual docket sheet for each action remanded;

(ii) a copy of the master docket sheet, if applicable;

(iii) the entire file for each action remanded, as originally received from the transferor district and augmented as set out in this Rule;

(iv) a copy of the final pretrial order, if applicable; and

(v) a "record on remand" as designated by the parties in accordance with 10.4(a).

[Former Rule 19 adopted May 3, 1993, effective July 1, 1993. Renumbered Rule 1.6 and amended September 1, 1998, effective November 2, 1998. Former Rule 1.6 redesignated in part and amended September 8, 2010, effective October 4, 2010.]

RULE 11.1 HEARING SESSIONS AND ORAL ARGUMENT

(a) Schedule. The Panel shall schedule sessions for oral argument and consideration of other matters as desirable or necessary. The Chair shall determine the time, place and agenda for each hearing session. The Clerk of the Panel shall give appropriate notice to counsel for all parties. The Panel may continue its consideration of any scheduled matters.

(b) Oral Argument Statement. Any party affected by a motion may file a separate statement setting forth reasons why oral argument should, or need not, be heard. Such statements shall be captioned "Reasons Why Oral Argument Should [Need Not] Be Heard" and shall be limited to 2 pages.

(i)* The parties affected by a motion to transfer may agree to waive oral argument. The Panel will take this into consideration in determining the need for oral argument.

(c) Hearing Session. The Panel shall not consider transfer or remand of any action pending in a federal district court when any party timely opposes such transfer or remand without first holding a hearing session for the presentation of oral argument. The Panel may dispense with oral argument if it determines that:

(i) the dispositive issue(s) have been authoritatively decided; or

(ii) the facts and legal arguments are adequately presented and oral argument would not significantly aid the decisional process.

Unless otherwise ordered, the Panel shall consider all other matters, such as a motion for reconsideration, upon the basis of the pleadings.

(d) Notification of Oral Argument. The Panel shall promptly notify counsel of those matters in which oral argument is scheduled, as well as those matters that the Panel will consider on the pleadings. The Clerk of the Panel shall require counsel to file and serve notice of their intent to either make or waive oral argument. Failure to do so shall be deemed a waiver of oral argument. If counsel does not attend oral argument, the matter shall not be rescheduled and that party's position shall be treated as submitted for decision on the basis of the pleadings filed.

(i) Absent Panel approval and for good cause shown, only those parties to actions who have filed a motion or written response to a motion or order shall be permitted to present oral argument.

(ii) The Panel will not receive oral testimony except upon notice, motion and an order expressly providing for it.

(e) Duty to Confer. Counsel in an action set for oral argument shall confer separately prior to that argument for the purpose of organizing their arguments and selecting representatives to present all views without duplication. Oral argument is a means for counsel to emphasize the key points of their arguments, and to update the Panel on any events since the conclusion of briefing.

(f) Time Limit for Oral Argument. Barring exceptional circumstances, the Panel shall allot a maximum of 20 minutes for oral argument in each matter. The time shall be divided among those with varying viewpoints. Counsel for the moving party or parties shall generally be heard first.

[Former Rule 16 adopted May 3, 1998, effective July 1, 1993. Renumbered Rule 16.1 and amended September 1, 1998, effective November 2, 1998. Amended April 2, 2001, effective April 2, 2001. Former Rule 16.1 redesignated and amended September 8, 2010, effective October 4, 2010.]

* So in original. No subdivision (ii) promulgated.

RULES 12 TO 15.   [RESERVED]

II. RULES FOR MULTICIRCUIT PETITIONS FOR REVIEW UNDER 28 U.S.C. § 2112(a)(3)

RULE 25.1 DEFINITIONS

The Panel promulgates these Rules pursuant to its authority under 28 U.S.C. § 2112(a)(3) to provide a means for the random selection of one circuit court of appeals to hear consolidated petitions for review of agency decisions.

An "Agency" means an agency, board, commission or officer of the United States government, that has received two or more petitions for review in a circuit court of appeals to enjoin, set aside, suspend, modify or otherwise review or enforce an action.

[Former Rule 20 adopted May 3, 1993, effective July 1, 1993. Renumbered Rule 25.1 and amended September 1, 1998, effective November 2, 1998. Amended September 8, 2010, effective October 4, 2010.]

RULE 25.2   FILING OF NOTICES

(a) Submitting Notice. An affected agency shall submit a notice of multicircuit petitions for review pursuant to 28 U.S.C. § 2112(a)(3) to the Clerk of the Panel by electronic means in the manner these Rules require and in accordance with the Panel's Administrative Policies and Procedures for Electronic Case Filing, except that the portion of Rule 3.2(d) requiring a courtesy copy is suspended in its entirety.

(b) Accompaniments to Notices. All notices of multicircuit petitions for review shall include:

(i) a copy of each involved petition for review as the petition for review is defined in 28 U.S.C. § 2112(a)(2);

(ii) a schedule giving

(A) the date of the relevant agency order;

(B) the case name of each petition for review involved;

(C) the circuit court of appeals in which each petition for review is pending;

(D) the appellate docket number of each petition for review;

(E) the date of filing by the court of appeals of each petition for review; and

(F) the date of receipt by the agency of each petition for review; and

(iii) proof of service (*see* Rule 25.3).

(c) Scope of Notice. All notices of multicircuit petitions for review shall embrace exclusively petitions for review filed in the courts of appeals within 10 days after issuance of an agency order and received by the affected agency from the petitioners within that 10–day period.

(d) Filing at the Panel. The Clerk of the Panel shall file the notice of multicircuit petitions for review and endorse thereon the date of filing.

(e) Filing With Each Circuit Clerk. The affected agency shall file copies of notices of multicircuit petitions for review with the clerk of each circuit court of appeals in which a petition for review is pending.

[Former Rule 21 adopted May 3, 1993, effective July 1, 1993. Renumbered Rule 25.2 and amended September 1, 1998, effective November 2, 1998. Amended September 8, 2010, effective October 4, 2010. Technical revisions effective July 6, 2011.]

RULE 25.3   SERVICE OF NOTICES

(a) Proof of Service. Notices of multicircuit petitions for review shall include proof of service on all other parties in the petitions for review included in the notice. Rule 25 of the Federal Rules of Appellate Procedure governs service and proof of service. The proof of service shall state the name, address and email address of each person served and shall indicate the party represented by each and the manner in which service was accomplished on each party. If a party is not represented by counsel, the proof of service shall indicate the name of the party and his or her last known address. The affected party shall submit proof of service for filing with the Clerk of the Panel and shall send copies thereof to each person included within the proof of service.

(b) Service on Clerk of Circuit. The proof of service pertaining to notices of multicircuit petitions for review shall certify the affected party has mailed or delivered copies of the notices to the clerk of each circuit court of appeals in which a petition for review is pending that is included in the notice. The Clerk shall file the notice with the circuit court.

[Former Rule 22 adopted May 3, 1993, effective July 1, 1993. Renumbered Rule 25.3 September 1, 1998, effective November 2, 1998. Amended September 8, 2010, effective October 4, 2010.]

RULE 25.4   FORM OF NOTICES; PLACE OF FILING

(a) Unless otherwise provided here, Rule 3.2 governs the form of a notice of multicircuit petitions for review. Each notice shall bear the heading "Notice to the United States Judicial Panel on Multidistrict Litigation of Multicircuit Petitions for Review," followed by a brief caption identifying the involved agency, the relevant agency order, and the date of the order.

(b) Rule 3.2(b) and (c) govern the manner of filing a notice of multicircuit petitions for review.

[Former Rule 23 adopted May 3, 1993, effective July 1, 1993. Renumbered Rule 25.4 and amended September 1, 1998, effective November 2, 1998. Amended September 8, 2010, effective October 4, 2010.]

RULE 25.5   RANDOM SELECTION

(a) Selection Process. Upon filing a notice of multicircuit petitions for review, the Clerk of the Panel shall randomly select a circuit court of appeals from a drum containing an entry for each circuit wherein a constituent petition for review is pending. Multiple petitions for review pending in a single circuit shall be allotted only a single entry in the drum. A designated deputy other than the random selector shall witness the random selection. Thereafter, an order on behalf of the Panel shall be issued, signed by the random selector and the witness,

(i) consolidating the petitions for review in the court of appeals for the circuit that was randomly selected; and

(ii) designating that circuit as the one in which the record is to be filed pursuant to Rules 16 and 17 of the Federal Rules of Appellate Procedure.

(b) Effective Date. A consolidation of petitions for review shall be effective when the Clerk of the Panel enters the consolidation order.

[Former Rule 24 adopted May 3, 1993, effective July 1, 1993. Renumbered Rule 17.1 September 1, 1998, effective November 2, 1998. Former Rule 17.1 redesignated and amended September 8, 2010, effective October 4, 2010.]

RULE 25.6 SERVICE OF PANEL CONSOLIDATION ORDER

(a) The Clerk of the Panel shall serve the Panel's consolidation order on the affected agency through the individual or individuals, as identified in Rule 25.2(a), who submitted the notice of multicircuit petitions for review on behalf of the agency.

(b) That individual or individuals, or anyone else designated by the agency, shall promptly serve the Panel's consolidation order on all other parties in all petitions for review included in the Panel's consolidation order, and shall promptly submit a proof of that service to the Clerk of the Panel. Rule 25.3 governs service.

(c) The Clerk of the Panel shall serve the Panel's consolidation order on the clerks of all circuit courts of appeals that were among the candidates for the Panel's random selection.

[Former Rule 25 adopted May 3, 1993, effective July 1, 1993. Renumbered Rule 25.5 and amended September 1, 1998, effective November 2, 1998. Former Rule 25.5 redesignated and amended September 8, 2010, effective October 4, 2010.]

III. CONVERSION TABLE

New to Old:

New Rule / Previous Rule		New Rule / Previous Rule	
1.1	1.1	9.1	1.6
2.1	1.2, 1.3, 1.4, 1.5	10.1	7.6
3.1	5.1	10.2	7.6
3.2	5.1.1, 5.1.2, 7.1	10.3	7.6
3.3	5.1.1, 5.1.2, 7.1	10.4	1.6
4.1	5.2	11.1	16.1
5.1	5.3	25.1	25.1
6.1	7.2	25.2	25.1, 25.2
6.2	7.2	25.3	25.3
6.3	6.2	25.4	25.1, 25.4
7.1	7.4	25.5	17.1
7.2	7.5	25.6	25.5
8.1	7.3		

Old to New:

Previous Rule / New Rule		Previous Rule / New Rule	
1.1	1.1	7.1	3.2, 3.3
1.2	2.1	7.2	6.1
1.3	2.1	7.3	8.1
1.4	2.1	7.4	7.1
1.5	2.1	7.5	7.2
1.6	10.4	7.6	10.1
5.1	3.1	16.1	11.1
5.1.1	3.2, 3.3	17.1	25.5
5.1.2	3.2, 3.3	25.1	25.1, 25.2, 25.4
5.1.3	-	25.2	25.2
5.2	4.1	25.3	25.3
5.3	5.1	25.4	25.4
6.2	6.3	25.5	25.6

[October 2010.]

ELECTRONIC CASE FILING ADMINISTRATIVE POLICIES AND PROCEDURES

1. DEFINITIONS.

1.1 "ELECTRONIC FILING SYSTEM" (ECF) refers to the United States Judicial Panel on Multidistrict Litigation's (the Panel's) automated system that receives and stores documents filed in electronic form. The program is part of the CM/ECF (Case Management/Electronic Case Files) software which was developed for the Federal Judiciary by the Administrative Office of the United States Courts.

1.2 "CLERK OF THE PANEL" means the official appointed by the Panel to act as Clerk of the Panel and shall include those deputized by the Clerk of the Panel to perform or assist in the performance of the duties of the Clerk of the Panel.

1.3 "FILING USER" is an individual who has a Panel-issued login and password to file documents electronically. In accordance with Rule 1.4 of the Rules of Procedure of the United States Judicial Panel on Multidistrict Litigation (the Panel Rules), every member in good standing of the Bar of any district court of the United States is entitled to practice before the Judicial Panel on Multidistrict Litigation.

1.4 "NOTICE OF ELECTRONIC FILING" (NEF) is a notice automatically generated by the Electronic Filing System at the time a document is filed with the system, setting forth the time of filing, the date the document is entered on the docket, the name of the party and attorney filing the document, the type of document, the text of the docket entry, the name of the party and/or attorney receiving the notice, and an electronic link (hyperlink) to the filed document, which allows recipients to retrieve the document automatically. A document shall not be considered filed for the purposes of the Panel's Rules until the filing party receives a system generated Notice of Electronic Filing with a hyperlink to the electronically filed document.

1.5 "PACER" (Public Access to Court Electronic Records) is an automated system that allows an individual to view, print and download Panel docket information over the Internet.

1.6 "PDF" (Portable Document Format). A document file created with a word processor, or a paper document which has been scanned, must be converted to portable document format to be filed electronically with the Panel. Converted files contain the extension ".pdf".

1.7 "TECHNICAL FAILURE" is defined as a failure of Panel owned/leased hardware, software, and/or telecommunications facility which results in the inability of a Filing User to submit a filing electronically. Technical failure does not include malfunctioning of a Filing User's equipment.

2. SCOPE OF ELECTRONIC FILING.

(a) All multidistrict litigation matters (MDLs) brought before the Panel under 28 U.S.C. § 1407 shall be assigned to the Electronic Filing System. Effective October 1, 2010, all MDLs, proceedings, motions, memoranda of law and other pleadings or documents filed with the Panel in new and existing dockets must be filed using CM/ECF unless otherwise specified herein.

(b) The filing of all MDL papers shall be accomplished electronically under procedures outlined in the Panel's CM/ECF User Manual.

(c) A party proceeding pro se shall not file electronically, unless otherwise permitted by the Panel. Pro se filers shall file paper originals of all documents. The clerk's office will scan these original documents into the JPML's electronic system, unless otherwise sealed.

3. ELIGIBILITY, REGISTRATION, PASSWORDS.

(a) Any attorney admitted to the Bar of any United States district court is eligible to practice before the Panel. Unless otherwise exempt as set forth herein, to become a Filing User, an attorney must register as a Filing User by completing the prescribed registration form and submitting it to the Clerk of the Panel.

(b) Registration as a Filing User constitutes consent to electronic service of all documents filed with or issued by the Panel in accordance with the Panel Rules.

(c) By submitting the online registration form, the Filing Users certify that they have read and are familiar with the Panel Rules and these administrative policies and procedures governing electronic filing and the method of training in the System used prior to becoming a Filing User. Filing users must also have a PACER account. An individual may register more than one Internet email address. The clerk's office will email the login and password to the attorney.

(d) Once the registration is processed by the clerk, the Filing User shall protect the security of the User password and immediately notify the clerk if the Filing User learns that the password has been compromised. Filing Users may be subject to sanctions for failure to comply with this provision. After registering, attorneys may change their passwords. If an attorney comes to believe that the security of an existing password has been compromised and that a threat to the System exists, the attorney must change his or her password immediately.

(e) Exemptions from mandatory electronic filing may be granted upon submission of a written request to the clerk. The written request shall include a supporting affidavit showing a substantial undue hardship. Final authority to grant such request is vested in the Clerk of the Panel or his/her designee.

(f)(1) Each attorney is responsible for keeping his/her contact information up to date. If an attorney is leaving a law firm and is the attorney of record on an existing case and representation in the case will remain with the law firm, withdrawal and substitution of counsel must be made prior to the attorney's termination in the law firm, for the following reason:

The attorney leaving the firm has an email address with the law firm he or she is leaving on record with the Panel. This email address may be disabled by the law firm as soon as the attorney terminates his/her employment. The electronic notices in CM/ECF will continue to go to the terminated attorney's email address at the former firm. If the email address is disabled at the law firm, the attorney will not receive the electronic notice. If a withdrawal/substitution of counsel has not been filed prior to the attorney leaving the firm, the law firm should not disable the email account of the attorney leaving the firm until another attorney in the firm enters his/her appearance. The law firm should designate someone in the firm to check this email account for CM/ECF notices until substitution of counsel has been filed with the Panel.

(2) If the attorney leaving the firm is taking active cases from the firm, the attorney needs to change his/her email address as soon as possible, otherwise the attorney will not receive electronic notices from CM/ECF. The email will continue to be sent to the former law firm's email address still on record. Procedures for changing an email address may be found in the Panel's CM/ECF User Manual.

4. ELECTRONIC FILING AND SERVICE OF DOCUMENTS.

(a) Electronic transmission of a document to the Electronic Filing System in accordance with these procedures, together with the transmission of a (System) Notice of Electronic Filing from the Panel with a hyperlink to the electronically filed document, constitutes filing of the document for all purposes of the Panel Rules of Procedure.

(b) Emailing a document to the clerk's office does not constitute filing the document. A document shall not be considered filed until the System generates a Notice of Electronic Filing (NEF) with a hyperlink to the electronically filed document.

(c) Before filing a scanned document with the court, a Filing User must verify its legibility.

(d) When a document has been filed electronically, the official record of that document is the electronic recording as stored by the Panel and the filing party is bound by the document as filed. A document filed electronically is deemed filed on the date and time stated on the Notice of Electronic Filing (NEF) from the Panel.

(e) Filing a document electronically does not alter the filing deadline for that document. Filing must be completed before midnight, **EASTERN TIME**, in order to be considered timely filed that day. However, if time of day is of the essence, the Clerk of the Panel may order a document filed by a certain time.

(f) Upon the filing of a document, a docket entry will be created using the information provided by the Filing User. The clerk will, where necessary and appropriate, modify the docket entry description to comply with quality control standards. In the event a Filing User electronically files a document in the wrong MDL or associated civil action, or the incorrect PDF document is attached, the Clerk of the Panel, or his/her designee, shall be authorized to strike the document from the record. A notice of the action striking a document from the record shall be served on all parties in the case.

(g) By participating in the electronic filing process, the parties consent to the electronic service of all documents, and shall make available electronic mail addresses for service. Upon the filing of a document by a Filing User, a Notice of Electronic Filing (NEF), with a hyperlink to the electronic document and an email message will be automatically generated by the electronic filing system, and sent via electronic mail to the email addresses of all parties who have registered in the MDL. In addition to receiving email notifications of filing activity, the Filing User is strongly encouraged to sign on to the electronic filing system at regular intervals to check the docket in his/her MDL and/or civil action.

(h) If the filing of an electronically submitted document requires leave of the Panel, such as a request to file out-of-time, the attorney shall attach the proposed document as an attachment to the motion requesting leave to file. If the Clerk of the Panel grants the motion, the document will be electronically filed without further action by the Filing User.

(i) A certificate of service must be included with all documents filed electronically. Such certificate shall indicate that service was accomplished pursuant to the Panel's electronic filing procedures. Service by electronic mail shall constitute service pursuant to Panel Rule 5.2.

A party who is not a registered CM/ECF participant with any United States federal court is entitled to a paper copy of any electronically filed pleading, document, or order pursuant to Panel Rule 5.1.1.(b). The filing party must therefore provide the non-registered attorney or party, including a terminated party or attorney, if appropriate, with the pleading, document, or order pursuant to Panel Rule 5.2. Under the Rule, they can be served with a paper copy of the electronically filed document, or they can consent in writing to service by any other method, including other forms of electronic service such as fax or direct email.

The following is a suggested certificate of service for electronic filing:

CERTIFICATE OF SERVICE

On [Date], I electronically filed this document through the CM/ECF system, which will send a notice of electronic filing to: [Attorney Name (attach list if necessary)]; and I [mailed] [hand delivered] [faxed] this document and the notice of electronic filing to: [Attorney/Party Name], [Address], [Parties Represented], [Civil Action(s)] (attach list if necessary).

/s/ [typed name of attorney]

Attorney's name

Law Firm Name (if applicable)

Address

Phone Number

Fax Number

Attorney's Email address

Attorney for:

5. ENTRY OF PANEL DOCUMENTS.

(a) A document entered or issued by the Panel will be filed in accordance with these procedures and such filing shall constitute entry on the docket kept by the Clerk.

(b) All signed orders will be electronically filed or entered. An order containing the electronic signature of a Panel Judge or the Clerk of the Panel shall have the same force and effect as if the Panel Judge or Clerk of the Panel had affixed a signature to a paper copy of the order and the order had been entered on the docket in a conventional manner.

(c) Orders may also be issued as "text-only" entries on the docket, without an attached document. Such orders are official and binding.

6. NOTICE OF PANEL ORDERS AND NOTICES.

Immediately upon the entry of an order or notice by the Panel, the clerk will transmit to Filing Users in affected cases in the MDL, in electronic form, a Notice of Electronic Filing (NEF), with a hyperlink to the electronic document. Electronic transmission of the NEF, along with a hyperlink to the electronic document, constitutes the notice required by Panel Rule 5.2. The clerk must give notice in paper form to a pro se party or an attorney who is not a Filing User to the extent notice is required.

7. ATTACHMENTS AND EXHIBITS.

Documents referenced as exhibits or attachments shall be filed in accordance with these administrative policies and procedures and the Panel's CM/ECF User Manual, unless otherwise ordered by the Panel. A Filing User shall submit as exhibits or attachments only those excerpts of the referenced documents that are directly germane to the matter under consideration by the Panel. Excerpted material must be clearly and prominently identified as such. Filing Users who file excerpts of documents as exhibits or attachments under these procedures do so without prejudice to their right to file timely additional excerpts or the complete document. Responding parties may timely file additional excerpts or the complete document that they believe are directly germane. The Panel may require parties to file additional excerpts or the complete document.

8. SEALED DOCUMENTS.

To ensure proper storage of a document, a document subject to a sealing order must be filed with the Panel on paper in a sealed envelope marked "sealed", citing thereon the MDL docket number and title and the associated case caption and case number; or by attaching thereto a paper copy of the Panel's order sealing the document or a copy of the NEF citing the entry of the court's order sealing the document. The clerk may require the document to be accompanied by a disk or CD–ROM containing the document in .pdf format. Only a motion to file a document under seal may be filed electronically, unless prohibited by law. The order of the Panel authorizing the filing of documents under seal may be filed electronically, unless prohibited by law or otherwise directed by the Panel. If a document is filed under seal pursuant to the E–Government Act of 2002, the filing party is nevertheless required to file a redacted copy for the public record along with the unredacted sealed document.

9. SPECIAL FILING REQUIREMENTS AND EXCEPTIONS.

9.1 Special Filing Requirements

The documents listed below shall be presented for filing on paper. The clerk may require the document be accompanied by a disk or CD–ROM containing the document in .pdf format:

Sealed

MDL dockets involving Qui Tam Cases (under seal)

9.2   Exceptions

All documents shall be filed electronically unless otherwise ordered by the Panel or specifically exempt herein.

10.   RETENTION REQUIREMENTS.

(a) A document that is electronically filed and requires an original signature other than that of the Filing User must be maintained in paper form by counsel and/or the firm representing the party on whose behalf the document was filed until one year after all periods for appeals expire. On request of the Panel, said counsel must provide the original document for review.

(b) The clerk's office may choose to discard certain documents brought to the clerk's office for filing in paper form after those documents are scanned and uploaded to the System (to include pro se filings). Therefore, counsel and pro se filers shall provide the Panel with a copy of the original documents with intrinsic value for scanning and maintain the original signature in accordance with 10(a).

11.   SIGNATURES.

(a) The user login and password required to submit documents to the Electronic Filing System serve as the Filing User signature on all electronic documents filed with the court. They serve as a signature for purposes of the Panel Rules and any other purpose for which a signature is required in connection with proceedings before the Panel.

(b) Each document filed electronically must indicate in the caption that it has been electronically filed. An electronically filed document must include a signature block in compliance with Panel Rule 7.1(e), and must set forth the name, address, telephone number, fax number, and email address. In addition, the name of the Filing User under whose login and password the document is submitted must be preceded by an "/s/" and typed in the space where the signature would otherwise appear. No Filing User or other person may knowingly permit or cause to permit a Filing User password to be used by anyone other than an authorized agent of the Filing User.

(c) A document requiring signatures of more than one party must be filed either by:

(1) electronically filing a scanned document containing all necessary signatures; or

(2) representing the consent of the other parties on the document; or

(3) identifying on the document the party whose signature is required and by the submission of a notice of endorsement by the other parties no later than three (3) business days after filing; or

(4) any other manner approved by the Panel.

(d) A non-filing signatory or party who disputes the authenticity of an electronically filed document with a non-attorney signature, or the authenticity of the signature on that document; or the authenticity of an electronically filed document containing multiple signatures or the authenticity of the signature themselves, must file an objection to the document within fourteen (14) days of service of the document.

(e) Any party challenging the authenticity of an electronically filed document or the attorney's signature on that document must file an objection to the document within fourteen (14) days of service of the document.

(f) If a party wishes to challenge the authenticity of an electronically filed document or signature after the fourteen (14) day period, the party shall file a motion to seek a ruling from the Panel.

12.   SERVICE OF DOCUMENTS BY ELECTRONIC MEANS.

12.1   Service

12.1.1   Filing User

Upon the electronic filing of a pleading or other document, the Panel's Electronic Case Filing System will automatically generate and send a Notice of Electronic Filing (NEF) to all Filing Users associated with that MDL and/or associated cases, along with a hyperlink to the electronic document. Transmission of the Notice of Electronic Filing with a hyperlink to the electronic document constitutes service of the filed document.

The NEF must include the time of filing, the date the document was entered on the docket, the name of the party and attorney filing the document, the type of document, the text of the docket entry, and an electronic link (hyperlink) to the filed document, allowing anyone receiving the notice by email to retrieve the document automatically. If the Filing User becomes aware that the NEF was not transmitted successfully to a party, or that the notice is deficient, i.e., the electronic link to the document is defective, the filer shall serve the electronically filed document by email, hand, facsimile, or by first-class mail postage prepaid immediately upon notification of the NEF deficiency.

12.1.2   Individual who is not a Filing User

A non-registered participant is entitled to receive a paper copy of any electronically filed document from the party making such filing. Service of such paper copy must be made according to the Panel Rules.

13. TECHNICAL FAILURES.

(a) If the site is unable to accept filings continuously or intermittently for more than one (1) hour occurring after 12:00 noon Eastern Time that day, the Clerk of the Panel shall deem the Panel's Electronic Case Filing web site to be subject to a technical failure.

(b) If a Filing User experiences a technical failure as defined herein, the Filing User may submit the document to the Clerk of the Panel, provided that the document is accompanied by a certification, signed by the Filing User, that the Filing User has attempted to file the document electronically at least twice, with those unsuccessful attempts occurring at least one (1) hour apart after 12:00 noon Eastern Time that day. The Clerk may require the document to be accompanied by a disk or CD–ROM which contains the document in .pdf format.

(c) The initial point of contact for a Filing User experiencing technical difficulty filing a document electronically will be the Panel's CM/ECF Help Desk at the numbers listed on the Panel's web site and in the CM/ECF User Manual.

(d) A Filing User who suffers prejudice as a result of a technical failure as defined herein or a Filing User who cannot file a time-sensitive document electronically due to unforeseen technical difficulties, such as the malfunctioning of a Filing User's equipment, may seek relief from the Clerk of the Panel.

14. PUBLIC ACCESS.

14.1 (a) A person may receive information from the Electronic Filing System at the Panel's Internet site by obtaining a PACER login and password. A person who has PACER access may retrieve docket sheets and documents (unless otherwise sealed or restricted) in MDL dockets and associated civil cases. Any case or document under seal shall not be available electronically or through any other means.

(b) If a case or document has been restricted, a PACER user may retrieve the docket sheet over the Internet, but only a Filing User who is counsel of record may retrieve restricted documents electronically. However, a restricted case or document will be available for viewing by the public at the clerk's office.

(c) Electronic access to electronic docket sheets and all documents filed in the System, unless sealed, is available to the public for viewing at no charge during regular business hours at the clerk's office. A copy fee for an electronic reproduction is required in accordance with 28 U.S.C. § 1932.

(d) Conventional copies and certified copies of electronically filed documents may be purchased at the clerk's office. The fee for copying and certifying will be in accordance with 28 U.S.C. § 1932.

14.2 Sensitive Information

Since the public may access certain case information over the Internet through the Panel's Electronic Filing System, sensitive information should not be included in any document filed with the court unless such inclusion is necessary and relevant. In accordance with these Administrative Policies and Procedures, if sensitive information must be included, certain personal and identifying information such as Social Security numbers, financial account numbers, dates of birth and names of minor children shall be redacted from the pleading, whether it is filed electronically or on paper.

The Panel recognizes that parties may need to include in the record a document containing information such as driver's license number; medical records, treatment and diagnosis; employment history; individual financial information; and proprietary or trade secret information.

To avoid unnecessary disclosure of private, personal or financial information, a party may:

(a) **RESTRICTED MDL DOCKETS OR DOCUMENTS.**

File a "Motion to Seal" or "Motion to Seal Document". The motion must state the reason and show good cause for restricting remote access to the case. If the motion is granted, remote access to documents will be limited to Filing Users who are counsel of record. However, the MDL docket sheet and/or documents will be available for viewing by the public at the clerk's office.

(b) **EXHIBITS.**

File an exhibit containing private, personal or financial information as an attachment to a pleading entitled "Notice of Filing Restricted Exhibit". The notice and the attached exhibit shall be filed as a separate docket entry, rather than as an attachment to the pleading supported by the exhibit. Remote public access to the notice and exhibit will be limited to Filing Users who are counsel of record. The notice and exhibit will, however, be available for viewing by the public at the clerk's office.

(c) **DOCUMENTS UNDER SEAL.**

(1) File a redacted copy of a pleading or exhibit containing private, personal or financial infor-

mation, whether electronically or on paper, while concurrently filing an unredacted copy under seal. This document shall be retained by the Panel as part of the record.

OR

(2) File a reference list under seal. The reference list shall contain the complete personal data identifier(s) and the redacted identifier(s) used in its (their) place in the filing. All references in the case to the redacted identifier(s) included in the reference list will be construed to refer to the corresponding complete identifier. The reference list must be filed under seal, and may be amended as of right. It shall be retained by the Panel as part of the record.

(d) **MOTION TO SEAL.**

File a motion to seal the document or MDL associated case. The motion must state the reason and show good cause for sealing the document or MDL associated case. If the motion to seal is granted, the document or case under seal will not be available electronically or through any other means.

It is the sole responsibility of counsel and the parties to ensure that all documents filed with the Panel comply with these Administrative Policies and Procedures, regarding public access to electronic case files. The Clerk will not review any document for redaction.

Counsel are strongly urged to share this information with all clients so that an informed decision about the inclusion, redaction, and/or exclusion of certain materials may be made.

[Effective May 2010.]

FEDERAL COURTS MISCELLANEOUS FEE SCHEDULES

COURT OF APPEALS FEE SCHEDULE

(Effective June 1, 2016)

The fees included in the Court of Appeals Miscellaneous Fee Schedule[1] are to be charged for services provided by the courts of appeals, including relevant services[2] provided by the bankruptcy appellate panels established under 28 U.S.C. § 158(b)(1).

- The United States should not be charged fees under this schedule, except as prescribed in Items 2, 4, and 5 when the information requested is available through remote electronic access.

- Federal agencies or programs that are funded from judiciary appropriations (agencies, organizations, and individuals providing services authorized by the Criminal Justice Act, 18 U.S.C. § 3006A, and bankruptcy administrators) should not be charged any fees under this schedule.

(1) For docketing a case on appeal or review, or docketing any other proceeding, $500.

- Each party filing a notice of appeal pays a separate fee to the district court, but parties filing a joint notice of appeal pay only one fee.

- There is no docketing fee for an application for an interlocutory appeal under 28 U.S.C. § 1292(b) or other petition for permission to appeal under Fed. R. App. P. 5, unless the appeal is allowed.

- There is no docketing fee for a direct bankruptcy appeal or a direct bankruptcy cross appeal, when the fee has been collected by the bankruptcy court in accordance with item 14 of the Bankruptcy Court Miscellaneous Fee Schedule.

- This fee is collected in addition to the statutory fee of $5 that is collected under 28 U.S.C. § 1917.

(2) For conducting a search of the court of appeals or bankruptcy appellate panel records, $30 per name or item searched. This fee applies to services rendered on behalf of the United States if the information requested is available through remote electronic access.

(3) For certification of any document, $11.

(4) For reproducing any document, $.50 per page. This fee applies to services rendered on behalf of the United States if the document requested is available through remote electronic access.

(5) For reproducing recordings of proceedings, regardless of the medium, $30, including the cost of materials. This fee applies to services rendered on behalf of the United States if the recording is available through remote electronic access.

(6) For reproducing the record in any appeal in which the court of appeals does not require an appendix pursuant to Fed. R. App. P.30(f), (or, in appeals before a bankruptcy appellate panel, pursuant to Fed. R. Bankr. P. 8018(e)), $83.

(7) For retrieval of one box of records from a Federal Records Center, National Archives, or other storage location removed from the place of business of the court, $64. For retrievals involving multiple boxes, $39 for each additional box. For electronic retrievals, $10 plus any charges assessed by the Federal Records Center, National Archives, or other storage location removed from the place of business of the courts.

(8) For any payment returned or denied for insufficient funds, $53.

(9) For copies of opinions, a fee commensurate with the cost of printing, as fixed by each court of appeals.

(10) For copies of the local rules of court, a fee commensurate with the cost of distributing the copies. The court may also distribute copies of the local rules without charge.

(11) For filing:

- Any separate or joint notice of appeal or application for appeal from the bankruptcy appellate panel, $5;

- A notice of the allowance of an appeal from the bankruptcy appellate panel, $5.

(12) For counsel's requested use of the court's videoconferencing equipment in connection with each oral argument, the court may charge and collect a fee of $200 per remote location.

(13) For original admission of attorney to practice, including a certificate of admission, $176. For a duplicate certificate of admission or certificate of good standing, $18.

1 Issued in accordance with 28 U.S.C. § 1913.

2 Item 13 does not apply to bankruptcy appellate panels.

DISTRICT COURT FEE SCHEDULE

(Effective June 1, 2016)

The fees included in the District Court Miscellaneous Fee Schedule[1] are to be charged for services provided by the district courts.

- The United States should not be charged fees under this schedule, with the exception of those specifically prescribed in Items 2, 4 and 5, when the information requested is available through remote electronic access.

- Federal agencies or programs that are funded from judiciary appropriations (agencies, organizations, and individuals providing services authorized by the Criminal Justice Act, 18 U.S.C. § 3006 and bankruptcy administrators) should not be charged any fees under this schedule.

1. For filing any document that is not related to a pending case or proceeding, $46.

2. For conducting a search of the district court records, $30 per name or item searched. This fee applies to services rendered on behalf of the United States if the information requested is available through electronic access.

3. For certification of any document, $11. For exemplification of any document, $21.

4. For reproducing any record or paper, $.50 per page. This fee shall apply to paper copies made from either: (1) original documents; or (2) microfiche or microfilm reproductions of the original records. This fee shall apply to services rendered on behalf of the United States if the record or paper requested is available through electronic access.

5. For reproduction of an audio recording of a court proceeding, $30. This fee applies to services rendered on behalf of the United States, if the recording is available electronically.

6. For each microfiche sheet of film or microfilm jacket copy of any court record, where available, $6.

7. For retrieval of one box of records from a Federal Records Center, National Archives, or other storage location removed from the place of business of the court, $64. For retrievals involving multiple boxes, $39 for each additional box. For electronic retrievals, $10 plus any charges assessed by the Federal Records Center, National Archives, or other storage location removed from the place of business of the courts.

8. For any payment returned or denied for insufficient funds, $53.

9. For an appeal to a district judge from a judgment of conviction by a magistrate judge in a misdemeanor case, $37.

10. For original admission of attorneys to practice, $176 each, including a certificate of admission. For a duplicate certificate of admission or certificate of good standing, $18.

11. The court may charge and collect fees commensurate with the cost of providing copies of the local rules of court. The court may also distribute copies of the local rules without charge.

12. The clerk shall assess a charge for the handling of registry funds deposited with the court, to be assessed from interest earnings and in accordance with the detailed fee schedule issued by the Director of the Administrative Office of the United States Courts.

For management of registry funds invested through the Court Registry Investment System, a fee at a rate of 2.5 basis points shall be assessed from interest earnings.

13. For filing an action brought under Title III of the Cuban Liberty and Democratic Solidarity (LIBERTAD) Act of 1996, P.L. 104-114, 110 Stat. § 785 (1996), $6,355. (This fee is in addition to the filing fee prescribed in 28 U.S.C. § 1914(a) for instituting any civil action other than a writ of habeas corpus.)

14. Administrative fee for filing a civil action, suit, or proceeding in a district court, $50. This fee does not apply to applications for a writ of habeas corpus or to persons granted in forma pauperis status under 28 U.S.C. § 1915.

15. Processing fee for a petty offense charged on a federal violation notice, $30.

1 Issued in accordance with 28 U.S.C. § 1914.

BANKRUPTCY COURT MISCELLANEOUS
FEE SCHEDULE

(Effective June 1, 2016)

The fees included in the Bankruptcy Court Miscellaneous Fee Schedule[1] are to be charged for services provided by the bankruptcy courts.

- The United States should not be charged fees under this schedule, with the exception of those specifically prescribed in Items 1, 3 and 5 when the information requested is available through remote electronic access.

- Federal agencies or programs that are funded from judiciary appropriations (agencies, organizations, and individuals providing services authorized by the Criminal Justice Act, 18 U.S.C. § 3006A, and bankruptcy administrators) should not be charged any fees under this schedule.

1. For reproducing any document, $.50 per page. This fee applies to services rendered on behalf of the United States if the document requested is available through electronic access.

2. For certification of any document, $11.
   For exemplification of any document, $21.

3. For reproduction of an audio recording of a court proceeding, $30. This fee applies to services rendered on behalf of the United States if the recording is available electronically.

4. For filing an amendment to the debtor's schedules of creditors, lists of creditors, or mailing list, $30, except:

- The bankruptcy judge may, for good cause, waive the charge in any case.

- This fee must not be charged if—

  - the amendment is to change the address of a creditor or an attorney for a creditor listed on the schedules; or

  - the amendment is to add the name and address of an attorney for a creditor listed on the schedules.

5. For conducting a search of the bankruptcy court records, $30 per name or item searched. This fee applies to services rendered on behalf of the United States if the information requested is available through electronic access.

6. For filing a complaint, $350, except:

- If the trustee or debtor-in-possession files the complaint, the fee must be paid only by the estate, to the extent there is an estate.

- This fee must not be charged if—

  - the debtor is the plaintiff; or

  - a child support creditor or representative files the complaint and submits the form required by § 304(g) of the Bankruptcy Reform Act of 1994.

7. For filing any document that is not related to a pending case or proceeding, $46.

8. Administrative fee:

- For filing a petition under Chapter 7, 12, or 13, $75.

- For filing a petition under Chapter 9, 11, or 15, $550.

- When a motion to divide a joint case under Chapter 7, 12, or 13 is filed, $75.

- When a motion to divide a joint case under Chapter 11 is filed, $550.

9. For payment to trustees pursuant to 11 U.S.C. § 330(b)(2), a $15 fee applies in the following circumstances:

- For filing a notice of conversion to a Chapter 7 case.
- For filing a motion to convert a case to a Chapter 7 case.
- For filing a motion to divide a joint Chapter 7 case.
- For filing a motion to reopen a Chapter 7 case.

10. In addition to any fees imposed under Item 9, above, the following fees must be collected:

- For filing a motion to convert a Chapter 12 case to a Chapter 7 case or a notice of conversion pursuant to 11 U.S.C. § 1208(a), $45.
- For filing a motion to convert a Chapter 13 case to a Chapter 7 case or a notice of conversion pursuant to 11 U.S.C. § 1307(a), $10.

The fee amounts in this item are derived from the fees prescribed in 28 U.S.C. § 1930(a).

If the trustee files the motion to convert, the fee is payable only from the estate that exists prior to conversion.

If the filing fee for the chapter to which the case is requested to be converted is less than the fee paid at the commencement of the case, no refund may be provided.

11. For filing a motion to reopen, the following fees apply:

- For filing a motion to reopen a Chapter 7 case, $245.
- For filing a motion to reopen a Chapter 9 case, $1167.
- For filing a motion to reopen a Chapter 11 case, $1167.
- For filing a motion to reopen a Chapter 12 case, $200.
- For filing a motion to reopen a Chapter 13 case, $235.
- For filing a motion to reopen a Chapter 15 case, $1167.

The fee amounts in this item are derived from the fees prescribed in 28 U.S.C. § 1930(a).

The reopening fee must be charged when a case has been closed without a discharge being entered.

The court may waive this fee under appropriate circumstances or may defer payment of the fee from trustees pending discovery of additional assets. If payment is deferred, the fee should be waived if no additional assets are discovered.

The reopening fee must not be charged in the following situations:

- to permit a party to file a complaint to obtain a determination under Rule 4007(b); or
- when a debtor files a motion to reopen a case based upon an alleged violation of the terms of the discharge under 11 U.S.C. § 524; or
- when the reopening is to correct an administrative error.
- to redact a record already filed in a case, pursuant to Fed. R. Bankr. 9037, if redaction is the only reason for reopening.

12. For retrieval of one box of records from a Federal Records Center, National Archives, or other storage location removed from the place of business of the court, $64. For retrievals involving multiple boxes, $39 for each additional box. For electronic retrievals, $10 plus any charges assessed by the Federal Records Center, National Archives, or other storage location removed from the place of business of the courts.

13. For any payment returned or denied for insufficient funds, $53.

14. For filing an appeal or cross appeal from a judgment, order, or decree, $293.

This fee is collected in addition to the statutory fee of $5 that is collected under 28 U.S.C. § 1930(c) when a notice of appeal is filed.

Parties filing a joint notice of appeal should pay only one fee.

If a trustee or debtor-in-possession is the appellant, the fee must be paid only by the estate, to the extent there is an estate.

Upon notice from the court of appeals that a direct appeal or direct cross-appeal has been authorized, an additional fee of $207 must be collected.

15. For filing a case under Chapter 15 of the Bankruptcy Code, $1167.

This fee is derived from and equal to the fee prescribed in 28 U.S.C. § 1930(a)(3) for filing a case commenced under Chapter 11 of Title 11.

16. The court may charge and collect fees commensurate with the cost of providing copies of the local rules of court. The court may also distribute copies of the local rules without charge.

17. The clerk shall assess a charge for the handling of registry funds deposited with the court, to be assessed from interest earnings and in accordance with the detailed fee schedule issued by the Director of the Administrative Office of the United States Courts.

For management of registry funds invested through the Court Registry Investment System, a fee at a rate of 2.5 basis points shall be assessed from interest earnings.

18. For a motion filed by the debtor to divide a joint case filed under 11 U.S.C. § 302, the following fees apply:

- For filing a motion to divide a joint Chapter 7 case, $245.
- For filing a motion to divide a joint Chapter 11 case, $1167.
- For filing a motion to divide a joint Chapter 12 case, $200.
- For filing a motion to divide a joint Chapter 13 case, $235.

These fees are derived from and equal to the filing fees prescribed in 28 U.S.C. § 1930(a).

19. For filing the following motions, $176:

- To terminate, annul, modify or condition the automatic stay;
- To compel abandonment of property of the estate pursuant to Rule 6007(b) of the Federal Rules of Bankruptcy Procedure;
- To withdraw the reference of a case or proceeding under 28 U.S.C. § 157(d); or
- To sell property of the estate free and clear of liens under 11 U.S.C. § 363(f).

This fee must not be collected in the following situations:

- For a motion for relief from the co-debtor stay;
- For a stipulation for court approval of an agreement for relief from a stay; or
- For a motion filed by a child support creditor or its representative, if the form required by § 304(g) of the Bankruptcy Reform Act of 1994 is filed.

20. For filing a transfer of claim, $25 per claim transferred.

21. For filing a motion to redact a record, $25 per affected case. The court may waive this fee under appropriate circumstances.

1 Issued in accordance with 28 U.S.C. § 1930.

JUDICIAL PANEL ON MULTIDISTRICT LITIGATION FEE SCHEDULE

(Effective June 1, 2016)

Following are fees to be charged for services to be performed by the clerk of the Judicial Panel on Multidistrict Litigation.[1]

No fees are to be charged for services rendered on behalf of the United States, with the exception of those specifically prescribed in items 1 and 3. No fees under this schedule shall be charged to federal agencies or programs which are funded from judiciary appropriations, including, but not limited to, agencies, organizations, and individuals providing services authorized by the Criminal Justice Act, 18 U.S.C. § 3006A.

(1) For every search of the records of the court conducted by the clerk of the court or a deputy clerk, $30 per name or item searched. This fee shall apply to services rendered on behalf of the United States if the information requested is available through electronic access.

(2) For certification of any document or paper, whether the certification is made directly on the document or by separate instrument, $11.

(3) For reproducing any record or paper, $.50 per page. This fee shall apply to paper copies made from either: (1) original documents; or (2) microfiche or microfilm reproductions of the original records. This fee shall apply to services rendered on behalf of the United States if the record or paper requested is available through electronic access.

(4) For retrieval of one box of records from a Federal Records Center, National Archives, or other storage location removed from the place of business of the court, $64. For retrievals involving multiple boxes, $39 for each additional box. For electronic retrievals, $10 plus any charges assessed by the Federal Records Center, National Archives, or other storage location removed from the place of business of the courts.

(5) For any payment returned or denied for insufficient funds, $53.

[1] Issued in accordance with 28 U.S.C. § 1932.

ELECTRONIC PUBLIC ACCESS FEE SCHEDULE

(Issued in accordance with 28 U.S.C. §§ 1913, 1914, 1926, 1930, 1932)

(Effective December 1, 2013)

The fees included in the Electronic Public Access Fee Schedule are to be charged for providing electronic public access to court records.

Fees for Public Access to Court Electronic Records (PACER)

(1) Except as provided below, for electronic access to any case document, docket sheet, or case-specific report via PACER: $0.10 per page, not to exceed the fee for thirty pages.

(2) For electronic access to transcripts and non-case specific reports via PACER (such as reports obtained from the PACER Case Locator or docket activity reports): $0.10 per page.

(3) For electronic access to an audio file of a court hearing via PACER: $2.40 per audio file.

Fees for Courthouse Electronic Access

(4) For printing copies of any record or document accessed electronically at a public terminal in a courthouse: $0.10 per page.

PACER Service Center Fees

(5) For every search of court records conducted by the PACER Service Center, $30 per name or item searched.

(6) For the PACER Service Center to reproduce on paper any record pertaining to a PACER account, if this information is remotely available through electronic access: $0.50 per page.

(7) For any payment returned or denied for insufficient funds, $53.

Free Access and Exemptions

(8) **Automatic Fee Exemptions.**

- No fee is owed for electronic access to court data or audio files via PACER until an account holder accrues charges of more than $15.00 in a quarterly billing cycle.

- Parties in a case (including pro se litigants) and attorneys of record receive one free electronic copy, via the notice of electronic filing or notice of docket activity, of all documents filed electronically, if receipt is required by law or directed by the filer.

- No fee is charged for access to judicial opinions.

- No fee is charged for viewing case information or documents at courthouse public access terminals.

(9) **Discretionary Fee Exemptions.**

- Courts may exempt certain persons or classes of persons from payment of the user access fee. Examples of individuals and groups that a court may consider exempting include: indigents, bankruptcy case trustees, pro bono attorneys, pro bono alternative dispute resolution neutrals, Section 501(c)(3) not-for-profit organizations, and individual researchers associated with educational institutions. Courts should not, however, exempt individuals or groups that have the ability to pay the statutorily established access fee. Examples of individuals and groups that a court should not exempt include: local, state or federal government agencies, members of the media, privately paid attorneys or others who have the ability to pay the fee.

- In considering granting an exemption, courts must find:

- that those seeking an exemption have demonstrated that an exemption is necessary in order to avoid unreasonable burdens and to promote public access to information;

- that individual researchers requesting an exemption have shown that the defined research project is intended for scholarly research, that it is limited in scope, and that it is not intended for redistribution on the internet or for commercial purposes.

- If the court grants an exemption:

  - the user receiving the exemption must agree not to sell the data obtained as a result, and must not transfer any data obtained as the result of a fee exemption, unless expressly authorized by the court; and

  - the exemption should be granted for a definite period of time, should be limited in scope, and may be revoked at the discretion of the court granting the exemption.

- Courts may provide local court information at no cost (e.g., local rules, court forms, news items, court calendars, and other information) to benefit the public.

Applicability to the United States and State and Local Governments

(10) Unless otherwise authorized by the Judicial Conference, these fees must be charged to the United States, except to federal agencies or programs that are funded from judiciary appropriations (including, but not limited to, agencies, organizations, and individuals providing services authorized by the Criminal Justice Act [18 U.S.C. § 3006A], and bankruptcy administrators).

(11) The fee for printing copies of any record or document accessed electronically at a public terminal ($0.10 per page) described in (4) above does not apply to services rendered on behalf of the United States if the record requested is not remotely available through electronic access.

(12) The fee for local, state, and federal government entities, shall be $0.08 per page until April 1, 2015, after which time, the fee shall be $0.10 per page.

JUDICIAL CONFERENCE POLICY NOTES

The Electronic Public Access (EPA) fee and its exemptions are directly related to the requirement that the judiciary charge user-based fees for the development and maintenance of electronic public access services. The fee schedule provides examples of users that may not be able to afford reasonable user fees (such as indigents, bankruptcy case trustees, individual researchers associated with educational institutions, 501(c)(3) not-for-profit organizations, and court-appointed pro bono attorneys), but requires those seeking an exemption to demonstrate that an exemption is limited in scope and is necessary in order to avoid an unreasonable burden. In addition, the fee schedule includes examples of other entities that courts should not exempt from the fee (such as local, state or federal government agencies, members of the media, and attorneys). The goal is to provide courts with guidance in evaluating a requestor's ability to pay the fee.

Judicial Conference policy also limits exemptions in other ways. First, it requires exempted users to agree not to sell the data they receive through an exemption (unless expressly authorized by the court). This prohibition is not intended to bar a quote or reference to information received as a result of a fee exemption in a scholarly or other similar work. Second, it permits courts to grant exemptions for a definite period of time, to limit the scope of the exemptions, and to revoke exemptions. Third, it cautions that exemptions should be granted as the exception, not the rule, and prohibits courts from exempting all users from EPA fees.